Lecture Notes in Computer Science 11701

More information about this series at http://www.springer.com/series/7409

Ilias O. Pappas · Patrick Mikalef ·
Yogesh K. Dwivedi · Letizia Jaccheri ·
John Krogstie · Matti Mäntymäki (Eds.)

Digital Transformation for a Sustainable Society in the 21st Century

18th IFIP WG 6.11 Conference on
e-Business, e-Services, and e-Society, I3E 2019
Trondheim, Norway, September 18–20, 2019
Proceedings

 Springer

Editors
Ilias O. Pappas 🆔
University of Agder
Kristiansand, Norway

Norwegian University of Science
and Technology
Trondheim, Norway

Yogesh K. Dwivedi 🆔
Swansea University
Swansea, UK

John Krogstie
Norwegian University of Science
and Technology
Trondheim, Norway

Patrick Mikalef 🆔
Norwegian University of Science
and Technology and SINTEF
Trondheim, Norway

Letizia Jaccheri 🆔
Norwegian University of Science
and Technology
Trondheim, Norway

Matti Mäntymäki 🆔
University of Turku
Turku, Finland

ISSN 0302-9743   ISSN 1611-3349 (electronic)
Lecture Notes in Computer Science
ISBN 978-3-030-29373-4   ISBN 978-3-030-29374-1 (eBook)
https://doi.org/10.1007/978-3-030-29374-1

LNCS Sublibrary: SL3 – Information Systems and Applications, incl. Internet/Web, and HCI

This Springer imprint is published by the registered company Springer Nature Switzerland AG
The registered company address is: Gewerbestrasse 11, 6330 Cham, Switzerland

Preface

This book presents the proceedings of the 18th International Federation of Information Processing (IFIP) Conference on e-Business, e-Services, and e-Society (I3E), which was held in Trondheim, Norway, during September 18–20, 2019. The annual I3E conference is a core part of Working Group 6.11, which aims to organize and promote the exchange of information and cooperation related to all aspects of e-Business, e-Services, and e-Society (the three Es). The I3E conference series is truly interdisciplinary and welcomes contributions from both academicians and practitioners alike.

The main theme of the 2019 conference was "Digital transformation for a sustainable society in the 21st century". In line with the inclusive nature of the I3E series, all papers related to e-Business, e-Services, and e-Society were welcomed.

The digitalization process and its outcomes in the 21st century accelerate transformation and the creation of sustainable societies. Our decisions, actions, and even existence in the digital world generate data, which offer tremendous opportunities for revising current business methods and practices, thus there is a critical need for novel theories embracing big data analytics ecosystems. The value of digital transformations that emerges through big data analytics ecosystems is an area that is receiving increased attention. The multiple actors of such ecosystems (e.g., academia, private and public organizations, civil society, and individuals) need to cooperate or collaborate in order to develop the necessary capabilities that will lead to the creation of value, as well as to business and societal change.

We need digital business models that will not just be more accurate or efficient, but that will also go beyond economic value, and address societal challenges generating shared value that impacts the society as a whole and its relevant actors individually. Thus, it is important to recognize that value can emerge through different means and can be captured through different measures. Creating shared value or co-creating value can lead to increased benefits for all actors taking part in digital transformation.

I3E 2019 brings together contributions from a variety of perspectives, disciplines, and communities for the advancement of knowledge regarding "Digital transformation for a sustainable society in the 21st century". Some organizations or entrepreneurs focus on driving business value and keeping ahead of competitors, while at the same time others can have a view of facilitating societal change, therefore generating value that impacts both them and the society overall. We call for research from different contexts that will contribute to the improvement of big data analytics ecosystems that emerge as drivers of digital transformation and sustainability. We seek to answer questions around the role of data actors, define data capacities and data availability, examine adoption at leadership and management level, and improve current approaches of data-driven sustainable development.

The Call for Papers solicited submissions in two main categories: full research papers and short research-in-progress papers. Each submission was reviewed by at least two knowledgeable academics in the field, in a double-blind process. The 2019 conference received 138 submissions from more than 30 countries from almost all continents (i.e., Asia, Africa, Europe, North America, South America, and Australia). Out of the 138 submissions, 69 papers were selected to be presented at the conference. Four of the accepted papers were not included in the final proceedings because the authors decided to withdraw them. Thus, the acceptance rate was 47.1%.

Following the conference, two special issues have been organized for selected best papers from I3E 2019. The two special issues are on the *Information Systems Frontiers (ISF)* journal and the *International Journal of Information Management (IJIM)*.

The final set of 65 full and short papers submitted to I3E 2019 that appear in these proceedings were clustered into 13 groups, each of which are outlined below.

The papers appearing in Part I address the area of e–business. In detail, the papers present works in electronic commerce and social commerce. Furthermore, adoption of mobile applications and mobile commerce is examined. Finally, three papers deal with consumer reviews in online environments.

The papers appearing in Part II address big data and analytics. In detail, the works here deal with the business and social value that stem from big data applications, as well as challenges of adopting big data analytics. Further, a spatio-temporal model is proposed for improved analytics. Also, the relation of data science and circular economy is examined.

The papers appearing in Part III address open science and open data. In detail, the papers discuss applications of open data in private and public organizations, as well as open science as means to improve the design of laboratory forensics.

The papers appearing in Part IV address Artificial Intelligence (AI) and the Internet of Things (IoT). In detail, the papers include a bibliometric analysis of the state of AI in national security, the adoption of AI by public organizations, and an Internet of Things business model.

The papers appearing in Part V address smart cities and smart homes. In detail, different cases of smart city enablers and smart home adoption are discussed, along with ways to offer incentives for energy saving. Finally, a software management architecture for smart cities is presented.

The papers appearing in Part VI address social media and analytics. In detail, several papers examine the business value of social media and how employees use social media after work. Also, a social media information literacy construct is proposed. Furthermore, several papers focus on social media analytics for online interactions, user engagement, and digital service adoption.

The papers appearing in Part VII address digital governance. In detail, the adoption and co-creation of e-government services is examined. Furthermore, the issues of transparency, traceability, personal data protection, and digital identity are examined in the context of developing economies.

The papers appearing in Part VIII address digital divide and social inclusion. In detail, digital inequalities are examined along with ways to reduce them. Also, three papers investigate the role of technology for people with ASD and older adults. Finally, the effect of the sharing economy on social inclusion and subjective well-being is examined.

The papers appearing in Part IX address learning and education. In detail, the papers here deal with e-learning environments and online programming courses. Also, ways to improve multi–campus courses are discussed. Further, a literature review on how technology enhances organizational learning is presented.

The papers appearing in Part X address security in digital environments. In detail, the two papers in this part deal with cybersecurity in the era of digital transformation.

The papers appearing in Part XI address the modeling and managing of the digital enterprise. In detail, the papers discuss business value in SMEs, success factors for dynamic enterprise risk management, and structural requirements for digital transformation of enterprises. Also, the role of chief digital officers is discussed for successful digital transformation, while a maturity model approach is proposed for assessing digital transformation of enterprises.

The papers appearing in Part XII address digital innovation and business transformation. In detail, the papers discuss knowledge transfer in innovation ecosystems, customer behavior that may lead to digital disruption, and present a taxonomy for better knowledge organization within personal process management.

The papers appearing in Part XIII address online communities. In detail, here is discussed how students between two countries can gain more skills and knowledge via online collaboration. Also, the power of virtual social communities to fight crime is discussed.

In addition to the aforementioned papers, we were delighted to welcome Prof. Jan vom Brocke, Dr. Lillian Røstad, and Prof. H. Raghav Rao as our keynote speakers.

Dr. Jan vom Brocke is Full Professor of Information Systems, the Hilti Endowed Chair of Business Process Management, and Director of the Institute of Information Systems at the University of Liechtenstein.

Dr. Lillian Røstad is head of the Cyber Security Advisory in Sopra Steria, and is responsible for building up Sopra Steria's services within Cyber Security in Scandinavia.

Dr. H. R. Rao was named the AT&T Distinguished Chair in Infrastructure Assurance and Security at The University of Texas at San Antonio College of Business in January 2016. He also holds a courtesy appointment as full professor in the UTSA Department of Computer Science.

The success of the 18th IFIP I3E Conference (I3E 2019) was a result of the enormous efforts of numerous people and organizations. Firstly, this conference was only made possible by the continued support of WG 6.11 for this conference series and for selecting Trondheim to host it in 2019, for which we are extremely grateful. We received many good-quality submissions from authors across the globe and we would like to thank them for choosing I3E 2019 as the outlet to present and publish their current research. We are indebted to the Program Committee, who generously gave up their time to provide constructive reviews and facilitate the improvement of the submitted manuscripts. We would like to thank the Department of Computer Science and the Faculty of Information Technology and Electrical Engineering at the Norwegian University of Science and Technology (NTNU) for hosting and supporting the conference. Finally, we extend our sincere gratitude to everyone involved in organizing the conference, to our esteemed keynote speakers, and to Springer LNCS as the publisher of these proceedings, which we hope will be of use for the continued development of research related to the three Es.

July 2019

Ilias O. Pappas
Patrick Mikalef
Yogesh K. Dwivedi
Letizia Jaccheri
John Krogstie
Matti Mäntymäki

Organization

Conference Chairs

Ilias O. Pappas	University of Agder and Norwegian University of Science and Technology (NTNU), Norway
Patrick Mikalef	Norwegian University of Science and Technology (NTNU) and SINTEF, Norway
Yogesh K. Dwivedi	Swansea University, UK
Letizia Jaccheri	Norwegian University of Science and Technology (NTNU), Norway
John Krogstie	Norwegian University of Science and Technology (NTNU), Norway

Program Committee Chairs

Ilias O. Pappas	University of Agder and Norwegian University of Science and Technology (NTNU), Norway
Patrick Mikalef	Norwegian University of Science and Technology (NTNU) and SINTEF, Norway
Yogesh K. Dwivedi	Swansea University, UK
Letizia Jaccheri	Norwegian University of Science and Technology (NTNU), Norway
John Krogstie	Norwegian University of Science and Technology (NTNU), Norway
Matti Mäntymäki	University of Turku, Finland

I3E2019 Keynote Speakers

Jan vom Brocke	University of Liechtenstein, Liechtenstein
Lillian Røstad	Head of Cyber Security Advisory, Sopra Steria, Norway
H. Raghav Rao	The University of Texas San Antonio, USA

Program Committee

Margunn Aanestad	University of Agder, Norway
Shahriar Akter	University of Wollongong, Australia
Peter Andre Busch	University of Agder, Norway
Khalid Benali	LORIA—Université de Lorraine, France
Djamal Benslimane	Université Claude Bernard Lyon 1, LIRIS Lab, France
Edward Bernoroider	WU Vienna, Austria
Lemuria Carter	University of New South Wales, Australia

Contents

Smart Cities and Smart Homes

Social Media and Analytics

Digital Divide and Social Inclusion

Learning and Education

Security in Digital Environments

Modelling and Managing the Digital Enterprise

Digital Innovation and Business Transformation

Online Communities

E-Business

Review of Theoretical Models and Limitations of Social Commerce Adoption Literature

Prianka Sarker, Hatice Kizgin, Nripendra P. Rana$^{(\boxtimes)}$,
and Yogesh K. Dwivedi

Emerging Markets Research Centre (EMaRC), School of Management,
Swansea University Bay Campus, Swansea SA1 8EN, UK
{937449,Hatice.Kizgin,n.p.rana,
y.k.dwivedi}@swansea.ac.uk,
ykdwivedi@gmail.com

Abstract. Social commerce is emerging as an important platform in e-commerce. It brings people to the comfort zone to buying and selling product that they cannot reach physically. The purpose of this research is to review the empirical research on social commerce published between 2012 to 2019. The paper mainly reviews the theories and models used in this area and limitations acknowledged by studies in social commerce area. The findings indicated that TAM, social support theory and S-O-R model are some of the most frequently used models. Also, use of biased sample, limited factors and cross-sectional studies are some of the most common limitations used across majority of studies.

Keywords: Social commerce · Literature review · TAM

1 Introduction

Social commerce is a new version of e-commerce that contains using social media that supports user contributions and social interactions to assist in the buying and selling of products and services online [1]. Yahoo is the first organisation who introduce social commerce concept in 2005. Following Yahoo; Facebook, Google, Instagram and many other social platforms adopted this concept and enhancing the businesses. Berkowitz [2] said that social commerce is how markets leverage social media to influence consumers' shopping behaviour, spanning product consideration, purchase intent, the transaction itself and post-transaction advocacy and retention. Social commerce is the digital presence of marketers, and it has been used depending on marketers' goals, interest and strategy. Carton [3] states that social commerce is a platform for buying and selling product through interaction between people. Social commerce is a potential online scale, reach and ease of sharing and connecting people. Social commerce brings people to the comfort zone to buying and selling a product that they cannot reach physically. On one side, it is fulfilling consumer's desire and another side it is developing the businesses. Increasing the demand and importance of social commerce, several studies have been conducted last few years in different aspects. For example, consumer behaviours on social commerce, consumer intention to buy, social commerce adoption, impulsive buying behaviour on social commerce, different factors that influence social commerce, social commerce online features. Several researchers have

© IFIP International Federation for Information Processing 2019
Published by Springer Nature Switzerland AG 2019
I. O. Pappas et al. (Eds.): I3E 2019, LNCS 11701, pp. 3–12, 2019.
https://doi.org/10.1007/978-3-030-29374-1_1

found different theories and model for developing social commerce. This paper attempts to review the past journal papers related to social commerce published between 2012 to 2019 and specifically empirical studies by nature. This study also discussed previous literature review papers to reduce the similarity of the research. For example, Busalim [4] conducted a systematic review of social commerce to explore the term of social commerce by reviewing the studies that related to social commerce published from 2010 to 2015. This study highlighted the understanding of customers' needs that influence the customer to stick with the same seller. Moreover, the study found that acquisition and retention are key success factors that need more investigation. Most of the studies focused on the intention of customers to buy in social commerce sites and transactional behaviour. Another systemic literature review has conducted by synthesising 407 papers from academic publications between 2006 and 2017. This study focused to reveal current social commerce researches, different research methods that used in social commerce, and future areas for social commerce researches [5]. Zhang [6] did the literature review conducted a systematic review of consumer behaviour on social commerce sites. This study particularly discussed theories and identify essential research methods. More importantly, this study draws upon the stimulus-organism–response model and the five-stage consumer decision-making process to propose an integrative framework for a holistic understanding of consumer behaviour. Hajli [7] studied on the framework of social commerce adoption. The findings from the model indicate that forums and communities, rating and reviews and referrals and recommendations are the primary constructs of social commerce adoption model. It was also found that trust is the on-going problem of e-commerce, and it can be developed through social commerce constructs. Altinisik and Yildirim [8] conducted a literature review on consumer adoption of social commerce and founded that social support theory, trust transfer theory, TAM and S-O-R model are used in five studies. China developed the highest number of studies, which is 14 in the context of social commerce adoption. The study also found that Social presence is the most frequent social factors where trust towards the website is the most frequent personal factor.

However, there is a lack in the literature review as regards of identifying most frequent used models, theories and Limitations in social commerce researches. Considering the discussion presented above, this study focuses mainly on two questions:

RQ1: what are the models/theories were used in past social commerce studies? RQ2: What are the most frequent Limitations that has mentioned in past studies? To finding those questions, this paper undertakes analysis and synthesis of existing research related to social commerce adoption. To achieve the aim, the remaining part of the paper is structured as followed: section two will describe the literature search and analysis approach. Section three will be described by different models, theories that have been found from previous literature. Section four discuss the identified limitations.

2 Systematic Literature Approach

This paper used the following keyword to find relevant article using Google scholar, Scopus, ScienceDirect, scholar database: "social commerce adoption" OR "consumer adoption of social commerce" OR "Consumers' behaviour on social commerce" OR "using intention of social commerce" OR "Influence Factors of social commerce" in order to identify the relevant article. The keyword search returned 110 papers. 25 papers were not relevant with this study and 16 papers were not accessible. However, we focused on 69 studies that directly relevant to individual consumer adoption of social commerce, consumer intention to use in social commerce and the factor that influence social commerce adoption.

3   Frequently Used Theories/Model in the Area of Social Commerce

Scholarly work has found social commerce adoption using various models and theories. The Table 1 below summarizes most frequent found models and theories.

Table 1. Models/Theories

Model/Theory	Freq	Citations
Technology Acceptance model (TAM)	17	Biucky et al. [9]; Cabanillas and Santos [10]; Chung et al. [11]; Dwairi et al. [12]; Gibreel et al. [13]; Gutama and Intani [14]; Hajli [15]; Hajli [16]; Huang and Benyoucef [17]; Jiang et al. [18]; Kim et al. [19]; Shin [20]; Shen [21]; Srinivasan [22]; Liang [22]; Wang and Yu [24]
Social support theory	11	Chen and Shen [25]; Hajli [7, 26]; Hajli et al. [27]; Li [28]; Liang and Turban [29]; Makmor and Alam [30]; Molinillo et al. [31]; Shanmugam et al. [32]; Sheikh et al. [33]; Tajvidi et al. [34]
Stimulus-Organism Response (S-O-R) model	7	Li [28]; Molinillo et al. [31]; Liu et al. [35]; Kim [36]; Wu and Li [37]; Xiang et al. [38]; Zhang et al. [39]
Theory of planned behaviour	6	Hajli [16]; Huang and Benyoucef [17]; Shin [20]; Lu et al. [40]; Farivar et al. [41]; Lin and Wu [46]
Trust transfer theory	4	Chen [25]; Bai et al. [43]; Ng [44]; Shi and Chow [45]
Relationship quality theory	4	Hajli [19]; Tajvidi et al. [34]; Zhang et al. [46]; Lin et al. [47]
Social exchange theory	4	Li [28]; Molinillo et al. [31]; Yang et al. [48]; Lin et al. [49]
Theory of Reasoned Action (TRA)	4	Huang and Benyoucef [17]; Kim and Park [57]; Teh et al. [58]; Akman and Mishra [59]
UTAUT (theory of acceptance and use of technology)	3	Nadeem et al. [50]; Yahia et al. [51]; Gatautis and Medziausiene [52]
Social learning theory	3	Chen [54, 55]; Li et al. [56]
Social identity theory	2	Farivar et al. [41]; Wang [60]

Models and theories with only one occurrence: Commitment-Trust Theory, Chen and Shen [10]; SCAM model, Hajli [15]; Holistic Theory, Liu et al. [39]; Social presence theory, Lu et al. [40]; Consumer behavior theory, Bai et al. [43]; EWOM model, Noori et al. [53]; Motivation theory, Yang et al. [48]; Communication Privacy Management (CPM) theory, Sharma and Crossler [61]; Keno model, Choi and Kim [62]; Push-Pull-mooring model, Li and Ku [63]; An integrated gratifications and motivational model (IGMM), Osatuyi and Qin [64]; Complexity theory, Pappas [65]; Utilitarian and hedonic motivation theory, Mikalef [66].

In discussion section we particularly picked up most significant and relevant articles to discuss. Technology acceptance model best known as TAM is the most used model in social commerce adoption. TAM has been adopted, adapted and extended in many various contexts. TAM has been used in 17 studies in social commerce context. TAM used to examine user preferences of social features on social commerce websites, drivers of social commerce, evaluating different factors of social commerce, Social interaction-based consumer decision-making model, Effects of antecedents of collectivism on consumers' intention to use social commerce, Social commerce adoption and the effects of perceived risk on social commerce adoption [9, 10, 12–15, 18–24]. Chung [11] used TAM alongside with commodity theory, psychological reactance theory, naive economic theory to utilise consumers' impulsive buying behaviour of restaurant products in social commerce context. TAM alongside with theory of planned behaviour was used in multiple studies. Hajli [16] evaluate social commerce constructs and consumer's intention to purchase. Huang and Benyoucef [17] has utilised TAM model along with TRA (theory of reasoned action) and TPB (The theory of planned behaviour). Shin [20] explore user experience in the adaptation of social commerce.

Social support theory is another popular theory in social commerce context. Social support theory has used in 11 studies to evaluate different contexts of social commerce adoption. Chen and Shen [25] explore consumers' decision making in social commerce context. Hajli [26] explore social support on relationship quality using social support theory. Li [28] explored social commerce constructs that influence social shopping intention using social support theory and S-O-R model. Makmor and Alam [30] evaluate the consumers' attitude towards adaptation of social commerce. Molinillo et al. [31] explore social commerce intention model to adaptation of social commerce. Sheikh et al. [33] explore the acceptance of social commerce in the context of Saudi Arabia. Stimulus–organism–response (S-O-R) model has been used in seven studies in social commerce context. Impulsive buying behaviour, customer motivation to participate in social commerce, consumer behaviour, marketing mix, and consumer value and consumer loyalty has used S-O- R model to examination those studies [35–39]. There are some other theories such as trust transfer theory, Relationship quality theory, Theory of Reasoned Action (TRA) and Social exchange theory has frequently used in the context of social commerce adoption. However, UTAUT, Social learning theory and social exchange theory occurs in three studies in social commerce context. There are some other theory and model such as Commitment-Trust Theory, SCAM, Holistic Theory, Social presence theory, Motivation theory, Communication Privacy Management (CPM) theory, Complexity theory, Utilitarian and hedonic motivation theory, Push-Pull-mooring model occurs in single studies where some models/theories has combined with other models/theories and some used along. However, those models/theories have contribution of exploration in different studies and played a vital role in several studies.

4   Research Limitations

Table 2 provides a summary of most frequent identified limitations in studies on social commerce adoption. The review finds sampling, single subjects are most frequent limitation in several studies. Furthermore, Limited factors, Cross sectional studies, use of specific model, method, and tools are the main limitations.

Table 2. Frequently mentioned Limitations

Limitations	Freq	Explanation	Citations
Single subject/biased sample	23	Sample based on only one or limited, community, culture, country, parson or age group	Dwairi [12]; Gibreel et al. [13]; Huang and Benyoucef [17]; Jiang [18]; Srinivasan [22]; Wang et al. [24]; Chen and Shen [25]; Hajli [27]; Molinillo et al. [31]; Sheikh et al. [33]; Tajvidi et al. [34]; Wu and Li [37]; Xiang et al. [38]; Zhang et al. [39]; Farivar [41]; Lin et al. [42]; Bai et al. [43]; Ng [44]; Zhang et al. [46]; Yang et al. [48]; Akman and Mishra [59]; Pappas et al. [65]; Braojos et al. [67]
Limited factors	15	Counted number of external constructs	Biucky et al. [9]; Chung [11]; Wang [24]; Chen and Shen [25]; Liu et al. [35]; Wu and Li [37]; Xiang [38]; Zhang et al. [39]; Farivar et al. [41]; Bai et al. [43]; Ng [44]; Shi and Chow [45]; Zhang et al. [46]; Yang et al. [48]; Pappas et al. [65]
Platform	11	Sample based on specific SNS platform	Gibreel et al. [13]; Huang and Benyoucef [17]; Hajli [26, 27]; Sheikh et al. [33]; Wu and Li [37]; Bai et al. [43]; Noori et al. [53]; Yahia et al. [51]; Gatautis and Medziausiene [52]; Braojos et al. [67]
Cross-sectional study	8	one-time cross-sectional study	Cabanillas and Santos [10]; Chung et al. [11]; Huang and Benyoucef [17]; Kim et al. [19]; Lu et al. [40]; Shi et al. [45]; Noori et al. [53]; Akman and Mishra [59]
Using specific model/theory	6	Specific type of model and theory	Sheikh et al. [33]; Liu [35]; Wu and Li [37]; Xiang et al. [38]; Farivar et al. [41]; Wang et al. [60]
Limited sample size	6	Small sample size	Cabanillas and Santos [10]; Gibreel et al. [13]; Molinillo et al. [31]; Zhang et al. [39]; Gatautis and Medziausiene [52]; Akman and Mishra [59]

Table 2 showing the most frequent limitation that has occurs in different studies during their studies. The table showing that 23 studies found a single subject and the biased sample is the most frequent limitation. The sample of the study based on a single community, culture, country, person age group. The major amount of study has been conducted in China, where researchers collected the data as Chinese cultural perspectives using Chinese social commerce platform such as WeChat, RenRen, Weibo etc. However, the finding does not generalise the other part of the world. The researchers suggested collecting the more diversified sample to adding more value and discard the bias. In this analysis, it has been founded that most sampling has collected from students and the age group from 18 to 35. However, few researchers suggested to collect the sample from an older generation to gain their perspective towards social commerce also, can be compared with the younger generation and older generation to find what exactly which generation demand from social commerce. The second highest mentioned limitation is limited factors. Cross-sectional studies have been founded in eight studies. It is described that the sample is collected from a single point of time. Moreover, most of the studies employed survey-based data collection with self-reported questionnaires that limit the overall perspective of the participant.

Moreover, researcher mostly used five and seven Likert scale to measure the data. Furthermore, the majority of studies have employed a quantitative approach [5]. However, the researcher suggested to employed qualitative methods for collecting the data. Such as Observation, interviews, focus group discussion session could be employed for future research, for quantitative approach researcher suggested to employed longitudinal studies which are the same data sources that repeatedly use for an extended period of time. The platform is an important aspect of social commerce studies. However, the researcher found that the perspective of one social commerce platform users cannot provide generalised other social commerce platform user perspective. As an example, WeChat only uses in China, so the collected data from WeChat only shows China's social commerce perspective. However, the researcher suggested that employees' multiple platforms collect the data and users who use different social commerce platform. This will enhance the broad understanding of various social commerce platform. This has been founded that TAM, social commerce theory, S-O-R model are used in most of the studies which have limited the findings of social commerce area. However, there are some model and theory that has used in fewer studies could be employed in future research. Such as theory of planned behaviour is used in six studies whereas UTAUT, Trust transfer theory employed in limited studies. However, the researcher suggested to employees those underrated theories and model for future research. This may produce a new understanding of the social commerce area. Few researchers suggested to employ larger sampling due to more understanding of social commerce context. There are some other, such as using different tools or techniques to analysis sampling. Such as SEM-PLS has used most frequently. Where the SPSS tool has mostly employed to measure that data, some of the studies applied Vikor, ANOVA, AMOS for analysis of the data. However, the researcher suggested using some other useful tools such as LISREL, LAS for measure future data.

5   Conclusion

This paper conducted a review of past literature on the area of social commerce in particular consumer adoption of social commerce. From this review, the study found that TAM is the most useful and most used model for this specific area. Moreover, S-O-R, Social support theory are equally important to investigate any research. Study Also Found some other theories that were used with some core model and theory and those are also an essential aspect of social commerce adoption. In most of the study found that data collection, sample size, specific culture and country are some frequent limitation. Moreover, using a single method, factor, tool and Technique create the limitation in the study. In terms of the limitation of this study, we analyse the journal paper studied from 2012 to 2019. Also, this paper did not include any books and conference papers. Furthermore, this research did not include any methodology analysis and future research analysis. The motivation of this study is to unfold the model/theories that have used most frequently in different studies. However, some model/theories are overlooking and has used one or two studies. Highlighting those underrated theories/model may discover different findings of social commerce. This study also highlighted the limitations. Future researches should reduce most of the limitations in social commerce studies, which may provide more information about the adoption of social commerce.

References

1. Shen, J., Eder, L.B.: An examination of factors associated with user acceptance of social shopping websites. Int. J. Technol. Hum. Interact. (IJTHI) **7**(1), 19–36 (2011)
2. Berkowitz, D.: Social Commerce Defined (2011). Heidi Cohen: https://heidicohen.com/social-commerce-defined/. Accessed 21 Feb 2019
3. Carton, S.: Social Commerce Defined (2011). Heidi Cohen: https://heidicohen.com/social-commerce-defined/. Accessed 21 Feb 2019
4. Busalim, A.H.: Understanding social commerce: a systematic literature review and directions for further research. Int. J. Inf. Manag. **36**(6), 1075–1088 (2016)
5. Han, H., Xu, H., Chen, H.: Social commerce: a systematic review and data synthesis. Electron. Commer. Res. Appl. **30**, 38–50 (2018)
6. Zhang, K.Z., Benyoucef, M.: Consumer behavior in social commerce: a literature review. Decis. Support Syst. **86**, 95–108 (2016)
7. Hajli, M.: A research framework for social commerce adoption. Inf. Manag. Comput. Secur. **21**(3), 144–154 (2013)
8. Altinisik, S., Yildirim, S.Ö.: Consumers' adoption of social commerce: a systematic literature review. Mugla J. Sci. Technol. **3**(2), 131–137 (2017)
9. Biucky, S.T., Harandi, S.R.: The effects of perceived risk on social commerce adoption based on TAM Model. Int. J. Electron. Commer. Stud. **8**(2), 173–196 (2017)
10. Liébana-Cabanillas, F., Alonso-Dos-Santos, M.: Factors that determine the adoption of Facebook commerce: the moderating effect of age. J. Eng. Tech. Manag. **44**, 1–18 (2017)
11. Chung, N., Song, H.G., Lee, H.: Consumers' impulsive buying behavior of restaurant products in social commerce. Int. J. Contemp. Hosp. Manag. **29**(2), 709–731 (2017)
12. Al-Dwairi, R.: Social commerce adoption among Jordanian youth: empirical study. Int. J. Bus. Inf. Syst. **26**(3), 277–296 (2017)
13. Gibreel, O., AlOtaibi, D.A., Altmann, J.: Social commerce development in emerging markets. Electron. Commer. Res. Appl. **27**, 152–162 (2018)
14. Gutama, W.A., Intani, A.P.D.: Consumer acceptance towards online grocery shopping in Malang, east Java, Indonesia. Agric. Soc.-Econ. J. **17**(1), 23 (2017)
15. Hajli, M.: An integrated model for e-commerce adoption at the customer level with the impact of social commerce. Int. J. Inf. Sci. Manag. (IJISM) 77–97 (2012)
16. Hajli, N.: Social commerce constructs and consumer's intention to buy. Int. J. Inf. Manag. **35**(2), 183–191 (2015)

17. Huang, Z., Benyoucef, M.: The effects of social commerce design on consumer purchase decision-making: an empirical study. Electron. Commer. Res. Appl. **25**, 40–58 (2017)
18. Jiang, G., Ma, F., Shang, J., Chau, P.Y.: Evolution of knowledge sharing behavior in social commerce: an agent-based computational approach. Inf. Sci. **278**, 250–266 (2014)
19. Kim, S., Noh, M.J., Lee, K.T.: Effects of antecedents of collectivism on consumers' intention to use social commerce. J. Appl. Sci. **12**(12), 1265–1273 (2012)
20. Shin, D.H.: User experience in social commerce: in friends we trust. Behav. Inf. Technol. **32**(1), 52–67 (2013)
21. Shen, J.: Social comparison, social presence, and enjoyment in the acceptance of social shopping websites. J. Electron. Commer. Res. **13**(3), 198 (2012)
22. Srinivasan, R.: Exploring the impact of social norms and online shopping anxiety in the adoption of online apparel shopping by Indian consumers. J. Internet Commer. **14**(2), 177–199 (2015)
23. Liang, T.P., Ho, Y.T., Li, Y.W., Turban, E.: What drives social commerce: the role of social support and relationship quality. Int. J. Electron. Commer. **16**(2), 69–90 (2011)
24. Wang, Y., Yu, C.: Social interaction-based consumer decision-making model in social commerce: the role of word of mouth and observational learning. Int. J. Inf. Manag. **37**(3), 179–189 (2017)
25. Chen, J., Shen, X.L.: Consumers' decisions in social commerce context: an empirical investigation. Decis. Support Syst. **79**, 55–64 (2015)
26. Hajli, M.N.: The role of social support on relationship quality and social commerce. Technol. Forecast. Soc. Chang. **87**, 17–27 (2014)
27. Hajli, N., Shanmugam, M., Powell, P., Love, P.E.: A study on the continuance participation in on-line communities with social commerce perspective. Technol. Forecast. Soc. Chang. **96**, 232–241 (2015)
28. Li, C.Y.: How social commerce constructs influence customers' social shopping intention? An empirical study of a social commerce website. Technol. Forecast. Soc. Chang. **144**, 282–294 (2017)
29. Liang, T.P., Turban, E.: Introduction to the special issue social commerce: a research framework for social commerce. Int. J. Electron. Commer. **16**(2), 5–14 (2011)
30. Makmor, N.B., Alam, S.S.: Attitude towards social commerce: a conceptual model regarding consumer purchase intention and its determinants. Int. J. Econ. Res. **14**(15), 431–441 (2017)
31. Molinillo, S., Liébana-Cabanillas, F., Anaya-Sánchez, R.: A social commerce intention model for traditional e-commerce sites. J. Theor. Appl. Electron. Commer. Res. **13**(2), 80–93 (2018)
32. Shanmugam, M., Sun, S., Amidi, A., Khani, F., Khani, F.: The applications of social commerce constructs. Int. J. Inf. Manag. **36**(3), 425–432 (2016)
33. Sheikh, Z., Islam, T., Rana, S., Hameed, Z., Saeed, U.: Acceptance of social commerce framework in Saudi Arabia. Telematics Inform. **34**(8), 1693–1708 (2017)
34. Tajvidi, M., Wang, Y., Hajli, N., Love, P.E.: Brand value co-creation in social commerce: the role of interactivity, social support, and relationship quality. Comput. Hum. Behav. (2017)
35. Liu, H., Chu, H., Huang, Q., Chen, X.: Enhancing the flow experience of consumers in China through interpersonal interaction in social commerce. Comput. Hum. Behav. **58**, 306–314 (2016)
36. Kim, J.B.: The mediating role of presence on consumer intention to participate in a social commerce site. J. Internet Commer. **14**(4), 425–454 (2015)
37. Wu, Y.L., Li, E.Y.: Marketing mix, customer value, and customer loyalty in social commerce: a stimulus-organism-response perspective. Internet Res. **28**(1), 74–104 (2018)

38. Xiang, L., Zheng, X., Lee, M.K., Zhao, D.: Exploring consumers' impulse buying behavior on social commerce platform: the role of parasocial interaction. Int. J. Inf. Manag. **36**(3), 333–347 (2016)
39. Zhang, H., Lu, Y., Gupta, S., Zhao, L.: What motivates customers to participate in social commerce? The impact of technological environments and virtual customer experiences. Inf. Manag. **51**(8), 1017–1030 (2014)
40. Lu, B., Fan, W., Zhou, M.: Social presence, trust, and social commerce purchase intention: an empirical research. Comput. Hum. Behav. **56**, 225–237 (2016)
41. Farivar, S., Turel, O., Yuan, Y.: Skewing users' rational risk considerations in social commerce: an empirical examination of the role of social identification. Inf. Manag. **55**(8), 1038–1048 (2018)
42. Lin, C.S., Wu, S.: Exploring antecedents of online group-buying: social commerce perspective. Hum. Syst. Manag. **34**(2), 133–147 (2015)
43. Bai, Y., Yao, Z., Dou, Y.F.: Effect of social commerce factors on user purchase behavior: an empirical investigation from renren.com. Int. J. Inf. Manag. **35**(5), 538–550 (2015)
44. Ng, C.S.P.: Intention to purchase on social commerce websites across cultures: a cross-regional study. Inf. Manag. **50**(8), 609–620 (2013)
45. Shi, S., Chow, W.S.: Trust development and transfer in social commerce: prior experience as moderator. Ind. Manag. Data Syst. **115**(7), 1182–1203 (2015)
46. Zhang, K.Z., Benyoucef, M., Zhao, S.J.: Building brand loyalty in social commerce: the case of brand microblogs. Electron. Commer. Res. Appl. **15**, 14–25 (2016)
47. Lin, J., Yan, Y., Chen, S.: Understanding the impact of social commerce website technical features on repurchase intention: a Chinese Guanxi perspective. J. Electron. Commer. Res. **18**(3), 225 (2017)
48. Yang, J., Sia, C.L., Liu, L., Chen, H.: Sellers versus buyers: differences in user information sharing on social commerce sites. Inf. Technol. People **29**(2), 444–470 (2016)
49. Lin, J., Luo, Z., Cheng, X., Li, L.: Understanding the interplay of social commerce affordances and swift Guanxi: an empirical study. Inf. Manag. **56**(2), 213–224 (2019)
50. Nadeem, W., Juntunen, M., Juntunen, J.: Consumer segments in social commerce: a latent class approach. J. Consum. Behav. **16**(3), 279–292 (2017)
51. Yahia, I.B., Al-Neama, N., Kerbache, L.: Investigating the drivers for social commerce in social media platforms: importance of trust, social support and the platform perceived usage. J. Retail. Consum. Serv. **41**, 11–19 (2018)
52. Gatautis, R., Medziausiene, A.: Factors affecting social commerce acceptance in Lithuania. Procedia-Soc. Behav. Sci. **110**, 1235–1242 (2014)
53. Noori, A.S., Hashim, K.F., Yusof, S.A.M.: The conceptual relation of electronic word-of-mouth, commitment and trust in influencing continuous usage of social commerce. Int. Rev. Manag. Mark. **6**(7S), 226–230 (2016)
54. Chen, A., Lu, Y., Wang, B.: Customers' purchase decision-making process in social commerce: a social learning perspective. Int. J. Inf. Manag. **37**(6), 627–638 (2017)
55. Chen, A., Lu, Y., Gupta, S.: Enhancing the decision quality through learning from the social commerce components. J. Glob. Inf. Manag. (JGIM) **25**(1), 66–91 (2017)
56. Li, Q., Liang, N., Li, E.Y.: Does friendship quality matter in social commerce? An experimental study of its effect on purchase intention. Electron. Commer. Res. **18**(4), 693–717 (2018)
57. Kim, S., Park, H.: Effects of various characteristics of social commerce (s-commerce) on consumers' trust and trust performance. Int. J. Inf. Manag. **33**(2), 318–332 (2013)
58. Teh, P.L., Ahmed, P.K., Tayi, G.K.: Generation-Y shopping: the impact of network externalities and trust on adoption of social commerce. Int. J. Electron. Bus. **12**(2), 117–141 (2015)

59. Akman, I., Mishra, A.: Factors influencing consumer intention in social commerce adoption. Inf. Technol. People **30**(2), 356–370 (2017)
60. Wang, T., Yeh, R.K.J., Yen, D.C.: Influence of customer identification on online usage and purchasing behaviors in social commerce. Int. J. Hum.-Comput. Interact. **31**(11), 805–814 (2015)
61. Sharma, S., Crossler, R.E.: Disclosing too much? Situational factors affecting information disclosure in social commerce environment. Electron. Commer. Res. Appl. **13**(5), 305–319 (2014)
62. Choi, S.B., Kim, J.M.: A comparative analysis of electronic service quality in the online open market and social commerce: the case of Korean young adults. Serv. Bus. **12**, 403–433 (2018)
63. Li, C.Y., Ku, Y.C.: The power of a thumbs-up: will e-commerce switch to social commerce. Inf. Manag. **55**(3), 340–357 (2018)
64. Osatuyi, B., Qin, H.: How vital is the role of effect on post-adoption behaviors? An examination of social commerce users. Int. J. Inf. Manag. **40**, 175–185 (2018)
65. Pappas, I.O., Kourouthanassis, P.E., Giannakos, M.N., Chrissikopoulos, V.: Explaining online shopping behavior with fsQCA: the role of cognitive and affective perceptions. J. Bus. Res. **69**(2), 794–803 (2016)
66. Mikalef, P., Giannakos, M., Pateli, A.: Shopping and word-of-mouth intentions on social media. J. Theor. Appl. Electron. Commer. Res. **8**(1), 17–34 (2013)
67. Braojos, J., Benitez, J., Llorens, J.: How do social commerce-IT capabilities influence firm performance? Theory and empirical evidence. Inf. Manag. **56**(2), 155–171 (2019)

Care About Your Customer:
A Use and Gratification Study Regarding
Co-creation and Customer Engagement
on Facebook

Patrick Cornelissen[1], Robin Effing[1,2(✉)], and Ton A. M. Spil[1]

[1] University of Twente, P.O. Box 217, 7500 AE Enschede, The Netherlands
`r.effing@utwente.nl`
[2] Saxion University of Applied Sciences, P.O. Box 70.000, 7500 KB Enschede,
The Netherlands

Abstract. Companies and their brands initiated various Co-creation practices on social media. Co-creation improves value for both companies and their customers. This study explored the customer perspective of interest for participating in such Co-creation opportunities on Facebook. Drawing upon the Use and Gratification Theory we investigated the intention of customers to take part in Co-creation on Facebook. We related people's Co-creation behaviour to the expectancy of satisfaction or reward for their actions. Customer Engagement is an additional concept that expresses the emotional attachment of customers to brands and companies. Underlying reasons were investigated why customers would consider taking part in Co-creation. The quantitative survey inquired customers about their expected Benefits, level of Customer Engagement and their intention for taking part in Co-creation with companies on Facebook. Our results showed that Customer Engagement can be considered as the most important predictor for the intention to Co-create instead of User Gratification. Hedonic Benefits are the most important drivers for User Gratification, playing a key role in the people's intention for taking part in Co-creation practices. Overall, people's intention for Co-creation on Facebook increases when they have a meaningful and pleasurable way of experiencing the companies' products that concern them.

Keywords: Social Media · Facebook · Social network sites ·
Customer Engagement · Consumer engagement · Co-creation ·
Use and Gratification Theory

1 Introduction

In 2019, Facebook exists 15 years and has more than 1.5 billion daily users. It was founded by Mark Zuckerberg from Harvard University for connecting with his fellow students in 2004 [1]. Facebook can be typified as a Social Networking Site. These sites give users the ability to make personal profiles and extend social life by befriending others [2]. Organizations can build a presence on Facebook since April 2006 and within two weeks over 4,000 organizations did so [3]. In Europe, over 307 million

© IFIP International Federation for Information Processing 2019
Published by Springer Nature Switzerland AG 2019
I. O. Pappas et al. (Eds.): I3E 2019, LNCS 11701, pp. 13–24, 2019.
https://doi.org/10.1007/978-3-030-29374-1_2

people are active on Facebook. More than 16 Million local business pages have been created since 2013 and next to brand pages many social influencers now promote companies and brands.

The idea behind a social network site such as Facebook is to connect people and companies for bridging and bonding purposes such as Co-creation. Co-creation leads to a unique value for customers, resulting in a personal experience and therefore worthwhile for customers to take part in [4]. As a result from Co-creation practices, companies can ask premium prices for their products which contribute to higher profits [4, 5]. Customers have various reasons to engage with companies and brands such as their desire or need for an emotional attachment with a company or Customer Engagement [6, 7]. Overall, people expect some kind of benefit from engaging and co-creating on Facebook [8, 9]. The Use and Gratification Theory can explain what benefits people expect and why they act [8–11]. However, this theory does not include a possible influence factor of Customer Engagement, emotional attachment or relationship. One previous study by Lee and Kim [8] did explore Co-creation on Social Media, but this study was limited to South-Korea and people that already took part in Co-creation. Furthermore, their study did not include Customer Engagement, which may be an important driver of Co-creation behaviour as well. Nambisan and Baron [9] did include Customer Engagement in their study but again among people that already Co-create.

Therefore, the main aim of this research is to understand why people want to start with Co-creation on Facebook. For this aim, we need to include Customer Engagement and emotional attachment regarding companies and brands. These may be important drivers of Co-creation next to the Perceived Benefits of receiving something in return. We want to refine a model of predictors and their effects on the intention to Co-create on Facebook. This paper explores people's willingness co-create with a company that is present on Facebook. Consequently, this study focuses on Perceived Benefits and Customer Engagement.

The remainder of this paper is structured as follows. First, this research shows a systematic literature review. In the next section, the research method is described including the data analysis approach. The results section is presenting the outcome of multi linear regression analysis. Finally, we present a discussion section including limitations and future research recommendations.

2 Systematic Literature Review

This part of the paper examines existing literature on relevant subjects. The review starts with the Use and Gratification Theory with existing studies are outlined and reviewed in how they explain Co-creation. Thereafter, Customer Engagement is explored in depth and Facebook, Co-creation and Customer Engagement are outlined together. These factors may be important to explain human behavior in general and more specifically Co-creation here. Afterwards the conceptual model is drawn based on the Use and Gratification Theory and Customer Engagement.

2.1   The Use and Gratification Theory

To understand why people would engage and/or Co-create on Facebook with a company, the Use and Gratification Theory is useful. Basically, people seek some sort of gratification for their actions [8–12]. Although this theory is not always explicitly used, the idea of fulfilling goals and needs in regard to using Social Media, engaging and Co-creation is mentioned more often [13–15]. Nambisan and Baron [9] explain why people engage and Co-create from a motivational perspective expecting a kind of gratification from Co-creation on virtual customer environments. There are four motivations as a base for people's action that lead to perceived benefits for the people involved.

First, Cognitive or learning benefits in order to improve usage of products and technologies. Second, Social Integrative benefits which creates a sense of community and one's own social identity. Third, Personal Integrative benefits which gives a sense of accomplishment. Fourth and last, Hedonic benefits which is about pleasure and intellectual stimulants from participating in discussions and such. These motivations of people improve engagement and Co-creation efforts. However, these authors looked into what people that already Co-create on a virtual customer site expect from their actions.

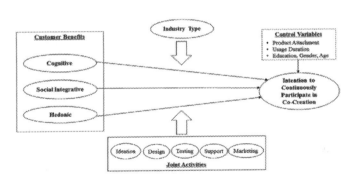

Fig. 1. Research model of Lee and Kim in [8]

Lee and Kim [8] explored why people intend to Continuously Co-create on corporate controlled Social Networking Sites such as Facebook and Twitter through a survey. They asked participants about their most important Co-creation activity, on the long-term and what they expected from their Co-creation. Lee and Kim use the Expectancy-value theory and additionally what value people derive from different Co-creation activities. These benefits are similar to the benefits in the Use and Gratification theory. (Fig. 1) Lee and Kim's [8] study did include Facebook as place for Corporate Social Networking Sites, their study was not specific to Facebook itself or Social Media outside a corporate managed domain. Additionally, it is restricted to South Korea as Lee and Kim note [8] as a limitation. Furthermore, they looked into long-term duration, instead of why people start to engage and Co-create.

3 Customer Engagement and Conceptual Model

Customer Engagement is an emotional attachment, a bond or a psychological state of mind towards a firm [5, 6, 14, 16]. Other views look at Customer Engagement as a behavioural manifestation and something that is relational in nature [7, 15, 17–19]. However, Customer Engagement is always a long term and interactive phenomenon between company and customer. People engage because they want to experience more value-in-use [6, 14, 15, 19, 20] or be entertained [6, 18]. But relevant here is the emotional or relationship value people expect from engaging with companies [6, 15, 21]. People may start to advocate or advertise on behalf of the company when they are engaged [22]. Engagement ranges from interaction, then participation and towards Co-creation itself as highest level [7] and people even start to help in production [17].

3.1 Underlying Dimensions of Customer Engagement

Customer Engagement is a very broad term in itself and often not well defined. However, this part explains the dimensions used in the survey more in depth. Importance is connected to one's own identity and goals [15], while in [9] importance is mentioned to perceived importance and product involvement. Lee and Kim [8] use importance in connection to the use of a product or service. Relevance is connected to possible benefits [9], but does not give a definition of relevance in itself. Likewise, Lee and Kim [8] do not define relevance of a product, but seem to connect this with the regular use or daily need of a product or service. Meaning, Nambisan and Baron [9] point out that meaning comes from long-term interactions with other community members. Sashi [22] too points at long term interactions, but this is focused on the company itself. However, Brodie et al. [7] mention that meaning comes from a connection to work or daily life in the broadest sense. Concern, again Lee and Kim [8] use this in relation to the use of products and services, but offer no definition or explanation on how a product may concern someone. Nambisan and Baron [9] mention concern in relation to product attachment, indicating an emotional reason. Overall, it is unclear where these underlying dimensions really differ from one and other. Importance and Relevancy appear more connected to the use of a product or service itself. While Meaning is related to long-term relationships and Concern seems to be affectional.

3.2 Facebook, Customer Engagement and Co-creation

These parts show where the subjects of Facebook, Customer Engagement and Co-creation overlap and relate to each other. People look for relationships with others and communities on Facebook [23], being able to receive information about friends and interests posted on profiles [11]. However, people can connect and relate to a shared object such as a company too [23]. Facebook gives companies and customers the ability to reach out and connect to each other [24]. People have various reasons to engage with companies, Muntinga et al. in [10] mention that people seek a kind of gratification. Similarly, Phua et al. [11] mention the need for gratification on Facebook such as socializing and entertainment. The interactive nature of Facebook strengthens the relationship value and community [25], which stimulates relationships to become long-term and emotional [26].

As a result, Facebook is an effective place to engage with customers. As people engage on Facebook with companies, they start to share content, comment on content and create their own content [24, 27, 28]. People are actually providing marketing work for the company such as word-of-mouth [24, 29]. Furthermore, people can provide support to others, test products or even help create them [8]. Customer Engagement and Co-creation are related to each other. While Co-creation may always be present, the active participation of Customer Engagement is not always there [13, 14]. People start to actively Co-create when they become engaged to the company [14, 15, 24, 30, 31]. Facebook allows people to interact through personalized profiles and possibly interact with a company of their choosing. The value of a product or a service also depends on the customer [32]. Co-creation can provide benefits for people and companies and people may intent to Co-create when they expect something in return.

3.3 Conceptual Model

From the Use and Gratification theory, the following conceptual model (Fig. 2) is drawn. People may be willing to Co-create when they expect benefits from that action. These benefits come from Cognitive, Social, Personal or Hedonic causes. Lee and Kim in [8] found that the control variables Usage duration, Education, Gender and Age were not significant and therefore left out in the survey of this study. They found that the control variable Product attachment is important, however, attachment is larger than a single product and can extend to a brand or a whole company. Therefore, Customer Engagement may be a better control variable then Product attachment as Customer Engagement extents to a whole company.

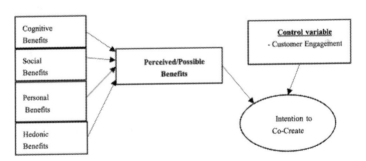

Fig. 2. Conceptual model

4   Methodology and Hypotheses

A structured literature review helped to find existing knowledge, theories and possible models [33, 34]. Furthermore, it helped to investigate what is known, where opportunities for research exist and what possible relationships are between subjects [35]. In Table 1 we present our keyword phrases and terms. These terms were then filtered on the last decade for the most recent studies, filtered on Business as the context for this study and the filter Highly Cited was used to extract the most important articles from these. In order to collect data for this research, a survey with Likert questions that allow reliability, precision and the correct scope was used [36]. The questions were designed based on Lee and Kim [8] and Nambisan and Baron [9] in order to ask people about their dispositions on User Gratification and Customer Engagement. These measures are then analysed with Reliability measures, Validity measures and a Factor Analysis to review if they accurately represent their intended constructs. After this a multi linear regression was conducted to test the hypotheses mentioned below. Finally, the results of the regression are used to create the analysis model to show where and how the constructs relate to one and other.

Table 1. Search results from keywords on web of science

Keywords	Total	Filtered	Included
Customer Engagement	18,966	16	8
Co-creation	22,722	83	8
Facebook	13,410	17	9
Facebook & Customer Engagement	328	8	6
Facebook & Co-creation	66	30	6
Co-creation & Customer Engagement	448	20	8
Facebook, Co-creation & Customer Engagement	22	22	7

Furthermore, to establish reliability and validity, Confirmatory Factor Analysis with an Oblique rotation is done to review the variables and their intended constructs as factors are expected to be correlated [37]. Additionally, Cronbach's Alpha, Composite Reliability, Convergent Validity and Divergent Validity are necessary statistics to establish reliability and validity of the measurements before modelling [37]. After this, single and multi linear regression are used to tests hypotheses and to build an appropriate model to reveal how constructs relate to each other. According to the Use and Gratification Theory, people expect certain benefits or values from their actions. Based on theory, as people expect higher Benefits from Co-creation on Facebook people will intend to co-create more on Facebook. Customer Engagement may be of influence on the benefits or a predictor for the intention to Co-create on Facebook in itself and therefore is expressed as a separate independent. From the use and Gratification Theory and Customer Engagement the following hypotheses are derived:

H1: Perceived Benefits increase the intention to Co-create.
- H1a: Perceived Cognitive Benefits increases the intention to Co-create.
- H1b: Perceived Social Benefits increases the intention to Co-create.
- H1c: Perceived Personal Benefits increases the intention to Co-create.
- H1d: Perceived Hedonic Benefits increases the intention to Co-create.

H2: Customer Engagement mediates the relationship between Perceived Benefits and the intention to Co-create.

H3: Customer Engagement increases the intention to Co-create.

5   Data Collection and Results

Data for this study has been collected through an online survey. The survey was spread through Facebook, LinkedIn and available student email lists of the university. The survey was sent on the 31st of August 2018. Some reminders were sent during the time the survey was active and the survey closed on the morning of the 17th of September 2018 with a total of n = 104 replies and imported to SPSS.

Since this research has a theoretical model to test, a Confirmatory Factor analysis was conducted with an Oblique (direct Oblimin) rotation as factors are expected to be correlated (see Table 2). Factors with a loading of 0.55 or greater are to be included for a sample size of 104. There are no cross-loading variables showing that all Factors are unique (CB2; PB3, PB4; HB3; CE1, CE2 have been removed).

Table 2. Results factor analysis

Factor	1	2	3	4	5	6
CB Q1	0,105	−0,060	0,757	0,057	0,022	−0,115
CB Q3	0,063	0,086	0,756	−0,043	0,024	0,109
CB Q4	−0,088	0,006	0,784	−0,009	0,022	−0,096
SB Q1	0,006	0,936	−0,048	−0,019	−0,030	−0,039
SB Q2	0,070	0,728	0,050	0,037	0,176	−0,056
SB Q3	−0,016	0,599	0,188	−0,215	0,001	0,013
PB Q1	0,042	0,262	−0,037	0,078	0,718	−0,005
PB Q2	−0,008	−0,138	0,100	−0,116	0,901	−0,042
HB Q1	0,015	−0,040	−0,057	−0,967	0,056	−0,036
HB Q2	0,056	0,117	0,053	−0,781	−0,028	−0,036
CE Q3	0,063	0,054	0,127	−0,050	−0,019	−0,827
CE Q4	0,002	0,004	−0,036	−0,018	0,027	−0,854
CC Q1	0,915	−0,055	0,053	−0,043	0,027	0,037
CC Q2	0,963	0,063	−0,041	0,023	0,011	0,011
CC Q3	0,886	−0,015	0,012	−0,024	−0,042	−0,095

Hedonic Benefits show to consist of an Enjoyable and Relaxing time and Fun and Pleasure, while problem-solving and idea-generation are not part of this construct. For the Customer Engagement questions in particular, the removed questions were about Importance and Relevancy of the use of a product or service. The included questions were about Meaning and Concern regarding products and services from the company. According to the factor analysis, Customer Engagement here is linked to long-term interactions and an emotional attachment instead of the use of a product itself.

In order to reduce measurement error, represent multiple facets of a concept and to optimize for prediction, Summated Scores were created based on the results from the Factor Analysis. (Table 2) For these scales, reliability and validity is verified in Table 3. Additionally, Divergent Validity was established in order to verify that the constructs are indeed different. With the constructs verified, it is then necessary to assess whether (multiple) linear regression can be done. Sample size requirements include N > 100 and preferably 15–20 observations per independent variable which are met. In addition, each scale needs to be normally distributed and the independents have to be correlated to the dependent both are shown to be so for all scales.

Table 3. Reliability and AVE for each factor

Factor	Construct	Included	A > 0.7	CR > 0.7	AVE > 0.5
1	Cognitive benefits	CB-Q1 CB-Q3 CB-Q4	0,845	0,810	0,586
2	Social benefits	SB-Q1 SB-Q2 SB-Q3	0,873	0,806	0,588
3	Hedonic benefits	HB-Q1 HB-Q2	0,917	0,870	0,773
4	Co-creation	CC-Q1 CC-Q2 CC-Q3	0,954	0,945	0,851
5	Personal benefits	PB-Q1 PB-Q2	0,836	0,796	0,664
6	Customer Engagement	CE-Q3 CE-Q4	0,896	0,828	0,706

Furthermore, this study analysed the four assumptions for linearity for each independent towards the dependent the Intention to Co-create existing out of: 1. Linearity of the phenomenon based on residual plot and plots of the independent towards the dependent itself. 2. Constant variance of error terms, using the residual plot and conducting Levene's tests in One-way ANOVA's. 3. Independence of error terms using the Durbin-Watson statistic. And lastly 4. Normality of error terms, using the Histogram and Normal Probability plot of residuals. Examining these assumptions showed that Hedonic Benefits and Customer Engagement at first failed to achieve the second Constant Variance of Error Terms criterium. But after stabilizing the dependent variable with a natural logarithmic all assumptions are met for all variables.

With the constructs showing reliability, validity and the assumptions for linear regression met, the hypotheses for each independent towards dependent is tested. The first part of the hypotheses is about the possible influence of the Perceived Benefits onto the intention to Co-create on Facebook. The second part about Customer Engagement as possible mediator or moderator and the third part about Customer Engagement as a separate predictor. Single linear regression shows that every Perceived Benefit has a statistically significant ($p < 0.001$) influence on the intention to Co-create, meaning that gratification does matter for the intention to Co-create and confirming the first set of hypotheses. Noteworthy is that Hedonics Benefits (0.502, t value of 5.862) and Cognitive Benefits (0.451, t value of 5.108) are the largest predictors. Social Benefits (0.380, t value of 4.153) and Personal Benefits (0.286, t value of 3.012) are smaller predictors of the intention to Co-create on Facebook.

Furthermore, Customer Engagement does not function as a mediator or moderator. Using it as such does not result in statistical significance and additionally results in multicollinearity issues in modelling which means that the second hypothesis is rejected. However, Customer Engagement does have a statistically significant ($p < 0.001$) influence on the intention to Co-create, confirming the third and last hypothesis. Moreover, Customer Engagement shows to have the largest influence (0.539, t value of 6.471) on the intention to Co-create among the predictors.

6 Analysis

The model was created and tested in SPSS through the Enter method and verified using the Stepwise method. Using all four benefits and Customer Engagement as predictors showed a lack of statistically significant betas and adjusted R squared for Cognitive, Personal and Social Benefits. Finally, Customer Engagement and Hedonic Benefits proofed to be predictors of the intention to Co-create.

In order to further verify this model, a split sample of 60%:40% was created randomly. Using the Enter method we verified Customer Engagement and Hedonic Benefits as significant predictors for both groups. Figure 3 shows the analysis model with the influence of each predictor on the intention to Co-create. Cognitive, Social and Personal benefits are not important in themselves to predict the intention to Co-create, perceived gratification is explained by Hedonic Benefits alone. Customer Engagement is a larger predictor than Hedonic Benefits, note that the included questions for Customer Engagement were about Product Meaning and Product Concern, both very relevant for Customer Engagement. People that find a company and its products meaningful and of concern to them are motivated to Co-create more than gratification does. The questions about Hedonic Benefits were about an Enjoyable and Relaxing time and a Fun and Pleasurable experience.

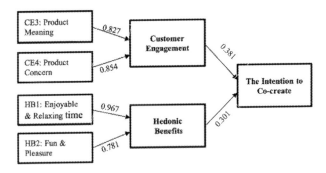

Fig. 3. Analysis model

7 Discussion

We delivered a predictive model for the intention to Co-create (Fig. 3). Results show that each separate benefit does improve the intention to Co-create, but remarkably, modelling showed that Hedonic Benefits are the most important and explain most of the perceived gratification. User Gratification does influence the intention to Co-create on Facebook, but not that much as Customer Engagement. Hedonic Benefits explains most of the gratification through the desire of people for an enjoyable and relaxing time. Customer Engagement functions as a separate independent factor. Hence, the factors Customer Engagement and Hedonic Benefits predict the intention to Co-create on Facebook.

Our results have various practical implications. In order to motivate customers to Co-create on Facebook, companies need to deliver Product Meaning and Product Concern. People are motivated by meaning, engagement with a company's products and by having fun while doing so for their intention to Co-creation. Customers want a meaningful experience in terms of long-term relationships with others, the company and its products. They want to feel an emotional connection with the company's products and want a pleasurable time. Gratification itself is not that important. Only Hedonic Benefits are significant as predictor in the model. Hedonic Benefits exists out of an Enjoyable and Relaxing time and a Fun and Pleasurable experience, while Problem Solving and Idea Generation are not fun for people here in contrast to previous studies [8, 9].

With regard to theory, the differences between the underlying dimensions are actually quite different based on factor analysis. Customer Engagement is a predictor on its own instead of a mediator or moderator as theory suggests. Moreover, the results show that Meaning and Concern are relevant underlying dimensions, while Importance and Relevancy are not. This is different from previous research that showed all dimensions to be important [8, 9]. The results mean that long-term relationships and an emotional attachment are important for Customer Engagement in this study.

Customer Engagement is about relationships and emotions, not about the use of a product or service. Intrinsic motivations with regards to meaning and concern may be more important than the extrinsic rewards gratification offers for Co-creation on Facebook. While Lee and Kim [8] did not use Customer Engagement as a possible predictor, we did and showed its importance. One could argue that meaning and concern are similar to benefits or gratification, but Factor Analysis showed that gratification and Customer Engagement are different constructs. Moreover, Discriminant Validity was established showing that Customer Engagement and Hedonic Benefits are separate constructs. In the end, Customer Engagement seems to be an important predictor for the intention to Co-create on Facebook and even better than gratification.

There are three important limitations regarding our findings. Firstly, we asked people about the intention to Co-create instead of participation data in Co-creation. For future research it may proof useful to consider what lies behind people's motivation for Co-creation. Secondly, while this research was carried out within Europe, other regions and other social media may provide different results. Finally, Co-creation could be studied in more detail when elaborating upon Meaning, Concern and intrinsic motivations over gratification and extrinsic motivations.

References

1. Kaplan, A.M., Haenlein, M.: Users of the world, unite! The challenges and opportunities of social media. Bus. Horiz. **53**, 59–68 (2010)
2. Hennig-Thurau, T., et al.: The impact of new media on customer relationships. J. Serv. Res. **13**, 311–330 (2010)
3. Waters, R.D., Burnett, E., Lamm, A., Lucas, J.: Engaging stakeholders through social networking: how nonprofit organizations are using Facebook. Publ. Relat. Rev. **35**, 102–106 (2009)
4. Cova, B., Dalli, D., Zwick, D.: Critical perspectives on consumers' role as "producers": broadening the debate on value co-creation in marketing processes. Mark. Theory. **11**, 231–241 (2011)
5. Grönroos, C., Voima, P.: Critical service logic: making sense of value creation and co-creation. J. Acad. Mark. Sci. **41**, 133–150 (2013)
6. Brodie, R.J., Ilic, A., Juric, B., Hollebeek, L.: Consumer engagement in a virtual brand community: an exploratory analysis. J. Bus. Res. **66**, 105–114 (2013)
7. Brodie, R.J., Hollebeek, L.D., Jurić, B., Ilić, A.: Customer engagement: conceptual domain, fundamental propositions, and implications for research. J. Serv. Res. **14**, 252–271 (2011)
8. Lee, A.R., Kim, K.K.: Customer benefits and value co-creation activities in corporate social networking services. Behav. Inf. Technol. **37**, 675–692 (2018)
9. Nambisan, S., Baron, R.A.: Virtual customer environments: testing a model of voluntary participation in value co-creation activities. J. Prod. Innov. Manag. **26**, 388–406 (2009)
10. Muntinga, D.G., Moorman, M., Smit, E.G.: Introducing COBRAs: exploring motivations for Brand-Related social media use. Int. J. Advert. **30**, 13–46 (2011)
11. Phua, J., Jin, S.V., Kim, J.(Jay): Gratifications of using Facebook, Twitter, Instagram, or Snapchat to follow brands: the moderating effect of social comparison, trust, tie strength, and network homophily on brand identification, brand engagement, brand commitment, and membership intention. Telematics Inform. **34**, 412–424 (2017)
12. Pappas, I.O., Papavlasopoulou, S., Kourouthanassis, P.E., Mikalef, P., Giannakos, M.N.: Motivations and emotions in social media: explaining users' satisfaction with FsQCA. In: Kar, A.K., et al. (eds.) I3E 2017. LNCS, vol. 10595, pp. 375–387. Springer, Cham (2017). https://doi.org/10.1007/978-3-319-68557-1_33
13. Etgar, M.: A descriptive model of the consumer co-production process. J. Acad. Mark. Sci. **36**, 97–108 (2008)
14. Payne, A.F., Storbacka, K., Frow, P.: Managing the co-creation of value. J. Acad. Mark. Sci. **36**, 83–96 (2008)
15. van Doorn, J., et al.: Customer engagement behavior: Theoretical foundations and research directions. J. Serv. Res. **13**, 253–266 (2010)
16. Schau, H.J., Muñiz, A.M., Arnould, E.J.: How brand community practices create value. J. Mark. **73**, 30–51 (2009)
17. Kunz, W., et al.: Customer engagement in a big data world. J. Serv. Mark. **31**, 161–171 (2017)
18. Dolan, R., Conduit, J., Fahy, J., Goodman, S.: Social media engagement behaviour: a uses and gratifications perspective. J. Strateg. Mark. **24**, 261–277 (2016)
19. Malthouse, E.C., Haenlein, M., Skiera, B., Wege, E., Zhang, M.: Managing customer relationships in the social media era: introducing the social CRM house. J. Interact. Mark. **27**, 270–280 (2013)
20. Hoyer, W.D., Chandy, R., Dorotic, M., Krafft, M., Singh, S.S.: Consumer cocreation in new product development. J. Serv. Res. **13**, 283–296 (2010)

21. Palmatier, R.W., Dant, R.P., Grewal, D., Evans, K.R.: Factors influencing the effectiveness of relationship marketing. J. Mark. **70**, 136–153 (2006)
22. Sashi, C.M.: Customer engagement, buyer-seller relationships, and social media. Manag. Decis. **50**, 253–272 (2012)
23. Kietzmann, J.H., Hermkens, K., McCarthy, I.P., Silvestre, B.S.: Social media? Get serious! Understanding the functional building blocks of social media. Bus. Horiz. **54**, 241–251 (2011)
24. Hanna, R., Rohm, A., Crittenden, V.L.: We're all connected: the power of the social media ecosystem. Bus. Horiz. **54**, 265–273 (2011)
25. Turri, A.M., Smith, K.H.: Developing affective brand commitment through social media. J. Electron. Commer. Res. **14**, 201–215 (2013)
26. Rolland, S.E., Parmentier, G.: The benefit of social media: Bulletin board focus groups as a tool for co-creation. Int. J. Mark. Res. **55**, 809 (2014)
27. Sorensen, A., Andrews, L., Drennan, J.: Using social media posts as resources for engaging in value co-creation: the case for social media-based cause brand communities. J. Serv. Theory Pract. **27**, 898–922 (2017)
28. Westberg, K., Stavros, C., Smith, A.C.T., Munro, G., Argus, K.: An examination of how alcohol brands use sport to engage consumers on social media. Drug Alcohol Rev. **37**, 28–35 (2018)
29. Huang, S., Chen, C.: How consumers become loyal fans on Facebook. Comput. Hum. Behav. **82**, 124–135 (2018)
30. Jaakkola, E., Alexander, M.: The role of customer engagement behavior in value co-creation: a service system perspective. J. Serv. Res. **17**, 247–261 (2014)
31. Nambisan, S.: Designing virtual customer environments for new product development: toward a theory. Acad. Manag. Rev. **27**, 392–413 (2002)
32. Pappas, I., Mikalef, P., Giannakos, M., Pavlou, P.: Value co-creation and trust in social commerce: an fsQCA approach. In: Proceedings 25th European Conference on Information Systems, pp. 2153–2168 (2017)
33. Bryman, A., Bell, E.: Business Research Methods. Oxford University Press, Oxford (2015)
34. Saunders, M., Lewis, P., Thornhill, A., Booij, M., Verckens, J.P.: Methoden en technieken van onderzoek. Pearson Education Benelux, Amsterdam (2011)
35. Wolfswinkel, J.F., Furtmueller, E., Wilderom, C.P.M.: Using grounded theory as a method for rigorously reviewing literature. Eur. J. Inf. Syst. **22**, 45–55 (2013)
36. Spector, P.E.: Summated Rating Scale Construction. Sara Miller McCune, SAGE Publications, INC., Iowa City (1992)
37. Hair Jr., J.F., Black, W.C., Babin, B.J., Anderson, R.E.: Multivariate Data Analysis. Pearson Education Limited, Essex (2014)

Exploring the Effects of Value Added Services on Perceived Value of Mobile Payment in the UK

Hassan Alhallaq[⊠], Muhammad Younas, Samia Kamal, and Bob Champion

Oxford Brookes University, Oxford, UK
hhallaq@gmail.com,
{m.younas,skamal,rchampion}@brookes.ac.uk

Abstract. Mobile payment (m-payment) apps have been introduced as an innovative alternative payment method that extends in-store payment options available to consumers. Despite being marketed as convenient and secure, recent research reports that m-payment uptake has gone far below earlier forecasts. This is due to consumers perceiving little added value relative to existing payment options, such as contactless cards. Augmenting m-payment with value added services (VAS) has been suggested as a way to add value to m-payment and boost demand. However, empirical investigation about the role and effect of VAS on consumers' perceptions of m-payment value remains scant. This study attempts to fill this gap by employing a deductive qualitative approach through the lens of perceived value theory, extended with perceived trust and risk. A total of 23 interviews were conducted with UK adopters and nonadopters of m-payment. The findings suggest that the perceived added value of the augmented m-payment service was mainly derived from utilitarian values associated with the additional functionalities offered by VAS. Additionally, the augmentation of m-payment has enhanced perceptions of trust in the service provider as a result of integrating additional features that tackle issues associated with the payment experience. This study advances knowledge of the concept of added value in the m-payment context and provides practical suggestions to m-payment providers for increasing the consumer perceived value.

Keywords: Mobile payment · Perceived value · Value added services

1 Introduction

The rapid technological advances in the past decade have changed the payments landscape worldwide. As a result, new payment instruments, such as mobile and wearable devices, have emerged as convenient and secure alternatives to traditional cards and cash payment methods for in-store payments. However, the success of these alternatives is heavily influenced by consumers' decisions to change their longstanding payment behaviours. Although mobile devices have achieved a massive success as reflected in penetration rates among consumers worldwide, their mobile payment (m-payment) apps appear to be lagging far behind. Recent market research reveals that

© IFIP International Federation for Information Processing 2019
Published by Springer Nature Switzerland AG 2019
I. O. Pappas et al. (Eds.): I3E 2019, LNCS 11701, pp. 25–36, 2019.
https://doi.org/10.1007/978-3-030-29374-1_3

proximity m-payment in the UK is far from mass adoption [1]. This is despite the fact that the main proximity m-payment wallet apps (Apple Pay, Android Pay, Samsung Pay) natively provided by the dominant global mobile handset manufacturers were commercially introduced within the past four years in the UK. Previous studies suggested that perceptions of risk involved in the use of proximity m-payment act as a strong barrier to adoption among UK consumers [2]. On the other hand, it has been repeatedly argued that consumers' reluctance to change their old payment habits is due to seeing no added value in m-payment as compared to traditional payment methods [3–5]. This appears to be particularly relevant to the case of the UK, where the increasing popularity of contactless cards has arguably made m-payment as a less valued alternative among consumers [6]. However, the way consumers would perceive m-payment added value has not been fully investigated by existing research.

Value maximization is regarded as the basic assumption in examining the consumer's eventual behaviour since potential adopters of new digital services play the dual role of technology users and consumers [7]. Therefore, with a set of multiple options, consumers often seek to maximize their utility or enjoyment from the consumption of a given market offering [8]. This implies that determinants of consumer choice decisions are subjectively evaluated on a net value basis perceived in a given option relative to other alternatives. Findings from previous research have concluded that augmenting the m-payment service with value added services (VAS) might add value to m-payment and promote demand [3, 4, 8]. Although these findings offer useful insights into the potential effect of VAS in increasing the value of m-payment, supporting empirical evidence confirming this effect among consumers is still lacking. This study aims to fill this gap by addressing the following research question: *What is the effect and role of VAS on the perceived value of m-payment from a consumer's perspective?* In doing so, we employed the perceived value theory extended with perceived trust in provider and perceived risk as our theoretical foundation. We conducted a qualitative investigation in the UK to explore how consumers perceive the added value of augmenting proximity m-payment apps with three exemplified VAS suggested by previous studies: instant account balance, loyalty cards integration, and cashback. Our key findings indicate that the perceived added value of the augmented m-payment app has been largely interpreted in terms of the additional convenience, monetary and trust benefits brought by the extra features of the VAS. These findings highlight the importance of addressing other activities involved in the payment experience. The remainder of this paper is organized as follows. In Sect. 2 we lay out the theoretical foundation of the study, followed by the research methodology in Sect. 3. The results and findings are presented in Sect. 4. In Sect. 5, the paper concludes with the research implications and provides directions for future research.

2 Theoretical Background and Related Work

Existing m-payment adoption research has offered a rich investigation into the factors that affect adoption decisions among consumers using well-established information systems (IS) theories, such as TAM (Technology Acceptance Model) and UTAUT (Unified Theory of Acceptance and Use of Technology) [10]. Although this body of research has been useful in terms of highlighting factors related to the characteristics of m-payment as a technology, some researchers argued that theories from other disciplines should be used to explore other factors pertinent to the adoption of m-payment as a new interactive payment experience that coexists with other widely used payment methods [e.g. 10, 11]. This study responds to this call by employing the perceived value theory, which has roots in marketing literature, as a suitable theoretical lens that fits the aim of investigation.

2.1 Perceived Value Theory and Its Determinants

Perceived value has been used to explain behavioural intentions towards different technologies [e.g. 7, 12]. Conceptually, perceived value has emerged in marketing literature as the trade-off between a combination of multiple determinants of benefits and sacrifices as perceived by consumers in a market offering [13]. As the definition suggests, value is subjectively weighed by consumers for what they receive against what they give to acquire and use a product. Following on previous value-based technology adoption research [e.g. 14, 15], we draw on the seminal PERVAL model of Sweeney and Soutar [16] and consider the determinants of benefits as functional, social, and enjoyment values. The functional value has been conceptualized as two separate utilitarian values that consumers derive from performance-related attributes and monetary gains perceived in a product or service [16]. While the performance aspect of functional value is derived from the convenience of fulfilling a task, monetary gains represent the time and money saved as a result of using mobile services [14]. Convenience value appears to be of a particular importance within the context of m-payment due to the ubiquity of the mobile phone [17]. Therefore, we define *convenience value* as the consumer's perceived utility from the ease of acquiring and using m-payment as a service accessible anytime and anywhere. Similarly, a positive relationship has been confirmed between perceived economic benefits and use of m-payment for in-store shopping [15]. Thus, we define *monetary value* as the consumer's perceived utility of the money savings resulting from the use of m-payment. Consumer behaviour research suggests that consumer's choice is influenced by experiential aspects represented in enjoyment and social values in addition to the utilitarian goals [18]. The enjoyment aspect of value, also termed as emotional or hedonic, is conceptualized as the product or service capability to arouse feelings or affective states [19]. We therefore define *enjoyment value* as the positive feelings that the consumer derives from interacting with m-payment apps. The social value reflects the extent to which a product or service enhances social self-image and interpersonal communication in a social setting [16, 19]. Previous studies have confirmed the influence of social value on perceived value of proximity m-payment [12]. In a similar vein, we define *social value* as a source of self-appreciation perceived from the impression conveyed by peers in a social context with regard to the use of m-payment. In addition, we augment the above determinants of value with *perceived trust* in service provider as a benefit and *perceived risk* as a nonmonetary sacrifice due to their profound effect on consumer intentions to transact using technology-based environments [20]. Since the interaction between consumers and m-payment providers lacks direct personal communication, trust beliefs in providers play an essential role in choosing their services.

The value created by perceived trust results from the benefits received through interacting with a competent and benevolent provider in addition to the role of trust in reducing uncertainties involved in service use [21]. Moreover, previous studies have shown that perceptions of risk exhibited a salient effect on the perceived value of m-payment [12, 15].

2.2   The Concept of Added Value

Different approaches have been suggested in marketing literature to increase the value of a market offering relative to competitors [22]. Zeithaml [13] broadly argues that added value can be achieved by increasing perceptions of benefits or reducing perceptions of sacrifices in a given product. On the other hand, Grönroos [23] has distinguished between core value brought by the core solution and added value resulting from the additional services. The author has also conceptualized additional services as the VAS offered along with the core service to enhance its perceived value and minimize the associated monetary and nonmonetary costs. In this sense, the concept of added value can be regarded as a multidimensional construct that includes both functional and emotional benefits as perceived by consumers [22]. Therefore, it could be argued that added value can be realized directly through perceived gains or indirectly as a result of reducing sacrifices or both. In this study, we explore how consumers perceive added value in proximity m-payment augmented with VAS through the lens of the theorized determinants of value extended with perceived trust and risk.

3   Methodology and Data Collection

The subjective nature of the concept of value and the relative newness of VAS in the m-payment context have led to the decision to use a qualitative research approach using semi-structured interviews. Qualitative methods have been suggested in IS research as a suitable approach for understanding the meanings a given system has for its users and unveil the processes involved in causal relationships [24]. Snowball sampling technique was utilized by asking participants invited through university research groups and social contacts to share the invitation with their contacts. The selection criteria were set to include participants who use a smartphone, regardless of previous m-payment experience, and were residents of the UK. The interview guide was first piloted with two PhD students and their comments were taken into consideration to clarify questions that had not been fully understood. A total of 23 interviews were conducted between November 2017 and April 2018, with an average duration of 37 min. Table 1 provides a summary of the characteristics of the participants.

The final interview guide comprised three sections. In the first section, participants were briefed about the aim of the study and asked general demographic questions. In the second section, participants were presented with the definition of each of the theorized determinants of perceived value followed by questions about their perceptions of the presented determinant in terms of using m-payment as a sole service. This method allowed participants to define each value determinant in their own words and contextualize their answers around the use scenarios of m-payment.

Table 1. Demographics of participants

Measure	Group	Number of participants	m-payment adopters
Age	18–24	4	1
	25–34	11	5
	35–44	6	None
	45–54	1	1
	55–60	1	None
Gender	Male	16	5
	Female	7	2
Occupation	Full-time employment	12	3
	Full-time student	10	4
	Retired	1	None

In the third section, three VAS have been chosen for this study based on suggestions from previous research and relevance to the UK market, namely instant account balance [3], loyalty card integration [9], and cashback rewards [25]. Following the introduction of the open banking initiative in the UK in January 2018, regulated third-party payment service providers will be able to provide account information services to consumers upon their consent [26]. It is thus of a great importance to understand how consumers would perceive value in future m-payment apps featuring instant account balance. The choice of loyalty card integration stemmed from the popularity of loyalty programs provided by high street retailers in the UK. Although some existing m-payment wallet apps offer the functionality of storing loyalty cards, understanding its effect on m-payment value is scarce. Finally, the cashback reward was chosen based on previous research suggesting that UK consumers are encouraged to use proximity m-payment apps that offer financial incentives [2]. Each of the suggested VAS was introduced to participants followed by questions about their perceptions of using m-payment augmented with the given value added service in terms of the value determinants. The purpose was to elicit their views about each of the suggested services individually. Interview recordings were transcribed and content-analysed using Nvivo 11 software. Data analysis involved labelling segments of the transcripts with descriptive codes that summarize the participant's views about the topic addressed in each segment. The codes were then categorized under the respective value theme that corresponded to one of the theorized value determinants. As coding and data collection took place simultaneously, the sampling continued until a data saturation point has been reached, where no new codes could be identified.

4 Results and Findings

Though the interview questions covered both the use of m-payment as a standalone service and m-payment augmented with VAS, this paper focuses on the results and findings of the latter. However, a summary of the findings relating to the use of m-payment as a sole service will be presented to contrast the effect of the VAS. More details about these findings can be found in our previous study [5].

4.1 Convenience Value

Most m-payment adopters have expressed their perception of convenience of proximity m-payment as a sole service in terms of the ubiquity of the mobile phone, the speed and ease of making m-payment, and the time and effort saved from not having to handle physical cards. Conversely, most nonadopters considered m-payment as more time consuming and less convenient compared to contactless card payment. Augmenting m-payment with an instant balance service was perceived by some participants as an added convenience for saving the time and effort needed to check the balance using different channels: *"it means that I don't have to go to different places to find the same information"* (P11). In addition, participants embraced the convenience of getting real-time balance updates after each purchase as compared to card payments that, in some instances, take longer to take effect. Integrating loyalty cards with m-payment was perceived by most participants as an added convenience value in terms of easier manageability of loyalty cards of different retailers in one place and reduced transaction time at check-out: *"you currently have to hand over two cards…so there is no question that it would factually speedup the process plus you would never forget them"* (P19). On the other hand, some participants noted that the need to scan a digital version of the loyalty card stored on the mobile phone does not offer much advantage in terms of convenience over scanning the physical card. They suggested that the integration should be seamless, where the m-payment app recognizes the retailer being paid for and transfers the points to the respective stored loyalty card. A few participants, who were familiar with cashback schemes, mentioned that having cashback integrated with a m-payment app would simplify the process of claiming cashback and locating deals through the app. In this sense, they recognized convenience in terms of the app's capability to contextually identify and suggest cashback deals based on location and payment patterns: *"…if I am in town deciding where to eat then my first thought would be my app to see if there are any offers that I can claim"* (P20).

4.2 Monetary Value

An overwhelming majority of the participants, regardless of their previous experience with m-payment, saw no monetary value from using proximity m-payment as a sole service. In contrast, participants perceived an added monetary value from seeing the account balance before making a payment as it would help to reduce 'blind' payments resulting from the absence of actual cash: *"Having lost cash, I and everyone I know has become a bit more lax with how they spend money … I think for me all of the savings come from an intuitive understanding of: do I have enough money to afford the treat of x today?"* (P7). Additionally, some participants anticipated that seeing the balance before and after the payment would help more with budgeting rather than being a means of direct money saving. However, participants who seemed to be organized in terms of their finances were hesitant to recognize any monetary gains from checking their balance before or after payments. The added monetary value that participants perceived in m-payment augmented with loyalty cards was based on simplifying the process of earning loyalty points. They mentioned that loyalty points are frequently missed because they often forget scanning loyalty cards at checkout. Having loyalty cards of different retailers visible alongside payment cards was observed as an efficient way to increase utilization of loyalty schemes: "*it would be easier for you to use them to collect points*" (P17). The cashback service was dominantly embraced by many participants as a financial incentive to use m-payment apps. The monetary value that participants perceived seems to outweigh their negative perceptions of reduced convenience from using the app: "*I suppose if it does make the paying process in anyway longer or more convoluted then ... it's definitely an inconvenience that I would put up to save a bit of money*" (P15). These findings demonstrate the potential high impact of monetary value on the perceived value of m-payment.

4.3   Enjoyment Value

Convenience related factors have generally emerged as the main drivers of enjoyment regardless of m-payment augmentation with VAS. The participants perceived enjoyment of m-payment as a frictionless and fast-paced experience. However, they perceived additional affective values based on the extra features of VAS. Receiving balance updates in real-time was regarded as an emotional benefit for being worry-free about their finances and eliminating the need to check balances through different channels: "*It would just make me have a greater quality of life, it would just be another thing that I don't have to do every week because I am already doing it every time I pay*" (P20). Likewise, simplifying the management of loyalty cards in one app and being rewarded with loyalty points were regarded as an additional positive emotional benefit of the app. On the other hand, participants were very enthusiastic about the attainable monetary gains of the cashback service: "*...I think getting the money back would certainly make you enjoy [m-payment] and it would give extra pennies to do other things that you would enjoy*" (P4). This finding suggests monetary value as another possible source of m-payment enjoyment.

4.4   Social Value

Participants were split over attaching a social value to the use of proximity m-payment as a sole service. While a few participants perceived that using m-payment would enhance their social image among their peers who use the service, many others argued that they don't pay much attention to how others think of them when it comes to how they pay. Some participants noted that they might care about impressions on others if they were younger. Although some of the participants mentioned that discussing one or more of the suggested VAS within their social groups might influence their perception about the service, however, they seemed to be reluctant to acknowledge any significant social value relating to their image per se. Compared to other value perceptions, the less significant interpretation of the social value could be attributed to the sensitivity of discussing financial matters in a social context, as was mentioned by one participant: "*I am British we don't talk about our money! Whether it would enhance their view of me or not I am not convinced that it would*" (P21).

4.5   Perceived Trust

Participants expressed their perceptions of trust in proximity m-payment providers in terms of the provider's business size as an indication of the popularity of their products, whether they are regulated by a local authority, or their reputation with regards to previous security breaches. Furthermore, the introduction of m-payment VAS has led to additional trust-enhancing perceptions in providers. Different measures were used by participants to describe the added trust value of augmenting m-payment apps with instant balance, mainly including the increased transparency about their financial information and making it easier to have balance information in a payment app: *"To put it all in the same place for you to view and use that does go to a level of trust for not hiding anything behind anything"* (P11). On the other hand, augmenting m-payment with loyalty schemes or cashback was considered as an indication of collaboration between m-payment providers and the retailers offering these incentives. In this context, the participants considered a m-payment app provider as more trustworthy since it is trusted by the retailers they are familiar with: *"It might make me more inclined to trust them because if they've got partnerships with major stores that is obviously even more legit than you would hope"* (P12). Additionally, addressing issues encountered with the payment experience in other payment methods, such as the absence of cash and the difficulty of managing multiple loyalty accounts, were perceived as additional trust-enhancing factors: *"I would tend to trust the provider more because I would think that they have looked up at what customers wanted"* (P16).

4.6   Perceived Risk

Nonadopters exhibited higher perceptions of risk on using m-payment as a sole service compared to adopters who repeatedly characterized the risks as avoidable. Three main themes have emerged under perceived risk: identity and payment information theft, privacy concerns, and the risk of running out of the phone battery. The growing news reports of data privacy breaches in recent years seem to have a significant impact on privacy concerns for many participants to use m-payment. This was also evident in perceptions of potential privacy issues associated with augmenting m-payment with instant balance and loyalty card integration. Many participants were reluctant to allow third-party m-payment providers access to their balance information due to their concerns about data misuse. They added that instant balance service is safe only if provided by their bank: *"If [the provider] has got access to what is your balance, then I probably want it to be my bank"* (P9). In contrast, some participants appeared to be more open to the service by relating the decision to share their balance information to the trustworthiness of the provider. This highlights the salient effect of trust in provider on reducing the perceived risks. Similarly, although most participants perceived little or no risks associated with the integrated loyalty cards service, one participant expressed his concerns about the possibility of making his shopping information available to the m-payment app provider: *"I don't necessarily want [the m-payment app provider] to know where I am with the GPS on my phone, how much I am spending through the data on my card, and what I am spending it on through the data on my loyalty card"* (P19). On the other hand, most participants perceived no additional risks associated with the cashback service. One participant stated that cashback gives him a reason to accept the risks he perceives in m-payment: *"It doesn't reduce the downside risk, but it adds something on the positive side to balance against it"* (P6).

4.7   Ranking of VAS

Having identified the participants' value perceptions of the proposed VAS, we sought to understand their most appealing value propositions in terms of the theorized value determinants. One approach was to ask them to rank the three VAS in order of preference and explain the reason of their choice. Table 2 summarizes the participants' main reasons for choosing the most preferred value added service.

Table 2. Participants' reasons for choosing the most preferred value added service

Top-ranked value added service	Number of participants	Reasons of choice	Value construct
Instant balance	8	Real-time account balance	Convenience
		Easier account management	Convenience
		Restore money tangibility	Convenience + Monetary
		Avoid overdraft	Monetary
Cashback	7	Easier to find deals	Convenience
		Saving money	Monetary
Loyalty cards integration	6	Easier loyalty management	Convenience
		Saving money	Monetary
None	2	No additional value	None

The instant balance was ranked as the most preferred value added service by the highest number of participants, closely followed by cashback and loyalty card integration. Two of the participants did not give any preference to any of the suggested VAS due to seeing no value that fits their needs. The relationship between the reasons and the related value constructs indicates that convenience and monetary values were the main drivers for choosing a given value added service. This finding further emphasizes the importance of utilitarian values in m-payment services.

5   Analysis and Discussion

5.1   Theoretical Implications

This study has provided a rich interpretation of the added value concept in m-payment context. The findings indicate that the added value of m-payment augmentation with VAS was mainly perceived through the dimensions of utilitarian values, i.e. convenience and monetary. Particularly, the added convenience value was perceived through the ability to achieve more with the m-payment app on top of a streamlined payment experience. Embedding more functionalities, such as the instant balance and loyalty accounts, into a frequently used payment app was seen as more time saving than accessing these services through separate channels. In addition, the suggested VAS were perceived to be solving usability issues associated with the payment activity, such as the visibility of paid money and the inconvenience of handling multiple loyalty cards. More interestingly, monetary value was only perceived from using the augmented m-payment service either directly from earning cashback or indirectly from simplifying ways of budgeting, collecting loyalty points, or finding cashback deals. Although this finding differs from earlier studies that conceptualize utilitarian values under a unified determinant [e.g. 12], differentiating between convenience and monetary values as two separate constructs has proved to be important since the monetary value has received no support in case of the sole m-payment service. Therefore, it could be argued that VAS do not only enhance existing perceived values of the core m-payment service but also create new values based on the additional features.

Perceptions of enjoyment value followed the same pattern of influence for the augmented and nonaugmented m-payment service. In both cases, enjoyment value was mainly derived as a consequence of convenience-related dimensions rather than being a main value determinant as indicated by previous studies [e.g. 15]. One possible explanation to this finding could be the pure utilitarian nature of m-payment services, where more emphasis is placed on fulfilling the payment task while the emotional aspect is recognized as a positive side effect of how the task was fulfilled [5]. Additionally, the added monetary value has also led to positive emotional aspects among some participants. No major changes were observed in terms of the influence of social value following the augmentation of m-payment service. In comparison with other value dimensions, participants appeared to be less encouraged to attach significant self-image aspects from using m-payment in general. Although this finding is in contrast with previous studies [e.g. 12, 15], however, our findings suggest that privacy and age-related considerations seem to inhibit noticeable social gains. Furthermore, the augmentation of m-payment with VAS has enhanced perceptions of trust in m-payment providers. Understanding consumer needs by adding extra features that simplify payment scenarios was perceived as a trust-enhancing factor. On the other hand, the augmentation of m-payment does not seem to reduce the perceived associated risks. However, almost all participants acknowledged that their perceptions of risk diminish with a trustworthy provider. Given that this association is confirmed by previous studies [e.g. 20], therefore, we can argue that augmenting m-payment with VAS may indirectly reduce perceptions of risk through enhancing perceptions of trust in provider.

5.2   Practical Implications

The findings of this study offer several implications for m-payment providers regarding how consumers perceive added value in m-payment services. First, m-payment providers should reconsider the concept of added value beyond the performance characteristics of the core payment service. Involving additional services that tackle issues associated with existing payment scenarios has proved to be pivotal in recognizing the added value of m-payment from a consumer's perspective as compared to existing payment methods. Second, more efforts are needed to understand consumer activities involved in the whole payment experience. As the findings suggest, different consumers exhibited different needs associated with their payment activities. Therefore, m-payment providers should invest in business initiatives that promote consumer engagement and value co-creation. Finally, to alleviate the negative impact of risk perceptions, more marketing efforts are needed to highlight the security advantages that m-payment solutions are built with relative to traditional payment methods.

5.3   Conclusion and Future Research

This study advances the existing body of knowledge about m-payment adoption using a value-based approach. The perceived value theory has been employed to understand the effect of m-payment VAS on the different determinants of value. In light of our findings, the added value perceived from m-payment augmentation with VAS was mainly interpreted in terms of convenience and monetary values in addition to enhanced trust perceptions in m-payment providers. The added enjoyment value was predominantly envisaged as a resulting emotional effect of convenience-related aspects rather than a substantial value determinant. Although the findings of this study present a rich account of the concept of added value in m-payment context, we suggest that these findings should be used to guide the development of future quantitative value-based m-payment studies due to the small sample size that characterizes this qualitative study. In addition, the current study was based on three pre-suggested VAS. Therefore, future research is encouraged to follow a more consumer-focused approach that derives possible VAS from participants based on their individual needs.

References

1. eMarketer: UK: Mobile Payments Still Looking to Grab a Foothold. https://www.emarketer. com/newsroom/index.php/uk-mobile-payments-grab-foothold. Accessed 12 Nov 2018
2. Slade, E., Williams, M., Dwivedi, Y., Piercy, N.: Exploring consumer adoption of proximity mobile payments. J. Strat. Mark. **23**(3), 209–223 (2015)
3. Hayashi, F.: Mobile payments: what's in it for consumers? Fed. Reserve Bank Kansas City Econ. Rev. **First Quarter**, 35–66 (2012)
4. Madureira, A.: Factors that hinder the success of SIM-based mobile NFC service deployments. Telematics Inform. **34**(1), 133–150 (2017)
5. Alhallaq, H., Younas, M., Kamal, S., Champion, B.: Understanding perceived value of mobile payments: a qualitative study. In: 24th UK Academy for Information Systems Conference Proceedings (2019)
6. Titcomb, J.: Mobile payments struggle to make impact on contactless card use. The Telegraph. https://www.telegraph.co.uk/technology/2017/04/14/mobile-payments-struggle-make-impact-contactless-card-use. Accessed 15 July 2017
7. Kim, H.W., Chan, H.C., Gupta, S.: Value-based adoption of mobile internet: an empirical investigation. Decis. Support Syst. **43**(1), 111–126 (2007)
8. Au, Y.A., Kauffman, R.J.: The economics of mobile payments: understanding stakeholder issues for an emerging financial technology application. Electron. Commer. Res. Appl. **7**(2), 141–164 (2008)

9. De Reuver, M., Verschuur, E., Nikayin, F., Cerpa, N., Bouwman, H.: Collective action for mobile payment platforms: a case study on collaboration issues between banks and telecom operators. Electron. Commer. Res. Appl. **14**(5), 331–344 (2015)
10. Dahlberg, T., Guo, J., Ondrus, J.: A critical review of mobile payment research. Electron. Commer. Res. Appl. **14**(5), 265–284 (2015)
11. Arvidsson, N.: Consumer attitudes on mobile payment services – results from a proof of concept test. Int. J. Bank Mark. **32**(2), 150–170 (2014)
12. Cocosila, M., Trabelsi, H.: An integrated value-risk investigation of contactless mobile payments adoption. Electron. Commer. Res. Appl. **20**, 159–170 (2016)
13. Zeithaml, V.A.: Consumer perceptions of price, quality, and value: a means-end model and synthesis of evidence. J. Mark. **52**, 2–22 (1988)
14. Pihlström, M., Brush, G.J.: Comparing the perceived value of information and entertainment mobile services. Psychol. Mark. **25**(8), 732–755 (2008)
15. de Kerviler, G., Demoulin, N.T.M., Zidda, P.: Adoption of in-store mobile payment: are perceived risk and convenience the only drivers? J. Retail. Consum. Serv. **31**, 334–344 (2016)
16. Sweeney, J., Soutar, G.: Consumer perceived value: the development of a multiple item scale. J. Retail. **77**(2), 203–220 (2001)
17. Zhou, T.: An empirical examination of continuance intention of mobile payment services. Decis. Support Syst. **54**(2), 1085–1091 (2013)
18. Holbrook, M.B., Hirschman, E.C.: The experiential aspects of consumption: consumer fantasies, feelings, and fun. J. Consum. Res. **9**(2), 132 (1982)
19. Sheth, J.N., Newman, B.I., Gross, B.L.: Why we buy what we buy. J. Bus. Res. **22**, 159–171 (1991)
20. Pavlou, P.: Consumer acceptance of electronic commerce: integrating trust and risk with the technology acceptance model. Int. J. Electron. Commer. **7**(3), 69–103 (2003)
21. Sirdeshmukh, D., Singh, J., Sabol, B.: Consumer trust, value, and loyalty in relational exchanges. J. Mark. **66**(1), 15–37 (2002)
22. de Chernatony, L., Harris, F., Dall'Olmo Riley, F.: Added value: its nature, roles and sustainability. Eur. J. Mark. **34**(1/2), 39–56 (2000)
23. Grönroos, C.: Value-driven relational marketing: from products to resources and competencies. J. Mark. Manag. **13**(5), 407–419 (1997)
24. Kaplan, B., Maxwell, J.: Qualitative research methods for evaluating computer information systems. In: Anderson, J.G., Aydin, C.E. (eds.) Evaluating the Organizational Impact of Healthcare Information Systems, pp. 30–55. Springer, New York (2005). https://doi.org/10.1007/0-387-30329-4_2
25. Apanasevic, T., Markendahl, J., Arvidsson, N.: Stakeholders' expectations of mobile payment in retail: lessons from Sweden. Int. J. Bank Mark. **34**(1), 37–61 (2016)
26. Zachariadis, M., Ozcan, P.: The API economy and digital transformation in financial services: the case of open banking. In: Working Paper. SWIFT Institute, London (2017)

Users' Behavioral Strategies Toward Mobile App Problems: Fight or Flight

Yavuz Inal[1]([⊠]) and Tuna Hacaloglu[2]

[1] Department of Information Science and Media Studies, University of Bergen,
Bergen, Norway
yvzinal@gmail.com
[2] Information Systems Engineering, Atilim University, Ankara, Turkey

Abstract. In this paper, we identify two distinct behavioral strategies for dealing with problems encountered in the use of mobile apps - fight or flight. In the fight strategy, individuals do not give up using an app when faced with a problem; rather, they experiment with different ways to cope with that problem, whereas the flight strategy refers to the user's decision to uninstall an app when they encounter a problem and/or their intention to use an alternative app. These strategies were identified from an analysis of documents, which forty-two users reported, and can be used to understand how users deal with encountered problems. The participants were asked to use a mobile app of their choice for one week and report the behavioral strategies they utilized to counter problems they experienced. According to the findings obtained from content analysis, the most reported complaints concerned the categories of interface design, functional error, feature request, and feature removal. The participants who complained about functional errors, frustrating features, and slow application speed stopped using the app (flight behavior) whereas those that were dissatisfied with the interface, a missing feature or the content of the app continued to use the app and tried to overcome the problems (fight behavior).

Keywords: User behavior · Behavioral strategy ·
Human-Computer interaction · Mobile interface design · Mobile apps ·
Fight or flight

1 Introduction

With rapid developments in technology, many new concepts have emerged in recent years to replace the term "computer" in the context of human-computer interaction. Mobile devices, being one of the technologies that people are most interacting with today, have an important place in this interaction [1]. Beyond communication, gaming or entertainment, it is possible to see mobile technologies in many areas from electronic commerce, banking and public services to information and communication systems [2]. Today, people have even begun to fear the absence of mobile phones, and there is a positive relationship between this fear and the duration of mobile device use [3]. Therefore, the analysis and evaluation of user behavior toward mobile apps, which are active parts of everyday life, play an essential role in the success of apps [4].

© IFIP International Federation for Information Processing 2019
Published by Springer Nature Switzerland AG 2019
I. O. Pappas et al. (Eds.): I3E 2019, LNCS 11701, pp. 37–49, 2019.
https://doi.org/10.1007/978-3-030-29374-1_4

Due to the growing popularity and trends toward widespread adoption of mobile devices, in recent years millions of apps have been developed for these devices. For example, according to Statista data, as of March 2017, there are 2.8 million apps for Android devices in Google Play Store and 2.2 million apps for iOS devices in Apple Store [5], and there is a greater adoption of smartphones and other mobile devices than PCs [6]. Thus, mobile apps have become the fastest growing part of the software world [7], and mobile app development continues to increase in popularity as an important area of work for software developers. Today, with the "Mobile-First" trend, software developers are expected to develop apps first for the mobile platform and then for computers [8]. However, mobile devices also have significant limitations, particularly concerning screen size, limited processing capacity, different design requirements, and the context in which they are used [9, 10]. Given all these limitations, it is clear that software developers need to pay more attention to the needs and expectations of users when developing mobile apps than desktop apps. In addition, the features of desktop apps and those of mobile apps significantly differ. These limitations and differences have also increased the importance of evaluating mobile apps [11].

Feedback and the evaluation by mobile app users are important sources of information [12, 13]. Studies have shown that features of mobile apps are a determinant of user behavior toward these apps [14–16]. User complaints regarding both the functional characteristics of an app [14] and its design and aesthetic appearance have a considerable influence on the user's decision to continue using it [17].

This study aimed to determine the problems encountered in mobile apps and the behavioral strategies adopted by users to overcome these problems. The data were collected from university students, who were active mobile app users. The findings of the study are expected to offer guidance to not only researchers but also mobile app developers and consultants.

Primary research questions of the study were addressed as below,

- What are the usability problems that the participants encountered while using mobile apps?
- What are the participants' behavioral strategies against the encountered mobile app problems?

2 Related Works

Mobile devices are one of the most important technological innovations of today [18]. With rapid evolution of these devices, mobile apps are gaining increasingly more attention [19]. Therefore, an important area of research is the identification of problems faced by users when using mobile apps and the analysis of the behavioral strategies they develop to counter these problems. However, in the literature, there are very few studies related to the assessment of user behavior, attitudes or their evaluation concerning mobile apps [20].

Chou et al. [21] examined the behavior and habits of users toward mobile apps in the context of expectance-confirmation theory. The authors gathered questionnaire data from university students and determined that the ultimate success of an app is related to the continued use of that app. In addition, they concluded that mobile apps that were considered useful and enjoyable positively influenced user satisfaction and users' tendency to continue using those apps. Similarly, Hsu and Lin [4] analyzed users' purchasing behavior of paid mobile apps based on the expectation confirmation model. The data collected from 507 users through a questionnaire showed that confirmation was positively associated with perceived value and satisfaction of users; therefore, the authors emphasized that confirmation was an important factor in using mobile apps. In addition, they determined that positive feedback given by other users for a mobile app had a positive effect on the purchasing behavior related to that app.

In another study [16] that aimed to determine mobile users' purchasing and information sharing behaviors, the effect of differences of the mobile platform, user interest in mobile apps, and last visits to mobile stores were investigated. The data was collected from 345 participants through a questionnaire. At the end of the study, it was reported that interest in a mobile e-commerce app was positively related to users' purchasing and information sharing behaviors. Wang et al. [22] focused on the factors that affect users' mobile app use based on the role of consumption values. The data was obtained from 282 mobile app users. It was found that functional, social, emotional and epistemic values had an important effect on the development of behaviors concerning app use. Similarly, Chang et al. [15] evaluated 12 different mobile apps in their analysis of factors that affect decisions to use mobile apps. The data gathered from 68 participants through a questionnaire revealed that users' needs and excitement regarding an app as well as its usability were influential factors in their decision to download and use that app.

Maghnati and Ling [23] conducted a study to determine the effect of experiential value on user attitudes toward mobile apps. User attitudes were examined under the experiential value categories of aesthetic, playfulness, service excellence, and customer return on investment. User attitudes were found to have a significant positive relationship with playfulness and customer return on investment, but not with aesthetic and service excellence. Similarly, Le and Nguyen [24] explored the effect of advertisements in mobile apps on user attitudes based on data collected from 206 participants using a questionnaire. Although many users were negative about advertisements in mobile apps, it was considered that the format and content of advertisements could be designed in a way that would appeal to users. In this context, the authors determined that "credibility" and "entertainment" in advertisements were the main factors that affected user attitudes toward advertisements.

Features of mobile apps are determinants of not only the attitudes of users toward these apps, but also the development of user perceptions and preferences. For example, Kim et al. [25] focused on the effects of "stickiness" and "word of mouth" on user perceptions concerning mobile app features. As a result of a survey conducted with 503 smartphone users, it was determined that user perceptions toward mobile app features were positively associated with the usability of apps. Furthermore, this resulted in increased "stickiness" and positive "word of mouth" intentions. Huy and vanThanh [26] identified the most popular mobile app paradigms and evaluated them from the perspective of developers, users, and service providers. From the users' point of view, it was determined that ease-of-use and functionality were very important in native mobile apps. In another study focusing on users' perspective on mobile apps, Bowen and Pistilli [14] investigated university students' preferences concerning the use of mobile apps. A total of 1,566 students studying at Purdue University were reached through a questionnaire. According to the data obtained, a significant number of participants used an Android phone or iPhone. The participants considered themselves to be moderate and advanced users, and were found to prefer native mobile apps because they are quicker and easier to use than the mobile Web.

User evaluation of mobile apps is critical to obtaining valuable information about the current state of apps, their place in the market, and their success. In this context, in addition to the feedback received from users through face-to-face interviews or questionnaires, user evaluation of apps in app stores provides important information [27]. Therefore, while some studies that analyzed user data in these environments used a manual analysis method, other studies proposed an automated evaluation system. For instance, Khalid et al. [27] investigated the most frequent complaints of users in relation to mobile apps. The authors manually reviewed a total of 6,390 user ratings for the 20 most popular iOS apps. The problems most users complained about were functional errors, feature requests, and app crashes. Fu et al. [13] proposed a system called WisCom to analyze user reviews of mobile apps. The authors stated that this system provided valuable information about the entire mobile app market by identifying inconsistencies in user ratings, the reasons why users like or dislike an app, and user preferences of different mobile apps.

3   Methodology

A total of 42 undergraduate university students enrolled in the Software Engineering, 29 male and 13 female, participated in the study. Different methods and techniques have been used in the research involving user evaluation of mobile apps. Some studies analyze feedback from users [e.g., 16, 25] while others assess user ratings on apps in app stores [e.g., 27]. In this study, descriptive quantitative analysis was used to engage in an in-depth analysis of user evaluation of mobile apps and to identify the adopted behavioral strategies.

3.1   Data Collection Procedure

It takes approximately eight minutes for users to learn how to use a new mobile app [28]. A large percentage of users decide whether to remove an app from their smart devices within three to seven days of first using that app [29]. In this context, the one-week timeframe from the moment that users learn how to use a mobile app is very critical for the success of that app in the market. This one-week period of use is considered to be sufficient to obtain the information necessary to evaluate a mobile app. Therefore, the participants in this study were given an assignment in a Human Computer Interaction Course, and asked to use a mobile app of their choice for one week. Then, they reported in detail the problems they encountered during the use of the app, as well as the behavioral strategies they adopted to counter these problems. The participants reported name of the mobile application that they evaluated, list of the usability problems that they countered, and their decisions regarding these problems in a document. The participants documented these issues as they happened and the reports were written using a word processor, and the participants sent their documents to the researchers via e-mail. The basic data used in the study was obtained through the descriptive quantitative analysis of the participants' documents.

Reaction to a problem in an app might depend on the type of app and users' needs. Users may have different tolerance towards various apps. Therefore, although the participants were completely free to choose the mobile app to evaluate, only free and hedonic-oriented apps were evaluated in the study because this may influence the features that an app offers as well as the participants' decision to uninstall it. Hedonic-oriented apps are type of mobile applications that are used for enjoyment, arousal and freedom [30]. This allowed for the coverage of a broader range of mobile apps through the assessment of different themes and types of hedonic-oriented apps and ensuring that the implications of research were more generalizable under this type of apps. Therefore, the types of mobile apps evaluated by the participants varied under 7 different themes such as photography, video, chat, sports, music, news and games.

3.2 Data Analysis

A content analysis was performed on the qualitative data collected from the participants. The mobile app problems reported by the participants were categorized using the 12 types of complaints determined by [27] based on user feedback (see Table 1). Each mobile app problem identified by the participants was included in one of these 12 categories and analyzed accordingly.

Table 1. Type of complaints identified by [27] and their description (p. 74)

Type of complaint	Description
App crashing	The app often crashed
Compatibility	The app had problems on a specific device or an OS version
Feature removal	A disliked feature degraded the user experience
Feature request	The app needed additional features
Functional error	The problem was app specific
Hidden cost	The full user experience entailed hidden costs
Interface design	The user complained about the design, controls, or visuals
Network problem	The app had trouble with the network or responded slowly.
Privacy and ethics	The app invaded privacy or was unethical
Resource heavy	The app consumed too much energy or memory
Uninteresting content	The specific content was unappealing
Unresponsive app	The app responded slowly to input or was laggy overall

Furthermore, behavioral strategies adopted by participants to handle the problems they identified were grouped into either 'fight' (continued to use) or 'flight' (abandoned the app). This made it possible to demonstrate the relationship between the problems encountered in mobile apps and the behavior exhibited. In the 'fight' strategy, individuals do not give up using an app when faced with a problem; rather, they experiment with different ways to cope with that problem. On the contrary, the flight strategy refers to the user's decision to uninstall an app when they encounter a problem and/or their intention to use an alternative app. Each mobile app problem included in one of the 12 complaint types were categorized as fight or flight.

4   Results

4.1   Problems Identified in Mobile Apps

Figure 1 presents the problems identified by the participants for the mobile apps they evaluated. Most of the participants complained about the interface design of mobile apps (Interface Design, n = 32, 76%). This category contained complaints, such as the app not being attractive or aesthetic, use of wrong color contrast, problems with size and alignment of images, font selection, and readability of texts. Visual design issues that affected the ease-of-use of the app were also included in this category. Functional errors in the app constituted another type of problems according to most of the participants (Functional Error, n = 29, 69%). Incorrect operation of buttons, certain operations giving constant errors, and some pages not responding were examples of this type of complaint.

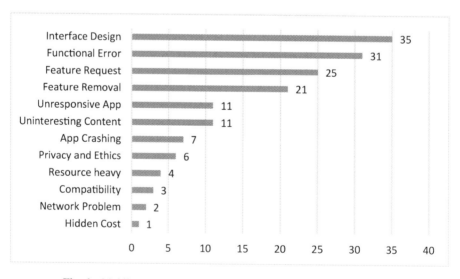

Fig. 1. Mobile app problems reported by the participants (percentage)

As the number of apps developed for mobile devices increases, user expectations and demands from these apps also increase. In this study, it was found that more than half of the participants complained about features they thought were missing in the mobile apps they evaluated (Feature Request, n = 21, 50%). The lack of an option to close a bank account, problems with bank integration, short duration of video recording, or lack of feedback within the app were among the reported issues.

Some of the participants were frustrated by the services, content or operations offered by the mobile apps (Feature Removal, n = 18, 43%), and they complained about the requirement to update the app, constant advertisements displayed in the app that forced the user to make a payment to close the window, and the recommendation to contact the management rather than describing the error in error messages.

The participants also referred to problems regarding the slow application speed generally, or in certain pages or operations, particularly on certain days of the week (Unresponsive App, n = 10, 24%). It is important that the content in apps is consistent with the features of the app and user expectations. However, concerning some of the mobile apps evaluated in this study, users had complaints regarding this situation (Uninteresting Content, n = 9, 21%). Examples given by the participants under this type of complaint were the app not presenting information that was needed and the content being limited and inadequate or including irrelevant information. Other mobile app issues identified by the participants include app crashes (App Crashing, n = 4, 10%), excessive use of battery, memory or internet (Resource Heavy, n = 4, 10%), violation of privacy and ethics (Privacy and Ethics, n = 3, 7%), and problems concerning the hardware or software specifications required by the app (Compatibility, n = 2, 5%).

4.2   Behavioral Strategies Adopted to Counter the Problems

The behavioral strategies developed by participants to counter the problems they faced when using the mobile apps were analyzed in detail. It was determined that the participants either responded by trying to find solutions to these problems (Fight) or abandoning the use of app and searching for an alternative (Flight). The methods used by the participants to cope with the problems are detailed in Table 2 according to the behavioral strategy.

Table 2. Behavioral strategies adopted by users to handle mobile app problems

	Users' behavioral strategies	n	%
Fight	Making an additional effort using the trial and error method	23	29
	Updating or reinstalling the app	9	12
	Sending feedback to the app developer(s)	5	6
	Contacting the customer services	5	6
	Seeking help within the app	2	3
Flight	Uninstalling the app	12	15
	Using the app less	9	12
	Seeking an alternative app	7	9
	Using the website of the app	6	8

The participants seemed to mostly prefer to make an additional effort to perform the operations they needed in the mobile app or to try to determine the causes of problems that confused them so that they would not trigger the same error in future use (50%, n = 21). This was followed by the behavior of updating or reinstalling the app (17%, n = 7). Other methods adopted by participants to tackle the app-related problems included sending feedback or complaining to the developer (12%, n = 5), contacting the customer services if it was an official app of a corporation (7%, n = 3), and searching for a help feature within the app (2%, n = 1).

Among the participants that adopted the behavior to abandon the app after facing problems, most preferred to uninstall the app (26%, n = 11). This was followed by reduced use of the app (19%, n = 8). The participants also reported that if they thought that the mobile apps, they were trying did not meet their expectations, they would use an alternative app designed for the same purpose to fulfill their needs (14%, n = 6). Finally, some of the participants stated that they resorted to the website version to perform the actions that were problematic on the mobile app (10%, n = 4).

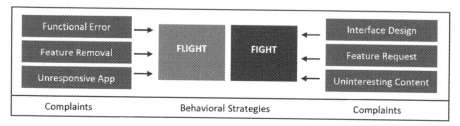

Fig. 2. Relationship between mobile app problems and behavioral strategies

In this study, the relationship between the mobile app problems identified and the behavioral strategies developed by the participants for these problems was also analyzed (see Fig. 2). The most reported complaints were considered to understand the participants' behavioral strategies properly, and rests such as app crashing, privacy and ethics, compatibility were ignored. It was found that the variety of the problems encountered during the use of mobile apps resulted in the differentiation of methods and behavioral strategies adopted to cope with these problems. For example, the majority of the participants that complained about functional errors (23 of 29, 79%), feature removal (11 of 18, 61%), or an unresponsive app (6 of 10, 60%) adopted the flight behavior by deciding not to use the app any more. On the other hand, those participants that were not happy with the interface design, ease-of-use, aesthetics (Interface Design, 25 of 32, 78%), lack of features (Feature Request, 15 of 21, 71%), or app content (Uninteresting Content, 5 of 9, 56%) exhibited the fight behavior, continuing to use the app and trying to overcome the problems. Other types of complaints addressed by the participants were not concentrated under any distinct behavioral strategy.

5   Discussion

The development of user-friendly mobile apps is a challenging process [31]. In addition to their unique features, mobile apps have many limitations [32, 33]. However, given the growing interest in mobile apps, competition in the industry, and the expectations of users, it is important that apps have features that will minimize user complaints.

5.1   Complaints About the Evaluated Mobile Apps

According to the results of the present study, the participants most complained about the interface design of mobile apps. They frequently emphasized problems concerning the aesthetic design and ease-of-use of the apps they evaluated. Mobile apps should be easy to use by target groups [34]. Individuals that do not have any difficulty using an app usually consider it user-friendly [35]. Research has shown that users assess the interfaces of mobile apps mostly based on their visual appearance [17], and the ease-of-use of an app is a decisive factor for preference of use [14, 26]. In this context, difficulty to understand how to use an app for the first time, uninteresting design, and visual problems are among issues to be considered in the development of mobile apps.

When mobile apps are being developed, they should be tested concerning different aspects, such as hardware, screen size, platform, and network connectivity [36, 37]. This will prevent potential users from encountering functional errors. However, considering that many developers manually test mobile apps due to the lack of automated testing tools for mobile apps and user testing [38], it is inevitable that users will experience functional problems in mobile apps. Huy and vanThanh [26] underlined the importance of the functionality of mobile apps from the point of view of users. Khalid et al. [27] determined that the most common complaints of users concerning mobile apps were functional errors. Similarly, in the current study, most of the participants complained about the functional problems they encountered in mobile apps.

In this study, some of the participants were also frustrated by and complained about some features or content of the mobile apps they evaluated, particularly in relation to the advertisements placed in apps. Advertisements are an important source of income for mobile app developers [39]. However, attention should be paid not to place advertisements in areas that would make it difficult for users to interact with the app and would interfere with their use of the app. Displaying a large number of advertisements is one of the main factors that negatively affects users' attitude toward an app [40]. Complex interaction provided by apps was another feature that displeased the participants. Mobile apps offer more interactivity with users compared to desktop apps [41], but it is important that this interaction is structured in a way that users can easily understand. Otherwise, users will not be able to use mobile app effectively.

In their research involving user evaluation of the usability of mobile apps, Fung et al. [42] found that the most frequent problems were inconsistencies regarding the content, the illogical presentation of information, and the lack of sufficient help concerning error messages. Similarly, among other problems, the participants reported that some of the necessary information was not included in the app while other content was unnecessary or outdated. Thus, although it is difficult to develop user-friendly mobile apps due to the small screen size [41], it is possible to avoid such problems by presenting the content appropriately for the limited size. Considering this constraint, it is critical to design mobile apps as simply and plainly as possible when, at the same time, ensuring that they fulfill their basic functions. Every new function and feature to be added to the app should also be carefully considered not to complicate the app and adversely affect its usability [33].

By their nature, mobile apps need to provide short and fast interaction [41]. It is not possible to talk about the advantages of mobile apps if users cannot access necessary information quickly [43]. Studies have also shown that speed is an important factor in user preference to use mobile apps [e.g., 14]. Furthermore, freezing, constant errors, slowness and excessive battery consumption are among the main problems that lead users to give negative feedback to mobile apps [40]. Similarly, in the current study, some of the participants identified slowness as one of the main problems with the apps they evaluated. Apps being generally slow or some of the pages and processes being slow, particularly on certain days of the week were among the reported issues.

5.2   Behavioral Strategies Against Problems Encountered

In a study investigating the responses of users in relation to an app not meeting their expectations and needs [40], the most utilized behavioral strategies were to uninstall the app immediately, remove it if it did not respond for longer than 30 s, tell their friends how bad it is, and complain about it in social media. In the current study, the participants developed two basic behavioral strategies to counter the problems with the mobile apps they evaluated; either trying to overcome the problem by continuing to use it, or giving up using the app and searching for alternatives.

Observing the relationship between the mobile app problems reported by the participants and the behavioral strategies they exhibited, it is clear that the types of problems differentiate the methods of handling the problems and the behavioral strategy adopted. The participants that chose the behavior to abandon the app often referred to functional errors, a feature that frustrated them, or the slow application speed. On the other hand, those participants that responded by continuing to use the app and trying to find some solution mostly mentioned problems with the interface design, ease-of-use, aesthetic characteristics, missing features or problems with the content of the app. Briefly, functional errors, disturbing features or slowness usually draw users away from the app. Although users that experienced design problems, missing features, or problematic content tended to give the evaluated apps another chance, the increasing competition in the mobile market and the availability of a large number of alternatives make it necessary to pay attention to such user complaints.

Users that are not satisfied with an app usually comment on it negatively to friends or colleagues [40]. Accordingly, an app with user-friendly features leads people to continue to use it and increase their possibility to recommend it to others [15, 25]. Some unsatisfied users not only remove an app but also make negative comments and reviews about the app, which can be influential in the download behavior of other users [44]. It is therefore important that mobile apps resolve both functional and design-related problems in order to have a larger share in the market, grow their target groups, and build a loyal customer base.

6   Conclusion, Limitations and Future Research

Today, mobile technologies continue to be used with increasing popularity. Accordingly, studies on the analysis of user behavior in the context of these technologies provide valuable findings. In this study, mobile app problems were examined from the point of view of university students, and the behavioral strategies they developed to counter these problems were also analyzed. The results revealed that the participants who encountered problems that made it difficult to use the app adopted the behavior to abandon the app whereas those that had complaints about design issues made more effort to continue to use the app. The data was collected from a limited number of participants. In terms of the generalizability of the findings, it is important that the data be obtained in a way to cover a broader group of participants. The participants were free to choose the app to evaluate, however we asked them to evaluate free and hedonic-oriented apps. Therefore, an assessment based on the other app types (such as utilitarian-oriented apps) was not possible. Therefore, it is important that future work consider both the number of participants and the types of mobile apps. As the continuation of the current work, we plan to undertake further research in view of these issues.

Acknowledgements. We thank Dr. Frode Guribye, who provided helpful comments on previous version of this document.

References

1. Gomez, R.Y., Caballero, D.C., Sevillano, J.L.: Heuristic evaluation on mobile interfaces: a new checklist. Sci. World J. (2014). Article ID 434326
2. El-Kiki, T., Lawrence, E.: Emerging mobile government services: strategies for success. In: 20th Bled eConference eMergence: Merging and Emerging Technologies, Processes, and Institutions, Bled, Slovenia, pp. 776–788 (2007)
3. Erdem, H., Türen, U., Kalkın, G.: Mobil telefon yoksunluğu korkusu (nomofobi) yayılımı: Türkiye'den üniversite öğrencileri ve kamu çalışanları örneklemi. Int. J. Inform. Technol. **10** (1), 1–12 (2017)
4. Hsu, C.L., Lin, J.C.C.: What drives purchase intention for paid mobile apps? – an expectation confirmation model with perceived value. Electron. Commer. Res. Appl. **14**, 46–57 (2015)
5. Statista (2017). https://www.statista.com/statistics/276623/number-of-apps-available-in-leading-app-stores/
6. Dunn, B.K., Galletta, D.F., Hypolite, D., Puri, A., Raghuwanshi, S.: Development of smart phone usability benchmarking tasks. In: 2013 46th Hawaii International Conference on System Sciences (HICSS), pp. 1046–1052 (2013)
7. Lee, G., Raghu, T.S.: Product portfolio and mobile apps success: evidence from app store market. In: Proceedings of the Seventeenth Americas Conference on Information Systems - All Submissions, p. 444 (2011)
8. Voas, J., Michael, J.B., van Genuchten, M.: The mobile software app takeover. IEEE Softw. **29**, 25–27 (2012)

9. Zhang, D., Adipat, B.: Challenges, methodologies, and issues in the usability testing of mobile applications. Int. J. Hum.-Comput. Interact. **18**(3), 293–308 (2005)
10. Hussain, A., Hashim, N.L., Nordin, N., Tahir, H.M.: A metric-based evaluation model for applications on mobile phones. J. ICT **12**, 55–71 (2013)
11. Miah, S.J., Gammack, J., Hasan, N.: Extending the framework for mobile health information systems research: a content analysis. Inf. Syst. **69**, 1–24 (2017)
12. Iacob, C., Harrison, R.: Retrieving and analyzing mobile apps feature requests from online reviews. In: 10th IEEE Working Conference on Mining Software Repositories, pp. 41–44 (2013)
13. Fu, B., Lin, J., Li, L., Faloutsos, C., Hong, J., Sadeh, N.: Why people hate your app - making sense of user feedback in a mobile app store. In: KDD 2013, pp. 1276–1284 (2013)
14. Bowen, K., Pistilli, M.D.: Student preferences for mobile app usage. In: EDUCAUSE Center for Applied Research (2012)
15. Chang, T.R., Kaasinen, E., Kaipainen, K.: What influences users' decisions to take apps into use? A framework for evaluating persuasive and engaging design in mobile apps for well-being. In: MUM 2012 (2012)
16. Taylor, D.G., Levin, M.: Predicting mobile app usage for purchasing and information-sharing. Int. J. Retail Distrib. Manag. **42**(8), 759–774 (2014)
17. Miniukovich, A., De Angeli, A.: Visual impressions of mobile app interfaces. In: NordiCHI 2014, pp. 31–40 (2014)
18. Baharuddin, R., Singh, D., Razali, R.: Usability dimensions for mobile applications - a review. Res. J. Appl. Sci. Eng. Technol. **5**(6), 2225–2231 (2013)
19. Kim, E., Lin, J.S., Sung, Y.: To app or not to app: engaging consumers via branded mobile apps. J. Interact. Advert. **13**(1), 53–65 (2013)
20. Harris, M.A., Brookshire, R., Chin, A.G.: Identifying factors influencing consumers' intent to install mobile applications. Int. J. Inf. Manag. **36**, 441–450 (2016)
21. Chou, C.H., Chiu, C.H., Ho, C.Y., Lee, J.C.: Understanding mobile apps continuance usage behavior and habit: an expectance-confirmation theory. In: PACIS 2013 Proceedings, p. 132 (2013)
22. Wang, H.Y., Liao, C., Yang, L.H.: What affects mobile application use? The roles of consumption values. Int. J. Mark. Stud. **5**(2), 11–22 (2013)
23. Maghnati, F., Ling, K.C.: Exploring the relationship between experiential value and usage attitude towards mobile apps among the smartphone users. Int. J. Bus. Manag. **8**(4), 1 (2013)
24. Le, T.D., Nguyen, B.T.H.: Attitudes toward mobile advertising: a study of mobile web display and mobile app display advertising. Asian Acad. Manag. J. **19**(2), 87–103 (2014)
25. Kim, S., Baek, T.H., Kim, Y.K., Yoo, K.: Factors affecting stickiness and word of mouth in mobile applications. J. Res. Interact. Mark. **10**(3), 177–192 (2016)
26. Huy, N.P., van Thanh, D.: Evaluation of mobile app paradigms. In: MoMM 2012, pp. 25–30 (2012)
27. Khalid, H., Shihab, E., Nagappan, M., Hassan, A.E.: What do mobile app users complain about? IEEE Softw. **32**, 70–77 (2015)
28. Flood, D., Harrison, R., Iacob, C., Duce, D.: Evaluating mobile applications: a spreadsheet case study. Int. J. Mob. Hum. Comput. Interact. **4**(4), 37–65 (2012)
29. Quettra Study (2016). https://xupler.com/2016/11/03/mobile-app-uninstall-ratewhats-considered-good-and-bad/
30. Hazarika, B., Khuntia, J., Parthasarathy, M., Karimi, J.: Do hedonic and utilitarian apps differ in consumer appeal? In: Sugumaran, V., Yoon, V., Shaw, M.J. (eds.) WEB 2015. LNBIP, vol. 258, pp. 233–237. Springer, Cham (2016). https://doi.org/10.1007/978-3-319-45408-5_28

31. Biel, B., Grill, T., Gruhn, V.: Exploring the benefits of the combination of a software architecture analysis and a usability evaluation of a mobile application. J. Syst. Softw. **83**, 2031–2044 (2010)
32. Heidmann, F., Hermann, F., Peissner, M.: Interactive maps on mobile, location-based systems: design solutions and usability testing. In: Proceedings of the 21st International Cartographic Conference (ICC), pp. 1299–1306 (2003)
33. Harrison, R., Flood, D., Duce, D.: Usability of mobile applications: literature review and rationale for a new usability model. J. Interact. Sci. **1**(1), 1 (2013)
34. Arsand, E., et al.: Mobile health applications to assist patients with diabetes: lessons learned and design implications. J. Diabetes Sci. Technol. **6**(5), 1197–1206 (2012)
35. Mattson, D.C.: Usability assessment of a mobile app for art therapy. Arts Psychother. **43**, 1–6 (2015)
36. Nimbalkar, R.R.: Mobile application testing and challenges. Int. J. Sci. Res. **2**(7), 56–58 (2013)
37. Gao, J., Bai, X., Tsai, W., Uehara, T.: Mobile application testing: a tutorial. Computer **47**, 46–55 (2014)
38. Joorabchi, M.E., Mesbah, A., Kruchten, P.: Real challenges in mobile app development. In: ACM/ IEEE International Symposium on Empirical Software Engineering and Measurement, pp. 15–24 (2013)
39. Leontiadis, I., Efstratiou, C., Picone, M., Mascolo, C.: Don't kill my ads! Balancing privacy in an ad-supported mobile application market. In: HotMobile 2012, San Diego, CA, USA (2012)
40. Apigee Survey: Users reveal top frustrations that lead to bad mobile app reviews (2012). https://apigee.com/about/press-release/apigee-survey-users-reveal-top-frustrations-lead-bad-mobile-app-reviews/
41. Holzinger, A., Errath, M.: Mobile computer web-application design in medicine: some research based guidelines. Univ. Access Inf. Soc. **6**(1), 31–41 (2007)
42. Fung, R.H.Y., Chiu, D.K.W., Ko, E.H.T., Ho, K.K.W., Lo, P.: Heuristic usability evaluation of University of Hong Kong Libraries' mobile website. J. Acad. Librariansh. **42**, 581–594 (2016)
43. Chae, M., Kim, J.: Do size and structure matter to mobile users? An empirical study of the effects of screen size, information structure, and task complexity on user activities with standard web phones. Behav. Inf. Technol. **23**(3), 165–181 (2004)
44. Inukollu, V.N., Keshamoni, D.D., Kang, T., Inukollu, M.: Factors influencing quality of mobile apps: role of mobile app development life cycle. Int. J. Softw. Eng. Appl. **5**(5), 15–34 (2014)

Examining the Influence of Mobile Store Features on User E-Satisfaction: Extending UTAUT2 with Personalization, Responsiveness, and Perceived Security and Privacy

Ali Abdallah Alalwan[1([☒])], Abdullah M. Baabdullah[2],
Nripendra P. Rana[3], Yogesh K. Dwivedi[4], and Hatice Kizgin[5]

[1] Amman College of Financial and Administrative Sciences,
Al-Balqa Applied University, Amman, Jordan
alwan.a.a.ali@gmail.com, Alwan_jo@bau.edu.jo
[2] Department of Management Information Systems,
Faculty of Economics and Administration,
King Abdulaziz University, Jeddah, Kingdom of Saudi Arabia
baabdullah@kau.edu.sa
[3] Marketing and Branding Research Centre, School of Management,
Bradford University, Bradford, UK
nrananp@gmail.com
[4] School of Management, Swansea University Bay Campus, Fabian Way,
Swansea SA1 8EN, UK
ykdwivedi@gmail.com
[5] School of Management, University of Bradford,
Emm Ln, Bradford BD9 4JL, UK
kizgin.hatice@gmail.com

Abstract. Despite the rapid growth in mobile stores (e.g., Apple Store, Google Play), scholarly research in this area is still in the early stages. In particular, there is a need for more empirical analysis of how the main features of these new systems shape the customer experience. This study aims to empirically identify and validate the key factors shaping users' satisfaction toward mobile stores. The conceptual model was proposed based on a group of the main factors from the extended Unified Theory of Acceptance and Use of Technology (UTAUT2), mobile interactivity, and perceived security and privacy. The empirical analysis was conducted in Jordan by collecting data from a convenience sample of users of mobile stores. Structural equation modelling was applied to test the current study's model. The results support the significant impact of performance expectancy, price value, hedonic motivation, personalization, responsiveness, and perceived security and privacy on user satisfaction. Discussion of the main limitations and future research directions are also provided.

Keywords: Mobile app stores · UTAUT2 · Mobile interactivity · E-satisfaction

© IFIP International Federation for Information Processing 2019
Published by Springer Nature Switzerland AG 2019
I. O. Pappas et al. (Eds.): I3E 2019, LNCS 11701, pp. 50–61, 2019.
https://doi.org/10.1007/978-3-030-29374-1_5

1   Introduction

The revolution in smartphone technologies and the rapidly growing number of smartphone users have led to mobile stores (e.g., Apple Store, Google Play) becoming increasingly important [20, 36]. According to a report published by [44], Apple Store alone contains more than 2.2 million applications that can be bought and downloaded by Apple platform users, while Google's Play Store hosts more than 2.8 million applications available to other kinds of smartphone user. By the end of 2017, 178.1 billion applications had been downloaded by smartphone users [45]. The importance of mobile stores is likely to increase further, as the number of smartphone users is expected to reach 5 billion in 2019 [45]. At the same time, the high engagement with social media and other digital applications will also increase the use of mobile stores [8, 9, 32, 41].

Prior studies [e.g. 2, 19, 24, 25] indicate a number of factors (such as the level usability, attractiveness, cost, personalization, and privacy) that are frequently reported to play a considerable role in shaping user satisfaction and intention to continue using mobile stores. Capturing a comprehensive picture of users' perception and experience with these digital stores could help practitioners better design the stores so that they cover the most important aspects from the users' perspective [16, 24]. Mobile stores have rarely been addressed by researchers from the customer and digital marketing perspectives [40]. Accordingly, empirical research on and validation of the most important aspects that shape customer satisfaction toward mobile stores are needed. The present study seeks to fill this gap. Moreover, issues relating to mobile stores have not been explored for Middle Eastern and Arab countries. Therefore, in order to advance understanding of mobile use in this region of the world, this study conducts empirical research on mobile users in Jordan.

The rest of this paper is structured as follows: Sect. 2 outlines the theoretical foundation and conceptual model; Sect. 3 explains the research methodology adopted to conduct the empirical analysis; Sect. 4 presents the results of structural equation modelling (SEM); Sect. 5 discusses the main empirical results along with practical and theoretical implications; and the final section presents the main limitations of the current study and suggested future research directions.

2   Literature Review

Due to its novelty, there is very limited literature on the customer's perspective of using mobile stores [20]. Most studies have focused on the technical and technological characteristics of mobile stores and related issues [15, 16, 24]. Chen and Liu [16] applied an observational approach to test three main characteristics: comment, static, and dynamic. Harman et al. [24] used an algorithm to identify the most important characteristics of mobile stores, such as price, download rank, and rate mean.

Iacob et al. [25] manually tested the most important features of mobile stores, finding that versioning, comparative feedback, price feedback, and usability are key mobile store characteristics that shape the user's experience. Based on the same manual method adopted by [25], other important features (namely, the quality, functionality, and aesthetics) were reported by [22] for the Google Play store. Chandy and Gu [15] examined the iOS App store using a Classification and Regression Tree and found that users pay considerable attention to the features related to number of apps, reviewing, rating mean, and ranking and rating statistics.

Among several studies that have addressed mobile stores from the user's perspective, Shen [43] demonstrated that the association between reputation sources and users' attitudes toward mobile stores is significantly predicted by the role of perceived risk. Liu et al. [30] also found that the sales volume of Google Play apps are largely predicted by the freemium strategy and the quality of the platforms. Security features (i.e., privacy protection, safe browsing, and malware prevention) were found by [33] to have a significant impact on the user's satisfaction toward the Google Play store.

Despite the contribution of such prior attempts to advance the current understanding about the important aspects of mobile stores, there has not yet been an attempt to examine mobile stores from the user's perspective. Moreover, there is a need for a solid theoretical foundation and a conceptual model that can capture the most important features from the user's perspective.

3   Conceptual Model

As this study concerns technology acceptance from the customer's perspective, the extended Unified Theory of Acceptance and Use of Technology (UTAUT2) was considered as the proposed conceptual model [4–6, 48]. UTAUT2 was based on the first version of Venkatesh et al.'s [48] model and considered to be more suitable for the customer context. Furthermore, the ability of UTAUT2 to predict individuals' behaviour and reaction toward several types of technology has been widely demonstrated [18, 39, 47].

Five factors from UTAUT2 – performance expectancy (PE), effort expectancy (EE), hedonic motivation (HM), price value (PV), and habit (HT) – were considered as key predictors of users' e-satisfaction (e-SATIS). Perceived privacy (PRV) and security (PS), which are critical aspects associated with mobile technology and mobile stores, were also considered in the current study model to predict users' e-satisfaction [14, 21]. Mobile store technology enjoys a high degree of interactivity [29], so two dimensions of mobile interactivity – responsiveness (RSP) and personalization (PRS) – were also proposed to have a direct effect on users' satisfaction. Figure 1 presents the conceptual model.

3.1   Performance Expectancy

Performance expectancy can be defined according to [48] as the cognitive and functional benefits captured by users of mobile stores. This construct has been largely found by prior literature on mobile technology to have an impact on customers' and users' intention and satisfaction [4–6, 47]. Therefore, users could be more satisfied with their experience with a mobile store if they perceive the store as more useful and productive for their daily life. Accordingly, the following hypothesis proposes:

H1: Performance expectancy will impact user e-satisfaction toward mobile stores.

3.2 Effort Expectancy

Effort expectancy is related to the customers' perception that the targeted applications are easy to use and understand [3, 48]. Users are more likely to be dissatisfied with their experience of using mobile stores if they feel that these stores are difficult to use. This assumption has been largely supported by prior studies that have tested applications similar to mobile technology [e.g., 10, 48]. Thus, the following hypothesis proposes:

H2: Effort expectancy will impact user e-satisfaction toward mobile stores.

3.3 Hedonic Motivation

As argued by [48], customer experience with new systems could be affected by the role of intrinsic motivation. Mobile stores provide users with a wide range of social and entertainment apps that could accelerate customers' feelings of pleasure, and hence to contribute to the level of customers' satisfaction, as reported by studies that have tested the role of hedonic motivation [e.g., 3, 4, 8, 9]. Accordingly, the following hypothesis proposes:

H3: Hedonic motivation will impact user e-satisfaction toward mobile stores.

3.4 Price Value

As proposed by [48], customers' satisfaction could be related to the financial cost of using new systems like mobile stores. Accordingly, customers will not be fully satisfied about their experience of using mobile stores if the perceived benefits are less than the financial costs. The role of price value has been demonstrated by a number of studies on mobile technology, such as [2] and [8]. Accordingly, the following hypothesis proposes:

H4: Price value will impact user e-satisfaction toward mobile stores.

3.5 Habit

Venkatesh et al. [48, p. 161] defined habit as "the extent to which people tend to perform behaviour automatically because of learning." Users seem to be highly attached to their smartphones and spend a considerable amount of time using and browsing mobile stores and downloading apps. They are more likely to have a habitual behaviour and accumulative knowledge and experience in using these apps. This, in turn, could positively impact on their experience of using mobile stores. Thus, the following hypothesis proposes:

H5: Habit will impact user e-satisfaction toward mobile stores.

3.6   Responsiveness

Perceived responsiveness captures how regularly and quickly users' questions and requests are addressed [51]. Furthermore, responsiveness can be viewed as the extent to which mobile stores provide users with relevant and pertinent information and responses to user questions and needs [26]. Therefore, it can be argued that the level of users' satisfaction is likely to be improved by increasing the level of responsiveness. Thus, the following hypothesis proposes:

H6: Responsiveness will impact user e-satisfaction toward mobile stores.

3.7   Personalization

Mobile technology, especially that related to smartphones, enjoys a high level of personalization that enriches the user's experience. Users of mobile technologies (e.g., mobile stores, mobile shopping) are more likely to be happy about their experience if more products, services, information, and applications are customized and tailored to their needs and requirements [1, 35, 36]. Accordingly, the level of users' satisfaction is likely to be increased by improving the level of personalization in mobile stores [29, 37, 38] and [31]. Thus, the following hypothesis proposes:

H7: Personalization will impact user e-satisfaction toward mobile stores.

3.8   Perceived Privacy

Perceived privacy is defined as the "user's perceptions about the protection of all the data that is collected (with or without users being aware of it) during users' interactions with an Internet banking system" [50]. Practically, to use mobile stores properly, users are requested to disclose their personal and financial information. Therefore, a level of perceived privacy is likely to motivate the usage of mobile stores and to enhance the level of users' satisfaction with their experience of mobile stores. Thus, the following hypothesis proposes:

H8: Perceived privacy will impact user e-satisfaction toward mobile stores.

3.9   Perceived Security

Perceived security can be articulated as "the extent to which a consumer believes that making payments online is secure" [49, p. 748]. The extent of protection and security in using mobile stores plays an important role not only in increasing users' intention to use such platforms but also in their satisfaction with these digital stores. Thus, the following hypothesis proposes:

H9: Perceived security will impact user e-satisfaction toward mobile stores.

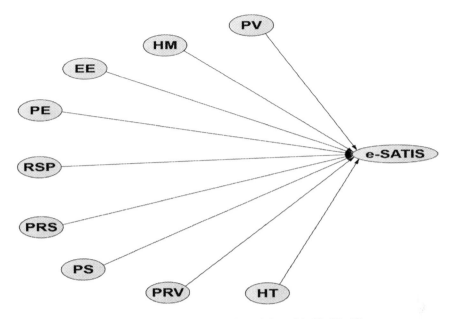

Fig. 1. Conceptual model [adapted from 14, 28, 29, 48]

4 Research Methodology

The empirical part of the current study was conducted in Jordan from November 2018 to the end of January 2019. It involved collecting data from 500 Jordanian users of mobile stores (Apple Store and Google Play). A self-administered questionnaire was developed and allocated to the targeted participants [11, 17]. The main model constructs were measured using well-validated scale items from prior literature. For example, all items from the UTAUT2 framework were adopted from [48], while the items of responsiveness and personalization were extracted from [27]. Perceived privacy and security were extracted from the scale used by [28], and e-satisfaction was tested using items derived from [7]. By using the back translation method suggested by [12], all items were translated into Arabic, the main language in Jordan. To ensure an adequate level of reliability, prior to the main survey a pilot study was conducted with a small sample of 25 users of mobile stores. Cronbach's alpha values for all constructs were above their recommended level of 0.70 [34].

5 Results

A two-stage SEM method was used to test the current study's model. The two-stage method has been widely used by a many high-impact journal papers, and it was considered to be more suitable for testing the goodness of fit and validating the constructs of the current study's model, as well as for testing the main research hypotheses [23].

In the first stage, the results of the SEM measurement model largely supported the level of goodness of fit. All of the fit indices had values within their suggested level, that is, goodness-of-fit index (GFI) = 0.901; adjusted goodness-of-fit index (AGFI) = 0.845; comparative fit index (CFI) = 0.965; normed chi-square (CMIN/DF) = 2.325; normed-fit index (NFI) = 0.932; and root mean square error of approximation (RMSEA) = 0.053 [13, 23, 46]. Likewise, all model constructs were found to have adequate values of composite reliability (CR) (>0.70) and average variance extracted (AVE) (>0.50). More specifically: PE (CR = 0.912; AVE = 0.721); EE (CR = 0.933; AVE = 0.777); RSP (CR = 0.984; AVE = 0.953); PV (CR = 0.866; AVE = 0.685); PS (CR = 0.903; AVE = 0.705); PRV (CR = 0.838; AVE = 0.635); E-SATIS (CR = 0.943; AVE = 0.847); HM (CR = 0.838; AVE = 0.622); PRS (CR = 0.778; 0.539); HT (CR = 0.971; AVE = 0.919).

The structural model results indicated that the model was able to predict about 0.54 of variance in user satisfaction (see Fig. 2). The model also adequately fit the observed data as all of its fit indices were found within their threshold values (CMIN/DF = 2.451; GFI = 0.90; AGFI = 0.832; CFI = 0.952; NFI = 0.921; RMSEA = 0.0601). Of the nine hypotheses, seven were confirmed. Figure 2 shows that the most significant factor predicting e-satisfaction was PE (γ = 0.49, p < 0.000), followed by PRS (γ = 0.32, p < 0.000), and then PRV (γ = 0.29, p < 0.000). PS was the fourth factor to significantly contribute to E-SATIS (γ = 0.20, p < 0.000). E-SATIS was also noticed to be significantly predicted by the role of RSP (γ = 0.19, p < 0.000), PV (γ = 0.14, p < 0.003), and HM (γ = 0.18, p < 0.000). On the other hand, neither EE (γ = -0.02, p < 0.775) nor HT (γ = −0.01, p < 0.877) have a significant relationship with e-satisfaction.

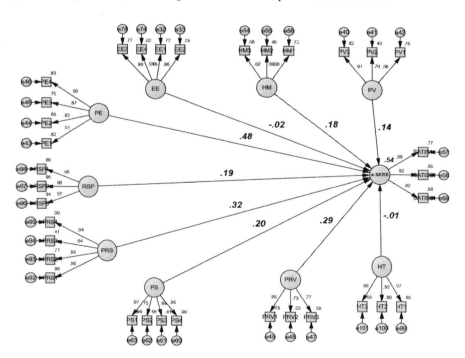

Fig. 2. Validation of the conceptual model

6   Discussion

This study aimed to capture an accurate picture of the main factors that could shape users' satisfaction toward mobile stores. The empirical results supported the proposed conceptual model, which was able to capture an adequate level of predictive validity with 0.54 of variance accounted in e-satisfaction. In addition, the model satisfactorily meets the criteria pertaining to model fitness.

The path coefficient analyses show that seven factors – PE, PRS, PRV, PS, RSP, HM, and PV – significantly contribute to E-SATIS. According to Fig. 2, the most powerful factor contributing to E-SATIS is PE. These results indicate that Jordanian users are drawn to and motivated by the level of utilitarian value in mobile stores. This could be because of the ability of these digital stores to help users find and download the requested apps using less time and effort. Moreover, it is likely that, because of the large number of useful apps available on these platforms, mobile stores are considered by users to be really useful and productive in their everyday lives.

As mobile stores require users to disclose and provide their own personal and financial information, both perceived privacy and security were the focus of attention of the participants in the current study. It is noticeable that users' satisfaction is largely shaped and predicted by the level of privacy and security in using mobile stores, which has been largely supported by prior mobile technology studies [e.g., 10, 28, 41, 42].

Satisfaction was also noticed to be increased among those users who perceive mobile stores to have a high degree of personalization. In research on digital marketing, it has been commonly argued and shown that customization is a key leverage of users' experience and satisfaction. The innovative features of mobile stores allow users to have a high level of customized buying experience, which in turn enriches the level of users' satisfaction. Users were also found to pay attention to the extent of responsiveness in mobile stores. This indicates that as long as users find a high level of correspondence between their needs, preferences, and lifestyles, and what is available in mobile stores, they will be more satisfied about their experience of using such digital platforms [9].

By the same token, users were found to pay a considerable attention to whether mobile stores are reasonably priced. To put this differently, users are more likely to be satisfied about their experience of using mobile stores if they see more monetary value from this experience. This was also demonstrated for Jordanian mobile banking users in a study conducted by [4]. The results of the current study also support the role of hedonic motivation in shaping users' satisfaction. This indicates that a high level of entertainment in the users' experience of mobile stores leads to a high level of satisfaction. This might be related to the degree of novelty that mobile stores enjoy. As mentioned above, mobile stores have high levels of personalization and responsiveness, which in turn contributes to the level of intrinsic utility.

6.1   Research Contribution

First, the significance of this study comes from the importance of mobile stores as a new technology requiring further research and analysis. Secondly, the topic of mobile stores has rarely been addressed from the user's perspective. Moreover, the vast majority of these limited studies have not adopted a systematic approach in proposing their models. Furthermore, there is as yet no study that has explored the subject of mobile stores in relation to Jordan. Accordingly, this study makes a number of theoretical contributions at different levels. It provides an accurate picture of the main factors that can shape user satisfaction toward mobile stores. The current model was developed and empirically validated, so it can be used in different contexts and countries to investigate how users perceive and use mobile stores differently.

7 Limitations and Future Research Directions

There are a number of limitations in the current study that could be addressed in future studies. Due to the word count restrictions, a limited and very short discussion has been provided. Accordingly, the hypotheses could be discussed in more detail in future studies. Although this study covers important aspects that could shape the user's satisfaction toward mobile stores, there are still other factors worth considering in future research. For instance, only two aspects of mobile interactivity (personalization and responsiveness) were tested in the current study, while other aspects (active control, ubiquitous connectivity, connectedness, and synchronicity) were ignored. Researchers interested in the area of mobile stores might consider these other factors. The technical features of mobile phone (e.g., phone brand and type, size of screen, battery capacity, memory) could also be considered by future studies as they have not been covered in the current study. This study has tested mobile stores in general, but it does not address the differences between Apple Store and Google Play. It would be worth conducting a comparison between these mobile stores to see how users' experiences and reactions are different from one store to another. Finally, the current study was purely quantitative, so a qualitative study could provide further and deeper understanding of the main factors that shape users' experience and satisfaction with mobile stores.

References

1. Alalwan, A.A.: Investigating the impact of social media advertising features on customer purchase intention. Int. J. Inf. Manag. **42**, 65–77 (2018)
2. Alalwan, A.A.: Mobile food ordering apps: an empirical study of the factors affecting customer e-satisfaction and continued intention to reuse. Int. J. Inf. Manag. **50**, 28–44 (2020)
3. Alalwan, A.A., Baabdullah, A.M., Rana, N.P., Tamilmani, K., Dwivedi, Y.K.: Examining adoption of mobile internet in Saudi Arabia: extending TAM with perceived enjoyment, innovativeness and trust. Technol. Soc. **55**, 100–110 (2018)
4. Alalwan, A.A., Dwivedi, Y.K., Rana, N.P.: Factors influencing adoption of mobile banking by Jordanian bank customers: extending UTAUT2 with trust. Int. J. Inf. Manag. **37**(3), 99–110 (2017)
5. Alalwan, A.A., Dwivedi, Y.K., Rana, N.P., Algharabat, R.: Examining factors influencing Jordanian customers' intentions and adoption of internet banking: extending UTAUT2 with risk. J. Retail. Consum. Serv. **40**, 125–138 (2018)

6. Alalwan, A.A., Dwivedi, Y.K., Rana, N.P., Williams, M.D.: Consumer adoption of mobile banking in Jordan: examining the role of usefulness, ease of use, perceived risk and self-efficacy. J. Enterp. Inf. Manag. **29**(1), 118–139 (2016)
7. Anderson, E.W., Sullivan, M.W.: The antecedents and consequences of customer satisfaction for firms. Mark. Sci. **12**(2), 125–143 (1993)
8. Baabdullah, A.M.: Consumer adoption of mobile social network games (M-SNGs) in Saudi Arabia: the role of social influence, hedonic motivation and trust. Technol. Soc. **53**, 91–102 (2018)
9. Baabdullah, A.M.: Factors influencing adoption of mobile social network games (M-SNGs): the role of awareness. Inf. Syst. Front. 1–17 (2018)
10. Baabdullah, A.M., Alalwan, A.A., Rana, N.P., Patil, P., Dwivedi, Y.K.: An integrated model for m-banking adoption in Saudi Arabia. Int. J. Bank Mark. **37**(2), 452–478 (2019)
11. Bhattacherjee, A.: Social Science Research: Principles, Methods, and Practices, 2nd edn. Anol Bhattacherjee, Florida (2012)
12. Brislin, R.: Comparative research methodology: Cross-cultural studies. Int. J. Psychol. **11**(3), 215–229 (1976)
13. Byrne, B.: Structural Equation Modeling with AMOS: Basic Concepts, Applications and Programming, 6th edn. Taylor & Francis Group, New York (2010)
14. Casaló, L.V., Flavián, C., Guinalíu, M.: The role of security, privacy, usability and reputation in the development of online banking. Online Inf. Rev. **31**(5), 583–603 (2007)
15. Chandy, R., Gu, H.: Identifying spam in the iOS app store. In: Proceedings of the 2nd Joint WICOW/AIRWeb Workshop on Web Quality, pp. 56–59. ACM (2012)
16. Chen, M., Liu, X.: Predicting popularity of online distributed applications: iTunes app store case analysis. In: Proceedings of the 2011 iConference, pp. 661–663. ACM, February 2011
17. Dwivedi, Y.K., Choudrie, J., Brinkman, W.P.: Development of a survey instrument to examine consumer adoption of broadband. Ind. Manag. Data Syst. **106**(5), 700–718 (2006)
18. Dwivedi, Y.K., Rana, N.P., Jeyaraj, A., Clement, M., Williams, M.D.: Re-examining the unified theory of acceptance and use of technology (UTAUT): towards a revised theoretical model. Inf. Syst. Front. 1–16 (2017). https://doi.org/10.1007/s10796-017-9774-y
19. Fu, B., Lin, J., Li, L., Faloutsos, C., Hong, J., Sadeh, N.: Why people hate your app: making sense of user feedback in a mobile app store. In: Proceedings of the 19th ACM SIGKDD International Conference on Knowledge Discovery and Data mining, pp. 1276–1284. ACM (2013)
20. Genc-Nayebi, N., Abran, A.: A systematic literature review: opinion mining studies from mobile app store user reviews. J. Syst. Softw. **125**, 207–219 (2017)
21. Gutierrez, A., O'Leary, S., Rana, N.P., Dwivedi, Y.K., Calle, T.: Using privacy calculus theory to explore entrepreneurial directions in mobile location-based advertising: identifying intrusiveness as the critical risk factor. Comput. Hum. Behav. **95**, 295–306 (2018)
22. Ha, E., Wagner, D.: Do android users write about electric sheep? Examining consumer reviews in Google play. In: 2013 IEEE 10th Consumer Communications and Networking Conference (CCNC), pp. 149–157. IEEE (2013)
23. Hair Jr., J.F., Black, W.C., Babin, B.J., Anderson, R.E.: Multivariate Data Analysis: A Global Perspective, 7th edn. Pearson Education International, Upper Saddle River (2010)
24. Harman, M., Jia, Y., Zhang, Y.: App store mining and analysis: MSR for app stores. In: Proceedings of the 9th IEEE Working Conference on Mining Software Repositories, pp. 108–111. IEEE Press (2012)
25. Iacob, C., Veerappa, V., Harrison, R.: What are you complaining about? A study of online reviews of mobile applications. In: Proceedings of the 27th International BCS Human Computer Interaction Conference, p. 29. British Computer Society (2013)

26. Johnson, G.J., Bruner II, G.C., Kumar, A.: Interactivity and its facets revisited: theory and empirical test. J. Advert. **35**(4), 35–52 (2006)
27. Kim, A.J., Ko, E.: Do social media marketing activities enhance customer equity? An empirical study of luxury fashion brand. J. Bus. Res. **65**(10), 1480–1486 (2012)
28. Kim, K.J., Jeong, I.J., Park, J.C., Park, Y.J., Kim, C.G., Kim, T.H.: The impact of network service performance on customer satisfaction and loyalty: high-speed internet service case in Korea. Expert Syst. Appl. Int. J. **32**(3), 822–831 (2007)
29. Lee, T.: The impact of perceptions of interactivity on customer trust and transaction intentions in mobile commerce. J. Electron. Commer. Res. **6**(3), 165–180 (2005)
30. Liu, C.Z., Au, Y.A., Choi, H.S.: Effects of freemium strategy in the mobile app market: an empirical study of Google play. J. Manag. Inf. Syst. **31**(3), 326–354 (2014)
31. Liu, Y.: Developing a scale to measure the interactivity of websites. J. Adv. Res. **43**(2), 207–216 (2003)
32. Marriott, H.R., Williams, M.D., Dwivedi, Y.K.: What do we know about consumer m-shopping behaviour? Int. J. Retail Distrib. Manag. **45**(6), 568–586 (2017)
33. Mei-Ling, Y.A.O., Chuang, M.C., Chun-Cheng, H.S.U.: The Kano model analysis of features for mobile security applications. Comput Secur. **78**, 336–346 (2018)
34. Nunnally, J.C., Bernstein, I.H., Berge, J.M.T.: Psychometric Theory. McGraw-Hill, New York (1967)
35. Pappas, I.O.: User experience in personalized online shopping: a fuzzy-set analysis. Eur. J. Mark. **52**(7/8), 1679–1703 (2018)
36. Pappas, I.O., Kourouthanassis, P.E., Giannakos, M.N., Chrissikopoulos, V.: Explaining online shopping behavior with fsQCA: the role of cognitive and affective perceptions. J. Bus. Res. **69**(2), 794–803 (2016)
37. Pappas, I.O., Kourouthanassis, P.E., Giannakos, M.N., Chrissikopoulos, V.: Sense and sensibility in personalized e-commerce: how emotions rebalance the purchase intentions of persuaded customers. Psychol. Mark. **34**(10), 972–986 (2017)
38. Pappas, I.O., Pateli, A.G., Giannakos, M.N., Chrissikopoulos, V.: Moderating effects of online shopping experience on customer satisfaction and repurchase intentions. Int. J. Retail Distrib. Manag. **42**(3), 187–204 (2014)
39. Rana, N.P., Dwivedi, Y.K., Lal, B., Williams, M.D., Clement, M.: Citizens' adoption of an electronic government system: towards a unified view. Inf. Syst. Front. **19**(3), 549–568 (2017)
40. Roma, P., Ragaglia, D.: Revenue models, in-app purchase, and the app performance: evidence from Apple's app store and Google Play. Electron. Commer. Res. Appl. **17**, 173–190 (2016)
41. Shareef, M.A., Baabdullah, A., Dutta, S., Kumar, V., Dwivedi, Y.K.: Consumer adoption of mobile banking services: an empirical examination of factors according to adoption stages. J. Retail. Consum. Serv. **43**, 54–67 (2018)
42. Shareef, M.A., Dwivedi, Y.K., Stamati, T., Williams, M.D.: SQ mGov: a comprehensive service-quality paradigm for mobile government. Inf. Syst. Manag. **31**(2), 126–142 (2014)
43. Shen, G.C.C.: Users' adoption of mobile applications: product type and message framing's moderating effect. J. Bus. Res. **68**(11), 2317–2321 (2015)
44. Statista: Mobile app usage: statistics and Facts (2018a). https://www.statista.com/topics/1002/mobile-app-usage/. Accessed 15 Dec 2018
45. Statista: Number of mobile app downloads worldwide in 2017, 2018 and 2022 (in billions) (2018b). https://www.statista.com/statistics/271644/worldwide-free-and-paid-mobile-app-store-downloads/. Accessed 15 Dec 2018
46. Tabachnick, B.G., Fidell, L.S., Ullman, J.B.: Using Multivariate Statistics. Pearson, Boston (2007)

47. Tamilmani, K., Rana, N.P., Prakasam, N., Dwivedi, Y.K.: The battle of brain vs. heart: a literature review and meta-analysis of "hedonic motivation" use in UTAUT2. Int. J. Inf. Manag. **46**, 222–235 (2019)
48. Venkatesh, V., Thong, J.Y., Xu, X.: Consumer acceptance and use of information technology: extending the unified theory of acceptance and use of technology. MIS Q. **36**(1), 157–178 (2012)
49. Vijayasarathy, L.R.: Predicting consumer intentions to use on-line shopping: the case for an augmented technology acceptance model. Inf. Manag. **41**(6), 747–762 (2004)
50. Wang, Y.S., Wang, Y.M., Lin, H.H., Tang, T.I.: Determinants of user acceptance of internet banking: an empirical study. Int. J. Serv. Ind. Manag. **14**(5), 501–519 (2003)
51. Zhao, L., Lu, Y.: Enhancing perceived interactivity through network externalities: an empirical study on micro-blogging service satisfaction and continuance intention. Decis. Support Syst. **53**(4), 825–834 (2012)

Towards Assessing Online Customer Reviews from the Product Designer's Viewpoint

Mate Kovacs$^{(\boxtimes)}$ and Victor V. Kryssanov

Ritsumeikan University, Nojihigashi 1-1-1, Kusatsu 525-8577, Japan
gr0370hh@ed.ritsumei.ac.jp, kvvictor@is.ritsumei.ac.jp

Abstract. Product reviews are a type of user-generated content that can be beneficial for both customers and product designers. Without quantifying the design knowledge present in product reviews, however, it is hard for the companies to integrate reviews into the design process. Several studies investigated review helpfulness in general, but few works explored the problem of review quality from the perspective of product designers. In this study, a theoretical model is presented and a system is proposed to assess the quality of online product reviews from the viewpoint of product designers. The system involves an original similarity-based metric to quantify the design information content of reviews on a continuous scale. Experiments are performed on a large number of digital camera reviews, with results indicating that the proposed system is capable of recognizing high-quality content, and would potentially assist companies in product improvement and innovation.

Keywords: eWOM · e-commerce · Review quality and helpfulness · Product design · Information overload

1 Introduction

EWOM (Electronic Word of Mouth) can provide valuable information about customer needs, as it offers potentially useful knowledge not just for customers, but also for product designers. Presently, manufacturing evolves to become more customer-driven and knowledge-based [4]. Customer intelligence extracted from online product reviews can help manufacturers to improve their products by incorporating relevant information into the design process [8]. Typically, companies use interviews and surveys to obtain feedback from customers. Design knowledge extracted from product reviews differs from and has a complementary function to customer intelligence collected by traditional methods [26,29]. The immense amount of reviews available at online platforms, however, makes it a challenging task for companies to obtain relevant information about product design. Popular and trending products often receive thousands of reviews from

© IFIP International Federation for Information Processing 2019
Published by Springer Nature Switzerland AG 2019
I. O. Pappas et al. (Eds.): I3E 2019, LNCS 11701, pp. 62–74, 2019.
https://doi.org/10.1007/978-3-030-29374-1_6

the customers, and review quality varies extensively through the large volume of reviews [13,25]. Addressing this issue, often called *information overload*, is essential to effectively utilize customer reviews for product and service enhancement [9].

A reason for many data-mining projects being abandoned is the poor quality of the data used [12]. Review quality is seldom discussed in opinion mining studies [2], even though often most of the reviews appear practically useless from the designer's standpoint. Many e-commerce platforms introduced helpfulness-voting, where users rate other users' reviews, based on their helpfulness. These votes, however, are unavoidably influenced by the Matthew effect, as customers usually only read and vote for the top reviews, which will, thus, remain on top [22]. In fact, this kind of helpfulness score is often argued to be an unreliable measure of actual helpfulness and review quality [3,5,25,28]. Another limiting factor of helpfulness-voting is the divergence between the helpfulness perceived by the customers and the helpfulness seen by the product designers [14]. Most of the studies dealt with review helpfulness only consider the customer's viewpoint, and limited work is available on quantifying design information of reviews to assist product designers and engineers.

The goal of the presented study is to reduce the information overload associated with customer reviews, and assess product review quality from the designers' standpoint in order to mine reviews that can potentially induce better design. The main contribution of this research is a theoretical model with a developed system using an original measure for quantifying review information at the design level without the need for manual feature engineering. Experiments are conducted on a large dataset of digital camera reviews, collected from Amazon US. Results obtained suggest that the proposed system can be used in practice effectively to assist companies in eliciting useful reviews.

The rest of the paper is organized as follows. Related work is presented in Sect. 2, while Sect. 3 describes the model and the system developed for assessing product review quality. Section 4 introduces the data used in this study. The experimental procedure is described in Sect. 5. Results obtained are interpreted, and the main findings are discussed in Sect. 6. Section 7 formulates conclusions and outlines future work directions.

2 Related Work

Some of the related literature formulate a classification problem of review helpfulness (as an aspect of review quality) [7,11,15], and other works treat it as a regression or ranking problem [3,16,24]. Most of the studies dealt with several types of features, such as product features (key attributes of products), sentiment values (e.g. positive or negative), linguistic cues (e.g. the number of nouns, grammatical rules, review length, readability features, etc.), and user information (e.g. reviewer reputation, gender). Qazi et al. [18] considered also the review type to develop a model for helpfulness prediction. The authors conducted experiments on 1500 hotel reviews with results suggesting that the number of concepts in a review, and the type of the review (regular, comparative, or suggestive) influences review helpfulness. Saumya et al. [21] found that besides features extracted from review texts, customer question-answer data improves the prediction of review helpfulness, as perceived by the customers. Krishnamoorthy [7] proposed a help-fulness prediction model based on review metadata, linguistic features, and also review subjectivity.

While the research on assessing review quality for product designers has been limited, there are still a number of notable studies dealing with the subject. Liu et al. [14] estimated the helpfulness of product reviews from the product designer's perspective, utilizing only the review text itself. The authors conducted an exper-iment to better understand what are the determinants of review helpfulness for product designers. Based on the results, four categories of features were identi-fied to be important. These are linguistic features (e.g. the number of words), product features (attributes of a specific product), information quality-based fea-tures (e.g. the number of referred products), and information-theoretic features (e.g. review sentiment). The authors used regression to predict the helpfulness of reviews, and found that extracting these features using only the review con-tent can help with identifying helpful reviews. Yagci and Das [26] argue that design intelligence helpful to both designers and customers can be extracted from product reviews. In their work, sentence-level opinion polarity determina-tion (with categories of negative, neutral, and positive) was used together with noun-adjective and noun-verb association rules to extract the probable cause of a certain opinion. In a later work, the authors introduced the design-level infor-mation quality (DLIQ) measure for assessing the volume and quality of design knowledge of product reviews [27]. Reviews were evaluated based on content (the total number of words), complexity (the total number of sentences and nouns), and relevancy (the total number of nouns matching predefined design features), and promising results were obtained for assisting businesses in product development.

Most of the previous work do not differentiate between the helpfulness seen by customers and by product designers. Furthermore, nearly all of the related studies required manual feature engineering to obtain product features, and used noun and noun phrase matching to extract them from the reviews. One of the biggest issues of such methods is that the same feature can be expressed in various ways (explicitly or implicitly, with different words and phrases, etc.), and pattern matching approaches cannot account for such cases. Moreover, the presence of a specific word does not necessarily guarantee high-quality content, as word context plays a critical role in its interpretation. In the next section, an approach capable of dealing with these issues is introduced.

3 Proposed Approach

3.1 Theoretical Model

The approach proposed in this study builds on the assumption that any word of a language can appear in any kind of document. More formally, depending on for whom the document is targeted (target population) and what is the subject of the document (domain), words of a language appear with certain probabilities, and have weights indicating their importance. Let us denote the set of all documents d as $D = \{d_1, d_2, ..., d_n\}$, and the vocabulary of all words w for language L as $L = \{w_1, w_2, ..., w_m\}$. Let us define a set of scalar weights $\Phi_V^T = \{\varphi_{V_1}^T, \varphi_{V_2}^T, ..., \varphi_{V_z}^T\}$, indicating the importance of words w for the domain V for a target population T. As follows,

$$(\forall V)(\forall T)[(\forall w)(w \in L) \wedge (\forall d)(d \in D)(\Diamond(w \in d)) \wedge (\exists \varphi_V^T)(\varphi_V^T \in \Phi_V^T)(w \rightarrow \varphi_V^T)], \tag{1}$$

where $\Diamond$ is the modal operator of possibility. For example, there is a chance that one encounters the word *sensor* in any kind of text, but if the domain is *digital cameras*, and the target population is the *product designer community*, this word has a high importance. If the domain-target combination is *programming-high school students*, the word *sensor* could still be important, but probably does not carry the same weight. On a similar note, the word *traditional* is probably not important for *digital cameras-product designer community*, but that does not mean it carries no information whatsoever about V and T, especially in the appropriate context. In fact, the underlying pragmatics will always have an impact on the interpretation of words. Word meaning in a natural language is defined by the context, and a huge part of the context depends on the domain and the target population. Thus, V and T also function as indicators of word meaning.

3.2 Review Quality Assessment

Based on the theoretical model proposed in Sect. 3.1, the inferential problem dealt with in this study is to approximate Φ_V^T for $T = product\ designer\ community$, and for a certain domain V. Then, review quality would be estimated by measuring the distance between a review and Φ_V^T. In the presented study, technical documents of domain V are analyzed for the definition of Φ_V^T, as texts, which are in the interest of product designers are assumed to contain a high volume of technical content. Figure 1 gives an overview of the proposed system for assessing review quality. There are two types of inputs involved, a database of technical documents, and a database of reviews, both from the same domain V.

Term Dictionary Formulation. A collection of technical documents representing the product domain is cleaned from "unwanted" content (e.g. author information, bibliography, etc.), and tokenized to build a corpus of preprocessed sentences. To obtain an approximation of the set Φ_V^T, the sentences are used to select a large number of words with weights attached to them, based on their importance. All words are first lemmatized to obtain their dictionary form (e.g. studying, study, studies all becomes study), and stopwords are eliminated. The word weights constituting the set Φ_V^T are calculated, based on the mean sentence-wise term frequency-inverse document frequency (tf-idf) scores of the

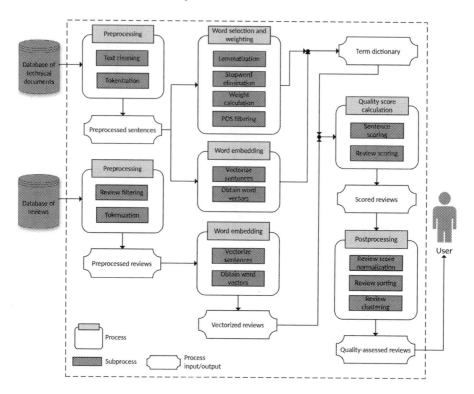

Fig. 1. The structure of the system proposed for assessing review quality

words. The statistical measure tf-idf is usually used to evaluate document-wise word importance. In this study, sentences are treated as individual documents, and the sentence-wise scores are averaged. Hence, the weight φ of word w is given by

$$\varphi(w) = \frac{1}{N} \sum_{i=1}^{N} f_{s_i}(w) \ln \left(\frac{N}{f_w(s)} \right), \tag{2}$$

where $f_{s_i}(w)$ is the frequency of word w in sentence s_i, $f_w(s)$ is the number of sentences containing w, and N is the total number of sentences in the corpus. As all word tokens are weighted by the above equation, irrelevant Part of Speech (POS) are to be filtered out from the sentences. In previous work, few nouns and noun phrases were typically considered for candidate features. In the proposed system, all adjectives, adverbs, verbs, nouns and noun phrases are considered with their corresponding importance weights.

The preprocessed sentences are also used to create word embeddings for representing the words in a continuous vector space. Most word embedding methods are not contextualized, meaning that the vector representations of words are static (one vector per word). However, as word meaning in a natural language is context-dependent, word vectors should change, depending on the context.

Embeddings from Language Models (*ELMo*) [17] uses an unsupervised, pre-trained deep bidirectional long short-term memory (BiLSTM) neural network model to compute contextualized word vectors in the following way:

$$ELMo_w = \gamma \sum_{j=0}^{L} b_j h_{w,j}, \tag{3}$$

where $h_{w,j}$ is the output of the jth layer L of the network for word w. The weight b_j is learned for each individual task (input sentence), and normalized by the softmax function. The parameter γ scales the word vectors for optimization. Since the model is initially pre-trained on a large amount of data, the network requires a single sentence to output context dependent vector representations of words. The ELMo embeddings obtained for all words are averaged for every unique word lemma remaining after POS filtering to acquire vectors describing V and T in the most accurate way possible. The selected words and their weights with their corresponding vector representations are stored together in a dictionary. These words will further be referred to as "terms".

Calculating Review Scores. The other input of the system is a database of product reviews. First, one-word and non-English reviews are filtered out from the database, and the remaining texts are tokenized. Next, the preprocessed reviews are vectorized with the same method as the technical documents (ELMo). As the embedding vectors are context dependent, even when product features or components are described in different ways, the corresponding phrases and sentences will still have similar vectors. The vector representations of reviews are used together with the term dictionary to compute the quality scores of the reviews. The procedure of score calculation is specified by Algorithm 1. For each review, the scores are calculated first on the word level, then on the sentence level and, lastly, on the review level. Cosine similarities are calculated between vectors **v** of the observed word w and terms t in the term dictionary to assess their closeness. The similarity scores computed are subtracted from 1 to get the cosine distance between the observed word and the terms, that is used as the exponent of term weights for the word scores. This means, each word w will receive as many scores as the number of terms t in the term dictionary, which are then summed up to compute the *word pertinence*:

$$pertinence(w) = \sum_{k=1}^{t} \varphi_k^{1-cos(\mathbf{v}_k,\mathbf{v}_w)}. \tag{4}$$

With Eq. 4, contributions of relevant words to the total score are much higher than irrelevant ones, and the dependence of word similarity the on context gets addressed. Sentence and review scores are defined as cumulated word pertinences and sentence scores, respectively. Thus, the final score of review r is obtained as

$$score(r) = \sum_{i=1}^{s}\sum_{j=1}^{w}\sum_{k=1}^{t} \varphi_k^{1-cos(\mathbf{v}_k,\mathbf{v}_j^i)}. \tag{5}$$

Algorithm 1. Calculate review quality scores

1: **procedure** CALCULATE SCORES(reviews,terms)
2:      **initialize** array *corpus_scores*
3:      **for all** review $\in$ reviews **do**
4:          **initialize** array *review_scores*
5:          **for all** sentence $\in$ review **do**
6:              **initialize** *sentence_score* $\leftarrow 0$
7:              **for all** word $\in$ sentence **do**
8:                  **if** word $\notin$ stopwords **then**
9:                      **initialize** *word_pertinence* $\leftarrow 0$
10:                     **for all** term $\in$ terms **do**
11:                         $\cos(\theta) = \frac{\mathbf{v}_{term} \cdot \mathbf{v}_{word}}{\|\mathbf{v}_{term}\|\|\mathbf{v}_{word}\|}$
12:                         *word_pertinence* $\leftarrow$ *word_pertinence* $+ \varphi_{term}^{1-\cos(\theta)}$
13:                     **end for**
14:                   *sentence_score* $\leftarrow$ *sentence_score* $+$ *word_pertinence*
15:                 **end if**
16:             **end for**
17:             **insert** *sentence_score* into *review_scores*
18:         **end for**
19:         **insert** *review_scores* into *corpus_scores*
20:     **end for**
21: **end procedure**

The reason for keeping the sentence-level scores is that knowing what sentences *s* contributed most to the final review score is often useful in practice.

Postprocessing. The computed raw quality scores are between 0 and theoretically, infinity. This means that normalization is necessary to obtain easily interpretable results, and to establish lower and upper bounds for the quality assessment of future reviews. Additionally, reviews are to be sorted in a descending order to help the end-user choosing high-quality reviews. Rather than defining a threshold value for when a review would become helpful, 1-dimensional K-means is used to cluster the review scores into potentially meaningful groups, and help the user with the elicitation of high-quality reviews. The number of clusters k is determined by the elbow method [20]. As k increases, there will be a point where the improvement of the model starts declining. At that point, the sum of squared distances of the datapoints to the nearest cluster creates an "elbow of an arm" when plotted. The location of this elbow point indicates the optimal number of k.

4   Data

In the presented study, the shared domain V of technical documents and product reviews is *digital cameras*. The reviews used are part of Amazon review data [6]. The data includes 7,824,482 reviews from the "Electronics" category, written by customers of Amazon.com in the period from 1996 to 2014. Reviews of digital cameras and closely related products (e.g. lenses, battery chargers, etc.) were selected, using product subcategory tags and product IDs. Reviews with sentences longer than 50 tokens are presumably reviews without punctuation, that would bias the review score and the overall results. Such reviews, for that reason, were eliminated from the dataset. The final review database used in the study consists of 300,170 product reviews, with 1,315,310 sentences in total. The technical text database was created from Wikipedia articles. Wikipedia contains a large quantity of technical information [23], and the articles are publicly available and downloadable from Wikimedia dumps[1]. All Wikipedia articles published until the 1st of Oct., 2018 were downloaded, and 1039 articles related to digital photography terminology, techniques, equipment, and product descriptions were extracted, using Wikipedia tags and other metadata. Unrelated parts of the articles (e.g. "References", "See also", "History", etc.) were later removed from the technical document database. The ELMo language model[2] used in this study has been pre-trained on the 1 Billion Word Benchmark dataset [1] for word vectors of 1024 dimensions.

5   Results

From the total of 24,134 sentences in the technical document database, 13,166 unique word lemmas were derived into the term dictionary. To give a few examples, the top 20 terms obtained are as follows: *mount, sensor, model, focus, shutter, series, aperture, flash, photography, system, frame, light, design, zoom, mode, speed, exposure, format, specification, iso.* To unbiasedly compute the elbow point of the sum of squared distances for different number of K-means clusters, the algorithm called "Kneedle" [20] is used. Figure 2 illustrates that the elbow point was detected at $k = 3$. Three clusters were, therefore, used to

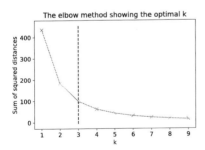

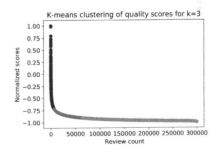

Fig. 2. Sum of squared distances for different number of k

Fig. 3. Distribution of normalized and clustered review quality scores, with different colors indicating the three clusters

---

[1] https://dumps.wikimedia.org.

[2] The pretrained ELMo model was obtained from AllenNLP (https://allennlp.org).

group the review quality scores. Figure 3 shows the distribution of the sorted (descending order) review quality scores normalized between $[-1, 1]$, clustered by K-means. The first cluster contains 6942 reviews with scores $[1.0, -0.72]$, the second includes 56,550 reviews with scores $(-0.72, -0.9]$, and the third has the rest of 236,678 reviews with scores $(-0.9, -1.0]$. Finally, Fig. 4 gives the distribution of sentence-wise quality scores normalized between -1 and 1.

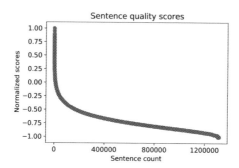

Fig. 4. Distribution of the normalized sentence quality scores

5.1   Comparision with Human Assessment

In order to predict the quality of a future review accurately, and to apply the system used in this study effectively in industrial settings, the system should utilize initially as many reviews as possible. However, this makes validation of the system a challenging task. As the scores define a ranking among the reviews, the three K-means clusters were labeled according to their ranks (1, 2, or 3, in the order of decreasing quality). 400 reviews were chosen randomly from each cluster to create the validation set of 1200 reviews.

The validation procedure used in this study is as follows. One review is chosen randomly from each cluster of the validation set, resulting in three reviews with a certain ranking among them established by the system. These reviews are then independently ranked by a human annotator (one of the authors), and Kendall's rank correlation coefficient is computed between the two rankings. The tau coefficient of Kendall measures the ordinal association between two rankings in the range of $[-1, 1]$ by

$$\tau = \frac{n_c - n_d}{n(n-1)/2}, \tag{6}$$

where n is the number of elements in each ranking, n_c is the number of concordant pairs, and n_d is the number of discordant pairs. $\tau = -1$ indicates a perfect inverse association, 1 implies 100% agreement, and 0 assumes no correlation between the rankings. Finally, the two-sided p-value for $H_0 : \tau = 0$ is computed to estimate the significance of the statistic. This process is repeated until every review is included in exactly one correlation calculation (400 iterations). The final correlation score is computed by taking the mean of all individual τ, and the p-values are combined by Fisher's method to obtain the significance of the averaged coefficients. The results have been obtained are as follows: the averaged correlation between the two rankings $\tau = 0.827$, significant at $p < 0.001$.

6   Discussion

Unsurprisingly, words in the term dictionary with higher weights are important features of domain V. However, there are words in the top few hundred terms, which are not necessarily features in the strict sense, nevertheless are quite significant, owing to their meaning and expected context in V. Examples of such terms include *capture, interchangeable, back, short, depth, integrate, dark, compensate,* etc.

Camera brands, series names, and product description-like facts about measurements (e.g. Canon, uhd, ias, dx, d500, ev, mm) are often encountered in product reviews. For example, the sentence "Has a superb AF-S DX NIKKOR 16–80 mm f/2.8-4E ED VR lens" is not very useful by itself, but the mere presence of these specification-like technical words would increase review score significantly. For this reason, the stopword list used in this study had to be extended with camera brand names, and all non-English words were also considered as stopwords.

The distribution of review scores (Fig. 3) reflects the fact that the number of reviews useful for the product designer community is very limited. The range of scores in the cluster with the highest review qualities is rather extensive. A reason for this is that reviews of topmost quality are highly detailed and particularly in-depth, yet extremely rare to encounter. The score range of the K-means clusters indicates that reviews with scores, for instance, 0 or −0.6 are still useful. Reviews in the second cluster can still be helpful for the product designers, but generally, these have a shorter review length, compared to the first cluster. The number of words and sentences in a review have been found to strongly correlate with review quality and helpfulness in the literature [10,19,28]. The same is observed in the results obtained in this study. As wordy reviews usually discuss more aspects of the product, these have high scores. While one could still find some useful information in the reviews from the third cluster, such reviews are very short, thus have low overall quality scores. A similar tendency can be observed for the sentence quality (Fig. 4), but the distribution of sentence scores is significantly more balanced. Accordingly, the transition between "high quality" and "low quality" is much more smooth and gradual, compared to the case of review qualities. This supports the validity of the idea of assessing quality scores not just on the review, but also on the sentence level. A few examples of review sentences with their corresponding scores are given in the next paragraph.

Evidently, there is an intersection between reviews important for the customers and those useful for the product designers. Product designers and more experienced customers would for example, both appreciate such a review sentence: "There are a few design and function annoyances (the silly sliding lens door, proprietary rechargable battery rather than AA batteries, and difficulty in achieving intended effects with large apertures in aperture priority mode) but overall this is a great little camera that produces great images" (computed score: 0.8). Likewise, there are reviews and sentences which are generally irrelevant, like "This camera is awesome" (computed score: -1.0). Reviews and sentences dealing with delivery, retailers, Amazon, etc. can be helpful for the customers, but not so for the designer community. Therefore, these sentences have lower scores, such as "I then received a bill in the mail for more than the camera was worth and when I contacted them about this they said it was b/c I did not send in the proper paperwork" (computed score: -0.75). Unfortunately, this kind of reviews can be excessively long, and so their overall review scores can be higher than a short review with at least one piece of useful information. Individual sentence scores can help to reveal such cases, and assist the user to properly evaluate reviews. Reviews dealing with existing problems would help designers to improve the product, e.g. "The focus ring is a little on the narrow side but usable and it took a little time to get used to the zoom and focus rings being reversed (zoom on far end of lens - focus closer to camera body), opposite of the Canon lenses" (score 0.5). On the other hand, reviews praising some attributes of a product could be used for product innovation and customer need assessment, for instance, "Super fast lens, great telephoto reach, numerous creative modes, intuitive and easy-to-use features are attributes of this camera and makes this an attractive alternative to carrying & switching different lenses for different photo shoots, or different subject compositions" (computed score: 0.56).

Even if a review involves only a small amount of relevant content, the information present could still be extremely significant. Thus, it can happen that a shorter review discussing only one attribute of a product is more useful than an in-depth review. Usually, this was the reason for the discrepancies between the human and system rankings. 52.88% of the ranking differences occurred between ranks 1 and 2, 45.19% between ranks 2 and 3, and 1.93% between ranks 1 and 3. Nevertheless, the obtained value of the correlation coefficient τ suggests that the system proposed in this study can efficiently differentiate between high- and low quality reviews. This suggests that besides eliciting potentially helpful reviews for product designers, the system can be used to obtain high-quality datasets for other data mining purposes, such as sentiment analysis, text summarization, etc.

7   Conclusions

In this work, the problem of online review quality was examined from the product designer's viewpoint. The presented study offers contributions both conceptually and methodologically to the field of review quality estimation. In order to deal with the information overload of online product reviews, a theoretical model was proposed, and a system was developed to quantify design knowledge in reviews without human involvement. Experiments were conducted on a large number of digital camera reviews from Amazon US, with results indicating that the system would potentially help companies improving their products, and to focus on customer-driven product innovation.

Future work should extend this study by using more technical documents for term dictionary development (such as product manuals), to obtain a better approximation of Φ_V^T. As sentence-wise quality assessment is more practical than focusing on entire reviews, a sentence-level review analysis tool could be developed to assist product designers in a user-friendly manner. Furthermore, a more refined evaluation of the proposed system is necessary to examine the validity of in-cluster rankings.

References

1. Chelba, C., Mikolov, T., Schuster, M., Ge, Q., Brants, T., Koehn, P.: One billion word benchmark for measuring progress in statistical language modeling. Computing Research Repository (CoRR), pp. 1–6 (2013)
2. Chen, C.C., Tseng, Y.D.: Quality evaluation of product reviews using an information quality framework. Decis. Support Syst. **50**(4), 755–768 (2011)
3. Danescu-Niculescu-Mizil, C., Kossinets, G., Kleinberg, J., Lee, L.: How opinions are received by online communities: a case study on Amazon.com helpfulness votes. In: Proceedings of the 18th International Conference on World Wide Web, pp. 141–150 (2009)
4. Ferreira, F., Faria, J., Azevedo, A., Marques, A.L.: Product lifecycle management in knowledge intensive collaborative environments. Int. J. Inf. Manag. **37**(1), 1474–1487 (2017)
5. Ghose, A., Ipeirotis, P.G.: Estimating the helpfulness and economic impact of product reviews: mining text and reviewer characteristics. IEEE Trans. Knowl. Data Eng. **23**(10), 1498–1512 (2011)
6. He, R., McAuley, J.: Ups and downs: modeling the visual evolution of fashion trends with one-class collaborative filtering. In: Proceedings of the 25th International Conference on World Wide Web, pp. 507–517 (2016)
7. Krishnamoorthy, S.: Linguistic features for review helpfulness prediction. Expert Syst. Appl. **42**(7), 3751–3759 (2015)
8. Ku, Y.C., Wei, C.P., Hsiao, H.W.: To whom should I listen? Finding reputable reviewers in opinion-sharing communities. Decis. Support Syst. **53**(3), 534–542 (2012)
9. Lee, H., Choi, K., Yoo, D., Suh, Y., Lee, S., He, G.: Recommending valuable ideas in an open innovation community: a text mining approach to information overload problem. Ind. Manag. Data Syst. **118**(4), 683–699 (2018)
10. Lee, S., Choeh, J.Y.: Predicting the helpfulness of online reviews using multilayer perceptron neural networks. Expert Syst. Appl. **41**(6), 3041–3046 (2014)
11. Liu, H., Hu, Z., Mian, A.U., Tian, H., Zhu, X.: A new user similarity model to improve the accuracy of collaborative filtering. Knowl.-Based Syst. **56**, 156–166 (2014)
12. Liu, Q., Feng, G., Wang, N., Tayi, G.K.: A multi-objective model for discovering high-quality knowledge based on data quality and prior knowledge. Inf. Syst. Front. **20**(2), 401–416 (2018)
13. Liu, Y., Huang, X., An, A., Yu, X.: Modeling and predicting the helpfulness of online reviews. In: Proceedings of the 2008 Eighth IEEE International Conference on Data Mining, ICDM 2008, pp. 443–452 (2008)

14. Liu, Y., Jin, J., Ji, P., Harding, J.A., Fung, R.Y.K.: Identifying helpful online reviews: a product designer's perspective. Comput. Aided Des. **45**(2), 180–194 (2013)
15. Malik, M., Hussain, A.: Helpfulness of product reviews as a function of discrete positive and negative emotions. Comput. Hum. Behav. **73**, 290–302 (2017)
16. Mukherjee, S., Popat, K., Weikum, G.: Exploring latent semantic factors to find useful product reviews. In: Proceedings of the 2017 SIAM International Conference on Data Mining, pp. 480–488 (2017)
17. Peters, M., et al.: Deep contextualized word representations. In: Proceedings of the 2018 Conference of the North American Chapter of the Association for Computational Linguistics: Human Language Technologies, pp. 2227–2237 (2018)
18. Qazi, A., Shah Syed, K.B., Raj, R.G., Cambria, E., Tahir, M., Alghazzawi, D.: A concept-level approach to the analysis of online review helpfulness. Comput. Hum. Behav. **58**(C), 75–81 (2016)
19. Salehan, M., Kim, D.J.: Predicting the performance of online consumer reviews. Decis. Support Syst. **81**(C), 30–40 (2016)
20. Satopaa, V., Albrecht, J., Irwin, D., Raghavan, B.: Finding a "kneedle" in a haystack: detecting knee points in system behavior. In: Proceedings of the 2011 31st International Conference on Distributed Computing Systems Workshops, pp. 166–171 (2011)
21. Saumya, S., Singh, J.P., Baabdullah, A.M., Rana, N.P., Dwivedi, Y.K.: Ranking online consumer reviews. Electron. Commer. Res. Appl. **29**, 78–89 (2018)
22. Singh, J., Irani, S., Rana, N., Dwivedi, Y., Saumya, S., Roy, P.: Predicting the "helpfulness" of online consumer reviews. J. Bus. Res. **70**, 755–768 (2017)
23. Talukdar, P.P., Cohen, W.W.: Crowdsourced comprehension: predicting prerequisite structure in Wikipedia. In: Proceedings of the Seventh Workshop on Building Educational Applications Using NLP, pp. 307–315 (2012)
24. Tang, J., Gao, H., Hu, X., Liu, H.: Context-aware review helpfulness rating prediction. In: Proceedings of the 7th ACM Conference on Recommender Systems, pp. 1–8 (2013)
25. Tsur, O., Rappoport, A.: Revrank: A fully unsupervised algorithm for selecting the most helpful book reviews. In: Proceedings of the Third International Conference on Weblogs and Social Media, ICWSM 2009 (2009)
26. Yagci, I.A., Das, S.: Design feature opinion cause analysis: a method for extracting design intelligence from web reviews. Int. J. Knowl. Web Intell. **5**(2), 127–145 (2015)
27. Yagci, I.A., Das, S.: Measuring design-level information quality in online reviews. Electron. Commer. Res. Appl. **30**, 102–110 (2018)
28. Yang, Y., Yan, Y., Qiu, M., Bao, F.: Semantic analysis and helpfulness prediction of text for online product reviews. In: Proceedings of the 53rd Annual Meeting of the Association for Computational Linguistics, ACL, pp. 38–44 (2015)
29. Yu, X., Liu, Y., Huang, X., An, A.: Mining online reviews for predicting sales performance: a case study in the movie domain. IEEE Trans. Knowl. Data Eng. **24**(4), 720–734 (2012)

Comparing Human Computation, Machine, and Hybrid Methods for Detecting Hotel Review Spam

Christopher G. Harris[(✉)]

School of Mathematical Sciences, University of Northern Colorado,
Greeley, CO 80639, USA
christopher.harris@unco.edu

Abstract. Most adults in industrialized countries now routinely check online reviews before selecting a product or service such as lodging. This reliance on online reviews can entice some hotel managers to pay for fraudulent reviews – either to boost their own property or to disparage their competitors. The detection of fraudulent reviews has been addressed by humans and by machine learning approaches yet remains a challenge. We conduct an empirical study in which we create fake reviews, merge them with verified reviews and then employ four methods (Naïve Bayes, SVMs, human computation and hybrid human-machine approaches) to discriminate the genuine reviews from the false ones. We find that overall a hybrid human-machine method works better than either human or machine-based methods for detecting fraud – provided the most salient features are chosen. Our process has implications for fraud detection across numerous domains, such as financial statements, insurance claims, and reporting clinical trials.

Keywords: Crowdsourcing · Human computation · Word of mouth · Web 2.0 · Machine learning · TripAdvisor · Review spam

1 Introduction

Consumers today have a vast amount of information at their fingertips when making a purchase decision. Despite the availability of a variety of resources, customers place a significant emphasis on the advice and recommendations of their peers; 4 of every 5 adults in the U.S. adults indicate they use online customer reviews before purchasing an item, with half of these (2 in 5) indicating they nearly always do [1]. Other industrialized nations also rely heavily on peer-generated online reviews (also called electronic word of mouth, or eWOM) before purchases [2–5]. This translates into a competitive advantage for retailers and service providers that maintain higher ratings and better reviews than their competitors; indeed, a one-star increase in a restaurant's Yelp review score translates into a 5 to 9 percent increase in revenue [6].

These high stakes create opportunity; some unscrupulous retailers have recognized an advantage to boost their own business or disparage their competitors, creating a market for generating fraudulent reviews. As many as a third of online reviews may be

© IFIP International Federation for Information Processing 2019
Published by Springer Nature Switzerland AG 2019
I. O. Pappas et al. (Eds.): I3E 2019, LNCS 11701, pp. 75–86, 2019.
https://doi.org/10.1007/978-3-030-29374-1_7

fraudulent [7, 8], with an estimate of 16% for Yelp [9] and a similar percentage estimated for unverified hotel review websites such as TripAdvisor [10].

In this paper, we focus on evaluating fraud in lodging reviews (also called *opinion spam* or *review spam*) on websites with unverified reviews. As with restaurant reviews, hotel reviews represent a complex mix of a product-related and a service-related good. Some websites contain only verified reviews; for example, Priceline and Booking only allow customers that purchased lodging through their website to contribute a review within a specified period (typically 28 days after the stay). Others, such as TripAdvisor, do not verify identities or stays. However, TripAdvisor branded sites make up the largest travel community in the world, reaching 350 million unique monthly visitors, with more than 570 million reviews and opinions covering more than 7.3 million accommodations, airlines, attractions, and restaurants [11].

A variety of methods have been employed in review spam detection. TripAdvisor claims to use a machine approach with 50 filters in its vetting process [12], but several recent, high-profile review spamming campaigns have demonstrated that their approach is not infallible. Humans are well-established judges in online fraud detection (e.g., [13, 14]), although they are considered poor at spotting deception [15]. Can a hybrid human-machine interface can outperform either of these models? We address this question in this paper.

The remainder of this article is organized as follows. In Sect. 2, we discuss related work in review spam detection. We describe our experiment methodology in Sect. 3, results and analysis in Sect. 4. We conclude and describe future research in Sect. 5.

2 Related Work

Efforts to detect fraudulent advertising claims has existed for centuries, with humans serving as the primary arbiters. The juries of many court systems worldwide are designed around this paradigm. In 2006 crowdsourcing gained prominence as a mechanism to perform small focused tasks in which humans outperformed machines; detecting fraudulent or misleading information using crowdworkers appeared to be a natural extension. Few studies to date, however, have used crowdworkers to detect online review spam (e.g. [16, 17]). Review spam detection provides an unusual scenario in the assessment of human-created data, since machine-based methods have been shown to outperform human judges. Review spam is created with the specific intent of misleading customers and is therefore difficult for humans to detect [18].

With the advent of natural language processing (NLP), machine-based techniques have been the primary focus in detecting review spam. These techniques can be divided into three basic forms: supervised learning, unsupervised learning, and semi-supervised learning. A comprehensive review of the various machine learning techniques applied to review spam can be found in [19].

Supervised learning is a popular technique in which the machine uses labeled training data to learn the class label (i.e., either "fake" or "genuine" review). Primarily using three types of learners – Logistic Regression (LR), Naïve Bayes (NB) and Support Vector Machine (SVM) – they make use of linguistic features in the review title and text, such as parts of speech (POS), Linguistic Inquiry and Word Count

(LIWC), and sentiment polarity. Ott et al. conducted a study of deceptive opinion spam limiting their scope to n-gram based features and achieved an accuracy with an SVM of 88% using unigram and bigram term frequency features for reviews on 1- and 2-star hotels [20] and 89% for bigrams for reviews on 4- and 5-star rated hotels [16]. Mukherjee et al. was only able to achieve an accuracy of 68% on Yelp data using the same approach [21]. Human judges were not able to outperform these classifiers on these same datasets, with the best judge achieving an accuracy of only 65%.

Unsupervised learning occurs when learning is from a set of unlabeled data and is often represented as clustering. It involves finding unseen relationships in the data that are not dependent on the class label. Few researchers to date have applied an unsupervised approach; Lau et al. achieved a true positive rate of 95% using an unsupervised probabilistic language model to detect overlapping semantic content among untruthful reviews on an Amazon review dataset [22], but their methods depend on having a large sample of fake reviews from which to build a language model.

Semi-supervised learning is a hybrid approach, in which learning occurs from both labeled and unlabeled data. It makes use of very little labeled data and a large amount of unlabeled data to determine the class label. This is ideal for online review spam because most data are unlabeled – in other words, there is rarely an oracle to tell if a review is genuine or fake. Although little research has applied the use of semi-supervised learning for review spam detection, results may yield better performance than supervised learning while reducing the need to generate large labeled datasets. To date, the best performer on review spam has been Li et al., who used a co-training algorithm and a two-view semi-supervised method to learn from a few positive examples and a set of unlabeled data [23]. They obtain a precision of 0.517, recall of 0.669 and an F-score of 0.583.

Little research to date in review spam has examined hybrid methods, in which the output of machine learning methods is then evaluated by humans before a final decision is made. Harris looked at bodybuilding supplement reviews in [16], first by examining the linguistic qualities identified by Yoo and Gretzel in [24] and then asking human evaluators to identify fake reviews. He found that human evaluators significantly improved their decision making by comparing each review against the dataset's linguistic features. In this study, we take a comparable approach – provide human evaluators with the linguistic qualities of the dataset, the machine recommendation, and then asking the evaluators to classify the data as either a genuine or fake review.

3 Detecting Hotel Review Spam

We seek to compare three different methods of identifying review spam – by non-expert human evaluation, by applying machine learning techniques, and by using a hybrid approach. We begin by constructing the dataset, describing the metrics, and then discussing the various methods and features from which review spam is assessed.

3.1   Dataset Construction

We wish to create a dataset containing a mix of genuine and fake reviews that appear to be drawn from TripAdvisor. We construct the dataset by selecting hotels on TripAdvisor from three markets: New York, London, and Hong Kong. We select these three markets as they have many international visitors which helps minimize cultural differences in language usage.

We create two pools of hotels in each market: those with high TripAdvisor ratings (a rating of four- and five- stars on TripAdvisor) and those with low TripAdvisor ratings (one- and two-star ratings). We filter out reviews in languages other than English and hotels that do not also appear on Booking.com. We eliminate those properties that have fewer than 300 Booking.com reviews.

From each of our 3 markets, we select five properties from the low-rated property pool and five from the high-rated property pool, comprising 30 properties in total. We randomly sample 90 Booking.com reviews from each property. The distribution of reviewer ratings from high-rated and low-rated properties differ as do the ratings in our samples. Booking.com verifies the reviewers have stayed at the property, therefore we assume that these reviews are genuine.

TripAdvisor scores hotels on a scale of 1 to 5 while Booking.com scores hotels in the range from 2.5 to 10; however, according to [25] a linear transformation can be made between the two. We transform the Booking.com score to a TripAdvisor score, rounded to the nearest half-star.

Using a conservative 10% estimate of fake reviews on travel websites mentioned in [12] as a guide, we then asked three non-experts to create 10 fake reviews for each of the 30 properties: 5 four- and five-star reviews (*boosting spam*) and 5 one- and two-star reviews (*vandalism spam*), which represent fake reviews used to either boost a given property or disparage a competing property, respectively. None of our fake review writers have stayed at any of the properties but are permitted to perform searches. They are asked to make the review "as convincing as possible" with respect to the type of review being asked (either high or low rating) and are asked to pay careful attention to the language used in all reviews for that property on the internet. For each property, the 10 fake reviews are then comingled with the 90 genuine reviews.

3.2   Metrics

We calculate accuracy, which is the number of correctly classified reviews divided by all reviews evaluated. We also calculate the precision and recall and the corresponding F-score. These are reported separately for the 15 high-rated hotels and the 15 low-rated hotels. We separately examine these metrics for boosting spam and vandalism spam.

3.3   Feature Extraction and Engineering

Identifying the correct features is essential for the review spam identification task. We apply the output obtained from the LIWC software [26] to derive a classifier, similar to the approach made by Ott et al. [17]. We constructed features for each of the 80 LIWC dimensions, which fall into four categories: linguistic (the average number of words per sentence, the rate of misspelling, use of exclamation marks, etc.), psychological (the use of language representing social, emotional, cognitive, perceptual and biological processes, as well as temporal and/or spatially-related terms), personal (references to work, leisure, money, religion, etc.) and construction (filler, connection, and agreement words). Additional details about LIWC and the LIWC categories are available at http://liwc.net.

In addition to LIWC, we also examine POS, term frequency and use bigram feature sets, with their corresponding language models, since bigrams performed best in a comparison made in [17]. We apply the Kneser-Ney smoothing method to provide absolute-discounting interpolation of n-gram terms [27].

3.4   Machine Approach

We use a supervised learning approach for our machine learning task, since we have the labels for all reviews. Using this dataset, we design a fully-supervised method using various features in the language. We use both Naïve Bayes (NB) and SVMs as our supervised methods.

NB assumes the features are conditionally independent given the review's category. Despite its inherent simplicity and the lack of applicability of the conditional independence assumption to the real world, NB-based categorization models still tend to perform surprisingly well [28].

$$P_{NB}(c|d) = \frac{P(c) \prod_{i=0}^{m} P(f_i|c)}{P(d)} \tag{1}$$

We use the Natural Language Toolkit (NLTK) [29] to estimate individual language models, for truthful and deceptive opinions.

SVMs [30] can make use of certain kernels to transform the problem to allow linear classification techniques to be applied to non-linear data. Applying the kernel equations arranges the data instances within the multi-dimensional space so that there is a hyperplane that separates the data into separate classes. We restrict our evaluation to linear kernels since these performed best in preliminary evaluations using our features. We use Scikit-learn [31] to train our linear SVM models on the POS, LIWC, and bigram feature sets. We normalize each LIWC and bigram feature to unit length before combining them.

To ensure all hotel reviews are learned using the same language model, we evaluated using a 5-fold nested cross validation (CV) procedure [32]. Each fold contains all reviews (boosting and vandalism, genuine and fake) from 12 hotels; thus, our model applies its learning on reviews from the remaining 3 hotels. This avoids some pitfalls of learning from an incomplete set of data, as is described in [33].

3.5   Human Computation Based Approach

For each of our 30 hotels, we randomly allocated our 100 reviews into 4 batches of 25 reviews. We hired 360 human assessors from Amazon Mechanical Turk (MTurk) to examine reviews from each batch of 25 presented in random order. To allow us to assess inter-annotator agreement, each hotel review was examined by three separate assessors. We created a simple web-based interface that displayed the title and text for each review, along with a prompt for the assessor to determine if the displayed review is genuine or fake. Assessors were paid $0.50 per batch; to provide an incentive for careful assessment, they were told that if they correctly classified all 25 hotels, they would be compensated an additional $0.50. We take the majority label for the 3 assessments for each review.

3.6 Hybrid Approach

To create a hybrid evaluation, we provide human assessors with the information ascertained by the machine approach. Along with each review, we provide the LIWC output for each feature for each review, the average LIWC output for all reviews for the 100 reviews, as well as the SVM and NB-determined classes using the best SVM and NB models. Human assessors recruited from MTurk were provided with the SVM- and NB-determined class and the LIWC output. They were asked to decide on whether each review was genuine or fake and had the opportunity to go along with the machine assessment or override it. They were provided the same payment and incentive as those in the human computation approach. As with the human computation approach, we take the majority label for the 3 assessments for each review.

4   Results and Analysis

Table 1 illustrates the results (accuracy, precision, recall, and F-score) obtained for both machine learning-based approaches, the human computation approach, and the hybrid approach.

From Table 1 we can observe that the hybrid approach does better (t-test) than the $SVM_{POS+LIWC+Bigrams}$ approach in accuracy, and for F-score of fake reviews. There was no difference for detection of genuine reviews for the hybrid method and the $SVM_{POS+LIWC+Bigrams}$ approach. The hybrid approach performs significantly better than the human computation approach (two-tailed t-test: $t(718) = 13.414$, $p < 0.001$ for F-score, $t(718) = 3.6116$, $p = 0.003$ for accuracy)

Initially this appears unsurprising; the hybrid approach provides the human assessor with the class decision (either fake or genuine) from the Naïve Bayes and SVM approaches and provides the LIWC feature information for the review that is being evaluated and the average for all reviews in the collection. With all this information, certainly a human decision maker's answer would have greater accuracy, precision and recall scores than the decision tool providing information. After all, one would expect that the information provided, the greater the confidence in the decision-making process.

Table 1. Classifier performance for our approaches. Machine learning approaches use nested 5-fold cross-validation. Reported precision, recall and F-score are computed using a micro-average, i.e., from the aggregate true positive, false positive and false negative rates.

Approach	Features used			Accuracy	P	R	F
	POS	LIWC	Bigrams				
NB	*		*	89.7%	48.8	70.0	57.5
NB		*	*	90.5%	52.0	71.0	60.0
NB	*	*	*	91.0%	53.5	73.3	61.9
SVM	*		*	93.4%	64.1	76.3	69.7
SVM		*	*	94.4%	68.8	81.7	74.7
SVM	*	*	*	94.9%	71.0	84.0	76.9
Human Comp				90.2%	50.6	74.7	60.3
Hybrid		*		95.1%	69.6	90.0	78.5

Upon closer examination, we find that this is true – to a point. Of the 3000 reviews evaluated, 271 were incorrectly classified according to the best Naïve Bayes approach (NB$_{POS+LIWC+Bigrams}$), 151 according to the best SVM approach (SVM$_{POS+LIWC+Bigrams}$), and 148 according to the Hybrid approach. However, we see in Fig. 1(a) the Hybrid approach misclassified 17 reviews (11%) in which it differed from the class label given by both SVM and NB but got correct 55 reviews (37%) in which both NB and SVM misclassified the review type. Therefore, the Hybrid approach was three times as likely to override the class decision from both machine learning approaches and make a correct decision as it was to override their decision and get the class label incorrect.

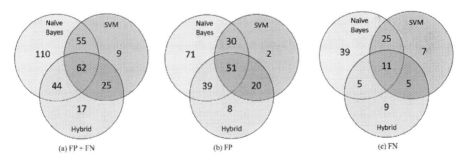

(a) FP + FN   (b) FP   (c) FN

Fig. 1. Venn diagrams showing counts of (a) all incorrectly labeled answers (False Positive and False Negative), (b) False Negative answers only and (c) False Negative answers for NB$_{POS+LIWC+Bigrams}$, SVM$_{POS+LIWC+Bigrams}$, and the Hybrid approaches.

The number of false positives (Fig. 1(b)) is considerably larger than the number of false negatives (Fig. 1(c)) for all three approaches. Comparing Fig. 1(b) and (c), we see that the best Naïve Bayes approach obtains a greater percentage of false positive decisions (i.e., it classifies more genuine reviews as fake than the converse) than the best SVM approach, indicating a slightly more "aggressive" approach towards classifying reviews as fake (a ratio of 2.4:1) than the best SVM approach (2.1:1). This, however, pales in comparison to the Human Computation approach (2.9:1) and the Hybrid approach (3.9:1). The relative aggressiveness of the human-based approaches may have to do with the incentives offered for correctly classifying reviews.

When the human decision-maker using the Hybrid model had to decide between the Naïve Bayes and SVM classes (i.e., when the two machine methods did not provided the same class label), they chose the Naïve Bayes 64% of the time and SVM 36% of the time. Had only the best SVM class labels have been offered and the humans classified the labels according to the SVM output, the 44 misclassified answers would have boosted Hybrid accuracy to 96.5% and obtained an F-score of 84.1 – a significant increase (two-tailed t-test: $t(718) = 9.156$, $p < 0.001$ for F-score, $t(718) = 2.289$, $p = 0.0224$ for accuracy)

We saw no distinguishable patterns between the 3 hotel markets we examined. However, we discovered that there was a discernable difference between detecting boosting spam and vandalism spam for high-rated and low-rated hotels. Table 2 illustrates the number of false negative classification errors (fake reviews classified as genuine) by hotel type and by review spam type. Figure 2 illustrates the relative proportion of false positive to false negative errors by approach. Overall, we observe that vandalism review spam on low-rated hotels were most difficult to detect (an average of $\frac{18}{75}$ or 24%, were not detected as review spam) whereas vandalism review spam for high-rated hotels was least difficult, with an average of $\frac{12}{75}$, or 16%, not detected.

Table 2. Number of false negative classification errors for each approach, broken down by hotel type and review spam type.

Hotel type	Review spam type	NB	SVM	Human Comp	Hybrid	Average	Total # fake reviews
High-rated	Boosting	17	16	13	12	14.5	75
High-rated	Vandalism	15	6	24	3	12.0	75
Low-rated	Boosting	26	7	18	5	14.0	75
Low-rated	Vandalism	22	19	21	10	18.0	75
All deceptive reviews		80	48	76	30	58.5	300

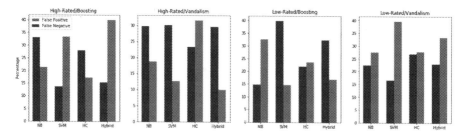

Fig. 2. Relative percentage of classification errors, comparing false positive and false negative values, by hotel type, review type, and approach.

In general, the best Naïve Bayes approach had a more difficult time with the low-rated hotels (i.e., those with one- and two-star ratings) while the best SVM and the Hybrid approaches had a more challenging time with boosting (positive) reviews on high-rated properties and vandalism (negative) reviews on low-rated properties. The human computation approach had a harder problem with vandalism on the low-rated properties and boosting on the high-rated properties. In part, this shows the influence of the best SVM approach on the Hybrid approach, but it also shows how language may also be a factor.

Next, we examine the output provided by the LIWC classifiers as this information is also provided to the assessors in the Hybrid approach. Spatial details were considerably more prominent in genuine reviews than in fake reviews, which supports the reality monitoring (RM) theory of Johnson and Raye [34]. This type of information provides more details about the room layout, bathroom configuration, etc. that can be verified by other guests. This also backs up other work (e.g. [35]) indicating that encoding spatial information into lies is challenging.

Emotion-laden terms, such as a description of the front desk staff's attitude, were more prominent in fake reviews – claims containing these experiences cannot be easily corroborated by other guests. We also noticed that fake reviews contained more external terms – providing background on their vacation, for instance – and less focus on terms that could be verified by others who stay in the same hotel.

Several other researchers have found that while deception is often associated with negative emotional terms (e.g., [36, 37]), the fake reviews were more extreme – the boosting review spam our study used contained more positive and fewer negative emotion terms whereas the vandalism review spam was just the opposite. This exaggeration of emotional terms was most readily picked up by the best SVM approach and least readily picked up by the Human Computation approach, showing how challenging it is for humans to associate strong emotional terms with fake reviews without guidance from machine techniques.

Regarding parts of speech, Gunther et al. [38] indicates that deceptive communications were characterized by fewer first-person singular pronouns, fewer third-person pronouns, more negative emotion words, fewer exclusive words, and more motion verbs. Our findings generally concur with this earlier work with one notable exception: in our study, deceptive reviews contained more first-person singular pronouns. This echoes the findings of Ott et al. [17], who speculated that the use of more first-person pronouns was an attempt to boost the writer's credibility by emphasizing that they were a participant and thus able correctly observe the situation.

One of the biggest indicators of a deceptive review was the generous use of punctuation, particularly exclamation marks. Both human and machine approaches detected this association. An examination of reviews of the 15 hotels on TripAdvisor and Booking.com indicates a much more prolific use of exclamation marks on the former.

It was challenging to analyze the performance of our human assessors, primarily because there were 360 used for each approach (720 total). Figure 3 illustrates the distribution of misclassification errors (false positive and false negatives) for each batch of 25 reviews for human computation and for hybrid approaches. Comparing these two bar graphs illustrates the value of the hybrid approach, as humans in both approaches were provided the same incentives. We note that false positive reviews were more prominent than false negative reviews because only 10% of reviews were fake. It is worth noting that many reviewers did not have a fake review in their batch, and therefore did not have a point of reference to know what constituted a fake review. This unfortunately raises a potential risk of confirmation bias [39].

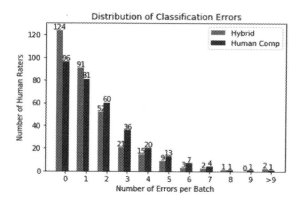

Fig. 3. Distribution of classification errors per batch, comparing human computation and hybrid methods.

5   Conclusion

We have conducted an empirical experiment in which we merged verified reviews for 15 hotel properties in 3 markets (New York, London, and Hong Kong), extracted 90 reviews for each hotel from Booking.com, and then merged them with 10 reviews we had non-experts write. Half of the review spam was boosting, or trying to positively influence the hotel's rating, while the other half was vandalism, or written to negatively influence a competitor's hotel – a growing area of review spam.

From these 3000 reviews, we employed four different methods to determine if each review was genuine or fake: two supervised machine learning methods (Naïve Bayes and SVM), human computation (using MTurk), and a hybrid method (also using MTurk) that allowed humans to make decisions using the class labels from the machine learning methods as well as LIWC output. While it is not surprising that the hybrid method outperformed either of the other methods, it was surprising that when humans were presented with too much information – particularly information that presented more than one possible decision – it negatively impacted human decision-making. Only when the additional information was presented in a non-conflicting manner did humans excel.

This study provided us with considerable data to evaluate, and we intend to do this with an extension of this study. We would also like to evaluate temporal aspects of reviews – the order in which they are posted – since the burstiness of reviews for a property can provide additional evidence of possible review spam.

Although this study was limited in scope to English-language reviews for five hotels, we believe that the overall findings of hybrid man-machine decision making can be extended to other situations outside of validating reviews, such as evaluating financial statements, investigating insurance claims, and evaluating the validity of clinical trials.

References

1. Smith, A., Anderson, M.: Online shopping and e-commerce, online reviews. Pew Research Center report (2016). https://www.pewinternet.org/2016/12/19/online-reviews/
2. Floh, A., Koller, M., Zauner, A.: Taking a deeper look at online reviews: the asymmetric effect of valence intensity on shopping behaviour. J. Mark. Manag. **29**(5–6), 646–670 (2013)
3. Burton, J., Khammash, M.: Why do people read reviews posted on consumer-opinion portals? J. Mark. Manag. **26**(3–4), 230–255 (2010)
4. Mikalef, P., Pappas, I.O., Giannakos, M.N.: Value co-creation and purchase intention in social commerce: the enabling role of word-of-mouth and trust. In: Americas Conference on Information Systems AMCIS (2017)
5. Mikalef, P., Giannakos, M.N., Pappas, I.O.: Designing social commerce platforms based on consumers' intentions. Behav. Inf. Technol. **36**(12), 1308–1327 (2017)
6. Luca, M.: Reviews, reputation, and revenue: the case of Yelp.com. In: Harvard Business School NOM Unit Working Paper (12–016) (2016)
7. Streitfeld, D.: The best book reviews money can buy. The New York Times **25** (2012)
8. Mukherjee, A., Liu, B., Glance, N.: Spotting fake reviewer groups in consumer reviews. In: Proceedings of the 21st International Conference on World Wide Web, pp. 191–200. ACM (2012)
9. Luka, M., Zervas, G.: Fake it till you make it: reputation, competition, and Yelp review fraud. Manage. Sci. **62**(12), 3412–3427 (2016)
10. Harris, C.: Decomposing TripAdvisor: detecting potentially fraudulent hotel reviews in the era of big data. In: 2018 IEEE International Conference on Big Knowledge (ICBK), pp. 243–251. IEEE (2018)
11. Comscore: Top 50 Multi-Platform Properties (Desktop and Mobile) April 2019. https://www.comscore.com/Insights/Rankings. Accessed 06 Nov 2019
12. Belton, P.: Navigating the potentially murky world of online reviews (2015). http://www.bbc.com/news/business-33205905. Accessed 06 Nov 2019
13. Vrij, A.: Detecting lies and deceit: pitfalls and opportunities in nonverbal and verbal lie detection. Interpersonal Commun. **6**, 321 (2014)
14. Lim, E.P., Nguyen, V.A., Jindal, N., Liu, B., Lauw, H.W.: Detecting product review spammers using rating behaviors. In: CIKM 2010 (2010)
15. Jindal, N., Liu, B.: Opinion spam and analysis. In: WSDM 2008 (2008)
16. Harris, C.G.: Detecting deceptive opinion spam using human computation. In: Workshops at the Twenty-Sixth AAAI Conference on Artificial Intelligence (2012)
17. Ott, M., Choi, Y., Cardie, C., Hancock, J.T.: Finding deceptive opinion spam by any stretch of the imagination. In: Proceedings of the 49th Annual Meeting of the Association for Computational Linguistics: Human Language Technologies, vol. 1, pp. 309–319. Association for Computational Linguistics (2011)
18. Bond Jr., C.F., DePaulo, B.M.: Accuracy of deception judgments. Pers. Soc. Psychol. Rev. **10**(3), 214–234 (2006)

19. Crawford, M., Khoshgoftaar, T.M., Prusa, J.D., Richter, A.N., Al Najada, H.: Survey of review spam detection using machine learning techniques. J. Big Data **2**(1), 23 (2015)
20. Ott, M., Cardie, C., Hancock, J.T.: Negative deceptive opinion spam. In: Proceedings of the 2013 Conference of the North American Chapter of the Association for Computational Linguistics: Human Language Technologies, pp. 497–501 (2013)
21. Mukherjee, A., Venkataraman, V., Liu, B., Glance, N.: What yelp fake review filter might be doing? In: Seventh International AAAI Conference on Weblogs and Social Media (2013)
22. Lau, R.Y., Liao, S.Y., Kwok, R.C.W., Xu, K., Xia, Y., Li, Y.: Text mining and probabilistic language modeling for online review spam detecting. ACM Trans. Manag. Inf. Syst. **2**(4), 1–30 (2011)
23. Li, F.H., Huang, M., Yang, Y., Zhu, X.: Learning to identify review spam. In: Twenty-Second International Joint Conference on Artificial Intelligence (2011)
24. Yoo, K.H., Gretzel, U.: Comparison of deceptive and truthful travel reviews. Inf. Commun. Technol. Tourism **2009**, 37–47 (2009)
25. Martin-Fuentes, E., Mateu, C., Fernandez, C.: Does verifying uses influence rankings? Analyzing Booking.com and TripAdvisor. Tourism Anal. **23**(1), 1–15 (2018)
26. Pennebaker, J.W., Boyd, R.L., Jordan, K., Blackburn, K.: The development and psychometric properties of LIWC2015 (2015)
27. Ney, H., Essen, U., Kneser, R.: On structuring probabilistic dependences in stochastic language modelling. Comput. Speech Lang. **8**(1), 1–38 (1994)
28. Coe, J.: Performance comparison of Naïve Bayes and J48 classification algorithms. Int. J. Appl. Eng. Res. **7**(11), 2012 (2012)
29. Loper, E., Bird, S.: NLTK: the natural language toolkit. arXiv preprint cs/0205028 (2002)
30. Kotsiantis, S.B., Zaharakis, I., Pintelas, P.: Supervised machine learning: a review of classification techniques. Emerg. Artif. Intell. Appl. Comput. Eng. **160**, 3–24 (2007)
31. Pedregosa, F., et al.: Scikit-learn: machine learning in Python. J. Mach. Learn. Res. **12**(Oct), 2825–2830 (2011)
32. Huang, C.M., Lee, Y.J., Lin, D.K., Huang, S.Y.: Model selection for support vector machines via uniform design. Comput. Stat. Data Anal. **52**(1), 335–346 (2007)
33. Krstajic, D., Buturovic, L.J., Leahy, D.E., Thomas, S.: Cross-validation pitfalls when selecting and assessing regression and classification models. J. Cheminform. **6**(1), 10 (2014)
34. Johnson, M.K., Raye, C.L.: Reality monitoring. Psychol. Rev. **88**(1), 67 (1981)
35. Vrij, A., et al.: Outsmarting the liars: the benefit of asking unanticipated questions. Law Hum Behav. **33**(2), 159–166 (2009)
36. Newman, M.L., Pennebaker, J.W., Berry, D.S., Richards, J.M.: Lying words: predicting deception from linguistic styles. Pers. Soc. Psychol. Bull. **29**(5), 665–675 (2003)
37. Toma, C.L., Hancock, J.T.: What lies beneath: the linguistic traces of deception in online dating profiles. J. Commun. **62**(1), 78–97 (2012)
38. Gunther, A.C., Perloff, R.M., Tsfati, Y.: Public opinion and the third-person effect. In: The SAGE Handbook of Public Opinion Research, pp. 184–191 (2008)
39. Yin, D., Mitra, S., Zhang, H.: Research note—when do consumers value positive vs negative reviews? An empirical investigation of confirmation bias in online word of mouth. Inf. Syst. Res. **27**(1), 131–144 (2016)

Why Consumers Do not Provide Online Reviews?

Daniele Doneddu[1,2(✉)] and Irina Novoshilova[3]

[1] School of Management, Swansea University, Swansea SA1 8EN, UK
d.doneddu@swansea.ac.uk
[2] SCIENTIA Group, Swansea, UK
[3] Faculty of Management, Law and Social Sciences, University of Bradford,
Bradford, UK
i.novozhilova@bradford.ac.uk

Abstract. In light of the very high popularity of electronic word of mouth in the form of products and services reviews on the internet and its critical importance for businesses, the aim of this research is to investigate why customers who buy skincare products do not engage in eWOM by not leaving reviews about these products online. This research adopts a qualitative nature, using semi-structured in-depth interviews. Respondents' group consists of the same amount of males and females who were asked questions regarding their electronic and traditional word of mouth experiences. Received responses demonstrate that laziness, lack of general interest in skin care and lack of feeling altruistic towards consumers online are the key factors preventing consumers from leaving reviews about skin care online.

Keywords: Online reviews · eWOM · Skincare

1 Introduction

Word of mouth communications help spreading information about products and services, boosting prospects' awareness [1, 2]. Firms attempt to trigger word of mouth activities and regulate its matters as much as they can [3].

Internet resources such as chat rooms, opinion sharing portals, social networking websites, email etc. have allowed word of mouth to expand into online space as consumers started sharing their experiences about products and services on the internet. This led to the creation of various internet communities. This process is referred to as electronic word of mouth (also known as word of mouse). Electronic word of mouth (eWOM) is "any positive or negative statement made by potential, actual, or former customers about a product or company, which is made available to a multitude of people and institutions via the Internet" [3].

A number of studies investigated why consumers engage in eWOM communications (see, amongst others, [3, 4]). However, limited number of studies investigated why consumers do not provide eWOM. Thus, the aim of this research is to explore the reasons why consumers do not provide eWOM. The findings will advance

© IFIP International Federation for Information Processing 2019
Published by Springer Nature Switzerland AG 2019
I. O. Pappas et al. (Eds.): I3E 2019, LNCS 11701, pp. 87–98, 2019.
https://doi.org/10.1007/978-3-030-29374-1_8

understanding of information dissemination online and allow companies to enhance their strategies to provide eWOM regarding their product/service.

2 Literature Review

2.1 Motivations to Provide EWOM

Based on the literature, the following five most common motivations to engage in eWOM have been identified [5]:

Altruism: A concept by which activity connected with disinterested concern for the well-being of others is understood. It correlates with the concept of selflessness - that is, with the sacrifice of their benefits in favour of the benefit of another person, other people, or in general - for the common good [6]. Thus, altruism can be described as a motivation with an aim to raise the welfare of one or more persons other than of oneself [7]. According to [8], altruism significantly influences brand communities on social media websites.

Self-enhancement: An individual's motivation to demonstrate one or more self-domains positively in order for other people to accept and favour them. It also helps to sustain self-esteem [9]. Humans usually lean towards self-enhancing, making it their vital motivation [10]. A study by Hennig-Thurau et al. [3] tested eleven motives to provide eWOM using a sample of 2083 German individuals who use various opinion-sharing platforms. Results indicated that self-enhancement is one of the most important motives for users to share their opinion on online platforms.

Venting Feelings: Believed to be beneficial for an individual. When emotions are expressed, it helps a person to go back to a more serene condition [11]. Based of research studies [12, 13], it is apparent that when a client is dissatisfied, they are unlikely to complain to a firm. Instead, they prefer to release their negative feelings through communicating their opinion to others. Lee and Hu [14] noted that frustrated clients are likely to make public complaint online.

Social Benefits: When consumers engage in online communication, they become part of the web-based group. Users may perceive this form of connection as a social benefit, as it allows them to get integrated into a new social network's structure. Therefore, it can be argued that users communicate through eWOM in order to be part of online groups. Consumers may leave messages on fora, reviews websites and other user generated resources to gain social benefits [3, 15]. Choi and Scott [16] found female social networks users were motivated to communicate on these platforms because they felt part of a community and because it supported their identification.

Economic Incentives: Some consumers engage in eWOM in order to receive economic incentives, such as discounts and electronic points vouchers granted after posting a review on the opinion platform or brand website [17]. Wirtz and Chew [18] conducted an experiment using 215 individuals. Results illustrated that those who received a financial incentive are more motivated to generate eWOM.

2.2 Information Sharing

There is a significant amount of studies researching why people engage in offline and online word of mouth. When it comes to the question why individuals refuse to post reviews online, it can be helpful to look at the broader picture. Posts, messages, other forms of expressing opinions are all essentially processes of information sharing.

In an internet context, information sharing is the core activity. Internet substantially consist of the data created and shared by the users. This means that all the individuals writing blog posts, interacting in online communities, chatting etc. are content creator or sharers. This category of users is defined as posters. Nevertheless, there is another type of online behavior, opposite to posters, referred to as lurking [19]. In fact, lurkers represent the largest part of the internet: >90% of the online users [20–22]. Lurking is not clearly defined by researches but it is normally connected to avoidance of posting and nonparticipation behaviour. Lurkers are described as passive or inactive, silent and those who do search for information and read online content but do not contribute themselves [19, 23].

When discussing reasons for lurkers to lurk, it is important to mention that lurking behaviour is triggered primarily by individuals' greater demand for information [24, 25]. Lurkers therefore do not write anything on online platforms because their demand for information is fulfilled without posting anything [22]. According to [26], lurking is a consequence of excessive amount of information users receive online. This overload may result in a person trying to avoid engaging into this turmoil.

In their study, Nonnecke and Preece [27] identified reasons for lurkers to lurk. They conducted semi-structured in-depth interviews with ten participants who were identified as online group members who behaved like lurkers. Interviewees named 79 reasons for not posting online and the researchers concluded that lurking cannot be solely defined as an absence of posting. Most voiced reasons for lurking included:

(1) Anonymity, privacy and safety. Users often want to remain anonymous when using the internet and are concerned about their personal data safety in case of sharing information in online spaces. People online can essentially choose who they want to be as they are unknown to others. Therefore, some users stress the issue of trust [28]. Bishop [29] also claims lurkers avoid posting due to the fear of losing privacy.

(2) Time and work related constraints. A situation when individuals claim not to have enough time to post or when they could not use their email as it was a work email.

(3) Message volume and quality. Interview participants mentioned that too low or too high amount of messages in the community prevent them from posting. Also, unsatisfactory quality of the information provided (such as off-topic conversations) turn user away from participating.

(4) Shyness over public posting. Despite the internet being largely anonymous and users not seen by each other, some individuals are still cautious and hesitant about posting. This was also supported by Katz [20].

3   Research Method

The study was conducted in the context of skincare product. As the aim of this research is to explore factors affecting providing eWOM, semi-structured interviews were chosen. 8 participants (4 males and 4 females), using convenience sampling, participated in this study. The full discussion guide can be provided upon request. In order to analyse interviews, NVivo software was used.

4   Research Findings

Here below we report some of the research findings in relation to our study.

4.1   Factors Preventing the Posting of a Review

In terms of factors preventing consumers from sharing their opinions online, interviewees' responses could be divided into two categories: (i) customer characteristics-specific and (ii) circumstance-specific reasons preventing from eWOM communication. Similar to Mangold, Miller and Brockway [30] and Wolny and Mueller [31], the researchers divided motives to engage in WOM into dependent on customer personal characteristics and context in which customer is situated.

(i) **Customer characteristics-specific.** 50% of the respondents reported that being lazy was their main reason for not leaving skin care reviews online. 25% also mentioned that they "could not be bothered" and did not care about leaving reviews after using a product. Some respondents specified that sharing their opinion online: "doesn't come to my mind" and "I never actually thought about leaving a review after buying anything".

Almost all interviewees expressed no interest in skin care products in general, as a topic. After saying that, they specified that this was actually the reason for not providing the internet with their skin care products opinion.

"…if there's anything I'm interested in, then I might leave my opinion as well. If I am very interested, for example a discussion about football, I leave some comments on football groups once or twice a week. So I don't leave reviews about skin care product because I am not interested in them."

Two respondents indicated that they do not leave reviews as they feel that their opinion wouldn't really matter due to high amount of other reviews online, consequently they do not see any reason to add on to other comments and repeating them.

"Cos there's so much out there that really my opinion wouldn't really matter because there's so much other people's opinions I would probably be saying the same thing as two hundred other women so I don't see any point of repeating other reviewers."

They also mentioned that they did not feel their opinion was needed and expressed the idea that companies would not even pay attention to their reviews. "I am not sure anyone would benefit from my opinion. If I was sure my opinion was needed or someone would use it, I would share, but otherwise, no"

One person repeatedly mentioned that they avoided leaving reviews due to considering it a waste of time. It is important to note that the two respondents expressing opinions about repeating the same concepts as other people and not feeling their opinion was important for anyone are themselves active skin care lurkers but they never leave any reviews about this or other product categories online.

"...Because for me it takes extra time and I feel that I would rather do something else in that extra time"

All above mentioned hindering factors were identified by the researchers as customer characteristics-specific because they come from the individuals' views and feelings, which were formed prior to the situation where they were expected to engage in electronic word of mouth. These are based on consumers' existing beliefs, interests and habits.

(ii) **Circumstance-specific**. Context specific factors affect individual's intentions to engage in electronic word of mouth. An example of this is a situation when a respondent mentioned not leaving a review when a firm's website or opinion platform is difficult to navigate or has irritating pop-ups. This can be marked as technological problems.

Cyber bullying was also named as one circumstantial factor that stops a person from sharing their opinion. However, only 3 persons demonstrated that they were influenced by other users online.

As mentioned above, three individuals shared their concern about posting their reviews online because they are not confident about sharing an opinion which is opposite to what is already published.

"If I consider leaving a review, I am worried that if it is negative, I might be the wrong one. I mean, what If I got a faulty, defective product which was just one in a batch, but generally it is good for the majority of people? Then I would feel wrong. I would feel like I would make a bad impact for the company. I would not like to mislead people with my negative emotions. So If I see that mostly people post positive reviews and I have a negative, I would probably doublethink."

"...So if my opinion fits others, I would go with the flow and if its contrary to others, then I would avoid posting it."

"...if you have bad experience about a product and everyone else's reviews say it's amazing, then as a person, it might stop you from saying something bad because you might think like - maybe I've made a mistake or I use that product wrongly. It could stop me and maybe make me think."

Furthermore, 75% of posting respondents stated that they would never leave a review if they have a neutral opinion about the product.

4.2 Other Findings

Level of Satisfaction. During the interviews it became apparent, that the level of satisfaction with a product or service determines participants' intentions to share their opinions online. 37.5% of respondents stated that they would only post reviews if they were extremely satisfied with the product and if it gave them outstanding results (specifically beauty products).

"If I have outstanding results, then I would post. But if it's negative or very negative I would not bother leaving my review."

"I think a very good experience would make me leave a review. If I want to leave a review, it's most likely going to be positive. So if I'm very happy with the product I'm more likely to leave a review."

Another 37.5% of interviewees reported they would only bother to leave their opinion if they had either a very negative or a very positive results.

"If the product is really excellent and it has affected me greatly I would definitely leave a positive review. And the same with a negative review - if I am extremely dissatisfied and the product was basically a disaster, then I will definitely post a negative review. So it's high ends of both sides, either very positive or extremely negative."

However, none of the participants demonstrated intentions to share neutral or just negative opinions on the internet.

"If I have nothing to say or if it is an everyday product and I feel no positive or negative emotions about it and I'm neutral, I would not really share that kind of opinion."

What Would Motivate Consumer to Leave Online Reviews. Respondents were asked about what they thought could motivate them to leave reviews and what they thought companies could do to trigger electronic word of mouth behaviour in them. One respondent mentioned that if he as a customer was given more attention from the company, he would be motivated to leave reviews.

"Sometimes probably just acknowledgement, recognition. Customers want to be heard, customers want to be noticed. So if there is a recognition, everyone would like to post reviews. Customers would like to see the reviews appreciated and maybe even shared. For example, ok here's a review of our customer John and here is what he thinks of our products. We're doing it, we are on it or something like that would be a good response of a company."

50% of interviewees mentioned that if they saw a message from a company asking them to leave their opinion online, if they realised their reviews mattered, they would be more likely to engage in eWOM.

"…I think that companies should let people know that their views count, because I think most people think that companies don't really care about their reviews. The company should ask in the advertising or maybe tell sales people when their products are sold, they should tell the customers to leave reviews because reviews matter."

"I think it's best if they can write on the package that they want people to leave reviews and that it's very important for them."

"Maybe if companies add the message to the advertising strategy that it is very important for them to get reviews so it's the kind of encourage customers to post reviews online"

Two respondents said that if they knew someone really needed their opinion and if they were asked to leave a review, they would definitely agree.

"…if someone asks me to do that if someone really wants me to do that I will be happy to do that."

"If I was sure my opinion was needed or someone would use it, I would share."

Economic incentives have been mentioned by seven out of eight participants as a motivating factor to leave a product review. In addition to that, one individual stressed that having received any form of incentive, they would take time writing a good quality, descriptive review.

"Something - incentives, samples. Does not have to be anything big, but something, gratification. In this case, I would leave a very detailed, good quality review with good explanation of my opinion."

"…getting some kind of incentive for example like on TripAdvisor, if you leave certain amount of reviews you get special status which brings you perks."

"I think giveaways would be a good idea, so if you buy something, leave a review and you would automatically enter a giveaway this would be stimulating to leave reviews."

They also mentioned that knowing that leaving review would result in company donating some money to charity would definitely make them leave reviews.

"They could also do something connected to charity. If, for example, they said that If I leave a review, they would donate some money to help animals or something like that, I would definitely participate."

5 Discussion

Preece et al. [22] claim that at least 90% of internet users are lurkers. However, interestingly, in our (albeit involving a limited sample) study the percentage of posters was quite high among the respondents, which is contrary to above mentioned study results. In addition to that, when it comes to skin care, despite every participant using it and almost everyone reading reviews about this type of product, they never post their opinions online. Surely, the type of product must be taken into consideration, as noted by Gunn [32] in her research on what factors hinder electronic word of mouth in tourism industry. Therefore, it can be concluded that electronic word of mouth behaviour is influenced by and depends on the category of the product. This, in turn, implies that consumers' interests play their role in determining whether they would lurk or post about certain things. This will be discussed more in another part of this chapter.

In Nonnecke and Preece's study of reasons for lurking one of the most mentioned reason for not posting included anonymity and privacy [27]. This is very well supported by the research findings, demonstrating that respondents do not provide their personal information. It is important to mention that interviewees emphasised safety concerns as the most serious factor. In this way, these concerns tie in with Nonnecke and Preece's case study which reported users' perturb about safety [33]. Gunn's research also demonstrated concerns about confidentiality and security as preventing factors for leaving reviews online [32].

Preece, Nonnecke and Andrews [22], after examining 219 lurkers, spotted reasons such as "other community members gave the same answer I would", "I don't feel I would able to contribute anything" and "have no necessity to post". This research expands this finding by contributing additional factors hindering electronic word of mouth communication. These are coming from personal characteristics of respondents, causing them not to think about leaving reviews online after buying anything, indicating that something stops that thought from coming to their mind.

Preece, Nonnecke and Andrews [22] concluded that lurking behaviour was mainly caused by interaction with online community as only 13.2% of surveyed people reported their intention to lurk from the beginning. However, participants of this research demonstrated that the majority of lurkers had no intention to post reviews about any products from the start. And although some respondents said their potential reviews could be influenced by people who had already posted their opinion, they indicated that deliberate avoidance of publishing a review or absence of initial intention to publish was present from the start.

In addition to that, interview participants were asked whether they thought other users online had any influence on them. Although the majority of respondents claimed to not be affected by already published reviews, several participants expressed their worry of other internet users' opinions. One participant mentioned that they would not like to post a review which is opposite to existing ones and two interviewees demonstrated doubt of posting a negative review as they were not sure the unsatisfying performance of product was caused by themselves. Such reasoning may be the result of uncertainty and lack of confidence in participants. This finding shows similarity to Gunn's [32] research which identified lack of confidence as one of the main obstacles preventing from posting reviews. Her research also marked technological problems as barriers to electronic word of mouth. Contrary to these results, only one person described technological problems as preventing from leaving reviews.

Altruism was found by many researchers to be among the most significant reasons for individuals to engage in both traditional and electronic word of mouth [3, 34, 35]. As mentioned in the previous chapter, desire to help others was a very strong motive for all the participants to engage in traditional word of mouth communication. However, such behaviour was only expressed by 25% of participants who indicated the same reason for sharing their product reviews online in our preliminary study. These results could be considered as slightly contradicting the existing research outcomes, as previously conducted studies demonstrated that unselfish concern about other users is motivating people to engage in eWOM, the current study only found this reason valid for traditional word of mouth.

According to Wirtz and Chew's [18] experiment, a degree of product or service satisfaction does not necessarily lead to word of mouth being produced. However, a later study by Velázquez, Blasco and Gil Saura [36] found out that higher customer satisfaction results in a higher chance of intention to engage in electronic WOM and particularly positive electronic word of mouth behaviour. This result supports the outcomes of this research as a large proportion of respondents mentioned that being extremely satisfied with the product or results it provided is highly likely to motivate them for leaving a review. The same proportion of interviewed individuals said that they would only leave a review if they are either very happy or very unhappy. This so-called U-shaped connection between clients' happiness with the product and their willingness to spread word of mouth was explained by Anderson [37] and Herr, Kardes and Kim [38] as either extremely satisfied or very dissatisfied customers have higher intentions to engage in word of mouth. Interesting outcome was that none of the respondents demonstrated intention to share just neutral or only negative experiences on review websites. This finding is once again supporting the previous works such as Anderson's [37], Velázquez, Blasco and Gil Saura's [36] and Herr, Kardes and Kim's [38]. Therefore, finding regarding satisfaction levels are correlating with the existing research.

These findings also support researches which identified venting feelings as a motivation to engage in both traditional and electronic word of mouth. Wetzer, Zeelenberg and Pieters' [39] found out that urge to release highly negative emotions such as anger played as a strong motivation to share negative word of mouth. Sundaram, Mitra and Webster [34] emphasised very positive experiences as a factor motivating to sharing reviews as well. However, some works have been found to be contrary to conducted research. According to Tong, Wang, Tan and Teo [40], consumers engage in WOM to take a revenge on a company which left them dissatisfied. This was not supported by research for this study as not many participants showed interest to companies and even those who did, showed only positive intentions.

Product involvement demonstrated to be high for all participants as they mentioned always asking people around them and checking online opinions prior to buying skin care. However, it is contrary to research results of Wolny and Mueller [31] indicating that higher product involvement leads to higher motivation to engage in electronic word of mouth. Although interviewees emphasise the importance of skin care for them, they do not express general interest in these types of products. Due to general lack of interest in the topic, electronic word of mouth communication is not triggered in case of our interviewed respondents.

A very important and new finding of this research is the factor of laziness. It was discovered in this research and has not been found in the previous literature on the topic. A large proportion (50%) of respondents named laziness as a reason stopping them from posting their opinion online.

Also, the researcher recruited an equal amount of males and females for the research in order to test whether sex influenced electronic word of mouth participation in the skin care category. This was done as other researchers recruited higher amount of females for data collection. Our results show that there is no difference between males and females regarding the interest, involvement or level of willingness to potentially participate in eWOM. Only one male demonstrated no lurking behaviour in the context of skin care.

6   Practical and Theoretical Implications

This research advances the understanding of information dissemination online by identifying reasons for consumers not to engage in eWOM communications. Knowing the reasons of consumers to avoid leaving reviews can help managers to create a strategy for engaging customers to give feedback about skin care on the internet. Based on the data analysis, the following recommendations will be made. Due to research result showing that altruism is mostly motivating consumers to communicate through traditional word of mouth, it is recommended for companies to create marketing campaigns targeting feelings of consumers, which could motivate them to help people they do not know - other consumers online. To that effect, it would be useful to show the importance of online reviews for a company, which could also trigger altruism towards a business in those customers who are naturally predisposed to it.

Another recommendation is to raise the general interest about skin care. Only something which interests customers will make them spend time creating and posting a review. This could be done by publishing more educational material on skin care and skin care products topic.

Business' website should have their own review section. The process of posting a review must be made simple, fast and safe. It must also look trustworthy, should not ask for telephone number or any sensitive data. It is important to demonstrate that the website complies with all data protection laws, presenting themselves a responsible and reliable business.

In order to motivate consumer to leave a review, it is crucial to show them that a company truly cares for them and their opinion. Interacting with reviewers, highlighting their opinions, sharing them with wider audience may inspire lurkers to participate and feel like a part of a community.

Finally, almost all participants mentioned that receiving economic incentives such as discounts, vouchers, coupons etc. can be a strong motivating factor to provide reviews.

7 Conclusion

The aim of this research was to investigate why customers who buy skincare products do not engage in eWOM by not leaving reviews about products online. After conducting semi-structured in-depth interviews and analysing collected data, several factors hindering sharing reviews about skin care were found. Finding of the research indicate that firstly, individuals avoid leaving skin care reviews due to lack of interest or general excitement about the topic. They also reported being lazy to leave reviews and showed lower amount of altruism towards online users, compared to people they know in real life. Half of the respondents appeared to be posting about other categories of products rather than skin care, meaning that measure could be taken to attract them to publish reviews about skin care products too.

References

1. Yin, D., Mitra, S., Zhang, H.: Research note—when do consumers value positive vs. negative reviews? An empirical investigation of confirmation bias in online word of mouth. Inf. Syst. Res. **27**, 131–144 (2016)
2. Mikalef, P., Pappas, I.O., Giannakos, M.N.: Value co-creation and purchase intention in social commerce: the enabling role of word-of-mouth and trust (2017)
3. Hennig-Thurau, T., Gwinner, K.P., Walsh, G., Gremler, D.D.: Electronic word-of-mouth via consumer-opinion platforms: what motivates consumers to articulate themselves on the internet? J. Interact. Mark. **18**, 38–52 (2004)
4. Mikalef, P., Giannakos, M.N., Pappas, I.O.: Designing social commerce platforms based on consumers' intentions. Behav. Inf. Technol. **36**, 1308–1327 (2017)

5. Ismagilova, E., Dwivedi, Y.K., Slade, E., Williams, M.D.: Electronic Word of Mouth (eWOM) in the Marketing Context: A State of the Art Analysis and Future Directions. Springer, Heidelberg (2017). https://doi.org/10.1007/978-3-319-52459-7
6. Shechter, M., Freeman, S.: Nonuse value: reflections on the definition and measurement. In: Pethig, R. (ed.) Valuing the Environment: Methodological and Measurement Issues, pp. 171–194. Springer, Dordrecht (1994). https://doi.org/10.1007/978-94-015-8317-6_7
7. Batson, C.D.: Why act for the public good? Four answers. Pers. Soc. Psychol. Bull. **20**, 603–610 (1994)
8. Lee, D., Kim, H.S., Kim, J.K.: The impact of online brand community type on consumer's community engagement behaviors: consumer-created vs. marketer-created online brand community in online social-networking web sites. Cyberpsychol. Behav. Soc. Netw. **14**, 59–63 (2011)
9. Alicke, M.D., Sedikides, C.: Self-enhancement and self-protection: what they are and what they do. Eur. Rev. Soc. Psychol. **20**, 1–48 (2009)
10. Fiske, S.T.: Social and societal pragmatism: commentary on augustinos, Gaskell, and Lorenzi-Cioldi. In: Representations of the Social: Bridging Research Traditions, pp. 249–253 (2001)
11. Parlamis, J.D.: Venting as emotion regulation: the influence of venting responses and respondent identity on anger and emotional tone. Int. J. Conflict Manag. **23**, 77–96 (2012)
12. Best, A., Andreasen, A.R.: Consumer response to unsatisfactory purchases: a survey of perceiving defects, voicing complaints, and obtaining redress. Law Soc. Rev. **11**, 701 (1976)
13. Tschohl, J.: Do yourself a favor: gripe about bad service. Am. Salesman **39**, 3–5 (1994)
14. Lee, C.C., Hu, C.: Analyzing hotel customers' E-complaints from an internet complaint forum. J. Travel Tourism Mark. **17**, 167–181 (2005)
15. Oliver, R.L.: Whence consumer loyalty? J. Mark. **63**, 33–44 (1999)
16. Choi, J.H., Scott, J.E.: Electronic word of mouth and knowledge sharing on social network sites: a social capital perspective. J. Theor. Appl. Electron. Commer. Res. **8**, 69–82 (2013)
17. Dalkir, K.: Knowledge Management in Theory and Practice. Routledge, Abingdon (2013)
18. Wirtz, J., Chew, P.: The effects of incentives, deal proneness, satisfaction and tie strength on word-of-mouth behaviour. Int. J. Serv. Ind. Manag. **13**, 141–162 (2002)
19. Edelmann, N.: Reviewing the definitions of "lurkers" and some implications for online research. Cyberpsychol. Behav. Soc. Netw. **16**, 645–649 (2013)
20. Katz, J.: Luring the lurkers. Slashdot (1998)
21. Nielsen, J.: Participation inequality: encouraging more users to contribute (2006). http://www.useit.com/alertbox/participation_inequality.html
22. Preece, J., Nonnecke, B., Andrews, D.: The top five reasons for lurking: improving community experiences for everyone. Comput. Hum. Behav. **20**, 201–223 (2004)
23. Nonnecke, B., Andrews, D., Preece, J.: Non-public and public online community participation: needs, attitudes and behavior. Electron. Commer. Res. **6**, 7–20 (2006)
24. Bartikowski, B., Walsh, G.: Attitude contagion in consumer opinion platforms: posters and lurkers. Electron. Mark. **24**, 207–217 (2014)
25. Wiertz, C., Charla, M., Ruyter, K.: Social capital production in a virtual P3 community. J. Consum. Res. **34**, 832–849 (2008)
26. Haythornthwaite, C.A.: Online knowledge crowds and communities (2009)
27. Nonnecke, B., Preece, J.: Why lurkers lurk. In: AMCIS 2001 Proceedings, p. 294 (2001)
28. Blanchard, A.L., Markus, M.L.: The experienced sense of a virtual community: characteristics and processes. ACM SIGMIS Database: DATABASE Adv. Inf. Syst. **35**, 64–79 (2004)

29. Bishop, J.: Transforming lurkers into posters: the role of the participation continuum. In: Proceedings of the Fourth International Conference on Internet Technologies and Applications (ITA 2011), pp. 1–11 (2011)
30. Glynn Mangold, W., Miller, F., Brockway, G.R.: Word-of-mouth communication in the service marketplace. J. Serv. Mark. **13**, 73–89 (1999)
31. Wolny, J., Mueller, C.: Analysis of fashion consumers' motives to engage in electronic word-of-mouth communication through social media platforms. J. Mark. Manag. **29**, 562–583 (2013)
32. Gunn, R.: Silent travlers: barriers to providing eWOM (2017)
33. Nonnecke, B., Preece, J.: Silent participants: getting to know lurkers better. In: Lueg, C., Fisher, D. (eds.) From Usenet to CoWebs: Interacting with Social Information Spaces, pp. 110–132. Springer, London (2003). https://doi.org/10.1007/978-1-4471-0057-7_6
34. Sundaram, D.S., Mitra, K., Webster, C.: Word-of-mouth communications: a motivational analysis. In: ACR North American Advances (1998)
35. Yoo, K.-H., Gretzel, U.: Influence of personality on travel-related consumer-generated media creation. Comput. Hum. Behav. **27**, 609–621 (2011)
36. Velázquez, B.M., Blasco, M.F., Gil Saura, I.: ICT adoption in hotels and electronic word-of-mouth. Academia Revista Latinoamericana de Administración **28**, 227–250 (2015)
37. Anderson, E.W.: Customer satisfaction and word of mouth. J. Serv. Res. **1**, 5–17 (1998)
38. Herr, P.M., Kardes, F.R., Kim, J.: Effects of word-of-mouth and product-attribute information on persuasion: an accessibility-diagnosticity perspective. J. Consum. Res. **17**, 454–462 (1991)
39. Wetzer, I.M., Zeelenberg, M., Pieters, R.: "Never eat in that restaurant, I did!": exploring why people engage in negative word-of-mouth communication. Psychol. Mark. **24**, 661–680 (2007)
40. Tong, Y., Wang, X., Tan, C.-H., Teo, H.-H.: An empirical study of information contribution to online feedback systems: a motivation perspective. Inf. Manag. **50**, 562–570 (2013)

Big Data Analytics

Big Data Readiness Index – Africa in the Age of Analytics

Anke Joubert, Matthias Murawski[✉], and Markus Bick

ESCP Europe Business School Berlin, Berlin, Germany
anke.joubert@edu.escpeurope.eu,
{mmurawski,mbick}@escpeurope.eu

Abstract. Big data promises to drive economic growth and development, but if not applied across borders it can lead to a greater digital divide. There are, however, no indexes measuring big data readiness on country level. Most existing indexes cover topics such as digitalization and focus on developed economies with a clear underrepresentation of Africa. Thus, the underlying question to answer is: what are the required components for an index measuring big data readiness in Africa? The design science approach is used to design the Big Data Readiness Index (BDRI). The BDRI is developed in line with the academic definition of big data under the five V's: volume, variety, velocity, veracity and value, and consists of 75 indicators, grouped into drivers that build up the five components. We apply this index to all African countries which yields, amongst others, country rankings that show relatively high BDRI levels for coastal countries such as South Africa, Kenya and Namibia as well as for islands such as Mauritius. Limitations and further development of the BDRI are discussed.

Keywords: Africa · Big data · Design science research · Readiness index

1 Introduction

Big data analytics has gained substantial interest among academics and business practitioners in the digital era and promises to deliver improved operational efficiency, drive new revenue streams, ensure competitive advantage and facilitate innovation, amongst other things [1, 2]. Big data is not only of interest to academics, but also to governments, businesses and the general public [3]. Fosso-Wamba et al. state that the topic 'big data' was searched on Google about 252 000 times in November 2011, whereas the peak is at 3.13 billion in March 2017 [4]. This shows not only the increasing interest in the subject of big data, but also indicates that the topic is not losing momentum.

The concept of data-driven decision making and automation through big data can be applied across various sectors including healthcare, security, services, manufacturing, retail and technology. In order to gain value, the concept of big data must be clearly defined and understood, both in terms of its benefits, application possibilities, as well as the shortcomings and risks involved - these include for example privacy concerns, human resource scarcity, infrastructure shortages and lack of institutional governance [1].

© IFIP International Federation for Information Processing 2019
Published by Springer Nature Switzerland AG 2019
I. O. Pappas et al. (Eds.): I3E 2019, LNCS 11701, pp. 101–112, 2019.
https://doi.org/10.1007/978-3-030-29374-1_9

As countries differ substantially across these fields, we believe it would be interesting to compare the structural, technological and institutional readiness for countries to adapt big data technologies in order to harvest the economic benefits. Most authors of published big data related literature up until 2015 are from China, followed by the USA, Australia, the UK and Korea [5]. Africa produces less than 1% of the world's research even though 12.5% of the world's population is from Africa [6]. This unequal geographic coverage of literature raises a vital question as to whether the lack of interest in African countries is due to a global big data divide or whether it is due to a lack of essential knowledge and proficiency to undertake big data related research within African countries.

Literature focusing on firm level e-business adaption shows that technology readiness has the strongest impact on facilitating assimilation of e-business in developing countries [7]. Lawrence and Tar [8] discuss issues hindering e-commerce in developing countries, concluding that the absence of basic infrastructure, socio-economic factors and inadequate government ICT strategies slows down adoption and growth. Furthermore, e-readiness does not have an established theoretical basis with the existing e-readiness measurement tools largely focusing on ICT, business and policy, underplaying the information access factor [9]. Thus, the lack of country level research in this field is established and leading to our research focus.

Furthermore, the Digital Transformation and Sustainability (DTS) model proposed by Pappas et al. [10] explains how different data actors and big data analytical capabilities interact to create sustainable societal value through critical factors such as a data-driven organisational culture, technology investment and technical and managerial skills. They mention the need for further research to focus on data capacities and availability in the digital society to take into account the capacity and availability of big data, as well as differences between countries, continents, and cultures [10].

In this paper, we will attempt to develop an index that can benchmark Big Data Readiness in the age of analytics. The focus area for data application will be the African continent. Establishing such an index will not only allow comparison between countries but will also set a benchmark of the indicators and topics which should be covered by an index measuring big data readiness. A new index covering Africa will help to fill the current gap in big data research for this region as well as the gap left by the existing indexes' limited African coverage. Based on this, we formulate the following research question:

What are required components for a big data readiness index (BDRI) and how could a comprehensive BDRI be designed?

As previously mentioned, the developed index will be applied to African countries with publicly available data. Before entering this empirical part, we start with a literature review which will yield a brief overview of big data. In the next step, Hevner's design science research approach [11] (outlined in the methodology section) will be applied as a baseline for constructing the index, including descriptions of the data collection, cleaning, weighting and normalization process. The section that follows includes an analysis of the BDRI by using data about African countries. The final section concludes by summarizing key findings and main contributions.

2 Theoretical Background

2.1 Introduction to Big Data

Big data analytics promises to deliver improved operational efficiency, drive new revenue streams, ensure competitive advantage and facilitate innovation, amongst other things [2, 12]. Fosso-Wamba et al. [4] summarize some descriptions of the impact of big data in previous literature as the *next big thing in innovation* [13]; *the fourth paradigm of science* [14]; *the next frontier for innovation, competition, and productivity* [15]; the *next management revolution* [16]; and that big data is *bringing a revolution in science and technology* [2].

There is no globally accepted definition for the term 'big data'. The complexity of defining this term was aggravated by a shared origin between academia, industry, the media and widespread public interest. The fact that various stakeholders provide diverse and even contradictory definitions, leads to the emergence of literature that attempts to establish a common definition.

The first concepts predominantly associated with big data are far from new and relate to data storage and data analysis. An early definition describes big data using the three V's: volume, velocity, and variety. This approach has been reiterated in various studies [16, 17]. Volume refers to the size of the data, whereas velocity refers to the speed of data generation and the frequency of data delivery. Variety takes the data types into consideration and highlights the fact that big data is generated from a large number of sources and formats that include structured and unstructured data [17].

A fourth V for value was subsequently suggested. Value implies that extracting economic benefits from the data is a key attribute of big data analytics [5, 18, 19]. A fifth V for veracity followed. The fifth V is sometimes referred to as verification in literature [20]. Veracity attempts to stress the importance of data quality and that trusting the various data sources is integral. This allows analysts and users to be sure that security measures and techniques are in place to assure trustworthy data analysis [4]. The use of inaccurate data will lead to biased and inconsistent results and recommendations. Both value and veracity are considered as important in this study, as without added value and trust towards the quality of the data used, the benefits of big data analytics deteriorate.

2.2 Big Data in Developing Countries

If not applied across borders, increased data generation and the availability of analytical tools, can lead to an even greater digital divide – where countries who successfully implement this will advance leaving the rest behind. The digital divide originated as a concept to describe the gap between countries that have and do not have access to computers and the internet. The digital divide does not only refer to physical access but also to skills and usage of technology. Van Dijk writes that "in terms of physical access the divide seems to be closing in the most developed countries; concerning digital skills and the use of applications the divide persists or widens" [21, p. 221].

A framework for ICT development strategies that can enable countries to participate competitively in the emerging digital economy shows an acute global shortage of high skilled staff needed to steer the emerging digital economy in both developed and developing countries [9]. Hilbert mentions that privacy concerns, human resource scarcity, infrastructure shortages, limited economic resources and institutions are areas that can be barriers to developing countries, keeping them from successful digitalization [22]. Although additional challenges exist that hinder developing countries to easily implement big data analytics, the positive impacts on developing countries' economies can be even greater. Thus, big data in itself can help alleviate the initial shortcomings that are barriers to the implementation of big data. For example, due to structural inconsistencies, statistical authorities in Ghana took 17 years to adopt the UN national accounting system. Afterwards, Ghana's GDP was 62% higher than previously estimated [23]. Some of the main opportunities big data can offer to developing countries are early warnings in times of crisis, detecting digital media and other anomalies, real-time awareness of data changes, a more honest representation of reality and real-time feedback. This can lead to early interventions for policies or programs that deliver different results than expected.

Bifet mentions that Global Pulse, a United Nations initiative launched in 2009, is using big data for the benefit of developing countries. This involves researching innovative techniques for real-time data analysis, detecting early emerging vulnerabilities and sharing open source real-time data among those integrated in the global network of Pulse Labs [24].

Some other interesting examples of how big data analytics is being applied to assist development include using machined roof counting to measure poverty in Uganda, using mobile phone data and airtime credit purchases to estimate food security in East Africa and mining citizen feedback data in order to gain input for government decision making in Indonesia [25]. These are only some of the many ongoing projects where big data analytics can be implemented for positive and productive outcomes in developing countries.

3   Research Design

3.1   Index Development Procedure

Developing an index will be approached in the same manner as designing an artefact in the context of design science research [11]. This approach is relevant as the BDRI is applicable to a technology related field. The index will be designed and evaluated accordingly. The seven steps of the design science approach will be applied to designing an index in the following manner (Fig. 1).

As described in the previous section, big data has been researched intensively and defined by many researchers. The definition as followed by this paper includes the five V's: volume, variety, velocity, veracity and value. Thus, the five V's also form the five components of the BDRI.

Each component is formed up by three drivers. These drivers are inspired by an analysis of existing digital related indexes such as the Enabling Digitalization Index (EDI), the Digital Evolution Index (DEI), the IMD World Digital Competitiveness (WDC) and the Networked Readiness Index (NRI) [26–30]. Certain components from

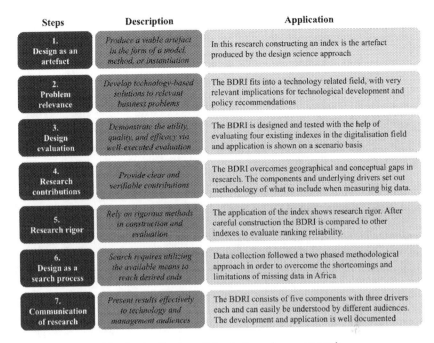

Steps	Description	Application
1. Design as an artefact	*Produce a viable artefact in the form of a model, method, or instantiation*	In this research constructing an index is the artefact produced by the design science approach
2. Problem relevance	*Develop technology-based solutions to relevant business problems*	The BDRI fits into a technology related field, with very relevant implications for technological development and policy recommendations
3. Design evaluation	*Demonstrate the utility, quality, and efficacy via well-executed evaluation*	The BDRI is designed and tested with the help of evaluating four existing indexes in the digitalisation field and application is shown on a scenario basis
4. Research contributions	*Provide clear and verifiable contributions*	The BDRI overcomes geographical and conceptual gaps in research. The components and underlying drivers set out methodology of what to include when measuring big data.
5. Research rigor	*Rely on rigorous methods in construction and evaluation*	The application of the index shows research rigor. After careful construction the BDRI is compared to other indexes to evaluate ranking reliability.
6. Design as a search process	*Search requires utilizing the available means to reach desired ends*	Data collection followed a two phased methodological approach in order to overcome the shortcomings and limitations of missing data in Africa
7. Communication of research	*Present results effectively to technology and management audiences*	The BDRI consists of five components with three drivers each and can easily be understood by different audiences. The development and application is well documented

Fig. 1. Application of the design science approach

each index could partially cover certain aspects of the five V's. These aspects were evaluated on a basis of relevance by referring to the definition as outlined in the literature review. Complementary drivers based on available data were added to give a global overview of big data. A total of 170 variables were collected and after analysis, taking missing values into account, and referring to the base definition, 75 variables were selected and aggregated in groups of five to build the fifteen drivers that form the basis of the final five components of the BDRI which is visualized in Fig. 2.

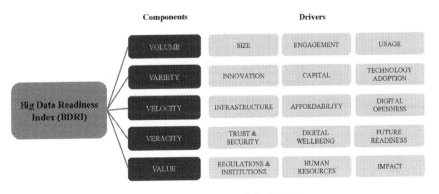

Fig. 2. Components of the BDRI

3.2   Data Collection

The data collection process followed a two phased methodological approach. In the first phase a comprehensive overview of the reviewed indexes' data sources was completed. This allowed an assessment of relevant available data to include in a BDRI, as well as ways to set up an index, measure outcomes, assign weights and normalize variables. It also indicated which first-hand sources cover all the African countries. Some of the sources [28, 29] could be reused to build up and define new components of the BDRI, but due to the limited coverage of Africa and the fact that big data requires other components not covered in the reviewed digitalization indexes, this was not exhaustive. This phase gave a broad overview that helped identify the gaps in data availability to construct the BDRI.

The second phase considered alternative sources to measure Africa's big data readiness. Due to data scarcity for some African countries, this phase had its obstacles. Dealing with data recency and missing values was a major part of the data cleaning process. This phase was successful in finding additional open data sources to help build the BDRI and also helped to verify and fill gaps for data collected in the first phase.

3.3   Evaluation of the Index

A thorough comparison of the created BDRI with the evaluated indexes(EDI, DEI, IMD WDC, and the NRI) was performed to function as a design evaluation. Even though the compared indexes have a less extensive coverage of Africa, these indexes provided the possibility to benchmark the countries that had been covered in similar topics and compare these rankings to the rankings of the BDRI. The evaluation concluded that the BDRI output is aligned with expectation and that the differences in rankings could be accounted for by the fact that the BDRI takes different features that relate to big data into account.

Hevner et al. state that scenarios can be applied as an evaluation technique for innovative artefacts. This is particularly relevant for new and complex artefacts which cannot be evaluated in one step [11]. Three scenarios that would be applicable use cases for the BDRI include governmental policy development, market entry analysis and institutional usage. The diverse scenarios illustrate research rigor through the wide range of usage possibilities and display how the development of the BDRI fits into the information system research framework.

4   Findings and Discussion

4.1   Country Rankings

We calculated the BDRI for all African countries. Ranking the countries by score allowed an analysis of the top performers. Figure 3 shows the top ten performers.

Rwanda (position 3) is the only country in the top 10 that is not a coastal country. Furthermore, three islands, Mauritius (position 1), the Seychelles (position 4) and Cape Verde (position 10) belong to the top performing BDRI countries in Africa. South

Fig. 3. BDRI - top 10 African countries

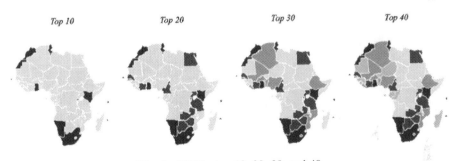

Fig. 4. BDRI - top 10, 20, 30, and 40

Africa, an influential economy in Africa, ranks in second position. Figure 4 shows the evolution of the BDRI.

Southern Africa is the top performing region, with Eastern Africa following in the top 20. The top 30 grows to include Nigeria and the neighboring Benin and Togo and coastal Liberia as well as Burkina Faso, Mali and Algeria in West Africa. Nigeria, one of Africa's largest economies, ranks at position 21. The top 40 fills the neighboring gaps in West Africa, with Guinea-Bissau as the only exception.

Looking at the location of the top performers, coastal countries perform well and neighbors can influence each other in terms of technology adoption.

Evaluating overall performance by component shows that volume produced the most unequal performance. This indicates a digital divide within Africa in terms of size, engagement and usage. On the opposite end, countries show less diverse performance in variety and veracity, yet this narrow spread has a low base. On average, velocity and value show a higher overall performance. Noteworthy positive outliers include Mauritius (usage), the Seychelles (usage and infrastructure) and South Africa (size, innovation and infrastructure). On the opposite end recurring negative outliers are Somalia, South Sudan and the Central African Republic.

4.2   Hierarchical Clustering Analysis

Hierarchical cluster analysis is an algorithm that groups similar objects together in clusters to get a set of clusters that are distinct from one another [31]. In order to perform this clustering, the raw data needs to be transformed into a distance matrix. A dendrogram was created, where the vertical axis represents the distance or dissimilarity between clusters, whereas the horizontal axis represents clusters in terms of size. Selecting a distance measure of one resulted in three clusters of similar size. The first cluster is expected to be more different to the second and third cluster that branches from the same clade of the dendrogram.

The countries are assigned to one of the three clusters in terms of similarity. We defined these three distinct groups as the countries *forging ahead* and thus outperforming the rest of Africa, the countries *gaining momentum* and thus catching up to big data implementation trends and the ones that are *lagging behind*.

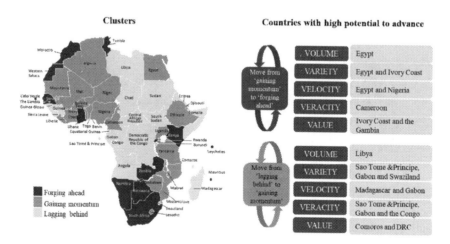

Fig. 5. Cluster analysis results

The map (Fig. 5) shows that the *lagging behind* cluster that requires the most intervention is the central geographical strip from Angola in the south to Libya in the north, as well as Sudan, Eritrea and Somalia on the Eastern coast. A small cluster in West Africa, consisting of Guinea-Bissau, Guinea and Sierra Leone, is also in need of large interventions to become technologically ready to gain value from big data.

4.3 Limitations and Next Steps

The major limitations of developing the BDRI for Africa was induced by missing data, aggregation methodology and the limited coverage of available indicators.

Data Scarcity. One of the major constraints to building an index for big data readiness in Africa is data scarcity. The limited data available makes analysis more difficult.

Aggregation Methodology. A major challenge was how to overcome aggregation where some indicators of the drivers were missing. There is little research on how to deal with aggregation as some indexes, such as the Digital Evolution Index (DEI) chose to cover countries based on data availability [26].

Limited Coverage. Some data that is available to include in indexes covering other countries was not available for Africa. After filling missing values using projections from data available in the past ten years, the following indicators still had a high number of missing values, making them unusable in the BDRI: Public private partnership investment in ICT consisted of 91% missing data and was thus only being available for five countries. Furthermore, software piracy rate has 86% missing values; patent applications 85%; commercial value of unlicensed software 74%; labor force with advanced education 72%; firms expected to give gifts to get a phone connection 63%; telephone faults cleared by next working day 60%; researchers in R&D 57% and average duration of power outages 52%.

Taking these three limitations into account, we include the following recommendations to help overcome these limitations, to improve the developed index and to expand its use in future research.

Look into Non-traditional Data Sources. Future studies can look beyond the traditional data sources. Data goes beyond tables of numbers and includes society's digital footprints created by cell phones, internet searches, personal transactions and other sources [32]. Pictures, sound and social media can also be used as data sources and are creative ways to capture the relevant data – especially on a continent where data capturing is limited. Together with alternative data sources, streamlined open data would be beneficial. Support and investment in platforms such as Open Africa could lead to increased published databases and higher coverage [33]. Africa has a population of 1.2 billion people of whom around 60% are young – thus Africa has a growing number of future digital natives who will be generating increasing amounts of data [32]. This indicates a great opportunity for non-public organizations to get involved in data collection, curation, labelling and help to increase open data sources. There are many other opportunities for data collection in Africa. Data collection should not only be the responsibility of the government but could also be an opportunity for start-ups. Kenyan and Namibian mobile-phone operators have made data records available to researchers to help combat malaria, which was used to compare caller movements with malaria outbreak data to predict where the disease might spread [34]. By looking into alternative sources of data, calling for more open data and by inviting the private sector to get involved, there is hope to ultimately eliminate the missing data issues on the African continent.

Expand BDRI Coverage. The BDRI could be expanded to cover countries outside Africa. We recommend covering other developing regions first, as the BDRI methodology is designed for measuring big data readiness specifically in developing countries.

Comparability. We recommend that the index is measured annually to create a basis for comparison. This will assure that country specific progress can be tracked, and the effectiveness of policy interventions can be compared over time. The inclusion of an in-depth country overview is also suggested.

Index Evaluation. At the current stage the BDRI is evaluated on a scenario basis. Users can be asked to use the index for their purposes and give feedback that could lead to redesign.

5 Conclusion

Big data has gained substantial interest among academics and business practitioners in the digital era, and with 2.41 billion searches for this term in July 2018 [35], this topic is not losing momentum. A new index, the Big Data Readiness Index (BDRI) that covers Africa extensively was developed in this paper. Data availability and limited research were key challenges, but the emergence of mobile technology which in Africa is double as high as global rates ensures higher big data potential [36]. The seven steps of the design science approach [11] were applied throughout design, development and evaluation of the BDRI. Research rigor is ensured through careful construction, comparison and evaluation of the ranking reliability. Finally, the BDRI is set up in an understandable format based on the five V's.

Looking at the rankings shows that coastal countries and islands perform best, Rwanda being the only non-coastal country in the top 10. Neighboring countries influence each other through clear diffusion patterns. Outlier detection shows noteworthy positive outliers within components such as Mauritius and the Seychelles in the value component and South Africa in some components from volume, variety and velocity. On the opposite end recurring negative outliers are Somalia, South Sudan and the Central African Republic. The hierarchical clustering analysis reinforces these results by classifying the central geographical strip as *lagging behind*. The larger distance between the *forging ahead* group and the other two clusters show that the top performers are far ahead in terms of big data readiness.

The development of the BDRI adds value in various ways. Firstly, by linking big data theory to propose a practical way to measure big data, we contribute to the development of, amongst others, 'big data analytics capability' [37]. Secondly, the BDRI covers Africa extensively, overcoming the geographical gap mentioned by scholars [5] and seen in underrepresentation of Africa in most existing digitalization indexes. Thirdly, no prior research could be found that explicitly focuses on measuring big data as all the reviewed indexes focused more on digitalization and ICT with the focus on firm level e-business.

African countries might have similar weaknesses and strengths and analysis will help countries to systematically review available policy options to foster data-driven opportunities and maximize big data driven growth and development. In this way, Africa will be able to overcome developmental challenges and play an increasing role in the age of analytics.

References

1. Grover, V., Chiang, R.H.L., Liang, T.-P., Zhang, D.: Creating strategic business value from big data analytics: a research framework. J. Manag. Inf. Syst. **35**, 388–423 (2018)
2. Keller, S.A., Koonin, S.E., Shipp, S.: Big data and city living - what can it do for us? Significance **9**, 4–7 (2012)
3. Agarwal, R., Dhar, V.: Editorial—big data, data science, and analytics: the opportunity and challenge for IS research. Inf. Syst. Res. **25**, 443–448 (2014)
4. Fosso Wamba, S., Akter, S., Edwards, A., Chopin, G., Gnanzou, D.: How 'big data' can make big impact: findings from a systematic review and a longitudinal case study. Int. J. Prod. Econ. **165**, 234–246 (2015)
5. Sivarajah, U., Kamal, M.M., Irani, Z., Weerakkody, V.: Critical analysis of big data challenges and analytical methods. J. Bus. Res. **70**, 263–286 (2017)
6. Duermeijer, C., Amir, M., Schoombee, L.: Africa generates less than 1% of the world's research; data analytics can change that. An in-depth analysis of the continent's research reveals promising developments – and strategies for continued improvement. https://www.elsevier.com/connect/africa-generates-less-than-1-of-the-worlds-research-data-analytics-can-change-that
7. Zhu, K., Kraemer, K.L., Xu, S.: The process of innovation assimilation by firms in different countries: a technology diffusion perspective on E-business. Manag. Sci. **52**, 1557–1576 (2006)
8. Lawrence, J.E., Tar, U.A.: Barriers to ecommerce in developing countries. Inf. Soc. Justice **3**, 23–35 (2010)
9. Mutula, S.M., van Brakel, P.: E-readiness of SMEs in the ICT sector in Botswana with respect to information access. Electron. Libr. **24**, 402–417 (2006)
10. Pappas, I.O., Mikalef, P., Giannakos, M.N., Krogstie, J., Lekakos, G.: Big data and business analytics ecosystems: paving the way towards digital transformation and sustainable societies. Inf. Syst. E-Bus. Manag. **16**, 479–491 (2018)
11. Hevner, A.R., March, S.T., Park, J., Ram, S.: Design science in information systems research. MIS Q. **28**, 75–105 (2004)
12. Chen, H., Chiang, R.H.L., Storey, V.C.: Business intelligence and analytics: from big data to big impact. MIS Q. **36**, 1165–1188 (2012)
13. Gobble, M.M.: Big data: the next big thing in innovation. Res. Technol. Manag. **56**, 64–67 (2013)
14. Strawn, G.O.: Scientific research: how many paradigms? https://er.educause.edu/-/media/files/article-downloads/erm1231.pdf
15. Manyika, J., Chui, M., Brown, B., Bughin, J., Dobbs, R., Roxburgh, C., et al.: Big data: the next frontier for innovation, competition, and productivity. https://www.mckinsey.com/business-functions/digital-mckinsey/our-insights/big-data-the-next-frontier-for-innovation
16. McAfee, A., Brynjolfsson, E.: Big data: the management revolution. Harv. Bus. Rev. **90**, 61–67 (2012)
17. Russom, P.: TDWI best practices report | Big data analytics | Transforming data with intelligence. https://tdwi.org/research/2011/09/best-practices-report-q4-big-data-analytics.aspx?tc=page0&tc=assetpg&tc=page0&m=1

18. Murawski, M., Bick, M.: Demanded and imparted big data competences: towards an integrative analysis. In: Proceedings of the 25th European Conference on Information Systems (ECIS), Guimarães, Portugal, 5–10 June 2017, pp. 1375–1390 (2017)
19. Günther, W.A., Rezazade Mehrizi, M.H., Huysman, M., Feldberg, F.: Debating big data: a literature review on realizing value from big data. J. Strateg. Inf. Syst. **26**, 191–209 (2017)
20. Opresnik, D., Taisch, M.: The value of big data in servitization. Int. J. Prod. Econ. **165**, 174–184 (2015)
21. van Dijk, J.A.G.M.: Digital divide research, achievements and shortcomings. POETICS **34**, 221–235 (2006)
22. Hilbert, M.: Big data for development: a review of promises and challenges. Dev. Policy Rev. **34**, 135–174 (2016)
23. Devarajan, S.: Africa's statistical tragedy. https://blogs.worldbank.org/africacan/africa-s-statistical-tragedy
24. Bifet, A.: Mining big data in real time. Informatica **37**, 15–20 (2013)
25. Decuyper, A., et al.: Estimating food consumption and poverty indices with mobile phone data (2014)
26. Chakravorti, B., Chaturvedu, R.S., Troein, C., Pagan, C., Filipovic, C., Beck, M.: Digital planet: how competitiveness and trust in digital economies vary across the world. https://sites.tufts.edu/digitalplanet/files/2017/05/Digital_Planet_2017_FINAL.pdf
27. Hermes, E., Enabling digitalization index 2018: measuring digitagility. http://www.eulerhermes.com/mediacenter/news/Pages/Enabling-Digitalization-Index-2018-Measuring-digitagility.aspx
28. International telecommunications union: ICT development index. https://www.itu.int/net4/ITU-D/idi/2017/#idi2017economycard-tab&AFG
29. World Economic Forum: The global information technology report: innovating in the digital economy. http://www3.weforum.org/docs/GITR2016/GITR_2016_full%20report_final.pdf
30. IMD World Competitiveness Centre: World digital competitiveness rankings 2017. https://www.imd.org/wcc/world-competitiveness-center-rankings/world-digital-competitiveness-rankings-2018/
31. Bock, T.: What is hierarchical clustering? https://www.displayr.com/what-is-hierarchical-clustering/
32. Sengeh, D.: Missing data: achieving the value of big data analytics in Africa. https://www.linkedin.com/pulse/missing-data-achieving-value-big-analytics-africa-david-sengeh
33. Open Africa: openAFRICA. https://africaopendata.org/dataset?q=&sort=score+desc%2C+metadata_modified+desc
34. The Economist: Off the map. https://www.economist.com/international/2014/11/13/off-the-map
35. Google Trends. https://trends.google.com/trends/?geo=US
36. Matinde, V.: Africa's missed opportunity in the multi-billion dollar mobile phone industry. https://www.idgconnect.com/idgconnect/opinion/1029329/africas-missed-opportunity-multi-billion-dollar-mobile-phone-industry
37. Gupta, M., George, J.F.: Toward the development of a big data analytics capability. Inf. Manag. **53**, 1049–1064 (2016)

Investigating Factors that Influence the Adoption of BI Systems by End Users in the Mining Industry in Southern Africa

Sunet Eybers$^{(\boxtimes)}$ ⓘ, Marie J. Hattingh ⓘ, and Liako Kuoe ⓘ

University of Pretoria, Private Bag X20, Hatfield 0028, South Africa
{sunet.eybers,marie.hattingh}@up.ac.za,
liakokuoe@gmail.com

Abstract. In an information society, information has become one of the most valuable asserts to an organisation. This is even more important in the mining industry in Africa where production lines are highly sensitive and decision makers are dependable on correct information to make decisions. One of the systems that can provide for the information needs of an organisation - Business Intelligence (BI) systems - unfortunately has a high failure rate. Some of the reasons can be attributed to technical issues (such as data structures, data warehouses), process issues (information retrieval processes and analysis), human issues (resistance to adoption) and the complex nature of BI.

This qualitative study investigated the adoption of BI systems by end users by considering the work environment and user empowerment as suggested by Kim and Gupta [1]. Data was gathered using semi-structured interviews considering both aspects of the work environment and user empowerment.

The findings of the study suggested that a strong bureaucratic culture and strict safety regulatory requirements inhibits job autonomy. Job autonomy in return has a negative impact on the willingness of end users to create their own BI reports. Poor management support and a lack of training in the utilisation of BI systems furthermore make it difficult for the ageing workforce to use all the advanced features of the BI systems and capabilities. Finally, end users felt a lack of empowerment to make business decisions and therefor lack motivation to use the system.

Keywords: BI systems · Mining · User empowerment · Work environment

1 Introduction

One of the many goals of a business is to seek profit through offering a market-leading product or service that yields profitable returns for shareholders, which in turn provides continuity and growth to a company [2]. Management is responsible for directing and making strategic decisions that will see an organisation operate in the most efficient and effective manner. On a daily basis, managers face a variety of challenges such as: leadership adjustment, talent management, technology, organisational culture and decision making [3]. Despite these daily challenges, managers need to constantly explore ways of improving the organisation's performance. Business Intelligence

© IFIP International Federation for Information Processing 2019
Published by Springer Nature Switzerland AG 2019
I. O. Pappas et al. (Eds.): I3E 2019, LNCS 11701, pp. 113–124, 2019.
https://doi.org/10.1007/978-3-030-29374-1_10

(BI) systems aims to assist management on challenges such as decision making, by providing timeous, accurate and reliable means of making informed decisions and predictions about the future [4]. The right strategic decisions can differentiate a product or service from its rivals, thus, increasing market share and competitiveness.

BI refers to the combination of operational data (which is usually raw data), processes, systems and applications to give business leaders competitive information that is crucial for decision making [5, 6]. BI helps executives to be more proactive by analysing the past to improve the future. It is predicted that by the year 2021, the growth of modern BI will double when compared to its mainstream counterparts, and that it will deliver greater business value [7]. However, organisations fail to achieve a return on their BI system implementation investments [1, 8–10].

Although organisations invest in BI for its recognised benefits, the actual realisation of BI benefits lies in the effective use of BI systems [11]. Service oriented BI has brought about new social and cognitive challenges such as the abandonment or sub-utilisation of the BI System [10]. Other challenges such as complex system implementation (due to multiple data source systems and multiple data owners for example), lack of alignment with business strategy and the absence of a clear project objective all contribute to the complexity of BI projects [10, 12, 13]. One way of addressing these challenges are to focus on BI system utilisation [10].

An end user's adoption and subsequent satisfaction to utilise a system has a direct impact on the benefits obtained from the system implemented [4]. This study focus on the factors that influence the adoption of BI systems by end users in the mining industry in South Africa (SA). Research on the successful adoption of BI systems in a SA context is emerging (see Sect. 2) and this paper aims to contribute to that body of literature.

The research question is *"How does end users influence the adoption of BI systems"*, particularly focusing on the impact of the user workplace environment, the attitude of end users towards the BI system and the willingness of users to utilise the BI system.

The paper outline is as follow: the first section considers current BI system utilisation success factors in SA context, the relationship between BI system adoption and end user satisfaction and subsequently BI system usage as a measure of BI system adoption. The research approach followed is presented in Sect. 4 followed by the discussion of the findings in Sect. 5. Sections 6 and 7 presents the conclusion and recommendations.

2 BI System Utilisation and Success in a South African Context

How BI systems are used in an organisation is dependent on the objectives each organisation aims to achieve [14]. BI systems are mainly used to analyse organisational data that is generated from operational activities for the customer relations purposes, process monitoring [15] and strategic purposes, to determine threats through the analyses of internal and external environments [16].

Dawson and Belle [17] conducted a study to understand the critical success factors (CSFs) most important to financial services in SA. Their study revealed that the most important CSFs were committed management support, business vision, user involvement and data quality. Eybers and Giannakopoulos [18] also looked at the CSFs South African organisations can use to improve their chances of BI project success by looking at different organisations. The results indicated that CSFs in BI implementations are somewhat generic. Organisational factors, project related factors, technical factors and environmental factors were the categories found in both academic literature and in responses from the interviewees [18]. An additional category was identified as "external factors", possibly indicating that some CSFs are industry specific [18]. Nkuna's [19] research was focused on the utilisation of a BI system as a key factor of BI system success. The findings suggested that perceived usefulness of a BI system will positively affect the intention to use a system, whilst perceived ease of use has a positive effect on perceived usefulness but has no influence on intention to use the BI system. Serumaga-zake [4] reported that user satisfaction played a mediating role between system and service quality with net benefits whilst information quality had no significant influence on perceived net benefits.

3   BI System Adoption and User Satisfaction

User satisfaction, as a result of end user system adoption contribute to the success of BI systems. User satisfaction, which is defined as: "an affective attitude towards a specific computer application by someone who interacts with the application directly" [11]. This measure is a subjective measure based on the BI user's perception of the BI system used, which can be influenced by a vast number of variables [5]. End user computing satisfaction (EUCS) is a five-factor measuring instrument developed by Doll and Torkzadeh (1988) cited in [11]. Its purpose is to measure satisfaction within the end user computing environment; however, [11] believes that the instrument can also be used to evaluate BI systems. The five factors of EUCS are; Content, accuracy, format, ease of use and timelines (Doll and Torkzadeh 1988) cited in [11]. These factors are important for management and stakeholders of BI systems as it contributes to a positive computing satisfaction.

Panahi [20] posited that user satisfaction is a factor of technological BI capabilities (i.e. data quality, functionality, access and flexibility), as well as organisational BI capabilities (i.e. comprehensive training, quality of support and the type of use). In Panahi's [20] research it was shown that the higher the technological factors are, the higher the user satisfaction was likely to be. This means that, for a BI implementation to be successful, the data, accessibility, functionality and flexibility need to be of highest quality. In addition to this finding, organisational BI capabilities also proved to be very significant in determining user satisfaction, thus BI success. Similarly, Serumaga-zake [4] findings also report system quality (i.e. availability, ease of use, accessibility, stability) and service quality (i.e. assurance, responsiveness and knowledge) as important factors to user satisfaction and BI success.

Isik et al. [5] refer to five BI satisfaction measures based on the BI system used, to evaluate BI success. These five measures are; user friendliness, timeous and precise decision making support and lastly the overall satisfaction of BI system users. The usage of the BI system, due its importance, is further explored in the next section.

3.1 BI Usage as a Measure of BI System Success

Between 10% and 20% of BI projects are abandoned or the implemented system is not utilized as intended. [10]. This highlights the importance to measure BI usage in order to determine BI success.

BI systems hold quality information that assists decision makers with insightful information that they can use for decision making. The measurement of the type of BI use (i.e. frequency or intensity of use) is therefore an important measure as it measures the realisation of meaningful use, which has a direct impact on productivity and success [21]. BI usage therefore has a direct impact on the ability to make decisions [21].

Jones and Straub [22] measured BI usage by considering six areas, namely; frequency of use, duration of use, extent of use, decision to use (use or not use), voluntariness of use (voluntary or mandatory), features used, and task supported. Similarly, Lee et al. (2003, cited in [11]) proposed four measures of system usage as; frequency of use, amount of time spent using the BI system, the actual number of times the system was used and diversity of usage. The study postulated that, if the system is used for a longer period of time, by a large number of users for various reasons of meaningful usage, the BI system is considered to be successful.

A number of frameworks/models have been published in academic literature investigating the influence of system end users on the adoption of BI systems. These include the BI system success model (Hackney et al. 2012), BI system success model [4], CSF framework for implementation of a BI system [12], Business Intelligence Extended Use (BIEU) model [21] and User Empowerment approach to IS Infusion [1].

The User Empowerment approach to Information System (IS) Infusion by Kim and Gupta [1] was selected as the theoretical underpinning for the study based on the strong focus on the system user. Although it focuses on IS, BI is perceived as a subset of IS and in many cases BI faces the same challenges as IS [8]. The model, as illustrated in Fig. 1, does not focus on technological factors or the external macro environmental characteristics but rather social aspects of IS system adoption. Due to space limitations, this paper will only report on the work environment and the user empowerment aspects.

The *work environment* aspect refers to the importance of the work environment in the psychological empowerment of end users toward the adoption of IS systems. This view is similar to the social cognitive theory as described by [4] which states that there is an interaction between human behavior and the environment. The approach suggests that the design of the work environment has an influence on a Business intelligence user's psychological empowerment. This framework focuses primarily on Information system (IS) users and not the general employees [1]. Perceived fit, job autonomy and climate for achievement are the main factors that influences an end users' view on work environment [1].

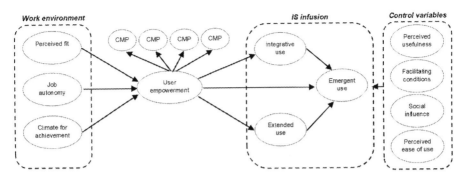

Fig. 1. A user empowerment approach to information systems infusion [1]

User empowerment is based on the theory of psychological empowerment as postulated by [23]. The user empowerment section contains four 'cognitions' or end user perceptions that influence an individual's character namely competence (CMP), impact (IMP), meaningfulness (MNG) and finally choice or self-determination (SDT) [1]. Each of these factors will be discussed further in section five.

4 Research Approach and Data Collection

The primary objective of this research is to investigate the influence of end user system adoption of BI systems in a mining firm in South Africa. Based on the objective, the study explores the "subjective views" of different BI users and are therefore qualitative in nature. This approach will allow the researcher to explore and to gain new insights as to how end user adoption influence BI implementations in an organisation.

Company X has two operating mining plants in the Northern Cape Province, South Africa. The mining operations are approximately 150 km apart. These mines are both open pit iron-ore mines.

The research focused on respondents from the Business Improvement department, Human Resources (HR) departments located at the two mines as well as the Head Office. Within each department, different levels of employees were targeted, including senior managerial level employees, HR and Business Improvement practitioners, general end users, business analysts. This diverse sample population represented the views of employees in their respective departments and locations. These two departments were an area of interest because in the past, they had implemented a number of BI projects in an effort to analyse and improve the productivity in the mine. A total of 30 participants were asked to participate in the research whilst 20 participants gave their consent.

Semi-structured interviews were conducted using the user empowerment approach to IS infusion [1] to cover various aspects of end user system adoption. The interview template consisted of three sections. The first section focused on soliciting demographic information of the interviewees. The second section aimed at understanding the work environment of the BI users. The third section of the interview focused on personal behaviors and attributes that influence BI system use.

After the construction of the interview template, a pre-test was conducted to test the appropriateness of questions and perform quality control. Two colleagues from the researcher's IT department completed the interview template during this process where after minor amendments were made.

The interview template was emailed to employees who were unable to attend face-to-face interviews. Due to geographic constraints, telephonic interviews were also conducted.

5 Discussion of Findings

The discussion section follows the outline of the user empowerment approach to information systems infusion [1] and include the work environment and user environment.

5.1 Work Environment

The work environment is influenced by the perceived fit of the technology to the task, the degree of job autonomy and the climate of achievement [1]. Each of these factors will be discussed in turn.

Perceived Fit of the BI System. The perceived fit between an application and the needs of the end user include the extent to which the system caters for basic end user needs as well as the provision of knowledge that can be actioned by a novice or expert user [1]. According to the findings, 50% of the respondents believe the BI system, in particular the systems are not integrated into their daily job tasks. 35% of users have a neutral feeling towards the BI system. 15% of the employees believe the BI systems fit fairly well into their daily tasks. Despite the neutral feeling towards the system, end users are optimistic towards the capabilities of the system. They believe the BI system compliments some of their work tasks. This was similar to findings in a study conducted by Nkuna [19] that there is a relationship between the perceived ease of use of systems and their perception of the system being suitable or appropriate for completing tasks. The job the users do have a great influence on whether employees find the system fitting or not. Employees working in the Business Improvement department stated that they felt the system fitted well in their work environment. This is mainly due to the nature of their work which include the ongoing task of finding ways to improve the business. Respondent 5 explained: *"We use the control charts in our daily caucuses to discuss previous performances and plans for the day"*.

HR employees on the other hand have a range of feelings on the system's fit to work. Most of the respondents felt that their BI system did not fit their job. The essence of this view is captured through respondent 16's response: *"I have to use my free time during lunch or after work if I want to use the tool"*. In support of the above view, Respondent 12 stated that: *"I don't often use it. The reports on the tool do not support my work"*.

In summary, the findings are:

- Using BI systems to support decision making is a fairly new process at the Mine. The importance of user oriented change management in new BI systems is acknowledged as a critical success factor of BI implementations by Eybers and Hattingh [24].
- 50% of the employees believe the BI systems does not fit well into their daily tasks, 35% of the employees perceive that the BI systems fits well into their daily tasks and 15% of the employees believe the BI systems fit fairly well into their daily tasks.

Job Autonomy. Kim and Gupta [1] hypothesize that job autonomy is another work environment factor that has a significant effect on user empowerment. The outcomes of the job are dependent on an individual's drive or initiatives rather than on instructions [1]. Job autonomy creates a care around a job which then enhances an individual's motivational disposition to use a system [1]. Based on this, the interviewees were then questioned about the BI system and whether or not they felt the system gave them the independence and freedom to conduct work on their own conditions.

Most of the respondents' views suggest that the nature of the Mine is not a conducive environment for job autonomy. Furthermore, respondents cited that their work was set around production targets and standard working procedures which makes job autonomy difficult. This view is captured Respondent 10: *"Most of the work we do is guided by standard work procedures. There are steps we have to follow to conduct work and we can't deviate from as that can put us at a health risk"*.

Emphasis on the lack of job autonomy, Respondent 9 stated: *"Guided by daily production targets therefore it is difficult to set own targets"*.

In summary, the findings are:

- In both the HR and the Business Improvement departments, employees felt that the mine's organizational structure does not allow for job freedom due to predefined set targets.
- Supervisors monitor employee performance and ensure targets are met which inhibits BI system users to make their own decisions.
- Legislation are strictly enforced by the Department of Mineral Resources through the Safety Act in SA. The act specify certain how certain tasks should be completed and therefore makes it difficult for job independence or freedom to perform work.
- Predefined BI reports prohibit the user to define their own reports.

Climate for Achievement. Climate for achievement is a social structure that provides a frame of reference for individuals' perceptions about the work environment [1]. It is the foundation of attitudes and beliefs and it informs the user on what is important and what is not. Interviewees were questioned about the BI system and whether or not they felt the system provided them with a platform to achieve more. The objective was to also understand if the mine had established ways of encouraging a culture of excellence and of achievement. Respondent 3 stated: *"The organisation does not really recognise us for using the tool"*. This was supported by Respondent 1 who indicated that they are unsure of the BI system capabilities: *"We do not know the capabilities of the BI system. We are not sure what it can do"*.

Employees have a need to achieve more but the organisation is not empowering them with the correct skillsets to achieve more. This is encapsulated in the following response by Respondent 6: *"I think I can do more with the system, but I am not sure"*. The following provide a summary of the findings:

- The BI users generally have a high appetite for achievement.
- Majority of BI users have basic BI skills, this makes it difficult to explore more of the system's functionality.
- There is a need to create an environment where employees feel empowered.
- Lack of senior management's support in using the system negatively affects the utilisation of the BI systems and technologies. Management support is crucial towards achieving a successful BI implementation [24, 25].

5.2   User Empowerment

User empowerment is a social construct that examines an individual's motivational orientation in relation to their work [1]. Motivation enables individuals to conduct work more effectively to improve work performances [1]. It is important for this research to examine the antecedents of user empowerment (competence, impact, meaningfulness and self-determination) and their influence on BI use. Each of these will be discussed in turn.

Competency of the User. Competence relates to self-efficacy. It is the degree of self-belief an individual has towards their own capabilities to effectively conduct tasks [23]. Most of the respondents believed that they were competent in conducting their jobs. They believe they have the adequate capabilities to effectively deliver work. Regarding their competency with the BI system, the respondents believed that their poor skill levels hindered their competency. They believe that their competency improved when they took an initiative to learn more (i.e. climate to achieve). Respondent 18 stated: *"I had no formal training. I am self-taught. The more I use the system the more I learn more about it."*

It was observed that users who have a climate to achieve are more competent than those with a lower climate to achieve. Training plays a pivotal role in improving employee competency. Trained users felt comfortable with the system and more competent. In support of this, Respondent 2 stated: *"We just started receiving training on using the system and now I am a bit confident"*.

As a result of the feedback received from respondents the following findings could be synthesized, similar to critical success factors identified by Eybers and Hattingh [24]:

- Employees believe that they are competent in conducting their work.
- Employees believe that their competency level will be reduced if they use the BI system.
- Employees believe that BI system training will improve their competency levels.
- Employees have limited basic skills to create their own reports.

Impact of System Usage. This antecedent to user empowerment reflects an individual's level of influence on work outcomes based on system use [1, 23]. In order to understand the BI system users' views on the impact of the system, the interviewees were questioned about their views on the impact they have on the organisation/respective departments, including the impact of using the BI system.

The results showed that users with great levels of influence are senior managers or supervisors. This is expected as they hold managerial roles. Management uses BI reports to make quick operational decisions. The high level of influence is attributed to that fact that they, as managers, are accountable for achieving production targets. Respondents from both HR and Business Improvement departments shared the same views that, the results produced by BI systems influences their actions. A Business Improvement respondent stated that: *"For short interval controls, the system results influence strategic actions". (Respondent 5)*

Similarly, an HR respondent stated:*"For HR reports such as absenteeism, the results influence strategic actions". (Respondent 16)*

In contrast, non-managerial employees believed they have a low influence on how work objectives can be achieved. Respondent 20 suggested:*"We can give suggestions to the supervisor",* whilst Respondent 14 felt: *"Do not have the power to influence operation".* The following findings could be synthesized:

- Senior managers or supervisors have a great level of influence.
- Lower level employees believe they have less influence on how work objectives can be achieved.

Meaningfulness of the System. Meaningfulness refers to the value a task has to an individual's personal development plans i.e. the level at which the tasks completed by an employee contribute towards their individual own goals, standards and beliefs [23]. The level of meaningfulness will affect the employee's determination thus influencing their motivation [26]. It relates to the harmonious relationship between the BI user's values/standards and the BI system's values [1]. In order to understand the BI users' orientation regarding meaning, the interviewees were questioned about the meaningfulness of regarding the BI system.

Some of the respondents felt that the system added some form of value. They believe in the system's objectives and aims. Although some respondents use the system only when needed, they still believe in the capabilities and values of the BI system. The respondents felt the system's objectives were aligned to their own values and standards. Those who just started using the system or those who knew little of the system still believed the system is an enabler and will influence them positively especially when the system is aligned to business requirements. This is evident in Respondent 2' statement: *"We just started using the system but believe it will assist us."*

A system that does not meet business requirements does not add value to its end users. It is therefore important that the views and requirements of end users are adhered to. The realisation of user requirements through the system's functionality creates value to its users. Respondent 5 supported this by stating: *"Our department defined the requirements, so it does bring a lot of value".* One user indicated a reluctance to change from old legacy solutions to using new BI systems. Users who have spent years building a solution using MS Excel are committed to and trust their own "systems".

The following findings could be synthesized:

- The business intelligence system can contribute to achieving business value. In areas where legacy systems are used, the value of the new BI system is compromised.
- Business value is achieved if reporting requirements are met and the system integrated into their daily work.

Self-determination. Self-determination relates to an individual's sense of choice [1, 26]. A lack of power to make choices gives employees a sense of autocratic leadership which they tend to be negative towards, this then leads to tensions and a decrease in self-esteem [26]. The interviewees were questioned about the choices they have when using the BI system. As seen with the results from analysing job autonomy in the previous section, users of the BI system believe they do not have much choice when it comes to deciding on their work tasks and schedules.

It is due to aspects such as committing to production targets, adhering to standard work procedures, mine safety controls, planned routine work and vertical organisational structures that make it difficult for employees to plan their own work schedules and deliverables. According to the respondents, self-determination is negatively influenced by routine work, standard operating procedures, organisational structures and target oriented tasks. Respondent 9 stated: *"I am guided by daily production targets therefore it is difficult to set my own targets"* confirmed by Respondent 10 who stated: *"Most of the work we do is guided by standard work procedures. There are steps we have to follow to conduct work"*. In summary, it can be concluded that BI users generally not empowered to take and be held responsible for business actions.

6 Conclusion

The study's findings identified numerous factors affecting the adoption of the BI system at a mining organisation. Factors related to the work environment suggests that the availability of a BI system that supports decision making is a fairly new concept at the mine. The user's perception of the BI system's ability to support their daily tasks were inconclusive. However, the majority of participants believed that the availability of data in the BI system could support them in performing daily tasks. The strong bureaucratic culture and nature of the mining work environment inhibits job autonomy. The environment is characterized by prescheduled tasks based on achieving clear set targets carefully managed by supervisors. The industry is furthermore regulated by prescriptive legislation which requires the creation of pre-defined reports for BI users leaving little room for the development of customized reports. The culture of the mining environment influences the climate for achievement. Although BI users have a high appetite for achievement their basic BI system skills inhibit them from achieving more using the BI systems. This is furthermore negatively influenced by the lack of senior management to acknowledge the benefits of using the BI systems.

The BI users in general were not empowered to utilise the BI system to its full potential. Factors pertaining to user empowerment suggested that BI users were generally not trained, and therefore didn't use, the advanced capabilities of BI systems and technologies. Even if they do get BI system training, study participants felt that they are not empowered to make business decisions.

7 Recommendations

The following recommendations are made: to improve BI implementations at the mine:

- Upskill workforce. The organization currently employ a relative older generation (above 40 years of age). These workers need to be trained in using specialized systems and technologies as part of BI systems.
- Create awareness. The mine needs to invest time and financial resources to create awareness of the availability, objectives and capabilities of BI systems.
- Management support. Mine managers, union leaders and supervisors should support the utilisation of BI systems and should set an example for using the BI systems.
- Suitable system for the task: Implement BI solutions in areas that can have a positive, visible impact on organisational performance.

References

1. Kim, H., Gupta, S.: A user empowerment approach to information systems infusion. IEEE Trans. Eng. Manag. **61**, 656–668 (2014)
2. Bagnoli, C., Biloslavo, R., Rusjan Figelj, R.: Managing dualities for efficiency and effectiveness of organisations. Ind. Manag. Data Syst. **113**, 423–442 (2013). https://doi.org/10.1108/02635571311312695
3. McAfee, A., Brynjolfsson, E.: Big data: the management revolution. Harv. Bus. Rev. **90**, 60–69 (2012)
4. Serumaga-zake, P.: The role of user satisfaction in implementing a Business Intelligence System. South Afr. J. Inf. Manag. **19**, 1–8 (2017)
5. Isik, O., Jones, M., Sidorova, A.: Business intelligence (BI) success and the role of BI capabilities. Intell. Syst. Account. Finance Manag. **18**, 161–176 (2012). https://doi.org/10.1002/isaf
6. Thamir, A., Poulis, E.: Business intelligence capabilities and implementation strategies. Int. J. Glob. Bus. **8**, 34–45 (2015)
7. Sallam, R., Howson, C., Idoine, C., Oestreich, T., Laurence, J.: Magic quadrant for business intelligence and analytics platforms. Gartner: https://www.gartner.com/home
8. Clavier, P., Lotriet, H., Van Loggerenberg, J.: A first step towards service-dominant logic as a new approach to overcome challenges in business intelligence. South Afr. J. Econ. Manag. Sci. **1**, 220–231 (2014). https://doi.org/10.5121/ijmpict.2012.3201
9. Katsikogiannis, G., Kallergis, D., Garofalaki, Z., Mitropoulos, S., Douligeris, C.: A policy-aware service oriented architecture for secure machine-to-machine communications. Ad Hoc Netw. **80**, 70–80 (2018). https://doi.org/10.1016/j.adhoc.2018.06.003
10. Díaz Pinzón, B.H., Villamarín García, J.M.: Key success factors to business intelligence solution implementation. J. Intell. Stud. Bus. **7**, 48–69 (2017)

11. Hou, C.: Examining the effect of user satisfaction on system usage and individual performance with business intelligence systems: an empirical study of Taiwan' s electronics industry. Int. J. Inf. Manag. **32**, 560–573 (2012). https://doi.org/10.1016/j.ijinfomgt.2012.03. 001

12. Yeoh, W., Koronios, A.: Critical success factors for business intelligence systems. J. Comput. Inf. Syst. Spring ABIINFORM Glob. **50**, 23–32 (2010). https://doi.org/10. 1080/08874417.2010.11645404

13. Lautenbach, P., Johnston, K., Adeniran-Ogundipe, T.: Factors influencing business intelligence and analytics usage extent in South African organisations. South Afr. J. Bus. Manag. **48**, 23–33 (2017). https://doi.org/10.4102/sajbm.v48i3.33

14. Vandenbosch, B., Huff, S.: Searching and scanning: how executives obtain information from executive information systems. MIS Q. **21**, 81–107 (1997)

15. Elbashir, M.Z., Collier, P.A., Davern, M.J.: Measuring the effects of business intelligence systems: the relationship between business process and organizational performance. Int. J. Account. Inf. Syst. **9**, 135–153 (2008). https://doi.org/10.1016/j.accinf.2008.03.001

16. Lönnqvist, A., Pirttimäki, V.: The measurement of business intelligence. Inf. Syst. Manag. **23**, 32–40 (2006). https://doi.org/10.1201/1078.10580530/45769.23.1.20061201/91770.4

17. Dawson, L., Van Belle, J.-P.: Critical success factors for business intelligence in the South African financial services sector. SA J. Inf. Manag. **15**, 1–12 (2013). https://doi.org/10.4102/ sajim.v15i1.545

18. Eybers, S., Giannakopoulos, A.: Identifying critical success factors for business intelligence systems. J. Comput. Inf. Syst. (2015). https://doi.org/10.1080/08874417.2010.11645404

19. Nkuna, D.: Business intelligence usage determinants: an assessment of factors influencing individual intentions to use a business intelligence system within a financial firm in South Africa (2011)

20. Panahi, P.: Business intelligence capabilities and user satisfaction. https://gup.ub.gu.se/file/ 143471. Accessed 03 Jan 2019

21. Grubljesic, T., Jaklic, J.: Conceptualization of the business intelligence extended use model. J. Comput. Inf. Syst. **55**, 72–82 (2015). https://doi.org/10.1080/08874417.2015.11645774

22. Jones, A.B., Straub Jr., D.W.: Reconceptualizing system usage: an approach and empirical test. Inf. Syst. Res. Inf. Syst. Res. **17**, 228–246 (2006). https://doi.org/10.1287/isre.l060. 0096

23. Spreitzer, G.M.: Psychological empowerment in the workplace: dimensions, measurement, and validation. Acad. Manag. Nurnnl. **18**, 42–1465 (1995). https://doi.org/10.2307/256865

24. Eybers, S., Hattingh, M.J.: Critical success factor categories for big data: a preliminary analysis of the current academic landscape. In: 2017 IST-Africa Week Conference (IST-Africa), pp. 1–11 (2017). https://doi.org/10.23919/ISTAFRICA.2017.8102327

25. Mikalef, P., Pappas, I.O., Krogstie, J., Giannakos, M.: Big data analytics capabilities: a systematic literature review and research agenda. Inf. Syst. E-Bus. Manag. **16**, 547–578 (2018). https://doi.org/10.1007/s10257-017-0362-y

26. Thomas, K., Velthouse, B.: Cognitive elements of empowerment: an "interpretive" model of intrinsic task motivation. Acad. Manage. Rev. **15**, 666–681 (1990)

Big Data Value Chain: Making Sense of the Challenges

Milla Wirén[1], Matti Mäntymäki[1(✉)], and A. K. M. Najmul Islam[2]

[1] Turku School of Economics, Turku 20014, Finland
{milla.wiren,matti.mantymaki}@utu.fi
[2] Department of Future Technologies,
University of Turku, Turku 20014, Finland
najmul.islam@utu.fi

Abstract. In this paper, we highlight how the value of data accumulates through the stages in a value chain. We introduce a Big data value chain where the value adding stages are decoupled from the technological requirements of data processing. We argue that through viewing the stages of value accumulation, it is possible to identify such challenges in dealing with Big Data that cannot be mitigated through technological developments. Our proposed Big Data value chain consists of eight stages that we subsequently cluster into three main phases, namely sourcing, warehousing and analyzing. In scrutinizing these three phases we suggest that the technologically immitigable challenges in sourcing relate to the veracity of data, and the challenges in warehousing concern ownership and power distribution. Finally, in the phase of analyzing the problems are manifold, including the black boxed nature of the algorithms, the problematics of standards of desirability, and the mandatory trade-offs. Our discursive article contributes to the literature discussing the value, utility and implications of Big Data.

Keywords: Big Data · Value chain · Big Data value chain ·
Big Data challenges · Data strategy

1 Introduction

According to a popular, yet highly controversial saying, data – especially the Big Data – is the new oil. However, while the analogue has its merits in terms of the value potential of Big Data for contemporary businesses, a deeper scrutiny of the analogue reveals certain discrepancies that can be used to explore the value chain and challenges of Big Data. For example, unlike oil, Big Data streams from seemingly unlimited sources, and as such, is to quite an extent continuously renewable. Second, unlike raw oil, raw data has no such consistent constitution, which would always yield value when refined [1] – a big portion of the raw data is merely useless. And thirdly, raw data has not emerged as a result of evolutionary processes guided by the immutable laws of nature, but is a creation of intentional and unintentional human agency, guided by the exactly same haphazardness that accompanies all human activities.

© IFIP International Federation for Information Processing 2019
Published by Springer Nature Switzerland AG 2019
I. O. Pappas et al. (Eds.): I3E 2019, LNCS 11701, pp. 125–137, 2019.
https://doi.org/10.1007/978-3-030-29374-1_11

These simple insights lead towards the focal discussion of this article. We map out the value chain of Big Data and identify the keychallenges associated with each stage of the value chain. We specifically focus on challenges that are particularly difficult to overcome with solely technological means. For example, the increasing sophistication of data processing algorithms notwithstanding, datafication of the entities from the physical, and particularly from the subjective realmsis prone to various errors and inaccuracies. Addressing these challenges essentially requires human judgement along the process of reaping the benefits of Big Data.

Far from being an unanimously defined concept [2], there is however an understanding of what types of contents the label 'Big Data' contains. The constitution of Big Data includes not only the traditional type of alphanumerical and relatively homogenous pre-categorized data found in institutional databases, but also the transsemiotic (images, sounds, scents, movements, digital action tokens, temperature, humidity to name a few) and highly heterogeneous data that is not categorized prior to its harvesting [3–7]. This latter type of data is sourced through sensor technology, from the intentional and unintentional interactions between humans and machines, from the surveillance systems, and from the automated digital transaction traces [2, 8–14]. As a result, of the increasing prowess of sourcing the data (i.e. datafication) and the equally increasing and cheapening computational capacity, the accumulation of data is extremely rapid, also resulting in the continuous change in its constitution. In short, Big Data is a constantly growing and changing nebulous and amorphous mass.

However, while the mass of existing Big Data is impossible to delineate, viewing the phenomenon from the perspective of its anticipated utility reveals a value chain spanning from datafication to potential business value creation. In this article, we identify eight stages of the value chain, discussed in more detail later, but named here as datafication, digitizing, connectivity, storage, categorizing, patterning, cross-analysis and personalization. Indeed, there are other proposals for the Big Data value chain [15], however, most of the existing value chain proposals delineate diverse technological stages required in rendering data useful. In this paper, we delineate the stages according to the increase in the value of the data, meaning that some of the stages include several technologies, and some technologies span more than one stage. In short, we decouple the technological requirements of processing data from the value adding activities in refining data.

The research question of this paper is twofold: (i) what types of challenges exist in different stages of the Big Data value chain, and (ii) which of these challenges are particularly difficult to mitigate without human-based intelligence and judgement? In order to explore these questions, the remainder of the article flows through first delving the eight stages and clustering them into three main phases to identify the relevant accompanying challenges, towards the conclusion listing the contributions, limitations and future research possibilities.

2 Big Data Value Chain

The process of obtaining insights from Big Data can be divided into three main stages, namely sourcing, warehousing, and analyzing data [16–18]. These stages have been rearranged and complemented, for example resulting in the stages of data acquisition, data analysis, data curation, data storage, and data usage [15]. These typologies are delineated from the perspective of technology, through clustering the stages along the technological requirements, a useful approach when the focus is on the side of technological developments needed for realizing the potential value of Big Data.

However, if we shift the focus beyond technology and zoom in to the actual value adding processes, the technology-driven boundaries do not match the boundaries between the stages of value add. Therefore, we propose another conceptualization of the Big Data value chain, where each of the stages differs from its neighbors in terms of its value accumulation potential. Our approach further divides the established three main stages and consists of the stages of datafication, digitizing, connectivity, storage, categorizing, patterning, cross-analysis and personalization, introduced next.

Datafication. The emergence of the phenomenon of Big Data is underpinned by the developments in technologies that enable datafying different types of entities. For example, the developments in the sensor technology have enabled producing data about movements, humidity, location, sounds, composition or smell to name a few [1]. On the other hand, the diffusion of digital devices and the accompanying increase in human-computer interaction is making it possible to deduce and produce data about the subjective preferences of the individuals, based on the traces of these interactions [2, 19–22]. These developments in the technologies enabling myriad forms of datafication are the core source of Big Data, and the first fundamental building block of the Big Data value chain.

Digitizing. As data is created from entities of a wide variety of ontological natures, capturing the data through analog technologies resulted in various data types, each requiring their own processing technologies. When all data is digitized, made into binary digits of zeroes and ones, in theory any machine capable of processing bits could process the data [23, 24] though in practice this is not yet the case. In terms of Big Data, the major value creating step is the homogenization of the data from the diverse sources, because it creates the foundation for cross-analyzing and -referencing data sets originating from very diverse sources.

Connectivity. Even if we had homogenous data from a variety of phenomena, without the capability to connect that data, each individual parcel of data would be relatively useless. However, with the emergence of the TCP/IP protocol and internet mandating how the data should be packaged, addressed, transmitted, routed and received, and the developments in the communications technologies, the uniform data from a diversity of sources can be transmitted somewhere to be pooled and accessed. The technologies enabling this are multiple and continuously developing. However, the value add transcends the technologies: while there are imperfections in the complex communications technologies and even in the very design of the internet [25], the idea of connectivity is a major value add by itself.

Storage. Even though digital data exists only in the form of zeroes and ones, it is not without a physical representation – quite the contrary, as storing the masses of data require hardware that enable accessing and processing the pooled homogenous data. The developments in the computational power and the cheapening of the storage capacity is critical for this value adding stage. However, the value itself emerges from the existence of these pools of data, which enables processing together data from the variety of sources. The technological solutions of data centers, data warehouses and data lakes are complex, however as with the stage of connectivity, the value add emerges from the mere possibility of having the data mass stored in pools fed and accessed from diverse points of entry [15].

Categorizing. Unlike data in the traditional data sources, one of the defining features of Big Data is its automated and autonomous accumulation, which in other words means that the data is not categorized on the way in [7]. Instead, any sense making of the vast data masses must begin – or at least be guided by – designing mechanisms and principles based on which the data can be categorized. This value adding stage of categorizing is the stage where the end use of the data needs to be accounted for, because of the generative nature of data [26]: not only can the data be categorized in many ways, but the same data may yield different utility depending on the context of its use [27]. This is the stage where the algorithms are essential. Due to the volume, variety, and velocity of data, human computational capabilities are insufficient for processing. Therefore, algorithmic processing capabilities are needed [3, 10, 28–30].

Patterning. The importance of the algorithms increases towards the end of the value chain. At the stage of patterning, the task is to identify patterns from the categorized masses of data. The patterns constitute the first stage in the value chain possessing to identify business value potential. Due to the volume and variety of the data, it is possible to identify patterns that may be invisible in smaller (in scope or quantity) data sets [31]. As an example, the customer behavior from CRM systems can be patterned to better understand the behavior of certain customer group.

Cross-analysis. Even more valuable than identifying novel patterns, is the ability to cross-analyze diverse patterns to seek correlations – for example through cross-analysing the data patterns of customer behavior against the patterns from marketing campaigns. Most of the current data use cases are grounded on this stage of data utility [13], which excels in creating generalized knowledge about a wide variety of phenomena. For example, through cross-analyzing the data from traffic accidents and driver demography, it is possible to find correlations between the age and gender of the drivers and accidents. This value adding stage also enables increasingly efficient customer segmentation for example in social media marketing. If certain preferences and demographic features are correlated, an offering can be marketed to the exact demography.

Personalization. The most value potential of Big Data is embedded in the final stage, namely personalization, which means that the data can be used for behavioral predictions [32, 33]. This value adding capability is built on first having such cross-analyzed patterns that reveal correlations, and then analyzing the behavioral datafied history of an individual against those correlations [2, 20]. Continuing the example in the previous stage, here the increase in value emerges from the possibility of harvesting the information of the driving behavior of an individual, and cross-analyzing that personal history with such generalized driving behavior patterns that correlate with an increase in accidents. Also, in terms of targeted marketing, at this stage it is possible to deduce the preferences on the level of the individual, based on the traces left in human-device interactions, and to personalize the offerings accordingly [19].

3   Challenges in the Big Data Value Chain

As our focus is on identifying such challenges that are particularly difficult to overcome through technological developments alone, we will not offer a comprehensive view on the current state-of-the-art in any of the underlying technologies. In other words, the boundary between what can and cannot be solved through technological developments is blurred and bound to a specific point of time.

The next subchapters cluster the aforementioned value chain into three phases familiar in other data value chain approaches, the first of which we refer to as sourcing to encompass datafication and digitizing, to be followed with warehousing consisting of connectivity and storage, and finally analyzing, covering the stages from categorization and patterning to cross-analyzing and personalization. Table 1 summarizes the discussion.

Table 1. Challenges in the Big Data value chain

Stage in the big data value chain	Cluster	Challenges	
Datafication	Sourcing	Veracity	
Digitizing			
Connectivity	Warehousing	Ownership, power distribution	
Storage			
Categorizing	Analyzing	Black boxes, standards of desirability	
Patterning			
Cross-analysis		Trade-offs	Privacy vs personalization
			Convenience vs independence
Personalization			Collective safety vs individual freedom
			Data security vs machine learning optimization
			Ease of outcomes vs validity of process

3.1 Challenges in Sourcing: Veracity

The validity of the end results of any data refining processes is dependent on the validity of the source data, and unlike with oil, the quality of the raw data varies vastly [1]. First, in digitizing existing data sets, the imperfections, biases, unintended gaps and intentional results of human curation of data also end up in the mass of Big Data [34]. In other words, such data that originates from times preceding the digital age, the acts of datafying and storing that data required a lot of work, which means that only a small part of all relevant data ended up in a form that yields itself to digitizing.

In a more limited scale, this applies also to such data that does exist in the traditional databases. Due to the costs embedded in storing data with pre-digital means, the databases hold pre-prioritized, pre-categorized data that someone has chosen at some stage to store. This means that such queries that require accounting for historical data can never be quite accurate, because most of what has been gone without a retrospectively datafiable trace, and the rest is already curated and thus subjected to human biases and heuristics [9]. This problem is referred to as veracity [35], which means coping with the biases, doubts, imprecision, fabrications, messiness and misplaced evidence in the data. As a result, the aim of measuring veracity is to evaluate the accuracy of data and its potential use for analysis [36].

However, the older databases are only one source of data, and the issue of veracity is not limited to it. Another source, the interactions between humans and digital devices [for example in using the mobile phones, browsing the internet or engaging in social media) is a vast torrent of data. Only Facebook generates more than 500 terabytes of data per day. The sheer volume and variability of such data presents its own problems in terms of technological requirements; however, the veracity of that data is even more problematic. As illustrated by Sivarajah, Irani, and Weerakkody [37] data from human-to-human online social interaction is essentially heterogenous and unclear in nature. Furthermore, malicious tools or codes can be used to continuously click on the performance-based ads creating fake data. There are bots that create traces mimicking human behavior. In addition, individuals vary in the level of truthfulness of their traceable activities. Part of the problems of veracity stem from the intentional human actions, which can be biased, misleading, and overall random. Furthermore, the samples of population participating in online interactions is skewed – not to even mention the geographical discrepancies emerging from the varying levels of technological penetration around the globe [1].

In turn, the data from the sensor technologies, surveillance systems and digital transaction traces does not suffer from similar biases such as intentional human actions. However, these sources have their own veracity issues. As the processes are automated, and not a priori prioritized, a portion of that data is irrelevant and useless. This challenge relates to cleaning data, i.e. extracting useful data from a collected pool of unstructured data. Proponents of Big Data analytics highlight that particularly developing more efficient and sophisticated approaches to mine and clean data can significantly contribute to the potential impact and ultimately value that can be created through utilizing big data [3]. At the same time, however, developing the tools and methods to extract meaningful data is considered an ongoing challenge [27].

The problem of veracity is partially mitigable through technological developments. With the development of data cleaning and mining technologies, it becomes easier to filter the vast data masses to extract the valuable nuggets. However, the inaccuracies resulting from the imperfect older data sources and the haphazardness of human action are fundamentally immitigable.

3.2 Challenges in Warehousing: Ownership and Power

The primary problems in connectivity and storage relate to technologies enabling the transmission, storing and accessing the vast data masses. However, not all problems are even in these stages solvable through technological progress. Scrutinizing data security highlights the issue, as it is only partially a technological question.

As argued by Krishnamurthy and Desouza [38], companies and organizations are facing challenges in managing privacy issues, thus hindering organizations in moving forward in their efforts towards leveraging big data. For example, smart cities, where collected data from sensors about people's activities can be accessed by various governmental and non-governmental actors [39]. Furthermore, the distributed nature of big data leads to specific challenges in terms of intrusion [40] and thus may lead to challenges to various threats such as attacks [41] and malware [42].

However, underpinning these data security capabilities is the question of data ownership. As Zuboff (2015) notes, one of the predominant features in digitalization is the lack of the possibility to not to opt-in as a data source – as the everyday life of an individual is embedded in the invisible digital infrastructures [23, 43, 44] the individuals have little control over the data exhaust being created about them.

The boundaries of ownership and control rights are a serious problem that surpasses the technological problems of ensuring the data security of specific data sets or applications. The issue of ownership is ultimately a question of data driven power distribution: the agents possessing not only the data sourcing capabilities but also the data sharing resources, are harnessing power to not only create business value but to have also socio-political influence [45].

3.3 Challenges in Analyzing: Black Boxes, Standards of Desirability and Tradeoffs

There are two major aspects to algorithms that pave the way for discussing the challenges, here dubbed as standards of desirability and black boxes. Firstly, the algorithms cannot come up with priorities or questions by themselves, but humans are needed to provide them, and secondly, as we need the algorithms because the human computational capacity cannot deal with the vast masses of digital data, the human computational capacity cannot follow the algorithmic processes dealing with those masses of data.

To begin with the problem of standards of desirability [46, 47], any question or task given to the algorithm to be processed must be underpinned by a set of goals that are to be reached. However, at any given moment of designing a goal there is no way of knowing whether that goal is still relevant or preferable at the time of reaching that goal: both the environmental circumstances and the internal preferences can have undergone changes. Especially, considering the generative nature of digital data [26] and the digital affordances [48], the data itself does not mandate a specific use or specific questions; instead the utility of the versatile data is dependent of the contextual fit and quality of the questions guiding the analyzing processes at any given time. However, as we know from both history and human focused research, we humans are far from infallible – the quality of questions, or the relevance of them is never guaranteed [49–53], which means that this challenge is immitigable through technological advances.

Secondly, as we cannot follow the algorithmic computational processes, we cannot detect if there are errors in the processes [34, 54] – ultimately the processes are black boxes. Furthermore, the black boxed nature of the outcomes does not end at the revelation of the outcomes of algorithmic processes: the outcomes of patterning and cross-analysis reveal correlations, and due to the sheer volume of the data masses there are high possibilities to find significant correlations between any pair of variables. This means that the identified correlations can be mere noise, unless supported by theoretical mechanisms(1]: unlike Anderson [55], McAfee et al. [9] claim, the scientists are not rendered obsolete, however the focal usefulness of scholars shifts from hunting correlations to understanding the underpinning theoretical causalities. The black boxes of algorithms reveal the black boxes of correlations, leaving it to humans to assess the relevance and validity of the outcomes.

Thirdly, the algorithmic analysis of Big Data creates such opportunities that require scrutinizing the accompanying tradeoffs. Newell and Marabelli [28] identify three, and next we introduce five. The tradeoffs next discussed are privacy-personalization, convenience-independence, collective security-individual freedom, data security-machine learning optimization, and ease of outcomes-validity of process.

Privacy vs Personalization. Reaping the benefits from the ultimate stage of the Big data value chain through providing personalized offerings means that the agent making the offerings has to have access to personal data – in other words, has to breach the privacy of the targeted customer to an extent [56, 57]. The ethical valence of this tradeoff needs to be considered contextually, meaning that there are both cases where the loss of privacy is easily offset by the benefits resulting from accessing the personalized service, and cases where the value of the personalized offering does not justify the breach to privacy [13, 58–60].

Convenience vs Independence. The more convenient it is to rely on a specific technology, for example the navigation devices and systems in cars and vessels, the more dependent on that technology one typically becomes. In a corporate use of Big Data and analytics, the widespread utilization of game analytics has even led into a situation where not using the technologies in decision-making is being referred to as "flying blind" and the use of analytics is considered as a necessity by game developers [61]. Taken together, there is an evident tradeoff between convenience and independence that requires acknowledging.

Collective Safety vs Individual Freedom. Newell and Marabelli [28] share a case where Facebook was accused for not reacting to a threatening post by a person who carried out the threat and shot an individual. This example highlights this tradeoff amply: it is possible with the help of Big Data and behavioural prediction to anticipate threats to collective security, however reacting on those threats a priori of incidents limits the freedom of the individual being detained before having committed anything.

Data Security vs Machine Learning Optimization. The different policies of EU and China in terms of access to data in developing artificial intelligence highlight this issue nicely. In Europe the priority is to protect the privacy and data security, which means that there is less data available for developing machine learning [62]. This results on the one hand the improved rights of the European citizens and on the other hand slower progress in developing artificial intelligence. In turn, China is investing heavily in developing artificial intelligence, for example facial recognition technologies through utilizing all available data from the ubiquitous mobile applications that billions of Chinese people use daily [63–65], resulting in less individual level data privacy, but competitiveness in the AI race.

Ease of Outcomes vs Validity of Process. Traditionally, the value of accounting information has resided in the transparent and accessible processes through which the financial information has been gathered and processed. The credibility of the ensuing financial figures has been built on the validity of these processes. However, with the increasing use of the automated accounting systems and algorithms, the outcomes are achieved faster, however through the black boxes of algorithms – the validity of the process of creating the end results is no longer visible [54]. This is again a choice for the humans: when and why does the swift outcome have more value, and when and why is it mandatory to be able to observe the processes?

4   Conclusion

This study was set out to explore (i) what types of challenges exist in different stages of the Big Data value chain, and (ii) which of these challenges are particularly difficult to mitigate without human-based intelligence?

By addressing this research question: our paper adds on the literature on the roles and interplay between algorithmic and human-based intelligence in reaping the benefits and business value from Big Data [66] with two specific contributions. First, we present a Big Data value chain decoupled from the technological underpinnings and grounded on the stages of value accumulation, and secondly, we highlight a set of such challenges in utilizing Big Data that cannot be mitigated through technological developments.

We advance the understanding of the value and utility of data by putting forward a Big Data value chain that consists of eight stages in three clustered phases: sourcing (datafication and digitizing), warehousing (connectivity and storage) and analyzing (categorizing, patterning, cross-analyzing and personalization). In the first cluster, the immitigable challenges reflect the problems of veracity whereas in the second one, the problems relate to ownership and power distribution. Finally, in the third cluster, the issues include the black-boxed nature of the algorithms and implications thereof, the need for standards of desirability, and five tradeoffs that require acknowledging.

By elaborating on these tradeoffs related to the Big Data value chain, our study adds
on the prior discussions related to data and privacy [2, 56, 57, 59, 60], strategic utility
of data [3, 4, 10, 12] reliability of data [1, 9] and data ownership [45].

Like any other piece of research, this study suffers from a number of limitations that
in turn call for additional research. First, due to its conceptual nature, empirical scrutiny
of our Big Data value chain is a self-evident area for future research. Second, since the
value chain can manifest itself differently across different contexts and under different
contingencies, future research focusing on contextual aspects of Big Data value chain
would be highly insightful [67]. Third, since the stages of the Big Data value chain
often consist activities undertaken various actors, it is relevant to consider how does
trust manifest itself among these actors [68], what kind of business ecosystems and
networks emerge for the utilization of big data, and how different actors strategize their
utilization of big data [69].

References

1. Condliffe, J.: China Turns Big Data into Big Brother. https://www.technologyreview.com/s/602987/china-turns-big-data-into-big-brother/. Accessed 2017
2. Vasarhelyi, M.A., Kogan, A., Tuttle, B.M.: Big Data in accounting: an overview. Account. Horiz. **29**, 381–396 (2015)
3. Wang, Y., Kosinski, M.: Deep neural networks are more accurate than humans at detecting sexual orientation from facial images (2017)
4. Varian, H.R.: Computer mediated transactions. Am. Econ. Rev. **100**, 1–10 (2010)
5. Davenport, T., Harris, J.: Competing on Analytics: Updated, with a New Introduction: The New Science of Winning. Harvard Business Press, Brighton (2017)
6. Barnaghi, P., Sheth, A., Henson, C.: From data to actionable knowledge: big data challenges in the web of things. IEEE Intell. Syst. **28**, 6–11 (2013)
7. Casti, J.L.: X-Events: The Collapse of Everything. Harper Collins, New York (2012)
8. March, J.G.: Bounded rationality, ambiguity, and the engineering of choice. Bell J. Econ. **9**, 587–608 (1978)
9. McAfee, A., Brynjolfsson, E., Davenport, T.H., Patil, D.J., Barton, D.: Big Data: the management revolution. Harv. Bus. Rev. **90**, 60–68 (2012)
10. Teece, D.J.: Research directions for knowledge management. Calif. Manag. Rev. **40**, 289–292 (1998)
11. Zuboff, S.: Big other: surveillance capitalism and the prospects of an information civilization. J. Inf. Technol. **30**, 75–89 (2015)
12. Thompson, J.D.: Organizations in Action: Social Science Bases of Administrative Theory. Transaction Publishers, Piscataway (2003)
13. Kosinski, M., Stillwell, D., Graepel, T.: Private traits and attributes are predictable from digital records of human behavior. Proc. Natl. Acad. Sci. U. S. A. **110**, 5802–5805 (2013). https://doi.org/10.1073/pnas.1218772110
14. Sivarajah, U., Irani, Z., Weerakkody, V.: Evaluating the use and impact of Web 2.0 technologies in local government. Gov. Inf. Q. **32**, 473–487 (2015)
15. Macaes,B.: Europe's AI delusion. Politico. https://www.politico.eu/article/opinion-europes-ai-delusion/. Accessed 2018
16. Yi, X., Liu, F., Liu, J., Jin, H.: Building a network highway for big data: architecture and challenges. IEEE Netw. **28**, 5–13 (2014)

17. Peterson, T.: Facebook will target ads to people based on store visits, offline purchases, calls to businesses. Marketing land. https://marketingland.com/facebook-will-target-ads-people-based-store-visits-offline-purchases-calls-businesses-224668. Accessed 2018
18. Van Dijck, J.: Datafication, dataism and dataveillance: Big Data between scientific paradigm and ideology. Surveill. Soc. **12**, 197–208 (2014)
19. Krishnamurthy, R., Desouza, K.C.: Big Data analytics: the case of the social security administration. Inf. Polity **19**, 165–178 (2014)
20. Weinberger, D.: Optimization over Explanation. Berkman Klein Center. https://medium.com/berkman-klein-center/optimization-over-explanation-41ecb135763d. Accessed 2018
21. Cárdenas, A.A., Manadhata, P.K., Rajan, S.P.: Big data analytics for security. IEEE Secur. Priv. **11**, 74–76 (2013)
22. Kallinikos, J., Constantiou, I.D.: Big data revisited: a rejoinder. J. Inf. Technol. **30**, 70–74 (2015)
23. Lyon, D.: Surveillance After Snowden. Wiley, Hoboken (2015)
24. Akter, S., Wamba, S.F., Gunasekaran, A., Dubey, R., Childe, S.J.: How to improve firm performance using big data analytics capability and business strategy alignment? Int. J. Prod. Econ. **182**, 113–131 (2016)
25. Labrinidis, A., Jagadish, H.V.: Challenges and opportunities with Big Data. Proc. VLDB Endow. **5**, 2032–2033 (2012)
26. Abbas, R., Michael, K., Michael, M.G.: The regulatory considerations and ethical dilemmas of location-based services (LBS) a literature review. Inf. Technol. People **27**, 2–20 (2014)
27. Sutanto, J., Palme, E., Tan, C.-H., Phang, C.W.: Addressing the personalization-privacy paradox: an empirical assessment from a field experiment on smartphone users. MIS Q. **37**, 1141–1164 (2013)
28. Newell, S., Marabelli, M.: Strategic opportunities (and challenges) of algorithmic decision-making: a call for action on the long-term societal effects of 'datification'. J. Strateg. Inf. Syst. **24**, 3–14 (2015)
29. Dinev, T., Hart, P., Mullen, M.R.: Internet privacy concerns and beliefs about government surveillance–an empirical investigation. J. Strateg. Inf. Syst. **17**, 214–233 (2008)
30. Simon, H.A.: Administrative behavior; a study of decision-making processes in administrative organization (1947)
31. Wu, X., Zhu, X., Wu, G.-Q., Ding, W.: Data mining with big data. IEEE Trans. Knowl. Data Eng. **26**, 97–107 (2014)
32. Shah, T., Rabhi, F., Ray, P.: Investigating an ontology-based approach for Big Data analysis of inter-dependent medical and oral health conditions. Clust. Comput. **18**, 351–367 (2015)
33. Smith, H.J., Dinev, T., Xu, H.: Information privacy research: an interdisciplinary review. MIS Q. **35**, 989–1016 (2011)
34. Mäntymäki, M., Hyrynsalmi, S., Koskenvoima, A.: How do small and medium-sized game companies use analytics? An attention-based view of game analytics, Information Systems Frontiers (In press)
35. Martines, J.: Forget Big Data-Little Data is Making Learning Personal
, WIRED 2019. https://www.wired.com/2016/11/forget-big-data-little-data-making-learning-personal/. Accessed 2019
36. Zicari, R.V.: Big data: Challenges and opportunities. Big Data comput. **564**, 103–128 (2014)
37. Yoo, Y.: Computing in everyday life: A call for research on experiential computing. MIS Q. **34**, 213–231 (2010)
38. Chen, H., Chiang, R.H., Storey, V.C.: Business intelligence and analytics: from big data to big impact. MIS Q. **36**, 1165–1188 (2012)
39. Brunsson, N.: The irrational organization (1985)

40. Quattrone, P.: Management accounting goes digital: will the move make it wiser? Manag. Account. Res. **31**, 118–122 (2016)

41. Tilson, D., Lyytinen, K., Sorensen, C.: Desperately seeking the infrastructure in IS research: Conceptualization of" digital convergence" as co-evolution of social and technical infrastructures. In: 2010 43rd Hawaii International Conference on Presented at the System Sciences (HICSS), pp. 1–10. IEEE

42. Huang, Z., Lei, Y., Shen, S.: China's personal credit reporting system in the internet finance era: challenges and opportunities. China Econ. J. **9**, 288–303 (2016)

43. Boyd, D., Crawford, K.: Critical questions for Big Data: provocations for a cultural, technological, and scholarly phenomenon. Inf. Commun. Soc. **15**, 662–679 (2012)

44. Davenport, T.H., Barth, P., Bean, R.: How Big Data is different. MIT Sloan Manag. Rev. **54**, 43 (2012)

45. Kahneman, D.: Thinking, Fast and Slow. Macmillan, London (2011)

46. Marwick, A.E., Boyd, D.: Networked privacy: how teenagers negotiate context in social media. New Media Soc. **16**, 1051–1067 (2014)

47. Liao, S.-H., Wu, C.-C., Hu, D.-C., Tsui, K.-A.: Relationships between knowledge acquisition, absorptive capacity and innovation capability: an empirical study on Taiwan's financial and manufacturing industries. J. Inf. Sci. **36**, 19–35 (2010)

48. Mäntymäki, M.: Does E-government trust in e-commerce when investigating trust? A review of trust literature in e-commerce and e-government domains. In: Oya, M., Uda, R., Yasunobu, C. (eds.) I3E 2008. ITIFIP, vol. 286, pp. 253–264. Springer, Boston, MA (2008). https://doi.org/10.1007/978-0-387-85691-9_22

49. Anderson, C.: The end of theory: the data deluge makes the scientific method obsolete. Wired Mag. **16**, 16–07 (2008)

50. Boncheck, M.: Little data makes big data more powerful. Harvard Business Review. https://hbr.org/2013/05/little-data-makes-big-data-mor. Accessed 2018

51. Kallinikos, J., Aaltonen, A., Marton, A.: The ambivalent ontology of digital artifacts. MIS Q. **37**, 357–370 (2013)

52. Wirén, M., Mäntymäki, M.: Strategic positioning in big data utilization: towards a conceptual framework. In: Al-Sharhan, Salah A., et al. (eds.) I3E 2018. LNCS, vol. 11195, pp. 117–128. Springer, Cham (2018). https://doi.org/10.1007/978-3-030-02131-3_12

53. Abawajy, J.H., Kelarev, A., Chowdhury, M.: Large iterative multitier ensemble classifiers for security of big data. IEEE Trans. Emerg. Top. Comput. **2**, 352–363 (2014)

54. Constantiou, I.D., Kallinikos, J.: New games, new rules: Big Data and the changing context of strategy. J. Inf. Technol. **30**, 44–57 (2015)

55. Aldama, Z.: China's big brother: how artificial intelligence is catching criminals and advancing health care. Post Magazine. http://www.scmp.com/magazines/post-magazine/long-reads/article/2123415/doctor-border-guard-policeman-artificial. Accessed 2017

56. Curry, E.: The Big Data value chain: definitions, concepts, and theoretical approaches. In: Cavanillas, J.M., Curry, E., Wahlster, W. (eds.) New Horizons for a Data-Driven Economy, pp. 29–37. Springer, Cham (2016). https://doi.org/10.1007/978-3-319-21569-3_3

57. Günther, W.A., Mehrizi, M.H.R., Huysman, M., Feldberg, F.: Debating big data: a literature review on realizing value from big data. J. Strat. Inf. Syst. **26**, 191–209 (2017)

58. Kaisler, S., Armour, F., Espinosa, J.A., Money, W.: Big data: issues and challenges moving forward. Presented at the 2013 46th Hawaii International Conference on System Sciences, pp. 995–1004. IEEE (2013)

59. Zittrain, J.L.: The generative internet. Harv. Law Rev. **119**, 1974–2040 (2006)

60. Weinberger, D.: Everything is Miscellaneous: The power of the New Digital Disorder. Macmillan, London (2007)

61. March, J.G.: Rationality, foolishness, and adaptive intelligence. Strat. Manag. J. **27**, 201–214 (2006)
62. Awad, N.F., Krishnan, M.S.: The personalization privacy paradox: an empirical evaluation of information transparency and the willingness to be profiled online for personalization. MIS Q. **30**, 13–28 (2006)
63. Autio, E., Nambisan, S., Thomas, L.D., Wright, M.: Digital affordances, spatial affordances, and the genesis of entrepreneurial ecosystems. Strat. Entrep. J. **12**, 72–95 (2018)
64. Lyytinen, K., Yoo, Y.: Ubiquitous computing. Commun. ACM **45**, 63–96 (2002)
65. Barbierato, E., Gribaudo, M., Iacono, M.: Performance evaluation of NoSQL big-data applications using multi-formalism models. Futur. Gener. Comput. Syst. **37**, 345–353 (2014)
66. Tilson, D., Lyytinen, K., Sørensen, C.: Research commentary—digital infrastructures: the missing is research agenda. Inf. Syst. Res. **21**, 748–759 (2010)
67. Mikalef, P., Pappas, I.O., Krogstie, J., Giannakos, M.: Big data analytics capabilities: a systematic literature review and research agenda. Inf. Syst. E-Bus. Manag. **16**(3), 547–578 (2018)
68. March, J.G.: Theories of choice and making decisions. Society **20**, 29–39 (1982)
69. Cadwallar, C., Graham-Harrison, E.: How Cambridge Analytica turned Facebook 'likes' into a lucrative political tool. The Guardian. https://www.theguardian.com/technology/2018/mar/17/facebook-cambridge-analytica-kogan-data-algorithm?CMP=share_btn_tw. Accessed 2018

A Spatio-Temporal Data Imputation Model for Supporting Analytics at the Edge

Kostas Kolomvatsos[1(✉)], Panagiota Papadopoulou[1],
Christos Anagnostopoulos[2], and Stathes Hadjiefthymiades[1]

[1] Department of Informatics and Telecommunications,
National and Kapodistrian University of Athens, Athens, Greece
{kostasks,peggy,shadj}@di.uoa.gr
[2] School of Computing Science, University of Glasgow, Glasgow, UK
christos.anagnostopoulos@glasgow.ac.uk

Abstract. Current applications developed for the Internet of Things (IoT) usually involve the processing of collected data for delivering analytics and support efficient decision making. The basis for any processing mechanism is data analysis, usually having as an outcome responses in various analytics queries defined by end users or applications. However, as already noted in the respective literature, data analysis cannot be efficient when missing values are present. The research community has already proposed various missing data imputation methods paying more attention of the statistical aspect of the problem. In this paper, we study the problem and propose a method that combines machine learning and a consensus scheme. We focus on the clustering of the IoT devices assuming they observe the same phenomenon and report the collected data to the edge infrastructure. Through a sliding window approach, we try to detect IoT nodes that report similar contextual values to edge nodes and base on them to deliver the replacement value for missing data. We provide the description of our model together with results retrieved by an extensive set of simulations on top of real data. Our aim is to reveal the potentials of the proposed scheme and place it in the respective literature.

Keywords: Internet of things · Edge computing ·
Missing values imputation · Clustering · Consensus

1 Introduction

Modern applications aiming at providing innovative services to end users are based on the management of responses in analytics queries. Such queries target to the provision of the results of data analysis that will facilitate knowledge extraction and efficient decision making. Any processing will be realized on top

© IFIP International Federation for Information Processing 2019
Published by Springer Nature Switzerland AG 2019
I. O. Pappas et al. (Eds.): I3E 2019, LNCS 11701, pp. 138–150, 2019.
https://doi.org/10.1007/978-3-030-29374-1_12

of data collected by various devices or produced by end users. If we focus on the Internet of Things (IoT), we can detect numerous devices capable of collecting data and interacting each other to support the aforementioned applications. IoT devices can send the collected/observed data to the edge infrastructure, then, to the Cloud for further processing. The envisioned analytics can be provided either at the Cloud or at the edge of the network to reduce the latency in the provision of responses. With this architecture, we can support innovative business models that could create new roads for revenues offering novel applications in close proximity with end users.

Edge nodes can interact with a set of IoT devices to receive the collected data and perform the processing that analytics queries demand. IoT devices create streams of data towards the edge nodes, however, due to various reasons these streams can be characterized by missing values. Missing values can be a serious impediment for data analysis [14]. Various methodologies have been proposed for handling them [11]: data exclusion, missing indicator analysis, mean substitution, single imputation, multiple imputation techniques, replacement at random, etc. To the best of our knowledge, the majority of the research efforts mainly focus on the 'statistical' aspect of the problem trying to provide a methodology for finding the best values to replace the missing one with the assistance of statistical methodologies. Their aim is to identify the distribution of data under consideration and produce the replacements.

In this paper, we go a step forward and propose a missing value imputation method based not only on a statistical model but also on the dynamics of the environment where IoT devices act. We deliver a technique that deals with the group of nodes as they are distributed in the space and the temporal aspect of the data collection actions. When a missing value is present, we rely on the peer IoT devices located in close proximity to conclude the envisioned replacements. The proximity is detected not only in relation with the location of the devices but also in relation with the collected data. We propose the use of a two layered clustering scheme and a data processing model based on a sliding window approach. The first clustering process is applied on the IoT devices spatial information while the second is applied on top of the collected data. Our aim is to identify the devices reporting similar multidimensional data for the same phenomenon enhanced by the correlation of each individual dimension in a successive step. We are able to combine two different techniques, i.e., an unsupervised machine learning model with a consensus based strategy to conclude the final replacements for any observed missing value.

The remaining paper is organized as follows. Section 2 reports on the prior work in the domain while Sect. 3 presents the problem under consideration and gives insights into our model. Section 4 discusses the proposed solution and provides formulations and our solution. Section 5 describes our experimental evaluation efforts and gives numerical results for outlining the pros and cons of our model. Finally, in Sect. 6, we conclude our paper by presenting our future research plans.

2   Prior Work

Data management in the IoT has received significant attention in recent years. The interested reader can refer in [9] for a review of the domain. IoT based large scale data storage in Cloud is studied by [4], where a review of acquisition, management, processing and mining of IoT big data is also presented. The authors of [8] discuss a comparison of Edge computing implementations, Fog computing, cloudlets and mobile Edge computing. The focus is also on a comparative analysis of the three implementations together with the necessary parameters that affect nodes communication (e.g., physical proximity, access mediums, context awareness, power consumption, computation time). Data storage and management is also the focus of [27]. The authors propose a model and a decision making scheme for storing the data in Cloud. The storage decision is delivered on top of a mathematical model that incorporates the view on the available resources and the cost for storing the envisioned data. Another storage framework is presented by [17]. The authors deal with structured and unstructured data combining multiple databases and Hadoop to manage the storage requirements. In [12], the authors propose a system to facilitate mobile devices and support a set of services at the Edge of the network. A controller is adopted to add the devices to the available clusters, thus, the system can have a view on how it can allocate the envisioned tasks. A storage model enhanced with a blockchain scheme is discussed in [30]. The proposed model aims at increasing the security levels for distributed access control and data management. In [10], the authors present a scheme for security management in an IoT data storage system. The proposed scheme incorporates a data pre-processing task realized at the edge of the network. Time-sensitive data are stored locally, while non-time-sensitive data are sent to the Cloud back end infrastructure. Another distributed data storage mechanism is provided by [35]. The authors propose a multiple factor replacement algorithm to manage the limited storage resources and data loss.

Missing data imputation is a widely studied subject in multiple application domains as it is a very important topic for supporting efficient applications. Moreover, imputation mechanisms can be applied over various types of values, e.g., over sensory data [16]. The simplest way to impute missing data is to adopt the mean of values; this technique cannot take into consideration the variance of data or their correlation [21] being also affected by extreme values. Hence, research community also focused on other statistical learning techniques to provide more robust models for missing data substitution. Statistical learning focuses on the detection of statistical dependencies of the collected data [19], [36]. One example is the imputation scheme based on Auto-Regressive Integrated Moving Average and feed forward prediction based method [7]. Any prediction model builds on top of historical values, thus, researchers have to take into consideration the prediction error and the demand for resources required for storing all the necessary historical observations. Usually, a sliding window approach is adopted to manage the most recent measurements, thus, to limit the demand for increased resources. When corrupted or missing data are identified, the calculated probability distribution is adopted for the final replacement [36]. Other efforts deal with the joint distribution on the entire data set. Such efforts assume a parametric density function (e.g., multivariate normal) on the data given with estimated parameters [15]. The technique of least squares provides individual univariate regressions to impute features with missing values on all of the other dimensions based on the weighted average of the individual predictions [2,25]. Extensions of the least squares method consist of the Predictive-Mean Matching method (PMM) where replacements are random samples drawn from a set of observed values close to regression predictions [3] and Support Vector Regression (SVR) [34]. Apart from linear regression models, other imputation models incorporate random forests [32], K-Nearest Neighbors (K-NN) [33], sequential K-NN [18], singular value decomposition and linear combination of a set of eigenvectors [22,33] and Bayesian Principal Component Analysis (BPCA) [23,24]. Probabilistic Principal Component Analysis (PPCA) and Mixed Probabilistic Principal Component Analysis (MPPCA) can be also adopted to impute data [36]. All the aforementioned techniques try to deal with data that are not linearly correlated providing a more 'generic' model. Formal optimization can be also adopted to impute missing data with mixed continuous and categorical variables [1]. The optimization model incorporates various predictive models and can be adapted for multiple imputations.

It becomes obvious that any data imputation process incorporates uncertainty related to the adopted decisions for substituting absent values. Fuzzy Logic (FL) and machine learning algorithms can contribute in the management of uncertainty and the provision of efficient schemes, especially when combined with other computational intelligence techniques. In [31], the authors proposes the use of a hybrid method having the Fuzzy C-means (FCM) algorithm combined with a Particle Swarm Optimization (PSO) model and a Support Vector Machine (SVM). Patterns of missing data are analysed and a matrix based structure is used to represent them. Other models involve Multi-layer Perceptrons (MLPs) [26], Self-Organizing Maps (SOMs) [6], and Adaptive Resonance Theory (ART) [5]. The advantages of using neural networks for this problem are that they can capture many kinds of relationships and they allow quick and easy modeling of the environment [20].

In our model, we aim to avoid the use of a scheme that requires a training process, thus, we target to save time and resources. The proposed approach is similar to the scheme presented in [19], however, we do not require a training process to build our model. We focus on the adoption of an unsupervised machine learning technique combined with a fast consensus model for the delivery of the replacement of a missing value. We aim to build on top of the spatio-temporal aspect of the collected data, i.e., the location where they are reported and the report time. We adopt a sliding window approach and use spatial clusters of the IoT devices. A second clustering process is realized on top of the collected data to detect the devices reporting similar information to the edge nodes. Based on this approach, we can handle a dynamic environment where nodes change their location. The data correlation between IoT devices is adopted to provide the basis for our consensus model in the proposed imputation method. Hence, any missing value is replaced on top of the 'opinion' of the IoT devices having the same 'view' on the phenomenon.

3   Preliminaries

Our scenario involves a set of Edge Nodes (ENs) where a number of IoT devices are connected to report the collected data. The proposed model aims to support the behaviour of ENs and provides a model for missing data imputation based on the data received by all the IoT nodes in the group. Without loss of generality, we focus on the behaviour of an EN and consider a set $\mathcal{N}$ of IoT devices i.e., $\mathcal{N} = \{n_1, n_2, \ldots, n_N\}$. IoT devices are capable of observing their environment, collect data and performing simple processing tasks. As their resources are limited, IoT devices should store only the necessary data. These data are updated while the remaining are sent to ENs or the Fog/Cloud for further processing. It is worth noticing that when IoT devices rely on the Fog/Cloud for the processing of data they enjoy increased latency [28].

We consider that data are received and stored in the form of multivariate vectors i.e., $\overrightarrow{x} = [x_1, x_2, \ldots, x_M]$ where M is the number of dimensions. Let D_i be the dataset stored in the ith EN. The EN should identify if the incoming data contain missing values and when this is true, it should apply the proposed imputation technique. We consider the discrete time $\mathbf{T}$. At $t \in \mathbf{T}$, the EN receives a set of multivariate vectors coming from the IoT devices, i.e., $\overrightarrow{x}_i = [x_{i1}, x_{i2}, \ldots, x_{iM}], i = 1, 2, \ldots, N$. The missing data can refer in: (i) the whole vector; (ii) specific dimensions of the reported vectors. When a value x_{jk} is absent, the EN should replace it with the result of our imputation function, i.e., $x_{jk} = f(\overrightarrow{x}_i), \forall i$.

$f()$ builds on top of a sliding window approach. The window W deals with the interval where data can be adopted to 'generate' the missing dimension(s). In addition, the EN maintains a set of clusters of nodes based on their spatial proximity. When nodes are static, our approach considers a 'static' clustering model. When IoT devices are mobile, we have to perform the clustering process at pre-defined intervals. In any case, this will add overhead in the performance of the system. We can reduce the overhead if we rely on an incremental clustering algorithm to save time and resources. The imputation function takes into consideration the location of nodes before it delivers the final result. This approach enhances the localized aspect of decision making adopted into our model. Afterwards, the imputation process is based on only the data coming from the devices located in close distance that are correlated with the data reported by the device where missing values are observed. The envisioned architecture is depicted by Fig. 1. It should be noted that we do not focus on IoT devices with 'special' requirements, e.g., sensors that record images performing advanced processing models.

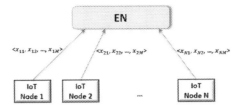

Fig. 1. The envisioned architecture.

4   The Proposed Model

Data Clustering and Correlation. The proposed model performs a hierarchical clustering, i.e., it creates clusters based on the spatial proximity of IoT devices and accordingly it delivers clusters based on the data proximity between the previously selected devices. For the clustering process based on the location of the devices, we can adopt any clustering algorithm (e.g., k-means or a subtractive method). Assume that this process returns the set $\mathcal{N}$ of the IoT devices (N IoT devices). The ith IoT device reports to the EN a data vector $\overrightarrow{x}_i^t = [x_{i1}, x_{i2}, \ldots, x_{iM}]$ at t. The EN performs the envisioned processing over the pre-defined window W. Hence, the EN has access to the $W \times M$ matrix $\overrightarrow{X} = \{\overrightarrow{x}_1^t, \overrightarrow{x}_2^t, \ldots, \overrightarrow{x}_N^t\}, \forall t \in [1, W]$. In each cell of this matrix, the EN stores the multidimensional vector reported by the corresponding IoT device at t. An additional vector $\mathbf{I}$ is adopted to store the ids of the involved devices. The discussed matrix can be characterized by 'gaps' in the collected values, i.e., the missing values that should be replaced.

We propose a second level of clustering as follows. For every $t \in [1, W]$, we perform clustering for N data vectors and store the corresponding ids. Figure 2 presents an indicative example. For the delivery of clusters, we adopt the Euclidean distance and the k-means algorithm. The distance between two vectors i and j will be delivered as follows: $\|\overrightarrow{x}_i - \overrightarrow{x}_j\| = \sqrt{(x_{i1} - x_{j1})^2 + (x_{i2} - x_{j2})^2 + \ldots + (x_{iM} - x_{jM})^2}$. The k-means algorithm is simple and adopts a set of iterations for concluding the final clusters. After the initial generation of k random multidimensional centroids $m_1, m_2, \ldots, m_k$, at each iteration, the algorithm assigns every vector to the closest centroid. The objective is to find the arg $\min_{\overrightarrow{X}_{row}} = \sum_{c=1}^{k} \sum_{\overrightarrow{x} \in \overrightarrow{X}_{row}} \|\overrightarrow{x} - m_c\|^2$. This is realized in the assignment step of the algorithm. In the update step, centroids are updated to depict the vectors participating in each cluster, i.e., $m_c = \frac{1}{|S_c|} \sum_{\overrightarrow{x} \in S_c}$ where S_i is the set of vectors participating in the cth cluster.

Let the ids of the IoT devices be annotated with n_i^{id}. At each t, we focus on the k clusters where ids are present. We consider that every cluster represents a 'transaction', thus, at each t we have to process k transactions. Every n_i^{id} is present in a cluster, thus, in a single transaction. In total, n_i^{id} will be present in W transactions. The ids present in each cluster vary. For instance, at $t = 1$, the

1st device (e.g., $n_1^{id} = XYZ$) can be present in the 2nd cluster together with two more peers, e.g., $n_5^{id} = YSZ$ and $n_3^{id} = BCD$, at $t = 2$, the 1st device can be present in the 3nd cluster, and so on and so forth. Figure 2 presents a clustering example.

Every transaction is an ID-set depicting the corresponding cluster. The presence of specific ids in an ID-set represents the correlation between the corresponding IoT devices as delivered by the clustering algorithm. When a missing value is present in a device, we consider the intersection of the ID-sets where the id of the device is present. The aim is to identify the devices that are in close data distance in W. Let $L_{n_i}^I$ be the intersection list for n_i. $L_{n_i}^I$ represents the intersection of W transactions; actually, we deliver nodes that are in the same cluster for αW transactions, $\alpha \in [0, 1]$. Together with $L_{n_i}^I$, we provide the list $L_{n_i}^C$ where the multidimensional correlation result between n_i and any other device present in $L_{n_i}^I$ is maintained. We detect the correlation between the corresponding dimensions in W. To produce $L_{n_i}^C$, we adopt the known Pearson Correlation Coefficient (PCC) for each dimension of vectors reported by two devices. The PCC is calculated for each device present in $L_{n_i}^I$ with the current device where a missing values is observed. Assume that we have to calculate the PCC for devices i and j. The final PCC is: $R_{PCC} = \sum_{l=1}^{M} r_{\vec{x}_{il}^t, \vec{x}_{jl}^t}, \forall t \in [1, W]$ with $r_{\vec{x}_{il}, \vec{x}_{jl}} = \frac{\sum_{t=1}^{W}(x_{il} - \overline{x_{il}})(x_{jl} - \overline{x_{jl}})}{\sqrt{\sum_{t=1}^{W}(x_{il} - \overline{x_{il}})^2}\sqrt{\sum_{t=1}^{W}(x_{jl} - \overline{x_{jl}})^2}}$ When applying the PCC in a single dimension, we get results in the interval $[-1, +1]$. In our case, due to the multiple dimensions, we get results in the interval $[-M, +M]$. Hence, the final format of $L_{n_i}^C$ is $L_{n_i}^C = \{R_{PCC}^{n_j}\}$ where j depicts the nodes present in $L_{n_i}^I$. When $R_{PCC}^{n_j} \to +M$ means that n_i and n_j exhibit a high positive correlation for all the envisioned dimensions while a strong negative correlation is depicted by $R_{PCC}^{n_j} \to +M$. The $L_{n_i}^C$ is sorted in a descending order and adopted to deliver the replacement of missing values as we report in the upcoming section.

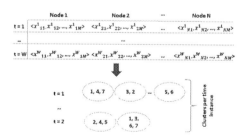

Fig. 2. An example of the envisioned clustering process.

Data Imputation. For substituting missing values, we rely on $L_{n_i}^I$ & $L_{n_i}^C$ and we adopt the linear opinion pool model. For each device present in $L_{n_i}^I$, we focus on the correlation with the device requiring the missing value imputation, say n_i. At first, we focus on the dimension where the missing value is present.

If multiple dimensions suffer, we adopt and iterative approach over the entire set of the dimensions under consideration. For each peer device in $L_{n_i}^I$, we rely on devices exhibiting a strong positive correlation with n_i. Let us focus on the subset C of correlated devices and the lth dimension. Our model proposes the use of the linear opinion pool scheme for the lth dimension in W. At first, we focus on the time instance t^* where the missing value is observed. At t^*, we have available $|C|$ values observed by the devices exhibiting a high correlation with n_i; each one has already observed a value for the lth dimension.

The linear opinion pool is a standard approach adapted to combine experts' opinion (i.e., devices) through a weighted linear average of the adopted values. Our aim is to combine single experts' opinions and produce the most representative value for the missing observation. We define a specific weight for each node in C to 'pay more attention' on its measurement, thus, to affect more the final aggregated result, i.e., the missing value substitution. Formally, $F(x_{1l}, \ldots, x_{|C|l})$ is the aggregation opinion operator (i.e., the weighted linear average), i.e., $y = F(x_{1l}, \ldots, x_{|C|l}) = \sum_{c=1}^{|C|} w_c x_{cl}$ where w_c is the weight associated with the measurement of the cth node such that $w_c \in [0, 1]$ and $\sum_{\forall c} w_c = 1$. Weights w_c are calculated based on the correlation with peer nodes depicted by $L_{n_i}^C$; $w_c = \frac{R_{PCC}^{n_j}}{\sum_{\forall n_j \in C} R_{PCC}^{n_j}}$. Weights are calculated on top of the correlation of all dimensions as we want to avoid any 'random' correlation events. Evidently, the mechanism assigns a high weight on the node that exhibits a high correlation with n_i. The final result y replaces the missing value observed at n_i.

5 Experimental Evaluation

Experimental Setup and Performance Metrics. We report on the performance of the proposed scheme aiming to reveal if it is capable of correctly substituting any missing value. Aiming at evaluating the 'proximity' of the replacement value with the real one, we adopt the Mean Absolute Error (MAE) and the Root Mean Squared Error (RMSE). MAE is defined as follows: $MAE = \frac{1}{|V|} \sum_{i=1}^{|V|} |v_i - \hat{v}_i|$ where $|V|$ is the number of missing values in our dataset (V denotes the set of the missing values), v_i is the actual and $\hat{v}_i$ is the proposed value. RMSE is defined as follows: $RMSE = \sqrt{\frac{1}{|V|} \sum_{i=1}^{|V|} (v_i - \hat{v}_i)^2}$. RMSE is similar to MAE, however, RMSE assigns a large weight on high errors. RMSE is more useful when high errors are undesirable.

We rely on three real datasets, i.e., (i) the GNFUV Unmanned Surface Vehicles Sensor Data Set [13]; (ii) the Intel Berkeley Research Lab dataset[1] and (iii) the Iris dataset[2]. The GNFUV dataset comprises values of mobile sensor readings (humidity, temperature) from four Unmanned Surface Vehicles (USVs). The swarm of the USVs is moving according to a GPS predefined trajectory. The

---

[1] Intel Lab Data, http://db.csail.mit.edu/labdata/labdata.html.
[2] http://archive.ics.uci.edu/ml/datasets/iris.

Intel dataset contains millions of measurements (temperature, humidity, light) retrieved by 54 sensors deployed in a lab. From this dataset, we get 15,000 measurements such that 15 sensors produced 1,000 measurements. Finally, the Iris dataset involves the classification of flowers into specific categories based on their attributes (e.g., sepal length).

We present results for our Clustering Based Mechanism (CBM) compared with an Averaging Mechanism (AM) and the Last Value Mechanism (LVM). The AM replaces any missing value with the mean of values reported by the peer devices at the same time interval. The LVM replaces missing values with the observation retrieved in the previous recording interval in the same device. At random time steps, we consider that a missing value is observed in a device selected randomly as well. We calculate the replacements for the considered schemes and compare them with the real ones to deliver the MAE and RMSE measurements. Our experiments deal with $W \in \{5, 10, 50\}$ and $M \in \{5, 50, 100\}$ trying to reveal the 'reaction' of our model to different window size and number of dimensions.

Performance Assessment. Our experimental evaluation involves a large set of experiments on top of the aforementioned datasets. In Fig. 3, we present our results for the GNFUV dataset (Left: MAE results; Right: RMSE results). We observe that our CBM exhibits the best performance when $W = 5$. Actually, it outperforms the AM (for $W \in \{5, 10\}$) and exhibits worse performance than the LVM (MAE results). When the RMSE is the case, the CBM outperforms both models when $W = 5$. A short sliding window positively affects the performance of our model as the EN decides on top of a low number of the envisioned clusters delivered for each t. The error of CBM increases as W increases as well. This also exhibits the capability of the CBM to deliver good results on top of a limited amount of data.

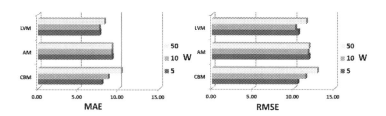

Fig. 3. MAE and RMSE for the GNFUV dataset.

In Fig. 4, we present our results for the Intel dataset. We observe that the CBM, again, for a short W exhibits the best performance compared to the remaining models. The CBM 'produces' 16% (approx.) less MAE compared to the AM and 35% (approx.) less MAE compared to the LVM (for ($W = 5$). When $W \to 50$, the CBM leads to 23% (approx.) more MAE than the AM and 2% (approx.) less MAE than the LVM. Similar results are observed for the RMSE which support the conclusion that the proposed model is more efficient when the EN is 'forced' to take decisions on top of a limited list of historical values.

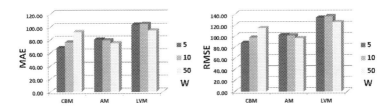

Fig. 4. MAE and RMSE for the Intel dataset.

In Fig. 5, we see our results for the Iris dataset. The CBM exhibits better performance than the AM but worse performance than the LVM. However, the results for the discussed models are very close. In general, the MAE for our CBM is in [0.51, 0.57] and the RMSE is in [0.63, 0.74]. Comparing our model with other schemes proposed in the literature, we focus on the comparative assessment discussed in [29]. There, the authors adopt the Iris dataset and provide performance results for the following missing values imputation algorithms: Mean, K-nearest neighbors (KNN), Fuzzy K-means (FKM), Singular Value Decomposition (SVD), bayesian Principal Component Analysis (bPCA) and Multiple Imputations by Chained Equations (MICE). The provided results deal with an RMSE in [5, 20] which is worse than the performance of the proposed CBM. Finally, in Fig. 6, we provide our results for the GNFUV dataset and for different M realizations. Concerning the MAE, the CBM performs better than the LVM for all M and the AM for $M = 5$. When $M > 5$, the AM exhibits the nest performance. A low number of dimensions lead to the best performance for the CBM. The CBM's MAE is around 0.5 while the RMSE is around 0.70.

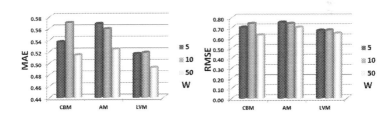

Fig. 5. MAE and RMSE for the Iris dataset.

Concluding the presentation of our results, we can note that in practical terms, the proposed CBM manages to efficiently replace the missing values when it deals with 'fresh' data and a low number of dimensions. The reason is that the CBM is affected by the clustering process which is applied on the multivariate data vectors. When the number of vectors and dimensions increase, there is a room for accumulating the distance of the vectors from the centroids, thus, we can meet vectors with high distance from centers affecting the final calculation of the substitution values.

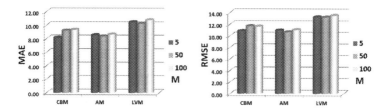

Fig. 6. MAE and RMSE for the GNFUV dataset and different dimensions.

6   Conclusions and Future Work

Missing values imputation is a significant task for supporting efficient data analysis, thus, efficient decision making. In the IoT, data can be collected by numerous devices transferred to the available edge nodes and the Cloud for further processing. Edge nodes can host the data and process them to deliver analytics limiting the latency. However, due to various reasons, the reported data can contain missing values. We propose a model for enhancing edge nodes behaviour to be capable of handling possible missing values. Our contribution deals with the provision of a two layered clustering scheme and a consensus methodology for the substitution of any missing value. Edge nodes take into consideration the observations retrieved by peer devices in close proximity that report similar data. The replacement values are calculated on top of the data of 'similar' devices weighted by the correlation between the device reporting the missing data and its peers. We provide the results of extensive simulations on top of real data and reveal the strengths of the proposed model. Our future research plans involve the definition of a more complex methodology taking into consideration the uncertainty behind the adoption of specific peer devices in the envisioned processing.

Acknowledgment. This work is funded by the H2020 research project under the grant agreement no 833805 (ARESIBO).

References

1. Bertsimas, D., et al.: From predictive methods to missing data imputation: an optimization approach. JMLR **18**, 1–30 (2018)
2. Bo, T., et al.: LSimpute: accurate estimation of missing values in microarray data with least squares methods. NAR **32**(3), e34–e34 (2004)

3. Buuren, S., Groothuis-Oudshoorn, K.: MICE: multivariate imputation by chained equations in R. JSS **45**(3), 1–67 (2011)
4. Cai, H., et al.: IoT-based big data storage systems in cloud computing: perspectives and challenges. IEEE IoT **4**(1), 75–87 (2017)
5. Carpenter, G., Grossberg, S.: Fuzzy ART: fast stable learning and categorization of analog patterns by an adaptive resonance system. Neural Netw. **4**, 759–771 (1991)
6. Catterall, et al.: Self organization in ad hoc sensor networks: an empirical study. In: 8th ICSSL (2002)
7. Chang, G., Ge, T.: Comparison of missing data imputation methods for traffic flow. In: ICTMEE (2011)
8. Dolui, K., Datta, K.S.: Comparison of edge computing implementations: fog computing. Cloudlet and mobile edge computing. In: IEEE GIoTS (2017)
9. Escamilla-Ambrosio, P.J., Rodríguez-Mota, A., Aguirre-Anaya, E., Acosta-Bermejo, R., Salinas-Rosales, M.: Distributing computing in the internet of things: cloud, fog and edge computing overview. In: Maldonado, Y., Trujillo, L., Schütze, O., Riccardi, A., Vasile, M. (eds.) NEO 2016. SCI, vol. 731, pp. 87–115. Springer, Cham (2018). https://doi.org/10.1007/978-3-319-64063-1_4
10. Fu, J.-S., et al.: Secure data storage and searching for industrial IoT by integrating fog computing and cloud computing. In: IEEE TII (2018)
11. Guan, N.C., Yusoff, M.S.B.: Missing values in data analysis: ignore or impute? EMJ **3**(1), e6–e11 (2011)
12. Habak, K., et al.: Femto clouds: leveraging mobile devices to provide cloud service at the edge. In: 8th IEEE CLOUD, pp. 9—16 (2015)
13. Harth, N., Anagnostopoulos, C.: Edge-centric efficient regression analytics. In: IEEE EDGE (2018)
14. He, Y.: Missing data analysis using multiple imputation: getting to the heart of the matter. CCQO **3**(1), 98–105 (2010)
15. Honaker, J., et al.: Amelia II: a program for missing data. JSS **45**(7), 1–47 (2011)
16. Jiang, N.: A data imputation model in sensor databases. In: Perrott, R., Chapman, B.M., Subhlok, J., de Mello, R.F., Yang, L.T. (eds.) HPCC 2007. LNCS, vol. 4782, pp. 86–96. Springer, Heidelberg (2007). https://doi.org/10.1007/978-3-540-75444-2_14
17. Jiang, L., et al.: An IoT-oriented data storage framework in cloud computing platform. IEEE TII **10**(2), 1443–1451 (2015)
18. Kim, L., et al.: Reuse of imputed data in microarray analysis increases imputation efficiency. BMC Bioinform. **5**(1), 160 (2004)
19. Ku, W., et al.: A clustering-based approach for data-driven imputation of missing traffic data. In: IEEE FISTA (2016)
20. Li, Y., Parker, L.: A spatial-temporal imputation technique for classification with missing data in a wireless sensor network. In: IEEE ICIRS (2008)
21. Little, R., Rubin, D.: Statistical Analysis with Missing Data. Wiley, Hoboken (1987)
22. Mazumder, R., et al.: Spectral regularization algorithms for learning large incomplete matrices. JMLR **11**, 2287–2322 (2010)
23. Mohamed, S., et al.: Bayesian exponential family PCA. In: ANIPS, pp. 1089–109 (2009)
24. Oba, S., et al.: A Bayesian missing value estimation method for gene expression profile data. Bioinformatics **19**(16), 2088–2096 (2003)
25. Raghunathan, T., et al.: A multivariate technique for multiply imputing missing values using a sequence of regression models. Surv. Methodol. **27**(1), 85–96 (2001)

26. Reznik, L., et al.: Signal change detection in sensor networks with artificial neural network structure. In: IEEE ICCIHSPS, pp. 44–51 (2005)
27. Ruiz-Alvarez, A., Humphrey, M.: A model and decision procedure for data storage in cloud computing. In: 12th IEEE/ACM CCGrid 2012 (2012)
28. Satyanarayanan, M.: A brief history of cloud offload: a personal journey from Odyssey through cyber foraging to cloudlets. MCC **18**(4), 19–23 (2015)
29. Schmitt, P., et al.: A comparison of six methods for missing data imputation. J. Biom. Biostat. **6**(1), 1 (2015)
30. Shafagh, H., et al.: Towards Blockchain-based auditable storage and sharing of IoT data. In: 9th ACM CCS Workshop (2017)
31. Shang, B., et al.: An imputation method for missing traffic data based on FCM optimized by PSO-SVR. JAT **2018**, Article ID 2935248, 21 p. (2018). https://doi.org/10.1155/2018/2935248
32. Stekhoven, D., Buhlmann, P.: MissForest: non-parametric missing value imputation for mixed-type data. Bioinformatics **28**(1), 112–118 (2012)
33. Troyanskaya, O., et al.: Missing value estimation methods for DNA microarrays. Bioinformatics **17**(6), 520–525 (2001)
34. Wang, X., et al.: Missing value estimation for DNA microarray gene Expression data by support vector regression imputation and orthogonal coding scheme. BMC Bioinform. **7**(1), 7–32 (2006)
35. Xing, J., et al.: A distributed multi-level model with dynamic replacement for the storage of smart edge computing. JSA **83**, 1–11 (2018)
36. Zhao, N., et al.: Improving the traffic data imputation accuracy using temporal and spatial information. In: ICICTA (2014)

The Role of Big Data in Addressing Societal Challenges: A Systematic Mapping Study

Farzana Quayyum[1]([⊠]), Ilias O. Pappas[1,2] [iD], and Letizia Jaccheri[1] [iD]

[1] Norwegian University of Science and Technology (NTNU),
Trondheim, Norway
farzanaq@stud.ntnu.no, letizia.jaccheri@ntnu.no
[2] University of Agder, Kristiansand, Norway
ilias.pappas@uia.no

Abstract. Big data has recently become the focus of academic and corporate investigation due to its high potential in generating business and social value. We have done a systematic mapping of the literature related to big data and its applications leading to social change through the lens of social innovation. The search strategy initially resulted in 593 papers, and after applying inclusion exclusion criteria a total of 156 papers were mapped; 59% of which were identified as empirical studies. This mapping investigated the publication frequency of the studies, research approach and contributions, research areas and article distribution per journal. We also address some challenges found from the mapping associated with the research topic. This mapping study will offer the basis for a reflection process among the researchers in this field and will allow us to develop a research agenda and roadmap of big data and its applications leading to social change.

Keywords: Big data · Data analytics · Social innovation · Social good · Social change · Societal transformation · Systematic mapping study

1 Introduction

The evolution of Information and Communication Technology drives the digitalization process in many aspects of peoples' daily lives, which generates huge amount of data every moment from a growing number of sources. In the last decade, the use of big data and their analytics has earned a lot of attention. In various fields of science, technology, and business, the merit of big data is undeniable. But from the social perspective, the potential use of big data is yet to be figured out by social sector organizations [1]. Several definitions of big data exist, and they typically refer to the 'three Vs' that characterize big data: volume, velocity, and variety, which have been extended including more characteristics of big data as explained a recent literature review [2]. Furthermore, several definitions of big data analytics exist [2], and they roughly refer to the combination of the data itself, the analytics applied to the data, and the presentation of results to generate value [3]. Thus, here we are interested in big data and their analytics.

© IFIP International Federation for Information Processing 2019
Published by Springer Nature Switzerland AG 2019
I. O. Pappas et al. (Eds.): I3E 2019, LNCS 11701, pp. 151–163, 2019.
https://doi.org/10.1007/978-3-030-29374-1_13

The potential of big data and analytics to generate social value seems clear [1], however the main focus of big data analytics research has been on business value [4]. Combining big data analytics with social innovation can be the solution to address this gap [5, 6]. Social innovation is defined as a novel solution to a social problem that is more effective, efficient, sustainable, or just than existing solutions and for which the value created accrues primarily to society as a whole rather than private individuals [7]. Social innovation can generate social good and lead to social change. Social good is typically defined as an action that provides some sort of benefit to the people of the society. The concept of social change refers to addressing the root causes of societal problems and changing them.

The terms social innovation, social good, social change, and societal transformation are related to each other. During this study our focus was on the applications of big data that have social impact and address social problems or challenges; so, to keep a broad and wide scope in this mapping review study we use all these terms.

Systematic literature reviews on big data applications have been conducted and investigate, among other things, big data dynamic capabilities [2], the operation and strategic value of big data for business [8], the impact of big data on business growth [9], the social economic value of big data [10]. Furthermore, there is an increasing number of studies that address both the business and social impact of big data as well as ways on how big data analytics can solve societal challenges, with evident examples the following recent special issues [1, 11]. However, to best of our knowledge there is no systematic mapping or literature review that focuses solely on how big data and their analytics can lead to societal transformation and social good.

A systematic mapping can help us to understand what conditions can enable successful solutions, combined with strategies, tactics, and theories of change that lead to lasting impact [5, 12, 13]. Furthermore, this mapping will allow capturing the needed capabilities, resources, and conditions that the big data actors need to develop or acquire in order to manage big data applications, increase social value and solve societal challenges and create a sustainable society. To contribute to the creation of sustainable societies, we have done this systematic mapping of the literature related to big data and their applications leading to social innovation and thus societal transformation.

The objective of this study is to offer a map of the research that has being done, thus offering the basis to develop a research agenda and roadmap of big data and analytics and their applications leading to societal transformation and change. We have followed the standardized process for systematic mapping studies [14]. Based on the primary search with search strings, a total of 593 unduplicated papers was retrieved. After applying some exclusion criteria, the number was reduced to 165 (based on titles), then 153 (based on abstracts) and finally 146 were selected from the search and later 10 more papers were added manually from Google scholar.

The relative newness and growing interest in the research field, argues the need for a mapping study to identify the focus and quality of research in using big data analytics for social challenges. To provide an up to date overview of the research results within the field, we came up with the following research questions:

RQ1: How the research about 'big data and social innovation' has changed over time (in the last decade)?

RQ2: How much of the research is done based on empirical studies and what type of empirical studies?

RQ3: What are the challenges or barriers for successful implementation of big data for societal challenges?

The paper proceeds as follows: Sect. 2 introduces the background of this study, Then, Sect. 3 explains the detailed procedure of the research method, Sect. 4 presents the results and findings of the mapping study, Sect. 5 discusses the findings in relation to the research questions, Sect. 6 concludes the paper presenting the implications of this study.

2   Background

2.1   Big Data

The digital and connected nature of modern-day life has resulted in vast amounts of data being generated by people and organizations alike. This phenomenon of an unprecedented growth of information and our ability to collect, process, protect, and exploit it has been described with the catchall term of Big Data [15]. Literature identifies 'big data' as the 'next big thing in innovation' [16], the next frontier for innovation, competition, and productivity [17]. The rationale behind such statements is that the 'big data' is capable of changing competition by "transforming processes, altering corporate ecosystems, and facilitating innovation" [18]. It can be acknowledged as a key source of value creation. Beyond improving data-driven decision making, it also is crucial to identify the social value of big data [4], and what are the role of big data and potential impact of it in the society.

2.2   Social Innovation

The term social innovation has largely emerged in the last few years and there is much discussion about it now. The field of social innovation has grown up primarily as a field of practice, made up of people doing things and then, sometimes, reflecting on what they do [19]. The term social innovation has not any fixed boundaries, as it cuts across many different sectors like public sector, the social benefit sector, technology sector, and many others. The social innovation process has been described by scholars in multiple contexts as it needs to be multidisciplinary and cross social boundaries, for its impact to reach more people [20–22]. Social innovations are ideas that address various social challenges and needs.

2.3   Big Data and Social Innovation

Big data contains a wealth of societal information and can thus be viewed as a network mapped to society; analyzing big data and further summarizing and finding clues and laws it implicitly contains can help us better perceive the present [23]. Data are an important element of social innovation. To initiate any innovative steps or to address any social challenge, data are needed. A deliberate and systematic approach towards social innovation through big data is needed as it will offer social value [5]. Since more data become available at a smaller cost, big data can be used as actionable information to identify needs and offer services for the benefit of the society and ensure aid to the individuals and society that generate them [13].

Following the importance of big data and social innovation, further work is needed to better define and understand how well society can benefit from big data to increase social value and lead to social good [4, 6]. From this mapping, we can contribute to the field of big data research from a social perspective. While presenting an overview of the present research status, we also want to identify if there are any obstacles and challenges in using big data analytics that the stakeholder might face in their way to employ big data for their social innovative solutions. Big data can empower policy-makers and entrepreneurs to provide solutions for social problems [6]. Identifying possible challenges and having a clear picture of the big data research in the social sector can also help stakeholders to prepare beforehand, to take advantage of the big data that are available, filter them and proceed to decisions that will help them innovate for social good and change.

3 Research Methodology

A systematic mapping study was undertaken to provide an overview of the research available in the field of big data analytics and social innovation leading to societal transformation, following the standardized process for systematic mapping studies [14] as illustrated in Fig. 1; along with guidelines from [24].

Fig. 1. The systematic mapping study process [14]

3.1 Data Sources and Search Strategy

In our primary search, we collected papers from all kind of sources including journals, conference papers, books, reports etc. This review was conducted in August 2018 and publications were searched from 2008 and onwards. We selected this timeframe as it is the time when these terms like big data and analytics, social innovation got the momentum. The systematic search strategy consisted of searches in seven online bibliographic databases which were selected based on their relevance with our search topic and these databases are also well known for good quality literature resources in the field. To obtain high-quality data, we searched in the following databases – Scopus,

ISI Web of Science, ACM Library, IEEE Xplore, SAGE, Emerald and Taylor & Francis. Then initial searches in the databases were conducted based on identified keywords (Table 1) related to this topic. The used search strings were:

Table 1. The keyword combination for initial search

"Big data"	AND	"Social innovation"
OR		"Societal transformation"
"Data analytics"		"Social good"
		"Social change"

3.2 Study Selection

The study selection process is illustrated in Fig. 2, along with the number of papers at each stage. Searching the databases using the search string returned 593 papers, resulting in 465 unduplicated papers. These were imported into EndNote X8. Due to the importance of the selection phase in determining the overall validity of the literature review, a number of inclusion and exclusion criteria were applied. Studies were eligible for inclusion if they were focused on the topic of big data and data analytics, and their applications to foster social innovation, and lead to social impact, change and transformation. We used "big data" and "data analytics" separate to broader our search as several studies employ big data analytics techniques but do not use the term big data.

The mapping included research papers published in journals, conference proceedings, reports targeted at business executives and a broader audience, and scientific magazines. In progress research and dissertations were excluded from this mapping, as well as studies that were not written in English. Given that our focus was on the social innovation and societal transformation that big data entails, we included quantitative, qualitative, and case studies. Since the topic of interest is of an interdisciplinary nature, a diversity of epistemological approaches was opted for.

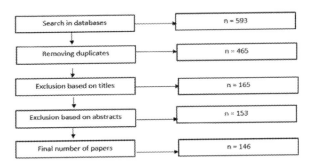

Fig. 2. The study selection process

3.3   Manual Search

Following the systematic search, a manual search was also conducted. Google Scholar was used to searching for papers manually. At this stage total 10 papers from Google scholar was added to our EndNote library and the final number of papers became 156.

3.4   Data Extraction

After the mapping, we finally ended up with 156 papers. We performed a systematic analysis and extracted data from the abstracts of the papers that we need to answer our research questions. We extracted data regarding the - publication frequency, publication source, research area, research type, empirical evidence and contribution type.

4   Results and Findings

RQ1: How the research about 'big data and social innovation' has changed over time (in the last decade)?

Publication Frequency. The analysis shows that relevant papers are published from 2012 or later, with their frequency increasing yearly. The study was conducted in August 2018, so the year 2018 is not complete. The findings (Fig. 3) verify that the momentum or applications of big data are becoming increasingly popular.

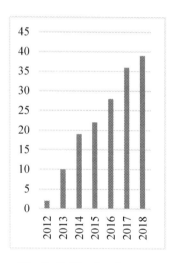

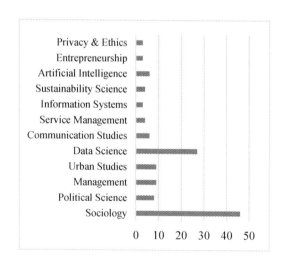

Fig. 3. Publication frequency

Fig. 4. Research areas

Research Areas. Next, we examined the research sectors of the published articles, to give an overview of the general categories. The findings are shown in Fig. 4.

Publication Sources. As mentioned in Sect. 3, our mapping includes research papers published in academic outlets; but we have considered reports also (e.g., Hitachi reviews) because a lot of evidence is published by companies and a lot of work on social innovation and big data is done by companies as well.

We have tried to figure out how many of the relevant scientific papers are published in journals, how many as conference papers and from other sources. The statistic is given in Fig. 5.

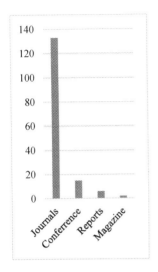

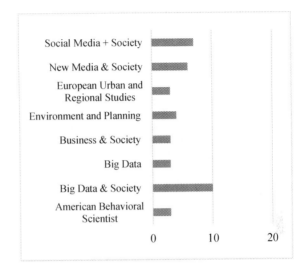

Fig. 5. Sources of publication   **Fig. 6.** Journals with a high number of relevant publications

Along with the sources of the relevant papers, we have also searched for the journals who published maximum number of papers about our research topic i.e. big data and social innovation. Here in Fig. 6, we mention a few journals with maximum number of published papers from our review.

RQ2: How much of the research is done based on empirical studies and what type of empirical studies?

Empirical Evidence. We primarily classified our reviewed papers as empirical and non-empirical papers. Non-empirical papers are conceptual papers. From the study, we see that majority (59%) of the paper s are based on empirical evidence. With this finding (Fig. 7), we also get the answer to our second research question.

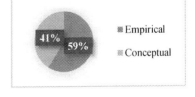

Fig. 7. Empirical and non-empirical studies

We then classified the empirical papers based on the type of study. The research types that have been assessed followed the guidelines from [25] include: (1) survey, (2) design and creation, (3) experiment, (4) case study, (5) action research, and (6) ethnography. We have also included 'Discussion' as a research type, inspired by [26]. We have added this last method as we felt that some papers are more suitable to categorize as a discussion paper. Discussion papers are also known as 'Expert opinion'.

After deciding about the research types, we counted the numbers for each type. The following figure shows which research types of the studies found from our mapping. Only the papers providing empirical evidence (92 papers) were included in Fig. 8, covering a total of 7 research methods.

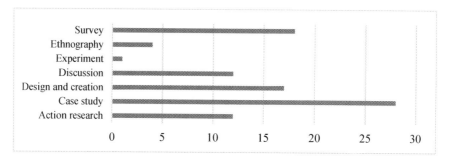

Fig. 8. Empirical evidence (research type)

Contribution Type. Every research paper has some contribution to the advancement of research in the relevant field by providing something new. To illustrate which types of contributions that have been made within the research area between, Fig. 9 was made. The figure shows the contribution type of papers. All 156 primary papers selected finally, in our mapping study are considered in this figure.

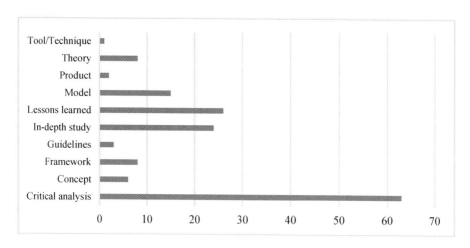

Fig. 9. Contribution types

We differ between 10 contribution types. Based on [25], we define six different knowledge outcomes including (1) product, (2) theory, (3) tool/technique, (4) model, (5) in-depth study and (6) critical analysis. We also adapt some more knowledge outcomes or contribution types since some contribution types from [27] can describe the contribution of some papers more precisely; including (1) framework, (2) lessons learned, (3) tool/guidelines and (4) concept.

RQ3: What are the challenges or barriers to the successful implementation of big data for societal challenges?

Studying the title and abstract of all 156 papers, it has been found that only 3 papers explicitly mentioned challenges regarding employing big data in their studies. The challenges we find from this study are mentioned below:

– Open data and privacy concern [28]
– Challenge around obtaining data [29]
– The prominence of marketing-driven software [30]
– The interpretation of unpredictability [30]

We expected challenges and barriers due to their importance to be mentioned in the abstract. Thus, there is little evidence to answer this research question through a systematic mapping study raising the need for more research in this area including more empirical studies.

5   Discussion

RQ1: How the research about 'big data and social innovation' has changed over time (in the last decade)?

From this mapping we have presented an overview of the research status on big data and social innovation that has been done in the last decade. As we could not find any prior systematic study on this topic, we cannot compare the results. But this mapping will now help other researchers to understand to social potential of big data research and applications. Our study proves that terms like big data and social innovation gained the attention of academic and business communities later than in 2010. It can be also seen that the number of researches and publications are increasing every year since then, which proves the importance and increasing attention big data and social innovation is getting day by day. Another study on big data [8] also stated that, "With regard to the literature review, 'big data' relevant journal articles have started appearing frequently in 2011. Prior to these years, the number of publications on the topic was very low. Publications on 'big data' related topics started only in 2008 (with 1 article) and then a steady increase in the number of publications in the following years".

From this mapping, we can see that many fields including social science, political science, information systems, urban management, communication, healthcare sector adapted big data for their applications. In the results section, we have presented the fields with major number of research studies, but there are also research fields we have found form the mapping where big data is being used; like- education, journalism, tourism, etc. Here notable that all these papers with applications of big data in different fields are directly or indirectly related to various social issues; which proves that big data applications have a big potential to be used for the good of the society not only for business or technology.

RQ2: How much of the research is done based on empirical studies and what type of empirical studies?

In our systematic mapping, more than half of the papers (59%) provide empirical evidence. As there was no previous mapping on this topic, we cannot say how much empirical work was done before. But when 59% of the studies are empirical it proves that the researchers of this field are contributing much. With their contributions, the quality of research is also improving. The major contribution of the research papers from our mapping was a critical analysis, both empirical and non-empirical. When analyzing different topics, the authors also presented their insights, research agenda, guidelines for future research, what lessons they learned and their opinions. The empirical studies also presented models, frameworks and tools that can be used in future research.

RQ3: What are the challenges or barriers to the successful implementation of big data for societal challenges?

In article [28], the authors reflected on various case related to big data challenges, including the challenge of maintaining data privacy and ethics when using all forms of big data for positive social change. The authors recommended exploring new formats for educating people about privacy/data protection risks to overcome data privacy challenges and to use templates to evaluate open data sources. In [29] authors investigate how the challenges around obtaining data to enforce new regulations are addressed by local councils to balance corporate interests with the public good. The authors stated that triangulating different sources of information is not always straightforward as the publicly available data might be partially obscured. In their case study, the authors recommend about platform economy to overcome the challenges regarding data collection. In [30], the authors examine the dominance of marketing-driven commercial tools for predictive analytics of data and their effectiveness to analyze data for completely different purposes such as law enforcement. Another challenge that [30] mentions is, the notions of predictability and probability remain contentious in the use of social media big data. The authors reflected upon the challenges and points to a crucial research agenda in an increasingly datafied environment.

5.1   Use of Keywords

We found some research papers relevant to our study, but they have not been included in the mapping as they do not use the keywords we searched with. For example, [31] use mobile call data to predict the geographic spread and timing of epidemics, and indeed they address a social challenge and has a significant societal impact. However, they do not use keywords regarding data analytics and societal impact, maybe because their focus is mainly on modeling and technical aspects. Instead their keywords include human mobility, mobile phones, epidemiology, dengue etc. Considering the importance of social implications of big data research as well as the interest of publication venues in contributing to societies [1], we suggest that future papers should take into account and report such implications in their abstract and keywords. We should note that indeed many papers discuss social implications, however they do not mention them in their abstracts, raising the need for a systematic literature review in the area. Thus, a more detailed analysis of the research articles can lead, among other things, to new combinations of keywords that will be able to better capture the current status regarding the impact of big data and analytics on societal challenges.

5.2 Limitation of the Study

Systematic mapping study approach is not without limitations [32]. For the validity of this review, threats of retrieval of papers need to be considered. Even though a systematic approach was used during this mapping, the selection of papers dealing with "big data" that we have included was based on our subjective judgment. Another limitation is, we have used only titles and abstracts to extract data. So, the categorizing and data extraction process depends on the quality of the abstracts. ICT-related research publications often do not use structured abstract [33] which results in poor accuracy when classifying papers based solely on abstracts. Following the standard procedure of systematic mapping, we did not include research articles in our study that do not use the keywords we searched with; even though some papers might be relevant to our topic.

6 Implication for Research and Practice

This systematic mapping study extends the big data research in several ways. Our work contributes to the social perspective that emphasizes the importance of adoption and applications of big data. This study can guide other researchers of this field to develop their agenda and roadmap for future research. The findings of this research show the type of contributions big data research is making in the industry; based on that future researchers can think what type of contributions we are lacking and make their research agenda on that. In this research, we have also identified the challenges of big data adoption in the social sector. Future researchers can explore more about these challenges and can investigate if there are other challenges. There is possible future research potential to address and propose solutions for these challenges; so that employing big data can be easier and more efficient for the stakeholders.

7 Conclusion

This paper presents findings of a systematic mapping study that researchers, social innovators, social entrepreneurs and all other stakeholders can use to unlock the power of big data for the benefit of the society. We have presented the current status that shows how research into big data and social innovation has increased over the last decade, attracting significant attention from across a wide array of disciplines. We have identified the major research areas where big data is getting significant attention; so future researchers can explore more about the impact of big data in those areas. This study also proves that the empirical ground of research in this field is strong; research is not only limited to case studies, but also other forms of research is being done like action research, critical analysis, designing and creating new products, etc. The key contribution this paper has made is offering the basis for a reflection process among the researchers in this field.

Acknowledgments. This work has received funding from the EU's Horizon 2020 research and innovation programme, under the Marie Sklodowska-Curie Grant Agreements No. 751550.

References

1. Pappas, I.O., Mikalef, P., Giannakos, M.N., Krogstie, J.: Big data and business analytics ecosystems: paving the way towards digital transformation and sustainable societies. Inf. Syst. E-Bus. Manag. **16**, 479 (2018)
2. Mikalef, P., Pappas, I.O., Krogstie, J., Giannakos, M.: Big data analytics capabilities: a systematic literature review and research agenda. Inf. Syst. E-Bus. Manag. **16**(3), 547–578 (2018)
3. Gantz, J., Reinsel, D.: The digital universe in 2020: big data, bigger digital shadows, and biggest growth in the far east. IDC iView IDC Anal. Future **2012**, 1–16 (2012)
4. Agarwal, R., Dhar, V.: Editorial—big data, data science, and analytics: the opportunity and challenge for IS research. Inf. Syst. Res. **25**, 443–448 (2014)
5. Pappas, I.O., Jaccheri, M.L., Mikalef, P., Giannakos, M.N.: Social innovation and social entrepreneurship through big data: developing a research agenda. In: 11th Mediterranean Conference on Information Systems (MCIS) (2017)
6. Desouza, K.C., Smith, K.L.: Big data for social innovation. Stanf. Soc. Innov. Rev. Summer **12**, 38–43 (2014)
7. Phills, J.A., Deiglmeier, K., Miller, D.T.: Rediscovering social innovation. Stanf. Soc. Innov. Rev. **6**(4), 34–43 (2008)
8. Wamba, S.F., Akter, S., Edwards, A., Chopin, G., Gnanzou, D.: How 'big data' can make big impact: findings from a systematic review and a longitudinal case study. Int. J. Prod. Econ. **165**, 234–246 (2015)
9. de Camargo Fiorini, P., Seles, B.M.R.P., Jabbour, C.J.C., Mariano, E.B., de Sousa Jabbour, A.B.L.: Management theory and big data literature: from a review to a research agenda. Int. J. Inf. Manag. **43**, 112–129 (2018)
10. Gunther, W.A., Mehrizi, M.H.R., Huysman, M., Feldberg, F.: Debating big data: a literature review on realizing value from big data. J. Strat. Inf. Syst. **26**(3), 191–209 (2017)
11. Tseng, F.M., Harmon, R.R.: The impact of big data analytics on the dynamics of social change. Technol. Forecast. Soc. Change **130**, 1–188 (2018)
12. Cajaiba-Santana, G.: Social innovation: moving the field forward. A conceptual framework. Technol. Forecast. Soc. Change **82**, 42–51 (2014)
13. Zicari R.V.: Big data: challenges and opportunities. Akerkar, R. (ed.) Big Data Computing. Chapman and Hall/CRC, Boca Raton (2014)
14. Petersen, K., Feldt, R., Mujtaba, S., Mattsson, M.: Systematic mapping studies in software engineering. EASE **8**, 68–77 (2008)
15. Cuquet, M., Vega-Gorgojo, G., Lammerant, H., Finn, R., Umair ul Hassan: Societal impacts of big data: challenges and opportunities in Europe. Cornell University Library (2017)

16. Gobble, M.M.: Big data: the next big thing in innovation. Res. Technol. Manag. **56**(1), 64–66 (2013)
17. Manyika, J., et al.: Big Data: The Next Frontier for Innovation, Competition and Productivity. McKinsey Global Institute (2011)
18. Brown, B., Chul, M., Manyika, J.: Are you ready for the era of 'big data'? McKinsey Q. **4**, 24–27+30–35 (2011)
19. Mulgan, G.: The theoretical foundation of social innovation. In: Nicholls, A., Murdock, A. (eds.) Social Innovation. Palgrave Macmillan, London (2012). https://doi.org/10.1057/9780230367098_2
20. Mulgan, G.: The process of social innovation. Innovations **1**(2), 145–162 (2006)
21. Herrera, M.E.B.: Creating competitive advantage by institutionalizing corporate social innovation. J. Bus. Res. **68**(7), 1468–1474 (2015)
22. Murray, R., Caulier-Grice, J., Mulgan, G.: The Open Book of Social Innovation. National Endowment for Science, Technology and the Art (NESTA), London, UK (2010)
23. Jin, X., Wah, B.W., Cheng, X., Wang, Y.: Significance and challenges of big data research. Big Data Res. **2**, 59–64 (2015)
24. Kitchenham, B.: Procedures for performing systematic reviews. Keele Univ. **33**, 1–26 (2004)
25. Oates, B.J.: Researching Information Systems and Computing: Sage Publications Ltd., Thousand Oaks (2006)
26. Zannier, C., Melnik, G., Maurer, F.: On the success of empirical studies in the international conference on software engineering. In: ICSE 2006, Proceedings of the 28th International Conference on Software Engineering, pp. 341–350 (2006)
27. Mathiassen, L., Chiasson, M., Germonprez, M.: Style composition in action research publication. MIS Q. **32**(2), 347–363 (2012)
28. Taylor, L., Cowls, J., Schroeder, R., Meyer, E.T.: Big data and positive change in the developing world. Policy Internet **6**, 418–444 (2014)
29. Ferreri, M., Sanyal, R.: Platform economies and urban planning: Airbnb and regulated deregulation in London. Urban Stud. **55**(15), 3353–3368 (2018)
30. Dencik, L., Hintz, A., Carey, Z.: Prediction, pre-emption, and limits to dissent: social media and big data use for policing protests in the United Kingdom. New Media Soc. **20**, 1433–1450 (2017)
31. Wesolowski, A., et al.: Impact of human mobility on the emergence of dengue epidemics in Pakistan. PNAS **112**, 11887–11892 (2015)
32. Kitchenham, B.A., Budgen, D., Pearl Brereton, O.: Using mapping studies as the basis for further research—a participant observer case study. Inf. Softw. Technol. **53**, 638–651 (2011)
33. Kitchenham, B.A., Pearl Brereton, O., Owen, S.: Length and readability of structured software engineering abstracts. IET Softw. **2**, 37 (2008)

Organizational Culture Challenges of Adopting Big Data: A Systematic Literature Review

Trygve Åse Lunde[1], Atilla Paul Sjusdal[1], and Ilias O. Pappas[1,2(✉)] 🅳

[1] University of Agder, 4639 Kristiansand, Norway
ilias.pappas@uia.no
[2] Norwegian University of Science and Technology, 7491 Trondheim, Norway

Abstract. The interest of adopting big data (BD) in organizations has emerged in recent years. Even though many organizations have attempted to adopt BD, the benefits gained by this investment has been limited, and organizations struggle to fully utilize the potential of BD. There has been done several studies on the different challenges and benefits that may occur during the process of adopting and using BD. One major factor that has been discussed in the literature to overcome such challenges has been organizational culture. This paper aims to provide a systematic literature review that reports the organizational culture's impact on BD adoption through the lens of different cultural dimensions. This paper identifies the different dimensions of organizational culture and dives into the specific challenges and potential strategies/techniques to combat these challenges. By reviewing these papers, we ended up with identifying four dimensions of organizational culture in the context of BD. The result of this paper aims to help practitioners and researchers to understand and combat the specific challenges surrounding organizational culture when adopting BD.

Keywords: Big data · Organizational culture · Data-driven culture · Systematic literature review

1 Introduction

Over the last decade, the business world has been shaken by a remarkable wave of digital disruption that is impacting the way organizations compete [1]. This is pushing today's societies into a continually expanding digitalized world, where information and knowledge gets available to more and more people. The different digital media platforms, digital services and technologies is changing the way societies are organized, and how their members interact with each other. Organizations are starting to realize that the massive amounts of data that are being generated, can provide them with a competitive edge [2]. Big data, however, are also challenging existing modes of business and well-established companies [2]. Solving this so that these technologies can be incorporated into competitive strategies has been a goal of academics and practitioners. The focus however has been on the technical aspect of BD, and less on the organizational changes [3]. This is causing organizations to have problems utilizing

© IFIP International Federation for Information Processing 2019
Published by Springer Nature Switzerland AG 2019
I. O. Pappas et al. (Eds.): I3E 2019, LNCS 11701, pp. 164–176, 2019.
https://doi.org/10.1007/978-3-030-29374-1_14

BD to improve their organizational performance [4], as it requires them to overcome several challenges, one of them being the organizational culture [5].

Organizational culture in relation to BD has been studied in the literature. Many of the papers highlight that organizational culture has a critical role in the success of BD initiatives and is often the main reason why BD initiatives fails, rather than technological factors [6, 7]. The primary focus for most of the papers has been on how organizations can handle the challenges and barriers that come with BD adoption, and how to gain the most from this adoption. This is where organizational culture is mentioned as being one of the most important factors for succeeding with BD adoption. Management support is also mentioned as an important component in relation to organizational culture since it requires training and new managerial skills.

BD adoption is not only technical platforms and skills but will also influence the organizational culture [8]. Thirathon et al. [9] specifically studied different factors that impacted big data analytics (BDA) with a focus on analytic culture and how much of an impact it had.

Organizational culture has a strong impact on various aspects of an organization, such as strategy, structure, and processes. Many of the obstacles in relation to BD, are more than likely to be related to organizational culture and not to data or technology [10]. This is also demonstrated in recent literature, where organizational culture has a critical role in the success of BD initiatives and is often the main reason why BD initiatives fails, rather than the technological factors [6, 7].

The literature exposed a need for knowledge surrounding organizational culture in the field of BD. By doing a systematic literature review on the topic, it could potentially bring a positive impact to the field of BD.

This paper is organized as follows. Firstly, it will present the research background where the different dimensions/concepts from BD and organizational culture will be defined. Secondly, it discusses the research method. Lastly, it presents and discusses the research findings.

2 Background

The goal of a BD investment is to enhance the organization's ability to make better decisions along with better decision execution processes. Making informed decisions is one of the building blocks of organizational success [11]. All organizations that have put effort and investment in BD should be able to harvest results via gaining a competitive advantage and improving their performance. However, to fully harness the full potential of big data, the organization also must develop, nurture and maintain an organizational culture that will have positive impact on BD [12]. This is important when around 80% of businesses have failed to implement their BD strategies successfully [11] and regardless of their efforts, many organizations have not been able to realize the potential of BD in an effective manner [13].

The notion of organizational culture is highly complex and hard to understand and describe. Definitions regarding organizational culture have been explained several times by management scholars, yet there is no consensus on a single definition [14]. Even though there are several definitions for organizational culture, it is often described in two different ways. Some suggest that organizational culture encompasses most of the areas of an organization, while others look at organizational culture as a glue that keeps an organization together [15, 16]. Yet organizational culture is often defined as: "a collection of shared assumptions, values, and beliefs that is reflected in its practices and goals and further helps its members understand the organizational functions" [17, 18].

One aspect of organizational culture in the context of BD is often referred to as organizational learning, which is a critical aspect of BD initiatives [3, 14, 19]. Gupta and George [14] defines organizational learning as: "a process through which firms explore, store, share and apply knowledge". Organizational learning opens the opportunity for employees to exploit the existing knowledge and expand their knowledge to adopt and compete in a continuously changing market [2]. By reconfiguring the resources according to the changes in the external environment, the organizations have better odds of having a sustained competitive advantage [20]. To gain a competitive advantage, the intangible resources, such as data-driven culture and organizational learning is just as important as the tangible resources, where the insights extracted from data are ought to be valued and acted upon [14]. Developing a data-driven culture requires the top management to select the strategy and design the organization structure according to the desired values and norms [10]. Additionally, organizations are more likely to use business analytics and big data effectively with a data-driven culture, where the leadership and employees understand the important and critical role of data in their organization [21, 22]. Further, Alharthi et al. [10] argues that many barriers related to BD is cultural, rather than technological. The lack of management's understanding of the value of BD may result in organizational resistance to BD, leading to the resistance to the development of a data-driven cultural and gaining the potential competitive advantage it carries.

Previous studies argue that BD itself does not give a competitive advantage, but rather developing capabilities that competitors struggle to match [14]. Creating BDA capabilities, a combination of certain tangible, human and intangible resources can lead to superior firm performance. Studies also examine technology management and suggest that it is related with BD decision making, while technological competency is required to facilitate the use of BD for analysis [6]. One of the defining features of BD is the unsuitability of existing processing techniques and how to store large amount of data to generate value from BD technology [23]. To generate value from BD and the technology used, organizations must develop or acquire analytic capabilities, which allows the organization to transform data to valuable information [9]. Dubey et al. [18] argues that organizational capability development is needed to fully exploit analytic capabilities. Furthermore, the complementary capability development highly depends on the organizational culture. Even though the analytic and technical capabilities are developed within an organization, executives still struggle to understand and implement BD strategies effectively [9]. One of the bigger challenges for managing BD, may not be the technology or data itself, but rather to use the human capital and culture to support these strategies [24].

3   Research Method

Reviewing previous literature is a key element in any academic work. The benefits of performing a systematic literature review is that it provides a framework/background in order to position new research activities [25]. There are an overwhelmingly amount of literature regarding every topic out there and reviewing all the literature concerning this topic will be difficult, but by using a systematic approach to review the literature, the level of quality will be higher and the process of reviewing the literature in a good manner will be achievable. By using such approach, it makes it less likely that the chosen literature is biased [25].

There are several ways of conducting a systematic literature review. Our literature review is based on the guidelines presented by Webster & Watson [26]. The process that has been used in this review is documented in the next section. The main objective of this study is to answer the following research question:

RQ: What is the current status regarding the impact of organizational culture on big data and analytics adoption?

When searching for relevant literature regarding our research question, we used seven databases. The databases we used were Wiley Online Library, SAGE journals, Taylor & Francis Online, Emeraldinsight, IEEE Xplore digital library, Sciencedirect and Scopus. By differentiating the use of databases, we ensure to obtain the literature required to perform a proper systematic literature review. In these databases, we used several search strings which included synonyms and other phrasing of the constructs used in the research question. The keywords used in the searches were not limited to title or abstract, but rather everywhere in the article. The phrases we decided to use were carefully selected by looking at different possibilities and synonyms that might increase the search result. This resulted in four different search strings which is presented in Table 1.

By using the different set of search strings presented in Table 1, we ended up with a plethora of gathered literature. The search strings we used and the total amount of articles for each search string and the number of articles that were used in systematic literature review.

Table 1. Search strings and results

Search strings	Results	Used articles
"Analytic Culture"	384	1
"Big Data" AND "Organizational Culture"	1455	10
"Data Analytics" AND "Organizational Culture"	817	1
"Data-Driven Culture"	218	7
Total results	2874	19

3.1 Selection Process

The literature was manually reviewed to conclude the relevance to this study by reviewing the title, abstract and full text and compare it to our research question. Therefore, we developed some inclusion and exclusion criteria for this review to assist us in evaluating the relevance of the articles to our research question and literature review. The articles that met the requirements in the inclusion criteria were used in the primary studies. The articles that included the exclusion criteria, were not used in the study. The inclusion and exclusion criteria are shown in Table 2.

Table 2. Inclusion and Exclusion criteria

Inclusion criteria	Exclusion criteria
Conference proceedings	Mentioning terms, but not related to our RQ
Focus on big data and relates to the RQ	Not peer-reviewed journals/conferences
Peer-reviewed journal	Books

The approach for gathering the literature were based on a concept centric approach, were we reviewed the concepts of the articles in relations to our research question. By using this approach, we eliminated several articles that had the search strings in their title or abstract but were not relevant to our study because of the wide range of research regarding these topics. We did not exclude "lower quality" journals because literature that is published in journals assumed to have less quality, may have established some new research that might assist this research in a positive manner. Watson and Webster [26] states that a literature review should not confined to one research methodology, one set of journals or one geographic region. By having this approach, we manage to look at literature that might not be published in the "top" journals but might have some contribution to the topic of interest.

By reviewing the titles of these articles, we looked at the relevance they had to our topic and research question. In this phase, we were open to articles that were not directly connected to our research question and accepted them when they were somewhat relevant. This was to ensure that we did not exclude any articles too soon.

In addition to the 19 articles we found, we rounded up the process by searching Google Scholar to see if there were any papers that were relevant to our systematic literature review that might not show up in the other searches. In this search process, we managed to find two papers that had a direct connected to our topic that we decided to include in this paper. The articles we included were Mikalef et al. [3] and Pappas et al. [2].

4   Findings

The findings of this literature review are presented in two parts. The first part is presented quantitatively. The second part is analyzing and interpreting the data from the selected studies to answer the research question. The main concepts discussed in the articles are BD and organizational culture. The different dimensions of both concepts are being discussed in the literature, however the level of focus on each paper varies. Most of the papers mentions organizational culture as an important factor in BD adoption, but few of them have organizational culture as a primary focus. The remaining papers that does, contribute more to the field of organizational culture, were they have more focus on the cultural part, even though it's in the context of BD. When analyzing the literature, we discovered that there were many challenges and sometimes solutions being presented in the articles. To make this a useful contribution, we decided to divide this into challenges and strategies for overcoming these.

4.1 Concept Matrix

The concept matrix was developed to get a figure that illustrate the dimensions discussed in the respective concepts in the literature (Fig. 1).

Articles \ Concepts	Big data				Organizational culture		
	Technology management	Big data analytics capabilities	Big data management capabilities	Big data analytic strategy	Organizational learning	Management	Data-driven culture
1. Alharthi et al., 2017	X			X		X	X
2. Dubey et al., 2019		X	X		X		
3. Ferraris et al., 2018			X				X
4. Thiraton et al., 2017		X	X				X
5. Dubey et al., 2017	X		X				X
6. Ylijoki & Porras, 2016							X
7. Grover et al., 2018			X	X	X	X	
8. Comuzzi & Patel, 2016			X	X			
9. Carillo et al., 2018			X				X
10. Jeble et al., 2018	X	X	X		X	X	X
11. Frisk, 2016		X	X	X	X		X
12. Shamim et al., 2018	X				X	X	X
13. Nguyen, N. 2018				X			X
14. Gupta & George, 2016	X	X	X		X		X
15. Adrian et al, 2016		X	X			X	
16. Côrte-real et al., 2019	X	X	X	X		X	X
17. Mikalef et al., 2017		X		X	X	X	X
18. Pappas et al., 2018		X			X		X
19. Tabesh et al., 2019	X	X		X		X	X
20. Cao & Duan, 2015	X	X				X	X
21. Duan et al., 2018	X		X	X		X	X

Fig. 1. Concept matrix

4.2 Organizational Culture's Impact on Big Data Adoption

Organizational culture through its assumptions, values, norms, and symbols has a strong impact on various aspects of an organization, such as strategy, structure, and processes [10]. This can be related to many of the obstacles that form when an organization is trying to adopt BD. These obstacles are likely to be related to organizational culture and not to data or technology [10]. Recent literature acknowledges this by expressing that organizational culture has a critical role in the success of big data initiatives and is often the main reason why big data initiatives fail, rather than technological factors [6, 7, 27]. Some go as far as saying that the main challenges for BD management is the organizational culture [4, 6]. This means that the impact BD investments has on an organization is usually driven by the culture and not the BD investment itself [9, 24], requiring that business analytics must become part of the organizational culture and all employees has to have a positive attitude towards it [28].

4.3 Challenges of Organizational Culture in Big Data Adoption

Most of the literature brings up several specific cultural challenges when adopting BD. The different challenges are categorized within the dimensions of the concept, organizational culture.

In a continuously changing environment, the ability to adapt and reconfigure the resources accordingly is crucial for organizations to maintain a competitive advantage [14]. One of the aspects that influences this ability is organizational learning. Organizational learning refers to the organization's ability to explore, store, share and apply knowledge [29, 30]. Due to the rapidly changing market conditions and innovations of new technologies, such as big data, the organizations are challenged to become more agile and adapt to the ever-changing market [14]. Another challenge that is presented is that the organizations need to adapt their organizational culture and adopt new procedures of organizational learning in order to benefit from big data.

Management challenges that may prevent companies from succeeding in BD initiatives include leadership and strategy [4]. Having top management support [7, 31, 32] and appropriate technical and management skills [33] is also important when trying to acquire success with big data initiatives. The behavior of top managers hat does not value data-driven decision making, will affect the decision patterns at all levels of the organization [11]. Obtaining full benefits from big data does also require aligning existing organizational culture and capabilities across the whole organization [34]. This can be a challenging task for the management. Overcoming leadership focus, harnessing talent, technology management and company culture [4], which are even bigger contributing factors than the technical ones [6], does also present a challenge. Concluding with the words of Gupta and George [14]: "the intelligence gleaned from data will be of little use to an organization if its managers fail to foresee the potential of newly extracted insights".

A data-driven culture is defined as "the extent to which organizational members (including top-level executives, middle managers, and lower-level employees) make decisions based on the insights extracted from data" [14]. The lack of data-driven culture is among the major reasons for the high failure rate of big data projects [35].

The organizations face the challenges of developing a data-driven culture that manifest a view of data-driven decision making as valuable to decrease the chance of resistance to the development of data-driven culture in order to benefit from big data. Further, developing a data-driven culture requires the management to base their decisions on data, rather than instinct [17] and change their attitude towards data-driven decision making [8]. This leads to the several challenges suggested by Ylijoki and Porras [8], where this challenge often requires the whole organizational culture to change as well as the decision-making process. The organizations ought to change the decision-making process for all members of an organization, including lower-level employees, middle-level managers and top-level executives [14].

4.4 Strategies for Overcoming Challenges of Organizational Culture in the Context of Big Data

Several strategies, techniques, requirements and suggestions to overcome these challenges are presented in the literature and identified in this study. These strategies, techniques, requirements and suggestions is presented within the respective dimension of the concept, organizational culture.

Regarding organizational learning, Bhatt and Grover [30] and Teece [19] argues that organizations need to make concerted efforts to use their existing knowledge to explore the new knowledge that is aligned with the changing market. Based on this knowledge, organizations can combine it with insight extracted from big data to generate value [14]. Shamim et al. [6] also points at the importance of developing a culture that is strongly change-oriented in order to utilize organizational learning.

First an organization needs to create and foster an organizational culture that is supportive of fact-based decision making and big data analytics. Developing a clear vision of how big data fits with the overall strategy of an organization should help accelerate and solidify the acceptance of this type of organizational culture. Once the vision is formulated, it must be translated into specific organizational processes and initiatives that rely on big data to improve organizational performance [10]. Successful cultural change of this nature can be achieved by documenting, implementing, and communicating a clear organizational vision in relation to big data ensuring top management commitment to this vision, and managing the drivers that influence organizational culture rather than trying to manage culture itself [36]. Adopting a design approach is also a way of enabling organizations to change their decision-making culture and increase the collaboration between different actors and [37] points at the influence of organizational culture in this process. Further, Côrte-real et al. [38] argues that organizations need to align their culture with a data-driven culture with a top-top approach, where strategy is top priority. Then it is followed by managerial and operational factors.

A culture that embraces data- and evidence-driven approaches to business decisions, and governance that delineates responsibility and accountability for data, are both catalysts for BDA value creation [24].

Prior studies in management strategy have identified organizational culture as a source of sustained firm performance [39–41]. Developing top management support is one of the critical success factors of big data implementation [32]. Commitment and support among management can significantly mitigate the cultural and technological barriers to BD strategies. This is done by commitment to big data projects that facilitates in generating a data-driven culture by sending signals to everyone in the organization [26]. Managers should also build multi skilled teams consisting of data scientists, engineers with technical knowledge and translators who are familiar with both technical and business languages. This can help managers interpret the generated insights before transforming them into business decisions [42]. This practice can over time create a rich culture of open communication that will help addressing BD challenges [11]. Further, aligning the existing organizational culture and capabilities across the whole organization [34] is another one. Companies must not only hire scientists who can translate big data into useful business information in order to have success. There also need to be a change in the managerial mindset, re-orient it to having a more digital and data-driven culture focus [34]. Managers must also "attend to the big data era" [43], resulting in becoming skilled in its methods and analytics, and learn to explore big data to develop the needed competitive advantage. Companies that manage to develop leadership teams with clear big data strategies, have clear goals, and can articulate the business case, would increase the likelihood of succeeding. Those teams can define what success is and have the ability to ask the right questions [24].

5 Discussion

The rise of big data has made the field very interesting for society, individuals and organizations. Organizations especially, are very interested in the potential big data can bring them, mostly because of the ever-increasing competition in today's marked. Publications discussing organizational culture`s effect on big data adoption is still in its early stage. This can be seen in this paper, where the oldest papers are from 2015. Our findings revealed that organizational culture is still a somewhat new aspect in the field of big data, the reason being that the majority of the papers only mentioned organizational culture as an important factor in the adoption of big data, and did not have it as one of the main focuses areas. Our findings also showed that the literature was very supportive of the notion that organizational culture played a critical role for organizations when trying to succeed with big data adoption. This demonstrated that there is a gap in the research about exactly how much organizational culture effect the big data adoption, and how one can strategically plan to cultivate an organizational culture that is fully supportive of big data, which will increase the benefit an organization get from big data.

Our findings revealed that a gap between the big data analytics investments and the ability to effectively derive business insights and increase the performance of the organization [43]. The impact of big data investments is predominantly driven by culture and not the BDA investments themselves [23]. Lack of such culture could be detrimental when trying to identify and generate the potential value big data has to offer [24].

Further, it is argued that being change-oriented and having focus on the existing knowledge is important in order to exploit new knowledge and organizational learning. The literature often mentions the leadership is an important factor for organizational learning, where the influence of the management and leadership is crucial. The organizations should be in constant change and be positive towards changing their procedures and routines accordingly to the changing environment [34, 45].

Organizations need to develop a data-driven culture in order to benefit from data. Duan et al. [46] also suggest that there is clear evidence that demonstrates the important role of data-driven as an emergent organizational culture in the context of big data. The literature suggested that the leadership must develop a vision for the change and implement procedures and routines that supports the vision. Even though organizations develop a clear vision, organizations tend to have less focus on the end state and goal, which may result in challenges regarding initiating the changes. This is often due to the focus on resource efficiency, which organizations may not predict [17]. Even though the cultural change must be initiated from the top leadership, the lower-level employees and medium-level managers must have a positive attitude towards the change.

Developing top management support was also demonstrated to be of great importance in our findings [31]. Organizational culture was also shown to be a source of sustained firm performance [38, 40, 41]. Aligning the existing organizational culture and its capabilities across the whole organization [34], while also having management educated in big data's methods and analytics, is needed. The management also need to change their managerial mindset, reorienting it to a more digital and data-driven culture focused one [34].

This study has some limitations, like any other systematic literature review. To avoid being biased in the selection process, we developed a research question, as well as inclusion and exclusion criteria. This may result in some relevant papers were excluded due the failure of meeting the requirements. Additionally, we limited the literature to conference proceedings and peer-reviewed articles which may leave out some useful research within this field.

6 Conclusion

The results showed that there is literature out there in support of the positive impact organizational culture has on BD. However, there is not many papers measuring this exactly, so a future study with the focus of measuring organizational culture and its impact on big data in organizations would be a valuable contribution. Furthermore, there are a need of research regarding changing the culture in order to align the culture with big data solutions.

The results of this review have implications for practitioners where organizations can identify the specific challenges that are brought with big data adoption. Additionally, there is several techniques, strategies or guidelines on how it can be combated. This study has also academic value where It summarizes the relevant literature that is discussing BD and organizational culture, which is a relatively new topic combined, but very timely and critical for understanding the cultural impact on big data adoption. Because of this topic being relatively new, some of the conclusion to draws from today's literature can be somewhat vague and hard for organizations to implement, this illustrates further that there is more research needed to be done on this topic.

Acknowledgments. This work has received funding from the European Union's Horizon 2020 research and innovation programme, under the Marie Sklodowska-Curie Grant Agreements No. 751550.

References

1. Weill, P., Woerner, S.L.: Thriving in an increasingly digital ecosystem. MIT Sloan Manag. Rev. **56**(4), 27–34 (2015)
2. Pappas, O.I., Mikalef, P., Giannakos, N.M., Krogstie, J., Lekakos, G.: Big data and business analytics ecosystems: paving the way towards digital transformation and sustainable societies. IseB **16**(3), 479–491 (2018). https://doi.org/10.1007/s10257-018-0377-z
3. Mikalef, P., Pappas, O.I., Krogstie, J., Giannakos, M.: Big data analytics capabilities: a systematic literature review and research agenda. Inf. Syst. e-Bus. Manag. (2017). https://doi.org/10.1007/s10257-017-0362-y
4. McAfee, A., Brynjolfsson, E.: Big data: the management revolution. Harvard Bus. Rev. **90**, 61–67 (2012)
5. Manyika, J., et al.: Big data: the next frontier for innovation, competition and productivity (2011). https://www.mckinsey.com/business-functions/digital-mckinsey/our-insights/big-data-the-next-frontier-for-innovation
6. Shamim, S., Zeng, J., Shariq, M.S., Khan, Z.: Role of big data management in enhancing big data decision-making capability and quality among Chinese firms: a dynamic capabilities view. Inf. Manag. (2018). https://doi.org/10.1016/j.im.2018.12.003
7. LaValle, S., Lesser, E., Shockley, R., Hopkins, M.: Big data, analytics and the path from insight to value. MIT Sloan Manag. **52**(2), 21–32 (2011)
8. Ylijoki, O., Porras, J.: Conceptualizing big data: analysis of case studies. Intell. Syst. Account. Finance Manag. **23**, 295–310 (2016). https://doi.org/10.1002/isaf.1393
9. Thirathon, U., Wieder, B., Matolcsy, Z., Ossimitz, L.-M.: Big data, analytic culture and analytic-based decision making - evidence from Australia. Procedia Comput. Sci. **121**, 775–783 (2017). https://doi.org/10.1016/j.procs.2017.11.100
10. Alharthi, A., Krotov, V., Bowman, M.: Addressing barriers to big data. Bus. Horiz. **60**, 285–292 (2017). https://doi.org/10.1016/j.bushor.2017.01.002
11. Tabesh, P., Mousavidin, E. Hasani, S.: Implementing big data strategies: a managerial perspective. Bus. Horiz. (2019). https://doi.org/10.1016/j.bushor.2019.02.001
12. Nguyen, L.T.: A framework for five big V's of big data and organizational culture in firms. In: Proceedings of the IEEE International Conference on Big Data (Big Data), Seattle, USA (2018)
13. Mazzei, M.J., Noble, D.: Big data dreams: a framework (2017)
14. Gupta, M., George, F.J.: Toward the development of a big data analytics capability. Inf. Manag. **53**, 1049–1064 (2016). https://doi.org/10.1016/j.im.2016.07.004
15. Iivari, J., Huisman, M.: The relationship between organizational culture and the deployment of systems development methodologies. MIS Q. **31**(1), 35–58 (2007)
16. Dowling, G.: Developing your company image into a corporate asset. Long Range Plan. **26**(2), 101–109 (1993)
17. Dubey, R., et al.: Can big data and predictive analytics improve social and environmental sustainability?. Technol. Forecast. Soc. Change (2017) https://doi.org/10.1016/j.techfore.2017.06.020

18. Dubey, R., et al.: Big data analytics and organizational culture as complements to swift trust and collaborative performance in the humanitarian supply chain. Int. J. Prod. Econ. **120**, 120–136 (2019). https://doi.org/10.1016/j.ijpe.2019.01.023

19. Jeble, S., Dubey, R., Childe, J.S., Papadopoulos, T., Roubaud, D., Prakash, A.: Impact of big data and predictive analytics capability on supply chain sustainability. Int. J. Logist. Manag. **29**(2), 513–538 (2018). https://doi.org/10.1108/IJLM-05-2017-0134

20. Teece, D., Pisano, G., Shuen, A.: Dynamic capabilities and strategic management. Strateg. Manag. J. **18**(7), 509–533 (1997)

21. Kiron, D., Prentice, P.K., Ferguson, R.B.: Innovating with analytics (cover story). MIT Sloan Manag. Rev. **54**(1), 47–52 (2012)

22. Cao, G., Duan, Y.: The affordances of business analytics for strategic decision-making and their impact on organizational performance. In: Proceedings of the Pacific Asia Conference on Information systems, Singapore (2015)

23. Comuzzi, M., Patel, A.: How organisations leverage big data: a maturity (2016)

24. Grover, V., Chiang, L.H.R., Liang, P.-T., Zhang, D.: Creating strategic business value from big data analytics: a research framework. J. Manag. Inf. Syst. **35**(2), 388–432 (2018). https://doi.org/10.1080/07421222.2018.1451951

25. Kitchenham, B., Charters, S.: Guidelines for performing systematic literature reviews in software engineering. EBSE technical report, Keele University and University of Durham

26. Webster, J., Watson, R.T.: Analyzing the past to prepare for the future: writing a literature review. MIS Q **26**(2), xiii–xxiii (2002)

27. Adrian, C., Abdullah, R., Atan, R., Jusoh, Y.: Towards developing strategic assessment model for big data implementation: a systematic literature review. Int. J. Adv. Soft Comput. Appl. **8**(3), 173–192 (2016)

28. Müller, S.D., Jensen, P.: Big data in the Danish industry: application and value creation. Bus. Process Manag. J. **23**(3), 645–670 (2017)

29. Grant, R.: Toward a knowledge-based theory of the firm. Strateg. Manag. J. **17**(2), 109–122 (1996)

30. Bhatt, G., Grover, V.: Types of information technology capabilities and their role in competitive advantage: an empirical study. J. Manag. Inf. Syst. **22**(2), 253–277 (2005)

31. Chen, D.Q., Preston, D.S., Swink, M.: How the use of big data analytics affects value creation in supply chain management. J. Manag. Inf. Syst. **32**(4), 4–39 (2015)

32. Halaweh, M., El Massry, A.: Conceptual model for successful implementation of big data in organizations. J. Int. Technol. Inf. Manag. **24**(2), 21–29 (2015)

33. Waller, M.A., Fawcett, S.E.: Data science, predictive analytics, and big data: a revolution that will transform supply chain design and management. J. Bus. Logist. **34**(2), 77–84 (2013)

34. Ferraris, A., Mazzoleni, A., Devalle, A., Couturier, J.: Big data analytics capabilities and knowledge management: impact on firm performance. Manag. Decis. (2019). https://doi.org/10.1108/MD-07-2018-0825

35. Ross, J.W., Beath, C.M., Quaadgras, A.: You may not need big data after all. Harv. Bus. Rev. (2013). https://hbr.org/2013/12/you-may-not-need-big-data-after-all

36. Rogers, P., Meehan, P., Tanner, S.: Building a winning culture [White paper]. Bain and Company (2006). http://growthtrilogy.com/bainweb/PDFs/cms/Public/BB_Building_winning_culture.pdf

37. Frisk, E.J., Bannister, F.: Improving the use of analytics and big data by changing the decision-making culture: a design approach. Manag. Decis. **55**(10), 2074–2088 (2017). https://doi.org/10.1108/MD-07-2016-0460

38. Côrte-Real, N., Ruivo, P., Oliveira, T., Popovic, A.: Unlocking the drivers of big data analytics value in firms. J. Bus. Res. **97**, 160–173 (2019). https://doi.org/10.1016/j.jbusres.2018.12.072

39. Barney, J.B.: Looking inside for competitive advantage. Acad. Manag. **9**(4), 49–61 (1995)
40. Teece, D.: Intangible assets and a theory of heterogeneous firms. In: Bounfour, A., Miyagawa, T. (eds.) Intangibles, Market Failure and Innovation Performance. Springer, Cham (2015). https://doi.org/10.1007/978-3-319-07533-4_9
41. Barney, J.B.: Organizational culture: can it be a source of sustained competitive advantage. Acad. Manag. **11**(3), 656–665 (1986)
42. Mayhew, H., Saleh, T., Williams, S.: Making data analytics work for you-instead of the other way around. McKinsey Q. (2016). https://www.mckinsey.com/business-functions/digital-mckinsey/our-insights/making-data-analytics-work-for-you-instead-of-the-other-way-around
43. Mishra, D., Luo, Z., Jiang, S., Papadopoulos, T., Dubey, R.: A bibliographic study on big data: concepts, trends and challenges. Bus. Process Manag. J. **23**(3), 555–573 (2017)
44. Carillo, A.D.K., Galy, N., Guthrie, C., Vanhems, A.: How to turn managers into data-driven decision makers: measuring attitudes towards business analytics. Bus. Process Manag. J. (2018). https://doi.org/10.1108/BPMJ-11-2017-0331
45. Kor, Y.Y., Mahoney, J.T., Michael, S.C.: Resources, capabilities and entrepreneurial perceptions. J. Manag. Stud. **44**(7), 1187–1212 (2007)
46. Duan, Y., Cao, G., Edwards, J.S.: Understanding the impact of business analytics on innovation. Eur. J. Oper. Res. (2018). https://doi.org/10.1016/j.ejor.2018.06.021

Exploring the Relationship Between Data Science and Circular Economy: An Enhanced CRISP-DM Process Model

Eivind Kristoffersen[1]([✉]), Oluseun Omotola Aremu[2], Fenna Blomsma[3],
Patrick Mikalef[1], and Jingyue Li[1]

[1] Norwegian University of Science and Technology, 7491 Trondheim, Norway
eivind.kristoffersen@ntnu.no
[2] The University of Queensland, Brisbane, QLD 4072, Australia
[3] Technical University of Denmark, 2800 Kgs Lyngby, Denmark

Abstract. To date, data science and analytics have received much attention from organizations seeking to explore how to use their massive volumes of data to create value and accelerate the adoption of Circular Economy (CE) concepts. The correct utilization of analytics with circular strategies may enable a step change that goes beyond incremental efficiency gains towards a more sustainable and circular economy. However, the adoption of such smart circular strategies by the industry is lagging, and few studies have detailed how to operationalize this potential at scale. Motivated by this, this study seeks to address how organizations can better structure their data understanding and preparation to align with overall business and CE goals. Therefore, based on the literature and a case study the relationship between data science and the CE is explored, and a generic process model is proposed. The proposed process model extends the Cross Industry Standard Process for Data Mining (CRISP-DM) with an additional phase of *data validation* and integrates the concept of *analytic profiles*. We demonstrate its application for the case study of a manufacturing company seeking to implement the smart circular strategy - predictive maintenance.

Keywords: Data science · Circular Economy ·
Predictive maintenance · Business analytics · CRISP-DM

1 Introduction

In recent years, the concept of Circular Economy (CE) has received significant attention from businesses, policymakers, and researchers as a way to promote sustainable development [25]. With the aim of decoupling value-creation from the consumption of finite resources, CE leverages a range of restorative, efficiency, and productivity oriented strategies to keep products, components, and materials in use for longer [16,17]. Nevertheless, the adoption of CE by the industry so far is modest [26,54,61]. This also holds for manufacturing companies. Although

© IFIP International Federation for Information Processing 2019
Published by Springer Nature Switzerland AG 2019
I. O. Pappas et al. (Eds.): I3E 2019, LNCS 11701, pp. 177–189, 2019.
https://doi.org/10.1007/978-3-030-29374-1_15

they play a vital role in the creation of value, little improvements are seen in their decoupling from linear consumption of resources.

In parallel, the emergence of new technologies as the Internet of Things, Big Data, and Artificial Intelligence - collectively known as Digital Technologies (DTs) - have encouraged a paradigm shift for industrial production, the 'Fourth Industrial Revolution'. These DTs are seen as one of the key enablers for a wider adoption and accelerated transition to CE [19,20]. Moreover, they form the operational building blocks of a more efficient and effective CE, the Smart CE.

The significance of DTs to transition to a CE however is argued to be more than a technical challenge [64]. First, it requires a clear data and business analytics strategy, the right people to effect a data-driven cultural change, and it demands the organization to appropriately structure their departments to align the analytics capability with their overall business strategy. Kiron and Shockley [36], concur and note that organizations have to develop data-oriented management systems both to make sense of the increasing volumes of data and, more importantly, for transforming the insights into business value and a competitive advantage. Supporting this transformation, by the use of analytics methods, is the data science process[1] [57]. However, there seems to be a gap between the output of these insights and the generation of business value [14,44,66]. As highlighted by extensive research, this is often due to the ineffective integration of data science methods within the organization [2,14,21,38,66].

Extant data science methodologies have not yet been scoped or demonstrated for the context of CE. For instance, the study [20] only presents the need for a process covering data collection, data engineering, algorithm development, and algorithm refinement within the CE without detailing how to operationalize it. Contributions are more commonly seen on topics such as service design [45], or the technical details of analyzing data, e.g., [11]. In this work, we recognize the importance of aligning an organizations analytics development with overall business and CE initiatives. The process discussed in this paper differs from previous contributions in three ways: First, it extends the Cross-Industry Standard Process for Data Mining (CRISP-DM) with an additional phase of *data validation*. Second, it consolidates an organization's analytics knowledge base by integrating the concept of *analytic profiles*. Third, the process is demonstrated for the context of CE by the case study of predictive maintenance (PdM) for an original equipment manufacturer (OEM). We use PdM as an example here as it is a prominent smart circular strategy (facilitating for extending the use-cycle, increasing the utilization and looping/cascading assets), allowing for generalization to other strategies.

The remainder of the work is detailed in following sections. Section 2 gives background on the data science and the concept of CE, thereafter Sect. 3 presents the research approach followed for this work. Section 4 presents the proposed CRISP-DM process model modifications, whilst Sect. 4.1 details the case study of PdM for CE. Finally, the paper is concluded and further work presented in Sect. 5.

---

[1] In this paper, we use the expressions process, method, and methodology interchangeable as a set of activities that interact to produce a result.

2   Background

2.1   Data Science

Data science is a multidisciplinary field encompassing tools, methods, and systems from statistics and data analytics (hereby referred to as analytics) applied to large volumes of data with the purpose of deriving insights for decision-making support [21,38,48,57,66]. As such, data science may include the collection and use of data to: *(i)* better understand the business operation and provide current state evaluation of performance, *(ii)* transform the organization from being reactive to proactive in business decision-making through use of predictive analytics, *(iii)* improve customer service through use of data to build a more coherent knowledge base and understanding of customer needs, and *(iv)* increase the efficiency, enhance the effectiveness and facilitate the implementation of CE concepts at scale (e.g., by optimizing circular infrastructures, business models, and products-service systems) [13,20,44,47,48].

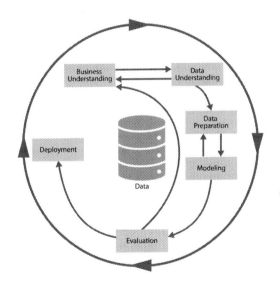

Fig. 1. Phases of the CRISP-DM process model [10]

Research shows that companies embracing data science have experienced noticeable gains in business development (i.e., productivity and profitability) [44,66]. However, the impact of data science is not limited to commercial endeavours alone. For instance, studies show improved sustainability for building energy management [46], predictive capabilities in supply chain management [66], health care services in the medical industry [50] and environmental impact of the manufacturing and process industry [29,34]. However, the effects for the CE is still largely unexplored.

To support the effective integration of data science within organizations, various methodologies have been proposed in the literature (e.g., KDD and SEMMA [22,59]). The most commonly used is the CRISP-DM process model created by IBM, reporting a use level of 43% followed by 28% of companies using their own methodology [53]. CRISP-DM is described in terms of a hierarchical and cyclic process model composed of six phases (see Fig. 1), each consisting of several generic tasks (e.g., clean data), specialized tasks (e.g., cleaning of numerical and categorical values) and process instances (i.e., how these tasks are operationalized through different actions, decisions and results). The methodology is designed to be generic, complete and stable, meaning that it should cover the whole analytics development process for all possible applications, and should be valid for yet unforeseen developments (e.g., new analytics modeling techniques) [10]. Despite the high reported level of use, the methodology appears to not be in active development. We recognize that IBM have later proposed an extension to CRISP-DM called the Analytics Solutions Unified Method (ASUM-DM) [30]. However, ASUM-DM differs only in the operational/deployment aspects of the process and describes the same phases for development. Therefore, given CRISP-DM's continued widespread adoption from practitioners and inherent generic, complete and stable design, we have chosen it as our reference model. As a stand-alone data science process, CRISP-DM has been successful within its bounds [67]. However, suggestions for the following shortcomings have been made [6,55] (the issues are addressed in Sect. 4):

(i) the lack of a good management view to track and communicate knowledge/insights,
(ii) the lack of assessment of analytics implementation feasibility (e.g. by leveraging a maturity assessment or gap analysis),
(iii) despite its widespread adoption, the process is not always understood by the wider business community, hence it is difficult to manage actual business value of the analyses,
(iv) the iterations do not loop back to the business level (prior to analytics modeling) for domain specific knowledge after the first two phases,
(v) and lack of control of added value.

2.2   Circular Economy

CE emerged as an umbrella concept in the 2010s as an approach to achieve sustainability [7], and encompass a range of strategies for narrowing, slowing and closing material and energy flows [8,18] as a means for addressing structural waste. Although the CE concept continues to grow and gain attention, it remains in an early stage of development. Therefore, a detailed definition of CE is still missing in the literature [24,31,35,41]. However, one of the most prominent definitions has been provided by the Ellen MacArthur Foundation [15,17], where CE is defined as a system *"that provides multiple value creation mechanisms, which are decoupled from the consumption of finite resources."*

CE strategies span from operational processes (i.e., restore, reduce, recirculate, and avoid) to more strategic, and business models related, strategies (i.e., reinvent, rethink, and reconfigure). DTs is highlighted by literature as an important enabler of CE strategies [4,9,19,49,51]. However, the adoption by industry is meager, and the research is still in a pre-paradigmatic stage [51]. Using DTs for the CE, Smart CE, promotes a sustainable ecosystem where assets (products, components, materials, and so on) are given virtual, or digital counterparts that allows for the sensing, communication, interaction, and exchange of data. By embedding software and analytics intelligence within or connected to these assets allows for easier manipulation and automation of the assets and of the environment, or system, in which they operate - enabling an increase of the systemic resource efficiency and productivity of the CE. This can for instance be seen with the data-driven maintenance strategy, or smart circular strategy, PdM [1,43,62]. PdM is a pertinent strategy for OEMs seeking to transition to the CE. OEMs offer one of the highest potential for environmental and economic impact of any sector [19]. In the European Union, material savings alone have been estimated to USD 650 billion for a full CE transition [15]. A gross part of this potential can be linked back to PdM by its three CE value drivers [19]:

Extending the life cycle: correct condition-assessment for need of and scheduling of appropriate life cycle extending operations,
Increasing utilization: reduce unplanned downtime and increased equipment effectiveness,
Looping the asset: improve insight and transparency into asset's condition and usage history.

Achieving a Smart CE requires companies to reconfigure and blend their existing value creation mechanisms with new innovative digital strategies. Blending digital strategies with value offerings require companies to become data-driven (i.e., decision-makers base their actions on data and insights generated from analytics, rather than instinct). Supporting this, Janssen et al. [33] argue that the quality of these evidence-based decisions depends largely on the quality of the inputs and the process that transforms these inputs into outputs - essentially the data science process.

3   Research Approach

The proposed process was developed based on an analysis of the *data understanding* and *data preparation* phases of the current CRISP-DM 1.0 step-by-step data mining guide [10] together with insights from company engagement under the CIRCit research project [12]. Given the exploratory nature of the research and the pre-paradigmatic stage of the field [51], case study research was chosen as the methodology for empirical investigation [69]. The case study research methodology is particularly suitable for the initial stage of investigation [31] as it help provide insights with relatively good understanding of the complexity and nature of the phenomenon [65]. Moreover, even a single case study can provide scientific development through a deep understanding of the problem and the capturing of experiences [23].

A research protocol was used in order to ensure reliability and validity of the findings, including case study design, data collection, data analysis, and formalization of results [69]. The company was selected based on a judgmental sampling technique [28]. First, the company should be from the manufacturing industry and have interest in, or experience with, the CE. Second, the company need to have sensory/operation data available for analytics and Smart CE investigation for this paper. To this regard, a Nordic OEM company manufacturing and servicing industrial cranes, who is particular interested in PdM, was contacted and accepted to participate in the project and case study. However, the company identity has been concealed here to protect their business interests.

Following the research protocol, data collection was performed through several semi-structured interviews to first gather general information about the context of the company before the operation data were exchanged and insights specific to analytics and PdM were collected. Following the collection of organizational and operation data, analytics investigation was performed to evaluate the potential PdM and set implementation requirements. Then, the last face of the protocol was conducted, looking for possible procedural improvements of the CRISP-DM model to meet the requirements from analytics.

4   An Enhanced CRISP-DM Process Model

Asset and process management research argue that data should be specifically structured for the intended use within the work flow [27,57]. Analytics research concur and note that insight is more obtainable when the data has been preprocessed for a specific domain of analysis [32,37,42,52,68]. To this effect, and to address the previous highlighted shortcomings, we propose an extended CRISP-DM process model. The proposed process model adds an additional phase called *data validation* (addressing issues (iv) and (v)), and argues for the integration of *analytic profiles* (addressing issues (i) and (iii)) as a core element of the process. Figure 2 illustrates the enhanced CRISP-DM process model developed.

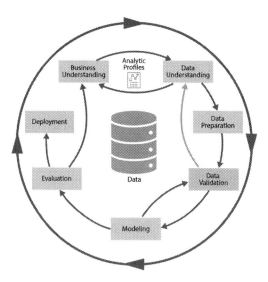

Fig. 2. An enhanced CRISP-DM process model

In CRISP-DM, there is no validation between the *data preparation* phase and the *modeling* phase against the specific business domain [6,48]. Specifically, once the data is prepared for modeling, only the criterion needed to ensure optimal analytics model performance are considered [48,67]. Thus, a complete understanding of whether the data which is prepared is a valid representation of the original problem is not guaranteed. General data preparation methods alter the original data, and there is often loss in information specific to the domain that should be monitored [5,48]. As such, this may result in sub-optimal solutions that miss the mark on the intended capturing of business value [55,63]. Therefore, we argue that data validation should be done by the re-involvement of the business entity, or domain experts, to validate that a proper understanding of the data and business problem have been reached, and include data preparation methods tailored for the given analytic profile. The data validation phase may result in a re-iteration of the data understanding and/or the data preparation phase(s) (indicated by a single arrow back in the diagram).

Analytic profiles are defined as structures that standardize the collection, application and re-use of analytics insights and models for key business entities [60]. As such, an analytic profile is an abstract collection of knowledge, mainly used in the business and data understanding phases, that lists the best practices for a particular analytics use case, or problem. Analytic profiles may have different levels of granularity depending in the use case and the organization's level of experience. However, information on the following elements should be included:

– **Use case description** defining the business goal (e.g., predict the remaining useful life of a crane),
– **Domain specific insights** important for the use case (e.g., knowledge about typical crane failures and causes),
– **Data sources** relevant for the use case (e.g., time-series data of crane operation and service data with failure modes),
– **Key Performance Indicators (KPIs)** or metrics for assessing the analytics implementation performance (e.g., crane failure rate, downtime and maintenance costs),
– **Analytics models and tools** with proven conformity for the given problem (e.g., long short-term memory networks and deep belief networks),
– **Short descriptions of previous implementations** with lessons learned (e.g., deep belief networks for backlash error prediction in machining centers [40]).

As per the CRISP-DM process level breakdown [10], analytic profiles can be regarded as a generic task particularly relevant between the business and data understanding phases (indicated by an analytic profile icon in the diagram). Through such a consolidation of the analytics knowledge base, organizations can more easily learn and reuse their own experience and the experience of others to catalyze the analytics development process. Furthermore, Kiron and Shockley [36] state that organizations should appropriately structure their resources to align their analytics capability with their overall business strategies. Therefore, we argue that analytic profiles should be build for all business strategies, or use cases, relying on insights from analytics.

4.1 Case Study: Predictive Maintenance for an Original Equipment Manufacturer

In this section we give detail to the strategy of PdM for the context of CE together with insights from the case study to validate the adaptations made to CRISP-DM. However, we only detail the structuring of data from the data understanding phase to the data validation phase. As such, we do not cover the whole analytics development process or the full contents of the analytic profile of PdM.

According to EN 13306:2010, predictive maintenance is defined as condition-based maintenance carried out following a forecast from analytics or known characteristics of the features of the degradation of an asset. It contrasts traditional, or non-predictive, maintenance actions that are only based on information of the current condition. Therefore, as PdM integrates multiple DTs (e.g. Internet of Things and Artificial Intelligence) it enables real-time access to detailed information about the assets' location, condition, and availability. This allows for augmenting human decision-making by predicting product health, wear, usage, and energy consumption [56]. This *"sense and respond"* capability is crucial for the CE as it allow for greater transparency of assets' actual condition throughout their life cycle, and enable triggering of appropriate life cycle extending operations for the OEM or service provider [58].

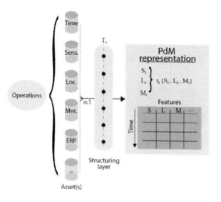

Fig. 3. Example structuring of data for a PdM analytic profile

The main goal of the analytics exploration was to evaluate the current status of analytics development towards the implementation of PdM within the company. For the case of a PdM analytic profile, the occurrence of faults or degradation and their influence during assets' life cycle are considered domain specific knowledge [3,5]. Therefore, the data must contain life cycle observations in which information or knowledge pertaining to the occurrence of faults, degradation, or process change can be inferred [39,52,62]. In general, this can be decomposed to sensor measurements S, location L, and maintenance logs M which describe the condition at various time steps. Figure 3 illustrates such a structuring of an asset's data in which its attributes are collected from multiple data sources, such as time, sensory/monitoring data, location, maintenance logs, and Enterprise Resource Planning (ERP) system data. The observation at an arbitrary time t_i describes the condition of the asset per set of attributes $t_i(S_i, L_i, M_i)$. This structuring ensures the data is useful for the intended analysis, and when combined with involvement from the business entity by domain experts makes up the *data validation* phase. However, the analytics exploration performed by the researchers showed that the current collected features were not sensitive enough to the failure categories required by PdM. This means that the provided data lacked in quality and did not contain the necessary level of detail of failure modes needed in order to predict impending failures. Consequently, the business goal and targeted analyses had to be changed to less advanced analyses. In this case, the goal was transferred to abnormality identification and the development of a method to evaluate the severity degree of the cranes. High severity degree means that the behaviour of the sample crane is different from the majority, thus is more likely to have impending failures. Also, it is not uncommon that important information, or observations, within the data might get 'lost', or disregarded, in the data preparation phase (due to misunderstanding of the business goal). Therefore, we argue that it is crucial for the success of data science initiatives to include a phase of data validation prior to modeling. In summary, the data validation phase ensures that modeling happens on the right data for the right reasons.

Following the data preparation and data validation phases, the standard CRISP-DM phases of *modeling, evaluation*, and *deployment* should be followed. In these phases, analytics methods are applied to, e.g., provide predictions or current state inferences of the manufacturing operation. This may include the accurate identification and prediction of impending failures, degradations, or abnormal behaviour, which can then be used for decision-making support or directive actions for operations management. Finally, when the process of PdM has been structured in such a way that it allows for standardized collection, application and re-use of its analytics insights.

Interviews with the case company revealed that such a structuring of the data and standardized use of analytic profiles had not been systematically integrated within the organization. In the intervention after the analytics exploration the researchers presented the results of their analyses with suggestions for how to appropriately structure their data science process model (e.g., how to link the abnormality identification with typical uses cases and KPIs). Feedback from the company showed the new data science process, especially with the active use of KPIs, could provide a better management view for easier communication of knowledge, tracking of business value and CE impact.

5   Conclusion and Future Work

This paper proposed an enhanced CRISP-DM process model and a case study discussing how to structure the data of the analytic profile of PdM for the context of CE. We addressed the issues (iv) and (v) (lack of iterations looping back to the business level and no control of added value) by introducing an additional phase of data validation. As such, we highlighted the importance of the re-involvement of the business entity, or domain experts, to include domain specific knowledge for structuring and validating the data prior to modeling. Furthermore, we partly addressed the issues (i) and (iii) (lack of good management view and difficulty in managing actual business value of analyses) by introducing analytic profiles as an integrative part of the process model. Motivated by the benefits of the Smart CE, we discussed how data science is fundamental for using DTs to increase the efficiency, enhance the effectiveness and facilitate the implementation of CE strategies. For future work, we aim to extend on the business analytics and CE connection to the data science process. Essentially, detailing the business understanding and data understanding phases with CE related business model scoping and analytics leverage assessment. Lastly, greater detail and empirical evaluation of the suggested CRISP-DM modification should be added.

Acknowledgment. The authors would like to thank the reviewers of this paper. Also, the authors would like to acknowledge that this work was conducted as part of the research project CIRCit (Circular Economy Integration in the Nordic Industry for Enhanced Sustainability and Competitiveness), which is part of the Nordic Green Growth Research and Innovation Programme (grant number: 83144), and funded by NordForsk, Nordic Energy Research, and Nordic Innovation.

References

1. Alaswad, S., Xiang, Y.: A review on condition-based maintenance optimization models for stochastically deteriorating system. Reliab. Eng. Syst. Saf. **157**, 54–63 (2017)
2. Amankwah-Amoah, J., Adomako, S.: Big data analytics and business failures in data-rich environments: an organizing framework. Comput. Ind. **105**, 204–212 (2019)
3. An, D., Choi, J.H., Kim, N.H.: Prognostics 101: a tutorial for particle filter-based prognostics algorithm using Matlab. Reliab. Eng. Syst. Saf. **115**, 161–169 (2013)
4. Antikainen, M., Uusitalo, T., Kivikytö-Reponen, P.: Digitalisation as an enabler of circular economy. Proc. CIRP **73**, 45–49 (2018)
5. Aremu, O.O., Salvador Palau, A., Hyland-Wood, D., Parlikad, A.K., McAree, P.R.: Structuring data for intelligent predictive maintenance in asset management. In: 16th IFAC Symposium on Information Control Problems in Manufacturing (2018)
6. Bahrepour, M.: The forgotten step in CRISP-DM and ASUM-DM methodologies. https://sharing.luminis.eu/blog/the-forgotten-step-in-crisp-dm-and-asum-dm-methodologies/. Accessed 08 Mar 2019
7. Blomsma, F., Brennan, G.: The emergence of circular economy: a new framing around prolonging resource productivity. J. Ind. Ecol. **21**(3), 603–614 (2017)

8. Bocken, N.M., Short, S.: Towards a sufficiency-driven business model: experiences and opportunities. Environ. Innov. Soc. Transitions **18**, 41–61 (2016)
9. Bressanelli, G., Adrodegari, F., Perona, M., Saccani, N.: The role of digital technologies to overcome circular economy challenges in PSS business models: an exploratory case study. Proc. CIRP **73**, 216–221 (2018)
10. Chapman, P., Clinton, J., Kerber, R., Khabaza, H., Reinartz, T., Shearer, C., Wirth, R.: CRISP-DM 1.0 Step-by-step data mining guide. Technical report (2000)
11. Cielen, D., Meysman, A., Ali, M.: Introducing data science: big data, machine learning, and more, using Python tools. Manning Publications Co. (2016)
12. CIRCit: Circit project page (2019). http://circitnord.com/
13. Dhar, V.: Data science and prediction. NYU Working Paper No. 2451/31635 (2012)
14. Domino Data Lab: Key factors on the journey to become model-driven - a survey report (2018)
15. MacArthur, E.: Towards a Circular Economy and Business Rationale for an Accelerated Transition. Ellen MacArthur Foundation, Cowes, UK (2013)
16. Ellen MacArthur Foundation: Delivering the circular economy: a toolkit for policymakers (2015)
17. MacArthur, E.: Growth within: a circular economy vision for a competitive Europe. Ellen MacArthur Foundation, Cowes, UK (2015)
18. Ellen MacArthur Foundation: Towards a circular economy: business rationale for an accelerated transition (2015). Accessed 25 Oct 2016
19. MacArthur, E.: Intelligent assets. unlocking the circular economy potential. Ellen MacArthur Foundation, Cowes, UK (2016)
20. MacArthur E.: Artificial intelligence and the circular economy. Ellen MacArthur Foundation, Cowes, UK (2019)
21. Elshawi, R., Sakr, S., Talia, D., Trunfio, P.: Big data systems meet machine learning challenges: towards big data science as a service. Big data research (2018)
22. Fayyad, U., Piatetsky-Shapiro, G., Smyth, P.: From data mining to knowledge discovery in databases. AI Mag. **17**(3), 37 (1996)
23. Flyvbjerg, B., Budzier, A.: Why your it project may be riskier than you think (2011)
24. Geng, Y., Doberstein, B.: Developing the circular economy in China: challenges and opportunities for achieving 'leapfrog development'. Int. J. Sustain. Develop. World Ecol. **15**(3), 231–239 (2008)
25. Ghisellini, P., Cialani, C., Ulgiati, S.: A review on circular economy: the expected transition to a balanced interplay of environmental and economic systems. J. Clean. Prod. **114**, 11–32 (2016)
26. Haas, W., Krausmann, F., Wiedenhofer, D., Heinz, M.: How circular is the global economy: an assessment of material flows, waste production, and recycling in the European Union and the world in 2005. J. Ind. Ecol. **19**(5), 765–777 (2015)
27. Haddar, N., Tmar, M., Gargouri, F.: A framework for data-driven workflow management: modeling, verification and execution. In: Decker, H., Lhotská, L., Link, S., Basl, J., Tjoa, A.M. (eds.) DEXA 2013. LNCS, vol. 8055, pp. 239–253. Springer, Heidelberg (2013). https://doi.org/10.1007/978-3-642-40285-2_21
28. Henry, G.T.: Practical Sampling, vol. 21. Sage (1990)
29. Ho, T.C., Mat, S.C.K.M.Z., San, L.H., et al.: A prediction model for CO_2 emission from manufacturing industry and construction in Malaysia. In: 2015 International Conference on Space Science and Communication (IconSpace). pp. 469–472. IEEE (2015)
30. IBM: Analytics solutions unified method - implementations with agile principles (2016). ftp://ftp.software.ibm.com/software/data/sw-library/services/ASUM.pdf

31. Jabbour, C.J.C., de Sousa Jabbour, A.B.L., Sarkis, J., Godinho Filho, M.: Unlocking the circular economy through new business models based on large-scale data: an integrative framework and research agenda. Technol. Forecast. Soc. Change **144** 546–552 (2017)

32. James, G., Witten, D., Hastie, T., Tibshirani, R.: An Introduction to Statistical Learning, vol. 112. Springer, New York (2013). https://doi.org/10.1007/978-1-4614-7138-7

33. Janssen, M., van der Voort, H., Wahyudi, A.: Factors influencing big data decision-making quality. J. Bus. Res. **70**, 338–345 (2017)

34. Kameswari, U.S., Babu, I.R.: Sensor data analysis and anomaly detection using predictive analytics for process industries. In: 2015 IEEE Workshop on Computational Intelligence: Theories, Applications and Future Directions (WCI), pp. 1–8. IEEE (2015)

35. Kirchherr, J., Reike, D., Hekkert, M.: Conceptualizing the circular economy: an analysis of 114 definitions. Resour. Conserv. Recycl. **127**, 221–232 (2017)

36. Kiron, D., Shockley, R.: Creating business value with analytics. MIT Sloan Manage. Rev. **53**(1), 57 (2011)

37. Kun, W., Tong, L., Xiaodan, X.: Application of big data technology in scientific research data management of military enterprises. Proc. Comput. Sci. **147**, 556–561 (2019)

38. Larson, D., Chang, V.: A review and future direction of agile, business intelligence, analytics and data science. Int. J. Inf. Manag. **36**(5), 700–710 (2016)

39. Lei, Y., Li, N., Guo, L., Li, N., Yan, T., Lin, J.: Machinery health prognostics: a systematic review from data acquisition to RUL prediction. Mech. Syst. Signal Process. **104**, 799–834 (2018)

40. Li, Z., Wang, Y., Wang, K.: A data-driven method based on deep belief networks for backlash error prediction in machining centers. J. Intell. Manuf. 1–13 (2017). https://doi.org/10.1007/s10845-017-1380-9

41. Lieder, M., Rashid, A.: Towards circular economy implementation: a comprehensive review in context of manufacturing industry. J. Clean. Prod. **115**, 36–51 (2016)

42. Lin, J., Keogh, E., Wei, L., Lonardi, S.: Experiencing sax: a novel symbolic representation of time series. Data Min. Knowl. Disc. **15**(2), 107–144 (2007)

43. Liu, B., Liang, Z., Parlikad, A.K., Xie, M., Kuo, W.: Condition-based maintenance for systems with aging and cumulative damage based on proportional hazards model. Reliab. Eng. Syst. Saf. **168**, 200–209 (2017)

44. McAfee, A., Brynjolfsson, E., Davenport, T.H., Patil, D., Barton, D.: Big data: the management revolution. Harvard Bus. Rev. **90**(10), 60–68 (2012)

45. Meierhofer, J., Meier, K.: From data science to value creation. In: Za, S., Drăgoicea, M., Cavallari, M. (eds.) IESS 2017. LNBIP, vol. 279, pp. 173–181. Springer, Cham (2017). https://doi.org/10.1007/978-3-319-56925-3_14

46. Molina-Solana, M., Ros, M., Ruiz, M.D., Gómez-Romero, J., Martín-Bautista, M.J.: Data science for building energy management: a review. Renew. Sustain. Energy Rev. **70**, 598–609 (2017)

47. Nath, P., Nachiappan, S., Ramanathan, R.: The impact of marketing capability, operations capability and diversification strategy on performance: a resource-based view. Ind. Mark. Manag. **39**(2), 317–329 (2010)

48. Newman, R., Chang, V., Walters, R.J., Wills, G.B.: Model and experimental development for business data science. Int. J. Inf. Manag. **36**(4), 607–617 (2016)

49. Nobre, G.C., Tavares, E.: Scientific literature analysis on big data and internet of things applications on circular economy: a bibliometric study. Scientometrics **111**(1), 463–492 (2017)

50. Ottenbacher, K.J., Graham, J.E., Fisher, S.R.: Data science in physical medicine and rehabilitation: opportunities and challenges. Phys. Med. Rehabil. Clin. N. Am. **30**(2), 459–471 (2019)
51. Pagoropoulos, A., Pigosso, D.C., McAloone, T.C.: The emergent role of digital technologies in the circular economy: a review. Proc. CIRP **64**, 19–24 (2017)
52. Peng, Y., Dong, M., Zuo, M.J.: Current status of machine prognostics in condition-based maintenance: a review. Int. J. Adv. Manuf. Technol. **50**(1–4), 297–313 (2010)
53. Piatetsky, G.: CRISP-DM, still the top methodology for analytics, data mining, or data science projects. In: KDD News (2014)
54. Planing, P.: Business model in novation in a circular economy reasons for non-acceptance of circular business models. Open J. Bus. Model Innov. **1**, 11 (2015)
55. Ponsard, C., Touzani, M., Majchrowski, A.: Combining process guidance and industrial feedback for successfully deploying big data projects. Open J. Big Data (OJBD) **3**(1), 26–41 (2017)
56. Porter, M.E., Heppelmann, J.E.: How smart, connected products are transforming competition. Harvard Bus. Rev. **92**(11), 64–88 (2014)
57. Provost, F., Fawcett, T.: Data Science for Business: What You Need to Know about Data Mining and Data-Analytic Thinking. O'Reilly Media Inc, Newton (2013)
58. Romero, D., Noran, O.: Towards green sensing virtual enterprises: interconnected sensing enterprises, intelligent assets and smart products in the cyber-physical circular economy. IFAC-PapersOnLine **50**(1), 11719–11724 (2017)
59. SAS: Semma. https://www.sas.com/en_gb/software/analytics-overview.html. Accessed 10 Apr 2019
60. Schmarzo, B.: Big Data MBA: Driving Business Strategies with Data Science. Wiley, Hoboken (2015)
61. Sousa-Zomer, T.T., Magalhães, L., Zancul, E., Cauchick-Miguel, P.A.: Exploring the challenges for circular business implementation in manufacturing companies: an empirical investigation of a pay-per-use service provider. Resour. Conserv. Recycl. **135**, 3–13 (2018)
62. Susto, G.A., Schirru, A., Pampuri, S., McLoone, S., Beghi, A.: Machine learning for predictive maintenance: a multiple classifier approach. IEEE Trans. Ind. Inf. **11**(3), 812–820 (2015)
63. Viaene, S.: Data scientists aren't domain experts. IT Prof. **15**(6), 12–17 (2013)
64. Vidgen, R., Shaw, S., Grant, D.B.: Management challenges in creating value from business analytics. Eur. J. Oper. Res. **261**(2), 626–639 (2017)
65. Voss, C.: Case research in operations management. In: Researching operations management, pp. 176–209. Routledge (2010)
66. Waller, M.A., Fawcett, S.E.: Data science, predictive analytics, and big data: a revolution that will transform supply chain design and management. J. Bus. Logistics **34**(2), 77–84 (2013)
67. Wirth, R., Hipp, J.: CRISP-DM: towards a standard process model for data mining. In: Proceedings of the 4th International Conference on the Practical Applications of Knowledge Discovery and Data Mining, pp. 29–39. Citeseer (2000)
68. Wood, D., Zaidman, M., Ruth, L., Hausenblas, M.: Linked Data. Manning Publications Co. (2014)
69. Yin, R.K.: Applied social research methods series case study research: design and methods (1984)

The Praxis of HR Analytics

Niels Netten[(⊠)], Sunil Choenni, and Mortaza S. Bargh

Creating 010, Rotterdam University of Applied Sciences,
3011WN Rotterdam, The Netherlands
{c.p.m.netten, r.choenni, m.shoae.bargh}@hr.nl

Abstract. The world changes and new digital solutions arise in a fast pace, requiring organizations to adapt fast to these changes and innovations. Consequently, the required skills and knowledge of employees to effectively contribute to the core business of an organization, are also subject to changes. Currently, Human Resource (HR) professionals cannot acquire a sufficient insight into organizations' human capital in order to align it with the current and future core processes of the organization. To acquire the necessary insights and knowledge, organizations see great potential in harnessing the wealth of data about their human capital and core processes. Hence, organizations have a great interest in HR Analytics, which is a rising field on the intersection of HR and big data. Despite the interest, there are only few efforts that focus on HR Analytics and its implementations. In this paper, we analyze the characteristics of the current HR function, present a framework that systematically exploits HR data in order to improve the HR function, and describe our implementation of parts of the presented framework. As such, our framework and its implementations can be regarded as a first step towards conducting HR Analytics in practice.

Keywords: HR Analytics · Framework · Big data

1 Introduction

Organizations have invested heavily in collecting and analyzing various data sets, such as those pertaining to their customers and the usage of their resources. The knowledge generated by these investments has resulted in different variants and architectures for Customer Relationship Management (CRM) systems and Enterprise Resource Planning (ERP) systems. The wealth of the data that organizations have today about their core processes and their human capital has triggered HR professionals to exploit this data for improving the HR function. This is partly due to the fact that organizations are subject to a fast-changing reality in which new digital solutions drive organizations to adapt fast to these changes. As a consequence, the required competencies of employees that are needed for the business performance of organizations are also subject to changes. Currently, HR professionals experience that, on the one hand, the development of the human capital and, on the other hand, the development of the core processes in organizations, are diverging. This induces a gap between the competencies of an organization's employees and what (skillset) is needed to adequately implement the core processes of the organization. Consequently, HR professionals are increasingly

© IFIP International Federation for Information Processing 2019
Published by Springer Nature Switzerland AG 2019
I. O. Pappas et al. (Eds.): I3E 2019, LNCS 11701, pp. 190–202, 2019.
https://doi.org/10.1007/978-3-030-29374-1_16

unable to adequately match the wishes and abilities of employees to the requirements of the core processes of organizations.

Concepts and techniques from the field of big data/data analytics may provide the desired insights in the gap and, more importantly, may inform organizations about how to bridge the gap. Realizing such applications, however, entails addressing a number of technical issues and challenges such as establishing efficient integration, storage and retrieval of large data volumes, as well as processing different types of data almost in real-time. It is also relevant to note that often the usage of big data does not fully coincide with the purpose for which the original data was collected. This entails a number of so-called soft challenges for using big data in (HR) practice. Relying on data gathered from various sources and for diverse purposes can result in, for example, violations of fundamental human rights, such as privacy and autonomy [1–3].

This paper aims at utilizing big data for improving the HR function in organizations. Specifically, our research question can be formulated as: *How can big data be utilized to bridge the gap between the skills and knowledge that employees of an organization have and the skills and knowledge that are needed within the organization in order to run the organization's core processes effectively?* This research question, which is originally posed by the HR professionals from the practice, is an emerging topic in the HR field. Our study can be classified on the intersection of HR and big data, referred to as HR Analytics. As pointed out in [4], the realization of HR Analytics is still in its childhood, despite many efforts made so far. We analyze the characteristics of HR Analytics and, on the basis of this analysis, present a framework for realizing HR Analytics. Two key findings of our analyses are: (a) typical HR needs must be considerably elaborated further in detail before being translated into required data analytics tasks such as classification, associations and profiling and (b) HR data is in practice scattered over various systems and a significant amount of effort is needed to integrate the corresponding data sets. The latter finding is in line with [5].

Although our framework consists of four main steps, the implementation part of this paper is primarily devoted to the first two steps. The goal of these steps is to map broad HR needs/concepts into a set of feasible data analytics tasks. For this purpose we present a number of tools in achieving this mapping and illustrate how these tools have been applied to two real life-cases.

We envision that in the near future HR analytics will be an integral part of the HR function. As such, HR analytics is going to restructure the HR function by providing HR professionals with the values of predefined and relevant indicators. These values can help HR professionals to take appropriate decisions for bridging the aforementioned gap. By means of the two real-life cases, we illustrate how the relevant indicators can be measured in practice.

The remainder of this paper is organized as follows. Section 2 reviews the contemporary HR function and reports our findings. Based on these findings, we propose in Sect. 3 a comprehensive framework for HR Analytics and elaborate on the implementations of the first two steps of the framework. Section 4 concludes the paper.

2   HR Analytics

Although there is an overwhelming number of papers related to HR Analytics, the term HR Analytics is relatively new [4]. In this section, we describe the state of the art of HR Analytics, discuss how HR Analytics restructures the HR function, and present some examples to illustrate the added value of HR Analytics. Finally, we describe a number of existing challenges involving HR data.

2.1   State of the Art

To improve their business functions, organizations take full advantage of the large amount of data that is available within or outside their organizations. However, this data exploitation is not the case for HR. So far, the HR field has focused mainly on descriptive analytics [6], a bit on predictive analytics [7], and very little on prescriptive analytics [8]. Yet, there is no widely accepted definition of HR Analytics. In [4], HR Analytics is regarded as a practice that is enabled by IT, focusing on the analysis and visualization of data, while [9] defines HR Analytics as a set of tools and technologies that provides a wide range of capabilities, ranging from simple reporting to predictive modelling.

In [10], a distinction is made between HR Analytics and HR Metrics. HR Metrics are the measures of key HR management outcomes. These measures are classified as efficiency, effectiveness or impact. In [10] is subsequently argued that HR Analytics is not about the measures, but rather represents the statistical techniques and experimental approaches that can be used to show the impact of HR activities. Despite this distinction between HR Metrics and HR Analytics in [10], definitional ambiguity still remains. In contrast to [10], we consider HR Metrics as a part of HR Analytics.

Regardless of the fact that there is a growing interest in and an abundance amount of literature about HR Analytics, the research and development on how to exploit relevant data to improve the HR function are still in its infancy. A search on Google Scholar on the terms "HR Analytics", for example, resulted in more than 80.000 hits. Nevertheless, very little and limited scientific evidence is found on the use and adoption of HR Analytics as mentioned in [4]. In [4] 60 papers were reviewed and only 14 of them were classified as scientific papers. There are a number of reasons why HR Analytics has not met the expectations so far. The main reason, as identified in [11], is that HR professionals do not understand big data analytics and big data analytics teams do not understand HR. In [4] an approach is proposed in which the central question that should be asked is: How HR data can be used to create, capture, leverage and protect value? Developing advanced concepts and techniques of big data may be helpful in answering this question. In our view, these concepts and techniques should be tailored to the HR domain in order to contribute to the solution of HR problems [12].

Given the current development stage of HR Analytics, we are in line with [4] about the need for doing more scientific research.

2.2   Restructuring the HR Function

A HR department's goal is to help the organization to deliver its strategy and objectives by effectively managing its human capital. To realize this goal, the HR function covers several areas, ranging from recruitment, learning and development to vitality.

Fast-changing circumstances in society create new questions that require up to date answers. Typical questions that must be addressed in contemporary HR departments are: What does our staff look like within 10 years if we do nothing? What interventions are needed to bridge the gap between the knowledge and skills of our employees and the competencies that are required in the future? Are we diverse enough? To what extent does our policy contribute to the sustainable employability of our employees? Up to now, HR professionals try to answer these questions by formulation a set of hypotheses and collecting the data needed to accept or reject these hypotheses. We note that a hypothesis does not necessarily answer a question but provides some insights that may help to find an answer. As it has been discussed in the literature, this traditional statistical approach suffers from some flaws [13]. For example, the hypotheses should be devised beforehand, which may be a time-consuming process as it requires advanced and in-depth knowledge of the field. Searching for interesting hypotheses can be accomplished by using contemporary (big) data analytics/data mining algorithms applied to all relevant data sets available.

An emerging area that is becoming part of the HR function is the so-called information provisioning [14]. In this area, the collection and analysis of employee data and the provision of the results to the organization are the main tasks. We argue that big data can strengthen the function of information provisioning.

There are many descriptions and definitions of big data in circulation, varying from formal to informal definitions. A common description of big data is based on the well-known 3 V's [15]. A formal definition of big data, on the other hand, considers it as inducing a model based on world observations/data stored in information systems. In this formal definition, we can distinguish three building blocks, namely: data from different systems, analysis techniques based on inductive reasoning, and models derived from big data [12]. To facilitate the design and implementation of these building blocks, a wide range of tools, concepts and algorithms are developed. Reliable employee data which is necessary to underpin the information provisioning are organized in the first building block. In the second building block, existing analytics algorithms are organized that must be tailored to extract those models that can answer the HR questions and needs. In the last building block, those tools are organized that can help interpreting the obtained models when answering the HR questions. Naturally, HR professionals should be able to interact with the latter building block.

2.3   Illustrative Examples

In large organizations, such as ministries or municipalities, a lot of money is invested in employees' professional development. However, employees often follow the same course or training in these organizations, without their job descriptions, abilities and personal wishes being taken into account. HR professionals, who currently cannot adequately tailor the wishes and abilities of individual employees to the needs of the organization, can use HR analytics to generate the profiles of employees. The resulting employee profile can be used by HR professionals to advise the employee about a suitable training to follow or to prepare the employee for a better fitting job.

Next, suppose the HR department of the Dutch Ministry of Justice and Security observing that crime in society becomes more technology-driven. This HR department, subsequently, experiences a skill gap in the organization because its staff are unable to cope with the criminal implications of new technologies. The organization, consequently, may require having employees with a law background in combination with cyber security skills. The questions that may arise are: how can the employer improve the skillset of its workforce? Which employees can best be chosen to follow an expensive in-depth training about new technologies? With HR Analytics the HR professional could obtain some indications that, for example, those employees with a background in financial law tend to adopt ICT skills more easily. The HR department, therefore, can focus on retraining these employees. This informed policy should help closing the observed gap significantly.

Another example is concerned with the change of the retirement pattern in the Dutch public sector, observing that more and more employees delay their retirement and change their contracts to part-time work. Note that in the Netherlands, retiring public sector employees have the option of postponing their retirement up to 5 years. After expiring these optional extra years, employees' retirement is obligatory. This retirement policy is based on the fact that, often, the retiring people are in key roles, hold key relationships, and are critical for ensuring the continuity of an organization's performance. However, it is also challenging to keep a potential successor waiting if the incumbent chooses not to retire at the time expected. Currently HR professionals use two indicators of age to estimate the collective retirement behaviors of their employees. To this end, HR Analytics can improve this estimation of the collective retirement behaviors by taking into account many additional indicators, such as recent changes in role, pay level, rates of the changes in pay, and incentive eligibility. This improved estimation allows HR professionals to be more effective in managing the retirement cycle and ensures that key roles have a successor ready just in time.

2.4   HR Data

Several processes may be distinguished in the HR function. For each of these processes, there are a number of data items that are collected in several HR Information Systems (HRIS). Examples of the collected HR data items are competence assessment, date of birth, disciplinary date and email traffic between employees. Often, these data items are scattered among different legacy HRIS. As has been pointed out by several scholars, legacy data sets are hard to integrate since they are noisy and incomplete; and their semantics are uncertain, see [16] for an overview. In addition, the silo mentality in organizations prevents HR-related data being combined [11].

Based on a prescriptive framework, Pape [5] prioritizes the data items that are important for HR analytics. Pape has selected a total of 298 descriptive and predictive HR analyses from the academic and professional literature (202); and interviewed HR analysts (96). From these analyses, Pape derives 126 data items and identifies top 30 data items influential in the identified HR processes. For identifying these top 30 data items, Pape uses a framework based on interviewing 24 HR professionals from 15 organizations. Six top data items in the derived top 30 list are location, role, function, manager ID, performance score and total other benefits. In [5] a further argument is made that collecting those data items is challenging for many HR departments.

For HR Analytics, the quality, accessibility and availability of data are crucial. As argued in [4, 5], an enormous effort is required to obtain the data that meets these aspects. Therefore, despite having many interesting HR questions (as raised in the previous sections) with a potential solution based on HR Analytics, it makes sense to choose a data set that is feasible to integrate and to exploit this data set to gain some of the insights needed by HR professionals. Thus, in a sense, HR Analytics is constrained by the efforts needed to build such an integrated data set.

2.5 Problem Statement

So far we have seen that there is a need by HR professionals to gain insight in tackling the main question of this contribution, namely: How to utilize big data to bridge the gap between the current and the desired skills and knowledge of employees within an organization? Actually, this is a very broad question as it includes many of the questions asked today by contemporary HR departments (see Sects. 2.2 and 2.3).

There are several issues in answering these questions raised. Firstly, the HR questions are open for various interpretations. Secondly, the HR questions are insufficiently elaborated upon for being translated to a set of data analytics solutions (such as association, clustering, profiling, or classification problems) [17]. Thirdly, it is unclear beforehand which efforts will be required to collect and integrate the proper data. Therefore, a systematic and specific approach is required to deal with such HR questions. In the next section, we present the main building blocks of such a systematic approach.

3   A Framework for HR Analytics

In this section we present a framework to realize HR Analytics in practice, as shown in Fig. 1. As concluded in [11], unfortunately HR professionals and big data analytics professionals do not understand each other well. This lack of understanding, as a consequence, may cause HR Analytics applications to fail and result in disappointments. Therefore, an essential part of our framework is to create a common understanding between these professionals. By means of the two real-life cases, we illustrate how to identify broad HR needs and make them into a set of feasible data analytics tasks and how the values of relevant indicators may be collected in practice. Although our framework consists of four steps, this paper primarily focuses on the implementation aspects of the first two steps of the framework. Due to page limitation, we excluded any implementations of the latter two steps. Issues related to these steps are common over many domains. For more discussion about this see, e.g., [16].

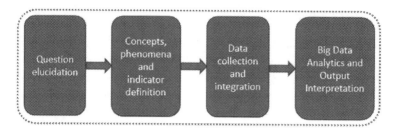

Fig. 1. Framework for HR-Analytics.

In the following subsections, we discuss each of the steps of the framework. In Sect. 3.1, we discuss how we use a multi-disciplinary approach [18] based on the method of design thinking to create consensus about the insights that are needed to contribute to the solution of our main question. In Sect. 3.2, we describe a route for mapping a broad HR notion/concept to concrete measurable indicators. Section 3.3 sketches the data collection and integration measures needed to acquire a clean and integrated data set for further analysis. Finally, Sect. 3.4 sketches the big data techniques to analyze the integrated data set and to interpret the analysis outcomes, i.e., the models.

3.1 Question Elucidation

In HR Analytics situations may arise where there is no consensus on what the main HR need (or problem) is, nor a common understanding of how (partial) problems should be tackled. A way to address these problems is to create either more consensus between the viewpoints of the stakeholders about the problem at hand and/or to create a shared understanding and acceptance of the cause-effect relations. Design Thinking [19] can contribute to resolving these uncertainties. It is rooted in product and service design, has been successfully applied to cases where people and organizations interact with technological processes. Particularly, in those cases where user needs are insufficiently documented and are hidden in tacit knowledge among poorly communicating stakeholders, Design Thinking is proven to be fruitful [20].

Design Thinking is a multi-disciplinary and participatory approach that encourages successive meetings in which various stakeholders (e.g., system developers and end-users) discuss their viewpoints and insights to answer the issue at hand. These meetings continue until a consensus is reached, i.e., a fitting solution arises from the viewpoints of the stakeholders involved [21].

As case studies, we have involved the HR professionals from the HR department of the Dutch Ministry of Justice and Security (case 1) and the HR department of the municipality of Rotterdam (case 2). By means of a number of lectures on HR Analytics provided by us to HR professionals, workshops and bilateral discussions between professionals of data analytics and HR, we elaborated our data analytics perspective in regard to the main research question of Sect. 2.5. In both cases the participants agreed that gaining insights in the development of the HR concepts of sustainable employability, diversity and job performance are important for the envisioned developments of the (core) processes of these organizations. Although these processes can be different for each HR department, one can distinguish a number of sub-processes that have similarities, for example, sub-processes that are needed for job applications.

Once an agreement about the relevant HR concepts is reached, it is worthwhile to work on these concepts and how to operationalize them based on the available and accessible data. In the next section, we describe and illustrate how the concepts of sustainable employability, diversity and job performance have been made operational.

3.2   Concepts, Phenomena and Indicator Definition

The second step of the framework involves the operationalization of the identified HR concepts. Based on a desktop research, some representative indicators that cover these concepts are searched for. In addition, the usefulness of these indicators must be determined by the HR professionals and big data analytics professionals involved. The first group indicates whether the indicator is representative enough and the latter group determines the quality of the attributes. For operationalization purposes, metrics for these representative indicators will be determined. The values of the indicators must be measured from the collected data.

Suppose, for diversity we have two indicators age and ethnicity. The age indicator can be expressed in years and measured reliably. Subsequently, a distribution function of the number of people in different age classes can be calculated. The ethnicity indicator is more difficult to measure because ethnicity must first be defined. Suppose we limit ourselves to the distinction between immigrants and non-immigrants, and we use a definition as proposed by Statistics Netherlands (abbreviated as CBS in Dutch). According to the definition of CBS, an immigrant is a person one of whose parents was not born in the Netherlands. The values for the indicator ethnicity are difficult to measure because organizations do not register the origin of their employees' parents.

The operationalization step of the sustainable employability concept was picked up in case 1 by two student groups of the Rotterdam University of Applied Sciences. The students got an assignment to develop a tool that gives HR professionals an insight into sustainable employability of employees, due to its importance for the HR department of the Dutch Ministry of Justice and Security. Based on desktop research, the students quickly discovered that sustainable employability is a broad notion. HR organizations tend to have different views about which topics are relevant to sustainable employability. Literature showed that the sustainable employability concept encompasses several HR topics such as (1) engagement and vitality, (2) work organization, (3) health, and (4) learning and development.

To limit the amount of work needed to define all indicators of these 4 HR topics of sustainable employability in the time given for the project, the students, in consultation with the HR professionals of the ministry, chose to further operationalize the topic of learning and development. This topic focuses on employees being more productive if they are working at the right level and if they are experiencing appropriate challenges. Involved and interested employees keep a close eye on developments in their field, gain new knowledge, and follow additional training courses. Involved employers offer room for this, because it pays off to invest in sustainable employability. Relevant indicators can show how many employees are at the right level and which employees should further develop themselves so that the organization can operate in a most optimal way.

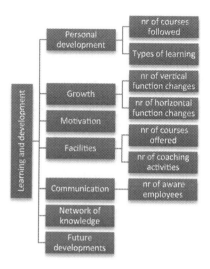

Fig. 2. From learning and development topic to measurable indicators

Figure 2 shows the operationalization of the learning and development concept. Some of the indicators in Fig. 2 measure organizational aspects (e.g., the amount of offered facilities) and others measure personnel aspects (e.g. motivation and personal development). Due to space limits, Fig. 2 shows only some of the values to be measured for the indicators. Next, the data collection and integration steps are needed to determine which data is available and useful per indicator.

3.3 Data Collection and Integration

The data about employees', for example, function, salary scale, performance appraisals, non-attendances, conducted training courses, is currently distributed among different legacy systems (i.e. database management systems). In the HR domain there exist many different Human Resource Information Systems (HRIS) for different HR purposes. The data varies from structured data, like salary information, to unstructured data, like paragraphs of natural language text about the performance appraisals of employees. Bringing this data together is a necessary step to measure the value of the indicators. To this end, employee data needs to be extracted from these legacy systems. Before the data is used as input for big data analytics, it is subjected to Ethical Impact Assessment (EIA) and Data Privacy Impact Assessment (DPIA) to determine, particularly, whether (or how) the secondary use of data is ethical and legal. Hereby one can revise the predefined indicators or to further anonymize the data.

Figure 3 depicts a schematic overview of the process for collecting and integrating data from multiple HR sources. The HR department of the Dutch Ministry of Justice &

Security uses multiple different HRISs. For example, P-direkt is the HR service provider for the Dutch national government, Leonardo is the ERP system for financial-logistics information, Coach Pool is an employee coaching system, Goodhabitz registers followed online training courses, Learning Management System (LMS) gives an insight into the skills/talents of employees, and MO contains data about employee surveys.

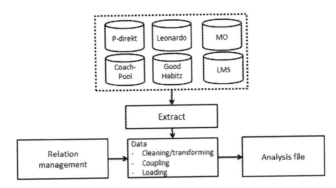

Fig. 3. Schematics of an approach to integrate data from different sources

The relation management module in Fig. 3 is used to clean (i.e., to remove those records with known wrong registrations from) the source files and combine the data (i.e., relate all available data to a unique event or class of employees). For example, to integrate the subjective MO survey data with the data from LMS (e.g., to find out whether satisfied employees have developed their talents and skills), it is required to exploit common attributes of employees. The module can also be used to deal with missing data. If the value of an attribute is (temporarily) unavailable, for example due to technological problems, it may be replaced with the value of a similar attribute that is measured at a slightly earlier or later point in time, while it, more or less, covers the same notion. This replacement is referred to as imputation.

To obtain the data set for analysis, it is usually required to have a unique identifying key that is present in all database systems. If such a key is not available or not desired because of, for example, privacy-regulations, then combining the datasets can be performed using a set of common attributes [1]. Based on this key or the attribute set, the data items of an employee from different sources are combined. The first step of the data integration process is to extract the same conceptual data from different database systems. In general, this is the so-called "micro data" on the person level.

3.4 Big Data Analytics and Output Interpretation

Over the years a wide range of techniques has been developed, resulting in many algorithms to analyze data. These algorithms are focused on performing a task such as classifying, associating, clustering and searching. For a certain task, various variants of techniques are usually available. For example, for a classification task, you may apply discriminant analysis, decision trees, regression, support vector machines or neural networks. Depending on the task and the given preconditions, an algorithm will be chosen and, if necessary, tailored. If, for example, it is very clear what characteristics should be classified, then discriminant analysis can be applied. If it is not clear which attributes need to be classified and there is a lot of data available, a neural network can be used to learn the classification task and generate a classification model. The challenge of using big data is to determine which tasks need to be performed in order to achieve meaningful results. Next, choosing an algorithm to perform the task is also a challenge. In the literature there are best practices and guidelines [12].

The interpretation of the results of big data is a challenging task. A reason for this is that it concerns statistical truths that apply to groups (e.g., a set of persons) and the fact that they are not always applicable to individuals. A statistical truth implies a distribution function of possible outcomes that only occurs with a very large group of observations (almost with an infinitive size). In addition, the dataset used contains only a limited number of variables that can partially describe the individual variation. Based on this, no conclusion can be drawn or no prediction can be made about individual cases. Such incorrect interpretations can lead to unjust decisions about individuals. In practice, however, this is often done to make (policy) decisions. In the end, each specific application domain has its own challenges in interpreting big data results. In HR data, which usually concerns personal data, privacy and security issues play an important role [. Guidelines and strategies for applying big data results in practice, while taking into account the mentioned challenges, are in their infancy.

4 Conclusion

Currently HR professionals face challenges when searching for an adequate answer to the question of how to match the wishes and abilities of individual employees to the requirements of the organization. To acquire the necessary insights and knowledge that can help HR professionals to minimize the gap or to anticipate an even greater gap, organizations see a great potential in harnessing the wealth of the data about their human capital and core processes. We argued that big data may provide new insights based on that data, referred to as HR Analytics in this contribution.

In this paper we analyzed the specific characteristics of HR Analytics and, on the basis of this analysis, presented a framework to realize HR Analytics in practice. Two key findings of our analyses are: (a) typical HR needs should be considerably further elaborated upon before being translated into data analytics tasks such as classification, associations and profiling and (b) HR data is scattered across various systems in practice and a significant amount of effort is needed to integrate the corresponding data.

This paper is primarily devoted to the first two steps in the presented framework. The goal of these steps is to operationalize broad HR needs into a set of feasible data analytics tasks. We presented a number of tools in achieving this goal and illustrated how these tools have been applied in practice. We envision that HR analytics will be an integral part of the HR function. As such, HR Analytics will restructure the HR function by informing HR professionals via relevant indicators. These indicators can help HR professionals to make appropriate decisions for bridging the mentioned gap.

References

1. Bargh, M., Choenni. R.: On preserving privacy whilst integrating data in connected information systems. In: 1st International Conference on Cloud Security Management, Seattle, USA (2013)
2. Kalidien, S., Choenni S., Meijer. R.: Crime statistics online: potentials and challenges. In Proceedings of the 11th Annual International Digital Government Research Conference on Public Administration (dg.o), pp. 131–137 (2010)
3. Prins, J.E., Broeders, D., Griffioen, H.M.: iGovernment: a new perspective on the future of government digitization. Comput. Law Secur. Rev. **28**(3), 273–282 (2012)
4. Marler, J.H., Boudreau, J.W.: An evidence-based review of HR analytics. Int. J. Hum. Resour. Manag. **28**(1), 3–26 (2017)
5. Pape, T.: Prioritising data items for business analytics: framework and application to human resources. Eur. J. Oper. Res. **252**, 687–698 (2016)
6. Smith, T.: HR Analytics: the what, why and how. Numerical Insights LLC (2013)
7. Cascio, W., Boudreau, J.: Investing in People: Financial Impact of Human Resource Initiatives. Ft Press, Upper Saddle River (2010)
8. Bordoloi, S.K., Matsuo, H.: Human resource planning in knowledge-intensive operations: a model for learning with stochastic turnover. Eur. J. Oper. Res. **130**(1), 169–189 (2001)
9. Bassi, L.: Raging debates in HR analytics. People Strat. **34**, 14–18 (2011)
10. Lawler III, E.E., Levenson, A., Boudreau, J.W.: HR metrics and analytics: use and impact. Hum. Resour. Plan. **27**, 27–35 (2004)
11. Angrave, D., Charlwood, A., Kirkpatrick, I., Lawrence, M., Stuart, M.: HR and analytics: why HR is set to fail the big data challenge. HRM J. **26**, 1–11 (2016)
12. Choenni, S., Netten, N., Bargh, M., Braak van den, S.: On the usability of big (social) data. In: IEEE International Conference on Parallel & Distributed Processing with Applications, Ubiquitous Computing & Communications, Big Data & Cloud Computing, Social Computing & Networking, Sustainable Computing & Communications, pp. 1167–1174 (2018)
13. Choenni, S., Bakker, R., Blok, H.E., de Laat, R.: Supporting technologies for knowledge management. In: Baets, W. (ed.) Knowledge Management and Management Learning, pp. 89–112. Springer, Heidelberg (2005). https://doi.org/10.1007/0-387-25846-9_6
14. Armadoul, K.: Data-driven HR-policy, research report. Bachelor thesis, RUAS (2017)
15. Kim, G., Trimi, S., Chung, J.: Big-data applications in the government sector. Commun. ACM **57**(3), 78–85 (2014)
16. Choenni, S., Bargh, M., Netten, N., Braak, van den, S.: Using data analytics results in practice: challenges and solution directions. In: ICT-Enabled Social Innovation for the European Social Model: A Multi-disciplinary Reflection and Future Perspectives from Internet Science, HCI and Socio-Economics (2019)
17. Netten, N., Bargh, M., Choenni, S.: Exploiting data analytics for social services: on searching for profiles of unlawful use of social benefits. In: Proceedings of the 11th International Conference on Theory and Practice of Electronic Governance, pp. 550–559. ACM (2018)

18. Choenni, S., van Waart, P., de Haan, G.: Embedding human values into information system engineering methodologies. In: Proceedings of ECIME 2011, 5th European Conference On Information Management and Evaluation, Como, Italy, pp. 101–108 (2011)
19. Dorst, K.: The core of 'design thinking' and its application. Des. Stud. **32**(6), 521–532 (1995)
20. Nonaka, I., Takeuchi, H.: The Knowledge Creation Company: How Japanese Companies Create the Dynamics of Innovation. Oxford University Press Inc., Oxford (1995)
21. Laudon, K.C., Laudon, J.P.: Management Information Systems. Prentice Hall, Upper Saddle River (1999)

Open Science and Open Data

Decision Tree Analysis for Estimating the Costs and Benefits of Disclosing Data

Ahmad Luthfi[1,2]([✉]) [ID], Marijn Janssen[1] [ID], and Joep Crompvoets[3] [ID]

[1] Faculty of Technology, Policy and Management,
Delft University of Technology, Jaffalaan 5, 2628 BX Delft, The Netherlands
{a.luthfi,m.f.w.h.a.janssen}@tudelft.nl
[2] Universitas Islam Indonesia, Yogyakarta, Indonesia
ahmad.luthfi@uii.ac.id
[3] Katholieke Universiteit Leuven, Leuven, Belgium
joep.crompvoets@kuleuven.be

Abstract. The public expects government institutions to open their data to enable society to reap the benefits of these data. However, governments are often reluctant to disclose their data due to possible disadvantages. These disadvantages, at the same time, can be circumstances by processing the data before disclosing. Investments are needed to be able to pre-process a dataset. Hence, a trade-off between the benefits and cost of opening data needs to be made. Decisions to disclose are often made based on binary options like "open" or "closed" the data, whereas also parts of a dataset can be opened or only pre-processed data. The objective of this study is to develop a decision tree analysis in open data (DTOD) to estimate the costs and benefits of disclosing data using a DTA approach. Experts' judgment is used to quantify the pay-offs of possible consequences of the costs and benefits and to estimate the chance of occurrence. The result shows that for non-trivial decisions the DTOD helps, as it allows the creation of decision structures to show alternatives ways of opening data and the benefits and disadvantages of each alternative.

Keywords: Decision tree analysis · Estimation · Costs · Benefits · Open data · Open government · Investments

1 Introduction

During the past decade, government institutions in many countries have been started to disclose their data to the public. The society expects that governments become open and that their becomes easy to re-use [1, 2]. The opening of the data by the governments can provide various opportunities including increased transparency, accountability but also to improve decision-making and innovation [3, 4]. However, opening of data is more cumbersome and many datasets remain closed as they many contain personal or sensitive data. Decisions to disclose are often made based on binary options like "open" or "closed" the data, whereas also parts of a dataset can be opened or datasets can be pre-processed in such a way that they can be opened data. A Decision tree analysis (DTA) can help decision-makers in estimating the investments needed to process data before releasing.

© IFIP International Federation for Information Processing 2019
Published by Springer Nature Switzerland AG 2019
I. O. Pappas et al. (Eds.): I3E 2019, LNCS 11701, pp. 205–217, 2019.
https://doi.org/10.1007/978-3-030-29374-1_17

The objective of this paper is to develop a decision tree analysis for open data (DTAOD) to estimate the costs and benefits of disclosing data. This will help us to gain insight into the potential of using DTA for supporting the opening of data. A decision tree is a decision support tool that uses a tree-like model of decisions and their possible consequences of conditional control statements [5, 6]. DTA is chosen as it can serve a number of purposes when complex problems in the decision-making process of disclosing data are encountered. Many complex problems in decision-making might be represented in the payoff table form [7]. Nevertheless, for the complicated problem related to investment decisions, decision tree analysis is very useful to show the routes and alternatives of the possible outcomes [6].

The developed DTA consists of the following four steps [8, 9], as follows: First, define a clear decision problem to narrow down the scope of the objective. Factors relevant to alternative solutions should be determined. Second, structure the decision variables into a decision-tree model. Third, assign payoffs for each possible combination alternatives and states. In this step, payoffs estimation is required to represent a specific currency of amount based on the experts' judgment. Fourth, provide a recommendation of decisions for the decision-makers.

This research can support decision-makers and other related stakeholders like business enablers and researchers, to create a better understanding of the problem structure and variants of opening data. Furthermore, this study contributes to the limited literature about decision support for disclosing data and it is the first work using DTA. This paper is consists of five sections. In Sect. 1 the rationale behind this research is described, Sect. 2 contains the related work of decision-making approaches to open data domain. In Sect. 3, the DTA approach is presented, including research method, related theories, and proposed steps in constructing DTA. Section 4 provides systematically the development of DTA. Finally, the paper will be concluded in Sect. 5.

2   Related Work

2.1   Overview of Methods for Deciding to Open Data

In the literature, there are various methods in analyzing to open data. Four types of approaches for decision-making of opening data were identified. First, an iterative decision-making process in open data using Bayesian-belief networks approach. Second, proposed guidance to trade-off the chances of value and risk effects in opening data. Third, a framework to weight the risks and benefits based on the open data ecosystem elements. Fourth, a fuzzy multi-criteria decision making (FMCDM) method to analyze the potential risks and benefits of opening data. The several related methods in analyzing to disclose data can be seen in Table 1.

Table 1. The overview in the literature

	Method	Overview and limitations
1	Iterative model of decision support for opening data [10, 11]	The use of Bayesian-belief networks approach is to construct the relational model of decision support in opening data. The outcomes of this model can be used to prevent the risks and still gain benefits of opening data
2	Trade-offs model [10, 12]	This method provides guidance for weighing the potential values and risks of opening data. Interview sections are based on some certain groups of government employees like civil servants and archivists. There is no specific methods nor algorithm found to develop the trade-off model
3	A framework of decision support in open data [13, 14]	A developed prototype is based on the following concept of open data ecosystems. The proposed model is exclusively for business and private organizations. There is no evaluation and assessment model introduced in this framework
4	A fuzzy multi-criteria decision making (FMCDM) [15, 16]	Fuzzy AHP has been implemented to a broader domain of studies. Fuzzy analytical hierarchy process (FAHP) is utilized by collecting input from experts' knowledge and expertise

However, none of these related existing approaches uses a method to analyze and estimate the possible costs-benefits of opening data for a specific problem. DTA can play a role in providing different steps and expectations of the decision-making process.

2.2   Theory of Decision Tree Analysis

DTA is introduced for the first time in the nineteen sixties and primarily used in the data mining domain. The main role of using this method is to establish classification systems based on multiple covariates in developing a prediction of alternative variables [7, 8]. This theory allows an individual or organizations to trade-off possible actions against another action based on the probabilities of risks, benefits, and costs of a decision-making process [8, 17]. In the case of opening data, DTA is used to identify and calculate the value of possible decision alternatives by taking into account the potential cost-adverse effects.

The existing literature provides insight into the advantages of using DTA the decision-making process. First, DTA can generate understandable the estimation process and is easy to interpret [8, 18]. Second, DTA is able to take into account both continuous and categorical decision variables [6, 8]. Third, DTA provides a clear indication of which variable is becoming the most important in predicting the outcome of the alternative decisions [9]. Fourth, a decision tree can perform a classification without requiring in-depth knowledge in computational [7, 8].

The use of DTA in this study can manage a number of variables of the costs and benefits in opening data. In this situation, DTA can support the decision-makers in deciding how to select the most applicable decision. Besides, this method is able to subdivide heavily skewed variable into a specific amount of ranges. Figure 1 shows the example of decision tree notation with alternatives of choices in the case of open data decision.

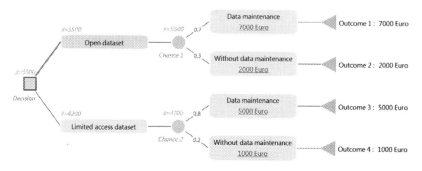

Fig. 1. An example of DTA

The objective of this decision tree illustrated in Fig. 1 is that the decision-makers are trying to find the expected monetary value (EMV) of probability decisions, namely open dataset and limited access to the dataset. The EMV is the probability-weighted average of the outcomes [6, 8]. The use of EMV in DTA can be defined in two main benefits. First, EMV helps decision-makers to understand the possible investments of alternative actions. Second, DTA supports selecting the most appropriate alternatives by weighing the costs of two alternative decisions.

In order to get the probability of an outcome in opening data case shows in Fig. 1, the probabilities along the branches of the tree need to be multiplied. Beforehand, we first should define that there are two alternative decisions in this case, namely: open the dataset or provide limited access to the dataset. Heavily skewed variable need to be subdivided into a specific amount of ranges. In this example, the ranges of the possible costs are between 0 to 10000 Euros. To obtain the expected monetary value from the example in Fig. 1, the probability-weighted average of the four outcomes is calculated by summing the data maintenance activity with the probability of each outcome. This, give the outcome $0.7 \times 7000 + 0.3 \times 2000 = 5500$ Euro. In a similar vein, the costs of the limited access alternative can be calculated $0.8 \times 5000 + 0.2 \times 0.2 \times 1000 = 4200$ Euro. In this example, the DTA shows that the investment needed to open a dataset is higher than the limited access to alternative decisions.

3   Research Approach

In this study, we use experts' judgment to assign payoffs possible consequences of the costs and benefits in opening data including the changes. The expert judgment is used because of their capability to interpret and integrate the existing complex problems in a domain of knowledge [19, 20]. To do so, we interviewed four experts from three post-graduate researchers and one professional with open government data and costs-benefits investment experiences consideration. There are some considerations in selecting the experts for this study. First, we select the experts based on their knowledge in the open data field. Second, best practices in estimating the costs and benefits investment in open data domain should take into account.

The selected experts use their understanding and reasoning processes as they refer to their experiences to make judgments [21, 22]. However, understanding the current issues and having logical reasons behind predicting costs and benefits in open data domain is not trivial. The costs and benefits estimation requires sufficient knowledge and complex experiences in a specific field [23]. There are some barriers and limitations of the expert judgments elicitation. First, during the elicitation process, the experts might possibly quantify the answers inconsistently because of the unclear set of questions from the interviewer. To cover this issue, we design a list of questions protocol as structured as possible and easy to comprehend by the experts. The use of specific terminologies in the field of open data, for instance, should be clearly defined. Second, the use of experts' judgment is potentially time-consuming and experts are often overconfidence that can lead to uncertainty estimation [19, 24]. To tackle this issue, we use aggregate quantitative review by subdividing heavily skewed variable into a specific amount of ranges.

3.1   Steps in Developing the DTA

In order to effectively manage and construct a decision tree based analysis, and to represent a schematic and structured way, in this paper we use four main steps in developing DTA [6, 8, 18], as follows: First, define a clear problem to narrow down the scope of the DTA. Relevant factors resulting in alternative solutions should be determined as well. This step could involve both internal and external stakeholders to seek the possible options for a better decision-making process.

Second, define the structure the decision variables and alternatives. The structure of the problems and influence diagram require to be interpreted into formal hierarchical modeling. In this step, organizations need to construct decision problems into tree-like diagrams and identify several possible paths of action and alternatives.

Third, assign payoffs and possible consequences. In this step, the EMV formula is required to help to quantify and compare the costs and benefits. EMV is a quantitative approach to rely on the specific numbers and quantities to perform the estimation and calculations instead of using high-level approximation methods like agree, somewhat agree, and disagree options. For this, experts' judgment is used to estimate the pay-off of possible consequences of the costs and benefits and to estimate the chance of occurrence.

Fourth, provide alternative decisions and recommendations. After successfully assigning payoffs the possible consequences and considering adjustments for both costs and benefits, decision-makers can select the most appropriate decision that meets the success criteria and fit with their budget. These steps will be followed when developed the DTAOD.

4   Developing the DTAOD: Step-by-Step

4.1   Step 1: Define the Problems

The problem of opening data consists of three main aspects. First, decision-makers have a lack of knowledge and understanding in estimating the costs and benefits of open data domain and its consequences. Second, decision-makers might consider how to decide on the opening of data. Too much data might remain closed due to a lack of knowledge of alternatives. Third, decision-makers have no means to estimate the potential costs and benefits of opening data.

4.2 Step 2: Structure the Decision Alternatives

The decision-making process in opening data can be time-consuming and might require many resources. To understand better the consequences of each possible outcome, decision-makers require simplifying the complex and strategic challenges. Therefore, the DTA presented in this paper can construct a model and structure the decision alternatives whether the data should be released or closed.

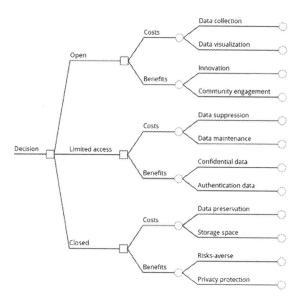

Fig. 2. Decision alternatives and possible paths

Figure 2 illustrates the decision alternatives and various types of possible paths in deciding the complex problems of opening data. We define three main decision nodes, namely "open", "limited access", and "closed". The first decision refers to the governments allow releasing their data to the public with less or without restrictions. Second, the limited access indicates that the level of openness is restricted to a specific group of user. Third, closed decision refers to the government should keep the data exclusively.

4.3 Step 3: Assign Payoffs and Possible Consequences

In this step, the assign numerical values to the probabilities including the action-taking place, and the investment value expected as the outcome will be carried out. In this paper, the assign payoffs represent the outcome for each combination in a table namely table of payoffs and possible consequences. This table uses costs terminology that represents the negative impact of a decision like value for the expense and potential lost revenue [8, 9]. While benefits-averse, indicate the positive influence to a decision like a net revenue stream, potential income, and other profit elements [7, 9]. The result of the assign payoffs and the possible consequences from the selected experts as presented in Table 2.

Table 2. Assign payoffs and possible consequences of the costs and benefits in opening data

Alternative decisions	Expert judgment (probability in percentage)					Expert judgment (invesment in Euro)						
	1	2	3	4	Mean	1	2	3	4	Mean	Total	Outcome
1. Open												
- Costs factors												
a. Data collection	65	67	58	62	63	15.500	16.200	16.500	16.600	16.200	30.238	46.438
b. Data visualization	35	33	42	38	37	14.250	15.500	12.100	14.300	14.038		44.276
- Benefits factors												
c. New knowledge	58	62	54	63	59	12.300	14.450	14.000	13.000	13.438	26.796	40.234
d. Community engagement	42	38	46	37	41	15.235	11.600	13.800	12.800	13.539		40.335
2. Limited access												
- Costs factors												
e. Data supression	66	58	54	55	58	16.000	16.500	17.000	14.500	16.000	32.725	48.275
f. Data maintenance	34	42	46	45	42	16.000	17.000	16.800	17.100	16.725		49.450
- Benefits factors												
g. Confidential data	55	65	44	45	52	18.000	17.600	17.700	18.200	17.875	35.000	52.875
h. Authentication data	45	35	56	55	48	18.500	17.500	16.850	16.500	17.338		52.338
3. Closed												
- Costs factors												
i. Data preservation	72	68	62	70	68	13.000	14.500	13.500	14.200	13.200	27.588	40.788
j. Storage space	28	32	38	30	32	16.000	15.850	12.200	13.500	14.388		41.976
- Benefits factors												
k. Risks-averse	52	56	57	60	56	9.300	10.500	12.000	10.000	10.450	22.513	32.963
l. Privacy protection	48	44	43	40	44	11.000	13.000	11.750	12.500	12.063		34.576

Table 2 presents the result of the assign payoffs between three alternative decisions, namely: "open", "limited access", and "closed". This table includes the expert judgment in estimating the probabilities of the costs and benefits, and the numerical values given to predict the investment of money in the euro currency. When the entire process of assign payoffs has completed, we can calculate the average numerical values of the costs and benefits percentages possibilities. For example, data collection factor might probability invests 63% of the revenue stream instead of a data visualization program (37%). This means, that the most significant money investment from this opening decision is data collection.

Data collection refers to a mechanism of gathering the dataset on the variables of interest from the holders or owners by using specific manners and techniques [25]. Data visualization, furthermore, refers to the action in presenting the dataset into an interactive and user-friendly interface and the ability to effectively capture the essence of the data [26]. Regarding the issue of the potential investment of money between data collection and data visualization, it is noticeable that deriving data from data providers can potentially cost expense higher than the visualizing the data. In addition, according to experts, data collection requires more than 16 K Euros on average of investments, which is higher than data visualization about (14 K). Therefore, the total costs for opening data decision from data collection and data visualization equal to approximate 30 K Euros. Figure 3 is the complete decision tree showing all alternatives.

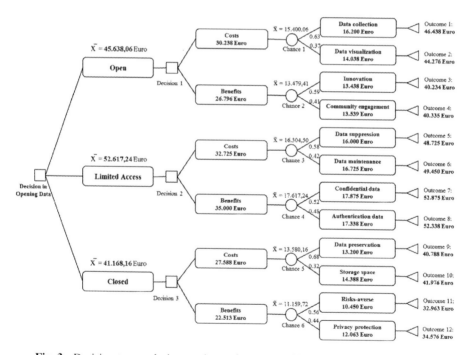

Fig. 3. Decision tree analysis to estimate the costs and benefits in open data domain

The process shown in the decision tree Fig. 3 results in the payoff result depicted in Table 2. From the constructed data, we are able to compare the costs and benefits of the three decision nodes. The number values stated on each sub-element indicate the prediction of money expenses. For example, to obtain the expected monetary value from an open decision, we have to do some structured ways. First, we need to know about the average costs of data collection and data visualization by calculating the probability and estimation of the amount. Here, we calculate (0,63 × 16.200 Euro) + (0,37 × 14.038 Euro) = 15.400,06 Euro. Second, we need to estimate the costs of the open data decision by adding up the value of data collection and data visualization whereby (16.200 Euro + 14.038 Euro) = 30.238 Euro. Third, we require estimating the outcome for each sub-costs factor. To do so, the amount of data collection and data visualization should be added to the potential total costs whereby (16.200 Euro + 30.238 Euro) = 46.438 Euro (outcome 1). Whereas, the outcome 2 is obtained from (14.038 Euro + 30.238 Euro) = 44.276 Euro. Finally, after we do the same way to the benefits of factors, we require estimating the total investment of the open decision. Before we calculate the process, it is important to compare the highest potential investment between the costs and benefits factors. The reason is to determine the highest priority of the potential investment between costs and benefits consideration. In this case, the highest probability is the costs factors (30.238 Euro) instead of its benefits (26.796 Euros). Therefore, the total average of expected monetary value (EMV) for "open" decision is equal to the EMV of the costs adding up to the total value of the costs whereby 15.400,06 Euro + 30.238 Euro = 45.638,06 Euro.

4.4   Step 4: Provide Decision and Recommendations

Based on the constructed decision tree analysis (in Fig. 3), the final step in developing decision tree analysis is making a decision and providing some recommendations presented in decision action plans. To provide the most suitable decision between the three alternatives (open, limited access, and closed) to the decision-makers, we take into consideration the weighting process of the costs and benefits affect in open data. Next, from the EMV results, the DTA can recommend a decision as to the highest priority that might influence the investment of institutional revenue streams. We classify the findings of the study into two parts, namely:

1. Possible Paths and with Total Payoffs

The first finding from the decision tree analysis is the possibility of the nodes and paths and its chances, as can be seen in Table 3. Every decision alternatives provide the estimation of payoffs in the euro currency. Based on these results, it can be concluded that the highest investment for the costs factor in open data domain is data maintenance where the cost almost 50 K euros. Data maintenance, in this case, is the sub-nodes of the limited access decision. Meanwhile, it is noticeable that the highest potential benefit by implementing the decision is confidentiality of the data where about 52 K Euros that would be a new benefit for the government institutions. In this case, the limited access decision one the hand can potentially have high costs and on the other hand, can result in high new revenues.

Table 3. Possible nodes, paths, and estimation payoffs

Terminal	Total payoff
Decision → Open → Decision 1 → Costs → Chance 1 → Data collection	46.438 Euro
Decision → Open → Decision 1 → Costs → Chance 1 → Data visualization	44.276 Euro
Decision → Open → Decision 1 → Benefits → Chance 2 → New knowledge	40.234 Euro
Decision → Open → Decision 1 → Benefits → Chance 2 → Community engagement	40.335 Euro
Decision → Limited access → Decision 2 → Costs → Chance 3 → Data suppression	48.725 Euro
Decision → Limited access → Decision 2 → Costs → Chance 3 → Data maintenance	49.450 Euro
Decision → Limited access → Decision 2 → Benefits → Chance 4 → Confidential data	52.875 Euro
Decision → Limited access → Decision 2 → Benefits → Chance 4 → Authentication data	52.338 Euro
Decision → Closed → Decision 3 → Costs → Chance 5 → Data preservation	40.788 Euro
Decision → Closed → Decision 3 → Costs → Chance 5 → Storage space	41.976 Euro
Decision → Closed → Decision 3 → Benefits → Chance 6 → Risks-averse	32.963 Euro
Decision → Closed → Decision 3 → Benefits → Chance 6 → Privacy protection	34.576 Euro

2. Expected Monetary Value (EMV)

The expected monetary value (EMV) resulted from the decision tree analysis shows that the limited access decision could gain the highest monetary value of about 52 K Euro. It is following the open decision in approximately 45 K Euro, and the decision to keep closed the data can contribute around 41 K Euro. The EMV of each decision is derived from the probability-weighted average of the expected outcome. Figure 4 presents the detailed of EMV result and ranges of the possible investment. This EMV result can recommend the decision-makers in estimating and quantifying the amount of money required includes the investment strategies.

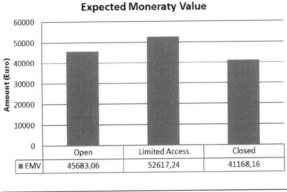

Decision	EMV	Range
Open	45.638,06 Euro	44.276 – 46.438 Euro
Limited Access	52.617,24 Euro	52.338 – 52.875 Euro
Closed	41.168,16 Euro	40.788 – 41.976 Euro

Fig. 4. The expected monetary value and investment ranges

5 Conclusion

Many government organizations are reluctant to disclose their data, because they have limited insight into the potential costs and possible adverse effects. Processing data or opening datasets partly can overcome this problem. However, this requires investments. In this study, we presented the DTAOD method to estimate the potential investments and merits of opening a dataset. This method was found to be useable by decision-makers to decide to disclose data. There are several advantages found in using DTAOD in this study. First, the decision tree can provide a better understanding of the possible outcomes of a decision alternative. Second, the proposed decision tree provides insight into selecting an informed decision. However, this is highly dependent on the alternatives that are formulated and included in the decision tree. Third, the decision tree is able to allocate the values in estimating the costs and benefits in open data domain based on expert judgments. This provides insight into the activities needed for opening data and the associated costs and benefits.

At the same time, using DTAOD might not be easy. First, during the assign payoff process, a small change in the quantification of numerical values can lead to a large chance in the entire structure of the decision tree. Second, the calculations are based on information from experts, but these might not be correct or biased towards openness or closeness. This result shows that the high and low of expected monetary values (EMV) of a decision will influence the decision made.

This study contributes to a better understanding of the problem structure and comes up with new insight in estimating the costs and benefits of releasing data for the policy-makers. In the future research, we recommend using a different method like paired comparison, multi-voting, and net present value (NPV) methods to quantify the assign payoffs as this study using a single expert judgment.

References

1. Lourenço, R.P.: An analysis of open government portals: a perspective of transparency for accountability. Gov. Inf. Q. **32**(3), 323–332 (2015)
2. Ubaldi, B.: Open government data: towards empirical analysis of open government data initiatives. OECD Working Papers on Public Governance, vol. 22, p. 60 (2013)
3. Zuiderwijk, A., Janssen, M.: Open data policies, their implementation and impact: a framework for comparison. Gov. Inf. Q. **31**(1), 17–29 (2013)
4. Janssen, M., Charalabidis, Y., Zuiderwijk, A.: Benefits, adoption barriers and myths of open data and open government. Inf. Syst. Manag. **29**(4), 258–268 (2012)
5. Zhou, G., Wang, L.: Co-location decision tree for enhancing decision-making of pavement maintenance and rehabilitation. Transp. Res. Part C **21**, 287–305 (2012)
6. Yuanyuan, P., Derek, B.A., Bob, L.: Rockburst prediction in kimberlite using decision tree with incomplete data. J. Sustain. Min. **17**, 158–165 (2018)
7. Song, Y.-Y., Lu, Y.: Decision tree methods: applications for classification and prediction. Shanghai Arch. Psychiatry **27**(2), 130–135 (2015)
8. Delgado-Gómez, D., Laria, J.C., Ruiz-Hernández, D.: Computerized adaptive test and decision trees: a unifying approach. Expert Syst. Appl. **117**, 358–366 (2019)
9. Adina Tofan, C.: Decision tree method applied in cost-based decisions in an enterprise. Procedia Econ. Financ. **32**, 1088–1092 (2015)
10. Luthfi, A., Janssen, M.: A conceptual model of decision-making support for opening data. In: Katsikas, Sokratis K., Zorkadis, V. (eds.) e-Democracy 2017. CCIS, vol. 792, pp. 95–105. Springer, Cham (2017). https://doi.org/10.1007/978-3-319-71117-1_7
11. Luthfi, A., Janssen, M., Crompvoets, J.: A causal explanatory model of bayesian-belief networks for analysing the risks of opening data. In: Shishkov, B. (ed.) BMSD 2018. LNBIP, vol. 319, pp. 289–297. Springer, Cham (2018). https://doi.org/10.1007/978-3-319-94214-8_20
12. Zuiderwijk, A., Janssen, M.: Towards decision support for disclosing data: closed or open data? Inf. Polity **20**(2–3), 103–107 (2015)
13. Buda, A., et al.: Decision Support Framework for Opening Business Data, in Department of Engineering Systems and Services. Delft University of Technology, Delft (2015)
14. Luthfi, A., Janssen, M., Crompvoets, J.: Framework for analyzing how governments open their data: institution, technology, and process aspects influencing decision-making. In: EGOV-CeDEM-ePart 2018. Donau-Universität Krems, Austria: Edition Donau-Universität Krems (2018)
15. Luthfi, A., Rehena, Z., Janssen, M., Crompvoets, J.: A fuzzy multi-criteria decision making approach for analyzing the risks and benefits of opening data. In: Al-Sharhan, S.A., et al. (eds.) I3E 2018. LNCS, vol. 11195, pp. 397–412. Springer, Cham (2018). https://doi.org/10.1007/978-3-030-02131-3_36
16. Kubler, S., et al.: A state-of the-art survey & testbed of fuzzy AHP (FAHP) applications. Expert Syst. Appl. **65**, 398–422 (2016)
17. Yannoukakou, A., Araka, I.: Access to government information: right to information and open government data synergy. In: 3rd International Conference on Integrated Information (IC-ININFO), vol. 147, pp. 332–340 (2014)

18. Yeoa, B., Grant, D.: Predicting service industry performance using decision tree analysis. Int. J. Inf. Manag. **38**(1), 288–300 (2018)
19. Beaudrie, C., Kandlikar, M., Ramachandran, G.: Using Expert Judgment for Risk Assessment. Assessing Nanoparticle Risks to Human Health (2016)
20. Veen, D., et al.: Proposal for a five-step method to elicit expert judgment. Front. Psychol. **8**, 1–11 (2017)
21. Walker, K.D., et al.: Use of expert judgment in exposure assessment: Part 2. Calibration of expert judgments about personal exposures to benzene. J. Expo. Anal. Environ. Epidemiol. **13**, 1 (2003)
22. Mach, K., et al.: Unleashing expert judgment in assessment. Glob. Environ. Change **44**, 1–14 (2017)
23. Rush, C., Roy, R.: Expert judgement in cost estimating: modelling the reasoning process. Concur. Eng. **9**, 271–284 (2001)
24. Knol, A., et al.: The use of expert elicitation in environmental health impact assessment: a seven step procedure. Environ. Health **9**(19), 1–16 (2010)
25. Kim, S., Chung, Y.D.: An anonymization protocol for continuous and dynamic privacy-preserving data collection. Futur. Gener. Comput. Syst. **93**, 1065–1073 (2019)
26. Xyntarakis, M., Antoniou, C.: Data science and data visualization. In: Mobility Patterns, Big Data and Transport Analytics, pp. 107–144 (2019)

Predicting Parking Demand with Open Data

Thomas Schuster and Raphael Volz[(⊠)] [iD]

University of Pforzheim, 75175 Pforzheim, Germany
{thomas.schuster,raphael.volz}@hs-pforzheim.de

Abstract. This paper focuses on demand forecasts for parking facilities. Our work utilizes open parking data for predictions. Several cities in Europe already publish this data continuously in the standardized DATEX II format. Traffic related information will become more ubiquitous in the future as all EU-member states must implement real-time traffic information services including parking status data since July 2017 implementing the EU directives 2010/40 and 2015/962. We demonstrate how to extract reliable and easily comprehensible forecast models for future-parking demand based on open data. These models find multiple use cases not only on a business planning level and for financial revenue forecasting but also to make traffic information systems more resilient to outages and to improve routing of drivers directing them to parking facilities with availability upon predicted arrival. Our approach takes into consideration that the data constitutes irregular time series and incorporates contextual information into the predictive models to obtain higher precision forecasts.

Keywords: Parking prediction · Machine learning · Data mining · Smart cities

1 Introduction

Congestion of transport systems is a major and increasing pain point in large cities. In the vision of smart cities this issue is tackled with "computerized systems comprised of databases, tracking, and decision-making algorithms" [1] instead of brick-and-mortar extensions of infrastructure. [2] cites multiple studies claiming that up to 30% of inner-city traffic can come from drivers searching for a free parking space.

To reduce this type of traffic bigger cities typically provide stationary car-park routing systems that indicate to drivers where spaces are currently available. A more modern approach is additional online publication of this data. While some cities, such as San Francisco, already provide app-based mobile information that can travel with the driver. This approach also incorporates current availability information directly into routing. For longer distance journeys a forecast of future availability is required, which can be determined using predictive models trained on historical parking demand information. Such predictive models are also useful in case of system outages providing a second means to assess the current status.

Predictive models for demand have also a great value for parking operators and can be used to develop forecasts of revenue [3] or to improve prices through performance pricing [4]. Recommendations for variable pricing of parking are around for a long time [5]. Understanding the demand of competitors is also beneficial to improve parking policies [6].

© IFIP International Federation for Information Processing 2019
Published by Springer Nature Switzerland AG 2019
I. O. Pappas et al. (Eds.): I3E 2019, LNCS 11701, pp. 218–229, 2019.
https://doi.org/10.1007/978-3-030-29374-1_18

With improved traffic management in mind, the European Commission has required member countries to contribute to the co-ordination of traffic management and development of seamless pan European services through the ITS directive 2010/40/EU. Among many other things this directive also mandates the publishing of traffic-related open data including parking status information for important cities and parking areas along highways.

This paper focuses on demand forecasts for parking facilities based on a continuous recording of the parking status updates of 42 parking facilities in Düsseldorf between March and August 2015. Working towards a benchmark of predictive model algorithms for parking demand predictions, we show that reliable and easy to understand forecast models for future parking demand can be mined from this open data using classical statistical learning approaches. Our approach takes into consideration that the data constitutes irregular time series and incorporates contextual information into the predictive models to obtain higher precision forecasts.

The paper is organized as follows: Sect. 2 describes the data set and its characteristics. Section 3 details our objectives and common assumptions for predicting parking. Section 4 reports on our results using linear regression as a technique that forms a baseline for comparison. Section 5 discusses our experiment with decision trees. Section 6 summarizes our findings and provides citywide results. We conclude in Sect. 7 with discussion of related work and our next steps.

2   The Data Set

2.1   Data Format, Source and Content

The European Commission has sponsored the development of the XML-based DATEX format to enable traffic-related information exchange. DATEX II version 2.3 published in December 2014 now also provides a standard data model for parking information[1]. This parking information is published in two separate files, one of which provides static information (metadata) such as name, typical capacity and location of a parking facility as well as categorization into city areas. The other file provides dynamic information that contains current status, capacity and demand, absolute number of parkers, as well relative occupancy and trend information both for single parking facilities and aggregates for city areas.

While individual parking facilities could publish their status using this format, it is more common for cities to aggregate the data from several parking facilities within its city limits to provide drivers with an overview of current availabilities. For example, Tampere (Finland) publishes the current parking status since February 2015 directly on the Web[2]. However, the EU delegated regulation mandates every member state to maintain national access points to such data that aggregates the data from various data providers in each country.

---

[1] http://www.datex2.eu/news/2014/12/01/datex-ii-version-23-available-now.

[2] http://wiki.itsfactory.fi/index.php/Tampere_Parking_DATEX2.

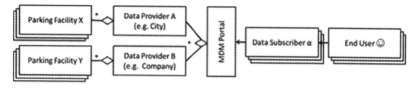

Fig. 1. A data flow of parking information through the MDM portal (Legend: ◇ aggregation)

In Germany this national access point is provided by the "Mobilitätsdatenmarkt-platz" (MDM portal)[3] and operated by the Bundesamt für Strassenbau (BaSt) on behalf of the ministry of transport. Figure 1 shows how traffic information flows from providers to subscribers and end users through this portal. Data sets of data providers are published on a secured URL endpoint by the MDM portal. Currently 6[4] German cities are providing parking demand information for their most important parking facilities. While data access may be restricted - and the MDM portal provides mechanisms for data providers to register data subscribers and provides access control - some cities such as Düsseldorf provide open[5] data. Each data provider of the MDM portal can individually choose a frequency in which the data is updated. For example, Düsseldorf updates its dynamic parking information every minute. Each update typically only contains the changes of parking demand since the last update, and some parking facilities might not have changes in that period. Hence, subscribers must maintain memory of the parking status across individual updates to get a complete up-to-date perspective since parking facilities might provide updates at a smaller frequency than the city and may not be providing any updates for longer periods of time during closing times or because of technical difficulties. The updates received therefore constitute highly irregular multivariate time series both at the level of single parking facilities and city aggregates. Our data set is based on minutely parking data that has provided by the city of Düsseldorf for 42 parking facilities on the MDM portal in the six months between March and August 2015.

2.2 Data Processing Implementation

We receive the dynamic parking information using a scheduled job (cron job) that polls the MDM portal URL endpoint(s) on a minutely basis. The DATEX message is then parsed and its content is appended to individual CSV files to create time series for each parking facility, parking area as well as one large CSV file that includes all updates received.

These CSV files are then read by data analysis scripts executed by the statistical software R [7]. In particular we use functions packages rpart [8] for decision tree fitting and zoo [9] to aggregate and plot the irregular time series that are found in the data.

---

[3] http://www.mdm-portal.de.

[4] As of September 2015: Aachen (only charging stations), Düsseldorf, Frankfurt am Main, Kassel, Magdeburg, and Wuppertal.

[5] Parties interested in accessing the data still need to register with the MDM portal and setup security certificates to receive data.

2.3   Data Characteristics

In total we have received 264.376 updates in 331 MB of XML data containing 2,6 million single changes in parking status across the 42 parking facilities in our data set. 7 of these parking facilities provide incorrect data, such as negative occupancies, or only a small number of data updates, for example updates that are several days apart, and are therefore excluded from further analysis.

The number updates provided by the remaining 35 parking facilities in scope varies greatly between 21.387 and 145.104 with a median of 75.499 observations per parking facility. Hence, the average parking facility provides a status update every 3½ minutes to the city of Düsseldorf.

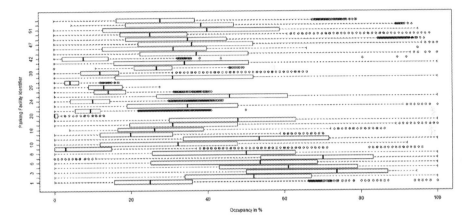

Fig. 2. Boxplot of parking facility occupancies (in %) in the data set

The box plot[6] Fig. 2 shows that the variance of occupancy is very high and also that the demand characteristics vary greatly between the different parking facilities. Hence, a robust predictive model is easier to obtain per parking facility than for the city level and the city level predictive model should be computed by aggregating the predictions made for individual parking facilities.

The data of individual parking facilities shows clear periodic patterns of demand, such as illustrated by Fig. 3 for two parking facilities side by side. The periodic pattern of Kunsthalle Düsseldorf is similar every day (with an increased demand on Saturdays) and demand is high in late evening hours, possibly due to the fact that parking is possible for 24 h and a reduced price is offered in the night. The parking facility is generally among the cheapest in the city and never really empty. Kö Gallerie, a prominent luxury store in the main shopping district located at Königsallee 60, shows a clear demand pattern centered around the afternoon and almost double demand on Saturdays. Demand is neglectable when the department store is closed in the night or on Sundays.

---

[6] A.k.a. box and whisker diagram showing from left to right: minimum, first quartile, median (thick line), third quartile and maximum as well as outliers (circles).

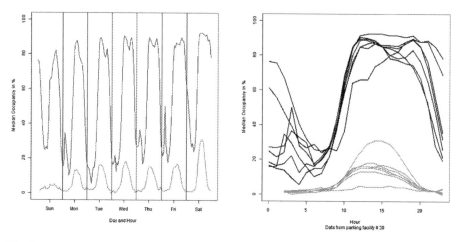

Fig. 3. Periodicity of parking demand with facility-specific temporal patterns (above #3 Kunsthalle (black) and below #39 Kö Gallerie (red)) (Color figure online)

3 Predicting Parking Demand

3.1 Objectives of Our Approach

Since our dataset is novel and the data has become publicly available just recently we want to establish a baseline with linear regression, a classical statistical supervised learning technique, and successively benchmark our results with other more recent machine learning and data mining approaches. In scope of this paper we will compare our linear regression baseline with decision trees, another well-known and broadly implemented regression technique.

The two main reasons for choosing those approaches is that both predictive models are very easy to comprehend for decision makers and can be implemented with few effort and computational demand either by a linear equation (linear regression) or nested if-else conditions (decision tree) in consumer apps or car information systems.

3.2 Decomposing Date and Time

As we have seen in Fig. 3 parking demand is typically periodic but exposes complex seasonality. The periodicity of different parking facilities is highly individual due to differences in opening and closing times and different intervals between data updates. System outages that can occur at any party involved in the data chain (see Fig. 1) create an additional source of irregularities in the data. Additionally, the timestamps of parking status have millisecond precision.

We therefore decompose the date and time information provided by the timestamp of each parking status update into variables for each component of time. Additionally, we determine the corresponding weekday for each date. *Hour* and *Weekday* are then used as input to the statistical learning algorithms, while all other components of time are ignored. We do not aggregate the data by hour to avoid biases.

3.3   Adding Contextual Information

[10] show that weather conditions influence parking demand. We therefore add hourly *rainfall* (in mm) and *temperature* (in degrees C°) data as recorded by the German national weather service (DWD) in its downtown Düsseldorf weather station. Hourly weather data is freely available[7] as part of the public mandate of DWD throughout Germany and world-wide from various data providers.

[11] discuss that public holidays influence electricity demand significantly. We therefore add binary information to the data set whether a given day is a *public holiday*, *school holiday* or a *Brueckentag*[8]. 35% of the observations in our data set are recorded on either one of these special days.

Both contextual data sets are available ahead of making predictions as 24 h weather forecasts and averaged historical weather observations as well as holiday calendars that are planned many years ahead (school holidays) or regulated by legislature (public holidays). We will compare how our predictive models perform with and without this contextual data.

3.4   Identifying the Dependent Variable

Parking facilities provide information on their status by transmitting both relative *occupancy* and absolute *occupied* spaces as well as *vacant* (available) spaces and their current *capacity* that fluctuates, for example due to ongoing renovations or by systematically opening and closing levels based on demand. Obviously, this information is redundant[9] and highly correlated.

Since the capacities of the parking facilities vary greatly, we choose to predict the absolute number of *occupied* spaces. *capacity* and the number of *long-term* parkers, that some garages report, are also independent variables in the predictive models.

3.5   Splitting Training and Test Data

We subset all 2.6 million observations into separate smaller data sets that single out observations per parking facility. Splitting the data sets into training and test data sets by months as often found in related work will lead to biases due to the different number of weekdays, length of months and occurrence of holidays. We therefore split the facility-specific data sets into 75% training and 25% test data in an algorithmic fashion[10] that preserves the relative ratios of the dependent variable in both data sets. The same training and test data sets are used to benchmark our approaches.

---

[7] http://www.dwd.de/WESTE (free registration of user account required).

[8] A *Brueckentag* is a single working day that fall between a public holiday and a weekend where many Germans take a day off from work.

[9] Occupancy = occupied/capacity and vacant = capacity − occupied.

[10] Using sample.split function offered by caTools (Tuszynski 2014).

3.6   Assessing Predictive Model Quality and Comparing Models

We assess the coefficient of determination R^2 for each predictive model on the training and test data. We indicate how well the models fit to the training data, and observe whether this fit deteriorates when making predictions on the unknown test data (indicated by a lower R^2).

To assess the overall quality of the model and compare model quality between experiments as well as between parking facilities we define the relative root mean-square deviation (*rRMSD*), which normalizes the well known *RMSD* by capacity. The $rRMSD_i$ is calculated for each parking facility i based on the predicted values $\hat{y}_t$ for times t of the dependent variable y (occupied) for all n different predictions as the square root of the mean of the squares of the deviations and normalized by the capacity of the parking facility k_i (1).

$$rRMSD_i = \frac{\sqrt{\sum_{t=1}^{n} \frac{(\hat{y}_t - y_t)^2}{n}}}{k_i} \tag{1}$$

The rRMSD allows comparing parking facilities with different capacities and denotes the relative prediction error of a predictive model (in % of capacity). rRMSD is an unbiased estimator like RMSD.

4   Linear Regression Models

We build similar linear regression models with ($\hat{y}_+$) and without ($\hat{y}_-$) contextual data for every parking facility. The regression model without context predicts the number of occupied parking spaces $\hat{y}_-$ based on the independent variables occurring in the linear equation v, where factor variables hour $\vec{h}$, weekday $\vec{w}$, and numeric variables of current capacity k and number of long-term parkers l are used as inputs, adjusted by the intercept c_-.

$$\hat{y}_- = v + c_- \\ v = \vec{c}_h \vec{h} + \vec{c}_w \vec{w} + c_k k + c_l l \tag{2}$$

The model with context predicts occupied parking spaces $\hat{y}_+$ in a similar fashion and adds numeric variables for temperature t, rainfall r as well as binary variables for Brueckentage b, school holidays s, and public holidays f, adjusted by the intercept c_+.

$$\hat{y}_+ = v + a + c_+ \\ a = c_t t + c_r r + c_b b + c_s s + c_f f \tag{3}$$

All coefficients c_i in Eqs. (2) and (3) are determined by the supervised learning task based on the training data, where factorial coefficients $\vec{c}_j$ will take different values for every factor. The coefficients will be different for every predictive model and adjust to the specific parking facility data.

For example, Table 1 shows the coefficients learned for parking facility Kö-Gallerie (#39) to occupied spaces $\hat{y}_+$ with the contextual information. The basic estimate c_+ of occupied parking spaces at 2 pm is 121. Thus, we expect 121 more cars to be present, while at 11 pm only a total of $121 - 28 = 93$ cars are expected.

Table 1. Excerpt of the linear regression model with context predicting occupied spaces $\hat{y}_+$ for parking facility Kö-Gallerie (#39)

(Factorial) coefficient		Estimate	Std. Error	t value
c_+		121.06	4.10	29.55
$\vec{c}_h$	hour3	16.92	24.91	0.68
	...			
	hour14	121.12	3.10	39.12
	...			
	hour23	−28.13	8.79	−3.20
$\vec{c}_w$	weekday1	56.45	0.90	62.71
	...			
	weekday6	134.28	0.88	152.03
c_k		−0.21	0.00	−60.13
c_t		0.49	0.03	15.81
c_r		0.63	0.39	1.62
c_f		−63.42	1.77	−35.87
c_s		−10.17	0.36	−28.40
c_b		120.63	2.21	54.70

Similarly, on Saturdays[11] we generally expect 134 more cars. Both higher temperatures c_t and rainfall c_r increase occupancy by one car for every 2 °C and 3 cars for every 2 mm of rain. 63 cars less can be expected on a public holiday and 10 cars less on school vacations while 120 more cars are parking on Brueckentage. The predictive model for Kö-Gallerie is robust and has a R^2 of 0.68 (without context) and 0.71 (with context) on the training data and 0.69/0.71 on the test data with a $rRMSD$ of 6.9% (without context) and 6.4% (context). Adding context provides a 4% improvement in prediction.

Table 2 reveals that R^2 the predictive models are generally robust on the test data. By comparing contextual and context-free predictions and excluding both best and worst models, it displays large deviations between 22% and 6.2% prediction error ($rRMSD$) for models without context that only slightly improve when context is added to 21% and 5.6%. In particular, context does not make bad models much better nor good models any worse. Overall adding contextual data provides 5.2% improvement in predictive quality on the capacity-weighted average of all linear regression models.

---

[11] Saturday is day 6 counting from 0 as Sunday, etc.

Table 2. Overall quality of linear regression models across 35 parking facilities

	$\widehat{y}_-$ (without context)			$\widehat{y}_+$ (with context)		
	Training R^2	Test R^2	rRMSD	Training R^2	Test R^2	rRMSD
2nd Worst $\widehat{y}_-$/$\widehat{y}_+$	0.53	0.53	14.6%	0.70	0.69	12.8%
Median $\widehat{y}_-$	0.8	0.8	10.4%	0.87	0.87	8.3%
Median $\widehat{y}_+$	0.42	0.41	11.2%	0.58	0.57	9.64%
2nd Best $\widehat{y}_-$/$\widehat{y}_+$	0.79	0.79	5.7%	0.88	0.88	4.3%

5   Decision Trees

The decision tree models [12] are trained with the same data set and input as the linear regression models, in particular we train two variants without (2) and with (3) contextual information. Whether input variables are used in the model depends on the results of the tree-fitting algorithm for the particular parking facility. Across all parking facilities, we obtain fits with the same parameters. To avoid overfitting to the data a minimum number of 30 observations must be in any terminal leaf node of the decision tree. We additionally avoid additional tree splits when the overall R^2 does not increase by at least $\frac{1}{1000}$.

The decision trees fitted from the training data for each parking facility are easy to understand but cumbersome to read and best-fitted for automated decision support. This is due to the fact that an average of 67 (maximum of 120) decision criteria are involved for trees trained on data with context. Figure 4 therefore only shows a sample tree that demonstrates important characteristics that are shared among the actual trees fitted to the training data. Top-level distinctions are typically made based on hour $\vec{c}_h$ and weekday $\vec{c}_w$ variables. Without considering any input variables, evaluating the tree would predict 107 occupied parking spaces. The first binary distinction is made based on whether the hour $\vec{c}_h$ is either before 10 am after 6 pm. If so, we should assume only 61 occupied spaces. If not, we can assume 137 occupied spaces.

These decisions are recursively refined while walking towards the leaves of the tree turning left when a condition is met and right if not until a leaf node is reached. For example, we assume 293 occupants between 1 pm and 4 pm on Saturdays, if our capacity is below 888 parking spaces.

Table 3 shows that the R^2 of the decision trees are also generally robust on the test data. We again exclude the best and worst models and observe smaller deviations between 14.6% and 5.7% prediction error (rRMSD) for models without context. Adding context generally improves the models and can observe between 12.8% and 4.3% prediction error. Adding contextual data provides a 15.6% improvement in predictive quality on the capacity-weighted average of all decision tree models.

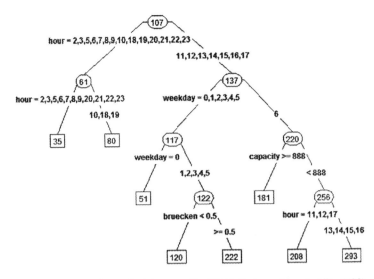

Fig. 4. Sample binary decision tree for Kö Gallerie parking facility (#39)

Table 3. Overall quality of decision tree models across 35 parking facilities

	$\widehat{y}_-$ (without context)			$\widehat{y}_+$ (with context)		
	Training R^2	Test R^2	rRMSD	Training R^2	Test R^2	rRMSD
2nd Worst $\widehat{y}_-/\widehat{y}_+$	0.53	0.53	14.6%	0.70	0.69	12.8%
Median $\widehat{y}_-$	0.8	0.8	10.4%	0.87	0.87	8.3%
Median $\widehat{y}_+$	0.42	0.41	11.2%	0.58	0.57	9.64%
2nd Best $\widehat{y}_-/\widehat{y}_+$	0.79	0.79	5.7%	0.88	0.88	4.3%

6   City-Wide Predictions and Overall Results

We define the citywide prediction error $rRMSD_{city}$ as a capacity-adjusted aggregate that normalizes the aggregated $rRMSD_i$ by the total capacity k_i across all n parking facilities:

$$rRMSD_{city} = \frac{\sum_{i=1}^{n} k_i \cdot rRMSD_i}{\sum_{i=1}^{n} k_i} \qquad (4)$$

Table 4 compares the overall prediction error $rRMSD_{city}$ across all 21.381 parking spaces in the data set. We can observe that contextual data generally improves prediction models in both approaches and provide a greater improvement to decision trees. Likewise, we can observe that decision tree models outperform linear regression models by 27.6% on the citywide level.

Table 4. Citywide prediction error **rRMSD$_{city}$**

	Linear regression	Decision tree	*Improvement*
$\hat{y}_-$ (without context)	**8.9%**	**7.2%**	*18.7%*
$\hat{y}_+$ (with context)	**8.4%**	**6.1%**	*27.6%*
Improvement	*5.2%*	*15.6%*	*31.4%*

We can generally confirm these improvements for every single predictive model although the improvements vary significantly across the individual parking facilities. Since *rRMSD$_{city}$* is smaller than the median prediction error we can conclude that our predictive models generally perform better for large parking facilities.

7 Conclusion

We have shown that robust predictive models for demand of parking facilities can be obtained from open parking status data and that classic regression techniques readily generate predictions with acceptable error rates while providing easy to understand models for decision makers and easy to implement equations and rules to implement decision-making algorithms. We have seen that contextual data related to (public and school) holidays and weather data can decrease prediction errors significantly and also show higher coefficients of determination R^2.

We are currently pursuing several directions to expand our results. First, we intend assessing the stability of the models with more data. This does include (a) stabilization with data of other cities with published DATEX II parking status and (b) addressing the challenges of irregularities by compensating failures in data provision with similar data providers.

We are currently benchmarking our results with other algorithms for multivariate time series with complex seasonality from the statistical community such as multivariate volatility models [13] as well as other supervised algorithms from the machine learning community that have been proposed for parking predictions such as wavelet neural networks [14].

Another direction for future research will be to develop an approach for short-term demand forecasts that considers the last known status as well as expected progressions from this status into the next couple of hours.

We will publish the data set after the anonymous review of this paper in an open data repository to provide a benchmark for parking prediction models since prior work on parking demand forecasts is based on proprietary data sets and our data set is the largest generally available dataset encompassing data from several parking facilities.

Acknowledgements. We thank the city of Düsseldorf to provide the data set openly and an anonymous company for providing technical assistance with the DATEX II format and providing us with access to the MDM portal.

References

1. Hall, R.E., Bowerman, B., Braverman, J., Taylor, J., Todosow, H., Von Wimmersperg, U.: The vision of a smart city. Brookhaven National Lab, Upton (2000)
2. Shoup, D.: The High Cost of Free Parking, Updated edn. Routledge, Chicago (2011)
3. Burns, M.R., Faurot, D.J.: An econometric forecasting model of revenues from urban parking facilities. J. Econ. Bus. **44**, 143–150 (1992)
4. Pierce, G., Shoup, D.: Getting the prices right. J. Am. Plan. Assoc. **79**, 67–81 (2013). https://doi.org/10.1080/01944363.2013.787307
5. Vickrey, W.: The economizing of curb parking space. Traffic Eng. Mag. **25**, 62–67 (1954)
6. Arnott, R.: Spatial competition between parking garages and downtown parking policy. Transp. Policy **13**, 458–469 (2006)
7. R Core Team: A language and environment for statistical computing. R Foundation for Statistical Computing, Vienna, Austria (2018)
8. Therneau, T.M., Atkinson, E.J.: An introduction to recursive partitioning using the RPART routines. Divsion of Biostatistics 61 (1997)
9. Zeileis, A., Grothendieck, G.: zoo: S3 infrastructure for regular and irregular time series. J. Stat. Softw. **14**, 1–27 (2005). https://doi.org/10.18637/jss.v014.i06
10. David, A., Overkamp, K., Scheuerer, W.: Event-oriented forecast of the occupancy rate of parking spaces as part of a parking information service. In: Proceedings of the 7th World Congress on Intelligent Systems (2000)
11. Livera, A.M.D., Hyndman, R.J., Snyder, R.D.: Forecasting time series with complex seasonal patterns using exponential smoothing. J. Am. Stat. Assoc. **106**, 1513–1527 (2011). https://doi.org/10.1198/jasa.2011.tm09771
12. Breiman, L.: Classification and Regression Trees. Routledge, Abingdon (2017)
13. Tsay, R.S.: Multivariate Time Series Analysis: With R and Financial Applications. Wiley, Hoboken (2014)
14. Ji, Y., Tang, D., Blythe, P., Guo, W., Wang, W.: Short-term forecasting of available parking space using wavelet neural network model. IET Intell. Transp. Syst. **9**, 202–209 (2014)

Towards an Ontology for Public Procurement Based on the Open Contracting Data Standard

Ahmet Soylu[1]([⊠]), Brian Elvesæter[1], Philip Turk[1], Dumitru Roman[1],
Oscar Corcho[2], Elena Simperl[3], George Konstantinidis[3],
and Till Christopher Lech[1]

[1] SINTEF Digital, Oslo, Norway
ahmet.soylu@sintef.no
[2] Universidad Politécnica de Madrid, Madrid, Spain
[3] University of Southampton, Southampton, UK

Abstract. The release of a growing amount of open procurement data led to various initiatives for harmonising the data being provided. Among others, the Open Contracting Data Standard (OCDS) is highly relevant due to its high practical value and increasing traction. OCDS defines a common data model for publishing structured data throughout most of the stages of a contracting process. OCDS is document-oriented and focuses on packaging and delivering relevant data in an iterative and event-driven manner through a series of releases. Ontologies, beyond providing uniform access to heterogeneous procurement data, could enable integration with related data sets such as with supplier data for advanced analytics and insight extraction. Therefore, we developed an ontology, the "OCDS ontology", by using OCDS' main domain perspective and vocabulary, since it is an essential source of domain knowledge. In this paper, we provide an overview of the developed ontology.

Keywords: Procurement · OCDS · Ontology

1 Introduction

Public entities worldwide are increasingly required to publish information about their procurement processes (e.g., in Europe, with EU directives 2003/98/EC and 2014/24/EU8) in order to improve effectiveness, efficiency, transparency, and accountability of public services [8]. As a result, the release of a growing amount of open procurement data led to various initiatives (e.g., OpenPEPPOL[1], CEN BII[2], TED eSenders[3], CODICE[4], Open Contracting Data Standard (OCDS)[5])

---

[1] https://peppol.eu.
[2] http://cenbii.eu.
[3] https://simap.ted.europa.eu/web/simap/sending-electronic-notices.
[4] https://contrataciondelestado.es/wps/portal/codice.
[5] http://standard.open-contracting.org.

© IFIP International Federation for Information Processing 2019
Published by Springer Nature Switzerland AG 2019
I. O. Pappas et al. (Eds.): I3E 2019, LNCS 11701, pp. 230–237, 2019.
https://doi.org/10.1007/978-3-030-29374-1_19

for harmonising the data being provided. XML formats and file templates are defined within these standards to make it possible to structure the messages exchanged by the various agents involved in electronic procurement. These standards are mostly oriented to achieve interoperability, addressing communication between systems, and hence they usually focus on the type of information that is transmitted between the various organizations involved in the process. The structure of the information is commonly provided by the content of the documents that are exchanged. Furthermore, there are no generalised standardised practices to refer to third parties, companies participating in the process, or even the main object of contracts. In sum, this still generates a lot of heterogeneity. Ontologies have been proposed to alleviate this problem [1,10]. Several ontologies (e.g., PPROC [5], LOTED2 [3], MOLDEAS [7], PCO [6]) have recently emerged, with different levels of detail and focus (e.g., legal, process-oriented, pragmatic). However, none of them has had a wide adoption so far.

In this context, OCDS is highly relevant due to its high practical value and increasing traction. It defines a common data model for publishing structured data throughout all the stages of a contracting process. It is document-oriented and focuses on packaging and delivering relevant data in an iterative and event-driven manner through a series of releases. However, in its current form, OCDS is a mere data structure. An ontology, beyond providing uniform access to heterogeneous procurement data, could enable integration with related data sets for advanced analytics and insight extraction. For instance, in the context of the EU project TheyBuyForYou[6] [8,10], we aim to integrate procurement and supplier data for improving effectiveness, efficiency, transparency, and accountability of public procurement through analytics and integrated data access.

To this end, in this paper, we report on the design and development of an ontology—the "OCDS ontology"—that uses the main perspective and vocabulary of OCDS, since it is an essential source of domain knowledge with high adoption.

2   Ontology-Based Approach

An ontology is a formal and shared specification of a domain of interest in a machine-readable format. One could consider the reasons behind choosing an ontology-based approach from knowledge representation and logical programming perspectives [2]. For the former, firstly, ontologies provide a commonly agreed terminology, that is a vocabulary and the semantic interpretation of the terms provided. Using a well-specified and unambiguous terminology enables the sharing and integration of data between disparate systems. Secondly, one could use a network of ontologies in a modular way to integrate different but related data sets without implementing yet another information model. For the latter, due to logical foundations of ontologies, one could infer new facts (i.e., implied information) through logical reasoning from the existing data (i.e., explicit information) and check the consistency of data.

---

[6] https://theybuyforyou.eu.

The adoption of ontology-based approaches is gaining momentum due to raising paradigms such as knowledge graphs (KG) [11] and ontology-based data access (OBDA) [4]. A KG represents real-world entities and their interrelations. Semantic KGs created by using ontologies and related technologies such as RDF and OWL benefit from high expressive and logical capabilities of ontologies for representing, exchanging, and querying data. OBDA approach is complementary in this respect, where an ontology defines a high-level global schema for existing data sources. For example, it could enable virtualising multiple heterogeneous data sources to a semantic KG without needing to alter original data sources through mappings between the underlying data sources and an ontology [9].

Our main interest and challenge in this context is to provide an ontology to allow uniform access to procurement data through a common terminology, which is based on a well-established standard, and to allow integrating procurement data with other related data sets. An example could be linking procurement data with company data for fraud analysis by detecting abnormal patterns in data.

3 OCDS Ontology

OCDS' data model is organised around a contracting process by gathering all the relevant information associated with a single initiation process in a structured form. Phases in this process include mainly planning, tender, award, contract and implementation information. An OCDS document may be one of two kinds: a release or a record. A release is basically associated to an event in the lifetime of a contracting process and presents related information, while a record compiles all the known information about a contracting process. A contracting process may have many releases associated but should have only one record.

Each release provides new information and may also repeat the previous information which still holds. A release document is composed of a number of sections. These are mainly: parties, planning, tender, awards, contract, and implementation. OCDS defines data fields for each section, and for some of those fields, it uses "open" or "closed" code lists, providing fixed and recommended lists of values respectively. There are also extensions defined by the OCDS or third parties for enabling publishing external data. We refer interested readers to the full OCDS specification for more details.

3.1   Development Process

We went through the reference specification of OCDS release and interpreted each of the sections and extensions including structured and unstructured information. The result is the first set of classes and properties forming an ontology for OCDS as depicted briefly in Fig. 1. Each ontology element is annotated with `rdfs:comment` and `rdfs:isDefinedBy` in order to provide a mapping to the corresponding OCDS fragment.

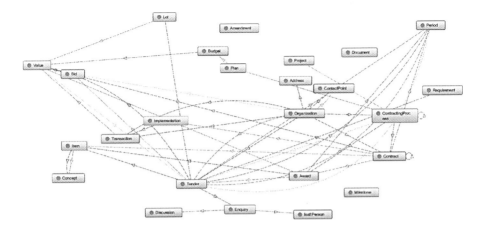

Fig. 1. OCDS ontology visualised with Protege OntoGraph plugin.

Though release reference seems to have a process-oriented perspective in some parts of the text, we avoided including process classes (except for the core class `ContractingProcess`), since the amount of information describing different processes is rather limited. We also avoided describing the release events for simplicity and assume that the ontology reflects the latest data available.

In line with Linked Data principles, we reused terms from external vocabularies and ontologies when appropriate. These include Dublin Core[7], FOAF[8], Schema.org[9], SKOS[10], and the W3C Organization ontology[11]. At this point, we have not used any cardinality restrictions, although OCDS provides some information on this. Finally, we used OWL annotation properties for specifying domain and ranges for generic properties in order to avoid any over restriction (i.e., `ocds:usesDataProperty`).

This edition of the OCDS ontology is available online in GitHub in two versions[12]: one version only with core OCDS terms and a second version with extensions (e.g., enquiries, lots, etc.).

3.2 Ontology Topology

In total, there are currently 24 classes, 62 object properties, and 80 datatype properties created from the four main OCDS sections and 11 extensions. In what follows, we zoom into each core class (i.e., directly mapping one of the OCDS sections) and discuss related classes and properties. The core classes are

---

[7] http://dublincore.org.
[8] http://xmlns.com/foaf/spec.
[9] https://schema.org.
[10] https://www.w3.org/2004/02/skos.
[11] https://www.w3.org/TR/vocab-org.
[12] https://github.com/TBFY/ocds-ontology/tree/master/model.

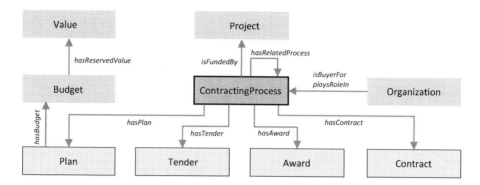

Fig. 2. ContractingProcess class and its neighbourhood.

`ContractingProcess`, `Plan`, `Tender`, `Award`, and `Contract`. Classes emerging from extensions are marked with "e" in the figures.

In Fig. 2, the neighbourhood of the `ContractingProcess` class is shown. A contracting process may have one planning and tender stage and multiple awards and contracts. The object property `hasRelatedProcess` has some subproperties originating from related process code list (e.g., `hasRelatedFrameworkProcess`, `hasRelatedParentProcess`, etc.). Process level title and description extension is used in the `ContractingProcess` class.

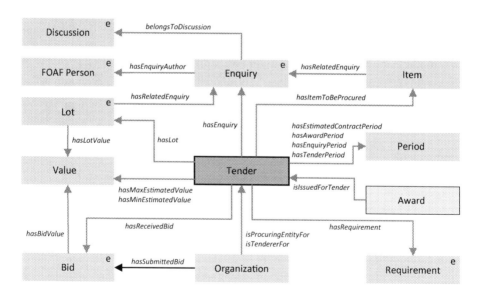

Fig. 3. Tender class and its neighbourhood.

The neighbourhood of the `Tender` class is shown in Fig. 3. Each tender may have multiple awards issued. The classes emerging from the tender

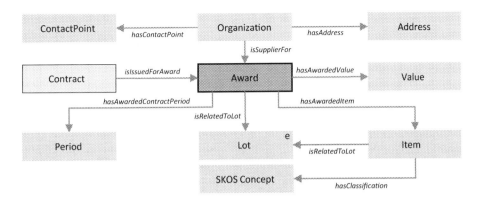

Fig. 4. Award class and its neighbourhood.

section and connected to the `Tender` class are `Value`, `Period`, `Award`, `Item`, and `Organization`. Several extensions are implemented, such as enquiries, lots, requirements, and bids, which map to the following classes: `Lot`, `Bid`, `Discussion`, `Enquiry`, `Requirement`, and `Person`.

In Fig. 4, the neighbourhood of the `Award` class is shown. There may be only one contract issued for each award. Other classes emerging from the award section and connected to `Award` class are `Value` and `Organization`. Lot extension also involves the `Award` class through the `isRelatedToLot` property. Item classifications (such as CPV – common procurement vocabulary) are realised through the use of SKOS Concept.

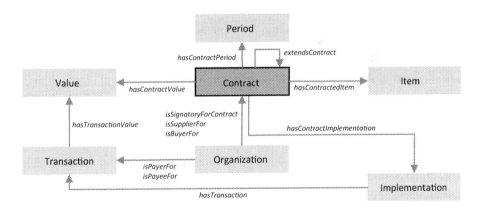

Fig. 5. Contract class and its neighbourhood.

Finally, the neighbourhood of the `Contract` class is shown in Fig. 5. It includes `Value`, `Item`, `Period`, and `Organization`. Multiple buyers extension is applied through extending the range of `isBuyerFor` property to the `Contract`.

Not all the classes and extensions implemented in the ontology are mentioned here. We refer readers to the OCDS specification and to the ontology documentation for more information regarding each class, OCDS mappings, datatype properties, extensions, and external vocabularies and ontologies used.

4   Conclusions

We developed an ontology derived from OCDS' schema and its extensions. We expect this to have a practical value and will be an important contribution for ongoing ontology development efforts, such as the upcoming eProcurement ontology[13]. Regarding future work, possible directions include the use of the Shapes Constraint Language (SHACL)[14] for validating RDF graphs based on the OCDS ontology (including cardinalities), development of a process ontology for procurement in combination with the OCDS ontology from a modular perspective, and extending the OCDS ontology to capture history (i.e., release events).

Acknowledgements. The work was partly funded by the EU H2020 projects TheyBuyForYou (780247) and euBusinessGraph (732003).

References

1. Alvarez-Rodríguez, J.M., et al.: New trends on e-Procurement applying semantic technologies: current status and future challenges. Comput. Ind. **65**(5), 800–820 (2014)
2. Baader, F., et al. (eds.): The Description Logic Handbook: Theory, Implementation, and Applications. Cambridge University Press, New York (2003)
3. Distinto, I., et al.: LOTED2: an ontology of European public procurement notices. Semant. Web **7**(3), 267–293 (2016)
4. Giese, M., et al.: Optique: zooming in on big data. IEEE Comput. **48**(3), 60–67 (2015)
5. Muñoz-Soro, J.F., et al.: PPROC, an ontology for transparency in public procurement. Semant. Web **7**(3), 295–309 (2016)
6. Necaský, M., et al.: Linked data support for filing public contracts. Comput. Ind. **65**(5), 862–877 (2014)
7. Rodríguez, J.M.Á., et al.: Towards a Pan-European e-procurement platform to aggregate, publish and search public procurement notices powered by linked open data: the moldeas approach. Int. J. Softw. Eng. Knowl. Eng. **22**(3), 365–384 (2012)
8. Simperl, E., et al.: Towards a knowledge graph based platform for public procurement. In: Garoufallou, E., Sartori, F., Siatri, R., Zervas, M. (eds.) MTSR 2018. CCIS, vol. 846, pp. 317–323. Springer, Cham (2019). https://doi.org/10.1007/978-3-030-14401-2_29
9. Soylu, A., et al.: Querying industrial stream-temporal data: an ontology-based visual approach. J. Ambient Intell. Smart Environ. **9**(1), 77–95 (2017)

---

[13] https://joinup.ec.europa.eu/solution/eprocurement-ontology.
[14] https://www.w3.org/TR/shacl.

10. Soylu, A., et al.: Towards integrating public procurement data into a semantic knowledge graph. In: Proceedings of the EKAW 2018 Posters and Demonstrations Session Co-Located with 21st International Conference on Knowledge Engineering and Knowledge Management (EKAW 2018), CEUR Workshop Proceedings, vol. 2262, pp. 1–4. ceur-ws.org (2018)
11. Yan, J., et al.: A retrospective of knowledge graphs. Front. Comput. Sci. **12**(1), 55–74 (2018)

Designing Laboratory Forensics

Armel Lefebvre$^{(\boxtimes)}$ and Marco Spruit

Department of Information and Computing Sciences, Utrecht University,
Princetonplein 5, 3584CC Utrecht, The Netherlands
{a.e.j.lefebvre,m.r.spruit}@uu.nl

Abstract. Recently, the topic of research data management (RDM) has emerged at the forefront of Open Science. Funders and publishers posit new expectations on data management planning and transparent reporting of research. At the same time, laboratories rely upon undocumented files to record data, process results and submit manuscripts which hinders repeatable and replicable management of experimental resources. In this study, we design a forensic process to reconstruct and evaluate data management practices in scientific laboratories. The process we design is named Laboratory Forensics (LF) as it combines digital forensic techniques and the systematic study of experimental data. We evaluate the effectiveness and usefulness of Laboratory Forensics with laboratory members and data managers. Our preliminary evaluation indicates that LF is a useful approach for assessing data management practices. However, LF needs further developments to be integrated into the information systems of scientific laboratories.

Keywords: Laboratory forensics · Reproducibility · Design science · Open science

1 Introduction

Research data management (RDM) is a pillar of sound data preservation and dissemination practices as encouraged by Open Science [1]. However, RDM has not (yet) reached the maturity of data management in the industry in terms of research, governance, and technology [2]. These ad-hoc RDM practices result in digital resources being inconsistently preserved in laboratories, thereby increasing the complexity of finding and accessing research data by laboratory members and external parties (e.g., reader, reviewer, another laboratory). Therefore, the consistent documentation of research processes, preservation, and dissemination of the artifacts created is still a complex challenge [3].

It can be argued that finding experimental data on storage systems in a laboratory is similar to finding any evidence on any computer. As the original author of the files, a quick scan of the file hierarchy is enough to recover most of the files mostly needed for a given purpose. For instance, finding a file to send with an e-mail does not require an advanced process to locate, verify, and validate the files to send to a correspondent.

In contrast, when laboratory members are responsible for storing research data, it may be difficult for a third party to interpret the file hierarchy and identify relevant files

© IFIP International Federation for Information Processing 2019
Published by Springer Nature Switzerland AG 2019
I. O. Pappas et al. (Eds.): I3E 2019, LNCS 11701, pp. 238–251, 2019.
https://doi.org/10.1007/978-3-030-29374-1_20

[4]. In a scientific laboratory, it is not uncommon that files created by a laboratory member need to be retrieved by others, for instance in the case a corresponding author has to respond to a request from another laboratory to access data [5]. At this point, the convenience of a simple file system becomes a significant limitation; the reason is that the understandability of the file structure largely depends on the efforts of the original authors to organize their folders and files.

Once experimental results have been published by a laboratory, the scientific community also benefits from available computational work. As noted by Peng [6], any attempt to reproduce published results require the availability of the original artifacts produced by the authors. In an era where computer technology has invaded scientific laboratories, few experimental works can avoid analytics software to study natural phenomena [7]. Still, the resulting publications often refer to a limited number of the original digital resources, if any [4]. Consequently, the reusability and replicability of published experiments remain challenging due to the lack of available original computational resources [8].

In this paper, we present the outcomes of a design science research (DSR) study focused on the design of a forensic approach which evaluates the functional repeatability and replicability of publications based on digital resources preserved on storage systems in a laboratory. The name of the approach is "Laboratory Forensics" as it combines digital forensic techniques on digital evidence. As further explained in Sect. 4, we aim at providing a set of artifacts that data managers and laboratory members can use to optimize the maximal availability of experimental evidence associated with scientific publications.

The main contribution of this work is a set of forensic techniques applicable to the extraction of experimental data from laboratories. Moreover, the outcomes of several forensic cases are evaluated with laboratory members and data managers in one university. By this, we show the feasibility and utility of laboratory forensics. The research question guiding this work is "How can digital forensics techniques be used to assess the reproducibility of scientific experiments?"

The paper is structured according to Hevner's DSR model [9]. More information about DSR is given in Sect. 2. Briefly, the structure of the paper revolves around DSR rigor, relevance, and design cycles. In the literature review section (Sect. 3); we present digital forensics and experimental systems, both of interest for the rigor cycle [9]. Then, in the Design section, we describe the outcomes of the evaluation of the laboratory forensics approach on four cases (i.e., publications). Finally, we discuss future research and conclude in Sect. 7.

2 Design Science Research

Design science research (DSR) addresses organizational problems by designing useful IT artifacts such as software, methods, models, or design theories [10]. Hevner [9] describes a design process which consists of three cycles named the relevance, design, and, rigor cycles. The three-cycle DSR aims to ground artifact design in rigorous construction and evaluation methods. Figure 1 shows a typical three-cycle model adapted to the study presented in this paper.

In DSR, the rigor cycle draws upon a body of knowledge named "knowledge base." There, design scientists describe the theories, processes, and evidence used to justify and evaluate a designed artifact. We explain further the domain and methods which are included in the rigor cycle in the next section. Similarly, we elaborate on the relevance cycle in the domain relevance section, where we give more details about the context of data management in scientific laboratories and the evaluation criteria adopted in this study.

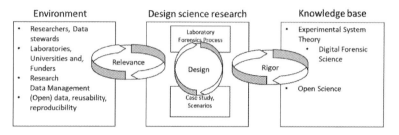

Fig. 1. The three cycles of a design science project, based on Hevner (2007)

3   Literature Review: The Rigor Cycle

In this section, we elaborate on two key aspects which drive our DSR study. First, we introduce digital forensics. Next, we briefly present a general view on the process and system of scientific experimentation.

3.1   Digital Forensics

Digital forensic science (DFS) has been defined as: "the use of scientifically derived and proven methods toward the preservation, collection, validation, identification, analysis, interpretation, documentation, and presentation of digital evidence derived from digital sources for the purpose of facilitating or furthering the reconstruction of events found to be criminal or helping to anticipate unauthorized actions shown to be disruptive to planned operations", p. 16 [11]. In other words, DFS employs an ensemble of techniques to transform digital resources into evidence usable by third parties in a convincing way. DFS often relates to (cyber) criminal activities. Hence the outcomes of DFS investigations serve judiciary systems by reporting on digital evidence found on computers involved in criminal activities [12]. As we will explain in the design section, the constraints of reliability and rigorous reporting found in DF investigations form a strong basis of rigor to transfer DF techniques to scientific laboratories. The reason to investigate laboratories with DF techniques is twofold: one is reactive (i.e., something happened) and another proactive. The former refers to the investigation of the preserved evidence underlying scientific publications to reconstruct past experiments. The latter refers to digital forensics readiness, a field of DF which prepare information systems to deal with external threats [13]. In the context of Open Science, this translates to evaluating the readiness of data management to comply with the production, proper preservation, and, dissemination of high-quality scientific data [14].

Table 1. Forensic processes all converge towards a stable set of activities

Step	Årnes	ENSFI	Casey	Candidate techniques [11]
1	Identification	Identify	Preparation and preservation	Audit analysis, case management
2	Collection	Acquire	Extraction and storage	Sampling, data reduction
3	Examination	–	Examination and reporting	Filtering, pattern matching
4	Analysis	Analysis	–	Statistical, timeline
5	Presentation	Report	Sharing, correlating and distributing	Documentation, impact statement

What can be seen from Table 1 is that the DFS process described by Årnes [15] is more refined than the two others. The reason is that Årnes makes a distinction between the examination and analysis phases. This distinction is facilitating the decomposition of the forensic process into clearly defined steps. Also, this distinction refines the categorization of candidate techniques that are used at each stage of the process suggested by Palmer. Candidate techniques are methods from other disciplines that belong to an analysis step in digital forensics [11].

According to Årnes, a DF investigation starts with the identification of the data sources. The next step, i.e., collection, is the actual extraction of the evidence from existing storage systems. Collection requires an image of the disk of interest to the investigators as it would be impractical and even hazardous (e.g., unexpected modifications of files) to investigate the laboratory storage in use. Once the evidence is isolated from a computer device, the examination phase locates potential evidence. After the investigators have recovered potential evidence, the analysis phase takes place. The last step, presentation, is the translation of the findings into a format that can be understandable by the practitioners.

3.2   Laboratories and Experimental Artifacts

Scientific laboratories are standard organizational settings encountered in natural sciences such as Physics, Chemistry, and Biology [16, 17]. At their core, laboratories are organizations producing scientific knowledge by designing and operating experimental systems. Experimental systems are closed systems that enable the observation of natural phenomena with an ensemble of equipment, theory, and human intervention [18].

Moreover, experimental systems produce intermediate products from experimental events that are not part of the (communicated) output. These products are, for instance, exports from data analysis software, manuscript's drafts, quality controls, interactions between technicians and researchers (i.e., experimenters) and, computer scripts. The association for computing machinery (ACM) has highlighted the need for a better assessment of the quality and availability of digital artifacts underlying publications [19]. The ACM classifies artifacts in two categories: functional and reusable [19]. Functional are artifacts that are consistent, documented, complete, and exercisable (i.e., runnable on a system).

4 Domain Relevance

4.1 Application Environment and Case Selection

In laboratories, scientists and technicians transform an object of study into data and data into scientific facts [20]. In science, facts are mainly communicated through scientific articles in journals which are presenting a curated version of experimental events [21]. Recently, journals developed new guidelines for more transparent reporting and enriched supplemental information [4]. Concurrently, public funding agencies encourage proper research data planning and management to foster high-quality data dissemination to mitigate the risks of poor RDM in laboratories. This trend presents several challenges for laboratories.

First, data management is not a priority, as it is often not rewarded by the academic system [22]. Second, as explained earlier, laboratories manipulate quite complex experimental processes to obtain results. As experimental processes rely on novel technology and people pushing forward the boundaries of a discipline, it is challenging to keep a record of the experimental evidence and activities produced during several years.

The case laboratory is a proteomics laboratory in the Netherlands that has produced over 400 publications in the last ten years. It makes this laboratory an ideal environment to design and evaluate our approach due to the complexity of the analyses done in the laboratory and a large number of authors (over 100) that worked or is currently working in the laboratory.

4.2 Evaluation Criteria

The criteria used to evaluate the outcomes of our LF approach are effectiveness and usefulness. First, we discussed the forensic results with two laboratory members, one experienced post-doc, acting as a data manager in the laboratory, and one a Ph.D. student who is the authors of one of the investigated publications. In addition, the outcomes of one forensic case were presented to 20 participants present at an RDM community event in February 2019. The participants were data managers, senior members of a data governance board, and members of RDM services at the University. Hence, both researchers and data managers could comment on the preliminary outcomes of the laboratory forensics approach presented in this paper.

The forensic cases are all publications originating from the investigated laboratory. The cases, i.e., publications, are selected primarily on the locality of the resources and their year of publication. For this study, we did not include any publication with multiple affiliations to limit the spreading of the files in separate laboratories. The publications are recent: CASE A and CASE C are from 2017, CASE B from 2018 and, CASE D from 2019. The reason is that the storage systems have been adapted recently, making the retrieval of older files an extra challenge due to their relocation which influenced critical meta-data such as date of creation to a large extent.

5   Design Iterations

The LF process, see Fig. 2, is designed by integrating digital forensic activities shown in Table 1 with evidence typically found in experimental science. The general idea is to merge meta-data collected from a file system in a laboratory (e.g., file names, date of creation, and date of modification) to software, methods and external sources found in the corresponding scientific article.

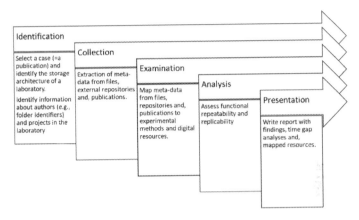

Fig. 2. An overview of the laboratory forensics process

To design our laboratory forensics approach, we first started with one publication, hereunder CASE A. The first design iteration was focused on adapting digital forensic techniques to the material available in on storage systems and their specific nature. The fact that (experimental) resources might be domain-specific made it necessary to redefine digital forensic activities which are increasing the likelihood of locating relevant material. Figure 2 shows the current iteration of the laboratory forensic process.

5.1   Laboratory Forensics in Action

A major challenge encountered during the investigation of CASE A was the low confidence that the files retrieved were related to the publication as much more (digital) material was generated by the instruments in the laboratory than necessary for the publication. This fact made the Annotated Experimental Resource Table (AERT) useful to guarantee that the files retrieved remain consistent with the resources reported in the investigated publication. The AERT is a spreadsheet containing all the methods described in the corresponding articles, the software and laboratory instruments used, and external resources such as an online database used by the experimenters. The AERT is helpful for systematic mapping of files and reported resources and excludes irrelevant material. We note that this mapping requires that LF investigators possess in-depth knowledge of storage systems and domain-specific knowledge (here in proteomics) (Table 2).

Table 2. The main activities of the laboratory forensics process

	Activity	Sub-activity	Example outcomes of CASE A
Identification	*Screen experimental report*	Identify laboratory employees	There are two authors in the author list and three laboratory members listed in the acknowledgment section
		Collect information about the editorial process and deposited data	The paper was published in June 2017. It was received by the journal three months earlier, in March 2017. One repository is used to deposit raw data
	Screen laboratory	Collect administrative data about current and former employees	One author is a principal investigator; two are postdocs. One member is a technician. One member with unknown status
		Determine storage systems architecture	There are several shared volumes used by the laboratory members. The data is shared between raw, users, and projects volumes
Collection	*Extract resources*	Extract experimental methods	There are two types of analyses reported in the paper, each with their own software and instrumentation. In CASE A, those are HDX-MS analysis and MS-MS analysis
		Extract experimental resources	In the publication of CASE A, we extracted: Waters nano-Acquity UPLC system, [...], Swiss-Model, Phyre2 server, [...] as a list of instruments and software
		Extract external repositories and supplemental information	In CASE A, files have been deposited on PRIDE a digital repository, and an access number is present in the additional information
	Make snapshots	Perform (targeted) snapshots of disk volumes	Select the user and project folders belonging to the laboratory members involved in the publication. Make a snapshot. For instance, in PowerShell (Windows) with the commands Get-ChildItem and Export-CSV

(continued)

Table 2. (*continued*)

	Activity	Sub-activity	Example outcomes of CASE A
Examination	*Process snapshots*	Consolidate snapshots	Merge user and project folders in one (tabular) data sets
		Reduce noise	Duplicates and system files are deleted from the consolidated snapshot
	Construct Annotated Experimental Resources Table (AERT)	Extract experimental methods	Determining what qualifies as an experimental method depends on the context of the analysis
		Link experimental resources to methods	The software is extracted for each method mentioning the use of the software
		Link laboratory instruments to methods	For a method, each instrument used can generate output with specific extensions (such as. RAW files in proteomics)
Analysis	*Map file paths*	Map files to AERT elements	File system meta-data might be inaccurate. Hence, cross-checking with elements in the AERT table is crucial not to include irrelevant files
	Filter file paths	Filter file paths referring to a publication	Not all files in a folder might belong to the analyzed publication; additional filtering is needed to exclude unnecessary files
	Estimate functional repeatability and replicability	Estimate Method coverage	An estimation of the number of methods reported in the publication that are covered by evidence left on the storage
		Estimate Software coverage	An indication of the number of software resources that are successfully identified from reading the file paths
		Estimate Instrument coverage	An indication of the number of laboratory instruments that are identified by the investigator

(*continued*)

Table 2. (*continued*)

	Activity	Sub-activity	Example outcomes of CASE A
Presentation	*Report findings*	Report file mappings and their confidence	We included the folders of the first and last author in our analysis and reported the folders used during the analysis
		Report functional repeatability	The extent to which preserved files are consistent, complete, and not fragmented
		Report functional replicability	The extent to which disseminated files are consistent, complete, and not fragmented
		Evaluate report with laboratory member(s)	We evaluated the report with one domain expert (laboratory member)

The goal of the LF approach is to present to research a report on the state of the storage in terms of reproducibility. To evaluate the functional repeatability and replicability, the following classification indicating the degree to which the preserved evidence corresponds to the requirements of completeness and consistency of the artifacts as described by the Association for Computing Machinery (ACM) [19]. The classification shown in Table 3, i.e., low, medium, high repeatability/replicability is diverging from the ACM is two ways. First, functional artifacts are divided in terms of locality: repeatable is used for resources preserved in the laboratory, and replicable is used for resources disseminated in supplemental information and digital repositories. Second, in terms of degree (low, medium, high) to account for varying scenarios.

Table 3. Findings from the first iteration on one publication (CASE A)

	Outcomes	CASE A	Comment
Identification	Number of laboratory members	5	Each user folder of laboratory member has to be mapped and investigated
	Number of external authors	2	Several authors from external research groups are listed. External authors do not have user folders. On the laboratory storage, authors are mentioned by name, identifier, or affiliations
	Editorial process duration	From 29/03/2017 until 28/06/2017	Filter project folders that were updated (i.e., modified date) at the time of submission

(*continued*)

Table 3. (*continued*)

	Outcomes	CASE A	Comment
Collection and examination	Number of methods*	4	Four method subsections are referring to computational work or laboratory instruments manipulated with software
	The number of software resources	10	There are ten software resources used (e.g., to preprocess and visualize data)
	Number of Instruments	5	Five laboratory instruments were used to generate raw data
	Number of files (local/deposited)	3011/15	In total, the consolidated mappings contain 3011 files on the storage and 15 files in the external repository
	Total file size	49.5 GB	The "weight" of digital evidence of the investigated publication is around 50 GB
	Time delta **	1486 days	The first file included as experimental data was modified more than four years before the last file included
Analysis	Corresponding software	5	Files corresponding to 5 software resources are located, which means five other software resources have no (explicit) traces left on the storage or online
	Corresponding instruments	4	One instrument could not be mapped to the digital evidence found
Presentation	Functional repeatability	MEDIUM	The evidence is complete and entirely consistent with the corresponding experimental report. However, files have not been aggregated in a project folder, which requires to investigate several folders across different folders to obtain the complete (computational) input
	Functional replicability	LOW	Only the necessary raw files of one method have been deposited. Direct replicability is therefore hindered by the absence of other artifacts which are necessary to replicate the results

* Computational methods, ** based on file system meta-data, not the exact duration of experiments

6 Evaluation of Laboratory Forensics Outcomes

We evaluated the usefulness of LF results with a member of the laboratory responsible for the storage infrastructure. We collected the impressions of our contact person after a short presentation of the forensic process and report of CASE A (see Table 3). The impressions formulated by the laboratory member indicate that our approach appears to be rigorous and convincing. The systematic classification of resources into instrument, methods, and software sheds new lights on the resources underlying a publication.

Next, the extent of the fragmentation of the files was not expected by our interviewee, which shows that the ability of an LF approach to gathering evidence beyond expected locations by users. Also, the communication of issues with a set of measurable indicators gives an overview of the strengths and weaknesses of data management for specific publications. A critical note was that the indicators and scoring method need further refinements and more transparency. For instance, the indicator of functional replicability should incorporate mandatory openness and non-mandatory openness. This distinction would help to distinguish scientific data dissemination imposed by publishers (mandatory) and self-motivated by researchers in the laboratory (non-mandatory).

Besides, we presented the outcomes of CASE A to the data management community meeting of our University in February 2019, attended by 20 participants. This presentation was meant to collect the impressions of people involved in data management services. There the main impressions of the participants are that although the approach is time-consuming, it seems worth to conduct such analyses to explain to researchers the importance of good data management practices. Even the fact that LF is challenging to accomplish is, by itself, a powerful example of problematic data management practices which data managers can use to engage with researchers about RDM practices. Further, to collect additional feedback about the effectiveness of the LF approach, we investigated three new cases to obtain better insights into alternative data management practices adopted by other laboratory members. The three additional cases are labeled case B, C, and D (see Table 4).

Table 4. Summary of the outcomes of additional cases

Outcome	CASE B	CASE C	CASE D
Size	1.2 GB	2.6 GB	136.9 GB
Number of preserved/deposited files	689/0	137/123	939/179
Corresponding software	2/8	1/5	2/6
Corresponding instruments	3/4	3/4	1/2
Functional repeatability	MEDIUM	MEDIUM	MEDIUM
Functional replicability	LOW	HIGH	MEDIUM

The second evaluation was driven by the question of whether a forensic analysis of a storage system in a laboratory retrieves more relevant evidence than laboratory members when they are asked for searching underlying evidence publications. To achieve that, we asked two laboratory members to collect data underlying a publication used in one of the four investigated cases. More, we asked the laboratory members, hereafter participants, to elaborate on their search strategy and judge the extent, according to them, of the repeatability and replicability of the article they received.

The participants reported located files in a word document or during a live demonstration. Their outcomes are consistent with LF assessment, which showed that relevant files are all preserved but fragmented on the storage (hence medium repeatability). Also, the participants expressed their difficulties in locating legacy data or data created by another laboratory member in the past. In that case, we found that the presence of a reference list of files created by the forensic investigation is essential to evaluate whether the participants retrieved the complete list of files or evidence was still not located.

7 Discussion and Conclusion

Throughout this study, we answered the following question: "How can digital forensics techniques be used to assess the reproducibility of scientific experiments?" A design science approach has delivered preliminary artifacts and evidence that laboratory forensics (LF) is a useful approach for evaluating storage systems in laboratories. Despite this, LF suffers from significant limitations in its current state. One limitation is that the LF process is yet to be further evaluated on a number of forensic cases in different environments to increase the rigor and reliability of LF investigations. These limitations are mainly due to the nature of reconstructing events from digital data [23] and the complicated extraction of experimental resources from publications. Moreover, access to storage systems in laboratories is needed, which might posit some additional challenges related to the privacy of the users. Despite the limitations of the current LF approach, LF has unique strengths compared to approaches for RDM such as post-publication curation of research data [3].

First, LF attempts to locate data despite reporting gaps and unavailable resources, unlike other studies relying on published material exclusively [4]. Collecting evidence from storage systems allows going beyond the written account of the events that occurred in a laboratory.

Second, an LF investigation actively seeks to reconstruct experiments to accurately report on which experimental resources are used, by whom and locate the underlying materials. This can serve as input for reproducibility studies, were retracing the full life cycle of scientific discoveries is a prerequisite for understanding all steps taken in an experiment to guarantee its reproducibility [24].

Last, the extraction of structured data about experimental methods, resources, and data together with evidence on storage systems might be of high value for designing ontologies representing a particular field of study [25] with a higher ability to manage the artifacts in use in laboratories and guarantee reproducible storage patterns.

To conclude, Laboratory Forensics demands further development, evaluation, automation, and tooling to become readily available for scientists and data managers. Hitherto, we have been able to show that in daily practices (digital) experimental resources are not preserved in a functionally repeatable and replicable way in the investigated laboratory. In short, laboratory forensics support the development of rigorous assessment of data management issues related to laboratory work. In upcoming research, we will further investigate the synergy of laboratory forensics with research data management practices.

References

1. European Commission: Access to and preservation of scientific information in Europe (2015). https://doi.org/10.2777/975917
2. Lefebvre, A., Schermerhorn, E., Spruit, M.: how research data management can contribute to efficient and reliable science (2018)
3. Bechhofer, S., Buchan, I., et al.: Why linked data is not enough for scientists. Futur. Gener. Comput. Syst. **29**, 599–611 (2013). https://doi.org/10.1016/j.future.2011.08.004
4. Federer, L.M., Belter, C.W., et al.: Data sharing in PLOS ONE: an analysis of data availability statements. PLoS ONE **13**, e0194768 (2018). https://doi.org/10.1371/journal.pone.0194768
5. Collberg, C., Proebsting, T.A.: Repeatability in computer systems research. Commun. ACM **59**, 62–69 (2016). https://doi.org/10.1145/2812803
6. Peng, R.D., Dominici, F., Zeger, S.L.: Reproducible epidemiologic research (2006). https://doi.org/10.1093/aje/kwj093
7. Stevens, H.: Life out of sequence: a data-driven history of bioinformatics. Univeristy of Chicago Press, Chicago (2013). https://doi.org/10.1080/14636778.2015.1025127
8. Ince, D.C., Hatton, L., Graham-Cumming, J.: The case for open computer programs. Nature **482**, 485–488 (2012). https://doi.org/10.1038/nature10836
9. Hevner, A.R.: A three cycle view of design science research. Scand. J. Inf. Syst. **19**, 87–92 (2007). https://aisel.aisnet.org/sjis/vol19/iss2/4
10. Gregor, S., Hevner, A.R.: Positioning and presenting design science for maximum impact. MIS Q. **37**, 337–355 (2013). https://doi.org/10.2753/MIS0742-1222240302
11. Palmer, G.: A road map for digital forensic research. In: Proceedings of the 2001 Digital Forensic Research Workshop Conference (2001). https://doi.org/10.1111/j.1365-2656.2005.01025.x
12. Casey, E., Katz, G., Lewthwaite, J.: Honing digital forensic processes. Digit. Investig. **10**, 138–147 (2013). https://doi.org/10.1016/j.diin.2013.07.002
13. Rowlingson, R.: A Ten Step Process for Forensic Readiness. Int. J. Digit. Evid. 2 (2004). https://doi.org/10.1162/NECO_a_00266
14. Ayris, P., Berthou, J.-Y., et al.: Towards a FAIR Internet of data, services and things for practicing open science. 3, 0 (2018). https://doi.org/10.2777/940154
15. Årnes, A.: Digital Forensics. Wiley, Hoboken (2017)
16. Franklin, A., Perovic, S.: Experiment in physics. In: Zalta, E.N. (ed.) The Stanford Encyclopedia of Philosophy. Metaphysics Research Lab, Stanford University (2016)
17. Weber, M.: Experiment in biology. In: Zalta, E.N. (ed.) The Stanford Encyclopedia of Philosophy. Metaphysics Research Lab, Stanford University (2018)
18. Radder, H.: Experimentation in the Natural Sciences. Presented at the (2012). https://doi.org/10.1007/978-94-007-4107-2_3
19. ACM: Artifact Review and Badging. https://www.acm.org/publications/policies/artifact-review-badging
20. Latour, B., Woolgar, S.: Laboratory Life the Construction of Scientific Facts. Princeton University Press, Princeton (1986)
21. Borgman, C.L.: Data, disciplines, and scholarly publishing. In: Learned Publishing, pp. 29–38. Wiley (2008). https://doi.org/10.1087/095315108X254476
22. Nosek, B.A., Alter, et al.: Promoting an open research culture (2015). https://doi.org/10.1126/science.aab2374

23. Mabey, M., Doupé, A., Zhao, Z., Ahn, G.-J.: Challenges, opportunities and a framework for web environment forensics. Advances in Digital Forensics XIV. IAICT, vol. 532, pp. 11–33. Springer, Cham (2018). https://doi.org/10.1007/978-3-319-99277-8_2
24. Huang, Y., Gottardo, R.: Comparability and reproducibility of biomedical data. Brief. Bioinform. **14**, 391–401 (2013). https://doi.org/10.1093/bib/bbs078
25. Hoehndorf, R., Dumontier, M., Gkoutos, G.V.: Evaluation of research in biomedical ontologies. Brief. Bioinform. **14**, 696–712 (2013). https://doi.org/10.1093/bib/bbs053

Artificial Intelligence and Internet of Things

The State of Artificial Intelligence Research in the Context of National Security: Bibliometric Analysis and Research Agenda

Samuel Fosso Wamba[1], Ransome Epie Bawack[1,2(✉)] (iD),
and Kevin Daniel André Carillo[1]

[1] Toulouse Business School, 20 Boulevard Lascrosses, 31068 Toulouse, France
ransome.bawack@tsm-education.fr
[2] Toulouse 1 University Capitole,
2 Rue du Doyen-Gabriel-Marty, 31042 Toulouse, France

Abstract. Artificial intelligence (AI) is a growing research topic in national security due to the growing need for peaceful and inclusive societies, as well as for the maintenance of strong institutions of justice. As e-societies continue to evolve due to the advancements made in information and communication technologies (ICT), AI has proven crucial to guarantee the development of security measures, especially against growing cyberthreats and cyberattacks. This relevance has been translated into an explosive growth of AI applications for the improvement of decision support systems, expert systems, robotics, surveillance, and military operations that aim at ensuring national security. However, there is no bibliometric research on AI in national security, especially one that highlights current debates on the topic. This paper presents an overview of research on AI and national security, with emphasis on the research focus areas and debates central to research on the topic. We analyzed 94 references collected from the Web of Science (WoS) Core Collection and used VOS viewer software to analyze them. Based on these analyses, we identified 7 focus areas and 8 debates on AI in national security. We also identified the state and evolution of research on the topic in terms of main journals, authors, institutions, and countries. Our findings help researchers and practitioners better understand the state of the art of AI research on national security, and guides future research and development projects on the topic.

Keywords: Artificial intelligence · National security · Military · Defense · Bibliometrics

1 Introduction

Artificial intelligence (AI) is a growing research topic in national security (NS) due to the rising need for peaceful and inclusive societies, as well as for the maintenance of strong institutions of justice. National security refers to a State's ability to protect and defend its citizens by preserving the principles, standards, institutions and values of its society [1]. This implies conscious and purposeful actions taken to defend citizens from both military and non-military threats, both in the physical and digital world. To this

© IFIP International Federation for Information Processing 2019
Published by Springer Nature Switzerland AG 2019
I. O. Pappas et al. (Eds.): I3E 2019, LNCS 11701, pp. 255–266, 2019.
https://doi.org/10.1007/978-3-030-29374-1_21

end, nations are investing huge amounts in AI research to achieve military, information, and economic superiority, as well as technological leadership [2].

For over 40 years, military power has been the main instrument used to enforce NS [1]. This power is often demonstrated by the ability to develop and use technologies in security actions. This has been the case with nuclear technology, aerospace, biotechnology, internet and cyber technology. Today, research efforts on technology for NS are turned towards AI, which refers to computational techniques that give technology artefacts the ability to act like intelligent beings [3].

AI's significant potential for NS is mostly due to advancements in machine learning. It promises unique opportunities for autonomy, speed, scaling, predictability, and explicability, all of which are essential for actions towards NS. This far, it has revolutionized intelligence, surveillance, reconnaissance, logistics, cybersecurity, command and control, autonomous vehicles, and lethal autonomous weapon systems (LAWS) [4]. However, there are several debates central to the use and consequences of using AI to ensure NS.

Ethical dilemmas on the framework within which AI should be used to enforce NS [5, 6] as well as in modern warfare [7, 8] are some of the most serious issues on using AI for IS. Also, it is becoming impossible for a State to ensure NS without considering the impact and implications this could have on other States [9]. This is due to the symbiotic relationship between national and global security, the latter evolving from the effects of globalization. This blurs the lines of territoriality in today's society, making NS a global concern.

AI researchers on NS in both the private sector and academia have made significant technical progress in the last five years at unprecedented speeds [4]. However, very little is known about the extent of this research in academic literature and the current debates they focus on that could help solve some of the issues on the topic at hand. Thus, we present an overview of academic research on AI in NS, with emphasis on the debates central to research on the topic. To this end, we use bibliometrics, which is an established method used to analyze specific research areas and draw meaningful insights that could guide future research and practice [10, 11].

There are recent studies that use bibliometrics to understand academic literature on global AI research [12], AI in health [13], and on sustainable AI [14]. To the best of our knowledge, there is no research that seeks to analyze current literature on AI in the context of NS especially using bibliometrics. Therefore, one of the main contributions we make for researchers and practitioners is to provide an overview of the structure and development of academic literature on AI in NS. Secondly, we reveal the trends and themes that lead the discussions and research on the topic. Thirdly, we identify current research gaps that could guide future research plans and inform practitioners or policymakers on current debates that could influence related policies.

Our work reveals the complexities of debates related to AI in NS especially given the implications and relative importance for global security in the physical and digital world. Thus, it helps both research and NS institutions manage and evaluate their research projects by setting the appropriate research priorities and allocating resources to match the current needs of the topic. In Sect. 2, we present our research methodology, followed by our results in Sect. 3, and then discussion and implications in Sect. 4.

2   Methodology

This study is based on a bibliometric analysis of AI research in the context of NS. Bibliometrics focuses on obtaining quantitative facts on written documents such as output, impact, and collaboration [15]. This approach has proven to be effective for capturing the temporal content of research topics and to identify research trends [12] like what we seek to do in this study. It has been used in information systems (IS) research and is found to be a complete and efficient assessment method of academic literature [16]. It has also been used to analyze and interpret existing IS literature in several contexts [8, 17].

The steps we used in our bibliometric analysis were adapted from the six steps proposed by Cuellar et al. [18]. This adaptation led to the following four steps: (i) define the academic field and the context of the study, (ii) identify and collect literature on the topic, (iii) conduct bibliometric analysis, and (iv) present and comment the results. Step four (4) is the results and discussion section of this paper.

2.1   Define the Academic Field and the Context of Study

The academic field concerned in this study is that of AI, and the context is that of NS. IS being a field that studies the link between people, processes and technology in relation to organizations and society, IS research can make significant contributions to discussions on the use of AI-based IS for NS.

2.2   Identify and Collect Literature on the Topic

We collected bibliometric data from the Web of Science (WoS) database. This database is one of the most commonly used databases for bibliometric analysis due to its huge journal coverage and reliability of references [19, 20]. Table 1 presents our search string and the results we obtained from the WoS core collection. The asterisk used next to the keywords enables the search query located and add any available literature with related keywords in the database. This search was conducted on May 6, 2019, at 9 pm. Thus, our analysis is based on the 100 publications obtained from the WoS search. We downloaded the complete bibliometric data in the WoS format for analysis.

Table 1. Web of Science search results

Search string	Time span	Results (from web of science core collection)
1. (TS = ("Artificial Intelligence*" AND "National Defense*")) AND LANGUAGE: (English) AND DOCUMENT TYPES: (Article)	All years	1
2. (TS = ("Artificial Intelligence*" AND "National Security*")) AND LANGUAGE: (English) AND DOCUMENT TYPES: (Article)	All years	4
3. (TS = ("Artificial Intelligence*" AND Military*)) AND LANGUAGE: (English) AND DOCUMENT TYPES: (Article)	All years	96
1 OR 2 OR 3	All years	100

2.3   Conduct Bibliometric Analysis

To conduct bibliometric analysis, we used the software called VOSviewer version 1.6.10. This tool is recognized for its ability to conduct sophisticated bibliometric analyses and provide reliable results with great visualizations to facilitate understanding [21]. With this software, we were able to conduct co-authorship, co-occurrence, citation, bibliographic coupling, and co-citation analyses based on the data we collected.

In the next section, we present the results of the bibliometric analysis, with emphasis on authors, institutions, countries, publications, research themes and trends that make up current discussions and debates.

3   Results

The results of this study are presented and discussed in two sections that answer the following questions: (i) what is the status and evolution of academic research on AI in the context of NS; (ii) what is the current research focus and trend driving debates on the topic?

3.1   What Is the Status and Evolution of Academic Research on AI in the Context of National Security?

The first papers in the WoS database related to AI in the context of NS were published in 1991. These papers discussed the applications of AI in expert systems (ES) [22] and decision support systems (DSS) [23]. Since then, one could barely find up to five academic research articles published on the topic each year until 2017 when 14 publications were recorded. About 51 of the 100 articles found were published between 2013 and May 2019. This shows the rising interest by academic researchers in this topic that has barely been researched for the past 30 years. Moreover, using the keywords "national security" and "national defense", we obtained only four results whereas we obtained 96 results when we searched the WoS database using the term "military" with AI. This confirms that indeed, the military applications of AI have been the main focus of academic researchers as concerns NS. 35 out of the 100 articles were published in the area of engineering, 31 in computer science, 18 in operations research management science, 13 in business economics, 11 in international relations, 7 in social issues, 6 in government law, and 5 in robotics, 4 in telecommunications, 3 in instruments instrumentation, 2 in material science, and 2 in oceanography.

At this point when the academic research on AI in NS is still at a nascent stage, it is important to identify the most influential authors, publications, and collaborations in this research area. This could help researchers and practitioners decide with whom to collaborate on such projects, and to identify key players with whom to develop strategic partnerships related to this issue. To respond to this question, we performed co-authorship, citation, and co-citation analyses on the bibliometric data. The co-authorship analysis was done by institution, and country. The citation analysis was done by document, source, author, organization, and country. The co-citation analysis was done by cited references, cited sources, and cited authors.

Co-authoring Research Institutions and Countries. This bibliometric analysis helps to interpret the structure of research collaboration networks on AI in NS. Hence, highlights the most influential countries and research institutions as well as the structure of research teams. Starting with the analysis of research institutions, the dispersion of literature on the topic is led by the United States Naval Institute – USN (3 documents, 83 citations) and the University of Oxford (3 documents, 6 citations). Only 13 out of 134 institutions have published at least two articles on AI in the context of NS.

There are three clusters of at least two institutions collaborating in this research area: cluster 1 consists of USN, Florida International University (2 documents, 92 citations), and the United States Army (2 documents, 12 citations). Cluster 2 consists of RAND Corporation (2 documents, 2 citations) and Stanford University (2 documents, 1 citation). Cluster 3 consists of the Chinese Academy of Science – CAS (2 documents, 9 citations) and the University of Chinese Academy of Science – UCAS (2 documents, 9 citations). Clusters 1 and 2 consists of US-based institutions while cluster 3 consists of Chinese institutions.

14 out of 32 countries identified in our analysis have published at least two papers on AI in NS. The three countries leading this research area are: USA (42 documents, 547 citations), England (12 documents, 47 citations), and China (10 documents, 137 citations). While China stands alone, England, Russia (2 documents, 1 citation) and the USA form an important research cluster, France (3 documents, 78 citations) and Singapore (3 documents, 1 citation) form another.

Publication, Journal, Reference and Author Citation and Co-citation Analysis. To identify the most influential publications, journals and references in this research area, we used citation and co-citation analysis to rank them by popularity.

We assume that the most cited publications and journals are the most influential ones. Table 2 presents the 10 most influential publications and their characteristics. 71 journals were found to have published research on AI in NS. Those that have published at least two papers include expert systems with applications (8 documents, 183 citations), Bulletin of the atomic scientists (6 documents, 1 citation), European journal of operational research (5 documents, 56 citations), IET Radar, Sonar & Navigation (3 documents, 9 citations), industrial robot an international journal (3 documents, 14 citations), interfaces (3 documents, 9 citations), and artificial intelligence (2 documents, 13 citations). The most cited references include are presented in Table 3. We were also able to identify the most cited authors in this research area and their research interests as presented in Table 4.

Table 2. Most cited papers in research on AI in national security

Article title	Authors	Year	# of citations	Journal
The use of Kalman filter and neural network methodologies in gas turbine performance diagnostics: a comparative study	Volponi, Allan J., et al.	2000	113	ASME Turbo Expo 2000: Power for Land, Sea, and Air
Virtual reality surgery: neurosurgery and the contemporary landscape	Spicer, M. A., & Apuzzo, M. L.	2003	87	Neurosurgery
Prognosis of bearing failures using hidden Markov models and the adaptive neuro-fuzzy inference system	Soualhi, Abdenour, et al.	2014	67	IEEE transactions on industrial electronics
Intelligent lessons learned systems	Weber, R., Aha, D. W., & Becerra-Fernandez, I.	2001	66	Expert systems with applications
Problem solving and knowledge inertia	Shu-hsien Liao	2002	41	Expert systems with applications
Probabilistic roadmap-based path planning for an autonomous unmanned helicopter	Pettersson, P. O., & Doherty, P.	2006	37	Journal of intelligent & fuzzy systems
Artificial intelligence technologies for robot assisted urban search and rescue	John G. Blitch	1996	35	Expert systems with applications
Case-based decision support system: architecture for simulating military command and control	Shu-hsien Liao	2000	34	European journal of operational research
Human–robot interaction: status and challenges	Thomas B. Sheridan	2016	32	Human factors
Virtual reality and telepresence for military medicine	Richard M. Satava	1995	31	Computers in biology and medicine

Table 3. Most cited references by researchers on AI in national security

Article	Authors	Year	# of citations	Type of publication
Superintelligence: paths, dangers, strategies. Oxford: Oxford University Press	Bostrom, N.	2014	4	Book
Governing lethal behavior in autonomous robots	Arkin, Ronald.	2009	3	Book
Swarming and the future of conflict	Arquilla, John, and David Ronfeldt	2000	3	Book

(*continued*)

Table 3. (*continued*)

Article	Authors	Year	# of citations	Type of publication
Artificial intelligence: a modern approach	Russell, Stuart, and Peter Norvig	1995	3	Book
Weapons, autonomous. An open letter from AI & robotics researchers	Signed by 20 (Hawking, Musk, Wozniak…)	2015	3	Open letter
Proceedings of IEEE international conference on neural networks	Kennedy, James, and R. C. Eberhart	1995		Conference proceedings

Table 4. Most cited authors by researchers on AI in national security

Author	# of citations	Research field
Vukobratovic M.	24	Robotics
Bostrom N.	9	Superintelligence
Good I.J.	9	Bayesian methods
McCulloch W.S.	9	Mathematical Biophysics
Kim J.	8	Theoretical AI
Laird J.E.	6	Cognitive architecture
Freedberg Jr Sydney J.	6	Art historian
Moffat J	6	Genetic interactions

3.2 What Is the Current Research Focus and Debates on AI in National Security?

The results in this section are based on bibliographic coupling and co-occurrence mappings. Bibliographic coupling was analyzed by document, source, author, organization, and country. Co-occurrence analysis was done by keywords (all, author-provided, and Keywords plus) and content analysis of the terms in the title and abstracts.

Research Focus of AI in the Context of National Security. To identify the main research topics on AI in the context of NS, we conducted keyword analysis through co-occurrences by concentrating on keywords provided by authors. This technique counts the number of co-occurrences of keywords and the greater the frequency, the greater the relevance of the topic. VOS viewer identified 359 keywords. Figure 1 illustrates the main keywords, the colors representing the clusters, the sizes representing the frequency, and the lines representing the links between keywords. The smaller the distance between the nodes, the stronger the relationship between them (how many times they occur together in the same paper). Figure 1 is based on a threshold of 2 occurrences, representing 25 keyword co-occurrences. The most common keywords leading the main clusters are: artificial intelligence (36 occurrences, lemon green), robotics (5 occurrences, red), autonomy (3 occurrences, purple), intelligent agents (3 occurrences, orange), drones (2 occurrences, sky blue), decision support systems (4 occurrences, blue), neural nets (2 occurrences, green).

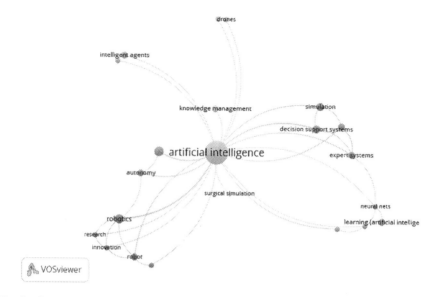

Fig. 1. Co-occurrence network of author keywords in publications. Related to AI in national security (Color figure online)

These clusters represent seven research focus area on AI in NS. Cluster 1 represents general AI research in the context of NS. Items in this cluster include artificial intelligence, decision support systems, economics, expert systems, future, military, models, simulation, and surgical simulation. Cluster 2 represents research that focuses on the learning capabilities of AI. The items in this cluster include classification, feature extraction, identification, learning (artificial intelligence), networks, neural nets, pattern recognition, performance, recognition. Cluster 3 represents research that focuses on the use of AI for decision support. Items in this cluster include decision support systems, decision-making, information, intelligence, intelligent agents, knowledge management, management. Cluster 4 represents the category of research that focuses on AI algorithms. Items in this cluster include algorithm, genetic algorithm, neural network, neural-networks, particle swarm optimization, and PID controller.

Cluster 5 represents research that focuses on the research and development of intelligent systems. The items in this cluster include innovation, intelligent control, research, robot, robotics, systems. Cluster 6 represents research that focuses on the applications of AI algorithms, systems or technologies in NS. Items in this cluster include algorithms, drones, robots, security, and state. Cluster 7 represents research on the use of machine learning for system autonomy. Items in this cluster include autonomy and machine learning.

Debates on AI in National Security. We identified current trends using KeyWords Plus analysis. KeyWords Plus is the result of Thomson Reuters editorial expertise in Science. The editors review the titles of all references and highlight additional relevant but overlooked keywords that were not listed by the author or publisher. This technique helps to uncover more papers that may not have appeared in the search due to changes in scientific keywords over time, showing the evolution of the field. 14 out of the 147 keyWords occur at least twice. The most recurrent are neural networks (3), algorithms (3) and systems (3).

KeyWords plus formed three clusters. Cluster 1 (3 items) includes Classification, Networks, Recognition. Cluster 2 (2 items) includes Algorithm and Identification. Cluster 3 (2 items) includes Future and Neural-networks. This depicts the growing interest in using neural network algorithms for identification, pattern recognition and classification of data for AI systems of the future.

Through the bibliographic coupling of documents, we were able to classify current AI research in the context of NS into eight research themes as presented in Table 2. The table shows how debates on AI have evolved since 1991 when the focus was on the applications of neural networks, till now that research focuses more on AI ethics, principles, and governance. We also notice that since 2017, world peace and conflict resolution became a major research theme thereby affirming the need for more research in this nascent theme.

Table 5. Research themes for AI in the context of national security.

Research theme	Start date	Description
AI ethics, principles, and governance	2018	Focuses on the ethics and control/laws governing the use of machines/robots/automated systems by governments for military or surveillance actions
World peace and conflict resolution	2017	Focuses on the challenges the military faces as technology and AI continues to spread. It emphasizes the fact that world peace is threatened by the democratization of technology. As a result, nations are losing their military control over the population. This research cluster investigates how nations can try to manage this situation
Robotics in modern warfare	2017	Focuses on how robotics is changing modern warfare, with emphasis on the legal and geopolitical implications. Advances are made on how autonomous systems and weapons like drones are using advanced combat techniques like swarming and hiving
Future & post-humanity	2017	Focuses on research related to the design of algorithms the and manufacturing of technologies for the future (post-humanity)
Human performance enhancement	2015	Focuses on using AI to enhance human performance and national defense strategies

(*continued*)

Table 5. (*continued*)

Research theme	Start date	Description
Expert systems	1996	Focuses on the use of intelligent knowledge-based expert systems for planning and analyzing military operations (activities and data)
Planning & control	1996	Focuses on research related to the use of AI to develop robust planning and workflow systems
Neural networks	1991	Focuses on research related to the use of neural networks (operational, financial, health...)

4   Discussion and Research Agenda

In this paper, we have investigated the state of AI research in the context of NS. We used bibliometric analyses to identify the key players in this research area, as well as their research focus and debates on AI research in NS. Due to the limited amount of academic research published in this area, we found this method most suitable to help identify key connections and relationships in the field in terms of authors, journals, research themes, research institutions, and even countries. Our results provide an overview of the research domain and provide information that could help researchers and practitioners plan their limited resources and develop strategic partnerships with the key players identified. It also informs on the key debates that influence decisions regarding using AI to ensure NS both in the digital and physical worlds. Therefore, from our results, we can arrive at the following conclusions.

AI in the context of NS is a very complex research area. This interdisciplinary research area involving over 12 major disciplines need is proof of this complexity This calls for the need to collect and integrate research on the topic in other to have a holistic view and to draw relevant conclusions for the conceptualization of AI for NS. Although this is a relatively young and growing research area, it is timidly rising as people get more aware of the dangers of AI and the rising NS issues worldwide. The fact that research on AI in NS started with applications in ES and DSS shows that the field of IS has a major role to play in this research area. Therefore, IS researchers need to get fully involved in this research field and contribute to how AI-enabled IS can contribute to ensuring NS.

As concerns the state and evolution of this research area, the facts reveal that there is still much to be done on this topic as it has not received the attention it deserves. The most cited papers in the 1990s focus on the use of AI in urban search and rescue, and in medicine. In this area of research was a publication in the year 2000 on neural networks. However, in recent years, the most cited paper was published in 2016 on the status and challenges of human-robot interactions. This shows the evolution of this research area from an application phase to an interaction phase. This explains the increasing number of debates on AI ethics and principles. Only 13 institutions, 14 countries and 71 journals have published academic research on AI in the context of NS. This is certainly not enough given how many disciplines can contribute to discussions on the topic. Thus, there is a need for more quality academic publications on the topic in well-recognized journals so that they can be more accessible to a wider audience. The most referenced publication is on the paths, dangers, and strategies of superintelligence. This is proof of the concerns people have on the use of AI technologies. The relevance of research on AI in NS was recognized by the United Nations in the sustainable development goals 2030 agenda where it features as part of goal 16 [24]. As 2030 approaches, academic researchers need to increase their efforts towards making meaningful contributions to the attainment of this goal.

As concerns current research focus and debates on AI in NS, we identified 7 major focus areas and 8 debates. The 7 focus areas are robotics, planning, governance, war, military, conflict resolution, community, internet, power, and organization. These focus areas cover both the physical and the digital world, showing that although much still needs to be done, researchers have identified these areas as key important to this research area. Table 5 describes the 8 debates in this research area from 1991 until now. All this information is especially important for State institutions when considering the use of AI in NS policies. They are also relevant to researchers seeking to use this information to provide answers or solutions to existing debates or open new ones. The literature also indicates the need for future research about the non-military-oriented use of AI for NS. For example, using technologies like blockchain, it could be interesting to investigate how people can connect with each other securely to ensure mutual protection before intervention from armed forces.

This paper has some limitations, particularly associated with bibliometrics. Firstly, some research papers might have been omitted as a result of the keywords used. To mitigate this risk, we used asterisks to increase the search sphere to related keywords. Secondly, our results are based on results from the WoS Core Collection database. Our work could be extended or complemented by analyzing other databases like Scopus or Google Scholar. Authors can also decide to evaluate published through other means or outlets such as conference proceedings, practice-oriented magazines, or doctoral theses. Perhaps there is more accessible research in these outlets, possibly published in other languages as well.

References

1. Segun, O.: National security versus global security. UN Chronicle: The Magazine of the United Nations (2014). https://unchronicle.un.org/article/national-security-versus-global-security
2. Allen, G., Chan, T.: Artificial intelligence and national security. Belfer Center for Science and International Affairs Cambridge, MA (2017)
3. Akgül, A.: Artificial intelligence military applications. Ankara Üniversitesi SBF Derg. **45**(1), 255–271 (2015)
4. Hoadley, D.S., Lucas, N.J.: Artificial Intelligence and National Security. Congressional Research Service (2018)
5. Cath, C., Wachter, S., Mittelstadt, B., Taddeo, M., Floridi, L.: Artificial intelligence and the 'good society': the US, EU, and UK approach. Sci. Eng. Ethics **24**(2), 505–528 (2018)
6. Teo, Y.-L.: Regulating Artificial Intelligence: An Ethical Approach (2018)

7. Garcia, D.: Lethal artificial intelligence and change: the future of international peace and security. Int. Stud. Rev. **20**(2), 334–341 (2018)
8. Johnson, J.: Artificial intelligence & future warfare: implications for international security. Def. Secur. Anal. **35**, 1–23 (2019)
9. Clopton, Z.D.: Territoriality, technology, and national security. U. Chi. L. Rev. **83**, 45 (2016)
10. Hicks, D., Wouters, P., Waltman, L., De Rijcke, S., Rafols, I.: Bibliometrics: the Leiden Manifesto for research metrics. Nat. News **520**(7548), 429 (2015)
11. King, J.: A review of bibliometric and other science indicators and their role in research evaluation. J. Inf. Sci. **13**(5), 261–276 (1987)
12. Niu, J., Tang, W., Xu, F., Zhou, X., Song, Y.: Global research on artificial intelligence from 1990–2014: spatially-explicit bibliometric analysis. ISPRS Int. J. Geo-Inf. **5**(5), 66 (2016)
13. Tran, B.X., et al.: Global evolution of research in artificial intelligence in health and medicine: a bibliometric study. J. Clin. Med. **8**(3), 360 (2019)
14. Larsson, S., Anneroth, M., Felländer, A., Felländer-Tsai, L., Heintz, F., Ångström, R.C.: Sustainable AI: an inventory of the state of knowledge of ethical, social, and legal challenges related to artificial intelligence (2019)
15. Corrall, S., Kennan, M.A., Afzal, W.: Bibliometrics and research data management services: emerging trends in library support for research. Libr. Trends **61**(3), 636–674 (2013)
16. Stewart, A., Cotton, J.L.: Does 'evaluating journal quality and the association for information systems senior scholars journal basket...' support the basket with bibliometric measures? AIS Trans. Replication Res. **4**(1), 12 (2018)
17. Renaud, A., Walsh, I., Kalika, M.: Is SAM still alive? A bibliometric and interpretive mapping of the strategic alignment research field. J. Strateg. Inf. Syst. **25**(2), 75–103 (2016)
18. Cuellar, M.J., Takeda, H., Vidgen, R.T., Truex, D.: Ideational influence, connectedness, and venue representation: making an assessment of scholarly capital. J. AIS **17**(1), 3 (2016)
19. Mongeon, P., Paul-Hus, A.: The journal coverage of web of science and Scopus: a comparative analysis. Scientometrics **106**(1), 213–228 (2016)
20. Garrigos-Simon, F., Narangajavana-Kaosiri, Y., Lengua-Lengua, I.: Tourism and sustainability: a bibliometric and visualization analysis. Sustainability **10**(6), 1976 (2018)
21. Van Eck, N.J., Waltman, L.: VOSviewer-Visualizing scientific landscapes. [Sl: sn]. Acesso em, vol. 12 (2017)
22. Woolsey, G.: On inexpert systems and natural intelligence in military operations research. Interfaces (Provid.) **21**(4), 2–10 (1991)
23. Dargam, F.C.C., Passos, E.P.L., Pantoja, F.D.R.: Decision support systems for military applications. Eur. J. Oper. Res. **55**(3), 403–408 (1991)
24. Keesstra, S.D., et al.: The significance of soils and soil science towards realization of the United Nations Sustainable Development Goals. Soil **2**(2), 111–128 (2016). https://doi.org/10.5194/soil-2-111-2016. https://www.soil-journal.net/2/111/2016/

Artificial Intelligence in the Public Sector: A Study of Challenges and Opportunities for Norwegian Municipalities

Patrick Mikalef[1,2(✉)], Siw Olsen Fjørtoft[1], and Hans Yngvar Torvatn[1]

[1] SINTEF Digital, S. P. Andersens Veg 5, 7031 Trondheim, Norway
{patrick.mikalef, siw.fjortoft, hans.torvatn}@sintef.no
[2] Norwegian University of Science and Technology, Sem Saelands Vei 7-9,
7491 Trondheim, Norway

Abstract. The value of Artificial Intelligence (AI) in augmenting or even replacing human decision-making in the organizational context is gaining momentum in the last few years. A growing number of organizations are now experimenting with different approaches to support and shape their operations. Nevertheless, there has been a disproportionate amount of attention on the potential and value that AI can deliver to private companies, with very limited empirical attention focusing on the private sector. The purpose of this research is to examine the current state of AI use in municipalities in Norway, what future aspirations are, as well as identify the challenges that exist in realizing them. To investigate these issues, we build on a survey study with respondents holding IT management positions in Norwegian municipalities. The results pinpoint to specific areas of AI applications that public bodies intend to invest in, as well as the most important challenges they face in making this transition.

Keywords: Artificial Intelligence · Business value · Public sector · Adoption · Empirical

1 Introduction

Artificial Intelligence (AI) can be defined as a set of technologies that simulate human cognitive processes, including reasoning, learning, and self-correction. Recent years have seen an increased interest in the potential uses of AI in private and public organizations [1]. The prevailing argument in applying AI technologies in such organizational settings is that it can enhance, and in some cases even replace, human decision-making and action [2]. This ability provides many opportunities to utilize human resources to more meaningful and less repetitive tasks, while at the same time improving efficiency, reducing errors, and slicing costs [3]. In fact, there have been several publications from academic and popular press to date regarding the potential of AI, which much discussions regarding how it can revolutionize the way organizations do business and interact with their customers [4]. Despite much promise however, and a strong wave of enthusiasm regarding the potential of AI, there is still very limited understanding regarding the status of AI adoption, the expectations of organizations, as well as the challenges they face when adopting and deploying such solutions [5]. This

© IFIP International Federation for Information Processing 2019
Published by Springer Nature Switzerland AG 2019
I. O. Pappas et al. (Eds.): I3E 2019, LNCS 11701, pp. 267–277, 2019.
https://doi.org/10.1007/978-3-030-29374-1_22

issue is particularly apparent in the public sector, where the competitive pressure that typically describes private companies is absent, and deployments are usually less swift [6].

The opportunities of applying AI technologies in the public domain have been documented extensively in several early studies [7]. These range from using chatbots to interact with citizens about procedures and other types of queries [8], to deploying sophisticated methods to identify fraud detection [9], and using autonomous vehicles in traditionally human-executed tasks [10]. Such uses of AI demonstrate that the public sector can benefit in many ways by such technologies when they are applied to key activities that are within the realm of their responsibilities. Nevertheless, despite much promise and a strong emphasis on AI applications from national and European bodies [11], we still have very limited understanding about what the status is in public bodies regarding adoption levels, what IT managers see as the most difficult hurdles to overcomes in order to make such objectives a reality, as well as what is the anticipated impact that AI will have on key performance indicators of public bodies [12]. Studies have shown that when it comes to technology adoption and challenges faced, public and private organizations have to overcome some common challenges but are also faced with distinct differences [13].

Building on this state of knowledge, and on the great promise that AI can produce for public organizations, this study seeks to explore the current level of adoption of AI in different areas of application pertinent to public organization activities. This research also seeks to highlight what are the key challenges public bodies face when routinizing such technologies, and to understand where public organizations see the greatest potential [14]. Exploring these aspects is crucial in order to direct investments and to deploy such technologies without any major hindrances. To empirically explore the research questions, we focus on Norwegian municipalities, and through a recent nation-wide survey present the outcomes from the answers received from IT managers. We selected municipalities as they typically have a broad range of activities that fall under their jurisdiction. Furthermore, the case of Norway is seen as well-suited as the degree of digitalization of public bodies is one of the highest word-wide, therefore being a good indicator of challenges, that other public bodies may face world-wide. The results provide us with an understanding of which are the priority areas that municipalities see as most important to deploy AI solutions, as well as what are the main constraints the currently face. This provides policy makers and practitioners with a clear view of what measures need to be taken to accelerate AI diffusion in the public sector through focused actions.

The rest of the paper is structured as follows. In Sect. 2 we overview the current state of knowledge regarding AI applications and highlight some key areas that have been documented in literature as being of increased significance for public bodies. We then proceed to discuss the context of Norwegian municipalities and the link to strategic direction set by the local and central government. Section 3 outlines the data collection process, the measures used to capture notions, as well as the demographics of respondents. Section 4 presents the findings from this exploratory study, illustrating the current state of adoption based on different functional areas, the planned level of deployments, as well as the most important challenges faced in realizing them. We conclude the paper with a discussion of the theoretical and practical implications of this work as well as some suggestions for future research.

2 Background

2.1 Business Value of Artificial Intelligence

Following the emergence of big data analytics and the rapid adoption of Internet-of-Things (IoT), Artificial Intelligence applications have seen a renewed interest building on the massive amounts of data collected and stored. This data has enabled practitioners to realize such AI applications, and grounded on advanced techniques such as deep learning and reinforcement learning. Unlike the previous decades where such massive data was located in the hands of research institutes, nowadays an increasing number of public and private organizations are in place to collect, store and analyze such data as a result of falling storage prices and increased processing capacity. This has sparked a new wave of enthusiasm in practitioners regarding the potential applications and the business value that AI applications can deliver [15]. Much has been written about the increased speed and accuracy that AI can deliver, and the large workload that can be assigned to such technologies. Recent studies emphasize that the role of AI in the contemporary economy is not to completely replace human labor, but rather to take over repetitive and manual tasks. Only by doing so will organizations be able to harness the skills in which humans excel in such as creative thinking and problem solving. Furthermore, other recent articles see AI and human cooperating harmoniously in a synergy called augmented intelligence. According to this view, AI applications can help enhance human tasks, automating many activities and serving as decision-making aids. Through this way organizations will be able to harness the complementary strengths of humans and machines.

Despite these claims, research on the business potential of AI is still at a very early stage [5, 16]. This is especially evident in relation to the public sector, which typically lags in technological adoption in comparison the private sector. To date, most academic literature has focused on potential applications of AI in the realm of public administration. For instance, a prominent example is that of chatbots for interactions with citizens, whereby human capacity to solve queries is automated. In another study, the use of AI for autonomous vehicles is examined, in which the task of internal resource management and delivery is assigned to unmanned vehicles or robots. Anecdotal claims suggest that such investments can reduce time needed to supple units with necessary resources, reduce human errors, and slice down costs. This application of AI has significant value in public institutions such as hospitals and medical centers, where consumables and critical equipment can be delivered on demand and without the need of human resources to be committed for such tasks. Extending on this, there has been a large discussion about the vast opportunities that open up with utilizing personnel in more meaningful and important tasks. Another important area where AI has been suggested to produce value for public administration is to automatize financial processes and detect fraud. Advanced techniques of vision computing are able to scan thousands of documents in a matter of seconds, register details of expenses and other financial information, and detect anomalies or potential fraud. In this way, AI not only contributes to increased speed in handling such financial information but is also less prone to human error in detecting errors or cases of potential fraud. While the academic and practice-based literature stresses the value of AI in tasks of public administration, to date we have little empirical evidence about if public bodies are actually deploying such solutions, and if so where. Furthermore, there is very little research regarding the plans of public organizations and which areas they see as the most likely to strengthen by means of AI investments. In the following sub-section, we discuss about the context of Norwegian municipalities and the strategic and operational decisions that guide their actions.

2.2   The Context of Norwegian Municipalities and Digitalization

The municipality is the lowest administrative and electoral level in Norway. Currently, there are 422 municipalities and size vary from a couple of hundred inhabitants to over 650,000 in Oslo. In terms of area, you have the same variation, the smallest municipality is 6 km^2 and the largest is 9700 km^2. Regardless of population or area, the municipalities must provide an equal service to the population. The municipalities have a diverse responsibility, ranging from basic welfare benefits such as schooling, kindergarten, social and medical assistance, child welfare, nursing home; to local roads, water, refuse collection, fire and rescue services; furthermore, the maintenance of churches and cemeteries, and cultural services such as operation of the cinema. Norway is focusing on good digital infrastructure. The Government has set a goal that by the year 2020, 90% of the households in the country will have at least 100 Mbit/s offer based on commercial development in the market. In the long term, the goal is for all households to have offers for high-speed broadband, also in areas where the population is low and less profitable with development. Expansion of access to fiber is also in full swing, in addition to mobile networks. From autumn 2019, the 5G technology is widely available to residents of Trondheim municipality, and 5G networks have been prepared in ten major Norwegian cities from 2020.

Internet access and bandwidth is a prerequisite for citizens and businesses to use public digital services. In addition, signals from sensors, welfare technology, traffic monitoring, and digital exchange of information, such as a «patient ready to leave hospital» - message, have become an integral part of municipal service production. In recent years, there has been an increased support for common digitization solutions for Norwegian municipalities. An example is SvarUt, which is a solution that conveys documents between sender and recipient via different channels. The municipalities and county authorities have had access since 2013. By the end of 2018, more than 400 municipalities, but also all county municipalities and 77 government agencies had adopted the solution. In 2018, approximately 7.5 million letters were sent through SvarUt in Norwegian municipalities and county municipalities. The potential for the number of shipments through SvarUt within one year is estimated at ten per capita, or approx. 53 million. But this is only one of many solutions to meet demands of more efficient municipal service production.

Three new common digitization solutions were offered to the municipalities in autumn 2018, DigiSos - a solution for being able to apply digitally for financial social assistance, DigiHelse - a solution that enables citizens to see agreements and have dialogue with the home service, and Minside- a service that provides residents access to all matters that they have with the municipality or the county municipality. These examples indicate that Norwegian municipalities to some extent have started a common digitalization to better citizen services. In our study we aim to examine the digital maturity and readiness for next level technologies, such as AI. One final thing that is worth taking note of is the ongoing merging of Norwegian municipalities. The Government has initiated a municipal reform in which 119 municipalities will be 47 new. This means a reduction from 422 to 356 municipalities from January 2020. More inhabitants per municipality and larger geographical distances can increase the demands of good digital services to the inhabitants - A factor that might promote further innovation in municipal service production.

3   Method

3.1   Sampling and Data Collection

To explore the questions raised in this study, we built on a survey-based research method aimed at key respondents within Norwegian municipalities. Key respondents included heads of the IT division, IT managers, and senior data scientists. The rationale of selecting respondents in these positions was that they are the most knowledgeable about the current status of AI investments in their organizations and are also the best informed about future areas of interest as well as challenged faced during implementations. To identify appropriate respondents, a search was conducted on the webpages of municipalities in Norway. These provide contact details for employees at different roles within the IT department, allowing us to locate those that fit the profile we were looking for better. A list of 83 respondents was compiles including some of the largest municipalities in Norway. Invitations were sent out to respondents via email, with a link to an online questionnaire. The questionnaire was designed in such a way so that it did not require more than 15 min to be filled out, and covered several areas relating to AI investments and future plans. After the initial invitation, two reminders were sent out within a two-week interval. The total number of complete responses received from this sample was 46, with 9 others being incomplete, and thus not retained for further analysis.

3.2   Sample Demographics

The final sample differed in several aspects, which provided an interesting dataset for further analysis. As planned, respondents held positions of senior management within the IT department, with the most frequent title being IT manager, digital transformation director, and department leader. With regards to AI adoption, the largest proportion of respondents indicated that their organization has not yet adopted AI, while from the rest, 10.9% had just started deploying AI within the year and another 19.6% had been using AI for 1–2 years. These results demonstrate that AI adoption in municipalities of Norway is still very low, and even those that have adopted some form of AI have only done so fairly recently. With regards to size, the sample varied significantly, with the largest proportion being municipalities with 500–1.000 employees, followed by a slightly smaller size-class of 100–500 (23.9%), while there were also some responses of the large municipalities with over 5.000 employees (13.0%). Respectively, the IT departments were fairly small, with the largest proportion being between 1–9 people (65.2%), followed by IT departments with 10–49 employees (26.1%), and a small number with 50–249 people (8.7%). These demographics are in alignment with the distribution of Norwegian municipalities, where there are primarily small municipalities and IT departments, and a smaller number of large ones (e.g. Oslo and Trondheim) (Table 1).

Table 1. Sample demographics

Factors	Sample (N)	Proportion (%)
Years using AI		
We do not use AI yet	31	67.4%
Less than 1 year	5	10.9%
1–2 years	9	19.6%
2–3 years	1	2.2%
How many people work in your organization?		
Less than 100	3	6.5%
100–500	11	23.9%
500–1.000	14	30.4%
1.000–2.500	8	17.4%
2.500–5.000	4	8.7%
More than 5.000	6	13.0%
How many people work in the IT department		
1–9	30	65.2%
10–49	12	26.1%
50–249	4	8.7%
More than 250	0	0.0%

4 Results

To analyze data, we used descriptive statistics and paired sample t-tests that were run through the software package IBM SPSS. The first part of the analysis involved examining the current state of AI use within municipalities. In order to examine potential areas of application within the context of public administration, we reviewed the relevant literature that discusses the most promising ways in which AI can be leveraged [17, 18]. The results depicted below illustrate the percentage of municipalities within our sample that have not used AI in the specific areas of application, as well as those that have initiated deployments. From the results depicted in the graph below we can see that the most popular applications of AI for municipalities in Norway include intelligent interaction agents with citizens (28.9%), real-time translations for meetings including speech-to-speech and speech-to-text (21.1%), as well as request processing and applications handling and automatizing data entry with 15.7% each. These results demonstrate a clear trend in using AI to interact with citizens primarily, and in assisting in tasks where additional aid is required, such as communication. On the other hand, there is a large proportion of municipalities that have still not adopted any form of AI (Fig. 1).

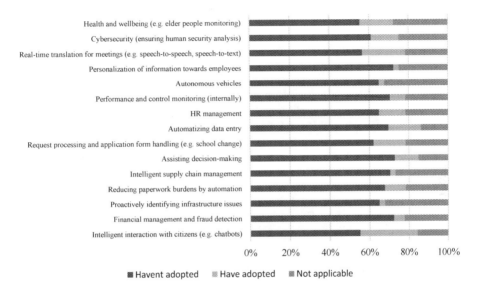

Fig. 1. Current levels of AI adoption in Norwegian municipalities by area of use

Extending on these findings, the next series of questions asked respondents to report the degree to which they plan to use AI in the future in the abovementioned areas. The reason for asking responses to evaluate future plans is to try to comprehend the types of investments they would be required to make and to propose policies and roadmaps to achieve desired objectives. Furthermore, future investment plans also are a good indication about where other public bodies or municipalities in other countries plan to increase their investments. To examine this, we asked respondents to whom these areas were applicable to assess the level to which they are planning to invest in AI technology to support them. Responses were marked on a 7-point Likert scale, with 1 denoting a very low intention to adopt, while 7 indicates a very high intention to implement AI for the particular task. From the results it is evident that some areas of AI use are of increased interest for municipalities. First and foremost, the use of intelligence interaction with citizens in the form of chatbots is regarded by respondents as a top priority to invest in for the near future. It is a frequent phenomenon that employees are overloaded with such requests and queries that can disrupt work and slow down other critical tasks. Since a lot of information on municipality websites requires effort to find, the use of chatbots to locate and provide this information in an easy way can free up the need for human resources in this task while at the same time provide increase citizen satisfaction with services. Similarly, request processing and application form handling was the area with the second highest interest for future adoption, with health and wellbeing services ranking as third. These results provide a clear view of where municipalities see the most value from AI in relation to the tasks that is within their realm of responsibilities. It also serves as a good roadmap to direct policy and funding to support such actions (Fig. 2).

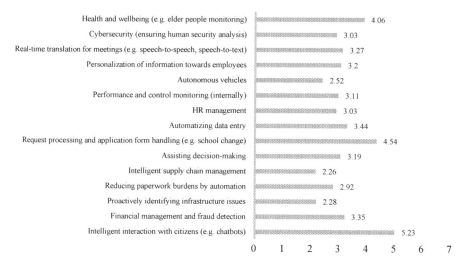

Fig. 2. Intention to adopt AI in Norwegian municipalities by area of use

The final part of our examination looked at the challenge's municipalities face when they adopt AI, or barriers that do not allow them to implement such solutions. In the categories presented below in Fig. 3, we asked respondents to evaluate on a 7-point Likert scale the extent to which each of the categories mentioned bellow was a significant barrier to adopt or implement AI technologies in their everyday operations. The scale ranged from 1, denoting that the specific factor was not an important inhibitor of adoption, to 7 which meant that it was an important hindering factor for implementing AI technologies. The results highlight that the challenges that are faced from municipalities range from both technical to organizational. The most important hindering factor is the inability to integrate systems and data, as well as to ensure that quality data are utilized to train AI. Almost as equally important are organizational factors including the lack of expertise with the necessary know-how, the limited financial resources, as well as organizational inertia. These outcomes demonstrate that if Norwegian municipalities aim to adopt AI, they need both structural reforms as well as financial capital to pursue these directions. In fact, respondents noted that the perception that AI is not necessary for public administration is not an issue for non-adoption, indicating that low levels of maturity to date are mostly a result of organizational or technical hindrances.

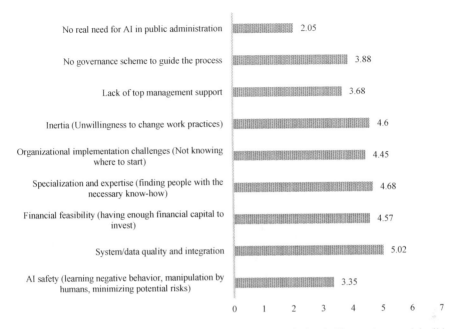

Fig. 3. Challenges in implementing and adopting AI technologies in Norwegian municipalities

5 Discussion

Artificial Intelligence has gained eminence over the past few years as a set of technological innovations that can potentially disrupt private and public organizations. There is a growing number of research and popular press articles claiming that AI will radically change the way we do business. Despite such claims about the potential of AI there is still very little empirical research concerning the level of use within organizations, and particularly for public bodies. The purpose of this study was to shed some light about the use and intended use of AI within public administration and particularly in Norwegian municipalities. Since the scope of activities of municipalities is to a large extent similar world-wide, areas of using AI, as well as challenges faced during adoption, or even barriers to adoption are likely to be the same also in other countries. To examine these issues, we conducted a survey study with a sample of municipalities in Norway, using senior IT managers as key respondents.

From a theoretical point of view our study contributes to literature by demonstrating the areas which public administration organizations such as municipalities are currently investing in or are planning to do so in the near future. It is important to understand in which areas AI will be central in in order to propose optimal methods for deploying such solutions and streaming adoption processes. As with any technological adoption, inertial forces and challenges are likely to delay implementation or reduce potential business value if appropriate measures are not taken at early stages of projects [19]. Therefore, such cases may serve as lessons learnt for future ventures where organizational know-how can be transferred and best-practices adopted. Furthermore, from a citizen's perspective, knowing what services would be best automated through AI can help create interfaces and AI-supported services that best fulfil citizen needs. It is critical to get feedback from users of these services in order not only to train AI applications but to design the provided services in a way that optimize satisfaction and ease-of-use. Furthermore, by knowing what the main challenges are it is possible to develop governance plans and strategies to facilitate adoption, use, and routinization of AI within the public administration sphere. While such governance practices are quite common for other types of information systems, in AI they are still non-existent.

From a practice-based perspective the outcomes of this study can help practitioners identify what the common challenges that they face are and form a knowledge exchange group [20]. Transferring such knowledge to other municipalities, and particularly those that are of a smaller size and with less resources can be particularly beneficial if they want to keep up with new emerging technologies. Furthermore, the outcomes can be used by policy makers in order to direct funding and assist municipalities with their deployments. With AI becoming an increasingly integral part of public administration, it is important that financial resources and policies are put into the right directions. Using such outcomes can help policy makers devise future frameworks and develop assistance plans for public bodies.

While this study used a small sample of Norwegian municipalities it does provide some insight of trends. We intend to expand the sample of municipalities and also survey other public bodies to examine the level of adoption and challenged faced. Furthermore, in extended reach the plan is to examine the readiness level of Norwegian municipalities in greater detail so that more concrete action plans can be formulated, and specific recommendations can be provided. We also encourage future researchers to examine how AI can be used to transform operations of public administration, and how deployments can be optimized in order to maximize derived value. It is important to understand how such novel technologies can shape and complement existing strategies [21].

References

1. Ransbotham, S., Gerbert, P., Reeves, M., Kiron, D., Spira, M.: Artificial intelligence in business gets real. MIT Sloan Management Review (2018)
2. Davenport, T.H., Ronanki, R.: Artificial intelligence for the real world. Harv. Bus. Rev. **96**, 108–116 (2018)
3. Li, B.-H., Hou, B.-C., Yu, W.-T., Lu, X.-B., Yang, C.-W.: Applications of artificial intelligence in intelligent manufacturing: a review. Front. Inf. Technol. Electron. Eng. **18**, 86–96 (2017)
4. Huang, M.-H., Rust, R.T.: Artificial intelligence in service. J. Serv. Res. **21**, 155–172 (2018)
5. Mikalef, P., Boura, M., Lekakos, G., Krogstie, J.: Big data analytics and firm performance: findings from a mixed-method approach. J. Bus. Res. **98**, 261–276 (2019)
6. Sun, T.Q., Medaglia, R.: Mapping the challenges of artificial intelligence in the public sector: evidence from public healthcare. Gov. Inf. Q. **36**, 368–383 (2019)
7. Wirtz, B.W., Müller, W.M.: An integrated artificial intelligence framework for public management. Public Manag. Rev. 1–25 (2018)

8. Park, D.-A.: A study on conversational public administration service of the Chatbot based on artificial intelligence. J. Korea Multimed. Soc. **20**, 1347–1356 (2017)

9. Herrera, J.L.L., Figueroa, H.V.R., Ramírez, E.J.R.: Deep fraud. A fraud intention recognition framework in public transport context using a deep-learning approach. In: 2018 International Conference on Electronics, Communications and Computers (CON-IELECOMP), pp. 118–125. IEEE (2018)

10. Hengstler, M., Enkel, E., Duelli, S.: Applied artificial intelligence and trust—the case of autonomous vehicles and medical assistance devices. Technol. Forecast. Soc. Chang. **105**, 105–120 (2016)

11. Cath, C., Wachter, S., Mittelstadt, B., Taddeo, M., Floridi, L.: Artificial intelligence and the 'good society': the US, EU, and UK approach. Sci. Eng. Ethics **24**, 505–528 (2018)

12. Goolsbee, A.: Public policy in an AI economy. National Bureau of Economic Research (2018)

13. Liu, S.M., Yuan, Q.: The evolution of information and communication technology in public administration. Public Adm. Dev. **35**, 140–151 (2015)

14. Mikalef, P., van de Wetering, R., Krogstie, J.: Big Data enabled organizational transformation: the effect of inertia in adoption and diffusion. In: Abramowicz, W., Paschke, A. (eds.) BIS 2018. LNBIP, vol. 320, pp. 135–147. Springer, Cham (2018). https://doi.org/10.1007/978-3-319-93931-5_10

15. McAfee, A., Brynjolfsson, E.: Machine, Platform, Crowd: Harnessing Our Digital Future. WW Norton & Company, New York (2017)

16. Mikalef, P., Boura, M., Lekakos, G., Krogstie, J.: Big data analytics capabilities and innovation: the mediating role of dynamic capabilities and moderating effect of the environment. Br. J. Manag. **30**, 272–298 (2019)

17. Duan, Y., Edwards, J.S., Dwivedi, Y.K.: Artificial intelligence for decision making in the era of Big Data–evolution, challenges and research agenda. Int. J. Inf. Manag. **48**, 63–71 (2019)

18. Mikhaylov, S.J., Esteve, M., Campion, A.: Artificial intelligence for the public sector: opportunities and challenges of cross-sector collaboration. Philos. Trans. R. Soc. A: Math. Phys. Eng. Sci. **376**, 20170357 (2018)

19. Mikalef, P., Krogstie, J.: Big Data governance and dynamic capabilities: the moderating effect of environmental uncertainty. In: Pacific Asia Conference on Information Systems (PACIS). AIS, Yokohama (2018)

20. Mikalef, P., Framnes, V.A., Danielsen, F., Krogstie, J., Olsen, D.H.: Big Data analytics capability: antecedents and business value. In: Pacific Asia Conference on Information Systems (2017)

21. Mikalef, P., Pateli, A.: Information technology-enabled dynamic capabilities and their indirect effect on competitive performance: findings from PLS-SEM and fsQCA. J. Bus. Res. **70**, 1–16 (2017)

Internet of Things Business Models: The RAWFIE Case

Panagiota Papadopoulou[(✉)], Kostas Kolomvatsos,
and Stathes Hadjiefthymiades

Department of Informatics and Telecommunications,
National and Kapodistrian University of Athens, Athens, Greece
{peggy, kostask, shadj}@di.uoa.gr

Abstract. Internet of Things (IoT) encompasses a wide range of devices and technologies which cumulatively shape a new environment with unprecedented business prospects. This paper aims to investigate the business potential of IoT, focusing on mobile IoT and IoT as a service. In this direction, it presents the case of RAWFIE, a H2020 project on a research and experimentation federated platform of mobile IoT testbeds and devices. The paper describes RAWFIE potential business models, analyzing them into their characteristics, based on the business model canvas, examining the possibilities as well as the challenges these entail, using a SWOT analysis, and testing them in a preliminary evaluation. The study offers research and practical insights as a starting point for business models of IoT as a service, focusing in the context of mobile IoT experimentation.

Keywords: Internet of Things · Mobile IoT · Business model · IoT as a service

1 Introduction

IoT is a very promising technology and is predicted to flourish within the next years. It is expected that 14.2 billion IoT devices will be in use in 2019 and they will reach 25 billion by 2021 [1]. Investments on IoT are predicted to reach $1.2 trillion in 2022 with a CAGR of 13.6% [2]. The IoT market is still in its infancy, with its potential yet to be revealed. IoT technologies offer vast opportunities for business models in almost every application domain. The introduction of mobile smart nodes further enhances the IoT potential for applications and business models. Mobile IoT involves moving devices equipped with processing and communication capabilities, which cover larger areas than 'typical' static IoT nodes. The movement of the devices intensively incorporates the spatial aspect in data gathering and processing. Mobile IoT applications are characterized by short and recurrent contact between IoT devices to perform assigned tasks [3]. Modern devices are equipped with wireless technologies facilitating the creation of a vast communication infrastructure, where mobile devices are connected, allowing for the creation of numerous applications. However, despite the extant literature on IoT business models, research on mobile IoT and related business models is scarce.

In this paper, we aim to explore the business potential of IoT, focusing on mobile IoT and its provision as a service. We examine mobile IoT business models based on

© IFIP International Federation for Information Processing 2019
Published by Springer Nature Switzerland AG 2019
I. O. Pappas et al. (Eds.): I3E 2019, LNCS 11701, pp. 278–290, 2019.
https://doi.org/10.1007/978-3-030-29374-1_23

the case of the RAWFIE (Road-, Air- and Water-based Future Internet Experimentation) EU H2020 project that provides research and experimentation facilities with a federation of unmanned mobile IoT devices (UAVs, USVs, UGVs) and testbeds. RAWFIE is examined from a business model perspective covering different variations of IoT as a service. RAWFIE business model is described using the Business Model Canvas and is further analyzed with a SWOT analysis, followed by a preliminary qualitative evaluation. The paper provides initial insights on mobile IoT business models and IoT as a service that can be of use to both researchers and practitioners.

The structure of the paper is as follows. Section 2 reviews related work while Sect. 3 presents the case of RAWFIE project. Section 4 describes the proposed business models, along their dimensions and characteristics, which are further analysed with a SWOT analysis presented in Sect. 5. Section 6 describes a preliminary evaluation of the proposed RAWFIE business models and Sect. 7 concludes the paper.

2 Background

A number of business models have been proposed in the IoT [4]. [5] build on top of the analysis of 55 IoT business model patterns in [6], focusing on the value creation steps that ensure the success of business models. The results indicate that business model patterns could be depicted by six components while defining two independent business model patterns, digitally charged products and sensors as a service. [7] present a business model framework for IoT applications. Based on the Business Model Canvas, they identify the building blocks that are relevant in an IoT business model, types of options that can be focused on within these building blocks and the relative importance of these building blocks and types. [8] has also proposed the use of Business Model Canvas for business models in the context of industrial IoT. The author presents the phases of the industrial Internet evolution and discusses the key elements in such a setting. [9] aim to develop a generic business model framework for IoT businesses through literature analysis and interviews. A set of case studies are adopted for testing purposes in IoT companies. The findings suggest that the capability for data analytics is an essential element for IoT service and open ecosystems help companies provide new integrated services and offer greater value for consumers. [10] study IoT business models discussing design challenges, i.e. diversity of objects, immaturity of innovation and unstructured ecosystems, and suggesting a design tool.

[11] propose a framework for designing business models for IoT in a structured and actionable way, based on 34 case studies. [12] propose a traditional value based business model applied for IoT applications, targeting how value is created and exchanged between actors. [13] propose an e3-value methodology applied to traditional business models for IoT applications, focusing on value proposition and target customers. [14] adopt a value net analysis for proposing a business model in IoT through a case study related to real-world traffic data generated by IoT services. [15] describe the use of a value based approach to business modeling of new solutions based on IoT and apply an e3-value methodology to demonstrate how a sustainable business model can be built for the IoT.

[16] studies existing business models and proposes a strategy for using business models in the development of IoT for China mobiles. The strategy includes four aspects, the improvement of high-quality network for IoT, the value proposition, the key partnerships and the key activities for launching the IoT product. [17] propose business models for the value and revenue creation in the IoT. Finally, [18] categorize business models for IoT in the manufacturing industries. The authors describe challenges like unprofitable environment, exploded market and need to extract more value in the existing business models for IoT and establish a framework for identifying different IoT business models.

3   RAWFIE Project

3.1   RAWFIE Aim and Scope

RAWFIE (Road-, Air-, and Water- based Future Internet Experimentation) (http://www.rawfie.eu) is a project funded by the European Commission (Horizon H2020 programme) under the Future Internet Research Experimentation (FIRE+) initiative. RAWFIE provides a platform for interconnecting multiple testbeds aiming at providing research facilities for mobile IoT devices, specifically unmanned vehicles UxVs, e.g., Unmanned Aerial Vehicles (UAVs), Unmanned Surface Vehicles (USVs), Unmanned Ground Vehicles (UGVs), for research experimentation in vehicular, aerial and maritime environments. The platform supports experimenters with smart tools for conducting and monitoring experiments in various domains of IoT.

RAWFIE project aims at delivering a federated infrastructure synthesized of heterogeneous testbeds and unmanned vehicles, operating in air, sea and ground. RAWFIE offers experimentation facilities that can accommodate diverse and complex experiments of various scales for testing and fine tuning mobile IoT technologies. RAWFIE operates as an Experimentation-as-a-Service model, providing a platform of testbeds, devices and specialized software tools for conducting experiments in mobile IoT. It enables experiments across three main axes; testing of hardware components, testing of software implementation of algorithms and network communication, and testing of dynamic re-routing of unmanned devices. RAWFIE includes testbeds in Greece, Spain, Germany and France. It also offers several types of UAVs, USVs and UGVs, which are either part of its testbeds or standalone. In addition, RAWFIE platform includes its own experiment toolset for designing and managing experiments.

There have been several research initiatives in the Future Internet Research & Experimentation (FIRE) open research environment, focusing on heterogeneous testbeds federations, such as Fed4FIRE, OneLab or WISEBED. While RAWFIE shares many similarities with some of these projects, it differs in the integrated use of UxV nodes in the testbeds. Federated testbeds mainly provide common access to several testbeds in the federation, which reduces the effort to conduct a test in another testbed. RAWFIE transfers this benefit to UxVs testbeds. It allows multidisciplinary experiments with potentially unlimited types of technologies, and offers a common platform for the management of a federation of testbeds, by providing a single point of access and a common software infrastructure, for the management, execution and analysis of experiments carried out using UxV resources which can be available at the different testbed facilities with minimal adaptations, as the platform can easily support the addition of new data formats for data exchange with UxV nodes.

3.2   RAWFIE Architecture

RAWFIE adopts a multi-tier architecture where each tier contains various components for the support of the mobile IoT vision. RAWFIE enables the implementation of a highly and easily extensible remote experimentation platform. The functionalities for the presentation of information to the experimenters, the implementation of the core parts of the business logic and the software interfaces for the integration of the different modules along with the data persistence are separated in different tiers. More specifically, the Testbed Tier undertakes the responsibility of providing functionalities for the actual control of the testbed resources (e.g. mobile IoT nodes) and the communication with the upper layers. It includes the software and hardware components that are needed to run the testbeds and UxVs. Testbeds comprise various software components related to the communication with the upper layers (i.e. Middle and Front-End Tier), the management of the infrastructure and the control of the UxVs.

Each testbed available through the RAWFIE federation is comprised of nodes of the same 'x' type (i.e. ground, air or water surface) that use the same communication protocols for the ease of their integration in a unified and fully controllable environment (i.e. testbed). A Web based Front-End Tier allows experimenters to have remote access to the platform, authorization and visualization of the information, and interaction with testbeds' resources. The front-end tier includes the services and tools that RAWFIE provides to the experimenters to define and perform the experimentation scenarios. The Middle Tier implements most of the business logic and, particularly, the communication between the Front-End and the Test-bed tiers. The Middle tier offers a set of components that 'transform' the 'commands' defined in the interface in the appropriate format to be consumed by the end devices and testbed components. It provides the software interfaces needed and includes useful software components related to security, trust, control and visualization aspects. This tier provides the infrastructure which enables the creation and integration of applications in the RAWFIE platform. RAWFIE middleware is a virtualized infrastructure, i.e., Infrastructure as a Service (IaaS), indicating the maturity and versatility of the developed RAWFIE layered architecture. The Data Tier is in charge of ensuring data persistence. It is a collection of repositories that store the different data types generated and collected by RAWFIE components. All the integrated testbeds and resources accessible from the federated facilities are listed in a central service. The Data tier manages information relevant to the testbeds and resources (i.e., location, facilities) as well information on the capabilities of a particular resource and its requirements for executing experiments e.g., in terms of interconnectivity or dependencies. The provided data repositories are accessed whenever an experimenter wants to retrieve information related to available testbeds and resources using the respective Front End tool. Data Tier provides a large, secure, cloud-based central repository in which collected data can be anonymized and made available to users.

RAWFIE follows the Service Oriented Architecture (SOA) paradigm: all components provide clearly defined interfaces, so that they can be easily accessed by other components or replaced by components with the same interface. The services are described in languages such as WSDL. Interaction with them is made possible by the use of remote service control protocols such as SOAP or the REST resource invocation style. Additionally, a message-based middleware (via a Message Bus) is used, providing a coherent communication model with distribution, replication, reliability, availability, redundancy, backup, consistency, and services across distributed heterogeneous systems. The message bus interconnects all components and all tiers. It is used for asynchronous notifications and method calls/response handling. As such, it can be used for transmitting measurements from producers (e.g., UxVs) to consumers pertaining to the Middle/Data tier (e.g., experiment monitoring or data repositories).

4 RAWFIE Business Model

In this section we proceed to further examine RAWFIE from a business model perspective. The description has been based on the Business Model Canvas, introduced by [19], a business model design template which provides a visual chart for documenting business models. The business model canvas contains nine building blocks for conceptualizing and describing a business model, in terms of value proposition, infrastructure, customers, and finances. Infrastructure is analysed into three building blocks, key activities, key resources and key partners. Customers are defined by three building blocks, customer segments, channels, customer relationships. Finances comprise two building blocks, cost structure and revenue streams. These nine business model building blocks, including value proposition, have been used as a tool for presenting the RAWFIE business model conceptualization.

RAWFIE platform provides a set of smart software tools to enable experimenters to remotely conduct and monitor experiments in the domains of IoT, including networking and sensing. RAWFIE federation allows for multiple types of experimentation, including testing with and among multiple and different mobile IoT devices. Experiments can involve different UxVs (e.g. UAVs) or different UxV types (e.g. UAVs with UGVs). Devices used in experimentations can be from different manufacturers and can be tested among different testbeds. The stakeholders can be the testbed providers, the unmanned vehicles/devices (UxVs) manufacturers and suppliers and the experimenters.

Another type of business model can emanate from the RAWFIE platform serving as a consolidator of testbeds and UxVs, an intermediary business entity which testbed providers and UxVs suppliers can join under various payment schemes. Intended RAWFIE customers-members can participate by paying a subscription or a commission based on their own revenue resulting from their use through the platform by RAWFIE customers. In this approach, testbed and device providers, who were previous RAWFIE stakeholders, become customers, extending RAWFIE business partnerships by adding new collaborations and new revenue channels. In this way, RAWFIE can be a mediator between infrastructure (testbed) and equipment (UxVs) providers and end user entities interested in using RAWFIE facilities. With such a business model, RAWFIE allows for a full implementation of Platform-as-a-Service, Infrastructure-as-a-Service and Experimentation-as-a-service. RAWFIE Business model canvas is depicted in Table 1 and is analysed in the following paragraphs.

4.1 Value Proposition

RAWFIE business models can be created providing a range of offerings for IoT experimentation across various domains to interested parties. The offerings can extend along three axes of providing (a) testbeds (b) IoT devices (i.e. UAVs, USVs and UGVs) and (c) software tools for experiments. These three RAWFIE assets can be offered either separately or in combination. For example, a device, or a set of devices, can be available for experimentation separately or jointly with the use of a particular testbed or with a set of specific testbeds. Therefore, RAWFIE has the potential to provide various value propositions to respective prospects. Regarding testbeds, RAWFIE can be an intermediary connecting testbed providers with research or other entities that seek to use such testbeds for experimentation purposes. The value proposition can be stronger by offering the option to find testbeds or additionally use the RAWFIE software platform for conducting experiments in the selected testbeds. In a similar vein, RAWFIE can serve as a mediator among device manufacturers and suppliers and entities that seek to use such devices for experimentation purposes. This business model can allow for the combination of different types of devices that can be requested or made available for rent or sale, for example, combining different UAVs, or combining UAVs and USVs. The value proposition can be strengthened by providing a marketplace in which participants have the possibility to buy and sell or rent unmanned vehicles or additionally use the RAWFIE software platform for conducting experiments with the selected devices. Furthermore, the value proposition can also include the matching of IoT devices with respective operators, such as UAV pilots, UGV drivers and USV captains. As an IoT device intermediary, RAWFIE can also offer its available UxVs in combination with providing the option for a selection of available testbeds to use for experimentation with these UxVs. Finally, in a full and more complex version, RAWFIE can operate as a hub for testbed providers, device manufacturers, device suppliers, unmanned vehicles operators and experimenters.

4.2 Customer Segments

RAWFIE is addressed to any entity that is interested in conducting experimentations with mobile IoT. Potential customers of RAWFIE business models can be universities or research institutions that can use RAWFIE to conduct experiments for academic purposes. Public organizations such as the police, the army, the fire brigade, local authorities and border control can also benefit from RAWFIE by using its devices or testbeds in order to test possible solutions for creating new services or improving the services they already offer. RAWFIE platform could also be a valuable tool for ecological and environment bodies and organisations in the pursuit of testing the efficiency and effectiveness of their ecology and environment protection plans.

Industrial customers, such as UAV, UGV and USV manufacturers and sensor manufacturers are undoubtedly one of the most important RAWFIE customer segments. RAWFIE would be of great value to them in several ways. On the one hand RAWFIE could be used for either testing their products as part of the design and manufacturing of new products or of the updating of existing ones. On the other hand, UxV and sensor manufacturers could be suppliers of RAWFIE infrastructure, by renting or selling their products for experimentation or for the platform itself.

Software developers specializing in IoT are also significant customers of RAWFIE, offering their products to the platform or using it for developing new software or upgrading existing one. Industrial customers also include electricity/water supply companies that would be interested in using RAWFIE for their planning and testing their mobile IoT-based operations, including energy saving processes.

4.3   Customer Relationships

Relationships have already been established with testbed providers, software developers and UAV, USV and UGV manufacturers and experimenters as part of the project scope. There partners are third parties that have been selected for receiving financial support through three open calls. Additional customer relationships can be established with testbed providers, device manufacturers and vendors, software developers and experimenters that seek to use RAWFIE for their activities.

Customer relationships can vary depending on the type of the exchange taking place between customers and RAWFIE. They can range from transactional relationships, for a single use of the RAWFIE infrastructure, in case of one experiment. to long-term relationships, for use of the RAWFIE facilities on a regular, recurring basis for a series of experiments. Customer relationships can also involve relationships that can be established among RAWFIE customers. This is the case of RAWFIE serving as an intermediary connecting RAWFIE customers, enabling them to establish relationships with other RAWFIE customers. Such relationships can be either transactional or long-term in case of partnerships that are formed within the platform for joint service provision.

4.4   Key Activities

RAWFIE key activities are largely horizontal across business model types. RAWFIE core activity can be considered to be the experimentation provision. This includes the activities of experiment planning, with the options of testbed booking, device booking and device operator booking if needed. Experiment design and execution services are also part of the core activity, including software testing. Platform management is also a RAWFIE key activity supporting its operation.

4.5   Key Partners

RAWFIE includes all actors from technology to facility provision and management. RAWFIE key partners are software developers, testbed owners and operators, device manufacturers and device operators. Specialized personnel for device service and maintenance as well as device insurance agencies can also be deemed as key partners.

4.6   Key Resources

RAWFIE key resources are needed for. Physical resources include the testbeds, the UAVs, USVs, UGVs available for experimentation, which can be part of the testbed infrastructure. Physical resources also comprise the software and hardware components needed to run the testbeds and the UxVs as well as for designing and executing the experiments. In addition, the facilities for the storage and maintenance of UxVs are part of the key resources required for RAWFIE being operational.

4.7   Channels

RAWFIE customers can be reached through online and offline channels. In the online setting, a main channel can be RAWFIE website and social media or presence in other relevant websites and social media. RAWFIE can seek communication and raise awareness through sharing mobile IoT expert interviews or publishing newsletters or other promotional material such as advertisements, articles and videos in related websites that are visited by potential customers in mobile IoT experimentation. Potential customers could also be attracted through organizing or participating in conferences, exhibitions and events on topics related to mobile IoT.

4.8   Revenue Streams

RAWFIE business models can induce revenue through various streams. Revenue models can be subscriptions or license, paid for using RAWFIE infrastructure or parts of it for a predefined time period. Another revenue model would be a transactional, pay-per-use scheme, with several versions. Under this scheme, customers can be charged per different basis depending on their intended use. A set of charge options could be available to select from, such as charge per experiment or charge per testbed. A charge per device could also be available, based on the number and the type of devices used. Charge per device can be applied either separately or in combination with charge per experiment or charge per testbed, depending on the use scenario.

Revenue can also come from RAWFIE partners participating in the platform as suppliers of testbeds, devices, or software, renting or even selling their products to other intended customers. Such RAWFIE partnerships can be another stream of revenue for RAWFIE business model, by partners paying a commission based on their own revenue resulting from their use of the platform for transacting with RAWFIE customers. These RAWFIE customers could also possibly be a source of revenue if they are charged a service fee for using RAWFIE platform for their transaction with RAWFIE partners.

4.9   Cost Structure

RAWFIE business models entail several costs. These can include the insurance cost for the devices and equipment, the license and training cost for the UxVs operators and the maintenance cost for the testbeds, the UxVs and the software platform. Customer acquisition costs should also be taken into account.

Table 1. RAWFIE business model canvas

Key Partners	Key Activities	Value Proposition	Customer Relationships	Customer Segments

• Testbed providers
• unmanned vehicles/devices (UxVs) manufacturers/suppliers
• Software developers
	• Planning for experiments
	• Testbed booking
	• Devices booking
	• Platform management
		• Platform for experimentation
		  - Testbeds
		  - Devices
		  - Software
		• Experiment design
		• Consolidator of testbeds and UxVs
			• Transactional relationships
			• Long-term partnerships
			• Collaborations among customers
				• Experimenters (universities, research institutions)
				• public organizations (police, army, fire brigade, local authorities, ecological bodies)
				• industries (UxV manufacturers, software developers, energy companies)

	Key Resources • Testbeds • UAVs, USVs, UGVs • Experimentation software tools • UxVs storage facilities • UxVs insurance • Licenses		**Channels** • Conferences • Exhibitions • Events • Website • Social media	

Cost Structure
• Insurance of devices
• Device operators license
• Testbed maintenance
• Device maintenance
• Software platform maintenance
• Customer acquisition

Revenue Streams
• Subscriptions
• License
• pay-per-use:
  - charge per experiment
  - charge per testbed
  - charge based on the number and the type of devices used

5   RAWFIE SWOT Analysis

Our study continues to a deeper understanding and assessment of the RAWFIE business potential through conducting a SWOT analysis, examining the strengths, weaknesses, opportunities and threats of RAWFIE business model, towards a complete view of our case.

5.1   Strengths

RAWFIE's main strength is its pioneering characteristics, as it is an innovative, unique platform for experiments with mobile unmanned IoT vehicles. Its innovation can be discerned into three intertwined pillars; a federation of testbeds for conducting experiments, a set of mobile unmanned devices and an experiment toolset. These are combined into an integrated experimentation environment, offering a collection of testbeds and devices and enabling users to design and conduct their own custom experiments with this equipment through easy-to-use tools. It provides interoperability of testbeds and devices, comprised of UAVs, UGVs and USVs, allowing for scalability and security and at the same time offering flexibility in experiment and device management with EDL based tools. It enables testing in the field, in real world conditions, including the weather, and in conjunction with the space and weight limitations of UxVs for mounting equipment such as sensors, cameras or batteries.

5.2   Weaknesses

RAWFIE is a new federation, with lack of experience. It may have to be enhanced in terms of functionality and equipment to reach maturity. In addition, because of its specialized nature, customer or user awareness of RAWFIE is limited and hard to raise. It can mainly be of interest to a niche market of academic or industrial entities active in mobile IoT and interested in relevant research and experimentation. There is also a difficulty of adaptability of the available IoT devices to the specific requirements of experiments. Energy requirements of mobile devices, and, in particular, the idle time needed between experiments for device charging and maintenance are weaknesses that could also hinder the successful implementation of RAWFIE business models. Another point of weakness is limitations associated with the specific availability of testbeds and devices and their management.

5.3   Opportunities

RAWFIE federation comes in a fruitful environment characterized by an increasing use of IoT in various domains. Mobile IoT, in particular, is still in its infancy, and receives a growing interest globally, creating a favorable setting for RAWFIE platform and services. The need for research and experimentation for IoT, especially mobile IoT, is strong, in both academia and industry. At the same time, there is a scarcity of IoT platforms offering similar functionality, combining testbeds, devices and tools for custom experiment design, execution and analysis. Mobile IoT as a service can facilitate experiments by supporting experimentation as a service, platform as a service, infrastructure as a service and software as a service. In this context, RAWFIE can be a powerful enabler of such service provision.

5.4   Threats

There are several threats that can potentially hinder RAWFIE business model success. First of all, the development of other competitive mobile IoT nodes platforms can shape a difficult setting for strategic differentiation. RAWFIE can also be threatened by the inadequacy of data storage and processing on autonomous IoT devices. Devices cannot yet accommodate powerful processing units, particularly in the case of UAVs that due to their nature have additional weight limitations. Similarly, storage capabilities are also limited, imposing the need for data transfer to cloud which is not always feasible in real time. The heterogeneity of devices as well as the technological immaturity of data exchange protocols can also be a problem in the expansion of the platform. Another setback can be the lack of an appropriate legal or regulatory framework that can prescribe the efficient use of unmanned mobile IoT nodes, particularly UAVs. This could also involve issues related to security and ethics, with respect to experiment and data management.

6   Evaluation

A preliminary study was carried out as a starting point for evaluating the proposed business models. We interviewed representatives of four testbeds that participated in RAWFIE as third parties receiving financial support from Open Call 1. The participants were asked if they would be interested in participating in the following business models: (1) a testbed agent, an intermediary for finding testbeds for conducting experiments; (2) an intermediary for finding testbeds for conducting experiments, (same as #1), with the additional option to also use the RAWFIE software tools for the experiments in the selected testbeds; (3) an intermediary for finding testbeds for conducting experiments, (same as #1), with the additional option to also find UxVs to use for the experiments in the selected testbeds; (4) as an intermediary for finding testbeds for conducting experiments, (same as #1), with the additional options (a) to use the RAWFIE software tools for the experiments in the selected testbeds and (b) to find UxVs to use for the experiments in the selected testbeds (combination of #2 and #3) and (5) a hub for testbed providers, UxV suppliers, UxV operators and experimenters, that could be used by anyone for finding testbeds, UxVs, UxV operators or experimenters, either separately or in any combination, for conducting experiments. Apart from experimenters finding testbeds and UxVs, this can include any participant collaboration, for example testbeds finding UxV suppliers.

The interviewees expressed a strong interest in participating in all proposed business models, with the first option being the most preferred one followed by the third and then options 2, 4 and 5. Although responses were all in favor of RAWFIE as a business model, they also included concerns about issues that should be taken into account. These referred to RAWFIE tools and the need to improve reliability in order to be able to deploy any experiment in a more stable and easy way. The need for full documentation and maintenance programs jointly with UxV manufacturers was also pointed out as a necessary part of an agreement. The concerns expressed against participating in a RAWFIE business model also involve the cost to hire personnel to run these tasks, the testbed organization position in the industry and facing possible legal barriers.

7 Conclusion

This paper approaches IoT from a business viewpoint through the case of RAWFIE project, analysing its business prospect through the business model canvas, describing the dimensions and characteristics of potential business models. The latter are further analyzed with a SWOT analysis and preliminarily evaluated through a limited scale qualitative study. RAWFIE comes in a promising setting with vast business possibilities thanks to the growth in IoT technologies and applications and the increasing interest in mobile IoT in diverse domains. Our preliminary findings are by no means complete or generalizable, yet they can be deemed as indicative of the potential of IoT business models and IoT as a service, with an emphasis in mobile IoT and experimentation. In that sense, our paper can serve as a starting point for studying IoT business models and mobile IoT as a service, for either academic or industrial purposes. Further research with more and refined IoT business models and empirical testing with input from all involved actors, such as IoT device manufacturers, is necessary to provide more insights towards this direction. In addition, future studies should include an in-depth analysis of mobile IoT as a service paradigm and the enabling of experimentation as a service based on providing IoT software, IoT infrastructure and IoT platform as a service.

Acknowledgement. This work is funded by the H2020 project under grant agreement No. 645220 (RAWFIE).

References

1. Gartner: Gartner Identifies Top 10 Strategic IoT Technologies and Trends (2018). https://www.gartner.com/en/newsroom/press-releases/2018-11-07-gartner-identifies-top-10-strategic-iot-technologies-and-trends
2. IDC:. IDC Forecasts Worldwide Technology Spending on the Internet of Things to Reach $1.2 Trillion in 2022 (2018). https://www.idc.com/getdoc.jsp?containerId=prUS43994118
3. Valarmathi, M.L., Sumathi, L., Deepika, G.: A survey on node discovery in mobile Internet of Things (IoT) scenarios. In: Proceedings of the 3rd International Conference on Advanced Computing and Communication Systems, Coimbatore, India (2016)
4. Chan, H.C.Y.: Internet of Things business models. J. Serv. Sci. Manag. **8**, 552–568 (2015)
5. Fleisch, E., Weinberger, M., Wortmann, F.: Business models and the Internet of Things. White Paper, Bosch Internet of Things & Services Lab (2014)
6. Gassmann, O., Frankenberger, K., Csik, M.: Geschäftsmodelle entwickeln: 55 innovative Konzeptemitdem St. Galler Business Model Navigator, Hanser Verlag (2013)

7. Dijkman, R.M., Sprenkels, B., Peeters, T., Janssen, A.: Business models for the Internet of Things. Int. J. Inf. Manag. **35**, 672–678 (2015)
8. Gierej, S.: The framework of business model in the context of industrial Internet of Things. In: Proceedings of the 7th International Conference on Engineering, Project, and Production Management (2017)
9. Ju, J., Kim, M.-S., Ahn, J.-H.: Prototyping business models for IoT service. Proc. Comput. Sci. **91**, 882–890 (2016)
10. Westerlund, M., Leminen, S., Rajahonka, M.: Designing business models for the Internet of Things. Technol. Innov. Manag. Rev. **4**, 5–14 (2014)
11. Turber, S., vom Brocke, J., Gassmann, O., Fleisch, E.: Designing business models in the era of Internet of Things. In: Tremblay, M.C., VanderMeer, D., Rothenberger, M., Gupta, A., Yoon, V. (eds.) DESRIST 2014. LNCS, vol. 8463, pp. 17–31. Springer, Cham (2014). https://doi.org/10.1007/978-3-319-06701-8_2
12. Liu, L., Jia, W.: Business model for drug supply chain based on the Internet of Things. In: Proceedings of the International Conference on Network Infrastructure and Digital Content (2010)
13. Fan, P.F., Zhou, G.Z.: Analysis of the business model innovation of the technology of Internet of Things in postal logistics. In Proceedings of Industrial Engineering and Engineering Management, pp. 532–536. IEEE Press (2011)
14. Berkers, F., Roelands, M., Bomhof, F., Bachet, T., van Rijn, M., Koers, W.: Constructing a multi-sided business model for a smart horizontal IoT service platform. In: 17th International Conference on Intelligence in Next Generation Networks (2013)
15. Glova, J., Sabol, T., Vajda, V.: Business models for the Internet of Things environment. Proc. Econ. Finan. **15**, 1122–1129 (2014)
16. Shi, X.: A research on Internet-of-Things-based business model of china mobile. In: International Conference on Logistics Engineering, Management and Computer Science (2014)
17. Bucherer, E., Uckelmann, D.: Business models for the Internet of Things. In: Uckelmann, D., Harrison, M., Michahelles, F. (eds.) Architecting the Internet of Things, pp. 253–277. Springer, Heidelberg (2011). https://doi.org/10.1007/978-3-642-19157-2_10
18. Leminen, S., Westerlund, M., Rajahonka, M., Siuruainen, R.: Towards IOT ecosystems and business models. In: Andreev, S., Balandin, S., Koucheryavy, Y. (eds.) NEW2AN/ruSMART-2012. LNCS, vol. 7469, pp. 15–26. Springer, Heidelberg (2012). https://doi.org/10.1007/978-3-642-32686-8_2
19. Osterwalder, A., Pigneur, Y.: Business Model Generation: A Handbook for Visionaries, Game Changers, and Challengers. Wiley, Hoboken (2010)

Smart Cities and Smart Homes

The Internet of Things as Smart City Enabler: The Cases of Palo Alto, Nice and Stockholm

Wouter H. N. Evertzen[1], Robin Effing[1,2(✉)],
and Efthymios Constantinides[1]

[1] University of Twente, P.O. Box 217, 7500 AE Enschede, The Netherlands
r.effing@utwente.nl
[2] Saxion University of Applied Sciences,
P.O. Box 70.000, 7500 KB Enschede, The Netherlands

Abstract. Due to rapid urbanization, city populations are rapidly increasing all over the world creating new problems and challenges. Solving some of these problems requires innovative approaches; one increasingly popular approach is to transform cities to Smart Cities. Smart Cities implement innovative approaches based on IoT technologies and convert many services to digital services. These services are implemented within the different components of a Smart City, helping city administrators to improve the life of the citizens, addressing different service, security and administrative challenges. The objective of this paper is to explore and determine how three well-known cities - Nice, Palo Alto and Stockholm - implemented the Smart City concept. The study indicates that a successful implementation of a Smart City model requires addressing a number of critical challenges: citizen involvement, business collaboration and strong leadership prove to be key success factors in the Smart City development process.

Keywords: Smart City · Smart City Strategy · Internet of Things · IoT ·
IoT infrastructure · E-government

1 Introduction

According to the United Nations [1], 55% of the world population lives in urban areas today, and this percentage is expected to increase to 68% by 2018. As a result, cities already are facing tremendous challenges related to issues like housing, mobility, logistics, energy consumption, air quality, quality of life, social inclusion, safety, public services and governance [2]. Cities are forced to search for and find solutions for these challenges in innovative and even groundbreaking ways. A strategy that is widely popular yet challenging in many ways, is to become a Smart City [3]. According to Yin et al. [4] a Smart City is a "systematic assimilation of technological infrastructures which builds on progressive data processing, with the objectives of making city governance more efficient, offer a higher quality of life for civilians, help businesses flourishing and protect the environment." Even though there is still not a city, that is universally recognized as a full-fledge Smart City, some cities are leading the way towards such a goal and provide examples of progress in this domain. It can be said that city attempts to become a real Smart City are made on a worldwide scale.

© IFIP International Federation for Information Processing 2019
Published by Springer Nature Switzerland AG 2019
I. O. Pappas et al. (Eds.): I3E 2019, LNCS 11701, pp. 293–304, 2019.
https://doi.org/10.1007/978-3-030-29374-1_24

The technologies often described as Internet of Things (IoT) could be seen as one of the key drivers behind the development of a Smart City. According to Giusto et al. [5], the IoT is a "communication paradigm which visualizes a near future, in which physical objects are equipped with microcontrollers, transceivers for digital communication and fitting protocol stacks that will make these objects able to communicate with each other and with the users". This technology develops fast with an estimated number of 20 to 50 billion devices connected in 2020 [6].

Smart Cities are seen as the future solution to urbanization problems. IoT-based infrastructures will allow cities to devise solutions addressing the earlier mentioned issues in an efficient and environmentally responsible way.

Since every city has its own unique problems and prioritizes its own city components, every city transforms into a Smart City in its own way. Research is mainly focused on implementation of IoT as a way for cities to become smart, but less attention is paid on differences of IoT implementation between cities and comparison of such strategies after implementation. The objective of this study is to contribute to better understanding of similarities and differences between cities during the Smart City implementation process using IoT. Therefore, the research question is: how do three globally leading Smart Cities implement the Internet of Things within different components of their city, in order to become a smarter city?

The study was carried out by conducting case studies in three cities, that are globally recognized as leading Smart Cities. By investigating how these cities successfully implement the IoT within their Smart City components, more insights will be gained on common success factors and common problems facing cities in the process of becoming smart.

2 Theoretical Framework

2.1 Smart Cities

Over the last few decades, the concept of a Smart City attracted wide interest and debate around the world. Part of the debate is about the extent to which technology and ICT should have a dominant role in the city to become smarter. According to Batty et al. [7], a Smart City is defined as "a city where Information and Communication Technologies (ICT) are blended with traditional infrastructures, organized and unified by using advanced digital technologies". Technology appears to be a common thread in most definitions within literature, but not the only aspect of importance. According to Hollands [8], a Smart City must be based on more than the use of ICT alone. This opinion seems to be supported by many different authors over the years, since most of the definitions found, are more integral than the one that Batty et al. [7] gave. According to Nam and Pardo [9], a Smart City consists of three core components: technology factors, human factors and institutional factors. Their vision states that "smart" can be identified as innovative and revolutionary developments, leaded by new technologies. However, it is the social aspect, rather than smart technologies that stands fundamental within a Smart City according to Nam and Pardo [9]. Even though these authors state that smart developments are leaded by new technologies, they do not designate technology as the core component within a Smart City. According to Caragliu, Del Bo and Nijkamp [10], a city is smart when "continuous economic growth and a high quality of life, with thoughtful handling of natural resources through participatory management, is inflamed by investments in human capital, social capital, traditional (transportation) and current (ICT) communication infrastructure". While the meaning of the word "smart" is interpreted differently within this definition, the underlying core components of a Smart City are highly similar to the ones given in the previous definition. Some researchers accept an even broader definition of a Smart City. According to Neirotti et al. [11], a Smart City should be capable of optimizing the practice and exploitation of tangible assets (e.g. transportation infrastructures, natural resources), as well as intangible assets (e.g. human capital, academic capital of firms). Zanella et al. [12] argue that "the final objective of a Smart City is to make better use of the public resources, in order to raise the quality of the services which are presented to the citizens, while lowering the operational expenditures of the civic administrations". While the concept of Smart City became broader over the years, including more integral approaches, researchers acknowledge the importance of using internet technology, and in particular IoT, as one of building blocks for a smart city. The most common of the components of smart cities we have identified are displayed in Table 1.

Table 1. Smart city components

Author(s)/ smart city domain	Environment	Mobility	Governance	Smart citizens	Energy	Buildings homes	Healthcare	Economy	Security
Al Nuaimi et al. [13]	x	x	x	x	x		x		x
Arasteh et al. [14]		x	x	x	x	x	x		x
Arroub et al. [2]	x	x	x			x		x	
Habibzadeh et al. [15]	x	x			x		x		
Khan et al. [16]	x	x	x	x				x	
Lombardi et al. [17]	x		x	x		x		x	
Nam & Pardo [9]	x	x	x	x	x		x		x
Neirotti et al. [11]	x	x	x	x	x	x		x	
Silva et al. [16]		x		x	x		x		
Talari et al. [18]	x	x				x	x		x
Venkat Reddy et al. [19]	x	x			x	x			
Yin et al. [4]	x		x	x				x	
Total of mentions	10	10	8	8	7	6	6	5	4

2.2   The Internet of Things

The concept of IoT is an increasingly popular concept in the literature; there are many different opinions, views and definitions on it. Giusto et al. [5] describe the IoT as a communication paradigm which visualizes a near future, in which physical objects are equipped with microcontrollers, transceivers for digital communication and fitting protocol stacks that will make these objects able to communicate with each other and with the users. Zanella et al. [12] state that "the intention of the IoT is to make the Internet even more engaging and omnipresent, by allowing easy entrance and communication with a large variety of devices so that it can support the development of a number of applications which make use of the possibly gigantic bulk and diversity of data produced by objects to present new services to citizens, companies and public administrations". According to Miorandi et al. [20], the IoT can be seen as an application whereby the Internet is used "for connecting physical items, that interact with each other and/or with humans in order to present a service that embraces the need to rethink about a new some of the traditional pathways commonly used in networking, computing and service management". As stated by Atzori et al. [21] the IoT should indeed be considered as part of the Internet of the future, which is expected to be dramatically different from the Internet we use today. According to these authors, the objective of the IoT is to enable communications with and among smart objects. The IoT interconnects a large variety of physical objects, enabling these objects to communicate with each other, as well as with users, without any human engagement.

Effective IoT implementation in cities requires a specific IoT infrastructure, supporting the complexity of different sensors set up in urban environments. Sensor-enabled smart objects demonstrate to be the essential feature for the interconnected infrastructures of the future [22]. According to Jin et al. [23], the IoT can be seen as the key technological enabler for the infrastructure of a Smart City. Sicari et al. [24] stated that, a flexible infrastructure is necessary within a Smart City, because of the large number of interconnected devices. Corici et al. [25] mention that an infrastructure where end device connectivity is monitored and IoT communication reliability is assured, is key for a Smart City. According to Joseph et al. [26], an IoT-infrastructure should ensure that the sub-systems of a Smart City are intelligent enough to communicate and work interconnected with each other. According to Rathore et al. [27], an IoT-based infrastructure is necessary to fulfill the needs of a Smart City and Gope et al. [28] argue that in future Smart Cities, devices should be connected to IoT-based infrastructure. According to Cheng et al. [29], to enable the IoT services, deployed within a Smart City, infrastructure should form a large scale IoT system with widely deployed IoT devices. IoT in Smart City development remained a central issue in the literature over the last decade and especially in recent years; in order to implement the IoT within Smart City components, an IoT-based infrastructure is indispensable. Therefore, it can be seen as the backbone for building a Smart City.

Many authors are modeling a Smart City infrastructure in layers that start with data generation [23, 30–33]. This data generation is used by an application and results into a service or processed data that serves an end-user. Sensors and devices collecting data and a using a dispersed network for transmission is another key part of the infrastructure [23, 30–34]. Data flows allow the formation of a layered and generic IoT-based infrastructure for Smart Cities. Berkel et al. [35] note that the baseline infrastructure for Smart Cities consists of four layers (Fig. 1). However, in practice, the entire system architecture is often more complex than shown in this layered infrastructure.

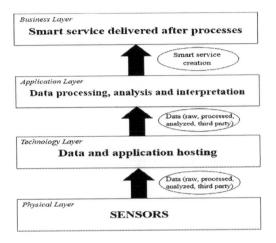

Fig. 1. Layers of an IoT based infrastructure

3 Methodology

We conducted an exploratory case study since we aim to discover underlying motivations, experiences and lessons from a few leading smart cities; professionals directly involved in prominent Smart City transformations were interviewed. We included the cases of Palo Alto, Nice and Stockholm. In the heart of Silicon Valley (US), Palo Alto is pioneering the concept of a Smart City for many people [36]. According to United Smart Cities (2017), Nice, at the Cote D'Azur in France, is recognized as a world pioneer and well-known Smart City. Stockholm is also seen as one of the top Smart Cities in the world [37–39], ranked 5th in The Top 10 Smartest Cities in the World [40]. The semi-structured interviews consisted of a total of 33 open-ended questions. The analysis included Axial coding.

4 Results

4.1 Palo Alto

"I cannot think of a single project that the city of Palo Alto is doing today, where technology is not on the table." [41] According to Palo Alto's CIO, technology is going to be one of the largest components of how to enable positive change in the future. Palo Alto stated to have over 300 distinctive systems and therefore, a whole array of services and technologies, that run everything within the city. From their record management system, to software that helps with medical information in their ambulances. "In order to have the IoT, which seems to be one of the major trends in the Smart City space, you got to have a solid, fast, high-quality core backbone infrastructure" [41]. The IoT-based infrastructure of Palo Alto was stated to be built of several critical elements. Data flows securely across this network. This includes everything from open-data, to analytics, visualizations and data-driven decision-making. This way, the data is opened-up and an ecosystem of participants exists. According to Palo Alto, a city cannot be smart without a data strategy. On top of that, sensors are embedded in physical pieces within the city's architecture. This architecture was not necessarily formalized into specific layers.

Palo Alto focuses on mobility, energy and sustainability as primary Smart City components. Mobility is a major challenge; "In many ways, probably that is the biggest Smart City area for the city of Palo Alto right now. It is everything from initiatives, to encourage people to not drive their car" [41]. They promote electric cars, bikes and scooters and try to make different forms of non-car transport available. Palo Alto also values the support of the emergences of autonomous vehicles. The second component was stated to be energy. "One of the things that makes Palo Alto unique in the United States, is that we are one of the few cities that provides all the utilities services. Electric, gas, water, waste-water. We even provide fiber internet. So, we have a lot of control over our utility's infrastructure" [41]. The city moved away from fossils and coals years ago and is therefore entirely carbon-free on the residential front. By having a smart energy grid rolled-out, Palo Alto connects every house, to gain rich information for optimizing their energy distribution. This information is also used for operations and repairs. The third component was stated to be sustainability in the environment. "In some ways, all the things I have already shared with you, are subscenes of that. Energy, transportation and digitization are all parts of the sustainability movement" [41]. Next to that, it also means water-management technology by using sensors in the water. Also, it includes distribution of electric vehicle chargers all over the community. Other examples were, gaining a better understanding of emissions and managing city buildings more energy-efficient.

A broad area of digital transformation was identified as key component. The city has deployed over 60 different digital experiences. "All our signatures are now done digitally. We do not have a lot of paperwork anymore; we digitize all our papers. We do not print as much as we used to. So, a big push on digital transformation and just better services. More efficient, more streamlined, more accurate and more managed services" [41]. In Palo Alto there were priorities set in city governance, talent management, budget allocation and leadership in order to realize smart city goals. "Even through your best tempts to get grants and loans and all the other kinds of mechanisms, there is just not enough money to do everything you want to do" [41]. Palo Alto stated several critical requirements for an IoT-based infrastructure. "Then, you have to have the mindset, the vision, the strategy and the governance. Those will be the additional layers on top of it" [41]. Next to those factors, human capital was also mentioned as an important factor for supporting the build of a Smart City, next to the IoT. According to Palo Alto, every city must decide whether becoming a Smart City is a mission they want to take on. "The best practice is to make sure that there is a strong supportable vision for it and then execute on it" [41].

4.2   Nice

"If we come back to how the Smart City of Nice was born, this is from political intentions to use digital innovation for developing the local economy of Nice" [42]. According to Nice, their IoT-based infrastructure consists of specific layers. It was also mentioned that public and private partnerships exist within the IoT-based infrastructure of Nice. The city of Nice is using the IoT to digitize existing services and to create new ones. "An IoT-based infrastructure is important for a Smart City, because it is a way to improve the performance of public services. Today we are living in a digital world. It is really important for cities to use an IoT-infrastructure to develop its services" [42]. On top of that, Nice agreed that an IoT-based infrastructure can be seen as the backbone for building a Smart City.

According to Nice, their primary Smart City components are: mobility, energy and environment. Next to that, the city plans developing the healthcare component as well. "Nice aims to be a good Smart City in all these components. So, I would say that Nice wants to be an innovative Smart City in developing these components" [42]. An example of how they already used the IoT to become a smarter city, is a high-tech tramway, that makes use of IoT-services within their mobility component. By means of an IoT-based mobile application, users can organize their trip. Also, drivers of the tramway can anticipate on technical problems and resolve them, because of real-time data presented by IoT-services. An example for their energy and environment components, are sensors that collect data about the environment by measuring the air quality. "In order to help business companies to use this data for developing new innovative services, enabling consumers to transform their energy habits" [42].

"One strength of Nice is, that they build their Smart City concept on the open-data perspective" [42]. However, in practice, not all data was always accessible. This was stated to be a real problem for the development of IoT-services. Next to this problem, the privacy and acceptance of citizens regarding IoT-services were experienced as important problems. A more general problem was experienced to be the public administration services in Nice. "It is a really bad problem we have in France, the public administration. If IoT-services could improve the process of public administration services, it would be good" [42]. According to Nice, the first requirement for an IoT-based infrastructure is technology-based. "You need it, to develop the infrastructure in order to implement the IoT" [42]. Next to that, the right digital capabilities need to be developed and enough storage space should be available. Other factors that are important for building a Smart City, next to the IoT, were stated to be: management and intention, funding and collaboration. "I think for developing innovations, build on IoT-technologies, we really need to improve the management of ecosystems of these technologies and how we can implement them" [42]. Therefore, the right intentions and management of local public actors are needed to build a Smart City. Within all of the focused components of Nice, private and public partnerships services were included. Nice does not only collaborate with big companies, but also with local startups. Together with these companies, the city of Nice creates smart solution services. "I think we also have to give chance to startups" [42]. Nice recommended other cities to assess citizen needs and to include citizens as co-actors within city projects, before developing these projects and corresponding technologies. Next to that, Nice recommended cities to care about citizen's privacy and their acceptance of the use and potential use of IoT-services. "When you use IoT-technologies, you collect a lot of personal and impersonal data and this data is sensitive" [42]. "The building of a Smart City depends on the main characteristics of its own territories and its managers. I do not think there is a universal model to build a Smart City" [42].

4.3 Stockholm

For Stockholm, an IoT-based infrastructure is extremely important for Smart Cities nowadays. "The reason though we are establishing this, is because we have a lot of challenges. We know that using the smart technologies can help us to be a better city, for the people that live there, work there and even the people that are visiting us" [43]. Stockholm did agree on the question whether an IoT-based infrastructure can be seen as the backbone for building a Smart City but were a bit hesitant to disclose details on how it was exactly layered. "There is no other part of our infrastructure that we can use to build a Smart City" [43]. Stockholm's main domains are: sustainability (green policies), smart locks, smart traffic and smart lighting. It was also stated that their environmental department is being active with smart technologies as well and that they are engaging in air pollution. "We need to be a fossil-free city within 2040" [43]. Several examples of how the IoT is used within Stockholm, in order to become a smarter city were given. "We have a lot of locks today that are electronic and used all over the world... a lock that you can open with an iPhone or a code for instance" [43]. For the smart traffic component, roads were equipped with sensors. Stockholm is actively using cameras in traffic, to obtain real-time data from cars, bicycles, pedestrians and public transportation and optimize the traffic lights operations. In a pilot project, next the use of LED-lighting in lampposts, these were equipped with sensors as well. These sensors are used among others for changing the light, measuring air pollution and measuring the wind temperature.

The data, generated from all the different projects described above, is shared and private companies are encouraged to establish new services using this data. "The city of Stockholm should establish the data that we can publish. The next step is to make the smart services. I hope that should be done by private companies and not by the city of Stockholm. By using the data from the sensors, we can establish new services" [43]. A new business model is a challenge: who is going to pay for it. A more important obstacle was stated to be the citizen security. "People are of course a little bit afraid when we use IoT-solutions" [43]. The development of an IoT-based infrastructure was seen as a continuous process. Stockholm stated that adaptability to a city's needs is the most important requirement for an IoT-based infrastructure. Also, technologies must meet security requirements. Apart from the IoT, citizens have a fundamental role within the Smart City development of Stockholm. It was stated that everything the city does, is for them. "When we work on the strategy, we asked a lot of citizens..., we also asked academia and the businesses" [43]. Stockholm views the Smart City development process as a democratic issue as well.

5 Discussion

Our findings show that there is not a single best approach for implementing IoT for creating a smart city. The approach is contingent on the specific characteristics of the city. IoT is the key enabling tool for smart cities; it can truly enrich the existing landscape of information technology in a city and deliver new open data and connections to the current information systems. Mobility and energy are the core challenges driving the smart city movement. These were shown as key fields of attention in both our literature findings and empirical results. IoT investments raise the need for additional security measures. A city can become vulnerable for hackers and terrorists as a result of connected sensors and devices that deliver a critical infrastructure. Without an underlying and fitting infrastructure, a city's desired Smart City vision is difficult to realize. Therefore, the IoT infrastructure is the backbone for a Smart City. Our cases have all reserved a major role for the IoT infrastructure. They all showed some form of layering. First, there is the use of sensors to obtain data (Physical Layer). Second, enough storage space is needed for storing and sharing data (Technology Layer). Third, in order to create new services, the data must be transformed (Application Layer). Finally, all cities spoke about the actual creation of new services, which confirms the Business Layer.

Even though the cases show how IoT can be implemented within various Smart City components, this paper emphasizes that a Smart City cannot be realized by using the IoT alone [8]. The social aspect of a city also matters [9]. Citizens and governance play a fundamental role within the Smart City development of each city. The needs, privacy, security and acceptance of citizens are seen as major challenges for every Smart City. This is because, all the Smart City objectives that are set by cities, are eventually aimed at the people that live and work there. Therefore, a strategy should be developed that includes citizens, businesses and universities and that is adaptable to their needs and those of the city. In order to create new and innovative services, collaboration with businesses is of great importance. During the Smart City development process, leadership must ensure that the needs of citizens are continuously strived for and collaborations are established. This should be done by setting the right priorities, maintaining the right intentions and aligning all parties involved.

There are some limitations that have to be taken into account for our study. During this research, semi-structured qualitative interviews were conducted. Interviews were conducted with a relatively small number of cities. There are many cities that are trying to become a Smart City worldwide. Therefore, the finding cannot easily be generalized for other smart cities (e.g. non-Western Cities). The underlying aim of our study was to describe three leading examples instead of trying to generalize findings. Smart Cities and the IoT are complex fields of expertise. Even though interest and objectivity has been demonstrated regarding these concepts, there is a lack of specific skills, knowledge, experiences and expertise compared to experts within these fields. Therefore, the quality and interpretation of the gathered data, might vary from the standpoint of specific fields (domains) of expertise. In the end, the future of a city is not dependent on IoT alone, but IoT is definitely playing a big part in innovation of the city.

References

1. United Nations: 68% of the world population projected to live in urban areas by 2050. https://www.un.org/development/desa/en/news/population/2018-revision-of-world-urbanization-prospects.html
2. Arroub, A., Zahi, B., Sabir, E., Sadik, M.: A literature review on smart cities: paradigms, opportunities and open problems. In: Proceedings - 2016 International Conference on Wireless Networks and Mobile Communications WINCOM 2016, pp. 180–186 (2016). https://doi.org/10.1109/WINCOM.2016.7777211. Green Commun. Netw.
3. Chourabi, H., et al.: Understanding smart cities: an integrative framework. In: Proceedings of the Annual Hawaii International Conference on System Sciences, pp. 2289–2297 (2012). https://doi.org/10.1109/HICSS.2012.615
4. Yin, C.T., Xiong, Z., Chen, H., Wang, J.Y., Cooper, D., David, B.: A literature survey on smart cities. Sci. China Inf. Sci. **58**, 1–18 (2015). https://doi.org/10.1007/s11432-015-5397-4
5. Giusto, D., Iera, A., Morabito, G., Luigi, A.: The Internet of Things. Springer, New York (2010). https://doi.org/10.1007/978-1-4419-1674-7
6. Perara, C., Zaslavsky, A., Christen, P., Georgakopoulos, D.: Sensing as a service model for smart cities supported by Internet of Things. Trans. Emerg. Telecommun. **25**, 81–93 (2014). https://doi.org/10.1002/ett
7. Batty, M., et al.: Smart cities of the future. Eur. Phys. J. Spec. Top. **214**, 481–518 (2012). https://doi.org/10.1140/epjst/e2012-01703-3
8. Hollands, R.G.: Will the real smart city please stand up? City **12**, 1–84 (2008). https://doi.org/10.1080/13604810802479126
9. Nam, T., Pardo, T.A.: Conceptualizing smart city with dimensions of technology, people, and institutions. In: Proceedings of the 12th Annual International Conference on Digital Government Research Conference on Digital Government Innovations Challenging Times - dg.o '11. 282 (2011). https://doi.org/10.1145/2037556.2037602
10. Caragliu, A., del Bo, C., Nijkamp, P.: Smart cities in Europe. J. Urban Technol. **18**, 65–82 (2011). https://doi.org/10.1080/10630732.2011.601117
11. Neirotti, P., De Marco, A., Cagliano, A.C., Mangano, G., Scorrano, F.: Current trends in smart city initiatives: some stylised facts. Cities **38**, 25–36 (2014). https://doi.org/10.1016/j.cities.2013.12.010
12. Zanella, A., Bui, N., Castelli, A., Vangelista, L., Zorzi, M.: Internet of Things for smart cities. IEEE Internet Things J. **1**, 1–12 (2014). https://doi.org/10.1109/JIOT.2014.2306328
13. Al Nuaimi, E., Al Neyadi, H., Mohamed, N., Al-Jaroodi, J.: Applications of big data to smart cities. J. Internet Serv. Appl. **6**, 1–15 (2015). https://doi.org/10.1186/s13174-015-0041-5
14. Arasteh, H., et al.: IoT-based smart cities: a survey. In: EEEIC 2016 - International Conference on Environment and Electrical Engineering, pp. 1–6 (2016). https://doi.org/10.1109/EEEIC.2016.7555867
15. Habibzadeh, H., Boggio-Dandry, A., Qin, Z., Soyata, T., Kantarci, B., Mouftah, H.T.: Soft sensing in smart cities: handling 3Vs using recommender systems, machine intelligence, and data analytics. IEEE Commun. Mag. **56**, 78–86 (2018). https://doi.org/10.1109/MCOM.2018.1700304
16. Silva, B.N., Khan, M., Han, K.: Towards sustainable smart cities: a review of trends, architectures, components, and open challenges in smart cities. Sustain. Cities Soc. **38**, 697–713 (2018). https://doi.org/10.1016/j.scs.2018.01.053
17. Lombardi, P., Giordano, S., Farouh, H., Yousef, W.: Modelling the smart city performance. Innovation **25**, 137–149 (2012). https://doi.org/10.1080/13511610.2012.660325

18. Talari, S., Shafie-Khah, M., Siano, P., Loia, V., Tommasetti, A., Catalão, J.P.S.: A review of smart cities based on the Internet of Things concept. Energies **10**, 1–23 (2017). https://doi.org/10.3390/en10040421
19. Venkat Reddy, P., Siva Krishna, A., Ravi Kumar, T.: Study on concept of smart city and its structural components. Int. J. Civ. Eng. Technol. **8**, 101–112 (2017)
20. Miorandi, D., Sicari, S., De Pellegrini, F., Chlamtac, I.: Internet of Things: vision, applications and research challenges. Ad Hoc Netw. **10**(7), 1497–1516 (2012). https://doi.org/10.1016/j.adhoc.2012.02.016
21. Atzori, L., Iera, A., Morabito, G.: The Internet of Things: a survey. Comput. Networks. **54**, 2787–2805 (2010). https://doi.org/10.1016/j.comnet.2010.05.010
22. Balakrishna, C.: Enabling technologies for smart city services and applications. In: Proceedings of the 6th International Conference on Next Generation Mobile Applications, Services and Technologies, NGMAST 2012, pp. 223–227 (2012). https://doi.org/10.1109/NGMAST.2012.51
23. Jin, J., Palaniswami, M., Gubbi, J., Marusic, S.: An information framework for creating a smart city through Internet of Things. IEEE Internet Things J. **1**, 112–121 (2014). https://doi.org/10.1109/JIOT.2013.2296516
24. Sicari, S., Rizzardi, A., Grieco, L.A., Coen-Porisini, A.: Security, privacy and trust in Internet of Things: the road ahead. Comput. Netw. **76**, 146–164 (2015). https://doi.org/10.1016/j.comnet.2014.11.008
25. Corici, A., et al.: Towards programmable and scalable IoT infrastructures for smart cities. In: 2016 IEEE Annual Conference on Pervasive Pervasive Computing and Communications Workshops (PerCom), pp. 1–6 (2016). https://doi.org/10.1109/PERCOMW.2016.7457132
26. Joseph, T., Jenu, R., Assis, A.K., Kumar, V.A.S., Sasi, P.M., Alexander, G.: IoT middleware for smart city: (an integrated and centrally managed IoT middleware for smart city). TENSYMP 2017 - IEEE International Symposium Technology Smart Cities, pp. 3–7 (2017). https://doi.org/10.1109/TENCONSpring.2017.8070054
27. Rathore, M.M., Paul, A., Ahmad, A., Jeon, G.: IoT-based big data. Int. J. Semant. Web Inf. Syst. **13**, 28–47 (2016). https://doi.org/10.4018/ijswis.2017010103
28. Gope, P., Amin, R., Hafizul Islam, S.K., Kumar, N., Bhalla, V.K.: Lightweight and privacy-preserving RFID authentication scheme for distributed IoT infrastructure with secure localization services for smart city environment. Futur. Gener. Comput. Syst. **83**, 629–637 (2018). https://doi.org/10.1016/j.future.2017.06.023
29. Cheng, B., Solmaz, G., Cirillo, F., Kovacs, E., Terasawa, K., Kitazawa, A.: FogFlow: easy programming of IoT services over cloud and edges for smart cities. IEEE Internet Things J. **5**, 696–707 (2018). https://doi.org/10.1109/JIOT.2017.2747214
30. Anthopoulos, L., Fitsilis, P.: From digital to ubiquitous cities: defining a common architecture for urban development. In: 2010 Proceedings of the 6th International Conference on Intelligent Environments IE 2010, pp. 301–306 (2010). https://doi.org/10.1109/IE.2010.61
31. Gaur, A., Scotney, B., Parr, G., McClean, S.: Smart city architecture and its applications based on IoT. Proc. Comput. Sci. **52**, 1089–1094 (2015). https://doi.org/10.1016/j.procs.2015.05.122
32. Jalali, R., El-Khatib, K., McGregor, C.: Smart city architecture for community level services through the Internet of Things. In: 2015 18th International Conference on Intelligence in Next Generation Networks, ICIN 2015, pp. 108–113 (2015). https://doi.org/10.1109/ICIN.2015.7073815
33. Rong, W., Xiong, Z., Cooper, D., Li, C., Sheng, H.: Smart city architecture: a technology guide for implementation and design challenges. China Commun. **11**, 56–69 (2014). https://doi.org/10.1109/CC.2014.6825259

34. Filipponi, L., Vitaletti, A., Landi, G., Memeo, V., Laura, G., Pucci, P.: Smart city: an event driven architecture for monitoring public spaces with heterogeneous sensors. In: Proceedings of the 4th International Conference on Sensor Technologies, SENSORCOMM 2010, pp. 281–286 (2010). https://doi.org/10.1109/SENSORCOMM.2010.50

35. Berkel, A.R.R., Singh, P.M., van Sinderen, M.J.: An information security architecture for smart cities. In: Shishkov, B. (ed.) BMSD 2018. LNBIP, vol. 319, pp. 167–184. Springer, Cham (2018). https://doi.org/10.1007/978-3-319-94214-8_11

36. Van Belleghem, S.: Is Palo Alto leading the way to a Smart City?. https://www.cbronline.com/internet-of-things/smart-cities/palo-alto-leading-way-smart-city/

37. Komninos, N.: The age of intelligent cities: smart environments and innovation-for-all strategies. Age Intell. Cities Smart Environ. Innov. Strateg. 1–278 (2014). https://doi.org/10.4324/9781315769349

38. Angelidou, M.: The role of smart city characteristics in the plans of fifteen cities. J. Urban Technol. **24**, 3–28 (2017). https://doi.org/10.1080/10630732.2017.1348880

39. Ching, T.-Y., Ferreira, J.: Smart cities: concepts, perceptions and lessons for planners. In: Geertman, S., Ferreira, J., Goodspeed, R., Stillwell, J. (eds.) Planning Support Systems and Smart Cities. LNGC, pp. 145–168. Springer, Cham (2015). https://doi.org/10.1007/978-3-319-18368-8_8

40. Luciano, M.: Top 10 Smartest Cities In The World. https://www.ecnmag.com/blog/2017/11/top-10-smartest-cities-world

41. Reichental, J.: Interview Jonathan Reichental, CIO Palo Alto (2018). City of P.A.

42. Attour, A.: Interview Amel Attour, smart city Nice University of Nice Sophia Antipolis (2018). University of N.S.A.

43. Johannesson, C.: Interview Claes Johannesson, smart city Stockholm, Projectleader (2018). City of S.

Smart Home Technology Acceptance: An Empirical Investigation

Davit Marikyan[✉], Savvas Papagiannidis, and Eleftherios Alamanos

Newcastle University Business School, 5 Barrack Road,
Newcastle upon Tyne NE1 4SE, UK
{d.marikyan2, savvas.papagiannidis,
eleftherios.alamanos}@newcastle.ac.uk

Abstract. Recent technological advances have contributed to the development of smart homes, embedded with artificial intelligence, which aim to provide tailored services to residents. Smart home technologies benefit people daily and improve the environment in the long-term perspective. Despite the great interest of the research community in smart homes, the adoption rate is still low. The purpose of this study is to develop the research model, which can explain the acceptance of smart homes by users. Along with the relationship of technology acceptance factors with use behaviour, this study analyses the importance of individuals' belief and values. Structural equational modelling has been employed to test the proposed hypotheses using a sample of 422 smart home users. The analysis revealed the significance of the relationships between values and perceived technology-fit, while the technology acceptance factors had a strong correlation with use behaviour leading to satisfaction.

Keywords: Technology acceptance model · Smart home technology · Smart technology · Use behaviour

1 Introduction

A smart home is defined as a "*residence equipped with computing and information technology, which anticipates and responds to the needs of the occupants, working to promote their comfort, convenience, security and entertainment through the management of technology within the home and connections to the world beyond*" [1]. The current research focuses mostly on the examination of benefits that smart homes make possible [2, 3]. However, compared to other technologies, the pervasive nature of smart homes undermines users' trust and raises concerns related to privacy. Technologies utilised in a private context have largely been overlooked in technology acceptance studies. Moreover, the examination of psychological factors of users, perceived outcomes of use and beliefs is of paramount importance as they may underpin the utilisation of such technologies [4]. Similarly, the use of technology in homes is heavily contingent on potential risks that users perceive in relation to personal data misuse and financial losses [1, 3, 5]. Therefore, studying technology acceptance from the perspective of potential risks and benefits perceived by users is more important when it comes to private spaces compared to public or mixed settings. This study will address

© IFIP International Federation for Information Processing 2019
Published by Springer Nature Switzerland AG 2019
I. O. Pappas et al. (Eds.): I3E 2019, LNCS 11701, pp. 305–315, 2019.
https://doi.org/10.1007/978-3-030-29374-1_25

the gap in the literature on the acceptance of technologies in private settings by pursuing two objectives. First, the study will examine the acceptance of technologies with the focus on users of smart homes. Second, the study will empirically investigate underlying attitudes towards technology utilisation, such as perceived benefits and risks.

2   Literature Review and Hypothesis Development

This study adopts the Task-Technology Fit (TTF) model as a baseline theoretical framework. The TTF model examines the dependence of users' behaviour on the perceived fit between technology functionality and task requirements of residents. The model assumes that a higher degree of fit indicates higher technology performance. Although the "fit" factor has been proved to be crucial in technology acceptance, the prior research has mostly studied it implicitly [6]. In this study, we combine TTF with perceived usefulness and perceived ease of use from the Technology Acceptance Model (TAM), which refer to the users' perception of technology performance [7].

2.1   Antecedents of Task-Technology Fit

TTF is defined as *"the degree to which technology assists an individual in performing his or her portfolio of tasks"* [6]. The theory that underlines task-technology fit suggests that individuals determine the fit between technology and task requirements based on their utilitarian and hedonic needs [6, 8]. The perception of the technology is dependent on the degree to which perceived values of the technology use satisfy individuals' needs [8, 9]. The essence of the hedonic value is the achievement of self-fulfilment. When it comes to the information systems context, hedonic value is defined as an individual's subjective perception of the extent to which a product or service brings fun and enjoyment [8, 10]. In contrast, utilitarian value implies an instrumental utility of technology use, such as enhanced task performance or efficiency [8]. Based on the above, we propose that there is a correlation between behavioural beliefs and users' perception of task-technology fit. Based on the literature on the smart home domain, smart home technology makes it possible to save on utility bills and improve the operational efficiency of daily tasks, thus satisfying users' utilitarian values [3, 5], as well as helping improve hedonic experiences by bringing fun and enjoyment [5]. Therefore, the first hypothesis states that:

H1: Utilitarian and Hedonic beliefs are positively correlated with consumers' perception of task technology fit.

There is a stream in the literature heavily focused on the perceived risks of using technology [11, 12]. Those risks can refer to two main categories: privacy and financial risks [11, 12]. Individuals perceive high risk when they are uncertain on the outcome of the technology use [13]. Following the definition, task-technology fit results from the consistency between the technology characteristics and an individual's belief that it is able to satisfy their requirements and assist in fulfilling particular tasks [8, 14]. Consequently, the perception that technology fits individuals' requirements can be inhibited by high perceived risks. In line with the research on the smart home domain, individuals have raised concerns that the use of technology may result in privacy intrusion, security breaches and the inability to reduce financial spending on energy consumption [1, 3, 5]. Therefore we hypothesise that:

H2: Financial and privacy risks are negatively correlated with an individual's perception of task technology fit.

2.2 The Effects of Task-Technology Fit

TTF has been used in combination with other technology acceptance models aiming to examine individuals' attitudes underlying technology adoption, the perception of performance and intention to continuously use technology [15–17]. The perception of fit between task and technology is an underlying factor of innovation adoption [15, 16]. The TTF model found implications in various contexts, including online learning systems, mobile insurance and mobile banking [16, 18]. When examining the adoption of online learning courses, users stressed the importance of task-technology fit in evaluating the usefulness and ease of use of online systems [16]. However, previous research found variance in the significance of TTF dimensions (i.e. data quality, authorisation, locatability, timeliness, training, compatibility, relationship with users and system reliability) for users. For example, Lee, Cheng [18] argued that data quality was the main factor underpinning the adoption of mobile insurance services. Another study found that the relationship between TTF and the impact of mobile banking performance varies across different age groups. Particularly, the effect was significant only for older respondents, but not for the younger generation [17]. Conflicting results in prior research can be explained by the difference in the purpose of online systems' use and users' IT skills. For example, TTF can play a more important role in the context of online learning, as online systems can be the only solution to achieve the task. When it comes to mobile banking, users are usually provided with other alternatives that aim to increase the convenience of the use of banking services. Secondly, TTF can be insignificant for younger users because they are more knowledgeable about the technology and more efficient in use. In addition, some studies focused on the outcomes of technology use in the form of satisfaction. The literature provides evidence of both an indirect and a direct effect of task-technology fit on satisfaction [19, 20]. The studies examining a direct relationship between TTF and satisfaction concluded that satisfaction is strongly and positively affected by perceived fit, and leads to continuous use intention [20, 21]. Based on the above, we hypothesise that:

H3: The perceived task technology fit is positively correlated with use behaviour and satisfaction.

There has been evidence in the literature about the correlation between TTF and PEOU [15]. The study compared the strength of the effect of constructs in two scenarios: (1) when TTF was examined as a stand-alone model and (2) when TTF was combined with TAM. The results demonstrated that TTF has a stronger effect when it was integrated with TAM constructs [15]. A similar finding was provided by another recent study that integrated TAM and TTF and concluded that an extended model has a better explanatory power [16]. Also, a higher effect of TTF was observed when the model was integrated with UTAUT constructs, such as effort expectancy and performance expectancy [22, 23]. Performance expectancy and perceived usefulness have a great deal of similarity. Similarly, both effort expectancy and perceived ease of use measure users' belief that using information systems is effortless [24]. By confirming a strong correlation between TTF constructs, effort expectancy and performance expectancy, the findings conclude that the combination of TTF with behavioural beliefs gives a better explanation of the utilisation and adoption of IT systems. Also, technology characteristics had an influence on effort expectancy, while performance expectancy was directly affected by TTF [23]. Based on the aforementioned, the next hypothesis states:

H4: The perceived task technology fit has a significant direct and indirect effect on (a) perceived usefulness and a direct effect on (b) perceived ease of use.

2.3 Perceived Usefulness and Perceived Ease of Use

Perceived usefulness is defined *"as the degree to which an individual believes that using the system will help him or her attain gains in job performance"* [24, 25]. Due to technology acceptance theories, such as TAM and UTAUT, perceived usefulness and perceived ease of use constructs have received wide attention in information systems research [7, 26]. The theories propose that the degree to which technology performance is perceived positively is dependent on the perception of the usefulness of the technology for users. Therefore, high perceived usefulness leads to use behaviour and influences the perception of the technology performance outcome [27]. Further research tested the construct in different cultural and geographical contexts and provided consistent results supporting the original findings [28, 29]. This means that perceived usefulness has an invariant effect on use behaviour. Based on the prior research, our next hypothesis is:

H5: Perceived usefulness is positively correlated with use behaviour.

Perceived ease of use can be defined *"as the degree of ease associated with the use of the system"* [24, 25]. Perceived ease of use refers to the key psychological belief underlying technology acceptance [25, 30]. Numerous studies have confirmed a significant relationship between perceived ease of use and behavioural intention in voluntary as well as mandatory settings [7, 26]. It was found that the construct has both an indirect and a direct relationship with the use behaviour. For example, it was found that perceived ease of use serves as one of the main motivational factors predicting the perceived relevance of information systems and technology satisfaction. Drawing upon the above, the next hypothesises of the paper is the following:

H6: Perceived ease of use is positively correlated with perceived usefulness.

2.4 Outcomes of Use Behaviour

A lot of attention has been paid to studying the relationship between technology use and satisfaction [31–33]. It was found that satisfaction plays a crucial role in technology adoption by consumers. Particularly, satisfaction acted as a mediator between the adoption of online platforms and actual use behaviour [34]. In the context of mobile internet services, satisfaction was used to examine the effect of user experience using a multidimensional construct. Experience represented the composite scale measuring hedonic, functional and overall performance expectations. The results of the study provided evidence that the strongest predictor of satisfaction was confirmed expectations, whereas the outcome of satisfaction is an intention to use services continuously [35]. A few studies tried to explain the antecedents of the individual's satisfaction by developing conceptual models [33]. However, there is inconsistency in the findings of research that examined the effect of technology use on stress and satisfaction [31]. While the general technology use construct was found to have a significant influence on satisfaction, there are contradictory findings when it comes testing the effect of the frequency of use [32]. Moreover, there was a variance in the level of satisfaction across respondents. For example, the literature provides evidence that the use of technology positively correlates with satisfaction levels [31]. Another stream of research argued that technology use positively correlates with the arousal of stress [36, 37]. For instance, a study focusing on technology acceptance in higher education found that technology use had a significant effect on anxiety, which led to dissatisfaction [38]. Drawing on the smart home literature, we propose that given the ability of smart homes to provide health-related, environmental and financial benefits, the technology use will more likely result in positive outcomes. Hence, we hypothesise the following:

H7: Smart home use is positively related to satisfaction.

3 Methodology

3.1 Data Collection and Sampling

The proposed model was examined using a quantitative approach. Before embarking on the collection of data, a pilot study was carried out with the purpose of testing the adequacy and feasibility of the data collection tools, the design of the questionnaire and the survey approach. The questionnaire comprised three parts. The first one contained screening questions which aimed to filter out respondents who had never used smart home technology. In the second part, individuals provided answers to general questions in order to build a descriptive profile of the survey respondents (i.e. socio-demographic data). In the third part of the questionnaire, respondents were provided with model-specific questions. The questionnaires were distributed online to consumers in the United States. The analysis was based on 422 responses. The sample was balanced in terms of gender with 53.6% of females and 46.4% of males. Out of those, 59.3% of the participants were married. The majority of the respondents were full-time employed (43.3%), had an annual income ranging from 25,000 to 74,999 US dollars (53.6%), had a college degree or were at least attending some college courses (50%) and living in urban or urbanized areas (71.3%). When it comes to age, the largest group, which constituted over 40%, were individuals from 60 to 69.

3.2 Measurement Items

For examining the research model, nine multi-item scales were adopted. To ensure content validity all scales derived from the prior literature and were validated. For the accuracy and precision of the measurement of latent variables, seven-point Likert scales were used [39]. *Antecedents of task-technology fit* were measured by privacy risk, financial risk, hedonic value and utilitarian value. *Privacy* and *financial risks* were adapted from the study by Featherman and Pavlou [11]. To measure privacy risk respondents were asked questions such as "What are the chances that using smart home technology will cause you to lose control over the privacy of your payment information?". Financial risk measurement included questions, like "What are the chances that you stand to lose money if you use smart home technologies?". The answers ranged from 1 = very low to 7 = very high. *Hedonic value* and *utilitarian value* items were adapted from the study by Babin et al. [9] and used the scale range from 1 = strongly disagree to 7 = strongly agree. The items, like "Using smart home technologies truly felt like an escape" measured hedonic value, and the statements like "I accomplished just what I wanted to during the use of smart home technologies" measured utilitarian value. *Task-technology fit* items were adopted from the study by Lin and Huang [40] (e.g. "Smart home technologies fit my requirements in daily life"), with answers ranging from 1 = strongly disagree to 7 = strongly agree. To examine the *outcomes of task-technology fit*, this study used (1) the *use behaviour* scale adapted from the study by Taylor and Todd [41] with the scale points from 1 = strongly disagree to 7 = strongly agree (e.g. "I believe I could communicate to others the consequence of using smart home technologies"), and (2) the *satisfaction* scale derived from the study by Spreng and Mackoy [42] measuring the overall experience of using smart home technologies by four scales (1 = very dissatisfied to 7 = very satisfied, 1 = very displeased to 7 = very pleased, 1 = very frustrated to 7 = very contented, 1 = terrible to 7 = very delighted). *Perceived usefulness* and *perceived ease of use* were measured using the adapted version of the scales developed by Venkatesh and Morris [43]. For measuring perceived usefulness respondents were asked to indicate the degree to which they agree with statements like "I would find smart home technologies useful in my daily life". Perceived ease of use was measured by statements such as "My interaction with smart home technologies is clear and understandable" using a scale ranging from 1 = strongly disagree to 7 = strongly agree.

3.3 Data Analysis

The analysis of data was in line with the strategy proposed by Hair Jr and Lukas [44]. SPSS v.24 and SPSS AMOS v.24 were employed to examine the relationships between variables. To ensure that the measured constructs meet construct validity and reliability requirements, confirmatory factor analysis was run. The CFA analysis showed a satisfactory model fit ($X^{(288)} = 605.198$ CMIN/DF = 2.101, CFI = .980, RMSEA = .0.51). As the results of the reliability test all indices were satisfactory, including the factor loading (> 0.8), construct reliability (C.R. > 0.8), average variance expected (AVE > 0.7) and Cronbach's α (>0.8) [44]. Also, a convergent validity test showed no validity concerns (Table 1).

Table 1. Convergent validity

		1	2	3	4	5	6	7	8	9
1	**UB**	0.891								
2	**PR**	−0.095	0.928							
3	**FR**	−0.086	0.821	0.877						
4	**HV**	0.764	−0.208	−0.173	0.942					
5	**UV**	0.792	−0.179	−0.162	0.903	0.929				
6	**TTF**	0.770	−0.244	−0.224	0.852	0.874	0.959			
7	**EoU**	0.787	−0.147	−0.171	0.797	0.787	0.745	0.932		
8	**PU**	0.736	−0.213	−0.178	0.864	0.845	0.869	0.815	0.936	
9	**Sat**	0.724	−0.264	−0.241	0.79	0.808	0.834	0.714	0.747	0.930

Note: Figure in the diagonal represents the square root of the average variance extracted (AVE); those below the diagonal represent the correlations between the constructs.

4 Results and Discussion

4.1 Path Analysis

The proposed model aimed to examine the factors underpinning the use of smart home technology and subsequent outcomes. The results of structural equation modelling showed that all model fit criteria were satisfactory and the model explained sufficient variance, as presented by R^2 coefficients in Table 2. All the hypotheses except 2a and 2b were supported.

Table 2. The results of hypothesis testing

Hypotheses	R^2	Standardised path coefficient	t-values
H1a: Hedonic value → Task technology fit	0.821	0.347	5.402[***]
H1b: Utilitarian value → Task technology fit		0.562	8.525[***]
H2a: Privacy risk → Task technology fit		−0.038	−0.794[ns]
H2b: Financial risk → Task technology fit		−0.042	−0.866[ns]
H3a: Task technology fit → Use behaviour	0.615	0.569	7.134[***]
H3b: Task technology fit → Satisfaction	0.723	0.732	13.752[***]
H4a: Task technology fit → Perceived usefulness	0.824	0.618	15.267[***]
H4b: Task technology fit → Perceived ease of use	0.590	0.768	20.397[***]
H5: Perceived usefulness → Use behaviour		0.235	2.968[**]
H6: Perceived ease of use → Perceived usefulness		0.343	8.759[***]
H7: Use behaviour → Satisfaction		0.146	2.827[**]

Note: SEM (H1–7): Model Fit $X^{2(307)}= 850.025$ CMIN/DF = 2.769, CFI = 0.966, RMSEA = 0.065

4.2 Discussion

Antecedents of Task-Technology Fit: The current study examined antecedents of task-technology fit in the form of hedonic and utilitarian values, and inhibiting factors, such as privacy risk and financial risk. As a result of testing relationships, the first hypothesis suggesting a significant effect of values on task-technology fit was supported. This means that prior beliefs about utilitarian and hedonic outcomes directly affect the perception of the match between users' household tasks and technology characteristics, and indirectly affect use behaviour. However, utilitarian value was found to have a stronger effect. A possible explanation could be that individuals are mostly concerned with the ability of smart home technology to reduce costs on energy, deliver operational convenience and reduce waste production [45]. Remarkably fewer studies confirmed that users tried to satisfy hedonic needs, such as fun and enjoyment when using smart homes [8, 9, 46]. This finding contributes to the current literature by shedding light on the relative importance of utilitarian and hedonic values in perceiving task-technology fit and their indirect influence on behaviour. Prior studies did not examine the relationship between values and task-technology fit [16, 23] and an indirect effect of values on use behaviour [8, 9, 46]. The second hypothesis suggesting the negative affect of perceived privacy and financial risks on task-technology fit was not supported. This contradicts the findings in the prior literature that showed evidence of the inhibiting role of perceived risks in technology acceptance and adoption [47].

The Effects of Task-Technology Fit: By supporting proposed hypotheses 3 and 4, the findings of the study confirm a significant correlation between task-technology fit, perceived usefulness, PEOU, use behaviour and satisfaction. First, the study provides evidence of a significant influence of task-technology fit on use behaviour, which is in line with the previous literature [15, 23]. This means that in order to use smart home technology, users must perceive the high relevance of technology characteristics and its capability to implement specific tasks in hand. Second, the study found a significant and strong effect of task-technology fit on perceived usefulness, which is consistent with previous research [22, 23]. Third, in line with the study conducted by Dishaw and Strong [15], PEOU is conditioned by the perception of high task-technology fit. Compared to the relationship between fit and perceived usefulness, the influence on PEOU is stronger. The potential interpretation is that users' requirement of smart home technology is to achieve higher efficiency of technology performance by simplifying daily routines [1, 5]. Fourth, the result of path analysis shows that perceived task-technology fit predicts satisfaction, which corresponds to the findings of the study by Lin [21] and contradicts the paper by Lu and Yang [48].

Perceived Usefulness, Perceived Ease of Use and Outcomes of Use Behaviour: The study supported hypotheses 5 and 6, confirming the direct effect of perceived usefulness on use behaviour, as well as an indirect effect of PEOU on use behaviour through perceived usefulness. Results of path analysis support the findings of prior literature [28, 29, 47]. The effect of perceived usefulness is weaker, which can be explained by the focus of the study on smart home technology. Smart home users try to make the performance of technology more efficient by decreasing the input of effort to implement household tasks [1, 5]. In addition, the results of path analysis make it possible to accept the seventh hypothesis, proposing a positive correlation between use behaviour and satisfaction. This is in contrast to other findings on the smart home domain that proved that the use of technology leads to dissatisfaction and stress [36, 37]. Contradictory findings can be explained by the difference in the conditions underpinning the technology use and settings. For example, the studies confirming that technology use caused dissatisfaction and stress focused on organisational settings, where the use of technology was not voluntary and was not aimed at satisfying individuals' needs [31]. In contrast, smart homes are used voluntarily, and the use is driven by hedonic or utilitarian needs. Hence, satisfaction is a more likely outcome.

5 Conclusion

The paper has examined the acceptance of smart home technologies by exploring the effect of behavioural belief factors and task-technology fit on use behaviour and satisfaction. This study addressed the gap in the literature on the acceptance of technologies in private settings by focusing on smart home users. The paper theorised and empirically investigated the relationship between underlying attitudes towards technology utilisation, such as perceived benefits and risks, the beliefs about technology performance and technology compatibility with users' requirements. The model produced robust results, supporting the relationships between the majority of the proposed constructs. The findings of the study add value to the current literature by providing insight into the acceptance of smart home technology. Secondly, the study contributes to the literature examining the acceptance of pervasive technology in private residential spaces from the perspective of users.

This paper is not without limitations. Research focusing on smart home technology is still scarce and to have a more comprehensive insight future research studies need to extend the model with additional constructs. For example, further research could examine the direct and indirect effect of normative beliefs on use behaviour. Also, this study has not tested the moderating role of psychological traits, which can potentially cause a variance in the strength of model relationships. Finally, future research could test the model in other geographical locations, which would help generalise the findings of the present study.

References

1. Aldrich, F.K.: Smart homes: past, present and future. In: Harper, R. (ed.) Inside the Smart Home, pp. 17–39. Springer, London (2003). https://doi.org/10.1007/1-85233-854-7_2
2. Chan, M., et al.: A review of smart homes—present state and future challenges. Comput. Methods Programs Biomed. **91**(1), 55–81 (2008)
3. Balta-Ozkan, N., et al.: Social barriers to the adoption of smart homes. Energy Policy **63**, 363–374 (2013)
4. Choe, E.K., et al.: Living in a glass house: a survey of private moments in the home. In: Proceedings of the 13th International Conference on Ubiquitous Computing. ACM (2011)
5. Marikyan, D., Papagiannidis, S., Alamanos, E.: A systematic review of the smart home literature: a user perspective. Technol. Forecast. Soc. Change **138**, 139–154 (2019)

6. Goodhue, D.L., Thompson, R.L.: Task-technology fit and individual performance. MIS Quart. **19**(2), 213–236 (1995)
7. Davis, F.D.: Perceived usefulness, perceived ease of use, and user acceptance of information technology. MIS Quart.: Manag. Inf. Syst. **13**(3), 319–339 (1989)
8. Van der Heijden, H.: User acceptance of hedonic information systems. MIS Quart. **28**(4), 695–704 (2004)
9. Babin, B.J., Darden, W.R., Griffin, M.: Work and/or fun: measuring hedonic and utilitarian shopping value. J. Consum. Res. **20**(4), 644–656 (1994)
10. Brown, S.A., Venkatesh, V.: Model of adoption of technology in households: a baseline model test and extension incorporating household life cycle. MIS Quart. **29**(3), 399–426 (2005)
11. Featherman, M.S., Pavlou, P.A.: Predicting e-services adoption: a perceived risk facets perspective. Int. J. Hum.-Comput. Stud. **59**(4), 451–474 (2003)
12. Pavlou, P.A.: Consumer acceptance of electronic commerce: integrating trust and risk with the technology acceptance model. Int. J. Electron. Commer. **7**(3), 101–134 (2003)
13. Bauer, R.A.: Consumer behavior as risk taking. In: Proceedings of the 43rd National Conference of the American Marketing Assocation, 15–17 June 1960, Chicago, Illinois, American Marketing Association (1960)
14. Goodhue, D.L.: Understanding user evaluations of information systems. Manag. Sci. **41**(12), 1827–1844 (1995)
15. Dishaw, M.T., Strong, D.M.: Extending the technology acceptance model with task–technology fit constructs. Inf. Manag. **36**(1), 9–21 (1999)
16. Wu, B., Chen, X.: Continuance intention to use MOOCs: integrating the technology acceptance model (TAM) and task technology fit (TTF) model. Comput. Hum. Behav. **67**, 221–232 (2017)
17. Tam, C., Oliveira, T.: Performance impact of mobile banking: using the task-technology fit (TTF) approach. Int. J. Bank Mark. **34**(4), 434–457 (2016)
18. Lee, C.-C., Cheng, H.K., Cheng, H.-H.: An empirical study of mobile commerce in insurance industry: task–technology fit and individual differences. Decis. Support Syst. **43** (1), 95–110 (2007)
19. Chen, Z.-J., Vogel, D., Wang, Z.-H.: How to satisfy citizens? using mobile government to reengineer fair government processes. Decis. Support Syst. **82**, 47–57 (2016)
20. Isaac, O., et al.: Internet usage, user satisfaction, task-technology fit, and performance impact among public sector employees in Yemen. Int. J. Inf. Learn. Technol. **34**(3), 210–241 (2017)
21. Lin, W.-S.: Perceived fit and satisfaction on web learning performance: IS continuance intention and task-technology fit perspectives. Int. J. Hum.-Comput. Stud. **70**(7), 498–507 (2012)
22. Abbas, S.K., et al.: Integration of TTF, UTAUT, and ITM for mobile banking adoption. Int. J. Adv. Eng. Manag. Sci. **4**(5), 375–379 (2018)
23. Zhou, T., Lu, Y., Wang, B.: Integrating TTF and UTAUT to explain mobile banking user adoption. Comput. Hum. Behav. **26**(4), 760–767 (2010)
24. Venkatesh, V., et al.: User acceptance of information technology: toward a unified view. MIS Quart.: Manag. Inf. Syst. **27**(3), 425–478 (2003)
25. Davis, F.D., Bagozzi, R.P., Warshaw, P.R.: User acceptance of computer technology: a comparison of two theoretical models. Manag. Sci. **35**(8), 982–1003 (1989)
26. Thompson, R.L., Higgins, C.A., Howell, J.M.: Personal computing: toward a conceptual model of utilization. MIS Quart. **15**(1), 125–143 (1991)
27. Shih, H.-P.: Extended technology acceptance model of Internet utilization behavior. Inf. Manag. **41**(6), 719–729 (2004)
28. Al-Gahtani, S.S., Hubona, G.S., Wang, J.: Information technology (IT) in Saudi Arabia: culture and the acceptance and use of IT. Inf. Manag. **44**(8), 681–691 (2007)

29. Venkatesh, V., Zhang, X.: Unified theory of acceptance and use of technology: US vs. China. J. Global Inf. Technol. Manag. **13**(1), 5–27 (2010)
30. Venkatesh, V., Davis, F.D.: A theoretical extension of the technology acceptance model: four longitudinal field studies. Manag. Sci. **46**(2), 186–204 (2000)
31. Román, S., Rodríguez, R., Jaramillo, J.F.: Are mobile devices a blessing or a curse? effects of mobile technology use on salesperson role stress and job satisfaction. J. Bus. Ind. Mark. **33**(5), 651–664 (2018)
32. Vlahos, G.E., Ferratt, T.W.: Information technology use by managers in Greece to support decision making: amount, perceived value, and satisfaction. Inf. Manag. **29**(6), 305–315 (1995)
33. Calisir, F., Calisir, F.: The relation of interface usability characteristics, perceived usefulness, and perceived ease of use to end-user satisfaction with enterprise resource planning (ERP) systems. Comput. Hum. Behav. **20**(4), 505–515 (2004)
34. Chiu, C.M., Chiu, C.S., Chang, H.C.: Examining the integrated influence of fairness and quality on learners' satisfaction and Web-based learning continuance intention. Inf. Syst. J. **17**(3), 271–287 (2007)
35. Deng, L., et al.: User experience, satisfaction, and continual usage intention of IT. Eur. J. Inf. Syst. **19**(1), 60–75 (2010)
36. Ahearne, M., Jelinek, R., Rapp, A.: Moving beyond the direct effect of SFA adoption on salesperson performance: training and support as key moderating factors. Ind. Mark. Manag. **34**(4), 379–388 (2005)
37. Sundaram, S., et al.: Technology use on the front line: how information technology enhances individual performance. J. Acad. Mark. Sci. **35**(1), 101–112 (2007)
38. Lepp, A., Barkley, J.E., Karpinski, A.C.: The relationship between cell phone use, academic performance, anxiety, and satisfaction with life in college students. Comput. Hum. Behav. **31**, 343–350 (2014)
39. Churchill, G.A., Iacobucci, D.: Marketing Research-Methodological Foundations, p. 14. Dryden Press, New York (2002)
40. Lin, T.-C., Huang, C.-C.: Understanding knowledge management system usage antecedents: an integration of social cognitive theory and task technology fit. Inf. Manag. **45**(6), 410–417 (2008)
41. Taylor, S., Todd, P.: Assessing IT usage: the role of prior experience. MIS Quart. **19**(4), 561–570 (1995)
42. Spreng, R.A., Mackoy, R.D.: An empirical examination of a model of perceived service quality and satisfaction. J. Retail. **72**(2), 201–214 (1996)
43. Venkatesh, V., Morris, M.G.: Why don't men ever stop to ask for directions? gender, social influence, and their role in technology acceptance and usage behavior. MIS Quart. **24**(1), 115–139 (2000)
44. Hair Jr., J.F., Lukas, B.: Marketing research, vol. 2. McGraw-Hill Education, Australia (2014)
45. Baudier, P., Ammi, C., Deboeuf-Rouchon, M.: Smart home: highly-educated students' acceptance. Technol. Forecast. Soc. Change (2018)
46. Turel, O., Serenko, A., Bontis, N.: User acceptance of hedonic digital artifacts: a theory of consumption values perspective. Inf. Manag. **47**(1), 53–59 (2010)
47. Martins, C., Oliveira, T., Popovič, A.: Understanding the Internet banking adoption: a unified theory of acceptance and use of technology and perceived risk application. Int. J. Inf. Manag. **34**(1), 1–13 (2014)
48. Lu, H.-P., Yang, Y.-W.: Toward an understanding of the behavioral intention to use a social networking site: an extension of task-technology fit to social-technology fit. Comput. Hum. Behav. **34**, 323–332 (2014)

Designing at the Intersection of Gamification and Persuasive Technology to Incentivize Energy-Saving

Böckle Martin$^{(\boxtimes)}$ and Yeboah-Antwi Kwaku

BCG Platinion, Design and Engineering, Berlin, Germany
{boeckle.martin,yeboah-antwi.kwaku}@bcgplatinion.com

Abstract. Gamified persuasive system design refers to design solutions at the intersection of gamification and persuasive technology aiming at influencing attitude and behavior change. Although both concepts have been successfully applied in many domains to increase end-user engagement and satisfaction, results are often mixed and highly context specific. Consequently, there is a dearth of knowledge on how to design those solutions and how they are perceived by different types of users within certain application contexts. Thus, this paper investigates the relationship between the HEXAD gamification user types and persuasive principles within the context of energy saving. First results reveal (n = 206) that, three out of six persuasive principles (*Reciprocity, Consistency & Commitment, Liking*) have been perceived as persuasive by identified HEXAD user types, which highlights the importance of such user types models. Finally, this paper contributes to the present body of gamification literature by providing a human computer interaction (HCI) perspective which highlights guidelines for designing gamified persuasive systems to incentivize energy-saving.

Keywords: Gamification · Persuasive technology · User-types ·
Persuasive principles · User-centered design

1 Introduction

In recent years, the use of information technology to foster the end-user engagement to enhance the individual level of energy conservation is becoming increasingly important [18, 32, 33]. Best practices for designing such solutions are being discussed within two research streams in the current body of persuasive literature:

Firstly, persuasive technology (PT), which aims to change human attitudes and behavior [16] where "computers function as persuasive tools (e.g., leading people through a process), social actors (e.g., rewarding people with positive feedback) and as a medium (e.g., providing people with experiences that motivate)" [10, p. 25]. Secondly, the research stream of gamification is focusing on the creation of playful experiences in order to increase overall engagement through the use of game design elements in non-game contexts [6]. This track has received great attention from researchers and practitioners and is being applied in many domains such as education [11], health [29], and crowdsourcing [24]. Gamification is still in its infancy, compared

© IFIP International Federation for Information Processing 2019
Published by Springer Nature Switzerland AG 2019
I. O. Pappas et al. (Eds.): I3E 2019, LNCS 11701, pp. 316–328, 2019.
https://doi.org/10.1007/978-3-030-29374-1_26

to the more established research stream of persuasive technology (PT), although both concepts share common aspects of aiming at influencing attitude and behavior through technology, as discussed in [14].

We believe that design solutions at the intersection of gamification and persuasive technology reveal promising potential. Solutions such as the consideration of different types of persuasive messages within gamified environments, particularly in combination with the gamification feedback mechanic, have often been neglected. Although, several game-design elements have been successfully applied to improve the overall end-user engagement, their effectiveness is often mixed, highly context specific and varies among different types of users [2]. This highlights the pitfalls of a "one size fits all" approach and the need for much more personalization in order to increase the end-user engagement of a broad range of individuals [3].

Though existing research refers to promising concepts of using personality traits for persuasive system design, there is a dearth of design knowledge which highlights best practices for the application of gamification user-types in specific application context, which also includes energy saving. Therefore, this paper aims to investigate the relationship between the HEXAD gamification user types [21] (*Philanthropist, Disruptor, Socializer, Free Spirit, Achiever and Player*) and the six persuasive principles of Cialdini [5] in order to highlight solutions, which aim to incentivize energy saving. This paper contributes to the present knowledge of human-computer interaction by answering the following research question:

> RQ: To which extent do the different HEXAD user-types respond to different persuasive principles when these are applied to the design of a persuasive system for energy saving?

Our results cover design solutions and supports researchers and practitioners in the creation of gamified persuasive system design in order to incentivize energy-saving. To the best of our knowledge, this is the first study which investigates the intersection and relationship between the HEXAD gamification user types and the six persuasive principles of Cialdini [5].

2   Research Background

2.1   Persuasive Technology and Principles

The research stream of persuasive technology was primarily introduced by the work of [9, 10] who proposed the term persuasive system design (PSD) and presented twenty-eight persuasive strategies, which have gained widespread acceptance and are based on the principles of Fogg [10]. Within this paper we focus on the six persuasive principles proposed by [5], which have gained considerable attention but have not been tested within the energy domain so far. Existing research has already paid attention to the relationship of game design elements and user types [8, 11]. This also includes articles on persuasive strategies and user type models [27], however the investigation of the relationship between the HEXAD gamification user types and the persuasive principles by Cialdini (2001) is currently missing and reveals promising potential for persuasive system design of energy-saving applications. The six persuasive principles will be explained in more detail:

- *Liking* refers to the phenomenon of "we say yes to people we generally like" [5]. According to [4], research has shown that people are more willing to purchase insurance policies from a salesperson with similarities in age, religion, politics or smoking habits.
- *Reciprocity* describes the norm that obligates people to repay in kind, a favor which they have received [5]. This principle is specifically strong and is also described as "give what you want to receive" [4, p. 75].
- *Scarcity* refers to the fact that "items and opportunities become more desirable to us if they become less available" [5, p. 80] and is described as people want more of what is less available [4].
- *Authority* highlights that axiom that "people defer to experts" [4, p. 77] meaning that if a request or statement is made by a legitimate authority, there is a propensity for people to accept the request or definitions of action "irrespective of the content of the act and without limitations of conscience" [23, p. 24].
- *Consistency and Commitment* reveals, that "people do as they said they would" [19, p. 1174]. This principle shows that the likelihood of people actively making choices is higher when the choices are "spoken out loud or written down actively" [4, p. 76] the choices become more powerful when they are made public.
- *Consensus* describes the principle of "people do as other people do" [19, p. 1174] and highlights that people "follow the lead of similar others" [4, p. 75]. The principle is also termed social validation [5] or social proof [4], meaning that if a group of individuals decide to go in a specific direction, others are more likely to follow because they perceive this direction to be more correct and valid [5].

2.2 Player Typologies

Generally, player types represent a useful concept for the definition of boundaries [22] in order to ensure the efficiency and effectiveness of the overall game design. Research shows that personality types play an important role and have an effect on player typologies, (e.g., BrainHex archetypes by [25]; or the HEXAD user types by [21]) as well as preferences and game design elements. The most frequently used player types, are the ones by Bartle [1], namely "Killer, Achiever, Socializer and Explorer", however these should not be generalized to gameful design as mentioned in [30], because their relation towards actual video games. Therefore, within this paper, we selected the HEXAD gamification user types framework, which has been developed to ensure gameful design with a high degree of personalization for mapping user types and game design elements. Within this paper we applied the HEXAD gamification user types framework consisting of the following six user types, described in Table 1:

Table 1. Gamification user types HEXAD [30, p. 231]

Philanthropists are motivated by purpose and meaning. This type of user is willing to give without expecting a reward
Socializers are motivated by relatedness. Their main goal is to interact with others and create social connections
Free spirits are motivated by autonomy and self-expression. Their aim is to create and explore
Achievers are motivated by competence. They are looking for challenges and are willing to improve themselves and learn new things
Players are motivated by extrinsic rewards. Independent of the type of activity, this user type does everything in order to obtain the rewards within the system
Disruptors are motivated by change. Generally, they tend to disrupt the system directly or through others to force negative and positive changes and test the system boundaries

Existing research presents the validation of player types (achievers, explorers, philanthropists, socializers) and their relationship to gamification mechanics inside an e-learning environment [11] with mixed results. Similarly, the work of [26] shows the connections between the big-five factor model ([12] FFM - openness, conscientiousness, extraversion, agreeableness, neuroticism) and the perceived persuasiveness towards selected persuasive principles to provoke behavior change of unhealthy drinking.

The study of [27] emphasizes the persuasiveness between the BrainHex typologies and persuasive strategies and includes the novel development of persuasive profiles. The authors suggest the following steps to the personalization of persuasive games towards their gamer types: "(1) Determine the gamer groups; (2) Decide on the design approach; (3) Map strategies to game mechanics" [27, p. 458]. The last step of "Map strategies to game mechanics" is actually covered by this paper and we highlight the importance of this mapping process.

3   Research Design

For the investigation of the relationship between the HEXAD gamification user types and the persuasive principles for energy saving, a survey with storyboards, which covers each of the persuasive principles within a predefined energy saving context, was designed. We came up with persuasive messages, which were then defined and integrated in the feedback mechanic of a mobile energy-saving application.

Two example storyboards are described in Fig. (1): On the left-hand side, the persuasive message for *Reciprocity (S1)* is designed as a reminder to invite more people to the energy-saving application after receiving a badge for the overall positive energy consumption. The user's willingness to act is expected to be higher after receiving an award from the system, which covers the principle of *Reciprocity*. The second example represents *Liking (S6)* where geographically close friends reduced their consumption by 30kWh. This is expected to persuade the friends to follow them and adopt a similar energy-consumption behavior. The following Table describes the persuasive message within the gamification feedback mechanic (Table 2):

Fig. 1. Sample story-board (Reciprocity – left; Liking – right)

Table 2. Persuasive messages within the storyboards

Reciprocity (S1): You just received the "Loyal Energy Saver Badge" for being a frequent system user. Please invite more users to the energy application through the e-mail form

Commitment and Consistency (S2): You defined your personal energy-saving goal up to +20% this month. You miss 5% to reach your goal. Try to reduce your energy consumption in the next days

Scarcity (S3): This is the last chance to receive the "Energy Saving Enthusiast Badge" this month. Score at least 50 points more this week in order to receive it

Authority (S4): According to the global energy authority, your current consumption is over average and very high. Follow their guidelines and try to reduce your current consumption by 30%

Consensus (S5): Four energy users from your neighborhood decreased their consumption by 25 kWh this month. Follow their profiles and consumption patterns in order to reduce your current consumption

Liking (S6): Four of your friends decreased their consumption by 30 kWh this month. Follow their profiles and consumption patterns in order to reduce your current consumption

In order to obtain feedback for each storyboard, the scale [7] for measuring the perceived persuasiveness has been added to the survey questions. The perceived persuasiveness is assessed on a seven-point Likert scale: (1 – strongly disagree; 7 – strongly agree) through the following questions: *(1) This system would influence me; (2) This system would be convincing; (3) This system would be personally relevant for me; (4) This system would make me reconsider my energy consumption habits.* The HEXAD gamification user types provide a questionnaire for the identification of those types, described in [30].

To answer our research question, we applied partial least square structural equation modeling (PLS-SEM), which provides approaches and techniques to investigate the relationship between the HEXAD gamification user types and the persuasive principles of [4], visualized in Fig. (2). Furthermore, to perform structural equation modeling

(SEM), we used SmartPLS, which provides solutions for path modeling [31]. The PLS-SEM model has been defined as following: As visualized in Fig. (2), each HEXAD user type on the left-hand side and persuasive principle on the right represents a latent variable. The values for the user types were collected through the HEXAD survey. On the right-hand side, the perceived persuasiveness for each principle has been listed. In order to investigate the relationship between user types and principles, each player type has been connected with each persuasive principle.

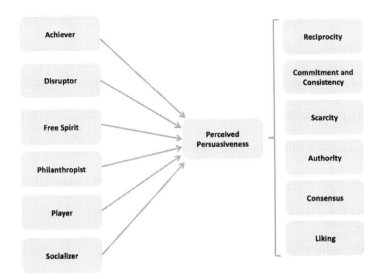

Fig. 2. PLS-SEM model

4   Results

Generally, to ensure model reliability in PLS-SEM we considered the following criteria for our collected data: Firstly, the Cronbach's α represents a standard indicator for reliability within PLS-SEM and revealed a value above 0.8 and therefore passes the threshold of 0.7. Secondly, the heterotrait–monotrait ratio (HTMT) represents an index for discriminant validity [15], which was below the threshold value of 0.85 for all the relationships. Thirdly, the average variance extracted (AVE) was above the recommended threshold of 0.5 for all the items we used. Results have been acquired through the micro-task platform Mechanical Turk (MTurk). Using this platform as a method for obtaining reliable results of end-user's responses is widely accepted [28] and has been used within a variety of studies with a human-computer-interaction (HCI) focus [27] as well as gamification research [17]. In order to provide high quality results, we followed best practices recommended by [13, 20] by setting a high approval rate (97% and above), combined with an approved number of HITs (5000 and above).

4.1 Demographic Information

We received 205 valid responses through Mechanical Turk from a diverse group of end-users. Results on demography highlight that 56% of end-users were male. The majority (53%) has an age between 26 and 35, whereas 52% had obtained a bachelor's degree. Furthermore, most of the end-users were from the USA (60%) and India (37%) (Table 3).

Table 3. Demographic information

Total responses (n = 205)	
Gender	Female (44%), Male (56%), Trans (0), Others (0)
Age	15–25 (18%), 26–35 (53%), 36–45 (11%), Over 45 (18%)
Education	Less than high school (2%), High school (14%), Graduate (11%), College diploma (8%), Bachelor's degree (52%), Master's degree (10%), Doctoral degree (1%), Other (2%)
Country	USA (60%), India (37%), Netherlands (0.5%), Germany (2%), Canada (0.5%)

4.2 Persuasive Principles

After defining the model, we applied the PLS algorithm, in order to reveal the path coefficient β, which explains the effect of one variable on another [31]. Furthermore, we bootstrapped the results and derived t-statistics, which provide the p-value for each of the calculated paths in order to understand the significance of this relationship, highlighted in Table (4):

Table 4. Path coefficients β (significant relationships - bold)

Persuasive principle	PHI	SOC	FRE	ACH	PLA	DIS
Reciprocity	−0.04	0.07	−0.09	−0.06	**0.17***	**0.15***
Commitment and consistency	0.12	0.09	**−0.24***	**0.17***	−0.00	**0.13***
Scarcity	−0.04	0.06	−0.00	0.106	0.01	0.08
Authority	0.01	0.12	0.08	0.04	−0.03	0.04
Consensus	−0.00	0.10	−0.01	0.02	−0.05	0.16
Liking	−0.12	0.07	−0.13	−0.07	0.12	**0.20***

Path coefficient beta (β) and the level of significance (p) between player types and persuasive strategies (*coefficient p < .05), PHI – Philanthropist, SOC – Socializer, FRE – Free Spirit, ACH – Achiever, PLA – Player, DIS - Disruptor

Reciprocity: Results show that the gamified persuasive principle *Reciprocity* only motivates end-users with a high tendency towards the *Player* (β = 0.17, p < 0.05) and *Disruptor* (β = 0.15, p < 0.05) user type. These results confirm that the *Player* type is motivated by extrinsic rewards like rewards, suggested and supported in [30], since S1 (storyboard) includes a badge within the gameful design. While the *Player* user type has a strong relationship towards rewards, *Disruptors* are motivated by change [30] and disrupt the system in a positive or negative way and try to push further [30]. Finally, end-users with a high tendency towards *Disruptors* ($\beta = 0.15$, $p < 0.05$) are motivated by the *Reciprocity* principle, which shows that the *Disruptor* user type is motivated by gamified reciprocity approaches and pushes towards change. The small preference by the user-type *Philanthropist*, *Socializer* and *Free Spirit* could have several reasons. *Socializers* tend to prefer social interactions and are motivated by relatedness, which has been less covered by the first storyboard (S1), representing *Reciprocity*. Furthermore, *Free Spirits* like to act by themselves [30], without external control, meaning that a feedback mechanic suggesting a call to action may not persuade this type of users, who are motivated by autonomy. Similarly, the *Philanthropist* user type is willing to give without expecting a reward, with a focus on purpose, and this is not addressed by the first storyboard.

Commitment and Consistency: Results of the Commitment and Consistency reveal that people with a high tendency towards the Achiever ($\beta = 0.17$, $p < 0.05$) and Disruptor ($\beta = 0.13$, $p < 0.05$) user type are motivated by this principle. According to [30], *Achievers* seek to progress within a system. This supports our results by referring to the goal-setting functionality within the defined gamification approach of S2. In addition, the *Disruptor* user type is motivated by this principle, which shows that goal-setting functionalities could enable end-users towards change. Finally, people with a high tendency towards *Free Spirit* are demotivated by this principle as the user-type is motivated by autonomy. Generally, this user-type prefers creativity tools, unlockable content or non-linear gameplay, which shows that persuasive principles could also have negative effects for a certain group of end-users. The principle has not been considered as motivating by the user-type *Philanthropist*, *Socializer* and *Player*. As the second storyboard (S2) does not include any social components, nor badges or scores, the results reflect the aim and design of the player types.

Scarcity, Authority and Consensus: Unfortunately, we could not identify any significant motivator between the persuasive principle *Scarcity* and the HEXAD user types. The *Scarcity* principle is based on the weakness for shortcuts of people. In the case of S3 the availability of certain badges should be equal to the quality and from a psychological perspective, the limited choice should increase the feeling to own the "Energy Saving Enthusiast". The reason for the low motivational effects by any of the HEXAD user types could be related to the setting of the storyboard, as the *Scarcity* effect may work better when end-users already own certain badges and scores and are aware of the value and impact of these game design elements, especially for the *Player* user type, who is motivated by extrinsic rewards. For the *Authority* principle, the user-type *Disruptor*, who is triggered by *change* could have shown a higher tendency towards this principle. Generally, the overall design of the *Authority* does not completely fit in with the rest of the user types and may only work in specific use cases (e.g., education), where people might listen to reminders from a higher instance (e.g., teacher). The *Consensus* principle is showing similar results, presented as a leaderboard with a list of geographically close neighbors and their improved energy-conservation profile. The system provided a feedback message that neighbors decreased their consumption by 30kWh and included a call to action titled "Start Following". Although, there were no tendencies from any of the HEXAD user types towards the *Consensus* principle, *Liking* follows a similar design, but uses friends instead of neighbors within the defined storyboard (S6) and reveals a significant relationship with the *Disruptor* user-type. This supports our assumption that motivational effects are higher when they are used within an environment where the end-users know each other, as demonstrated by the result of the *Liking* principle. This also includes the awareness of already collected rewards, scores including their impact and value after an intense usage of the application.

Liking: Results show that the *Liking* principle motivates people with a high tendency towards the *Disruptor* user type ($\beta = 0.2$, $p < 0.05$), which confirms that end-users prefer environments with people they know compared to the *Consensus* principle where we did not identify any significant results. Although, *Liking* has been preferred by people with a high tendency towards the *Disruptor* user type which shows that people with those characteristics prefer positive change and to push further, the *Socializer* user type did not show any preferences for S6. This could be due to several reasons: Firstly, the usage of the design element *Leaderboard* is more preferred by the *Player* user type, described in [30] and people with a high tendency towards *Socializers* prefer the interaction itself [30].

5 Discussion and Limitations

For the identified persuasive principles (*Reciprocity, Commitment & Consistency, Liking*), which reveal a significant relationship with the HEXAD user types, we came up with the following design guidelines (Table 5) to offer the opportunity to personalize and design for certain groups of users. The design guidelines consist of well-known game design elements and text messages, provided by the system within the feedback mechanic, which are used in combination with a call to action button:

Generally, we identified four HEXAD user types (*Disruptor, Player, Achiever, Free Spirit*), which reveal a high tendency of perceived persuasiveness towards three principles (*Reciprocity, Commitment & Consistency, Liking*) and came up with design guidelines for gamified energy saving applications.

In addition, we confirm and highlight the importance of user-type models within the design of gamified persuasive system for energy-saving. Although our approach reveals promising results, there are few limitations to consider. First, we used static storyboards which represent the six persuasive principles by [4] and asked end-users about the perceived persuasiveness. Although, storyboards represent a valid method to investigate preferences for certain types of users, persuasive principles may be more effective if they are used in a real-world application, especially when gamification elements are used. Especially, the everyday usage would probably reveal the strength and weaknesses of each strategy in a more meaningful way. For instance, the *Achiever* user type prefers levels or progression. Persuasive principles may show it's potential to the full extent if the end-users find themselves in a certain context, which can't be represented by storyboards in general (e.g., already collected certain amount of score, badges or situations where end-users find themselves in situations like crossing the next

Table 5. Design guidelines

Reciprocity (Player, Disruptor)
DG1: After receiving several extra badges or rewards by the application, the system provides access to new functionalities (e.g., advanced usage analytics) and asks the end-users to apply (call to action) those within their daily usage
Reciprocity (Player, Disruptor)
DG2: The system offers extra points and asks end-users to set (call to action) their personal consumption goals for their current month
DG3: The system offers extra badges and asks end-users to use a certain device (e.g., light) in a more efficient way (call to action) in order to change their present energy consumption behavior
Commitment and Consistency (Achiever, Disruptor)
DG4: The application offers goal-setting functionalities in combination with levels and status ("e.g., energy-saving starter – energy-saving enthusiast etc.) and reminds end-users about their consumption goals, status, progression and suggest incentives in order to reach the next level (call to action - e.g., apply this well-known energy-saving tip and receive additional 50 points)
DG5: The system reminds end-users about their past energy-saving behavior and comes up with new challenges in order to tackle them and improve their current consumption
DG6: The system provides several options for end-users to set their level of importance for reaching defined consumption goals and sends reminders and incentives in case of any negative deviations (e.g., reducing power for the fridge has been set as very important by you; reduce it now). Energy-saving goals are connected to certificates and status within the application
Liking (Disruptor)
DG7: The system reminds end-users that friends also apply the following best practice energy saving tip (e.g., use different light bulbs – update them now and receive extra points)
DG8: The application lists energy-saving profiles based on consumption metrics of friends and asks the user to adapt to similar behavior patterns and recommends actions and incentives ("e.g., follow your friends and reduce consumption by installing a smart thermostat). This functionality also includes a voting system for nominating friends who perform best
DG9: The system offers group functionalities like closed groups, chats and visualizations where consumption behaviors and tips can be shared with other friends. Energy-saving tips include voting functionalities

level or stage within the application). Certain contexts and the efficiency of persuasive principles within these contexts are not only difficult to measure, but also the collection of results through MTurk may reveal cultural aspects, which cannot be considered, for example energy-saving behaviors may differ remarkable between different countries or cultures. Finally, future research should pay attention to existing energy-consumption behaviors and how these can be incorporated into the design to provide more contextual guidelines by considering different cultures, gender and age groups.

6   Conclusion

This paper explores design possibilities at the intersection of gamification and persuasive technology (PT) within the energy-saving domain by investigating the relationship between the HEXAD gamification user types and the six persuasive principles, proposed by Cialdini [4]. The main contribution is therefore twofold: Firstly, we identified which user types show a high tendency towards the designed storyboard of the six persuasive principles in order to inform researchers and practitioners for designing more personalized gamified applications with persuasive elements in text format. Furthermore, we derived design guidelines which reveal best practices for designing consumption-focused environments in order to provide a more general perspective. Secondly, we validated the usage of persuasive principles of Cialdini [4] within gamified environments, which has not been investigated so far and thus contribute towards the present body of human-computer interaction (HCI) knowledge. Furthermore, we identified several design solutions where HEXAD user-types show significant values for the perceived persuasiveness of the gamified persuasive system designs. Although only three out of six persuasive principles show significant results towards certain HEXAD gamification user types, we think that designing at the intersection of gamification and persuasive technology offers manifold opportunities, which has been researched very little. Consequently, this paper has a high explorative character and represents a showcase that demonstrates how to combine persuasive text messages within game design elements to incentivize energy-saving.

References

1. Bartle, R.: Hearts, clubs, diamonds, spades: players who suit MUDs. J. MUD Res. 1(1), 19 (1996)
2. Böckle, M., Micheel, I., Bick, M., Novak, J.: A design framework for adaptive gamification applications. In: Proceedings of the HICSS-51, Waikoloa, Hawaii, USA, pp. 1227–1236 (2018)
3. Böckle, M., Novak, J., Bick, M.: Towards adaptive gamification: a synthesis of current developments. In: Proceedings of the Twenty-Fifth European Conference on Information Systems (ECIS), Portugal, pp. 158–174 (2017)
4. Cialdini, R.B.: Harnessing the science of persuasion. Harvard Bus. Rev. 79(9), 72–81 (2001)
5. Cialdini, R.B.: The science of persuasion. Sci. Am. Mind 284, 76–84 (2004)
6. Deterding, S., Dixon, D., Kahled, R., Nacke, L.: From game design elements to gamefulness: defining gamification. In: Proceedings of the 15th International Academic MindTrek Conference: Envisioning Future Media Environments, pp. 9–15, Tampere, Finland (2011)
7. Drozd, F., Lehto, T., Oinas-Kukkonen, H.: Exploring perceived persuasiveness of a behavior change support system: a structural model. In: Bang, M., Ragnemalm, E.L. (eds.) PERSUASIVE 2012. LNCS, vol. 7284, pp. 157–168. Springer, Heidelberg (2012). https://doi.org/10.1007/978-3-642-31037-9_14
8. Ferro, S.L., Walz, P.S., Greuter, S.: Towards personalised, gamified systems: an investigation into game design, personality and player typologies. In: Proceedings of the 9th Australasian Conference on Interactive Entertainment, pp. 1–6, Melbourne, Australia (2013)
9. Fogg, B.J.: Persuasive computers: perspectives and research directions. In: Proceedings of CHI 1998, pp. 225–231, Los Angeles, USA (1998)
10. Fogg, B.J.: Persuasive Technology: Using Computers to Change What We Think and Do. Morgan Kaufmann Publishers, Burlington (2002)

11. Gil, B., Cantador, I., Marczewski, A.: Validating gamification mechanics and player types in an e-learning environment. In: Conole, G., Klobučar, T., Rensing, C., Konert, J., Lavoué, É. (eds.) EC-TEL 2015. LNCS, vol. 9307, pp. 568–572. Springer, Cham (2015). https://doi.org/10.1007/978-3-319-24258-3_61

12. Goldberg, L.R.: An alternative description of personality: the big-five factor structure. J. Pers. Soc. Psychol. **59**, 1216–1229 (1990)

13. Goodman, K.J., Cryder, E.C., Cheema, A.: Data collection in a flat world: the strengths and weaknesses of mechanical turk samples. J. Behav. Decis. Making **26**, 213–224 (2012)

14. Hamari, J., Koivisto, J., Pakkanen, T.: Do persuasive technologies persuade? - a review of empirical studies. In: Spagnolli, A., Chittaro, L., Gamberini, L. (eds.) PERSUASIVE 2014. LNCS, vol. 8462, pp. 118–136. Springer, Cham (2014). https://doi.org/10.1007/978-3-319-07127-5_11

15. Henseler, J., Ringle, M.C., Sarstedt, M.: A new criterion for assessing discriminant validity in variance-based structural equation modeling. J. Acad. Mark. Sci. **43**(1), 115–135 (2015)

16. IJsselsteijn, W., de Kort, Y., Midden, C., Eggen, B., van den Hoven, E.: Persuasive technology for human well-being: setting the scene. In: IJsselsteijn, Wijnand A., de Kort, Yvonne A.W., Midden, C., Eggen, B., van den Hoven, E. (eds.) PERSUASIVE 2006. LNCS, vol. 3962, pp. 1–5. Springer, Heidelberg (2006). https://doi.org/10.1007/11755494_1

17. Jia, Y., Xu, B., Karanam, Y., Voida S.: Personality-targeted gamification: a survey study on personality traits and motivational affordances. In: Proceedings of CHI 2016, pp. 2001–2013, San Jose (2016)

18. Johnson, D., Horton, E., Mulcahy, R., Foth, M.: Gamification and serious games within the domain of domestic energy consumption: a systematic review. Renew. Sustain. Energy Rev. **73**, 249–264 (2017)

19. Kaptein, M., Van Halteren, A.: Adaptive persuasive messaging to increase service retention: using persuasion profiles to increase the effectiveness of email reminders. Pers. Ubiquit. Comput. **17**, 1173–1185 (2013)

20. Kittur, A., Chi, E.H., Suh, B.: Crowdsourcing user studies with mechanical turk. In: Proceedings of CHI 2008, Florence, Italy (2008)

21. Marczewski, A.: User types. In: Even Ninja Monkeys Like to Play: Gamification, Game Thinking & Motivational Design, pp. 69–84. CreateSpace Publishing Platform (2015)

22. Meder, M., Plumbaum, T., Albayrak, S.: Learning gamification design – an usability first approach for the enterprise infoboard experiment. In: Proceedings of the GamifIR Workshop, Pisa, Italy (2016)

23. Milgram, S.: Obedience to Authority. Travistock, London (1974)

24. Morschheuser, B., Hamari, J., Koivisto, J.: Gamification in crowdsourcing. In: Proceedings of HICSS 49, USA (2106)

25. Nacke, L.E., Bateman, C., Mandryk, R.L.: BrainHex: preliminary results from a neurobiological gamer typology survey. Entertainment Comput. **5**(1), 288–293 (2014)

26. Orji, R., Nacke, L.E., Di Marco, C.: Towards personality-driven persuasive health games and gamified systems. In: Proceedings of CHI 2017, Denver, USA, pp. 1015–1027 (2017)

27. Orji, R., Vassileva, J., Mandryk, R.L.: Modeling the efficacy of persuasive strategies for different gamer types in serious games for health. User Model. User-Adap. Inter. **24**(5), 453–498 (2014)

28. Paolacci, G., Chandler, J.: Inside the turk: understanding mechanical turk as a participant pool. Curr. Dir. Psychol. Sci. **23**(3), 184–188 (2014)

29. Pereira, P., Duarte, E., Rebelo, F., Noriega, P.: A review of gamification for health-related contexts. In: Marcus, A. (ed.) DUXU 2014. LNCS, vol. 8518, pp. 742–753. Springer, Cham (2014). https://doi.org/10.1007/978-3-319-07626-3_70

30. Tondello, F.G., Wehbe, R.R., Diamond, L., Busch, M., Marczewski A., Nacke, L.: The gamification user types hexad scale. In: Proceedings of CHI Play 2016, pp. 229–243 (2016)
31. Wong, K.K.: Partial least squares structural equation modeling (PLS-SEM) techniques using SmartPLS. Mark. Bull. **24**(1), 1–32 (2013)
32. Lounis, S., Neratzouli, X., Pramatari, K.: Can gamification increase consumer engagement? a qualitative approach on a green case. In: Douligeris, C., Polemi, N., Karantjias, A., Lamersdorf, W. (eds.) I3E 2013. IAICT, vol. 399, pp. 200–212. Springer, Heidelberg (2013). https://doi.org/10.1007/978-3-642-37437-1_17
33. Peham, M., Breitfuss, G., Michalczuk, R.: The ecogator app: gamification for enhanced energy efficiency in Europe. In: Proceedings of the Second International Conference on Technological Ecosystems for Enhancing Multiculturality, pp. 179–183, Salamanca, Spain (2014)

D2C-SM: Designing a Distributed-to-Centralized Software Management Architecture for Smart Cities

Amir Sinaeepourfard[1]([✉]), Sobah Abbas Petersen[1], and Dirk Ahlers[2]

[1] Department of Computer Science,
Norwegian University of Science and Technology (NTNU), Trondheim, Norway
{a.sinaee, sobah.a.petersen}@ntnu.no
[2] Department of Architecture and Planning,
Norwegian University of Science and Technology (NTNU), Trondheim, Norway
dirk.ahlers@ntnu.no

Abstract. Smart city innovations can enhance the quality of citizens' life through different smart technology management solutions, including resource management, data management, and software management. Nowadays, there are two primary proposals for smart technology management architectures in smart city environments, centralized, and distributed-to-centralized. The distributed-to-centralized schema architecture has several advantages. These advantages emerge from the contribution of distributed (e.g., Fog and cloudlet), and centralized (e.g., Cloud) technologies. For instance, decreasing network communication traffic and its latencies, improving data quality, and upgrading the security and privacy levels. In this paper, we develop our proposed Distributed-to-Centralized Data Management (D2C-DM) architecture and suggest novel contributions. First, we describe a new fully hierarchical software management architecture for smart cities based on Fog, cloudlet, and Cloud technologies. This Distributed-to-Centralized Software Management (D2C-SM) architecture can provide different software and services layers (including local, historical, and combined) through using distinct data types gathered from physical (e.g., sensors and smartphones) and non-physical (e.g., simulated data, and external databases) data sources in the smart city. Second, we envisage that our proposed D2C-SM can fit the software requirements of the Zero Emission Neighborhoods (ZEN) center. Thereafter, we use three different use cases of the ZEN center to depict the easy adaptation of our proposed ICT architecture, including D2C-SM and D2C-DM architectures.

Keywords: Smart city · Software management · Data management ·
Centralized Software Management (CSM) ·
Distributed-to-Centralized Software Management (D2C-SM) ·
Centralized Data Management (CDM) ·
Distributed-to-Centralized Data Management (D2C-DM) ·
Fog-to-Cloud Data Management (F2C-DM) ·
Fog-to-cloudlet-to-Cloud Data Management (F2c2C-DM)

© IFIP International Federation for Information Processing 2019
Published by Springer Nature Switzerland AG 2019
I. O. Pappas et al. (Eds.): I3E 2019, LNCS 11701, pp. 329–341, 2019.
https://doi.org/10.1007/978-3-030-29374-1_27

1 Introduction and Motivation

Smart city concepts have been proposed by multiple researchers in recent decades to enhance the citizens' quality of life by various smart technology management solutions (such as management of resource, data, and software) between end-users, city planners, and technological devices (e.g., sensors) [1, 2]. By those solutions, data are such primary feeds for smart cities and play a vital role for the smart cities developments. The data provide a massive opportunity for a city to be smart and agile through the different types of services for a city. Moreover, the services use data to build their service scenarios for the smart city stakeholders' requirements by the appropriate information according to the contextual state, or some high-level knowledge discovered from different data analysis techniques. Therefore, we highlight that data and software management is one of the most significant and challenging issues ICT use in smart cities.

From the beginning, many smart technology management solutions in smart cities have been discussed by centralized facilities based on Cloud technologies [1, 2]. Various benefits that can be gained by using Cloud technologies. For instance, Cloud technologies provide (almost) unlimited resources capacity for a set of data processing and data storage, etc. [1–3]. However, there are several disadvantages with forwarding all data and services to Cloud technologies, including appraising the level of data quality, security, and privacy, and undesirable network communication latencies, etc. [4, 5]. Hence, the advent of edge computing has been added novel issues to the smart technology management solutions in smart cities [4–6]. For edge-dominant systems, the old smart technology management solutions and development will not work for software development life cycles, data life cycles, etc. [6–8]. Thereafter smart technology management solutions go beyond to ideas of distributed-to-centralized facilities to manage data, software, resources and so on. The core idea of distributed-to-centralized is to make contributions between the edge of networks (as a place which is nearest to the data sources) and centralized schemas (as a place which is furthest to the data sources, but possibly closer to data consumers and processing) through a unified strategy [9–12].

In this paper, we extend our proposed ICT architecture based on D2C-DM architecture for smart cities [9, 10, 13]. Several contributions have suggested in the paper to expand the ICT architecture through more detailed use cases in cities and focus on applicability to scenarios of software management. First, we draw a novel fully hierarchical software management architecture for smart cities based on Fog, cloudlet, and Cloud technologies. This new Distributed-to-Centralized Software Management (D2C-SM) architecture can generate different services layers (including local, historical, and combined) through using distinct data types gathered from physical (e.g., sensors) and non-physical (e.g., simulated data, and external databases) data sources in the smart city. Second, as our first discussion, we envisage that our proposed D2C-SM can fit the software's requirements of the Zero Emission Neighbourhoods (ZEN) center [14]. Thereafter we use three different use cases of the ZEN center to depict the efficiency of our proposed ICT architecture, including D2C-SM and D2C-DM architectures.

The rest of the paper is structured as follows. Section 2 introduces the related work of different smart technology management (such as resource management, data management, and software management) with a focus on software management strategies in the smart city. Section 3 describes a particular smart city project in Norway (ZEN center), and its pilots. Section 4 explains the main insight of the Information and Communication Technology (ICT) architecture for ZEN center, including D2C-DM and D2C-SM. In addition, we propose a novel D2C-SM architecture for ZEN center (based on Fog, cloudlet, and Cloud technologies) as well as the smart city. Section 5 discusses three different use cases of ZEN pilots to illustrate easy adaption of the D2C-DM and D2C-SM architecture. Finally, Sect. 6 concludes the paper.

2 Related Work

Several smart technology management solutions suggest managing the resources, software, and data in the smart city. Those solutions make the interconnection between end-users to city planners, and technological devices in smart cities to develop the citizens' quality of life [1–5, 9–13, 15] and can also be understood as a collaboration of citizens and technology [16].

There are two main views to design the smart technology management solutions in smart cities as shown below, centralized and distributed-to-centralized.

- The centralized schema architectures are developed so that data is produced from many different data sources spread across the city but data is stored and reached from a centralized platform, mostly using Cloud technologies [1, 2]. This approach also exists in a partially decentralized or federated systems, often focused on database structures and replication, or separation of responsibility across systems [17, 18].
- The distributed-to-centralized schema architectures use both potentials of centralized and distributed schema for processing and storage at the same time. For instance, this combined architecture highlights that the distributed technologies (such as Fog [5, 19], cloudlet [20], etc.) can contribute to centralized technologies (e.g., Cloud) at the same time to provide user requirements (e.g., data and software) from the smallest scale of the city to largest scale of the city.

With a focus on software management architectures in the smart city, a majority of the proposed architectures go beyond the Centralized Software Management (CSM) architectures which also centralizes the data management schemes [1, 2]. For instance, in [1, 2], the author designed an information framework for the smart city. This information framework used centralized schema architecture to organize data and software from city to cloud environments. This means that all applications and services obtain the data from a centralized cloud-computing platform through Centralized Data Management (CDM) architecture. Although the data is collected from different sources spread among the city, the data is accessible from a centralized platform, usually in the cloud. Alternatively, few proposals mentioned that a distributed schema for resource (few examples in [5, 19]) and data management (few examples in [9–13]) in smart cities by using distributed technologies such as Fog [5, 19], and cloudlet [20]; In addition, none of them have an explicit focus on software management architecture. One exception is found in [21] where the author explicitly address some initial issues related to a new health service model by using the potential of Fog (only sensors data considered in this example), and cloud technologies.

To sum up, we can highlight that almost all the available software management architectures for smart cities have the following limitations:

- Almost all the software management architectures have been designed through or for centralized technologies (few examples in [1, 2]);
- There are new schools of thought to propose a distributed-to-centralized software architecture by the contribution of Fog (sensors data) and cloud technologies (e.g., [21]) but they are not mature enough;
- There is no proposed architecture to fit D2C-DM with D2C-SM architecture concerning using all data types and formats (including physical, and non-physical data sources) from distributed (the smallest scale of a city) to centralized (largest scale of a city) schema in smart cities.

For all discussed reasons, first, we suggest a novel hierarchical D2C-SM architecture by using Fog, cloudlet, and Cloud technologies for the smart city. In addition, this D2C-SM architecture can be matched with our proposed D2C-DM architecture [9, 10, 13]. Second, we envisage that this architecture can cover many of the above limitations. Finally, this architecture can be fitted to the idea of the ZEN center and its pilots [14].

3 Our Scenario Description: The ZEN Center

The ZEN Center is an example of smart cities projects in Norway. The ZEN center has a plan to develop the idea of the Zero Emission Building (ZEB) further towards neighborhoods [22]. The ZEN objectives have been to scale from buildings to neighborhood to reach the "zero energy" ambition. In addition, the European Union made a plan for buildings to reach the "nearly zero energy" level approximately in 2020 [14, 23]. In [13, 24], as shown in Fig. 1, the ZEN conceptual levels are depicted by three levels from the smallest scale of the city to the largest scale of the city, micro-, meso-, and macro. Furthermore, the ZEN center concentrates on meso-level of a city (neighborhoods) [14], constituting of varieties of city elements within buildings, streets, etc. The ZEN center has eight different pilot projects in distinct cities in Norway [14].

Six different work packages are defined by the ZEN center to fulfil its objectives [14]. The main tasks of this paper are in the work package on "ZEN Data Management and Monitoring: Requirements and Architecture" [14]. In [24], the authors mentioned that an efficient data management and monitoring is required for the ZEN center and its pilot projects. Two main roles are defined [24]. The first role is concerned with monitoring and evaluation and includes tracking the progress and success of ZEN along a set of important dimensions, identified through key performance indicators (KPIs). The next role is operational to support the work packages and pilots in the implementation of the project.

Our main responsibility for the ZEN center is to design a comprehensive ICT architecture for ZEN center and its related pilots. The ICT architecture includes different architectures (including data management, software management, etc.) to organize the ICT requirements for the ZEN center and its pilots concerning the ZEN business requirements and future requirements of the citizens in a smart city. In our previous work [9, 10, 13], we proposed a D2C-DM architecture to manage all produced data of the ZEN center and its pilots, from physical data sources (e.g., sensors) to non-physical data sources (e.g., simulated data). Then, in this paper, we start to draw a novel architecture for software management in the smart city, from distributed to centralized schema. Plus, we add this D2C-SM architecture to our ZEN ICT architecture.

4   The ICT Architecture for the ZEN Center

The conceptual background of the ICT architecture is structured into two main axes, "Time" and "Location," as depicted in Fig. 1. In addition, the current proposal of our ICT architecture constitutes different inline architectures, including "data management architecture" and "software management architecture." Also, in [9, 10, 13], we presented the different data types (consisting of the ZEN center and smart city) and technology layers (including Fog, cloudlet, and Cloud technologies) are required for the ZEN ICT architecture.

The bottom-up ICT architecture is designed to range from the very small scale to very large scale of the city. In addition, the proposed ICT architecture illustrates that the bottom layer (Fog-Layer) across the city has the lowest latency of the network communications and the limited resources capacities in terms of the processing and storage capabilities. Moving upwards from bottom to top makes the undesired level of the network latencies, while the capabilities of processing and storage will be improved.

This section is organized into two main subsections. First, we describe our previous works to design the D2C data management architecture for the ZEN center based on Fog, cloudlet, and Cloud technologies [13]. Second, we propose a novel software management architecture for the ZEN center based on the same technologies.

4.1   The D2C-DM Architecture for ZEN Center

In our previous work [13], we drew a fully hierarchical distributed (from sensors and IoT devices) to centralized (Cloud computing technologies) data management architecture for smart cities to organize smart city data types (including "real-time", "last-recent", and "historical") as well as ZEN center data types (consisting of "context", "research", and "KPIs") through the bottom-up ICT architecture.

As shown in Fig. 1, the F2c2C-DM architecture proposed data according to its age, ranging from real-time to historical data; and the data location and scope. The F2c2C-DM architecture [13] proposes the following three layers of architecture from Fog-Layer, to cloudlet-Layer, and Cloud layer. Those layers are covered by different data management strategies (including distributed and centralized):

- Distributed data management: is the nearest neighbor to the end-users and IoT devices in the smart city and ZEN center pilots. Two different distributed technologies (including Fog and cloudlet) are used to handle the distributed data management for our proposed architecture. The core idea of the Fog and cloudlet are quite similar. This core idea is that the Cloud services could run closer to the users and data sources. Although, the main difference between Fog and cloudlet technologies is that the Fog uses the potential of available physical devices (such as traffic lights) in a city [5, 19], but the cloudlet installs new physical device(s), namely "data center in a box", at the edge of the network [20].

The distributed data management can provide facilities to do a set of processing and storage at the edge of networks. In [7], a data lifecycle model is proposed for the smart city (namely is SCC-DLC). This model offers three main blocks and their related phases as described below concisely.

- Data Acquisition Block: The main responsibility of this block for the distributed data management is to collect all the available data (from physical and non-physical data sources) across the city. In addition, this block aims to prepare the collected data for the Processing and/or Preservation block concerning the capacity of the Fog and cloudlet resources in a city. This block has different phases as shown below:

  1. "Data Collection" phase aims to collect different data types and formats across to the city by the available physical (such as sensors and IoT devices) and non-physical data (such as simulated data) sources. To apply this in our F2c2C-DM architecture, the Fog technology is responsible to handle physical data sources and cloudlet technology is active to add non-physical data sources in a city.
  2. "Data Filtering" phase provides different types of facilities to perform different levels of optimizations (e.g., data aggregation, and cleaning) for the collected data in a city. In our architecture, a set of different algorithms can be defined within Fog and cloudlet technologies in each/all the local-domains to make optimization for the collected data concerning their resource capacities in each layer of Fog and cloudlet.
  3. "Data Quality" phase has the intention to appraise the quality level of collected data. Plus, this phase can provide the facility to control the levels of security and privacy. To implement it in our architecture, a set of several different algorithms can be applied in each/all the local-domains by Fog and/or cloudlet technology.
  4. "Data Description" phase has potential to do tagging data with some additional information and description of data (metadata), including data production time, data expiry time, data ownership, and so on. The Fog and cloudlet can handle this data description for physical and non-physical data sources locally.

- Data Preservation Block: The main task of this block for the distributed data management is to store the collected data in local storage media for short-term (e.g., public data) and/or long-term (e.g., private data) usage purposes regarding the storage capacities of the data sources across the city. This block consists of four main phases as shown below:

  1. "Data Classification" phase able to organize data (e.g., sorting and/or clustering data) for efficient storage at Fog and/or cloudlet layer.

    2. "Data Archive" phase uses the capabilities of the local storage media at Fog and/or cloudlet layer to store the collected data for short and long terms consumption.

    3. "Data Dissemination" phase brings a facility at Fog and/or cloudlet layer to publish data for public or private access through user interfaces.

– Data Processing Block: The main objective of this block for the distributed data management is to establish a set of processing somewhere close to the data sources at Fog and/or cloudlet layer. This block includes two main phases:

    1. "Data Process" phase prepares a set of processes to transform raw data into more sophisticated data/information at Fog and/or cloudlet layer.

    2. "Data Analysis" phase offers analysis or analytic approaches for extracting further value and knowledge at Fog and/or cloudlet layer.

- CDM: Normally, Cloud computing technologies are responsible for CDM tasks. The Cloud layer is located at the top level of the F2c2C-DM architecture. The Cloud technology offers the highest level of resources for the computing and storage that is positioned far away from the data sources and end-users. Furthermore, the Cloud can organize a variety of complex tasks (for instance, data processing) that sometimes cannot be organized in the lower layers (Fog and cloudlet) across the city.

4.2   The D2C-SM Architecture for ZEN Center

The ZEN center aims to provide several ICT applications/services/tools for the researchers, and partners regarding their requirements in the early future [14, 24]. By December 2018, there was a total of 18 tools available at ZEN center and their related pilots as described in [25]. Hence, the ZEN applications/services/tools must utilize a variety of data sources with different data types and formats from distributed to centralized through our proposed F2c2C-DM architecture.

As explained in Sect. 4.1, the F2c2C-DM architecture provided data according to its age, ranging from real-time to historical data; and the data location and scope. It means data can be available from the smallest scale of the city (e.g., room/building of pilots) to the largest scale of the city (e.g., the city through Cloud technologies). Thereafter, we envisage that we can design a new architecture for software management from distributed to centralized schema at cross-layers of our ZEN ICT architecture.

As shown in Fig. 1, we propose a D2C-SM on the right side of the ICT architecture. The D2C-SM architecture has been fitted to the D2C-DM architecture that highlights all that data (form real-time, to last-recent, and historical data) is available from the bottom (smallest scale of the pilot city location) to top (largest scale) of the cross layers of our ICT architecture. Our proposed D2C-SM architecture has three main layers to generate varieties of applications/services/tools as described below.

- "Local Services" layer: Developers can use the locally stored data (the smallest data scale of the pilot city location) across the Fog, and cloudlet layers to create different types of services (including critical and private) in this layer as shown below.

- Critical Services: The developers can build critical services (e.g., healthcare, fire, and accident) in a city at this layer. It means the service can be launched in this layer through the lowest network communication latencies.
- Private Services: The developers can generate exclusive and privacy-aware services by using the private/locally stored data in this layer that is physically very close to the data sources and end-users. Thereafter, we can enhance data privacy levels through this kind of private services.

- "Historical Services" layer: This layer uses the largest scale of stored data (cloud data storages) from all data sources (including physical and non-physical) in all city pilots. In addition, this layer can also contribute to other data sources that are out of the scope of the ZEN center. For instance, data sources from other Cloud service providers, etc.

- "Combined Services" layer: This layer provides the facility for developers to use all data from distributed to centralized schema. For instance, in [21], the authors explained a particular medical application that needs to get data from medical sensors (real-time, local, and private data) as well as Cloud data (historical, large scale, and public data). Normally, this kind of services uses the history and background of particular data types in Cloud and then this data can be mixed with the local/real-time data to provide efficient services for the end-users.

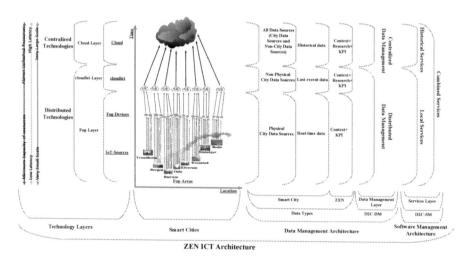

Fig. 1. An ICT architecture for ZEN center by using Fog, cloudlet, and Cloud technologies

5   The ZEN Center Use Cases

This section is organized into three primary subsections along with three different ZEN pilots in a micro-, meso-, and macro-level (from building, to neighborhood, and city) to illustrate the easy adaptation of the D2C-SM and D2C-DM architectures through ICT architecture as shown in Fig. 1.

5.1   The Micro-level (Use Case: The Living Lab)

The Living Lab is one building as a test facility located at NTNU in Trondheim, Norway [14]. The Living Laboratory is occupied by real persons using the building as their home and their consumption of novel building technologies, including smart control of installations and equipment, the interaction of end-users with the energy systems, and other aspects.

In the first example, we will use the living lab pilot (micro-level) as a case to illustrate the potential of our proposed D2C-DM and D2C-SM architectures:

- With focus on our proposed data management architecture (D2C-DM), as shown in Fig. 2, the living lab is at the micro level (only building level). The data in the living lab pilot is currently produced by different numbers of sensors (IoT-Sources) at the micro level. At the micro level, Fig. 2 shows that the researchers can deal with context data (as real-time data) to build their research data concerning KPIs data and their requirements. Finally, for any future usage, the researchers can store the newly generated data (their research data) in the cloudlet technology. Also, the researchers have the possibility to store this in the local storage media (for instance their available storage at micro or/and meso level).
- With focus on software management architecture (D2C-SM), the developers can reach to the locally stored data (including real-time and last-recent data) through Fog and cloudlet technologies. Thereafter, the developers can create local services (including critical and private) concerning the business and users' requirements and data privacy issues.

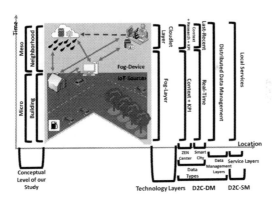

Fig. 2. ZEN ICT architecture through the living lab scenario (one building case study)

5.2   The Meso-level (Use Case: Campus Evenstad)

The campus Evenstad pilot is located in a rural area of Stor-Elvdal municipality [14]. The campus consists of seventeen buildings on 61,000 m^2 of land. The campus provides a facility for administration, education, and sport, student housing and building operation. This campus aims to optimize energy production.

In the second example, we will use the campus Evenstad pilot (meso-level) as a case to illustrate the ICT architecture adaptation as described below.

- With a focus on data management architecture (D2C-DM), as depicted in Fig. 3, the campus scope is in the meso level (including building and their neighborhoods level). Figure 3 illustrates that the huge number of data is generated by the different IoT-Sources of seventeen buildings and their related neighborhoods. The researchers can then use the context data (real-time data) to build their research data concerning KPIs and can store this data in their local storage media and their related cloudlet storages. Note that all data types (including context, research, and KPIs) of the Evenstad pilot are supposed to be for online access interface by different researchers through cloudlet technologies.
- With a focus on software management architecture (D2C-SM), the developers can have access to the locally stored data through Fog and cloudlet technologies to build their local services through the open data platform.

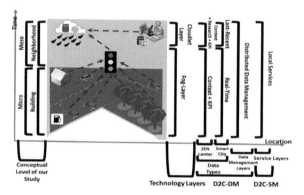

Fig. 3. ZEN ICT architecture through the Campus Evenstad scenario (neighborhood case study)

5.3   The Macro-level (Use Case: Smart City)

In the macro level, the ZEN partners might request to collect all data from each/all pilots of the ZEN centers by a single request. Therefore, we can use the potential of the Cloud technologies to keep all context, research, and KPIs data in their repositories for any future process and requirement. Consequently, all partners or other data stake-holders of the ZEN center can get access to the interface to use all obtained data from the pilots. In addition, many software and services can be launched by all obtained data (including historical, real-time, and last-recent data) at this level as depicted in Fig. 4.

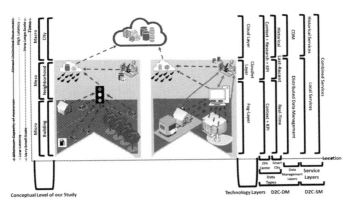

Fig. 4. ZEN ICT architecture through the smart city case study

6   Conclusion

In this paper, we further developed our proposed ICT architecture (including data management and software management architecture) for the ZEN center based on a distributed hierarchical schema by using Fog-to-cloudlet-to-Cloud technologies. The main points of this development are as following:

- We illustrated that the potential of D2C-DM architecture could make data accessible from the smallest scale of a city to the largest scale;
- The availability of data in all levels of a city provides desirable advantages to generate varieties of applications/services/tools across different layers of distributed to centralized schema;
- We proposed a novel software management architecture to make different service layers (including local, historical, and combined) in each/all cross layers of distributed to centralized schema;
- We envisage that D2C-DM and D2C-SM can adapt to ZEN center as well as other smart city environments.

As a part of our future work, we will discover more options related to developing our ZEN ICT architecture and its related inline architecture (including D2C-DM, and D2C-SM).

Acknowledgment. This paper has been written within the Research Centre on Zero Emission Neighborhoods in smart cities (FME ZEN). The authors gratefully acknowledge the support from the ZEN partners and the Research Council of Norway.

References

1. Jin, J., Gubbi, J., Marusic, S., Palaniswami, M.: An information framework for creating a smart city through Internet of Things. IEEE Internet Things J. **1**, 112–121 (2014)
2. Gubbi, J., Buyya, R., Marusic, S., Palaniswami, M.: Internet of Things (IoT): a vision, architectural elements, and future directions. Future Gener. Comput. Syst. **29**, 1645–1660 (2013)

3. Hu, X., Ludwig, A., Richa, A., Schmid, S.: Competitive strategies for online cloud resource allocation with discounts: the 2-dimensional parking permit problem. In: 35th IEEE International Conference on Distributed Computing Systems (ICDCS), pp. 93–102. IEEE (2015)
4. Rao, T.V.N., Khan, A., Maschendra, M., Kumar, M.K.: A paradigm shift from cloud to fog computing. Int. J. Sci. Eng. Comput. Technol. **5**, 385 (2015)
5. Bonomi, F., Milito, R., Zhu, J., Addepalli, S.: Fog computing and its role in the Internet of Things. In: Proceedings of the First Edition of the MCC Workshop on Mobile Cloud Computing, pp. 13–16. ACM (2012)
6. Bass, L., Clements, P., Kazman, R.: Software Architecture in Practice. Addison-Wesley Professional (2003)
7. Sinaeepourfard, A., Garcia, J., Masip-Bruin, X., Marin-Tordera, E., Yin, X., Wang, C.: A Data LifeCycle model for smart cities. In: International Conference on Information and Communication Technology Convergence (ICTC), pp. 400–405. IEEE (2016)
8. Sinaeepourfard, A., Garcia, J., Masip-Bruin, X., Marín-Tordera, E.: Towards a comprehensive Data LifeCycle model for Big Data environments. In: Proceedings of the 3rd IEEE/ACM International Conference on Big Data Computing, Applications and Technologies, pp. 100–106. ACM (2016)
9. Sinaeepourfard, A., Krogstie, J., Petersen, S.A.: A Big Data management architecture for smart cities based on Fog-to-Cloud data management architecture. In: Proceedings of the 4th Norwegian Big Data Symposium (NOBIDS) (2018)
10. Sinaeepourfard, A., Krogstie, J., Petersen, S.A., Gustavsen, A.: A zero emission neighbourhoods data management architecture for smart city scenarios: discussions toward 6Vs challenges. In: International Conference on Information and Communication Technology Convergence (ICTC). IEEE (2018)
11. Sinaeepourfard, A., Garcia, J., Masip-Bruin, X., Marin-Tordera, E.: Fog-to-Cloud (F2C) data management for smart cities. In: Future Technologies Conference (FTC) (2017)
12. Sinaeepourfard, A., Garcia, J., Masip-Bruin, X., Marin-Tordera, E.: Data preservation through Fog-to-Cloud (F2C) data management in smart cities. In: IEEE 2nd International Conference on Fog and Edge Computing (ICFEC), pp. 1–9. IEEE (2018)
13. Sinaeepourfard, A., Krogstie, J., Abbas Petersen, S., Ahlers, D.: F2c2C-DM: A Fog-to-cloudlet-to-Cloud Data Management Architecture in Smart City. In: IEEE 5th World Forum on Internet of Things (WF-IoT), IEEE, Limerick, Ireland (2019)
14. https://fmezen.no/
15. Tei, K., Gurgen, L.: ClouT: cloud of things for empowering the citizen clout in smart cities. In: IEEE World Forum on Internet of Things (WF-IoT), pp. 369–370. IEEE (2014)
16. Ahlers, D., Driscoll, P., Löfström, E., Krogstie, J., Wyckmans, A.: Understanding smart cities as social machines. In: Proceedings of the 25th International Conference Companion on World Wide Web, pp. 759–764. International World Wide Web Conferences Steering Committee (2016)
17. Khan, Z., Anjum, A., Kiani, S.L.: Cloud based big data analytics for smart future cities. In: Proceedings of the 2013 IEEE/ACM 6th International Conference on Utility and Cloud Computing, pp. 381–386. IEEE Computer Society (2013)
18. Ahlers, D., Akerkar, R.A., Krogstie, J., Opdahl, A.L., Tessem, B., Zhang, W.: Harnessing mobility data in cities: a case study from the Bergen region (2018)
19. Xiong, Z., Feng, S., Wang, W., Niyato, D., Wang, P., Han, Z.: Cloud/fog computing resource management and pricing for blockchain networks. IEEE Commun. Mag. **6**(3), 4585–4600 (2018)

20. Bilal, K., Khalid, O., Erbad, A., Khan, S.U.: Potentials, trends, and prospects in edge technologies: fog, cloudlet, mobile edge, and micro data centers. Comput. Netw. **130**, 94–120 (2018)
21. Masip-Bruin, X., Marín-Tordera, E., Alonso, A., Garcia, J.: Fog-to-cloud computing (F2C): the key technology enabler for dependable e-health services deployment. In: Mediterranean Ad hoc Networking Workshop (Med-Hoc-Net), pp. 1–5. IEEE (2016)
22. https://www.zeb.no/
23. Hestnes, A.G., Eik-Nes, N.L.: Zero Emission Buildings. Fagbokforlaget, Bergen (2017)
24. Ahlers, D., Krogstie, J.: ZEN data management and monitoring: requirements and architecture. Technical reports (2017)
25. Abbas Petersen, S., Krogstie, J.: Intermediate ICT coordination and harmonization guidelines. Technical reports (2019)

Social Media and Analytics

Use of Social Media by b2b Companies: Systematic Literature Review and Suggestions for Future Research

Yogesh K. Dwivedi[1], Elvira Ismagilova[2], Nripendra P. Rana[1(✉)], and Vishanth Weerakkody[2]

[1] Emerging Markets Research Centre, School of Management, Swansea University, Swansea, UK
{y.k.dwivedi,n.p.rana}@swansea.ac.uk
[2] Faculty of Management, Law and Social Sciences, University of Bradford, Bradford, UK
{e.ismagilova,v.weerakkody}@bradford.ac.uk

Abstract. Social media plays an important role in the digital transformation of businesses. This research provides a comprehensive analysis of the use of social media by b2b companies. The current study focuses on a number of aspects of social media such as: the effect of social media; social media tools; social media use; adoption of social media use and its barriers; social media strategies; and measuring the effectiveness of the use of social media. This research provides a valuable synthesis of the relevant literature on social media in the b2b context by analysing and discussing the key findings from existing research on social media. The findings of this study can be used as an informative framework on social media for both academics and practitioners.

Keywords: Social media · B2B · Literature review

1 Introduction

The Internet has changed social communications and social behaviour, in turn leading to the development of new forms of communication channels and platforms [1]. Social media plays an important role in the digital transformation of businesses. Whereas, in the past, social networks were used to provide information about a company or brand, nowadays businesses use social media to support their marketing aims and strategies to improve consumer's involvement, relationship with customers and to get useful consumers' insights [2]. Business to consumer (b2c) companies widely use social media and enjoy its benefits such as an increase in sales, brand awareness, and customer engagement to name a few [3].

More recently, business to business (b2b) companies started using social media as part of their marketing strategy. Even though b2b companies are benefitting from social media used by marketers, it is argued that research on that area is still in the embryonic stage and future research is needed [4–6].

© IFIP International Federation for Information Processing 2019
Published by Springer Nature Switzerland AG 2019
I. O. Pappas et al. (Eds.): I3E 2019, LNCS 11701, pp. 345–355, 2019.
https://doi.org/10.1007/978-3-030-29374-1_28

The topic of Social media in the context of b2b companies has started to attract attention from both academics and practitioners. This is evidenced by the growing number of research output within academic journals and conference proceedings. Some studies provided a comprehensive literature review on social media use by b2b companies [4, 7], but focused only on the adoption of social media by b2b or social media influence, without providing the whole picture of the use of social media by b2b companies. Thus, this study aims to close this gap in the literature by conducting a comprehensive analysis of the use of social media by b2b companies. The findings of this study can provide an informative framework for research on social media in the context of b2b companies for academics and practitioners.

The remaining sections of the study are organised as follows. Section 2 offers a brief overview of the methods used to identify relevant studies to be included in this review. Section 3 synthesises the studies identified in the previous section and provides their detailed overview. Section 4 presents limitations of current studies on social media use by b2b companies and outlines directions for future research. Finally, Sect. 5 discusses the key aspects of the research, outlining limitations of the current research and proposing direction for future research.

2   Literature Search Method

This study used a keyword search based approach for identifying relevant articles [8, 9]. Keywords such as "Advertising" OR "Marketing" OR "Sales" AND TITLE ("Social Media" OR "Web 2.0" OR "Facebook" OR "LinkedIn" OR "Instagram" OR "Twitter" OR "Snapchat" OR "Pinterest" OR "WhatsApp" OR "Social Networking Sites") AND TITLE-ABS-KEY ("B2B" OR "B to B" OR "Business to Business" OR "Business 2 Business") were searched via the Scopus database. Only results in English language were included. All studies were processed by the authors in order to ensure relevance and that the research offered a contribution to the social media in the context b2b discussion. The search and review resulted in 70 articles and conference papers that formed the literature review for this study. The selected studies appeared in 33 separate journals and conference proceedings, including Industrial Marketing Management Journal, Journal of Business and Industrial Marketing and Journal of Business research.

3   Literature Synthesis

The studies on the use of social media by b2b companies were divided into the following themes: effect of social media, social media tools, social media use, adoption and barriers of social media use, social media strategies, and measuring the effectiveness of the use of social media (see Table 1). The following subsections provide an overview of each theme.

Table 1. Themes in social media research (b2b context)*

Theme	Studies
Effect of social media	[10–15]
Social media tools	[16–18]
Social media use	[19–22]
Adoption of social media use	[5, 23–26]
Social media strategies	[27–30]
Measuring effectiveness of use of SM	[5, 31]

* Note: just some studies out of 70 were included in this review due to the page limit. The full list of studies can be requested from authors.

3.1 Effect of Social Media

Some studies focus on the effect of social media for b2b companies which include customer satisfaction, value creation, post sales service behavior, sales, building relationships with customers, brand awareness, intention to purchase, knowledge creation, perceived corporate credibility, acquiring of new customers, salesperson performance and employee brand engagement. For example, Agnihotri et al. [10] investigated how the implementation of social media by b2b salesperson affects consumer satisfaction. Salesperson social media use is defined as a "salesperson's utilization and integration of social media technology to perform his or her job" [10]. The study used data of 111 sales professionals involved in b2b industrial selling to test the proposed hypotheses. It was found that a salesperson's use of social media will have a positive effect on information communication, which will, in turn, lead to improved customer satisfaction with the salesperson. Also, it was investigated that information communication will be positively related to responsiveness, which impacts customer satisfaction.

Another study by Kho [32] states the advantages of using social media by B2B companies, which include faster and more personalised communications between customer and vendor, which can improve corporate credibility and strengthen the relationships. Thanks to social media companies can provide more detailed information about their products and services. Kho [32] also mentions that customer forums and blog comments in b2b environment should be carefully monitored in order to make sure that inappropriate discussions are taken offline and negative eWOM communications should be addressed in a timely manner.

Another group of studies investigated the effect of social media on the level of sales. For example, Itani et al. [13] use theory of reasoned actions to develop a model that tests the factors affecting the use of social media by a sales person and its impact. By collecting data from 120 salespersons from different industries and using SmartPLS to analyse the data, it was found that attitude towards social media usefulness did not affect the use of social media. It was found that social media use positively affects competitive intelligence collection, adaptive selling behaviour which in turn influenced sales performance. The study conducted by Rodriguez et al. [15] examines the effect of social media on b2b sales performance by using social capital theory and collecting data from 1699 b2b salespeople from over 25 different industries. By employing SEM

Amos the study found that social media usage has a positive significant relationship with selling companies' ability to create opportunities and manage relationships. The study also found that social media usage has a positive and significant relationship with sales performance (based on relational measurers of sales that focus on behaviours that strengthen the relationship between buyers and sellers), but not with outcome-based sales performance (reflected by quota achievement, growth in average billing size, and overall revenue gain).

Some researchers argued that social media can influence brand awareness. For instance, Hsiao et al. [12] investigated the effect of social media in fashion industry. By collecting 1395 posts from lookbook.nu and employing regression analysis it was found that inclusion national brand and private fashion brands in the post increased the level of popularity which lead to purchase interest and brand awareness.

Meire et al. [14] investigated the impact of social media on acquiring B2B customers. By using commercially purchased prospecting data, website data and Facebook data from beverage companies the study conducted an experiment and found that social media us an effective tool in acquiring B2B customers.

Agnihotri et al. [11] proposed theoretical framework to explain the mechanisms through which salespeople's use of social media operates to create value, and propose a strategic approach to social media use to achieve competitive goals. The proposed framework describes how social media tools can help salespeople perform service behaviours leading to value creation.

3.2   Adoption of Social Media

Some scholars investigated factors affecting the adoption of social media by b2b companies. For instance, Lacka and Chong [23] investigated factors affecting the adoption of social media by b2b companies from different industries in China. The study collected the data from 181 respondents and used the Technology Acceptance Model with Nielsen's Model of Attributes of System Acceptability as a theoretical framework. By using SEM Amos for analysis the study found that perceived usability, perceived usefulness, and perceived utility positively affect the adoption and use of social media by b2b marketing professionals. The usefulness is subject to the assessment of whether social media sites are suitable means through which marketing activities can be conducted. The ability to use social media sites for B2B marketing purposes, in turn, is due to those sites learnability and memorability attributes.

Lashgari et al. [24] studied the adoption and use of social media by using face-to-face interviews with key managers of four multinational corporations and observations from companies' websites and social media platforms. It was found that the elements essential in forming the B2B firm's social media adoption strategies are content (depth and diversity), corresponding social media platform, structure of social media channels, the role of moderators, information accessibility approaches (public vs. gated-content), and online communities. These elements are customised to the goals and target group the firm sets to pursue. Similarly, integration of social media into other promotional channels can fall under an ad-hoc or continuous approach depending on the scope and the breadth of the communication plan, derived from the goal.

Another study by Müller et al. [25] investigated factors affecting the usage of social media. By using survey data from 100 polish and 39 German sensor suppliers, it was found that buying frequency, the function of a buyer, the industry sector and the country does not affect the usage of social media in the context of sensor technology from Poland and Germany. The study used correlation analysis and ANOVA.

Shaltoni [26] applied technology organisational environmental framework and diffusion of innovations to investigate factors affecting the adoption of social media by b2b companies. By using data from marketing managers or business owners of 480 SMEs, the study found that perceived relative advance, perceive compatibility, organizational innovativeness competitor pressure and customer pressure influence the adoption of social media by b2b companies. The findings also suggest that many decision makers in b2b companies think that internet marketing is not beneficial, as it is not compatible with the nature of b2b markets.

While most of the studies focused on the antecedents of social media adoption by b2b companies, Michaelidou et al. [5] investigated its perceived barriers. By using data from 92 SMEs the study found that over a quarter of B2B SMEs in the UK are currently using SNS to achieve brand objectives, the most popular of which is to attract new customers. The barriers that prevent SMEs from using social media to support their brands were lack of staff familiarity and technical skills. Innovativeness of a company determined the adoption of social media.

3.3 Social Media Strategies

Another group of studies investigated types of strategies b2b companies apply. For example, Cawsey and Rowley [27] focused on social media strategies of b2b companies. By conducting semi-structured interviews with marketing professional from France, Ireland, UK and USA it was found that enhancing brand image, extending brand awareness and facilitating customer engagement were considered the most common social media objective. The study proposed b2b social media strategy framework which includes six components of a social media strategy: (1) monitoring and listening (2) empowering and engaging employees (3) creating compelling content (4) stimulating eWOM (5) evaluating and selecting channels (6) enhancing brand presence through integrating social media.

Kasper et al. [28] proposed the Social Media Matrix which helps companies to decide which social media activities to execute based on their corporate and communication goals. The matrix includes three parts. The first part is focusing on social media goals and task areas, which were identified and matched. The second part consists of five types of social media activities (content, interaction/dialog, listening and analysing, application and networking). The third part provides a structure to assess the suitability of each activity type on each social media platform for each goal. The matrix was successfully tested by assessing the German b2b sector by using expert interviews with practitioners.

McShane et al. [33] proposed social media strategies to influence online users' engagement with b2b companies. Taking into consideration fluency lens the study analysed Twitter feeds of top 50 social b2b brands to examine the influence of hashtags, text difficulty embedded media and message timing on user engagement, which was evaluated in terms of likes and retweets. It was found that hashtags and text difficulty are connected to lower levels of engagement while embedded media such as images and video improve the level of engagement.

Another study by Swani et al. [30] aimed to investigate message strategies which can help in promoting eWOM activity for b2b companies. By applying content analysis and Hierarchical Linear Modeling the study analysed 1143 wall post messages from 193 fortune 500 Facebook accounts. The study found that b2b account posts will be more effective if they include corporate brand names and avoid hard sell or explicitly commercial statement. Also, companies should use emotional sentiment in Facebook posts.

Most of the studies investigated the strategies and content of social media communications of b2b companies. However, the limited number of studies investigated the importance of CEO engagement on social media in companies strategies. Mudambi et al. [29] emphasise the importance of CEO of b2b companies to be present and active on social media. The study discusses the advantages of social media presence for CEO and how it will benefit the company. For example one of the benefits for CEO can be perceived as being more trustworthy and effective and non-social CEOs, which will benefit the company in increased customer trust. Mudambi et al. [29] also discussed the platforms CEO should use and posting frequencies depending on the content of the post.

3.4   Social Media Use

Most of the studies employed context analysis and surveys to investigate how b2b companies use social media. For example, Vasudevan and Kumar [22] investigated how b2b companies use social media by analysing 325 brand posts of Canon India, Epson India, and HP India on Linkedin, Facebook and Twitter. By employing content analysis the study found that most of the post has a combination of text and message. More than 50% of the posts were about product or brand centric. The study argued that likes proved to be an unreliable measure of engagement, while shares were considered more reliable metric. The reason was that likes had high spikes when brand posts were boosted during promotional activities.

Müller et al. [21] investigated social media use in the German automotive market. By suing online analysis of 10 most popular car manufacturers online social networks and surveys of 6 manufacturers, 42 car dealers, 199 buyers the study found that Social Media communication relations are widely established between manufacturers and (prospective) buyers and only partially established between car dealers and prospective buyers. In contrast to that, on the business-to-business (b2b) side, Social Media communication is rarely used. Social Online Networks (SONs) are the most popular Social Media channels employed by businesses. Manufacturers and car dealers focus their Social Media engagement, especially on Facebook. From the perspective of prospective buyers, however, forums are the most important source of information.

Moore et al. [20] investigated the use of social media between b2b and b2c salespeople. By using survey data from 395 sales professional from different industries they found that B2B sales managers use social selling tools significantly more frequently than B2C managers and B2C sales representatives while conducting sales presentations. Also, it was found that B2B managers used social selling tools significantly more frequently than all sales representatives while closing sales.

Katona and Sarvary [19] presented a case of using social media by Maersk-the largest container shipping company in the world. The case provided details on the programme launch and the integration strategy which focused on integrating the largely independent social media operation into the company's broader marketing efforts.

Keinänen and Kuivalainen [16] investigated factors affecting the use of social media by b2b customers by conducting an online survey among 82 key customer accounts of an information technology service company. Partial least squares path modeling was used to analysed the proposed hypotheses. It was found that social media private use, colleague support for using SM, age, job position affected the use of social media by b2b customers. The study also found that corporate culture, gender, easiness to use and perception of usability did not affect the use of social media by b2b customers.

3.5 Measuring Effectiveness of Social Media

It is important for a business to be able to measure the effectiveness of social media by calculating return on investment (ROI). ROI is the relationship between profit and the investment that generate that profit. Some studies focused on the ways companies can measure ROI and the challenges they face. For example, Gazal et al. [31] investigated the adoption and measuring of the effectiveness of social media in the context of US forest industry by using organizational-level adoption framework and TAM. By using data from 166 companies it was found that 94% of respondents do not measure the ROI from social media use. The reason is that the use of social media in marketing is relatively new and companies do not possess the knowledge of measuring ROI from the use of social media. Companies mostly use quantitative metrics (number of site visits, number of social network friends, number of comments and profile views) and qualitative metrics (growth of relationships with the key audience, audience participation, moving from monologue to dialogue with consumers.

Another study by Michaelidou et al. [5] found that most of the companies do not evaluate the effectiveness of their SNS in supporting their brand. The most popular measures were the number of users joining the groups/discussion and the number of comments made.

3.6 Social Media Tools

Some studies proposed tools, which could be employed by companies to advance their use of social media. For example, Mehmet and Clarke [17] proposed Social Semiotic Multimodal (SSMM) framework that improved analysis of social media communications. This framework employs multimodal extensions to systemic functional linguistics enabling it to be applying to analysing non-language as well as language constituents of social media messages. Furthermore, the framework also utilises expansion theory to identify, categorise and analyse various marketing communication resources associated with marketing messages and also to reveal how conversations are chained together to form extended online marketing conversations. This semantic approach is exemplified using a Fairtrade Australia B2B case study demonstrating how marketing conversations can be mapped and analysed. The framework emphasises the importance of acknowledging the impact of all stakeholders, particularly messages that may distract or confuse the original purpose of the conversation.

Yang et al. [18] proposed the temporal analysis technique to identify user relationships on social media platforms. The experiment was conducted by using data from Digg.com. The results showed that the proposed techniques achieved substantially higher recall but not very good at precision. This technique will help companies to identify their future consumers based on their user relationships.

4 Limitations and Future Research Directions

Studies on social media in the context of b2b companies have the following limitations. First, studies investigated the positive effect of social media such as consumer satisfaction, consumer engagement, and brand awareness. However, it will be interesting to consider the dark side of social media use such as an excessive number of request on social media to salespeople, which can result in the reduction of the responsiveness. Second, a limited number of studies discussed the way b2b companies can measure ROI. Future research should investigate how companies can measure intangible ROI, such as eWOM, brand awareness, and customer engagement [34]. Also, future research should investigate the reasons why most of the users do not assess the effectiveness of their SNS. Furthermore, most of the studies focused on likes, shares, and comments to evaluate social media engagement. Future research should focus on other types of measures. Third, studies were performed in China [23, 35], USA [36–38], India [21, 22, 39], UK [5, 37, 40]. It is strongly advised that future studies conduct research in other countries as findings can be different due to the culture and social media adoption rates. Future studies should pay particular attention to other emerging markets (such as Russia, Brazil, and South Africa) as they suffer from the slow adoption rate of social media marketing. Some companies in these countries still rely more on traditional media for advertising of their products and services, as they are more trusted in comparison with social media channels [41, 42]. Lastly, most of the studies on social media in the context of b2b companies use a cross-sectional approach to collect the data. Future research can use longitudinal approach to advance understanding of social media use and its impact over time.

5 Conclusion

The aim of this research was to provide a systematic review of the literature on the use of social media by b2b companies. It was found that b2b companies use social media, but not all companies consider it as part of their marketing strategies. The studies on social media in b2b context focused on the effect of social media, antecedents and barriers of adoption of social media, social media strategies, social media use, and measuring the effectiveness of social media.

The summary of the key observations provided from this literature review is the following:

- Facebook, Twitter and LinkedIn are the most famous social media platforms used by b2b companies.
- Social media has a positive effect on customer satisfaction.
- In systematically reviewing 70 publications on social media in the context of b2b companies it was observed that most of the studies use online surveys and online content analysis.
- Companies still look for ways to evaluate the effectiveness of social media.
- Innovativeness has a significant positive effect on companies' adoption to use social media.
- Lack of staff familiarity and technical skills are the main barriers affect adoption of social media by b2b.

This research has a number of limitations. First, only publications from the Scopus database were included in literature analysis and synthesis. Second, this research did not use a meta-analysis. To provide a broader picture of the research on social media in b2b context and reconcile conflicting findings of the existing studies future research should conduct a meta-analysis. It will advance the knowledge of the social media domain.

References

1. Ismagilova, E., Dwivedi, Y.K., Slade, E., Williams, M.D.: Electronic word of mouth (eWOM) in the marketing context: A state of the art analysis and future directions. Springer (2017)
2. Alalwan, A.A., Rana, N.P., Dwivedi, Y.K., Algharabat, R.: Social media in marketing: a review and analysis of the existing literature. Telematics Inform. **34**, 1177–1190 (2017)
3. Barreda, A.A., Bilgihan, A., Nusair, K., Okumus, F.: Generating brand awareness in online social networks. Comput. Hum. Behav. **50**, 600–609 (2015)
4. Salo, J.: Social media research in the industrial marketing field: review of literature and future research directions. Ind. Mark. Manag. **66**, 115–129 (2017)
5. Michaelidou, N., Siamagka, N.T., Christodoulides, G.: Usage, barriers and measurement of social media marketing: an exploratory investigation of small and medium B2B brands. Ind. Mark. Manag. **40**, 1153–1159 (2011)
6. Juntunen, M., Ismagilova, E., Oikarinen, E.-L.: B2B brands on Twitter: engaging users with a varying combination of social media content objectives, strategies, and tactics. Ind. Mark. Manag. (2019)
7. Pascucci, F., Ancillai, C., Cardinali, S.: Exploring antecedents of social media usage in B2B: a systematic review. Manag. Res. Rev. **41**, 629–656 (2018)
8. Ismagilova, E., Hughes, L., Dwivedi, Y.K., Raman, K.R.: Smart cities: advances in research —an information systems perspective. Int. J. Inf. Manag. **47**, 88–100 (2019)
9. Williams, M.D., Rana, N.P., Dwivedi, Y.K.: The unified theory of acceptance and use of technology (UTAUT): a literature review. J. Enterp. Inf. Manag. **28**, 443–488 (2015)
10. Agnihotri, R., Dingus, R., Hu, M.Y., Krush, M.T.: Social media: influencing customer satisfaction in B2B sales. Ind. Mark. Manag. **53**, 172–180 (2016)

11. Agnihotri, R., Kothandaraman, P., Kashyap, R., Singh, R.: Bringing "social" into sales: the impact of salespeople's social media use on service behaviors and value creation. J. Pers. Selling Sales Manag. **32**, 333–348 (2012)

12. Hsiao, S.-H., Wang, Y.-Y., Wang, T., Kao, T.-W.: How social media shapes the fashion industry: the spillover effects between private labels and national brands. Ind. Mark. Manag. (2019)

13. Itani, O.S., Agnihotri, R., Dingus, R.: Social media use in B2b sales and its impact on competitive intelligence collection and adaptive selling: examining the role of learning orientation as an enabler. Ind. Mark. Manag. **66**, 64–79 (2017)

14. Meire, M., Ballings, M., Van den Poel, D.: The added value of social media data in B2B customer acquisition systems: a real-life experiment. Decis. Support Syst. **104**, 26–37 (2017)

15. Rodriguez, M., Peterson, R.M., Krishnan, V.: Social media's influence on business-to-business sales performance. J. Pers. Selling Sales Manag. **32**, 365–378 (2012)

16. Keinänen, H., Kuivalainen, O.: Antecedents of social media B2B use in industrial marketing context: customers' view. J. Bus. Ind. Mark. **30**, 711–722 (2015)

17. Mehmet, M.I., Clarke, R.J.: B2B social media semantics: analysing multimodal online meanings in marketing conversations. Ind. Mark. Manag. **54**, 92–106 (2016)

18. Yang, C.C., Yang, H., Tang, X., Jiang, L.: Identifying implicit relationships between social media users to support social commerce. In: Proceedings of the 14th Annual International Conference on Electronic Commerce, pp. 41–47. ACM (2012)

19. Katona, Z., Sarvary, M.: Maersk line: B2B social media—"it's communication, not Marketing". Calif. Manag. Rev. **56**, 142–156 (2014)

20. Moore, J.N., Raymond, M.A., Hopkins, C.D.: Social selling: a comparison of social media usage across process stage, markets, and sales job functions. J. Mark. Theory Pract. **23**, 1–20 (2015)

21. Müller, L., Griesbaum, J., Mandl, T.: Social media relations in the german automotive market. In: IADIS International Conference ICT, Society and Human Beings, pp. 19–26. IADIS Press (2013)

22. Vasudevan, S., Kumar, F.J.P.: Social media and B2B brands: An indian perspective. Int. J. Mech. Eng. Technol. **9**, 767–775 (2018)

23. Lacka, E., Chong, A.: Usability perspective on social media sites' adoption in the B2B context. Ind. Mark. Manag. **54**, 80–91 (2016)

24. Lashgari, M., Sutton-Brady, C., Solberg Søilen, K., Ulfvengren, P.: Adoption strategies of social media in B2B firms: a multiple case study approach. J. Bus. Ind. Mark. **33**, 730–743 (2018)

25. Müller, J.M., Pommeranz, B., Weisser, J., Voigt, K.-I.: Digital, social media, and mobile marketing in industrial buying: still in need of customer segmentation? empirical evidence from Poland and Germany. Ind. Mark. Manag. **73**, 70–83 (2018)

26. Shaltoni, A.M.: From websites to social media: exploring the adoption of Internet marketing in emerging industrial markets. J. Bus. Ind. Mark. **32**, 1009–1019 (2017)

27. Cawsey, T., Rowley, J.: Social media brand building strategies in B2B companies. Mark. Intell. Planning **34**, 754–776 (2016)

28. Kasper, H., Koleva, I., Kett, H.: Social media matrix matching corporate goals with external social media activities. In: Simperl, E., et al. (eds.) ESWC 2012. LNCS, vol. 7540, pp. 233–244. Springer, Heidelberg (2015). https://doi.org/10.1007/978-3-662-46641-4_17

29. Mudambi, S.M., Sinha, J.I., Taylor, D.S.: Why B-to-B CEOs should be more social on social media. J. Bus. Bus. Mark. **26**, 103–105 (2019)

30. Swani, K., Milne, G., Brown, P.B.: Spreading the word through likes on Facebook: evaluating the message strategy effectiveness of Fortune 500 companies. J. Res. Interact. Mark. **7**, 269–294 (2013)

31. Gazal, K., Montague, I., Poudel, R., Wiedenbeck, J.: Forest products industry in a digital age: factors affecting social media adoption. Forest Prod. J. **66**, 343–353 (2016)
32. Kho, N.D.: B2B gets social media. EContent **31**, 26–30 (2008)
33. McShane, L., Pancer, E., Poole, M.: The influence of B to B social media message features on brand engagement: a fluency perspective. J. Bus. Bus. Mark. **26**, 1–18 (2019)
34. Kumar, V., Mirchandani, R.: Increasing the ROI of social media marketing. MIT sloan Manag. Rev. **54**, 55 (2012)
35. Niedermeier, K.E., Wang, E., Zhang, X.: The use of social media among business-to-business sales professionals in China: how social media helps create and solidify guanxi relationships between sales professionals and customers. J. Res. Interact. Mark. **10**, 33–49 (2016)
36. Guesalaga, R.: The use of social media in sales: individual and organizational antecedents, and the role of customer engagement in social media. Ind. Mark. Manag. **54**, 71–79 (2016)
37. Iankova, S., Davies, I., Archer-Brown, C., Marder, B., Yau, A.: A comparison of social media marketing between B2B, B2C and mixed business models. Ind. Mark. Manag. (2018)
38. Ogilvie, J., Agnihotri, R., Rapp, A., Trainor, K.: Social media technology use and salesperson performance: a two study examination of the role of salesperson behaviors, characteristics, and training. Ind. Mark. Manag. **75**, 55–65 (2018)
39. Agnihotri, R., Trainor, K.J., Itani, O.S., Rodriguez, M.: Examining the role of sales-based CRM technology and social media use on post-sale service behaviors in India. J. Bus. Res. **81**, 144–154 (2017)
40. Bolat, E., Kooli, K., Wright, L.T.: Businesses and mobile social media capability. J. Bus. Ind. Mark. **31**, 971–981 (2016)
41. Ali, Z., Shabbir, M.A., Rauf, M., Hussain, A.: To assess the impact of social media marketing on consumer perception. Int. J. Acad. Res. Account. Financ. Manag. Sci. **6**, 69–77 (2016)
42. Olotewo, J.: Social media marketing in emerging markets. Int. J. Online Mark. Res. **2**, 10 (2016)

Social Media Reporting and Firm Value

Abdalmuttaleb Musleh Al-Sartawi[(✉)] and Allam Hamdan

Ahlia University, Manama, Bahrain
amasartawi@hotmail.com, ahamdan@ahlia.edu.bh

Abstract. Technologies are changing how stakeholders, and investors access and capture data. Social Media has had a dramatic impact on how firms communicate with investors and stakeholders about their financial and sustainability reporting, giving them an edge over their competitors. The aim of this paper is to investigate the relationship between social media reporting and firm value of the GCC listed firms. To answer to research questions, the researchers collected cross-sectional data from a sample of 241 firms listed in the financial stock markets of the GCC for the year 2017. Additionally, an Index was used to calculate the total level of social media disclosure. The findings show that the 84% of firms in the GCC countries use social media, while 70% of these firms use SM for reporting. The results indicate that enhanced reporting levels through various social media channels significantly influence value of firms. These results have implications for GCC listed firms as it is important to examine how they can utilize social media to enhance their reporting process.

Keywords: Social media reporting · Tobin's Q · Sustainability reporting · GCC countries

1 Introduction

Technologies are changing how stakeholders, and mainly, investors access and capture a firm's data. Firms are recognizing the importance of the data they own and that the way it is used can provide them with an edge over their competitors. Social Media (SM), in particular, has had a dramatic impact on how firms engage in dialogue with investors as it allows in producing immediate and large quantities of data in many forms including videos, images, and audios. SM is based on the technological and ideological foundations of Web 2.0 which allows the creation and exchange of user generated content [18], unlike the Web 1.0 which is a set of static websites that do not provide interactive content.

While many firms are still using paper-based means and static websites (Web 1.0) to disclose information to stakeholder, others are jumping on the trending social media bandwagon (Web 2.0). Offering a variation in the way information reach investors will ensure that firms are being heard. In April 2013, the Securities and Exchange Commission issued a report stating that firms can use SM tools such as Facebook and Twitter to announce key information in compliance with Regulation Fair Disclosure [29]. Based on the Canadian Investor Relations Institute [11], the role of social media in financial and sustainability reporting is increasing as firms that may have primarily

© IFIP International Federation for Information Processing 2019
Published by Springer Nature Switzerland AG 2019
I. O. Pappas et al. (Eds.): I3E 2019, LNCS 11701, pp. 356–366, 2019.
https://doi.org/10.1007/978-3-030-29374-1_29

used social media for marketing purposes are now expanding their scope to include investors. Similarly, [22] claim that the use of internet-based communications by firms, mainly social media, is growing rapidly. Whereas, firms ignoring SM will be disadvantaged within the investment community [3].

These developments have considerable implications for accounting practices due to the demand of stakeholders for instant access to wide-ranging information related to a firm's governance, performance, finances, operations, and practices [22]. Therefore, amidst these significant developments the incentive for this paper is imminent, as it is important to examine how social media can be utilized to enhance the reporting process. [1] believes that the disclosure process should encompass the formal as well as the informal communications and interactions with the various stakeholders, and not simply sharing a single and static annual report on the firm's website. [7] found that institutional investors analyze firms and make recommendations based on information they find on social media searches.

Consequently, by improving the quality of communication and reducing information costs, firms may reduce the cost of their capital [5]. According to [23], that firms which aim to increase their value might choose a disclosure position which will allow their higher position to be disclosed, as opposed to firms with lower performance, which will choose a disclosure position to legitimize their performance. It enhances transparency by disclosing symmetrical information and reducing the costs associated with the agency problem, thus adhering to the principles of corporate governance [6]. This paper, henceforth, defines social media reporting as the public reporting of financial, operating and sustainability information by firms through social media.

Despite the importance of such a research paper, there are negligible studies that provide evidence on the relationship between social media reporting and firm value, certainly none related to the GCC countries. Therefore, this explanatory paper attempts to develop a better understanding of the effects of social media reporting on the firms listed in the GCC stock markets, whereby the main purpose is to determine whether information transparency has an impact on firm value, with a particular emphasis on Tobin's Q. This paper extends on previous research which focused on website-based disclosure through Web 1.0 and delves into social media reporting through Web 2.0.

From a theoretical perspective, this paper contributes to the literature by addressing a new and important topic within the context of the study. Moreover, from a practical perspective, the paper offers implications for firms to utilize social media to improve transparency and enhance their reporting process. This paper offers another contribution by proposing a Social Media Reporting Index (SMRI), based on the framework of prior studies relevant to web-based disclosure such as [4, 23]. As such, this paper's research questions are: What is the level of SM reporting in the GCC countries? And, what is the relationship between SM reporting and firm value.

The GCC is selected as a context to study due to its unique environment in relation to the advancements in technology. They have recently introduced their own corporate governance codes to enhance the social and regulatory environments, hence attracting more investors by encouraging voluntary disclosure. According to its geographical location, the GCC is at the heart of the Middle East, providing quick and efficient access to every market in the region. It has, therefore, become an intended destination for many foreign investors. These investors ask for financial information and carry on with certain decisions whether to continue with a certain company or not, and this is provided through social media.

The GCC countries such as Saudi Arabia and UAE are among the world's leading nations in terms of social-media growth and use, driven by smartphone ownership, high levels of internet penetration and a large, digitally savvy youth population [17]. Another study, [8], states that in the GCC, consumers and investors believe that social media encourages consumer-centric and transparent approaches, and is an instant platform to get news and information. Moreover, they believe that it offers for a cheap means of communication despite that SM poses a threat to traditional media by taking a piece of their market shares. This willingness to accept SM in business provides an interesting perspective for investigating the level of SM usage by firms and its relation to firm value.

2   Literature Review

Social media has boomed as a platform that people use to create content, share, network, and interact at a phenomenal rate. SM such as Facebook, Twitter, YouTube refer to technology-facilitated dialogue conducted through platforms including blogs, wikis, content sharing, social networking, and social bookmarking. According to [27], many firms are using social media as another outlet for their external and internal corporate communication about sustainability.

The value of SM is engagement. Corporate social media facilitates firm-directed, one-to-many communications that bypass traditional media and allow a firm to broadcast its intended message to a large network of stakeholders which is instantly made visible to all [20]. [24] found out that Chief Financial Officers believe that their decisions which are related to disclosures have high implications. Therefore, [19], claim that the recent changes in technology, capital markets and the media affect and are affected by firms' disclosure policies, whereby regulators as well as companies are starting to embrace social media as a viable disclosure channel for important information such as sustainable development activities. [12] claim that most large global corporations report at least some sustainability performance data annually through social media. Social media can, hence, be leveraged as to convey the firm policy and assist in their mission to support the United Nation's sustainable development goals.

[22] argue that social media provide investors, who have no direct channel of communication with the management, a voice to question decisions that give management incentives to take action. The use of SM for disclosure enables interaction between the stakeholders, and not merely between the stakeholders and the firms. This adds a new dimension to corporate reporting, as what had been previously found regarding investors' reactions to corporate reporting cannot be applied to their reactions in today's dynamic environment [19]. [27] argue that the level of commitment to sustainability reported through social media may yield important insights regarding the firm's business strategy. For example, a firm's mission statement may directly reference sustainability-related values. [10] argues that as investors and other stakeholders depend on SM for firm news and investment advice, firms that fail to take part in the conversation will be singled out for remaining silent. Hence, the previous researches

which focused more on Web 1.0 need to be extended methodically to include more relevant issues such as SM disclosure on sustainable development activities.

SM channels are more widely available to investors and allow for interaction between users via postings and comments [14]. Firms usually choose SM as a part of their overall strategy to for online disclosure which aims to create a positive reputation and increase their value [25]. Firms also use SM as part of their strategy to reduce information asymmetry, increase transparency, and reduce agency-related costs [8]. Agency losses normally arise when there is a conflict between the desires or goals of the principal (shareholder) and the agent (manager), and it is difficult or expensive for the shareholder to determine what the manager is actually doing [14]. The agency theory hence attempts to reduce agency losses by specifying mechanisms such as tying their compensation with shareholder returns.

Increased transparency is often achieved through voluntary disclosure. Therefore, to let the shareholders know what they are doing, managers need to reach stakeholders through different medium. [13] claim that managers know that shareholders aim to control their behavior through monitoring activities. Consequently, managers have incentives to disclose more information to show shareholders that they are acting optimally. Managers might opt to disclose information through SM due to the wide-range of benefits it offers such as low cost, timely information, and a wide-reach two-way communication platform. More transparency and better disclosure are associated with equality among investors, less insider trading and lowers uncertainty in investment decisions [25]. For example, when the CEO of Netflix posted on Facebook that Netflix's monthly online viewing is more than one billion hours, the stock price increased in one day by 6.2% [30]. This indicates that SM disclosure has a direct influence on stock price, and by extension firm value.

[8] argued that social media channels, mainly Twitter, reduces information asymmetry, as other researchers [9] found that by increasing the dissemination of the same information leads to a reduction in information asymmetry. According to [4] enhancing voluntary disclosure can motivate top managers to improve firm value because of increased pressure from the intensive monitoring of outside shareholders. As market values depend on investor confidence presumably through increased and transparent disclosure, market evaluation could be measured using Tobin's Q. Tobin's Q is computed as the ratio of the market value of the firm's outstanding debt and equity divided by the book value of assets [16]. A prior study by [21] used Tobin's Q to examine the relationship between corporate disclosure and performance, and they reported a positive and significant association between the two variables.

Several researches have attempted to explore social media reporting; however, as this is a new trend, these studies mainly focus on the literature, SM adoption, and the determinants of social media reporting [10, 19, 25, 30]. From these studies, we can assume that the topic of SM as a disclosure platform is gaining momentum, and this paper offers a contribution by taking part in the conversation. However, what differentiated this paper from previous studies is that this study empirically investigates the relationship between SM disclosure and firm value. This paper, therefore, hypothesizes that: There is a relationship between social media reporting and firm value measured through Tobin's Q.

3 Research Methodology

The empirical study of the current research depended on a sample which consisted of all the listed firms in the GCC stock exchange markets for the year 2017. The required data were gathered from 241 companies out of 289 companies listed under financial sector. The financial sector was chosen for the study due to the large size of the banking industry in the GCC countries. The GCC countries are gradually undergoing a shift in their economies, from oil-dependent economies to more diversified economies, focusing mainly on the financial sector as the largest non-oil contributor to their GDPs. Table 1 shows the sample distribution according to country and industry type (Banks, Insurance and Investment).

Table 1. Sample distribution according to country and industry

Industry	KSA	UAE	QAT	BAH	KUW	Per industry	
Banks	11	33	8	7	8	67	28%
Insurance	32	31	4	5	7	79	32%
Investment	7	19	4	10	55	95	40%
Per country	**50**	**83**	**16**	**22**	**70**	**241**	**100%**

Consequently, the study applies a two-stage process to measure (1) the level of usage of Social Media (SM) in UAE firms as well as (2) the level of Social Media Reporting of those firms. Therefore, some firms might use social media, but not for reporting financial and sustainability information. These were excluded from the study.

The first stage involved measuring the social media usage by GCC listed firms. In order to measure the percentage of usage of SM, the study use the binary data method, i.e., if a firm uses any type of social media platform (Facebook, Twitter, Instagram, Snapchat, YouTube, LinkedIn, others) it received a score of 1. However, if the firm did not use any form of SM platform it received a score of 0. Similarly, the second stage involved measuring the level of SMR for firms using SM in stage 1. So, if a firm used SM to report financial/sustainability information it received a score of 1, and if a firm did not use its SM to report financial/sustainability information it received a score of 0. Accordingly, the Index for each firm was calculated by dividing the total earned scores of the firm by the total maximum possible scours appropriate for the firm. To secure the data on the social media applications and channels from any updates or changes during the time of the study, all information, hyperlinks and images were downloaded and saved as HTML files beforehand. Below formula shows the way of calculating the SMR index.

$$SMR = \sum_{i=1}^{} \frac{di}{n}$$

Where:

di: disclosed item equals One if the bank meets the checklist item and zero otherwise.

n: equals maximum score each bank can obtain.

To test the hypothesis, the following regression model was developed using SMR as an independent variable, and Tobin's Q as the criterion variable. Additionally, the study used firm age, firm size and financial leverage as control variables (Table 2).

Model

$$TQ = \beta_0 + \beta_1 SMD_i + \beta_2 LFSZ_i + \beta_3 LVG_i + \beta_4 AGE_i + \varepsilon_i$$

Table 2. Study variables

Code	Variable name	Operationalization
Dependent variable		
TQ	Market value add	Total Market Value/Total Assets Value
Independent variables –:		
SMR	Social media reporting %	Total scored items by the company/Total maximum scores
Control variables:		
LFSZ	Firm size	Natural logarithm of Total Assets
LVG	Leverage	Total liabilities/Total Assets
AGE	Firm age	The difference between the establishing date of the firm and the report date

4 Data Analysis

4.1 Descriptive Statistics

Table 3 reports the descriptive analysis of the independent, dependent and control variables. The overall mean of Tobin's Q was 1.07 by GCC firms with a minimum of 0.68 and maximum of 2.55 indicating that the majority of the firms are overvalued as their stocks are higher than the replacement costs of their assets. This proxy exposes the potential of added value of the firm as viewed by the market as a reflection of its performance. Therefore, if Tobin's Q is greater than 1, it indicates that the firm has a market value exceeding the price of the replacement of its assets. With regards social media usage, show the show that the overall level of firms in the GCC countries that use social media was 84%, which is considered as a moderate level of usage of SM. Additionally, the results show that of the 84% of firms that use SM, 70% use SM for financial and sustainability disclosure, which again indicates a moderate level of disclosure through SM.

In addition to the dependent and independent variables, the descriptive statistics for control variables show that the mean of firm size was 84, 43,579, with a minimum of 4,

06,832 and a maximum 3,412,461.54, implying large firms. As according to Table 5 firm size was not normally distributed due to the significance of the Kolmogorov-Smirnov test being less than 5%, so natural logarithm was used in the regression analysis to reduce skewness and bring the distribution of the variables nearer to normality. Moreover, the mean leverage of the firms was approximately 42%, with a minimum of 4% and a maximum of 87%, indicating that most GCC firms have a medium level of debts. Finally, firm age ranges from 2 to 64 with a mean of 33.45.

Table 3. Descriptive Statistics for continues variables

Variables	N	Minimum	Maximum	Mean	Std. Deviation
TQ	241	0.68	2.55	1.07	0.09025
Firm size	241	406832.3	3412461.54	8443579	220268.40264
LVG	241	0.04	0.87	0.4254	0.26508
AGE	241	2	64	33.45	13.004

Descriptive Statistics for non-continuous variables

Variables	Achieved		Not achieved	
	Number	Percentage	Number	Percentage
SMR	89	70%	38	30%
SML	96	84%	18	16%

4.2 Testing Regression Assumptions

A Variance Inflation Factor (VIF) test was used to check the data for multicollinearity. The VIF scores for each variable, both independent and dependent, are reported in Table 4. The results indicate that since no VIF score exceeded 10 for any variable in the model, while no Tolerance score was below 0.2. So, it was concluded that there is no threat of multicollinearity.

Table 4. Collinearity statistics test

Model	Tolerance	VIF
SMR	.717	1.107
Firm size	.805	1.206
LVG	.733	1.080
AGE	.826	1.098

In addition to test for homoscedasticity and linearity, an analysis of residuals, plots of the residuals against predicted values as well as the Q-Q and scatter plots were conducted. Therefore, wherever there was a problem of heteroskedasticity the data were transformed. Autocorrelation test was not conducted in this research as the data used are cross-sectional.

Table 5. Kolmogorov-Smirnov test

	Statistics	Sig.
Tobin's Q	2.137	0.165
SMR	2.009	0.381
Firm size	2.044	0.003
LVG	2.095	0.540
AGE	2.113	0.347

Finally, the Kolmogorov-Smirnov test used to assess the normality of the collected data for the variables. As Table 5 illustrates, a significance level of more than 5% for all the variables except for firm size indicates that the data are normally distributed. With regards to firm size however, the variable was adjusted using natural logarithm.

4.3   Testing the Hypotheses

Table 6 reports the findings of the regression analysis. The findings indicate that the model was reflecting the relationship between the variables in a statistically appropriate way. According to the table, the model has an adjusted R2 of 0.303 which shows that the model explains approximately 30% of the variation in the Tobin's Q amongst the GCC listed firms. Additionally, the probability of the F-statistic with a significance 0.026 means that the independent variables are significant in interpreting the dependent variable, Tobin's Q.

Table 6. Regression analysis

Variables	Beta	T. test	Sig.
SMR	.432	8.678	.008***
Firm size	.277	2.683	.187
LVG	−.056	−.938	.207
AGE	−.184	−1.546	.000***
R^2		.303	
F		16.283	
Prob. (F)		.026	

*Prob. < 10%, **Prob. < 5%, ***Prob. < 1%

The main hypothesis of the study states that there is a relationship between the level of social media reporting and firm value (Tobin's Q) by firms listed in the GCC stock exchange markets. The result indicates that there is a significant and positive relationship between the level of SMR and firm value, that is, the higher the level of disclosure, the higher the Tobin's Q. This is in line with the studies conducted by [5] who suggest that the level and quality of disclosure affect firm value. Another study conducted in the MENA region [2] found a positive relationship between disclosure and firm value. This indicates that investors and other stakeholders react positively to information about the sustainable development activities that firms undertake towards achieving their sustainable goals. However, an earlier study conducted by [15] in the Middle East found no relationship between disclosure and firm value, which could be due to the lack of control for the endogeneity of the disclosure variable in relation to Tobin's Q. One reason for this could be the potential of SM as a two-way communication platform that allows timely dissemination of information to investors, shareholders and other stakeholders. This way all parties involved transmit information instantaneously, which helps them in making well-informed decisions. Furthermore, firms are able to receive instant feedback from their stakeholders which helps managers in making improvements, accordingly, thus satisfying all parties involved and reducing costs related to agency.

With regards to the control variables, the study found a significant and positive relationship between firm value and age. Based on [28] who also found a positive association between age and firm value, investors have a higher level of confidence and trust in older firms due to their experience and maturity. On the other hand, this contradicts the study by [26] who claim that firm value declines as investors learn about the firm's profitability or as their uncertainty resolves over time. Finally, the results show no relationship between firm value and the other control variables, firm size and leverage.

5 Conclusion and Recommendations

The paper aimed to address several research questions: (1) the level of social media usage by GCC listed firms, (2) the level of social media reporting (SMR) by GCC listed firms and (3) the relationship between social media reporting and firm value of the GCC listed firms. To answer to research questions, the researchers collected data from a sample of 241 firms listed in the financial stock markets of the GCC for the year 2017. Due to the nature of the data collected which is cross-sectional only one year was chosen to gauge the data at a specific point in time.

The findings show that the 84% of firms in the GCC countries use social media, while 70% of these firms use SM for financial and sustainability disclosure. The results also confirm the hypothesis that enhanced disclosure levels through various social media channels of GCC listed firms significantly influence the firm value of these firms. This indicates that investors react positively to firms which engage in sustainable development activities, and communicate this clearly to stakeholders. In the days of Web 1.0, firms used to simply publish their annual reports as PDFs online, thus failing to capture the opportunities of two-way communication. However, when firms follow a similar approach to their utilization of social media, it is considered as a wasted potential. This paper recommends that firms give their information disclosure a face, whereby they listen to stakeholders more than they talk. Firms can, therefore, get insights, new ideas, complaints as well as warning signs to change.

From a theoretical standpoint, these results have implications for both social media reporting literatures and value relevance literatures in the GCC countries. From a practical perspective, this study provides contributions to GCC's government, policymakers and regulators with regards to a trending issue such as the modern disclosure tools that could be used by firms to increase transparency and reduce the agency problem. Policy makers and regulators in the GCC can make use of information from this research in setting new policies on social media disclosure in line with the Securities and Exchange Commission which recognized the potential of SM as a platform for reporting.

This paper suggests having a study that further investigates the relationship between social media reporting and other types of performance such as financial and sustainability performance. Future studies could also investigate the level of corporate social responsibility disclosure or intellectual capital of firms on social media.

References

1. Adams, C.A.: The international integrated reporting council: a call to action. Crit. Perspect. Account. **27**, 23–28 (2015)
2. Al-Akra, M., Ali, M.J.: The value relevance of corporate voluntary disclosure in the Middle East: the case of Jordan. J. Account. Public Policy **31**(5), 533–549 (2012)
3. Alexander, R.M., Gentry, J.K.: Using social media to report financial results. Bus. Horiz. **57** (2), 161–167 (2014)
4. Al-Sartawi, A.: Corporate governance and intellectual capital: evidence from Gulf cooperation council countries. Acad. Account. Finan. Stud. J. **22**(1), 1–12 (2018)
5. Al-Sartawi, A.: Does institutional ownership affect the level of online financial disclosure? Acad. Accounti. Finan. Stud. J. **22**(2), 1–10 (2018)
6. Al-Sartawi, A., Sanad, Z.: Institutional ownership and corporate governance: evidence from Bahrain. Afro-Asian J. Finan. Account. **9**(1), 101–115 (2019)
7. Arab Social Media Report (2015). http://sites.wpp.com/govtpractice//~/media/wppgov/files/arabsocialmediareport-2015.pdf
8. Blankespoor, E., Miller, G.S., White, H.D.: The role of dissemination in market liquidity: evidence from firms' use of Twitter'. Account. Rev. **89**(1), 79–112 (2014)
9. Bushee, B.J., Core, J.E., Guay, W., Hamm, S.J.: The role of the business press as an information intermediary. J. Account. Res. **48**(1), 1–19 (2010)
10. Cade, N.L.: Corporate social media: how two-way disclosure channels influence investors. Account. Organ. Soc. **68**, 63–79 (2018)
11. CIRI (2012). The role of social media in performance reporting: A discussion brief. The Canadian Institute of Chartered Accountants. https://www.cpacanada.ca/-/media/site/business-and-accounting-resources/docs/role-of-social-media-in-performance-reporting-a-discussion-brief-2012.pdf?la=en&hash=394D1825712E8FC2F1ED7DBC68747B12F1E2225C
12. Clark, A.: Selling sustainability, 5 February 2008. Accessed 2 June 2019. http://www.climatebiz.com/blog/2008/02/06/selling-sustainability
13. Dolinšek, T., Tominc, P., Lutar Skerbinjek, A.: The determinants of internet financial reporting in Slovenia. Online Inf. Rev. **38**(7), 842–860 (2014)
14. Eisenhardt, K.M.: Agency theory: an assessment and review. Acad. Manag. Rev. **14**(1), 57–74 (1989)
15. Hassan, O.A., Romilly, P., Giorgioni, G., Power, D.: The value relevance of disclosure: Evidence from the emerging capital market of Egypt. Int. J. Account. **44**(1), 79–102 (2009)
16. Himmelberg, C.P., Hubbard, R.G., Palia, D.: Understanding the determinants of managerial ownership and the link between ownership and performance. J. Finan. Econ. **53**(3), 353–384 (1999)

17. Internet World Stats: CIA World Factbook: Middle East Media.org. (2018). https://www. zdnet.com/article/whats-driving-middle-easts-rush-to-social-media/
18. Kaplan, A.M., Haenlein, M.: Users of the world, unite! the challenges and opportunities of social media. Bus. Horiz. **53**(1), 59–68 (2010)
19. Lardo, A., Dumay, J., Trequattrini, R., Russo, G.: Social media networks as drivers for intellectual capital disclosure: evidence from professional football clubs. J. Intell. Capital **18** (1), 63–80 (2017)
20. Lee, L.F., Hutton, A.P., Shu, S.: The role of social media in the capital market: evidence from consumer product recalls. J. Account. Res. **53**(2), 367–404 (2015)
21. Lishenga, L., Mbaka, A.: The link between compliance with corporate governance disclosure code and performance for Kenyan firms. Net J. Bus. Manag. **3**(1), 13–26 (2015)
22. Lodhia, S., Stone, G.: Integrated reporting in an internet and social media communication environment: conceptual insights. Aust. Account. Rev. **27**(1), 17–33 (2017)
23. Meek, G.K., Roberts, C.B., Gray, S.J.: Factors influencing voluntary annual report disclosures by US, UK and continental European multinational corporations. J. Int. Bus. Stud. **26**(3), 555–572 (1995)
24. Miller, G.S., Skinner, D.J.: The evolving disclosure landscape: how changes in technology, the media, and capital markets are affecting disclosure. J. Account. Res. **53**(2), 221–239 (2015)
25. Mohamed, E., Basuony, M.: The use of social media for corporate disclosure by companies listed in the GCC. Inf. Technol. Manag. Soc. ITMSOC–Trans. Innov. Bus. Eng. **1**(1), 14–20 (2016)
26. Pástor, Ľ., Pietro, V.: Stock valuation and learning about profitability. J. Finan. **58**(5), 1749–1789 (2003)
27. Reilly, A.H., Hynan, K.A.: Corporate communication, sustainability, and social media: it's not easy (really) being green. Bus. Horiz. **57**(6), 747–758 (2014)
28. Susanti, N., Restiana, N.G.: What's the Best Factor to Determining Firm Value? J. Keuangan dan Perbankan **22**(2), 301–309 (2018)
29. U.S. SEC: SEC Says Social Media OK for Company Announcements if Investors Are Alerted (2013). https://www.sec.gov/news/press-release/2013-2013-51htm
30. Zhou, M., Lei, L., Wang, J., Fan, W., Wang, A.G.: Social media adoption and corporate disclosure. J. Inf. Syst. **29**(2), 23–50 (2014)

Social Media Information Literacy – What Does It Mean and How Can We Measure It?

Matthias Murawski[1(⊠)], Julian Bühler[1], Martin Böckle[1], Jan Pawlowski[2], and Markus Bick[1]

[1] ESCP Europe Business School Berlin, Berlin, Germany
{mmurawski,jbuehler,mboeckle,mbick}@escpeurope.eu
[2] Ruhr West University of Applied Sciences, Mülheim an der Ruhr, Germany
Jan.Pawlowski@hs-ruhrwest.de

Abstract. In times of increasing importance of social media services, we have to rethink information literacy. One of the key assumptions of existing information literacy constructs is "static" information, meaning that information does not change. But compared to traditional and mostly unidirectional media services such as printed newspapers or television, this does not reflect the reality of a social media context. Here, information can be characterized as "dynamic", meaning that, for example, every user can easily modify information before sharing it (again). A measurement construct covering these novel aspects of information literacy is missing, so far. Thus, the main objective of this paper is to develop a rigor and updated construct to measure and quantify social media information literacy of an individual social media user. We selected a comprehensive construct development framework that guided us through the investigation, and which includes qualitative as well as quantitative analyses. The outcome is a theoretically grounded and empirically derived social media information literacy (SMIL) construct. The paper ends with a discussion of potential future research directions.

Keywords: Construct development · Information literacy · Social media · Social media information literacy (SMIL)

1 Introduction

In an increasingly digital environment, social media services have become a key channel for individuals to share information and news [1], but are understood and used heterogeneously [2]. Compared to traditional and mostly unidirectional media services (such as printed newspapers or television), these services change the characteristic of distributed information towards being dynamic. Particularly the concept of user-generated content (UGC) implies that users can easily modify information, thus allowing them to add their own opinions or even change the meaning dynamically [e.g., 3, 4].

But besides social media advantages such as high transportation velocity and network effects that help spread important information among large user groups, also disadvantages can be observed. One major disadvantage of social media services and

I. O. Pappas et al. (Eds.): I3E 2019, LNCS 11701, pp. 367–379, 2019.
https://doi.org/10.1007/978-3-030-29374-1_30

the related UGC is that no trusted authority exists which verifies the quality of information distributed through the services' networks. For example, it is relatively easy to produce misleading or false information, which is often referred to as fake news [5]. Fake news are omnipresent in today's world and have the potential to cause massive social and monetary damage on every level, i.e., from an individual to a political or societal level [6]. In this context, the recent announcement of the French president Macron to introduce a law to ban fake news on the internet during French election campaigns [7] and a similar law that came into effect in Germany at the beginning of 2018 [8] emphasize the relevance of this topic. Another trend with increasing importance regarding UGC is electronic word-of-mouth (eWOM), meaning that (potential) consumers exchange information regarding products or brands in social media environments [9, 10].

Obviously, from the perspective of an individual social media user, these developments require certain competencies on how to deal with information [11]. The established term for this is *information literacy* which contains, among others, the ability to assess the credibility of information and the reliability of sources [12]. Although a relatively large body of knowledge on information literacy exists, two gaps related to this topic can be identified. First, most definitions and conceptual works of information literacy still consider information as "static", thereby ignoring its "dynamic" character which is one key feature of information in the social media context. Second, there is a lack of rigor measurement construct development. This statement counts for both general information literacy constructs as well as more specific constructs, i.e., those that consider a certain context such as social media. For instance, *metaliteracy* [13, 14] as an enhanced information literacy concept that aims at covering the dynamic aspects of information in a social media context is based on conceptual work but does not provide any rigor measurement items. Both gaps hinder accurate academic progress (e.g., in terms of empirical studies) as this would require a precise definition and valid measurement items. Thus, the research question of this paper is *what comprises information literacy in the social media context and how can we measure it?*

Our main objective is to answer this question by developing a rigor measurement construct of what we call *social media information literacy* (SMIL). We have selected the established construct development guideline of MacKenzie et al. [15], which serves as the methodological framework of our study. Starting with developing a conceptual definition of SMIL and the identification of respective items, several stages are proceeded to ensure content validity and general scale validity, thereby conducting both qualitative as well as quantitative methods. Our main contribution is a rigor construct to measure information literacy of an individual social media service user. In other words, we develop a way to quantify social media information literacy.

The structure of this paper is as follows. First, the concept of information literacy and its current state of research are briefly outlined. After that, the development of the SMIL construct according to the step-by-step guideline of MacKenzie et al. [15] is presented. The paper ends with a discussion of future research opportunities and applications of the SMIL construct.

2 Information Literacy and Social Media

Since the rapid increase and the abundance of published information online, research regarding *information literacy* (IL) is becoming increasingly important. The term has gained momentum but also reveals limitations in new application areas, such as social media, where UGC is changing dynamically. Research endeavors have shown that similar literacy concepts exist with blurring borders between the definitions of terms and their goals. For example, Pinto et al. [16, p. 464] define IL as "the skills, competencies, knowledge and values to access, use and communicate information". Godwin [17, p. 267] suggests that IL refers to "recognizing appropriate information, collaborating, synthesizing and adapting it wisely and ethically". These definitions also represent that current attempts of defining IL are diverse and aligned to a specific context such as *education* [18] or *work* [12]. The term information literacy is often used in combination with *media* [19, 20], *online* [21, 22] or *computer* [23, 24], as well as using the term of IL *skills* [25] and IL *competencies* [26]. Existing IL models are usually described with corresponding tasks (e.g., search information, use information, etc.). This 'task perspective' is the predominant approach in studies about information literacy and can be linked to the life cycle model of information management of Krcmar [27]. This model contains five views: managing (1) demand for information, (2) information sources, (3) information resources, (4) supply of information, and (5) application of information and is often used as the structural basis for related research.

Traditional models on IL mainly ignore specific features and characteristics of social media. One of the few conceptual works of IL in the context of social media is the *7i framework* [28, 29] that consists of seven sub-competencies: (1) Information needs; (2) Information sources; (3) Information access and seeking strategy; (4) Information evaluation; (5) Information use; (6) Information presentation; (7) Information process & finding reflection [29]. Although numbered, Stanoevska-Slabeva et al. [29, p. 9] emphasize that there is no strict sequence: "teachers and pupils [...] also frequently switched in an interactive manner back and forth among the sub-competences before moving to the next sub-competence in the sequence. For example, if the evaluation of the found information (sub-competence 4) reveals that more information is needed, than the process was rather started from the beginning in order to refine the information needs (sub-competence 1) or went back to refine the information access and retrieval strategy (sub-competence 3)." Although the 7i framework seems to be a comprehensive approach at first glance, one limitation is that it is "only" derived from literature but not developed according to rigor construct development procedures.

Another more holistic approach is the concept of *metaliteracy*. According to Jacobson and Mackey [13], metaliteracy is envisioned as a "comprehensive model for information literacy to advance critical thinking and reflection in social media, open learning setting and online communities" [13, p. 84] and expands the standard literacy concept. This new term unifies related literacy concepts (e.g., media literacy, visual literacy etc.) and provides a so-called meta-perspective because current environments are much more social, open, multimodal and enriched with media combined with collaborative functionalities. Jacobson and Mackey [13] apply their model to teaching including the following elements: (1) Understand Format Type and Delivery Mode, (2) Evaluate User Feedback as Active Researcher, (3) Create a Context for User generated Information, (4) Evaluate Dynamic Content Critically, (5) Produce Original Content in Multiple Media Formats, (6) Understand Personal Privacy, Information Ethics and Intellectual Property Issues, and (7) Share Information in Participatory Environments [13, p. 87], which is again in line with the general structure of information management suggested by Krcmar [27]. However, similar to the case of the 7i framework, a rigor measurement construct for metaliteracy is not suggested, which constitutes a barrier of empirical investigations in this regard.

3   Construct Development

Based on the roots of construct development [30], the most recent guideline with a focus on IS is the paper of MacKenzie et al. [15]. Compared to other approaches which have been applied recently [31, 32], one of the key benefits of the guideline of MacKenzie et al. [15] is a comprehensive description of how to develop an appropriate conceptual definition of the focal construct (before starting with content validity checks that is often the first step in other guidelines). This is very important for our project as we find that current definitions of information literacy do not reflect the dynamic character of information. Thus, the development of a clear and concise updated definition of information literacy is the basis of our study. Furthermore, MacKenzie et al. [15] discuss often underutilized but useful techniques for providing evidence, e.g., regarding content validity. Therefore, we have selected the guidelines of MacKenzie et al. [15] as our core paper and their suggested steps serve as the basis for our study.

3.1   Conceptualization (Step 1)

Step 1 refers to a summary of factors authors should consider in the conceptualization phase, based on a literature review of previous theoretical and empirical research as well as a review of literature with a focus on related constructs. To get an overview of current measurements of social media skills and competencies in the fast growing body of social media literature, we conducted such a literature review and applied the guidelines proposed by Webster and Watson [33]. To define the scope at the beginning of the review, an initial explorative search using Google Scholar and other scientific databases (i.e., Scopus, ScienceDirect, ACM, Proquest, JSTOR and EBSCO) was conducted to find out about current approaches of how to measure social media skills or competencies and to identify them through the appropriate search query. After reading and analyzing initial search results and testing several combinations of keyword on Scopus, we conducted a search query with the following string:

```
information literacy AND social media OR construct* OR
measure*
```

To include the full range of publications, we applied the truncation (asterisk character) at the keywords *construct* and *measure* and considered all variation of these terms such as plural or verb forms. A portfolio of 88 core articles were retrieved to reach the ultimate goal of the process which is to *develop a conceptual definition of the construct*. The retrieved papers are part of a very heterogenous academic field ranging from *educational* and *bibliographic* studies to articles dealing with *work*. We did not narrow down the scope of literacy initially, but considered articles that refer to aspects such as *metaliteracy, transliteracy* [34], or *reading literacy* [35]. An individual analysis of all articles followed for the purpose of identifying literacy definitions used by the various authors. We could identify information literacy definitions made by authors or references to such definitions given in other papers for 59 publications. We proceeded with an iterative word-by-word analysis of the definitions to extract 23 major keywords in the first iteration and 18 in the second iteration that were repetitively used. We ultimately condensed these keywords to certain clusters that describe the treatment of information in general or with special regard to social media, characterize the treatment, or address influencing factors. Based on the clustered keywords, we finalize the first step (conceptualization) of the agenda of MacKenzie et al. [15] by giving the definition displayed in Fig. 1.

We followed the objective of a concise definition and, hence, aggregated common terms to clusters, i.e., we combined related terms like *select information* and *retrieve information* to the topic of *obtaining information*. *Communication of information* in the context of SMIL is understood as a unidirectional, but also a bidirectional exchange of information with the help of social media services. Signature examples would be a tweet and response on Twitter, or comment and reply below a YouTube video. The literature review suggests that *re-evaluation* should be perceived as a self-contained cluster that can be differentiated from *evaluation* by adding additional interactive exchange between users and integration of their feedback.

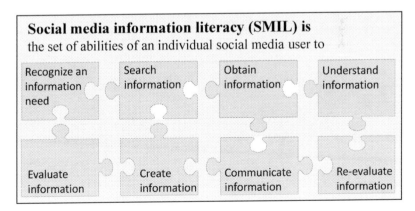

Fig. 1. Definition of social media information literacy (SMIL)

372   M. Murawski et al.

3.2 Development of Measures (Steps 2 and 3)

The first set of items stems from two sources. First, we screened the literature we had selected for the literature review (see 3.1) for measurement items. Second, we derived further items from our own SMIL definition which is in line with the recommendations of MacKenzie et al. [15]. In total, we generated 40 items.

According to the procedure described in the core paper, we then aimed at analyzing content validity of the items. Most content validity checks are of qualitative nature, e.g., interviews. However, a limitation lies in the very subjective answers of such approaches. We therefore applied the more quantitative approach of Hinkin and Tracey [36] in which a rater has to assess the 'fit' of each item to the components of a construct; in our case the eight SMIL components. Given the 40 items, this is a very inconvenient approach for the raters, as it results in 320 decisions (40 items times 8 SMIL components) to be made by one respondent. Similar to Hinkin and Tracey [36], we conducted the survey as part of official lectures in master's programmes at our affiliation (a business school located in Germany) to ensure enough time for responding. By this, we were able to collect 79 completed surveys which is above the recommended benchmark of n = 50 [36] for this type of content validity check.

We then applied one-way repeated measures ANOVA calculations to assess whether the eight steps are significantly different from each other for each item. We found for 14 out of the 40 items that there were steps not significantly different from another step. These cases were discussed among the authors of this paper, and with further department members during a research seminar. Based on this, we decided to rephrase some of the items to improve clarity as suggested by Wieland et al. [37], and, in turn, improve the content validity of our set of items. Table 1 lists the resulting set of 40 items.

Table 1. Overview of 40 SMIL items

Code	Phrase
REC_1	I am able to recognise the information I need
REC_2	I am able to realize my need for information
REC_3	I am able to recognize the information I do not need
SEA_1	I am able to decide where and how to find the information I need
SEA_2	I am able to technically access information
SEA_3	I am able to apply appropriate search strategies (e.g., use of meaningful keywords)
SEA_4	I am able to limit search strategies (e.g., date, hashtag, user)
SEA_5	I am able to choose appropriate sources when searching for information
OBT_1	I am able to collect information
OBT_2	I am able to retrieve information
OBT_3	I am able to choose appropriate information
UND_1	I am able to interpret information
UND_2	I am able to find consensus among sources

(continued)

Table 1. (*continued*)

Code	Phrase
UND_3	I am able to understand the intention of information
UND_4	I am able to identify points of agreement and disagreement among information sources
UND_5	I am able to understand type and delivery mode of information
EVAL_1	I am able to evaluate the relevance of information
EVAL_2	I am able to evaluate the credibility of information
EVAL_3	I am able to evaluate the accuracy of information
EVAL_4	I am able to evaluate the quality of information
EVAL_5	I am able to identify if information is a fake
EVAL_6	I am able to identify if information is a rumour
CREAT_1	I am able to rephrase information to clarify its meaning
CREAT_2	I am able to create context for information
CREAT_3	I am able to modify identified information
CREAT_4	I am able to merge information
CREAT_5	I am able to change the scope by reducing information
CREAT_6	I am able to enrich identified information
CREAT_7	I am able to design information
COMM_1	I am able to display information for a given audience
COMM_2	I am able to share information with others
COMM_3	I am able to provide feedback
COMM_4	I am able to communicate information safely and securely
COMM_5	I am able to exchange information
COMM_6	I am able to provide constructive criticism to other users
REVAL_1	I am able to use reflective practices in order to re-evaluate information
REVAL_2	I am able to evaluate users' reaction on my content
REVAL_3	I am able to evaluate information from interaction with other users
REVAL_4	I am able to reconsider my existing evaluation of information
REVAL_5	I am able to identify the benefits of re-evaluating information

According to MacKenzie et al. [15], the next, fourth step would be specifying the research model. Because of the limited space of a research-in-progress paper, we decided to integrate the illustration of the model specification (step 4) with the data collection (step 5) and scale evaluation and refinement (step 6). We thus present the final model in the end of Sect. 3.3 highlighting the initial model of step 4 and the changes made during the scale evaluation.

3.3   Scale Evaluation and Refinement, and Model Specification (Step 5 and 6)

Decisions about the investigated sample are especially crucial for testing a newly specified model [15]. For consistency, we decided to address a larger number of participants with similar characteristics compared to the initial target group of master students we asked during the item generation step. But we expanded the target area to a second UK-based business school to gather a data set of students with even more heterogeneous backgrounds, which allows us to control for cross-cultural differences. This data set of 96 valid responses account for approximately one-third of the overall sample for this stage. The remaining two-thirds (n = 186 valid responses) were collected with the help of the *Amazon Mechanical Turk*[1] (MTurk) crowdsourcing platform, making our overall sample more diverse by adding answers from various countries around the world such as the USA and India. After reliability checks, the final sample we could use for the scale evaluation consists of 282 participants with an average age of 34.09 years. This is a sample size large enough to perform an exploratory factor analysis (EFA) which is suggested by MacKenzie et al. [15] as a suitable method to evaluate an item scale. The 160 male and 114 female respondents— 8 decided not to disclose their gender—needed 8.42 min to fill in the questionnaire that was distributed.

We again asked to rate the 40 items (see Table 1) on the same 5-Point Likert scale and transferred the raw data to IBM SPSS for further analyses. The main focus lay on the EFA calculation that included all 40 item ratings of all 282 responses. This method can be used to associate a number of correlated and measured items to superordinate factors. We initially used Eigenvalues of 1 or above as the standard threshold for factor extraction and rotated the factors using the Varimax method. This approach revealed some rather unprecise item-factor relations though with only some clear extracted factors. Following our conceptualization, we could expect eight unique factors, but based on the Eigenvalues, we received only seven factors. However, relevant indicators such as a good KMO value of .949, a significant Bartlett test, communalities of 0.464 for the weakest items or above, and ultimately 58.22% of the variance explained indicated a reasonable model specification. Therefore, we proceeded with the refinement as referred to in step 6 of the core paper.

First, we fixed the number of factors to be extracted to eight as operationalized in the model. The variance explained raised to 60.63% accordingly. Second, we iteratively eliminated items with low overall factor loadings, including two items associated with *search information*, SEA1 and SEA5, COMM4 (*communicate information*), or REVAL1 (*re-evaluate information*). Second, we further deleted items from the set that revealed high cross loadings towards multiple factors, e.g. CREAT1 and CREAT2 linked to *create information*. Finally, we decided to eliminate at this point all three items that are supposed to form *obtain information* due to unsolvable cross loadings with other items that form other factors. This led to a reduced item set with 19 out of 40 initial items at this stage of our research. The figure below (Fig. 2) contains all 40 original items and their factors as our conceptual SMIL model and—highlighted in different shapes—those eliminated during our EFA calculation.

---

[1] Accessible at https://www.mturk.com.

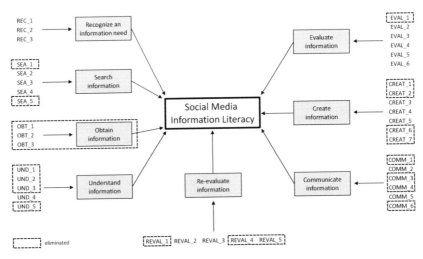

Fig. 2. SMIL model

3.4   Discussion of the Developed Model

Our results allow two key interpretations based on the initially derived model. The EFA results correspond with the forecasted factors to a certain extent as seven of eight factors could be identified. However, the results also reveal some cross loadings suggesting interrelations of items between factors. As a prominent example, all three items forming *obtain information* show rather weak loadings overall, and they load on three different factors. Thus, we decided to eliminate the entire factor and its associated items for now. As one next step though, we plan to reanalyze the cross loadings to integrate these items to potential rearranged superordinate factors.

EFA results allow additional in-factor interpretations as individual analyses per factor items yield two sub-factors instead of one main factor. Considering the example of *evaluate information*, items *EVAL1* and *EVAL4* form one sub-factor whereas *EVAL2*, *EVAL3*, *EVAL5* and *EVAL6* form another. Content-wise, the first sub-factor can be linked to a level of higher abstraction, i.e., general evaluation of the information itself and its quality. In contrast, the second sub-factor refers to a more detailed level of evaluation such as credibility, accuracy, or the specific focus on fake news. Similarly, *communicate information* revealed two distinctive sub-factors instead of a single factor. One can be summarized as communication actions referring to information handling (COMM1 & COMM2), e.g., "display" or "share" information, and the second sub-factor addresses the communication and interaction with a recipient (COMM3 & COMM6), e.g., providing "feedback" or "constructive criticism". These findings pave the way for extending the originally postulated model with second order constructs.

4 Contributions, Implications and Future Work

We provide a construct which solves the issue of a more or less dispersed topic by providing rigor in the design and development of the measurement scale for information literacy in social media. Existing approaches dealing with enhanced information literacy concepts such as metaliteracy [13, 14] or the 7i framework [28, 29] do not cover a rigor measurement construct development. Our scale is valid for every individual social media user; both in the private and business context.

Second, we introduce new ways of mapping our construct to existing theoretical concepts in the field of IS research. A natural link exists towards the life cycle model of information management of Krcmar [27]. More specifically, considering the research stream of technology acceptance, *experiences* are often solely linked to the time users spend to work and familiarize with a system, e.g., in TAM2 [38], UTAUT [39] or its successor UTAUT2 [40]. In these models, experience is measured simplistically with a tripartite ordinal scale. Our scale, however, also contributes in a new and unexpected, but more eligible way to the measurement of experience in the social media environment. Information literacy of social media users can serve as a novel criterion of experience in addition to, exclusively, time.

Initial practical implications can be derived as well from our construct development. From the perspective of several stakeholders, our research can contribute to their decision taking. For example, educational institutions such as universities can use it to adjust and optimize the measurement of students' digital competencies (SMIL) [41]. Additionally, companies in general can capitalize from the construct in a similar way as it gives them an instrument, they can use to identify potential fields for employee trainings.

Intended future applications of our SMIL model are primarily related to research on fake news. There are several potential ways of applying the construct on individuals to assess their competencies in social media services to inform about possible threats, impacts and create the awareness of misleading information in those networks. This is in line with the call of Lazer et al. [6] to empower individuals to deal with fake news. Empowering requires understanding of the status quo (i.e., the individual SMIL level), and our model paves the way for future ways of its measurement. Upcoming research projects could likely integrate the SMIL construct into holistic models addressing, amongst others, work-related performance categories [42]. Moreover, the developed scale informs existing roles on different levels (e.g., social media managers) in the business context. Related questions could ask for a minimum SMIL level for a specific occupation or role. At the same time this includes the measurement and assessment of success for teaching social media literacy practices to students [29], e.g., when investigating how curricula respond to the call of Fichman et al. [43] to support students in understanding "how social media works".

References

1. Kaplan, A.M., Haenlein, M.: Users of the world, unite! the challenges and opportunities of social media. Bus. Horiz. **53**, 59–68 (2010)
2. Bühler, J., Bick, M.: Name it as you like it? keeping pace with social media something. Electron. Markets **28**, 509–522 (2018)
3. Baur, A.W., Lipenkova, J., Bühler, J., Bick, M.: A novel design science approach for integrating Chinese user-generated content in non-Chinese market intelligence. In: Proceedings of the 36th International Conference on Information Systems (ICIS), Fort Worth (TX), USA (2015)
4. Mikalef, P., Sharma, K., Pappas, I.O., Giannakos, M.N.: Online reviews or marketer information? an eye-tracking study on social commerce consumers. In: Kar, A.K., et al. (eds.) I3E 2017. LNCS, vol. 10595, pp. 388–399. Springer, Cham (2017). https://doi.org/10.1007/978-3-319-68557-1_34
5. Allcott, H., Gentzkow, M.: Social media and fake news in the 2016 election. J. Econ. Perspect. **31**, 211–236 (2017)
6. Lazer, D.M.J., et al.: The science of fake news. Science **359**, 1094–1096 (2018)
7. Fouquet, H., Mawad, M.: Macron Plans to Fight Fake News With This Law. https://www.bloomberg.com/news/articles/2018-06-06/macron-fake-news-bill-shows-challenges-of-misinformation-fight
8. Nicola, S.: How Merkel Is Taking on Facebook and Twitter. https://www.bloomberg.com/news/articles/2018-01-04/how-angela-merkel-is-taking-on-facebook-twitter-quicktake-q-a
9. Hennig-Thurau, T., Gwinner, K.P., Walsh, G., Gremler, D.D.: Electronic word-of-mouth via consumer-opinion platforms: what motivates consumers to articulate themselves on the Internet? J. Interact. Mark. **18**, 38–52 (2004)
10. Ismagilova, E., Dwivedi, Y.K., Slade, E., Williams, M.D.: Electronic Word of Mouth (eWOM) in the Marketing Context. Springer, Cham (2017). https://doi.org/10.1007/978-3-319-52459-7
11. Ilomäki, L., Paavola, S., Lakkala, M., Kantosalo, A.: Digital competence – an emergent boundary concept for policy and educational research. Educ. Inf. Technol. **21**, 655–679 (2016)
12. Jinadu, I., Kaur, K.: Information literacy at the workplace: a suggested model for a developing country. Libri **64**, 61–74 (2014)
13. Jacobson, T.E., Mackey, T.P.: Proposing a metaliteracy model to redefine information literacy. Commun. Inf. Lit. **7**, 84–91 (2013)
14. Mackey, T.P., Jacobson, T.E.: Reframing information literacy as a metaliteracy. Coll. Res. Libr. **72**, 62–78 (2011)
15. MacKenzie, S.B., Podsakoff, P.M., Podsakoff, N.P.: Construct measurement and validation procedures in MIS and behavioral research: integrating new and existing techniques. MIS Quart. **35**, 293–334 (2011)
16. Pinto, M., Doucet, A.-V., Fernández-Ramos, A.: Measuring students' information skills through concept mapping. J. Inf. Sci. **36**, 464–480 (2010)
17. Godwin, P.: Information literacy and Web 2.0. Is it just hype? Program **43**, 264–274 (2009)
18. Lau, W.W.F., Yuen, A.H.K.: Developing and validating of a perceived ICT literacy scale for junior secondary school students: pedagogical and educational contributions. Comput. Educ. **78**, 1–9 (2014)

19. Somabut, A., Chaijaroen, S., Tuamsuk, K.: Media and information literacy of the students who learn with a digital learning environment based on constructivist theory. In: Proceedings of the 24th International Conference on Computers, India (2016)
20. Austin, E.W., Muldrow, A., Austin, B.W.: Examining how media literacy and personality factors predict skepticism toward alcohol advertising. J. Health Commun. **21**, 600–609 (2016)
21. Allen, M.: Promoting critical thinking skills in online information literacy instruction using a constructivist approach. Coll. Undergrad. Libr. **15**, 21–38 (2008)
22. Peterson-Clark, G., Aslani, P., Williams, K.A.: Pharmacists' online information literacy: an assessment of their use of Internet-based medicines information. Health Inf. Libr. J. **27**, 208–216 (2010)
23. Punter, R.A., Meelissen, M.R.M., Glas, C.A.W.: Gender differences in computer and information literacy: an exploration of the performances of girls and boys in ICILS 2013. Eur. Educ. Res. J. **16**, 762–780 (2017)
24. Scherer, R., Rohatgi, A., Hatlevik, O.E.: Students' profiles of ICT use: identification, determinants, and relations to achievement in a computer and information literacy test. Comput. Hum. Behav. **70**, 486–499 (2017)
25. Al-Aufi, A.S., Al-Azri, H.M., Al-Hadi, N.A.: Perceptions of information literacy skills among undergraduate students in the social media environment. Int. Inf. Libr. Rev. **49**, 163–175 (2017)
26. Pinto, M., Fernández-Pascual, R.: Information literacy competencies among social sciences undergraduates: a case study using structural equation model. In: Kurbanoğlu, S., Špiranec, S., Grassian, E., Mizrachi, D., Catts, R. (eds.) ECIL 2014. CCIS, vol. 492, pp. 370–378. Springer, Cham (2014). https://doi.org/10.1007/978-3-319-14136-7_39
27. Krcmar, H.: InformationsManagement. Springer, Heidelberg (2015). https://doi.org/10.1007/978-3-662-45863-1
28. Müller, S., Scheffler, N., Seufert, S., Stanoevska-Slabeva, K.: The 7i framework - towards a measurement model of information literacy. In: Proceedings of the 21st Americas Conference on Information Systems (AMCIS), Puerto Rico (2015)
29. Stanoevska-Slabeva, K., Müller, S., Seufert, S., Scheffler, N.: Towards modeling and measuring information literacy in secondary education. In: Proceedings of the 36th International Conference on Information Systems (ICIS), Fort Worth (TX), USA (2015)
30. Churchill, G.A.: A paradigm for developing better measures of marketing constructs. J. Mark. Res. **16**, 64–73 (1979)
31. Lewis, B.R., Templeton, G.F., Byrd, T.A.: A methodology for construct development in MIS research. Eur. J. Inf. Syst. **14**, 388–400 (2005)
32. Schmiedel, T., Vom Brocke, J., Recker, J.: Development and validation of an instrument to measure organizational cultures' support of business process management. Inf. Manag. **51**, 43–56 (2014)
33. Webster, J., Watson, R.T.: Analyzing the past to prepare for the future: writing a literature review. MIS Quart. **26**, xiii–xxiii (2002)
34. Brage, C., Lantz, A.: A re-conceptualisation of information literacy in accordance with new social media contexts. In: The 7th International Multi-Conference on Society, Cybernetics and Informatics (IMSCI), pp. 217–222. Orlando, FL, USA (2013)
35. Fahser-Herro, D., Steinkuehler, C.: Web 2.0 literacy and secondary teacher education. J. Comput. Teach. Educ. **26**, 55–62 (2010)
36. Hinkin, T.R., Tracey, J.B.: An analysis of variance approach to content validation. Organ. Res. Methods **2**, 175–186 (1999)
37. Wieland, A., Durach, C.F., Kembro, J., Treiblmaier, H.: Statistical and judgmental criteria for scale purification. Supply Chain Manag.: Int. J. **22**, 321–328 (2017)

38. Venkatesh, V., Davis, F.D.: A theoretical extension of the technology acceptance model. Four Longitudinal Field Stud. Manag. Sci. **46**, 186 (2000)
39. Venkatesh, V., Morris, M.G., Davis, G.B., Davis, F.D.: User acceptance of information technology: toward a unified view. MIS Quart. **27**, 425–478 (2003)
40. Venkatesh, V., Thong, J.Y., Xu, X.: Consumer acceptance and use of information technology: extending the unified theory of acceptance and use of technology. MIS Quart. **36**, 157–178 (2012)
41. Murawski, M., Bick, M.: Demanded and imparted big data competences: towards an integrative analysis. In: Proceedings of the 25th European Conference on Information Systems (ECIS), pp. 1375–1390, Guimarães, Portugal (2017)
42. Alessandri, G., Borgogni, L., Truxillo, D.M.: Tracking job performance trajectories over time: a six-year longitudinal study. Eur. J. Work Organ. Psychol. **24**, 560–577 (2015)
43. Fichman, R.G., Santos, B.L., Zheng, Z.: Digital innovation as a fundamental and powerful concept in the information systems curriculum. MIS Quart. **38**, 329–353 (2014)

The Role of Tweet-Related Emotion on the Exhaustion – Recovery from Work Relationship

Konstantina Foti[1(✉)], Despoina Xanthopoulou[2],
Savvas Papagiannidis[1], and Konstantinos Kafetsios[3]

[1] Newcastle University Business School, Newcastle upon Tyne NE1 4SE, UK
{k.foti2,savvas.papagiannidis}@ncl.ac.uk
[2] Aristotle University of Thessaloniki, 541 24 Thessaloniki, Greece
dxanthopoulou@psy.auth.gr
[3] University of Crete, 741 00 Rethymnon, Greece
kafetsik@uoc.gr

Abstract. This study examined the relationship between work-related exhaustion and the recovery experiences of psychological detachment and relaxation during leisure, and the moderating role of emotion (positive & negative) when using Twitter during and after work. Participants were asked to rate their emotion based on the tweets they posted each day, together with their exhaustion at work and their recovery experiences at the end of the day. Results from the multilevel analyses showed that experiencing positive emotion when tweeting at work buffered the negative relationship of exhaustion and psychological detachment, but not relaxation. Negative emotion did not moderate the relationship significantly. The results show that social media can play a significant role in the recovery process and offer interesting insights both for employees and organisations.

Keywords: Emotion · Exhaustion · Psychological detachment · Relaxation · Twitter

1 Introduction

Employees deal with several demands on a daily basis at work. Research has shown that employees need to adequately unwind and recover from job demands daily as this prevents further energy depletion and keeps them physically and mentally healthy [1, 2]. So far, research examined how specific activity types (e.g. work-related, household, physical, social and low effort) associate with recovery. However, due to major changes introduced by the progress of Information and Communication Technologies (ICTs), many of the activities that employees engage in today are digital, take place online and relate to social media. Existing research on ICTs and recovery paid attention on the medium, such as smartphones [3], on the Internet use [4], or on social media use in general [5, 6], thus, neglecting the nature of the social media experience and its role on recovery. To address this gap in the literature, we examined active social media use and the impact the nature of the experience while using social media as a new context may

© IFIP International Federation for Information Processing 2019
Published by Springer Nature Switzerland AG 2019
I. O. Pappas et al. (Eds.): I3E 2019, LNCS 11701, pp. 380–391, 2019.
https://doi.org/10.1007/978-3-030-29374-1_31

have on the process of recovery from work. Specifically, we investigated the moderating role of emotion (positive & negative) by tweets posted during and after work on the exhaustion–recovery experiences relationship. The study adds to the literature by integrating the role of social media in the recovery process. Importantly, we advance our understanding of the conditions under which social media use is more likely to be beneficial or detrimental for the daily recovery. By investigating the moderating role of emotion elicited by the social media activity, we bring out the conditions under which tweeting at work and during leisure may help (or impede) exhausted employees to detach from work and relax during their off-job time.

2 Daily Exhaustion and Recovery from Work

Recovery is the process where employees unwind and refill the resources used at work [7]. Following the effort-recovery model [8], investing effort to deal with job demands leads to physio-psychological activation and acute responses, such as exhaustion (i.e., the state of energy depletion from job demands) [9]. Hence, employees recover when demands are no longer present, which allows for their physio-psychological systems to return to baseline. In this context, recovery can occur by taking breaks between work tasks (i.e., internal), and at leisure time (i.e., external).

Engaging in off-job activities that enable recovery experiences, employees can "recharge their batteries" and feel recovered [10–13]. This is because recovery experiences facilitate replenishing those resources that employees invested at work and even gain additional resources [14]. From the four recovery experiences (i.e. psychological detachment, relaxation, control & mastery) [7], this study focuses on psychological detachment and relaxation, that are considered the most central. Psychological detachment refers to switching off from work, while relaxation is a state of low activation [7].

Exhaustion was found to correlate negatively to psychological detachment and relaxation [7]. Also, exhausted employees were less likely to detach psychologically from work [2]. When feeling exhausted, employees are unable to meet job demands due to lack of energy and as such they fail to meet performance goals [15]. As a result, exhausted employees are more likely to continue working during leisure [16] to compensate for performance failures and as such, they are less likely to detach from work and relax. Also, exhausted employees are less likely to relax during their leisure time. Exhaustion due to prolonged exposure to work stressors exposes employees to extended activation of their functional systems [8]. At the same time, resource depletion due to exhaustion impedes employees from investing resources in activities that can help them experience relaxation and recover [7, 17].

Hypothesis 1: Exhaustion is negatively associated with psychological detachment and relaxation during leisure.

3   Social Media and the Recovery Process

The rapid growth of social media has introduced major changes in everyday life. Social media refer to "web-based services that allow individuals, communities, and organizations to collaborate, connect, interact, and build community by enabling them to create, co-create, modify, share, and engage with user-generated content that is easily accessible" [18]. Today, there are approximately three billion people globally logging onto social media, spending an average of two hours per day [19]. Research so far has presented social media as a double-edged sword. On the one hand, using social media actively helps individuals reduce stress, increases life satisfaction, reduces loneliness and enhances well-being [20–22]. Interacting with co-workers on social media after work promotes job satisfaction, as social media help employees keep their work tasks under control and bond with their colleagues [5]. Spending personal time on the Internet during work can help employees take a mental break and re-charge their batteries resulting in higher work engagement in the subsequent hour [6]. Taking a break from work using your smartphone was found to relate to higher levels of happiness by the end of the working day [23]. On the other hand, digital breaks from work were found to inhibit recovery [24], while extensive social media use at work results in lower work engagement [6]. Using Facebook passively (e.g., content consumption, without engagement or content creation) was related to lower life satisfaction and well-being [25]. Nevertheless, the association between social media and recovery experiences remains untangled.

Previous research has provided mixed results on the effect of social media use on recovery. These mixed findings may be due to the fact the previous studies mainly assessed the social media use. Hence, the present study focuses on the quality of the social media use instead, as experienced by the users. To this end, we investigated the role of emotion from actively engaging with the social media platform of Twitter at work and leisure. In this study, we employed the popular social networking micro-blogging service Twitter. Users share up to 280-character long text messages called tweets. Twitter attracts 321 million monthly users of all age groups [26], tweeting about various topics. The vast majority of users tweet about their lives on the go since 80% of them access the platform via their smartphone [27]. The advantages of Twitter, in terms of frequency of use, diversity of its population and speed of information, make it ideal for this study.

4   The Moderating Role of Emotion from Twitter

Social media in general, and Twitter in particular, offer a broad variety of services (e.g. networking, communication, content creation, etc.). By being active in Twitter, users may have variant experience and may satisfy different needs online (e.g. entertainment, information seeking, etc.). Thus, it is essential not to focus solely on social media use, but to examine what people are actually experiencing while using social media and how these experiences are affecting the recovery process. We argue that the emotion experienced while posting on Twitter at work and at leisure can moderate the impact of work exhaustion on recovery experiences. Emotion is an important component of everyday communication in both offline and online human interactions [28, 29]. Emotion can be described as "multi-component response tendencies that unfold over relatively short time spans" [30]. Compared to moods – which are more diffused and last longer – emotion is triggered by specific causes and has a limited duration [31]. Here, we adopt a two-dimensional structure composed of the orthogonal dimensions of positive and negative emotion [32].

Negative emotion refers to negative valence, such as distress and sadness. Research has shown that negative emotion narrows thought-action repertoires [33] and depletes individuals' personal resources [34] - a process detrimental to employee recovery [14]. Negative emotion also triggers reactivity. In this way, individuals' load reactions remain activated [8], which hampers exhausted employees from recovery experiences. Based on these arguments, we hypothesise:

Hypothesis 2: Negative emotion from tweets moderates the negative relationship between exhaustion and recovery experiences (i.e., psychological detachment and relaxation), where the relationship is stronger when negative emotion is high than when it is low.

Positive emotion refers to positive valence, such as happiness, alertness and excitement. Experiencing positive emotion broadens thought-action repertoires and helps employees build resources [33, 35, 36]. Positive emotion can down-regulate the negative impact of negative emotion on well-being [34]. Thus, when employees post tweets that elicit positive emotion, they gain resources that may help them counteract they negative impact of exhaustion on recovery experiences. Put differently, when exhausted employees experience higher (vs. lower) positive emotion by actively using Twitter, they are more likely to detach from work and relax because they gain resources that can be used for recovery purposes. Thus, we hypothesize:

Hypothesis 3: Positive emotion from tweets moderate the negative relationship between exhaustion and recovery experiences (i.e., psychological detachment and relaxation), where the relationship is weaker when positive emotion is high than when it is low.

5 Method

5.1 Procedure and Sample

A convenience sample was employed, consisted of full- and part-time employees that use Twitter. The participants completed an online questionnaire at the end of the working day, for a maximum of 5 working days. A bespoke system was built to retrieve the tweets employees posted. Participants reported their emotion about the tweets they posted on that day, together with questions about exhaustion at work, and psychological detachment and relaxation at leisure. Participation was voluntary and the data was gathered confidentially. As a participation incentive, respondents were offered to be included in a raffle for Amazon coupons at the end of the data collection.

The final study sample consisted of 33 employees ($N = 285$ study points), of which 16 (48.5%) were women, and posting on average 3.4 tweets per day ($SD = 1.5$). Participants employed full-time were 97% of the sample, with mean tenure in their current position of 7 years ($SD = 5$). Their mean age was 38 years ($SD = 8.4$). The sample was heterogeneous in terms of jobs: 16 participants (50%) were working in education, 6 (18.8%) in technology and the rest were employed in sales, consulting, entertainment and administrative sectors. Their contract hours were on average 38 h per week ($SD = 7.5$), while their actual working hours were on average 46 h per week ($SD = 11$). All participants held a university degree, with 15 (45.5%) holding a master's degree, 11 (33.3%) holding a PhD and 7 (21.2%) a bachelor's degree.

5.2 Measures

The diary study assessed each participant's (positive and negative) emotion for different tweets they posted and their daily levels of exhaustion at work and psychological detachment and relaxation during leisure. Because of the demanding nature of diary studies [37] and to minimise participant burden, the variables were measured with the use of abbreviated and one-item scales [38].

Emotion from Tweets. The momentary emotional experience elicited by each tweet was measured with items from the Positive and Negative Affect Schedule (PANAS) [32]. Participants were presented with a list of 8 PANAS descriptors (5 positive and 3 negative) and were asked to indicate the extent to which these adjectives described how they felt with regard to each tweet ("This tweet made me feel…"). All items were rated on a 5-point scale, ranging from (1) "not at all" to (5) "to a great extent". The items measuring positive emotion were 'happy', 'energetic', 'proud', 'interested' and 'attentive'. Cronbach's alphas ranged from .86 to .89 across the study points. The items measuring negative emotion were 'nervous', 'upset' and 'sad'. Mean Cronbach's alpha was $\alpha = .68$ (ranged from .55 to .76). Reliabilities for the emotion sub-scales were calculated on a tweet-basis (where reliability was measured for all the first tweets of the first day, then second tweets of the first day, etc.).

Daily Work-Related Exhaustion. Two items from the Shirom-Melamed Burnout Measure (SMBM) were used to assess exhaustion: "Today at work, I felt exhausted" and "Today at work, I felt burned out". Items were scored on a 5-point scale ranging from (1) "totally disagree" to (5) "totally agree". The inter-item correlations ranged from .51 to .78 across the study days, suggesting high internal consistency.

Daily Recovery Experiences. Psychological detachment and relaxation were measured using items from the Recovery Experience Questionnaire [7], as adapted to measure daily recovery experiences [39]. Two items were used to measure psychological detachment: "during leisure, I forgot about work" and "during leisure, I didn't think about work at all." Inter-item correlations ranged from .66 to .96 across the study days. Relaxation was measured with the item: "after work, I used the time to relax". The items used for the purposes of this study were selected based on their factorial (Bakker et al., 2015) and face validity. Response options were based on a 5-point scale, ranging from (1) "totally disagree" to (5) "totally agree".

6   Strategy of Analysis

Data were collected at the tweet-level ($N = 285$), the day-level ($N = 5$) and the person-level ($N = 33$). Given that both antecedent and outcome variables were assessed at the day-level, and since we were interested in overall emotional experiences, data related to tweets (i.e., positive and negative emotions) were averaged to the day-level. Participants reported their emotion from tweeting for an average of 3.5 tweets per day (min = 1; max = 6 tweets/day). We tested a two-level model, with daily measurements (level-1) nested in employees (level-2). All relationships were modelled at the within-person level of analysis. According to Maas and Hox's [40] rule of thumb, there is a need for at least 30 cases at the highest level of analysis in order to perform robust multilevel analyses with fixed slopes, making the sample of the study sufficient. Predictor and moderating variables were centred around the person mean, to capture within-person variations. The total sample was split into two samples based on the time the tweets were posted: one for the tweets posted at work ($N = 32$ participants & $N = 95$ study points), and one for the tweets posted after work ($N = 21$ participants & $N = 40$ study points). Hypotheses were tested for each sub-sample separately. Analyses were performed with MLwiN 3.00 [41]. For significant interaction effects, the simple slopes test was performed with the online calculation tool by Preacher, Curran and Bauer [42].

7   Results

7.1   Preliminary Analyses and Descriptive Statistics

First, we examined if the variance of the day-level dependent variables could be explained by both levels of analysis, by estimating the interclass correlation coefficient. Also, for each dependent variable a deviance difference test ($\Delta\chi^2$) was conducted to test whether a model that accounted for two-levels (i.e., days nested in employees) fit the data better than a model with one level. Results indicated that the two-level model fit the data better than the one-level model, both for the sample for tweets posted at work and for the sample for tweets posted at leisure. For tweets posted at work, results showed that 57% of daily psychological detachment ($\Delta-2x$ log = 13.48, $df = 1$, $p < .05$) and 67% of daily relaxation ($\Delta-2x$ log = 8.84, $df = 1$, $p < .05$) could be attributed to within-person changes. For tweets posted during leisure, results showed that 22% of daily psychological detachment ($\Delta-2x$ log = 20.8, $df = 1$, $p < .05$) and 61% of daily relaxation ($\Delta-2x$ log = 4.42, $df = 1$, $p < .05$) is attributable to within-person changes, meaning that multilevel modeling is appropriate for testing the study hypotheses. The means, standard deviations, and correlations between the study variables for the tweets posted at work ($N = 32$ participants & $N = 95$ study points) and for the tweets posted at leisure ($N = 21$ participants & $N = 40$ study points) are presented in Table 1.

Table 1. Means, standard deviations and within-person correlations of the study variables for tweets at work and at leisure.

Variables	M work	SD work	M leisure	SD leisure	1	2	3	4	5
1. Exhaustion	2.41	1.10	2.39	1.20	–	−.23	.26	−.05	−.46**
2. Positive emotions	3.49	0.90	3.17	1.10	−.13	–	−.18	−.02	.14
3. Negative emotions	1.22	0.52	1.27	0.52	−.01	−.25*	–	−.20	−.11
4. Psychological detachment	2.54	1.18	2.99	1.53	−.10	.20	−.19	–	.48**
5. Relaxation	3.01	1.20	3.00	1.43	−.44**	.19	−.05	.47**	–

Note. N = 32 participants and N = 95 study points for tweets posted at work. N = 21 participants and N = 40 study points for tweets posted at leisure. Correlations above the diagonal concern tweets posted at leisure, and below the diagonal concern tweets posted at work. The Mean and Standard Deviation for tweets at work and tweets at leisure are also presented. ** $p < .01$, * $p < .05$.

Table 2 presents the results from the multilevel analyses predicting psychological detachment, and Table 3 the multilevel analyses predicting relaxation. According to Hypothesis 1, daily exhaustion was expected to relate negatively to both psychological detachment and relaxation. As shown in Tables 2 and 3, this hypothesis was rejected since no significant interaction found between exhaustion and the experiences of psychological detachment and relaxation.

According to Hypothesis 2, negative emotion from tweets was expected to boost the negative relationship between exhaustion and recovery experiences. Results regarding the negative emotion related to tweets during work did not support a significant interaction effect either on psychological detachment ($\beta = -0.25$, SE = 0.43, $t = -0.58$, *ns;* Table 2) or on relaxation ($\beta = -0.18$, SE = 0.46, $t = -0.40$, *ns;* Table 3). Also, results regarding negative emotion from tweets posted during leisure did not support the moderating role of negative emotion either on the relationship between exhaustion and psychological detachment ($\beta = 0.20$, SE = 1.09, $t = 0.18$, *ns;* Table 2), nor on the relationship between exhaustion and relaxation ($\beta = 0.35$, SE = 1.13, $t = 0.31$, *ns;* Table 3). Thus, Hypothesis 2 was rejected.

According to Hypothesis 3, positive emotion from tweets was expected to buffer the negative relationship between exhaustion and recovery experiences. Results showed that positive emotion from tweets posted during work indeed moderated the exhaustion – psychological detachment relationship ($\beta = 0.63$, SE = 0.32, $t = 1.99**$, $p < .01$; Table 2) significantly, but not the exhaustion – relaxation relationship ($\beta = 0.07$, SE = 0.35, $t = 0.19$, *ns;* Table 3). Results for the tweets posted during leisure did not support the moderating role of positive emotion from tweets either on the relationship between exhaustion and psychological detachment ($\beta = -0.88$, SE = 0.64, $t = -1.38$, *ns;* Table 2) or on the relationship between exhaustion and relaxation ($\beta = 0.49$, SE = 0.76, $t = 0.65$, ns; Table 3).

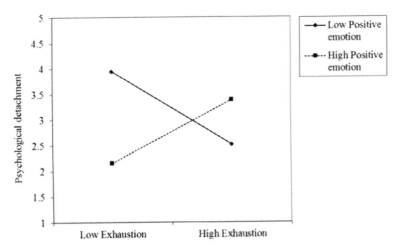

Fig. 1. Interaction effect of exhaustion and positive emotion from tweets on change in psychological detachment

We probed the significance of the simple slopes [42], to examine the pattern of the significant interaction effect of exhaustion and positive emotion on detachment. When positive emotion from tweets was low, exhaustion related negatively to detachment (estimate = −2.27, SE = 1.1, z = −2.07, p < .05; Fig. 1), but was not related when positive emotion was high (estimate = 2.13, SE = 1.13, z = −1.88, ns; Fig. 1), partially supporting Hypothesis 3.

Table 2. Multilevel analysis for day-level psychological detachment

Tweets posted during work	Est.	SE	t
Intercept ($\gamma 0$)	2.60	0.17	15.49**
Exhaustion ($\gamma 1$)	−0.07	0.14	−0.49
Positive emotions ($\gamma 2$)	−0.28	0.22	−1.27
Exhaustion × Positive emotions ($\gamma 3$)	0.63	0.32	1.99**
Intercept ($\gamma 0$)	2.56	0.17	15.04**
Exhaustion ($\gamma 1$)	−0.06	0.14	−0.41
Negative emotions ($\gamma 2$)	−0.15	0.24	−0.62
Exhaustion × Negative emotions ($\gamma 3$)	−0.25	0.43	−0.58
Tweets posted during work	Est.	SE	t
Intercept ($\gamma 0$)	2.89	0.32	9.10**
Exhaustion ($\gamma 1$)	−0.09	0.15	−0.61
Positive emotions ($\gamma 2$)	−0.05	0.33	−0.15
Exhaustion × Positive emotions ($\gamma 3$)	−0.88	0.64	−1.38
Intercept ($\gamma 0$)	2.86	0.31	9.30**
Exhaustion ($\gamma 1$)	−0.17	0.16	−1.09
Negative emotions ($\gamma 2$)	0.27	0.46	0.58
Exhaustion × Negative emotions ($\gamma 3$)	0.20	1.09	0.18

Note. N = 32 participants & N = 95 study points for tweets posted at work. N = 21 participants & N = 40 study points for tweets posted at leisure. **p < .01

Table 3. Multilevel analysis for day-level relaxation

Tweets posted during work	Est.	SE	t
Intercept ($\gamma0$)	3.04	0.17	18.34**
Exhaustion ($\gamma1$)	−0.28	0.15	−1.82
Positive emotions ($\gamma2$)	−0.23	0.25	−0.92
Exhaustion × Positive emotions ($\gamma3$)	0.07	0.35	0.19
Intercept ($\gamma0$)	3.04	0.16	18.64**
Exhaustion ($\gamma1$)	−0.23	0.15	−1.50
Negative emotions ($\gamma2$)	−0.02	0.26	−0.08
Exhaustion × Negative emotions ($\gamma3$)	−0.18	0.46	−0.40
Tweets posted during work	Est.	SE	t
Intercept ($\gamma0$)	3.00	0.25	11.87**
Exhaustion ($\gamma1$)	−0.71	0.21	−3.43**
Positive emotions ($\gamma2$)	−0.38	0.45	−0.86
Exhaustion × Positive emotions ($\gamma3$)	0.49	0.76	0.65
Intercept ($\gamma0$)	3.02	0.26	11.69**
Exhaustion ($\gamma1$)	−0.68	0.20	−3.44**
Negative emotions ($\gamma2$)	−0.24	0.58	−0.41
Exhaustion × Negative emotions ($\gamma3$)	0.35	1.13	0.31

Note. $N = 32$ participants & $N = 95$ study points for tweets posted at work. $N = 21$ participants & $N = 40$ study points, for tweets posted at leisure. ** $p < .01$

8   Discussion, Implications and Future Research

In this diary study, we examined the moderating role of positive and negative emotion elicited from tweets (during and after work) on the relationship between daily work-related exhaustion and the recovery experiences of psychological detachment and relaxation during leisure. In contrast to our expectations, daily exhaustion from work was not found to associate directly to psychological detachment or relaxation. However, multilevel analyses showed that the positive emotion elicited by the social media activity moderated the recovery process. As expected, in line with the broaden-and-build theory [33, 43], when employees are experiencing positive emotion when posting on Twitter, the negative impact of exhaustion on psychological detachment from work is buffered. Contrary to expectations, positive emotion elicited from tweeting were not found to buffer the impact of exhaustion on relaxation, while negative emotion did not significantly strengthen the negative impact of exhaustion on recovery experiences.

The study contributes to the literature, by providing a better understanding of the exhaustion – recovery experiences relationship when taking into consideration the emotional experiences in the social media context. Our results contribute to the discussion on the impact of social media on recovery from work, by showing that the quality of the social media activity and specifically the experience of positive emotion is relevant for the recovery process. Taking into consideration that recovery is crucial for healthy and productive employees that help organisations flourish, understanding recovery when using social media has also practical implications. Organisations can allow social media use at work, as it can buffer the negative impact of job demands on employees. As research has shown, recovery can be supported by intervention programmes [44]. Work trainings could include the topic of social media use at work to help employees reflect on their use and benefit from it on the level of recovery and well-being.

Our study has some limitations. First, the study does not comprise an exhaustive framework for all potential factors that may determine the social media-recovery relationship. Future research could replicate the study, while introducing new factors, to shed more light on the impact of social media on recovery. One such is examining the effects discrete emotions may have on recovery. Next, the sample size was relatively small. While the sample size was adequate for the purposes of the study [40], future research can benefit from larger sample sizes. Finally, this study was conducted in the Twitter setting, excluding other social media. This may place constraints to the generalisability of the findings. However, the study did not focus on Twitter use per se, but on the quality of experience when using Twitter. Future research could replicate our framework by adopting other social media. To conclude, the quality of social media experience can have an impact on the job demands-recovery relationship. Future research is needed to focus on the quality of social media experience and its implication on employee well-being.

References

1. Demerouti, E., Bakker, A.B., Geurts, S.A., Taris, T.W.: Daily recovery from work-related effort during non-work time. In: Current Perspectives on Job-Stress Recovery, pp. 85–123. Emerald Group Publishing Limited (2009)
2. Sonnentag, S., Arbeus, H., Mahn, C., Fritz, C.: Exhaustion and lack of psychological detachment from work during off-job time: moderator effects of time pressure and leisure experiences. J. Occup. Health Psychol. **19**(2), 206–216 (2014)
3. Derks, D., Bakker, A.B.: Smartphone use, work-home interference, and burnout: a diary study on the role of recovery. Appl. Psychol.-Int. Rev. **63**(3), 411–440 (2014)
4. Quinones, C., Griffiths, M.D.: The impact of daily emotional demands, job resources and emotional effort on intensive Internet use during and after work. Comput. Hum. Behav. **76** (C), 561–575 (2017)
5. Robertson, B.W., Kee, K.F.: Social media at work: the roles of job satisfaction, employment status, and Facebook use with co-workers. Comput. Hum. Behav. **70**, 191–196 (2017)
6. Syrek, C.J., Kühnel, J., Vahle-Hinz, T., De Bloom, J.: Share, like, twitter, and connect: ecological momentary assessment to examine the relationship between non-work social media use at work and work engagement. Work Stress **32**(3), 209–227 (2018)
7. Sonnentag, S., Fritz, C.: The recovery experience questionnaire: development and validation of a measure for assessing recuperation and unwinding from work. J. Occup. Health Psychol. **12**(3), 204–221 (2007)
8. Meijman, T.F., Mulder, G.: Psychological aspects of workload. In: Handbook of Work and Organizational Psychology, vol. 2 (1998)
9. Xanthopoulou, D., Meier, L.L.: Daily burnout experiences. In: Burnout at Work: A Psychological Perspective, vol. 5. p. 80 (2014)

10. Sonnentag, S.: Work, recovery activities, and individual well-being: a diary study. J. Occup. Health Psychol. **6**(3), 196 (2001)

11. Oerlemans, W.G.M., Bakker, A.B.: Burnout and daily recovery: a day reconstruction study. J. Occup. Health Psychol. **19**(3), 303–314 (2014)

12. ten Brummelhuis, L.L., Trougakos, J.P.: The recovery potential of intrinsically versus extrinsically motivated off-job activities. J Occup. Organ Psychol. **87**(1), 177–199 (2014)

13. Sonnentag, S., Zijlstra, F.R.H.: Job characteristics and off-job activities as predictors of need for recovery, well-being, and fatigue. J. Appl. Psychol. **91**(2), 330–350 (2006)

14. Hobfoll, S.E.: Conservation of resources: a new attempt at conceptualizing stress. Am. Psychol. **44**(3), 513 (1989)

15. Taris, T.W.: Is there a relationship between burnout and objective performance? a critical review of 16 studies. Work Stress **20**(4), 316–334 (2006)

16. Peterson, U., Demerouti, E., Bergström, G., Åsberg, M., Nygren, Å.: Work characteristics and sickness absence in burnout and nonburnout groups: a study of Swedish health care workers. Int. J. Stress Manag. **15**(2), 153 (2008)

17. ten Brummelhuis, L.L., Bakker, A.B.: A resource perspective on the work–home interface: the work–home resources model. Am. Psychol. **67**(7), 545 (2012)

18. McCay-Peet, L., Quan-Haase, A.: What is social media and what questions can social media research help us answer? In: The SAGE Handbook of Social Media Research Methods, vol. 13 (2017)

19. https://blog.globalwebindex.net/chart-of-the-day/daily-time-spent-on-social-networks/

20. van Ingen, E., Rains, S.A., Wright, K.B.: Does social network site use buffer against well-being loss when older adults face reduced functional ability? Comput. Hum. Behav. **70**, 168–177 (2017)

21. Wang, J.-L., Jackson, L.A., Gaskin, J., Wang, H.-Z.: The effects of Social Networking Site (SNS) use on college students' friendship and well-being. Comput. Hum. Behav. **37**, 229–236 (2014)

22. Matook, S., Cummings, J., Bala, H.: Are you feeling lonely? the impact of relationship characteristics and online social network features on loneliness. J. Manag. Inf. Syst. **31**(4), 278–310 (2015)

23. Rhee, H., Kim, S.: Effects of breaks on regaining vitality at work: an empirical comparison of 'conventional' and 'smart phone' breaks. Comput. Hum. Behav. **57**, 160–167 (2016)

24. Kim, S., Park, Y., Niu, Q.: Micro-break activities at work to recover from daily work demands. J. Organ. Behav. **38**(1), 28–44 (2017)

25. Wenninger, H., Krasnova, H., Buxmann, P.: Activity matters: investigating the influence of Facebook on life satisfaction of teenage users (2014)

26. https://s22.q4cdn.com/826641620/files/doc_financials/2018/q4/Q4-2018-Selected-Company-Financials-and-Metrics.pdf

27. Wang, W., Hernandez, I., Newman, D.A., He, J., Bian, J.: Twitter analysis: studying US weekly trends in work stress and emotion. Appl. Psychol.: Int. Rev. **65**(2), 355–378 (2016)

28. Derks, D., Fischer, A.H., Bos, A.E.: The role of emotion in computer-mediated communication: a review. Comput. Hum. Behav. **24**(3), 766–785 (2008)

29. Pappas, I.O., Kourouthanassis, P.E., Giannakos, M.N., Chrissikopoulos, V.: Shiny happy people buying: the role of emotions on personalized e-shopping. Electron. Markets **24**(3), 193–206 (2014)

30. Fredrickson, B.L.: The broaden-and-build theory of positive emotions. Philos. Trans. R. Soc. B: Biol. Sci. **359**(1449), 1367 (2004)

31. Gray, E.K., Watson, D., Payne, R., Cooper, C.: Emotion, mood, and temperament: similarities, differences, and a synthesis. In: Emotions at Work: Theory, Research and Applications for Management, pp. 21–43 (2001)

32. Watson, D., Clark, L.A., Tellegen, A.: Development and validation of brief measures of positive and negative affect: the PANAS scales. J. Pers. Soc. Psychol. **54**(6), 1063–1070 (1988)
33. Fredrickson, B.L.: The role of positive emotions in positive psychology: the broaden-and-build theory of positive emotions. Am. Psychol. **56**(3), 218 (2001)
34. Fredrickson, B.L., Mancuso, R.A., Branigan, C., Tugade, M.M.: The undoing effect of positive emotions. Motiv. Emot. **24**(4), 237–258 (2000)
35. Fredrickson, B.L., Levenson, R.W.: Positive emotions speed recovery from the cardiovascular sequelae of negative emotions. Cognit. Emot. **12**(2), 191–220 (1998)
36. Xanthopoulou, D., Bakker, A.B., Demerouti, E., Schaufeli, W.B.: A diary study on the happy worker: how job resources relate to positive emotions and personal resources. Eur. J. Work Organ. Psychol. **21**(4), 489–517 (2012)
37. Bolger, N., Davis, A., Rafaeli, E.: Diary methods: capturing life as it is lived. Ann. Rev. Psychol. **54**(1), 579–616 (2003)
38. Ohly, S., Sonnentag, S., Niessen, C., Zapf, D.: Diary studies in organizational research. J. Pers. Psychol. (2010)
39. Bakker, A.B., Sanz-Vergel, A.I., Rodríguez-Muñoz, A., Oerlemans, W.G.M.: The state version of the recovery experience questionnaire: a multilevel confirmatory factor analysis. Eur. J. Work Organ. Psychol. **24**(3), 350–359 (2015)
40. Maas, C.J., Hox, J.J.: Sufficient sample sizes for multilevel modeling. Methodology **1**(3), 86–92 (2005)
41. Charlton, C., Rasbash, J., Browne, W., Healy, M., Cameron, B.: MLwiN Version 3.00. Bristol: Centre for Multilevel, Modelling University of Bristol (2017)
42. Preacher, K.J., Curran, P.J., Bauer, D.J.: Computational tools for probing interactions in multiple linear regression, multilevel modeling, and latent curve analysis. J. Educ. Behav. Stat. **31**(4), 437–448 (2006)
43. Weiss, H.M., Cropanzano, R.: Affective events theory: a theoretical discussion of the structure, causes and consequences of affective experiences at work (1996)
44. Querstret, D., Cropley, M., Fife-Schaw, C.: Internet-based instructor-led mindfulness for work-related rumination, fatigue, and sleep: assessing facets of mindfulness as mechanisms of change: a randomized waitlist control trial. J. Occup. Health Psychol. **22**(2), 153 (2017)

Winning of Hearts and Minds: Integrating Sentiment Analytics into the Analysis of Contradictions

Jennifer Ferreira, Denis Dennehy[(✉)], Jaganath Babu,
and Kieran Conboy

Lero—Irish Software Research Centre, National University of Ireland Galway,
Galway, Ireland
Denis.Dennehy@nuigalway.ie

Abstract. Interactions in open source communities are often informal, and enacted through online discussion forums. While discussion and associated sentiment is critical to sustaining open source communities, they have not been studied to date. To address this gap in knowledge, this study uses sentiment analytics to illuminate the frequency of 2,364 discursive manifestations of contradictions through the theoretical lens of Activity Theory (AT). The study contributes to current discourse on contradictions by demonstrating the importance of dialectical contradictions as a driving force for learning, change, and sustaining open source communities. Implications for research and practice provide opportunities for revising current business methods and practices, which inevitably have implications for a sustainable society in the 21st century.

Keywords: Activity Theory · Contradictions · Sentiment analytics · Open source

1 Introduction

OSS[1] development is a knowledge-intensive activity that involves software developers, who are usually geographically dispersed, using online forums to coordinate their work activities [1–3]. These online forums are communication channels where software developers express their emotions concerning their degree of satisfaction [4] concerning a specific piece of software code (known as a patch) that is peer reviewed. Peer review is an important quality assurance mechanism in the OSS community but is less well understood when compared to other aspects of OSS development [5].

As the online forums facilitate peer reviews and interactions between members of the open source community, it offers a rich source of insights into community practices and social norms [3]. Previous research on online forums focused on discovering knowledge sharing practices [6], information seeking behaviours among developers

---

[1] OSS is a type of computer software in which source code is released under a license in which the copyright holder grants users the rights to study, change, and distribute the software to anyone and for any purpose (Laurent, AMS, 2004).

© IFIP International Federation for Information Processing 2019
Published by Springer Nature Switzerland AG 2019
I. O. Pappas et al. (Eds.): I3E 2019, LNCS 11701, pp. 392–403, 2019.
https://doi.org/10.1007/978-3-030-29374-1_32

[7], identifying active contributors [8], and the sentiment of members within the community [4, 9–12]. Research has shown that sentiment affect quality, productivity, creativity, group rapport, and job satisfaction [13]. Understanding the sentiment of software developers is important for project managers as it provides a better understanding of the social factors that affect the project and the corrective actions required to improve sentiment [4, 5].

OSS development is also a highly collaborative activity [2], requiring creativity and problem-solving skills, which are influenced by emotion [14]. Further, the sustainability of open source communities requires software developers to maintain healthy relationships with their peers in order to ensure their input and support [15]. It would therefore seem logical that the sentiment of project members plays an important role in the success or failure of a project, however project managers find it difficult to keep track of their people's feelings [1].

As OSS projects are notoriously subject to contradictions (i.e. tensions, conflict, breakdown in communication), we use Activity Theory (AT) to examine contradictions because AT anticipates this [16]. Contradictions are "historically accumulating structural tensions within and between activity systems" and are a fundamental concept in AT [17, p. 137]. The identification of contradictions helps practitioners to focus their efforts on the root causes of problems. This collaborative analysis can lead to the creation of a shared vision for the solution of the contradictions [18]. [19] propose four distinct types of contradictions which they associate with discursive manifestations, namely, (i) double binds, (ii) conflicts, (iii) critical conflicts, and (iv) dilemmas. In this manner, discursive manifestations can be associated with a type of contradiction and with its resolution.

We argue that a greater scrutiny of discursive manifestations is necessary in the study of open source communities for three key reasons.

First, by illuminating discursive manifestations of contradictions rich insights into the social norms and practices of open source communities will be revealed. This is important as organisations in the 21st century play an active role in shaping the structure and direction of open source communities [20].

Second, there is a noticeable absence of research that progress from simply applying sentiment analytics [1, 4, 5] to advancing the accumulative body of knowledge via theoretical development. This lack of cumulative tradition [21, 22] resonates with the issue of 'fragmented adhocracy', which has previously overshadowed IS research [23–25]. By grounding the study in AT, we theorise how sentiment analytics can be used to provide a deeper understanding contradictions.

Third, in the context of online forums that are used by open source communities, [26] makes a call for a serious expansion of our understanding of organisations, work, and learning. This study answers this call, by examining sentiment in the context of collaborative work.

Using AT as the theoretical lens is pertinent in this study for three key reasons, namely (i) understanding context in which the words are used is important as it strongly influences accuracy [27, 28] and AT is oriented at understanding the activity in context [29]. AT acknowledges contradictions as a means of understanding and change [17, 30], a concept that is not explicit in other social theories [31]. Hence, we make the claim that it is more useful to integrate sentiment analytics with the analysis of discursive manifestations. In doing so, rich insights into how emotions permeate work and contradictions, that influence how people work on daily basis is revealed. Therefore, through the lens of AT the overarching aim of this study is to

> "Explore how sentiment analytics can illuminate discursive manifestations of contradictions in the context of open source communities".

The paper is structured as follows. First, a review of literature on contradictions from the perspective of AT is presented. Next, the method used to extract and clean data for the purpose of analysis is outlined. Then, key findings and analysis is presented. Followed by discussion and implications for practice, academia, and society. The paper ends with conclusions, limitations and future action.

2 Activity Theory

Contemporary thinking on AT, known as third-generation AT emerged from the seminal work of [32] who acknowledges the systemic relations between an individual and their environment, by highlighting the influential nature and interrelatedness of the larger social context.

A fundamental concept of AT is the notion of contradictions, which occur within an activity and/or between multiple interrelated activities and promote dialectical transformation [17, 33]. While the term 'contradiction' may be considered by some as a weakness, from the perspective of AT, they are a sign of richness and an opportunity to develop in the activity system [33, 34]. Contradictions are seen as the sources of learning and can become the driving force for change and development in a system, if they are addressed [16]. Essentially contradictions are 'motors of change' [35]. Contradictions can occur either inside the key constructs (e.g. community) or between them, or they may occur in networks of activity systems [17, 36]. Contradictions can be identified through their manifestations, which include, disturbances, errors, problems, rupture of communication, breakdowns, and clashes [17, 37, 38]. However, contradictions may not be obvious, openly discussed, or be culturally or politically challenging to confront [35, 39]. Researchers must therefore rely on indirect methods to make visible the contradictions and to explain the genesis of their development [40].

More recently, discursive manifestations of contradictions in organisational change efforts have been studied [19, 40]. Table 1 lists four distinct types of contradictions that [19] associate with discursive manifestations and its resolutions.

Table 1. Types of discursive manifestations of contradictions

Manifestation	Features	Linguistic cues
Double bind	Facing pressing and equally unacceptable alternatives in an activity system: Resolution: practical transformation (going beyond words)	"We", "us", "we must", "we have to" pressing rhetorical questions, expressions of helplessness
Critical conflict	Facing contradictory motives in social interaction, feeling violated or guilty Resolution: finding new personal sense and negotiating a new meaning	Personal, emotional, moral accounts narrative structure, vivid metaphors "I now realise that…"
Conflict	Arguing, criticising Resolution: finding a compromise, submitting to authority or majority	"No", "I disagree", "this is not true", "this I can't accept"
Dilemma	Expression or exchange of incompatible evaluations Resolution: denial, reformulation	"On the one hand [.. .] on the other hand"; "yes, but" "I didn't mean that", "I actually meant"

Double bind is typically expressed "first by means of rhetorical questions indicating a cul-de-sac, a pressing need to do something and, at the same time, a perceived impossibility of action" [19]. Occurs when a person or group engages in interactions that raise paradoxical and contradictory demands, which make it difficult to step back from their current activities, and consequently create feelings of helplessness. A double bind is typically a situation which cannot be resolved by an individual alone [19]. Resolution requires making practical changes that are transformative and collective actions that go beyond words but is often accompanied with expressions such as "let us do that", "we will make it" [19, 40].

Critical conflict are situations 'in which people face inner doubts that paralyse them in front of contradictory motives unsolvable by the subject alone' [19, p. 374]. These critical conflicts are very emotionally and morally charged, which makes it difficult, or even impossible, for them to be resolved solely by the subjects involved (*ibid*). The discourse is also marked by vivid metaphors [40]. Resolution occurs 'via a renegotiation of meaning for the subject who was accompanied by the collective in order to allow the former to gain critical distance from their experience and to give it new meaning' (*ibid*, p. 282).

Conflict takes the form of resistance, disagreement, argument and criticism, and occurs "when an individual or a group feels negatively affected by another individual or group, i.e. because of a perceived divergence of interests, or because of another's incompatible behaviour" [41, p. 1]. [19] observed that people engaged in a conflict tend to argue and to criticise each other. Conflicts are resolved through compromise or submitting to authority or the majority [40].

Dilemma is an 'expression or exchange of incompatible evaluations, either between people or within the discourse of a single person' and is most often expressed in the form of hesitations, such as "yes, but" [19]. It is typically reproduced rather than resolved, often with the help of denial or reformulation (i.e. I didn't mean that).

3   Methodology

This section outlines the process we used to analyse sentiment and discursive manifestations pertaining to discussions via the DPDK[2] community platform between 28th Feb and 4th May 2018. As sentiment analysis tools require customisation for the context of software development [42–44] we customised two popular sentiment analysis dictionaries – '*Opinion Lexicon*' and '*Comparative Words*'. To analyse the sentiment in the message body content, we followed a similar approach to [9] where the message body is split into tokens and using a rule-based algorithm in combination with two dictionaries, assigned a positive, neutral, or negative score. The assigned sentiment scores ranged from 'Strong negative' (−20), Weak negative (−10), Neutral (0), Positive (+10), and Strong positive (+20). A token is assigned a score according to the matching word found in the dictionaries and the overall sentiment of a message was computed as the sum of all scores assigned to the tokens contained in that message. The research method consists of three inter-related phases, namely, (i) data extraction, (ii) data preprocessing, and (iii) data analysis.

Phase 1 Data Extraction: Comprised of extracting messages from the dpdk-dev mailing list archived at http://mails.dpdk.org/archives/dev/. A total of 13,461 messages were extracted in RAR file format.

Phase 2 Data Pre-processing: Executed using Python scripts, messages were converted from RAR file format into CSV file format and messages dated outside the release cycle removed. This resulted in 8,585 messages being included in this study. The message content was cleaned for analysis using regular expressions to ensure that only the message body and natural language remained. All message headers, code, file paths, and non-alphanumeric symbols/characters were removed. This activity was critical to reduce any instances of misclassification [1]. The remaining text was then converted into DataFrame format (tabular data structure in Python) for compatibility purposes with the sentiment analysis algorithm.

Phase 3 Data Analysis: As domain-specific terms influence sentiment analysis [1], the research team collaborated with members of the open source community to refine the dictionaries and data in an iterative manner. The natural language dictionary was augmented with domain-specific language of the open source community to include the following terms, 'NIT' (e.g. OK but a small problem),

---

[2] The main features of the DPDK review process include, (i) hosting software code in a public repository, (ii) a mailing list where registered members 'submit' code, (iii) code is reviewed publicly on the mailing list, and (iv), successfully reviewed code is merged into the main repository for scheduled releases.

'NACK' (e.g. Not accepted by the community), and 'LGTM' (e.g. Looks good to me). Also, as noted by [19], their categorisation of manifestations is not exhaustive. Therefore, the linguistic cues unique to the open source community studied are included in the analysis of discursive contradictions, namely, 'NIT' (e.g. Dilemma), and 'NACK' (e.g. Critical conflict). These findings are presented in the next section.

4 Findings and Analysis

We investigate sentiment around 'nack' and analyse the underlying discursive manifestations of contradictions, these are generally viewed by the community as wasted time and effort (i) of the developer who developed the patch, and (ii) of the community members who review the patch.

Sentiment Analysis: Figure 1 illustrates the sentiment score plotted against time, during which activities (e.g. scoping, pre-merge code, bug fix, test, and release) are completed as part of the release cycle. The red bars are the dates that 15 'nacks' occurred during the release cycle - 5 in March, 8 in April, and 2 in May.

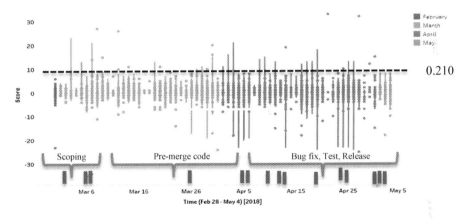

Fig. 1. Sentiment score plotted against time (Color figure online)

Analysis of the sentiment reveals that the overall sentiment is minimally positive (0.210). A number of positive and negative outliers are present at the start and end of release cycle. The underlying reason for these is that initially a patch will have errors/defects but following a series of reviews and revisions, the quality of the patch improves, as does sentiment of the community. As overall sentiment is minimally positive, these findings challenge the assumptions of the community that messages containing 'nack' should have strong negative sentiment. This indicates that the 'nack' messages can also contain positive sentiment that can have a neutralising effect on the overall sentiment score.

This finding is supported by the distribution of sentiment scores represented in Fig. 2 below. The sentiment score distribution that is normally distributed and the mode is zero. This indicates that the majority of discussions were neutral due to the technical nature of the conversations for each review.

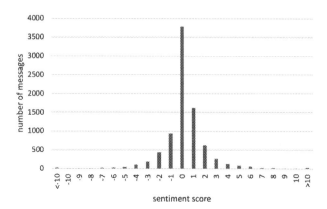

Fig. 2. Frequency distribution of sentiment scores

Table 2 provides a summary of the statistics for the 18.05 release cycle. These findings support the previous analysis such as the 'mean' progressing from −0.12 in Feb to +0.21 in April.

Table 2. Summary statistics of release cycle

	Feb	Mar	Apr	May	Release cycle
Number of messages	85	2884	5224	392	8,585
Mean sentiment score	−0.12	0.34	0.15	0.11	0.21
Standard deviation	2.98	2.56	2.56	2.38	2.55
% of messages with a sentiment score within 1 standard deviation	89%	86%	87%	83%	86%

To further investigate the underlying sentiment of 'nack' messages, the discursive manifestations of contradictions are analysed.

Analysis of Contradictions: Table 3 below shows that a 'nack' can manifest as different types of contradictions – critical conflict, conflict, and dilemma – indicating that there are subtle differences around instances of 'nack' that require further investigation. For example, in the following excerpt from an email message (2nd Mar), "*The proposed patch is a workaround that doesn't address the underlying issue, thus NACK unless proven otherwise:)*" we start to understand why sentiment around 'nack' are not strongly negative. Firstly, a smiley emoji at the end of the sentence indicates that the author is not adversarial with this comment. Secondly, the author rejects the patch, but leaves it to the community to prove that this patch is still useful for solving the "underlying issue", which implies this is a conditional 'nack' and the author is willing to retract it. In another excerpt (12th Apr), "*So, as it is, it's a NACK from me, but let's work together on something better:)*" a positive sentiment is displayed by the author who encourages the community to work towards a better solution, despite the rejection of the patch.

Table 3. Discursive manifestations of contradictions

Manifestation	Examples in context of this study	Frequency
Double bind	"We must guarantee" "We must allocate" "We can work around that" "We need to know how" "We must consider a solution" "We must send comments"	1,380
Critical conflict	"I am sorry; I have to NACK because the change is not explained" "I can't agree with this statement" "I'm very unhappy about the…" "No, we must use…"	933
Conflict	"I disagree with this final assessment" "I bet your teacher would disagree with that statement with one single paragraph in your book reports - taste is hard to debate, but you have gone the extreme route with only the bare minimum blank lines and that is not good" "Looks like you assume that the device is always plugged in while the DPDK application starts, this is not true"	10
Dilemma	"I don't like it. It's a NACK from me, but let's work together on something better" "Two nits I think we could add a note" "Self-nack on this patch" "On second thoughts, self-nack" "Does it mean a NACK?" "We would like 2 or 3 more days on this before we can 'ACK' 'NACK' this patch" "Yes, but I have already…" "NACK, I am looking into it"	41
	Total	2,364

5   Discussion and Implications

The study revealed that although 'nack' is considered by the community to be extremely negative, 7 cases of 'self-nack' occurred. Rather than categorise 'self-nack' as a critical conflict manifestation, in the context of this study it is categorised as a 'dilemma'. The reasoning for this is that a person who contemplates a 'self-nack' is faced with the dilemma of being ridiculed or rewarded by their peers, depending on when and why the 'self-nack' is initiated. The analysis of sentiment and contradictions collectively challenge the assumptions of the open source community, namely, that the community is overly negative due to the online platform that is used to communicate feedback on patch reviews, and that all instances of 'nack' are really negative and considered 'bad'. Further, from the perspective of AT, our analysis highlighted that events that are perceived as "bad" are indeed opportunities for innovation, improved dialogue within the community, and better collaboration between all stakeholders of the open source ecosystem. Also, rather than view a 'nack' as a waste of time, resources, and finances, it can be used as an opportunity to create events (on/offline) that can build cohesion in the open source community and contribute to the overall health and sustainability of the community.

The findings from this study have important implications for software development research in academia, industry, and the wider society.

Implications for Industry: First, understanding the pattern of communication is important because it provides an opportunity for management and project teams to stabilise the flow of work and patch reviews during the various activities (i.e. scoping) of a release cycle. Second, sentiment and contradictions provides insight into the emotional states of software developers and holds much promise for better management of people involved in software development projects in general. Third, it is a strategic advantage for organisations involved in open source projects to understand the circumstances of a 'nack' in order for corrective action to be taken.

Implications for Academia: First, as all data analysis tools have limitations, researchers need to not only assess the suitability of such tools for their research project, but also need to carefully understand the social context of the research in order to draw meaningful and actionable insights that enable organisational change. A second implication, which is related to the first, is that sentiment analysis, by itself, does not provide rich contextual data to drive organisational change (i.e. at project level). Supplementing this approach with a robust theoretical framework such as AT provides researchers with the opportunity to analyse and conceptualise complex real-world situations where the interrelationship between communities of people (open source community), mediating tools (online forum), and a cultural-historical setting co-evolve (new members join or leave the open community). Third, analysing the natural language used in the mailing list, from the perspective of discursive manifestations provides rich insights into the internal dynamics of online communities, which we know are not well understood [c.f. 6].

Implications for a Sustainable Society: As social sustainability is a key dimension of sustainability [45], the role of big data and analytics can have positive and negative implications for society [46]. Remote working is recognised as a key strategy for a sustainable society as it reduces travel, which in turn reduces carbon emissions. The tools used in this study have a meaningful role to play in enabling sustainable work practices as part of a larger suite of technologies that enable and support distributed work. Combining sentiment analysis with analysis of contradictions are useful indicators of the social well-being of individuals and teams, as well as maintaining the social structure of communities [47]. For example, these indicators can provide companies with opportunities to develop interventions that improve the quality of life and well being of its employees and their families, which in turn would reduce health care costs, as prevention is better than a cure [46].

6 Conclusion, Limitations, and Future Action

Obtaining accurate sentiment from mailing lists remains a key challenge [2] but can be mitigated by customising sentiment analysis tools for the context of the study [42]. The research demonstrates that it is feasible to extract and analyse data from mailing lists with high accuracy. We presented sentiment analysis as a mechanism for extracting (i) sentiment expressed in mailing list patch review comments, and (ii) the four types of discursive manifestations and their frequency during the release cycle. While a limitation of the study is that one release cycle is not representative of the DPDK online community, the study does present opportunities for future work in order to gain a deeper understanding of the relationship between discursive manifestations of contradictions and sentiment, as well as the propensity of individual reviewers over time. Future work will indeed focus on multiple release cycles during a full year and/or compare sentiment across multiple projects. This study highlights the importance of not only considering sentiment as quantitative values but to take into consideration the context of the sentiment values and how discourse can directly and indirectly have a positive or negative impact on people within the activity system.

Acknowledgements. This work was supported with the financial support of the Science Foundation Ireland grant 13/RC/2094 and co-funded under the European Regional Development Fund through the Southern & Eastern Regional Operational Programme to Lero | The Irish Software Research Centre (www.lero.ie).

References

1. Tourani, P., Jiang, Y., Adams, B.: Monitoring sentiment in open source mailing lists: exploratory study on the apache ecosystem. In: Proceedings of 24th Annual International Conference on Computer Science and Software Engineering, pp. 34–44. IBM Corp. (2014)
2. Mistrík, I., Grundy, J., van der Hoek, A., Whitehead, J.: Collaborative software engineering: challenges and prospects. In: Mistrík, I., Grundy, J., Hoek, A., Whitehead, J. (eds.) Collaborative software engineering, pp. 389–403. Springer, Heidelberg (2010). https://doi.org/10.1007/978-3-642-10294-3_19
3. Bird, C., et al.: Mining email social networks. In: Proceedings of the 2006 International Workshop on Mining Software Repositories, pp. 137–143. ACM (2006)
4. Guzman, E., Azócar, D., Li, Y.: Sentiment analysis of commit comments in GitHub: an empirical study. In: Proceedings of the 11th Working Conference on Mining Software Repositories, pp. 352–355. ACM (2014)
5. Rigby, P.C., German, D.M., Storey, M.A.: Open source software peer review practices: a case study of the apache server. In: Proceedings of the 30th International Conference on Software Engineering, pp. 541–550. ACM (2008)
6. Sowe, S.K., Stamelos, I., Angelis, L.: Understanding knowledge sharing activities in free/open source software projects: an empirical study. J. Syst. Softw. **81**(3), 431–446 (2008)
7. Sharif, K.Y., et al.: An empirically-based characterization and quantification of information seeking through mailing lists during open source developers' software evolution. Inf. Softw. Technol. **57**, 77–94 (2015)

8. Guzzi, A., et al.: Communication in open source software development mailing lists. In: Proceedings of the 10th Working Conference on Mining Software Repositories, pp. 277–286. IEEE Press (2013)

9. Rousinopoulos, A., Robles, G., González-Barahona, J.: Sentiment analysis of free/open source developers: preliminary findings from a case study. Electron. J. Inf. Syst. **13**(2), 1 (2014)

10. Pletea, D., Vasilescu, B., Serebrenik, A.: Security and emotion: sentiment analysis of security discussions on GitHub. In: Proceedings of the 11th Working Conference on Mining Software Repositories, pp. 348–351. ACM (2014)

11. Paul, R., Bosu, A., Sultana, K.Z.: Expressions of Sentiments During Code Reviews: Male vs. Female. arXiv preprint arXiv:1812.05560 (2018)

12. Sinha, V., Lazar, A., Sharif, B.: Analyzing developer sentiment in commit logs. In: Proceedings of the 13th International Conference on Mining Software Repositories, pp. 520–523. ACM (2016)

13. De Choudhury, M., Counts, S.: Understanding affect in the workplace via social media. In: Proceedings of the 2013 Conference on Computer Supported Cooperative Work, pp. 303–316. ACM (2013)

14. Carver, J., et al.: Gender, sentiment and emotions, and safety-critical systems. IEEE Softw. **35**(6), 16–19 (2018)

15. Ozer, M., Vogel, D.: Contextualized relationship between knowledge sharing and performance in software development. J. Manag. Inf. Syst. **32**(2), 134–161 (2015)

16. Hasan, H., Banna, S.: The unit of analysis in IS theory: the case for activity. Inf. Syst. Found. **191** (2012)

17. Engeström, Y.: Expansive learning at work: toward an activity theoretical reconceptualization. J. Educ. Work **14**(1), 133–156 (2001)

18. Engestrom, Y.: Activity theory as a framework for analyzing and redesigning work. Ergonomics **43**(7), 960–974 (2000)

19. Engeström, Y., Sannino, A.: Discursive manifestations of contradictions in organizational change efforts: a methodological framework. J. Organ. Change Manag. **24**(3), 368–387 (2011)

20. Germonprez, M., Levy, M.: Is it egalitarianism or enterprise strategy? Exploring a new method of innovation in open source (2015)

21. Metcalfe, M.: Theory: seeking a plain English explanation. JITTA: J. Inf. Technol. Theor. Appl. **6**(2), 13 (2004)

22. Weick, K.E.: Theory construction as disciplined imagination. Acad. Manag. Rev. **14**(4), 516–531 (1989)

23. Fitzgerald, B., Adam, F.: The status of the IS field: historical perspective and practical orientation (2000)

24. Banville, C., Landry, M.: Can the field of MIS be disciplined? Commun. ACM **32**(1), 48–60 (1989)

25. Hirschheim, R., Klein, H.K., Lyytinen, K.: Exploring the intellectual structures of information systems development: a social action theoretic analysis. Acc. Manag. Inf. Technol. **6**(1), 1–64 (1996)

26. Engeström, Y., Kerosuo, H.: From workplace learning to inter-organizational learning and back: the contribution of activity theory. J. Workplace Learning **19**(6), 336–342 (2007)

27. Aue, A., Gamon, M.: Customizing sentiment classifiers to new domains: a case study. In: Proceedings of Recent Advances in Natural Language Processing (RANLP), vol. 1, no. 3.1, pp. 2–1 (2005)

28. Turney, P.D.: Thumbs up or thumbs down? Semantic orientation applied to unsupervised classification of reviews. In: Proceedings of the 40th Annual Meeting on Association for Computational Linguistics, pp. 417–424. Association for Computational Linguistics (2002)

29. Cole, M., Engeström, Y.: A cultural-historical approach to distributed cognition. In: Distributed Cognitions: Psychological and Educational Considerations. Cambridge University Press, Cambridge. pp. 1–46 (2014)

30. Ilyenkov, E.: Dialectical Logic: Essays on its History and Theory. Progress Publishers, Moscow and Pacifica, CA (1974)

31. Karanasios, S., Allen, D.: Mobile technology in mobile work: contradictions and congruencies in activity systems. Eur. J. Inf. Syst. **23**(5), 529–542 (2014)

32. Engestrom, Y.: Learning by Expanding. Orienta-Konsultit Oy, Helsinki (1987)

33. Karanasios, S., Riisla, K., Simeonova, B.: Exploring the use of contradictions in activity theory studies: an interdisciplinary review (2017)

34. Karanasios, S.: Toward a unified view of technology and activity: the contribution of activity theory to information systems research. Inf. Technol. People **31**(1), 134–155 (2018)

35. Allen, D.K., et al.: How should technology-mediated organizational change be explained? a comparison of the contributions of critical realism and activity theory. MIS Q. **37**(3), 835–854 (2013)

36. White, L., Burger, K., Yearworth, M.: Understanding behaviour in problem structuring methods interventions with activity theory. Eur. J. Oper. Res. **249**(3), 983–1004 (2016)

37. Helle, M.: Disturbances and contradictions as tools for understanding work in the newsroom. Scand. J. Inf. Syst. **12**(1), 7 (2000)

38. Kuutti, K.: Activity theory as a potential framework for human-computer interaction research. In: Context and Consciousness: Activity Theory and Human-Computer Interaction, pp. 17–44. MIT Press (1995)

39. Capper, P., Williams, B.: Enhancing evaluation using systems concepts. American Evaluation Association (2004)

40. Dionne, P., Bourdon, S.: Contradictions as the driving force of collective and subjective development group employment programmes. J. Educ. Work **31**, 1–14 (2018)

41. De Dreu, C.K.W., Van De Vliert, E.: Introduction: using conflict in organizations (1997)

42. Lin, B., et al.: Sentiment analysis for software engineering: how far can we go? In: 2018 IEEE/ACM 40th International Conference on Software Engineering (ICSE), pp. 94–104. IEEE (2018)

43. Novielli, N., Girardi, D., Lanubile, F.: A benchmark study on sentiment analysis for software engineering research. In: Proceedings of the 15th International Conference on Mining Software Repositories, pp. 364–375. ACM, New York (2018). https://doi.org/10.1145/3196398.3196403

44. Jongeling, R., Datta, S., Serebrenik, A.: Choosing your weapons: on sentiment analysis tools for software engineering research. In: 2015 IEEE International Conference on Software Maintenance and Evolution (ICSME), pp. 531–535 (2015). https://doi.org/10.1109/ICSM.2015.7332508

45. Moos, M., Andrey, J., Johnson, L.C.: The sustainability of telework: an ecological-footprinting approach. Sustain.: Sci. Pract. Policy **2**(1), 3–14 (2006)

46. Pappas, I.O., et al.: Big data and business analytics ecosystems: paving the way towards digital transformation and sustainable societies (2018)

47. Rogers, D.S., et al.: A vision for human well-being: transition to social sustainability. Curr. Opin. Environ. Sustain. **4**(1), 61–73 (2012)

Analyzing Customer Engagement Using Twitter Analytics: A Case of Uber Car-Hailing Services

Saroj Bijarnia[✉], Richa Khetan, P. Vigneswara Ilavarasan, and Arpan K. Kar

Department of Management Studies, Indian Institute of Technology Delhi, Vishwakarma Bhawan, New Delhi 110016, India
saroj.bijarnia91@gmail.com, richa.khetan18@dmsiitd.org, {vignes,arpankar}@iitd.ac.in

Abstract. Nowadays, most of the organizations and businesses develop online services, which add value in their business and even increase their customer base. Social Media has changed the dynamics of digital marketing. Social media gives power to customers to post, share, and review content. Customers can directly interact with other customers and companies. In this paper, we will analysis huge user-generated content which can be used by organizations for their customer engagement strategies. The purpose of this study is to derive insights using Twitter Analytics on Twitter data to understand how businesses use Twitter for customer engagement strategies. Data collected from Twitter. The present paper uses descriptive and content analysis techniques for analyzing the tweets. The analysis will help in identifying the gaps in the priorities of the stakeholders. With the right customer engagement strategies, companies can make benefits.

Keywords: Twitter Analytics · Customer engagement · Sharing economy

1 Introduction

The concept of Customer engagement has gained attention in recent years by both practitioners and academics [21]. Organizations today need to build an emotional connection with their customers for performing better. This business communication between the brand and its customers referred to as customer engagement [5]. The outcome is a customer base with more brand loyalty and awareness and hence better revenues for the company. Companies today use various methods like personalized discounts, feedback collection, social campaigns, which could be either offline or online. However, with the major shift towards technology, companies have now extensively started using social media for engaging with their customers, for Example, blogs, microblogging sites, Video sites, social sites [22].

The competition among the players and the service providers on online services are rising. Companies always need to come up with new ideas, features, and discounts, etc. They also need to pay special attention to their customer service, as being an online

© IFIP International Federation for Information Processing 2019
Published by Springer Nature Switzerland AG 2019
I. O. Pappas et al. (Eds.): I3E 2019, LNCS 11701, pp. 404–414, 2019.
https://doi.org/10.1007/978-3-030-29374-1_33

platform, they receive instant criticisms or gratifications. Social media platforms widely used for expressing such emotions by users. In the long run, customer loyalty can contribute by continuous engagement and providing differentiated service.

Twitter has gained immense popularity and is being used in all fields like political campaigns, marketing purposes, branding, public sensitization, etc. [16]. Twitter is being used by users and service providers extensively for discussions and opinions. So, it very important to analyze, visualize, and summarize the Twitter conversations for finding the new insights in respective of customer engagement [16, 23]. The reason why marketers should concern about Twitter conversations because tweets from customers and service providers can influence the sentiments of customers towards their brands. Keeping this in mind, the purpose of this study is to explore the Customer engagement behavior of Uber in India and the users of this service, in the Twitter platform. Uber, a US-based company, is one of the leaders in sharing economy in the global market [18]. As a business that runs from a digital platform, Uber follows many customer engagement methods. We aim to understand the strategy that Uber applies to ensure customer loyalty and hassle-free customer service. So, we attempt to address the following research objectives (RO) based on Uber as a case study using Twitter data.

RO1: Using social media analytics to learn about customer engagement of businesses.

RO2: Examine customer engagement behavior of Uber in India using Twitter data.

In this paper, Sect. 2 describes literature. Section 3 is talking about methodology and findings. Section 4 describes managerial implications, and in the end, Sect. 5 gives limitations and future work.

2 Literature Review

Social media users generate a massive amount of user data. Social media term means online portals and websites where people can share information, interest, and even can give opinions [8]. Social media and engagement connected as social media engagement mean communication or interaction. There are several studies on social media and engagement [9–12]. Armstrong and Hagel [13] highlighted that engagement through social media for marketers can be beneficial. Even now, it becomes a new business communication way where marketers and customers can get engaged in conversations [14]. Existing literature shows many insights about engagement on social media [3–6]. It is also relieved that on social media customer engagement is easier. Boyd et al. [14] studied retweet behavior and tried to connect with customer engagement. Harrigan et al. [15] highlight customer engagement in respective of tourism brands based on social media. Ibrahim et al. [16] collected data from Twitter and studied to determine how different types of engagement with customers affect customer sentiments. Social media conversations also affect brand value of businesses. Ahujaa and Shakeel [1] talk about customer engagement for this purpose; they used word clouds and further did sentiment analysis for Jet Airways. There are few studies, which uses social media data for customer engagement [24, 27]. Twitter has been used as a social media platform for customer engagement [2, 7].

The sharing economy has changed the way of consuming goods and services [25]. Kumar et al. [26] give insights for service enablers, i.e., how resources and focus between service providers and customers can be balanced. Most of the current literature addresses, what are the motives of a consumer to participate in collaborative services tangibly [25]. Based on the literature, we find out that there is no study in sharing economy domain where customer engagement measured on Twitter data conversations.

3   Methodology and Findings

3.1   Data Collection

The collection of tweets from Twitter was done using R programming and using TwitteR package. Tweets having #Uber_India, #uberindia and @mentions of Uber_-India, UberINSupport, Uber_Support collected over three months from October 2017 to December 2017. The tweets collected were then segregated into two categories. First is tweets by users in which the tweets collected from the same handles. The tweets having @mentions of Uber but not posted by Uber were separated and were taken to be tweeted by the customers. Second is Tweets by Uber. The tweets which had been tweeted by the Uber company handles were chosen to be tweets by Uber. Post removing duplicates, we had 46,618 tweets by Uber and 41,135 tweets by the users.

3.2   Data Preprocessing

The data preprocessing involved steps like removing URLs, @usernames, numbers and punctuations and common English stop words like the, are, is, Uber, etc. Stemming of the document and stripping the white spaces have done [19]. The "tm" package in R programming was used to achieve this. The result was a set of tweets with only the words that have relevance and can contribute to the analysis.

3.3   Data Analysis

The analysis was done separately for both types of categories of tweets, i.e., the tweets by the users and the tweets by the Uber as the objective was to understand the customer engagement of Uber, the activities and reactions of the users to the service provided by Uber. For this purpose, Descriptive analytics of the tweets done in the form of the word cloud and content analysis [20].

Tweets by Users: The purpose of analyzing the tweets by users is to understand their essential requirements and their satisfaction from the services of Uber.

Word Cloud: As a part of the analysis, the most common words used by the users found out in the form of a word cloud (Fig. 1). The size of the word is proportional to its usage. It shows that words like "driver," "help," "app," "charge" dominate the picture. Some other words which stand out are "issue," "cancel," "refund," "support" etc. which seem to portray an image of users facing issues with the service and looking out for help. The critical topics of discussion are related to payment, security, ride, bookings, and customer service, which tells that users generally use Twitter to post the issues or they may have faced and looked for support and resolution from the company.

Sentiment Analysis: Sentiment analysis would help us to understand the dominating sentiments of the users towards Uber in their tweets.

(a)   (b)

Fig. 1. (a) Word Cloud for user tweets (b) Word Cloud for Uber tweets customer replies

Figure 2 shows the sentiment analysis of the tweets by the users. It shows that the highest percentage is for trust, followed by anticipation and sadness. Users were looking for a trust factor while availing any services. About the sentiments, even though the positive sentiment is slightly more than negative, there is still a large percentage which falls under negative sentiment which cannot be ignored.

Topic Modeling: Topic modeling discovers abstract "topics" in a set of documents which are in the form of a cluster of words. For this purpose, we have used the Latent Dirichlet Allocation (LDA) model [17]. For this study, 50 such topics of 15 words each found. From the word cloud, we could understand that the users gave priority to customer service. However, to further understand the most common reasons for their issues or the topics of discussion among them, these topics were manually classified under three categories i.e. customer service, information sharing, and criticism.

A. *Customer Service:* Customer service, we can divivde into two categories i.e. technical and non-technical (Table 1).

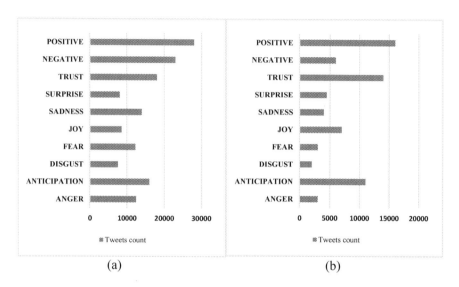

Fig. 2. (a) Sentiment analysis of user tweets (b) Sentiment analysis of Uber tweets

Table 1. Classification of customer services

Category	Attribute	Description
Technical	Application/account related	Tweets that talked about the Uber application and account related issues like login, bookings, etc.
	Payment	Problems related to payment and payment methods like being overcharged, Paytm associated problems, etc.
	Fares and promo	Issues related to the charge and promotion offers given like Fares incorrectly charged, promo code did not work as expected
Non-technical	Safety	About problems or threat of any kind, the passengers must have faced during the journey
	Quality of customer service	Problems with the customer service they receive, which includes the time duration of customer query resolution, experience of the customer in this duration, follow-ups due to the delay, etc.
	Diversifications	Issues with the different services under Uber, for example, Uber Eats, Uber Pool, Uber Auto, etc.

B. News/Information Sharing: Customers share the current trending information about the organization like the change in leadership, organizational expansion, mergers or acquisitions, etc. A loyal customer is interested to know about the brand and expects continuous communication about the organizational strategies.

C. Criticism: Customers directly criticize the services of the company when they face issues with the services in any form. They may sometimes not be as generous with their complaints. Others Mostly dealing with collaborations, feedback received, etc. which are few.

On classification, the results were obtained as shown in Table 2. It observed that a vast majority of tweets (72%) dealt with customer service, be it for technical or non-technical issues. This shows that users use Twitter extensively for seeking issue solution. Among these, a significant chunk of the topics related to the quality of customer service (20%) and issues related to payment (13%) and driver (13%). This reinstates the importance of customer service. Customers look for quicker and a hassle-free solution to their problems. Any issues about the duration taken for customer service, constant reminders from the customer's end, unsatisfactory resolution, etc. reflect poorly on the quality of customer care. Customers are also open with their criticisms (13%) and not as transparent about appreciations.

Tweets by Uber: These are the Tweets posted by Uber. Which, we can divide into three major types. First is Customer Replies. These are the replies to individual customers and looks to either provide a solution to their issue, request for further information to solve the problem or give some information to a user query. Second is retweets. Many of the positive comments by the users and feedbacks are retweeted by Uber and broadcasted to their followers to increase their brand value and marketing. Tweets by customers provide a more significant impact and help in increasing their customer base.

In the end, third is Tweets by Uber for Customer Engagement. These were the tweets by Uber which aims at establishing constant engagement with the customers, be it in terms of providing promos, running a contest, talking about a social cause, etc. Sentiment analysis of all Uber Tweets shown in Fig. 2. On analyzing the tweets, it observed that the percentage of tweets in each of the categories mentioned above found to be as given below in Table 3. Most of the tweets are customer replies, followed by retweets and then tweets by Uber for establishing customer engagement. We analyzed these three categories in detail for more insights into customer enagagement. Which discussed in below subsequent subsections.

A. Customer Replies

Word Cloud: Among the tweets of customer replies, a word cloud was formed to understand the most common words in use. The results have shown in Fig. 1. It saw that words like "Please," "Help," "Sorry" is prominent, which shows that they are amicable and apologetic in their response to the issues. Other words such as "email," "app," "section," "register," etc. show the solutions given for the issues faced by users. The customer replies as expected, mostly dealt with providing customer care services.

Table 2. Classification of user tweets

Types of tweets			Percentage
Customer service	Technical	Application and account related	9%
		Payment	13%
		Promo, Fares	7%
	Non-technical	Safety/security	7%
		Quality of customer service	20%
		Driver	13%
		Diversifications	4%
News/information sharing			9%
Criticism			13%
Others			7%

Sentiment Analysis: Further, sentiment analysis was done to understand the polarity of response by Uber. On examining Fig. 3, the fact that sentiment adopted by Uber towards the user is highly positive. The trust factor is very high, while emotions like disgust and fear are the least. These results show that Uber tries to build trust among its customers, knowing that it is of utmost importance to them. The language they use for interaction is also very positive.

Topic Modeling: A topic modeling for the tweets was done, with an output of 15 topics containing ten words each. Each of these topics divided into four types of replies. Viriya et al. [7] used a six type of reply model. However, in our study, we have removed the chit-chat and the positive comment categories as they do not fit in our data. The four types of replies can be explained as below:

Table 3. Classification of Uber tweets

Categories	% of tweets
Customer replies	81.8
Customer engagement	7.2
Re-tweets	11

i. Information: The purpose of the reply is to provide the users with useful information he/she needs.
ii. Apology: The purpose of the response is to apologize for a mistake. Such reactions are crucial when providing customer support and typically contain apologetic and supportive words, such as 'sorry,' 'apology,' etc.
iii. Question & inquiry: The purpose of the reply is to ask the user a question or request specific information.
iv. Gratitude: The purpose of the reply is to offer gratitude or thank to the user. It was seen that the maximum types of responses were for information (47%), followed by an apology (24%). The other two were less frequent, i.e., gratitude (18%), inquiry and question (12%).

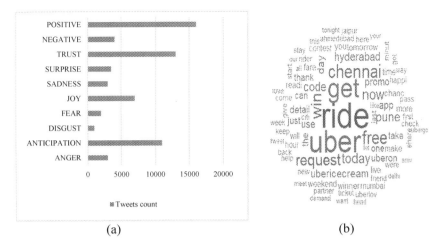

(a)   (b)

Fig. 3. (a) Sentiment analysis for customer replies of Uber (b) Word Cloud for customer engagement of Uber

Since we had seen earlier that maximum tweets by users were related to issues and customer service, the replies by Uber are in sync with that. Most of their responses dealt with providing information to the customer, be it about their issues and how to resolve them or proactive information. Also, a large section of the tweets was for apologizing and empathizing with the customers for their unhappiness and inconvenience they may have faced.

B. Retweets: Uber retweets many positive comments and appreciations they receive from the customers. It acts as online word-of-mouth; hence, customers get more influenced. It acts as a recommendation by the customers and helps in increasing their customer base and building new relationships. It is these retweets that make a tweet go viral in the online media. Therefore this is a great strategy used by businesses to improve their brand presence. Also, retweeting user tweets makes them feel good and post similar compliments in the future. Retweeting again helps in building the brand image. While Uber retweets customer comments, they also frequently request the customers to retweet their tweets to increase their reach. This action is usually a part of a contest or to promote it. This strategy, along with providing information to the existing followers, also helps in generating new customers.

C. Tweets by Uber for Customer Engagement: These tweets are the contents created by Uber for customer engagement. It may be in the form of contests that involve interactions by customers, providing information about the organization or services, talking about collaborations, and social issues.

Word Cloud: A word cloud created (Fig. 3) and it shows that, apart from the names of the cities in which Uber has its operations, words like "free," "ride," "win," "code," "contest," "promo" show relevance. These words suggest that promotion campaigns are widely run to ensure users embrace the service. The reason could be because the customers in India are very price sensitive. Campaigns like "ubericecream" also seem to have been well promoted. Since we wanted to understand in-depth how Uber engaged with its customers so, further, the tweets divided into three categories, which explained below:

Organizational Content: These directed towards the organization and shares news about organizational growth, plans, and corporate social responsibility, etc. They help to build an image of the brand in the minds of the customers.

Promotional Content: These deal with promotional campaigns to increase their business and provide information related to the products and prices. The aim is that the customers accept the product and use it.

Relational Content: These are information which is of considerable significance to the customer and shows the sensitive side of the organization. The primary objective here is to build a long lasting relationship with the customer by keeping them engaged.

Instead of finding the topics of discussion using topic modeling, the 4598 tweets by Uber were categorized into these three categories manually to get a more realistic picture. It observed that a significant portion of the tweets dedicated to promotional content (86%) followed by relational content (13%) and organizational content (less than 1%). It shows that Uber focuses highly on promotions. They regularly give offers in the form of free rides, rate cuts, credit points, etc. This strategy is essential as the users in India are price sensitive, and there are several players in the market offering competitive prices. Such promotions become crucial for such industries. Lastly, the organizational content, as expected, is low. They share details about the organization and its leadership, but the number deficient. An overall picture from the analysis shown below (Table 4), which gives a comparison of the results obtained using Social Media Analytics of the two perspectives of customer engagement.

4   Discussion and Managerial Implications

Post studying the tweets by users and by Uber, it can be said that users give high importance to the trust factor when availing the services of a cab aggregator. Safety is of utmost importance. The quality of customer service provided by a company is a major factor that determines if a customer would be loyal to them and continue using their services. Uber should keep these in mind in their social engagement strategy. Since customers have shown dissatisfaction for the customer care service provided, Uber should make it their focus area. A discontented customer tends to become a negative influencer which could pose a problem for Uber. Most of the issues arise for payments or driver related issues. These should be made a priority if the target is to reduce the number of problems faced by the customers over time.

The current activity by Uber in social media is mostly in line with the customer requirement as the majority of their tweets are catering to customer service, issue judgement, positive and polite. However, they still need to improve the quality in terms of quicker resolution and better communication. Apart from this, Uber should also post more information about the organization as it would make customers feel more connected. They should seek more feedback from the customers. Uber has excellent promotional and customer engagement programs.

5 Limitations and Future Research

The study was initiated to explore the Customer Relationship Management (CRM) of Uber. However, we faced issues with segregating the tweets into the different stages of CRM – Customer Acquisition, Retention, and Advocacy. A large number of tweets made it difficult to classify them manually. Using topic modeling also did not help resolve this as the topics do not give a clear picture of the content talked. A new way of trying to explore this could be done which would help organizations to reflect upon their existing CRM models. The scope of this study has been limited to India and could be expanded globally. In our study, the drivers have not been taken into consideration enough though they form a large customer segment for Uber. A survey of the drivers could have been done to analyze the relationship of the organization with the drivers. This survey would increase the extent of the study to incorporate all the stakeholders. The scope of this study can be further expanded to study the retweets in-depth, which would help identify the influencers and the correlation between retweets and various stages of CRM.

Table 4. Comparison of the two perspectives

Analysis method	Tweets by users	Tweets by UBER
Word cloud	Words related to issues faced with respect to payments, ride, driver etc. are highlighted	Words that dominate are related to customer issue resolution
Sentiment analysis	Emphasis given to trust and safety Positive sentiment slightly more than negative. However, a large percentage is still negative which shows that a large segment of customers are dissatisfied	Emphasis given to safety and tries to re-install trust in the mind of the customers Highly positive for customer service which shows that Uber maintains a positive behavior in their interaction
Topic modelling	Mostly related to customer issues Top complaints: • Customer service quality • Payments related • Driver related	For customer service most topics were for providing information or apology in one form of the other For customer engagement, highly focused on promotions and campaigns

References

1. Ahujaa, V., Shakeel, M.: Twitter presence of jet airways-deriving customer insights using netnography and word clouds. Proc. Comput. Sci. **122**, 17–24 (2017)
2. Díaz-Martín, A.M., Rozano, M., Menéndez-Benito, H.D.: Using Twitter to engage with customers: a data mining approach. Internet Res. **25**(3), 416–434 (2015)
3. Arsenault, P.: Using social media for effective customer service. Vermont Connect. **35**, 20–31 (2014). Article 3
4. Sashi, C.M.: Customer engagement, buyer-seller relationships, and social media. Manag. Decis. **50**(2), 253–272 (2012)

5. Peltier, J.W., Schultz, D.E.: Social media and consumer engagement: a review and research agenda. J. Res. Interact. Mark. **10**(4), 268–287 (2016)
6. Vivek, S.D., Beatty, S.R., Morgan, R.M.: Customer engagement: exploring customer relationships beyond purchase. J. Mark. Theor. Pract. **20**(2), 122–146 (2014)
7. Taecharungroj, V.: Starbucks' marketing communications strategy on Twitter. J. Mark. Commun. **23**(6), 552–571 (2017)
8. Hansen, D., Shneiderman, B., Smith, M.A.: Analyzing Social Media Networks with NodeXL: Insights from a Connected World. Morgan Kaufmann, Burlington (2010)
9. Chae, B.: Insights from hashtag #supplychain and Twitter analytics: considering Twitter and Twitter data for supply chain practice and research. Int. J. Prod. Econ. **165**, 247–259 (2015)
10. Ebner, M., Lienhardt, C., Rohs, M., Meyer, I.: Microblogs in Higher Education a chance to facilitate informal and process-oriented learning? Comput. Educ. **55**(1), 92–100 (2010)
11. Meske, C., Stieglitz, S.: Adoption and use of social media in small and medium-sized enterprises. In: Harmsen, F., Proper, H.A. (eds.) PRET 2013. LNBIP, vol. 151, pp. 61–75. Springer, Heidelberg (2013). https://doi.org/10.1007/978-3-642-38774-6_5
12. Golbeck, J., Grimes, J.M., Rogers, A.: Twitter use by the U.S. Congress. J. Am. Soc. Inf. Sci. Technol. **61**(8), 1612–1621 (2010)
13. Armstrong, A., Hagel, J.: The real value of online communities. In: Knowledge and Communities, pp. 85–95 (2000)
14. Boyd, D., Golder, S., Lotan, G.: Tweet, tweet, retweet: conversational aspects of retweeting on Twitter. Paper presented at the Proceedings of the 43rd Hawaii International Conference on System Sciences (2010)
15. Harrigan, P., Evers, U., Miles, M., Daly, T.: Customer engagement with tourism social media brands. Tourism Manag. **59**, 597–609 (2017)
16. Ibrahim, N.F., Wang, X., Bourne, H.: Exploring the effect of user engagement in online brand communities: evidence from Twitter. Comput. Hum. Behav. **72**, 321–338 (2017)
17. Blei, D.M., Ng, A.Y., Jordan, M.I.: Latent dirichlet allocation. J. Mach. Learn. Res. **3**(Jan), 993–1022 (2003)
18. Wallsten, S.: The competitive effects of the sharing economy: how is uber changing taxis? (2015)
19. Clark, E., Araki, K.: Text normalization in social media: progress, problems and applications for a pre-processing system of casual English. Proc. Soc. Behav. Sci. **27**, 2–11 (2011)
20. Krippendorff, K.: Content Analysis: An Introduction to its Methodology. Sage, London (2004)
21. Brodie, R.J., Hollebeek, L.D., Juric, B., Ilic, A.: Customer engagement: conceptual domain, fundamental propositions, and implications for research. J. Serv. Res. **14**, 252–271 (2011)
22. Wirtz, B.W., Schilke, O., Ullrich, S.: Strategic development of business models: implications of the Web 2.0 for creating value on the internet. Long Range Plan. **43**(2–3), 272–290 (2010)
23. Weiguo, F.W., Gordon, D.M.: The power of social media analytics. Commun. ACM **57**(6), 74–81 (2014)
24. Ashley, C., Tuten, T.: Creative strategies in social media marketing: an exploratory study of branded social content and consumer engagement. Psychol. Mark. **32** (2015). https://doi.org/10.1002/mar.20761
25. Milanova, V., Maas, P.: Sharing intangibles: uncovering individual motives for engagement in a sharing service setting. J. Bus. Res. **75**, 159–171 (2017). https://doi.org/10.1016/j.jbusres.2017.02.002
26. Kumar, V., Lahiri, A., Dogan, O.: A strategic framework for a profitable business model in the sharing economy. Ind. Mark. Manag. **69** (2017). https://doi.org/10.1016/j.indmarman.2017.08.021
27. Liu, L., Lee, M., Liu, R., Chen, J.: Trust transfer in social media brand communities: the role of consumer engagement. Int. J. Inf. Manag. **41**, 1–13 (2018). https://doi.org/10.1016/j.ijinfomgt.2018.02.006

Aggressive Social Media Post Detection System Containing Symbolic Images

Kirti Kumari[1], Jyoti Prakash Singh[1], Yogesh K. Dwivedi[2],
and Nripendra P. Rana[2(✉)]

[1] National Institute of Technology Patna, Patna, India
{kirti.cse15,jps}@nitp.ac.in
[2] School of Management, Swansea University, Swansea, UK
ykdwivedi@gmail.com, nrananp@gmail.com

Abstract. Social media platforms are an inexpensive communication medium help to reach other users very quickly. The same benefit is also utilized by some mischievous users to post objectionable images and symbols to certain groups of people. This types of posts include cyber-aggression, cyberbullying, offensive content, and hate speech. In this work, we analyze images posted on online social media sites to hurt online users. In this research, we designed a deep learning based system to classify aggressive post from a non-aggressive post containing symbolic images. To show the effectiveness of our model, we created a dataset crawling images from Google search to query aggressive images. The validation shows promising results.

Keywords: Cyber-aggression · Cyberbullying ·
Online Social Networks · Convolutional Neural Network ·
Augmentation

1 Introduction

With the emergence of the web-based popular Online Social Networks (OSN) such as Instagram[1], Facebook[2], Vine[3], these are exponentially increasing the user-generated content, that can reach billions of people in mere of a second. These sites make a user find people with common interests, share enormous real-time information, and eases business. In spite of these benefits, there are many detrimental outcomes associated with OSN such as Internet harassment, Cyber-aggression [4], Cyberstalking [12], Cyberbullying [23], and many more. Among them, Cyber-aggression is a growing and serious problem for online users. Cyber-aggression is defined as aggressive or hostile behavior that uses electronic media to cause harm to other people [8,9,13,14]. Cyber-aggression could occur

---

[1] www.instagram.com.

[2] www.facebook.com.

[3] https://vine.co/.

© IFIP International Federation for Information Processing 2019
Published by Springer Nature Switzerland AG 2019
I. O. Pappas et al. (Eds.): I3E 2019, LNCS 11701, pp. 415–424, 2019.
https://doi.org/10.1007/978-3-030-29374-1_34

in various form like, written/verbal aggression (e-mails, instant messaging, chats, verbal post, etc.), visual-based aggression (posting, sending or sharing embarrassing images or video).

Cyber-aggression crosses all physical borderline. The Internet has abundantly opened up the global platform to users who access it on a wide-range of devices. Some users use free to post or send whatever they want on an online platform without bearing in mind how that content can inflict pain and sometimes cause severe psychological and emotional injuries. Online users can hide their identities through the Internet too easily [7]. The social networking site such as ask.fm[4] allow the users to post with hiding their identity. As a result, the experiences of a victim may be unnoticed, and the activities of a bully may remain uncontrolled. Even if bullies are recognized, many individuals are unaware of responding properly to these instances. Cyber-aggression can be continual phenomenon because of the easily available, and access of the Internet make viral and exposing the victims to an entire virtual world. It makes them feel sick and worthless. Although any age-group of social networking user could be affected by Cyber-aggression, teenagers and youngsters are the most affected people. Cyber-aggression on teenagers and youngsters have been shown to cause both mental and psychological issues. Most of the time, kids and teenagers use online social sites only with curiosity irrespective of knowing the potential risks [22]. Recent studies have reported that teenagers make generous use of image and video sharing online sites (e.g., Instagram, Vine) [18]. In particular, visual (image and video) content now accounts for more than 70 % of all web contents[5]. All together, there has been a substantial rise in using image and video content for Cyber-aggression [25] and it has been declared that Cyber-aggression grows bigger and meaner with photos and video [10]. The reality is that cyberbullying is one such issue that only becomes more severe if it is ignored. Therefore, it must be monitored at an earlier stage. The severity of the problem needs immediate attention from a technical point of view because manual detection is not scalable as well as time-consuming. Automated tools need to be developed, which can be helpful in automated monitoring [30] that can minimize the mental and physical health issues on users.

Therefore, this motivated us to develop an automated tool to detect the cases of Cyber-aggression so that users can feel safe and secure and get unconditional support. Identifying the Cyber-aggression on social media is a very challenging task due to several reasons, e.g., various form of post, multi-lingual text, the non-standard writing style of online users, etc. Most of the existing works [2–5,15,20,24,29] have solved Cyber-aggression issues based on text. Some recent works [9,28] tried to solve Cyberbullying issues related to the image-based post. Hosseinmardi et al. [9] built a model to predict Cyberbullying incidents on the Instagram network based on initial user data such as the post of an image with associated text caption, and the number of followers & followings. Singh et al.

---

[4] https://ask.fm/.

[5] https://www.recode.net/2015/12/7/11621218/streaming-video-now-accounts-for-70-percent-of-broadband-usage.

[28] built a model to identify Cyberbullying incidents on the Instagram network with visual and text features. To the best of our knowledge, no previous work has been proposed to detect Cyber-aggression on the image-based post, especially on symbolic images. We analyze aggressive post of several social media such as Facebook, Twitter, and Instagram and found that some post only the image part of the post are aggressive that contain direct aggression or indirect aggression in the form of symbolic aggression where bullies target the user to humiliate, insult, and to make fun of or mock them. We mainly considered those type of image where the post is having both types of direct or indirect aggression. The last decade has provided considerable research on the causes and effects of text-based aggression on social media, but there is no research has been done on a symbolic type of aggression related to the image-based post. Due to a scarcity of aggressive image based post, we created a dataset crawling images from Google search to query aggressive images.

The current approach focused on the image content of the detection of Cyber-aggression on OSN. We target to detect Cyber-aggression because it may lead to Cyberbullying events in the near future. Our method is tested on the dataset of 3600 images. We propose a deep Convolutional Neural Network (CNN) for identification of Cyber-aggression on social media. The fundamental idea of CNN is to consider features extraction and classification task as collaboratively trained task. The idea of using deep CNN (many layers of convolutions and pooling) to extract a hierarchical representation of the input sequentially. For generalization purpose, we augmented the image and used a dropout layer in between the two convolutional layers. Our main contributions can be summarized as:

- Creation and labeling of Cyber-aggressive posts containing symbolic images from Google search to query aggressive images.
- A deep Convolutional Neural Network based system to classify images containing symbolic aggression and no-aggression.

The remainder of the paper is organized as follows: Sect. 2 presents related works in Cyber-aggression detection while Sect. 3 presents our proposed framework for Cyber-aggression detection. The finding of the proposed system is presented in Sect. 4. Finally, we conclude the paper and discusses future work directions in Sect. 5.

2   Related Works

Cyber-aggression is widely recognized as a social challenge from the last few years, especially for teenagers and youngsters [26]. Recently, a number of researches have been proposed to address Cyber-aggression over online platforms. In this section, we briefly discuss some of the potential works proposed in this domain.

A number of works [4–6] performed Cyber-aggression classification on English text whereas [2,3,15,20,24,29] performed Cyber-aggression classification on multi-lingual text. The Cyber-aggression classification performed by [4] on twitter. They found that when user and network-based features are combined with text-based features gave better accuracy. They got overall precision and recall of 0.72 and 0.73 respectively for four classes classification: Bully, Aggression, Spam, and Normal tweets. Chavan and Shylaja [5] detected Cyber-aggression on unknown social media. They used the Term Frequency-Inverse Document Frequency (TF-IDF), and n-gram features, Support Vector Machine (SVM) and logistic regression as a classifier. They reported the best Area Under Curve (AUC) score was 0.87. Chen et al. [6] detected aggressive tweets using Convolutional Neural Network (CNN) based on a sentiment analysis method. They found the accuracy of 0.92. Raiyani et al. [20] used dense system architecture on the multi-lingual text. Their system was suffered from false positive cases, and they removed the words that are not found in the vocabulary. Julian and Krestel [21] used ensemble learning and data augmentation techniques. They augmented training dataset using machine translation of three different languages. Their system is not stable, especially for Hindi dataset for the same domain it was performed well, but for other domain, it fails to classify the tweets with good accuracy. Aroyehun and Gelbukh [2] used various deep learning models such as Long Short Term Memory (LSTM), CNN, and FastText as word representation. Their system was not clearly classified covertly aggressive comments from overtly aggressive comments with significant accuracy. Modha and Majumder [15] used various deep learning models such as LSTM, CNN, Bidirectional LSTM, and FastText as word representation and machine learning classifiers. They used ensemble learning based on majority voting scheme. Samghabadi et al. [24] used ensemble learning based on various machine learning classifiers such as logistic regression, SVM and word n-gram, character n-gram, word embedding, sentiment, etc., as a feature set. Srivastava et al. [29] identified online social aggression on Facebook comment and Wikipedia toxic comments using stacked various LSTM units followed by Convolution layer and Fasttext as word representation. They achieved 0.98 AUC for Wikipedia toxic comment classification. For code-mixed English dataset, they achieved a weighted F1 score of 0.63 for the Facebook domain and 0.59 for the Twitter domain.

Very few researchers [9,28] have begun using visual characteristics to identify Cyberbullying. Hosseinmardi et al. [9] anticipated the Cyberbullying event taking into account visual characteristics and using original user data such as picture, caption, number of followers and followings, but visual characteristics do not help. By integrating textual and visual characteristics, Singh et al. [28] identified Cyberbullying. Their sample of practice is very small and high adverse words in the dataset predominated. Most of the work performed in the Cyber-aggression domain is concentrated on the text in particular. Very few operates with image-based post on the detection of Cyber-aggression. Best of our knowledge, there is no work on symbolic aggression classification.

3 Methodology

To automatically detect Cyber-aggression in OSN, we propose a Convolutional Neural Network (CNN) approach. In the following subsections, we describe the details of the dataset in Subsect. 3.1. The deep CNN based model is described next in Subsect. 3.2.

3.1 Data Collection and Labelling

We analyze the aggressive post containing images used by Internet users of multiple social media sites such as Facebook, Twitter, and Instagram, etc., and discovered that users of these sites usually use aggressive symbolic images to insult, harass, and humiliate other Internet users. We gathered some images from these social media (Facebook, Twitter, and Instagram). Because of the scarcity of marked information to make machine learning classifiers to identify the post contains aggression, we use Google Search to query aggressive images; specifically, we used some keywords such as aggressive images, Cyber-aggressive images, bullying pictures, etc. These images are manually filtered based on the clarity of decidable for a level of aggression, and then finally, we got a total of 3600 images. Three graduate students volunteered to annotate the images. They individually annotated the images into three classes of aggression: high aggression, medium aggression, and no aggression. We considered only those images on which at least two students agreed. The images which are having physical threats are labelled as high aggressive images, images which are having indirect aggression are labelled as medium aggressive images, and the images which do not have any threat are labelled as not aggressive images. The details of our dataset can be seen in Table 1.

Table 1. Description of Cyber-aggressive image dataset

Image class	Number of sample
no_aggression	1566
midium_aggression	1080
high_aggression	954
total images	3600

3.2 Proposed Model

The Convolutional Neural Network (CNN) is a deep neural network architecture that can take the image as an input and extract essential features in their hidden layers to do the classification task. In the proposed model, we used six layers of convolution, followed by three dense layers. We used max-pooling layer after every two convolution layer. We also used dropout between each of the CNN

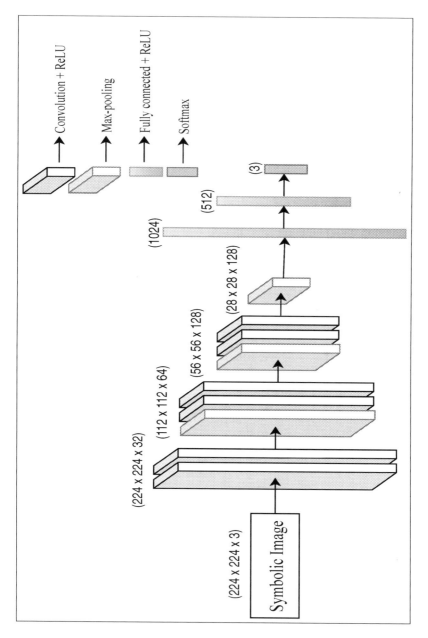

Fig. 1. Overview of the proposed CNN based architecture

as well as dense layers. The overall architecture for the proposed CNN based model can be seen from Fig. 1. We first converted all the images into an equal size, i.e., $224 \times 224 \times 3$. For the normalization of pixel values, the pixel matrix of the image is divided by the maximum pixel value, i.e., 255 and given to the CNN layers. We used 32, 32, 64, 64, 128, and 128 filters each of size 3×3 in the first, second, third, fourth, fifth, and sixth convolution layer respectively. After applying all the convolution operation, we flatten the feature vector and then passes it into the dense layers as can be seen in Fig. 1.

The detailed explanation of the CNN model can be seen in [11]. The normalized matrix is then used by the proposed system to train and test the model. In every cases, out of total data samples, 75% of them were used for training, and the remaining 25% samples were used for testing the performance of the models. In the hidden layers, ReLU activation function and softmax activation function at the output layer used. The model performed best with categorical cross-entropy as a loss function, the learning rate 0.001, batch size 10, and an epoch of 100. Table 2 listed all the hyper-parameters used during our experiments.

Table 2. Hyper-parameters setting for the proposed model

Description	Values
Filter region size	3×3
Feature map	32, 32, 64, 64, 128, 128
Pooling size	2×2
Activation function	ReLU, Softmax
Dropout rate	0.2
Learning rate	0.01
Batch size	10
Epoch	100

4   Results and Discussions

The findings of our current strategy to symbolic image-based Cyber-aggression detection are described in this section. Precision, recall, and weighted F1-score are the performance metrics used. The result of the proposed Convolutional Neural Network on the dataset after image augmentation tabulated in Table 3. The proposed model achieved a precision of 0.86, 0.91, and 0.93 for no-aggression, medium-aggression, and high-aggression class, respectively. The corresponding recall values are 0.95, 0.89, and 0.79. The weighted F1-score for no-aggression, medium-aggression, and high-aggression class are 0.91, 0.90, & 0.86 respectively. We also experimented with VGG-16 [27], which generally perform well for image classification in several scenarios [1, 16, 17, 19]. In VGG-16 experimentation, we

Table 3. Results of detection of Cyber-aggressive images

Approach	Image class	Results		
		Precision	Recall	F1-score
VGG-16	no_aggression	0.67	0.87	0.76
	midium_aggression	0.74	0.63	0.68
	high_aggression	0.76	0.52	0.62
	weighted average	**0.72**	**0.71**	**0.70**
CNN	no_aggression	0.86	0.95	0.91
	midium_aggression	0.91	0.89	0.90
	high_aggression	0.93	0.79	0.86
	weighted average	**0.90**	**0.89**	**0.89**

trained the last two layers of VGG-16, and all other layers marked as non-trainable. The VGG-16 model achieved 0.70 weighted F1-score, whereas our CNN based model, which is a lesser number of layers in compare to VGG-16, got 0.89 weighted F1-score. As shown in Table 3, our model can currently identify 93 out of 100 cases of predicted high-aggression post.

One of our major contributions is the creation of labelled dataset for aggressive symbolic images. There is no such labelled dataset exist which contains symbolic images for Cyber-aggression detection task. Therefore, we collected symbolic images from different online social sites and then labelled them into three classes of aggression. Next contribution is the development of Convolutional Neural Network based model, which is six layers of convolution and performed well for image classification. Our model can able to classify the images with good F1-score of around 90% whereas the VGG-16 model achieved F1-score of 0.70.

5   Conclusion and Future Work

In this article, we presented a deep Convolutional Neural Network based approach to identify aggressive posts containing symbolic images. We used six layers of convolution, followed by three dense layers and got weighted F1-score of 89% for aggressive post-identification. We explored the existing models of VGG-16 [27] to compare the performance of the pre-trained model for this task and found that our CNN based model performed better than VGG-16 which has more number of layers in compare to our model. One of the major limitations of the current research is that it only considers the symbolic images ignoring any textual contents associated with those images that may be more correct informative content for identifying the aggression on symbolic images. In the future, the textual contents can be exploited along with the symbolic images to make this system more robust and more accurate.

Acknowledgements. The first author would like to acknowledge the Ministry of Electronics and Information Technology (MeitY), Government of India for the financial support during the research work through Visvesvaraya Ph.D. Scheme for Electronics and IT.

References

1. Alam, F., Imran, M., Ofli, F.: Image4Act: online social media image processing for disaster response. In: Proceedings of the 2017 IEEE/ACM International Conference on Advances in Social Networks Analysis and Mining 2017, pp. 601–604. ACM (2017)
2. Aroyehun, S.T., Gelbukh, A.: Aggression detection in social media: using deep neural networks, data augmentation, and pseudo labeling. In: Proceedings of the First Workshop on Trolling, Aggression and Cyberbullying (TRAC-2018), pp. 90–97 (2018)
3. Arroyo-Fernández, I., Forest, D., Torres-Moreno, J.M., Carrasco-Ruiz, M., Legeleux, T., Joannette, K.: Cyberbullying detection task: the EBSI-LIA-UNAM system (ELU) at COLING 2018 TRAC-1. In: Proceedings of the First Workshop on Trolling, Aggression and Cyberbullying (TRAC-2018), pp. 140–149 (2018)
4. Chatzakou, D., Kourtellis, N., Blackburn, J., De Cristofaro, E., Stringhini, G., Vakali, A.: Mean birds: detecting aggression and bullying on Twitter. In: Proceedings of the 2017 ACM on Web Science Conference, pp. 13–22. ACM (2017)
5. Chavan, V.S., Shylaja, S.: Machine learning approach for detection of cyber-aggressive comments by peers on social media network. In: 2015 International Conference on Advances in Computing, Communications and Informatics (ICACCI), pp. 2354–2358. IEEE (2015)
6. Chen, J., Yan, S., Wong, K.C.: Verbal aggression detection on Twitter comments: convolutional neural network for short-text sentiment analysis. Neural Comput. Appl., 1–10 (2018). https://doi.org/10.1007/s00521-018-3442-0
7. Dadvar, M., Trieschnigg, D., de Jong, F.: Experts and machines against bullies: a hybrid approach to detect cyberbullies. In: Sokolova, M., van Beek, P. (eds.) AI 2014. LNCS (LNAI), vol. 8436, pp. 275–281. Springer, Cham (2014). https://doi.org/10.1007/978-3-319-06483-3_25
8. Grigg, D.W.: Cyber-aggression: definition and concept of cyberbullying. J. Psychol. Couns. Sch. **20**(2), 143–156 (2010)
9. Hosseinmardi, H., Rafiq, R.I., Han, R., Lv, Q., Mishra, S.: Prediction of cyberbullying incidents in a media-based social network. In: 2016 IEEE/ACM International Conference on Advances in Social Networks Analysis and Mining (ASONAM), pp. 186–192. IEEE (2016)
10. Kornblum, J.: Cyberbullying grows bigger and meaner with photos, video. Eschool News (2008). https://www.eschoolnews.com/2008/07/15/cyber-bullying-grows-bigger-and-meaner-with-photos-video/
11. Krizhevsky, A., Sutskever, I., Hinton, G.E.: ImageNet classification with deep convolutional neural networks. In: Advances in Neural Information Processing Systems, pp. 1097–1105 (2012)
12. League, A.D.: Glossary of cyberbullying terms. adl. org (2011). http://www.adl.orgleducationlcurriculurnconnectionslcyberbullyingjglossary.pdf
13. Machackova, H., Dedkova, L., Sevcikova, A., Cerna, A.: Bystanders' supportive and passive responses to cyberaggression. J. Sch. Violence **17**(1), 99–110 (2018)

14. Modecki, K.L., Barber, B.L., Vernon, L.: Mapping developmental precursors of cyber-aggression: trajectories of risk predict perpetration and victimization. J. Youth Adolesc. **42**(5), 651–661 (2013)
15. Modha, S., Majumder, P., Mandl, T.: Filtering aggression from the multilingual social media feed. In: Proceedings of the First Workshop on Trolling, Aggression and Cyberbullying (TRAC-2018), pp. 199–207 (2018)
16. Nguyen, D.T., Ofli, F., Imran, M., Mitra, P.: Damage assessment from social media imagery data during disasters. In: Proceedings of the 2017 IEEE/ACM International Conference on Advances in Social Networks Analysis and Mining 2017, pp. 569–576. ACM (2017)
17. Nguyen, D.T., Alam, F., Ofli, F., Imran, M.: Automatic image filtering on social networks using deep learning and perceptual hashing during crises. arXiv preprint arXiv:1704.02602 (2017)
18. Pater, J.A., Miller, A.D., Mynatt, E.D.: This digital life: a neighborhood-based study of adolescents' lives online. In: Proceedings of the 33rd Annual ACM Conference on Human Factors in Computing Systems, pp. 2305–2314. ACM (2015)
19. Paul, R.: Classifying cooking object's state using a tuned VGG convolutional neural network. arXiv preprint arXiv:1805.09391 (2018)
20. Raiyani, K., Gonçalves, T., Quaresma, P., Nogueira, V.B.: Fully connected neural network with advance preprocessor to identify aggression over Facebook and Twitter. In: Proceedings of the First Workshop on Trolling, Aggression and Cyberbullying (TRAC-2018), pp. 28–41 (2018)
21. Risch, J., Krestel, R.: Aggression identification using deep learning and data augmentation. In: Proceedings of the First Workshop on Trolling, Aggression and Cyberbullying (TRAC-2018), pp. 150–158 (2018)
22. Rybnicek, M., Poisel, R., Tjoa, S.: Facebook watchdog: a research agenda for detecting online grooming and bullying activities. In: 2013 IEEE International Conference on Systems, Man, and Cybernetics (SMC), pp. 2854–2859. IEEE (2013)
23. Salawu, S., He, Y., Lumsden, J.: Approaches to automated detection of cyberbullying: a survey. IEEE Trans. Affect. Comput. (2017). https://doi.org/10.1109/TAFFC.2017.2761757
24. Samghabadi, N.S., Mave, D., Kar, S., Solorio, T.: RiTual-uh at TRAC 2018 shared task: aggression identification. arXiv preprint arXiv:1807.11712 (2018)
25. Seiler, S.J., Navarro, J.N.: Bullying on the pixel playground: investigating risk factors of cyberbullying at the intersection of children's online-offline social lives. Cyberpsychol.: J. Psychosoc. Res. Cyberspace **8**(4) (2014). http://dx.doi.org/10.5817/CP2014-4-6
26. Servance, R.L.: Cyberbullying, cyber-harassment, and the conflict between schools and the first amendment. Wis. Law Rev. **6**, 1213–1244 (2003)
27. Simonyan, K., Zisserman, A.: Very deep convolutional networks for large-scale image recognition. arXiv preprint arXiv:1409.1556 (2014)
28. Singh, V.K., Ghosh, S., Jose, C.: Toward multimodal cyberbullying detection. In: Proceedings of the 2017 CHI Conference Extended Abstracts on Human Factors in Computing Systems, pp. 2090–2099. ACM (2017)
29. Srivastava, S., Khurana, P., Tewari, V.: Identifying aggression and toxicity in comments using capsule network. In: Proceedings of the First Workshop on Trolling, Aggression and Cyberbullying (TRAC-2018), pp. 98–105 (2018)
30. Van Royen, K., Poels, K., Daelemans, W., Vandebosch, H.: Automatic monitoring of cyberbullying on social networking sites: from technological feasibility to desirability. Telematics Inform. **32**(1), 89–97 (2015)

Digital Payment Adoption in India: Insights from Twitter Analytics

Prabhsimran Singh[1(✉)], Yogesh K. Dwivedi[2],
Karanjeet Singh Kahlon[3], Nripendra P. Rana[2], Pushp P. Patil[2],
and Ravinder Singh Sawhney[4]

[1] Department of Computer Engineering and Technology,
Guru Nanak Dev University, Amritsar, India
prabh_singh32@yahoo.com
[2] School of Management, Emerging Market Research Center (EMaRC),
Swansea University, Swansea, UK
y.k.dwivedi@swansea.ac.uk, nrananp@gmail.com,
pushpppatil@gmail.com
[3] Department of Computer Science, Guru Nanak Dev University,
Amritsar, India
karankahlon@gndu.ac.in
[4] Department of Electronics Technology, Guru Nanak Dev University,
Amritsar, India
sawhney.ece@gndu.ac.in

Abstract. Ever since demonetization happened in India on November 8, 2016, there has been a steady improvement in the use of digital payments. The usage trend has become exponential in the last 15 months across the digital payment methods (DPMs) in India. Government of India is promoting this landmark change of Indian financial system through Digital India initiative. Both national and international corporates, established as well as startups are investing heavily in DPMs to promote their products and services among Indian consumers. The promotion of DPMs also includes the use of social media marketing. Social media (especially Twitter) is being extensively used by companies to make the consumer aware about their services and promote themselves. The consumers do get motivated to try and use their services but they also share their grudges on Twitter. This paper aims to analyze DPMs adoption in India using Twitter as a tool. This study collected 172996 tweets over a period of four months and analyzed using a mix of conventional as well novel social media analytics techniques. Our analysis highlights the critical factors that drive and inhibit the use of DPMs in India. Further, our state wise analysis clearly differentiates about DPM adoption rate from high to low in all states of India.

Keywords: Digital payment · Mobile payment · Sentiment analysis · Social media analytics · Twitter

1 Introduction

With advancement in technology, the life of mankind has become both comfortable and convenient [1]. The one such technology that has revolutionized our lives is Internet [2]. One sector that has seen a complete makeover due to advancements in internet is

© IFIP International Federation for Information Processing 2019
Published by Springer Nature Switzerland AG 2019
I. O. Pappas et al. (Eds.): I3E 2019, LNCS 11701, pp. 425–436, 2019.
https://doi.org/10.1007/978-3-030-29374-1_35

the financial (Banking) sector, which has experienced a paradigm shift from use of traditional currency notes to use of digital payment methods (DPMs) [3, 4]. The availability coupled with ease of use of mobile devices has taken DPMs to next level of banking that is, because of the additional capabilities that it offers in term of mobility and portability [2, 5, 6]. Nowadays smart phones have become integral part of our life and the ease of use of the android apps shared by the various e-marketers (such as Amazon, Paytm mall, Domino's) are making users hooked to the technology in performing their day to day activities including financial transactions [1]. DPMs such as mobile payments or mobile wallets are becoming popular amongst users (especially youth) as these platforms provide direct transactions through smartphones [4, 7].

Currently, transactions through DPMs are estimated around $3,598,226 million of global GDP and are expected to be almost double i.e. $6,686,650 million by 2023 [8]. With advantages such as transparency, better services, better delivery system, gradually more and more people are adopting DPMs. However, they have not been able to reach to their optimum potential in many developing as well as developed countries apart from few exceptions [6, 9]. Given the above, this paper explores the potential of DPMs in India using Twitter as a tool. The reason for choosing Twitter is its ease of use among social media, which is becoming an important part of people's life [10]. The statistics suggest that an average person spends two and half hours daily on social media sites [11]. So, social media provides an ideal platform for both vendors and consumers (having common interest) to interact virtually [12]. It has been examined that the social media is being used by consumers who wish to express the acceptance or rejection of services. It has been suggested that vendors also utilize the potential of social media to promote their services and products [13, 14].

The paper is structured as follows: Sect. 2 discusses the related work including DPMs, its background, its brief history with Indian context and importance of social media in our life. Section 3 gives details of our research methodology for this research work, followed by implementation and results in Sect. 4. Section 5 discusses the results and finally, we conclude in Sect. 6.

2   Review of Literature

Digital payment is a mode of making financial transactions using electronic medium and devices such as smart mobile phones and laptops [15]. DPMs provide convenient and time saving option as compared to traditional banking system [16]. In addition to this DPMs also provide various benefits to individuals (like ease of handling of cash, security from thefts) and nation (like removing corruption and black money). Since 1990's, E-banking started becoming popular among educated users, however, the popularity and usage were restricted to users of mostly developed countries. By 2010, digital payments gained popularity all around the world and started getting adopted in many developed as well as developing countries as the data communication took up the pace [17]. With the availability of cheap and affordable data services as well as mobile devices, M-banking became more popular than its predecessor i.e. E-banking, as it eliminated the requirement of relying on a PC device or a Laptop with internet connection to make payments [18–20].

In India, DPMs saw an exponential growth after demonetization by the Government of India (GOI) on 8th November, 2016 [21]. GOI promoted the DPMs as a part of Digital India Initiative which helped them in enhancing transparency, reduction in tax envision and improving public delivery system [22]. Most of the time when we talk about consumer oriented DPMs, it's the mobile payment systems (like M-banking) [23]. In Mobile based DPMs, the payments or the transactions are made using mobile devices having technologies like Near Field Communication (NFC) etc. [24, 25]. Portability and mobility are the major contributors in making Mobile based DPMs more popular than traditional DPMs (E-banking etc.) [26]. India currently has 530 million smart phones [27] and approximately 478 million users are using Internet on these mobile gadgets [28]. With Indian digital payment industry poised to reach $700 billion by 2022 wherein Mobile based DPMs are expected to be playing a major role [29].

Nowadays Social Media has become an Integral part of our social life including routine daily chores [10]. Everyday people spend hours on social media to discuss and interact with like-minded people. In short, social media provides a perfect platform for people all around the world to discuss topics of common interest such as sports, entertainment and even digital payments [30, 31]. Even the firms are aware of this fact, and hence various studies indicate that 96.43% of firms utilize the potential of social media to promote their services and products through social media marketing [13, 14]. Important studies indicate that almost 80% of users on social media access information regarding sales and offers/deals related to promotion of various products [32]. This effective communication through the virtual world plays a crucial role in building a strong relationship between the user and the firm [33].

Despite the potential of DPMs in India and the numerous advantages it is offering to people in India, it has failed to reach its optimal potential in terms of its adoption by the Indian consumers. This difference in perception and execution has motivated us to take this research and carry out our analysis using data from Twitter. Through this research article, we try to the best of our understanding, to answer the following research questions: (a) What are the factors that influence the people to adopt DPMs? (b) What are all the factors that inhibit consumers to adopt DPMs? Both these questions will be answered through analysis of the collected tweets posted by people on Twitter during our sampling period of 4 months.

3 Research Methodology

As mentioned earlier, to accomplish our research goals, the entire task has been divided into four phases. In phase-1, data was fetched from Twitter using Twitter API [34]. Since the collection of data is in unstructured json format, it becomes crucial to convert it into the structured format (excel format). So, in phase-2, we convert this unstructured data into structured format. Though, the data gets converted into structured format; still it contains a lot of noise and other redundant stuff (like web links etc.). Hence, it is essential to preprocess the data as these ambiguities can lead to superfluous results [35, 36]. Phase-3 deals with data preprocessing, where we accomplish the entire task of preprocessing using R-Language [37]. Finally, in phase-4, the processed structured data is ready to be used to perform analysis using various social media analytics techniques [38, 39].

4   Implementation and Results

The entire implementation of moderating the processed data collected from previous step has been done in R-Language using various text mining libraries. Towards better understanding of the readers, this section is further divided in various sub-sections, with each giving in depth details of each analysis.

4.1   Data Collection

As previously explained, we fetched data for our experimentation from Twitter using specific #hashtags (#DigitalPayment OR #CashlessPayment OR #Epayment OR #Mpayment OR #MobileMoney OR #MobilePayment). In total, we collected 1,72,996 tweets 88,373 unique users over a period of four months (March 1, 2018 to June 30, 2018). This time duration was selected because March is the last month of Indian financial year while, the first quarter of the new financial year consists of other three months (April, May and June) and most of the financial activities take place during this duration. Since, the aim of this paper is to do detailed analysis of DPMs in the Indian context; hence, tweets were only collected from India. The detail of monthly tweets collection is shown in Fig. 1, while Fig. 2 shows categories of collected tweets regarding DPMs. Similarly, Table 1 shows detailed tweet statistics.

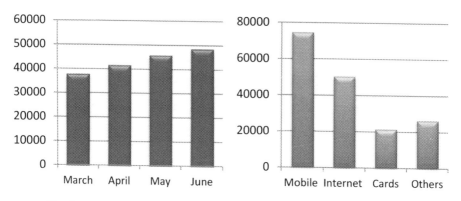

Fig. 1. Tweet collection details   **Fig. 2.** Tweet categorization details

Inference: The above stats clearly indicate the popularity of DPMs is rising among Indian people. Moreover, a major chunk of tweets were related to mobile payments and mobile wallets. Internet banking was second most popular DPM followed by cards (Credit and Debit cards). The rest of the tweets were related to other DPMs, bank promotions, government initiatives etc. Overall, the DPMs are becoming popular among Indian people. Further, more and more people are adopting this mechanism for making financial transactions with mobile payments and mobile wallets, being the most convenient and popular choice.

Table 1. Tweet statistics

	March	April	May	June
Total tweets	37616	41427	45632	48321
Max tweets in a day	2076	2646	2548	2977
Min tweets in a day	92	63	71	106
Total unique senders	14371	21674	25423	26905
Average tweets per sender	2.617	1.911	1.794	1.795
Average tweet per month	1213.41	1380.90	1472	1610.70

4.2 (#) Hashtag Analysis

Hashtags depicts what is trending on Twitter [40, 41]. In total, we collected a total of 2,01,594 Hashtags out of that we only retained unique 60,567 hashtags. With 24,647 occurrences, #DigitalIndia was the most used hashtag. The association among top ten hashtags is shown in Table 2. The diagonal represents the occurrence for each hashtag, while other columns represent the amount of association with other hashtags.

Table 2. Association among different hashtags

	#DigitalIndia	#Cashless	#MobileMoney	#NarendraModi	#Transform	#GoDigital	#DigitalPayment	#Benefits	#Offers	#Secure
#DigitalIndia	24647	467	19	1001	362	19	214	257	427	246
#Cashless	467	3905	16	89	31	20	181	32	154	118
#MobileMoney	19	16	2296	21	34	29	31	23	125	53
#NarendraModi	1001	89	21	2154	34	42	14	38	53	17
#Transform	362	31	34	34	1615	18	37	24	67	33
#GoDigital	19	20	29	42	18	4540	16	54	22	42
#DigitalPayment	214	181	31	14	37	16	2413	51	74	137
#Benefits	257	32	23	38	24	54	51	1099	101	61
#Offers	427	154	125	53	67	22	74	101	1231	87
#Secure	246	118	53	17	33	42	137	61	87	1297

Inference: We observed that most of the collected hashtags were related to digital and cashless payments (#DigitalIndia, #Cashless, #MobileMoney, #GoDigital, #Digital-Payment). Since Prime Minister of India advocated heavily for digital payment systems, #NarendraModi and #Modi also featured in top hashtags. Since people get attractive offers from various vendors, #Benefits and #Offers were also among popular hashtags. Hashtags such as #Reliable and #Secure depict that people find these services secure and can rely upon. However, many users also used the hashtags with #CyberSecurity emphasizing the need for bigger encryption security for the transaction policies [42]. Overall, the hashtags depict a mixed but biased positive attitude among all the users.

4.3   Sentiment Analysis

Sentiment analysis deals with extraction of sentiment from given piece of information regarding a particular entity [43–45]. It is widely considered as the most effective tool to map public opinion. The ultimate aim here is to detect the polarity of the view i.e. positive or negative for a given entity (tweets in our case). Figure 3 below shows the results of polarity analysis while Fig. 4 shows the treemap of positive and negative words.

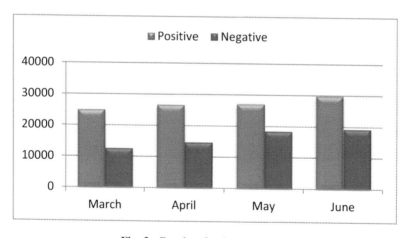

Fig. 3. Results of polarity analysis

Inference: For the entire duration of four months, the positive polarity maintained its upper edge over the negative polarity, indicating the positive opinion of people using the digital technologies. However, there was a constant growth in number of negative tweets from March (33%) to June (40%), indicating that more people posted negative tweets in the later part of our sample period depicting their anger and displeasure after availing services from respective vendors.

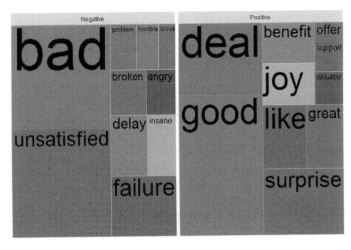

Fig. 4. Treemap of positive and negative words

4.4   Network Analysis

The use of network analysis approach is to detect prominent communities taking part in discussion regarding a particular entity [46]. The result of network analysis is shown in Fig. 5. There are three prominent communities and a minor community.

Fig. 5. Results of community analysis (Color figure online)

Inference: Figure 5 clearly depicts that there are three main communities. The blue nodes indicate the community of people who are posting positive tweets in favor of DPMs. This community is largest among the lot representing overall positive attitude among people regarding DPMs. The red nodes indicate the people who are posting negative tweets regarding DPMs. These are the people who are not willing to use DPMs and are critical of its efficacy. The green nodes indicate the community of people who were earlier supporting DPMs, but later started posting negative tweets after their experience with these activities might have went wrong. These people were once committed users of DPMs, but due to some technical issues or bad experiences turned against DPMs. Finally, we have the users, who are continuously switching among all three communities; these people are indicated with yellow nodes.

4.5 Geo-Location Analysis

Location based analysis is considered the most critical tool for mapping public response in an area of large demography towards an entity [47–49]. For a diverse country like India, location based analysis becomes even more crucial. Due to Twitter privacy policy, all the tweets were not geo-tagged. Hence, only geo-tagged tweets are considered for this analysis. The result of location based analysis is shown in Fig. 6. Similarly, Fig. 7 shows the top five cities with maximum DPM usage.

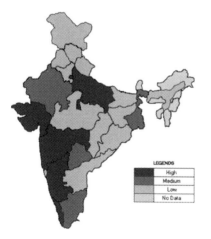

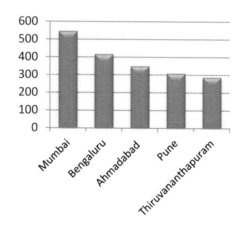

Fig. 6. Result of geo-location analysis   **Fig. 7.** Top cities with highest DPM usage

Inference: The results evidently point out that DPM usage is not uniform in India and more users are concentrated mainly in the south western states. The strong reasons for this asymmetry is due to these states being economically developed and having higher literacy rate. Maharashtra being the commercial capital of India tops the table with the highest number of users, closely followed by New Delhi. A closer analysis of top states shows that most people in these areas have access to mobile phone with internet and their higher literacy rates are significant factors in DPMs adoption.

5 Discussion

Through this study, we tried to analyze the DPMs among Indian people employing Twitter as a tool. We applied different social media analytic techniques for identifying the various reasons that promote or oppose that usage of DPMs in India. Different social media techniques provided different insights but were really influential in depicting the possible factors that promote or oppose the usage of DPMs. Our results clearly showed that tweets related to mobile payments and mobile wallets constituted 43% (74,678) of the total tweets, indicating "mobility" and "ease of use" being the promoting factors that people get using these hand held devices. Another factor detected by us is the "cost of use" associated with the use of DPMs. This factor acts as a promoter in case of mobile payments where people not just make free transactions but also get benefits like cashbacks and offers [50] while it acts as an opposing factor in case of internet banking and credit/debit cards where people need to pay an addition service fees [51]. Similarly, "security" was another factor which was ambiguous playing the dual role of promoting as well as opposing factor. Some people felt secured with the use of DPMs for making financial transactions while there were people who demanded more secure and reliable transaction policies for DPMs. Even GOI is stressing on security factor, making it mandatory for mobile wallets to send SMS alerts and email for every transaction, so that more and more people can adopt these mechanisms [52]. The geo-location analysis shows that the DPM usage is not uniform in India. The two possible reasons for this are Information and Communications Technology (ICT) infrastructure and literacy rate. In India, a major chunk of population lives in rural areas where the education and infrastructure level are not at all at par with urban areas. This is a major hindrance in adoption of DPMs in these rural areas. So overall, mobility, ease of use, cost of use (Offers and Promotions), security, education and ICT infrastructure were the main promoting factors, while security, reliability, cost (Extra Service Charges) and lack of ICT infrastructure were the main opposing factors that created a negative opinion among people of India.

6 Conclusions

Technology is changing at a fast pace and it is making the life of mankind more comfortable and relaxing. DPM is one such area where technology has contributed extensively to completely transform it. The way of performing financial transactions has totally changed with introduction of E-Banking and M-Banking. Now, one can make transaction with just a click of button. Given this huge potential, still DPMs fail to reach its optimum potential. The aim of this research article was to analyze the adoption of DPMs in India using Twitter as a Tool. The analysis shows that though there has been a highly positive attitude among people but the number of users with negative opinion increases during later part of our sampling period due to the difficulties faced by the users. The main factors that promoted DPMs were mobility, ease of use, security, offers by the various wallets and better service. In contrast, the main factors which went against the adoption of DPMs were lack of security, inadequate infrastructure backup and unreliability. Another important finding of this research article is that DPMs are not uniformly used throughout India with the south western states dominating its use. The main reasons for this asymmetry are possibly higher literacy rate, financial strength and availability of mobile devices with internet connections.

Though we were able to get some valuable insights from this research about adoption of DPMs in India, it still leaves some open questions for researchers to carry forward their research in this area. These issues mainly include the reasons for polarization among supporters of DPMs. Similarly, why people are more intended towards mobile based DPMs as compared to other DPMs? All these questions need to be addressed in future work, which will help to understand the perception of bigger user base about DPMs' adoption in India.

References

1. Grover, P., Kar, A.K., Ilavarasan, P.V.: Understanding nature of social media usage by mobile wallets service providers–an exploration through SPIN framework. Proc. Comput. Sci. **122**, 292–299 (2017)
2. Patil, P.P., Dwivedi, Y.K., Rana, N.P.: Digital payments adoption: an analysis of literature. In: Kar, A., et al. (eds.) Digital Nations – Smart Cities, Innovation, and Sustainability, I3E 2017. Lecture Notes in Computer Science, vol. 10595, pp. 61–70. Springer, Cham (2017). https://doi.org/10.1007/978-3-319-68557-1_7
3. Patil, P.P., Rana, N.P., Dwivedi, Y.K.: Digital payments adoption research: a meta-analysis for generalising the effects of attitude, cost, innovativeness, mobility and price value on behavioural intention. In: Elbanna, Amany, Dwivedi, Y.K., Bunker, D., Wastell, D. (eds.) TDIT 2018. IAICT, vol. 533, pp. 194–206. Springer, Cham (2019). https://doi.org/10.1007/978-3-030-04315-5_14
4. Kapoor, K.K., Dwivedi, Y.K., Williams, M.D.: Examining the role of three sets of innovation attributes for determining adoption of the interbank mobile payment service. Inf. Syst. Front. **17**(5), 1039–1056 (2015)
5. Jack, W., Suri, T.: Mobile money: the economics of M-PESA (No. w16721). National Bureau of Economic Research (2011)
6. Patil, P.P., Rana, N.P., Dwivedi, Y.K.: Digital payments adoption research: a review of factors influencing consumer's attitude, intention and usage. In: Al-Sharhan, S., et al. (eds.) Challenges and Opportunities in the Digital Era, I3E 2018. Lecture Notes in Computer Science, vol. 11195, pp. 45–52. Springer, Cham (2018). https://doi.org/10.1007/978-3-030-02131-3_6
7. Grover, P., Kar, A.K.: User engagement for mobile payment service providers–introducing the social media engagement model. J. Retail. Consum. Serv. (2018). https://doi.org/10.1016/j.jretconser.2018.12.002
8. Statista. https://www.statista.com/outlook/296/100/digital-payments/worldwide
9. Augsburg, C., Hedman, J.: Value added services and adoption of mobile payments. In: Proceedings of the Sixteenth International Conference on Electronic Commerce, p. 27. ACM, August 2014
10. Kapoor, K.K., Tamilmani, K., Rana, N.P., Patil, P., Dwivedi, Y.K., Nerur, S.: Advances in social media research: past, present and future. Inf. Syst. Front. **20**(3), 531–558 (2018)
11. Statista. https://www.statista.com/statistics/433871/daily-social-media-usage-worldwide/
12. Singh, P., Dwivedi, Y.K., Kahlon, K.S., Sawhney, R.S., Alalwan, A.A., Rana, N.P.: Smart monitoring and controlling of government policies using social media and cloud computing. Inf. Syst. Front. 1–23 (2019). https://doi.org/10.1007/s10796-019-09916-y

13. Alalwan, A.A., Rana, N.P., Dwivedi, Y.K., Algharabat, R.: Social media in marketing: a review and analysis of the existing literature. Telematics Inf. **34**(7), 1177–1190 (2017)
14. Dwivedi, Y.K., Kapoor, K.K., Chen, H.: Social media marketing and advertising. Mark. Rev. **15**(3), 289–309 (2015)
15. Singh, N.K., Sahu, G.P., Rana, N.P., Patil, P.P., Gupta, B.: Critical success factors of the digital payment infrastructure for developing economies. In: Elbanna, A., Dwivedi, Y., Bunker, D., Wastell, D. (eds.) Smart Working, Living and Organising, TDIT 2018. IFIP Advances in Information and Communication Technology, vol. 533, pp. 113–125. Springer, Cham (2019). https://doi.org/10.1007/978-3-030-04315-5_9
16. Siu, N.Y.M., Mou, J.C.W.: Measuring service quality in internet banking: the case of Hong Kong. J. Int. Consum. Mark. **17**(4), 99–116 (2005)
17. Sahu, G.P., Singh, N.K.: Paradigm shift of indian cash-based economy to cash-less economy: a study on Allahabad City. In: Kar, A., et al. (eds.) Digital Nations – Smart Cities, Innovation, and Sustainability, I3E 2017. Lecture Notes in Computer Science, vol. 10595, pp. 453–461. Springer, Cham (2017). https://doi.org/10.1007/978-3-319-68557-1_40
18. Baabdullah, A.M., Alalwan, A.A., Rana, N.P., Patil, P., Dwivedi, Y.K.: An integrated model for m-banking adoption in Saudi Arabia. Int. J. Bank Mark. **37**(2), 452–478 (2019)
19. Alalwan, A.A., Dwivedi, Y.K., Rana, N.P.: Factors influencing adoption of mobile banking by Jordanian bank customers: extending UTAUT2 with trust. Int. J. Inf. Manag. **37**(3), 99–110 (2017)
20. Sharma, S.K., Sharma, M.: Examining the role of trust and quality dimensions in the actual usage of mobile banking services: an empirical investigation. Int. J. Inf. Manag. **44**, 65–75 (2019)
21. Singh, P., Sawhney, R.S., Kahlon, K.S.: Sentiment analysis of demonetization of 500 & 1000 rupee banknotes by Indian government. ICT Express **4**(3), 124–129 (2018)
22. Digital India. https://digitalindia.gov.in/content/about-programme
23. Oliveira, T., Thomas, M., Baptista, G., Campos, F.: Mobile payment: understanding the determinants of customer adoption and intention to recommend the technology. Comput. Hum. Behav. **61**, 404–414 (2016)
24. Slade, E., Williams, M., Dwivedi, Y., Piercy, N.: Exploring consumer adoption of proximity mobile payments. J. Strateg. Mark. **23**(3), 209–223 (2015)
25. Slade, E.L., Dwivedi, Y.K., Piercy, N.C., Williams, M.D.: Modeling consumers' adoption intentions of remote mobile payments in the United Kingdom: extending UTAUT with innovativeness, risk, and trust. Psychol. Mark. **32**(8), 860–873 (2015)
26. Schierz, P.G., Schilke, O., Wirtz, B.W.: Understanding consumer acceptance of mobile payment services: An empirical analysis. Electron. Commer. Res. Appl. **9**(3), 209–216 (2010)
27. Smartphones in India. https://yourstory.com/2017/10/india-530m-smartphone-users-2018
28. Mobile Internet Users in India. https://www.bloombergquint.com/business/mobile-internet-users-in-india-seen-at-478-million-by-june-says-report#gs.31o483
29. Digital Payment Industry in India. https://www.orbisresearch.com/reports/index/digital-payment-systems-market-in-india-drivers-opportunities-trends-and-forecasts-to-2022
30. Singh, P., Kahlon, K.S., Sawhney, R.S., Vohra, R., Kaur, S.: Social media buzz created by# nanotechnology: insights from Twitter analytics. Nanotechnol. Rev. **7**(6), 521–528 (2018)
31. Whiting, A., Williams, D.: Why people use social media: a uses and gratifications approach. Qual. Market Res.: Int. J. **16**(4), 362–369 (2013)
32. Singh, J.P., Irani, S., Rana, N.P., Dwivedi, Y.K., Saumya, S., Roy, P.K.: Predicting the "helpfulness" of online consumer reviews. J. Bus. Res. **70**, 346–355 (2017)
33. Sharma, N., Patterson, P.G.: The impact of communication effectiveness and service quality on relationship commitment in consumer, professional services. J. Serv. Mark. **13**(2), 151–170 (1999)

34. Twitter API. https://www.nuget.org/packages/TweetinviAPI/
35. Liu, Y., Chen, Y., Wu, S., Peng, G., Lv, B.: Composite leading search index: a preprocessing method of internet search data for stock trends prediction. Ann. Oper. Res. **234**(1), 77–94 (2015)
36. García, S., Luengo, J., Herrera, F.: Data Preprocessing in Data Mining. Springer, Heidelberg (2016). https://doi.org/10.1007/978-3-319-10247-4
37. R-Language. https://www.r-project.org/about.html
38. Stieglitz, S., Dang-Xuan, L.: Emotions and information diffusion in social media—sentiment of microblogs and sharing behavior. J. Manag. Inf. Syst. **29**(4), 217–248 (2013)
39. Grover, P., Kar, A.K., Dwivedi, Y.K., Janssen, M.: Polarization and acculturation in US Election 2016 outcomes–Can twitter analytics predict changes in voting preferences. Technol. Forecast. Soc. Chang. **145**, 438–460 (2018)
40. Chae, B.K.: Insights from hashtag# supplychain and Twitter Analytics: Considering Twitter and Twitter data for supply chain practice and research. Int. J. Prod. Econ. **165**, 247–259 (2015)
41. Aswani, R., Kar, A.K., Ilavarasan, P.V., Dwivedi, Y.K.: Search engine marketing is not all gold: insights from Twitter and SEOClerks. Int. J. Inf. Manag. **38**(1), 107–116 (2018)
42. Miao, M., Jiang, T., You, I.: Payment-based incentive mechanism for secure cloud deduplication. Int. J. Inf. Manag. **35**(3), 379–386 (2015)
43. Singh, P., Sawhney, R.S., Kahlon, K.S.: Forecasting the 2016 US presidential elections using sentiment analysis. In: Kar, A., et al. (eds.) Digital Nations – Smart Cities, Innovation, and Sustainability, I3E 2017. Lecture Notes in Computer Science, vol. 10595, pp. 412–423. Springer, Cham (2017). https://doi.org/10.1007/978-3-319-68557-1_36
44. Ou, G., et al.: Exploiting community emotion for microblog event detection. In: EMNLP, pp. 1159–1168 (2014)
45. Mohammad, S.M., Turney, P.D.: Emotions evoked by common words and phrases: using mechanical turk to create an emotion lexicon. In: Proceedings of the NAACL HLT 2010 Workshop on Computational Approaches to Analysis and Generation of Emotion in Text, pp. 26–34. Association for Computational Linguistics, June 2010
46. Herdağdelen, A., Zuo, W., Gard-Murray, A., Bar-Yam, Y.: An exploration of social identity: the geography and politics of news-sharing communities in Twitter. Complexity **19**(2), 10–20 (2013)
47. Amirkhanyan, A., Meinel, C.: Density and intensity-based spatiotemporal clustering with fixed distance and time radius. In: Kar, A., et al. (eds.) Digital Nations – Smart Cities, Innovation, and Sustainability, I3E 2017. Lecture Notes in Computer Science, vol. 10595, pp. 313–324. Springer, Cham (2017). https://doi.org/10.1007/978-3-319-68557-1_28
48. Singh, P., Sawhney, R.S., Kahlon, K.S.: Twitter based sentiment analysis of GST implementation by Indian government. In: Patnaik, S., Yang, X.S., Tavana, M., Popentiu-Vlădicescu, F., Qiao, F. (eds.) Digital Business. Lecture Notes on Data Engineering and Communications Technologies, vol. 21, pp. 409–427. Springer, Cham (2019). https://doi.org/10.1007/978-3-319-93940-7_17
49. Singh, J.P., Dwivedi, Y.K., Rana, N.P., Kumar, A., Kapoor, K.K.: Event classification and location prediction from tweets during disasters. Ann. Oper. Res. 1–21 (2017)
50. Business Today. https://www.businesstoday.in/sectors/banks/paytm-payments-bank-account-interest-rate-offer-free-imps-neft-rupay-debit-card-transaction/story/264971.html
51. Times of India. https://timesofindia.indiatimes.com/business/india-business/sbi-atm-online-cash-transaction-fees-change-from-june-1-all-you-need-to-know/articleshow/58942912.cms
52. Times of India. https://timesofindia.indiatimes.com/gadgets-news/rbi-sets-new-rules-to-protect-consumers-from-fraud-transactions-on-paytm-phonepe-or-other-mobile-wallets/articleshow/67453118.cms

Digital Governance

Adoption of Transactional Service in Electronic Government – A Case of Pak-Identity Service

Muhammad Mahboob Khurshid[1]([✉]) [iD], Nor Hidayati Zakaria[2],
Ammar Rashid[3], Yunis Ali Ahmed[4],
and Muhammad Noman Shafique[5]

[1] School of Computing, Faculty of Engineering, Universiti Teknologi Malaysia,
Johor Bahru, Malaysia
mehboob.khursheed@vu.edu.pk
[2] Azman Hashim International Business School, Universiti Teknologi Malaysia,
Kuala Lumpur, Malaysia
hidayati@utm.my
[3] College of IT, Ajman University, Ajman, UAE
a.rashid@ajman.ac.ae
[4] Faculty of Computing, SIMAD University, Mogadishu, Somalia
yunisali@simad.edu.so
[5] Dongbei University of Finance and Economics, Dalian, China
shafique.nouman@gmail.com

Abstract. Governments around the world are using information and communication technologies to offer both simple information portals and transactional services. A less than one-third of the electronic government (e-government) initiatives focused on the provision of transactional services and understanding on studies related to the adoption of such services using domain-specific adoption theories/models are scarce. Therefore, the objective of this study is to understand the adoption of transactional service system, i.e. 'Pak-Identity' by employing a domain-specific model, i.e. Unified Model of Electronic Government Adoption (UMEGA). A UMEGA model with four new constructs is validated using data gathered from 441 citizens from all over Pakistan. A survey was conducted among citizens using simple random sampling technique. The collected data were analyzed employing variance-based structure equation modelling, i.e. partial least squares technique in SmartPLS 3.0 to test the formulated hypotheses. Findings indicate that (1) facilitating conditions is the predictor of effort expectancy, (2) performance expectancy, trust, and herd behaviour are the predictors of attitude, (3) price value, grievance redressal, and attitude are the predictors of behavioural intention to use e-government service. Surprisingly, effort expectancy, facilitating conditions, social influence, and perceived risk are found to be the nonsignificant predictors of adoption of e-government service. Interestingly, new constructs and new relationships are exposed, i.e. trust and herd behaviour on attitude, and price value and grievance redressal on behavioural intention. Moreover, a 55% variance in effort expectancy, 65% variance in attitude, and 40% variance in behavioural intention to adopt e-government has been found. Implications for the academics and managers are also outlined.

© IFIP International Federation for Information Processing 2019
Published by Springer Nature Switzerland AG 2019
I. O. Pappas et al. (Eds.): I3E 2019, LNCS 11701, pp. 439–450, 2019.
https://doi.org/10.1007/978-3-030-29374-1_36

Keywords: Electronic Government (E-Government) · Transactional service ·
UMEGA · Behavioural intention · Adoption · Factors

1 Introduction

Governments around the world are using information and communication technologies
(ICTs) in order to upsurge effectiveness and efficiency in their services. Moreover,
governments are providing services to their citizens using ICTs. In this connection, the
conceptualization of the provision of services by the government to the public using
ICTs is referred to as e-government [1]. On the one hand, there are several substantial
benefits of e-government, such as increasing transparency, delivery of services, public
engagement in different government decisions, and corruption reduction. However, on
the other hand, several barriers of human, technical and organizational nature (such as
active inter- and intra-organizational communication, monetary constraints, strong
political will and support, awareness issues, security, and privacy concerns, and skills
and abilities, hinder the implementation of e-government successfully [2].

Significant efforts are being undertaken by the countries (about 98%) around the
world to develop e-government portals which provide simple information; however,
less than one-third of these efforts are related to the provision of transactional services
[3]. Besides, the ratio of successfully completed e-government projects is only 15% [4,
5]. One of the arduous issues in e-government transactional services is its adoption and
diffusion [2]. Scholars are increasingly focusing on understanding the factors of
adoption of e-government transactional service systems in primary and secondary
stakeholders, particularly in developing countries [1] since such services are successful
in developed countries [5]. Therefore, this research aims to investigate the factors
affecting the citizens' adoption of e-government transactional services in Pakistan.
Policy-makers in the government need to understand the adoption factors and instrumentalize related policies. This study can bring new insights for policy-makers to
understand and increase the citizen's adoption of e-government from a transactional
service perspective.

2 Overview of E-Government Transactional Service – The 'Pak-Identity'

The 'Pak-Identity' is one of the e-government transactional service system developed
and launched by National Database and Registration Authority (NADRA), Pakistan
through which online application facilities are provided to the Pakistani citizens for
obtaining identity documents. It is a one-stop e-government service through which ten
different identity documents can be applied online by the public such as identity card
for local citizens (CNIC), National Identity Card of Overseas Pakistanis (NICOP),
Pakistan Origin Card (POC), Family and Child Registration Certificates. These identity
documents are then delivered to the citizens by mail.

3   Theoretical Foundations

This study focuses on evaluating e-government adoption from a transactional service perspective (i.e. Pak-Identity system) using Unified Model of Electronic Government Adoption (UMEGA) developed by Dwivedi, Rana, Janssen, Lal, Williams and Clement [1]. The decision to choose UMEGA lies on the facts that (1) it is purely developed in electronic-government context, (2) it explains between 77% variance in EE, 49% variance ATT, and 80% variance in the behavioural intention to e-government systems usability, (3) the model is developed after extensive study on previously nine competing models on assessing individuals' adoption of technology, (4) studies have reported UMEGA to be the superior performing model in e-government studies and to measure adoption [6].

The UMEGA model is extended by adding four additional factors relevant to the context that may give a better understanding of the influencing factors on the adoption of e-government. To the best of our knowledge, no study was carried out so far that has empirically investigated the factors of adoption of e-government by employing UMEGA and examining additional factors, i.e. trust, herd behaviour, price value, and grievance redressal factors and hence, make a novel contribution to the adoption studies. Moreover, two new relationships are proposed, empirically investigated, and proved, i.e. the influence of trust and herd behaviour on attitude.

4   Literature Review/Hypotheses Development

4.1   Performance Expectancy (PE)

Previous studies reveal that PE is the most influential determinant to measure the innate probabilities of individuals in involving or adopting a new information system/technology (IS/IT) [7, 8]. It has been accredited that improved job performance is a critical inducement for adopting IT/IS [5]. Moreover, the influence of PE on behavioural intention has been failed in a study conducted by Krishnaraju, Mathew and Sugumaran [9]. Therefore, successes and failures of PE construct have suggested the reconceptualization of PE and hence investigated its influence on adoption through attitude by Dwivedi, Rana, Janssen, Lal, Williams and Clement [1]. Based on these facts, we hypothesize that:

H1: There is a positive and significant relationship between PE and ATT toward using Pak-Identity.

4.2   Effort Expectancy (EE)

Actual and potential users would be willing to adopt an IS/IT if it is believed to be simple and easy to use despite its usefulness in their jobs [1]. Therefore, users will be intended to use a system if it is simple and effortless such that they need not make any hard efforts in using it. However, no support was found to have an influence of EE on the adoption of e-government in a study conducted by Lallmahomed, Lallmahomed and Lallmahomed [10]. In contrast, effort expectancy has been proposed to influence attitude in UMEGA [1]. Align with the UMEGA model, the hypothesis is proposed as:

H2: There is a positive and significant relationship between EE and ATT toward using Pak-Identity.

4.3   Social Influence (SI)

People live in a social system. They influence or motivate each other/one another to use an IS/IT. Social influence construct is regarded as one's self-instructed beliefs of others about system usage. It is a construct used to measure the users' beliefs of an IS/IT about what other people (like peers, friends, and family members) would be thinking as much important to use that IS/IT. Social influence is the most influential factor affecting individuals' attitudes to accept and use e-government systems [1, 6] and hence, is hypothesized as:

H3: There is a positive and significant relationship between SI and ATT toward using Pak-Identity.

4.4   Facilitating Conditions (FC)

An individual does not seem to have adequate technical and organizational facilities to use an IS/IT and hence will not be able and intend to use it. Thus, the higher the availability of technical resources and knowledge, the higher its adoption of e-government systems and services. Align with these studies; we also conceptualize that FC has a positive and significant effect on adoption of e-government system [5, 6, 10]. Moreover, the influence of this factor on EE has also been conceptualized, hypothesized, and validated in previous studies [1, 6]. Thus, the following two hypotheses have been framed:

H4: There is a positive and significant relationship between FC and BI toward using Pak-Identity.
H5: There is a positive and significant relationship between FC and EE toward using Pak-Identity.

4.5   Perceived Risk (PR)

Individuals may not use or limit their interactions with a government system because of the risks or losses associated with it. Perceived risks are the security concerns or anxieties, such as revealing their identities and making transactions online in using e-government systems. These and such other types of anxieties or uncertainties will restrict them to adopt e-government systems. Perceived risk is found to be the significant negative predictor that influences attitudes towards using e-government technologies. Thus, we hypothesize that:

H6: There is a negative and significant relationship between PR and ATT toward using Pak-Identity.

4.6   Trust (TRST)

Trust is a complex and multilayered concept spanning across varied disciplines; thus; it is defined according to the context and discipline. However, generally, trust is taken as a trust in internet technologies [10, 11]. Trust is considered an e-government service to be trustworthy, secure, reliable, and accurate. Trust has also been found to be the significant positive predictor of adoption of e-government [6, 12, 13]. However, this construct has also been found to be a significant predictor of attitude at pre-usage [14] and post-usage stages [14, 15]. We hypothesize trust as the significant positive predictor of building citizens' attitudes towards e-government adoption:

H7: There is a positive and significant relationship between TRST and ATT toward using Pak-Identity.

4.7   Herd Behaviour (HB)

Herd behaviour is conceptualized as an individual's followings in adopting an IS/IT even when his or her private information suggests doing the opposite [16]. HB is a self-observation about the behaviour of other people in adopting an IS/IT and does not depend on what others think [17]. Thus, the more the users are observatory about the practices of others in adopting technology, the more they adopt it. Therefore, we hypothesize HB as an indirect predictor of behavioural intention towards using e-government service, i.e. Pak-Identity, through attitude:

H8: There is a positive and significant relationship between HB and ATT toward using Pak-Identity.

4.8   Price Value (PV)

An individual will be inclined to use e-government system or service if its benefits are higher as compared to its monetary cost [7]. This construct is considered for having a significant role in the studies related to technology adoption as well as e-government studies [10]. Based on the evidence from previous literature on e-government, it is hypothesized that:

H9: There is a positive and significant relationship between PV and BI toward using Pak-Identity.

4.9   Grievance Redressal (GR)

Grievance redressal is defined as a mechanism/system to address the disputes between a consumer and a service provider. Since there may arise some legal disputes between the government and the citizens while making transactions by the public and resolution of such disputes is necessary, provision of grievance redressal is quite necessary. Grievance redressal has been very effective in developing countries like India, that have contributed to creating positive impacts on individuals' use of services [18, 19]. Previous research has evidenced that grievance redressal bears a significant positive predictor of m-wallets use intentions [20]. Thus, in this study, grievance redressal has been hypothesized as:

H10: There is a positive and significant relationship between GR and BI toward using Pak-Identity.

4.10   Attitude (ATT)

Attitude is described as the degree to which a unit of adoption has a positive evaluation of the behaviour in question. Most recent studies, including [1, 21] have postulated the role of attitude in measuring adoption of IS/IT. Moreover, the attitude has also been investigated to influence behavioural intention to use e-government [6]. Thus, we hypothesize attitude as (Fig. 1):

H11: There is a positive and significant relationship between ATT and BI toward using Pak-Identity.

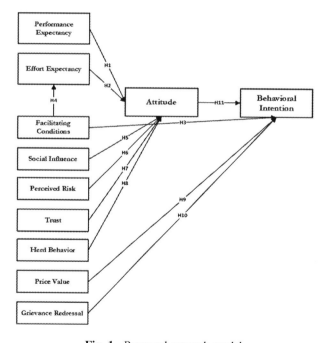

Fig. 1. Proposed research model

5   Methods

We employed partial least squares - structure equation modeling (PLS-SEM) technique using SmartPLS 3.0 to analyze the collected data and test the hypotheses. Moreover, a simple random sampling technique was adopted to collect data from citizens [22].

A questionnaire was designed by adapting scales from previous studies to examine the research question. The items of the constructs were based on previous studies in which they had already been used and tested. These studies included [1, 6, 12, 20, 23]. A survey was undertaken among citizens to seek substantial insights after investigating the influencing factors on the adoption of e-government service, i.e. Pak-Identity facilitated by NADRA. A self-administered online questionnaire was set up to collect data. A total number of 441 respondents participated in this survey, whereas the data collection took place three months long. The questionnaire was divided into two parts, including demographic questions and questions about all the constructs. Each construct consisted of a minimum of three items and respondents were asked to provide their opinions in one of the predefined choices like 'Extremely Disagree', 'Disagree', 'Neutral', 'Agree', and 'Extremely Agree'. A small introduction about e-government transactional service, i.e. Pak-Identity, was presented before the respondents to give them an introduction about the service understudied.

The questionnaire also comprised of ordinal questions concerning the age group, education, occupation, and age of the respondents. No extrinsic incentive or reward scheme was introduced to the respondents to increase their participation in this survey except a voluntary will. Since a significant percentage (i.e. 75%) of the respondents was well-educated, participated in the survey, we are sure about citizens' high degree of competencies to answer the questions. Therefore, we are confident that the respondents are suitable for the study.

6   Findings

Of the study population, 143 are females, and 298 are males. A total number of 112 participants are of having 12-year of schooling, 176 are of having 14-year of schooling, 123 are postgraduates, and qualification level of 29 participants is postgraduate research. A total number of 188 are students who participated in this research survey, 28 are unemployed, 28 are self-employed, 121 are employees of private-sector, and 76 are employees of public-sector. A total number of 206 participants are 18–24 years old, 104 are 25–29 years old, 67 are 30–34 years old, 40 are 35–39 years old, 15 are 40–44 years old, 2 are 45–49 years old, 4 are 50–54 years old, 3 are 55–59 years old and no participant is above 59 years of age.

6.1   Measurement Model

We have assessed the measurement model by applying reliabilities and validities tests such as Cronbach's Alpha, composite reliability, convergent validity, average variance extracted (AVE), and discriminant validity. Following the recommendations of Hair, Hult, Ringle and Sarstedt [24], the threshold values of Cronbach's Alpha (α), composite reliability, and indicator's reliability have been set to greater than 0.7 whereas the threshold value of AVE has been set to greater than 0.5. All the values are above the threshold values and demonstrated in Table 1.

Table 1. Reliability and validity statistics

Constructs	Items	Cronbach's α	Composite reliability	AVE
Performance Expectancy (PE)	3	0.918	0.948	0.859
Effort Expectancy (EE)	3	0.899	0.937	0.833
Social Influence (SI)	3	0.857	0.912	0.776
Facilitating Conditions (FC)	3	0.859	0.914	0.780
Perceived Risk (PR)	3	0.919	0.944	0.849
Trust (TRST)	3	0.939	0.961	0.891
Herd Behaviour	3	0.829	0.897	0.745
Price Value (PV)	3	0.885	0.928	0.810
Grievance Redressal (GR)	3	0.923	0.951	0.867
Attitude (ATT)	3	0.958	0.973	0.923
Behavioural Intention (BI)	3	0.903	0.939	0.837

Finally, we check for the construct's discriminant validity [24]. Table 2 presents the results of the evaluation for discriminant validity test. We have detected no anomalies using this test (see Table 2). Overall, our constructs show excellent measurement properties in terms of reliabilities and validities.

Table 2. Fornell-Larcker criterion

	PE	SI	FC	ATT	BI	HB	EE	GR	PR	PV	TRST
PE	0.927										
SI	0.677	0.881									
FC	0.667	0.739	0.883								
AT	0.670	0.640	0.631	0.961							
BI	0.667	0.507	0.470	0.569	0.915						
HB	0.594	0.558	0.622	0.691	0.494	0.863					
EE	0.769	0.738	0.742	0.652	0.565	0.619	0.912				
GR	0.621	0.461	0.468	0.496	0.508	0.432	0.531	0.931			
PR	0.101	0.169	0.196	0.105	0.053	0.239	0.152	0.083	0.922		
PV	0.563	0.622	0.646	0.565	0.408	0.552	0.602	0.288	0.206	0.900	
TRST	0.656	0.644	0.629	0.703	0.531	0.631	0.589	0.457	0.080	0.592	0.944

6.2   Structural Model

In the structural model, the coefficient of determination (R^2) and the significant values (p values) are assessed. The R^2 value of EE is 0.551, ATT is 0.647, and R^2 value of BI is 0.404 (see Table 4). It is found that there is a high explanatory variance of EE, ATT, and BI. The p-values (less than 0.05) of the hypothesized relationships are considered as significant values and lead to the acceptance of a hypothesis (Table 3).

Table 3. Testing of hypotheses

Path	β	T statistics	p-values	Remarks
H1: PE → ATT	0.151	2.185	0.029	Supported
H2: EE → ATT	0.098	1.304	0.193	Not-Supported
H3: FC → BI	0.065	0.956	0.339	Not-Supported
H4: FC → EE	0.742	17.592	0.000	Supported
H5: SI → ATT	0.122	1.834	0.067	Not-Supported
H6: PR → ATT	−0.041	1.387	0.166	Not-Supported
H7: TRST → ATT	0.276	4.354	0.000	Supported
H8: HB → ATT	0.308	5.503	0.000	Supported
H9: PV → BI	0.095	1.974	0.049	Supported
H10: GR → BI	0.285	4.060	0.000	Supported
H11: ATT → BI	0.333	4.995	0.000	Supported

$p < 0.05$

Table 4. Coefficient of determination (R^2)

Endogenous variables	R^2	T statistics	p-values
Attitude	0.647	13.063	0.000
Behavioural intention	0.404	5.780	0.000
Effort expectancy	0.551	8.912	0.000

This study has found seven out of eleven hypotheses supported since the p-values are less than 0.05. The most striking results attained from the analysis are that PE does have an influence on ATT, FC on EE, GR on BI, TRST on ATT, HB on ATT, PV on BI, and ATT does influence behavioural intention to use e-government service. The results that PE influences on ATT, FC on EE, TRST on ATT, HB on ATT, PV on BI, GR on BI, and ATT influences on BI are aligned with the previous studies [1, 6, 12, 20, 23]. Moreover, the influence of EE on BI is not supported in this study which is aligned the earlier studies [6, 10] whereas it contradicts with the assumption of the base theory, i.e. UMEGA [1]. On the other hand, the influence of SI on ATT is supported in one study [6] whereas it is not supported in another study [10]. Surprisingly, although PR is negatively influencing, it is not supported in this study, whereas it has been proved to have a significant negative influence on ATT [1, 6]. The results are more attractive such that 55% of variance has been explained in effort expectancy and 64.7% of variance has been explained in attitude whereas 40.4% of the variance is explained in behavioural intention to use e-government.

7 Discussion and Implications

This research is conducted, including the citizens of all domains. It can be deduced from the research that a UMEGA model, which has been extended according to the context, can be used to identify directions for policy-makers to increase the citizens' intentions to use e-government transactional services which are then lead to its wide use. Identification of these insights and, in return, improvement in e-government policies will lead to achieving high-level benefits such as transparency, access to information, efficient delivery of services, and citizens' engagement.

Being H1 to be accepted postulates that the relationship between performance expectancy and attitude is strong. Thus, users' perceptions of performance would play a vital role in constructing positive attitudes, which will then lead to high intention in using e-government services. Policy-makers should take actions in making e-government services user-friendly and beneficial in citizens' daily lives, such as applying online and obtaining identity documents at home without making long journeys.

H4 is also accepted, which evidences that the availability of technical and organizational infrastructure would affect the users' attitudes positively through minimizing the efforts in using e-government services. Accordingly, policy-makers should make policies to arrange for training and support to users at the organizational level, internet facilities, and unique customer access outlets [1]. Moreover, they should invest more in developing public-private partnerships and hire analysts/designers so that easy to use and easily understandable applications can be developed in applying for identity documents.

Users perceptions about trust in e-government services are also contributing towards building attitudes, which would then lead to upsurge the intentions to use services since H7 is accepted. The e-government services should be reliable, secure, and trustworthy, which would shape the users' attitudes in using them. Therefore, the responsible authorities should concentrate on shaping users' beliefs by ensuring citizens' security and privacy concerns. Multiple authentications while making payment transactions for obtaining identity documents can be implemented for this purpose [10].

The empirical analysis in this study also supports hypothesis H8. Accordingly, herd behaviour, which is the user's self-observations about using technology or service by other people, is the predictor in forming attitudes. Users will articulate their attitudes if they are observing Pak-Identity a dominant service in the society since a large number of people will be using it. Therefore, policy-makers should make such policies through which use of e-government service should be largely discernible to the society (e.g. elevating awareness campaigns) [1].

Pak-Identity service requires the internet, computers, and other equipment for the printing, uploading, and downloading scanned documents (e.g. forms, photographs). Users would be inclined to use e-government transactional services if it is a good substitute for perceived benefits over incurred costs. Hypothesis H9 is accepted, which postulates that price value is a significant positive predictor of behavioural intention. Thus, policy-makers should make policies which help in delivering inexpensive technological services or the service that requires less equipment to the maximum extent.

A novelty in this research is the introduction of grievance redressal to investigate its influence on behavioural intention to use e-government transactional service i.e. Pak-Identity. This study reveals the hypothesis H10 'supported' by the empirical analysis. Legal disputes between the service providers and users should be resolved timely and transparently (e.g. payment clearance for applying identity documents). Moreover, safe and secure service would form users' behavioural intention to use it [20]. For this purpose, a continuous monitoring system/mechanism should be observed by top officials.

Hypothesis H11 postulates a strong positive linkage between attitude and behavioural intention to use e-government transactional service i.e. Pak-Identity. Thus, policy-makers should instrumentalize in increasing attitudes (by demonstrating benefits to the users), which will lead to increasing intentions.

8 Conclusion, Limitations, and Future Directions

To sum up, our work has investigated the predictors of adoption of e-government by employing UMEGA model since studies on the adoption of transactional services in e-government by applying domain-specific theories/models are scarce. The evidence from this study intimate that adoption of e-government is influenced by some factors determined by impacts on citizens' attitude and behavioural intention. The findings prove that performance expectancy, trust, and herd behaviour are influencing factors of attitude, facilitating conditions of effort expectancy whereas grievance redressal, price value, and attitude are influencing factors of behavioural intention to use e-government transactional service, i.e. Pak-Identity. The model has explained 55% of the variance in effort expectancy, 65% of the variance in attitude, and 40% of the variance in behaviour intention to use e-government by the citizens. Our study provides suitable bases for a new way to conduct adoption studies on e-government using UMEGA [1]. These findings add to a vast growing body of knowledge on e-government adoption, which has particular implications for the academics and managers.

Limitation of the survey id that respondents/citizens are limited to e-government users in Pakistan only and care should be exercised when generalizing these results to other countries. Moreover, future researchers are invited to conduct studies on other e-government transactional services where difference/comparison of factors in adopting various e-government transactional services can make more significant insights for the policy-makers. Since the model underperformed concerning the explained variance of behavioural intention as compared to UMEGA, future researchers should investigate some other factors which can accelerate the citizens' behavioural intention to use e-government.

References

1. Dwivedi, Y.K., Rana, N.P., Janssen, M., Lal, B., Williams, M.D., Clement, M.: An empirical validation of a unified model of electronic government adoption (UMEGA). Gov. Inf. Quart. **34**, 211–230 (2017)
2. Palvia, S., Anand, A.B., Seetharaman, P., Verma, S.: Imperatives and challenges in using e-government to combat corruption: a systematic review of literature and a holistic model. In: Americas Conference on Information Systems. Association for Information Systems, Boston (2017)
3. Taheri, F., Mirghiasi, S.R.: Presenting a typology of users satisfaction model from electronic government. Int. Acad. J. Organ. Behav. Hum. Resour. Manag. **3**, 11–26 (2016)
4. Heeks, R., Bailur, S.: Analyzing e-government research: Perspectives, philosophies, theories, methods, and practice. Gov. Inf. Quart. **24**, 243–265 (2007)

5. Ali, U., et al.: Innovative citizen's services through public cloud in Pakistan: user's privacy concerns and impacts on adoption. Mob. Netw. Appl. **24**, 47–68 (2019)
6. Verkijika, S.F., De Wet, L.: E-government adoption in sub-Saharan Africa. Electron. Commer. Res. Appl. **30**, 83–93 (2018)
7. Venkatesh, V., Thong, J.Y.L., Xu, X.: Consumer acceptance and use of information technology: extending the unified theory of acceptance and use of technology. MIS Quart. **36**, 157–178 (2012)
8. Venkatesh, V., Morris, M.G., Davis, G.B., Davis, F.D.: User acceptance of information technology: toward a unified view. MIS Quart. **27**, 425–478 (2003)
9. Krishnaraju, V., Mathew, S.K., Sugumaran, V.: Web personalization for user acceptance of technology: an empirical investigation of e-Government services. Inf. Syst. Front. **18**, 579–595 (2016)
10. Lallmahomed, M.Z., Lallmahomed, N., Lallmahomed, G.M.: Factors influencing the adoption of e-Government services in Mauritius. Telematics Inf. **34**, 57–72 (2017)
11. Abu-Shanab, E.A.: E-government familiarity influence on Jordanians' perceptions. Telematics Inf. **34**, 103–113 (2017)
12. Alzahrani, L., Al-Karaghouli, W., Weerakkody, V.: Investigating the impact of citizens' trust toward the successful adoption of e-government: a multigroup analysis of gender, age, and internet experience. Inf. Syst. Manag. **35**, 124–146 (2018)
13. Rehman, M., Kamal, M.M., Esichaikul, V.: Adoption of e-Government services in Pakistan: a comparative study between online and offline users. Inf. Syst. Manag. **33**, 248–267 (2016)
14. Venkatesh, V., Thong, J.Y.L., Chan, F.K.Y., Hu, P.J.-H., Brown, S.A.: Extending the two-stage information systems continuance model: incorporating UTAUT predictors and the role of context. Inf. Syst. J. **21**, 527–555 (2011)
15. Zuiderwijk, A., Cligge, M.: The acceptance and use of open data infrastructures-drawing upon UTAUT and ECT. In: Electronic Government and Electronic Participation: Joint Proceedings of Ongoing Research, Ph.D. Papers, Posters and Workshops of IFIP EGOV and EPart 2016, p. 91. IOS Press (2016)
16. Banerjee, A.V.: A simple model of herd behavior. Quart. J. Econ. **107**, 797–817 (1992)
17. Sun, H.: A longitudinal study of herd behavior in the adoption and continued use of technology. MIS Quart. **37**, 1013–1041 (2013)
18. Rana, N.P., Dwivedi, Y.K., Williams, M.D., Weerakkody, V.: Adoption of online public grievance redressal system·in India: toward developing a unified view. Comput. Hum. Behav. **59**, 265–282 (2016)
19. Rana, N.P., Dwivedi, Y.K., Williams, M.D., Lal, B.: Examining the success of the online public grievance redressal systems: an extension of the is success model. Inf. Syst. Manag. **32**, 39–59 (2015)
20. Kumar, A., Adlakaha, A., Mukherjee, K.: The effect of perceived security and grievance redressal on continuance intention to use M-wallets in a developing country. Int. J. Bank Market. **36**, 1170–1189 (2018)
21. Dwivedi, Y.K., Rana, N.P., Jeyaraj, A., Clement, M., Williams, M.D.: Re-examining the unified theory of acceptance and use of technology (UTAUT): towards a revised theoretical model. Inf. Syst. Front. **21**, 719–734 (2017)
22. Zikmund, W.G., Babin, B.J., Carr, J.C., Griffin, M.: Business research methods. Cengage Learning (2013)
23. Vinnik, V.: User adoption of mobile applications: Extension of UTAUT2 model. Master of Science in Economics and Business Administration, Norwegian School of Economics (2017)
24. Hair, J.F., Hult, G.T.M., Ringle, C.M., Sarstedt, M.: A Primer on Partial Least Squares Structural Equation Modeling (PLS-SEM). SAGE Publications, Inc., Thousand Oaks (2017)

Governments' Perspective on Engaging Citizens in the Co-creation of E-Government Services: A Meta-synthesis of Qualitative Case Studies

Anupriya Khan[1], Satish Krishnan[1(✉)], and A. K. M. Najmul Islam[2]

[1] Indian Institute of Management Kozhikode, Kozhikode, India
{anupriyak09fpm, satishk}@iimk.ac.in
[2] University of Turku, Turku, Finland
najmul.islam@utu.fi

Abstract. The innovative and improved delivery of public services is largely contingent on the co-creation process. Noting that engaging citizens in the development and delivery of e-government services is challenging and that limited attention is given to the process of facilitating citizen participation, this study intends to explore (a) governments' perception of the co-creation; and (b) how governments can facilitate citizen participation in the development of e-government services. Through a meta-synthesis of qualitative case studies, this study identifies factors that are crucial for enabling co-creation, and develops a process view of the co-creation of e-government services to provide a holistic understanding on how the process of co-creation can be facilitated by the government and how the citizens could be engaged. The study thus contributes to the literature on e-government and public administration by improving the understanding of co-creation phenomenon, and suggests the mechanisms to improve citizen participation for the benefit of practitioners and policy makers.

Keywords: Co-creation · Citizen participation · Open innovation ·
E-government service · Meta-synthesis · Qualitative case study

1 Introduction

Enid Mumford [1] admitted that work systems function towards enhancing human experience when the interests, needs, and values of different stakeholders are well integrated (p. 20). She held a strong belief in favor of the use of computers and information systems in all areas to enhance the quality of human life. E-government is a remarkable example of such information system. Governments across many countries are now investing effort and significant amount of money to develop e-government systems to deliver and improve public services [3].

Mumford also endorsed the participatory approach to the design and development of computer-based work systems [1]. A participatory design approach not only enables users to impart their skills and knowledge but also renders an opportunity for learning and knowledge sharing for the benefit of both designers and users. It further empowers

© IFIP International Federation for Information Processing 2019
Published by Springer Nature Switzerland AG 2019
I. O. Pappas et al. (Eds.): I3E 2019, LNCS 11701, pp. 451–463, 2019.
https://doi.org/10.1007/978-3-030-29374-1_37

users by creating a sense of ownership within them and encourages acceptance of new systems [2]. The participatory approach involves interaction between stakeholders that allows system developers to gain understanding on the diverse objectives, needs, and characteristics of various groups, which, in turn, help in defining and validating requirement specifications [3]. Apparently, it bestows several benefits on stakeholders working towards the design and improvement of products, systems, and services. For instance, the participatory approach can better match the individual's needs with the services provided, and enhance the usability, reliability, and security of the systems [3].

Similar thought is observed to be echoed in the concept of co-creation. Since its inception in service management and marketing literature [4], the concept of co-creation is widely been adopted and studied in the fields of public administration and e-government [5, 6]. Despite that the new studies are being emerged on co-creation, there is a substantial lack of consensus on its definition. This is largely due to its close association with the vast field of public administration [7] that produces research in several directions with difference in theoretical positions. For the purpose of this study, we describe co-creation as the "involvement of outside, non-typical, stakeholders in the initiation, design, implementation, and/or evaluation of a public service" [8]. Governments around the world are allegedly beginning to try out or implement co-creation practices in the development of public services [7]. The co-creation may increase government transparency, generate innovative and efficient public services, solve social problems and challenges, and help connect citizens and the government to provide higher levels of public value [4, 9].

The motivation for co-creation often is linked to its potency of generating higher levels of public value. The concept of "public value" is highly debated and discussed in the literature, yet there is no widely agreed upon definition of it [7]. However, in general, public value can be considered to be created at a societal level. In other words, "it is something that emerges when people use or create something" [7, p. 89]. It is worthy to note that public service delivery is rapidly changing; it is growing as more open and collaborative, and less top-down driven. This generates a new paradigm where new technologies, such as e-government and open government, empower stakeholders to create new services that are meaningful and valuable to them. Nevertheless, the current research suggests that citizens are hardly involved in co-creation of public services. Their direct participation appears to be almost non-existent [10, 12]. In most cases, the e-government development is followed through a techno-centric approach, instead of participatory approach [3]. Therefore, it becomes imperative to gain understanding of how to facilitate the co-creation process for enabling an effective and efficient public service delivery.

The government is believed to play a crucial role in engaging citizens in the process of the co-creation of e-government services [13]. Governments may perceive their citizens as consumers or as participants. Such perception would largely decide the actions the government would take towards co-creation. Accordingly, to enhance our understanding of co-creation, specifically the process of engaging citizens in co-creation, there is a need to explore (1) what governments perceive about co-creation; and (2) how they facilitate the citizen participation. Although prior studies have analyzed and consolidated the benefits of co-creation by reviewing the literature, little is known about the process of facilitating the citizen participation in the co-creation of e-government services. Hence, in an attempt to develop an in-depth understanding of the co-creation from governments' perspective, we conducted a meta-synthesis of 10 qualitative case studies. A meta-synthesis refers to "an exploratory, inductive research design to synthesize primary qualitative case studies for the purpose of making contributions beyond those achieved in the original studies" [14, p. 523]. The meta-synthesis can offer a holistic understanding of a phenomenon, reveal important insights, and help build a theory. Analyzing the selected studies by the meta-synthesis approach, we propose a process view of the co-creation that entails how the process of co-creation can be facilitated by the government and how the citizens could be engaged. We, therefore, contribute to the literature on e-government and public administration by improving the understanding of the process of co-creation, and suggest the mechanisms to facilitate citizen participation for the benefit of practitioners and policy makers.

2   Background

2.1   Co-creation

With the development of the new forms of public service delivery, specifically the co-creation of public service, the understanding of public value is appeared to be shifting. Though the concept of "public value" is applied and discussed in many studies, there is hardly a consensus as to what this term actually entails. The study by Bryson et al. [15] provides a thorough overview of the different predominant views on public value. Amongst those, the most commonly held view is given by Mark Moore, who believes that "the task of a public sector manager is to create public value" [17], and managers would be able to create public value by aligning different factors in a "strategic triangle" [16]. Stoker [18] suggests another notion of public value. He supports the idea of networks, and contends that public value can be delivered by interacting and engaging with stakeholders [18]. He also argues that the created "public value" could change over time [18]. These examples indicate how the understanding of public value has been shifted. Now, researchers have started arguing that public value is not something which is static; instead, it can be developed at societal level from some service or activity [7]. This is further supported by Ostrom [19], one of the distinguished authors dealing with public value, who noted that public value can emerge through a process of co-production. Osborne [20] also acknowledged that public services can be created by any actor, and public value can be generated through interactions between service user and service provider [4].

Another phenomenon that nearly resembles the concepts of public value and co-production is the concept of co-creation [7]. Alike public value, co-creation is also conceptualized in the literature in different ways. We contend that the essence of co-creation is deemed to rest upon the concept of open innovation. Being stemmed from the private sector, open innovation aims to enlarge the knowledge base by involving outsiders into decision making; sharing skills and expertise with outsiders; and innovating thorough a collaborative approach [22, 23]. Participation and engagement are fundamental while exploring the philosophical understanding of the term "open" [24]. The principles of open innovation are thus perceived to be closely related to the participatory approach of governance [25]. In case of public sector, open innovation have the potential to co-create public policy and services that are desired by the public. Citizens and governments collaborate and share the responsibility for resources, decision making, and the management of public services; this essentially discards the notion that the responsibility of designing and providing public services lies with only governments [21]. Citizen participation is now a core component of the process. E-government services are evolving and inclusiveness of citizens is a necessary prerequisite for improving the public services [26, 27].

2.2   Meta-synthesis

Synthesis of knowledge is important considering that it is the accumulation of knowledge from the research evidence of the extant studies on which the foundation of science rests [28, 29]. Meta-studies (i.e., the analysis of the analysis) being grounded in the evolutionary process of knowledge building thus can offer significant insights into a phenomenon [14]. Broadly, the array of synthesis activities in organizational and management research can be classified into (1) aggregation synthesis; (2) interpretation synthesis; and (3) translation synthesis, with each having distinct ways of approaching a synthesis of knowledge [14].

Aggregation synthesis is grounded in positivist and quantitative tradition. A meta-analysis provides an understanding of research synthesis as aggregation [52], and is viewed as an effective and efficient approach of testing a theory or establishing a predictive theory [28, 30, 31]. For a meta-analysis, prior study results become the primary data. The empirical findings that are dispersed across time and publications are then statistically synthesized [32, 34–37]. Against this, some researchers follow an inductive form of knowledge synthesis that goes beyond the deductive logic of classical positivism and provides interpretations across the existing qualitative studies. As opposed to the quantitative aggregation, the purpose of which is to generate prediction, interpretation synthesis refers to the accumulation of primary evidence for producing interpretive explanation. The synthesis involves the extraction and analysis of insights generated within the primary studies. Through this process, it seeks to identify categories and patterns that emerge across the studies with an attempt to preserve the integrity of original studies [14]. The goal is to make a theoretical contribution by taking into account the local contexts [38]. Lastly, the research synthesis as translation is rooted in a constructivist paradigm and especially applied in medical science, health care, or social and political policy [39]. Within this perspective, synthesis of knowledge is contingent on data that are viewed as "constructed entities" and the goal is to develop "the informed and meaningful reconstruction of how the study's participants constructed their own understandings" [14, p. 526].

In case of interpretation synthesis, the data, analysis, and the consequent insights are considered as separate entities. And, this qualitative evidence of the case studies are collected and subsequently synthesized to build a theory. In this study, the objective is to perform a synthesis without violating the essence and integrity of the qualitative case study research. Therefore, we contend that it would be reasonable to follow the perspective of interpretation synthesis to best carry out a meta-synthesis.

2.3   Meta-synthesis of Qualitative Case Studies

A case study approach for a research is useful to answer the questions of why or how [38]. Case studies demonstrate how particular practices are developed and carried out in particular organizations, and contribute to theory building [40]. Further, qualitative case studies create the scope of studying the research question in depth that could lead to unexpected, but interesting findings, which can form the basis for hypotheses to be empirically examined in future research [38]. Within the broader array of case study research, there directions are apparent ranging from inductive, interpretive case studies to more indicative, comparative case study research used to build theory in a post-positivist fashion [38, 41–43]. A case study research usually focuses on a specific phenomenon, and researchers conducting the case study research seek to understand it completely. Rather than controlling variables the case study researchers observe all the variables, study the interactions among variables, and explore the contextual conditions pertinent to the phenomenon under study [38, 41, 42]. Case study research has the ability to include a variety of data sources and methodologies that produce in-depth qualitative findings in specific contexts [38, 44].

A meta-synthesis is defined as "an exploratory, inductive research design to synthesize primary qualitative case studies for the purpose of making contributions beyond those achieved in the original studies" [14, p. 527]. Essentially, it is a meta-study because it involves the accumulation of the evidence from prior case studies, and it extracts, analyzes, and synthesizes the prior evidence. Therefore, a meta-synthesis does not advocate the reuse of the original primary data collected by the case researchers [14]. Instead, a meta-synthesis is conducted on the insights constructed by the original researchers of the primary studies with respect to their own understanding and interpretation.

3   Research Design

3.1   Framing the Research Question

This study aims at exploring the process of co-creation of e-government services and understanding the role of the government in facilitating citizen participation. Consistent with our research objective, we choose to frame our research questions as: How does the government facilitate the co-creation of e-government services? How does the government motivate citizens to participate in the development of e-government services?

3.2   Locating Relevant Research

The important step in our study was to identify the bodies of research that are relevant for our meta-synthesis interest. Given the volume of studies in the field of e-government, it was challenging to formulate search keywords pertaining to our research question. As some terms can be expressed in several forms, we decided to combine different keywords related to e-government, participation, and qualitative case study methodology. Finally, we based the search in Scopus and ABI/INFORM digital libraries using keywords ("electronic government" OR "e government" OR "egovernment" OR "digital government" OR "open government" OR "public e-service") AND ("participation" OR "engage" OR "collaborative" OR "open data" OR "involvement" OR "participatory" OR "co creation" OR "co production" OR "co operative" OR "co design") AND ("qualitative" OR "case" OR "interview" OR "focus group"). The first set of keywords about e-government was used as a selection criterion in the *Title* of the articles and other keywords were used as a selection criterion in topic *Title*, *Keywords*, and *Abstract*. This yielded a total of 319 studies published in journals and conference proceedings between January 2001 and March 2019.

Table 1. Summary of the selected articles

Studies	Description	Country
Chatwin and Arku [13]	Explores the motivation, capabilities and constraints, and the influence of the institutional environment on the co-creation of an open government action plan	Ghana
Gascó-Hernández et al. [45]	Discusses how the training interventions can increase awareness among citizens, improve users skills, and potentially engage them in the open government	Spain, Italy, and USA
Axelsson et al. [33]	Discusses the importance of citizen participation and involvement in developing public e-services	Sweden
Nam [46]	Performs a SWOT analysis to understand the challenges around open government and meaningful civic participation	Korea
Pilemalm et al. [48]	Explores inter-organizational and cross-sector collaborations for participative development of e-government systems and analyses the challenges	Sweden
Olphert and Damodaran [3]	Focuses on socio-technical and participatory approach to the development of e-government systems, and explores the enabling conditions and benefits of such participatory approach	United Kingdom
Chan and Pan [47]	Focuses on how to identify and engage the relevant stakeholders in e-government implementation	Singapore
Oostveen and Besselaar [49]	Applies participatory design principles to involve users in the design of infrastructural system prototype	Europe
McBride et al. [7]	Explores institutional dimensions that can facilitate open government and citizen participation	USA
Safarov [11]	Discusses factors that are important for driving the co-creation of open government data driven public services	Netherlands, Sweden, and UK

To find the relevant studies amongst these 319 studies, we first went through their abstracts to have an overview of the studies. Most articles except 48 were identified as false positives and excluded due to the lack of relevance. These 48 articles were then thoroughly studied to assess whether they pertain to our research questions. Finally, the articles that were found to discuss the co-creation and open government phenomenon from citizens' perspective, or the articles that did not employ qualitative case study research, or case studies that were quantitative in nature were excluded. Therefore, within the subset of 48 articles, we finally identified 10 articles for our meta-synthesis. A brief description of these articles is presented in Table 1.

4   Analysis

4.1   Analysis on a Case-Specific Level

Hoon suggested that before embarking on the meta-synthesis, an analysis has to be carried out on a case-specific level [14]. That is, each case study under synthesis has to be explored individually as a first step towards executing the meta-synthesis. As the current study intends to understand how citizens can be engaged in the co-creation of e-government services, we explored each case study in terms of the factors that drive the co-creation. At the same time, to capture the role of the government in facilitating citizen participation, we specifically identified factors that are important for the government to enable the phenomenon of co-creation and investigated the process of achieving such collaboration. As suggested by Hoon [14], and Miles and Huberman [44], we developed a network by establishing relationships among the relevant factors for each case study. Such technique helps to map each case into a case-specific network of variables that could generate the underlying theme for the phenomenon of interest. For instance, one case-specific network suggests that "intrinsic motivation" of the government influences the way governments facilitate the co-creation of e-government.

4.2   Synthesis on a Cross-Study Level

As the next step towards carrying out the meta-synthesis, we moved from case-specific level analysis to cross-study level analysis. The case-specific networks developed in the previous step are the foundation to further understand how the studies under synthesis are connected or different [14]. Thus, the factors that were identified in each of the case studies and represented through the case-specific network were now compared and assessed for their commonalities across studies. To elaborate, we observed (1) how and which components of the case-specific networks were similar across the studies under synthesis; (2) how the factors were different across the case-specific networks; (3) if the relationships between the factors could hold across the studies; and (4) if new set of relationships can be formed by merging the case-specific networks. This process resulted into an integrated network called as meta-causal network that established relationships among the broad factors identified throughout the studies under synthesis. The meta-causal network shown in Fig. 1 provides a process view of the co-creation of e-government systems from governments' perspective.

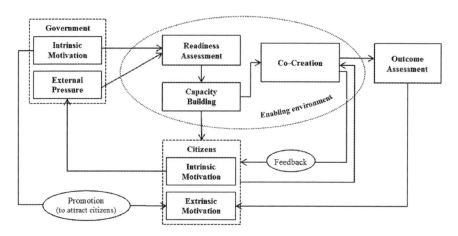

Fig. 1. The process view of the co-creation of e-government services

5   Discussion

This study, through a meta-synthesis of qualitative case studies, provides some crucial insights into the process of co-creation in e-government services. Specifically, our aim was to investigate the co-creation from governments' perspective whereby we explored (1) governments' perception of the co-creation, and (2) how they facilitate citizen participation in the co-creation of e-government services. The meta-causal network (Fig. 1) that emerged from the meta-synthesis of the selected case studies renders a holistic view in that direction. It represents the process view of the co-creation of e-government services that delineates how the co-creation of e-government services is initiated and facilitated.

The co-creation of e-government services or the participatory approach to the development of e-government can be initiated by the government or the citizens. We first describe the process of co-creation when the government becomes pioneer. In such instances, usually the government could be internally motivated to engage citizens while developing public services. It could be the commitment towards enhancing public value and serving the communities, and/or the willingness to rebuild trust between the government and its constituents that could motivate the government to take the initiative, as discussed in the case study by [13]. Further, the perceived benefits of the co-creation can also incentivize the government internally to take up the participatory approach. **Internal motivation** of the government thus has been observed as a main driver of co-creation [7, 13].

Once motivated, the government may embark on assessing its readiness. This is a crucial step that eventually determines the success of the government initiatives in most cases. **Readiness assessment** includes the assessment of technological, financial, and human resources. Most case studies under the synthesis discussed the importance of technological infrastructure in influencing the co-creation phenomenon [7, 13, 45]. If the technological infrastructure is weak in a locality, and the government portal is not accessible and lacks user-centred design and interactive functionalities, it is highly unlikely that it would encourage the citizens to participate in the e-government service development and delivery [3, 45]. Further, the financial resources are also necessary for the co-creation as the implementation of systems, the development of new services, and the organization of the whole process often require huge financial support [7, 13]. Human resources include the ability of the public managers and employees, more specifically their skills and knowledge of designing, implementing, and managing an e-government initiative [45]. Not only are the technical and managerial skills and experience of public employees important but the technical skills of citizens also matter for the co-creation. This is closely linked to the next tenet of the process view of co-creation, namely, capacity building.

The importance of **capacity building** is cited in most of the case studies under synthesis [3, 7, 13, 45, 46]. Capacity building for the government encompasses several facets ranging from developing technical skills and knowledge, to developing communication skills to engage citizens, to building innovative leadership. An innovative leader can look for opportunities and have strategic action plan for motivating and engaging citizens. Similarly, proper communication with citizens can motivate them to participate in developing e-government services. For that, many researchers emphasized the requirement of citizen communication system [13]. Case studies suggest the need for proper training interventions for the public employees to address any gap in their capability [13, 45]. Capacity building also indicates the need for improving skills and knowledge of citizens for the success of e-government.

The process view of co-creation as presented in Fig. 1 shows that once the government assesses its resources and capability required for developing e-services and engaging citizens, the government can participate in the co-creation of e-government services. Nonetheless, before that, it is necessary that the government makes citizens aware of the e-government services that require participation from citizens. Analysing its importance, the need for public awareness activities is discussed in many of the case studies. The government has to inform citizens, through town hall meetings or radio shows or workshops, the utility of the particular e-service, the values of participating in e-government, and the existence of incentives, if any [11]. Public awareness activities become more significant, especially when the citizens do not initiate the process of co-creation. The goal is to convince citizens and sensitize them so that they become motivated to participate in e-government [45].

While interacting with citizens, the government has to understand the user need at the same time. Many a time, when governments take the initiative, they opt for implementing an e-service that they feel comfortable and convenient without assessing the citizen demand of solving real problems. Heeks [50, p. 162] indicates this as "an opportunity which could be seized" in opposite to "a problem that needs to be solved". The decision has to be driven by the citizen demand or need [33]. The lack of citizen focus becomes detrimental for the success of e-government.

We discussed so far the process of co-creation that was initiated by the government. As stated previously, the citizens may also initiate the process. When there is increased awareness from citizens about their rights and responsibilities, they have particular demand for enhancing public value, and they are intrinsically motivated, then they could cast pressure on the government for creating e-services [13]. Such **intrinsic motivation** of citizens may act as the **external pressure** for the government in the process of co-creation of e-government services. Once both the stakeholders—the government and the citizenry are motivated either intrinsically or extrinsically, the phenomenon of co-creation takes place. Further, to have sustained citizen engagement, a feedback mechanism could be beneficial whereby the citizens can receive constructive feedback on their participation [47]. It is worthy to note that it may not always be possible for the government to directly engage citizens in every e-government service development. The role of intermediary becomes significant in that case, indicating the need for stakeholder identification and management by the government [49].

In addition, it is to be noted that the **enabling environment** has significant role in facilitating the co-creation. The institutional environment such as the political environment and the legislative acts [11], and the economic factors [45] could affect the availability of technological, financial, and human resources, and determine the readiness and the ability of the government.

This meta-synthesis study contributes to the literature on the co-creation and e-government by providing a holistic understanding of the process of co-creation of e-government services. We integrate the co-creation process initiated by the government with that initiated by the citizens. We contend that governments' perception of the co-creation largely determines the way they conduct. If governments realize the benefits of engaging citizens in the e-government service development, they are motivated to initiate and participate in such participatory development process. Apart from the perceived benefits, their commitment towards serving the communities plays a major role in facilitating the co-creation. Further, to engage citizens, we discuss the mechanisms that are emerged from the case studies under synthesis. In particular, we emphasize the need for promoting e-government initiatives, developing public awareness activities, facilitating training interventions, developing effective communication systems, building innovative leadership, and providing technological and related resources to citizens. In essence, the proposed process view of co-creation would enable researchers, practitioners, and policy makers to develop insights into the important parameters enabling the co-creation of e-government services for effective and efficient public service delivery.

The major limitation of this study is that it relies on published articles and conference proceedings. In an ideal scenario, any synthesis has to be exhaustive by including maximum number of eligible literature [30, 51]. In this meta-synthesis, we discarded dissertations and unpublished research studies. Nevertheless, this increased the scientific rigor of the meta-synthesis considering the acceptance of peer-reviewed publications.

6   Concluding Remarks

The effective and efficient delivery of public services is largely dependent on citizen participation for co-creating e-government services. Nevertheless, minimal participation of citizens is witnessed in the development and delivery of e-government services. Realizing the importance of engaging citizens to facilitate the co-creation, this study entails the role and the perceptions of the government through a meta-synthesis of qualitative case studies. A process view of the co-creation of e-government services is proposed to delineate how governments can facilitate citizen participation in the co-creation of e-government services to enhance the public value. We believe that this process view would enhance the understanding of researchers, practitioners, and policy makers about the process of co-creation in the context of e-government, and encourage future empirical research.

References

1. Mumford, E.: Designing human systems for new technology: the ETHICS method. Manchester Business School, Manchester (1983)
2. Mumford, E.: Participation in systems design - what can it offer? In: Shackel, B., Richardson, S. (eds.) Human Factors for Informatics Usability, pp. 267–290. Cambridge University Press, Cambridge (1991)
3. Olphert, W., Damodaran, L.: Citizen participation and engagement in the design of e-government services: the missing link in effective ICT design and delivery. J. Assoc. Inf. Syst. 8(9), 491–507 (2007)
4. Osborne, S., Radnor, Z., Strokosch, K.: Co-production and the co-creation of value in public services: a suitable case for treatment? Public Manag. Rev. 18(5), 639–653 (2016)
5. Cordella, A., Paletti, A.: Value creation, ICT, and co-production in public sector: bureaucracy, opensourcing and crowdsourcing. In: Proceedings of the 18th Annual International Conference on Digital Government Research, pp. 185–194. ACM, Staten Island (2017)
6. Uppström, E., Lönn, C.-M.: Explaining value co-creation and co-destruction in e-government using boundary object theory. Gov. Inf. Quart. 34(3), 406–420 (2017)
7. McBride, K., Aavik, G., Toots, M., Kalvet, T., Krimmer, R.: How does open government data driven co-creation occur? Six factors and a 'perfect storm'; insights from Chicago's food inspection forecasting model. Gov. Inf. Quart. 36(1), 88–97 (2019)
8. Toots, M., McBride, K., Kalvet, T., Krimmer, R.: Open data as enabler of public service co-creation: exploring the drivers and barriers. In: Proceedings of the International Conference for E-Democracy and Open Government, Krems, Austria, pp. 102–112 (2017)
9. Voorberg, W., Bekkers, V., Tummers, L.: A systematic review of co-creation and co-production: embarking on the social innovation journey. Public Manag. Rev. 17(9), 1333–1357 (2015)
10. Safarov, I., Meijer, A., Grimmelikhuijsen, S.: Utilization of open government data: a systematic literature review of types, conditions, effects and users. Inf. Polity 22(1), 1–24 (2017)
11. Safarov, I.: Institutional dimensions of open government data implementation: evidence from the Netherlands, Sweden, and the UK. Public Perform. Manag. Rev. 42, 1–24 (2018)
12. Styrin, E., Luna-Reyes, L.F., Harrison, T.M.: Open data ecosystems: an international comparison. Transforming Gov.: People Process Policy 11(1), 132–156 (2017)
13. Chatwin, M., Arku, G.: Co-creating an open government action plan: the case of Sekondi-Takoradi metropolitan assembly, Ghana. Growth Chang. 49(2), 374–393 (2018)
14. Hoon, C.: Meta-synthesis of qualitative case studies: an approach to theory building. Organ. Res. Methods 16(4), 522–556 (2013)
15. Bryson, J., Crosby, B., Bloomberg, L.: Public value governance: moving beyond traditional public administration and the new public management. Public Adm. Rev. 74(4), 445–456 (2014)

16. Bryson, J., Sancino, A., Benington, J., Sørensen, E.: Towards a multi-actor theory of public value co-creation. Public Manag. Rev. **19**(5), 640–654 (2017)
17. Moore, M.: Public value as the focus of strategy. Aust. J. Public Adm. **53**(3), 296–303 (1994)
18. Stoker, G.: Public value management. The Am. Rev. Public Adm. **36**(1), 41–57 (2006)
19. Ostrom, E.: Metropolitan reform: propositions derived from two traditions. Soc. Sci. Quart. **53**, 474–493 (1972)
20. Osborne, S.: From public service-dominant logic to public service logic: are public service organizations capable of co-production and value co-creation? Public Manag. Rev. **20**(2), 225–231 (2018)
21. Osborne, S., Strokosch, K.: It takes two to tango? Understanding the co-production of public services by integrating the services management and public administration perspectives. Br. J. Manag. **24**, 31–47 (2013)
22. Möslein, K.: Open innovation: Actors, tools and tensions. In: Huff, A., Möslein, K., Reichwald, R. (eds.) Leading Open Innovation, pp. 69–86. MIT Press, Cambridge (2013)
23. Seltzer, E., Mahmoudi, D.: Citizen participation, open innovation, and crowdsourcing: challenges and opportunities for planning. J. Plann. Lit. **28**, 3–18 (2013)
24. Yu, H., Robinson, D.: The new ambiguity of open government. UCLA Law Rev. Discourse **59**, 180–208 (2012)
25. Baka, V.: Co-creating an open platform at the local governance level: how openness is enacted in Zambia. Gov. Inf. Quart. **34**(1), 140–152 (2017)
26. Cornwall, A.: Democratising Engagement What the UK Can Learn from International Experience. Demos, London (2008)
27. Griffiths, S., Foley, B., Prendergast, J.: Assertive citizens: new relationships in the public services. Social Market Foundation, London (2009)
28. Hunt, M.: How Science Takes Stock: The Story of Meta-Analysis. Russell Sage, New York (1997)
29. Hunter, J.E., Schmidt, F., Jackson, G.: Meta-Analysis: Cumulating Research Findings Across Studies. Sage, Beverly Hills (1982)
30. Aytug, Z.G., Rothstein, H.R., Zhou, W., Kern, M.C.: Revealed or concealed? Transparency of procedures, decisions, and judgment calls in meta-analyses. Organ. Res. Methods **15**, 103–133 (2012)
31. Cooper, H.: Research Synthesis and Meta-Analysis: A Step-by-Step Approach, 4th edn. Sage, Thousand Oaks, CA (2010)
32. Aguinis, H., Pierce, C.A., Bosco, F.A., Dalton, D.R., Dalton, C.M.: Debunking myths and urban legends about meta-analysis. Organ. Res. Methods **14**, 306–331 (2011)
33. Axelsson, K., Melin, U., Lindgren, I.: Exploring the importance of citizen participation and involvement in e-government projects: practice, incentives, and organization. Transforming Gov.: People Process Policy **4**(4), 299–321 (2010)
34. Carlson, K.D., Ji, F.X.: Citing and building on meta-analytic findings: a review and recommendations. Organ. Res. Methods **14**, 696–717 (2011)
35. Dalton, D.R., Dalton, C.M.: Meta-analyses: some very good steps toward a bit longer journey. Organ. Res. Methods **11**, 127–147 (2008)
36. Glass, G.V.: Integrating findings: the meta-analysis of research. Rev. of Res. Educ. **5**, 351–379 (1977)
37. Schmidt, F.L.: Meta-analysis: a constantly evolving research integration tool. Organ. Res. Methods **11**, 96–113 (2008)
38. Yin, R.: Case Study Research: Design and Methods, 3rd edn. Sage, Thousand Oaks (2009)

39. Tranfield, D., Denyer, D., Smart, P.: Towards a methodology for developing evidence-informed management knowledge by means of systematic review. Br. J. Manag. **14**(3), 207–222 (2003)
40. Scapens, R.W.: Researching management accounting practice: the role of case study methods. Br. Acc. Rev. **22**(3), 259–281 (1990)
41. Eisenhardt, K.M.: Building theories from case study research. Acad. Manag. Rev. **14**, 532–550 (1989)
42. Eisenhardt, K.M., Graebner, M.E.: Theory building from cases: opportunities and challenges. Acad. Manag. J. **50**, 25–32 (2007)
43. Sigglekow, N.: Persuasion with case studies. Acad. Manag. J. **50**, 20–24 (2007)
44. Miles, M.B., Huberman, A.M.: Qualitative Data Analysis: An Expanded Sourcebook, 2nd edn. Sage, Thousand Oaks (1994)
45. Gascó-Hernández, M., Martin, E.G., Reggi, L., Pyo, S., Luna-Reyes, L.F.: Promoting the use of open government data: cases of training and engagement. Gov. Inf. Quart. **35**, 233–242 (2018)
46. Nam, T.: Challenges and concerns of open government: a case of Government 3.0 in Korea. Soc. Sci. Comput. Rev. 33(5), 556–570 (2015)
47. Chan, C.M., Pan, S.L.: User engagement in e-government systems implementation: a comparative case study of two Singaporean e-government initiatives. J. Strateg. Inf. Syst. **17**, 124–139 (2008)
48. Pilemalm, S., Lindgren, I., Ramsell, E.: Emerging forms of inter-organizational and cross-sector collaborations in e-government initiatives: implications for participative development of information systems. Transforming Gov.: People Process Policy **10**(4), 605–636 (2016)
49. Oostveen, A.-M., Besselaar, P. V.: From small scale to large scale user participation: A case study of participatory design in e-government systems. In: Proceedings of the Eighth Conference on Participatory Design Artful Integration Interweaving Media Materials and Practices, PDC 2004, Toronto, Canada, pp. 173–182 (2004)
50. Heeks, R.: Implementing and Managing eGovernment: An International Text. Sage, London (2006)
51. Kisamore, J., Brannick, M.T.: An illustration of the consequences of meta-analysis model choice. Organ. Res. Methods **11**, 35–53 (2008)
52. Rousseau, D., Manning, J., Denyer, D.: Evidence in management and organizational science: assembling the field's full weight to scientific knowledge through synthesis. Acad. Manag. Ann. **2**, 475–515 (2008)

Blockchain Technology for Enabling Transparent and Traceable Government Collaboration in Public Project Processes of Developing Economies

Ebizimoh Abodei[1], Alex Norta[1]([envelope]) [ORCID], Irene Azogu[2], Chibuzor Udokwu[1], and Dirk Draheim[3] [ORCID]

[1] Blockhain Technology Group, Tallinn University of Technology,
Akadeemia tee 15a, 12618 Tallinn, Estonia
ebizimohabodei@gmail.com, alex.norta.phd@ieee.org, cjobuzor@gmail.com
[2] Department of Public Policy, University of Regina,
2155 College Ave, Regina, SK S4P 4V5, Canada
ina679@uregina.ca
[3] Information Systems Group, Tallinn University of Technology,
Akadeemia tee 15a, 12618 Tallinn, Estonia
dirk.draheim@taltech.ee

Abstract. Infrastructural development is a significant determinant of economic growth. It remains an elusive pursuit for many developing economies suffering from public infrastructural project failures. Although the causes of these failures are identifiable, they remain persistent. Government corruption has been identified as the primary cause of project failures amidst a host of other causal factors, spurred by the ambiguity in public service administration. These factors heighten capital expenditures and hence, the need for more transparent systems in public infrastructural project planning and -delivery. This research uses a case-study methodology to examine the importance of public involvement in addressing the causes of failures in public infrastructural project planning and -delivery. Using Nigeria as a case, the findings from conducted interviews and a document review support the proposition of a technologically collaborative approach in addressing the causes of public infrastructural project failures. The institutionalization of transparency-enhancing blockchain systems are vital in government and public involvement in the processes of public infrastructural project planning and -delivery.

Keywords: Collaborative public governance ·
Public infrastructural development · Policy · Administration ·
Blockchain technology · Smart contracts

1 Introduction

Many public infrastructure projects in developing countries suffer failures that result in declining economic growth and societal underdevelopment. Projects

I. O. Pappas et al. (Eds.): I3E 2019, LNCS 11701, pp. 464–475, 2019.
https://doi.org/10.1007/978-3-030-29374-1_38

that measure a country's growth and economic standard are identified as the building blocks of development. From previous research, it is evident that factors impeding the success of public infrastructural projects are common in developing nations. Identified as recurring factors, some of them include corruption, non-transparency, unaccountability, and budget overruns, inadequate monitoring, change in government and political interferences, and poor communication between different stakeholders [14, 22, 42]. Although these causal factors are identifiable, they have still not been addressed, and thus, developing countries are in a perpetual state of economic regress, or stagnation. Additionally, these infrastructural development projects are very costly and considered a loss for citizens with high expectations for public service delivery.

Over the last decade, Nigeria has budgeted an average of 28% on capital expenditure projects to improve public infrastructure development for better living conditions. Still, the government has not been able to deliver its promises to citizens due to many inconsistencies in the delivery system. For instance, even after over 40 years of independence, Nigeria only has 15% paved roads[1]. As a result, there has been a drastic reduction of public trust in government, stakeholders have also been discouraged from investing in the nation's economy, which leaves a negative mark on governance. Thus, the question remains, how can developing countries such as Nigeria overcome these challenges?

The complexities and challenges with managing the process of project delivery has attracted various technological solutions. One of such attraction is blockchain technology [40], a disruptive innovation with a wide range of applications to provide better management systems in many sectors by constituting trust, transparency, and traceability. The dynamic grouping of different actors/companies with cross-dependencies requires a decentralized system where trust is decisive. Blockchain technologies for decentralized networks and its different use-cases, present novel solutions leading to the creation of a digital society where information- and communication technologies are geared towards the provision of solutions to societal problems.

This paper explores the factors that plague public project processes in developing nations, while using Nigeria as a case study. Thus, Sect. 2 presents related work and Sect. 3 details the chosen research methodology. Next, Sect. 4 presents the case selection, subject description and result presentation. Section 5 discusses the research findings. In, Sect. 6 we discuss limitations and future work. We finish the paper with a conclusion in Sect. 7.

2 Related Work

The term *collaboration* is a focus in public governance and also in diverse fields including environmental management, conflict resolution, private sector, education, and research. The wide application of this yields several definitions based on the purpose served. In connection to public governance, collaboration stems

---

[1] https://tradingeconomics.com/nigeria/roads-paved-percent-of-total-roads-wb-data.html.

from *public participation* and is a new paradigm of democratic governance in the field of public administration [18] in reaction to previous government failures [3]. Collaboration is also a model for problem solving in this digital- and post-industrial age [6]. Collaboration as a need in society is not addressed adequately by elected officials [12]. Furthermore, the bureaucracy, complexities and multifaceted challenges of contemporary governance are more visible [19]. Though the earliest forms of public participation comprise the representation of political party members [35], government is seeking now more active and deliberative ways of public engagement in diverse spheres.

Much of the scientific literature in collaborative public governance focuses on single-case studies concentrating on sector-specific collaborative management for solving individual problems within the public sector. The first public collaborative networks are centered on delivering public inclusion in federal agencies' decision-making processes in response to increasing public frustration on futile efforts in maintaining the government's status quo [35]. The growing importance of public participation attracts research for the involvement of citizens in planning and decision-making processes, relaying the assurance of more widely accepted programs, policies and projects [17].

Collaborative public governance presents several valuable theories compared to traditional forms of governance. One of such arguments is *collaborative advantage* argued by scholars as a decisive factor towards widely accepted public policies and decisions [10,15,25], stating that problems in public governance are very complex to resolve only by public officials. Additionally, [7,8] introduce the theory of *collective intelligence* and *crowd wisdom* with the idea that collaborative public governance networks harness the collective intellect embedded in public circles. Individuals are imperfect and often let emotions cloud their judgments [37]. Nevertheless, despite these limitations, when all imperfect judgments are accumulated and aggregated rightly, collective intelligence is often excellent. Extending these notions further, citation [7] also introduces the concept of *non-expert knowledge* as a benefit to public participatory networks by explaining the inclusion of citizens accompanies non-expert, or non-mainstream knowledge in the creative problem-solving process.

Theories in collaborative public governance are also related to public participation theories, relaying the values and benefits of engaging and involving citizens in the public decision-making process [26]. Public participation improves public policy decision quality, minimizes cost and delays [13]. In study [13], the authors observe that unilateral decisions by public officials suffer delays in implementation due to resistance, controversy, and litigation, while in some cases, these decisions are never implemented. Resolutions with public participation sustain delays in reaching a consensus; conversely, implementation runs smoothly and quickly. Furthermore, unilateral decisions are highly consequential in the long run as policies and projects are frustrated by citizens. Although time and cost do not only measure efficiency, decisions with public participation remain sustained by future users with expressions of trust for government.

While most studies view collaborative public governance positively, some literature emphasizes the difficulties in managing the complexity of the process [32], e.g., there is the problem of ethnic rivalry. The study [5] argues that how a particular ethnic group presents a project idea may divide between the minorities and the mainstream. Research in [9] warns that there is a lack of empirical evidence that reveals the successes of public participation and points to the fact that negotiating can culminate into high levels of argument, slows down projects and frustrates project managers. Citation [1] sees collaborative public governance as consensus-seeking, where a consensus is usually not reached, and the government still reserves the authority to make the final decision.

Although some project managers argue that public consultation in project execution is professionally hazardous, the importance of civic engagement is still paramount. First, there is the case of stronger plans and increased chances of proper implementation when there is public inclusion. In [23], it is argued that public participation ensures that local knowledge is embedded in project plans and culminate better ideas as a result of continuous exchange of information between the public and project managers. Governance refers to the rules and forms that guide collective decision-making where the focus is on decision-making. Thus, governance focuses on groups of individuals, organizations, or systems of an organization making decisions [36].

3   Research Methodology

Initially, we present a problem statement of public infrastructural project delivery in developing economies. Then, a potential solution is suggested as collaborative public management. Although backed by peer-reviewed literature and theories, this proposition still has to be tested and validated. Thus, part of the research covers the testing of that proposition commencing by selecting the case and providing the research questions for the study. We conduct case study-based research [33] for data collection and analysis. For the remainder, Sect. 3.1 describes the case study design and Sect. 3.2 explains the sample selection for semi-structured interviews.

3.1   Case-Study Design

The selection of our case is based on the consideration of cross-case characteristics with developing economies to allow for a generalization of theoretical propositions [20]. The research is qualitative and includes both primary- and secondary data-collection methods to ensure the validity of the study triangulation [41]. Documents are reviewed, and semi-structured interview questions are instrumental to collect primary data. For data analysis, we employ a tool-based thematic analysis using the open-source R software package RQDA (R Qualitative Data Analysis) [16]. We follow the six (6) phase data analysis guide [27] for using RQDA.

3.2 Survey-Sample Selection

The sample size for data collection is ten respondents, from different regions of the case. The selection of respondents is based on their knowledge and experience in the research domain. Three (3) experts stem from the private sector, five (5) are public service officials and two (2) are members of the public.

The survey starts by exploring existing public participatory methods, evaluating their relevance and effectiveness. Our research extends to identifying and understanding the challenges and causes of public infrastructural project failure. This is essential, because exploring how government collaboration can improve public infrastructural project success, first requires identifying the common problems and causes of failures. The research questions also examine how government collaboration improves the success rate of public infrastructure projects and increases economic growth in the long run. We investigate this by measuring the efficiency, benefits, and suitability of the network in addressing the identified challenges tied to public infrastructure-project delivery.

4 Case Selection, Subject Description and Results

In Sect. 4.1, we present the detailed description of the case and subjects. Next, Sect. 4.2 presents the results of this research. Finally, in Sect. 4.3, we map blockchain technology into solving problems that currently exist in public-private partnership (PPP) projects.

4.1 Case and Subject Description

The selected case for this study is Nigeria – a typical example of a developing country with a high population and considerably large economy. The case selection allows to extend our research findings to a broad range of developing economies. Nigeria is commonly compared with developing economies including South Africa, Saudi Arabia, Brazil, Ghana, Malaysia, India, Ghana, Nepal, and Bangladesh. The case reflects a wide range of developing economies and suffers numerous public infrastructural failures over the years.

Many researchers argue that Nigeria's poor state of infrastructural development is due to the military rule for many years. The advent of democracy in 1999 has only seen the rise in corruption and alienation of the populace due to allegations that massive rigging has marred the various elections held in the country. The leadership does not truly reflect the votes of the people and this is also manifested in the poor state of infrastructural development that results in a decline of the economy. These events stem from gross failures by the government in project delivery, aided by little, or no public participation in the decision-making process. To provide a vivid meaning of project failure, the project lead advisor of the United Nations Industrial Development Organization adequately explains: *"In project management, a project fails not only when the project delivery refuses to meet the use or the needs of the project, or when the project's product refuses to satisfy the end-user, but when the project is not accomplished within the allowed time frame, project budget, scope defined for the project and even when the outcome of the project is rejected by the stakeholder."*

In Nigeria, about 60–80% of projects fail. According to Vanguard Newspaper in the country, dated 24th Aug 2015[2], project managers have claimed that the nation achieves only a 39% success on projects.

4.2   Result Presentation

This section presents the findings from our semi-structured interviews. With thematic analysis we found the following specific topic themes:

- level of economic development,
- rate of project delivery/success,
- importance of public involvement,
- current participatory approach,
- collaboration as a potential solution,
- measuring efficiency and effectiveness,
- challenges with using the Web/Internet.

Level of Economic Development. The state of economic development in Nigeria is deplorable. Results endorse the fact that Nigeria is in a perpetual state of economic stagnation and a significantly low pace of economic growth. Responses are disparate due to regional economic inequality. The results also show that the causes of the slow-, or low economic growth are chiefly due to corrupt practices by the government, tribalism, a high rate of public infrastructural failures, and poor communication between the government and public.

Rate of Project Delivery/Success. The success rate of public infrastructural projects as described by respondents is below average. The causes of failures include organizational bureaucracy and complexities, government instability, market fluctuations, poor implementation and monitoring processes, tribalism and public exclusion from the process of planning and delivery.

Importance of Public Involvement. Respondents consider public participation to play a significant role in infrastructural project delivery. Although elusive and not widely practiced in Nigeria, we identify key criteria to allow for the implementation of a stable participatory process. Respondents mention that public policies and decisions are accepted where the government only implements relevant policies. Citizens take it as a duty to checkmate government activities due to the transparent system with an increased public contribution to project success. Assuring project success is shared and citizens take ownership of public programs. Accruing more importance, the quality of decisions increases due to the sampling of a wider pool of knowledge.

---

[2] https://www.vanguardngr.com/2015/08/60-of-projects-fail-in-nigeria-unido/.

Current Participatory Approach. Public participation methods are notable in infrastructural project planning and delivery. The common approach is in town hall meetings and public opinion hearings. The expectations of citizens with the current techniques are unactualized, contributing to the reduced public interest in the process with lacking trust and confidence in governance. Thus, participation is merely a constitutional theory. Current methods are deemed unproductive for several reasons including the size of the population, power dynamics, and non-transparency.

Collaboration as a Potential Solution. Inferences suggest that public participation in the process of infrastructural project planning and delivery accompany a positive impact. As a more comprehensive solution alongside the implementation, government officials mention the following as secondary additions: a collaborative network, punitive measures, stronger monitoring institutions and stringent legal actions against corrupt practices by public servants. Emphasizing the need for collaboration and an open system, one respondent opined: *"Transparency is the bedrock of any system that will address the current challenges in project delivery."*

Measuring Efficiency and Effectiveness. One commonality from inferences is that the impact of the proposed collaborative network is evident, fostered by transparent systems that curb corrupt practices, e.g., blockchain technology. The assessment of impact can only be performed after the implementation, and there is currently no specific metric for evaluating productivity.

Challenges in Using the Web/Internet. The internet remains a luxury in Nigeria and most citizens have little, or no accessibility to web services. Information technology (IT) literacy, the cost and level of internet coverage are specified as the most common challenge with using the Web/Internet as a participatory approach. Nonetheless, there is a widespread view that the government has the resources to address these challenges.

4.3   Mapping Blockchain Technologies to PPP Problems

We propose a blockchain-based technical solution in Table 1 to address the problems identified in Sect. 4.2. A blockchain-based collaborative tool for managing public project execution addresses issues including project complexity, corruption, inadequate project monitoring by providing a system that enables trust and transparency. We also provide the references of blockchain technologies and smart-contract based projects that provide solutions similar to the proposals provided in the table.

Table 1. Mapping PPP problems onto blockchain-technology solutions.

Problem theme	Findings	Blockchain technology	Application and impact
Level of economic development	Inadequate communication between the government and public	Digital Signature, Consensus	e-Participation tool based on blockchain enables the identification of citizens using unique digital signatures. Agreement reached through such platform cannot be manipulated by any party [21]
Rate of project delivery/success	High rate of project failure caused by corruption, bureaucracy and project complexity	Smart Contract, Cryptocurrency, Consensus	Smart contracts enable transparency in terms of project execution. Payments for project execution is performed when certain conditions in the smart contract (project conditions) are met [11,34]
Importance of public involvement	Benefits derived in knowledge sharing. Transparency renders government more accountable	Consensus, Smart Contract	Consensus allows participants to contribute based on defined messages. Smart contract enables traceability and accountability since every activity is visible on blockchains [4]
Current participatory approach	Current methods are ineffective, do not influence project outcomes or decisions	Digital Signature, Smart Contract	A blockchain-based collaborative platform provides the possibility for people to express their ideas on specific government projects [39]
Collaboration as a potential approach	Collaboration is not a complete solution	NA	NA
Measuring efficiencies and effectiveness	No metric for measurement of project success	Smart Contract	Smart contract shows project milestones, providing the status of projects for tracking and monitoring, even after completion [38]
Challenges with using the Web/Internet	Low rate of internet users	NA	NA

5   Discussions

While we refer the reader to [2] for the extended version of this research, investigating the causes of infrastructure project failures reveals various factors that are disjointed. Studying the factors holistically, it is apparent that a transparent system in project delivery fosters better management and accountability. Furthermore, an essential finding in this paper is that a one-for-all solution does not adequately address all the problems. It is vital to engage the public in the planning and delivery processes of infrastructure projects.

With the above as a background, we start by suggesting a consensus-driven collaborative network based on blockchain-based technology. This approach is particularly useful for security, authentication and transparency reasons [24], to prevent the participatory process from being hijacked by stakeholders with adverse interest/intent. The collaborative network is also purposed to gain novel insight from the public, engaging them to identify the most critical needs and, eventually, gain trust, commitment, and share the responsibility of project delivery. The application of blockchain technology in governance is not a new idea [30,31], with the use of digital signatures, e.g., with the Estonian state as an example. Thus, citizens securely communicate with their representatives, reach a consensus on project messages and track the process of implementation in the network – instituting transparency and accountability.

In [40], the authors discuss, the potentials of a blockchain-based contract and procurement-management systems in delivering a seamless and transparent stream of project activities. Blockchain technology enables interaction between the government and citizens and [40] provides potential components to address corruption further, producing a complete solution to redress project failures. In Nigeria for instance, the contract bidding and procurement processes have been negated by nepotism and corruption. These have resulted in delays in infrastructure-project deliveries.

These additional blockchain components prove valuable in identifying gridlocks during the planning and implementation process. To extend this thought, smart contracts manage project contracts and release payments according to rules-based operations. The cross verification of the process by all participants prevents exploitation and strengthens confidence in a blockchain-technology system [28]. Smart contracts are especially useful in the procurement of service and materials, supply-chain management, providing integrity in the bidding process by reducing redundancy, marginal cost, corruption and conflict of interests due to transparency [29]. Additionally, payments can be initiated automatically using cryptocurrency to contractual parties when the prescribed requirements are met to prevent insolvency and late payments.

In summary, governance transparency plays a vital role in ensuring trust and accountability. To this effect, blockchain technology offers tangible gains such as confidentiality, disintermediation, provenance tracking, non-repudiation, multiparty aggregation, change tracing, traceability, and recordkeeping. Instrumentally, blockchain technology establishes transparent systems in infrastructure project delivery and renders it easier for a broad set of stakeholders, including the public, to monitor the whole process from start to finish.

6   Limitions and Future Directions

It is undeniable that the approach presented in this paper is accompanied by some challenges due to the specific digital divide in developing countries. Thus, to ensure the inclusiveness of some groups of citizens that are unable to participate, other methods of participation should be considered such as the broad use of mobile devices that are widely adopted in developing countries. Finally, it is vital to implement a robust legislative and regulative framework to serve as a background and guide for the collaborative network, in order to preserve government commitment in the participatory process.

One limitation of this research can be drawn directly from the criticisms of single case study-based research. Secondly, the paper proposes a solution to problems but fails to investigate the feasibility of its implementation. Another significant limitation of this study is the issue of external validity, or generalisability. In future work, a related field of study is the development of a blockchain-based collaborative framework for public infrastructural project planning and -delivery.

7   Conclusion

The barriers to successful infrastructure-project delivery are plenteous and encapsulated in government corruption. The multifacetedness of corruption undermines the success of most proposed solutions and hence, failures in project delivery remain persistent. Further studying the underlying factors driving corruption, we identify government non-transparency and lack of communication with the public as the main causes of project failures in the long run. As a strategy to institute communication between the government and citizens, and transparent systems, a consensus-driven collaborative network based on blockchain is recommended. To address the failure factors directly and also provide a comprehensive solution, other blockchain-based technologies such as smart contracts, digital signatures, diverse consensus algorithms, and crypto-currencies are suggested as additional components of such a collaborative network.

References

1. Abram, S., Cowell, R.: Learning policy - the contextual curtain and conceptual barriers. Eur. Plann. Stud. **12**(2), 209–228 (2004)
2. Adobei, E.: Enabling government - public collaboration in public project processes in developing economies - a case study of Nigeria, Master thesis, Tallinn University of Technology (2018). https://digi.lib.ttu.ee/i/file.php?DLID=10947&t=1
3. Ansell, C., Gash, A.: Collaborative governance in theory and practice. J. Public Adm. Res. Theor. **18**(4), 543–571 (2008)
4. Baliga, A.: Understanding blockchain consensus models. In: Persistent (2017)

5. Beebeejaun, Y.: The participation trap: the limitations of participation for ethnic and racial groups. Int. Plan. Stud. **11**(1), 3–18 (2006)
6. Brabham, D.C.: Crowdsourcing as a model for problem solving: an introduction and cases. Convergence **14**(1), 75–90 (2008)
7. Brabham, D.C.: Crowdsourcing the public participation process for planning projects. Plan. Theor. **8**(3), 242–262 (2009)
8. Brabham, D.C.: Using Crowdsourcing in Government. Collaborating Across Boundaries Series. IBM Center for the Business of Government, Washington, DC (2013)
9. Brody, S.D.: Measuring the effects of stakeholder participation on the quality of local plans based on the principles of collaborative ecosystem management. J. Plan. Educ. Res. **22**(4), 407–419 (2003)
10. Bryson, J.M., Ackermann, F., Eden, C.: Discovering collaborative advantage: the contributions of goal categories and visual strategy mapping. Public Adm. Rev. **76**(6), 912–925 (2016)
11. Buterin, V., et al.: A next-generation smart contract and decentralized application platform. White Pap. **3**, 37 (2014)
12. Cooper, T.L., Bryer, T.A., Meek, J.W.: Citizen-centered collaborative public management. Public Adm. Rev. **66**, 76–88 (2006)
13. Creighton, J.L.: The Public Participation Handbook: Making Better Decisions Through Citizen Involvement. Wiley, Hoboken (2005)
14. Damoah, C.A., Akwei, C., Mouzughi, Y.: Causes of government project failure in developing countries - focus on ghana. In: Conference Proceedings of the 2015 British Academy of Management Conference (2015)
15. Doberstein, C.: Designing collaborative governance decision-making in search of a 'collaborative advantage'. Public Manag. Rev. **18**(6), 819–841 (2016)
16. Estrada, S.: Qualitative analysis using R: a free analytic tool. Qual. Rep. **22**(4), 956–968 (2017)
17. Fisher, R., Ury, W.L., Patton, B.: Getting to Yes: Negotiating Agreement Without Giving In. Penguin (2011)
18. Frederickson, H.G.: Toward a theory of the public for public administration. Adm. Soc. **22**(4), 395–417 (1991)
19. Fung, A.: Varieties of participation in complex governance. Public Adm. Rev. **66**, 66–75 (2006)
20. Gerring, J.: Case Study Research: Principles and Practices. Cambridge University Press, Cambridge (2006)
21. Hanifatunnisa, R., Rahardjo, B.: Blockchain based e-voting recording system design. In: Proceedings of TSSA 2017 - The 11th International Conference on Telecommunication Systems Services and Applications, pp. 1–6. IEEE (2017)
22. Ikediashi, D.I., Ogunlana, S.O., Alotaibi, A.: Analysis of project failure factors for infrastructure projects in Saudi Arabia: a multivariate approach. J. Constr. Dev. Countries **19**(1), 35 (2014)
23. Innes, J.E.: Information in communicative planning. J. Am. Plan. Assoc. **64**(1), 52–63 (1998)
24. Jacobovitz, O.: Blockchain for identity management. The Lynne and William Frankel Center for Computer Science Department of Computer Science, Ben-Gurion University, Beer Sheva (2016)
25. Johnston, E.W., Hicks, D., Nan, N., Auer, J.C.: Managing the inclusion process in collaborative governance. J. Public Adm. Res. Theor. **21**(4), 699–721 (2010)

26. King, C.S., Feltey, K.M., Susel, B.O.: The question of participation: toward authentic public participation in public administration. Public Adm. Rev. **58**(4), 317–326 (1998)
27. Maguire, M., Delahunt, B.: Doing a thematic analysis: a practical, step-by-step guide for learning and teaching scholars. AISHE-J: All Irel. J. Teach. Learn. High. Educ. **9**(3), 3351–33514 (2017). http://ojs.aishe.org/aishe/index.php/aishe-j/article/viewFile/335/553
28. Mason, J.: Intelligent contracts and the construction industry. J. Leg. Aff. Dispute Resolut. Eng. Constr. **9**(3), 04517012 (2017)
29. Mathews, M., Robles, D., Bowe, B.: BIM+ blockchain: a solution to the trust problem in collaboration? Dublin Institute of Technology (2017)
30. Maupin, J.: The G20 countries should engage with blockchain technologies to build an inclusive, transparent, and accountable digital economy for all. Technical report, Economics Discussion Papers (2017)
31. Nordrum, A.: Govern by blockchain - Dubai wants one platform to rule them all, while Illinois will try anything. IEEE Spectr. **54**(10), 54–55 (2017)
32. Rigg, C., O'Mahony, N.: Frustrations in collaborative working: insights from institutional theory. Public Manag. Rev. **15**(1), 83–108 (2013)
33. Runeson, P., Höst, M., Rainer, A., Regnell, B.: Case Study Research in Software Engineering - Guidelines and Examples. Wiley, Hoboken (2012)
34. Sidhu, J.: Syscoin: a peer-to-peer electronic cash system with blockchain-based services for e-business. In: Proceeding of ICCCN 2017 - The 26th International Conference on Computer Communication and Networks, pp. 1–6. IEEE (2017)
35. Nancy Perkins Spyke: Public participation in environmental decisionmaking at the New Millenium: structuring new spheres of public influence. BC Envtl. Aff. L. Rev. **26**, 263 (1998)
36. Stoker, G.: Public value management: a new narrative for networked governance? Am. Rev. Public Adm. **36**(1), 41–57 (2006)
37. Surowiecki, J.: The Wisdom of Crowds. Anchor (2005)
38. Turk, Ž., Klinc, R.: Potentials of blockchain technology for construction management. Proc. Eng. **196**, 638–645 (2017)
39. Van der Elst, C., Lafarre, A.: Bringing the AGM to the 21st Century: Blockchain and Smart Contracting Tech for Shareholder Involvement. ECGI Law Series 258 (2017)
40. Wang, J., Peng, W., Wang, X., Shou, W.: The outlook of blockchain technology for construction engineering management. Front. Eng. Manag. **4**(1), 67–75 (2017)
41. Yin, R.K.: Case Study Research and Applications: Design and Methods. Sage Publications, Thousand Oaks (2017)
42. Zuofa, T., et al.: Project failure: the way forward and panacea for development. Int. J. Bus. Manag. **9**(11), 13 p. (2014)

Aspects of Personal Data Protection from State and Citizen Perspectives – Case of Georgia

Mariam Tsulukidze[1], Kartin Nyman-Metcalf[2], Valentyna Tsap[2(✉)],
Ingrid Pappel[2], and Dirk Draheim[2]

[1] Information Systems Group, Tallinn University of Technology,
Akadeemia tee 15a, 12618 Tallinn, Estonia
`mariam.tsulukidze@taltech.ee`
[2] e-Governance Academy, Rotermanni 8, 10111 Tallinn, Estonia
`katrin.nyman-metcalf@ega.ee`,
`{valentyna.tsap,ingrid.pappel,dirk.draheim}@taltech.ee`

Abstract. This paper aims to investigate the process of personal data protection in Georgia within the frame of e-governance, focusing on available legal and technological protecting mechanisms, their practical usage and importance for realizing principles of good governance in the state. The scope of this research is defined by the protection of state databases containing citizen's personal data. Its key legal and technological aspects are identified and analyzed. The potential of proper data protection to act as the enabler of e-governance services success is also evaluated. We explore the defense mechanisms of Georgian governmental entities by conducting interviews with seven experts from the Personal Data Protection Inspectorate and other public entities handling citizens' data. We study citizens' perception of data safety and the citizens' knowledge of existing monitoring mechanisms through analysis of over 400 responses that we have received to our survey. We also analyze and assess the influence of these factors on the success of e-governance and its broad diffusion. Finally, guidelines and recommendations are formulated for raising citizens' awareness on the data protection mechanisms to be used in future theoretical and practical considerations.

Keywords: e-government · Personal data protection · Citizens' awareness · Georgia

1 Introduction

A recent resolution by United Nations titled "The right to privacy in the digital age" [14] has for the first time asserted the applicability of internationally recognized human rights including right to privacy in the online world in the same manner they stand applicable to the offline activities of the states. Resolution stressed the importance of government commitment to guarantee citizen data privacy. It encouraged member states to take active measures for establishing digital environment which will be reflecting internationally recognized fundamental rights and freedoms of individuals.

© IFIP International Federation for Information Processing 2019
Published by Springer Nature Switzerland AG 2019
I. O. Pappas et al. (Eds.): I3E 2019, LNCS 11701, pp. 476–488, 2019.
https://doi.org/10.1007/978-3-030-29374-1_39

Ever-increasing importance of the data safety is also reflected in the rapid establishment of personal data protection inspectorates and DPAs (Data Protection Authorities) within and outside of European Union.

After proclaiming its aspiration to become a member of the EU, Georgia, one of the EaP (Eastern Partnership) states, has taken responsibility to get compliant with data privacy requirements. Upon signing the Association Agreement in 2014, [2] Georgia has undertaken the obligation to harmonize legislation with European standards regarding users' rights, personal data security and protection along with promoting e-government initiatives and supporting their active use between governments, businesses, and citizens. While a number of positive reforms have been made in this direction recently, unfortunately, many of the obstacles are still to be overcome, available services differ in level of security for the processed personal data from one public entity to another and user turnout remains low for their majority.

Therefore, we are aiming to investigate how Georgian government entities are adapting to the new data protection approaches in practice on the premise that achieving high security standard is vital to successful implementation of e-governance. We will examine the current state of electronic databases in Georgian public institution to find out whether they comply with internationally accepted standards and guidelines. Furthermore, we will look into citizens' level of awareness about data protection mechanisms and, additionally, try to better understand the motives behind citizens' distrust, offer potential solutions for changing public perception and pose as motivator for the future researchers to broaden the understanding of this issue.

To address named matters and specify the scope of this paper, below-presented questions have been formulated:

RQ1: How are Georgian government entities adopting to current data protection approaches in practice?

RQ2: What is the citizens' level of awareness about data protection mechanisms and how to define it as a factor of e-governance success in Georgia?

We proceed as follows. In Sect. 2 we explain the methods we have used within this research. Section 3 elaborates on the theoretical concepts that support personal data protection. In Sect. 4, we discuss the importance of interconnections between Data Protection and e-Governance. Section 5 reports on our findings and is divided into two subsections that reflect state and citizen perspective. Section 6 serves as a field for discussion and analyses the outcomes. The paper is summarized with a conclusion in Sect. 7.

2 Methodology

Analyzing specifications of citizens' data safety in Georgian administrative e-environment called for gathering in-depth observational evidence and therefore qualitative research methods were given priority. We have used expert interviews conducted with state officials to investigate practical adaptation of data protection mechanisms by Georgian governmental entities. Online surveys have been distributed for understanding citizens' perception of personal data safety and their awareness of existing monitoring mechanisms.

Seven expert interviews have been conducted in total from five different administrative institutions during face-to-face meetings. Respondents were either head of the specific institutions or employees designated on personal information safety. All interviews were conducted in Georgian language and transcribed, translated and then coded afterwards. Interviews were semi-structured and allowed going beyond pre-written framework. Respondents were permitted to follow up, expand and stir focus towards the matter which emerged in the course of conversation.

Assessing citizens' awareness level about data-protective mechanisms requires first-hand empirical evidence and therefore, multiple-choice questionnaires have been drafted and distributed online, targeting citizens of Georgia for getting an insight into their perspective. To increase the credibility of outcomes, goals and motivations for collecting data were outlined explicitly at the beginning of survey and it was made sure that participants clearly understood the contextual framework.

To be in line with its explorative nature, this research will outline new insights into the security of publicly-held personal data; recommendations and potential solutions for existing problems will be suggested with an aim to lay down grounds for future reforms.

3 Theoretical Background

This section portrays an overview of restricted access theory of privacy which is considered suitable for addressing data privacy challenges that accompany technological developments. The theory is relevant in the context of digitally processed personal information as it allows formulating consistent data safety policy and proposes balanced interconnection between the interests of e-states and individuals.

The origins of restricted access theory can be traced back to 1980 s' in the hypotheses of authors such as Allen [1] and Gavison [6] however, it was only in later works of Moor [9, 10] when these original incentives were elaborated and conveyed into a functional theory.

Moor based concept of privacy on three pillars of non-intrusion, non-interference and restricted access to one's personal data. The theory defines privacy as "a matter of the restricted access to persons or information about persons" [10] and goes on to suggest that it is achieved in a situation where individuals and their data are protected from intrusion, observation and surveillance. Moor puts emphasis on a general term "situation" here to broaden the scope of circumstances to which the theory can apply; it can be interpreted as daily interactions, activities or storing and using personally identifiable information in digital databank [9].

Restricted access approach suggests creating different zones of protection for each private situation to ensure that personal information is only accessed by authorized people, at right times and for predefined purposes. Necessary means for establishing zones of privacy for electronically stored data include technological solutions such as proper filters, firewalls or authentication requirements [11]. Moor suggests that when protected zones are built properly in digital environment individuals enjoy the higher level of privacy compared to traditional paper recordkeeping practices. This is because computing allows restraining all the unnecessary encounters and keeps the list of authorized personnel to the bare minimum.

The given concept obliges governments to apply appropriate restrictions to personal information which was accumulated upon introducing e-services so that users can feel protected from violation of their normative privacy while they harvest benefits of the digital world. Establishing zones of privacy and employing proper technological mechanisms for their realization has the potential to make e-services even more secure than their traditional counterparts [9, 10].

4   e-Governance and Data Protection

Incorporating ICTs into public administration has amplified state capabilities to generate and process massive amounts of personal information simultaneously, which led to establishing e-governance and ultimately more citizen-oriented public services.

Data processing by the public sector has several peculiarities which make preventing privacy invasion a rather intricate and obscure matter. First and foremost, states collect data on the legal grounds which not only deviates the submission costs towards the citizens but also deprives them of ability to refuse such collection. Unlike the private sector, governments are not encouraged by the market stimulus to set boundaries for the amount of gathered personal information and hence, are inclined to assign less importance to the mere fact of data collection [7]. Third aspect and perhaps the most crucial one comes with the fact that anonymizing or pseudonymizing sensitive information is often unfeasible or even prohibited for administrative purposes and sensitive information which allows identifying an individual is kept in the state repositories so long that it can even outlive the data subject [15].

However, multiple empirical studies have found a strong correlation between adequate data protection and e-governance success which serves to counterbalance above described tendencies. Irrespective of their initial proclivities, governments become bound to secure personal information in order to invoke public trust towards e-services they offer. Citizens refrain from using e-portals unless the state has proven to treat their data in a rational, transparent and predictable manner. Skeptical attitude towards security of digital transactions and apprehension that electronically gathered data will be used for illicit purposes were named as prominent reasons for citizens' reluctance in adopting e-governing initiatives by number of published studies and articles [5, 8, 12].

A 2011 study which was conducted in the Netherlands proved that even when people trust good intentions of government and believe that state officials will not misuse confided information, they abstain from using e-services if they are concerned about potential external interventions from third parties [4]. This shows that users' distrust in government capabilities to protect their data from malicious actors also has the potential to hinder e-governance adaptation.

To harvest benefits of digital services, states are challenged to invoke institution-based trust among citizens. This is to be achieved by clearly defining data protection policies, implementing privacy-enhancing technological solutions and ensuring secure and private transmissions of personal information. Research has shown that when the privacy-related concerns are adequately mitigated, users become less sensitive to risk considerations. Potential threats which would otherwise paralyze their actions no longer hold them back from submitting even sensitive personal data through electronic channels. Therefore, it can be deduced that broad diffusion of e-services cannot be attained unless citizens deem them trustworthy, which turns data protection into the essential prerequisite for e-governance success [3].

5 Data Protection in Georgia – Results

This section presents our finding with regards to the research goals we have set within this study. The Subsect. 5.1 elaborates on the details of interviews we have conducted with experts to reveal how Georgia is adapting to the new data protection standards while Subsect. 5.2 gives a comprehensive analysis of citizens' surveys responses that reflect level of their awareness on data protection mechanisms.

5.1 State Perspective

This subsection portrays current situation in Georgian public sector with regard to the personal data protection. Empirical data presented in this section was gathered during face to face interviews with experts. In order to evaluate to what extent Georgian governmental entities have managed to implement legal and technological mechanisms for data protection in practice, Office of the Personal Data Protection Inspector was approached at the very beginning of this research. Consultation at the Office of Data Protection Inspector alluded to the differences in technological maturity between different organizations within the public sector. Therefore, additional interviews were conducted in four organizations which were selected to represent diverse segments of the spectrum, some with higher e-governing capacity (Public Service Hall and Public Service Development Agency) and others which lack some prominent features of e-governance (Public schools and Social Service Agency).

Personal Data Protection Inspectorate of Georgia was founded by the end of 2013 and its core competencies include: conducting audits of data controllers, consulting organizations on matters related to data protection, addressing citizen inquiries and raising overall level of awareness regarding information security. The conducted interviews covered all these activities and the outcomes were coded into six categories each of which is elaborated below.

Document Management Systems. A representative from the Office of Data Protection Inspector pointed out that while Georgian state authorities differ in their level of e-governance adaptation, they all employ technological means for storing/processing personal data to some extent. Although state entities with only paper-based administration no longer exist, governing through the application of fully paperless management has not occurred either.

As it was discovered during the interviews, implementing electronic systems in administrative bodies preceded adaptation of data protection standards and regulations by a decade in Georgia. Software developments for document management started out as a sporadic and idiosyncratic process, lacking trans-organizational cooperation and considerations for system interoperability. As a result, a number of these systems turned out inadequate to ensure proper security level for personal information which is demanded by later enacted law on Personal Data Protection. Furthermore, these systems proved unviable for incorporating secure data exchange channel between agencies from the architectural standpoint.

To tackle this challenge, the government has elaborated unified minimal standard for document management systems, [16] allowing administrative bodies to adapt any software they deemed appropriate as long as its technical features met certain requirements, permitting system interoperability and secure data processing. Such supportive measures have had positive impact on existing conjuncture and up to 70% of public institutions now employ one out of three information management systems created by either Ministry of Internal Affairs (named "e-FLOW"), Ministry of Justice (named "DES") or Ministry of Finance (named "eDocument"). There is still around 30% of institutions which have developed software tailored to their own peculiarities. Thus, they are obliged to incorporate proper technological means to become compliant with abovementioned security and interoperability standards.

Data Exchange. Matter of interoperability between three dominant document management systems which were mentioned earlier ("e-FLOW", "DES" and "eDocument") stands as a challenge to be overcome until this time. As three different respondents from Public Schools explained potential complications in practice are avoided by having the data subject place direct inquiry to the institution which possesses needed information.

As the representative of Personal Data Protection Inspector's Office explained, there is no preferred method of data exchange defined by the legislation. The law demands that transmitted data must be protected from unlawful disclosure regardless of the employed means for the transaction. This gives authorities discretion to agree upon any secure way of information sharing. The representative of the Inspectorate named two most frequent ways for data exchange in practice. Usually, organizations give out citizens' data based on written inquiries they receive from other state entities where legal basis for the request is indicated.

Alternatively, for instance, *"Database for administrative offences is controlled and maintained by the LEPL (Legal Entity of Public Law) under the Ministry of Internal Affairs of Georgia and number of public and private organizations have digital access to this database according to their needs and legally supported interests. Such practices are quite common and this is only one example out of many".*

Access Control Mechanisms. When it comes to legal regulations concerning electronically processed personal data, the only requirement Georgian law on Personal Data Protection asserts is to maintain detailed records of every manipulation. It does not inquire from data controllers to draft written policy for data processing or establish authentication mechanisms such as individual usernames and passwords for every employee who accesses the database. As a respondent from Data Protection Inspectors' Office explained this factor prevents Inspectorate from officially obligating state entities to implement this mechanism. However, based on the previous experience it can be asserted that this is always one of the recommendations the inspectorate gives to the data controllers during monitoring and in practice, a number of public entities have built their databases with personified accounts and access restrictions for their employees.

The representative of Public Service Development Agency gave more credibility to this statement by describing implemented access control mechanisms:

"Rights and obligations are outlined for each individual employee and everyone is given adequate access to the personal data reflective of his or her responsibilities in the agency. Software users can only access the system through a software module that is protected by user and password and needs to be changed regularly."

Audit Trail Logs. The legal requirement to implement automatic logging mechanism in databases containing citizens personal information is actively enforced and monitored by Data Protection Inspectorate in practice. The absence of automated audit trails already provides a legal basis for reprimanding and penalizing data controller even without a recorded case of data mishandling and disclosure. Inspectorate has accumulated a myriad of cases regarding automated logging while conducting provisions of state institutions. In practice, government entities often start building the technological framework for depicting "footprints" on personal data in the midst of inspection to avert anticipated financial sanctions.

The representative of Data Protection Inspector's Office mentioned that in many cases database software which was incorporated into administrative processing before enacting the law on Personal Data Protection does not permit technical implementation of audit trail logging mechanism. Therefore, state institutions are compelled to abandon old systems and implement new software/build them from the scratch which demands time and human resources and is proved to be quite costly depending on the organizations' capacity. As a result, getting compliant with legal requirements is a lengthy process in public sector and there are still institutions which violate data processing standards until this time.

Filling Systems Catalogues. Filing systems catalogues are electronic documents published on the web-page of Personal Data Protection Inspector's Office depicting the list of data categories processed by every data controller in Georgia, public and private institutions alike. They are filled out electronically by data controller authority and entail database description, legal grounds for processing, retention period of the data, categories of data, data subjects etc. Completed catalogues are overviewed by Data Protection Inspector and in case of mistakes, organizations are instructed to correct erroneous entries before they are made available to the broader public.

Citizen Inquiries. One of the responsibilities of Personal Data Protection Inspector's Office is representing the interests of data subjects and acting as the mediator between citizen and data controller authority. With respect to this competency, a respondent from the Inspectors' Office asserted that amount of citizen inquires has increased at least five times for the past couple of years. For instance, Data Protection Inspectorate lawyers now review 20 to 30 cases per day which is a significant growth compared to the year of 2015 when daily consultations amounted to single digit numbers.

5.2   Citizen Perspective

After having scrutinized security features of governmental databases in preceding subsection, users' perception of data safety in Georgian public sector will be evaluated below.

Overall 419 responses were received which serve to bring light to citizens' awareness level about data protection mechanisms employed in public sector (See Table 1).

The conducted survey consisted of 12 questions and aimed at understanding citizens' perceptions, factual knowledge, opinions, concerns and overall attitudes towards the matters posed in this study. Survey was anonymous and participants' personal information has not been gathered. Below the interview questions are presented:

Cumulative analysis of responses to the first, fourth, seventh and eighth questions suggest that while the majority of the respondents are familiar with the existence of digital data repositories within the public sector, only a few of them appear to have sufficient information on legal means they can use to oversee the processes and even fewer seem to have practiced those tools in real life. However, dominant replies to these questions have indicated growing interest on this matter among the general public.

Latter interpretation also goes in line with interview findings as representative of Data Protection Inspectorate has similarly highlighted a recent increase in citizen inquiries to their institution. Majority of the respondents confirmed being informed about the existence of Personal Data Protection Inspectorate and many of those who learned about the institution for the first time with this survey demonstrated being open to the possibility to use its services in future which is undisputedly a positive tendency. However, far lesser number of respondents seem to be aware of what is probably the strongest tool at their disposal for direct monitoring – placing inquiries at public institutions regarding how their personal data is being handled. Such deficiency of citizen awareness about existing monitoring mechanisms can decrease public trust towards government processes and result in low engagement rate for e-services as it was confirmed by studies discussed in earlier chapters of this research [4].

Second, third and fifth questions delved into subjective attitudes of the participants towards publicly-held personal data processing. Interpreting their responses leads to the conclusion that the considerable number of respondents doubt that electronic data processing in Georgian public sector complies with optimal standards and guidelines. While this apprehension seems to limit respondents' acceptance rate towards e-governing initiatives to some extent, it does not appear to affect their overall trust towards government to the point where they would refrain from using e-services altogether.

The dominant pattern of responses for these questions suggests that although governmental entities are believed to provide more effective protection for personal data compared to the private ones, the public sector still fails to measure up to the standards demanded by the general public in this regard. Thus, as it was already stated in earlier chapters, a gap between social and technical standards of data security can lead to major implications for e-governing initiatives if not addressed adequately by the state [8].

Table 1. Survey results.

Please specify your age

18-25	26-35	36-45	46-55	56-65	66<
125	91	71	58	44	30

Do you know how is your personal data stored in state institutions? On paper or electronically?

Yes, in both forms	Yes, electronically	Yes, on paper	I don't know because it is not important for me	I don't know
223	72	13	16	95

Which form would you prefer for your personal data to be stored in state institutions from the security perspective?

Hard to choose because neither are safe in my opinion	On paper as I consider it to be safer	They are both safe in my opinion	Electronically as I consider it to be safer	Other
202	27	86	95	9

Which sector to you trust more to process your personal data lawfully, public or private?

Public organizations	Private organizations	Neither protect as they should	I don't know	protect
141	29	156	62	31

How well-aware are you of the mechanisms used for keeping your data safe at public organisations?

Very well aware	Somewhat aware	Somewhat aware but it would like to know more	Not at all aware, it's beyond my sphere of interest	Other
19	61	197	139	3

Do you trust state institutions that they are processing your data in a good faith?

Yes, absolutely	I trust them but it would be better to also monitor it	I don't trust them because I have no way of monitoring	I don't trust them because of other reason
41	219	136	23

What do you consider to be the biggest issue when it comes to processing your data electronically by the state?

State entities failing to adhere to data safety regulations	Officials have possibility to view my data	State giving my data to third parties	Systems are not secure enough technially	Other
54	110	88	155	12

Do you know that from any state organization you can inquire to whom your data has been disclosed? Have you ever submitted such request?

I knew by I've never made an inquiry	I didn't know but I might use it further	I didn't know, unlikely with use it further	I knew and inquired before
153	210	42	14

Have you heard of the Office of Personal Data Protection Inspector and its functions? Have you ever used its services?

I knew and used them before	I knew but never used them	I didn't know, unlikely with use them further	I didn't know but I might use them further
15	218	52	134

Have you had an experience of public institution violating data protection standards? (disclosed your data, refused to correct inaccurate recordings etc.)

Yes, I have experienced it myself	No, an I've never heard of anyone with this experience	No, but I heard of people who have	Other
7	214	193	5

Do you support implementing new e-solutions in Georgia such as e-voting of e-prescriptions for instance?

I support and would become a user	I support but I'm not sure if would use them myself	I don't support since e-systems are not transparent	I don't support due to lack of safety guarantees	Other
189	43	50	126	11

Which factor would you say has the biggest potential to increase citizens' trust towards electronic services in Georgia?

Increasing data protection standard by Government institution	Increasing computer literacy and access to internet across the whole country	Informing citizens regarding existing safety mechanisms	Enabling citizens to monitor the way government treats their data	Other
140	60	152	61	6

Analyses of the responses for sixth and ninth questions give insights to participants' perception of the most urgent issues related to digital data processing in Georgian public sector. More than third of total participants seem to believe that the lack of technical security mechanisms in data repositories is the biggest threat to publicly-held personal data at the moment. A study from the Netherlands from 2011 which was discussed earlier demonstrated that citizen skepticism towards state capability to provide adequate protection for their personal data makes them reluctant to use e-services [5]. As named study suggested, despite existing general trust towards good intentions of the public entity, when latter fails to offer proper level of data protection from third parties citizens withhold from using electronic channels of communication and give preference to the conventional methods to receive available public services.

Finally, tenth and eleventh questions focused on evaluating the prospect of e-governing initiatives in Georgia. The idea of more technology-heavy public sector appears to cause nonhomogeneous attitudes among survey participants. A noteworthy number of respondents confirmed their support for digital channels of communication offered by the government owing to their efficiency, convenience and user-oriented nature. The remaining segment of participants however, reacted negatively to the possibility of digitalized public services due to transparency and security hazards. Analyzing these outcomes with regard to the responses from previous questions once again reaffirms the conclusion that although a considerable number of citizens are willing to adopt e-services, the circle of users is prone to remain limited due to circulating concerns on information security in the society.

6 Outcomes and Discussion

Main insights gathered within the frames of this research suggest that state entities need to prioritize achieving personal information security for e-services they offer. At the same time, considerable attention must be paid to increasing level of citizens' awareness on monitoring mechanisms at their disposal. Below-presented recommendations were formulated to suggest solutions for current challenges and facilitate accomplishing responsibilities state of Georgia has undertaken by Association Agreement with EU:

- Implementing legislative amendments to include clear-cut obligations for data controllers on matters such as introducing a written policy on information security or enforcing access control mechanisms, in order to harmonize existing law in force with internationally accepted standards and guidelines;
- Elaborating centralized governmental strategy for incorporating technological mechanisms such as audit trail logging in electronic databases to accelerate reforms and guarantee homogeneity of personal data protection across the whole public sector;
- Fostering interoperability and creating protected data exchange channels in between governmental institutions to ensure secure circulation of citizens data between state institutions;
- Adhering to the concept of 'privacy by default' while building digital infrastructure for e-services and improving work ethics of the public servants with respect to citizens' personal information privacy by the means of thematic training together with continuous monitoring of their activities inside personal information databases;
- Providing citizens with tools for direct and real-time monitoring of how their personal data is being handled by various public entities to increase the element of system accountability;

- Conducting active information campaigns to raise citizens awareness on matters related to personal information processing and monitoring tools at their disposal in order to refute existing misconceptions and invoke public trust towards digital data processing in public sector.

7 Conclusion

Empirical data gathered from the interviews with state officials allowed a thorough investigation of matters posed in the first question of this research. Georgian public sector has shown significant effort towards getting compliant with internationally accepted data security standards. Several positive reforms have been made in this regard, be it adopting the law on personal data safety or implementing technological solutions for establishing secure and interoperable state network.

However, a number of pertinent issues still prevail from legal as well as technological perspective which prevent Georgian public sector from harvesting the benefits of the secure digital environment. List of these issues include: absence of necessary legal requirements to guarantee safety for personal data, unsatisfactory level of technological security in majority of state entities, absence of proper access control policies and audit trail monitoring mechanisms and lack of system accountability component within state databases. All these factors place data security in Georgian public sector at its preliminary stage of development. As this research has indicated Georgian governmental entities still have not adapted to the number of suggested data protection approaches which continues to hinder country's association with EU standards and its values (RQ1).

Formulating the response to the second question of this research called for gathering first-hand empirical data from citizens by the means of online questionnaires. Interpreting their outcomes has led to the conclusion that knowledge of existing data protection mechanisms and practical monitoring tools is rather limited and fractional for a sizable number of polled citizens. However, both sources of data used for this research have confirmed growing interest of the public in matters related to personal data protection which has the potential to serve as the catalyst for future improvements in this regard.

According to the survey outcomes concerns related to personal information safety in public sector seem to have a certain deterrent effect on respondents' willingness to utilize e-services. While such apprehensions are unlikely to exclude usage of digital services entirely, they prove capable of impeding board diffusion of e-governing initiatives among the citizens of Georgia (RQ2).

Limitations of the presented study concern nonprobability sampling methods which were chosen for identifying studied subset of Georgian citizens. Convenience sampling which was applied for selecting study participants included collecting data by posting the questionnaire on social media platforms and spreading it via electronic channels of communication. Therefore, responses had been gathered only from those who were conveniently available and willing to participate. Such non-systematic approach to respondent recruiting limits sample representativeness and impedes generalizing outcomes to the entire population however, it can be justified by exploratory nature of this study. Since it aims to gather a preliminary overview of the observed phenomenon, while making generalizations might be desirable, it is still a secondary consideration for this type of research [13].

Increasing importance of personal data security creates myriad of possibilities for future research on this topic, especially along the lines of newly emerged General Data Protection Directive. Since the presented case was limited to exploring the current state of personal data safety in Georgian public sector, future research should be conducted on the effects of GDPR on non-EU countries as sufficient empirical evidence accumulates for observation and analysis. Further explanatory research can also be conducted for understanding reasons behind the problems which were exposed by this study. As a logical continuation of presented work, it would provide generalizable explanations for issues such as citizens' distrust and resistance to digital data processing in public sector.

References

1. Allen, A.L.: Uneasy Access: Privacy for Women in a Free Society, pp. 1–25. Rowman & Littlefield, Lanham (1988)
2. Association agreement between the European Union and the European Atomic Energy Community and their Member States of the one part and Georgia, on the other part. Opened for signature 27 June 2014, [entered into force 1 July 2016]. OJ L 261/4. https://eur-lex.europa.eu/legal-content/en/TXT/PDF/?uri=CELEX:22014A0830(02). Accessed 11 June 2019
3. Bélanger, F., Carter, L.: Trust and risk in e-government adoption. J. Strateg. Inf. Syst. **17**(2), 165–176 (2008)
4. Beldad, A., De Jong, M., Steehouder, M.: I trust not therefore it must be risky: determinants of the perceived risks of disclosing personal data for e-government transactions. Comput. Hum. Behav. **27**(6), 2233–2242 (2011)
5. Beldad, A., van der Geest, T., de Jong, M., Steehouder, M.: A cue or two and I'll trust you: determinants of trust in government organizations in terms of their processing and usage of citizens' personal information disclosed online. Gov. Inf. Quart. **29**(1), 41–49 (2012)
6. Gavison, R.: Privacy and the limits of law. Yale Law J. **89**(3), 421–471 (1980)
7. Järvsoo, M., Norta, A., Tsap, V., Pappel, I., Draheim, D.: Implementation of information security in the EU information systems. In: Al-Sharhan, S., et al. (eds.) Challenges and Opportunities in the Digital Era. I3E 2018. Lecture Notes in Computer Science, vol. 11195, pp. 150–163. Springer, Cham (2018). https://doi.org/10.1007/978-3-030-02131-3_15
8. Jho, W.: Challenges for e-governance: protests from civil society on the protection of privacy in e-government in Korea. Int. Rev. Adm. Sci. **71**(1), 151–166 (2005)
9. Moor, J.H.: The ethics of privacy protection. Libr. Trends **39**, 69–82 (1991)
10. Moor, J.H.: Towards a theory of privacy in the information age. ACM SIGCAS Comput. Soc. **27**(3), 27–32 (1997)
11. Reidenberg, J.: The use of technology to assure internet privacy: adapting labels and filters for data protection. Tex. Law Rev. **3**(2), 553 (1997)
12. Tsap, V., Pappel, I., Draheim, D.: Key success factors in introducing national e-identification systems. In: Dang, T.K., Wagner, R., Küng, J., Thoai, N., Takizawa, M., Neuhold, E.J. (eds.)

FDSE 2017. LNCS, vol. 10646, pp. 455–471. Springer, Cham (2017). https://doi.org/10.1007/978-3-319-70004-5_33

13. Sue, V.M., Ritter, L.A.: Conducting Online Surveys, pp. 33–35. Sage Publications, Thousand Oaks (2012)

14. United Nations, General Assembly: Resolution A/RES/69/166 on the Right to Privacy in the Digital Age (2014). https://undocs.org/pdf?symbol=en/A/RES/69/166. Accessed 11 June 2019

15. Wu, Y.: Protecting personal data in e-government: a cross-country study. Gov. Inf. Quart. **31** (1), 150–159 (2014)

16. საქართველოს _მთავრობის _დადგენილება _№64 [2012] სახაზინო _(საბიუჯეტო) დაწესებულებებში _საქმისწარმოების _ავტომატიზებული _სისტემის _მინიმალური _სტანდარტის _დამტკიცების _შესახებ [№64 Decree of the Government of Georgia on Approving Minimum Standard for Automated Document Management Systems in State Budget Institutions]. Government of Georgia. Tbilisi (2012)

Prioritizing Digital Identity Goals – The Case Study of Aadhaar in India

Umar Bashir Mir[(✉)], Arpan K. Kar, M. P. Gupta, and R. S. Sharma

Indian Institute of Technology Delhi, New Delhi 110016, India
mirumar.iitd@gmail.com

Abstract. Identity is one of the basic building blocks of the Fourth Industrial Revolution, and as the capability of digital technologies improves drastically in the last decade, identity in digital form has become unavoidable. Identity entitles an individual to various services like voting, education, employment, insurance, healthcare etc. Yet there are around 1 billion people in the world at present that do not possess any form of official identity. Lack of identity has a significant impact on people living in rural areas, especially women, children, and financially backward families. In recently released Sustainable Development Goal-16 by the UN, it has been recommended that by 2030, every individual should be given a legal identity. India's digital identity program –Aadhaar is one significant contribution in this direction considering its coverage. Rolling out a national identity scheme needs a considerable budget, time and most importantly, domain knowledge for smooth implementation. This paper attempts to identify the overarching goals of Aadhaar. The study also ranks goals based on their significance. The research uses focus group for data collection along with secondary data. The research in total identified nine primary goals with uniqueness, privacy and security as the high priority goals and scalability and future-proofing of technology as low priority goals. Total Interpretive Structural Modeling (TISM) has been used to identify the significance of each goal. This study could be taken as a starting point by other nations that are desirous of having a similar biometric identity program for its citizens.

Keywords: Aadhaar · Biometrics · CSF · Digital identity · E-governance · MCDM · TISM · India

1 Introduction

Identity of a person or a group is the mixture of their characteristics, emotions, behavior, beliefs and personality and in online space is called digital identity (DI). DI is an old concept and existed since the early days of Internet. It is a multidimensional concept and philosophically 'identity' explains 'who am I?'. It is formed of attributes that make an individual unique and distinguishable from the rest of the population [1]. The World Economic Forum (WEF) defines DI as "collection of individual attributes that describe an entity and determine the transactions in which that entity can participate" [2].

In the past, researchers have explored use of information technology for effective e-governance initiatives [3], governance of Internet of Things [4] and performance

© IFIP International Federation for Information Processing 2019
Published by Springer Nature Switzerland AG 2019
I. O. Pappas et al. (Eds.): I3E 2019, LNCS 11701, pp. 489–501, 2019.
https://doi.org/10.1007/978-3-030-29374-1_40

assessment e-government projects [3, 5, 6]. Disruptive technologies have significantly shifted transactions from offline to online mode giving rise to an era where performing transactions anonymously has become almost impossible [7]. Performing transactions over digital networks demands a secure and fool-proof mechanism for creating, exchanging and storing identities of an entity online [7]. Traditional identity documents are not compatible with today's digital needs there is a need to have trusted and secure digital identities that would facilitate faceless transaction online [8, 9]. Digital identities can have positive socio-political and economic impact for a country especially emerging ones if designed and implemented properly across different application areas [10].

The continuous evolution of the digital economy worldwide mandates individuals to be uniquely identifiable to be part of the growing digital economy. In this direction, the United Nations set a target of providing "legal identity" to each by 2030 (SDG-16). Perceiving the transformational capability of new age ID systems for the distribution of essential services to the people, World Bank launched ID4D project with the aim of "providing an identity and delivering digital ID-enabled services to all."

Considering the fact that at present 24% of the developing countries do not possess any kind of DI system and only 3% have a basic identity scheme which could be used in both online and offline sphere, this study is need of the hour [11]. Countries that do not have any national level identity program will need guidelines to follow such that, "identity for all" objective is achieved. Aadhaar is the shining example to follow at present for benchmarking the objectives of DI scheme. This study attempts to decode success of Aadhaar system and tries to answer following research questions:

- What are the critical success factors (CSFs) of Aadhaar?
- How to prioritize CSFs of Aadhaar based on their significance?

This paper aims to identify CSFs of Aadhaar and rank each factor based on their significance, TISM methodology has been adopted for evaluating expert's opinions.

The subsequent sections of this paper are organized as follows: Sect. 2 highlights the need of digital identity systems and presents Aadhaar as a case study for this research. Section 3 presents the theoretical aspects of this study. Section 4 focuses on the research questions and gaps identified in the domain. Section 5 introduces focus group members and TISM methodology for ranking CSFs identified in Sect. 3. Finally, implications of this research are discussed followed by the conclusion.

2   Literature Review

With population more than 1.3 billion, India is the second most populous country in the world and it became the first country to roll out digital identity scheme on such a large scale for its citizens [11]. DI and its management have been in focus among the research community in recent past, most of the research on DI systems have focused on the implication side of it [12–14].

Extensive literature in the form of reports and studies is available which highlights that management of DI is still in its infancy stage, full potential of the digital economy could be accomplished only after having a sophisticated system in place for the issuance, storing and management of digital identities [15]. It's because the online communications possess a significant level of risk, and security measures to deal with these risks in present DI management systems is not enough. This asymmetry results in a lack of confidence in the digital transaction [16]. Many governments across the world are taking initiatives to address this asymmetry and have initiated programs at national level to provide digital identities to its citizens that are verifiable and secure [17]. Examples of some of the countries that have a digital identity system in place are Canada, UK, Sweden, Estonia, Nigeria, and Argentina.

Nations around the world want to develop a connected and interoperable global digital economy with digital identities at the core [18]. Because of the high variance among national DI systems in terms of their scope and functionality, developing an effective and efficient DI system is subject to multiple risks in terms of time, budget, adoption, implementation, security and utility [19].

With the improvements in biometric precision, biometrics is becoming the vital part of an identity systems, traits like retina, face, voice and iris could be used for identification purpose [20]. Any trait could be used for identification purpose if it is universal, unique, permanent, and recordable. Because of its unique features, it has found application in various areas like security [21], healthcare and attendance [22], surveillance [21], and law [23].

2.1 Aadhaar–A Case Study from India

Aadhaar is an initiative by the Government of India that is meant to provide every resident of India a unique identity number. It addresses 'identity gap' of India [24]. This unique identity number is tightly coupled with individual's biometrics like their photograph, fingerprint's of both hands and iris scan [25]. This Aadhaar number is used by both private and public sector platforms as proof of address where ever required. Supreme Court in 2013 ruled out that Aadhaar is not mandatory for enrolling in any government programs. However, Aadhaar Bill was passed by the Lok Sabha in 2016 which allows use of Aadhaar for delivery of various subsidies through Direct Benefit Transfer (DBT), and other benefits and services [26]. Aadhaar has made the existing welfare schemes more effective and efficient by targeting beneficiaries directly. The Aadhaar platform is indicative of the changing forms of a state and citizen relation in which the citizens are regularly redefined as customers of government for services [27]. Main purpose of Aadhaar is to provide unique identification and authentication service and is achieved with the help of biometrics [24]. Aadhaar is a twelve digit random number linked with the biometrics of a resident e.g. photo, fingerprints of hands, iris scan and demographic details e.g. date of birth, gender etc. [30]. India has issued Aadhaar cards to more than 1 billion residents [14].

Inclusion of biometrics in Aadhaar has helped to deal with the gaps in the existing systems–to ensure legal identity and to extend social protection schemes. Aadhaar is aligned with the main elements of SDGs-16 [17] i.e. right to identity and development of a sound system to guarantee social protection by preventing leakages and mismanagement in various welfare schemes, absence of identification documents, scalability, lack of trusted platform for financial transactions and the presence of large number of fake beneficiaries [28].

3   Theoretical Lens

This study attempts to identify the overarching latent goals of India's digital identity system–Aadhaar, under the backdrop of extensively used theory called Critical Success Factors Theory.

3.1   Critical Success Factors Theory

The concept of "Critical Success Factors" was first introduced by Rockart in 1979 [29]. Initially used mostly in the context of project management and gradually it has found its application in other different domains like smart cities [30], supply chain [31], business intelligence [32]. CSFs define fundamental zones of action in which positive outcomes are essential for a specific organization to achieve its primary goal, these are the conditions, qualities or factors that must go right for the success of an organization.

We did comprehensive literature review of various secondary data; research papers related to digital identity, Aadhaar, Estonia digital identity, e-governance, and SSN from Scopus database were taken into consideration for this study. Apart from research articles, we also considered official reports from government especially UIDAI and news articles published by some of the leading online news portals. A total of forty key factors were identified that are refined regrouped and classified into fifteen generic themes out of which nine were selected as CSFs (also known as overarching goals) by experts. This addresses our first research question, to identify CSFs of Aadhaar. These nine CSFs are shown in Table 1 and are used for further analysis.

Table 1. CSFs of Aadhaar

Sl. No.	Factors
1.	Building it as a platform
2.	Future-proofing of technology
3.	Data security & privacy
4.	Scalability
5.	Inclusion
6.	Uniqueness of IDS
7.	Cost optimization
8.	Speed
9.	Resident convenience

4   Research Questions

To the best of our knowledge, there is no such study found in the existing research which has attempted to identify and rank the CSFs of any digital identity system like Aadhaar. Majority of the research on biometric identities explores its utilitarian aspects and privacy and security concerns [35]. Hence, the motivation for this research is to analyze India's digital identity program–Aadhaar. The flow of this research is shown in the Fig. 1.

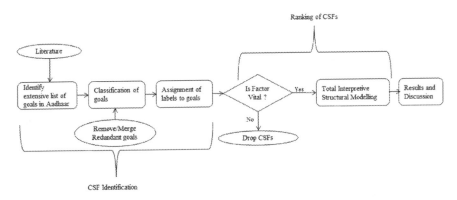

Fig. 1. Research flow diagram

5 Research Methodology

This study used focus group methodology to identify the significance level of each goal, it is a well-established systematic technique for synthesizing the opinions of domain specific experts on specific issues. This method is extremely useful in investigating different beliefs and thoughts on a particular issue in detail in presence of a moderator who oversees and records the deliberations [33].

In this study, focus group of eight-members was formed. Each member had direct association with Aadhaar and had experience of more than fifteen years; they were selected and approached using personal connections. Details of the focus group participants are shown in Table 2:

Table 2. Focus groups details

No. of participants	8
Duration of interview (minutes)	45 (approx.)
Male: Female	6 : 2
Indian Administrative Service officer (IAS)	3
Management professional	2
Dy. Director General (DDG)	1
Secretary	1
Senior govt. official	1
Minimum experience (years)	15

5.1   Focus Group Protocol

Focus group discussion started with a short welcome note, and all members were appreciated for their participation in the discussion. One of the authors moderated the session and was accompanied by an assistant responsible for taking notes, and before the discussion was started, every member of the group was requested to submit a consent form. The consent form had details like discussion being recorded in writing (taking notes) and digitally (audio), and all transcripts to be kept anonymous. For the sake of confidentially, each participant had a nameplate in front of them showing their first name only. Lastly, the moderator emphasized the objective of the focus group, which was to identify the overarching goals (CSFs) of Aadhaar and then determining the relative significance of each goal corresponding to other goals.

5.2   Identification of Overarching Goals of Aadhaar

Identification of relevant constructs empowers the decision makers to visualize the impact of actions [34]. Goals identified from the secondary data sources were evaluated by focus group participant; based on the consensus of the participants, some identified goals were clubbed, dropped, renamed, and some new were added. This method has subdued the duplicity in goals and has improved overall knowledge of the study. The final list of overarching goals is mentioned in Table 3.

5.3   Total Interpretive Structural Modeling – TISM

TISM, which is the modified version of ISM – method that is used to convert unclear and ambiguous mental representations into clear visible models [35]. Both TISM and ISM has been used extensively in the literature, [36, 37] and in this study it is used to rank overarching goals of Aadhaar system.

Table 3. Coding and labeling scheme of identified goals

Sl.No	Goal	Label	Code
1.	Building it as a platform	Platform	F1
2.	Future-proofing of technology	Future-proofing	F2
3.	Data security and privacy	Security and privacy	F3
4.	Scalability	Scalability	F4
5.	Inclusion	Inclusion	F5
6.	Uniqueness of IDS	Uniqueness	F6
7.	Cost optimisation	Cost	F7
8.	Speed	Speed	F8
9.	Resident convenience	Convenience	F9

TISM generates a hierarchical model by multiple pairwise comparisons using ISM methodology introduced by Warfield in 1974 [35]. In this study, a six steps TISM method is followed and is described as follows:

1. Identification of overarching goals of Aadhaar.
2. Based on expert's inputs, determine contextual relationships among factors identified in step 1 and develop Structural Self-Interaction Matrix (SSIM).
3. Develop Reachability Matrix (RM) from SSIM and check for transitive relations.
4. Do level partitioning on RM
5. Develop canonical matrix based on the final stage of partitioning matrix.
6. Finally, convert canonical matrix into hierarchical diagraph in which factors (i.e. Goals) are represented by nodes and edges represent relationship (i.e. significance of goals) among nodes.

To determine contextual relation between factors, the following four symbols are used and have following interpretation: V: if i helps in j and j does not help in i; A: if i does not help in j but j helps in i; X: if both i and j help each other and O: if i and j do not help each other.

Table 4. Structured self-interaction matrix

	F9	F8	F7	F6	F5	F4	F3	F2
F1	A	A	A	A	A	V	A	V
F2	A	A	A	A	A	X	A	
F3	V	V	V	A	V	V		
F4	A	A	A	A	A			
F5	A	A	A	A				
F6	V	V	V					
F7	X	X						
F8	X							

Step by step implementation of TISM methodology adopted for prioritization is explained below:

Step 1: A total of forty key factors were identified that are refined regrouped and classified into fifteen generic themes out of which nine were selected for this study (see Table 3).

Step 2: A focus group of eight members were employed to analyses the significance of nine CSFs and their relationships with each other. The association between factors is evaluated using "yes" or "no" queries. The final Self-interaction matrix is shown in see Table 4.

Step 3: All the identified relations are represented in the binary matrix called reachability matrix (see Table 5). Each entry in the matrix represents a relationship between two goals.

Step 4: All entries in the RM are checked for additional transitive relations that are not covered already. In our case, no additional transitive relations were discovered.

Table 5. Reachability matrix (binary)

	F1	F2	F3	F4	F5	F6	F7	F8	F9
F1	1	1	0	1	0	0	0	0	0
F2	0	1	0	1	0	0	0	0	0
F3	1	1	1	1	1	0	1	1	1
F4	0	1	0	1	0	0	0	0	0
F5	1	1	0	1	1	0	0	0	0
F6	1	1	1	1	1	1	1	1	1
F7	1	1	0	1	1	0	1	1	1
F8	1	1	0	1	1	0	1	1	1
F9	1	1	0	1	1	0	1	1	1

Step 5: For each goal from the reachability matrix, three sets are obtained, i.e. reachability set, antecedent set, and intersection set of reachability and antecedent set that form partitioning matrix (see Table 6). A particular goal is assigned a level if the intersection set is same as the reachability set for that particular goal. Once a goal is assigned a level, it is removed from the subsequent iterations. This process is repeated until each goal is assigned a level. In this study, a total of six iterations were performed.

Step 6: Finally, the partitioning matrix is converted into TISM hierarchy model as shown in Fig. 2. This model is drawn from bottom to top where bottom level goals are most significant and top level goals are less significant. Uniqueness (level 6) is at the bottom of TISM hierarchical model which signifies it is the most significant goal whereas future-proofing and scalability (level 1) are at the top level and are considered as less significant.

Partitioning is applied multiple times till level of each factor is identified; it took six iterations to identify level of each factor in Table 6.

Table 6. Final partitioning matrix

Element	Reachability	Antecedents	Intersection	Levels
F1	{F1, F2, F4}	{F1, F3, F5, F6, F7, F8, F9}	{F1}	II
F2	{F2, F4}	{F1, F2, F3, F4, F5, F6, F7, F8, F9}	{F2, F4}	I
F3	{F1, F2, F3, F4, F5, F7, F8, F9}	{F3, F6}	{F3}	V
F4	{F2, F4}	{F1, F2, F3, F4, F5, F6, F7,F8, F9}	{F2, F4}	I
F5	{F1, F2, F4, F5}	{F3, F5, F6, F7, F8, F9}	{F5}	III
F6	{F1, F2, F3, F4, F5, F6, F7, F8, F9}	{F6}	{F6}	VI
F7	{F1, F2, F4, F5, F7, F8, F9}	{F3, F6, F7, F8, F9}	{F7, F8, F9}	IV
F8	{F1, F2, F4, F5, F7, F8, F9}	{F3, F6, F7, F8, F9}	{F7, F8, F9}	IV
F9	{F1, F2, F4, F5, F7, F8, F9}	{F3, F6, F7, F8, F9}	{F7, F8, F9}	IV

In the final step, partitioning matrix is transformed into TISM hierarchical model (see Fig. 2). The result of this TISM model will enable concerned authorities to focus on the most important elements first while developing a digital identity solution.

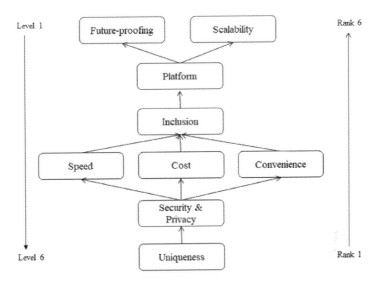

Fig. 2. Prioritization of CSFs of Aadhaar

6   Discussion

This section highlights the insights derived from this research. It can be observed that developing a biometric enabled digital identity system is a complex task and we need to take all stakeholders into consideration for successful development and implementation of the project. Most existing identity systems in place are functional identity systems– primarily developed for a particular use case like voter ID. Some of the high risks associated in developing a country level digital identity system are accurate budget calculation, securing assets, manpower with desirable skills, and availability of required technology, policy documentation, and maintenance of the overall system. To avoid risks which could cause project failure an extensive action plan is must to have. To the best of our knowledge, we have not found any research in existing academic research literature related to the ranking and identifying significance of goals of Aadhaar.

The findings depict that uniqueness with level six is the most significant goal followed by security and privacy that is at level five. This could easily be explained as these three are the fundamentals of any identity system and the same was reciprocated by the experts. Any identity system would lose its utility and robustness if any of these are compromised. Speed, cost and convenience share level four and equal significance; these are factors which would define the efficiency aspect of the Identity system and the performance of the system would be measured in their terms. Inclusion at level three is followed by platform that is at level two which signifies inclusion is slightly more significant as compared to platform, scalability and future-proofing of technology; this is because of the fact that India is a country of diversities and exclusion has been a long-standing foe for Government plans focusing on growth. So, inclusion received a special focus and was closely associated with the performance based factors that featured on the previous level; it plays a critical role of making Aadhaar into a successful platform which is on the next level and encompasses factors like infrastructural requirements and service delivery supply-chain. Scalability and future-proofing of the technology are both at level one and they focus on the future of this platform keeping in view the rapid growth of population and the changing nature of utilities or services expected out of the platform.

6.1 Implications of the Study

It is always a good practice to take successful system as a reference when developing similar one for different audience. It has been estimated that the total cost of a typical digital identity system is in-between £100–250 million [38]. Hence, it is important to analyze each risk beforehand and have measures to avoid or mitigate these types of risks. Further, digital identity could save £5–10 billion by avoiding identity related frauds [38].

The results of this study support the concept of stakeholder engagement in public schemes and for focusing at the CSFs analyzed during the overall development process. They are also consistent with the previous research that highlighted that confidentiality must be enforced over enrolment [39, 40]; also security and privacy are the second most important goal in the hierarchy.

Regarding the methodological contribution, this study is the first of its kind to employee TISM for ranking a gigantic project in Indian context –Aadhaar and the experience gained through the methods and techniques implemented may be helpful in other studies on analyzing large scale government initiatives.

The practical implications of this study relate to the concept of using hierarchical ranking model in devising a real life digital identity project. The listed CSFs (see Table 1) can help concerned authorities like governments to make policies which have the possibility of creating significant impact on the target. It shows the significance of each CSFs which will be valuable information while making feasibility analysis in terms of time required to develop an identity system, budget required, technological requirements, skill set of manpower, longevity of project, robustness of identity system and overall management of the project.

7 Conclusion

In this research, we identified the factors that are critical for a digital identification system. India's digital identity program – Aadhaar has been studied as a case study in this paper using CSFs theory as baseline. A total of nine CSFs are identified with the help of expert's opinion and ranked using TISM methodology which resulted in the hierarchical model as shown in Fig. 2.

The findings depict that uniqueness with level six is the most significant goal followed by security and privacy that is at level five. Scalability and future-proofing of the technology are the least significant goals both at level one. Speed, cost and convenience share level four and equal significance. Inclusion at level three is followed by platform that is at level two which signifies inclusion is slightly more significant as compared to platform, scalability and future-proofing of technology.

The results of this study will act as a reference for the countries that are yet to develop a digital identity program for its inhabitants. We hope this research will motivate researchers across the globe to conduct similar research on other digital identity program and develop a ranking hierarchy which is valid universally. Directions for future research are to validate the results of this study on some more identification programs and use the ranking model in designing practical digital identity systems.

References

1. Olson, E.T.: Personal Identity. Stanford Encyclopedia of Philosophy (2015). https://plato.stanford.edu/entries/identity-personal/. Accessed 21 Apr 2019
2. Mcwaters, R.J.: A blueprint for digital identity the role of financial institutions in building digital identity. In: World Economic Forum, Future of Financial Services Series, pp. 1–108, August 2016
3. Singh, H., Kar, A.K., Ilavarsana, P.V.: Assessment of e-governance projects: an integrated framework and its validation. In: Proceedings of the Special Collection on eGovernment Innovations in India, pp. 124–133 (2017)
4. Chatterjee, S., Kar, A.K.: Regulation and governance of the Internet of Things in India. Digit. Policy Regul. Gov. 20(5), 399–412 (2018)
5. Singh, H., Kar, A.K., Ilavarsana, P.V.: Performance assessment of e-government projects: a multi-construct, multi-stakeholder perspective. In: Proceedings of the 10th International Conference on Theory and Practice of Electronic Governance, pp. 558–559 (2017)
6. Mishra, A., Misra, D.P., Kar, A.K., Babbar, S., Biswas, S.: Assessment of open government data initiative - a perception driven approach. In: Kar, A., et al. (eds.) Digital Nations – Smart Cities, Innovation, and Sustainability, I3E 2017. Lecture Notes in Computer Science, vol. 10595, pp. 159–171. Springer, Cham (2017). https://doi.org/10.1007/978-3-319-68557-1_15
7. Rifkin, J.: The Age of Access: The New Culture of Hypercapitalism Where All of Life Is a Paid-For Experience. Putnam Publishing Group, New York City (2001)
8. Baym, N.K.: Personal Connections in the Digital Age, 2nd edn. Polity Press, Malden (2015)
9. Al-Khouri, A.M.: Digital identity: transforming GCC economies. Innov. Manag. Policy Pract. 16(2), 184–194 (2014)
10. McKinsey: Digital Identification : A Key To Inclusive Growth (2019)
11. BankWorld: World Development Report 2016: Digital Dividends. The World Bank (2016)
12. Herbert Kubicek, T.N.: Different countries-different paths extended comparison of the introduction of eIDs in eight European countries. Identity Inf. Soc. 3(1), 235–245 (2010)
13. Agrawal, S., Banerjee, S., Sharma, S.: Privacy and security of Aadhaar: a computer science perspective. Econ. Polit. Wkly. 52(37), 1–23 (2017)
14. Dixon, P.: A failure to "Do No Harm" – India' s Aadhaar biometric ID program and its inability to protect privacy in relation to measures in Europe and the U.S. Health Technol. 7, 539–567 (2017)

15. OCED: Digital identity management: enabling innovation and trust in the internet economy. The Organisation for Economic Co-operation and Development (OECD) (2011)
16. Bertino, R.F.E., Paci, F.: Privacy-preserving digital identity management for cloud computing. IEEE Comput. Soc. Tech. Comm. Data Eng. **31**, 21–27 (2009)
17. UN: "SDG," UNDP (2016). https://www.un.org/sustainabledevelopment/peace-justice/. Accessed 08 Feb 2019
18. Atick, J.: Digital identity: the essential guide. ID4Africa Identity Forum (2016). http://www.id4africa.com/prev/%0Aimg/Digital_Identity_The_Essential_Guide.pdf
19. Leo, F.B., Goodstadt, F., Connolly, R.: The Hong Kong e-identity card: examining the reasons for its success when other cards continue to struggle. Inf. Syst. Manag. **32**(1), 72–80 (2015)
20. Hoang, B., Caudill, A.: Biometrics. IEEE Emerging Technology Portal, pp. 3–5 (2012)
21. Rao, U.H., Nayak, U.: Physical security and biometrics. In: Rao, U.H., Nayak, U. (eds.) The InfoSec Handbook, pp. 293–306. Apress, Berkeley (2014). https://doi.org/10.1007/978-1-4302-6383-8_14
22. Marohn, D.: Biometrics in healthcare. Biometric Technol. Today **14**(9), 9–11 (2006)
23. Jain, A.K., Ross, A., Prabhakar, S.: An introduction to biometric recognition. IEEE Trans. Circ. Syst. Video Technol. **14**(1), 4–20 (2004)
24. Gelb, A., Clark, J.: Performance lessons from India's universal identification program. CGD Policy Pap. **20**, 1–12 (2013)
25. Weinberg, J.T.: Biometric identity. Commun. ACM **59**(1), 30–32 (2016)
26. T.E. Times: Government Notifies Aadhaar Act, The Economic Times (2016). https://economictimes.indiatimes.com/news/economy/policy/government-notifies-aadhaar-act/articleshow/51585001.cms?from=mdr. Accessed 06 Apr 2019
27. Jayal, N.G.: A' democratic deficit: citizenship and governance in the era of globalisation. In: Choudhary, K. (ed.) Globalisation. Governance Reforms and Development in India. Sage Publications, New Delhi (2007)
28. Bhatia, A., Bhabha, J.: India' s Aadhaar scheme and the promise of inclusive social protection. Oxford Dev. Stud. **0818**(December), 1–16 (2017)
29. Bullen, C.V., Rockart, J.F.: A primer on critical success factors. Rise Manag. Comput. **69**, 1220–1281 (1981)
30. Chatterjee, M.G.S., Kar, A.K.: Critical success factors to establish 5G network in smart cities: inputs for security and privacy. J. Glob. Inf. Manag. **25**(2), 15–37 (2017)
31. Shankar, R., Gupta, R., Pathak, D.K.: Modeling critical success factors of traceability for food logistics. Transp. Res. Part E **119**(August 2017), 205–222 (2018)
32. Yeoh, W., Popovič, A.: Extending the understanding of critical success factors for implementing business intelligence systems. J. Assoc. Inf. Sci. Technol. **67**(1), 134–147 (2016)
33. Krueger, R.A.: Focus Groups: A Practical Guide for Applied Research, 4th edn. Sage, Thousand Oaks (2009)
34. Dunn, R.C., Henning, T.F.P., Muruvan, S., Feng, W.A.: The development of a benchmarking tool for monitoring progress towards sustainable transportation in New Zealand. Transp. Policy **18**(2), 480–488 (2011)
35. Sushil, S.: Interpreting the interpretive structural model. Glob. J. Flex. Syst. Manag. **13**(2), 87–106 (2012)
36. Kumar, H., Singh, M.K., Gupta, M.P.: A policy framework for city eligibility analysis: TISM and fuzzy MICMAC-weighted approach to select a city for smart city transformation in India. Land Use Policy **82**(February 2018), 375–390 (2018)

37. Dubey, R., Ali, S.S.: Identification of flexible manufacturing system dimensions and their interrelationship using total interpretive structural modelling and fuzzy MICMAC analysis. Glob. J. Flex. Syst. Manag. **15**(2), 131–143 (2014)
38. I. Identity: Digital Identity in the UK : The cost of doing nothing, April 2018
39. Mali, N.V., Avila-Maravilla, M.A.: Convergence or conflict? In: Proceedings of 11th International Conference on Theory and Practice of Electronic Governance - ICEGOV 2018, pp. 443–448 (2018)
40. Belanche-gracia, D., Casaló-ariño, L.V., Pérez-rueda, A.: Determinants of multi-service smartcard success for smart cities development : a study based on citizens' privacy and security perceptions. Gov. Inf. Q. **32**(2), 154–163 (2015)

Digital Divide and Social Inclusion

Digital Inequalities: A Review of Contributing Factors and Measures for Crossing the Divide

Eli Hustad(✉) , June Lithell Hansen, Andreas Skaiaa,
and Polyxeni Vassilakopoulou

University of Agder, Kristiansand, Norway
{eli.hustad,junelhl7,oandsl7,polyxenv}@uia.no

Abstract. This literature review focuses on the digital divide in contemporary technologically and economically advanced societies. Prior research shows that the digital divide entails more than physical accessibility and points to issues of technology acceptance and actual use. Recurring digital divide factors outside socioeconomic characteristics were identified in the articles reviewed. These factors relate to personality traits, motivation and digital skills. The factors can be used as the basis for a personality model for understanding acceptance and use of technology complementing models related to economic and social resources. Furthermore, measures for crossing the divide are traced in the literature and organized in three key intervention domains related to policy, training and design. The findings of this review can be a foundation for further research orienting researchers within the domain.

Keywords: Digital divide · ICT access · ICT acceptance · Digitalization · Motivation · Personality · Skills

1 Introduction

Citizens are increasingly expected to participate online using information and communications technologies (ICT) in order to utilize digitalized services. The continuous effort to digitalize society poses a challenge for individuals who are not fully capable of using the digital tools necessary for accessing online services. This can have severe consequences for citizen groups who may feel partially excluded or completely left out of society because of their inability to adapt to digitalization.

Phenomena of digital inequalities are referred to with the term *digital divide* signifying the gap between individuals, households, businesses or geographic areas regarding opportunities to access and use ICTs and the Internet for a variety of activities [1, 2]. According to Van Dijk [3], digital inequality concerns have shifted from unequal motivation and physical access to inequalities of skills and usage. In terms of physical access, the divide seems to be closing in the developed countries, but inequalities in digital skills and application use persist. In the past, the digital divide literature was mostly driven by policy-oriented reports that focused on access. Scientific research in the domain foregrounded the multifaceted nature of digital inequality beyond access; researchers pointed to issues related to knowledge, economic and social resources, attributes of technology such as performance and reliability, and utility

© IFIP International Federation for Information Processing 2019
Published by Springer Nature Switzerland AG 2019
I. O. Pappas et al. (Eds.): I3E 2019, LNCS 11701, pp. 505–519, 2019.
https://doi.org/10.1007/978-3-030-29374-1_41

realization [4–6]. Investigations go mostly beyond questions of access (the so-called "first-level digital divide") to examining factors that affect people's ability to make good use of digital resources.

Understanding how digital inequalities emerge in settings that are advanced in terms of technological infrastructure and economy and finding ways to address such inequalities is today more important than ever. The digital divide is a serious threat to civil society in an era where public services go digital. For instance, daily activities such as paying bills, filling in application forms, filing tax returns, are all expected to be carried out electronically There are high expectations for active citizens' role based on online services [7, 8]; hence, we need to be constantly in the lookout for digital inequalities ensuring fairness and inclusiveness.

Our study identifies, analyses, and integrates a critical mass of recent research on the digital divide focused on places where the technological infrastructures and economies are advanced. To ensure a robust result, we performed a systematic literature review [9] guided by the following question: *What are the key research findings of the factors that contribute to the digital divide in contemporary technologically and economically advanced settings?* Our contribution is threefold. First, we identify recurring digital divide factors and we map these factors to different groups of people that are threatened by digital inequality in modern societies. Second, we present different measures proposed in the literature and organize them in three key intervention domains. Finally, as a third contribution, we identify areas for future research providing a foundation for researchers to aim to engage with the domain.

The remainder of the paper is organized as follows. First, we present the method used for selecting and analyzing the articles for this review. Then we offer a synthesis of our findings related to digital divide factors and related measures and present them in a concise concept matrix. We continue by discussing the implications for further research and we end with overall concluding remarks.

2   Research Approach

The systematic literature review was performed by following the process proposed by Kitchenham [9]. This structured approach encompasses three main steps: (a) planning the review, where a detailed protocol containing specific search terms and inclusion/exclusion criteria is developed, (b) conducting the review, where the selection, appraisal and synthesis of prior published research is performed and (c) reporting the review, where the write-up is prepared. We used these steps as our methodological framework. In addition, we utilized principles suggested by Webster and Watson [10] for the analysis of the articles included in the review. Following these principles, we identified key concepts and created a concept-centric matrix that provides an overview of the literature reviewed.

To identify and select research articles to be reviewed, a set of search terms and a set of inclusion/exclusion criteria were used. The search terms consisted of the words Digital and Divide. We decided to search for any combination of these two words in the abstract, title and keywords of published articles instead of searching for the string "Digital Divide" which can be too restrictive. Moreover, we conducted backward and forward searches to review relevant citations. The primary search was performed in Scopus and we used Google Scholar for our backward and forward searches.

Inclusion and exclusion criteria were established to reduce selection bias, guarantee the quality of the papers selected and increase the validity of our review. Peer-reviewed, empirical papers, written in English, published within information systems research between 2010 and 2018 were included. Conceptual papers that lacked empirical evidence, reviews, and papers focusing on the digital divide in developing countries were excluded. Our intention was to obtain an overview of empirical research on the digital divide in settings that are technologically and economically advanced. To ensure covering the mainstream journals in information research we searched within the basket of eight [11], and additionally, the Communications of the Association for IS (CAIS), Information and Organization and Information Technology & People. Furthermore, we searched for articles in all Association of Information Systems (AIS) conferences and the Hawaiian International Conference on System Sciences (HICSS). The search yielded 165 unique articles in total. The next step was to read the titles and abstracts of the articles identified checking their relevance to the research question. For this step, the exclusion criteria were used. Specifically, we excluded papers that only casually mentioned the digital divide but had a different focus, literature reviews and conceptual papers and papers focused on developing countries. After this step, 53 papers were shortlisted and used as a basis for a backward and forward search which yielded 9 additional papers. For the backward and forward search, we decided to include papers based on topic relevance only without restrictions for the publication outlet. Finally, the full text of each one of the shortlisted papers was assessed for relevance applying the inclusion-exclusion criteria to the full content. Additionally, the quality of the research reported was assessed. For the quality assessment, each article´s method description was checked for rigorousness. After this step, a final corpus of 17 articles was defined (Table 1). Figure 1 provides an overview of the selection process.

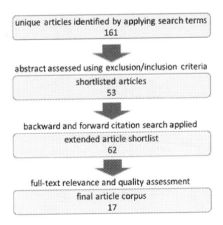

Fig. 1. The literature selection process.

Table 1. List of selected articles

#	Reference
1	Abdelfattah, B. M., Bagchi, K., Udo, G., & Kirs, P. (2010). *Understanding the Internet Digital Divide: An Exploratory Multi-Nation Individual-Level Analysis.* Paper presented at the 16th American Conference on Information Systems (AMCIS 2010). Proceedings. Paper 542
2	Niehaves, B., & Plattfaut, R. (2010). *The Age-Divide in Private Internet Usage: A Quantitative Study of Technology Acceptance.* Paper presented at the 16th American Conference on Information Systems (AMCIS 2010). Proceedings. Paper 407
3	Hsieh, J. P.-A., Rai, A., & Keil, M. (2011). Addressing digital inequality for the socioeconomically disadvantaged through government initiatives: Forms of capital that affect ICT utilization. *Information Systems Research, 22*(2), 233–253
4	Wei, K.K., Teo, H.H., Chan, H. C., & Tan, B. C. (2011). Conceptualizing and testing a social cognitive model of the digital divide. *Information Systems Research, 22*(1), 170–187
5	Chang, S.-I., Yen, D. C., Chang, I.-C., & Chou, J.-C. (2012). Study of the digital divide evaluation model for government agencies–a Taiwanese local government's perspective. *Information Systems Frontiers, 14*(3), 693–709
6	Ghobadi, S., & Ghobadi, Z. (2015). How access gaps interact and shape digital divide: a cognitive investigation. *Behaviour & Information Technology, 34*(4), 330–340
7	Niehaves, B., & Plattfaut, R. (2014). Internet adoption by the elderly: employing IS technology acceptance theories for understanding the age-related digital divide. *European Journal of Information Systems, 23*(6), 708–726
8	Friemel, T. N. (2016). The digital divide has grown old: Determinants of a digital divide among seniors. *New media & society, 18*(2), 313–331
9	Alam, K., & Imran, S. (2015). The digital divide and social inclusion among refugee migrants: A case in regional Australia. *Information Technology & People, 28*(2), 344–365
10	Racherla, P., & Mandviwalla, M. (2013). Moving from access to use of the information infrastructure: A multilevel sociotechnical framework. *Information Systems Research, 24*(3), 709–730
11	Ebermann, C., Piccinini, E., Brauer, B., Busse, S., & Kolbe, L. (2016). *The Impact of Gamification-Induced Emotions on In-car IS Adoption – The Difference between Digital Natives and Digital Immigrants.* Paper presented in the 49th Hawaii International Conference on System Sciences *(HICSS 2016)* (pp. 1338–1347). IEEE
12	Fox, G., & Connolly, R. (2018). Mobile health technology adoption across generations: Narrowing the digital divide. *Information Systems Journal, 28*(6), 995–1019
13	Chipeva, P., Cruz-Jesus, F., Oliveira, T., & Irani, Z. (2018). Digital divide at individual level: Evidence for Eastern and Western European countries. *Government Information Quarterly, 35*(3), 460–479
14	Quan-Haase, A., Williams, C., Kicevski, M., Elueze, I., & Wellman, B. (2018). Dividing the grey divide: Deconstructing myths about older adults' online activities, skills, and attitudes. *American Behavioral Scientist, 62*(9), 1207–1228
15	Szeles, M. R. (2018). New insights from a multilevel approach to the regional digital divide in the European Union. *Telecommunications Policy, 42*(6), 452–463

(*continued*)

Table 1. (*continued*)

#	Reference
16	Reisdorf, B. C., & Rikard, R. V. (2018). Digital rehabilitation: a model of reentry into the digital age. *American Behavioral Scientist, 62*(9), 1273–1290
17	de Carvalho, C. V., Olivares, P. C., Roa, J. M., Wanka, A., & Kolland, F. (2018). *Digital Information Access for Ageing Persons.* Paper presented at the 18th International Conference on Advanced Learning Technologies (ICALT 2018) (pp. 345–347). IEEE

3 Results

This section presents the literature review results. Recurring digital divide factors are identified and presented for the different population groups threatened by digital inequality. Furthermore, measures for addressing the challenge of the digital divide are described and organized in three key intervention domains. The key findings of the literature review are summarized in the concept matrix which is presented in Table 2. A comprehensive overview of all the papers reviewed is included in Appendix 1.

3.1 Factors Contributing to the Digital Divide

In settings with advanced infrastructures and economy, physical access is not a key source of digital inequalities anymore and the studies that examine issues of unequal access show that this gap is closing (with the exception of special population groups such as prisoners). Nevertheless, there is still a stark difference between access and acceptance. Several of the studies reviewed combine established technology acceptance theories and models with concepts related to the characteristics and preferences of individuals and pragmatic constraints related to access. Going beyond socioeconomic demographics, a number of personal contributing factors were identified: *(a) motivation, (b) personality traits* (e.g. openness, extraversion, conscientiousness), *(c) digital skills.* Many of the studies reviewed focus on particular groups of people. Specifically, a significant part of the literature is focused on the elderly who are also referred to as "digital immigrants" (as opposed to digital natives that have been interacting with digital technology since childhood). Additionally, several studies are focused on specific marginalized population groups such as prisoners and refugees. In the paragraphs that follow, we present the research findings organizing them according to the different groups studied.

Elderly Population. Although digital technologies have been around for several decades, some of the elderly members of society have difficulties learning about and adopting digital tools and services. Hence, targeted efforts are needed for fully integrating senior citizens in the knowledge society [12]. This is not a physical access problem because, for the senior citizens that do not own computers or mobile devices, access is provided in libraries and community centers. This group has problems with the actual use of digital technologies [13]. Elderly people may *want to stay connected* and learn new digital skills, but at the same time, they tend to feel overwhelmed [14]. Still, they do engage in a wide range of online activities despite having limited *skills*, and some are eager to learn as they go [14]. Unwillingness to adopt digital technologies by the elderly was found to stem from *mistrust, high-risk perceptions, and desire for privacy* [15]. Research also shows that not all seniors have the same stances towards digital technologies [14]. Overall older people are a heterogeneous group, and it is important not to overlook their differences (for instance in digital skills and use of social media). Niehaves and Plattfaut [16] used the unified theory of acceptance and use of technology (UTAUT) and the model of adoption of technology in households (MATH) to explain internet acceptance and usage by the elderly. These models were able to predict how the elderly could be encouraged to learn to use technology. Performance expectancy (ease of use) was found to be the main driver for internet usage among senior citizens.

Marginalised Population Groups. Language barriers as for instance, in the case of refugees, can cause social exclusion and may hinder the process of ICT assimilation throughout society. Alam and Imram found in their research that even though refugees and immigrants in the US are motivated to learn about new technology, many were not able to do so for three main reasons: unaffordable cost, language barriers and lack of skills [17]. They showed that *refugees* think that technology is helpful for finding new jobs or facilitating social engagement but barriers such as expenses and problems with access prevent them from using the Internet [17]. Reisdorf and Rikard [18] focus on the challenges of paroles that are released from prison and argue that very little research on the digital divide focuses on complete nonusers, bringing into attention the problems that paroles encounter on release from *prison* after lengthy periods of nonuse [18]. They propose a model of digital rehabilitation that addresses both online and offline arenas in the rehabilitation of prisoners. The model fills a gap in prisoner rehabilitation that usually only targets offline arenas and issues, while the digital realm is often disregarded [18].

General Population. In the general population, socioeconomic factors including educational level relate to the digital inequalities [19]. A study conducted by Chipeva and colleagues [20] combined the extended unified theory of acceptance and use of technology (UTAUT2) with the big five personality traits (openness, extraversion, agreeableness, conscientiousness, and neuroticism) to investigate factors that relate to the digital divide. The study is interesting because it goes beyond the socio-demographic characteristics of individuals showing the influence of *attitudes and personality traits*. Additionally, the study showed the impact of cultural differences by identifying factors that differ across Bulgarian and Portuguese cultures. Performance expectancy and habit turned out to be the strongest predictors of ICT acceptance, also, the personality characteristics of openness, extraversion, and agreeableness were found to be significant predictors of ICT acceptance [20]. Unreasonably high expectation and specific personality traits are found to have a negative impact on ICT acceptance [21] while individual characteristics such as gender, language, race, household and area of residence (rural or urban) do not seem to have an impact [22]. Nevertheless, Hsieh and colleagues suggest that demographic factors such as ethnic background and education that have been shown to explain the high acceptance of ICT can also explain the nonuse of ICT [23]. Socio-economically disadvantaged people are affected by digital inequalities. Two individuals might have equal access to digital technologies, but a difference in skills can create digital inequalities [24]. Abdelfattah argues that socio-economic status among groups can cause inequality and some groups may be disadvantaged because they are too far embedded in older systems, which makes it difficult for them to adopt newer ICTs [25].

Table 2. Concept matrix

	Papers reviewed																
	1	2	3	4	5	6	7	8	9	10	11	12	13	14	15	16	17
Type of inequality																	
ICT access	x	x	x	x	x	x	x	x	x	x						x	
ICT acceptance	x	x	x	x	x	x	x	x	x	x	x	x	x	x			
Digital divide contributing factors																	
Motivation		x	x			x	x	x			x		x	x			
Personality traits						x			x				x	x			
Digital skills	x	x		x	x	x	x	x				x		x	x	x	x
Digital divide remedies																	
Policy measures		x	x	x	x	x	x		x	x			x		x		
Education/training				x	x	x			x			x			x	x	x
Design tailoring								x			x	x	x	x			

3.2 Overcoming the Digital Divide

Policy-making is considered instrumental for closing the digital gap [20]. Szeles [19] suggests a mix of regional and national policy measures to bridge the digital gap in EU countries [19]. These measures include: stimulating regional economic growth, strengthening tertiary education, increasing R&D expenditure, discouraging early leaving from education. Effective evaluation mechanisms make it easier to develop new policies in the public sector and can contribute to addressing the digital divide [26]. This makes it possible for policy-makers to take action by implementing various initiatives to bridge the divide among certain sectors of society, such as elderly people and socio-economically disadvantaged groups [23]. Policies that leverage existing communities, social structures, and local actors can help in reducing digital inequalities [27]. Such policies can stimulate public/private partnerships with grassroots organizations that already have "hooks" in local communities. Policy measures should allow room for local adaptations, as contextual and local elements seem to play a role for technology users and could influence policy success [27].

Van Dijk suggests that proper training and education might help mitigate the inequalities of the digital divide [3]. Furthermore, information campaigns also have a significant role to play. The digital divide can be narrowed if vendors engage in trust building campaigns targeting the elderly [15]. In addition, social networks, friends and family are important for supporting the training of disadvantaged people in technologies. Digital literacy programs targeting senior citizens can help them develop the necessary skills and abilities to use digital mobile devices so that they could be part of the Digital Society [12, 15]. Friemel's study [28], conducted in Switzerland, finds that internet usage among the elderly was encouraged by family members and friends and that a private learning setting was more effective and was preferred over a professional learning approach. Overall, prior research has shown that senior citizens appreciate very much digital literacy programs and have positive perceptions of the digital abilities they develop [12]. Looking at the specific marginalized population group of prisoners, Reisdorf and Rikard [18] also point to the importance of training and call for more research on digital skills development and interventions to mitigate digital exclusion experienced during imprisonment.

Chipeva and colleagues [20] address the concrete level of conceptualizing and developing ICT solutions and point to the importance of taking into account individual differences for creating proper stimuli to different user groups. This makes the role of appropriate design for overcoming the digital divide a center of attention. Their findings show that it is important to emphasize ICT usefulness and performance rather than ease of use as performance expectancy is the strongest antecedent of behavioral intention while effort expectancy does not have the same strong role. Similarly, Quan-Haase and colleagues emphasize the need for tools and applications to be specifically developed to support the elderly in their current activities [14] as opposed to tools that are not related to their everyday practices. Overall, research points to the importance of functionalities that suit the needs of specific user groups to stimulate ICT acceptance.

4   Discussion and Implications for Future Research

Prior research shows that the digital divide is related to socioeconomic characteristics and also personality traits, motivation and digital skills. Digital inequalities in the technologically and economically advanced societies have shifted from unequal physical access to inequalities in actual usage. Although the physical access divide seems to be closing, inequalities in use persist. Measures for crossing the divide range include policy interventions, training and design. The findings of this review can be a foundation for further research orienting researchers within the domain. Several questions remain unanswered related to the digital divide in our societies thus further studies are needed. Several future research topics were suggested by the authors of the papers reviewed. Further work should be undertaken to *investigate different national, social and cultural settings* [13, 20, 24] across geographical contexts [16]. Future research should pay attention to how *institutional and environmental factors* at the macro level may influence individuals' ability and motivation to access and use technology [27]. Furthermore, further research is needed to *extend established models with new variables*. Future investigations may add variables to social theories [16, 22, 23, 28], personal traits models [20, 21], and capital theory [23]. Future research should consider testing other psychological variables [13] and socio-economical aspects [18, 23] to develop a more fine-grained understanding of the association between digital divide variables and ICT acceptance [15, 16, 20, 23]. Additionally, further work is required to *research the effect of interventions* to avoid the exclusion of citizens from the digital realm addressing inequalities [17, 18, 24].

5   Conclusion

Remaining cautious of digital inequalities is critical in our digitalization era. These inequalities are manifested not just in terms of access issues but also, in terms of what citizens can actually do with digital technologies. Understanding how digital inequalities emerge and finding ways to address them, needs to be a key premise for the development of e-societies. Researchers largely agree that the digital divide should be defined in terms that go beyond accessibility to access and actual use and that a personality model can help us to understand acceptance and use of technology complementing models related to economic and social resources. Such a personality model can include personality traits (e.g. openness, extraversion, conscientiousness) and also, motivation, and digital skills. Concerted action at the policy level, training initiatives and tailored design catering for the most vulnerable user groups can all contribute in closing the gap. The findings of this literature review can provide a foundation for further research development and a basis for researchers to orient themselves within the domain and position their own work.

Appendix 1

See Table 3.

Table 3. Overview of key elements of the reviewed articles

#	Author(s)	Year	Research objectives	Findings	Future research directions
1	Abdelfattah et al.	2010	Aims to identify factors of the digital divide that separate the digitally deprived from frequent internet users. The study covers both developed and developing nations	Socio-economics, demographic variables, use of media channels, and religion (to some extent) influence the digital divide; most factors differ between the digitally deprived and frequent users of the Internet	More research on the influences of self-perceptions, traditional media, religion, and word-of-mouth on the digital divide; additional research on the factors that contribute to the digital divide extremes
2	Niehaves & Plattfaut	2010	Aims to identify factors that influence senior citizens' internet usage and non-internet usage; uses UTAUT and digital divide theory as a theoretical lens	An extended UTAUT model with digital divide variables was useful for analyzing private internet usage; performance expectancy (ease of use) was found to be the main driver for senior citizens' internet usage	Comparative studies in other national/social/cultural settings; longitudinal studies on senior citizens' internet usage; further testing of psychological variables by modifying UTAUT

(continued)

Table 3. (*continued*)

#	Author(s)	Year	Research objectives	Findings	Future research directions
3	Hsieh et al.	2011	Aims to understand the inequality between the socio-economically disadvantaged and the socio-economically advantaged to inform public policy; uses capital theory as a theoretical lens	The disadvantaged realized greater gains in cultural capital, social capital and habitus than the advantaged; intention to use ICT was influenced by intrinsic and extrinsic motivations for habitus and self-efficacy of cultural capital but not by social capital	Research on how the socio-economically disadvantaged can effectively convert their ICT usage into economic, health, social and educational benefits; extend the capital framework with economic capital (e.g., affordability of training and infrastructure); utilize and extend social theories
4	Wei et al.	2011	Examines digital inequalities among students as: digital access divide, digital capability divide (capability to exploit IT), and digital outcome divide (learning and productivity)	Generates insights into the relationships between the three levels of the divide; provides an account of the effects of the digital divide	Understand other effects of the digital divide and how governments can use interventions to avoid citizen exclusion from the digital realm
5	Chang et al.	2012	Aims to identify the digital divide and measure its different levels among local governments in Taiwan	A model of five dimensions was developed to enable local government assess pros and cons of digitalization; the model addresses government agencies	Use the model as a point of departure for studies on other countries or city governments in Taiwan; identify new dimensions for customizing the model
6	Ghobadi & Ghobadi	2015	Focuses on inequalities in ICT access and in particular on motivational, material, skill, and usage gaps; demonstrates interactions and linkages between these gaps	Provides a theoretical model which includes 22 concepts and the linkages between them; contributes insights about dynamics shaping the digital divide and develops new concepts related to gaps	Use the theoretical model for future research on the digital divide; conduct studies on the digital divide in different cultures that develop interventions to reduce the digital divide

(*continued*)

Table 3. (*continued*)

#	Author(s)	Year	Research objectives	Findings	Future research directions
7	Niehaves & Plattfaut	2014	Focuses on the age-related digital divide; identifies important influencing factors regarding internet usage	Combines the UTAUT model and MATH with socio-demographical variables to explain the variance of internet adoption among the elderly	Conduct research on other geographical settings; repeat the research with larger sample size; conduct studies on e-inclusion to explore and theorize social context
8	Friemel	2016	Focuses on internet usage among the elderly, the so-called "gray divide" (seniors 65+)	Old seniors (70+) are partially excluded, gender differences found to disappear; family encouragement found to have a strong influence on internet usage	Investigate the influence of social networks; conduct social network analysis to reveal new concepts for analyzing the digital divide among seniors
9	Alam & Imram	2015	Examines the factors that influence refugee adoption of digital technology and its relevance to their social inclusion in Australia	A digital divide exists among refugee groups related to inequalities in physical access to and use of digital technology, the skills necessary to use technologies effectively and the ability to pay for services	Investigate how education, period of stay and gender influence the digital divide among refugee groups; Examine whether this digital divide is unique to the region under study or applies to wider Australian society
10	Racherla, & Mandviwalla	2013	Investigates antecedents of access and use at the individual and collective level focusing on "horizontal support" and "universal service" information infrastructures	The human and technological elements underlying individual access are embedded within institutional elements that enable and constrain use. A multi-level framework is suggested showing the influenced of both micro and macro factors	Connecting macro level institutional and environmental factors with the individuals' ability and motivation to access and use technology. Develop a process theory. Research new measures of interconnectedness that take into account the identities and varied communities afforded by digital world

(*continued*)

Table 3. (*continued*)

#	Author(s)	Year	Research objectives	Findings	Future research directions
11	Ebermann et al.	2016	Investigates differences in gamification-induced emotions among digital natives and digital immigrants and their relationship to IS adoption	Findings indicate that digital natives feel more pleasure, dominance and arousal than digital immigrants after being confronted with the hedonic part of a dual-purpose IS (used in cars)	Recommends future research to analyze the impact of game mechanisms on participants' emotional states in a realistic field setting
12	Fox & Connolly	2018	Explores factors driving resistance to mobile health technologies among older adults. Uses protection motivation theory and social cognitive theory	Unwillingness to adopt mobile health technologies stems from mistrust, high risk perceptions, and desire for privacy. Remedies include inclusive design and efforts to improve self-efficacy, privacy, literacy, and trust	Recommends future research that builds upon data on actual adoption instead of adoption intentions
13	Chipeva et al.	2018	Explores the digital divide by focusing on the individual level analysing data collected in Bulgaria and Portugal. Uses both socio—demographic characteristics of individuals, and attitudes and personality traits	Combines the extended unified theory of acceptance and use of technology (UTAUT2) with the big five personality traits (openness, extraversion, agreeableness, conscientiousness, and neuroticism) in a model. Identifies differences across Bulgarian and Portuguese cultures	Expand research by (a) using other personality frameworks, (b) examining the impact of personality on more specific IS types, (c) studying different age and professional groups, (d) studying other cultural contexts, (e) detecting changes over time through a longitudinal investigation
14	Quan-Haase et al.	2018	Develop a fine-grained understanding of older adults′ online activities, skills and attitudes, based on 41 in-depth interviews with adults aged above 65 years	A typology of older adults that includes Reluctants, Apprehensive, Basic Users, Go-Getters, and Savvy Users was developed. A nonlinear association between skill levels and online engagement was identified	Investigate if people embedded in networks of savvy users see themselves as more adept and empowered. Use surveys to further validate the typology. Perform longitudinal research to disentangle cohort-based from generational differences

(*continued*)

Table 3. (*continued*)

#	Author(s)	Year	Research objectives	Findings	Future research directions
15	Szeles	2018	Analyses regional and country-level determinants of the regional digital divide in the EU based on 2001–2016 data.	Bridging the digital divide requires a mix of regional and national measures that include: regional economic growth stimulation, strengthening tertiary education, increasing R&D expenditure, discouraging education dropout	This is a complex phenomenon with multiple facets, so further longitudinal research across levels can bring valuable insights
16	Reisdorf & Rikard	2018	Develops a new model of digital rehabilitation integrating digital divide theories and existing models of rehabilitation and reentry	Rehabilitation and reentry frameworks need to move away from only focusing on the offline realm and rather focus on the relationships between online and offline realms	Examine digital exclusion experienced by returning citizens based on length of sentence, age, previous engagement with digital technologies. Further investigate the current use of ICTs in reentry practices and related reentry outcomes
17	de Carvalho et al.	2018	The article analyses the results of a European-wide digital literacy development initiative for senior citizens	The results of the initiative reflect a very positive perception of the seniors on digital abilities. The training was much appreciated. The duration of the course has been deemed as too short	Points to the need of fully integrating senior citizens in the Knowledge Society

References

1. Pick, J., Sarkar, A.: Theories of the digital divide: critical comparison. In: 49th Hawaii International Conference on System Sciences (HICSS), pp. 3888–3897. IEEE (2016)
2. OECD: Understanding the digital divide, Paris, France (2001)
3. Van Dijk, J.: The Evolution of the Digital Divide: The Digital Divide Turns to Inequality of Skills and Usage. Digital Enlightenment Yearbook, pp. 57–75 (2012)
4. DiMaggio, P., Hargiattai, E., Celeste, C., Shafer, S.: Digital inequality: from unequal access to differentiated use. In: Social Inequality, pp. 355–400. Russell Sage Foundation (2004)
5. Van Dijk, J.A.: Digital divide research, achievements and shortcomings. Poetics **34**(4–5), 221–235 (2006)

6. Van Deursen, A.J., Helsper, E.J.: The third-level digital divide: who benefits most from being online? In: Communication and Information Technologies Annual, pp. 29–52. Emerald Group Publishing Limited (2015)

7. Axelsson, K., Melin, U., Lindgren, I.: Public e-services for agency efficiency and citizen benefit—findings from a stakeholder centered analysis. Gov. Inf. Quart. **30**(1), 10–22 (2013)

8. Vassilakopoulou, P., Grisot, M., Aanestad, M.: Enabling electronic interactions between patients and healthcare providers: a service design perspective. Scand. J. Inf. Syst. **28**(1), 71–90 (2016)

9. Kitchenham, B.: Procedures for performing systematic reviews. Keele University Technical report, UK, TR/SE-0401(2004), pp. 1–26 (2004)

10. Webster, J., Watson, R.T.: Analyzing the past to prepare for the future: writing a literature review. MIS Quart. **26**(2), xiii–xxiii (2002)

11. AIS: Association for Information Systems. Senior Scholars' Basket of Journals. https://aisnet.org/page/SeniorScholarBasket. Accessed 29 Jan 2019

12. de Carvalho, C.V., et al.: Digital information access for ageing persons. In: 18th International Conference on Advanced Learning Technologies (ICALT 2018), pp. 345–347. IEEE (2018)

13. Niehaves, B., Plattfaut, R.: The age-divide in private internet usage: a quantitative study of technology acceptance. In: Proceedings of 16th American Conference on Information Systems (AMCIS 2010), Paper 407 (2010)

14. Quan-Haase, A., et al.: Dividing the grey divide: deconstructing myths about older adults' online activities, skills, and attitudes. Am. Behav. Sci. **62**(9), 1207–1228 (2018)

15. Fox, G., Connolly, R.: Mobile health technology adoption across generations: narrowing the digital divide. Inf. Syst. J. **28**(6), 995–1019 (2018)

16. Niehaves, B., Plattfaut, R.: Internet adoption by the elderly: employing IS technology acceptance theories for understanding the age-related digital divide. Eur. J. Inf. Syst. **23**(6), 708–726 (2014)

17. Alam, K., Imran, S.: The digital divide and social inclusion among refugee migrants: a case in regional Australia. Inf. Technol. People **28**(2), 344–365 (2015)

18. Reisdorf, B.C., Rikard, R.V.: Digital rehabilitation: a model of reentry into the digital age. Am. Behav. Sci. **62**(9), 1273–1290 (2018)

19. Szeles, M.R.: New insights from a multilevel approach to the regional digital divide in the European Union. Telecommun. Policy **42**(6), 452–463 (2018)

20. Chipeva, P., et al.: Digital divide at individual level: evidence for Eastern and Western European countries. Gov. Inf. Quart. **35**(3), 460–479 (2018)

21. Ebermann, C., et al.: The impact of gamification-induced emotions on in-car is adoption - the difference between digital natives and digital immigrants. In: 49th Hawaii International Conference on System Sciences (HICSS 2016), pp. 1338–1347. IEEE (2016)

22. Abdelfattah, B.M., et al., Understanding the internet digital divide: an exploratory multi-nation individual-level analysis. In: Proceedings of 16th American Conference on Information Systems (AMCIS 2010), Paper 542 (2010)

23. Hsieh, J.P.-A., Rai, A., Keil, M.: Addressing digital inequality for the socioeconomically disadvantaged through government initiatives: forms of capital that affect ICT utilization. Inf. Syst. Res. **22**(2), 233–253 (2011)

24. Ghobadi, S., Ghobadi, Z.: How access gaps interact and shape digital divide: a cognitive investigation. Behav. Inf. Technol. **34**(4), 330–340 (2015)

25. Abdelfattah, B.M.: Individual-multinational study of internet use: the digital divide explained by displacement hypothesis and knowledge-gap hypothesis. In: Proceedings of 18th American Conference on Information Systems (AMCIS 2012), Paper 24 (2012)

26. Chang, S.-I., et al.: Study of the digital divide evaluation model for government agencies–a Taiwanese local government's perspective. Inf. Syst. Front. **14**(3), 693–709 (2012)
27. Racherla, P., Mandviwalla, M.: Moving from access to use of the information infrastructure: a multilevel sociotechnical framework. Inf. Syst. Res. **24**(3), 709–730 (2013)
28. Friemel, T.N.: The digital divide has grown old: determinants of a digital divide among seniors. New Media Soc. **18**(2), 313–331 (2016)

A Review of the State-of-the-Art of Assistive Technology for People with ASD in the Workplace and in Everyday Life

Lina J. Wali[1] and Filippo Sanfilippo[2]($\boxtimes$) (iD)

[1] Department of Science and Industry Systems,
University of South-Eastern Norway (USN), Post box 235,
3603 Kongsberg, Norway
[2] Department of Engineering Sciences, University of Agder (UiA),
Jon Lilletuns vei 9, 4879 Grimstad, Norway
filippo.sanfilippo@uia.no

Abstract. Autism, also known as autism spectrum disorder (ASD), is an incurable brain-based disorder that refers to a wide range of complex neurodevelopment disorders characterised by marked difficulties in communication and social skills, repetitive behaviour, highly focused interests and sensory sensitivity. Autism can present challenges for affected people at the work environment and in everyday life. The barrier for individuals with ASD increases further with changing environmental situations. Individuals with ASD have limited abilities to isolate their *Five senses* and often experience over- or under-sensitivity to sounds, touch, tastes, smells, light, colours or temperatures. In this perspective, individuals with autism may experience extraordinary challenges during a regular day for most people, especially in non-conductive crowded environments like workplaces.

This work presents a survey of the state-of-the-art implementation as well as research challenges of assisting technology for people with ASD in the workplace and in everyday life. An overview of relevant key technologies and methods is outlined by focusing both on the therapeutic perspective as well as on the technological viewpoint. The aim of this paper is to provide a better understanding of the design challenges and to identify important research directions in this increasingly important area.

Keywords: Autism · Assistive technology · ASD

1 Introduction

Once considered a rare disorder, *Autism or autism spectrum disorder* (ASD) is nowadays a major public health problem affecting about 1% of the world population [46]. Nevertheless, numerous medical research works regarding the cause, prevention, treatment and cure of ASD, the medical area is still very restricted

© IFIP International Federation for Information Processing 2019
Published by Springer Nature Switzerland AG 2019
I. O. Pappas et al. (Eds.): I3E 2019, LNCS 11701, pp. 520–532, 2019.
https://doi.org/10.1007/978-3-030-29374-1_42

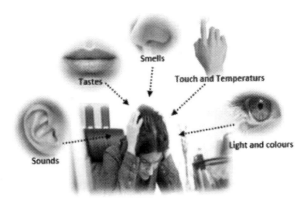

Fig. 1. The underlying idea of this work is to provide an overview of the state of the art in the area of assistive technology for people with *Autism or autism spectrum disorder* (ASD) in the workplace and in everyday life by considering different sensor channels, such as sounds, touch, tastes, smells, light, colours or temperatures.

to specific facilitation techniques and interventions [40]. As a result, there is a population of individuals with autism having a variety of ages, genders and individual needs. This variety mostly depend on different ways of facilitation in one or several areas throughout the individuals' lives. One of these areas is work or work environments where adults with ASD are facing daunting challenges. There is a good indication, that the challenges which individuals with autism face at work because of changing environmental situations are one of the causes of their remarkable unemployment rate of 80+% [19]. Employment is an essential aspect of life for individuals including those with ASD [24]. "Work facilitates economic independence, engendering a sense of purpose and accomplishment, providing opportunities for socialisation and a mechanism through which to contribute to society" [41]. Hence, an unemployment rate of 80+% of a group of people that currently constitutes 1% of the world population is very alarming. Nevertheless, in recent years, people with ASD have received improved attention from the labour market including some well-known employers such as Freddie Mac, Microsoft, SAP, Willis Towers Watson, Walgreens [23]. In parallel, there is a growing international interest in the use of assistive technology to support people with ASD and other impairments with life skills/independence [28].

Sensory sensitivity differences may be experienced by people with autism due to limited abilities to isolate their *Five senses* and often encounter over- or under-sensitivity to sounds, touch, tastes, smells, light, colours or temperatures. Therefore, individuals with autism may experience extraordinary challenges during a regular day for most people, especially in non-conductive crowded environments like workplaces. This paper aims at providing an overview of the state of the art in the area of assistive technology for people with ASD in the workplace and in everyday life by considering different sensor channels, as shown in Fig. 1. It can be extremely difficult to design technologies that fully engage the autistic user experience, especially when considering the impact of potential sensory

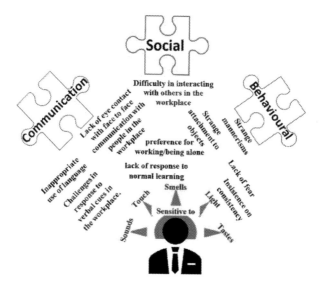

Fig. 2. Autism spectrum disorders are defined by social, communication and behavioural impairments and are associated with a range of symptoms [13].

impairments and multi-sensory integration. To support this kind of thoughtful assisting technologies, relevant key techniques and methods are presented by focusing both on the therapeutic perspective as well as on the technological viewpoint. On the basis of current trends, relevant design challenges are considered to identify the corresponding research directions in this increasingly important area.

The paper is organised as follows. A review of the related research work from a therapeutic perspective is given in Sect. 2. In Sect. 3, we focus on the description of the technological perspective. In Sect. 4, existing systems for obtaining an inclusive workplace are surveyed. A discussion is presented in Sect. 5. Finally, conclusions and future works are discussed in Sect. 6.

2 Medical Perspective

2.1 A Brief Background Related to ASD

Autism is a lifelong incurable brain-based disorder that refers to a group of complex neurodevelopment disorders resulting in a substantial burden for individuals, families and society [48]. It is primarily characterised by social-communication challenges and restricted repetitive behaviours, activities and interests [43], as shown in Fig. 2 [13].

Autism is caused by changes in the brain without knowing exactly why the changes occur. Researchers associate the development of autism to genetics and environmental factors such as infection during the pregnancy, premature birth, older age of parents and toxins in the environment [32]. However, the exact cause of autism is currently unknown, but still investigated. Different numbers are presented regarding the prevalence of ASD. According to *Centers for Disease Control and Prevention* (CDC)s' website, between 1%–2% of the world population in average has ASD [16]. Data show a steady rise of autism which has sparked fears of an autism epidemic. Only in the U.S., 1 in 59 children had a diagnosis of ASD by age 8 in 2014, a 15% increase over 2012 [16]. There are disagreements and different opinions and theories among researchers regarding the underlying cause of the more frequent occurrence of autism. According to numerous researches, the bulk of the increase stems from a growing awareness of autism and lower threshold for diagnosis, and expanded definition of ASD [47]. While according to other experts, the trend among parents in those past years of getting children in an older age is one of the causes. As the studies have shown older men and women are more likely than young ones to have a child with autism [31]. On the other hand, Dr. Stephanie Seneff, a senior research scientist at the Massachusetts Institute of Technology (MIT)'s Computer Science and Artificial Intelligence Laboratory, connects this rise to a particular toxic in the environment called Glyphosate and according to her by 2025, half the children born in the United States will be diagnosed with autism [3].

Autism occur in a spectrum, with a variety of different symptoms ranging from mild to severe, characteristics and level of intelligence quotient (IQ) as shown in Figs. 3 and 2. To help individuals with autism developing fundamental skills for good functioning throughout life, mental health professionals used to classify the autism spectrum into several different types. The primary types consisted of three groups as shown in Fig. 3:

- Asperger's syndrome. The individuals within this group, have a variety of symptoms milder than classical autism, specifically, in communication context and often tends to be normal or to above intelligent and able to handle their daily life;
- Pervasive developmental disorder not otherwise specified (PDD-NOS). The individuals within this group include the ones with more severe autism than Asperger's syndrome, but not as severe as autistic disorder;
- Autistic disorder or classical autism. This includes the same types of symptoms as Asperger's and PDD-NOS, but at a more intense level.

However, because of the confusion among professionals, family and teachers about the different types, it was concluded in 2013 to only use the term "Autism spectrum disorder" and herewith, based on their characteristics and impairments, individuals with ASD can be diagnosed as low, medium or high functioning. Regardless, it is not unusual to hear the former terms being used nowadays since the they are still widely adopted by professionals and other people in general.

The symptoms usually occur early and can be dedicated at 18 months or younger [26]. Hence, a reliable diagnosis can often be made at the age of 2 to 3. However, in many cases, the child does not receive a final diagnosis until later [2,42]. The primary cause for this is the absence of medical or lab tests

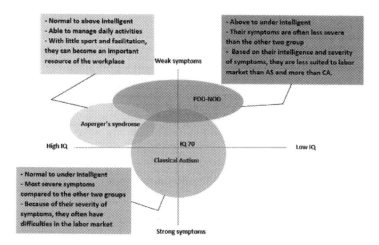

Fig. 3. The three sub-types of ASD vary in the severity of their symptoms and mental impairments [13].

for diagnosing ASD [11]. So, instead of blood tests, brain scans or any other physical tests, the mental health professionals rather depend on observations of the child and feedback from the parents or carers [11]. Besides, the fact that ASD has an extensive range of symptoms makes the diagnostic process more complex, challenging and time consuming. This is unfortunate since "a growing body of evidence supports the value of early diagnosis and treatment with evidence-based interventions, which can significantly improve the quality of life of individuals with ASD as well as of their families. Particularly noteworthy are early interventions that occur in natural surroundings and can be modified to address age-related goals throughout the lifespan" [17].

2.2   Challenges in Everyday Life and at the Workplace for People with ASD

People with autism often possess sought-after abilities and a desire to work. Also, they often have sought after valuable characteristics in the labour market such as mathematical acuity, exceptional computer skills, concentration skills, photographic and long-term memory, or tolerance for repetitive activities [21]. In addition, they tend to be known for being honest, reliable and displaying perseverance which can result productivity in the workplace. Even their impairment in social skills and communication, as shown in Fig. 2, can often lead to positive outcomes in the workplace by avoiding unnecessary social interactions [21]. Presently, there are numerous successful individuals with autism working in different areas such as math, computer science and art [10]. This proves that many other people with ASD can achieve great achievments with the right support and guidance.

However, the main challenge is the large variation of ASD due to enormous individual differences and complexities of each individual [27], as shown in Fig. 3. It is widely accepted that the heterogeneity in the functional level within ASD is greater than in other clinical groups, and that the identification of severity and additional difficulties is crucial to obtain personalised diagnoses. Addressing the challenges is therefore demanding and requires cutting edge expertise and collaboration between experts, local people and local authorities. Despite, the great variation of ASD, some of the symptoms are commonly observed among people with autism, some of which are in: cognitive and intellectual abilities, sensory processing, language and gestures, reciprocal conversation, movement and motor skills, eye contact, imagination, abstract and symbolic play, mental simulation, perception, affect and empathy, problem solving skills, executive functions, responses to sensory stimulation, adaptation to changes, generalization of learnt skills, anxiety management, cooperative working, managing phobias/fears such as loud noises, dogs, thunderstorm and vacuum cleaners, distinguishing between important and unimportant events/aspects [7]. As we can tell from the common symptoms, many of them are related to sensory challenges.

It is estimated that over 90+% of people with ASD have sensory processing disorders (SPD) [8]. In fact, hyper- or hyporeactivity to sensory input or unusual interest in sensory aspects of the environment is now included in the Diagnostic and Statistical Manual of Mental Disorders, Fifth Edition (DSM-5)'s diagnostic criteria [8]. As a result, people with autism can be susceptible to changes and disadvantaged regarding employment [44]. For many people, habits, rituals and routines are a part of everyday life including their workday. People can become uneasy if the daily routine change while individuals with autism can have an unusual or more intense reaction. The case is the same or worse when it comes to environmental changing situations. A brighter light intensity, sound or smell in the background which most people would ignore can lead to anxiety or meltdown for people with autism. This is particularly demanding when it comes to crowded environments like workplaces where individuals with autism recognise stressful situations. By avoiding these problems, people with autism can have a better life quality and much more energy and willingness to do activities of daily living including better work productivity and performance. Fortunately, there are tools dealing with different aspects of the routine or habits challenges. However, assistive tools for reducing stress and increasing situational awareness are crucially needed but still missing [37].

3   Technological Perspective

In existing literature, different works have been done to develop assistive technology interventions for people with ASD. However, they primarily focus on children, while only a few of them target adolescents or adults. Personal digital assistants (PDAs) are supported by emerging researches as assistive tools for cognition among people with various brain injuries such as intellectual disability, mental illness and Alzheimer's disease [21]. In recent years, this is motivated by the fact that PDAs such as smartphones and tablets have been developed into multi-functional devices that can incorporate advanced task managers. This makes PDAs a convenient tool for communication, a source for finding support, recording and editing videos and being a dynamic and growing source of information in academia [21]. These devices may be especially suitable for people with ASD since it is observed that people with ASD generally prefer instruction and support provided by computers rather than directly by another person [1]. Multiple studies support the use of PDAs for people with ASD at the workplace based on various strategies (e.g. time, task, task-training, social interactions and behavioural management) used in school and transitional settings [21].

Further, various studies confirm the challenges for people with ASD due to environmental changes and how they negatively affect their work performance and productivity. Some works suggest the idea that people with neurological conditions can be successfully supported by smart homes. This approach assumes that the needs and aspirations of people with ASD from the technological interventions are fully understood and integrated in the design [14]. However, the current approaches that can provide a customised work environment such as smart buildings or cities are both complex and expensive [22]. In contrast, there are some inexpensive assistive systems such as noise blocking, active noise cancelling (ANC), or noise reduction headphones [34]. These systems are widely used by people with ASD in the workplace and in everyday life. A brief description of each of them along with a comparison of advantages and disadvantages from the perspective of an individual with autism is depicted in[1].

4   Existing Systems for an Inclusive Workplace

Instead of isolating, an inclusive workplace is a work environment where the individuals are valued, integrated and included within their work force independently of their gender, background, religion and disability. Assistive technology can have a remarkable contribution to the inclusion of people with disability in the workplace. Thus, research in this area is essential for developing new assistive technologies for obtaining an inclusive workplace. In this perspective, supporting sensory needs in the workplace among people with ASD is of primary importance. There is a good body of literature and research that show how people with autism face challenges regarding sensory sensitivity [12,33]. However, research about coping strategies and assistive technology used in the workplace is still limited.

Relevant studies related to different sensory channels are outlined in the following of this section. Challenges, missing gap and further proposals of different technological strategies that have potential for successful implementation in a conductive workplace are grouped according to the different senses and presented. Finally, a review of the current promising assistive robotics technologies for interventions in an inclusive workplace is also outlined.

---

[1] https://medium.com/musings-from-mars/headphones-f1b64cfae7d1.

4.1 Touch

People with autism often tend to be sensitive to touch or close contact. This includes animals, food plants, textiles, other objects/materials and especially contact with other people. Thus, it is often easier for individuals with autism to relate to technological devices instead of direct contact with other people. In this context, the use of technological devices like computers, tablets and smart phones has been essential in many areas such as entertainment, education or school and therapeutically purposes. However, research on the use of this technology by workers with ASD is slight [20,21]. According to the literature, this technology is primarily adopted for autistic children. A few studies show positive outcomes of using iPads and iPods as an assistive technology for autistic adults and adolescents [9,25,29]. A few works [20,21] in this field focus on the use of a tablet as an assisive technology in the workplace. According to the work presented in [20], "Reducing the need for personal supports among workers with autism using an iPod touch as an assistive technology delayed randomised control trial". According to the same study, workers among the 50 autistic participants who were trained to use iPods in the beginning of their job required significant fewer hours of job coaching support. However, the participants in this study consisted of only high functioning adults with no intellectual, verbal communication or severe sensitive impairment.

4.2 Eye Sight

Individuals with autism often suffer from light sensitivity regardless of whether its source is natural or artificial. Sustained exposure to visual stimuli may cause pain, headache and in worst cases meltdown. Concentration challenges is also reported when exposed to fluorescent lighting or bright sunlight [6]. From a visual perspective, computerised smartglasses are being developed as an assistive technology for daily activities for children and adults with autism spectrum disorder (ASD) [36]. While smartglasses may be able to help with educational and behavioral needs, their usability and acceptability for children with ASD is largely unknown. Even less it is known when considering the workplace environment.

4.3 Sound

When considering sound, remote-microphone (RM) technology is employed to facilitate self-hearing [30] and distance communication [39]. The individual and group data from the last study suggest that RM technology may improve auditory function in children with ASD. However, no studies have been performed regarding the workplace environment to the best of the authors' knowledge. To complement this aspect, sensory headphones (sound blocking, active noise cancelling (ANC), or noise reduction headphones) are also adopted. Even though these devices are generally inexpensive, there are several drawbacks, such as feedback not available, no data shearing features, the possibility that individuals can feel overwhelmed while wearing them.

4.4 Taste

Regarding the sense of taste, only a few studies can be found in the literature. In [4], olfactory and taste functioning in individuals with autism were considered to characterise chemosensory processing. In general, this aspect may be also relevant when considering the workplace of people with ASD during breaks or lunches.

4.5 Smell

When considering smell, a mechanistic link between olfaction and ASD is proven in [35]. This aspect my be very relevant when considering specific workplaces, such as food manufactures or chemical manufacturers.

4.6 Multi-sensor Channels

The barriers to inclusion at the workplace for people with ASD may increase further with changing environmental situations. Deviations in multi-sensor channels may lead to increased stress. The intervention plans to instill positive behaviour support (PBS) suggest that a customised environment can minimise the impacts due to these variations. In this perspective, our research team previously proposed a novel framework which leverages the information from multi-sensor channels in a combined manner to customise the environment so that situational awareness (SA) can be improved [37]. The proposed framework allows for monitoring the environment by combining the information from different sensor channels including both personal sensors (i.e. on board of a mobile device) as well as environmental sensors/actuators (i.e. embedded in smart-buildings). In this preliminary work, a case study was considered through the development of a prototype for a mobile application and by reporting results on a scale model of a smart workplace with customisable environment.

4.7 Robotics Technologies for Interventions in an Inclusive Workplace

Robots have been shown to provoke proactive social behaviour in individuals with ASD, especially with children [15,18,38]. Robot therapy for autism has been explored as one of the first application domains in the field of socially assistive robotics (SAR), which aims at developing robots that assist people with special needs through social interactions [38]. Regarding multi-sensorial stimuli, an interactive robotic framework that delivers emotional and social behaviours for multi-sensory therapy for children with autism spectrum disorders was presented in [5]. The framework comprises emotion-based robotic gestures and facial expressions, as well as vision and audio-based monitoring system for quantitative measurement of the interaction. Special aspects of interacting with children with autism with multi-sensory stimuli and the potentials for personalised therapies for social and behavioural learning were considered. However, research on the use of this technology by workers with ASD is still slight. This technology has great potential, especially when considering to combine it with the previously mentioned technologies.

5   Discussion

The most common existing assistive technologies for people with ASD in the workplace can mainly be divided in to two groups. The first group include PDAs and is mostly used for the purpose of reducing the need of personal sport and being able to manage different tasks independently. PDAs are pocket-size, easily accessible and economical when compared to other solutions. There are numerous features and several apps [45] which can turn the device in to a personal assistive technology device based on their needs. However, the learning process of people with ASD when using them might be both time-consuming and costly for the employer. In addition, research about their affect for adolescents or adults in the workplace and in everyday life is limited [20].

On the other had, the second group includes a few approaches and solutions to deal with environmental changing situation to improve productivity of individuals with autism at the workplace and in everyday life. One of the most promising approach that could turn the office workplace into a customised conductive workplace is the development of smart building or cities, but this is both complex and expensive. The other solutions, such as the sensory headphones, are more economical and easy to develop from a technical point of view. However, they are only based on one sense (the hearing sense), provide no feedback data, have no data sharing features and therefore cannot provide a conductive work environment for people with ASD.

6   Conclusion

In this work, an overview of the state of the art of technological solutions for assisting people with autism spectrum disorder (ASD) in the day-to-day work was presented by considering different sensor channels. Relevant key technologies and methods were presented by focusing both on the therapeutic perspective as well as on the technological viewpoint. Relevant design challenges were considered to identify the corresponding research directions in this increasingly important area. When considering the current solutions and works in the area, there is a remarkable gap of research and there is little evidence to suggest that all individuals with ASD have access to appropriate assistive technologies.

Assistive technology for people with ASD in the workplace and in everyday life is still at its infancy. However, there are strong results which can be used to build further upon from both a therapeutic perspective as well as on the technological viewpoint. One of the fundamental targets of this paper is to further increase efforts world-wide on realising the large variety of application possibilities offered by the current technology as a stepping-stone for new research and development within this field. This effort is also supported by our ongoing research [37].

References

1. Aliee, Z.S., Jomhari, N., Rezaei, R., Alias, N.: The effectiveness of managing split attention among autistic children using computer based intervention. Turk. Online J. Educ. Technol.-TOJET **12**(2), 281–302 (2013)
2. Barbaro, J., Dissanayake, C.: Autism spectrum disorders in infancy and toddlerhood: a review of the evidence on early signs, early identification tools, and early diagnosis. J. Dev. Behav. Pediatr. **30**(5), 447–459 (2009)
3. Beecham, J.E., Seneff, S.: Is there a link between autism and glyphosate-formulated herbicides? J. Autism **3**(1), 1 (2016)
4. Bennetto, L., Kuschner, E.S., Hyman, S.L.: Olfaction and taste processing in autism. Biol. Psychiatry **62**(9), 1015–1021 (2007)
5. Bevill, R., et al.: Interactive robotic framework for multi-sensory therapy for children with autism spectrum disorder. In: Proceedings of the 11th ACM/IEEE International Conference on Human-Robot Interaction (HRI), pp. 421–422 (2016)
6. Bogdashina, O.: Sensory Perceptual Issues in Autism and Asperger Syndrome: Different Sensory Experiences-Different Perceptual Worlds. Jessica Kingsley Publishers, London (2016)
7. Bozgeyikli, L., Raij, A., Katkoori, S., Alqasemi, R.: A survey on virtual reality for individuals with autism spectrum disorder: design considerations. IEEE Trans. Learn. Technol. **11**(2), 133–151 (2018)
8. Chang, Y.S., et al.: Autism and sensory processing disorders: shared white matter disruption in sensory pathways but divergent connectivity in social-emotional pathways. PloS One **9**(7), e103038 (2014)
9. Coffin, A.B., Myles, B.S., Rogers, J., Szakacs, W.: Supporting the writing skills of individuals with autism spectrum disorder through assistive technologies. In: Cardon, T.A. (ed.) Technology and the Treatment of Children with Autism Spectrum Disorder. ACPS, pp. 59–73. Springer, Cham (2016). https://doi.org/10.1007/978-3-319-20872-5_6
10. Connect, L.: 20 incredibly successful people on the autism spectrum. https://www.abadegreeprograms.net/successful-people-on-the-autism-spectrum/. Accessed 17 Oct 2018
11. Connect, L.: Screening & diagnosis. https://www.cdc.gov/ncbddd/autism/screening.html. Accessed 17 Oct 2018
12. Corbett, B.A., Schupp, C.W., Levine, S., Mendoza, S.: Comparing cortisol, stress, and sensory sensitivity in children with autism. Autism Res. **2**(1), 39–49 (2009)
13. Lichtenstein, D.: Behind the autism spectrum (2014). https://www.scienceinschool.org/2012/issue24/autism
14. Dewsbury, G., Linskell, J.: Smart home technology for safety and functional independence: the UK experience. NeuroRehabilitation **28**(3), 249–260 (2011)
15. Dickstein-Fischer, L.A., Crone-Todd, D.E., Chapman, I.M., Fathima, A.T., Fischer, G.S.: Socially assistive robots: current status and future prospects for autism interventions. Innov. Entrepreneurship Health **5**, 15 (2018)
16. Center for Disease Control and Prevention: Data & statistics (2019). https://www.cdc.gov/ncbddd/autism/data.html. Accessed 17 Oct 2018
17. Elder, J.H., Kreider, C.M., Brasher, S.N., Ansell, M.: Clinical impact of early diagnosis of autism on the prognosis and parent-child relationships. Psychol. Res. Behav. Manag. **10**, 283 (2017)

18. Feil-Seifer, D., Matarić, M.J.: Toward socially assistive robotics for augmenting interventions for children with autism spectrum disorders. In: Khatib, O., Kumar, V., Pappas, G.J. (eds.) Experimental Robotics. Springer Tracts in Advanced Robotics, vol. 54, pp. 201–210. Springer, Heidelberg (2009). https://doi.org/10.1007/978-3-642-00196-3_24

19. Frank, F., et al.: Education and employment status of adults with autism spectrum disorders-a cross-sectional-survey. BMC Psychiatry 18(1), 75 (2018)

20. Gentry, T., Kriner, R., Sima, A., McDonough, J., Wehman, P.: Reducing the need for personal supports among workers with autism using an iPod touch as an assistive technology: delayed randomized control trial. J. Autism Dev. Disord. 45(3), 669–684 (2015)

21. Gentry, T., Lau, S., Molinelli, A., Fallen, A., Kriner, R.: The Apple iPod touch as a vocational support aid for adults with autism: three case studies. J. Vocat. Rehabil. 37(2), 75–85 (2012)

22. Hancke, G.P., Hancke Jr., G.P., et al.: The role of advanced sensing in smart cities. Sensors 13(1), 393–425 (2012)

23. Nezich, H.: More companies hiring employees with autism spectrum disorder (2017). http://www.who.int/mediacentre/factsheets/fs282/fr/. Accessed 25 Oct 2018

24. Hendricks, D.: Employment and adults with autism spectrum disorders: challenges and strategies for success. J. Vocat. Rehabil. 32(2), 125–134 (2010)

25. Hillier, A., Greher, G., Queenan, A., Marshall, S., Kopec, J.: Music, technology and adolescents with autism spectrum disorders: the effectiveness of the touch screen interface. Music Educ. Res. 18(3), 269–282 (2016)

26. Johnson, C.P., Myers, S.M., et al.: Identification and evaluation of children with autism spectrum disorders. Pediatrics 120(5), 1183–1215 (2007)

27. Lombroso, P.J., Ogren, M.P., Jones, W., Klin, A.: Heterogeneity and homogeneity across the autism spectrum: the role of development. J. Am. Acad. Child Adolesc. Psychiatry 48(5), 471–473 (2009)

28. Mintz, J., Gyori, M., Aagaard, M.: Touching the Future Technology for Autism? Lessons from the HANDS Project, vol. 15. IOS Press (2012)

29. Nepo, K., Tincani, M., Axelrod, S., Meszaros, L.: iPod touch® to increase functional communication of adults with autism spectrum disorder and significant intellectual disability. Focus Autism Other Dev. Disabil. 32(3), 209–217 (2017)

30. Ni Chuileann, S.J., Quigley, J.: Recognizing voice: the child with autism spectrum disorder. J. Assistive Technol. 10(3), 140–152 (2016)

31. Parner, E.T., et al.: Parental age and autism spectrum disorders. Ann. Epidemiol. 22(3), 143–150 (2012)

32. Ratajczak, H.V.: Theoretical aspects of autism: causes-a review. J. Immunotoxicol. 8(1), 68–79 (2011)

33. Robertson, A.E., Simmons, D.R.: The relationship between sensory sensitivity and autistic traits in the general population. J. Autism Dev. Disord. 43(4), 775–784 (2013)

34. Rowe, C., Candler, C., Neville, M.: Noise reduction headphones and autism: a single case study. J. Occup. Ther. Schools Early Interv. 4(3–4), 229–235 (2011)

35. Rozenkrantz, L., et al.: A mechanistic link between olfaction and autism spectrum disorder. Curr. Biol. 25(14), 1904–1910 (2015)

36. Sahin, N.T., Keshav, N.U., Salisbury, J.P., Vahabzadeh, A.: Second version of google glass as a wearable socio-affective aid: positive school desirability, high usability, and theoretical framework in a sample of children with autism. JMIR Hum. Factors 5(1), e1 (2018)

37. Sanfilippo, F., Raja, K.: A multi-sensor system for enhancing situational awareness and stress management for people with ASD in the workplace and in everyday life. In: Proceedings of the 52nd Hawaii International Conference on System Sciences (HICSS 2019), Maui, Hawaii, United States of America, pp. 4079–4086 (2019)
38. Scassellati, B., Admoni, H., Matarić, M.: Robots for use in autism research. Ann. Rev. Biomed. Eng. **14**, 275–294 (2012)
39. Schafer, E.C., et al.: Assistive technology evaluations: remote-microphone technology for children with autism spectrum disorder. J. Commun. Disord. **64**, 1–17 (2016)
40. Schall, C.M.: Positive behavior support: supporting adults with autism spectrum disorders in the workplace. J. Voc. Rehabil. **32**(2), 109–115 (2010)
41. Scott, M., Falkmer, M., Falkmer, T., Girdler, S.: Evaluating the effectiveness of an autism-specific workplace tool for employers: a randomised controlled trial. J. Autism Dev. Disord. **48**, 1–16 (2018)
42. Shattuck, P.T., et al.: Timing of identification among children with an autism spectrum disorder: findings from a population-based surveillance study. J. Am. Acad. Child Adolesc. Psychiatry **48**(5), 474–483 (2009)
43. Texas Health and Human Services Commission: What is autism spectrum disorder? (2016). https://hhs.texas.gov/services/disability/autism/what-autism-spectrum-disorder. Accessed 9 Oct 2018
44. Tomczak, M., Wójcikowski, M., Listewnik, P., Pankiewicz, B., Majchrowicz, D., Jdrzejewska-Szczerska, M.: Support for employees with asd in the workplace using a bluetooth skin resistance sensor-a preliminary study. Sensors **18**(10), 3530 (2018)
45. Alcoholics Anonymous of Western Australia: Autismapps. https://www.autism apps.org.au/. Accessed 17 Oct 2018
46. World Health Organisation: Facts and statistics (2014). http://www.who.int/mediacentre/factsheets/fs282/fr/. Accessed 30 Oct 2018
47. Wright, J.: The real reasons autism rates are up in the US (2017). https://www.scientificamerican.com/article/the-real-reasons-autism-rates-are-up-in-the-u-s/. Accessed 17 Oct 2018
48. Xu, G., Strathearn, L., Liu, B., Bao, W.: Prevalence of autism spectrum disorder among US children and adolescents, 2014–2016. Jama **319**(1), 81–82 (2018)

Understanding the Value of Using Smartphones for Older Adults in China: A Value-Focused Thinking Approach

Shang Gao[1(✉)] ⓘ, Ying Li[2], and Hong Guo[3]

[1] School of Business, Örebro University, Örebro, Sweden
shang.gao@oru.se
[2] School of Business Administration,
Zhongnan University of Economics and Law, Wuhan, China
liying0912@qq.com
[3] Department of Computer Science,
Norwegian University of Science and Technology, Trondheim, Norway
homekuo@gmail.com

Abstract. This study aims to explore the values of using smartphones in older adults' daily lives in China. The value of using smartphones can be seen as the benefits associated with the use of smartphones in peoples' daily activities. By employing the Value-Focused Thinking (VFT) approach, this study investigates what fundamental objectives and means objectives are important with the daily use of smartphones for older adults in China. Based on the data collected from the interviews, we developed a means-ends objective network describing the values of using smartphones for older adults in China. According to the results, maximizing well-being, maximizing life efficiency, maximizing safety, and maximizing digital inclusion are identified as the fundamental objectives to maximize values of using smartphones for older adults in China.

Keywords: Using smartphones · Older adults ·
The Value-Focused Thinking (VFT) approach · Means-ends objective network ·
Value

1 Introduction

Today, smartphones have become an inseparable part of peoples' daily lives. A smart phone is a mobile phone with more advanced computing capability and connectivity than basic feature phones (e.g., calling, texting). It allows users to make mobile shopping, make mobile payments, watch videos, and so on. Smartphones have the potential to enhance the quality of peoples' lives [8, 9]. For instance, smartphones come with social network functionality built in, which enable users to keep in touch with their friends and relatives on different social media sites (e.g., Twitter, Facebook, Wechat [7], and Instagram). Moreover, smartphones also come with music and video players built in, which enable users to listen to their favorite music, and watch video clips and TV shows. In [22], the authors found that using smartphones could enhance older adults' ability in different physical, mental, and social dimensions of life through

© IFIP International Federation for Information Processing 2019
Published by Springer Nature Switzerland AG 2019
I. O. Pappas et al. (Eds.): I3E 2019, LNCS 11701, pp. 533–544, 2019.
https://doi.org/10.1007/978-3-030-29374-1_43

enhancing their knowledge, facilitating their communication with friends, enabling their participation in social networks, and so on.

Most countries in the world are experiencing an increase in terms of the medium age of population. The ageing of the population is one of the major challenges most countries have to face over the next few decades [23]. Although the Internet and smartphones are playing increasingly important roles in connecting people of all ages to news, information and services, older adults face challenges when they are using smartphones. There are barriers to older adults' use of mobile phones, including the lack of computer literacy, economic barriers, and privacy concerns. The term older adult has been defined in a variety of ways in different articles, which ranges from over 40 to over 75. The distinction of "older" depends upon the specific context under consideration. We defined older adult as people over the age of 65 in this study.

Although some previous studies (e.g., [11, 16]) have been reported on various benefits of using smartphones, little is known about the values of using smartphones from the perspectives of ageing population in China. Most previous research tended to focus on the use and adoption of smartphones [13, 14], and application development on smartphones (e.g., [21]). One of the effective ways in gaining a better understanding of the use of smartphones by older adults is to identify the values of using smartphones by engaging older smartphones users. This research intends to bridge the research gap in the values of using smartphones among older adults in China.

The objective of this study is to explore the values of using smartphones for older adults in China. The proposed research question is: what are the values of using smartphones for old adults. To address this, we employed the value-focused thinking (VFT) to identify the values of using smartphones with older adults in China. This is helpful to make the use of smartphones for older adults with maximized values.

The rest of the paper is organized as follows. We present the literature review in Sect. 2. Section 3 illustrates the research method. Section 4 describes the application of the methodology and results of this study. We discuss the findings of the study in Sect. 5. Section 6 concludes this research and points out some future research directions.

2   Literature Review

The literature related to this research is discussed in this section.

2.1   Aging Society in China

Due to the effects of one child policy in China, China's population is growing old at a faster rate than almost all other countries. The percentage of Chinese above the retirement age (i.e., 60 years old) is expected to reach 39 percent of the population by 2050. Various technologies are being designed to enhance older adults' quality of life [4]. Among the various kinds of new technologies, the smartphone is the one of most commonly used products by older adults in their daily lives. Smartphones can be a powerful tool to tackle some challenges of older adults [1]. Smartphones are able to provide personalized health care and social services for older adults. However, the use of new technologies is not straightforward for older adults. For instance, it was found that anxiety was associated with using smartphones [6].

2.2   Research on the Use of Smartphones

Research work has been carried out by researchers in studying various aspects related to the use and adoption of smartphones [10]. In [3], Chen et al. combined TAM [5] and innovation diffusion theory (IDT) [25] to study and explain the adoption of smartphones in logistics. Self-efficacy was a strong predictor of behavioral intention through attitude. Based on a study on the performance of mobile applications, Huang et al. [15] indicated that smartphones could become a suitable substitute of traditional computers. But, the performance of the applications on smartphones is poorly understood.

Although significant effort has been done to explore the use and adoption of smartphones, there are not many studies on the values of using smartphones for older adults. The samples used in previous research are relatively young. In [26], Sheng et al., examined the values of the use of mobile technology in a leading publishing company by interviewing 12 sales representatives and district managers from the publishing company. Concerning the research on the use of new technologies by older adults, most previous research [29] tends to focus on the use and adoption of computers and Internet by older adults. Lee et al. [19] examined users' constraints of using computers at various age stages.

An examination of the current literature reveals that few studies have addressed the use and adoption of smartphones by older adults. Pheeraphuttharangkoon et al. [24] investigated the use and adoption of smartphones with older adults in the UK. However, the sample size with people over 50 years old was quite small in their study. In [13], the authors explored the adoption of smartphones with older adults in China and found that social influence, observability, compatibility, performance expectancy and perceived enjoyment, were important determinants for the use and adoption of smartphones with older adults in China.

Despite the increasing attention on the adoption of smartphones with older adults, there is few studies focusing on the values of using smartphones with older adults. Therefore, to bridge the research gap, this study aims to investigate the values of using smartphones from the perspectives of older adults in China.

3   Research Methodology

The value focused thinking approach is a decision technique and defines a method which can help identify values and structure the identified values systematically [18]. These objectives which are of concern by users during the decision-making process make up the value portfolio. It offers the preconditions of each decision from decision-makers' perspectives [17]. VFT approach can reach a means-ends objective network of fundamental objectives and means objectives.

In this study, we aim to get insights of the essential activities that must occur to maximize the values of using smartphones from the perspectives of older adults in China. Therefore, it is believed that VFT is an appropriate approach to address the research question. The VFT approach has been applied to the research in information systems, such as creativity in understanding users' privacy and security concerns with

SNS [2], understanding the values of MOOCs in education from students' perspectives [12], the values of live game streaming [30], the values of blockchain based games [20], and strategic implications of mobile technology [26].

The VFT approach is chosen to answer the proposed research question 'what are the values of using smartphones from the perspectives of older adults in China?' and to assist in identifying value objectives.

The application of the VFT methodology in exploring older adults' perspectives on the value of using smartphones can result in a value map which helps us understand their user behavior and promote the digitalization among them. The VFT approach is designed to identify what is important and how this can be achieved as it focuses on what the decision-maker cares about [17, 26].

In this study, we employ VFT approach as follows (see Fig. 1):

Step 1: Identify older adults. According to the defined age for older adults in Sect. 1, we choose people more than 65 years old as our interviewees and gather information about the value estimated by them to help us gain an insight of the use of smartphones among them.

Step 2: Develop a list of the initial value objectives and convert them into a common form. Several techniques such as wish lists, problems, shortcomings, and alternatives can help conclude the possible objectives from the insights and make them easier to comprehend.

Step 3: Identify the objectives and distinguish the fundamental objectives from means objectives. Fundamental objectives are the ends that decision makers valued in a specified context, while means objectives are methods to reach the ends. In the process of distinguish means objectives from fundamental objectives and build their relationships, Keeney suggested using the question "why is that important" [18]. For each value objectives, the question will result into two types of possible responses. One is that this objective is one of the essential reasons for interest in the situation, and it is the fundamental for decision making. That is called fundamental objective. Another response is that the objective is important because of its implications for other objectives, which is called means objectives [28].

Step 4: Build the means-end objective network on the basis of the third step. The network provides a model describing the specified relationships between fundamental objectives and means objectives. According to this, analysts could find out how fundamental objectives can be achieved via means objectives. And the relationships presented in the network can help analysts better understand the complex value system of decision makers.

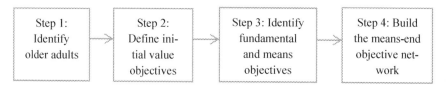

Fig. 1. Steps of VFT approach

4 Application of the Methodology

4.1 Data Collection

The data were collected from face to face interviews conducted from 15th January 2019 to 31st January 2019 in two cities in two different provinces in China. We sent interview invitations to twenty older adults in China who had some experience in using smartphones during the first week of January 2019. Eleven of them agreed to participate in the research and the face to face interviews were recorded. The VFT approach was applied to discover the values of using smartphones from the perspectives of older adults in China.

All participants were more than 65 years old who had some experience in using smartphones. Thus, it is believed that the interviewees were aware of the use of smartphones and would have some thoughts to be shared regarding the values of using smartphones.

4.2 Identifying the Value Objectives

By following the VFT approach, we interviewed the participants with the probing questions below:

"What are the benefits of using smartphones, and why is that important?"
"What difficulties have you experienced in using smartphones?"
"What kind of supports have you received to use smartphones?"
"Do you have some expectations on using smartphones?"

By asking these questions, we primarily discovered the objectives of older adults' usage of smartphones and formed an initial list of objectives. Then, we asked participants "why is that important" to get a further understanding of the initial list of objectives. The interviewees needed to consider and review the decision of using smartphones and the whole process. Until they have arrived at the most important value, fundamental objectives could be seized and distinguish fundamental objectives from means objectives. Objectives can be classified into means objectives and fundamental objectives. Means objectives contributed to the achievement of fundamental objectives. Finally, a means-end objective network was draw to present the relationships between these objectives.

4.3 The Fundamental Objectives and Means Objectives

Two researchers firstly conducted coding of four interviews, and identified fundamental objectives and means objectives from the interview material independently. Then the coding results had been compared, with 90% of the coding in the same. Some ambiguities caused by oral and written expression had been discussed. After an agreement was reached, one researcher coded the remaining data from the interviews. Once all coding has been completed, three researchers reviewed all the coding results to merge duplicate values and remove the extra values. The results of the identification of value objectives were showed in Table 1.

Table 1. The fundamental objectives

Fundamental objectives	Evidences from the interviews
Maximize well-being	• I enjoy the interactions with my relatives and friends using various applications on smartphones • I achieve a sense of fulfillment due to the use of smartphones
Maximize life efficiency	• I can check the time and weather on the phone which help me better plan my daily activities • I can pay bills and shop online with the Ali-pay and Wechat which are convenient and can save my time
Maximize safety	• When I hang out, I can use my smartphone to tell my children where I am and what I am doing to make sure that I am safe • By checking the weather by using smartphones, I can avoid going out in a bad weather condition
Maximize digital inclusion	• I want to integrate into the digital society by using smartphones • My children and my friends help me using smartphones

Maximize Well-Being. Improving the well-being of older adults is the ultimate goal of the whole society. It involves the effort from the society, governments and individuals. Using smartphones enables older adults to engage in more activities, gain more practical information, and receive more cares from others. Older adults living apart from their children would cause many potential social problems. For instance, older adults may suffer intense loneliness. Using smartphones would help them diminish their loneliness and enjoy their lives in the society.

Maximize Life Efficiency. Using smartphones among older adults is becoming more and more common in China although there are still many problems to be addressed. It offers many useful features for older adults. For example, they can check the time and weather on the phone, which help them better plan their daily activities. What's more, as the mobile payment getting more and more popular in China, old adults are encouraged to use mobile payments when possible. And some older adults also do mobile shopping with the assistance from others. The use of smartphones increases their life efficiency.

Maximize Safety. Health problem is one of the most important issues among older adults living independently. Their children would like to pay close attention to their health conditions and daily routines. Older adults can reach their children easily by using application on smartphones. For example, older adults can inform their children via sending instant voice messages by using smartphones. The location information of older adults can be tracked by using location-based applications on smartphones.

Maximize Digital Inclusion. The use of smartphones can be seen as a mean to help older adults integrate into the digital society. Along with the development and advancement of digital technologies, there are many concerns with the use and adoption of smartphones among older adults. The data collected from the interviews also indicated that the social influence from others gave impetus to the efforts toward the digital inclusion.

The means objectives are the ways to achieve the fundamental objectives. From the initial means objectives, we did another coding to assure the result is detailed and without any redundancy. Table 2 summarizes 12 means objectives and evidences from the interviews.

Table 2. The means objectives

Means objectives	Evidences from the interviews
Customize apps for older adults	• There are many features I never use on my smartphone • I wish there would be more voice-enabled mobile applications
Assure user-friendly interface	• When using a smartphone, text on the screen are too small and I always find it difficult to see the text • The ringtone volume on my smartphone is too low so that sometimes I would miss the phone call
Reduce language barriers	• I grew up during the period where education was hardly offered in China • Since I am unable to read the text message, I prefer to receive voice messages via applications on my smartphone
Simplify the operation	• I cannot always remember how to operate the apps on my smartphone in an appropriate manner • The operation of smartphone is too complex for older adults like me, for example, to run an application, I have to touch screen several times
Receive help from others	• My grandchildren helped me use my smartphone • When I have questions on the use of smartphones, my children can give me assistance
Meet needs from older adults	• Nowadays, it is difficult to find interesting TV programs for older adults on TV. However, I can find my favorite operas in different video applications on my smartphones • There are many applications on my smartphone that I never use while sometimes I cannot find what I need on my smartphone
Enable easier to use	• Touching screen is not easy to use. I prefer to have a smartphone with a physical keyboard • Straightforward operations on a smartphone would motivate me to have a continuous intention to use the smartphone
Increase communication	• Using smartphones enables me to communicate with my relatives and friends more frequently • I can talk with my relatives and friends quite often by using application on my smartphone
Enrich activities for older adults	• My friends often organize activities by posting group messages on Wechat • I often listen to music and watch videos in various applications on my smartphone
Get information from multiple sources	• I can read news and feeds by using applications on my smartphone • I can be informed with important and useful information via various apps on my smartphone

(continued)

Table 2. (*continued*)

Means objectives	Evidences from the interviews
Minimize loneliness	• I can share my moments and daily activities easily with my relatives and friends via Wechat on my smartphone. Thus, I feel being socially connected with them • When I am alone or boring, I often check posting from my relatives and friends on Wechat
Maximize care	• My children often message me via apps to show their care • Although my children don't live in the same city with me, they often talk to me by making video calls via their smartphones

4.4   The Means-Ends Objective Network

Based on the identified fundamental objectives and means objectives structured in this study and the relationship between the two types of objectives, a means-ends objective network was developed (see Fig. 2) [27]. The developed network indicated that using smartphones was able to provide many values for older adults in China although there were some barriers for older adults to use smartphones in an efficient manner. Using smartphones provides a new opportunity for older adults to be connected in the digital society. It helps them strengthen the tie with their relatives and friends. Moreover, it also helps them engage in different online communities. There are many hobby groups for older adults on Wechat, such as dancing groups and hiking groups. They can use Wechat on their smartphones to organize different activities. In addition, they are able

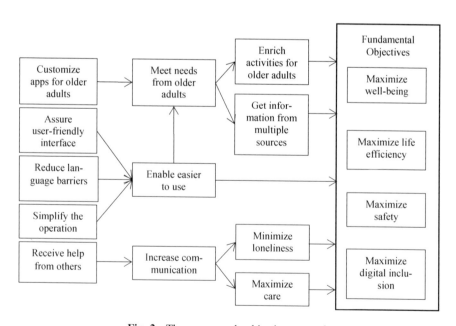

Fig. 2. The means-ends objective network

to keep updated with or subscribe the latest news by using different apps on their smartphones. Besides this, some older adults have enthusiasm to learn skills with the use of smartphones (e.g., using mobile shopping and mobile payment) which enable them to keep connected with the new technologies.

5 Discussion on the Findings

This study used a qualitative research approach to understand the values of using smartphones from older adults' perspectives in China (e.g., what do older adults expect with the use of smartphones), and developed a means-ends objective network that depicts these values and their relationships. This study contributed to the literature on the use of smartphones. It contributed to the existing literature on using VFT approach to explore the values of using smartphones for older adults in China.

Some features of smartphones need to be further enhanced. Older adults did not use many apps on their smartphones in a right manner although many apps were designed to make their lives' easier, safer and more efficient. It helps them enrich their retirement life and improve their well-beings. For instance, there were many apps on the smartphones that were not used by older adults, such as healthcare applications and fitness applications, which aimed to help older adults manage their health conditions. But these values were nearly never indicated in the interviews with older adults.

Along with the development of new digital technologies, some older adults were under the social pressure to keep up to date with the digitalization and increase their digital inclusion. Various assistances from people around older adults have an important role in promoting the use of smartphones among older adults. This is in line with the findings in [24]. It can help them reduce social pressure and eliminate the difficulties with the use of smartphones.

The findings from this research also offered some practical implications. It is important to get older adults involved in the development of applications on smartphones. The results indicated that older adults were interested in using smartphones. They wanted the developed applications on smartphones easier to use. Thus, it is believed that they want to express their opinions on the developed applications on smartphones before using them. Furthermore, the governmental sectors need to work on more initiatives on helping older adults using smartphones. Most respondents in this study wanted to be included in the digital society. However, some of them were not good at using smartphones. If the governmental sectors can organize some training sessions for using smartphones in older adults' communities, it would facilitate the learning process of using smartphones for older adults. As a result, it would be more likely to maximize the values of using smartphones for older adults. The social security service sectors can invest additional resources in developing customized information-oriented applications for older adults on smartphones. Then, it would be easier for older adults to get access relative information on their smartphones.

6 Conclusion and Future Research

This study investigated the values of using smartphones in peoples' daily lives from the perspectives of older adults in China by using VFT approach. Based on the data collected from the interviews, we developed a means-ends objective network describing the values of using smartphones for older adults in China. The developed network included twelve means objectives and four fundamental objectives. The results indicated that using smartphones for older adults in China entailed fundamental objectives such as increased well-being, increased digital inclusion, increased awareness of safety, and increased life efficiency. The derived fundamental objectives in this study can serve as factors in assessing the success of using smartphones in older adults' daily lives in China.

We are also aware of some limitations of this study. The sample size of this study was quite small. Therefore, the generalizability of the results to other users remains to be determined. Secondly, the participants of this study were only from two provinces in China. Although they can represent older adult users of smartphones to some extent, they may not reflect the total population of older adults in China. Thirdly, the process of identifying values might be subjective. And there might be a potential age-gap between the interviewers and the interviewees. Last but not least, there are other possible research methodologies could be used to examine the values of using smartphones for older adults.

We plan to refine the means-ends objective network by collecting additional data from older adults in China. Furthermore, we also plan to expand the research by identifying the values of using smartphones from older adults' perspectives in some other countries.

References

1. Barnard, Y., Bradley, M.D., Hodgson, F., et al.: Learning to use new technologies by older adults: perceived difficulties, experimentation behaviour and usability. Comput. Hum. Behav. **29**(4), 1715–1724 (2013)
2. Barrett-Maitland, N., Barclay, C., Osei-Bryson, K.-M.: Security in social networking services: a value-focused thinking exploration in understanding users' privacy and security concerns. Inf. Technol. Dev. **22**(3), 464–486 (2016)
3. Chen, J.V., Yen, D.C., Chen, K.: The acceptance and diffusion of the innovative smart phone use: a case study of a delivery service company in logistics. Inf. Manag. **46**(4), 241–248 (2009)
4. Chen, K., Chan, A.H.: The ageing population of China and a review of gerontechnology. Gerontechnology **10**(2), 63–71 (2011)
5. Davis, F.D.: Perceived usefulness, perceived ease of use and user acceptance of information technology. MIS Q. **13**(3), 319–340 (1989)
6. Elhai, J.D., Levine, J.C., Dvorak, R.D., et al.: Fear of missing out, need for touch, anxiety and depression are related to problematic smartphone use. Comput. Hum. Behav. **63**, 509–516 (2016)

7. Gao, S., Krogstie, J.: Understanding business models of mobile ecosystems in China: a case study. In: The Proceedings of the 7th International Conference on Management of Computational and Collective IntElligence in Digital EcoSystems (MEDES 2015). ACM (2015)
8. Gao, S., Krogstie, J., Chen, Z., et al.: Lifestyles and mobile services adoption in China. Int. J. E-Bus. Res. (IJEBR) **10**(3), 36–53 (2014)
9. Gao, S., Krogstie, J., Siau, K.: Adoption of mobile information services: an empirical study. Mobile Inf. Syst. **10**(2), 147–171 (2014)
10. Gao, S., Krogstie, J., Siau, K.: Developing an instrument to measure the adoption of mobile services. Mobile Inf. Syst. **7**(1), 45–67 (2011)
11. Gao, S., Krogstie, J., Thingstad, T., et al.: A mobile service using anonymous location-based data: finding reading rooms. Int. J. Inf. Learn. Technol. **32**(1), 32–44 (2015)
12. Gao, S., Li, Y., Guo, H.: Understanding the value of MOOCs from the perspectives of students: a value-focused thinking approach. In: Al-Sharhan, S.A., et al. (eds.) I3E 2018. LNCS, vol. 11195, pp. 129–140. Springer, Cham (2018). https://doi.org/10.1007/978-3-030-02131-3_13
13. Gao, S., Yang, Y., Krogstie, J.: The adoption of smartphones among older adults in China. In: Liu, K., Nakata, K., Li, W., Galarreta, D. (eds.) ICISO 2015. IAICT, vol. 449, pp. 112–122. Springer, Cham (2015). https://doi.org/10.1007/978-3-319-16274-4_12
14. Hoehle, H., Venkatesh, V.: Mobile application usability: conceptualization and instrument development. MIS Q. **39**(2), 435–472 (2015)
15. Huang, J., Xu, Q., Tiwana, B., et al.: Anatomizing application performance differences on smartphones. In: Proceedings of the 8th International Conference on Mobile Systems, Applications, and Services, pp. 165–178. ACM (2010)
16. Hubert, M., Blut, M., Brock, C., et al.: Acceptance of smartphone-based mobile shopping: mobile benefits, customer characteristics, perceived risks, and the impact of application context. Psychol. Mark. **34**(2), 175–194 (2017)
17. Keeney, R.L.: Creativity in decision making with value-focused thinking. Sloan Manag. Rev. **35**(4), 33 (1994)
18. Keeney, R.L.: Value Focused Thinking - A Path to Creative Decisionmaking. Harvard University Press, Cambridge (1992)
19. Lee, B., Chen, Y., Hewitt, L.: Age differences in constraints encountered by seniors in their use of computers and the internet. Comput. Hum. Behav. **27**(3), 1231–1237 (2011)
20. Li, Y., Gao, S.: Understanding the values of blockchain based games from users' perspectives: a value-focused thinking approach. In: 18th Wuhan International Conference on E-Business (WHICEB 2019), Wuhan, China, 24–26 May 2019. Association for Information Systems (2019)
21. Mata, P., Chamney, A., Viner, G., et al.: A development framework for mobile healthcare monitoring apps. Pers. Ubiquit. Comput. **19**(3–4), 623–633 (2015)
22. Morris, M.E., Aguilera, A.: Mobile, social, and wearable computing and the evolution of psychological practice. Prof. Psychol.: Res. Pract. **43**(6), 622 (2012)
23. Peacock, S.E., Künemund, H.: Senior citizens and Internet technology. Eur. J. Ageing **4**(4), 191–200 (2007)
24. Pheeraphuttharangkoon, S., Choudrie, J., Zamani, E., et al.: Investigating the adoption and use of smartphones in the UK: a silver-surfers perspective. In: the 22nd European Conference on Information Systems (ECIS2014) (2014)
25. Rogers, E.M.: Diffusion of Innovations. Free Press, New York (1995)
26. Sheng, H., Nah, F., Siau, K.: Strategic implications of mobile technology: a case study using value-focused thinking. J. Strateg. Inf. Syst. **14**(3), 269–290 (2005)

27. Sheng, H., Nah, F.F.H., Siau, K.: Value-focused thinking and its application in MIS research. J. Database Manag. **18**(3), I–V (2007)
28. Sheng, H., Siau, K., Nah, F.F.-H.: Understanding the values of mobile technology in education: a value-focused thinking approach. ACM SIGMIS Database **41**(2), 25–44 (2010)
29. Wagner, N., Hassanein, K., Head, M.: Computer use by older adults: a multi-disciplinary review. Comput. Hum. Behav. **26**(5), 870–882 (2010)
30. Yang, X., Gao, S.: Understanding the values of live game streaming: a value-focused thinking approach. In: 16th Wuhan International Conference on E-Business (WHICEB 2017), Wuhan, China, 26–27 May 2017, pp. 394–401. Association for Information Systems (2017)

Adoption and Use of Tablet Devices by Older Adults: A Quantitative Study

Uchenna Ojiako[✉], Jyoti Choudrie, Ukamaka Nwanekezie,
and Chike-Obuekwe Chikelue

Business School, University of Hertfordshire, Hatfield AL10 9EU, UK
uchenna.ojiako18@gmail.com, j.choudrie@herts.ac.uk,
makmek2004@yahoo.com, chikejunior424@gmail.com

Abstract. Information and communication technologies have become essential for everyday activities. Recently, ubiquitous or mobile computing is the new trend whereby information and services can be accessed anywhere and anytime. However, not all groups of society are taking advantage of its benefits, of which the older population is one of such groups. This study aims to identify and evaluate the factors that influence the adoption, use and diffusion of tablet devices within the older population (aged 50 and above) in UK. From an online survey of 203 completed responses, Compatibility, Perceived Usefulness, Perceived ease of use, Trust, Attitude and Perceived behavioral control were identified as factors that affect the adoption and use of tablet devices. This study also provides the implications of the research to academia, industry and policy makers.

Keywords: Older adults · Mobile technology · Tablet devices · Digital divide · United Kingdom

1 Introduction

Information and Communication Technologies (ICTs) currently plays a major role in the exponential growth and development of political, social and economic aspect of many nations [5]. It offers several benefits to individuals including online shopping, online banking and online social networks [6]. For demographic groups of society, particularly older adults who are the focus of this study, it offers benefits such as independence and connectedness, which can improve their quality of life [15]. However, there are still many who are not accepting and using ICT, which has let to a digital divide [29]. Digital divide is the term used to describe the inequality existing among people with physical access to digital technologies and those with limited or no access to digital technologies [18]. A demographic group affected by the digital divide is the older adult population [29].

Currently, countries around the globe are facing aging populations and concurrently, technology is evolving, thus, this situation highlights the importance of digitally including the older population. The United Kingdom (UK) is one of such countries facing an ageing population and also the digital divide. For instance, with respect to the digital divide, the Office for National Statistics (ONS) found that about 4.8 million

Published by Springer Nature Switzerland AG 2019
I. O. Pappas et al. (Eds.): I3E 2019, LNCS 11701, pp. 545–558, 2019.
https://doi.org/10.1007/978-3-030-29374-1_44

adults in UK had never used the Internet as at the year 2017 [24]. In addition, in a report published by Age UK, nearly 3.8 million people aged 65+ are non-users of the Internet while 59% of those aged 75+ are also non-users [1]. In terms of the ageing population official statistics data revealed that in UK, the proportion of individuals aged 65 and over increased from 14.2% to 18% between the years 1976 to 2016 [24]. While, the proportion of those aged 15 and under decreased from 24.5% to 18.9% between 1976 and 2016. Furthermore, in economic terms, the older population is of immense importance as government policies are removing barriers to employment that has led to organisations employing older adults [13]. Moreover, due to the medical advances and a better quality of life it has been predicted that this ageing society is likely to continue over the next decades, which further suggests that special attention should be paid to the older generation [24]. Also, the digital inclusion of older adults can be beneficial to UK's society especially with organisations currently using technological artifacts for conducting work-related activities, and the older population becoming the fastest growing proportion of the workforce [13].

Furthermore, ICTs are evolving leading to new innovations that now makes daily activities quicker, convenient and cheaper [6]. One of such innovations is ubiquitous or mobile computing, which has made information accessible anytime and anywhere. It is anticipated that this form of computing will be more effective in reducing the digital divide because of its capability of combining the integral benefits of wireless Internet and interactivity with its own unique characteristics namely, mobility, portability and flexibility [11, 27]. One of the devices that have made this form of computing a reality is the tablet device. Tablet devices are also making a significant impact in encouraging the use of the Internet and ICT generally among the older population. For instance, tablet devices have plateaued over the years and changed the way older adults use the Internet [23]. Specifically, older adults aged 65–74 years using tablets to go online more than trebled in recent years in the UK, going from 5% in 2012 to 17% in 2013. However, this percentage remains low compared with younger age groups (e.g., 37% of adults aged 25–34 years used tablets to go online in the last 3 months) [20]. The presence of ICTs has led to many daily activities becoming digital; thus, converting many societies into an Electronic society (e-society). However, for the e-society to be successful, it is essential that all citizens adopt and use technology, which as stated earlier is not occurring within the older adults population; thus a motivating reason for conducting this study. The adoption and use of ICTs especially mobile computing like the tablet devices is a growing research topic because it helps access the successful diffusion of technology in the society. However, there is limited study on the reasons older adults adopt and use tablet devices. Therefore, this study aims to identify and evaluate the factors that influence the adoption, use and diffusion of tablet devices within the older population (aged 50 and above) in UK. To achieve this aim, the following research questions were formed:

(a) Is there an age difference in the adoption and use of tablet devices?
(b) What are the factors enabling or hindering the adoption and usage of tablet devices especially among the older population

To familiarise readers with the content of this paper, the following is provided. This section introduced the research problem, aims and research questions. This is followed by a background of the study, conceptual framework and hypotheses. The research approach, analysis and findings, discussions and limitations of this study are then provided. The conclusion and implications of this research draws the paper to a close.

2 Background of Study

2.1 Mobile Technologies

Ubiquitous or mobile technology enables faster and easier access to the Internet [11, 27]. For this study, the tablet device has been selected as an example of mobile technology considering that this particular device has become commonplace in modern society especially UK [2]. The tablet device is among one of the various mobile technologies that has made it possible to access information anytime and anywhere. It combines the features of a computer and a mobile phone to form a unique device [4]. These devices potentially offer numerous benefits some of which include continuous connectivity, as well as the provision of a means for multitasking [27]. Originally, the tablet device was intended as a supplement to desktop and laptop computers [21]. However, in recent times, this device has begun to replace the desktops and laptops. Research has shown that most individuals are currently moving from laptops and desktops towards smartphones and tablets. For instance, there was a decrease in the number of people accessing the Internet via laptop/desktop computer from 81% in 2014 to 71% in 2015 [21]. Meanwhile, between the same period, the percentage of people accessing the Internet via smartphones and tablet devices increased by 4% and 6% respectively. Additionally, the rate of the adoption and usage of the tablet device especially among older adults has increased over time. For instance, the number of 65–74 years old going online with a tablet device in the UK, increased by 9% between the years 2013 to 2015 [21]. Thus, to summarise, the popularity of the tablet has led to it being used in various areas of society including the educational, social and medical sectors.

2.2 The Digital Divide

As ICTs including mobile technology are expanding, and the ageing of population continues to progress, there is an increasing need for studies relating to the adoption of technologies among older adults. Over the last decades, there has been an increment in life expectancy in the UK and it is further projected that by 2036, over half of the local areas in UK will experience a 25% increase in the population of citizens aged 65 and over [22]. The digital divide is one of the negative consequences of the presence of ICT in society and has led to numerous debates among academia and policy makers. Consequently, the older population is one of the marginal groups negatively affected by the digital divide [5, 29]. Some of the reasons attributed to the lack of engagement among the older population include the difficulties encountered in embracing the changes that these technologies have brought to society especially considering most of these adults were not raised with technology [6]. Furthermore, Choudrie et al. [5] reckons that some health issues such as vision impairment, memory loss and arthritis prevent older adults from using technology, which has led to their exclusion from the e-society. Therefore, these identified issues have affected ICT adoption pattern in this group. Furthermore, most of the times, older adults prefer to sustain their independence for as long as is possible [5, 29]. However, age-related deficiencies among other factors can challenge the achievement of this independence desired by older adults. Devices such as tablet computers might be a solution for some of these challenges because these devices provide convenient and prompt access to several benefits [4]. These benefits include sustaining connections with family and friends as well as using the current healthcare systems. This will in turn reduce loneliness and isolation normally experienced by older adults [29]. Moreover, considering that the functioning of modern society now depends heavily on technology, it is important that every member of the society adopt technology, which highlights the importance of bridging the digital divide. Additionally, with the ageing of nations, older adults are of immense importance to the economy and society at large. Therefore, these older adults need to feel included, valuable and part of society. This further emphasises the importance of ensuring that the older population engage in the current technology adoption and usage trend. This will in turn ensure healthy and successful ageing in these adults as well as secure the future of the economy [6].

Having discussed the background of the study, the following discusses the development of the conceptual framework and hypotheses formulation.

3   The Conceptual Framework and Hypotheses Formation

In information system (IS) research, there is an emerging need to understand why people behave in certain ways when it comes to adopting and using technology. To ensure the selection of suitable constructs, studies on mobile technologies were reviewed to identify the theories that have been employed in addressing this subject area. Generally, since the inception of mobile technology, studies have been carried out to address the adoption of mobile technologies in various sectors. For instance, in 2011, an empirical study investigating the use of mobile technology to conduct mobile commerce and financial services also emerged [12]. This study combined attributes from Roger's diffusion of innovation theory with attributes from knowledge-based trust to assess mobile banking adoption [12]. Result from this study showed that perceived relative advantage, ease of use, compatibility, competence and integrity have significant impact on attitude towards adopting mobile banking. Result also indicated that attitude has a significant influence on behavioural intention to adopt mobile banking [12]. Furthermore, with respect to tablet devices, Moran et al. [16] in their study employed a modified UTAUT model to examine the implementation of tablet device in a higher education institution. Findings from this study showed that performance expectancy, self-efficacy, effort expectancy and attitude were significant predictors of behaviour intention. However, social influence and anxiety were not significant in predicting behaviour intention [16]. Moreover, some studies assessing the adoption of tablet device from the consumer's perspective have also been carried out. For example, Hur et al. [10] conducted a study in South Korea to explore the factors that influence a consumer's intention to use a tablet device. This study applied a modified TAM model and analysed the data gathered using partial least squares (PLS) analysis. Result indicated that perceived usefulness and enjoyment have a positive impact on attitude while; social influence and attitude have a positive impact on intention to use tablets [10]. Following the review of previous theories, this study built upon the decomposed theory of planned behaviour (DTPB) and trust theory in developing the conceptual framework. Subsequently, each of the constructs selected for the study along with the relevant hypothesis associated with it is discussed in details below:

Compatibility (COMP): This is the extent to which an innovation conforms to an individual's existing values, past experiences and needs [28]. This means that potential adopters of technology often require the new technology to be compatible with their existing lifestyle or cultural norm otherwise; this will result in a slower or none adoption rate [12]. Moreover, a few studies have highlighted the significance of compatibility in determining attitude and intention to adopt technology [12, 30]. However, consistent with the rationale and application in DTPB, the compatibility construct is linked to the attitude variable. In addition, to address this compatibility construct, the following hypothesis (H1) was created.

H1: Compatibility has a significant effect on an individual's attitude towards adopting and using a tablet device.

Perceived Usefulness (PU): This construct refers to the extent to which using technology will increase productivity and aid in the achievement of a desired goal [10]. For this research, perceived usefulness is used as an antecedent of attitude. To test the perceived usefulness construct, the following hypothesis (H2) was generated.

H2: Perceived usefulness will significantly influence an individual's attitude towards adopting and using a tablet device.

Perceived Ease of Use (PEOU): The usability of ICT is an important factor considered by users especially older adults during the process of adoption decision-making [5]. For clarification purposes, usability is defined as the ease with which a technological artefact is learnable and usable [19]. In the light of this, the perceived ease of use of the tablet device is an important aspect to examine in this study. Thus, for this study, perceived ease of use is posited as a determinant of attitude. To address this construct, the following hypothesis (H3) was developed.

H3: Perceived ease of use will significantly influence an individual's attitude towards adopting and using a tablet device.

Trust (TRU): Trust was also identified as a relevant construct for this study because it is a fundamental factor when apprehension, risk and uncertainty are concerned. In this case, it is related to the belief that technology in the form of tablet devices will be safe to use as well as the belief that it will do what it is expected to do. Furthermore, previous studies have found that trust is a key factor for assessing technology adoption and use pattern especially among the older population [26, 33] Considering this, the trust construct is used as an antecedent of attitude towards using and the intention to use a tablet device. To measure this construct, it was divided into trusting beliefs, institutional based trust and disposition to trust [26]. The following hypotheses (H4 and H5) were generated.

H4: An individual's perception of trust significantly affects his/her attitude towards adopting and using a tablet device.
H5: An individual's perception of trust significantly affects his/her intention to adopt and use a tablet device.

Attitude (ATT): Attitude is defined as an individual's response towards a concept or performing certain behaviour. It is a person's salient belief regarding the consequences of carrying out an action [31]. In addition, in terms of age and technology adoption, attitude has been identified as a key determinant of behaviour [17]. Thus, this study identified attitude as a relevant construct and it is used as a determinant for intention behaviour. In addition, to assess this construct, the following hypothesis (H6) was created.

H6: An individual's attitude towards using a tablet device directly influences his/her intention to adopt and use the device.

Subjective Norm (SN): Subjective norm was also identified as a suitable construct for this research. This construct postulates that a person's behaviour is based on the influence of important people in their life [31]. This means that if a person perceives that people important to them think they should act in a particular way, then, they are motivated to comply. This study posits SN as a determinant of intention to use. In line with this, the following hypothesis (H7) was developed.

H7: Subjective norm has a significant effect on an individual's intention to adopt and use a tablet device.

Perceived Behavioural Control (PBC): This construct refers to the level of one's perception with regards to the access to resources and opportunities required for performing a specific behaviour. The rationale behind this construct is that a person's behaviour is often dependent on how much resources as well as confidence the person has at their disposal to perform the required action [31]. In this study, this construct is used as a determinant of the intention to use. Considering this, the hypothesis (H8) was thus generated to address this construct.

H8: Perceived behavioural control has a direct effect on an individual's intention to adopt and use a tablet device.

Intention to Use Tablet Device (INT): The intention to perform any action is often dependent on attitude, subjective norm and perceived behavioural control [10, 31]. However, to account for the issue of apprehension often linked with adopting technology, this study included trust along with ATT, SN and PBC in the examination of intention behaviour. Furthermore, an individual's need to carrying out their intentions given the opportunity usually results in the actual behaviour [31]. Therefore, for this study, intention behaviour is the direct antecedent of actual behaviour. Considering the above discussion on intention and actual use, the following hypothesis (H9) was created.

H9: An individual's intention behaviour towards a tablet determines their actual use of the tablet.

Having provided details on the selected constructs and relating hypotheses, the conceptual framework for this study is presented in Fig. 1.

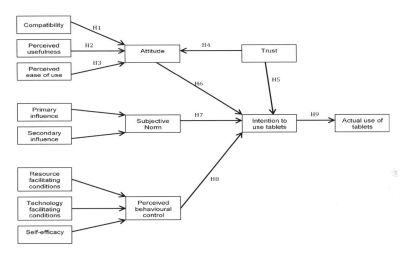

Fig. 1. The framework for tablet device adoption (FTDA).

4   Research Approach

A quantitative approach was employed to collect data for this research using survey questionnaires. The questionnaire contained mainly close-ended questions and was divided into five sections. In addition, a reflective measurement model was employed and the measurement items for each construct were adopted from previous studies with some modification to suit the research context. This study also used a 7-point Likert scale (1 = strongly disagree to 7 = strongly agree) to measure the constructs. To acquire data, the sample site selected for this study was the Hertfordshire County of UK, which is the second most populated area in the east of England with a population of approximately 1.2 million people as at 2015 [9]. Moreover, statistics obtained from the Office for National Statistics (ONS) showed that the proportion of those aged 50 years and over living in the County is about 35% [25]. Thus, it was based on these details as well as its proximity to the researcher that Hertfordshire County was selected as a suitable site for the study.

Furthermore, to measure how suitable the questionnaire is in achieving the intended purpose, the questionnaire was pre-tested using a panel consisting of 20 experts. These experts consisted of academics (7), industrial specialist (4) and the prospective target population (9). This was then followed by a pilot study, which was carried out using a combination of non-random sampling method including snowball and purposive sampling technique. Moreover, the survey questionnaire was distributed both in paper and online form in order to boost the response rate and reach the target population. Data was collected between the periods of 4th of May 2016 to 15th of July 2016. Initially, the snowball method involved the recruitment of already established contacts via emails and word-of-mouth. These selected contacts were then used to recruit more participants from their own established contacts and this led to the snowball sampling technique employed. Following this, 455 questionnaires were distributed purposively in some household in Hertfordshire. This resulted in 203 completed responses consisting of 168 softcopies and 35 hardcopies. Furthermore, according to Dillman et al. [7], for a pilot study to make an impact, it is the recommended number of responses should be between 100 and 200 responses. Thus, based on this, the number of responses (203) collected for this pilot study is considered suitable.

5   Analysis and Findings

5.1   Descriptive Statistics

To verify if there was a difference in tablet usage, younger adults (18 – 49 years old) and the older adults (50 years and over) were targeted. In surveys, bias can arise due to the sampling strategy and or non-response. To minimise this bias, this study applied a weight adjustment technique, which was done by using the data analysis tool SPSS version 23. From the result, the participants for this study consisted of 114 (56.2%) females and 89 (43.8%) males. In terms of age, participants were split into seven age groups including 18–29 years old, 30–39 years old, 40–49 years old, 50–59 years old, 60–69 years old, 70–79 years old and 80+ years old. Result based on these age groups showed that 38 (18.7%) of the respondents were 18-29 years old, 30 (14.8%) were 30–39 years old, 17 (8.4%) were 40–49 years old, 26 (12.8%) were 50–59 years old, 58 (28.6%) were 60-69 years old and 70–79 and 80+ age groups were 34 (16.7%) and 0 (0%) respectively. Moreover, results showed that out of the 203 respondents, 56.7% used a tablet device, 26.6% did not use a tablet device and had no intention of using one while 16.7% did not currently use a tablet device but had the intention to purchase one. Furthermore, for users of tablets, 55.7% belonged to the older group (50 years and over) while 44.3% belonged to the younger group (18–49 years). This result indicated and confirmed the suggestion of BBC [2] that the use of the tablet device has significantly influenced the number of citizens going online especially among the older adults. Furthermore, results also showed that compared to other age groups, the highest adopters of tablet devices belonged to the 60–69 years age group (31.4%) while the highest non-adopters were from the 70–79 years age group with 37%.

Additionally, in terms of education, it was found that the highest percentage of tablet device adopters belonged to those who had a Bachelor's degree with 31.3%. In terms of gender, women adopted tablet devices more than men with 57.4% of adopters representing women while 42.6% representing men. This suggests that there could be a connection between gender and tablet device adoption. In terms of health, it was observed that the better the health status, the more likely the adoption of a tablet device.

This suggestion was based on the finding that 56.5% of adopters indicating that their health status was excellent while 35.7%, 6.1% and 1.7% of adopters indicated that their health status was good, fair and poor respectively.

5.2 Path Analysis

To ensure reliability and validity of constructs, Cronbach's alpha, rho_A, composite reliability and average variance extracted (AVE) were employed. As a rule of thumb, the acceptable value for Cronbach's alpha, rho_A, composite reliability should be greater than or equal to 0.7 respectively while the acceptable value for AVE should be greater than or equal to 0.5 [8]. Based on this recommendation, the values found for each of the measurement test exceeded 0.7, 0.7, 0.7 and 0.5 respectively.

Using SmartPLS 3.0, path analysis for all age group was conducted in order to determine the path coefficient (β). Furthermore, bootstrapping was applied to the PLS analysis using 0.05 level of significance and this generated t-values and corresponding p-values. From the result, it was observed that PBC had the strongest influence on INT with $\beta = 0.382$, $t = 2.954$ and $p = 0.003$. This was followed by ATT with $\beta = 0.314$, $t = 2.461$ and $p = 0.014$. However, SN was considered insignificant in predicting the intention to use tablets with $\beta = -0.043$, $t = 0.464$ and $p = 0.643$. TRU also was considered insignificant in determining the intention to use with $\beta = 0.108$, $t = 1.206$ and $p = 0.228$. Result indicated that PEOU had the strongest impact on ATT with $\beta = 0.293$, $t = 4.128$ and $p = 0.000$. Additionally, COMP, PU and TRU proved to be significant in determining the ATT with values ($\beta = 0.258$, $t = 2.913$ and $p = 0.004$), ($\beta = 0.286$, $t = 3.375$ and $p = 0.001$) and ($\beta = 0.183$, $t = 3.362$ and $p = 0.001$) respectively.

5.3 Multi-group Analysis

Multi-group analysis (MGA) was also performed in order to compare the age group categories (younger and older group). Among the older and younger group, PBC had the strongest influence on the INT to use tablet with ($\beta = 0.360$, $t = 2.265$ and $p = 0.024$) and ($\beta = 0.455$, $t = 2.091$ and $p = 0.037$) respectively. Additionally, both groups showed that SN and TRU were insignificant in determining INT. Furthermore, it is noteworthy that among the older group, PEOU ($\beta = 0.384$, $t = 5.186$ and $p = 0.000$), PU ($\beta = 0.375$, $t = 4.214$ and $p = 0.000$) and TRU ($\beta = 0.127$, $t = 2.651$ and $p = 0.008$) were significant in determining ATT while COMP ($\beta = 0.147$, $t = 1.600$ and $p = 0.110$) was insignificant in relation to ATT.

For the younger group, result indicated that TRU ($\beta = 0.255$, $t = 2.063$ and $p = 0.040$) and COMP ($\beta = 0.378$, $t = 2.080$ and $p = 0.038$) were significant in determining ATT. Meanwhile, PEOU ($\beta = 0.143$, $t = 1.107$ and $p = 0.269$) and PU ($\beta = 0.223$, $t = 1.722$ and $p = 0.086$) were insignificant in determining ATT.

Additionally, ATT was significant in determining INT among the older group ($\beta = 0.302$, $t = 1.983$ and $p = 0.048$) while it was insignificant among the younger group ($\beta = 0.374$, $t = 1.646$ and $p = 0.100$).

5.4   Coefficient of Determination

Coefficient of determination (R^2) is used to determine the extent an independent variable can explain a dependent variable. The closer the value is to 1, the better the fit, thus, R^2 values that range from 0.5 and above are often recommended [8, 32]. Based on this, R^2 derived for the key dependent variable (intention to use tablets) is 0.527. This implies that the FTDA framework can explain about 52.7% of the variability in respondents' intention to use tablets. This value indicates the sufficiency of FTDA in predicting behaviour intention with regards to tablet devices. Additionally, the R^2 value for the attitude variable is 0.868, which means that about 86.8% of the respondents' attitude formation can be explained by their perception of the tablet device in terms of compatibility, trust, perceived ease of use and perceived usefulness.

6   Discussions and Limitations of Study

The following limitations should be noted when interpreting and making generalisations about the results.

6.1   Limitations of Study

The limitations of this study are specified to provide clarity on the level of generalisation that can be drawn from the results. Firstly, in ensuring the feasibility of completing the study within the required timeframe, data was collected from Hertfordshire County, UK, which reduces the applicability of the result to one part of UK. Therefore, future research should consider assessing the adoption of tablet devices in other parts of the Country. In addition, data collection for the quantitative study utilised a purposive and snowball sampling technique. Although, bootstrapping and weight adjustments were applied to the data in order to make up for the sampling variances. However, these sampling techniques are non-probability method, which reduces the extent of generalisation that can be drawn from the results of this study. Therefore, it is recommended that an alternative method be used for future studies. Overall, considering these limitations, it is suggested that caution should be taken when interpreting the results of this study.

6.2   Age Difference in the Adoption and Use of Tablet Devices

A study by Broady et al. [3] suggested that although older adults may not use technology as much as the younger adults however, the negative stereotypes of older adults being technophobic and incapable of using ICT is now outdated. Evidence of this was found in this study that given the right device, this stereotyping of older adults has faded. Specifically, a comparison between the younger adults (18–49 years old) and the older adults (50+ years) was conducted and the derived result indicated that the older group (55.7%) adopted the tablet device more than their younger counterpart (44.3%). This finding almost agrees with Magsamen-Conrad et al. [14] who found that there was a significant generational difference in the use of tablets. Furthermore, older adults' use of the tablet device more than their younger counterpart might be because the design of the tablet device has some ageing specific features, which makes it a suitable device for the older adults. For instance, most tablet devices have large screen size, which will be suited for older adults who are visually impaired. In addition, its mobility feature will be suited for older adults who have mobile issues or back problem or basically require being comfortable while using any device. Consequently, this result further confirms that there is an age-related digital divide [5, 29] however, with regards to tablets, the older adults are on the positive side of the divide. This further provides evidence that a tablet device offers a better chance of ensuring that older adults are digitally included. Subsequently, in the category of those planning to adopt tablets, 44.1% of this category belongs to the 50+ years age group. This indicates a willingness on the part of older adults to use ICT, which coincides with the finding of Broady et al. [3] that older adults are not technophobic especially with respect to the tablet device. Furthermore, the general result including all age group revealed that PBC and ATT were significant in determining INT. This finding is consistent with previous ICT adoption and use studies [17, 31] that revealed that factors such as ATT and PBC often affects an individual's intention to adopt. Subsequently, the theories were further tested to assess whether there was a difference between the young and old in terms of the hypothesised constructs. To achieve this, a multi-group analysis (MGA) was employed to compare both groups. It was observed that both groups shared some similarities in factors that determine ATT and subsequently, INT. For example, within the two groups, PBC was significant in determining INT and TRU was significant in determining ATT. This finding is similar to a study by Broady et al. [3] where it was suggested that similar factors influence younger and older adults. Furthermore, in this study, it was also observed that the two groups shared some differences with regards to the hypothesised constructs. For instance, ATT was found significant in determining INT among the older group but was not significant among the younger adults. Moreover, among the older group, PU and PEOU were significant in determining ATT. This finding almost agrees with the work of Hur et al. [10] where it was found that PU and perceived enjoyment significantly impacted on ATT. In addition, COMP was found significant in determining ATT among the young group but was not significant among the older group.

7 Conclusions

This study aimed to identify and evaluate the factors that influence the adoption, use and diffusion of tablet devices within the older population (aged 50 and above) in UK. To achieve this aim, a conceptual framework (FTDA) was developed and tested using data collected quantitatively. From the results of this study, the following conclusions and recommendations were obtained. Firstly, the findings of the study sufficiently demonstrated that the FTDA model proposed was appropriate in predicting intention behaviour and attitude towards adopting and using tablet devices. This was deduced from the R^2 values of 52.7% and 86.8% respectively. Furthermore, the digital divide research has shown some considerable variation in the way older adults adopt and use technology in comparison to their younger counterpart. For instance, Selwyn [29] highlighted that older adults are usually on the negative side of the digital divide and this issue has resulted in debates among academia and policy makers. Furthermore, this significant variation with regards to older adults adoption of ICT is currently a social problem and might sooner or later affect the economy at large. This is because there is an increase in the number of older people in the labour market as a result of the ageing of populations [24] and simultaneously, technology continues to penetrate everyday activities including organisations. Thus, older adults adoption and use of technology is of importance in the growth and development of a stable economy. In the light of this, the result of this study showed that in terms of tablet devices, older adults are on the positive side of the digital divide. Thus, it can be concluded that the use of tablet devices is a potential solution for reducing the digital divide when it comes to older adults participation in the information society.

7.1   Implications of Research

The findings from this study have numerous implications for academia, industry and policy-makers. Therefore, the following provide details on the implications of the study with respect to the three categories mentioned.

For academia, past research have focused on the presence of the digital divide and its effect on modern society. Some of these studies have examined the age-related digital divide especially from the perspective of older adults. Therefore, this study contributes to the theoretical and empirical research on the digital divide as well as studies on older adults adoption and use of technology. Moreover, this study offers an insight on the factors that influence the adoption and use of tablet devices especially from the perspective of older adults residing in UK.

For policymakers, considering that policymakers often look for cost-effective schemes that will help provide support to older adults without compromising their safety. Meanwhile, for example, this study found that tablet device has the potential of helping older adults remain independent and socially included, which in turn might lead to an improvement in their quality of life. Thus, these finding from this study offer information that policymakers might manipulate to facilitate citizens adoption and use of ICT, which in turn could influence its successful diffusion in the UK.

Furthermore, for industry, the result of this study also has some implications for the developers of technology especially with respect to designing suitable technology for older adults. For instance, it was noted that age-related changes in health impacts on the adoption of technology. Thus, developers of technology should pay attention to the usability features of the technology in order to encourage the older adults' market segment.

References

1. Age UK. https://www.ageuk.org.uk/globalassets/age-uk/documents/reports-and-publications/later_life_uk_factsheet.pdf?dtrk=true. Accessed 13 Feb 2018
2. BBC News. http://www.bbc.co.uk/news/technology-27205172. Accessed 25 Apr 2017

3. Broady, T., Chan, A., Caputi, P.: Comparison of older and younger adults' attitudes towards and abilities with computers: Implications for training and learning. Br. J. Educ. Technol. **41**(3), 473–485 (2010)
4. Burford, S., Park, S.: The impact of mobile tablet devices on human information behaviour. J. Doc. **70**(4), 622–639 (2014)
5. Choudrie, J., Ghinea, G., Songonuga, V.N.: Silver surfers, e-government and the digital divide: an exploratory study of UK local authority websites and older citizens. Interact. Comput. **25**(6), 417–442 (2013)
6. Damant, J., Knapp, M., Freddolino, P., Lombard, D.: Effects of digital engagement on the quality of life of older people. Health Soc. Care Community **25**(6), 1679–1703 (2017)
7. Dillman, D.A., Smyth, J.D., Christian, L.M.: Internet, Phone, Mail, and Mixed-Mode Surveys: The Tailored Design Method, 4th edn. Wiley, Hoboken (2014)
8. Hair, J.F., Black, W.C., Babin, B.J., Anderson, R.E., Tatham, R.L.: Multivariate Data Analysis, 7th edn. Pearson Education Limited, Harlow (2014)
9. Herts Insights. http://atlas.hertslis.org/profiles/profile?profileId=79&geoTypeId=16&geoIds=E10000015#iasProfileSection4. Accessed 25 Apr 2017
10. Hur, W.M., Kim, H., Kim, W.M.: The moderating roles of gender and age in tablet computer adoption. Cyberpsychol. Behav. Soc. Netw. **17**(1), 33–39 (2014)
11. Leung, L.: Using tablet in solitude for stress reduction: an examination of desire for aloneness, leisure boredom, tablet activities, and location of use. Comput. Hum. Behav. **48**, 382–391 (2015)
12. Lin, H.F.: An empirical investigation of mobile banking adoption: the effect of innovation attributes and knowledge-based trust. Int. J. Inf. Manag. **31**(3), 252–260 (2011)
13. Lusardi, A., Mitchell, O.S.: Baby boomer retirement security: the roles of planning, financial literacy, and housing wealth. J. Monet. Econ. **54**(1), 205–224 (2007)
14. Magsamen-Conrad, K., Upadhyaya, S., Joa, C.Y., Dowd, J.: Bridging the divide: using UTAUT to predict multigenerational tablet adoption practices. Comput. Hum. Behav. **50**, 186–196 (2015)
15. Mitzner, T.L., et al.: Older adults talk technology: technology usage and attitudes. Comput. Hum. Behav. **26**(6), 1710–1721 (2010)
16. Moran, M., Hawkes, M., Gayar, O.E.: Tablet personal computer integration in higher education: applying the unified theory of acceptance and use technology model to understand supporting factors. J. Educ. Comput. Res. **42**(1), 79–101 (2010)
17. Neves, B.B., Amaro, F., Fonseca, J.R.: Coming of (old) age in the digital age: ICT usage and non-usage among older adults. Sociol. Res. Online **18**(2), 1–14 (2013)
18. Niehaves, B., Plattfaut, R.: Internet adoption by the elderly: employing IS technology acceptance theories for understanding the age-related digital divide. Eur. J. Inf. Syst. **23**(6), 708–726 (2014)
19. Nielsen, J.: Usability 101: Introduction to Usability (2003)
20. Ofcom. https://www.ofcom.org.uk/__data/assets/pdf_file/0020/58223/2014_adults_report.pdf. Accessed 30 Jan 2017
21. Ofcom. https://www.ofcom.org.uk/__data/assets/pdf_file/0024/26826/cmr_uk_2016.pdf. Accessed 30 Jan 2017
22. Ofcom. https://www.ofcom.org.uk/about-ofcom/latest/media/media-releases/2017/rise-social-seniors. Accessed 04 Mar 2018
23. Ofcom. https://www.ofcom.org.uk/research-and-data/multi-sector-research/cmr/cmr-2018/summary. Accessed 26 Feb 2019
24. ONS. https://www.ons.gov.uk/businessindustryandtrade/itandinternetindustry/bulletins/internetusers/2017. Accessed 12 Feb 2018
25. ONS. https://www.nomisweb.co.uk/query/asv2htm.aspx. Accessed 25 Apr 2017

26. Pappas, I., Mikalef, P., Giannakos, M., Pavlou, P.: Value co-creation and trust in social commerce: an fsQCA approach. In: Proceedings of the 25th European Conference on Information Systems (ECIS), Guimarães, Portugal, pp. 2153–2168 (2017)
27. Park, S.: Always on and always with mobile tablet devices: a qualitative study on how young adults negotiate with continuous connected presence. Bull. Sci. Technol. Soc. **33**(5–6), 182–190 (2013)
28. Rogers, E.M.: Diffusion of Innovations, 4th edn. The Free Press, New York (1995)
29. Selwyn, N.: Apart from technology: understanding people's non-use of information and communication technologies in everyday life. Technol. Soc. **25**(1), 99–116 (2003)
30. Shaikh, A.A., Karjaluoto, H.: Mobile banking adoption: a literature review. Telematics Inform. **32**(1), 129–142 (2015)
31. Taylor, S., Todd, P.A.: Understanding information technology usage: a test of competing models. Inf. Syst. Res. **6**(2), 144–176 (1995)
32. Vinzi, V.E., Trinchera, L., Amato, S.: PLS path modeling: from foundations to recent developments and open issues for model assessment and improvement. In: Esposito Vinzi, V., Chin, W., Henseler, J., Wang, H. (eds.) Handbook of Partial Least Squares: Concepts, Methods and Applications. Springer Handbooks of Computational Statistics, pp. 47–82. Springer, Heidelberg (2010). https://doi.org/10.1007/978-3-540-32827-8_3
33. Vroman, K.G., Arthanat, S., Lysack, C.: "Who over 65 is online?" Older adults' dispositions toward information communication technology. Comput. Hum. Behav. **43**, 156–166 (2015)

Reciprocity and Social Exchange in the Sharing Economy

Dinara Davlembayeva$^{(\boxtimes)}$, Savvas Papagiannidis,
and Eleftherios Alamanos

Newcastle University Business School, Newcastle upon Tyne NE1 4SE, UK
d.davlembayeva2@newcastle.ac.uk,
{savvas.papagiannidis,eleftherios.alamanos}@ncl.ac.uk

Abstract. This study pursued two objectives: (1) it comprehensively investigated the role of the factors facilitating social exchange, reciprocity expectation and social value in use behaviour, and (2) it examined the effect of the sharing economy on social inclusion and subjective well-being. The data were collected from 487 users of different sharing economy platforms in the United States. Structural equation modelling was employed to analyse the correlation of the examined variables. The results demonstrated the positive effect of egoistic belief, reciprocity norm, social value, and the negative effect of identification on the use of the sharing economy. In addition, strong relationships between use behaviour and outcomes were identified. Future research suggestions are provided.

Keywords: Sharing economy · Social exchange · Social capital ·
Factors of use behaviour · Subjective well-being · Social inclusion

1 Introduction

The sharing economy is an emergent socio-economic system that has been growing fast, affecting the values and purchasing behaviour of consumers [1]. However, the academic literature exploring the driving forces of collaborative consumption is still scarce, providing little empirical evidence of the consumers' perspective on the phenomenon [2, 3]. The observed effect of the sharing economy on individuals' preferences signals the need for further empirical investigation of consumer behaviour in the context of the new socio-economic system.

Given the above, this study aims to address three main gaps in the literature. First, due to the socio-economic nature of the sharing economy, the literature has been split into two streams – the economic and the social one –each of which focuses on different drivers of the system development and the users' motives for participation [4]. Due to the divergent focuses of the two streams of the literature, the role of the key drivers of collaborations, such as psychological (e.g. expected reciprocity) and social factors, has not been explored. The second gap refers to the tendency of the previous research to collect data from consumers of particular platforms, such as the Airbnb accommodation sharing system and the Uber ridesharing service [5, 6]. In addition, the comprehensiveness of the current research is limited by the focus on single factors, such as trust,

I. O. Pappas et al. (Eds.): I3E 2019, LNCS 11701, pp. 559–569, 2019.
https://doi.org/10.1007/978-3-030-29374-1_45

price and cultural values [7, 8]. Thirdly, due to the focus on the wider scale of the sharing economy impact (i.e. institutional change and environmental sustainability) [9, 10], the users' perceived benefits of collaborative consumption in terms of access to society, resources and well-being have not been explored. To address the above gaps, there are three main objectives of the paper: (1) to examine psychological factors of collaborations, (2) to employ an overarching approach to examine key social factors driving collaborations in different sharing economy segments, and (3) to provide empirical evidence of the effect of the sharing economy on perceived social inclusion and well-being.

2   Literature Review and Hypotheses

2.1   Sharing Economy: Definition and Theoretical Foundation

The literature revolves around two main approaches of conceptualising practices carried out in the sharing economy. Botsman and Rogers [11] define collaborative consumption as an act of *"swapping, sharing, bartering, trading and renting being reinvented through the latest technologies and peer-to-peer marketplaces"*. This definition places purely commercial (e.g. renting and trading) and non-compensated practices (e.g. sharing, swapping) of resources redistribution under one umbrella. In contrast, Belk [12] postulates that collaborative consumption is different from sharing, gift-giving and commodity exchange. The latter three concepts are differentiated by the type of reciprocity and ownership control over sharable objects. Sharing and gift-giving are socially bonding practices. They are carried out without the obligation or expectation of immediate return [13, 14], whereas commodity exchange denotes mutual and immediate reciprocity. In addition, sharing enables temporary access to a resource for use, such as Couchsurfing communities that offer free accommodation for travellers. Gift-giving and commodity exchange provide a complete transfer of resources ownership from one person to another [14]. For example, the Freecycle community makes it possible to prolong the lifecycle of used items by gifting them to other members of the platform. However, commodity exchange resembles a marketplace transaction, excluding social relations between parties. The exchange is immediate and negotiated, without lingering returns. Finally, collaborative consumption denotes compensated practices, which embrace different types of ownership control. It is defined as an act of *"people coordinating the acquisition and distribution of a resource for a fee or other compensation"* [12]. Despite the economic outcomes of relations, it is people, rather than the market, that regulate transactions.

From the theoretical perspective, collaborative consumption can be explained by the social exchange framework. Social exchange is defined as *"the exchange of activity, tangible or intangible, and more or less rewarding or costly, between at least two persons or more"* [15]. There are three main premises of social exchange. First, social exchange is contingent on social capital, which refers to social entities, such as norms, values, rules, trust, expectations, obligations and information channels, to name a few. These social entities enable the functioning of social groups by both facilitating and inhibiting social relations and their consequences [16–19]. Second, social exchange results from the subjective evaluation of the costs and rewards of exchange with the purpose of ensuring reciprocal relations. The third premise of social exchange is that the value of rewards and the fairness of costs incurred by transactions is dependent on individuals' perception, thus it is a subjective process [15, 20]. In line with the above, collaborative relations in the sharing economy represent the effect of factors facilitating or hindering social exchange, the outcome of the evaluation of expected benefits and costs resulting from the lack of reciprocity.

2.2   Hypothesis Development

Social Capital Factors
To examine the facilitating role of social capital factors in collaborative relations, we used the framework developed by Nahapiet and Ghoshal [16]. The framework by Nahapiet and Ghoshal [16] was developed for organisational settings, which was later adapted to a private context [17, 21]. Given the context of the study, we adopted the later version of the framework for the hypothesis development.

Structural Social Capital Factor: Structural social capital represents properties of social systems, facilitating social interaction and helping develop social networks [19]. Structural social capital enables the development of bonding ties within communities representing direct relationships between community members. *Bonding ties* are characterised by strong connections resulting from the repeated interactions of parties [18]. There is evidence that social ties have both direct and mediated effects on collaborative practices [17, 21, 22]. Bonding ties have an indirect effect on behaviour through interpersonal trust [21]. Several studies tested the direct influence of connections on the use of online communities [17, 22]. However, the significance of the factors was not confirmed in the context of accommodation sharing [2]. The inconsistency of findings in the previous literature could be due to the difference in the strength of ties, rather than the frequency. Hence, the first hypothesis states that:

> *H1: Bonding social ties have a positive effect on the use of sharing economy platforms.*

Cognitive Social Capital Factor: Cognitive social capital represents resources enabling shared cognition, representation and interpretation of things and events [16, 17]. *Shared vision* underpins the work of communities by uniting their members through common goals, ideas and rules of conduct. Shared vision enables effective interpersonal communication, facilitates understanding and stimulates individuals' contribution to communities [21]. This social capital factor was studied in the context of collective practices [2, 17, 21]. It was found that the factor had an indirect relationship with use behaviour through interpersonal trust [21]. However, another study provides opposite results suggesting that shared vision negatively affects behaviour. Conflicting results require a further examination of the effect of shared vision on use behaviour:

> *H2: Shared vision has a positive effect on the use of sharing economy platforms*

Relational Social Capital Factors: Relational social capital represents relationship characteristics facilitating the development of relations, such as cooperative norms, interpersonal trust, obligations/expectations to cooperate and social identification with other group members [16, 18, 19]. *Identification* is defined as *"one's conception of self in terms of the defining features of self-inclusive social category"* [23]. Identification reflects the sense of belonging, loyalty and commitment to communities [16]. Previous literature gives an account of the indirect effect of identification on individuals' behaviour [3, 24]. Particularly, identification with social groups had a positive effect on the perception of encouragement and usefulness of social networking websites, which further lead to actual use [24]. Given the above, we hypothesise that:

H3: Identification has a positive effect on the use of sharing economy platforms

The literature on the sharing economy has strongly discussed the association between *pro-environmental beliefs and norms* and collaborative consumption [25, 26]. Sustainability was found to be the key factor driving the intention to share accommodation and use online marketplace platforms [27]. Theoretically, the above findings are supported by the value-belief-norm theory by Stern [28]. This theory argues that biospheric, altruistic and egoistic values activate the beliefs in adverse consequences, which affect the formation of personal norms underpinning pro-environmental behaviour. *Biospheric belief* refers to the belief that the environment is under threat and requires urgent actions to be protected. Altruistic belief is associated with pro-social values, while egoistic belief causes the resistance to protecting the environment due to the belief that pro-environmental behaviour can harm oneself [28]. Drawing on the above, this study hypothesises that:

H4: (a) altruistic and (b) biospheric beliefs have positive effects on the use of sharing economy platforms; (c) egoistic beliefs have a negative effect on the use of sharing economy platforms.

The *reciprocity norm* represents the two factors of social capital (i.e. *obligations* and *norms*), which refers to the obligations to reciprocate and the belief that the act of exchange should always be reciprocated [20]. Relationships in the sharing economy are built upon two forms of reciprocity, which are negotiated and generalised ones. It was found that knowledge sharing in virtual communities was motivated by expected reciprocity [29]. Similarly, in market-based transactions, individuals' engagement in collaborations is contingent on the perception of reciprocal rewards [30]. Based on the above-mentioned discussion, the fifth hypothesis states that:

H5: Reciprocity norm has a positive effect on the use of sharing economy platforms

Perceived Social Values

According to Holbrook and Corfman [31], *perceived social value* refers to the belief that certain events or the attainment of objects represent symbolic meaning and help achieve a certain status/role in the society. Individuals may be driven by personal needs to establish social relationships and engage in exchange [32, 33]. For example, one of the drivers of participation in the sharing economy is the development of social networks through repeated interactions with other peers [27, 34]. Also, the engagement in collaborative practices may help individuals to establish identity with the group [32, 33, 35, 36]. The development of social identity may help members receive the benefits of their group and establish the image that is favourable by the society. Based on the above:

> H6: Perceived social values have a positive effect on the use of sharing economy platforms.

The Outcomes of Using Sharing Platforms
In the context of this study, the outcomes of the use of sharing platforms reflect the degree to which people satisfy their goals [10, 27, 37]. There are two forms of potential sustained benefits of collaborations in the sharing economy, which refer to social inclusion and subjective well-being. *Social inclusion* happens when people get access to economic benefits and resources, access to social services, feel integrated with the society at the interpersonal (i.e. family, social network) and legal levels (i.e. equal citizens in society) [38]. *Subjective well-being* results from the subjective evaluation of one's own standard of living and perceived level of happiness [39]. Both subjective well-being and social inclusion may result from social network development, identification with a community, the access to goods and services which otherwise would not be available, the development of self-confidence, and the engagement in meaningful activity for the society and the environment [25, 40]. Hence this study posits that:

> H7: The use of sharing economy platforms has a positive effect on (a) social inclusion and (b) subjective wellbeing.

3   Methodology

Considering the focus of the study, the utilisation of online questionnaires as a data collection tool was deemed appropriate. An independent company was involved in the distribution of questionnaires to respondents in the United States. Former and current users of platforms were eligible to participate. The questionnaire was designed in a way to ensure confidentiality and gather respondents' profiles, such as social and demographic data. The final sample of respondents comprised 487 people, which made it possible to run a statistical analysis of the correlation of the proposed variables [41]. The sample consisted of 48.7% male and 51.3% female respondents with almost half of them being over 50 years old (49.3%). The majority of the respondents were either full-time (57.5%) or part-time (12.1%) employed, had a college graduate degree (34.3%), received an annual income between 50,000 and 74,999 US dollars (26.1%) or over 100,000 US dollars (25.1%).

The questionnaire included 57 items related to eleven main constructs. The items for social capital derived from adapted scales measuring bonding social ties [29], shared vision, [21, 42], identification [29], the reciprocity norm [17, 43, 44] and three types of pro-environmental beliefs [45]. Social value scale originated from the study by

Rintamäki, Kanto [46], while use behaviour derived from the IS literature [47–50]. The items for social inclusion were adopted from Richardson and Le Grand [51], and subjective well-being was measured by the scale developed by Diener *et al.* [52]. The responses were measured by a 7-point Likert scale with anchors between "1 - strongly disagree" to "7 – strongly agree".

SPSS v.24 and SPSS Amos v.24 were employed to analyse the collected data. To test the validity and reliability of the constructs, we ran the confirmatory factor analysis by following the guidelines suggested by Hair [41]. The results of the CFA analysis were satisfactory ($\chi 2(1484) = 3748.23$, CMIN/DF = 2.526, CFI = 0.926, RMSEA = 0.056). Factor loading (>0.7), average variance extracted (AVE > 0.5), construct reliability (C.R. > 0.7) and Cronbach's α (>0.7) confirmed the reliability of the measurements [41]. The result of the convergent validity test showed no validity issues (Table 1). To test the relationship between constructs, the structural equation modelling was conducted using Amos v.24.

Table 1. Convergent validity test

	1	2	3	4	5	6	7	8	9	10	11
SI	.77										
ST	.04	.94									
Rec	.29	.67	.90								
ID	.16	.79	.85	.91							
SV	.12	.80	.80	.87	.90						
AB	.32	.34	.49	.43	.40	.84					
BB	.28	.27	.43	.34	.34	.81	.85				
SV	.28	.66	.75	.83	.77	.46	.43	.86			
EB	.16	−.43	−.30	−.40	−.43	.06	.01	−.35	.88		
US	.54	.40	.61	.54	.53	.41	.38	.66	−.02	.82	
WB	.37	.57	.67	.70	.63	.48	.47	.79	−.24	.71	.88

Notes: Diagonal figures represent the square root of the average variance extracted (AVE) and the figures below represent the between-constructs correlations

4 Results and Findings

Considering The model fit indices were satisfactory, confirming the consistency of the proposed model with the collected data and the ability to examine paths' significance (Table 2). The model explained 57.6% of the variance for the behaviour of sharing economy users, 28.3% of the variance for the feeling of being socially included and 54.8% for the perception of their subjective well-being. The coefficients of path analysis are provided in Table 2.

Table 2. The results of the test of hypotheses

H	Path			Coef.	(t-test)
H1	Social ties	—>	Use behaviour	−0.031	(−0.478 ns)
H2	Shared vision	—>	Use behaviour	0.087	(1.019 ns)
H3	Identification	—>	Use behaviour	−0.23	(−2.024*)
H4a	Altruistic belief	—>	Use behaviour	0.009	(0.118 ns)
H4b	Biospheric belief	—>	Use behaviour	0.029	(0.373 ns)
H4c	Egoistic belief	—>	Use behaviour	0.219	(4.907***)
H5	Reciprocity	—>	Use behaviour	0.357	(4.399***)
H6	Social value	—>	Use behaviour	0.631	(8.041***)
H7a	Use behaviour	—>	Social inclusion	0.532	(10.186***)
H7b	Use behaviour	—>	Subjective well-being	0.74	(13.985***)

Method: ML; SEM Model fit: $\chi2(1501) = 4011.336$, CMIN/DF = 2.672, CFI = 0.918, RMSEA = 0.059

The paper examined the influence of eight antecedents on use behaviour: social ties, shared vision, identification, reciprocity, biospheric, egoistic and altruistic beliefs and social value (H1 – H6). Hypotheses 1, 2, 4a-b were not supported, suggesting that social ties, shared vision, biospheric and altruistic beliefs do not underpin the behaviour of sharing economy users. The paper gives insight into the relationship between use behaviour and social ties, which have been studied in the prior literature providing controversial findings (e.g. [2, 17, 22]). The finding of this paper demonstrates that the strength of social ties does not condition the use of sharing economy platforms. Similarly, users' participation in the sharing economy is not dependent on the views that they share with other members of sharing platforms. Previous research providing contradictory results partially explains this finding [29]. Shared vision had a different effect on the behaviour of different platform users. Therefore, future research should test the effect of the construct by controlling for the type of activity and platform. When it comes to the effect of biospheric and altruistic beliefs, the insignificant effect on use behaviour is consistent with the study by Möhlmann [53]. The author concluded that pro-environmental beliefs are not significant for monetary-based practices, such as accommodation and car sharing. A possible explanation could be that values driving behaviour are dependent on the type of sharing economy practice.

As a result of the study, hypotheses 3, 5, 4c, 6 and 7a-b were supported, confirming a positive relationship between identification, egoistic belief, reciprocity norm and social value. The effect of reciprocity norm was moderate and significant, supporting the findings of the prior literature on the domain of collaborative consumption and online exchange practices [2, 30]. This finding supports the assumption that individuals' participation in collaborative practices is triggered by the expectation of either immediate or delayed reciprocation in the exchange of resources. A significant path between egoistic belief and use behaviour is inconsistent with the majority of the prior literature [24, 28]. However, it is logical considering that the insignificant effect of biospheric and altruistic beliefs was established. The plausible interpretation is that individuals are driven by personal needs that can go against social values, such as the contribution to the societal well-being and environment. When it comes to the relationship between identification and use behaviour, the results are negative, which contradicts evidence in the research on the social exchange domain [3, 24]. This means that transactions in the sharing economy are not conditioned by a strong feeling of belonging to the sharing economy community, pride and collective self-esteem. Of all paths examining the antecedents of use behaviour, social value was found to be the strongest predictor of participation in the sharing economy. This finding suggests that the belief in fair allocation of resources among members of the community, the development of social relationships, the consistency of practices with individuals' lifestyle and image motivate collaborative consumption [3, 34, 36].

Significant relationships between use behaviour, social inclusion and subjective well-being confirm that the participation in the sharing economy enables them to feel integrated with the society in terms of access to economic, social and legal resources, as well as achieving higher standards of living. The findings are consistent with the prior literature postulating a positive correlation between subjective well-being and collective-oriented practices [54].

5 Conclusion

The paper makes three contributions to the literature on the sharing economy domain. First, following the social exchange framework, the paper has investigated the role of social capital factors, the norm of reciprocity and values that shed light on the collective orientation of individuals engaging in collaborative relations. The study provides a comprehensive analysis of the effect of three types of factors facilitating social exchange that represent structural social capital, relational social capital and cognitive social capital [16, 17]. The second contribution is that the study provides an insight into the drivers of the participation in the sharing economy by exploring the effect of social capital factors that have been controversial in the prior literature. The third contribution is that the paper empirically investigates the outcomes of the participation in the sharing economy, such as subjective well-being and perceived social-inclusion that have been a debatable topic in the previous research.

The paper has some limitations deriving from the adopted research design. Firstly, future research may adopt a longitudinal approach, that would make it possible to observe the dynamics in the perception of social inclusion and well-being over a certain time-span. Secondly, given the insignificance of some social factors and a positive relationship between egoistic belief and use behaviour, future research could examine the effect of utilitarian and monetary factors, such as price value, price sensitivity and price perception. Thirdly, to test the application of the model in other contexts, future studies could collect data in countries with different cultural values, beliefs and norms underpinning behaviour.

References

1. Wallenstein, J., Shelat, U.: What's Next for the Sharing Economy? Boston Consulting Group (2017)
2. Kim, S., et al.: Examining the influencing factors of intention to share accommodations in online hospitality exchange networks. J. Travel Tour. Mark., 1–16 (2017)
3. Barnes, S.J., Mattsson, J.: Understanding collaborative consumption: test of a theoretical model. Technol. Forecast. Soc. Change **118**, 281–292 (2017)
4. Davlembayeva, D., Papagiannidis, S., Alamanos, E.: Mapping the economics, social and technological attributes of the sharing economy. Inf. Technol. People (2019)
5. So, K.K.F., Oh, H., Min, S.: Motivations and constraints of Airbnb consumers: findings from a mixed-methods approach. Tour. Manag. **67**, 224–236 (2018)
6. Boateng, H., Kosiba, J.P.B., Okoe, A.F.: Determinants of consumers' participation in the sharing economy: a social exchange perspective within an emerging economy context. Int. J. Contemp. Hosp. Manag. (2019)
7. Wu, X., Shen, J.: A study on airbnb's trust mechanism and the effects of cultural values—based on a survey of Chinese consumers. Sustainability **10**(9), 3041 (2018)
8. Lindblom, A., Lindblom, T., Wechtler, H.: Collaborative consumption as C2C trading: analyzing the effects of materialism and price consciousness. J. Retail. Consum. Serv. **44**, 244–252 (2018)
9. Retamal, M.: Product-service systems in Southeast Asia: business practices and factors influencing environmental sustainability. J. Clean. Prod. **143**, 894–903 (2017)
10. Fremstad, A.: Does craigslist reduce waste? Evidence from California and Florida. Ecol. Econ. **132**, 135–143 (2017)
11. Botsman, R., Rogers, R.: What's mine is yours: how collaborative consumption is changing the way we live. Collins London (2011)
12. Belk, R.: You are what you can access: sharing and collaborative consumption online. J. Bus. Res. **67**(8), 1595–1600 (2014)
13. Sahlins, M.D.: Stone Age Economics, vol. 130. Transaction Publishers, Piscataway (1974)
14. Belk, R.: Sharing. J. Consum. Res. **36**(5), 715–734 (2010)
15. Homans, G.C.: Human Behavior: Its Elementary Forms. Harcourt, Brace, New York (1961)
16. Nahapiet, J., Ghoshal, S.: Social capital, intellectual capital, and the organizational advantage. Acad. Manag. Rev. **23**(2), 242–266 (1998)
17. Wasko, M.M., Faraj, S.: Why should I share? Examining social capital and knowledge contribution in electronic networks of practice. MIS Q. **29**, 35–57 (2005)
18. Coleman, J.S., Coleman, J.S.: Foundations of Social Theory. Harvard University Press, Cambridge (1994)
19. Putnam, R.D.: Tuning in, tuning out: the strange disappearance of social capital in America. PS: Polit. Sci. Polit. **28**(4), 664–684 (1995)
20. Blau, P.M.: Exchange and Power in Social Life, 352 p. Wiley, New York (1964)
21. Tsai, W., Ghoshal, S.: Social capital and value creation: the role of intrafirm networks. Acad. Manag. J. **41**(4), 464–476 (1998)
22. Ellison, N.B., Steinfield, C., Lampe, C.: The benefits of Facebook "friends:" social capital and college students' use of online social network sites. J. Comput.-Mediat. Commun. **12**(4), 1143–1168 (2007)
23. Bagozzi, R.P., Dholakia, U.M.: Intentional social action in virtual communities. J. Interact. Mark. **16**(2), 2–21 (2002)
24. Kwon, O., Wen, Y.: An empirical study of the factors affecting social network service use. Comput. Hum. Behav. **26**(2), 254–263 (2010)

25. Hong, S., Vicdan, H.: Re-imagining the utopian: transformation of a sustainable lifestyle in ecovillages. J. Bus. Res. **69**(1), 120–136 (2016)
26. Aptekar, S.: Gifts among strangers: the social organization of freecycle giving. Soc. Probl. **63** (2), 266–283 (2016)
27. Tussyadiah, I.P.: Factors of satisfaction and intention to use peer-to-peer accommodation. Int. J. Hosp. Manag. **55**, 70–80 (2016)
28. Stern, P.C.: New environmental theories: toward a coherent theory of environmentally significant behavior. J. Soc. Issues **56**(3), 407–424 (2000)
29. Chiu, C.-M., Hsu, M.-H., Wang, E.T.: Understanding knowledge sharing in virtual communities: an integration of social capital and social cognitive theories. Decis. Support Syst. **42**(3), 1872–1888 (2006)
30. Shiau, W.-L., Luo, M.M.: Factors affecting online group buying intention and satisfaction: a social exchange theory perspective. Comput. Hum. Behav. **28**(6), 2431–2444 (2012)
31. Holbrook, M.B., Corfman, K.P.: Quality and value in the consumption experience: Phaedrus rides again. Perceived Qual. **31**(2), 31–57 (1985)
32. Belk, R.W.: Possessions and the extended self. J. Consum. Res. **15**(2), 139–168 (1988)
33. Solomon, M.R.: The role of products as social stimuli: a symbolic interactionism perspective. J. Consum. Res. **10**(3), 319–329 (1983)
34. Lampinen, A., Huotari, K., Cheshire, C.: Challenges to participation in the sharing economy: the case of local online peer-to-peer exchange in a single parents' network. IxD&A **24**, 16–32 (2015)
35. Belk, R.W.: Extended self in a digital world. J. Consum. Res. **40**(3), 477–500 (2013)
36. Böcker, L., Meelen, T.: Sharing for people, planet or profit? Analysing motivations for intended sharing economy participation. Environ. Innov. Soc. Transit. **23**, 28–39 (2017)
37. Tussyadiah, I.P.: An exploratory study on drivers and deterrents of collaborative consumption in travel. In: Tussyadiah, I., Inversini, A. (eds.) Information and Communication Technologies in Tourism 2015, pp. 817–830. Springer, Cham (2015). https://doi.org/10.1007/978-3-319-14343-9_59
38. Huxley, P., et al.: Development of a social inclusion index to capture subjective and objective life domains (phase II): psychometric development study. Health Technol. Assess. **16**(1), 1–248 (2012)
39. Diener, E.: Subjective well-being: the science of happiness and a proposal for a national index. Am. Psychol. **55**(1), 34 (2000)
40. Yang, S., et al.: Why are customers loyal in sharing-economy services? A relational benefits perspective. J. Serv. Mark. **31**(1), 48–62 (2017)
41. Hair, J.F.: Multivariate Data Analysis, 7edn. Prentice Hall, Harlow (2014)
42. Leana, C.R., Pil, F.K.: Social capital and organizational performance: evidence from urban public schools. Organ. Sci. **17**(3), 353–366 (2006)
43. Morales, A.C.: Giving firms an "E" for effort: consumer responses to high-effort firms. J. Consum. Res. **31**(4), 806–812 (2005)
44. Suh, A., Shin, K.-S.: Exploring the effects of online social ties on knowledge sharing: a comparative analysis of collocated vs dispersed teams. J. Inf. Sci. **36**(4), 443–463 (2010)
45. Snelgar, R.S.: Egoistic, altruistic, and biospheric environmental concerns: measurement and structure. J. Environ. Psychol. **26**(2), 87–99 (2006)
46. Rintamäki, T., et al.: Decomposing the value of department store shopping into utilitarian, hedonic and social dimensions: evidence from Finland. Int. J. Retail Distrib. Manag. **34**(1), 6–24 (2006)
47. Ajzen, I., Fishbein, M.: Understanding Attitudes and Predicting Social Behaviour (1980)
48. Taylor, S., Todd, P.A.: Understanding information technology usage: a test of competing models. Inf. Syst. Res. **6**(2), 144–176 (1995)

49. Riemenschneider, C.K., Harrison, D.A., Mykytyn, P.P.: Understanding IT adoption decisions in small business: integrating current theories. Inf. Manag. **40**(4), 269–285 (2003)
50. Venkatesh, V., Thong, J.Y., Xu, X.: Consumer acceptance and use of information technology: extending the unified theory of acceptance and use of technology (2012)
51. Richardson, L., Le Grand, J.: Outsider and insider expertise: the response of residents of deprived neighbourhoods to an academic definition of social exclusion. Soc. Policy Adm. **36** (5), 496–515 (2002)
52. Diener, E., et al.: New well-being measures: short scales to assess flourishing and positive and negative feelings. Soc. Indic. Res. **97**(2), 143–156 (2010)
53. Möhlmann, M.: Collaborative consumption: determinants of satisfaction and the likelihood of using a sharing economy option again. J. Consum. Behav. **14**(3), 193–207 (2015)
54. Burroughs, J.E., Rindfleisch, A.: Materialism and well-being: a conflicting values perspective. J. Consum. Res. **29**(3), 348–370 (2002)

Learning and Education

Technology-Enhanced Organizational Learning: A Systematic Literature Review

Michail N. Giannakos[1]([✉]) [iD], Patrick Mikalef[1] [iD],
and Ilias O. Pappas[1,2] [iD]

[1] Norwegian University of Science and Technology, 7491 Trondheim, Norway
michailg@ntnu.no
[2] University of Agder, 4639 Kristiansand, Norway

Abstract. E-Learning systems are receiving ever increasing attention in, academia, businesses as well as in public administrations. Managers and employee who need efficient forms of training as well as learning flow within the organization, do not have to gather in a place at the same time, or to travel far away for attending courses. Contemporary affordances of e-learning systems allow them to perform different jobs or tasks for training courses according to their own scheduling, as well as collaborate and share knowledge and experiences that results rich learning flow within the organization. The purpose of this article is to provide a systematic review of empirical studies in the intersection of e-learning and organizational learning in order to summarize the current findings and guide future research. Forty peer-reviewed articles were collected from a systematic literature search and analyzed based on a categorization of their main elements. This survey identifies five major directions Technology-Enhanced Organizational learning has been focused during the last decade. Future research should leverage on big data produced from the platforms and investigate how the incorporation of advanced learning technologies (e.g., learning analytics, personalized learning) can help increasing organizational value.

Keywords: Organizational learning · E-learning · Literature review ·
Learning environments

1 Introduction

E-Learning covers the integration of Information and Communication Technology (ICT) in environments with the main goal to foster learning [1]. The term E-Learning is often used interchangeably with the term Technology-Enhanced Learning (TEL), to portray several modes of such environments (i.e., online, virtual learning environments etc.). The digitalization of resources and processes enables flexible ways to foster learning across the different sections and personnel inside an organization. Learning has long been associated in the past with formal or informal education and training. However organizational learning is much more than that. It can be defined as "the process of improving actions through better knowledge and understanding" [2]. Organizational learning is extremely important in an organization, since it is associated with the process of creating value from an organizations' intangible assets; it combines

© IFIP International Federation for Information Processing 2019
Published by Springer Nature Switzerland AG 2019
I. O. Pappas et al. (Eds.): I3E 2019, LNCS 11701, pp. 573–584, 2019.
https://doi.org/10.1007/978-3-030-29374-1_46

notions from several different domains, such as organizational behavior, human resource management, artificial intelligence and information technology [3].

In this work, we define Technology-Enhanced Organizational Learning (TEOL) as "the utilization of digital technologies to enhance the process of improving actions through better knowledge and understanding in an organization". During the last years, there is a significant body of research focusing in the intersection of TEL and organizational learning (i.e., TEOL) [4, 9, 10]. However, there is systematic work that summarizes and conceptualizes the results in order to reinforce the swift of enterprises that want to move from information-based to knowledge-based enterprises [3]. Thus, the study addresses the following research questions:

- What is the current status of Technology-Enhanced Organizational Learning research, seen through the lens of areas of implementation (e.g., industries, public sector), technologies used, and methodologies (e.g., types of data and data analysis techniques employed)?

Our motivation for this work is based on the emerging developments in the area of learning technologies, creating momentum for their adoption in organizations. The purpose of this paper is to provide a review of research on the Technology-Enhanced Organizational Learning research in order to summarize the findings and guide future studies. This study can provide a springboard for other scholars and practitioners, especially in the area of knowledge-based enterprises, to examine TEL approaches by taking into consideration the prior and ongoing research efforts.

The rest of the paper is organized as follows. In the Sect. 2 we present the related background work; the Sect. 3 describes the methodology used for the literature review describing how the studies were selected and analyzed. The Sect. 4 presents the research findings derived from the data analysis based on the specific areas of focus. Finally, in the Sect. 5, the authors discuss the results and make suggestions for future work.

2   Background

Switching from the information-based enterprise to the knowledge-based enterprise is a major challenge for today's companies [3]. Uni-directional learning flows, such as formal and informal training, is surely important but not sufficient to cover the needs enterprises face [4]. To uphold enterprises' competitiveness, enterprise staff have to operate in highly intense information and knowledge-oriented environments. Traditional learning approaches fail to substantiate learning flow on the basis of daily evidence and experience. Thus, novel, ubiquitous and flexible learning mechanisms are needed, placing the human (e.g., employees, managers, civil servants etc.) at the center of the information and learning flow and bridging traditional learning with experiential, social and smart learning.

Organizations consider the lack of skills and competences as being the major knowledge-related factors hampering innovation today [3]. Thus, the implementation of solutions supporting informal, everyday and work training (e.g., social learning, VR/AR solutions etc.) in order to develop individual staff competences as well to upgrade the competence affordances at the organization level.

TEOL has been delivered primarily in the form of web-based learning [3]. More recently, the TEL tools portfolio is rapidly expanding to make more efficient joint use of novel learning concepts, methodologies and technological enablers to achieve more direct, effective and lasting learning impact. Employing virtual learning environments, mobile-learning solutions and AR/VR technologies and head-mounted displays so trainees are empowered to follow their own training pace, learning topics and assessment tests that fit their needs [6, 34, 35]. The spread of use of social networking tools has also brought attention to the contribution of social and collaborative learning [17, 38].

Contemporary learning systems supporting adaptive, personalized and collaborative learning, expand the toolset available in TEOL and contribute to the adoption, efficiency and general prospects of the introduction of TEL in the organization [19]. During the last years, TEOL has put particular emphasis in the form of sharing internal and external to the enterprise knowledge, with systems that leverage collaborative learning and social learning functionalities [25, 32]. This is the essence of Computer Supported Collaborative Learning (CSCL), CSCL literature has developed a framework that combines individual learning, organizational learning and collaborative learning, facilitated by establishing adequate learning flows and emerges effective learning in an enterprise learning [5], in Fig. 1.

Fig. 1. Representation of the combination of enterprise learning and knowledge flows (adapted from [5]).

Establishing efficient knowledge and learning flows is a prime target for future data-driven enterprises [3]. Considering the involved knowledge, the human resources and their required skills in an enterprise, a clear need for continuous, flexible and efficient learning exists. This can be achieved by contemporary learning systems and practices, that provide high adoption, smooth usage, high satisfaction and alignments with the current practices of the enterprise. Since, the required competences in an enterprise are evolving over time, the development of competence models needs to be agile and leverage on state-of-the art technologies that align with organization's processes and models. Therefore, with this paper we attempt to provide a review of the TEOL research in order to summarize the findings and guide the development of organizational learning in future enterprises as well as future studies.

3   Methodology

To answer the research questions, the authors decided to conduct a systematic review of the literature by following transparent procedure adopted in the field of information systems and software engineering in order to minimize potential researcher biases and support reproducibility [7].

3.1   Articles Collection

Several procedures were followed to ensure high quality review of the literature of TEOL. A comprehensive search of peer-reviewed articles was conducted through February 2019, (short papers, posters, dissertations and reports were excluded), based on a relatively inclusive range of key terms: "organizational learning" "elearning", "organizational learning" "e-learning", "organisational learning" "elearning" and "organisational learning" "e-learning". The term "elearning" (also written as e-learning) was selected, since it's an umbrella term that always captures articles that use different terminology (e.g., learning technology, educational technology, technology enhanced learning). Publications were selected from 2010 onwards, since after 2010 we saw tremendous advancements (e.g., MOOCs, learning analytics, personalized learning) in the area of learning technologies. A wide variety of databases were searched, including the SpringerLink, Wiley, ACM Digital Library, IEEE Xplore, Science Direct, SAGE, ERIC, AIS eLibrary and Taylor & Francis. The search process uncovered 2.347 peer-reviewed articles.

3.2   Inclusion and Exclusion Criteria

The selection phase determines the overall validity of the literature review, and thus it's important to define specific inclusion and exclusion criteria. As Dybå and Dingsøyr [8] specified, the quality criteria needs to cover three main issues (i.e. rigour, credibility, and relevance) that needs to be considered when evaluating the quality of the selected studies. We applied eight quality criteria informed by the proposed Critical Appraisal Skills Programme (CASP) and related works [8]. You can see those criteria in Table 1.

Table 1. Quality Criteria

1.	Does the study clearly address the research problem?
2.	Is there a clear statement of the aims of the research?
3.	Is there an adequate description of the context in which the research was carried out?
4.	Was the research design appropriate to address the aims of the research?
5.	Does the study clearly determine the research methods (subjects, instruments, data collection, data analysis)?
6.	Was the data analysis sufficiently rigorous?
7.	Is there a clear statement of findings?
8.	Is the study of value for research or practice?

Therefore, studies were eligible for inclusion if they were focused on TEOL. The aforementioned criteria were applied in stage 2 and stage 3 of the selection process (Fig. 2), when the researcher had to assess the papers based on their titles and abstracts, and the full papers.

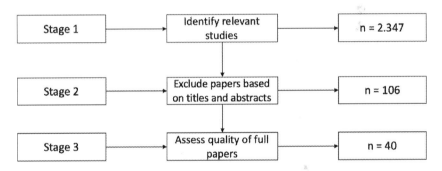

Fig. 2. Stages of the selection process

3.3 Analysis

Each collected study was analyzed based on the following elements: study design (e.g., experiment, case study), area (e.g., IT, healthcare), technology (e.g., wiki, social media), population (e.g., managers, employees), sample size, unit of analysis (individual, firm), data collections (e.g., surveys, interviews), research method, data analysis and the main research objective of the study. It is important to highlight, that the articles were coded based on the reported information, different authors reported information in different level of granularity (e.g., an online system vs the name of the system), while in some case the information was missing from the paper. Overall the authors did their best to code the article as accurately and complete as possible.

4 Findings

In this section, Table 2 presents the detailed results. Analysis of the studies was performed using non-statistical methods considering the variables reported in Table 2. This section follows by an analysis and discussion of the categories.

Table 2. Table captions should be placed above the tables.

Study	Study Design	Area/Topic	Technology	Population	Sample	Unit of analysis	Data Collect.	Method	Analysis	Objectives
[9]	Survey	ND	Web	Mixed	222	Individ	Surv	Quant	SEM	ItU
[10]	Survey	MGM	generic	mg	380	Individ	Surv	Quant	Reg	Sat
[11]	Survey	Telec	generic	empl	128	Individ	Surv	Quant	SEM	Sat
[12]	Exp	Bsn	Online	stud	143	Individ	Surv	Quant	A-VA	Flearn
[13]	Survey	IT	Online	empl	500	Individ	Surv	Quant	Reg	OV
[14]	Survey	Univ.	Web	stud	832	Individ	Surv	Quant	SEM	OV
[15]	Exp	IT	Web	empl	24	Individ	Surv	Quant	Descr	Per
[16]	Exp	IT	Web	empl	24	Individ	Surv/Int	Mixed	Descr	Per
[17]	Exp	IT	Podcast	empl	26	Individ	Surv/Int	Mixed	CA	ItU
[18]	CaseST	Cons.	ABAP	empl	12	Session	Int	Quall	Descr	Per
[19]	Survey	Cons.	Web	clients	222	Individ	Surv	Quant	SEM	ItU
[20]	Survey	ND	m-learn	mg.em	342	Individ	Surv	Quant	Descr	Usage
[21]	Survey	ND	collabor	ND	130	Individ	Surv	Quant	SEM	Per
[22]	Survey	Health	KRS	empl	800	Individ	Surv	Quant	SEM	ItU
[23]	CaseST	Public	OERs	civil	68	Individ	Int/FG	Quall	CA	Barr.
[24]	Survey	Ent	generic	empl	317	Firm	Surv	Quant	SEM	Per
[25]	Exp	ND	social	empl	28	Individ	Surv	Quant	Descr	Per
[26]	Survey	Ent	smart	mg	120	Individ	Surv	Quant	SEM	ItU
[27]	Exp	Bsn	e-portf.	stud	7	Individ	Surv	Quant	Descr	Flearn
[28]	CaseST	Autom	collabor	empl	3	Firm	Int/FG	Quall	Descr	Usage
[29]	CaseST	IT	collabor	empl	202	Individ	Surv	Quant	Reg	Per
[30]	CaseST	ND	generic	empl	126	Individ	Int	Mixed	CA	Flearn
[31]	CaseST	ND	Wiki	res	16	Individ	Surv	Quant	Descr	Flearn
[32]	Survey	Ent	social	empl	97	Individ	Surv	Quant	SEM	Flearn
[33]	Survey	IT	Podcast	empl	12	Individ	Int	Quall	CA	ItU
[34]	Survey	ND	generic	learn	12	Firm	Int	Quall	CA	align
[35]	CaseST	IT	SL	ND	16	Individ	Int	Quall	CA	feas
[36]	CaseST	MGM	Web	ND	22	Individ	Surv/log	Quant	Descr	Usage
[37]	Survey	several	smart	empl	342	Individ	Surv	Quant	SEM	ItU
[38]	Survey	ND	generic	learn	83	Individ	Surv	Quant	SEM	ItU
[39]	Survey	Telec	Online	empl	294	Individ	Surv	Quant	A-VA	Usage
[40]	Survey	IT	generic	empl	550	Individ	Surv	Quant	Descr	feas
[41]	CaseST	Health	Web	empl	40	Individ	log	Quant	Descr	Usage
[42]	CaseST	ND	generic	empl	15	Individ	Int	Quall	CA	Usage
[43]	Survey	Electr.	generic	empl	379	Individ	Surv	Quant	SEM	Flearn
[44]	Survey	ND	generic	empl	120	firm	Surv	Quant	SEM	Benef
[45]	Exp	IT	Web	empl	24	Individ	Surv/Int	Mixed	Descr	Per
[46]	Survey	Telec	generic	ND	297	Individ	Surv	Quant	SEM	Sat
[47]	Survey	ND	Web	civil	439	Individ	Surv	Quant	SEM	ItU
[48]	CaseST	IT	generic	empl	93	Individ	Surv	Quant	SNA	Flearn

Survey, Survey study; Exp,- Experiment; CaseSt, Case Study; ND, Non-Defined; MGM, Management; Telec, Telecommunication; Bsn, Business; Univ, University; Cons., Consulting; Public, Public Sector; Ent., Enterprise; Web, Web-based; KRS, knowledge repository system; OERs, Open Educational Resources; SL, Second Life, mg, Managers; empl, employees; stud, students; res, Researchers; learn, learning specialists; Indiv., Individual; Surv, Surveys; Int, Interviews; FG, Focus Groups; Log, Log files; Reg, Regression Analysis; Descr, Descriptive Statistics; A-VA, Analysis of variances/covariance; CA, Content Analysis; ItU, Intention to Use; Sat, Satisfaction; OV, Organizational Value; Per, Performance; Flearn, foster learning; Benef, Benefits; align, alignment; feas, feasibility; Barr, Barriers

4.1 Sample Size and Population Involved

The categories related to the sample of the articles, include the number of participants in each study (size), their background (e.g., managers, employees) and the area/topic the study was conducted. The majority of the studies involve employees (24), with few studies involve managers (3), civil servants (2), learning specialists (2), clients and researchers. Regarding the sample size, approximately half of the studies (19) have been conducted with less than 100 participants, few (9) can be considered large scale studies (more than 300 participants) and few (8) can be considered small scale (less than 20 participants). When it comes to the area/topic the study was conducted, most of the studies (9) were conducted in the context of the IT industry, but also having a good coverage of other important areas (i.e., healthcare, telecommunications, business, public sector). Interestingly, there are several studies that either didn't define the area or they were implemented in a generic context (e.g., participants from different sections or companies).

4.2 Research Methods

When assessing the status of research of an area, one of the most important aspects is the methodology used. By "method" in Table 1, we refer to the distinction among quantitative, qualitative, and mixed research. In addition to the method, in our categorization protocol we also "study design", referring to the distinction among survey study (i.e., gathers data by asking a group of participants), experiment (i.e., creation of situations to record beneficial data) and case study (i.e., closely studies a group of individuals).

Based on this categorization, we can see from Table 2 that the majority of the papers are quantitative (29) and qualitative (7) with few studies (4) utilizing mixed methods. Regarding the study design, most of the studies were survey studies (22), 11 were the case studies and fewer were experiments (7). The unit of analysis in most of the studies was the individual participant (35), with fewer studies having the firm as the unit of analysis and one study the training session. Regarding the measures used on the studies, most of them utilized surveys (32), followed from interviews (11), with few studies using field notes from focus groups (2) and log files from the systems (2). We only had 6 studies were the researchers used different measures to triangulate or extend their findings. The majority of the articles used Structural Equation Modeling (SEM) (15) to analyze their data, with 11 studies employing descriptive statistics, 7 content analysis, 5 regression analysis or analyses of variances/covariance and 1 study using social network analysis (SNA).

4.3 Technologies

Concerning the technology used, most of the studies (12) didn't study a specific system, but they referred in their investigation to a generic e-learning or technological solution. Several studies (8) named web-based learning environment, without describing the functionalities of identifying the system. The rest of the studies focused on online learning environment (3), collaborative learning systems (3), social learning systems (2), smart learning systems (2), podcasting (2) and the rest of the studies used a specific system (e.g., a wiki, mobile learning system, ABAP, e-portfolios, second life).

4.4 Research Objectives

Concerning the research objectives of the studies, we can separate them in six main categories. The first category focuses intention of the employees to use the technology (9), the second focuses in the performance of the employees (8), the third focuses in the value/outcome of the organization (2), the fourth focuses in the actual usage of the system (6), the fifth in employees satisfaction (3) and the sixth in the ability of the proposed system to foster learning (7). In addition to the six aforementioned categories, we also saw studies focusing in potential barriers for TEOL in the organization [23], the various benefits associated with the successful implementation of TEOL [44], the feasibility [35, 40] and the alignment of the proposed innovation with the other processes and systems in the organization [34].

5 Discussion and Conclusion

After reviewing the 40 identified articles in the area of TEOL, we can agree on the importance of the affordances offered from different e-learning technologies, as well as, the importance of the relationship between TEOL and employees satisfaction and performance, and benefits associated with organizational value and outcome. TEOL provides employees, managers and even clients opportunities to learn in a more differentiated manner, compared to the formal learning form. However, how the organization adopts these capabilities and leverages on them to achieve its goals is a complex and challenging procedure.

Several studies [7, 22, 26] focused on the positive effect of perceived managerial support, perceived usefulness, perceived ease of use and other Technology Acceptance (TAM) related constructs of the e-learning system in supporting all the three levels of learning (i.e., individual, collaborative and organizational). Another interesting dimension highlighted from many studies [12, 21, 31] is the role of socialization in the adoption and usage of the e-learning system. Building connections and creating a shared learning space in the e-learning system is critical [12]. This is consistent with the expectancy-theoretical explanation of the social context impacts on employees motivation to participate in learning [7, 26].

Organizational learning literature suggests that e-learning may be more appropriate for the acquisition of certain types of knowledge than others (e.g. procedural vs. declarative, or hard-skills vs. soft-skills), however there is no empirical evidence for that [12]. However, the literature highlights the importance of integrating organizational, individual, and social perspectives [25] in TEOL. In addition, for the development TEOL approach, the organization needs to consider the alignment of individual learning needs, organizational objectives, and social networking [25]. To achieve this, it is advisable for the organization to define the expected objectives and technologies that have the capacity to support them, and enrich them with self-directed and socially constructed learning practice in the organization [25].

5.1 Status of TEOL Research

The current review suggests that, while the efficient implementation of TEOL entails certain challenges, there is also a great potential for employees' performance and organizational outcome and value overall. There are also opportunities for improving organizations learning flow that might not be feasible for formal learning and training. Overall the research conducted during the last decade in TEOL has focused on the following directions:

1. **Investigating the Affordances of Different Technologies in Different Organizations**
   In particular focusing in aspects of how easy to use or useful the technology is, or how well aligned/integrated to other systems and processes within the organization. In addition, studies focused on how different learning technologies (e.g., smart, social, personalized etc.) contribute to organizational learning in different contexts and needs.
2. **Enriching the Learning Flow and Learning Potential in Different Levels**
   How different factors contribute to different levels of organizational learning, and practices to address individual, collaborative and organizational learning within the structure of the organization.
3. **Identifying Critical Aspects for Successful TEOL**
   There is a considerable amount of mainly qualitative studies, focusing on potential barriers of TEOL implementation as well as risks and requirements associated with the feasibility. In the same vain, there was an emphasis in the importance of alignment of TEOL (in both processes and technologies) within the organization.
4. **Implementing Employee-Centric TEOL**
   In most of the studies, the main objective was to increase employee's adoption, satisfaction and usage of the learning system. In addition, several studies focused on TEOL's ability to increase employee's performance as well as to increase knowledge flow and foster learning.
5. **Achieving Goals Associated with the Value Creation of the Organization**
   A considerable number of studies, that utilized the firm as a unit of analysis (and not the individual employee) focused on TEOL's capacity to increase organizational value and customer value.

5.2 Implications and Future Work

Several implications for TEOL were revealed through this literature review. First, most of the studies agree that employees/trainees experience is extremely important for the successful implementation of TEOL. Thus keeping them in the design and implementation cycle of TEOL will increase the adoption and satisfaction as well as reduces the risks and barriers. Another important implication relates with the qualities of the technologies, easy to use, useful and social technologies result more efficient TEOL. Thus it's important for the organization to incorporate these functionalities in the platform and reinforce them within appropriate content and support. This should not only benefit learning outcomes, but it can also provide the networking opportunities for employees to broaden their personal networks, that are often lost when companies move to e-learning.

A number of suggestions for further research have emerged from reviewing prior and ongoing work on TEOL. One recommendation for future researchers is to clearly describe the TEOL approach by providing detailed information for the technologies and materials used, as well as the organizations. This will allow us to conduct meta analyses and identify potential effects of firm's size or area on the performance and other aspects related with organizational value. Future work should also focus on collecting and triangulating different types of data from different sources. The reviewed studies have been conducted using mainly survey data and limited usage of data coming from the platforms, thus the interpretations and triangulation between the different types of the collected data were limited.

Acknowledgments. This work has received funding from the Norwegian Research Council under the project FUTURE LEARNING (number: 255129/H20) and Xdesign (290994/F20).

References

1. Rosenberg, M.J., Foshay, R.: E-learning: strategies for delivering knowledge in the digital age. Perform. Improv. **41**(5), 50–51 (2002)
2. Fiol, C.M., Lyles, M.A.: Organizational learning. Acad. Manag. Rev. **10**(4), 803–813 (1985)
3. El Kadiri, S., et al.: Current trends on ICT technologies for enterprise information systems. Comput. Ind. **79**, 14–33 (2016)
4. Manuti, A., Pastore, S., Scardigno, A.F., Giancaspro, M.L., Morciano, D.: Formal and informal learning in the workplace: a research review. Int. J. Train. Dev. **19**(1), 1–17 (2015)
5. Goggins, S.P., Jahnke, I., Wulf, V.: Computer-Supported Collaborative Learning at the Workplace. Springer, New York (2013). https://doi.org/10.1007/978-1-4614-1740-8
6. Muller Queiroz, A.C., et al.: Immersive virtual environments in corporate education and training. In: AMCIS (2018)
7. Kitchenham, B., Charters, S.: Guidelines for performing systematic literature reviews in software engineering (2007)
8. Dybå, T., Dingsøyr, T.: Empirical studies of agile software development: a systematic review. Inf. Softw. Technol. **50**(9–10), 833–859 (2008)
9. Cheng, B., Wang, M., Moormann, J., Olaniran, B.A., Chen, N.S.: The effects of organizational learning environment factors on e-learning acceptance. Comput. Educ. **58**(3), 885–899 (2012)
10. Mitić, S., Nikolić, M., Jankov, J., Vukonjanski, J., Terek, E.: The impact of information technologies on communication satisfaction and organizational learning in companies in Serbia. Comput. Hum. Behav. **76**, 87–101 (2017)
11. Navimipour, N.J., Zareie, B.: A model for assessing the impact of e-learning systems on employees' satisfaction. Comput. Hum. Behav. **53**, 475–485 (2015)
12. Yanson, R., Johnson, R.D.: An empirical examination of e-learning design: the role of trainee socialization and complexity in short term training. Comput. Educ. **101**, 43–54 (2016)
13. Iris, R., Vikas, A.: E-Learning technologies: a key to dynamic capabilities. Comput. Hum. Behav. **27**(5), 1868–1874 (2011)

14. Alsabawy, A.Y., Cater-Steel, A., Soar, J.: IT infrastructure services as a requirement for e-learning system success. Comput. Educ. **69**, 431–451 (2013)
15. Jia, H., Wang, M., Ran, W., Yang, S.J., Liao, J., Chiu, D.K.: Design of a performance-oriented workplace e-learning system using ontology. Expert Syst. Appl. **38**(4), 3372–3382 (2011)
16. Wang, M., Vogel, D., Ran, W.: Creating a performance-oriented e-learning environment: a design science approach. Inf. Manag. **48**(7), 260–269 (2011)
17. Wei, K., Ram, J.: Perceived usefulness of podcasting in organizational learning: the role of information characteristics. Comput. Hum. Behav. **64**, 859–870 (2016)
18. Bologa, R., Lupu, A.R.: Organizational learning networks that can increase the productivity of IT consulting companies. A case study for ERP consultants. Expert Syst. Appl. **41**(1), 126–136 (2014)
19. Cheng, B., Wang, M., Yang, S.J., Peng, J.: Acceptance of competency-based workplace e-learning systems: effects of individual and peer learning support. Comput. Educ. **57**(1), 1317–1333 (2011)
20. Lee, J., Kim, D.W., Zo, H.: Conjoint analysis on preferences of HRD managers and employees for effective implementation of m-learning: The case of South Korea. Telematics Inform. **32**(4), 940–948 (2015)
21. Choi, S., Ko, I.: Leveraging electronic collaboration to promote interorganizational learning. Int. J. Inf. Manag. **32**(6), 550–559 (2012)
22. Tsai, C.H., Zhu, D.S., Ho, B.C.T., Wu, D.D.: The effect of reducing risk and improving personal motivation on the adoption of knowledge repository system. Technol. Forecast. Soc. Change **77**(6), 840–856 (2010)
23. Stoffregen, J.D., et al.: Barriers to open e-learning in public administrations: a comparative case study of the European countries Luxembourg, Germany, Montenegro and Ireland. Technol. Forecast. Soc. Change **111**, 198–208 (2016)
24. López-Nicolás, C., Meroño-Cerdán, Á.L.: Strategic knowledge management, innovation and performance. Int. J. Inf. Manag. **31**(6), 502–509 (2011)
25. Wang, M.: Integrating organizational, social, and individual perspectives in Web 2.0-based workplace e-learning. Inf. Syst. Front. **13**(2), 191–205 (2011)
26. Lee, J., Choi, M., Lee, H.: Factors affecting smart learning adoption in workplaces: comparing large enterprises and SMEs. Inf. Technol. Manag. **16**(4), 291–302 (2015)
27. Wang, S., Wang, H.: Organizational schemata of e-portfolios for fostering higher-order thinking. Inf. Syst. Front. **14**(2), 395–407 (2012)
28. Siadaty, M., Jovanović, J., Gašević, D., Jeremić, Z., Holocher-Ertl, T.: Leveraging semantic technologies for harmonization of individual and organizational learning. In: Wolpers, M., Kirschner, P.A., Scheffel, M., Lindstaedt, S., Dimitrova, V. (eds.) Sustaining TEL: From Innovation to Learning and Practice. LNCS, vol. 6383, pp. 340–356. Springer, Heidelberg (2010). https://doi.org/10.1007/978-3-642-16020-2_23
29. Subramaniam, R., Nakkeeran, S.: Impact of corporate e-learning systems in enhancing the team performance in virtual software teams. In: Al-Masri, A., Curran, K. (eds.) Smart Technologies and Innovation for a Sustainable Future. Advances in Science, Technology & Innovation (IEREK Interdisciplinary Series for Sustainable Development), pp. 195–204. Springer, Cham (2019). https://doi.org/10.1007/978-3-030-01659-3_22
30. Kaschig, A., et al.: Knowledge maturing activities and practices fostering organisational learning: results of an empirical study. In: Wolpers, M., Kirschner, P.A., Scheffel, M., Lindstaedt, S., Dimitrova, V. (eds.) EC-TEL 2010. LNCS, vol. 6383, pp. 151–166. Springer, Heidelberg (2010). https://doi.org/10.1007/978-3-642-16020-2_11

31. Khalili, A., Auer, S., Tarasowa, D., Ermilov, I.: SlideWiki: elicitation and sharing of corporate knowledge using presentations. In: ten Teije, A., et al. (eds.) EKAW 2012. LNCS (LNAI), vol. 7603, pp. 302–316. Springer, Heidelberg (2012). https://doi.org/10.1007/978-3-642-33876-2_27

32. Qi, C., Chau, P.Y.: An empirical study of the effect of enterprise social media usage on organizational learning. In: PACIS, p. 330 (2016)

33. Wei, K., Sun, H., Li, H.: On the driving forces of diffusion of podcasting in organizational settings: a case study and propositions. In: PACIS, p. 217 (2013)

34. Costello, J.T., McNaughton, R.B.: Integrating a dynamic capabilities framework into workplace e-learning process evaluations. Knowl. Process Manag. 25(2), 108–125 (2018)

35. Mueller, J., Hutter, K., Fueller, J., Matzler, K.: Virtual worlds as knowledge management platform–a practice-perspective. Inf. Syst. J. 21(6), 479–501 (2011)

36. Hung, Y.H., Lin, C.F., Chang, R.I.: Developing a dynamic inference expert system to support individual learning at work. Br. J. Educ. Technol. 46(6), 1378–1391 (2015)

37. Lee, J., Zo, H., Lee, H.: Smart learning adoption in employees and HRD managers. Br. J. Educ. Technol. 45(6), 1082–1096 (2014)

38. Hester, A.J., Hutchins, H.M., Burke-Smalley, L.A.: Web 2.0 and transfer: trainers' use of technology to support employees' learning transfer on the job. Perform. Improv. Q. 29(3), 231–255 (2016)

39. Gal, E., Nachmias, R.: Online learning and performance support in organizational environments using performance support platforms. Perform. Improv. 50(8), 25–32 (2011)

40. Kim, M.K., Kim, S.M., Bilir, M.K.: Investigation of the dimensions of workplace learning environments (WLEs): development of the WLE measure. Perform. Improv. Q. 27(2), 35–57 (2014)

41. Rober, M.B., Cooper, L.P.: Capturing knowledge via an "Intrapedia": a case study. In: 2011 44th Hawaii International Conference on System Sciences, pp. 1–10. IEEE, January 2011

42. Michalski, M.P.: Symbolic meanings and e-learning in the workplace: the case of an intranet-based training tool. Manag. Learn. 45(2), 145–166 (2014)

43. Joo, Y.J., Lim, K.Y., Park, S.Y.: Investigating the structural relationships among organisational support, learning flow, learners' satisfaction and learning transfer in corporate e-learning. Br. J. Educ. Technol. 42(6), 973–984 (2011)

44. Liu, Y.C., Huang, Y.A., Lin, C.: Organizational factors' effects on the success of e-learning systems and organizational benefits: an empirical study in Taiwan. Int. Rev. Res. Open Distrib. Learn. 13(4), 130–151 (2012)

45. Wang, M., Ran, W., Liao, J., Yang, S.J.: A performance-oriented approach to e-learning in the workplace. J. Educ. Technol. Soc. 13(4), 167–179 (2010)

46. Lin, C.Y., Huang, C.K., Zhang, H.: Enhancing employee job satisfaction via E-learning: the mediating role of an organizational learning culture. Int. J. Hum.-Comput. Interact. 35(7), 584–595 (2019)

47. Lai, H.J.: Examining civil servants' decisions to use Web 2.0 tools for learning, based on the decomposed theory of planned behavior. Interact. Learn. Environ. 25(3), 295–305 (2017)

48. Škerlavaj, M., Dimovski, V., Mrvar, A., Pahor, M.: Intra-organizational learning networks within knowledge-intensive learning environments. Interact. Learn. Environ. 18(1), 39–63 (2010)

E-Assessment in Programming Courses: Towards a Digital Ecosystem Supporting Diverse Needs?

Aparna Chirumamilla$^{(\boxtimes)}$ ⓘ and Guttorm Sindre ⓘ

Department of Computer Science,
Norwegian University of Science and Technology,
Trondheim, Norway
{aparnav, guttors}@ntnu.no

Abstract. While a number of advantages have been discussed on e-learning/e-assessment tools, little research has been reported on programming courses. Today, the different types of questions have been used in exams based on course type, e.g., Text-based questions, mathematical questions, and programming questions. All these question types require supporting plug-ins for e-assessments. In this study, we provide our practical experience on programming exams in Inspera Assessment and Blackboard Learn, especially focusing on Parsons problems (drag-and-drop questions) and code writing questions. Our findings indicate that currently, tools have basic support for programming exams, and also there is a low-level integration between the tools. However, the adaptability of any exam system could depend on the interoperability between the platforms and external plugins. Hence, more improvements can be made with the implementation of e-assessments in digital ecosystems while it requires a lot of changes internally and outside institutions. In the paper, we will explain how a digital ecosystem within e-assessment could improve assessments and how it supports diverse needs of programming exams.

Keywords: Digital ecosystem · e-Assessments · Programming exams · Parson problems · Code writing

1 Introduction

Many universities are transitioning from pen and paper exams to e-exams [1]. At the same time, formative e-assessment is receiving increased attention [2]. With automated self-tests where students can get immediate feedback, it is possible to have rapid feedback cycles scale to large and distributed classes without overloading the teaching staff. However, e-assessment systems need to be well adapted to user needs, supporting appropriate assessment tasks for the intended learning outcomes. The development of good test items is often time-consuming, so universities could save effort and increase quality if tests could be shared across countries and learning institutions [3]. Also, it would be interesting to share data and metadata, e.g., about the performance of various student groups, for benchmarking and adaptive testing.

A digital ecosystem is a business ecosystem based on an organizational network in the context of digital technology [4–6]. Digital ecosystems are formed based on digital

© IFIP International Federation for Information Processing 2019
Published by Springer Nature Switzerland AG 2019
I. O. Pappas et al. (Eds.): I3E 2019, LNCS 11701, pp. 585–596, 2019.
https://doi.org/10.1007/978-3-030-29374-1_47

objects (digital content, products, ideas, software, hardware, infrastructure) that are interchanged and shared between independent actors [7]. The potential advantages of digital ecosystems in e-learning were outlined more than a decade ago [8, 9]. An e-learning ecosystem is the learning community, together with the enterprise, united by a learning management system (LMS) and it is formed by three categories of components: content providers, consultants, and infrastructure [8]. For the e-assessment aspects of such an ecosystem, sharing of content (e.g., tests and test items) and metadata (e.g., anonymized student scores on test items, to assess difficulty) would be a key ingredient. In addition, easy development and good availability of plug-ins to support various needs in e-assessment would be essential. Traditional monolithic systems might have the ambition that customers find all the features they require within the system. However, user needs will be quite diverse, related to different disciplines and learning outcomes, pedagogical approaches, assessment types, different devices to be used, students with special needs, languages and cultures, and different national rules and regulations of assessments, grading and collection of personal information. In addition, the system should be able to evolve quickly to cater for new needs [10], e.g., new learning methods, test types, technology.

Although monolithic systems may include many features, these will tend to be features that a sufficient number of mainstream customers require, while more specialized needs will not be supported. Moreover, they tend to become heavy and slow to respond to changes. If an e-learning system has an open, well-documented API, this could allow for plug-ins from other vendors, or from universities themselves, with niche expertise to quickly develop functionality supporting specific needs. Our research questions for this paper are: *RQ1: To what extent does e-learning/e-assessment tools support e-assessment tasks specifically needed in programming courses? RQ2: In what ways could a digital ecosystem within e-assessment make for improved assessments?*

In the case study performed we look in most detail at the tools used in the authors' own university, which we had the opportunity to try out in detail, whereas other related tools were only studied via documentation available on the internet. The rest of the paper is structured as follows: Sect. 2 provides some background on question types in programming and identifies two question types for which the support (or lack of support) will be specifically investigated in the case study – namely Parsons problems [11] and code writing questions [12]. Section 3 then looks at the support for these question types in typical e-assessment/e-learning tools, with most detailed focus on the tools used in the authors' university, namely Blackboard Learn and Inspera Assessment. Section 4 then discusses whether the progress towards digital ecosystems with open API's could help improve the support for more diverse needs in e-assessment. Finally, Sect. 5 concludes the paper.

2   Question Types for E-Assessment in Programming

Programming exams may contain many different types of questions [13]. The below list provides some broad categories:

- Conceptual questions: These are questions that do not directly involve code, but focus on the recall and understanding of concepts, e.g., "What is a key difference between a list and a set?" (possibly a multiple choice question) or "Explain the concept of polymorphism and its utility?" (possibly a free text question)

- Code tracing: The code is given, and the candidate's task is to explain what the code does. Within this category, questions may vary from those requiring only brief answers, e.g., "What will be the output of this program?", to more detailed ones, e.g., "Explain what this program does, line by line."
- Code writing: It is explained what a program is supposed to do, and the candidate's task is to write the code.
- Code completion: It is explained what a program is supposed to do, and some code is provided, but not fully complete. The candidate's task is then to fill in or select missing parts, or to rearrange code lines in the correct order.
- Error detection: It is explained what a program is supposed to do, and some faulty code is provided. The candidate's task is then to identify the mistakes, possibly also to propose corrections.

As indicated by Sheard et al. [14], code writing appears to be the most used question type in programming exams, followed by code tracing. Writing and tracing tasks can be seen as opposites, i.e., write all the code vs. write no code (rather understand the code which is given). Completion and error detection tasks as somewhere in between those two extremes, requiring both understanding of the code already given, and ability to write some extra code: the missing parts to be added to completion tasks, the corrections to be proposed for error detection tasks.

A detailed analysis of all possible question types would be prohibitively time-consuming, so here we choose to focus on two specific question types, namely Parsons problems [11] and code writing questions [12]. The reason for choosing these two types is that they are quite specific for the discipline of programming, whereas other question types could more easily be supported by generic question types found in most e-assessment and e-learning systems. For instance, conceptual questions could be implemented as free-text short answer tasks or multiple choice questions. The same applies to code tracing questions, where the brief answer variety might typically be given as multiple choice, fill-in-number or fill-in-text depending on the output, while the longer variety could be a free-text answer or a sequence of fill-in fields showing the changes of variable content during execution. Code completion tasks (other than Parsons problems) could be implemented by e.g. multiple choice, fill-in, or pull-down menus for each missing code fragment, and error detection could again be short answer, fill-in (for proposed corrections) or multiple choice (selecting between real errors and distractors).

What are then the particularities of the two mentioned question types? *Parsons problems* [11] are coding problems where it is explained what some piece of code is supposed to do, and the code lines are given, but in jumbled order. It is then the candidates' task to rearrange them in the right order. This question type has attracted a lot of research interest [15–18] because it reduces cognitive load for the students (e.g., recall of syntax, avoiding typing mistakes), yet still tests their visual-spatial abilities, constructive skills in solving a problem and constructing a solution from available building blocks. Since building blocks are larger (entire code lines rather than character by character on the keyboard), each question can be solved faster, thus potentially achieving better topical coverage in the exam set as a whole. Also, quick solution and automated feedback make such problems interesting for digital learning resources with self-testing features, for instance, the interactive e-book [19] makes extensive use of such problems among its exercises. Questions in Parsons problems can be made easier by providing hints [20] or more difficult by adding distractors [18], they can be one-dimensional (most common) or two-dimensional [21], the latter relevant with programming languages where indents have semantic significance (e.g., Python).

A common way of implementing Parsons problems digitally would be as drag-and-drop questions – a featured question type in many e-learning/e-exam applications. Drag and drop questions may test students' higher order thinking skills, i.e., algorithmic problem-solving skills [22, 23]. The recent research has been progressed more towards the visual programming language (VPL) that allows users to create programs using drag-and-drop genre [24]. However, its use in e-exam applications will normally not have been made with programming tasks in mind, rather tasks such as placing names in the correct positions on a background picture (e.g., Latin names of body parts for an anatomy exam, names on countries on a map for a primary school Geography exam). Hence, standard tool support for drag-and-drop questions may not be ideal for Parsons problems in programming.

Code writing tends to be a key element of programming exams, and most would agree that doing these tasks with pen and paper is not particularly authentic. Switching to a digital interface will make the task more similar to real work – but not necessarily fully authentic, as there may be various ambition levels to the tool support. For instance, students may be able to type the code in the test interface, but this could be in an editor with specific support for code writing (more authentic) or in a generic text input window with few functional features (less authentic). Also, students might be able to compile and run the code (more authentic), or not (less authentic). Sometimes, the more authentic, the better – but not always. A problem with the ability to compile, run, and test the code during an exam, for instance, is that students will then spend more time on each programming task – due to the need to debug and rerun if something was not working. More time on each task would give poorer coverage of the learning outcomes, especially if tool usage was not among the specified learning outcomes for the course. An ideal e-exam tool should therefore have a wide range of support for code writing tasks, anything from writing in a fairly simple editor without the ability to run, to professional tool support for code editing, testing and debugging.

3   Analysis of Mainstream Tool Support

As shown in [25], there are many tools for e-assessment of programming, but many of these are standalone applications or cloud tools not integrated with official university information systems. This section looks at mainstream tool support for Parsons problems and code writing problems, with special focus on Blackboard Learn and Inspera Assessment, which happen to be the mandatory tools in the authors' university for formative and summative e-assessment, respectively. The first subsection looks at Blackboard Learn, the second at Inspera Assessment, and the third makes a quick review of some other tools.

3.1 Blackboard Learn

Blackboard Learn is the current LMS for the authors' university. It is used for communication between teaching staff and students during the semester, e.g., course info and announcements, learning resources, exercises (if not graded), etc. It is not compulsory to use it for everything, so teaching staff could use supplementary tools, in addition, for instance, for students' automated self-testing. However, it would be convenient both for teachers and students if course tasks are seamlessly supported through Blackboard, so that they avoid confusing and time-consuming switches between tools [26].

Support for Parsons problems in Blackboard turns out to be limited. Drag and drop questions do not exist, so such questions would instead have to be approximated by other question types. Obvious candidates might be *ordering questions* or *jumbled sentence questions*. Ordering questions would show the code lines in a shuffled order, then let the user assign ordinal numbers to each in input fields beside the code lines. This is not entirely ideal for the purpose. For instance, code lines are not repositioned, so the resulting code is not easily read. Reordering requires changing the ordinal numbers of all code lines affected, whereas a modern drag and drop interface might solve this by repositioning fewer lines. Jumbled sentence questions would give a series of input fields, where each would yield a drop-down menu when clicked, with all the code lines as alternatives. The student would then have to make a multiple choice selection for each input field. This would appear somewhat better than the ordering question since at least the code would be shown in the wanted order when selections had been made. However, reordering would have the same issues as with the ordering questions, and if the task contains many code lines, the drop-down menus will be long and clumsy.

Specific support for Code writing problems in Blackboard does not exist, beyond generic essay and short answer question forms meant for natural language text, or using file upload questions (e.g., student could write the code in a separate tool more fit for programming, and then upload the file to Blackboard).

3.2 Inspera Assessment

When it comes to Parsons problems, Inspera Assessment does support drag and drop questions. The resulting interface for the student while solving the task is therefore more elegant than what can be achieved in Blackboard, though there are some issues with the user interface. The task has to be made with separate drop areas for each code line, rather than one big drop area where the order is given by relative positioning. This means that the student still has to reposition several code lines in cases where a better interface might have gotten away with just repositioning one line and having other lines yield place. Especially, if trying to make two-dimensional Parsons problems, the snapping feature may behave a little counter-intuitively, since it is not determined by the position of the mouse pointer, rather the middle of the drag object (mouse pointer would be more natural, or the left edge of the drag object). Parsons problems become very time-consuming for the teacher to develop in Inspera, since all the drag areas must be created manually one by one and filled with solution (and possibly distractor) code lines, and then linked to the correct drop areas, also manually created one by one. Especially for two-dimensional Parsons problems, this takes quite a lot of time. An illustration of a two-dimensional Parsons problem for Python, as implemented in Inspera, is shown in Fig. 1. For space reasons, the natural language explanation of what the code was supposed to do is omitted, showing only the interactive part of the screen. The candidate's task would be to drag each code line into the correct position in the grid (the function heading def deriv(poly): going upper left), both concerning vertical order and horizontal indenting, as indents have semantic significance in Python. In Inspera Assessment, the 28 drop areas must be created one by one, hand positioned in the grid and adjusted for size, hence quite time-consuming for the question author.

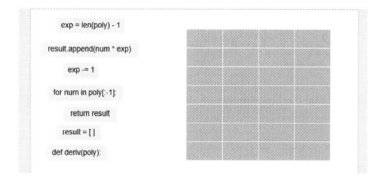

Fig. 1. Two-dimensional Parson problem for Python.

For code writing tasks, Inspera has a dedicated question type called "Programming". Notably, the student is not able to compile and run the code during the exam, nor is staff able to run it afterwards in connection with grading, so this type of task is manually graded. However, it does support the following features:

- A monotype font suitable for code, and syntax highlighting for some much used programming languages
- Other syntax related support, such as automatically giving an end parenthesis for each start parenthesis, and automatically making indents where appropriate, for instance in Python if the previous code line ended with a colon.

All in all, then, Inspera Assessment has better question type support both for Parsons problems and code writing than what Blackboard has, but still with substantial limitations. The user interaction for drag and drop questions is somewhat tedious for students, especially if reordering, and for teacher authoring of questions it is even more tedious. For code writing questions, both have the shortcoming that the code will not run and must be manually graded, and Blackboard does not even have syntactic support. Hence, both Blackboard and Inspera could clearly be made much more usable for handling these question types if there were plugins specifically targeting them.

3.3   Other Tools

Table 1 gives a summary of the possible support for Parsons problems and code writing problems in various tools. In addition to Inspera and Blackboard, other tools worth looking at are the e-exam tool WISEflow (a competitor to Inspera) and general LMS tools Canvas and Moodle (competitors to Blackboard). The authors gathered information about these tools from web-documentation since they do not have direct access for these tools in their institution. Our findings show that Blackboard does not support drag-and-drop functionality while all the other tools support this feature. However, these tools only support the basic functionality of drag-and-drop into text and image, which is not ideal for Parson problems. Code writing is supported in Inspera and Moodle, moreover it seems Moodle has better support than Inspera. Both Moodle and Inspera support code writing with syntactic support (e.g., indentation and code highlighting). In addition, Moodle has an external plugin, Coderunner that allows students to run their programs during exams and teachers to run programs in order to grade student's answers. Limitations of the functionalities in tools can be improved further by third-party extensions and plugins with the adoption of digital ecosystems.

Table 1. Tool support summarized.

Tool	Parsons problems	Code writing	Import/export questions	Plugins
Blackboard	Lacks drag&drop	No specific support (free text)	QTI, LTI	LTI, Google Apps SafeAssign
Inspera	Has drag&drop, but not ideal	Only syntactic support for code [27]	QTI, LTI	Atlassian Jira
Canvas	Hasdrag&drop but not ideal	No specific support (free text)	QTI, LTI	LTI, Facebook, Google Drive, Twitter, Tinychat Google Docs, Kaltura, LinkedIn, Canvasdocs
WISEflow	Hasdrag&drop but not ideal	No specific support (free text)	QTI, Canvas, Moodle XML, Blackboard V6-9	
Moodle	Hasdrag&drop but not ideal	Syntactic support, Code runner support	QTI, LTI, GIFT Moodle XML, XHTML, LTI	SEB Quiz Access, Coderunner Rule, LTI, Turnitin, Plagiarism

4   Towards a Digital Ecosystem

Tools like those discussed in Sect. 3 can import/export questions in the QTI (Question and Test Interoperability) format [28]. So for authoring of drag-and-drop questions (which was somewhat cumbersome in Inspera), a possible way to improve the support would be to make a stand-alone authoring tool that could generate questions as QTI files, then to be uploaded to Inspera, for instance as suggested by [29]. In Blackboard, such an authoring tool would not be of much use, since the question type is not supported. Hence, Blackboard would need an integrated plugin supporting the question type, and an integrated plugin would probably appear better for the user of Inspera, too, especially for students solving the tasks, since the user interface could then be improved with custom features for Parsons problems. A plugin might also be a possible solution for better support of code writing questions in both tools (e.g., for the student, ability to compile and test the code during the exam; for the teacher, support for automated testing and grading of delivered code).

Currently, Inspera offers REST-based APIs to enable the third-party developers to integrate the additional functionalities and a Custom Interaction API that allows customers to build specialized question types. It supports stimuli elements with JavaScript and mathematical tools such as Geogebra and Desmos. These specialized question types can still be exchanged through QTI specification and the IMS Global Assessment Custom Interactions specification.

As the digitization of the exams increased, the need for technology for exams is also rapidly increasing. However, the usability of a digital exam system highly depends on the simplicity of the system. Also, users are sometimes forced to use several systems, not well integrated. For instance, in the authors' own university Blackboard is actively used as an LMS while Inspera is used as an assessment tool. The key requirements from teachers in the computer science department at our university that are ecosystems related include:

- Teachers want to have some exercises using the Inspera UI rather than Blackboard's, to give the students more accurate exam practice. Preferably, students should then be able run Inspera via Blackboard, so that Blackboard could still automatically register who has delivered the exercise.
- Concerning the import and export of contents, teachers may want to use last year's exam questions as exercise questions the next year. However, while Inspera can export questions in QTI 2.1 format, Blackboard (at least the version in our university) for some reason only seems to support the older QTI 1.2 standard.

In a well functioning software ecosystem, the platform system would have open APIs for external third-parties to develop plug-ins on top of the platform. This type of solution has several advantages over monolithic exam systems. García-Holgado and García-Peñalvo [30] explained that technological ecosystems could be considered as a framework to develop technological solutions where information and the human factor are the centre of the system. One of the main advantages with such an ecosystem is the flexibility it provides to institutions to integrate new software components within their workflows to support emerging needs.

The key requirements from teachers could be fulfilled to some extent with the current plug-in support by Inspera: (i) Integrate contents and external tools into LMS. Inspera supports sharing of the contents through the IMS Learning Tools Interoperability™ (LTI) plugin. LTI is an interoperability specification which facilitates full integration between Inspera and Blackboard. With LTI support, Inspera can be launched as a tool from Blackboard, which allows students to take exams directly through Blackboard. This feature is currently supported in Canvas, Blackboard, and Moodle [31]. (ii) Sharing of the contents across e-learning platforms. Issues with import and export questions can be reduced with more updates in the versions of interoperability specifications of platforms and tools [32]. In [30], the authors addressed the problem of sharing questions across departments in university in the e-learning context. They argued that although the technological ecosystem provides tools to facilitate communication between departments, employees are not utilizing the tools.

Presently, Inspera only supports sharing questions among teachers in the same university – for wider sharing, one must export and import. Of course, one deterrent against easier sharing could be increased fear for question leakage, i.e., confidential exam questions being disclosed to candidates before the exam. However, it mostly seems to come down to lacking features, and a natural tendency to prioritize the basic features first: support for each autonomous teaching staff for making the exam in their course, rather than to support a wider community of teachers within a discipline in making larger question bases that can be shared and continuously quality assured and updated.

However, Inspera also has some frustrating shortcomings on the single course level. In Norway, the law says that complaint graders shall not know the grades or viewpoints of the original graders. However, in Inspera it was impossible to hide given scores on the tasks. This meant that complaint graders could not do their grading in Inspera, but instead had to receive pdf screenshots of student answers, and then had to score manually even tasks like multiple choice, that would have been auto-scored in Inspera – with higher work-load and increased risk of error as a result. Fixing such issues will of course have a higher priority for the next release than more ambitious ideas supporting disciplinary communities. In Norwegian universities, Inspera must also be integrated with FS (Common Student System), a legacy system used for the administration of students in universities. Both the LMS and the e-exam system will fetch information from FS (e.g., which students are enrolled, registered for the exam, etc.) and send information back to FS (e.g., grades). The legacy system is not directly seen by students or teachers, but by administrative personnel – for instance it also contains the link between anonymous candidate numbers used during exams and the students' identities.

The implementation of digital exam ecosystems involves a higher degree of complexity due to the integration of different components that should evolve both individually and collectively. Although the REST APIs aids the developer, lack of the framework and design patterns makes the integration with plug-ins more difficult. A framework for technological ecosystems will consider all aspects related to integration, interoperability, and the evolution of the components [33] thus forms the well-developed open ecosystem. Several frameworks and methods were discussed in the literature. For instance, A framework can be designed using architectural patterns using the Business Process Model and Notation (BPMN) [30]. García et al. proposed a service-based framework connecting Moodle LMS and Basic LTI (BLTI) [33]. Consequently, it could ease commercial vendors and free software developers to make plugins supporting the authoring, solving, and grading of various question types.

5 Conclusion

Several advantages have been discussed in literature about e-assessments, and today many tools are available for course management and assessments. Although many e-learning/e-assessment tools are available, only a few support programming exams. In the paper, we discussed our practical experience with programming questions in Blackboard Learn and Inspera Assessment tools, particularly focusing on Parsons problems (i.e., drag - and–drop questions) and code writing questions. Our observations revealed that currently Inspera, Moodle, Canvas, WISEflow supports drag-and-drop questions but not ideal for programming using Parson problems. Also, there is a low-level integration between Inspera and Blackboard for programming exams. The improvements can be made further with the transition of a monolithic digital exam system to digital exam ecosystem by opening APIs though it requires a lot of changes internally and outside institutions. However, open APIs alone cannot be able to improve e-assessments, without the support of frameworks, and architectural designs that explain software updates, security policies, access permissions etc. Though many papers discussed ecosystem phenomenon in e-learning, its implementation on the digital exam is still in infancy. This paper has initiated the concept of the ecosystem in the digital exams area focusing on programming exams.

The paper still has some limitations: It discussed only details of the tools used in authors' university, Inspera and Blackboard, since they have direct access to only these tools. Currently, there are many tools available for digital assessment; the study of every tool would require more time for research and cost (to buy licenses for tools). Moreover, students and teachers are adapted to the tools they use, so it is more convenient to receive their feedback. The findings from this study are based on the author's practical experience. Hence, this study can be improved in the future by more quantitative and qualitative research in academia and industries, especially on the perspective of a digital ecosystem.

References

1. Fluck, A.: An international review of eExam technologies and impact. Comput. Educ. **132**, 1–15 (2018)
2. Spector, J.M., et al.: Technology enhanced formative assessment for 21st century learning (2016)
3. Veiga, W., et al.: A software ecosystem approach to e-learning domain. In: Proceedings of the XII Brazilian Symposium on Information Systems on Brazilian Symposium on Information Systems: Information Systems in the Cloud Computing Era-Volume 1. Brazilian Computer Society (2016)

4. Stanley, J., Briscoe, G.: The ABC of digital business ecosystems. arXiv preprint arXiv:1005. 1899 (2010)
5. Nachira, F., Dini, P., Nicolai, A.: A network of digital business ecosystems for Europe: roots, processes and perspectives. Introductory Paper, 106. European Commission, Bruxelles (2007)
6. Jansen, S., Cusumano, M.A.: Defining software ecosystems: a survey of software platforms and business network governance. In: Software Ecosystems: Analyzing and Managing Business Networks in the Software Industry, p. 13 (2013)
7. Kallinikos, J., Aaltonen, A., Marton, A.: The ambivalent ontology of digital artifacts. MIS Q. **37**(2), 357–370 (2013)
8. Uden, L., Wangsa, I.T., Damiani, E.: The future of E-learning: E-learning ecosystem. In: 2007 Inaugural IEEE-IES Digital EcoSystems and Technologies Conference, DEST 2007 (2007)
9. Oskar, P.: Software ecosystems and e-learning: recent developments and future prospects. In: Proceedings of the International Conference on Management of Emergent Digital EcoSystems, France, pp. 427–431. ACM (2009). ISBN 978-1-60558-829-2
10. Marti, R., Gisbert, M., Larraz, V.: Technological learning and educational management ecosystems. Thirteen characteristics for efficient design. In: EdMedia+ Innovate Learning. Association for the Advancement of Computing in Education (AACE) (2018)
11. Parsons, D., Haden, P.: Parson's programming puzzles: a fun and effective learning tool for first programming courses. In: Proceedings of the 8th Australasian Conference on Computing Education, vol. 52. Australian Computer Society, Inc. (2006)
12. Sheard, J., et al.: Assessment of programming: pedagogical foundations of exams. In: Proceedings of the 18th ACM Conference on Innovation and Technology in Computer Science Education. ACM (2013)
13. Simon, et al.: Introductory programming: examining the exams. In: Proceedings of the Fourteenth Australasian Computing Education Conference, vol. 123. Australian Computer Society, Inc. (2012)
14. Sheard, J., et al.: Exploring programming assessment instruments: a classification scheme for examination questions. In: Proceedings of the Seventh International Workshop on Computing Education Research. ACM (2011)
15. Denny, P., Luxton-Reilly, A., Simon, B.: Evaluating a new exam question: Parsons problems. In: Proceedings of the Fourth International Workshop on Computing Education Research. ACM (2008)
16. Helminen, J., et al.: How do students solve parsons programming problems?: an analysis of interaction traces. In: Proceedings of the Ninth Annual International Conference on International Computing Education Research. ACM (2012)
17. Ericson, B.J., Margulieux, L.E., Rick, J.: Solving parsons problems versus fixing and writing code. In: Proceedings of the 17th Koli Calling International Conference on Computing Education Research. ACM (2017)
18. Harms, K.J., Chen, J., Kelleher, C.L.: Distractors in Parsons problems decrease learning efficiency for young novice programmers. In: Proceedings of the 2016 ACM Conference on International Computing Education Research. ACM (2016)
19. Guzdial, M., Ericson, B.: CS Principles: Big Ideas in Programming. RuneStone Academy (2014)
20. Morrison, B.B., et al.: Subgoals help students solve Parsons problems. In: Proceedings of the 47th ACM Technical Symposium on Computing Science Education. ACM (2016)
21. Ihantola, P., Karavirta, V.: Two-dimensional parson's puzzles: the concept, tools, and first observations. J. Inf. Technol. Educ. **10**, 119–132 (2011)

22. Kalelioğlu, F.: A new way of teaching programming skills to K-12 students: Code.org. Comput. Hum. Behav. **52**, 200–210 (2015)
23. Lee, Y.Y., Chen, N., Johnson, R.E.: Drag-and-drop refactoring: intuitive and efficient program transformation. In: Proceedings of the 2013 International Conference on Software Engineering, San Francisco, CA, USA, pp. 23–32. IEEE Press (2013)
24. Tsai, C.-Y.: Improving students' understanding of basic programming concepts through visual programming language: the role of self-efficacy. Comput. Hum. Behav. **95**, 224–232 (2019)
25. Gupta, S., Gupta, A.: E-Assessment tools for programming languages: a review. In: Proceedings of the First International Conference on Information Technology and Knowledge Management (2018)
26. Forment, M.A., Guerrero, M.J.C., González, M.Á.C., Peñalvo, F.J.G., Severance, C.: Interoperability for LMS: the missing piece to become the common place for Elearning innovation. In: Lytras, M.D., et al. (eds.) WSKS 2009. LNCS (LNAI), vol. 5736, pp. 286–295. Springer, Heidelberg (2009). https://doi.org/10.1007/978-3-642-04754-1_30
27. Inspera Assessment. Programming - Knowledge Base - Inspera. https://inspera.atlassian.net/wiki/spaces/KB/pages/57311556/Programming
28. IMS Global. Question and Test Interoperability (QTI): Overview. https://www.imsglobal.org/question/qtiv2p2/imsqti_v2p2_oview.html
29. Jørgensen, J., Kvannli, S.: Efficient generation of Parsons problems for digital programming exams in Inspera, Department of Computer Science. NTNU, Trondheim (2019)
30. García-Holgado, A., García-Peñalvo, F.J.: Architectural pattern to improve the definition and implementation of eLearning ecosystems. Sci. Comput. Program. **129**, 20–34 (2016)
31. Inspera Assessment. Assessment technology standards. http://www.inspera.com/standards
32. Dagger, D., et al.: Service-oriented e-learning platforms: from monolithic systems to flexible services. IEEE Internet Comput. **11**(3), 28–35 (2007)
33. García Peñalvo, F.J., et al.: Opening learning management systems to personal learning environments. J. Univers. Comput. Sci.: J. UCS **17**(9), 1222–1240 (2011)

Reflection on How to Write the Learning Outcomes for an Online Programming Course for Teachers

Hege Annette Olstad[(✉)] and Majid Rouhani

Department of Computer Science (IDI),
Norwegian University of Science and Technology (NTNU),
7491 Trondheim, Norway
{hege.a.olstad,majid.rouhani}@ntnu.no

Abstract. The EU Commission for Higher Education through the Bologna Process declaration has put into action a series of reforms. One of the reforms is the development of learning outcomes in the *European Credit Transfer and Accumulation System (ECTS)*. One part of these reforms requires European universities to identify and describe learning outcomes students will achieve after attending a course or program. There is no exact way of writing the learning outcomes, and there seems to be an indistinctly use of terms when explaining outcomes [1]. This can naturally cause some possible confusions in relation to what the learning outcomes should consist of, and make it difficult to write the learning outcomes for a course or a program. The purpose of this paper is to promote some explanations and clarifications that can ease the writing of the learning outcomes. The research question is How to write meaningful learning Outcomes? This paper presents a reflection on how the learning outcomes might be written. It is taken into account recommendations from relevant literature and framework intended for Europe. In this paper, the online course Applied Programming for Teachers is an example of how meaningful learning outcomes may be written with a focus on digital competence.

Keywords: Learning outcome · Competence · Digital competence · Pedagogical- and didactic competencies · Online course

1 Introduction

Right competencies are essential for companies but are equally important for students, to perform a particular profession. Higher education systems strive to produce graduates with the right competencies whatever field of study. On the other hand, students are not always aware of the competencies they developed during their education [2], which can lead to students with low confidence [3].

Some researchers suggest that learning outcomes could be used as a learning resource to make students aware of competencies they can gain. Learning outcomes are statements of what a learner knows, understands, and can do when completing a learning process. In this way, the students with knowledge of where they are going and what is expected of them at the end of a course. In addition, learning outcomes can be

© IFIP International Federation for Information Processing 2019
Published by Springer Nature Switzerland AG 2019
I. O. Pappas et al. (Eds.): I3E 2019, LNCS 11701, pp. 597–608, 2019.
https://doi.org/10.1007/978-3-030-29374-1_48

used as a reflection tool for students to create awareness of achievements throughout a course or program [2]. To archive this, learning outcomes must be identified and clearly articulated to the students [4], and to be used productively by students, it needs to be emphasized, explained and exemplified [2].

The identification and description of competence areas is the first step towards the writing of the learning outcomes [5, p. 4], but one problem is that courses and programs in Higher Education often use different terms when describing the learning outcomes. Competence is also a term used for learning outcomes, together with learning objectives, aims, and objectives. The indistinctly use of terms might be challenging when it comes to writing the learning outcomes, select learning outcomes that are appropriate and reflect the particular purpose, and the context in question [1].

There might be several competencies students can achieve through a course or a program. Which competencies a course or program will give depends on the content of the course [2]. Further, there seems to be essential to understand the complexity of each competency, since some may be transversal key competencies. Transversal key competencies consist of several underlying competencies like language, mathematics, learning to learn and cultural awareness. In the course Applied Programming for Teachers, there are listed several competencies students will achieve by attending this course. One competence listed is *Good digital competence*, and this is a typical example of transversal key competencies. Digital competence is an important key competence which also is listed by the European Parliament as one of eight competencies for lifelong learning [5, p. 1].

In this paper, we will give an example of how the learning outcomes could be written reflecting on previous studies with digital competence as the starting point. The paper is organized as follows. Next section presents a literature review on related work and positions the paper in the context of learning outcomes in the area of digital competencies. Section 3 presents a description of the method and case. Sect. 4 presents the results combined with a discussion. This chapter outlines some examples of how the existing learning outcomes can be changed to approximate recommendations identified in the literature review. Sect. 5 present a conclusion and further work.

2   Literature Review

2.1   Clarification of the Terms

An aim is usually a definition of overall achievements that teachers, courses, or program are trying to reach. It tells participants what the course or a session is about and how to ensure that students have achieved knowledge about this in a final test or exam. Learning objectives were earlier stated as the observable and measurable behaviors that learners should show as a result of participating. Today learning objectives provide more broad-based learning outcomes as goals that are intended to arise as a result [6]. The learning outcomes, on the other hand, are pointed out as broader intuitive and user-friendly because this describes students' expected knowledge and skills and what is expected that they will be able to do as a result of engaging in the learning process [7, 8]. When students demonstrate what they can do at the end of a course or program, it shows that they have specific competencies. It is the focus on competencies that brings in the concept of learning outcomes. The term competence is widely used throughout Europe, and in several countries substitutes the term learning outcomes [9].

There are many different definitions and interpretations with the term competence, that can create some confusion when operating internationally. Fortunately, in *The European Qualifications Framework* (EQF), it is pointed towards a shared approach where competence means: "the proven ability to use knowledge, skills and personal, social and/or methodological abilities, in work or study situations" [10, p. 11].

What students know, understand and are able to demonstrate after completion the process of learning is stated in the learning outcomes, and learning outcomes are validated by their relationship to competencies [9, p. 31]. The shared approach creates a mutual relationship between learning outcomes and competence [11]. Compared to competence, learning outcomes are more distinct. Even if learning outcomes and competencies substitutes each other the term learning outcomes seems clearer. Therefor learning outcomes are easier to use than competence when describing what students are expected to know, understand and/or be able to demonstrate at the end of a module or program. The "fuzziness" of competence disappears in the clarity of learning outcomes. The characteristics of successful courses are that they consist of a clear idea of what can be achieved at the end [11].

2.2 Competence

As mentioned in the introduction, the identification of competencies is the first step towards writing the learning outcomes. One competence may have several specific outcomes within knowledge and skills, so a course typically contains more outcomes than competencies [6, p. 31].

Digital competence is one of eight key competencies for lifelong learning in the 2006 European Recommendation on Key Competencies, and is defined broadly as:

> "the set of knowledge, skills, attitudes (thus including abilities, strategies, values and aware-
> ness) that are required when using ICT and digital media to perform tasks; solve problems;
> communicate; manage information; collaborate; create and share content; and build knowl-
> edge effectively, efficiently, appropriately, critically, creatively, autonomously, flexibly, ethi-
> cally, reflectively for work, leisure, participation, learning, socializing, consuming, and
> empowerment." [5, p. 43]

Digital competence is seen as a transversal key competence because it also consists of several underlying competencies like language, mathematics, learning to learn and cultural awareness. This competence is also related to the so-called 21st century skills which all citizens should hold to ensure their active participation in society and the economy [5, p. 1].

For teachers, digital competence is more complex and is also seen up against 21st-century competencies. The most prominent 21st-century competencies found in international frameworks that have been shown to offer benefits in multiple areas of life are associated with critical thinking, communication, collaboration, and creativity and innovation [7]. Based on the literature and previous studies in this field, it is identified four competencies (learning competency, educational competency, social competency, and technological competency) that are theorized as core competencies for teachers' innovative teaching.

The term innovative teachers are adopted as a result of teachers' responsibility to attract student's interest and attention in new ways. Innovative teaching is a necessity for all teachers in order to meet the educational needs of the new generations [8].

2.3   Teachers Digital Competence

The technological competence is critical because technology creates great opportunities for teachers to inspire curiosity, imagination, and their students' interest. Competence refers to that teachers are aware of how to integrate educational technologies, provoke critical thinking, and deepen student understanding. Teachers also need to be able to find the necessary information among information available on the internet, to integrate this information which often coming from multiple sources, and to effectively use this information to solve teaching problems [13]. Taking in concern the definition of digital competence (also referred to as core competencies, key competence, and generic competence), the definition indicates that being digitally competent involves more than having technical skills. Technical skills and the ability to use specific tools are only two of many underlying competencies within digital competence. However, digital competence for teachers include more than technological competence and is more complex than citizens' average use and other professional groups. While teachers need to hold basic competencies, they also need pedagogical- and didactic judgments based on how technology can expand the learning possibilities for students in certain subjects [14]. This leads to the term pedagogical digital competence (PDC) and includes a pedagogical aspect of digital competence into consideration [15].

The main characteristic of PDC is thus the ability to develop/improve pedagogical work by means of digital technology in a professional context, primarily in web course/online teaching. However, PDC involves all kinds of pedagogical work in professional contexts where digital technology is used and adds a wider sense to PDC. There are three levels to PDC, and their internal relationship. First, there is on a micro-level an interaction level which involves the pedagogical interaction with students. Second, there is a meso-level, which is on a course level and involve design and implementation of courses, and infrastructure of education which can typically contain integration of resources. Third and last is the macro-level which is on an organizational level. This level focuses on educational management and the development of the organization. Strategic pedagogical leadership is a central component of PDC on all three levels, and the complexity of PDC makes this a competence that can be defined in different ways. Which competence a course will lead to will depend on methodological choices of theories of learning, but it is always something that finds expression in concrete action. Regardless of theory applied PDC can always be evaluated, documented and developed. In principle developed PDC always results in better support for students' learning [15].

Based on this, PDC can be defined as: *"The concept of pedagogical digital competence refers to the ability to consistently apply the attitudes, knowledge and skills required to plan and conduct, and to evaluate and revise on an ongoing basis, ICT-supported teaching, based on theory, current research and proven experience with a view to supporting students' learning in the best possible way."* [15, p. 48].

2.4   Writing the Learning Outcomes

The *European Qualifications Framework for Lifelong Learning* defines learning outcomes as a statement of what a learner knows, understands and can do when completing a learning process. What a student knows, understand and can do are defined in terms of knowledge, skills, and competence. [9, p. 17]. The same definition is used in *Defining, writing and applying learning outcomes: A European Handbook* [5, p. 29]. One of the basic theories in the European Handbook is Bloom's taxonomy. Bloom's taxonomy is an important theory that have influenced the thinking about learning outcomes and progression. A central focus in this taxonomy is action verb, and good learning outcomes will be described with action verbs that identifies what action the student should be able to perform. The action verbs are made solely associated with the cognitive dimension of learning, but it is important to avoid ambiguous verbs. Examples of ambiguous verbs are "know", "understand", "enjoy", "determine" and "appreciate". Examples of precise words are "identify", "distinguish between", "assemble", "adjust" and "solve" [9, p. 49]. Even if a framework might ease the writing of the learning outcomes, outlining knowledge, skills, and competence as the main elements, there are still some challenges. First, one needs to be careful about treating outcomes of learning as information bits that can be selected and combined at will. This can ignore the extent to which knowledge, skills, and competence are related and interdependent and lead to neglect of the conditions [9, p. 45]. Second, it might be challenging to select learning outcomes that are appropriate and reflect the particular purpose and context in question [1].

Bloom's taxonomy has been reviewed and adjusted several times, but some describe the original Bloom's taxonomy from 1956 as a good starting point for writing the learning outcomes [7]. The taxonomy is a hierarchical level categorization of cognitive learning, where one moves from basic knowledge and comprehension to increasingly complex skills. The action verbs associated with each level of this taxonomy is a good starting point for writing the learning outcomes. Table 1 shows in the left column the levels of the taxonomy, while the right column is the verb. A good learning outcome will have a verb that identifies what students should be able to do, and under what conditions they should be able to demonstrate this.

Table 1. Bloom's taxonomy [7, p. 70]

Keywords	
I. Knowledge: Remembering information	Define, identify, label, state, list, match
II. Comprehension: explaining the meaning of information	Describe, paraphrase, summarize, estimate
III. Application: using abstracts in concrete situation	Determine, chart, implement, prepare, solve, use, develop
IV. Analysis: breaking down a whole into component parts	Point out, differentiate, distinguish, discriminate, compare
V. Synthesis: putting parts together to form a new and integrated whole	Create, design, plan, organize, generate, write
VI. Evaluation: making judgments about the merits of ideas, materials or phenomena	Appraise, critique, judge, weigh, evaluate, select

According to Bloom's taxonomy, well-written learning outcomes will consist of verbs that identify what action the students should be able to perform, under which conditions students should demonstrate the mastery, and how the mastery may be evaluated [7].

Knowledge is stated as one of three elements in the written learning outcomes, and when describing the knowledge, it should consist of words like define, identify, label, state, list, and match. Comprehension, application, analysis, synthesis are all levels that refer to the element skills [7]. Each level includes verbs that should be mentioned in the learning outcomes as shown in the right column in Table 1. The last element in the learning outcomes, competence, is when students use knowledge and skills in work or study situations [10]. The main distinction between competencies and true learning outcome is that the learning outcomes are written so that it can be measured or assessed. For example, to state that a student will understand or know some facts or topics are good objectives, but it is not easily measured [7]. Having in mind that objective is road-based learning outcomes as goals that are intended to arise as a result [6]. Readers are referred to the *Taxonomy of educational objectives: the classification of educational goals* [16], for a detailed explanation of Bloom's taxonomy.

In the introduction, it was pointed out that students need specific outcomes to reflect on throughout and after a course. The written learning outcomes are important for the students throughout a course to be able to identify which way they are going. The learning outcomes are also important for students after a course to be made aware of the competencies that they have developed during a course. Without, the learning outcomes it would be like planning a journey and don't know where to go before the journey start, you may end up somewhere you do not want to be [6]. However, it is worth mention that students are unlikely to seek out, read or reflect on the learning outcomes unless they are specifically encouraged to do so by teachers, or communicated through assessment practices [4].

3   Description of Method and Case

The purpose of this research is to promote some explanations and clarifications that can ease the writing of the learning outcomes. This case study is organized according to the pattern identified in relevant literature, frameworks, and standards common for European countries. Findings in the literature are compared to the learning outcomes as it is written in the course Applied Programming for Teachers today. Each element used in this research is examined separately before considering all of the elements together.

As explained in the introduction, this is not a close examination of the learning outcomes for the course in this research but outlines some example on how to write the learning outcomes, and where to start.

The Norwegian University of Science and Technology (NTNU) have created a Development Guide for study plans and course descriptions that is a standard requirement specification for all studies. The Development guide points out that the description of the learning outcomes on a course level should be more concrete and measurable than the descriptions on a program level. This because it is the sum of all courses in a program that ensure that the total learning outcomes of a program are covered. Further, the Development guide provides some example on how to write the learning outcomes focusing on knowledge and skills. One example is that formulation such as "The candidate understands key theories within…" should rather be described as "The candidate shows good understanding of theories within…". Another example is the use of active verb with explicit subjects and rather write "candidate understand" instead of "it is understood" [17]. The Development guide offers no explanation of what each category knowledge, skills, and competence are or why each of them is important but is a table divided into the three categories knowledge, skills, and competence. Several institutes at NTNU have developed forms based on this guide. Here one can fill in information related to the course or program, and the learning outcomes are one part of the form. The form does not explain what each category knowledge, skills, and competence are or why each of them is important. The form is also used in the description of the learning outcomes in the course Applied Programming for Teachers.

Applied Programming for Teachers is one of two online courses for teachers within ICT Programming. These two courses build on each other where the first one is Basic programming for teachers. The second course, Applied Programming for Teachers, will give students a deeper understanding of basic programming and how this can be applied to solve issues within different subject areas. The learning objective of the second course is to provide in-service teachers with insight on how to use programming to create digital solutions. This course focuses on the knowledge students need to become a teacher, and how they can ease students learning process and understanding of programming. Further, it gives guidance to programming in school and other subjects and activities where programming is used to support learning. The course currently has 83 participants, but this will more than double for the next year. The course has already received applications from 320 qualified applicants, of which 200 of these will be invited to participate in the course. Table 1 shows the description of the learning outcomes as it is written today. Here the teacher started on the top of the form describing the knowledge, the skills and finally the competencies.

Table 2. Learning outcomes: applied programming for teachers

Knowledge	• Detailed knowledge of constructions and structures in modern programming
	• Knowledge of programming languages, tools and methodology, both pedagogically oriented solutions and solutions that are used professionally
	• Basic understanding of the software's function in electronics and robots
	• Basic insight into the technique and methods for testing and misfire in major program projects

(continued)

Table 2. (*continued*)

Skills	• Develop and test programs with some complexity
	• Utilize modern programming tools and assess their suitability in teaching and learning
	• Identify and evaluate programming that should be included in simple technological solutions, understand the difficulty, scope and suitability in a teaching situation
	• Understand how creativity and collaboration can be utilized to promote programming learning
Generic competence	• Convey knowledge of programming and the didactics of the subject to others, both written and oral
	• Discuss, describe and evaluate solutions with some complexity
	• Plan varied work tasks and programming projects, focusing on creativity and social learning
	• Evaluate ethical issues related to programming
	• Demonstrate good digital competence

The First author in this paper is currently a Pd.D. candidate in Computer Science, with the aim to highlight what competencies students hold after completing higher IT education. The second author is the primary teacher and responsible for the subject Applied Programming for Teachers and is also responsible for writing the learning outcomes in this course. In this research, the first author has done the writing and review of the literature. Together we have discussed challenges that may arise when writing the learning outcomes and gone through the learning outcomes as they are today for this course. The discussion outlined that without any clear guideline on what knowledge, skills, and competence could consist of and where to start, it is challenging to write the learning outcomes. One competence often mentioned in 21st-century education, and essential for teaching today is digital competence. This is the competence that will be discussed further in this paper related to the learning outcomes.

4   Result and Discussion

A starting point for writing the learning outcomes pointed out in the literature is to identify competencies students can achieve by attending a course or a program. One competence students will hold after attending the course Programming for teachers is stated to be *Demonstrate good digital competence*. This statement raises questions like how can good digital competence be demonstrated, and what is good digital competence? First, digital competence consists of several underlying competencies because it is a transversal key competence [5]. To stat that participants get digital competence by attending one course could be a little ambitious, but may be suited better for a program. Second, to demonstrate something will be connected to skills, and under what condition students should demonstrate the mastery [7]. The digital competence for teachers is in additional transversal because it includes pedagogical- and didactic judgments. When pedagogical- and didactic judgments are included the existence of other underlying competencies occur. An underlying competence may be more suited for Applied Programming for Teachers. Example of one underlying competence that might suit the course is technological competence, which includes how to integrate educational technologies, provoke critical thinking, and deepen student understanding. Further, this provides skills such as synthesis and analyze. For example, to integrate information from multiple sources requires the ability to plan and organize, in another word synthesis. To be able to integrate information from multiple sources also requires the skill analyze because the information from several sources needs to be compared. Also, competencies on a micro level can be included like pedagogical interaction with students. The micro level will also lead to strategic pedagogical leadership competence [15]. Given that the course focuses on the knowledge students need to become a teacher, and how they can ease students learning process and understanding of programming, it also leaves students with the tree competencies *Learning competence, Educational competence*, and *Social competence*.

When it comes to knowledge and skills, there seem to be significant differences between the recommendations given by Cedefop [9] and Blooms Taxonomy described by Hartel and Foegeding [7], and the Development guide provided by NTNU [17]. While Cedefop [9] and Hartel and Foegeding [7] refer to words like know and understand as ambiguous verbs, the Development guide recommends these verbs. Thus, it may seem that the Development guide is somewhat indistinct. First, the Development guide recommends ambiguous verbs, and second, it points out that the description of learning outcomes on a course level should be more concrete and measurable than the specifications on a program level. This may lead to some confusions because ambiguous verbs may appear to be a contradiction to something that should be precise. Further, the Development guide does not offer a description of where to start when writing the learning outcomes, and the focus on competence is very limited. Since the various competencies require students to hold specific knowledge and specific skills, competencies are the first step towards writing the learning outcomes [5, p. 49].

When it comes to the knowledge listed in Table 2, this also seems to be ambiguous, if we are to follow the verb described in Bloom's taxonomy. Statements like knowledge of, detailed knowledge of, basic understanding, and basic insight, are all words that not easily are measurable. At the same time, words like this can ignore the relationship with subsequent ability and competence [9, p. 45]. Knowledge is information students should remember, and consists of action verbs like define, identify, label, state, list, and match. When students prove that they are capable of doing some of this action, they show that they possess the knowledge the course is meant to provide. Since what is listed within knowledge in Table 2 do not consist of action verb the knowledge may not be sufficiently described as it is today. Two examples here are *Detailed knowledge of constructions and structures in modern programming* and *Basic insight into the technique and methods for testing and misfire in major program prospects.* The first example could be replaced with *Identify constructions and structures in modern programming*. The second example could be replaced with *State misfire in major program projects, technique and methods for testing.* To state that a student will understand or know some fact or topic is a good objective but are not fitted as learning outcomes [8]. Words like know and understand is too ambiguous and might create some confusion about what's actually learned.

Also, the element skills might be confusing for students in this course, and especially *Understand how creativity and collaboration can be utilized to promote programming learning*. Again, understand together with knowledge of some facts or topic could be a good objective for the course, but may not fit for describing what student actually can do. Creativity is a valid term to use and is also one of the mentioned in teachers' digital competence [12]. In Table 2, however, creativity is described as something students should understand instead of with an action verb that typical shows that students can demonstrate creativity. This might be more appropriate if this skill were described with words like putting parts together to form a new and integrated whole, or in other words, design. Using verbs from Bloom's taxonomy, this skill could be written, for example, as *Design programming learning through creativity and collaboration.*

The writing of the learning outcomes for this course might have been challenging because the competencies that are described sounds more like knowledge and skills except for *Digital competence*. Example of skills are the words plan, evaluate and convey listed under the element competencies, in Table 2. These are all action verbs connected to skills and might be more suitable for this purpose. There are listed several competencies in the learning outcomes for the course Applied Programming for Teachers and one competence will typically have several specific outcomes. Looking at the amount of knowledge and skills in Table 2, compared to competencies listed, might be the first sign that this might not be an adequate learning outcomes. In the learning outcomes five competencies are listed, four types of knowledge and four types of skills. This is less than two outcomes for each competence. Also, as mentioned earlier, since this is a course for teacher's competencies attached to pedagogical- and didactic judgment might be more appropriate. Descriptions of pedagogical work in professional contexts or strategic pedagogical leadership might be better choices than *Good digital competence* for the course Applied Programming for Teachers. This involves all kinds of pedagogical work in professional contexts where digital technology is used. It may also be advisable to look more closely at the remaining competencies listed in Table 2. Here it can be recommended to take into account what competencies are and are not, and Bloom's Taxonomy described briefly in Sect. 2.4 Writing the learning outcomes.

Plan varied work tasks and programming projects, focusing on creativity and social learning, seems more like skills. Also, the competence Discuss, describe, and evaluate solutions with some complexity, is more connected to skills than it is a core competence. To be able to state that students have a specific competence, they who write the learning outcomes need to know what is expected within that competence. For example, reviewing relevant literature showed that digital competence is a complex competence because it consists of several underlying competencies. It is also recommended to look into the content of the course and identify if the content is suitable for the competencies that will be listed in the learning outcomes [2].

5   Conclusions and Further Work

This research shows that writing meaningful learning outcomes can be challenging, even with a development guide. A development guide needs a description of the meaning of each element knowledge, skills and competence, and where to start. Without this description, there is a risk of neglecting the relationship and interdependent between knowledge, skills, and competence, as seen in this case. For the course Applied Programming for Teachers, several competencies listed in Table 2 are identified as skills, and this might be the reason for the use of ambiguous descriptions listed in knowledge and skills.

Today only the Good digital competence appears as a pure competence, but it may be too broad for a single course. Further, digital competence might not be appropriate because it does not reflect the particular purpose and context in question. Since this is a course for teachers, it should include pedagogical- and didactic competencies. Also, competencies on a micro level like pedagogical interaction with students, strategic pedagogical leadership and learning competence, educational competence, and social competency, may be appropriate for the course Applied Programming for Teachers.

The identification of competencies student can gain by attending a course is the first step towards the development of the learning outcomes [5, p. 4]. It is indicated through the literature that there is a need for knowing what is expected within each competence listed, and then look into the course content and identify if this suits the competence. Further, words like know and understand are challenging to measure and asses. This indicates that several of the descriptions listed in Table 2 are too ambiguous. The description of the learning outcomes as it is written today may give unclear dependencies between knowledge, skills, and competencies. The description may also create confusions among students when it comes to where they are going and what is expected that they can do at the end of the course. The examples given Sect. 4 Result and discussion might provide some guidelines on how to write the learning outcomes.

This paper has not completed a full evaluation of the learning outcomes for the course Applied Programming for Teachers but given some example, based on a review of relevant literature. Further work should evaluate the learning outcomes as a whole for this course, and identify competencies through the course content. As mentioned in the introduction, students' reflection on learning outcomes will promote students with knowledge of where they are going and what they can do at the end of a course. Further work should, therefore, also investigate ways to use the learning outcomes for reflection, to better prepare students for employability through the competencies they gain.

References

1. Adam, S.: An introduction to learning outcomes. In: EUA Bologna Handbook: Making Bologna Work. European University Association, Berlin (2007)
2. St Jorre, T., Oliver, B.: Want students to engage? Contextualise graduate learning outcomes and assess for employability. J. High. Educ. Res. Dev. **37**(1), 44–57 (2018)

3. Ciarocco, N.J., Strohmetz, D.B.: The employable skills self-efficacy survey: an assessment of skill confidence for psychology undergraduates. J. Scholarsh. Teach. Learn. Psychol. **4**(1), 1–15 (2018)

4. Janosik, S.M., Frank, T.E.: Using ePortfolios to measure student learning in a graduate preparation program in higher education. Int. J. ePortfolio **3**(1), 13–20 (2013)

5. Ferrari, A.: Digital competence in practice: an analysis of frameworks. Institute for Prospective Technological Studies. Technical Report by the Joint Research Centre of the European Commission. Publications Office of the European Union, Luxembourg (2012)

6. Mckimm, J.: Setting learning objectives. J. Br. Hosp. Med. **70**(7), 406–409 (2009)

7. Hartel, R.W., Foegeding, E.A.: Learning: objectives, competencies, or outcomes? J. Food Sci. Educ. **3**, 69–70 (2004)

8. Shephard, K.: Higher education for sustainability: seeking affective learning outcomes. Int. J. Sustain. High. Educ. **9**(1), 87–98 (2008)

9. The European Centre for the Development of Vocational training (Cedefop): Defining, writing and applying learning outcome: a European Handbook. Publications Office of the European Union, Luxembourg (2017)

10. European Parliament and Council of EU: The European Qualifications Framework for Lifelong Learning (EQF) (2008)

11. Kennedy, D., Hyland, A., Ryan, N.: Learning outcomes and competencies. In: Kennedy, D., Hyland, A., Ryan, N., Gemlich, V., Balissa, A. (eds.) Using Learning Outcomes: Best of the Bologna Handbook, vol. 33, pp. 59–76. Dr. Josef Raabe Verlag, Berlin (2009)

12. Ananiadou, K., Clario, M.: 21st century skills and competences for new millennium learners in OECD countries. OECD Education Working Papers, no. 41. OECD Publishing, Paris (2009)

13. Zhu, C., Cai, Y.: What core competencies are related to teachers' innovative. Asia-Pacific J. Teach. Educ. **41**(1), 9–27 (2013)

14. Krumsvik, R.: Digital competence in Norwegian teacher education and schools. Högre utbildning **1**(1), 39–51 (2011)

15. From, J.: Pedagogical digital competence—between values, knowledge and skills. High. Educ. Stud. **7**(2), 43–50 (2017)

16. Bloom, B., et al.: Taxonomy of Educational Objectives: The Classification of Educational Goals, vol. 1. David McKay Co., Inc., New York (1956)

17. The Norwegian University of Science and Technology (NTNU): Veiledning for utvikling av studieplaner og emnebeskrivelser ved ntnu (2016). https://innsida.ntnu.no/documents/portlet_file_entry/10157/Veiledning-utvikling-studieplaner-emnebeskrivelser.pdf/e35dfeec-cd97-435b-b411-4f70051deb2a?status=0. Accessed April 2019

Autonomous and Collaborative e-Learning in English for Specific Purposes

Ivana Simonova[(⊠)] [iD]

University of Jan Evangelista Purkyne, Usti nad Labem, Czech Republic
ivana.simonova@ujep.cz

Abstract. The paper deals with the process of acquiring professional vocabulary and grammar in English for Specific Purposes (ESP) in pre-service teacher preparation. The main objective of the research was to (1) discover how much students learn in the ICT-enhanced process of instruction, where autonomous work and collaborative learning are applied so that to build preconcepts and reconstruct misconceptions in ESP; (2) detect the sources students exploited towards acquiring the learning content. The research was conducted at the Faculty of Education, University of Jan Evangelista Purkyne, Usti nad Labem, Czech Republic. Research sample consists of 62 probands enrolled in bachelor and master study programmes English Language and Literature and Teaching English Language and Literature. The research process is structured into three phases, and didactic tests are applied after each of them. Moreover, types of sources students used for acquiring the learning content were monitored and analyzed. Six hypotheses were tested and results showed statistically significant increase in knowledge after each phase.

Keywords: Higher education · ESP · English for Specific Purposes ·
English grammar · Professional vocabulary · e-Learning · Pre-service teacher

1 Introduction

Fast technical and technological development produces outcomes which accelerate changes in sustainable societies. All fields of life are impacted, including education. Teaching and learning methods, roles of teachers and learners, competencies required from them, educational environment and other factors are continuously under the process of development. Since their very beginning, information and communication technologies (ICT) have been contributing to this process. They provide tremendous opportunities for revising current approaches and practices in the field of education and implementing appropriate methodologies in the teacher education, i.e. both in the pre-service teacher preparation and in-service teacher training, which consequently changes ways how learners acquire new knowledge.

In the Czech Republic, the master degree in pedagogy and one subject as minimum is required from teachers at all school levels. Moreover, as the role of English language as lingua franca is more and more important in the current globalized world, teaching English as a foreign language has a key role in education. And, to acquire English for Specific Purposes, i.e. the language of profession, is highly required. In compliance

© IFIP International Federation for Information Processing 2019
Published by Springer Nature Switzerland AG 2019
I. O. Pappas et al. (Eds.): I3E 2019, LNCS 11701, pp. 609–620, 2019.
https://doi.org/10.1007/978-3-030-29374-1_49

with these demands, the pre-service teacher preparation needs to be efficient both in the field of methodology and English language. Considering these requirements, autonomous and collaborative learning (instead of others) can be applied to reach this objective, and ICT have the potential to enhance the process.

Reflecting the above mentioned, the main objective of this article is to present, analyze and discuss results of research focused on acquiring English professional vocabulary and grammar within English for Specific Purposes (ESP) with pre-service teachers at the Faculty of Education (FE), University of Jan Evangelista Purkyne (UJEP), Usti nad Labem, Czech Republic.

2   Theoretical Background

The process of acquiring English professional vocabulary and grammar within English for Specific Purposes (ESP) with pre-service teachers applies autonomous work, collaborative learning, ICT support towards *building preconcepts and re-constructing misconceptions.*

Before the research started, all participants reached a similar level of general English knowledge and hardly any experience in ESP. As stated by Comenius in the 17th century [1], the chance of remembering information which comes to the brain is much higher, if it is subjectively considered important and emotionally supported by the learner, if it is sensed by more than one sense at the same time, if it is associated with anything known before, as well as discovered by the learners themselves. As continuously adjusted to the newly developed knowledge and learner's experience, the more frequently the information is recalled, the more it differs from the primary preconcept [2]. Learner's memory can be improved by exploiting efficient learning strategies which reflect individual strengths and arrange the information to be acquired in appropriate order [3]. Moreover, other factors may impact the process of learning, e.g. stressful environment, learner's tiredness, boredom – extremely high levels decrease learner's quality of remembering, whereas mild levels support this process [4]; feelings of success and/or failure [5]; personal goals, and also the quality of sleep, when each information in memory network is predisposed to interfere, and the key consolidation comes when sleeping [6].

Irrespective the previous length of institutional education, learners' preconcepts may not be correct. However, learners consider them valid until enough evidence is collected to change their understanding. This phase may take a long period, in some cases till the adult age [7]. The exploitation of mixed-method approach (autonomous work, collaborative learning, ICT support application and others) in the pre-service teacher preparation is expected to assist the di10dactic modification of preconcepts and misconceptions which were developed within learner's previous studies of English language.

The benefit of working together is fairly obvious and *collaborative learning* approach works to provide students opportunities to engage with each other in thoughtful learning through peer interaction. This strategy addresses both the professional and social skills simultaneously. It is reported to be highly successful because of its need for interdependence in all levels, providing students with the tools to effectively learn from each other. And, it is a team approach where the success of the group depends on activities in which students team together to explore a significant question as well as upon everyone pulling his or her weight. Collaborative learning can be synonymous with social constructivism where collaboration leads to co-constructing new knowledge and meaning [8].

Learner's *autonomous work* is part of the process of autonomous, also called self-directed, learning. This is defined as an approach, in which individuals take responsibility for their learning; constructivist approach is applied in which students actively participate in the process of understanding within the learning context; learners focus on and control of learning rather than a teacher, and they also regulate and control their own learning activities [9]. In other words, it is the learner who takes responsibility for his/her own learning, sets goals, chooses language learning strategies, monitors progress, and evaluates his/her successful acquisition.

Generally, *information and communication technologies* (ICT) work as a supportive tool in all learner's activities, including the search for sources (study materials), as applied in this research.

To sum up, the main contribution of the research is that the autonomous work and collaborative learning supported by ICT are exploited simultaneously within learning ESP. Similar, but not identical approaches were applied by e.g. Huang et al. [10] who researched the autonomy in English language teaching of novice secondary school teachers, by Zao [11] who focused on the ability of autonomous learning with college students, or Chen and Yu [12] who conducted a longitudinal case study of changes in students attitudes and participation in collaborative learning.

3   Methodology

3.1   Research Objective

The main objective was to (1) discover how much students learn in the ICT-enhanced process of instruction which includes autonomous work and collaborative learning towards building preconcepts and re-constructing misconceptions in ESP, particularly in acquiring professional vocabulary and grammar; (2) detect the sources students exploited towards acquiring the learning content.

3.2   Research Sample

Totally 62 probands participated in the research. They all were enrolled in study programmes of English and literature, and teaching English and literature. Nearly half of them (29) were males (46%), the age of 40 students (65%) was in the range of 19 – 23 years, the age of 22 students (35%) was in the range of 24 – 36 years. Their level of general English was defined by the results of entrance exam as B2 of Common European Framework of Reference for Languages (CEFR) level as minimum [13]. Within CEFR, six levels are distinguished: Basic user: A1 (breakthrough, or beginner), A2 (waystage, or elementary); Independent user: B1 (threshold, or intermediate), B2 (wantage, or upper intermediate); Proficient user: C1 (effective operational proficiency, or advanced), C2 (mastery, or proficiency).

At the Faculty of Education (FE), University of Jan Evangelista Purkyne (UJEP), Usti nad Labem, Czech Republic, the amount of applicants exceeds the amount of those who can enroll the above mentioned study programmes. Therefore, the process of entrance exams is very competitive and only the best applicants succeed, reaching the B2 level as minimum. English general vocabulary and grammar are developed through all subjects, as they all are taught in English. Moreover, students attend six courses of Practical Language (PL) during the bachelor study programme, where all language skills are under the focus and particularly direct communication activities are conducted. During the semester (14 weeks long) students attend two face-to-face lessons per week (45 min each). So that to support the level of professional language (ESP), professional vocabulary and grammar from the field of linguistics and literature are acquired. Students also have online courses for each subject available in the LMS Moodle providing them with additional materials for reading, practising and testing their knowledge through autonomous learning. For the bachelor the exam the C1 level of CEFR is required.

3.3 Research Process, Methods and Tools

Reflecting their previous experience in learning English, participants had their preconcepts built for general English whereas their knowledge of ESP (i.e. professional vocabulary, grammar, professional stylistics etc.) was being developed step-by-step since the beginning of their bachelor studies. So as to avoid forming misconceptions, authentic sources are exploited as study materials to help construct their knowledge in the ESP field as well. As the theory of constructivism claims knowledge (preconcept) is not passively accepted but actively built in the process of cognition [14] and learning activities intentionally change learners' preconcepts and correct potential misconceptions [7]. Therefore, in this research, students' task was to actively search for the sources (professional texts) through autonomous work; however, they could collaborate/cooperate during this process, and ICT were expected to support students' activities.

The research process was structured into three phases.

Within the first phase, when *learners preconcepts were monitored,* when the pretest was administered on the first face-to-face lesson of PL before the process of acquiring new learning content started. Students received a list of 44 grammar phenomena in the electronic form. They were to write a simple sentence containing each phenomenon in appropriate context. The choice of grammar phenomena reflected the required starting level of English knowledge at the beginning of the first year of university study which is B2 of CEFR. The terminology of phenomena was both in English and Czech language. Reflecting the minimum required starting level of English knowledge for the students in the research sample, the phenomena were divided in two groups which followed the CEFR requirements for A2 (elementary level) and B1 (intermediate level) groups:

On A2 level, 20 phenomena were listed (G1-20): Irregular Noun in plural; Uncountable Noun; Comparative or Superlative form of Adverb; Present Simple tense;

Present Continuous; Past Simple Past Continuous; Future action expressed by Will, Going to, Present Continuous; Present Perfect Simple; Present Perfect Continuous; Past Perfect; Past Perfect Continuous; Modal verbs; There is/There are; Would rather; Had better.

On B1 level, other 24 phenomena were included (G21-44): three types of Conditional sentences; Future Perfect Simple; Future Perfect Continuous; Wish clauses for the Present and Past; expressing the Purpose; Time clause for future actions; Relative clause; word order in Indirect speech; Sequence of tenses; Subject with Infinitive structure; Object with Infinitive structure; Modal verb with Past Infinitive; Gerund or Infinitive form; Have Something Done structure; Used to with Infinitive; Used to with -ing form; Make/Do sentences; Who/What question; Question tags; So am I/Neither am I. Time for completing the appropriate sentences was 70 min. After the lesson, the list was submitted to the Learning Management System (LMS) Moodle. Each sentence was assessed by the teacher (one point per correct sentence; maximum test score was 20 points for G1-20 part, and 24 points for G21-44 part). These results are called the pretest scores further on.

Within the second phase, after receiving teacher's feedback on pretest results towards *rebuilding misconceptions,* autonomous learning was applied: students searched for, found, and read sources (professional texts) relating to their field of study and work, i.e. professional books, articles in journals, manuals, novels, stories etc. Based on student's decision and equipment, the search for sources could be supported by latest technologies and devices. The reading focused on the 44 listed grammar phenomena, and when one was found, the whole sentence containing the appropriate grammar phenomenon and professional vocabulary was added to the list, including the reference to the source. So as to create as good as possible list of sentences, students were allowed (or even encouraged) to use both printed and e-sources for reading and to exploit various learning aids, e.g. a presentation created by the teacher which provided the summary with comments on all required grammar phenomena and few samples, any grammar book or student's book with exercises and the key, web pages relating to learning English, printed and e-dictionaries etc. Moreover, students were allowed (and encouraged) to conduct discussions, both in the LMS or on social networks, to consider the appropriateness (in/correctness) of single sentences, to share sources and methods of searching for single phenomena. Thus the misconceptions could have been corrected (re-constructed) and new concepts built.

The total time for completing the list was six weeks; then, it was submitted through the LMS and assessed by the teacher as post-test1. Identically to the pretest, one point per correct sentence was scored (maximum score was 20, resp. 24 points). The teacher provided feedback to each student – correct and incorrect sentences were distinguished and links to study materials with further explanations were provided to the student. As the amount of sentences was high, the feedback was sent within two weeks, one month before the end of semester as minimum. Advanced students completed the list of sentences in the time shorter than six weeks, so the "first come first served" principle in providing the feedback was applied by the teacher. Then, student's task was to study the feedback and continue the process of acquiring the grammar; and if needed, to contact the teacher for further support. As the online courses in LMSs were available through computers, notebooks, smartphones and other mobile devices, the blended learning approach was applied combining face-to-face lessons and autonomous work supported by latest devices and technologies.

Within the third phase, after autonomous learning and receiving teacher's feedback on post-test1 results towards *rebuilding misconceptions*, student's final knowledge was tested at the end of semester in the form of face-to-face post-test2. The task was to write simple sentences using professional vocabulary and showing each grammar phenomenon in the context. This task was rather difficult because not only the knowledge of grammar phenomena, their structure and spelling, but also the context and professional vocabulary were required. No didactic aids were allowed during the testing. Identically to the pretest and post-test1, one point per correct sample was scored (maximum score was 20, resp. 24 points). This result is called the post-test2 score [15].

3.4 Hypotheses

Reflecting the above described theory, research process and objective, six hypotheses were set, considering the learning content in three categories: G1-44, G1-20, G21-44:

H1: A statistical significant difference between pretest and post-test1 scores in the category of grammar phenomena G1-44 exists.

H2: A statistical significant difference between pretest and post-test1 scores in the category of grammar phenomena G1-20 exists.

H3: A statistical significant difference between pretest and post-test1 scores in the category of grammar phenomena G21-44 exists.

H4: A statistical significant difference between post-test1 and posttest2 scores in the category of grammar phenomena G1-44 exists.

H5: A statistical significant difference between post-test1 and posttest2 scores in the category of grammar phenomena G1-20 exists.

H6: A statistical significant difference between post-test1 and posttest2 scores in the category of grammar phenomena G21-44 exists.

4   Results

Totally, 2,728 sentences should have been provided, however, four sentences were missing. In fact, 2,724 sentences were submitted. Data were structured according to the tests they were collected from, i.e. pretest, post-test1 and post-test2, and the categories, i.e. G1-44 (all phenomena), G1-20 (A2 level according to CEFR) and G21-44 (B1 level according to CEFR) phenomena. The Wilcoxon Signed Rank test was applied to calculate the paired differences between the tests; Z-values were exploited to verify/falsify each hypothesis on significance level $\alpha = 0.05$. Results are structured into two parts: (1) descriptive statistics and (2) testing hypotheses.

4.1   Descriptive Statistics

Results of descriptive statistics are displayed in Table 1. They present the values of total amount of respondents (N), Mean, Standard Deviation (SD), Minimum and

Maximum score, Score range, Median, Mode and results of two tests of normality data distribution (Shapiro-Wilk W test and Kolmogorov-Smirnov test).

As clearly seen mainly from the Mean values, the increase in test scores was detected in all three categories of grammar phenomena (G1-44, G1-20, G21-44) when comparing pretest to posttest1 scores as well as posttest1 to posttest2 scores.

Table 1. Descriptive statistics G1-44, G1-20, G21-44.

	G1-44			G1-20			G21-44		
	Pretest	Post1	Post2	Pretest	Post1	Post2	Pretest	Post1	Post2
N	62	62	62	62	62	62	62	62	62
Mean	29.34	35.60	36.14	14.66	18.06	18.24	11.03	16.11	16.75
SD	8.5496	6.5352	8.8352	3.7326	2.3738	2.2881	6.0434	5.0085	4.5075
Min	4	18	7	6	6	6	2	5	7
Max	42	44	43	20	20	20	22	23	23
Range	38	26	36	14	14	14	20	18	16
Median	32	37	31	15	19	19	11	17	18
Mode	–	37	30	15	19	19	3	22	18
Shap.-Wilk.	0.9203 (R)	0.9287 (R)	0.9445 (R)	0.9340 (R)	0.7208 (R)	0.6770 (R)	0.9331 (R)	0.9440 (R)	0.937 (R)
Kolm.-Smir.	0.1699 (R)	0.1581 (R)	0.1162 (R)	0.1054 (CNR)	0.2661 (R)	0.2749 (R)	0.1361 (R)	0.1145 (R)	0.1246 (R)

Shap.-Wilk.: Shapiro-Wilk W test; Kolm.-Smir.: Kolmogorov-Smirnov test; R: Reject normality; CNR: Cannot reject normality; (Source: own)

4.2   Testing Hypotheses

Hypotheses were tested in two steps: (1) the results of hypotheses H1, H2 and H3 comparing the differences between pretest and post-test1 scores are presented; (2) the results of hypotheses H4, H5 and H6 considering the differences between post-test2 and post-test2 scores are displayed.

Grammar Phenomena G1-44. First, the paired difference for pretest score and post-test1 score was calculated for grammar phenomena G1-44 by Wilcoxon Signed Rank test. Reaching the Z-value = 6.7541, the hypothesis *H1 was verified* ($\alpha = 0.05$; probability level = 0.000000). This result means that statistically significant difference was discovered between the pretest and post-test1 scores.

Second, the paired difference for post-test1 and post-test2 score was calculated for grammar phenomena G1-44 by Wilcoxon Signed Rank test. Reaching the Z-value = 3.8248, the hypothesis *H4 was verified* ($\alpha = 0.05$; probability level = 0.000131). This result means that statistically significant difference was discovered between the post-test1 and post-test2 scores.

Grammar Phenomena G1-20. First, the paired difference for pretest score and post-test1 score was calculated for grammar phenomena G1-20 by Wilcoxon Signed Rank test. Reaching the Z-value = 6.6667, the hypothesis *H2 was verified* ($\alpha = 0.05$; probability level = 0.000000). This result means that statistically significant difference was discovered between the pretest and post-test1 scores.

Second, the paired difference for post-test1 and post-test2 score for the FE group was calculated for grammar phenomena G1-20 by Wilcoxon Signed Rank test. Reaching the Z-value = 2.6381, the hypothesis H5 *was verified* (α = 0.05; probability level = 0.008337). This result means that statistically significant difference was discovered between the post-test1 and post-test2 scores.

Grammar Phenomena G21-44. First, the paired difference for pretest score and post-test1 score was calculated for grammar phenomena G21-44 by Wilcoxon Signed Rank test. Reaching the Z-value = 6.2706, the hypothesis *H3 was verified* (α = 0.05; probability level = 0.000000). This result means that statistically significant difference was discovered between the pretest and post-test1 scores.

Second, the paired difference for post-test1 score and post-test2 score was calculated for grammar phenomena G21-44 by Wilcoxon Signed Rank test. Reaching the Z-value = 3.7282, the hypothesis *H6 was verified* (α = 0.05; probability level = 0.000193). This result means that statistically significant difference was discovered between the post-test1 and post-test2 scores. Z-values and p-values are displayed in Table 2.

Table 2. Z-values and p-values. (Source: own).

	G1-44		G1-20		G21-44	
	Dif. pre-post1	Dif. post1-post2	Dif. pre-post1	Dif. post1-post2	Dif. pre-post1	Dif. post1-post2
z-score	6.7541	3.8248	6.6667	2.6381	6.2706	3.7282
p-score	0.000000	0.000131	0.000000	0.008337	0.000000	0.000193
Hypothesis	H1 verified	H4 verified	H2 verified	H5 verified	H3 verified	H6 verified

Paired difference: Dif.

To sum up, in G1-44 category the results show the statistically significant increase in post-test1 score compared to pretest (+6.26); and further significant increase was detected in post-test2 score compared to post-test1 (+0.54). In G1-20 category the results show the statistically significant increase in post-test1 score compared to pretest (+3.40); and further significant increase was detected in post-test2 score compared to post-test1 (+0.18). In G21-44 category the statistically significant increase was even higher in post-test1 compared to pretest (+5.08); and further significant increase was discovered in post-test2 score compared to post-test1 (+0.64). When total differences between pretest and post-test2 scores are compared, the increase of +6.80 was calculated in G1-44 category, the increase of +3.580 was detected in G1-20 category, and the increase of +5.725 in G21-44 category. Test scores are displayed in Fig. 1.

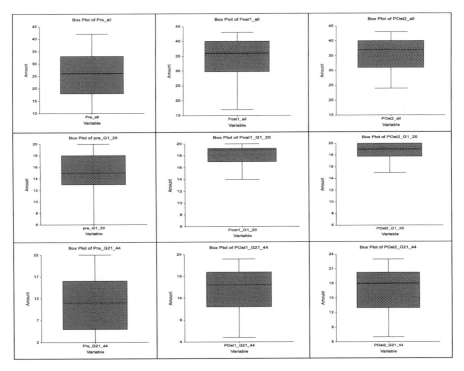

Fig. 1. Test scores in pretest, post-test1, post-test2 in categories G1-44 (All), G1-20, G21-44 (Source: own).

4.3   Types of Authentic Sources

Another feature under the focus was the type of source students exploited for searching sentences. Sources were structured according to two main types (electronic, or printed) and ten sub-types (Table 3).

Table 3. Types of sources exploited for searching for sentences (Source: own).

Electronic sources	Printed sources
Type 1: Electronic book dealing with the professional topic reflecting student's field of education, or work	**Type 6:** Printed book dealing with the professional topic reflecting student's field of education, or work
Type 2: Electronic book – fiction, long, e.g. novels	**Type 7:** Printed book – fiction, long, e.g. novels
Type 3: Electronic book – fiction, short, e.g. stories	**Type 8:** Printed book – fiction, short, e.g. stories
Type 4: Electronic article dealing with the professional topic reflecting student's field of education, or work	**Type 9:** Printed article dealing with the professional topic reflecting student's field of education, or work
Type 5: Electronic sources not listed above	**Type 10:** Printed sources not listed above

In total, out of 2,724 sentences submitted by all students; 70.34% of sentences were collected from fine literature – fiction (long novels); 49.69% of sentences were collected from printed sources and 20.65% from electronic ones. From the above listed ten types of sources (see Table 3), no occurrences of types 5 and 10 were detected (Fig. 2).

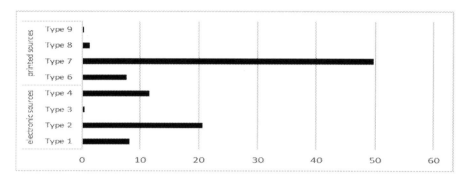

Fig. 2. Frequency of sources used in the research (Source: own).

5   Discussions and Conclusions

To sum up, all hypotheses were verified proving statistically significant differences in test scores. When briefly considering this result, it is obvious the applied approach works efficiently in teaching/learning English professional vocabulary and grammar through autonomous work, collaborative learning enhanced by ICT and exploiting authentic sources.

There may be several reasons supporting the result, none of them working separately – they are interconnected, each of them contributing to reaching the learning objective.

First of all, when considering the types of sources used for collecting appropriate samples, out of 2,724 sentences submitted by all students more than 70% of sentences were collected from fine literature – fiction (long novels), 50% of them from electronic sources and 20% from printed books. These statistics clearly reflect the fact the probands are students of study programmes English language and literature and Teaching English language and literature – despite being members of Y generation, living in the e-society and exploiting ICT in a large extent as the whole generation does, they still read printed books.

Second, starting B2 level is appropriate for working with authentic sources in ESP – students can ground in the preconcepts built within general English and develop them further on.

Third, students' previous experience in using ICT for educational purposes, which naturally differs according to the field studied [15], was reflected in the preference of printed sources.

Fourth, irrespective of the starting level of English knowledge, some students had problems with terminology, i.e. they did not know the names of single grammar phenomena, neither in Czech, nor in English.

Fifth, student's motivation to learning English language and individual ability to learn autonomously produce strong impact on the whole process.

Last but not least, being aware of the fact that the task required in post-test2 was difficult, as the application of new knowledge always is, the low(er) test scores in post-tests2 in all categories is not so surprising.

As summarized by Uskov et al. [16], student's personal characteristics, particularly motivation to learn but also learning style preferences, effort to learn, level of starting knowledge, appropriateness of didactic means used in the process of (blended) teaching/learning, are the main criteria which play substantial role, whatever type of learning we have in mind. Carey et al. [17] evaluated the validity of teaching English grammar to pre-service teachers and proved the positive contribution of ICT for this purpose. Identical approach was demonstrated by Pinto-Llorente et al. [18] who conducted a quantitative study (N = 358 students aged 29 – 58 years) focused on the process of improving grammatical competence. Students mainly highlighted the learning autonomy in learning ESL (English as Second Language) – pace, time, and exercises for practising single phenomena in authentic context. Authors also proved that students' knowledge of English grammar, including theoretical rules, improved. Additionally, according to Liu et al. [19] a new learning pattern based mainly on the collaborative learning in the flipped environment can be (instead of others) applied in English classes on the higher education level.

Even though the main didactic principles are identical for centuries [20], new methodological approaches and fast development of latest technologies offer both the teachers and learners new ways how to reach learning contents. Reflecting this state, teachers are to master new skills and their role is changing. However, teachers will always work as an important factor in the process of acquiring the new knowledge, irrespective of the extent the technologies will take within the process of instruction. And, for every learner, irrespective their year of birth, the interest, motivation, engagement in any activity within the process of learning will play the crucial role.

Acknowledgements. This paper is supported by IG projects N. 43101 16 2003-43 01 and 43101 16 2004-43 01 on Teaching ESP within pre-service teacher preparation.

References

1. Comenius (Komensky), J.A.: Analyticka didaktika. [Analytical didactics]. State Pedagogical Publishing, Praha (1947)
2. Gais, S., Born, J.: Declarative memory consolidation: mechanisms acting during human sleeps. Learn. Mem. **11**, 679–685 (2004)
3. Doulik, P.: Geneze dětských pojetí vybraných fenoménů. [Genesis of learners' concepts of selected phenomena]. Acta Universitatis Purkynianae 107. Studia paedagogica. UJEP, Usti nad Labem (2005)

4. Payne, J.D., Nadel, L.: Sleep, dreams, and memory consolidation: the role of the stress hormone cortisol. Learn. Mem. **11**, 671–678 (2004)
5. Hangen, E., Elliot, A.J., Jamieson, J.P.: Highlighting the difference between approach and avoidance motivation enhances the predictive validity of performance-avoidance goal reports. Motiv. Emot. **42** (2018). https://doi.org/10.1007/s11031-018-9744-9. Accessed 08 Mar 2019
6. Mitru, G., Millrood, D.L., Mateika, J.H.: The impact of sleep on learning and behavior in adolescents. Teach. Coll. Rec. **104**, 704–726 (2002)
7. Skoda, J., Doulik, P.: Psychodidaktika [Psychodidactics]. Grada, Praha (2011)
8. Teacherswithapps. https://www.teacherswithapps.com/the-differences-in-cooperative-learning-collaborative-learning/. Accessed 18 Apr 2019
9. What is autonomous learning. IGI Global, Disseminator of Knowledge. https://www.igi-global.com/dictionary/autonomous-learning/2014. Accessed 16 Apr 2019
10. Huang, J.: Autonomy in English language teaching. Chin. J. Appl. Linguist. **42**(1), 3–20 (2019). https://doi.org/10.1515/CJAL-2019-0001
11. Zhao, D.: The cultivation of College students' English Autonomous learning ability based on "Internet plus". In: Conference proceedings of 2018 International Workshop on Advances in Social Sciences (IWASS 2018), pp. 706–709 (2019). https://doi.org/10.25236/iwass.2018.149
12. Chen, W.T., Yu, S.L.: A longitudinal case study of changes in students' attitudes, participation, and learning in collaborative writing. System **83**, 83–96 (2019). https://doi.org/10.1016/j.system.2019.03.005
13. Common European Framework of Reference for Languages: learning, teaching and assessment (CEFR). Cambridge University Press (2001). https://rm.coe.int/1680459f97. Accessed 14 Apr 2019
14. Wheatley, G.H.: Constructivist perspectivists on science and mathematics learning. Sci. Educ. **75**(1), 9–22 (1991)
15. Simonova, I.: Enhancing learning success through blended approach to learning and practising English grammar: research results. In: Cheung, S.K.S., Kwok, L., Kubota, K., Lee, L.-K., Tokito, J. (eds.) ICBL 2018. LNCS, vol. 10949, pp. 69–80. Springer, Cham (2018). https://doi.org/10.1007/978-3-319-94505-7_5
16. Uskov, V.L., Bakken, J.P., Penumatsa, A., Heinemann, C., Rachakonda, R.: Smart pedagogy for smart universities. In: Uskov, V.L., Howlett, R.J., Jain, L.C. (eds.) SEEL 2017. SIST, vol. 75, pp. 3–16. Springer, Cham (2018). https://doi.org/10.1007/978-3-319-59451-4_1
17. Carey, M., Christie, M., Grainger, P.: What benefits can be derived from teaching knowledge about language to preservice teachers? Aust. J. Teach. Educ. **40**(9), 16–30 (2015). https://doi.org/10.14221/ajte.2015v40n9.2
18. Pinto-Llorente, A.M., Sanchez-Gomez, M.C., Garcia-Penalvo, F.J., Casillas-Martin, S.: Students' perceptions and attitudes towards asynchronous technological tools in blended-learning training to improve grammatical competence in English as a second language. Comput. Hum. Behav. **72**, 632–643 (2017)
19. Liu, T., Chen, Z., Lesgold, A.M., Feng, X., Wang, C.: Novelty blended learning pattern and its application in English language teaching. In: ICDTE 2017: International Conference on Digital Technology in Education. ACM International Conference Proceedings Series Volume, Part F, vol. 131203, pp. 7–12 (2017)
20. Comenius (Komensky), J.A.: Didactica magna. Dedictvi Komenskeho, Praha (1930)

User Experience Evaluation in eModeration: The Case of Higher Education Institutions in Developing Countries

Corné J. van Staden ⓘ, Jan H. Kroeze$^{(\boxtimes)}$ ⓘ, and Judy A. van Biljon ⓘ

School of Computing, University of South Africa, Science Campus, 28 Pioneer Ave, Florida Park, Roodepoort 1709, South Africa
{vstadcjl,kroezjh,vbiljja}@unisa.ac.za

Abstract. While the need for the moderation of examination scripts as part of quality assurance is globally undisputable, moderation associated risks and challenges are more pronounced in developing countries. eModeration (online moderation of examination scripts) can improve the user experience of an examination moderation process while lowering the risk of losing scripts and delaying the moderation process. Various factors could contribute to resistance against implementing and adopting eModerate systems in Higher Education Institutions, ranging from human factors to technical issues and organisational resistance to change. The focus of this study is on the human factors involved in eModeration, i.e. the factors influencing the user experience when using eModeration. The research uses a design science research methodology, which includes the design, development and testing of a User Experience Evaluation Framework for eModeration. The contribution of this paper is the demonstration of how eModeration (e-Service) is relevant to Higher Education management, as well as the provision of some insights regarding eModerators' user experience of an existing system. The resultant artifact is a validated User Experience Evaluation Framework for eModeration, which can be used to improve human experience of electronic moderation with an emphasis on improving the quality of educational assessment practices in developing countries.

Keywords: e-Service Moderation · User experience · Usability

1 Introduction

The role of computing has changed over the years, especially in the Higher Education (HE) environment. There are indications of an emerging trend in research regarding electronic moderation, but Higher Education Institutions (HEIs) face certain challenges with the implementation and use of systems for online moderation of examination scripts (eModeration) ranging from technical obstacles regarding internet access, file size and infrastructure problems to human factors. More specifically, HEIs are faced with the challenge of finding eModeration systems, which provide an acceptable user experience level within the constraints of a developing country such as South Africa where moderation is an integral part of ensuring standards.

© IFIP International Federation for Information Processing 2019
Published by Springer Nature Switzerland AG 2019
I. O. Pappas et al. (Eds.): I3E 2019, LNCS 11701, pp. 621–633, 2019.
https://doi.org/10.1007/978-3-030-29374-1_50

The traditional method of moderation of examination scripts involves the distribution of hard copies of the actual marked examination scripts to moderators using courier delivery or postal services, which is expensive, time consuming and not always effective [1]. The motivation for this study stems from HEIs' need to consider alternative modes of distribution when they employ Information Communication Technology (ICT) as an e-Service solution towards improving effectiveness, efficiency and resilience. Resilience, namely the ability of systems to cope with external shocks and trends [2] is an important consideration in HEI's. User experience is a critical part of making any information system – including eModerate systems used in HEIs – more acceptable and resilient, but the evaluation of these eModeration systems are lacking. Therefore, the research question for this paper is: how will the implementation of a User Experience Evaluation Framework for eModeration influence eModeration practices (e-Services) within the context of Higher Education Institutions in South Africa? This paper addresses the knowledge gap by reporting on the empirical evaluation of a User Experience Evaluation Framework for eModeration implemented in South Africa. The contribution is an updated eModeration Framework together with new insights on the challenges of implementing a resilient eModeration system in a developing country, which is moving away from traditional methods of moderation. The e-Service under discussion in this paper will be that of an eModerate system while the e-Society will be management and eModerators in HEIs.

The paper is structured as follows: the literature review is followed by sections on the methodology and the research results respectively. The findings are discussed and the resultant framework is explained before presenting the contribution of this paper.

2   Literature Review

2.1   eModeration

In contrast to online assessment and automated marking, which have been researched in depth and applied in various HEIs successfully, electronic examination script moderation is still a relatively new phenomenon, and related software applications are limited and not widely used. This paper focuses on this relatively under-researched area.

Different online assessment technology tools exist which allow HEIs to assess their students making use of electronic technology [3]. Although little effort has been made to adopt these innovative technologies where HEIs are still using traditional assessment methods [4], the need to enhance student learning in tertiary institutions is playing a role to accelerate the conversion from paper-based to digital methods [4, 5]. Similarly, the need to optimise moderation processes prompts the transformation from traditional paper-based moderation methods to electronic examination script moderation in HEIs. Digital systems could overcome the challenges that are typical of a developing country, such as slow and unreliable postal services, expensive courier systems, the involvement of distant international experts and feedback to students enquiring about their marked scripts.

The concept of eModeration is used in various contexts, for example, mentoring and discussions between lecturers and students on digital platforms [3, 6–12]. Adie's studies [13] on social moderation focus on lecturers acting as eModerators who purposefully develop agreements on standards, quality and consistency of assessment judgement across different programmes. Adie [14] further proposes a theoretical framework for online professional discussion. Grainger, Adie and Weir [15] use social moderation meetings to discuss the methods which members are supposed to use during assessments, for example, using a criteria sheet to ensure a common understanding of accountability and justification, as well as to build a community. Adie [16] recommends that moderation forums can also be used in online moderation meetings to support the collaborative professional development of teachers and the formation of a common understanding of quality in students' work.

Moderation forums focus on sharing meaning where, for example, more than one marker is used to mark the same assessment to ensure consistency and to facilitate discussions between lecturers and markers [16, 17]. In this paper eModeration refers to a specific type of peer review, defined as: "the electronic moderation (quality assurance/critical reading) of summative examination scripts by external moderators in a virtual learning environment" [18]. Within the context of peer moderation, electronic moderation of examination scripts involves the use of some electronic moderation systems to electronically moderate examination scripts [19, 20]. Peer electronic moderation involves different users, for example, internal examiners (users who grade the assessment initially) and external examiners (users who grade the assessment externally – eModerator), as well as management who can be deans or examination officers involved in the moderation process. The focus of peer moderation is not between lecturer and student but between external examiners and management. External examiners judge the internal examiners' grading using an eModerate system. Management oversees the process of eModeration using the eModerate system to track the progress of the moderation process, to peruse the feedback received from the external moderators, and to intervene and take action where necessary. The e-Service under discussion in this paper will be that of an eModerate system, while the e-Society will be management and eModerators in HEI. The user experience that is under investigation is that of both the eModerator and management.

An eModerate system is supposed to provide the user with an interface that can be used to electronically assess and re-grade marked examination scripts of students at HEIs. The marked scripts that need to be moderated should be scanned and uploaded from the original, hand-written examination scripts of students with the internal markers' allocated marks. The eModerate system should allow the institution requesting moderation to upload the scanned scripts to, for example, a module site in a virtual learning environment, where the eModerator will have secure access to the documentation. Once the eModerator has finished with the electronic control (confirmation or re-grading) of the marked scripts, he/she must be able to upload the documents back onto the same system for the Higher Education Institution (HEI) requesting the moderation to download and view. Some advantages of using an eModerate system are the ability to track the moderation process; cost effectiveness; the fact that it can be done anytime and anywhere; and the electronic availability of moderated examination script(s) for future reference [20].

Not only is it important to complete the task of eModeration in a flexible, efficient and cost-effective way, but it is also important to evaluate the users' experience of the eModerate system used to moderate examination scripts electronically. According to Preece, Sharp and Rogers [21], user experience is complex and draws from different fields, such as interactive design, information architecture and usability, amongst others. eModerate systems allow users to interact with the system at any time and place. According to the International Organization for Standardization's standard 9241–210 (human-centred design for interactive systems), user experience is described as "[a] person's perceptions and responses resulting from the use and/or anticipated use of a product, system or service. User experience includes all the user's emotions, beliefs, preferences, perceptions, physical and psychological responses, behaviours and accomplishments that occur before, during and after use. User experience is a consequence of brand image, presentation, functionality, system performance, interactive behavior and assistive capabilities of the interactive system, the user's internal and physical state resulting from prior experiences, attitudes, skills and personality, and the context of use" [22].

A particular challenge regarding user experience relates to how the measurement of all instrumental and non-instrumental aspects or qualities are associated with the design process [23, 24]. The measurement of instrumental and non-instrumental aspects will provide feedback on the user's use and acceptance of products or services, referred to as the user's emotional reaction to the product or service. Another aspect of user experience concerns the situation in which a product or service is used [8, 24–27]. Roto [28] extends the scope by including factors such as infrastructure, services, people and the technology context. The process used to improve the usability of an artifact involves an iterative design cycle [24] which promotes effectiveness and efficiency of the task to be performed, as well as the satisfaction of the user [29]. Usability goals are objective [21, 30], while user experience aspects are more subjective [21, 22].

There has been a shift in determining a product's success from only considering usability aspects to including aspects such as product interaction, individual disposition and context, which in turn affect the user experience of a particular product [31]. For the purpose of this paper, usability will be viewed as a concept embedded in user experience [32]. The researchers also view satisfaction as a shared attribute of both user experience and usability. User experience involves more than a product's utility and usability—the subjective nature of user experience is affected by the user's internal state and, furthermore, the context and the perceived image of the product's instrumental and non-instrumental qualities [23, 33–36]. According to Tullis and Albert [37] user experience includes three observable and measurable characteristics: the "user" who is involved, the user who is "interacting with a product or system" via an interface, and the user's "experience".

Ensuring effective and efficient moderation practices in HEI's is a challenge in developing countries where resource constraints impact the effectiveness, efficiency and safety of examination scripts' distribution and storage systems. According to Abdelnour-Nocera and Densmore [38] information and communication technologies for development (ICT4D) as a field is concerned with the use of ICT to support poor and marginalized people in social, political and economic spheres. Many HEI's in developing countries operate under financial and knowledge resource constraints and thus fall in the application domain for ICT4D research.

ICT can be used as a platform for development [39] and resilience is the key to the sustainability of ICT systems in developing countries [40]. Resilience has three primary foundations namely robustness, self-organisation and learning and six secondary enablers namely redundancy, rapidity, scale, diversity, flexibility and equality [2, 41]. This study supports resilience through the conversion of a manual system where scripts could get lost or stolen in transit to eModeration which greatly reduces the risk of losing scripts. The resulting framework was implemented and evaluated in a developing country and can thus be used to assist managers and users to evaluate the user experience in order to ensure sustained moderation and consistently high tertiary standards.

The constructs associated with user experience is measured by non-instrumental (non-task-orientated usability) qualities and instrumental (task-orientated user experience) qualities [20]. The proposed User Experience Evaluation framework also considers the eModerators' willingness to adopt to eModeration and produce digital content.

The constructs associated with user experience [23, 28, 42, 43] were mapped onto eModeration aspects, which guided the design and development of the questionnaire used during the survey. The data gathered during the survey was used to "determine which user experience constructs would be relevant" with regard to a User Experience Evaluation Framework for eModeration [20]. Through the literature review and research process the following key constructs were taken into consideration in terms of eModeration user experience for the study: system (eModeration web application), context (eModeration in Private Higher Education Institutions (PHEIs)) and user (eModerator and management) [19, 44]. The following theoretical approaches of other relevant studies were applied in this study: the concepts and principles used in user experience frameworks in the fields of user experience of audio players [33], interacting with products in an online environment [45] and mHealth [46]. The principals used by these indirectly related frameworks guided the design and development of the conceptual User Experience Evaluation Framework for eModeration [1]. After the design of the concept framework and presentation to the academic community the framework was used in the context of PHEIs to ensure that the framework will support academic assessment practices related to moderation.

3   Research Approach

The Design Science Research approach used in the study is an adaptation of Hevner's conceptual framework for Design Science Research in Information Systems [47]. This approach was appropriate for the design and development of a User Experience Evaluation Framework for eModeration, given its four evaluation and iteration phases used to construct a validated artifact. The various iterative steps of evaluation and construction/refinement of Design Science Research, therefore, guide the research process to ensure relevance and rigour of the design principles [47–51].

In the first phase a literature review was conducted using context analysis to determine the relevance of the field of study. The initial design and development of a conceptual framework were based on insights gained from the literature study. In the second phase the aim was the formative evaluation of the initial artifact design (ex ante evaluation), resulting in a refined artifact. During the third phase, which is the main focus of this paper, the second version of the framework was validated, and the results of this ex post evaluation were used to further refine the artifact before it was validated and improved in a final phase.

The research was conducted at Midrand Graduate Institute (MGI), a Private Higher Education Institution (PHEI) in South Africa, which changed its name in 2016 to Pearson Institute of Higher Education. The targeted participant population was moderators selected from all the faculties in the institution. Participants were formally approached via email to take part in the research. No incentives were offered to any participant and participation was voluntary. Although all 75 of the moderators of the institution (MGI) were invited to take part in the research, only 30 of the eModerators participated in the survey (phase two). During the third phase two moderators per faculty were selected and invited to be interviewed. Only six out of the 30 eModerators volunteered to be interviewed during phase three. English was used as language to conduct the interviews and each interview lasted on average 20 to 30 min. The participants were not close to the researcher and for that reason interviews were conducted using *Skype* if face-to-face interviews could not be conducted.

A case study strategy, which concerns the interpretation of qualitative data collected, was used to generate data. An interpretive philosophical worldview was used because it allows contemplative reflection on the participants' views. The data generation methods used during the third phase include interviews with eModerators from different faculties. Interviews were designed using open-ended questions.

The evaluation criteria used to evaluate the artifact were selected after thorough consideration of various aspects. For example, the evaluation criteria had to be independent of the artifact type [52]. Hevner et al. [47] also indicate that artifacts should be evaluated using criteria relevant to the requirements of the context in which the artifact is implemented. Participants had to evaluate the framework using the following evaluation criteria [47, 53]: simplicity, generality, exactness, clarity, completeness and relevance of the three levels (Environmental, eModeration requirements and eModeration User Experience constructs levels).

Prior to the interview a diagrammatical representation of the framework, as well as a detailed explanation of the constructs, was emailed to the eModerators. The interviews were transcribed by an independent person. Interviews were conducted using the telephone and Skype as tools. Notes were also made during the interview process. To verify the correctness of data the captured responses were emailed back to the interviewees for confirmation and clarification to determine if the researchers understood the answers to questions correctly, using thematic analysis [54]. The comments and responses from the eModerators were coded into a structure in which themes emerged across the subset of data. Common themes were defined, grouped together and named accordingly. The comments, feedback and responses from the participants (eModerators) were used to refine the User Experience Evaluation Framework for eModeration.

4 Results and Findings

As mentioned by Mahlke and Thüring [33], user experience evaluations should be based on non-instrumental qualities, effect and emotion. In this paper the findings were reached by using principles of user experience heuristics identified by Hassenzahl and Monk [55], as well as Väänänen-Vainio-Mattila and Wäljas [35].

Based on the questions related to the **adequacy and appropriateness,** of the three identified levels of the framework, the eModerators agreed that there is no need to add an additional level. One participant (D) indicated that, if an extra level were to be added, it would make the framework to complex and confusing, while Participant F commented: "Would not add another level as the three levels cover all aspects of eModeration". Only Participant E highlighted a specific theme namely 'context'. The participant found it difficult to understand how and where the construct 'context' should appear in the framework. The comment was taken into consideration with the refinement of the framework and more details were added to the evaluation criteria associated with 'context'. The 'context' construct is included under the user experience level and includes "characteristics of module assessment" as requested by Participant E.

Under the environmental level, eModerators were asked if the framework could be used in other organisations besides PHEIs. Organisations are a construct under the environmental level. According to Participant A, who is also an expert in eLearning systems, "…the criteria could also be applied to any system as both a quality assurance and user experience evaluation framework". Participant D indicated that "[p]ublic HEIs… colleges, schools and any other academic institution[s] having access to internet might also benefit, especially where external moderators are needed", and Participant E agreed. Participant C, however, was of the following opinion: "No, I think it is customised for Higher Education Institutions only". Participant F identified the possibility of using the framework not only for moderation purposes, but also in instances where documents require quality assurance. As a result, it was decided to use "Higher Education Institutions" in general instead of differentiating between Public and Private HEIs to facilitate the inclusion of colleges, schools and other academic institutions. Embedded within the 'user' construct are roles and responsibilities. Participant C expressed the following opinion: "Within the environment level, my opinion is that constitutional regulations and policies might also influence this level. I am not sure, however, if such regulations exist and are prescribed and enforced by the Department of Higher Education". Academic institutions in South Africa, and specifically HEIs, are governed by the country's Department of Higher Education, which prescribes and requires HEIs to externally moderate all exit level modules [56]. However, each HEI has its own set of policies and procedures incorporating regulatory requirements. Instead of covering policies under the environmental level, it was included and incorporated under the eModeration requirements level. To conclude, two themes emerged under the environmental level: the framework could be used in more than one type of academic institution and it could be used for other purposes, not only for moderation of examination scripts. It was agreed by the participating eModerators that the environmental level was appropriate with respect to simplicity, generality, clarity and relevance.

Under the eModeration requirements level, IT support emerged as an additional theme. IT support includes hardware, software and people. The roles and responsibilities of IT support were included under 'users', but the tasks associated with provision of IT support were included as an additional construct during the refinement of the framework. Participant A recommended that, if an institution cannot afford it to appoint an individual to take the full responsibility of 'IT support', these roles be assigned to the eModeration systems operator. Participant C also recommended that "system maintenance and upgrades" be added under support.

Participants were of opinion that the evaluation criteria discussed under the eModeration requirements level were clearly explained and comprehensive. A theme that emerged under the eModeration requirements level relates to the distribution of login details to be sent automatically via email to eModerators instead of a developer emailing the manager to communicate the details to them. Participants considered the eModeration requirements level to be adequate with respect to exactness, simplicity, comprehensiveness and relevance. Participant D commended the uploading process: "The upload process works smoothly; I was quite amazed by the effectiveness." It is thus important to note that, when evaluating an eModerate system, users should make sure that the system makes provision for users to upload documents easily and that the process is effective.

The eModeration user experience construct level was divided into two categories: instrumental and non-instrumental qualities [32, 34, 57]. The participants agreed that the constructs were relevant, clearly explained, complete and comprehensive enough for the eModeration user experience level. Participant C indicated: "I would add an item such as system maintenance under the heading of error prevention", which was consequently added under the element of system maintenance during the refinement of the artifact. Overall, the participants agreed that the framework presents a relevant solution to a very practical problem, as indicated: "Perfect for external moderation! Very useful for internal moderation as well to keep track and record of each semester's examination results and moderation". Figure 1 represents the revised User Experience Evaluation Framework for eModeration after refinement based on feedback received during interviews with eModerators.

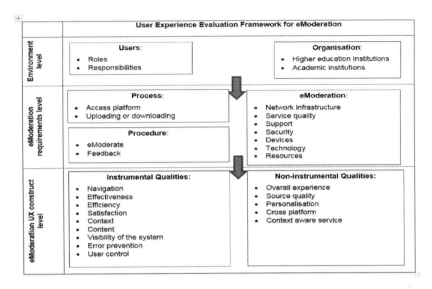

Fig. 1. User experience evaluation framework for eModeration

The eModerators were satisfied with the instrumental and non-instrumental qualities identified in the artifact. The third evaluation phase of the User Experience
Evaluation Framework for eModeration provided useful feedback to refine the artifact.
IT support was added to the conceptual framework as extra user roles and responsibilities with a separate IT support element under the eModeration requirements level. In
conclusion, the interviews with eModerators provided useful feedback to incorporate
into the refinement of the User Experience Evaluation Framework for eModeration
before it was evaluated in the last phase to validate the artifact with an external
institution (the results of which fall outside the scope of this paper). A more detailed
discussion on the eModeration Framework can be found in Van Staden [58].

5   Conclusion

This paper makes a theoretical contribution by responding to the need for research on
user experience and by presenting an evidence based artifact to guide and evaluate the
implementation of an eModeration system. The proposed User Experience Evaluation
Framework for eModeration is the artifact that expands existing theoretical framework
to describe eModeration in the field of higher education. The User Experience Evaluation Framework for eModeration also contributes to the solution of a local relevant
problem in a developing country, specifically with respect to improving resilience as
well as providing an e-Service to educators. This framework supports all the primary
foundations of resilience, namely robustness, self-organisation and learning. This
framework can also guide the transformation from manual moderation to electronic
moderation, with the focus on the use of ICT as a productive tool (eModerate system)
used by eModerators and management to fit their objective to produce digital content

(electronic examination scripts). The paper explained how e-Services can be used by educators to improve human experience of electronic moderation with an emphasis on improving the quality of educational assessment practices in developing countries. The authors trust that the proposed framework could be used to facilitate and improve quality control in tertiary assessment practices, while contributing on a theoretical level to Information Systems knowledge regarding human-computer interaction and user experience in eModeration.

Acknowledgements. This work is based on the research supported by the South African Research Chairs Initiative of the Department of Science and Technology and National Research Foundation of South Africa (Grant No 98564).

References

1. Van Staden, C.J.: IT moderation going green! In: Proceedings of SAICSIT 2010 Conference, pp. 1–3. UNISA Production Printers, Bela Bela, Limpopo, South Africa (2010). https://doi.org/10.1145/1899503.1899559
2. Heeks, R., Ospina, A.V.: Conceptualising the link between information systems and resilience: a developing country field study. Inf. Syst. J. **29**(1), 70–96 (2018)
3. Dennick, R., Wilkonson, S., Purcell, N.: Online eAssessment: AMEE guide no. 39. Med. Teach. **31**(3), 192–206 (2009)
4. Guàrdia, L., Crisp, G., Alsina, I.: Trends and challenges of e-assessment to enhance student learning in higher education. In: Cano, E., Ion, G. (eds.) Innovative Practices for Higher Education Assessment and Measurement, pp. 295–415. IGI Global, Hershey, PA, USA (2017)
5. Whitelock, D.: Activating assessment for learning: are we on the way with Web 2.0? In: Lee, M.J.W., McLoughlin, C. (eds.) Web2.0-Based e-Learning: Applying Social Informatics for Tertiary Teaching. Information Science Reference, pp. 319–342. IGI Global, Hershey, PA. The Open University, UK (2010)
6. Salmon, G.: E-moderating: The Key to Teaching and Learning Online. Kogan Page, London (2003)
7. Salmon, G.: E-tivities: The Key to Active Online Learning. Taylor & Francis Group, New York (2013)
8. Greatorex, J.: Moderated e-portfolio evaluation. Evaluation and Validation Assessment Directorate, UCLES (2004)
9. Bridge, P., Appleyard, R.: A comparison of electronic and paper based assignment submission and feedback. Br. J. Educ. Technol. **39**(4), 644–650 (2008). https://doi.org/10.1111/j.1467-8535.2007.00753.x
10. Morgan, A.: eModeration: contextualising online learning in undergraduate nurse education. Asian J. Nurs. **11**(1), 48–53 (2008)
11. Vlachopoulos, P.: The nature of e-moderation in online learning environments. In: Proceedings of LICK 2008 Symposium, pp. 48–57. Napier University TESEP, Edinburg (2008). http://www.napier.ac.uk/transform

12. Wichmann, A., Giemza, A., Hoppe, U.: Effects of awareness support on moderating multiple parallel e-discussions. In: Computer Supported Collaborative Learning Practices, CSCL2009, pp. 646–650. ISLS (2009)
13. Adie, L.: An investigation into online moderation. Assess. Matters **3**, 5–27 (2011)
14. Adie, L.: Towards a theoretical framework for online professional discussions. J. Learn. Des. JLD **7**(3), 54–66 (2014)
15. Grainger, P., Adie, L., Weir, K.: Quality assurance of assessment and moderation discourses involving sessional staff. J. Assess. Eval. High. Educ. **41**(4), 548–559 (2016). https://doi.org/10.1080/02602938.2015.1030333
16. Adie, L.: Changing assessment practices: the case for online moderation. In: AARE 2008 Proceedings of International Educational Research Conference, pp. 1–14. Australian Association of Research in Education, AARE, Brisbane (2009)
17. Adie, L., Lloyd, M., Beutel, D.: Identifying discourses of moderation in higher education. J. Assess. Eval. High. Educ. **38**(8), 968–977 (2013)
18. MGI: Assessment Policy, Midrand (2010)
19. Van Staden, C.J., Van Biljon, J.A., Kroeze, J.H.: Adopting eModeration: understanding the user experience in the organisation. In: 8th European Conference on IS Management and Evaluation, ECIME 2014 Conference, Ghent, Belgium, pp. 356–365 (2014)
20. Van Staden, C.J., Van Biljon, J.A., Kroeze, J.H.: eModeration: towards a user experience evaluation framework. In: SAICSIT 2015 Proceedings of the 2015 Annual Research Conference of the South African Institute of Computer Scientists and Information Technologists. ICPS ACM. Article 39, Stellenbosch, Western Cape, South Africa (2015). http://dx.doi.org/10.1145/2815782.2815821
21. Preece, J., Sharp, H., Roger, Y.: Interaction Design, 3rd edn. Wiley, Chichester (2011)
22. ISODIS9241-210.: Ergonomics of human systems interaction – part 210: human-centred design for interactive systems (formerly known as 13407). International Organisation of Standards (2010)
23. Hassenzahl, M., Tractinsky, N.: User experience – a research agenda. Behav. Inf. Technol. **25**(2), 91–97 (2006). https://doi.org/10.1080/01449290500330331
24. Van Schaik, P., Van Aranyi, G.: Research - white paper: model-based user-experience. Teesside University (2014)
25. Law, E., Kort, J., Roto, V., Hassenzahl, M., Vermeeren, A.P.O.S.: Towards a shared definition of user experience. In: Proceedings of Computer-Human Interaction CHI 2008 Special Interest Group, Florence, Italy, pp. 2395–2398. Association for Computing Machinery ACM (2008)
26. Law, E., Roto, V., Hassenzahl, M., Vermeeren, A., Kort, J.: Understanding, scoping and defining user experience: a survey approach. In: Proceedings Computer Human Interaction CHI 2009 User Experience, Boston, MA, USA, pp. 719–728. Association for Computing Machinery ACM Special Interest Group for Computer-Human Interaction SIGCHI (2009)
27. Law, E.: The measurability and predictability of user experience. In: Conference Proceedings of EICS 2011, Pisa, Italy, pp. 1–10. ACM, New York (2011)
28. Roto, V.: Web browsing on mobile phones – characteristics of user experience. Doctoral dissertation. University of Technology, Helsinki (2006)
29. Van Der Peijl, J., Klein, J., Grass, C., Freudenthal, A.: Design for risk control: the role of usability engineering in the management of use-related risks. J. Biomed. Inform. **45**, 795–812 (2012)

30. Vermeeren, A.P.O.S., Law, E., Roto, V., Obirist, M., Hoonhout, J., Väänänen-Vainio-Mattila, K.: User experience evaluation methods: current state and development needs. In: Proceedings of the Workshop on Recommendation and Personalization in Electronic Commerce, International Conference on Adaptive Hypermedia and Adaptive Web Based Systems, Reykjavik, Ireland, pp. 530–531 (2010)
31. McCarthy, J., Wright, J.: Technology as Experience. MIT Press, Cambridge (2007). https://doi.org/10.1145/1015530.1015549
32. Väätäjä, H., Koponen, T., Roto, V.: Developing practical tools for user experience evaluation: a case from mobile news journalism. In: Proceedings of ECCE 2009 European Conference on Cognitive Ergonomics beyond the Product – Understanding Activity and User Experience in Ubiquitous Environments, article 23, Helsinki, Finland. ACM (2009)
33. Mahlke, S., Thüring, M.: Studying antecedents of emotional experiences in interactive contexts. In: Proceedings of CHI 2007, Conference on Human Factors in Computing Systems, vol. 1, pp. 915–918. CHI, San Jose (2007)
34. Hassenzahl, M.: User experience (UX): towards an experiential perspective on product quality. In: Proceedings of the 20th International Conference of the Association Francophone d'Interaction Homme Machine, Proceedings of IHM, Metz, pp. 11–15 (2008)
35. Väänänen-Vainio-Mattila, K., Wäljas, M.: Development of evaluation heuristics for web service user experience. In: Proceedings of Computer-Human Interaction CHI EA 2009, 27th International Conference on Extended Abstracts on Human Factors in Computing Systems, pp. 3679–3684, Boston, MA, USA. ACM (2009)
36. Nielsen-Norman-Group: User satisfaction vs. performance metrics (2012). http://www.nngroup.com/articles/satisfaction-vs-performance-metrics/
37. Tullis, T., Albert, B.: Measuring the User Experience: Collecting, Analyzing and Presenting Usability Metrics, 2nd edn. Morgan Kaufman Elsevier, Waltham (2013)
38. Abdelnour-Nocera, J., Densmore, M.: A review of perspectives and challenges for international development in information and communication technologies. Ann. Int. Commun. Assoc. 41, 250–257 (2017)
39. Marais, M.A.: ICT4D and sustainability. In: Eng, P.H., Mansell, R. (eds.) The International Encyclopedia of Digital Communication and Society, vol. 1. (2015). Major Reference Works
40. Heeks, R.: ICT4D 2.0: the next phase of applying ICT for international development. Computer 41(6), 26–33 (2008)
41. Heeks, R.: Information and Communication Technology for Development (ICT4D). Routledge, Abingdon (2017)
42. Paluch, K.: User experience design blog: commentary on strategy and design of interactive products (2006). http://www.montparnas.com/articles/what-is-user-experience-design/
43. Rubinoff, R.: How to quantify the user experience. APA, Chicago (2009)
44. Van Staden, C.J., Van Biljon, J.A., Kroeze, J.H.: Using a user experience evaluation framework for eModeration. In: Olugbara, O., Millham, R., Heukleman, D. (eds.) Proceedings of IEEE ICTAS 2017, Durban, South Africa, pp. 15–21 (2017)
45. Schulze, K., Krömker, H.A.: A framework to measure user experience of interactive online products. In: Proceedings of MB 2010 Conference, article 14, Eindhoven, Netherlands. Association for Computing Machinery ACM, New York (2010). https://doi.org/10.1145/193144.1931358
46. Ouma, S.: M-health user experience framework for the public healthcare sector. Ph.D. dissertation, Nelson Mandela Metropolitan University NMMU (2013)
47. Hevner, A.R., March, S.T., Ram, S.: Design science in information systems research. MIS Q. 28(1), 75–105 (2004)

48. Hevner, A.R.: A three cycle view of design science research. Scand. J. Inf. Syst. **19**(2), 87–92 (2007)
49. Sonnenberg, C., vom Brocke, J.: Evaluations in the science of the artificial – reconsidering the build-evaluate pattern in design science research. In: Peffers, K., Rothenberger, M., Kuechler, B. (eds.) DESRIST 2012. LNCS, vol. 7286, pp. 381–397. Springer, Heidelberg (2012). https://doi.org/10.1007/978-3-642-29863-9_28
50. Gregor, S.: The nature or theory in information systems. MIS Q. **30**, 611–642 (2006)
51. Gregor, S., Jones, D.: The anatomy of a design theory. J. Assoc. Inf. Syst. **8**(5), 312–335 (2007)
52. Aier, S., Fischer, C.: Criteria for progress of information systems design theories. IseB **9**(1), 133–172 (2011)
53. Rossmann, M., Vessey, I.: Towards improving the relevance of information systems research to practice: the role of applicability checks. MIS Q. **32**(1), 1–22 (2008)
54. Braun, V., Clarke, V.: Using thematical analysis in psychology. Qual. Res. Psychol. **3**(2), 77–101 (2006). https://doi.org/10.1191/1478088706qp063oa
55. Hassenzahl, M., Monk, A.: The inference of perceived usability from beauty. Hum.-Comput. Interact. **25**(3), 235–260 (2010)
56. SAQA: Criteria and guidelines for assessment of NQF registered unit standards and qualifications. SAQA, Pretoria (2010)
57. van Staden, C.J., van Biljon, J.A., Kroeze, J.H.: eModeration: the validation of a user experience evaluation framework. In: Wu, T.-T., Huang, Y.-M., Shadieva, R., Lin, L., Starčič, A.I. (eds.) ICITL 2018. LNCS, vol. 11003, pp. 241–252. Springer, Cham (2018). https://doi.org/10.1007/978-3-319-99737-7_25
58. Van Staden, C.J.: User experience evaluation of electronic moderation systems: a case study at a private higher education institution in South Africa. Doctoral dissertation, University of South Africa, School of Computing (2017)

Computational Linguistics and Its Implementation in e-Learning Platforms

Marcel Pikhart[(⊠)]

Faculty of Informatics and Management, University of Hradec Kralove,
Rokitanskeho, 50003 Hradec Kralove, Czech Republic
marcel.pikhart@uhk.cz

Abstract. We have experienced in the past few years massive use of various kinds of e-Learning methodology, such as m-learning and blended learning etc. Despite this ubiquitous implementation of these modern approaches, we still lack their proper use regarding their full exploitation in the virtual learning environment. M-learning platforms are ubiquitous, however, they lack the potential which is given to us from computational linguistics, deep learning, and artificial intelligence. The paper attempts to highlight this fact and brings this neglected topic to the attention of the creators and designers of these mobile apps because their potential is much greater and we should put our undivided attention to this issue if we want to improve the technology which we use.

Keywords: Artificial intelligence · Computational linguistics · e-Learning · m-Learning · Blended learning · Corpus linguistics · Natural language processing · Deep learning

1 Literature Review

In the past few years, we have experienced a vast increase in the use of mobile devices used for various purposes such as communication, learning, teaching, data processing, planning, etc. [4, 10, 14, 15, 17, 24, 26, 30, 35, 40]. Mobile devices are present and used every day and everywhere, regardless the society and culture globally [2, 5, 31, 39, 40, 44]. Traditional desktops have seen a decline recently and, on the contrary, mobile apps and tools have experienced a dramatic rise [16, 19, 28, 39]. The number of the users is increasing year on year in a dramatic pace, and all these aspects of modern society must be reflected by the professionals responsible for the development of the area of smart learning, e-Learning, hybrid learning, etc. [8, 18].

In education, this rise described above is very similar and follows the same trend [12, 13, 45–47], i.e. more and more people are using computers and smart devices on a daily basis [7], not only for basic communication with the tutor but as – potentially – a very efficient tool for educational purposes [11, 20, 21, 25, 27, 29].

It is mostly the young generation which cannot imagine its life without these tools of everyday life. Educational professionals and IT professional have a unique chance to use this opportunity and implement these modern tools into educational process on a larger scale.

© IFIP International Federation for Information Processing 2019
Published by Springer Nature Switzerland AG 2019
I. O. Pappas et al. (Eds.): I3E 2019, LNCS 11701, pp. 634–640, 2019.
https://doi.org/10.1007/978-3-030-29374-1_51

Despite all the facts, the topic of the use of artificial intelligence and computational linguistics in e-Learning is basically non-existent, not only in theory in academic papers but also in practice of the use of mobile apps. The opportunities of the use and implementation of computational linguistics and artificial intelligence are vast and it is a question why this topic still lacks attention of the creators of various online learning courses, i.e. e-Learning tools and platforms.

Naturally, there are many apps which have implemented the computational linguistics practice, deep learning and artificial intelligence, however, the trend in e-learning and m-Learning is still rather old fashioned, i.e. these platforms are still used more like repository warehouses for data and texts to be studied and don't use their full potential, i.e. information analysis through modern means of artificial intelligence. The possibilities are vast, however, still neglected, and this paper brings this topic into attention of the creators and professionals who are active in IT business and therefore responsible for the implementation of the modern tools into various technological aspect of human communication, interaction and learning [7, 23, 25, 27].

The efficiency of the use of e-Learning, m-Learning, blended learning, etc., has already been proven significantly [32–34] and it must be taken into consideration so that it is added to traditional approaches in educational processes [41–43] and mostly in language acquisition of grammar and vocabulary [3, 22, 36–38].

The use of e-Learning tools is so ubiquitous in our universities and other educational institutions that it is complicated to acknowledge the fact that a systematic approach to creation of the courses is still missing and the implementation of artificial intelligence into these courses is still more or less non-existent.

2 Computational Linguistics in e-Learning

Computational linguistics has been used for decades, not only by linguistics but also by IT specialists, however, the massive use of this extremely useful tool is still expected and this paper is an attempt to urge this process. The use of artificial intelligence and computational linguistics in mobile platforms has been proven to be extremely useful in the learning process [1, 6, 9] as the student receives updated motivation based on their progress in the learning process.

Computational linguistics uses very efficient tools of data analysis which can be very beneficial when creating larger texts, assessing of the progress of students, creating more systematic approach to the learning process by analysing big data and using data mining so that the input is more optimised and the output more targeted to the current needs of the users of the app or mobile platform [23].

The most important use of these modern tools is in data processing based on the development of the situation, i.e. the progress of the information is important for further information processing. For example, if the students use a mobile platform, they are provided with the information based on their previous information processing - if the student is tested and makes mistakes, they will be provided with the information which still contains the yet not acquired information until it is acquired properly. This beneficial tool supported by computational linguistics is simple, however, brings incredible progress if implemented in the learning platforms which are already in use.

When using computational linguistics and even artificial intelligence, we are equipped with the tools we never had available and these tools bring many opportunities to data processing and management that must be used and exploited as much as possible.

3 Research

The research was conducted by the author of the paper into the use of any kind of artificial intelligence in e-learning platforms which are currently used in our universities, such as the Blackboard and Moodle. These environments are extremely popular both in the creators of curricula and the users, i.e. university students because they provide us with comfortable tools which can be used easily without the need to attend the classes physically.

The author of the research has access to both platforms (Blackboard and Moodle) because he is a teacher at two Czech universities which use both of them. The subjects varied but were mostly language classes (English and German), finance, and economics.

The research was qualitative and was conducted in January 2019. Data were collected by analysis and comparison of the online courses of the given universities. The author visited online courses as a fictitious student, the data were collected, and researched the contents and structure of the classes. The total number of the university courses which were researched was 46, equally spread through Blackboard and Moodle, from both universities which both have more than 15,000 students and are considered to be the major educational institutions in the Czech Republic.

4 The Result of the Research and Discussion

The research results are extremely surprising. Forty-six online university courses were researched, however, none of them uses any kind of artificial intelligence, deep learning or computational linguistics methodology. The most surprising is that even language courses did not use any of these tools.

The e-Learning platforms were used only as text repositories without any interactive environment which could be fostered by the use of computational linguistics and other kinds of artificial intelligence. Even the tests were just online tests without any interaction with the student based on their previous progress during their studies. Both platforms were used but not appropriately and it is also due to the lack of these basic tools in themselves. Neither Blackboard nor Moodle, even if they are used massively in our universities, do not provide efficient computational linguistics tools which would process the information and create an adapted course based on the needs of the users.

It is difficult to accept that in the year 2019 when artificial intelligence progress and computational linguistics findings are vast and unprecedented, we still lack any sign of this progress implemented in e-Learning, even if we know that the implementation of these basic technological tools for data processing would change the learning process positively and the progress would be enormous.

It is crucial to redesign all e-Learning courses with the use of artificial intelligence as it will move the traditional learning process a few levels higher compared to the current situation and it will also provide us with a dramatic improvement in our competiveness. Big data and machine learning will also provide us with indispensable tools for data analysis which will help us to create more targeted and personally oriented webs, apps, tests, learning contents, etc. These are crucial improvements in the educational paradigm and IT professionals with the cooperation with educators are now fully responsible for this challenge.

5   Conclusion

The author of the paper claims that the use of electronic platforms with the implementation of computational linguistics and deep learning is not at all sufficient and is rather a misunderstanding of modern technological tools which equip us with so many opportunities. They are merely used as a classic pen and paper tests and simple electronic communication tools. If we do not move forward, both designers and creators of these course in favour of artificial intelligence and computational linguistics, we can never succeed and it will present a potential threat to our global competitiveness and sustainability.

The paper attempts to show the absolute lack of the use of artificial intelligence and computational linguistics in our universities e-Learning platforms and claims that it is one of the biggest problems in the further development of educational processes. It also ought to stimulate professionals who are in IT industry such as the creators of various apps and platforms to enhance the need to implement artificial intelligence into these tools.

Acknowledgements. The paper was created with the support of SPEV 2019 at the Faculty of Informatics and Management of the University of Hradec Kralove, Czech Republic. The author would like to thank the student Jan Sprinar for his help when collecting the data of the research.

References

1. Alpaydin, E.: Machine Learning: The New AI. MIT Press, Cambridge (2016)
2. Alghabban, W.G., Salama, R.M., Altalhi, A.H.: Mobile cloud computing: an effective multimodal interface tool for students with dyslexia. Comput. Hum. Behav. **75**, 160–166 (2017)
3. Balula, A., Marques, F., Martins, C.: Bet on top hat – challenges to improve language proficiency. In: Proceedings of EDULEARN15 Conference, Spain, Barcelona, 6–8 July 2015, pp. 2627–2633 (2015)
4. Berger, A., Klímová, B.: Mobile application for the teaching of english. In: Park, J.J., Loia, V., Choo, K.-K.R., Yi, G. (eds.) MUE/FutureTech -2018. LNEE, vol. 518, pp. 1–6. Springer, Singapore (2019). https://doi.org/10.1007/978-981-13-1328-8_1
5. Bidaki, M.Z., Naderi, F., Ayati, M.: Effects of mobile learning on paramedical students' academic achievement and self-regulation. Future Med. Educ. J. **3**(3), 24–28 (2013)
6. Buckland, M.: Information and Society. MIT Press, Cambridge (2017)

7. Cheung, S.K.S.: A case study on the students' attitude and acceptance of mobile learning. In: Li, K.C., Wong, T.L., Cheung, S.K.S., Lam, J., Ng, K.K. (eds.) Technology in Education. Transforming Educational Practices with Technology. Communications in Computer and Information Science, vol. 494, pp. 445–454. Springer, Heidelberg (2015). https://doi.org/10.1007/978-3-662-46158-7_5

8. Chinnery, G.: Going to the MALL: mobile assisted language learning. Lang. Learn. Technol. **10**(1), 9–16 (2006)

9. Clark, A., et al.: The Handbook of Computational Linguistics and Natural Language Processing. Blackwell, Chichester (2010)

10. Dupalova, P.: Hodnocení aplikací na mobilní zařízení zaměřující se na samostatné studium slovní zásoby v anglickém jazyce (2014). https://otik.uk.zcu.cz/bitstream/11025/24285/1/Graduate%20Thesis_Petra%20Dupalova.pdf. Accessed 16 Feb 2019

11. Elfeky, A.I.M., Masadeh, T.S.Y.: The effect of mobile learning on students' achievement and conversational skills. Int. J. High. Educ. **5**(3), 20–31 (2016)

12. Gideon, A.: Influence of time-on-phone on undergraduates academic achievement in Nigerian universities. Am. J. Educ. Res. **5**(5), 564–567 (2017)

13. Klimova, B.: Teacher's role in a smart learning environment—a review study. In: Uskov, V. L., Howlett, R.J., Jain, L.C. (eds.) Smart Education and e-Learning 2016. SIST, vol. 59, pp. 51–59. Springer, Cham (2016). https://doi.org/10.1007/978-3-319-39690-3_5

14. Klimova, B.: Assessment in the eLearning course on academic writing – a case study. In: Wu, T.-T., Gennari, R., Huang, Y.-M., Xie, H., Cao, Y. (eds.) SETE 2016. LNCS, vol. 10108, pp. 733–738. Springer, Cham (2017). https://doi.org/10.1007/978-3-319-52836-6_79

15. Klímová, B., Berger, A.: Evaluation of the use of mobile application in learning English vocabulary and phrases – a case study. In: Hao, T., Chen, W., Xie, H., Nadee, W., Lau, R. (eds.) SETE 2018. LNCS, vol. 11284, pp. 3–11. Springer, Cham (2018). https://doi.org/10.1007/978-3-030-03580-8_1

16. Klimova, B., Poulova, P.: Mobile learning and its potential for engineering education. In: Proceedings of 2015 I.E. Global Engineering Education Conference (EDUCON 2015), pp. 47–51. Tallinn University of Technology, Estonia, Tallinn (2015)

17. Klimova, B., Poulova, P.: Mobile learning in higher education. Adv. Sci. Lett. **22**(5/6), 1111–1114 (2016)

18. Klimova, B., Simonova, I., Poulova, P.: Blended learning in the university English courses: case study. In: Cheung, S., Kwok, L., Ma, W., Lee, L.K., Yang, H. (eds.) ICBL 2017. LNCS, vol. 10309, pp. 53–64. Springer, Cham (2017). https://doi.org/10.1007/978-3-319-59360-9_5

19. Kukulska-Hulme, A., Shield, L.: An overview of mobile assisted language learning: from content delivery to supported collaboration and interaction. ReCALL **20**(3), 271–289 (2008)

20. Lameris, A.L., Hoenderop, J.G.J., Bindels, R.J.M., Eijsvogels, T.M.H.: The impact of formative testing on study behaviour and study performance of (bio)medical students: a smartphone application intervention study. BMC Med. Educ. **15**, 72 (2015)

21. Lee, P.: Are mobile device more useful than conventional means as tools for learning vocabulary? In: Proceedings of the 8th International Symposium on Embedded Multicore/Mangcore SoCs, pp. 109–115. IEEE (2014)

22. Lewis, B.: The Lexical Approach. LTP, London (1993)

23. Lopuch, M.: The effects of educational apps on student achievement and engagement (2013). http://www.doe.virginia.gov/support/technology/technology_initiatives/e-learning_backpack/institute/2013/Educational_Apps_White_Paper_eSpark_v2.pdf. Accessed 2 Mar 2018

24. Luo, B.R., Lin, Y.L., Chen, N.S., Fang, W.C.: Using smartphone to facilitate English communication and willingness to communicate in a communicative language teaching classroom. In: Proceedings of the 15th International conference on Advanced Learning Technologies, pp. 320–322. IEEE (2015)
25. Males, S., Bate, F., Macnish, J.: The impact of mobile learning on student performance as gauged by standardised test (NAPLAN) scores. Issues Educ. Res. **27**(1), 99–114 (2017)
26. Mehdipour, Y., Zerehkafi, H.: Mobile learning for education: benefits and challenges. Int. J. Comput. Eng. Res. **3**(6), 93–101 (2013)
27. Miller, H.B., Cuevas, J.A.: Mobile learning and its effects on academic achievement and student motivation in middle grades students. Int. J. Scholarsh. Technol. Enhanc. Learn. **1** (2), 91–110 (2017)
28. Moher, D., Liberati, A., Tetzlaff, J., Altman, D.G.: The PRISMA group. Preferred reporting items for systematic review and meta-analysis: the PRISMA statement. PLoS Med. **6**, e1000097 (2009)
29. Muhammed, A.A.: The impact of mobiles on language learning on the part of English Foreign Language (EFL) university students. Procedia – Soc. Behav. Sci. **136**, 104–108 (2014)
30. Oz, H.: Prospective English teachers' ownership and usage of mobile device as m-learning tools. Procedia-Soc. Behav. Sci. **141**, 1031–1041 (2013)
31. Pew Research Center. Mobile fact sheet (2018). http://www.pewinternet.org/fact-sheet/ mobile/. Accessed 16 Feb 2019
32. Pikhart, M.: Sustainable communication strategies for business communication. In: Soliman, K.S. (ed.) Proceedings of the 32nd International Business Information Management Association Conference (IBIMA), Seville, Spain, 15–16 November 2018, pp. 528–53. International Business Information Management Association (2018). ISBN 978-0-9998551-1-9
33. Pikhart, M.: Intercultural business communication courses in European universities as a way to enhance competitiveness. In: Soliman, K.S. (ed.) Proceedings of the 32nd International Business Information Management Association Conference (IBIMA), Seville, Spain, 15–16 November 2018, pp. 524–527. International Business Information Management Association (2018a). ISBN 978-0-9998551-1-9
34. Pikhart, M.: Multilingual and intercultural competence for ICT: accessing and assessing electronic information in the global world. In: 11th International Conference on Multimedia and Network Information Systems, MISSI 2018. Advances in Intelligent Systems and Computing, vol. 833, pp. 273–278 (2019). 11th International Conference on Multimedia and Network Information Systems, MISSI 2018, Wroclaw, Poland 12–14 September 2018 (2018b). ISSN 2194-5357. https://doi.org/10.1007/978-3-319-98678-4_28
35. Pikhart, M.: Technology enhanced learning experience in intercultural business communication course: a case study. In: Hao, T., Chen, W., Xie, H., Nadee, W., Lau, R. (eds.) SETE 2018. LNCS, vol. 11284, pp. 41–45. Springer, Cham (2018). https://doi.org/10.1007/978-3-030-03580-8_5
36. Sandhya, K., Smitha, J., Asha, J.V.: Mobile learning apps in instruction and students achievement. IJIM **11**(1), 143–147 (2017)
37. Schmitt, N., McCarthy, M.: Vocabulary: description, acquisition and pedagogy. Cambridge University Press, Cambridge (2008)
38. Shih, R.C., Lee, C., Cheng, T.F.: Effects of English spelling learning experience through a mobile LINE APP for college students. Procedia – Soc. Behav. Sci. **174**, 2634–2638 (2015)
39. Statcounter: Mobile Operating System Market Share Worldwide. http://gs.statcounter.com/ os-market-share/mobile/worldwide/#monthly-200901-201812. Accessed 16 Feb 2019

40. Sung, Y.T., Chang, K.E., Liu, T.C.: The effects of integrating mobile devices with teaching and learning on students' learning performance: a meta-analysis and research synthesis. Comput. Educ. **94**, 252–275 (2016)
41. Tayan, B.M.: Students and teachers' perceptions into the viability of mobile technology implementation to support language learning for first year business students in a Middle Eastern university. Int. J. Educ. Lit. Stud. **5**(2), 74–83 (2017)
42. Teodorescu, A.: Mobile learning and its impact on business English learning. Procedia – Soc. Behav. Sci. **180**, 1535–1540 (2015)
43. Tingir, S., Cavlazoglu, B., Caliskan, O., Koklu, O., Intepe-Tingir, S.: Effects of mobile devices on K–12 students' achievement: a meta-analysis. J. Comput. Assist. Learn. **33**(4), 355–369 (2017)
44. West, M., Vosloo, S.E.: UNESCO Policy Guidelines for Mobile Learning. UNESCO, Paris (2013)
45. Wu, Q.: Learning ESL vocabulary with smartphones. Procedia – Soc. Behav. Sci. **143**, 302–307 (2014)
46. Wu, Q.: Designing a smartphone app to teach English (L2) vocabulary. Comput. Educ. (2015a). https://doi.org/10.1016/j.compedu.2015.02.013
47. Wu, Q.: Pulling Mobile Assisted Language Learning (MALL) into the mainstream: MALL in broad practice. PLoS ONE **10**(5), e0128762 (2015)

ICT-Based Challenges of Repurposing a Single-Campus Course to Multi-campus Settings: A Pragmatic Case Study

Abdullah Bahmani$^{(\boxtimes)}$ ⓘ, Rune Hjelsvold ⓘ,
and Birgit Rognebakke Krogstie ⓘ

The Norwegian University of Science and Technology (NTNU),
Trondheim, Norway
{Abdullah.Bahmani,Rune.Hjelsvold,
Birgit.R.Krogstie}@ntnu.no

Abstract. Studies show that the integration of ICT in education is suffering from some barriers at student, teacher, and university level. This also holds for multi-campus education, as ICT is one of the main ingredients for sharing education among campuses. In this study, through a pragmatic case study at the context of a Scandinavian multi-campus university and with the help of activity theory, we examined the challenges of offering a single-campus course to students at multiple campuses by using ICT for lecture sharing, without further adjustments. Data for this study is collected from different sources (teachers, teaching assistants, and students) through interviews and observations and from an online questionnaire. Our findings suggest that repurposing a single-campus course to a multi-campus one without having clear and pre-defined rules poses some challenges for the different stockholders and influences their relations, resulting in negative impacts on teaching and learning processes and teacher and students' satisfaction. Therefore, we conclude that there should be careful planning with a clear set of rules, including technology training and preparation for teaching staff, students, and technical staff. Staff structure may also need to be modified to accommodate the additional needs for technical support.

Keywords: ICT · Lecture video streaming · Multi-campus education · Challenges · Activity theory

1 Introduction

There are several studies dealing with the integration of ICT in education [1–6]. Despite the number of studies on ICT and education, our understanding of how multi-campus education can be mediated by ICT is still limited [7–11]. Multi-campus education differs from MOOC, or Massive Open Online Course, which provides education for a massive number of learners at any geographical location without "the need to satisfy formal entry requirements" [12]. Multi-campus education as a learning environment provides education for students at each campus, aiming to increase the learning quality by having collaboration among people from different campuses. Offering multi-campus education in universities, particularly those that have multiple

© IFIP International Federation for Information Processing 2019
Published by Springer Nature Switzerland AG 2019
I. O. Pappas et al. (Eds.): I3E 2019, LNCS 11701, pp. 641–653, 2019.
https://doi.org/10.1007/978-3-030-29374-1_52

campuses dispersed in different geographical locations, promises new opportunities to students, teachers, and universities [7, 13–15]. Therefore, multi-campus education deserves more attention.

Much of the research on multi-campus education is concerned with the implementation process and provides insight into how to use different ICT devices for multi-campus courses and their pros and cons [7, 8, 13, 14, 16–18]. Only a few studies have investigated issues relating to the application of ICT in multi-campus education like [19–21]. Research to date has not determined a fuller picture on the issues, in particular, those related to offering a single-campus course in a multi-campus setting. In our previous research [22] we tried to understand the challenges of repurposing single-campus courses to the multi-campus setting by observing five different cases at a Scandinavian multi-campus university. This study examines an in-depth analysis of one of these case studies in which a course – delivered in the single-campus mode for several semesters – was repurposed to a multi-campus setting. We will be using the activity theory and will analyze both qualitative and quantitative data. In this case, the repurposing mainly happened through the use of ICT; and only minor modifications were done otherwise. This posed some challenges to the course stakeholders and influenced their outcome. The research questions that we explicitly address in this study are the following:

- First, what are the challenges caused by extending a single campus course to a multi-campus setting with the use of ICT?
- Then, how are different teaching staff (teachers and TAs), students, technical staff, administrative rules affected by these challenges?
- Finally, what are the necessary actions to take, when planning for a multi-campus course?

The significance of the contributions of this paper is threefold: First, it helps the readers to get an overview of multi-campus course delivery with the presence the ICT to share education among different campuses. Second, it increases the readers' awareness, particularly the administration in multi-campus universities, about the impacts on different elements of the multi-campus education activity. Third, this paper heightens our practical and theoretical awareness of the importance of examining both technological and human/social aspects of multi-campus education.

2 Literature Review

2.1 ICT in Education

These days, ICT is an indispensable part of our lives, and we can see its footprints in all aspects of our life, such as in business [23], health [24], retail and marketing [25], money [26], and banking [27]. Regardless of a dynamic role in society, ICT, however, has fewer usage in education [28].

According to Bingimlas [2], computers found their way into schools at the beginning of the 1980s. Some researchers proposed that ICT will be an essential portion of education in the future, such as [2, 29]. They believed that ICT could play an active role in learning and teaching activities [2, 29] and that ICT will provide inter-action, flexibility, and innovation [30]. However, ICT integration in education has just been considered "a simple matter of putting computers in classrooms" [30]. Some researcher argued that, so far, ICT has had a minor impact on education regardless of the vast amount of money spent on ICT in education [6, 31].

In response to the question "Why ICT has a minor role in education?", Bingimlas [2] classified the related barriers into teacher-level (lack of teachers' confidence and competence, resistance to change and negative attitudes), and school-level (lack of time, effective learning, accessibility, and technical support) [2]. Dubé, et al. [32] reported teachers' stress as an obstacle when confronted with the new technology. Some studies focus on challenges at the student-level (lack of technical skill, lack of academic advisors, lack of feedback from the teacher, lack of interaction with other students and teachers) [1].

2.2   ICT and Multi-campus Universities

[33] distinguished between four broad types of multi-campus universities in terms of their size, structure, and relationship between their campuses. One of the unique challenges that Groenwald [33] identified for leaders in multi-campus universities is the quality assurance in campuses, particularly having curricula and courses with the same quality in all parts. In the context of this study, we are interested in multi-campus education to address this challenge.

Two options for having multi-campus education are replication and integration. The former refers to a situation where universities provide all the courses and programs in all campuses, while the latter refers to a flexible model of education that campuses can have collaboration with each other to share the courses or even study programs running from one to others [34]. There are several reasons for why universities offer multi-campus education. Reasons include equal access to the study programs for stu-dents living in different places, bringing students and university staff with different experiences together in a single united place [34], multi-mode of learning with flexible course delivery option for the students, preparation for the workplace by studying in online learning mode [7] reducing the costs, and having more students [15].

According to Ebden [7], multi-campus integration requires ICT support. Some studies reported the use of ICT devices for synchronous [35, 36] and asynchronous [8, 14] multi-campus education. Besser [37], however, believed that it is not just about installing devices and using them. He recommended that there should be careful planning for technical and physical set-up, support for the teachers, and think of change in teaching strategies. Reilly et al. [38] proposed a teachers' development program through a community of practice.

The literature also shows that multi-campus education raises a new set of related challenges [7]. This includes the lack of ICT knowledge of teachers and students [20], logistical barriers, lack of interaction between teacher and students [21], students' engagement [39], remote students' feeling of isolation [40], lack of rules [16, 41, 42] and careful planning [43], technical failure and lack of sufficient technical support [7, 39, 44]. The existing literature discusses some of the challenges in multi-campus education, but no prior study gives a holistic view of the process and related challenges.

In this research, therefore, through a pragmatic case study and with the help of the activity theory, we examined the related challenges and their impacts on different stakeholders in the education process. In addition, we identified the necessary actions to consider when planning for offering a multi-campus course.

2.3 Theoretical Framework

In this study, we adopted the activity theory [45] and, in particular, the activity system [46], as it gives a holistic understanding of a "real-world situation." The activity system has six elements (Tools, Subjects, Object, Rules, Community, and Division of Labor) as shown in Fig. 1. A critical and central part

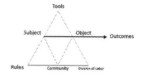

Fig. 1. Activity system

of the activity theory is contradictions. Contradictions may arise when an external force modifies an element of the activity system, which causes potential imbalances among the elements. Some studies have used the activity theory (particularly the complete activity system) in the education context [5, 47, 48].

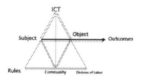

Fig. 2. An imbalance in the activity system

Offering a single-campus course in a multi-campus setting implies a need to employ ICT devices to provide multi-campus education. Based on the activity system, the integration of ICT into the single-campus education activity is an external force that brings an imbalance to the system. The presence of new tools affects elements of the system and their relations and consequently, the outcome of the activity system, as shown in Fig. 2.

3 Research Approach

3.1 Pragmatic Case Study

This paper adopts a pragmatic case study [49]. In pragmatic studies, researchers try to have an experiment to gain the experience and then interpret the result. It is a mixed method [50] approach, which includes (a) qualitative data; (b) quantitative data, and (c) interpretations of data made in a scientific, theoretical, empirical and peer-reviewed context.

3.2 Case Setting

Recently, a Scandinavian university has been merged with several colleges situated at different geographical places. The merger is intended to result in improved quality of teaching and research that extends the sum of the parts. This means that multi-campus courses and study programs should utilize and combine the strengths of each campus. Sometimes, however, the resources are unevenly distributed among the campuses. In the case of one course offered on two campuses in Fall 2018, there was a lack of academic staff at one campus. Accordingly, it was decided to repurpose the course to the multi-campus setting with the help of ICT, as shown in Fig. 3. Mediasite [51] was used for this course, providing unidirectional video streaming with a close to 30-s delay. This setup was chosen because there were already Mediasite installations present and available without the need for additional investments in ICT. Two TAs were hired to help the process of teaching and learning at both campuses. They had constant communication with each other via a specific social network, SMS, and phone call as well as the internal mail service. Both TA were master's students.

Fig. 3. The multi-campus setup

3.3 Data Collection and Analysis Methodology

In this study, we used qualitative as well as quantitative data () from multiple sources (a teacher, TAs, and students). The data was gathered from interviews, observation, and an online questionnaire. Data triangulation helped us to validate and align the findings. Having different types of data gathered through different methods from multiple sources can help us to have a complete picture of the question we have under our investigation [52]. The semi-structured interviews with the teaching staff were done in December 2018. The length of interviews was varying from 30 min to one hour. The recorded voice files were transcribed and then analyzed with Nvivo 12.0 pro.

Students (n = 200) from both campuses were invited to participate in an online questionnaire. The quantitative data were analyzed in line with the qualitative to align the findings. Forty-eight students completed the questionnaire. Written observations with a lesser degree analyzed to confirm and complete the overall data.

4 Results

The analysis of the interviews and questionnaire data unveiled challenges and tensions that can be considered as contradictions in the course viewed as an activity system:

Contradictions with Rules. The lack of specific rules for multi-campus education in the university was a challenge for the teacher. The teacher did not receive any specialized training for multi-campus teaching.

[**TEACHER**] *"All the material was new. I was not sure that I would finalize all the stuff."*

No supplemental information or activities were offered to the students to prepare them for the new setting. 54% of all students identified that they were informed about course setting by the teacher in the first session. Also, 37% believed that they should have been given more information about the setting in advance, and some (20%) asked for a more thorough introduction. 8% of them specified that they did not feel a noticeable change in the teaching style, and 11 percent asked for more changes. TAs did not receive training either.

[TA] *"I wasn't really informed about that...I guess I got sort off thrown into it from the start".*

TAs complained about the changes in logistics and GDPR. Changes in the logistics, in particular, the place of the class resulted in checking the devices before the session starts. Also, because of GDPR, the time of class had to be specified in advance, and it reduced the flexibility of the session length.

Contradictions with Tools. There was a strong contradiction with tools for the teacher. The department had decided to repurpose a regular course, which previously had been offered for several semesters in a single-campus style. There was no technology training for the teacher. This was crucial in the presence of technical failure, as it stopped the lecture and made the teacher to be stressed and lose the focus on the teaching.

[TEACHER] *"It [technical failure] is very important because when you are teaching... I get distracted, I get stressed, and it affects my teaching."*

Of all students, 39% confirmed that the technical failure happened in a few sessions, and 30% noticed that the teacher lost the focus on teaching. 29% did "agree" or "strongly agree" that the teacher should be trained for the new setting. Students also lost their attention while there were technical failures. This is confirmed by 13% of students in total. TAs also confirmed technical failure as a challenge for the process of teaching and learning.

[TA] *"Where we had problems with the microphone not picking up, and lots of noise in the background, and stuff like that."*

Besides, some lecture time was wasted because of technical failures (confirmed by 8% of students) and lack of tools in the classroom, particularly the lack of good microphone coverage in the main campus to ensure comprehensible audio playback at the remote campus.

[TEACHER] *"I didn't have microphone, so I repeated the question."*

In the main campus, a camera was installed to record the teacher and lecture room to give the remote students a feeling of "social presence" and engage them in the lecture. However, some students (9%) had a problem with the class engagement, and it was not as what they expected. Therefore, they asked for *"more class discussions"*. 9% of the main campus students reported that they opposed being recorded on the video. The new setup for the course hurt 12% of students; 8% percent stated that they needed to change their learning habit because of the multi-campus setting. From the viewpoint of the TAs, this negative impact originated from the technical failures:

[TA] *"because it [was] demotivating to sit there with a bad image and terrible sound and just have to force yourself through the course."*

The new setting also influenced TAs' work. They had to be in touch in order to be sure about the connection between the campuses. They did not get any training for the additional tools, and in many cases, they had to contact the technical staff. Technical staff also had problems with cross-campus communication tools. The technical staff did not have sufficient knowledge and skills to handle the technical problems when needed. TAs confirmed this challenge. Furthermore, in the TAs' point of view, the permission level of a person from technical staff, who showed up in the classroom to solve the problems was also critical.

[TA] *"So at least make sure that there is one person with the right qualifications and admin right to fix the system if something is not working correctly."*

Furthermore, the new tools influenced the relationship between teacher and students. Because of the technology, it was impossible to have a direct interaction between the lecturer and the main campus students on one side and the remote campus students on the other.

[TEACHER] *"It was not possible to have a dialogue, so it is hard to have any interaction with* [remote campus]. *It misses out something."*

Students also identified some challenges in their relationship with the teacher. 23% reported that they could not participate in the class discussion and 19% did not have the same amount of attention from the teacher in comparison with single-campus courses. The TAs also confirmed this:

[TA] *"for the students I think the experience of being on the remote campus is probably a lot less interesting ... Because there is definitely a distance there that is hard."*

Because of a unidirectional setup, remote students had to relay their question the local TA to be sent to the teacher via the TA at the main campus. This process was not only frustrating to the TAs, but it also took TAs' time:

[TA] *"When students had questions. I had to make sure that the questions were sent up to* [Main campus] *and to the lecturer and make sure that they got the answer."*

Contradiction with the Division of Labor. There was no local academic staff on the remote campus, and it was a challenge for the teacher to observe and assess the remote students.

[TEACHER] *"I cannot be in two places at the same time. Then I would need some other academic person at the other place to do this thing."*

The TAs complained about their role as it was different from what they expected.

[TA] *"it is a fairly passive role, more of an administrative job, not so much of a teaching job."*

Being busy with the logistics, the TAs were not able to create a productive relationship with the student, helping them in their course material, exercise, and class activities. Students confirmed this, and not a single student did receive help from the TAs. Even though the TAs had communications, they were facing some challenges in their communication because there was no rule for the TAs' communication, and they did not receive any training.

The unavailability of the technical staff during the sessions was another challenge for the TAs. Students (11%) admitted that it is good to have someone from technical support staff in the classroom to solve the problems as soon as possible.

> [TA] *"The media center has not been available to actually help us with those problems during the lecture itself."*

5 Discussion

This study aimed at identifying the challenges of integrating ICT into a traditional course to offer it in a multi-campus mode. We used activity theory as a "lens" to analyze both the qualitative and the quantitative data. It helped us to identify the elements of the related activity system and their relationships. With the help of activity theory, we, therefore, could determine the probable contradictions which are the results of changes in any elements.

For the first research question, we found that there were some challenges related to the rules, tools and the division of the labor.

Contradictions with Rules: Several reports have shown that the lack of rules is a challenge for multi-campus courses [16, 41, 42]. Our findings support their work as in our case, after the merger, rules at the university level were not updated to cover multi-campus activities. This includes the lack of ICT strategies, which is in line with the work of Stensaker et al. [4]. We also found that external rules such as GDPR can be a challenge as it reduced the flexibility course delivery in our case.

Contradiction with Tools: There were some challenges related to tools such as inadequate infrastructure, poor audio/video quality, technical failure, lack of interaction with remote students. These are consistent with the work of Divanoglou et al. [39].

Contradiction with Division Labor. We found that lack of local academic staff was a source of a challenge for the teacher, especially for students' observation and examination. Our finding also shows that to keep the link between campuses alive, TAs were responsible for logistics and technology. They, therefore, had much less time for assisting the teacher and students in the process of education. Unavailability of technical staff in case of having technical problems was another challenge which agrees with the findings of other researchers Ebden [7, 39].

With respect to the second research question, lack of rules to cover multi-campus activities resulted in the selection of inadequate and inappropriate tools for lecture sharing. Video-streaming tools did not support two-way discussion between two campuses. So remote students did not have live interaction with the teacher. It made TAs have constant communication with each other to relay remote students' question to the teacher. This took much of the TAs time with the students, so the TAs could not establish productive relationships with teacher and students.

Lack of ICT-strategies resulted in starting the semester without having technical training and preparation for teaching staff and students. It was critical when there were technical problems, which made the teacher be stressed and distracted students from their learning. Our findings show that lack of local staff in the remote campus made teacher worry about the students' progress and outcome.

Concerning the third research question, we learned that the rules should be updated to cover multi-campus activities. Rules should contain technical and pedagogical training and preparation for teaching staff and students in the new learning spaces, which is in agreement with Andrews and Klease [20]. Also, there should be a "well-defined institutional ICT-strategy," which supports ICT initiatives together with multi-campus activities. This can help in the selection of adequate and appropriate technology and infrastructure. This is in line with Stensaker et al. [4]. We also learned that TAs should be offered technical training to deal with some of the minor technical problems. However, in order to solve more complex technical problems, there should be technical staff to specifically assigned to support the multi-campus courses. The availability of technical staff to deal with difficulties may help TAs to establish a productive teacher-TA-student relationship. Furthermore, the presence of local academic staff for students' observation and evaluation seems to be necessary.

5.1 Implication for Theory

The theoretical contribution of this paper is an addition to the stock of cases for which activity theory can usefully be applied, demonstrating how the use of activity systems as an analytic device for in-depth analysis of multi-campus education. The activity system gave us a holistic overview and helped explain some complicated challenges.

5.2 Implication for Practice

Having done this research, we have acquired first-hand experiences and knowledge about the challenges of offering a single campus course for more than one. The findings from this study help in offering multi-campus courses in the mentioned university as they are planning for more multi-campus courses. These findings help the university to be aware of potential challenges to try to address them well in advance. For example, by updating the rules, the university can have some training and preparation steps for the teachers and students. It will help the teachers to modify their teaching method to cover students in the remote campus. Furthermore, other higher education institutions planning to organize their education similarly may find the results useful. This is particularly relevant at this point of time after many countries have seen a wave of mergers of universities and colleges into multi-campus institutions.

5.3 Limitations of the Research

Our research has a limitation in terms of scale, as in our case, the course was repurposed to cover only two campuses, though we believe that in case of having more campuses, some parts of findings can be generalized. Also, this research has a limitation in the size of the students' sample as 48 out of 200 students completed the online questionnaire.

6 Conclusion

Our study shows how repurposing a single-campus course to a multi-campus setting posed some challenges to the teacher such lack of ICT skill, lack of interaction, and by posing an extra burden. This was stressful, making the teacher lose the focus on the teaching process. Time was also wasted in dealing with technical problems and inadequate infrastructure. Besides that, students had problems with tools, and they were not properly prepared for the new setup. Technical problems distracted them from the class. Remote campus students did not have direct interaction with the teacher, so they were not deeply engaged in the lecture. The TAs, who in most cases assist with teaching-related tasks, had to take responsibilities related to logistics and technology, spending time on the technology set up and technical failure handling. They had to have constant communication to monitor the link between campuses and to relay remote students' questions to the teacher. Technical staff faced some challenges with the new setup as in some cases, they did not have enough technical skills, or they lacked the right permission level.

Our research shows that multi-campus education is not just connecting two campuses by using ICT. There should be careful planning for multi-campus courses. The universities should provide clear and sufficient rules for using ICT in the classroom, particularly for multi-campus courses. The roles should be defined clearly, especially for the teacher and the TAs, so they know what to do when there are difficulties. To observe and reduce the burden of the teacher, there should be local teaching staff that students can contact in case of having difficulties with the lectures or course material. Teachers, students, TAs, and even technical staff should be prepared for the new setting. The division of work for staff should be modified if the universities want to support the multi-campus courses efficiently.

References

1. Frederick, G.R., Schweizer, H., Lowe, R.: After the in-service course: challenges of technology integration. Comput. Sch. **23**(1–2), 73–84 (2006)
2. Bingimlas, K.A.: Barriers to the successful integration of ICT in teaching and learning environments: a review of the literature. Eurasia J. Math. Sci. Technol. Educ. **5**(3), 235–245 (2009)
3. Law, N., Chow, A.: Teacher characteristics, contextual factors, and how these affect the pedagogical use of ICT. In: Law, N., Pelgrum, W.J., Plomp, T. (eds.) Pedagogy and ICT Use, pp. 181–219. Springer, Heidelberg (2008). https://doi.org/10.1007/978-1-4020-8928-2_6
4. Stensaker, B., Maassen, P., Borgan, M., Oftebro, M., Karseth, B.: Use, updating and integration of ICT in higher education: linking purpose, people and pedagogy. High. Educ. **54**(3), 417–433 (2007)

5. Hu, L., Webb, M.: Integrating ICT to higher education in China: from the perspective of activity theory. Educ. Inf. Technol. **14**(2), 143 (2009)
6. Cubeles, A., Riu, D.: The effective integration of ICTs in universities: the role of knowledge and academic experience of professors. Technol. Pedag. Educ. **27**(3), 339–349 (2018)
7. Ebden, M.: We're on a steep learning curve: the benefits and challenges of multi-campus university course delivery. Res. Dev. High. Educ.: Reshaping High. Educ. **33**, 267–277 (2010)
8. Anderson, A., Date-Huxtable, E.: ICT-assisted multi-campus teaching: principles and practice to impact equity of experience for students. Changing Demands, Changing Directions. Proceedings Ascilite Hobart 2011 (2011)
9. Dinye, A.: Managing multi-campus Universities in Ghana: a comparative analysis of university for development studies (UDS) and Presbyterian University College, Ghana (PUCG). University of Ghana (2016)
10. Fisher, M.B., Hill, A.J.: Eportfolio adoption and implementation in a multiple campus University environment–a reflection on opportunities and challenges in learning and teaching at the Australian Catholic University (2014)
11. Cox, S.R.: Technology to enhance in-class discussions and student participation at a multi-campus program. Curr. Pharm. Teach. Learn. **11**, 719–722 (2019)
12. Boyatt, R., Joy, M., Rocks, C., Sinclair, J.: What (Use) is a MOOC? In: Uden, L., Tao, Y.H., Yang, H.C., Ting, I.H. (eds.) The 2nd International Workshop on Learning Technology for Education in Cloud, pp. 133–145. Springer, Heidelberg (2014). https://doi.org/10.1007/978-94-007-7308-0_15
13. Vines, R.L., Bruner, J.: Addressing course accessibility through collaboration and technology. In: EdMedia + Innovate Learning, pp. 568–573. Association for the Advancement of Computing in Education (AACE) (2008)
14. Moridani, M.: Asynchronous video streaming vs. synchronous videoconferencing for teaching a pharmacogenetic pharmacotherapy course. Am. J. pharm. Educ. **71**(1), 16 (2007)
15. Kobayashi, V.: Transformations in higher education: online distance learning. Educ. Perspect. **35**(1), 6–11 (2002)
16. Downey, M., Brown, M.: The challenge of equivalence: meshing food technology with blended learning across campuses and modes (2009)
17. Liu, X.: Research on science and technology innovation of multi-campus universities in China (2007)
18. Yates, K., Birks, M., Woods, C., Hitchins, M.: #Learning: the use of back channel technology in multi-campus nursing education. Nurse Educ. Today **35**(9), e65–e69 (2015)
19. Bower, M., Dalgarno, B., Kennedy, G.E., Lee, M.J., Kenney, J.J.C.: Design and implementation factors in blended synchronous learning environments: outcomes from a cross-case analysis. Comput. Educ. **86**, 1–17 (2015)
20. Andrews, T., Klease, G.: Challenges of multisite video conferencing: the development of an alternative teaching/learning model. Australas. J. Educ. Technol. **14**(2), 88–97 (1998)
21. Whelan, R.: Use of ICT in education in the South Pacific: findings of the Pacific eLearning observatory. Distance Educ. **29**(1), 53–70 (2008)
22. Hjelsvold, R., Bahmani, A.: Challenges in repurposing single-campus courses to multi-campus settings. Læring om læring **3**(1), 20–25 (2019)
23. Gërguri-Rashiti, S., Ramadani, V., Abazi-Alili, H., Dana, L.P., Ratten, V.: ICT, innovation and firm performance: the transition economies context. Thunderbird Int. Bus. Rev. **59**(1), 93–102 (2017)
24. Haluza, D., Jungwirth, D.: ICT and the future of health care: aspects of health promotion. Int. J. Med. Inf. **84**(1), 48–57 (2015)

25. Pederzoli, D.: ICT and retail: state of the art and prospects. In: Ricciardi, F., Harfouche, A. (eds.) Information and Communication Technologies in Organizations and Society, pp. 329–336. Springer, Cham (2016). https://doi.org/10.1007/978-3-319-28907-6_22
26. Reiss, D.G.: Is money going digital? An alternative perspective on the current hype. Finan. Innov. **4**(1), 14 (2018)
27. Casolaro, L., Gobbi, G.: Information technology and productivity changes in the banking industry. Econ. Notes **36**(1), 43–76 (2007)
28. Tsolakidis, C.: ICT in Education: The Dawn of a New Era or the Development of an Accessory. University of Aegean, Kefalonia (2004)
29. Bates, A.W.: Managing Technological Change: Strategies for College and University Leaders. The Jossey-Bass Higher and Adult Education Series. Jossey-Bass Publishers, San Francisco (2000). ERIC
30. Zhou, J.: A study of academic staff development in Chinese higher education institutions. King's College London, University of London (2005)
31. Carnoy, M.: ICT in education: possibilities and challenges. Lección inaugural del curso académico (2004–2005)
32. Dubé, L., Bourhis, A., Jacob, R.: Towards a typology of virtual communities of practice. Interdisc. J. Inf. Knowl. Manag. **1**, 69–94 (2006)
33. Groenwald, S.L.: The challenges and opportunities in leading a multi-campus university. J. Prof. Nurs. **34**(2), 134–141 (2018)
34. Harman, G., Harman, K.: Institutional mergers in higher education: lessons from international experience. Tert. Educ. Manag. **9**(1), 29–44 (2003)
35. Szeto, E.: Bridging the students' and instructor's experiences: exploring instructional potential of videoconference in multi-campus universities. Turk. Online J. Educ. Technol. TOJET **13**(1), 64–72 (2014)
36. Freeman, M.: Video conferencing: a solution to the multi-campus large classes problem? Br. J. Educ. Technol. **29**(3), 197–210 (1998)
37. Besser, H.: Issues and challenges for the distance independent environment. J. Am. Soc. Inf. Sci. **47**(11), 817–820 (1996)
38. Reilly, J.R., Vandenhouten, C., Gallagher-Lepak, S., Ralston-Berg, P.: Faculty development for E-learning: a multi-campus community of practice (COP) approach. J. Asynchronous Learn. Netw. **16**(2), 99–110 (2012)
39. Divanoglou, A., Chance-Larsen, K., Fleming, J., Wolfe, M.: Physiotherapy student perspectives on synchronous dual-campus learning and teaching. Australas. J. Educ. Technol. **34**(3), 88–104 (2018)
40. Lakhal, S., Bateman, D., Bédard, J.: Blended synchronous delivery mode in graduate programs: a literature review and its implementation in the Master Teacher Program. Collected Essays Learn. Teach. **10**, 47–60 (2017)
41. Brick, J., d'Arbon, T., Robson, J.: Putting the TOE into the shark-infested waters of electronic distance education: the development of a multi campus unit and learning package using Lotus Learningspace. In: Conference on the Proceedings of the Australasian Society for Computers in Learning in Tertiary Education 1998, pp. 87–96 (1998)
42. Weitze, C.L., Ørngreen, R.: The global classroom model simultaneous campus-and home-based education using videoconferencing. Electron. J. E-learn. **12**(2), 215–226 (2014)
43. Buchan, J., Swann, M.: A bridge too far or a bridge to the future?: A case study in online assessment at Charles Sturt University. Australas. J. Educ. Technol. **23**(3), 408 (2007)
44. Halabi, A., Tuovinen, J., Maxfield, J.: Tele teaching accounting lectures across a multi campus: a student's perspective. Acc. Educ. **11**(3), 257–270 (2002)
45. Vygotsky, L.S.: Mind in Society: The Development of Higher Psychological Processes. Harvard University Press, Cambridge (1980)

46. Engestrom, Y.: Learning by Expanding: An Activity-Theoretical Approach to Developmental Research. Cambridge University Press, Cambridge (1987)
47. Kaptelinin, V., Nardi, B.: Activity theory as a framework for human-technology interaction research. Mind, Cult. Act. **25**(1), 3–5 (2018). https://doi.org/10.1080/10749039.2017.1393089
48. Isssroff, K., Scanlon, E.: Using technology in higher education: an activity theory perspective. J. Comput. Assist. Learn. **18**(1), 77–83 (2002)
49. Fishman, D.: The Case for Pragmatic Psychology. NYU Press, New York (1999)
50. Teddlie, C., Tashakkori, A.: Foundations of Mixed Methods Research: Integrating Quantitative and Qualitative Approaches in the Social and Behavioral Sciences. Sage, Thousand Oaks (2009)
51. Mediasite. "mediasite" (2019). https://www.mediasite.com/. Accessed 29 Mar 2019
52. Kaplan, B., Duchon, D.: Combining qualitative and quantitative methods in information systems research: a case study. MIS Q. **12**, 571–586 (1988)

From Theory to Practice: Teaching Assistants' Role in Multi-campus Education

Abdullah Bahmani$^{(\boxtimes)}$ and Rune Hjelsvold

The Norwegian University of Science and Technology (NTNU),
Trondheim, Norway
{Abdullah.Bahmani,Rune.Hjelsvold}@ntnu.no

Abstract. Teaching Assistants (TAs) are an indispensable part of higher education. TAs have two identities simultaneously: those of a student and of a teacher. However, the role of TAs' may not be clearly defined, resulting in a role ambiguity. In this study, we have researched the TAs' role in multi-campus education. Data for this research was collected through interviews with eight TAs at a Scandinavian multi-campus university who took a multi-campus TA role for the first time. This paper summarizes these TAs' work tasks in multi-campus courses. Their tasks included setting up technology, dealing with technical problems, and communicating with other TAs in the course. Our study suggests that TAs' challenges may be reduced if technical staff is caring for ICT equipment and technical problems, if direct interaction is provided between teacher and students, and if local teaching staff is involved in the activities at the remote campus.

Keywords: Teaching Assistant · Multi-campus course · Activity theory ·
Relevance theory · Role theory

1 Introduction

TAs are an integral part of higher education. According to Webster et al. [1], the role of TA in higher education is the result of a more extensive development of backup role in public welfare services like health, social and education. In higher education, it is more common for a course to be offered with the help of one or more TAs. For instance, in China, around 210K people were working in Chinese universities as TAs in 2000 [2]. TAs are essential for higher education as they help the academic staff, and teach between one-third and half of the undergraduate courses ([3] as cited in [4]).

Despite the importance of the TAs' role in higher education, yet, there is no clear-cut definition for the role of TAs [5, 6]. Some studies investigated the TA's role in higher education [7–10]. However, with the advent of multi-campus universities, our understanding of the TAs work and responsibility in multi-campus courses is remarkably limited. To address this gap, this study tries to examine the role of TAs at a Scandinavian multi-campus university who for the first time participated in multi-campus courses. As the number of multi-campus courses increase at the university level, new responsibilities arise. Our aim of doing this research is to identify the new responsibilities of the TAs in the multi-campus setting and to study potential impacts

© IFIP International Federation for Information Processing 2019
Published by Springer Nature Switzerland AG 2019
I. O. Pappas et al. (Eds.): I3E 2019, LNCS 11701, pp. 654–664, 2019.
https://doi.org/10.1007/978-3-030-29374-1_53

on the TAs' relationship with other actors, such as teachers and students. Also, we aim to address the challenges which arise from the differences between TAs' role in the single- and multi-campus settings. Therefore, the research questions that we explicitly are trying to address in this study are:

- RQ1. To what extent does the TA role in multi-campus courses differ from a single-campus course TA role?
- RQ2. How can the challenges raised from these differences be addressed?

The significance of our contributions in this paper is threefold: First, it tries to differentiate the role of TAs in multi-campus courses from the single-campus setting. This is important, as there is little research considering the TA's role in multi-campus courses, and its differences from traditional courses. Second, it raises the reader's attention about the multi-campus TA role when assigning tasks other than what an actual TA has, as it may cause negative influence on the Student-TA-Teacher relationship. Third, it provides a theoretical and practical evaluation of the existing literature.

2   Literature Review

The TA role was introduced in the 1950s in the US [2]. According to Gilmore et al. [11] it is for more than 50 years that TAs have taught up to half of the undergraduate courses. Edmond and Hayler [12] reported that the role of TAs was the result of an agreement in reducing the burden of the teachers. Raaper [13] defined TAs as postgraduate students who are hired by higher education institutions to teach part-time while. Often, a TA is also a doctoral student, and in some cases, a master's student. Edmond [14] believed that having a dual identity (student and teacher) in higher education makes it arduous to establish a "professional identity" for TAs. This can be a reason why there is an increase in the roles and responsibilities of the TAs [7–10, 15]. For example, Warhurst et al. [9] reported that besides the increase in the number of TAs in Scotland, their roles are also expected to change significantly.

Having role ambiguity and increase in their responsibilities, TAs have some concerns and challenges in their student- and teacher-life. Cho et al. [16] classified their concerns into class control, external evaluation, role, time, and communication. Gardner and Parrish [17] identified the following challenges that TAs are facing: Lack of preparation, difficulties in balancing the time for research and teaching, lack of pedagogical knowledge, and reliance on previous class experience. Lueddeke [18] warned about assigning TAs in the classroom without proper preparation and training. The literature frequently recommends TA training, preparation, and pre-hiring assessment, but there is currently no rigorous program to do so. According to Smith and Smith [19], it is needed to recruit TAs through a process similar to the one for new academic staff, as currently TAs are chosen from students by a faculty member.

In the literature, researchers consider two kinds of relationship for the TAs: TA-students and TA-teacher. The abovementioned challenges and concerns for the TAs may result in an inefficient interaction between TA and students affecting the students' learning quality and their perception. Equally important, a poor experience in teaching, may hurt the development of the TAs' teaching skill, satisfaction, and motivation and may result in the TA losing the interest in pursuing an academic position [20].

While Smith and Smith [19] studied the change of the TA role in an online course, there is little research on the multi-campus TA role. In this study, we will try to explore the TA role with the help of activity theory [21], analyses their role by the relevance theory and the role theory. Moreover, we will summarize their expectations with some recommendation in the conclusion section.

3   Theoretical Framework

In this study, in order to identify the role of TAs and their responsibilities in a multi-campus course, we adopted the activity theory [21], in particular, the activity system [22] as it is shown in Fig. 1. It provides a holistic view of a "real-world condition."

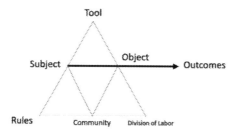

Fig. 1. Activity system

Based on the *Activity System,* an external force changing one or some elements of the system, may result in *contradictions* (e.g., incompatible evaluations, restrictions, disagreement, etc.) within and between the elements. TAs, as a part of the *community* in the activity system, help the teacher and students in the teaching and learning process. Extending a single campus course to the multi-campus setting brings some new responsibilities and consequently challenges to TAs as discussed later in this paper.

To identify the relevance of the tasks assigned to the TAs in our case, we used the relevance theory. As shown in Fig. 2, Gorayska and Lindsay [23], defined the relevance as follows:

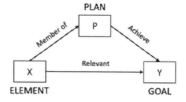

Fig. 2. Definition of Relevance adopted from *Gorayska and Lindsay* [23]

"X is <u>relevant</u> to Y if Y is a GOAL and X <u>is</u> an ELEMENT of some PLAN which is sufficient to achieve that GOAL." Therefore, *"X is <u>irrelevant</u> to Y if Y is a GOAL and X is **NOT** an ELEMENT of any PLAN which is sufficient to achieve that GOAL."*

Wilks [24] involved an AGENT to the definition of relevance: *"SOMETHING is relevant to SOMEONE (who seeks to achieve some GOAL).* Therefore, the definition of relevance in the presence of an agent is shown in Fig. 3.

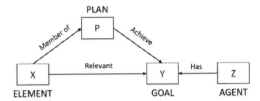

Fig. 3. Definition of Relevance with the presence of an Agent adopted from Gorayska and Lindsay [23]

According to Gorayska and Lindsay [23], goal is known motivation, which includes *"aims, objectives, wishes, desire, interests, intentions, and wants."*. Goals are reachable by an array of known actions. These actions include *"methods, strategies, and procedures,"* which altogether shape the plans. Plans contain elements, which are *"operations, actions, and related necessities"* to achieve the goals. Each element is acquired from the knowledge source to support practical actions.

Moreover, we also used the role theory to analyze the process of taking a role theory and the result of assigning different tasks to TAs. Rizzo, et al. [25] defined the organizational role as *"a position within an organizational structure that comes with a specified set of tasks or responsibilities"*. Therefore, a person who is assigned to a role is expected to do a specific set of tasks related to that role [26]. However, managers or employers do not often specify the roles accurately [27] resulting in reducing or expanding the activities related to the roles and consequently to role conflict and role ambiguity [28]. Role conflict means the role owner is asked to perform some tasks, which is inconsistent or incompatible with each other. Role ambiguity rises when there are no clear borders for the role, which means that the role owner does not know which tasks, are related to his or her role. Role conflict, in turn, leads to role strain [29]. It means that the role owner has difficulty in fulfilling the given role. Moreover, according to Van Maanen and Schein [30], people must negotiate on the role while they are taking a role. According to Deutsch [31], negotiating on a role can happen when both parties have the same power to persuade their ambitions to reach their goals.

Based on the abovementioned theories and definitions, when somebody has a role, he or she has a goal to achieve. Also, there are some elements and requirements which are already planned to lead this person to his or her goal. So, an element is relevant to a goal, if it is a member of the "plan" and it helps to achieve the goal. Hence, in our case, AGENT is a person with a TA role whose GOAL is helping the teacher and students in the education process, as well as acquiring experience in teaching as a future teacher.

The role of a TA is planned to consist of those elements (as their tasks) and related prerequisites, which help them to reach their GOAL.

In this study, to address the research questions, we used this theoretical framework to analyze our data.

4 Research Methodology

Recently, a Scandinavian university has been merged with several state colleges to become a multi-campus university. Leaders of the university, as Groenwald [32] already discussed, have been facing a challenge related to quality assurance. They have been trying to find a solution, which provides equal access to resources such as courses and curricula with the same quality for students at different campuses. To address this challenge, so far, there have been some initiatives to extend existing courses from a single-campus style to a multi-campus setting to extend the course offering to students at other campuses [33]. The technical solution was nearly the same in all cases, based on unidirectional video streaming of lectures held by a single teacher at the main campus to students gathered in a classroom at the other campus. For each of these courses, one or two TAs were recruited at each campus to setting up and monitoring the video stream and help the teachers and students as well.

In this study, in order to reach our aim, we had a semi-structured interview with eight TAs (four doctoral students and four master's students) who assisted in multi-campus courses, in Fall 2018. As there had not been so many multi-campus courses at the university level before, these TAs were among the first ones to act as multi-campus TAs. The participants had already been involved in single-campus courses, and they were familiar with the related responsibilities. Questions asked to the TAs only addressed the new responsibilities in the multi-campus setting. We did not ask any question about the single-campus TA role for comparing as it was already known by the literature, and participants had already had experience in a single-campus setting. Interviews were done either in-person at each campus or through Skype meetings. The interviews varied in length from 20 to 30 min. The recorded files were then transcribed and qualitative data analyzed with Nvivo 12. We used activity theory to specify the role of TAs and their relationships with other stakeholders in the context of a multi-campus course. The relevance theory helped us to examine the relevance of the new responsibilities with the actual role of a TA in a multi-campus setting. The role theory also helped us to analyze the challenges posed by the new responsibilities and specify TAs expectations to fulfill the differences between two different course settings.

5 Findings

Concerning the activity theory for single-campus courses, a TA can be considered a part of the *community* element and thereby will be having a direct relationship to the teacher as subject and students as object and the related responsibilities defined based on these relationships. The TA helps teacher and students in the teaching and learning process, as shown in Fig. 4.

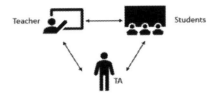

Fig. 4. TAs' relationships in single-campus courses

In our multi-campus setting, as shown in Fig. 5, the TAs had more complex relationships with other elements. Therefore, they were assigned some new and additional tasks. These tasks were related to setting up technology, dealing with technical failure, and communicating with other TA(s) to exchange the status of the link between campuses and to relay remote campus students' question to the teacher at the main campus.

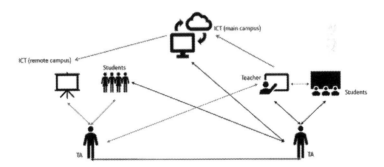

Fig. 5. TAs' relations in multi-campus courses

Participants in our study took the TA role in two different ways. Those who were master's student assigned to the TA role by the administration after sending the application form, while the teachers assigned doctoral students to the role as a part of their duty work. As an organizational role, the tasks of TAs were not clearly identified. Also, none of the TAs received any formal training and preparation for the role of TA in the multi-campus course. Before and after taking the TA role, they did not negotiate over the assigned tasks:

> **[TA]** *"I got sort off thrown into it from the start." "I was not really informed about that. I got to learn that after I was chosen for the position."*

TAs identified that their role was not a practical role:

> **[TA]** *"It was more of an administrative job, not so much of a teaching job. I did not help the students with understanding the course."*
> **[TA]** *"my entire duty was into the administration to look into administration kind of work."*

The main reason for having such a role is that they were mostly busy with irrelevant tasks such as followings:

Technology Setup. In our multi-campus setting, in order to share the lecture from the main campus to the remote one, TAs had to show up in the lecture room 10–15 min before the sessions, to set up the technology devices, make sure the link between the campus was stablished, and the audio and video were being transferred between the campuses seamlessly.

[TA] *"I had to come in a reasonable time [15–20 min earlier] to make sure that everything was set up and running."*

Deal with Technical Problems. During the lectures, TAs had to keep an eye on the technical equipment connecting the campuses:

1. To deal with minor technical problems and provide the necessary equipment.

   [TA] *"I will be in the class whole time, in case there are some problems with the transmission." "That would be more on the technical level. Make sure that everything works. Making sure that there are no technical issues. Also providing the necessary equipment on all campuses to make sure that this works.*

2. To contact technical support staff to inform the technical problems to come and solve:

   [TA] *"Make sure that there are people available if something happens, which was the problem we had." "When we had technical issues with the streams not starting, the hard part was to make technical contact with their maintenance unit up in* [main campus].*"*

Communicate with Other TA(s). TAs on the same course but at different campuses had to have constant communication with each other:

1. To exchange the link status and technical problems.

   [TA] *"It was more communication if there was something wrong with the stream ...; the automatic tracking camera is not always turned correctly. That kind of stuff."*

2. To relay the remote students' questions to the teacher on the main campus.

   [TA] *"When students had questions to me, then I had to make sure that the questions were sent up to* [main campus] *TA and to the lecturer (or guest lecturer) and make sure that they got the answer.*

The tasks mentioned above are crucial for a successful outcome of multi-campus teaching. The responsibility to handle these tasks was not assigned to anybody else. Therefore, assigned to these tasks, TAs had to give them higher priority than other tasks. This created a role conflict for the TAs. It was difficult for them to balance their tasks. Consequently, they did not have as much time to interact with students as they were expecting.

[TA] *"you spend a lot more time coordinating and just making sure that pure technical aspects of the course are working, like the live stream, rather than actually interacting with the students and having that one-to-one interaction."*

These tasks made the TA role challenging for our participants. All of them indicated that if they had a choice, they would not choose a multi-campus TA role. As a potential improvement, they suggested that hired TAs were properly introduced to the particularities of the multi-campus TA role before recruiting, and that a training and preparation assistance was offered before the semester. In addition, they asked for the presence of technical staff who can care for the technology and who can handle technology-related difficulties. TAs having a local teaching staff in a remote campus preferred not to spend time on communication with other TA in the course for remote students' questions. They also expected the university to install technology that would provide a multi-directional link between campuses, which does not need for TAs' communication.

6   Discussion

Our findings show that there were no changes to the TA recruitment process, but there are new and challenging responsibilities assigned to them. TAs, who were doctoral students, were assigned to the courses as a part of their duty work. Master's students were selected by a faculty member as mentioned by Smith and Smith [19], which is common in TAs hiring. None of the TAs were offered any training for the new tasks and responsibilities and were operating based on their knowledge and experience, which is in agreement with the work of Lueddeke [18].

In this study, the process of the TAs role taking caused some friction between the TA and the university. Firstly, because the role responsibilities were not clearly communicated to the TAs when they were hired (role ambiguity). Secondly, because during the semester, TAs were assigned to different types of tasks that, each required a specific level of time and effort (role conflict). Finally, because the TAs had no means for renegotiating the TA terms once they were hired (role-taking).

There are similarities between the role of TAs in this study, and those described by Smith and Smith [19], as TAs were mostly busy with non-teaching tasks like dealing with logistics and technology. For example, technology setup and dealing with technical failure are time-consuming and demanding tasks for multi-campus TAs. They could solve some minor problems, but the complex ones were too demanding, knowledge wise, and time wise (role strain). To solve these role conflicts, TAs suggested the presence of technical staff or a facilitator who has just responsibilities other than TAs'.

TAs in main and remote campuses also had to have constant communication to exchange the status of the link between campuses. So, they had to spend much of their time on monitoring technology to make sure the audio and video streamed smoothly between campuses. Relaying the remote students' question to the teacher was another task that TAs were given. Remote campus TAs had to spend time to make sure that the question was transferred to the teacher via the TA in the main campus. To solve this problem, there is a need for a multi-directional link between campus that remote students can have direct interaction with a teacher in the main campus. Also, the presence of a local teaching staff who can help remote students is another solution. These tasks are not related to ordinary TAs' role. First, these tasks were not already planned for the role, and there were not the required prerequisites like training and preparation. Second, the mentioned tasks were not on the list of tasks that lead a TA to achieve his or her goal: helping the teacher and students in the education process and prepare for future as a would-be teacher.

Our findings show that having a role in the education process, like a teacher, and a role related to other tasks such as logistics and technology brings role conflict to TAs. It was difficult for doctoral students to make a balance in terms of time and effort between their research and different assigned tasks as TA (role strain). This finding is in line with Gardner and Parrish [17]. Also, our finding supports the work of Lowman and Andreoli Mathie [20], as TAs were busy with non-teaching tasks, they could not establish a productive relationship with the students to help them in their learning process. TAs' tasks in multi-campus courses hindered them from having excellent practical experience in teaching as a would-be teacher.

6.1 Implication for Theory

The theoretical contribution of this paper is giving an account to the activity theory in identifying a role and its relationships in the context. Also, in this paper, the combination of the relevance and role theory helped us to find the relevance of the tasks to a role.

6.2 Implication for Practice

Multi-campus universities can use our findings if they want to assign TAs for multi-campus courses. Our findings can help them not to assign the tasks which are not relevant to a TA role and prevent the possible negative impacts or at least provide some training and preparation steps to make them ready for the new style of TA role.

6.3 Limitations of the Research

Our research has a limitation in terms of scale, as we covered courses share between two campuses. However, we believe that in the case of more campuses, some parts of our findings can be generalized. Also, this research has a limitation in the size of the participants, as there were just eight TAs who took the multi-campus TA role.

7 Conclusion

In this study, we showed that as the role of TAs is not well-defined, TAs may be assigned a variety of tasks that are not handled by others. Several new tasks needed to be taken care of to ensure successful multi-campus courses, including administrative and technical support tasks. These tasks included setting up technology, dealing with technical problems, and communicating with other TAs in the course. It may seem easier for a multi-campus university to assign such unrelated tasks to TAs rather than having to add them to the administrative and technical support staff. As demonstrated in the cases studied in this paper, such an approach puts a heavy burden on the TAs. This extra burden can impair the Students-TA-Teacher relationship and thereby have a negative impact on the teaching and learning outcome.

To overcome these challenges, universities should provide some other roles in the classroom, letting the TAs maintain their traditional roles – i.e., supporting the local students in their learning. Alternatively, the universities should offer a training or preparation step to allow them to become familiar with the new role and let them make a choice. Finally, universities can install technology, which support a multi-directional connection between the campuses that students can have direct interaction with the teacher on the other campus to reduce the extra burden on the TAs.

References

1. Webster, R., Blatchford, P., Bassett, P., Brown, P., Martin, C., Russell, A.: Double standards and first principles: framing teaching assistant support for pupils with special educational needs. Eur. J. Spec. Needs Educ. **25**(4), 319–336 (2010)
2. Chandrakar, C.L., Bentao, Y.: From learning theory to academic organisation: the institutionalisation of higher education teaching assistant position in China. Int. J. High. Educ. **7**(3), 124–134 (2018)
3. Ericksen, S.: Teaching Fellows, Memo to the Faculty 13. Centre for Research on Learning and Teaching, University of Michigan, Ann Arbor (1965)
4. Crewe, L.: Arena symposium: teaching assistants: graduate teaching assistant programmes: the challenge ahead. J. Geogr. High. Educ. **20**(1), 83–89 (1996)
5. Kerry, T.: Towards a typology for conceptualizing the roles of teaching assistants. Educational Review **57**(3), 373–384 (2005)
6. Smith, P.H.: The paradox of higher vocational education: the teaching assistant game, the pursuit of capital and the self. Educ. Rev. **70**(2), 188–207 (2018)
7. Graves, S.: New roles, old stereotypes–developing a school workforce in English schools. Sch. Leadersh. Manag. **34**(3), 255–268 (2014)
8. Webster, R., Russell, A., Blatchford, P.: Reassessing the Impact of Teaching Assistants: How Research Challenges Practice and Policy. Routledge, Abingdon (2012)
9. Warhurst, C., Nickson, D., Commander, J., Gilbert, K.: 'Role stretch': assessing the blurring of teaching and non-teaching in the classroom assistant role in Scotland **40**(1), 170–186 (2014)
10. Tucker, S.: Perceptions and reflections on the role of the teaching assistant in the classroom environment. Pastor. Care Educ. **27**(4), 291–300 (2009)
11. Gilmore, J., Maher, M.A., Feldon, D.F., Timmerman, B.: Exploration of factors related to the development of science, technology, engineering, and mathematics graduate teaching assistants' teaching orientations. Stud. High. Educ. **39**(10), 1910–1928 (2014)
12. Edmond, N., Hayler, M.: On either side of the teacher: perspectives on professionalism in education. J. Educ. Teach. **39**(2), 209–221 (2013)
13. Raaper, R.: 'Peacekeepers' and 'machine factories': tracing graduate teaching assistant subjectivity in a Neoliberalised University. Br. J. Sociol. Educ. **39**(4), 421–435 (2018)
14. Edmond, N.: The role of HE in professional development: some reflections on a foundation degree for teaching assistants. Teach. High. Educ. **15**(3), 311–322 (2010)

15. Minondo, S., Meyer, L.H., Xin, J.F.: The role and responsibilities of teaching assistants in inclusive education: what's appropriate? J. Assoc. Pers. Severe Handicaps **26**(2), 114–119 (2001)
16. Cho, Y., Kim, M., Svinicki, M.D., Decker, M.L.: Exploring teaching concerns and characteristics of graduate teaching assistants. Teach. High. Educ. **16**(3), 267–279 (2011)
17. Gardner, G.E., Parrish, J.: Biology graduate teaching assistants as novice educators: are there similarities in teaching ability and practice beliefs between teaching assistants and K–12 teachers? Biochem. Mol. Biol. Educ. **47**(1), 51–57 (2019)
18. Lueddeke, G.R.: Training postgraduates for teaching: considerations for programme planning and development. Teach. High. Educ. **2**(2), 141–151 (1997)
19. Smith, K., Smith, C.: Non-career teachers in the design studio: economics, pedagogy and teacher development. Int. J. Art Des. Educ. **31**(1), 90–104 (2012)
20. Lowman, J., Andreoli Mathie, V.: What should graduate teaching assistants know about teaching? Teach. Psychol. **20**(2), 84–88 (1993)
21. Vygotsky, L.S.: Mind in Society: The Development of Higher Psychological Processes. Harvard University Press, Cambridge (1980)
22. Engeström, Y., Miettinen, R., Punamäki, R.-L.: Perspectives on Activity Theory. Cambridge University Press, Cambridge (1999)
23. Gorayska, B., Lindsay, R.: The roots of relevance. J. Pragmat. **19**(4), 301–323 (1993)
24. Wilks, Y.: Relevance must be to someone. Behav. Brain Sci. **10**(4), 735–736 (1987)
25. Rizzo, J.R., House, R.J., Lirtzman, S.I.: Role conflict and ambiguity in complex organizations. Adm. Sci. Q. **15**, 150–163 (1970)
26. Rogers, D.L., Molnar, J.: Organizational antecedents of role conflict and ambiguity in top-level administrators. Adm. Sci. Q. **21**(4), 598–610 (1976)
27. Kahn, R.L., Wolfe, D.M., Quinn, R.P., Snoek, J.D., Rosenthal, R.A.: Organizational Stress: Studies in Role Conflict and Ambiguity. Wiley, Hoboken (1964)
28. Ebbers, J.J., Wijnberg, N.M.: Betwixt and between: role conflict, role ambiguity and role definition in project-based dual-leadership structures. Hum. Relat. **70**(11), 1342–1365 (2017)
29. Goode, W.J.: A theory of role strain. Am. Sociol. Rev. **25**, 483–496 (1960)
30. Van Maanen, J.E., Schein, E.H.: Toward a Theory of Organizational Socialization. JIP Press, New York (1977)
31. Deutsch, M.: The Resolution of Conflict: Constructive and Destructive Processes. Yale University Press, New Haven (1977)
32. Groenwald, S.L.: The challenges and opportunities in leading a multi-campus university. J. Prof. Nurs. **34**(2), 134–141 (2018)
33. Hjelsvold, R., Bahmani, A.: Challenges in repurposing single-campus courses to multi-campus settings. Læring om læring **3**(1), 20–25 (2019)

Security in Digital Environments

Demographic Factors in Cyber Security: An Empirical Study

Shweta Mittal[(⊠)] and P. Vigneswara Ilavarasan

Department of Management Studies, Indian Institute of Technology, Delhi, India
fl2shwetam@iima.ac.in, vignes@iitd.ac.in

Abstract. Despite high quality information systems security in place, organizations are vulnerable to cyber-attacks due to lapses in the human behavior. The present paper explores the importance of human factors in cyber security using an online survey data. It uses the work of Parson, Calic, Pattenson, Butavicius, McCormac and Zwaans [23] in measuring the human aspects of cyber security (leaving printouts, links from known source, website access, information in website, password complexity, links from known source, plugging USB in public places) and their linkages with the demographic factors (age, work experience, academic discipline, qualification, and place). ANOVA was used on a sample size of 165. It was found that demographic profile of employees and students significantly differ in their perception towards the cyber security. The paper has suggestions for information security awareness training programmes to handle the inadequacies.

Keywords: Demographics · ANOVA ·
Human Aspects of Information Security Questionnaire · Cyber security

1 Introduction

Humans can cause risk to cyber security, as any technical security solution or operation can fail due to the human error. Information security threats cannot be stopped, evaded, noticed or eradicated by completely relying on technological solutions [14, 15, 36]. Behavior of computer users' can pose danger to an organization's computer system. Human behaviors can probably put the organization at danger by unintentionally or intentionally revealing the passwords to others, providing sensitive information by clicking on embedded web site links, or putting unknown media into work computers. Research has found that human is the weakest link in safe guarding the organization's information security system [13]. Computer users' immature and unintentional behaviors are the reason behind information security breaches [24, 28, 39]. The data of the current research states that 95% of security breaches incidents are due to human errors. A technological system doesn't guarantee a secure environment for information [30]. It needs to be collaborated with mature human behaviors. [35] enquired about information security and cyber security, though they are related but can be compared. Information security consists of availability, integrity, and confidentiality. Cyber security also comprises of humans in their personal capacity and society at large. In

I. O. Pappas et al. (Eds.): I3E 2019, LNCS 11701, pp. 667–676, 2019.
https://doi.org/10.1007/978-3-030-29374-1_54

organizations, security on both the fronts can be established by collaboration of technology and human behaviors [37].

Information security breaches can cost heavily to organizations and can also affect their reputation [29]. Many studies suggest that employees' information security awareness plays an important role to attenuate the risk associated with their behavior in organizations [1, 3]. Organizations invest heavily in technological aspects of information security and tools but still security breaches incidents continue due to the lack of attention to employees in organizations [16].

Cyber security is of paramount importance to individuals and organizations to safeguard important and sensitive information about the clients. The researchers have found that different human characteristics lead to low security practices and are more prone to be a part of cybercrimes, still the work is limited in this area [11]. The research has suggested that information security awareness (ISA) is important in lowering the risks linked with information security breaches [3, 31]. Humans are consistently being called as "the first line defense" against the information security threats [12, 26]. We have used the Human Aspects of Information Security Questionnaire (HAIS-Q) developed by [23] to understand the different aspects of cyber security factors with respect to demographics.

Through a survey of 165 respondents comprising of students, working professionals at India, Bangladesh and other places, we make the following contributions.

- We used the HAIS-Q questionnaire and found that knowledge, attitude and behavior (KAB) model didn't hold well in our population.
- We deducted the constructs like password sensitivity, password complexity, links from known source, links from unknown source, and etc. with the reliability 0.60 and above.

We expand on the work of [23] by using ANOVAto delineate the linkage between demographic factors and cyber security.

The paper consists of seven sections. The first section introduced the paper. The section two shares the theoretical background of the research. The section three discusses the importance of demographics. The section four presents the methodology. The fifth section covers the analysis and findings of the study. The sixth section discusses the findings. The final section concludes the paper with suggestions for future work.

2   Theoretical Background

In today's scenario, dangers associated with information security pose major challenges for most of the organizations, as these dangers have dire consequences, including corporate liability, loss of credibility, and monetary damage [7]. In organizations ensuring information security has become an utmost managerial priority as well as responsibility [5, 21, 27]. Research on the human perspective of information security have focused on the employee behaviors and have found the factors that lead to risk the information security. The employees can risk the information security because of their ignorance, mistakes, and deliberate acts [10, 19, 20]. Organizations are organizing technological systems to safeguard their information and technological resources, but still they depend on their employees. Employees who are consistently using information and technology resources take certain roles and responsibilities in protecting those resources, so we are interested in what demographic factors are responsible for ensuring these roles and responsibilities.

Thus, we can understand how much the demography differences of employees understand the need and impact of information security. If the demography differences of employees are not reflecting information security behavior, then the organizations need to tailor the training programs to influence or cultivate positive attitude towards cyber security.

3 Demographics and Hypotheses

Demographics include number of characteristics in a human population. We have focused on the following demographic characteristic: age, place, qualification, academic discipline, work experience and sector working presently. These represent demographic characteristics which we analyzed how cyber security varies according to the differences in age, place, qualification, academic discipline, work experience and sector working presently. [9] found liberal arts students to be more susceptible to attacks than other majors. [22] however, suggested demographics were not conclusive in predicting attack susceptibility. There are few researches showing how demographics influence cyber security behaviors. [38] found that younger people were significantly more likely to engage in the poor security practice of password sharing. [34] found that age is an important demographic predictor in organizations. To this, the prior research states that increasing age has lower attitudes towards its usage [18], and acceptance behavior [8]. The reasoning for this could be that older people have less computer experience, less open to change, and relatively are not good in managing computer related documents. Further, older employees are more inclined to social activities than in knowledge acquisition [6]. This could be another reason for older employees being insensitive towards leaving the printouts. Individuals with lesser job tenure are more inclined towards learning new things [25, 32, 33]. This rationale could be the probable reason that employees with lesser experience are more susceptible to clicking the links from known source, may be thinking that there could be some new knowledge or information. Research clearly shows that education level (EL) is directly associated to knowledge skills, and has positive effect related to behavior [2, 17]. Thus, through this reasoning we can say that PhD qualified people have an intention to share or contribute new learning enters the information in website, forgetting that it could be detrimental to organization's security. Further, different places and academic discipline have different information security issues.

The following research questions were investigated:

1. Is there a difference in 'Leaving print outs' across different age groups?
2. Does the links from known source vary according to the work experience?
3. Is there difference in 'Website accesses across different academic disciplines?
4. Does the cyber security (information in website) vary according to the qualification?

5. Is there a difference in password complexity across different places?
6. Is there a difference in clicking links from unknown sources across different places?
7. Is there a difference in plugging USB in public places across different places?

4   Research Methodology

This research expanded the work done by the [23] on human aspects of information security (HAIS). This research will help in comprehending different aspects of cyber security with respect to demographic differences. We used Parson & team's HAIS questionnaire. In order to examine the questions, Analysis of Variance (ANOVA) was used to test the differences across different groups.

4.1   Data Collection

The data were collected from the employees and students of India, Bangladesh and other countries. We used the electronic version of the questionnaire and sent the link to the participants. This helped the respondent to answer the questions at any time and place, and this way we accelerated the process of data collection. With the aid of Google, we received 200 questionnaires electronically. Thirty-five questionnaires were not considered because of their incongruent responses. Finally, we received 165 questionnaires for data analysis.

4.2   Sample

The sample of 165 consisted of working (78.3%) and non-working (19.3%) professionals from India (70.5%), Bangladesh (26%) and other countries (3%). A total of 81% of respondents were Male. The mean age was 29.41 years, with an average experience of 5.74 years. The sample was composed of arts and commerce (8.4%), management and social science (55.4%), science (4.2%) and engineering (29.5%) backgrounds. It comprised of undergraduate (30.7%), post graduate (59.0%) and PhD (9.6%).

5   Measures

We used the HAIS-Q questionnaire and extracted eighteen constructs with the reliability 0.60 and above. The deducted constructs with reliability are given in Table 1.

5.1   Data Analysis and Results

Cyber Security: Leaving Printouts
A one-way ANOVA was conducted to understand the perception of respondents towards leaving printouts, in accordance to their age. Leaving printouts perceptions varied according to the age at $p < .05$ for the four conditions [$F_{(3,157)} = 2.89$,

Table 1. Reliability of the constructs

Focus area	Sub area	Reliability
Password sensitivity	It's acceptable to use my social media passwords on my work accounts	0.71
	It's safe to use the same password for social media and work accounts	
	I use different password for my social media and work accounts	
Password complexity	A mixture of letters, numbers and symbols is necessary for work passwords	0.60
	I use a combination of letters, numbers and symbols in my work passwords	
Attachments from unknown source	I am allowed to open email attachments from unknown senders	0.64
	It's risky to open an email attachment from an unknown sender	
	I don't open email attachments if the sender is unknown to me	
Links from known sources	I am allowed to click on any links in emails from people I know	0.62
	It is always safe to click on links in emails from people I know	
Links from unknown source	Nothing bad can happen if I click on a link in an email from an unknown sender	0.64
	If an email from an unknown sender looks interesting, I click on a link within it	
Download file	I am allowed to download any files onto my work computer if they help me to do job	0.75
	I download any files onto my work computer that will help me get the job done	
Website access	While I am at work, I shouldn't access certain websites	0.61
	Just because I can access a website at work, doesn't mean that it's safe	
Information in website	I am allowed to enter any information on any website if it helps me do my job	0.72
	If it helps me to do my work it doesn't matter what information I put on a website	
Social media privacy	I must periodically review the privacy settings on my social media accounts	0.62
	It's good idea to regularly review my social media privacy settings	
	I don't regularly review my social media privacy settings	
Work information on social media	I can post what I want about my work on social media	0.68
	It's risky to post certain information about my work on social media	

(continued)

672   S. Mittal and P. V. Ilavarasan

Table 1. (*continued*)

Focus area	Sub area	Reliability
Laptop care	When working in a café, it's safe to leave laptop unattended for a minute	0.79
	When working In a public place, I leave my laptop unattended	
Public Wi-Fi and sensitive files	I am allowed to send sensitive work files via a public Wi-fi network	0.64
	It's risky to send sensitive work files using a public Wi-fi network	
	I send sensitive work files using public Wi-fi network	
Strangers and sensitive file	When working on a sensitive document, I must ensure that strangers can't see my laptop	0.85
	It's risky to access sensitive work files on a laptop if strangers can see my screen	
	I check that strangers can't see my laptop screen if I'm working on a sensitive document	
Disposing the sensitive printouts	Sensitive printouts can be disposed of in the same way as non-sensitive ones	0.75
	Disposing of sensitive print-outs by putting them in the rubbish bin is safe	
	When sensitive print-outs need to be disposed of, I ensure that they are shredded or destroyed	
Plugging USB in public places	If I found a USB stick in a public place I shouldn't plug into my work computer	0.76
	If I find a USB stick in a public place nothing bad can happen if I plug it into my work computer	
	I wouldn't plug a USB stick found in a public place into my work computer	
Leaving printouts	I am allowed to leave print-outs containing sensitive information on my desk overnight	0.66
	It's risky to leave print-outs that contain sensitive information on my desk overnight	
Reporting of suspicious acts	If I see someone acting suspiciously in my workplace, I should report it	0.72
	If I ignore someone acting suspiciously in my workplace nothing bad can happen	
	If I saw someone acting suspiciously in my workplace, I would do something about it	
Security behavior of colleagues	Nothing bad can happen if I ignore poor security behavior by a colleague	0.80
	If I notice my colleague ignoring security rules, I wouldn't take any action	

p = .037]. Post hoc comparisons using the Turkey B test indicated that the mean score for the age range (>25 and ≤ 27) (M = 4.52) and (≤ 25) (M = 4.16) was significantly different than the age range (>32 and ≤ 50) (M = 3.94).

Cyber Security: Links from Known Source

We found that Links from known source vary according to the experience of employees in organization by conducting one-way ANOVA at the p < .05 for the four conditions [F (3,159) = 3.727, p = .013]. Post hoc comparisons taking the Turkey B test indicated that the mean score for the work experience (≤ 2) (M = 2.97) was significantly different than the work experience (2 and ≤ 3) (M = 3.56) and (>8 and ≤ 28) (M = 3.57).

Cyber Security: Website Access

Again, by applying ANOVA we found website access perception was different for the academic discipline at p < .05 for the four conditions [F (3,156) = 4.19, p = .001]. The mean score of the academic discipline Arts and Commerce (M = 3.32) was significantly different from Management and Social Science (4.06), Science (4.32) and Engineering (4.57) by using Turkey B test of Post hoc comparisons.

Cyber Security: Information in Website

Information in website varied according to the qualification by using one-way ANOVA at the p < .05 for the three conditions [F (2,159) = 4.79, p = .01]. The mean score for the PhD qualified people (M = 2.94) was different from Post Graduates (3.72) and Undergraduate (3.72) by Turkey B test.

Cyber Security: Password Complexity and Links from Known Source

Password complexity and links from known source didn't vary according to the place. We used one-way ANOVA to get the results.

Cyber Security: Plugging USB in Public Places

Plugging USB in public places varied according to their place by applying ANOVA. Plugging USB in public places was significantly different according to the place at the p < .05 for the three conditions [F (2,158) = 3.09, p = .048]. The mean score for other Places (M = 4.80) significantly varied from Bangladesh (M = 4.06) and India (M = 4.31) by using Turkey B test.

6 Discussion and Findings

The results clearly states that there is a need to increase security awareness, and it has been found that security awareness training is the most cost- effective form of security control [4]. Precisely, from the results, we can advocate that the culture of cyber security needs to be cultivated by providing training and workshops by laying emphasis that if cyber security is not kept in mind it could be detrimental to their work. Age differences show different behavior towards cyber security (leaving printouts). The people in the age range of (>32 and ≤ 50) are prone towards leaving important printouts on their table. It is imperative that organization or colleges orient these people how leaving these important papers could be harmful to the information framework of their respective companies. Employees who have an experience of (≤ 2) should be provided with a training that by clicking any links in email could harm their data. These trainings would make them cautious and vigilant towards link in email. People specifically from Bangladesh should be sensitize through trainings that picking up and plugging in USB drives can unknowingly open their organization to an internal attack of virus. The results also concluded that the students from arts and commerce are more inclined in accessing websites which could be harmful. They require an orientation programme to address towards the safety of their data by avoiding the access to certain websites. Further, the PhD students' needs a training to be aware of entering any information in website could have adverse effects on cyber security framework. These results clearly point that age, work experience, place, academic discipline and qualification differences require tailored training programes to cyber security issues. Building on this, human intervention like putting the important print outs in the file, avoiding certain websites, entering any information in website, picking up and plugging in USB drives, forming simple passwords and clicking any links in email could make the cyber security robust in the organization.

7   Conclusion

The organizations should adopt proper information security training, which in turn brings the information security awareness, which is an important parameter for security assurance. This study examined the relationship between cyber security issues (leaving printouts, links from known source, website access, information in website, password complexity, links from known source, plugging USB in public places) with demography differences (age, work experience, academic discipline, qualification, and place) to understand which are the significant relationship between demography and cyber security. It was found that demographic profile of employees and students significantly differ in their perception towards the cyber security. Our findings have important implication for organization that students and employee's perception towards cyber security varies in accordance to their difference in age, work experience, qualification, education and place. It can help organization identifying cyber security strength and weakness across demography and can assist in developing the tailored information security training programmes for the respective employees and students.

7.1   Future Directions

Building on the present study, future research could examine the human aspect of information security and organization security culture. Future research can also consider the different aspects of personality traits of human beings.

References

1. Abawajy, J.: User preference of cyber security awareness delivery methods. Behav. Inf. Technol. **33**(3), 237–248 (2014)
2. Agarwal, R., Prasad, J.: Are individual differences germane to the acceptance of new information technologies? Decis. Sci. **30**(2), 361–391 (1999)
3. Arachchilage, N.A.G., Love, S.: Security awareness of computer users: a phishing threat avoidance perspective. Comput. Hum. Behav. **38**, 304–312 (2014)
4. Albrechtsen, E., Hovden, J.: Improving information security awareness and behaviour through dialogue, participation and collective reflection. An intervention study. Comput. Secur. **29**(4), 432–445 (2010)
5. Brancheau, J.C., Janz, B.D., Wetherbe, J.C.: Key issues in information systems management: 1994-1995 SIM Delphi results. MIS Q. **20**(2), 225–242 (1996)
6. Carstensen, L.L., Issacowitz, D.M., Charles, S.T.: Taking time seriously: a theory of socioemotional selectivity. Am. Psychol. **54**, 165–181 (1999)
7. Cavusoglu, H., Cavusoglu, H., Raghunathan, S.: Economics of IT security management: four improvements to current security practices. Commun. Assoc. Inf. Syst. **14**(1), 3 (2004)
8. Chung, J.E., Park, N., Wang, H., Fulk, J., McLaughlin, M.: Age differences in perceptions of online community participation among non-users: an extension of the Technology Acceptance Model. Comput. Hum. Behav. **26**(6), 1674–1684 (2010)
9. Darwish, A., El Zarka, A., Aloul, F.: Towards understanding phishing victims' profile. In: 2012 International Conference on Computer Systems and Industrial Informatics, pp. 1–5. IEEE, December 2012
10. Durgin, M.: Understanding the importance of and implementing internal security measures. SANS Institute Reading Room (2007). (https://www2.sans.org/reading_room/whitepapers/policyissues/1901.php)
11. Egelman, S., Peer, E.: Scaling the security wall: developing a security behavior intentions scale. In: Proceedings of the 33rd Annual ACM Conference on Human Factors in Computing Systems, pp. 2873–2882. ACM, April 2015
12. European Union Agency for Network and Information Security (ENISA). The new users' guide: how to raise information security awareness (EN) (2010)
13. Furnell, S., Clarke, N.: Power to the people? The evolving recognition of human aspects of security. Comput. Secur. **31**(8), 983–988 (2012)
14. Furnell, S.M., Jusoh, A., Katsabas, D.: The challenges of understanding and using security: a survey of end-users. Comput. Secur. **25**(1), 27–35 (2006)
15. Herath, T., Rao, H.R.: Protection motivation and deterrence: a framework for security policy compliance in organisations. Eur. J. Inf. Syst. **18**(2), 106–125 (2009)
16. Ifinedo, P.: Understanding information systems security policy compliance: an integration of the theory of planned behavior and the protection motivation theory. Comput. Secur. **31**(1), 83–95 (2012)
17. Igbaria, M., Parasuraman, S.: A path analytic study of individual characteristics, computer anxiety and attitudes toward microcomputers. J. Manag. **15**(3), 373–388 (1989)
18. Igbaria, M., Zinatelli, N., Cragg, P., Cavaye, A.L.: Personal computing acceptance factors in small firms: a structural equation model. MIS Q. **21**, 279–305 (1997)
19. Lee, J., Lee, Y.: A holistic model of computer abuses within organizations. Inf. Manag. Comput. Secur. **10**(2), 57–63 (2002)
20. Lee, S.M., Lee, S.G., Yoo, S.: An integrative model of computer abuse based on social control and general deterrence theories. Inf. Manag. **41**(6), 707–718 (2004)

21. Lohmeyer, D.F., McCrory, J., Pogreb, S.: Managing information security. McKinsey Quart. Spec. Ed. **2**, 12–16 (2002)
22. Mohebzada, J.G., El Zarka, A., Bhojani, A.H., Darwish, A.: Phishing in a university community: two large scale phishing experiments. In: 2012 International Conference on Innovations in Information Technology (IIT), pp. 249–254. IEEE, March 2012
23. Parsons, K., Calic, D., Pattinson, M., Butavicius, M., McCormac, A., Zwaans, T.: The human aspects of information security questionnaire (HAIS-Q): two further validation studies. Comput. Secur. **66**, 40–51 (2017)
24. Parsons, K.M., Young, E., Butavicius, M.A., McCormac, A., Pattinson, M.R., Jerram, C.: The influence of organizational information security culture on information security decision making. J. Cogn. Eng. Decis. Making **9**(2), 117–129 (2015)
25. Porter, C.E., Donthu, N.: Using the technology acceptance model to explain how attitudes determine Internet usage: the role of perceived access barriers and demographics. J. Bus. Res. **59**(9), 999–1007 (2006)
26. PricewaterhouseCoopers (PWC). Security awareness: turning your people into your first line of defence (2010)
27. Ransbotham, S., Mitra, S.: Choice and chance: a conceptual model of paths to information security compromise. Inf. Syst. Res. **20**(1), 121–139 (2009)
28. Schultz, E.: From the Editor-in-Chief: the human factor in security. Comput. Secur. **24**(6), 425–426 (2005)
29. Safa, N.S., Ismail, M.A.: A customer loyalty formation model in electronic commerce. Econ. Model. **35**, 559–564 (2013)
30. Safa, N.S., Sookhak, M., Von Solms, R., Furnell, S., Ghani, N.A., Herawan, T.: Information security conscious care behaviour formation in organizations. Comput. Secur. **53**, 65–78 (2015)
31. Safa, N.S., Von Solms, R., Furnell, S.: Information security policy compliance model in organizations. Comput. Secur. **56**, 70–82 (2016)
32. Taylor, S., Todd, P.: Assessing IT usage: the role of prior experience. MIS Q. **19**, 561–570 (1995)
33. Venkatesh, V., Morris, M.G.: Why don't men ever stop to ask for directions? Gender, social influence, and their role in technology acceptance and usage behavior. MIS Q. **24**, 115–139 (2000)
34. Venkatesh, V., Morris, M.G., Davis, G.B., Davis, F.D.: User acceptance of information technology: toward a unified view. MIS Q. **27**, 425–478 (2003)
35. Von Solms, R., Van Niekerk, J.: From information security to cyber security. Comput. Secur. **38**, 97–102 (2013)
36. Vroom, C., Von Solms, R.: Towards information security behavioural compliance. Comput. Secur. **23**(3), 191–198 (2004)
37. Werlinger, R., Hawkey, K., Botta, D., Beznosov, K.: Security practitioners in context: their activities and interactions with other stakeholders within organizations. Int. J. Hum Comput Stud. **67**(7), 584–606 (2009)
38. Whitty, M., Doodson, J., Creese, S., Hodges, D.: Individual differences in cyber security behaviors: an examination of who is sharing passwords. Cyberpsychol. Behav. Soc. Netw. **18**(1), 3–7 (2015)
39. Wood, C.C., Banks Jr., W.W.: Human error: an overlooked but significant information security problem. Comput. Secur. **12**(1), 51–60 (1993)

Identifying Security Risks of Digital Transformation - An Engineering Perspective

Anh Nguyen Duc[1]([⊠]) [iD] and Aparna Chirumamilla[2]

[1] Business School, University of South Eastern Norway,
Bø i Telemark, Norway
Anh.Nguyen.duc@usn.no
[2] IDI, Norwegian University of Science and Technology, Trondheim, Norway
aparna.vegendla@ntnu.no

Abstract. Technological advancements continue to disrupt how organizations compete and create value in almost every industry and society. The recent digital transformation movement has expanded the reliance of companies and organizations in software technologies, such as cloud computing, big data, artificial intelligence, internet-of-things, and also increase the risk associated with software usage. This work aims at identifying security risks associated with these technologies from an engineering management perspective. We conducted two focused groups and a literature review to gather and discuss the list of security risks. The findings have implications for both practitioners to manage software security risks and future research work.

Keywords: Digital transformation · Cybersecurity ·
Software vulnerability · Internet-of-Things · Cloud computing ·
Big data · Artificial intelligence

1 Introduction

Technological changes continue to disrupt how organizations compete and create values in almost every industry and societies. Recent trending technologies, such as cloud computing, big data, artificial intelligence, and internet-of-things have expanded the reliance of organizations in data and data processing software. Many companies have experienced an organizational process so-called "digital transformation" to explore these new digital technologies and to exploit their benefits [13,16]. However, this process is not risk-free. Before realizing the potential benefits of adopting such technologies, digital strategy makers should be aware of pitfalls that might impact the digital transformation process [10].

Cybersecurity is recognized as a significant cross-cutting concern that influences various aspects of digital transformation, from the choice of technology to

© IFIP International Federation for Information Processing 2019
Published by Springer Nature Switzerland AG 2019
I. O. Pappas et al. (Eds.): I3E 2019, LNCS 11701, pp. 677–688, 2019.
https://doi.org/10.1007/978-3-030-29374-1_55

the financial outcomes [36]. The Center for Strategic and International Studies estimates that *"the likely annual cost to the global economy from cybercrime is more than 400 billion US dollars"* [28]. A recent industrial survey shows that almost 60% of respondents experienced a phishing attack in 2015, and in 30% of these organizations, it is occurring on a daily basis [9]. While considering software technology to adopt, it is increasing demand on securing safety and security of organizations' data [3]. However, securing software is not a simple task, due to not only the emergence and evolution of software technologies, but also the peer pressure of digital transformation movement. While many organizations recognize the importance of cybersecurity, it is still a limited understanding of the actual effort on identifying and managing risks of cybersecurity [9]. Towards a risk management framework for digital transformation, such as [8], we aim at providing an overview of cybersecurity risks in digital transformation. Instead of looking at organizational or managerial factors, the work focuses on engineering aspect. Our research question is:

RQ: What are engineering-level security risks relevant to a digital transformation process?

From an academic perspective, this paper contributes to business research about digital transformation by a list of security concerns in emerging technologies. From a practitioner's perspective, the list can be used as a checklist for further analysis when an organization wants to adopt one or many digital technologies.

The paper is organized as follows. Section 2 presents the terminology of security. Section 3 describes our research methodology. Section 4 presents technology-specific security challenges. Section 5 discusses the finding and concludes the paper.

2   Terminologies of Security

In the software-driven world, it is common to consider security as a quality or non-functional attribute of a software system. Software security is about making software behave correctly in the presence of a malicious attack [17]. Software security is always relative to the data and services being protected, the skills and resources of adversaries, and the costs of potential assurance remedies; security is an exercise in risk management [4,17]. Several distinguishable terms about software security that are relevant to this work include:

- Vulnerability: a part of the software source code that possesses some weakness in specification, development and operation which will allow any external user to exploit it for any malicious activity.
- Error: a mistake caused by developers of the software is called an error.
- Fault: a piece of source code which on execution causes a failure to occur. It is a hidden programming error caused by programmers.
- Failure: It is the deviation of software from its normal functioning. Software, when exploited or targeted for attack is denied from performing its intended functionality.

– Attack: It is the event that exposes the software's inherent errors. The individuals breaking into the system or program for any malicious activity are termed as attackers.

The general objective of (software) security includes (1) availability, (2) integrity, and (3) confidentiality [33]. Federal Information Processing Standard 199 defines the security categories, security objectives, and impact levels to which SP 800-60 maps information types [33]. The security categories are based on the potential impact on an organization when certain events occur, as shown in Table 1.

Table 1. The three objectives of security

Security aspect	FIPS 199's definitions [33]
Confidentiality	A loss of confidentiality is the unauthorized disclosure of information
Integrity	A loss of integrity is the unauthorized modification or destruction of information
Availability	A loss of availability is the disruption of access to or use of information or an information system

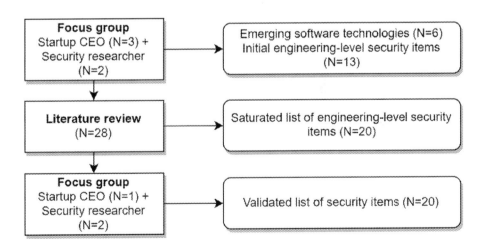

Fig. 1. Research methodology

3   Research Methodology

The research approach adopted in this study is interpretivism [2]. Security risk during digital transformation is subjective to managers and decision makers.

To collect the relevant security risks for organizations, we performed focused groups and literature review. Focused groups are successfully used to collect ideas and initiate the process of further investigation of software engineering phenomenon [34]. We invited managers, strategic decision makers of software companies, software startups and researchers in both engineering and business areas to participate. The first meeting included five participants from both software industry and academia. During this meeting, we identified a list of emerging software-relevant technologies that organization might adopt in their digital transformation process. We also came up with an initial list of security risks that participants were aware of.

The major data collection approach in this work is a literature review. Due to the time limitation, we did not adopt any systematic literature or mapping study [24]. Moreover, the focus of this work is not exhaustively coverage of security risks but raising the awareness of security as a cross-cutting concern in digital transformation. We searched with the string: ("security" or "risk management") AND ("big data" or "artificial intelligence" or "mobile apps" or "digital transformation" or "cloud computing" or "internet-of-things"). We collected risk items from articles that are recent (preferable articles published after 2010), from known journals and conferences, and articles with high citations. The review is stopped when we can add no more new risk items. The final list of risks was extracted from 28 articles given in the Reference section.

The second focused group was dedicated to discussing the relevance of identified security risks. Although there are different opinions on the importance of each risk items in a specific context, we were consensus on the relevance of all identified risks for the digital transformation process. The research process is illustrated in Fig. 1.

4   Security Risks in Software-Relevant Technologies

The first focused group resulted in thirteen security risk items (65% of the risk items from the literature review), showing that participants were aware of security risks to a good extent. The final list includes 20 unique risk items that will be presented according to software technologies below. Some risks that occur in more than one technology will be presented in one category.

4.1   Mobile Security

Current smartphone devices provide lots of the capabilities of traditional personal computers (PCs) and, also, offer a large selection of connectivity options, and inclusion of a wide variety of sensors such as biometric, GPS, compass, gyroscope, barometer, and camera. Although these smartphone functions are more useful for users, often they are vulnerable to attacks. In recent year, researchers have recognized the importance of mobile security [5, 22, 25]. The investment in mobile application's security has steadily increased [27]. Compared to the traditional computing environment, mobile presents some unique risks due to its configurations [22]:

- Resource-limited security mechanisms: Mobile devices have strict resource constraints in both computational and power capabilities due to their mobility and small size. Therefore, while complex security algorithms may scale in standard non-constrained desktop environments, they can be less effective in resource-constrained mobile environments.
- Varied use cases of mobile attacks: Compared to traditional computer attacks, the case of botnets is not as straightforward [22]. Some of the traditional attacks on hosted servers include spam, denial of service extortion, sensitive data theft, and phishing. However, as much sensitive data such as login credentials are stored on mobile devices, attackers may still wish to target them for harvesting data. Moreover, a mobile device is a one-stop-shop for hackers to steal voice/SMS/data communications, track their physical locations in real-time via GPS functionality, and even eavesdrop on non-cellular conversations via the device's microphone. Mobile devices may also act as bridges, allowing penetration of an enterprise's network [22].
- Platform obscurity: While many mobile platforms are based on commodity operating systems (e.g., Android vs. iOS), they can look significantly different from a security perspective. Besides, different platforms often associate with their ecosystems of mobile apps and communities with different security mechanisms [18]. In addition, platforms are often intentionally restricted from modification and instrumentation due to mobile carrier agreements and regulatory requirements.
- Diverse set of testing configurations Hundreds of different mobile devices are on the market, produced by different vendors, and with different software features and hardware components [20]. Mobile applications, while running on different devices, may behave differently due to variations in the hardware or O.S. components. Hence the protection of mobile devices includes thorough security tests of various combinations of operational environments and mobile devices' configurations.
- Attacks via varied communication channels: Viruses can spread not only through internet downloads or memory cards, but they can also spread through Bluetooth, AirDrop (iPhone-specific communication) or even voice recognition [25,26]. For instance, a virus can send unsolicited messages over Bluetooth to smartphones and access unauthorized information.

4.2 Cloud Storage Security

Via different cloud business models[1], organizations are now largely depending on cloud computing for storage, processing and analysis of their data [39]. Despite the affordable cost and easy-to-use as two major motivations for cloud computing, there can be serious threats to security if no proper governance is provided:

- Limited control of third-party services: It is more and more important that customer's data and computation tasks should be kept confidential from both

---

[1] https://www.ibm.com/cloud/learn/iaas-paas-saas.

cloud providers and other customers who are using the service. User's private or confidential information should not be accessed by anyone in the cloud computing system, including application, platform, CPU, and physical memory. Whether adopting public or hybrid cloud environments, a loss of visibility in the cloud can mean the limited control on data security.

- Exposing data to public: Shifting stored data from local computers to cloud servers also means that the data now might be searchable and exploitable by public users [29]. Data stored in an IaaS environment can be encrypted to decrease the risk of private data becoming public. However, this is not always as easy as it sounds as the level encryption always depends on the type of encryption method. Moreover, there are other security-relevant challenges of searching, retrieving, and sorting encrypted data [1,29].
- Expensive on-cloud data auditing: The data owners would less control to ensure data integrity of outsourced data storage than local storage. Moreover, a large amount of cloud data and the users constrained computing capabilities to make data correctness auditing in a cloud environment is expensive and even formidable [29].
- Exploitable Application programming interfaces (APIs): Cloud vendors provide their customers with a range of APIs, which can also be a source of security threats. They may have been deemed to be initially, and then at a later stage be found to be insecure in some way. This problem is compounded when the client company has built its own application layer on top of these APIs. The security vulnerability will then exist in the customer's own application. This could be an internal application, or even public facing application potentially exposing private data.

While in-house storage infrastructure is entirely under the control of the company, cloud services delivered by third-party providers do not offer the same level of granularity with regards to administration and management. Although private cloud services could be more secure than legacy architecture, there is still a potential cost for data breaches and downtime.

4.3 Securing Big Data

Big Data is defined via the three V: the magnitude of data (volume), the structural heterogeneity of datasets (variety) and the rate at which data are generated (velocity) [12]. Security issues could not be discussed without the context of Big data processes and infrastructures for data management and analytic [6,32].

- Risks of switching database models Switching from relational databases to NoSQL databases should be done with a careful evaluation due to the differences of security mechanisms between these two types of databases. For instance, in Cassandra[2] databases, nodes in a cluster can communicate freely and no encryption or authentication is used [23,37]. Moreover, all communication between the database and its clients is unencrypted. It is shown that

---

[2] http://cassandra.apache.org/.

NoSQL has not been designed with security as a priority, so developers or security teams must add a security layer to their organisations.

– Outsourcing data control: Big data administrators may decide to mine data without permission or notification [37]. Whether the motivation is curiosity or criminal profit, the adopted security tools need to monitor and alert on suspicious access no matter where it comes from. If the big data owner does not regularly update security for the environment, they are at risk of data loss and exposure, as seen in Cloud Computing models (Sect. 4.2).

– Efficient mechanisms for volume and velocity: The sheer size of a big data installation, terabytes to petabytes, is too big for routine security audits. Moreover, most big data platforms are cluster-based, this introduces multiple vulnerabilities across multiple nodes and servers. Besides, classical method to make sure data integrity is that getting all data blocks from the server and has been verified by client [23]. However, this way is inapplicable on big data space. Hence, auditing big data is an active research topic recently [14].

4.4   Security and Internet-of-Things

Internet-of-things refers to a systems of sensing devices, hubs, gateways, and servers that provides services on top of a networked of connected devices [21]. Internet-of-things implies the compositions of multiple hardware, communication and software technologies that we have mentioned in the previous sections. Here we describe security issues that is specific for the whole Internet-of-things systems [3,31,35] (Table 2).

Table 2. Security concerns across layer of IoT systems

IoT layer	Typical security concerns
Application layer security	Authentication, access control, security audit, etc.
Network layer security	Wireless network security, secure routing, firewall, content analysis, etc.
Physical layer security	Attack detection, intrusion response, cryptography, virus control, etc.

– Cross-layer security approaches: Sensing layers could be a subject to physical attacks, including invasive hardware attacks, side-channel attacks, and reverse-engineering attacks [11]. Application layers, including cloud computing, big data, can be compromised by malicious code, such as Trojans, viruses, and runtime attacks (see Sects. 4.2 and 4.3). Communication protocols are subject to protocol attacks, including man-in-the-middle and denial-of-service attacks [30].

- Flexible system architecture [3]: IoT systems would require multiple and diverse security protocols and standards in order to support (i) multiple security objectives (e.g., secure communications, DRM), (ii) interoperability in different environments (e.g., a handset that needs to work in both 3G cellular and wireless LAN environments), and (iii) security processing in different layers of the network protocol stack. The overall security architecture should be flexible enough to adapt easily to changing requirements.
- Hardware-based versus software-based security solutions [31]: There is a rich body of literature on security architectures for Internet-of-Things systems, mainly due to the broad range of devices considered as embedded systems. On one hand, hardware-based security solutions might be complex and expensive for low-end embedded systems. On the other hand, software-based isolation of components might not satisfy security and performance requirements.

4.5 Security and Artificial Intelligence (AI)

There have been increasing scientific discussions about AI and cybersecurity [19]. Research shows that 60% of surveyed people think AI could be positively used to find attacks before they do damage. AI's strength is its ability to learn and adapt to its current environment and the threat landscape. If deployed correctly, AI would be able to consistently collect intelligence regarding new threats, attempted attacks, successful breaches, blocked or failed attacks and learn from all of it. However, AI could also be configured to learn the specific defenses and tools that it runs up against, which will allow it to be able to better breach them in the future. Viruses could be created that host this type of AI, which produces malware that can bypass even more advanced security implementations. Moreover, hackers do not even need to tamper with the data itself, and they could work out the features of code that a model is using and mirror it with their own code they are using with malicious intent so the algorithm is not able to catch it.

4.6 Security and Digital Transformation

Digital transformation, lead by organizational strategy, is causing explosive growth in digital organizations [10]. It is creating new ways to engage customers, collaborate with partners, and achieve operational efficiency. We discuss here the security risk at the business level:

- Securing adopted technologies: These are technologies mentioned above, including smartwatches, health bands, smart home devices, smart cars and voice assistants, artificial intelligence, big data analytics, etc. These products and services need to be provided with suitable security controls mechanisms (detail in Sects. 4.1 to 4.5) to handle the vulnerabilities, threats and attacks for these technologies.
- Business-driven risk management: Risk management techniques are used to identify information risks arising out of business processes. In digital business,

processes are dynamic and evolve, which traditional risk modeling can not handle. Moreover, digital businesses depend on using data and assets, which increase the risk profile—for example, the use of consumer data for digitizing retail.

– Evolving user behaviors: The digital world is built around the consumer or user. The user is given the tools to make a choice. The user can define the level of engagement, such as sharing location information to get relevant services. Traditional security models treat users as the weakest link. This means that, now, the weakest element has the most power.

– Regulation support: Regulations are changing to support digital business and control standards for managing risk and privacy. A good example is the General Data Protection Regulation (GDPR). Compliance assurance and sustenance need to transform to adapt to the relevant changes.

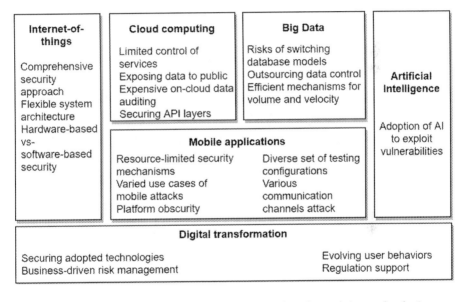

Fig. 2. An overview of security risks associated with emerging technologies

5   Discussion and Conclusions

Digital transformation is recognized as a complex issue, which managers need to balance between achieving organizational agility and other objectives [7]. While there exists research about organizational and managerial risks of digital transformation [7,38], to the best of our knowledge we found no previous research on engineering-level risks of cybersecurity for digital transformation. Similar research about product engineering, for instance, is about risk management at system architecture level [15].

While digital transformation is considered as strategy-driven actions with risk-taking becoming a cultural norm [10], we found that strategic decision-makers were aware of technical risks associated with the technologies they would adopt. Organizations transform their business by taking advantage of technologies such as mobility, Internet-of-Things and cloud computing, there are security risks in digital transformation to consider. In business models that rely on the quality of offered software-based services and products, cybersecurity has a direct impact on both value creation and financial aspects.

Based on focused groups and literature review, this paper presents a list of security risks for emerging software-based technologies. As shown in Fig. 2, the security risks were presented according to the technology stack. The adoption of these technologies in digital transformation can be assisted by this list to reduce the negative impact of software vulnerabilities on business activities. The findings from this study are based on limited empirical evidence. Hence, we do not claim for the comprehensiveness of the list. Future research can adopt surveys or case studies to investigate cybersecurity concerns of digital transformation systematically. Last but not least, this work treats digital transformation at a conceptual level. Future work can explore in detail the process of transforming, i.e., possible effect before, during, and after the transformation.

Acknowledgments. This work was co-funded under the Vietnam national project entitled *"Towards the development of secured Operating Systems and App Stores for e-Goverment solutions"*. The project is led by MQ Solution (https://mqsolutions.vn/).

References

1. Behl, A., Behl, K.: An analysis of cloud computing security issues. In: 2012 World Congress on Information and Communication Technologies, pp. 109–114, October 2012. https://doi.org/10.1109/WICT.2012.6409059
2. Creswell, J.W.: Research Design: Qualitative, Quantitative, and Mixed Methods Approaches. SAGE Publications, Thousand Oaks (2014)
3. Duc, A.N., Jabangwe, R., Paul, P., Abrahamsson, P.: Security challenges in IoT development: a software engineering perspective. In: Proceedings of the XP2017 Scientific Workshops, Cologne, Germany, XP 2017, pp. 11:1–11:5. ACM, New York (2017). https://doi.org/10.1145/3120459.3120471
4. Felderer, M., Büchler, M., Johns, M., Brucker, A.D., Breu, R., Pretschner, A.: Chapter one - security testing: a survey. In: Memon, A. (ed.) Advances in Computers, vol. 101, pp. 1–51. Elsevier, January 2016. https://doi.org/10.1016/bs.adcom.2015.11.003
5. Furnell, S.: Handheld hazards: the rise of malware on mobile devices. Comput. Fraud Secur. **2005**(5), 4–8 (2005). https://doi.org/10.1016/S1361-3723(05)70210-4
6. Gandomi, A., Haider, M.: Beyond the hype: big data concepts, methods, and analytics **35**(2), 137–144. https://doi.org/10.1016/j.ijinfomgt.2014.10.007
7. Hess, T., Matt, C., Benlian, A., Wiesböck, F.: Options for formulating a digital transformation strategy **15**(2), 123–139 (2016)

8. InfoQ: Guide to digital transformation. define, price, and plan a digital transformation (part 1). https://www.infoq.com/articles/Digital-Transformation-Guide-1

9. ISACA: State of Cybersecurity: Implications for 2016 - An ISACA and RSA Conference Survey. Technical report, ISACA (2016)

10. Kane, G., Palmer, D., Phillips, A., Kiron, D., Buckley, N.: Strategy, not technology, drives digital transformation. MIT Sloan Manag. Rev. Deloitte Univ. Press, 1–25 (2015)

11. Koushanfar, F., Sadeghi, A., Seudie, H.: EDA for secure and dependable cybercars: challenges and opportunities. In: DAC Design Automation Conference 2012, pp. 220–228, June 2012. https://doi.org/10.1145/2228360.2228402

12. Laney, D.: 3D data management: controlling data volume, velocity, and variety. BibSonomy. https://www.bibsonomy.org/bibtex/742811cb00b303261f79a98e9b80 bf49

13. Lankshear, C., Knobel, M.: Digital Literacies: Concepts, Policies and Practices, vol. 30. Peter Lang Publishing, Bern (2008)

14. Liu, C., Ranjan, R., Yang, C., Zhang, X., Wang, L., Chen, J.: MuR-DPA: top-down levelled multi-replica merkle hash tree based secure public auditing for dynamic big data storage on cloud. IEEE Trans. Comput. **64**(9), 2609–2622 (2015). https://doi.org/10.1109/TC.2014.2375190

15. Masuda, Y., Shirasaka, S., Yamamoto, S., Hardjono, T.: Risk management for digital transformation in architecture board: a case study on global enterprise. In: 2017 6th IIAI International Congress on Advanced Applied Informatics (IIAI-AAI), pp. 255–262. https://doi.org/10.1109/IIAI-AAI.2017.79

16. Matt, C., Hess, T., Benlian, A.: Digital transformation strategies **57**(5), 339–343. https://doi.org/10.1007/s12599-015-0401-5

17. McGraw, G., Potter, B.: Software security testing. IEEE Secur. Priv. **2**(5), 81–85 (2004). https://doi.org/10.1109/MSP.2004.84

18. Mohamed, I., Patel, D.: Android vs iOS security: a comparative study. In: 2015 12th International Conference on Information Technology - New Generations, pp. 725–730. https://doi.org/10.1109/ITNG.2015.123

19. Morel, B.: Artificial intelligence and the future of cybersecurity. In: Proceedings of the 4th ACM Workshop on Security and Artificial Intelligence, Chicago, Illinois, USA, AISec 2011, pp. 93–98. ACM, New York. https://doi.org/10.1145/2046684.2046699

20. Muccini, H., Francesco, A.D., Esposito, P.: Software testing of mobile applications: challenges and future research directions. In: 2012 7th International Workshop on Automation of Software Test (AST), pp. 29–35, June 2012. https://doi.org/10.1109/IWAST.2012.6228987

21. Nguyen-Duc, A., Khalid, K., Shahid Bajwa, S., Lønnestad, T.: Minimum viable products for internet of things applications: common pitfalls and practices **11**(2), 50. https://doi.org/10.3390/fi11020050

22. Oberheide, J., Jahanian, F.: When mobile is harder than fixed (and vice versa): demystifying security challenges in mobile environments. In: Proceedings of the Eleventh Workshop on Mobile Computing Systems & Applications, Annapolis, Maryland, HotMobile 2010, pp. 43–48. ACM, New York (2010). https://doi.org/10.1145/1734583.1734595

23. Okman, L., Gal-Oz, N., Gonen, Y., Gudes, E., Abramov, J.: Security issues in NoSQL databases. In: 2011 IEEE 10th International Conference on Trust, Security and Privacy in Computing and Communications, pp. 541–547, November 2011. https://doi.org/10.1109/TrustCom.2011.70

24. Okoli, C.: A guide to conducting a standalone systematic literature review **37**(1). https://doi.org/10.17705/1CAIS.03743

25. Penning, N., Hoffman, M., Nikolai, J., Wang, Y.: Mobile malware security challeges and cloud-based detection. In: 2014 International Conference on Collaboration Technologies and Systems (CTS), pp. 181–188, May 2014. https://doi.org/10.1109/CTS.2014.6867562

26. Petracca, G., Sun, Y., Jaeger, T., Atamli, A.: AuDroid: preventing attacks on audio channels in mobile devices. In: Proceedings of the 31st Annual Computer Security Applications Conference, Los Angeles, CA, USA, ACSAC 2015, pp. 181–190. ACM. https://doi.org/10.1145/2818000.2818005

27. Polla, M.L., Martinelli, F., Sgandurra, D.: A survey on security for mobile devices. IEEE Commun. Surv. Tutor. **15**(1), 446–471 (2013). https://doi.org/10.1109/SURV.2012.013012.00028

28. Ponemon: Cost of a Data Breach Study: Global overview. Technical report. IBM (2018)

29. Ren, K., Wang, C., Wang, Q.: Security challenges for the public cloud. IEEE Internet Comput. **16**(1), 69–73 (2012). https://doi.org/10.1109/MIC.2012.14

30. Rostami, M., Koushanfar, F., Karri, R.: A primer on hardware security: models, methods, and metrics. Proc. IEEE **102**(8), 1283–1295 (2014)

31. Sadeghi, A., Wachsmann, C., Waidner, M.: Security and privacy challenges in industrial Internet of Things. In: 2015 52nd ACM/EDAC/IEEE Design Automation Conference (DAC), pp. 1–6, June 2015. https://doi.org/10.1145/2744769.2747942

32. Sagiroglu, S., Sinanc, D.: Big data: a review. In: 2013 International Conference on Collaboration Technologies and Systems (CTS), pp. 42–47. https://doi.org/10.1109/CTS.2013.6567202

33. Sharing (LLIS), LLI: FIPS Pub 199: Standards for Security Categorization of Federal Information and Information Systems, February 2004

34. Singer, J., Sim, S.E., Lethbridge, T.C.: Software engineering data collection for field studies. In: Shull, F., Singer, J., Sjøberg, D.I.K. (eds.) Guide to Advanced Empirical Software Engineering, pp. 9–34. Springer, London (2008). https://doi.org/10.1007/978-1-84800-044-5_1

35. Sun, X., Wang, C.: The research of security technology in the Internet of Things. In: Jin, D., Lin, S. (eds.) Advances in Computer Science, Intelligent System and Environment. Advances in Intelligent and Soft Computing, vol. 105, pp. 113–119. Springer, Heidelberg (2011). https://doi.org/10.1007/978-3-642-23756-0_19

36. Teoh, C.S., Mahmood, A.K.: National cyber security strategies for digital economy. In: 2017 International Conference on Research and Innovation in Information Systems (ICRIIS), pp. 1–6. https://doi.org/10.1109/ICRIIS.2017.8002519

37. Terzi, D.S., Terzi, R., Sagiroglu, S.: A survey on security and privacy issues in big data. In: 2015 10th International Conference for Internet Technology and Secured Transactions (ICITST), pp. 202–207, December 2015

38. Fitzgerald, M., Kruschwitz, N., Bonnet, D., Welch, M.: Embracing digital technology: a new strategic imperative. MIT Sloan Manag. Rev. **55**(2), 1–12 (2014)

39. Wu, J., Ping, L., Ge, X., Wang, Y., Fu, J.: Cloud storage as the infrastructure of cloud computing. In: 2010 International Conference on Intelligent Computing and Cognitive Informatics, pp. 380–383, June 2010. https://doi.org/10.1109/ICICCI.2010.119

Modelling and Managing the Digital Enterprise

Creating Business Value from Cloud-Based ERP Systems in Small and Medium-Sized Enterprises

Eli Hustad[1]([✉]) [iD], Dag H. Olsen[1], Emeli Høvik Jørgensen[2],
and Vegard Uri Sørheller[3]

[1] University of Agder, Kristiansand, Norway
{eli.hustad,dag.h.olsen}@uia.no
[2] Equinor, Stavanger, Norway
emelijorgensen@gmail.com
[3] Accenture, Oslo, Norway
vegard.u.sorheller@gmail.com

Abstract. This qualitative study focuses on how small- and medium-sized enterprises (SMEs) can realize benefits and create information technology (IT) value by investing in cloud enterprise resource planning (ERP) systems. We interviewed 19 respondents from cloud providers and cloud clients and found that their SMEs experienced both benefits and challenges when implementing cloud ERP systems. The digital value was obtained through work process automatization, fast updates of system functionalities, enhanced security of data storage, and increased access to critical business data from multiple digital units. Challenges in realizing these benefits related to organizational compliance with standard solutions and the need for organizational changes for employees to optimize system usage. The SMEs preferred an informal process for realizing benefits and creating digital value from the system. In contrast, the providers wanted to integrate benefits realization as part of their formal implementation methodology. Based on frameworks identified in the literature, we integrate a benefits realization model with an information systems value model to understand how SMEs realize benefits and create business value from cloud ERP systems. We contribute to the SME literature and explain the value creation process for SMEs implementing cloud ERP systems.

Keywords: Cloud-based ERP system · SaaS · Benefits realization · IS business value

1 Introduction

Enterprises face an increasingly turbulent and competitive business environment, and advanced information systems (IS) functionality is essential to stay competitive and profitable. Obtaining and maintaining state-of-the-art IS functionality is challenging for any company, but it is particularly challenging for small- and medium-sized enterprises (SMEs) because of their limited human and financial resources [1, 2].

© IFIP International Federation for Information Processing 2019
Published by Springer Nature Switzerland AG 2019
I. O. Pappas et al. (Eds.): I3E 2019, LNCS 11701, pp. 691–703, 2019.
https://doi.org/10.1007/978-3-030-29374-1_56

SMEs make up more than 99% of the enterprises in market economies, provide more than 50% of the employment in industrialized countries and contribute significantly to economic development [3]. Thus, the survival and growth of SMEs are crucial to the income and welfare of citizens—in any industrialized country. It is, therefore, important for SMEs to utilize new technology innovatively and realize its potential benefits [1].

Cloud computing is a promising way to effectively provide advanced IS functionality to SMEs [4]. The *software-as-a-service* model offers SMEs advanced enterprise system functionality as a subscription service over the Internet [5]. Customers can utilize state-of-the-art enterprise resource planning (ERP) systems without investing in servers or human IT capabilities, making such systems feasible even for small companies [6, 7]. However, there is still a lack of knowledge about how SMEs realize value from such technology [8]. We have, therefore, explored how cloud-based ERPs are implemented in SMEs. To guide our investigation, we have addressed the benefits and challenges of cloud-based ERPs and explored how SMEs realize the benefits of this technology. We conducted a qualitative study comprising interviews with both providers of cloud-based ERP systems and SMEs using cloud-based ERP systems. The study was guided by the following research question: How do SMEs generate benefits and create business value from cloud ERP systems? The paper is organized as follows: The next sections present related work on cloud computing and benefits realization. Then, we present the research method, followed by the results, a discussion, and implications. Finally, we offer concluding remarks.

2   Background

Cloud services have recently gained popularity among enterprises. Such services vary from small applications to large business-critical systems, platforms, and infrastructure. Cloud providers give customers access to a wide variety of IT services over the Internet, freeing them from the restrictions of locally installed software and local infrastructure or traditional application service providers (ASPs) [9]. They also make it feasible for small companies to implement advanced IT functionality that they could not acquire otherwise due to limited resources and a lack of IT capability [10].

Cloud services are the modern operating model for ERP systems. Cloud-based ERP systems can be defined as ERP software distributed over the internet, and such systems are usually accessed via a browser. Cloud-based solutions allow customers to acquire an ERP system without having to manage hardware, software, or updates, while also reducing upfront system costs. Cloud-based ERP solutions offer functionality similar to that of terrestrial systems; however, their infrastructure (software, hardware, etc.) is delivered and managed by the suppliers [11].

The literature has identified several benefits related to cloud ERP systems, such as time savings, reduced costs, scalability, updates, and easy access [4, 12, 13]. Some scholars have posited that many of these benefits materialize by themselves when a company implements an ERP in the cloud [14], while others maintain that many important benefits do not materialize without deliberate benefits management processes [15, 16]. It is, therefore, important to understand how the benefits from SaaS ERP can be fostered. Further, evidence suggests that many IT projects fail to realize their planned benefits and that success depends on certain inhibitors and facilitators [17]. The term *benefits management* can be defined as "the process of organizing and managing such that the potential benefits arising from the use of IT/IS are actually realized" [18, p. 36]. The approach emphasizes that benefits only appear through changes made by individuals or groups of users and that these changes must be identified and managed to succeed. Benefits management and change management are, therefore, closely related [19]. Realizing the maximum value of IT investments depends particularly on three competencies: benefits planning, change management, and benefits realization. This last competency requires companies to conduct organizational changes, especially when implementing such extensive systems as ERPs.

In this paper, we have utilized Ward and Daniel's [18] benefits management model to understand why and how potential benefits are realized [18]. The model consists of five steps in an iterative process: (1) identifying and structuring benefits, (2) planning benefits realization, (3) executing benefits realization, (4) evaluation and reviewing results, and (5) potential for further benefits. The stages in the benefits realization model are necessary to better achieve the potential benefits of the IT investment. They relate to the organization's ability to achieve value from the IT investment. In addition, we wanted to combine the benefits realization model with an IS business value model; it is important to understand how businesses create value from their IT investments by embedding benefits management into the IS value creation process.

There are a number of IS business value models, such as Schryen's IS business value model [20], Soh and Markus' IT business value process model [21], and Melville et al.'s IT business value model [22]. Since Ward and Daniels' benefits management model is a process model, and our findings are consistent with this perspective, we argue that a process model will best capture how benefits realization contributes to IS value creation. We have, therefore, integrated the benefits management model stages into Soh and Markus' [21] value creation process model [21] to get a better understanding of our findings (see Fig. 1).

3   Research Approach

We conducted an inductive qualitative study in Norway comprising semi-structured interviews as the primary empirical data source. In total, 19 interviews were carried out. The informants were drawn from two different providers offering cloud-based ERP systems (8 informants) and nine SMEs that use these solutions (11 informants). The companies involved operate in different business domains, including logistics, travel industry, health care, manpower and recruiting services, IT business, and voluntary organizations. The informants from the providers were working as senior consultants, while the informants participating from the SMEs had company roles such as CIO, project manager, financial director, administrative leader or accounting controller. The interviews were mostly conducted face-to-face at the companies' sites. A few interviews were conducted through Skype. The interviews lasted approximately 1 h and were taped and fully transcribed. The interviews were largely dialogue-based [23] (the interview guide is presented in the Appendix). Secondary data sources included internal project documents.

The empirical material was systematized and reduced [24]. Then, long statements were condensed to shorter quotes to filtrate the essence of the text, and sequences in the text were interpreted to generate themes [25]. We combined previous research studies documented in the literature (e.g., studies focusing on cloud ERP implementation, IT value models, and concepts from benefits realization models) with our empirical findings to gain a broader understanding of how SMEs can generate digital value by implementing cloud-based ERP systems. The insight from the two provider organizations and some of their SME customers allowed the generation of thick descriptions and rich insight into the implementation of cloud-based ERP systems and perceptions of IT value creation. The content of the interviews had a retrospective character, and the findings represent stories and events from both ongoing and completed cloud ERP projects in which the informants are or were involved.

4   Results

The interviews focused on the benefits of cloud ERP systems and how SMEs can realize these benefits and create value from these investments.

All respondents emphasized that cloud-based ERPs simplify and automate several work processes and manual tasks through standardization and making employees work more intelligently. Several SME informants also noted that the ERP system was easy and intuitive to use, and that user support was easily available due to a large number of users. One of the provider informants explained that cloud-based ERP systems are better than on-premise systems regarding automatization: "cloud-based systems are easier to keep updated with new functionality, and thus it is possible to achieve more automation."

We also found a difference in the degree of automation the system supported and that the SMEs had different expectations regarding enhancing and creating new processes. Some of the SMEs sought to automate a number of manual processes, while others sought to automate as many processes as possible and integrate the ERP system with other systems to ensure inter-system communication. These SMEs had higher expectations of the system and a better understanding of how the system could be exploited. In addition, they expected more from the providers regarding process awareness and support to realize maximum automation and optimization of work processes. The main benefits identified from the study are summarized in Table 1.

None of the SMEs stated that they performed planned benefits realization processes. Nevertheless, several *informal* benefits realization steps were activated. These steps were not standardized as a part of the implementation methodologies applied by the vendors. Table 2 briefly summarizes the benefits realization steps the SMEs performed. The steps are based on Ward and Daniel's [18] benefits realization model, which identifies which activities are performed in each step.

Table 1. Benefits of cloud-based ERP systems in SMEs.

Themes of benefits identified	Explanations
Simplifying and automatizing work processes	Work processes are standardized, automated, and simplified based on "best practice"
Future-oriented technology	The system develops over time through new solutions, technology, and modern digital designs
Security	ERP systems are offered by professional providers that take security seriously
Cost reduction	The system reduces customers' costs, releases resources, shifts responsibility for the IT infrastructure to the provider, and reduces the need for internal IT competencies
Continuous updating	System updates happen automatically for all users
Saving time	The system supports fast implementation, automatized processes, and diversity of units (e.g., mobile units)
Availability	The system is available through a web browser and several mobile units

Most of the SMEs explained their needs and expectations to their provider, who provided feedback on how the system would support these requirements. In some cases, the provider explained this during the sales meeting, and the SMEs got a sense of the benefits they could achieve by adopting the system. However, most of the SMEs had not documented their expectations and had no appointed person responsible for following up on these benefits. One of the two providers was interested in implementing benefits realization as part of its future methodology and suggested that the SMEs chart their expected benefits. The other provider had developed a value proposal to present to the customer. This value proposal was a summary of the benefits customers could achieve based on information provided during the sales process. Since none of the SMEs had a prepared plan for realizing benefits, it became difficult to explain how the realization of benefits was performed.

The most challenging issue in the benefits management process was activating organizational change. Though cloud ERP systems are easy to implement, employees still need to change their routines and work processes to optimize the system. One consultant highlighted this: "The most challenging thing is the people working in the company. No doubt about that. The employees are worried about doing something wrong in the system before they get to know it properly. That is easy to overcome. But there are people that do not want to change. There is a quite big group that has this personality." SMEs might choose to implement a cloud ERP system because of its ease of implementation; however, to realize the benefits, various change activities may be necessary. As one informant shared: "With regard to the amount of time spent in the implementation, we see that we are well below compared to traditional systems. But that does not mean that customers are able to learn the system faster. You need to focus on this after the implementation." Furthermore, several consultants pointed out the difficulty of changing a business' mindset when shifting from an on-premise system to a cloud-based system: "When establishing a cloud-based system, then we need to inform employees that we are using a cloud-based system. So, the biggest challenge is to get the employees to realize the benefit." This explains the importance of informing the entire business about the benefits of the system and the process to understand the value of the change. The findings indicated that some SMEs felt they lost control of their own systems when they moved to a cloud solution and became part of a larger cloud ERP user community. A consultant from one of the providers believed that this challenge is especially true for businesses with strong IT departments, as members of IT departments may express strong resistance if they feel that they are losing control and power. Moreover, customers may feel that they lose control when processes become automated, as they cannot access each of the steps. One of the consultants pointed out that this is a common challenge for accountants who have worked in their own way for a long time. A willingness to change and the ease of implementation were perceived as benefiting by the implementing company, indicating the degree of maturity: "If you succeed or not, depends very much on the maturity of the company." However, this problem was considered to be larger in a cloud-based environment than in an on-premise ERP environment.

Some of the SMEs emphasized that the implementation methodology was not entirely appropriate for their business. They thought the methodology was very good for implementing the system itself but felt that it did not support or suggest any process or benefit improvements. As a result, they did not change their processes as they originally wanted.

However, the enterprises had to adapt to the system to get the most out of it. The SMEs had different approaches to managing the organizational changes to achieve maximum system benefits, but there were some similarities. Specifically, all SMEs performed employee training. Some did this together with the provider, while others performed training internally.

One of the consultants from the provider side pointed out that it is difficult to give concrete figures on the benefits of cloud ERP systems as the quantification of concrete benefits depends on several prerequisites. The consultant noted that such quantification is not impossible; however, it requires industry knowledge and an understanding of how the customer's company works. Some of the consultants pointed out that evaluating benefits was a natural task at the end of the project when they discussed with the customers how the implementation had turned out. Based on these conversations, the consultants would write a "lessons learned" report to support future improvement.

One of the partners of the providers worked to make benefits realization an integral part of the process, such that they followed up with customers following implementation. The providers pointed out that the many benefits of a cloud-based ERP system are easy to evaluate informally following an implementation. These benefits include, among other things, increased work process efficiency, the lack of need for an IT infrastructure, and the release of resources. One of the SME informants emphasized how they obtained efficiency gains: "[Efficiency] was easy to observe. With the new system, it is easy to handle a bulk of [transactions] at the same time. So, instead of spending one minute per customer, then we use five minutes for 100 customers." Some informants also mentioned that they had meetings with the provider both along with the way and after the implementation when a review of whether the goals were reached or not was conducted. Some informants mentioned that, even though they did not formulate a benefits realization plan, they had clear goals for what they wanted to get out of the implementation. These goals were discussed after the implementation. In general, few evaluation activities were carried out, but various goals were evaluated informally in project status meetings. Though the effects were not measured, several of the SMEs informally noted the benefits of the implementation.

The SMEs under study were satisfied with the implementation of the systems and regarded them as successful. Moreover, they noted that several of the benefits of a cloud-based ERP system manifested after extended use. These benefits were often associated with streamlining and automating processes, improving utilization of the system, and developing skills through learning by doing. It took time to explore all the system's functions; therefore, it was easier for users to identify new benefits and potential benefits when they had more experience. Both of the providers experienced that their customers achieved more benefits when using the system on a continuous basis: "Some of the values are already realized after three to four months in the project. While other values take more time to realize [because of higher task complexity]."

None of the SMEs formally identified potential extended benefits. Some noted that they were constantly working to optimize and become more effective, but that these efforts were not necessarily in the context of the cloud-based ERP system. In some cases, employees offered requests for improvements, but this was not a pre-planned event.

The providers and the SMEs had different perspectives on benefits realization. The following quote from an SME illustrates this: "We are not the kind of organization that develops measurable benefits before we conduct a project. We have some hypotheses and some resolute goals we want to achieve and follow up. But we do not have a systematically structured plan. We are not so fond of the benefits realization concept at all, especially if we need to pay for it." Moreover, the SMEs thought that the benefits of the system were clear and that there was no need for a formal realization approach: "The benefits were very clear when we implemented a new cloud-based ERP system, even if they were not documented and measured." In addition, the SMEs were not familiar with the concept of benefits realization: "I think there are many terms for this, but people do not always use the same term. We are always operating to make everyday life better, but we may not call it benefits realization. We aim to change the system to get something better, nothing worse." The providers had a somewhat different opinion on this, arguing that it was important to be aware of benefits realization approaches to obtain better value from the system, as illustrated in the following quotes: "I think customers could have used the system better by being more aware of benefits realization." Furthermore: "You could certainly get paid for having a benefits realization plan for projects. It should be a responsibility both with us and the customer, where we are responsible for initiating and telling the customer that it could be a good idea."

Table 2. Benefit realization plans and actions for cloud-based ERP systems in SMEs.

Benefits realization	Explanations
Identification and focus on benefits	Several of the SMEs identified benefits through dialogues with the provider, sometimes developing a value proposal
Planning of benefits realization	None of the SMEs had developed a formal benefit realization plan
Executing the benefits realization plan	None of the SMEs had a formal benefit realization plan to execute; however, some practiced change management
Evaluation of benefits	Informal evaluation through dialogues with the provider and observation of use
Potential for extended benefits	None of the SMEs formally identified potential for extended benefits; however, some were working on optimizing and increasing the effectiveness
Perspective on benefit realization	The SMEs did not see the need for a formal benefit realization focus, while the providers were more receptive towards this idea

5   Discussion and Implications

We have explored how SMEs aim to generate benefits and create value from their cloud ERP systems. In addition, we have identified challenges in obtaining benefits and creating value.

Previous literature has identified organizational change as a key challenge. When an organization adopts a cloud-based ERP system, it leads to a number of business process changes [26]. Organizational change is crucial for realizing benefits and is an important part of the benefits management process. Companies must learn to handle processes and data differently. The literature describes that the challenges for organizational change are greater among larger businesses than among SMEs, as fewer SME employees facilitate personal follow-ups [27]. This can explain why few of the SMEs experienced an organizational change to be a challenge.

The results of this study are partly consistent with previous literature. Both the literature and the results revealed by the providers identified organizational change as a central challenge, as companies must change their thinking and their processes from previous systems. We found that the companies underestimated change management in the benefits and value creation process when implementing a cloud-based ERP system. As a sales tactic, consultants often argue that implementation is fast. This may cause customers to believe that changes will be rapid and require little effort.

The SMEs under study did not follow a *formalized* benefits realization approach; thus, no benefits realization approach was institutionalized as a formal and standardized process in their organization. There were several reasons for this. Some thought it was more expensive than necessary, while others believed that the benefits of a cloud-based ERP system were so clear that there was no need for a formal benefits realization approach. If an IT project goes according to plan, it may achieve the desired benefits. However, if companies focus only on tangible benefits, they may miss other important benefits [18, 28].

The ERP literature points out that benefits realization has always had a low priority among SMEs [29, 30]. There may be several reasons for this. For example, evaluating IT investments and benefits realization may be seen as too extensive and complex and not worth implementing [28, 31]. Furthermore, the benefits realization effort is perceived to be too expensive [28]. Finally, SMEs feel that they have too little time to implement procedures and that the extent of the implementation is too small to justify the benefits realization measures [31].

On the other hand, the benefits realization literature suggests that the value gained from benefits realization is greater than the cost of implementing the measures [18]. One of the basic assumptions in the literature on information systems is that IT has no inherent value [19]. To realize and sustain benefits, any potential benefits must first be identified together with the necessary organizational changes. Ownership and responsibility for the realization of each benefit must be established, and the ways in which the benefits are to be realized must be planned in detail. Introducing benefits management significantly increases the likelihood of achieving a full range of benefits. Benefits management also supports a clear understanding of how an organization's personnel should work together to achieve the desired benefits [19]. We found that the informants believed that benefits realization was better suited for larger businesses than for SMEs. However, Peppard et al. [19] demonstrated that small businesses also benefit greatly from a focus on benefits realization [19].

Several of the studied SMEs identified potential benefits with the help of the suppliers. One of the providers developed a value proposition that specified potential benefits, and this value proposition was reviewed at the end of the project to evaluate whether the project had been successful. Apart from this, however, none of the SMEs developed any plans for how to realize benefits. Without such plans, it is hard to see how companies can realize the benefits effectively. Some researchers have asserted that, if SMEs choose the right system, they can realize some benefits without further benefits realization planning [29]. However, other researchers have posited that the benefits do not come automatically and that they need to be managed actively [19].

Our findings indicate that some of the potential benefits of a cloud-based ERP investment in SMEs are considered too obvious to necessitate a benefits realization plan. Nevertheless, we believe that SMEs can better achieve the potential benefits of the system by implementing such an approach and that a benefits realization plan can help them realize all benefits more effectively. If an enterprise saves time and resources without a clear plan for how to exploit these savings, it will not achieve any business value [19].

As mentioned in the background section, we wanted to utilize the IS value model developed by Soh and Markus [21]. This model depicts the link between IT investments and organizational performance. This can be perceived as a chain of necessary conditions, such that enhancing organizational performance requires IT impacts, which, in turn, require IT assets and IT investments. In this context, IT investments mean investments into the cloud ERP system, any required new infrastructure, human resources, and management capabilities [20]. IS assets consist of IT, human resources, and, in our context, the cloud ERP system. IS impacts refer to one or more of the following benefits: improved operational efficiency of processes, new/improved products or services, and strengthened organizational intelligence and dynamic organizational structure [21, 22].

Benefits management will help develop and explicate the potential benefits of an ERP system and clarify how to manage the process of achieving this value. The benefits management process is an important means to contribute to the IT conversion process, the IT use process, and the competitive process geared toward realizing the full range of potential value. We conceptualize how benefits management can be integrated into the IS value model in Fig. 1 and illustrate its contribution to IS value creation in the discussion below.

We argue that the lack of benefits management is a serious limitation when SMEs adopt cloud-based ERPs. SMEs do not realize the full range of benefits and, therefore, miss a substantial portion of the potential value. The first benefits management stage, *Identifying and structuring benefits*, builds the rationale for adopting cloud-based ERPs and, therefore, improves the likelihood of securing appropriate financial and human resources for the implementation process. The second stage, *Planning benefits realization*, prepares the organization for performing the required organizational changes. The third stage, *Executing the benefits realization plan*, involves implementing the plan in practice. We, therefore, suggest that the first three stages of Ward and Daniel's [18] framework support the IT conversion and the IT use processes and help the organization achieve appropriate IT assets and impacts. Figure 1 combines the IS value model and benefits management into a framework to illustrate how SMEs create value from their IT investments by integrating benefits management into the value creation process.

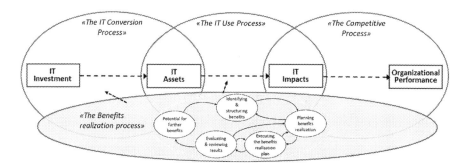

Fig. 1. Framework for understanding how SMEs realize benefits and create value from IT investments (e.g., ERP cloud systems; adapted from Ward and Daniel and Soh and Markus [18, 21]).

6   Conclusion

We have explored how cloud-based ERPs create digital value in SMEs. SMEs experience several benefits and challenges related to cloud-based ERP systems and a lack of benefits management. The digital value was achieved through the automatization of work processes, fast system updates, enhanced security of data storage, and increased availability of business-critical data. Organizational change was difficult to implement and was the most important challenge in the benefits management process. We found that the SMEs had no formal benefits management processes and that they preferred an informal process for creating digital value from the cloud ERP system. In contrast, the providers wanted to integrate benefits realization as part of their formal implementation methodology. Without such plans, it is hard to see how companies can realize benefits effectively. The main contribution is a conceptualization of how benefits management can be integrated into the IS value model. We thus propose that the benefits management process would be a valuable addition to Soh and Markus' [21] IT value creation model.

This research has several limitations. It was performed in one country with a small number of informants and, therefore, has limited generalizability. Further research should explore this pertinent issue in other contexts, using the present research as a basis for subsequent quantitative studies to provide generalizable results.

Appendix – Interview Guide

1. What do you think are the most significant benefits when implementing a cloud-based ERP system?
2. What do you think are most challenging when implementing a cloud-based ERP system?
3. Did you experience any challenges in the implementation process and how did you handle the challenges?
4. Did your organization carry out any activities to prepare the employees? (training, competence building, etc.)
5. Did you have a meeting with the supplier where you discussed what benefits you could possible achieve from the system?
6. Did you create a plan or strategy to achieve expected benefits?

   - If no: why not?
   - If yes: Can you elaborate on the plan and strategy in the organization?

7. Did you evaluate the achievement of the benefits during the implementation process?
8. Do you know if the various benefits were measured quantitatively during or after the implementation?
9. Did a specific employee have the responsibility for making sure that the benefits were realized?
10. Did you have a follow-up plan after the implementation regarding achieving the expected benefits?
11. Did you achieve specific benefits after the system went live? Would you say that you achieved more benefits than previously assumed?
12. Have you made new goals after the system went live – regarding how you can better utilize the system? Ex. become more effective?
13. Were there any gains you did not realize?

14. Did you have to change processes to adapt to the system?
15. What were typical changes you had to make?
16. Did someone have responsibility to take care of executing the changes?
17. How did you experience the willingness to change among employees?
18. Did you assess whether the implementation was successful/unsuccessful?
19. How was success considered?

References

1. Chan, C.M., Teoh, S.Y., Yeow, A., Pan, G.: Agility in responding to disruptive digital innovation: case study of an SME. Inf. Syst. J. **29**(2), 436–455 (2019)
2. Zach, O., Munkvold, B.E., Olsen, D.H.: ERP system implementation in SMEs: exploring the influences of the SME context. Enterp. Inf. Syst. **8**(2), 309–335 (2014)
3. OECD: Enhancing the Contributions of SMEs in a Global and Digitalised Economy. 24 (2017)
4. Seethamraju, R.: Adoption of software as a service (SaaS) enterprise resource planning (ERP) systems in small and medium sized enterprises (SMEs). Inf. Syst. Front. **17**(3), 475–492 (2015)
5. El-Gazzar, R., Hustad, E., Olsen, D.H.: Understanding cloud computing adoption issues: a Delphi study approach. J. Syst. Softw. **118**, 64–84 (2016)
6. Kranz, J.J., Hanelt, A., Kolbe, L.M.: Understanding the influence of absorptive capacity and ambidexterity on the process of business model change–the case of on-premise and cloud-computing software. Inf. Syst. J. **26**(5), 477–517 (2016)
7. Gupta, S., Misra, S.C., Kock, N., Roubaud, D.: Organizational, technological and extrinsic factors in the implementation of cloud ERP in SMEs. J. Organ. Change Manag. **31**(1), 83–102 (2018)
8. Grubisic, I.: ERP in clouds or still below. J. Syst. Inf. Technol. **16**(1), 62–76 (2014)
9. Demi, S., Haddara, M.: Do cloud ERP systems retire? An ERP lifecycle perspective. Procedia Comput. Sci. **138**, 587–594 (2018)
10. Wamuyu, P.K.: Use of cloud computing services in micro and small enterprises: a fit perspective. Int. J. Inf. Syst. Proj. Manag. **5**(2), 59–81 (2017)
11. Vithayathil, J.: Will cloud computing make the Information Technology (IT) department obsolete? Inf. Syst. J. **28**(4), 634–649 (2018)
12. Al-Johani, A.A., Youssef, A.E.: A framework for ERP systems in SME based on cloud computing technology. Int. J. Cloud Comput.: Serv. Archit. **3**(3), 1–14 (2013)
13. Gallardo, G., Hernantes, J., Serrano, N.: Designing SaaS for enterprise adoption based on task, company, and value-chain context. IEEE Internet Comput. **22**(4), 37–45 (2018)
14. Haddara, M., Paivarinta, T.: Why benefits realization from ERP in SMEs doesn't seem to matter? In: 44th Hawaii International Conference on in System Sciences (HICSS 2011), pp. 1–10. IEEE (2011)
15. Badewi, A., Shehab, E., Zeng, J., Mohamad, M.: ERP benefits capability framework: orchestration theory perspective. Bus. Process Manag. J. **24**(1), 266–294 (2018)
16. Ashurst, C., Hodges, J.: Exploring business transformation: the challenges of developing a benefits realization capability. J. Change Manag. **10**(2), 217–237 (2010)
17. Coombs, C.R.: When planned IS/IT project benefits are not realized: a study of inhibitors and facilitators to benefits realization. Int. J. Proj. Manag. **33**(2), 363–379 (2015)

18. Ward, J., Daniel, E.: Benefits Management: Delivering Value from IS & IT Investments. Wiley, Chichester (2006)
19. Peppard, J., Ward, J., Daniel, E.: Managing the realization of business benefits from IT investments. MIS Q. Exec. **6**(1), 1–11 (2007)
20. Schryen, G.: Revisiting IS business value research: what we already know, what we still need to know, and how we can get there. Eur. J. Inf. Syst. **22**(2), 139–169 (2013)
21. Soh, C., Markus, M.L.: How IT creates business value: a process theory synthesis. In: International Conference on Information Systems (ICIS), pp. 29–41 (1995)
22. Melville, N., Kraemer, K., Gurbaxani, V.: Information technology and organizational performance: an integrative model of IT business value. MIS Q. **28**(2), 283–322 (2004)
23. Myers, M.D., Newman, M.: The qualitative interview in IS research: examining the craft. Inf. Organ. **17**(1), 2–26 (2007)
24. Miles, M.B., Huberman, A.M.: Qualitative Data Analysis: An Expanded Sourcebook. Sage, Thousand Oaks (1994)
25. Kvale, S., Brinkmann, S.: Interviews: Learning the Craft of Qualitative Research Interviewing. Sage, Los Angeles (2009)
26. Lenart, A.: ERP in the cloud – benefits and challenges. In: Wrycza, S. (ed.) SIGSAND/PLAIS 2011. LNBIP, vol. 93, pp. 39–50. Springer, Heidelberg (2011). https://doi.org/10.1007/978-3-642-25676-9_4
27. Gupta, S., Misra, S.C., Singh, A., Kumar, V., Kumar, U.: Identification of challenges and their ranking in the implementation of cloud ERP: a comparative study for SMEs and large organizations. Int. J. Qual. Reliab. Manag. **34**(7), 1056–1072 (2017)
28. Lin, C., Pervan, G.P.: A review of IS/IT investment evaluation and benefits management issues, problems and processes. In: van Grembergen, W. (ed.) Information Technology Evaluation Methods and Management, pp. 2–24. IGI Global, Pennsylvania, USA (2001)
29. Haddara, M., Zach, O.: ERP systems in SMEs: a literature review. In: Proceedings of the 44th Hawaii International Conference on System Sciences, pp. 1–10. IEEE (2011)
30. Hawking, P., Stein, A., Foster, S.: Revisiting ERP systems: benefit realisation. In: Proceedings of the 37th Annual Hawaii International Conference on System Sciences, pp. 1–10. IEEE (2004)
31. Thomas, G., Seddon, P.B., Fernandez, W.J.P.P.: IT project evaluation: is more formal evaluation necessarily better? In: Proceedings of the Pacific Asia Conference on IS (PACIS 2007), p. 111 (2007)

Critical Success Factors for Dynamic Enterprise Risk Management in Responsive Organisations: A Factor Analysis Approach

Brenda Didi-Quvane, Hanlie Smuts[✉], and Machdel Matthee

University of Pretoria, Pretoria, South Africa
Brenda.Didi-Quvane@mmiholdings.co.za,
{hanlie.smuts,machdel.matthee}@up.ac.za

Abstract. Globalisation and technology advancements have disrupted the organisational landscape and with the proliferation of new technology; risk management is fundamental to transforming the business especially considering the dynamic nature of the digital society organisations now exist in. However, the challenge faced by the enterprise risk management (ERM) function operating in such a dynamic and transformative environment, is the capability to continuously innovate, evolve and transform its risk management processes to meet the needs of the organisation. Questionnaire survey research examined the relative importance of 18 critical success factors for dynamic ERM. Factor analysis revealed that the appropriate grouping of the 18 critical success factors (CSFs) are ERM charter, ERM processes, and ERM business alignment. These findings should empower organisations to identify risk management processes influencing agility in the risk management practise applied.

1 Introduction

Globalisation and technology advancements have disrupted the organisational landscape. In a time of extraordinary economy and market disturbances, as well as changing market conditions, organisations are faced with the challenge of being competitive and having to meet customer requirements [1]. Organisational flexibility is defined in terms of an organisation's response to change, as well as the ability to judge environmental change and respond readily [2]. Therefore, organisations are required to be fast moving, rapidly creating new products through the use of different exponential technologies and methods, while possessing the capabilities to respond to aggressive competitors, quickly navigate volatile markets and successfully penetrate new markets [3]. The ability of an organisation to be responsive to changing conditions requires that it addresses ambiguity which may be generated through innovative initiatives and market change [4]. The reliance of risk management practices to aid in these decision making processes and addressing ambiguity, are therefore vital, taking into account uncertainty and its effect on achieving the organisation's objectives [5].

Although attempts have been made to solve this more dynamic risk management capability problem by suggesting the integration of the risk management processes with the agile development processes, the proposed integration model lacked guidelines on

© IFIP International Federation for Information Processing 2019
Published by Springer Nature Switzerland AG 2019
I. O. Pappas et al. (Eds.): I3E 2019, LNCS 11701, pp. 704–717, 2019.
https://doi.org/10.1007/978-3-030-29374-1_57

how to actually conduct risk management in a dynamic and responsive environment [6]. Therefore, in order to guide such responsive organisations towards more dynamic risk management, this research study considers the following research question: *what is the relative importance of critical success factors that will enable dynamic ERM in responsive organisations?* We will reflect on this research question by considering ERM in general, the nature of responsive organisations and the role of CSFs towards more dynamic risk management.

The remainder of the paper is structured as follows: in Sect. 2 we provide the background to the study presenting an overview of risk management, as well as risk management principles, processes and models. The approach to this study is discussed in Sect. 3 where after we provide an overview of quantitative findings in Sect. 4. In Sect. 5 we present the CSFs for dynamic risk management in responsive organisations and conclude in Sect. 6.

2 Background

In a progressively digital world, organisations are faced with challenges to sustain or establish a competitive advantage in the market and stay ahead of competitors [7, 8]. Responsive organisations are designed, structured and operate differently from the traditional organisations. Dynamic, exponential and disruptive thinking have been introduced in these organisational environments with goals of experiencing exponential growth [9]. How an organisation is structured and operates informs the organisations ERM practices. Therefore, to perform effective risk management, constant alignment should exist between the organisation and enterprise risk function [3, 10], with ERM integrated into the organisations decision making processes. As a decision making tool, ERM should be aligned to the organisation with specific focus on the organisation's processes, in order to assist in the active and effective management of risk across the business [11]. ERM defines a "process that combines the organisation's entire risk management activities in one integrated, holistic framework to achieve a comprehensive corporate perspective" [4, 12, 13].

Several existing ERM frameworks are used by organisations. The Committee of Sponsoring Organisations of the Treadway Commission (COSO) [14] and the ISO31000 [11], are well known risk frameworks. COSO addresses the need for organisations to improve their approach to managing risk to meet the demands of an evolving business environment. With the adoption of COSO, organisations should be able to understand risk impacting the outcome of the business strategy and objectives. ISO3100 is currently best practice for risk management frameworks and incorporates best practice from COSO [13]. It provides a generic guideline for risk management, not intending to impose uniformity of risk management practices. ISO 31000 includes a detailed list of the suggested principles for risk management, and has an open system model to fit multiple needs and context. Both COSO and ISO consider the important influences that culture and biases carry in decision-making and risk management practices, but no guideline is given on how responsive organisations operating in dynamic and changing environments, can implement more dynamic risk management practices [12, 13].

Furthermore, adequate risk management capabilities are needed when operating in an environment of uncertainty [9, 15]. This is opposed to the current systematic and linear risk management approach applied [16], that is in line with the organisational structure of the traditional organisation which is linear in nature [17, 18]. Responsive attributes will guide organisations towards implementing essential components for managing risk.

In the next sections we present a high level synopsis of ERM and responsive organisations, as well as an overview of CSFs in the context of ERM.

Enterprise Risk Management

Organisations of all forms, types and sizes face a range of risks that can affect the achievement of the organisation's objectives. These organisational objectives can relate to a range of organisational activities, such as operations and processes reflected in terms of strategic, operational, financial and reputational outcomes and impacts [19]. An enterprise wide approach to risk management draws together these impacts to provide a structured approach to consider the potential impact of all types of risks on all processes, activities, stakeholders, products and services [20]. Stakeholders, both external and internal to the organisation, are now much more concerned with risk [20], understanding that adequate risk management capabilities are needed when operating in an environment of uncertainty [15].

Before an organisation select the most effective strategy or decision, it needs to understand the risks being taken when seeking to achieve objectives and it needs to assess the organisations exposure, risk profile, financial position and acceptable risk and reward trade-off [13]. Therefore, for the ERM to be effective, it must be directly connected to company strategy, and designed to recognise events that could have an impact on organisational performance as defined by its strategic objectives [19]. A successful ERM initiative can affect the likelihood and consequences of risks materializing, as well as deliver benefits related to better informed strategic decisions, successful delivery of change and increased operational efficiency [4, 19]. Other benefits include reduced cost of capital, more accurate financial reporting, competitive advantage, improved perception of the organisation and better marketplace presence and enhance informed decision making ability [19, 21].

As organisations attempt to gain maximum benefit from ERM in the current dynamic organisational environments, we consider the nature of responsive organisations in the next section.

The Nature of Responsive Organisations

The development of new technology influences the design of organisations and their ways of work [22]. For organisations to thrive in an environment of continuous and often unanticipated change, they are required to quickly adapt by reshaping the culture of the organisation, reforming business practices to cater for more collaborative and robust management, provide for the increased use of iterative practices and consider rigorous change management [1, 23, 24]. The shift in organisational design principles from old to new distinguishes speed, flexibility, integration and innovation as key success factors [22]. Therefore, organisational attributes that provide for flexibility is needed in an environment that is continuously changing [3, 25].

To consider the nature of responsive organisations, we reviewed various definitions of responsiveness from the literature in order to identify the essential attributes embedded within those definitions as shown in Table 1. For each responsive organisation attribute, we provide a brief description, as well as the references for the particular attribute. The purpose of Table 1 is to guide the CSF identification towards responsiveness.

Table 1. Attributes of responsive organisations

Responsive organisation attribute and references	Description
Slimmer, flatter and adaptable organisational structure [26, 27]	Employing organisational structures that are lean and foster flexibility; an organisation with fewer layers of management (flat), is able to respond more flexibly to business challenges
Robust learning, knowledge and adaptation processes [26, 27]	Ability to integrate working and learning, focus on life-long learning and learn and work effectively both as individuals and in teams
Disposal of non-core activities [26]	Outsourcing, separation from core business or selling off of non-core activities
Delegation and decentralisation [26]	Assignment of decision making to the customer interface, with few management layers between customers and decision points, utilising more lateral communication
Fast moving and non-linear eco-system [28, 29]	Risk management in a dynamic and rapidly growing organisation must be differently defined and executed
Measurement of output [2, 26]	Assessment and remuneration based on output rather than position in the organisation, as well as measurement of organisational agility
Responsive to various stakeholders [25, 30–32]	Customising engagement to the individual customer, suppliers and community
Access to skill [26, 30]	Skills capacity planning and acquisition of skills to enable response to diverse customer needs
Cohesion and high degree of readiness [33, 34]	React purposefully and within an appropriate timescale, to significant events, opportunities or threats (especially from the external environment) to bring about or maintain competitive advantage; handle disturbances in an organic fashion
Diversity of employees [26]	Extent to which resources contrast in their competence and attitudes, market value, and their work, life style and learning preferences
Culture of trust [3, 34]	Create a collaborative environment where failure is not feared

According to Table 1, responsive organisations represent flexible organisational structures with few levels of management that enable clear accountability and decision-making. Responsive organisations operate with a high degree of readiness to purposefully address any business- or external environment changes, grounded in a culture of trust. Employees are highly skilled with a strong focus on continuous learning and assessed on output. These findings are confirmed by the all-encompassing definition presented by Dove [4, 27]: "an effective integration of response ability and knowledge management in order to rapidly, efficiently and accurately adapt to any unexpected (or unpredictable) change in both proactive and reactive business/customer needs and opportunities without compromising with the cost or the quality of the product/process".

For responsive organisations, the challenge now faced by the ERM function is the question of linearity, where risk management processes are planned, and methodically and systematically applied [17]. Risk management agility within organisations is not easily attained due to organisation-wide functions and processes still functioning and operating in a linear manner [17, 35]. Traditionally, risk management has always followed a more linear approach to the identification, assessing, managing and monitoring of risks, providing drawn-out projections of emerging risks and tracking currents risks within the control environment of a stretched period of time [25]. Therefore, adequate risk management capabilities are needed when operating in an environment of uncertainty and risk management should be the product of both responsiveness and capability [15].

In order to identify CSFs for dynamic ERM in responsive organisations, we consider ERM CSF categories in the next section.

Risk Management Critical Success Factors

CSFs refer to a limited number of characteristics, conditions, or variables that have a direct and significant impact on the effectiveness, efficiency, and viability of an organisation [21]. Activities associated with CSFs must be performed at the highest possible level of excellence to achieve the intended overall objectives [36]. The main principle of ERM is that it delivers value to the organisation [13]. In order for an organisation to understand the characteristics of ERM and what it is to deliver on, ERM practices operate on a set of principles [2]. Such principles define the essential features of ERM, describing what ERM should be in practice, while including information on what ERM should deliver on [13]. Furthermore, such principles point to a systematic process that involves activities of communicating and consulting, establishing the context and assessing, treating, monitoring, reviewing, recording and reporting of risk [11, 20].

Table 2. Critical success factors for enterprise risk management in responsive organisations

Critical success factor	References
Adequate internal reporting of framework effectiveness	[18, 21, 37]
Appropriate and timeous communication of framework modification	[11, 18, 20, 38]
Clear risk management framework development and implementation accountability	[18, 38, 39]
Consider internal and external organisational context	[15, 20, 40]
Continuous suitability-checking of risk management framework	[18, 39]
Creates value for the organisation	[13, 20, 38, 41]
Effectiveness agility and resilience dependent	[12, 18, 40]
Embedded in organisational decision making	[21, 37, 41]
Facilitation of continual improvement and enhancement of the organisation	[38, 41]
Foster skills diversity and expertise	[18, 39, 40]
Integral part of organisational processes	[21, 37–39]
Integration of risk management within overall risk management system	[39, 42]
Iterative and responsive to change	[18, 39, 40]
Joint practitioner and business contingency planning	[21, 38]
Regular review of risk management policy and framework in response to changes	[2, 37, 39]
Risk indicators tracking directly aligned to business performance indicators	[18, 38, 42]
Risk management practice should accommodate changing organisation	[38, 40, 43]
Systematic, planned and structured approach	[20, 21]

By considering the factors identified in the sections above and the literature, we extracted 18 relevant CSFs depicted in Table 2. Key decisions in an organisation are informed by a range of possible outcomes, and these outcomes are rarely binary. The CSFs depicted in Table 2 point to a well-developed capability to identify, measure, manage and monitor risks across the organisation e.g. adequate internal reporting, risk indicator tracking, timeous communication to and involvement of all stakeholders, as well as a structured approach. Furthermore, the dynamic nature and the ability to adapt to changing risks and varying business cycles, are reflected in CSFs such as effectiveness agility, responsive to change and accommodation of a changing organisation. Explicit consideration of risk and risk management are supported by value creation, the identification of new risks using internal and external information and ultimately moving from prevention of risks to exploit risk. In addition, these CSFs should also accommodate emerging risks and other non-quantifiable risks as a result of extreme internal or external organisational events [21].

3 Research Approach

Our overall objective of this paper was to provide CSFs for dynamic ERM in responsive organisations. These CSFs empower organisations to identify risk management processes influencing agility in the risk management practise applied. Eighteen CSFs as identified from the literature are given in Table 2. However, it is necessary to investigate these factors with respect to relative importance and underlying groupings: Are these CSFs equally important? Can these CSFs be reduced to fewer essential factors?

In order to answer these questions, we chose quantitative research, namely factor analysis, to determine the underlying patterns amongst these CSFs. We utilised survey research as a research strategy with the selection of a large sample of participants from a pre-determined population of interest [44]. By choosing survey as a research strategy, it allowed us to obtain the same kind of data from a large group of people, in a standardised manner [45]. We utilised an on-line questionnaire for data collection as a questionnaire enabled the collection of a large data set over a short period of time [46]. The attributes of responsive organisations (Table 1) and the CSFs defined (Table 2) were included in the design of the on-line questionnaire. After the online questionnaire was pilot tested to ensure that all items were clear and meaningful, respondents had to provide data on their role and years of experience. They also had to rate the 18 CSF statements using a 5-point Likert rating scale.

Specific criteria and rationale were used in identifying the research participants for the online questionnaire i.e. risk practitioners working in a risk function, professionals working in a business function that engages with the risk fraternity, and professionals with a business strategy understanding. Convenience sampling was used where research participants are of the target population that meet certain practical criteria, such as easy accessibility, geographical proximity, availability at a given time, or the willingness to participate [47]. A web link to the questionnaire, was emailed to the identified target audience, which comprised of 319 research participants representing various organisational structures and business sectors. The total number of respondents (refer profile in Table 3) for the questionnaire was 183, yielding a response rate of 57%.

Table 3. Profile of questionnaire respondents

Respondent profile	% of respondent profile	Respondent role	% of respondent role	Respondent tenure	% of respondent tenure
Risk practitioner	35.6%	Executive	7.9%	<5 years	10.1%
		Senior Manager	23.6%	5–10 years	16.3%
Professional (engaging with risk)	45.8%	Middle Manager	29.1%	11–20 years	51.1%
		Junior Manager	5.6%	21–30 years	16.9%
Professional (strategic role, engaging with risk)	18.6%	General staff	27.5%	31–40 years	5.1%
		Specialist	6.2%	40 years above	0.6%

remains relevant for the organisation through measuring its effectiveness, as well as continuously checking the suitability of the risk management framework. This process of continuous optimization is achieved by consciously *considering the internal and external organisational context.* This comprehensive monitoring and alignment of the ERM charter, relates to the next CSF with fairly strong association (0.722) as any changes in the internal or external environment, reporting, measurement or accountability, will trigger a *regular review of the risk management policy and framework in response to changes.* This CSF also points to the fact that an organisation must ensure that their ERM remain relevant and aligned in times of any change impacting the organisation. The last CSF in factor 1, also with the lowest association of 0.705, is *integration of risk management within overall risk management system.* ERM involves establishing actions to respond to risk and implement adequate internal controls with which to limit the possibility of occurrence or consequences of risk, if it materialized. In order to ensure efficiency in achieving objectives, the process must be coherent and convergent, integrated to objectives, activities and operations carried out within the organization. The entire ERM system must be managed. ERM charter update is required whenever the organisation changes its strategic objectives, or when the risk policy changes.

Factor grouping 2, *ERM processes,* consists of 7 CSFs with *integral part of organisational processes* and *embedded in organisational decision making* depicting the highest association (0.817 and 0.800 respectively). A dynamic approach to ERM calls for preventing losses, as well as regarding risks as a source of competitive advantage. This approach requires that all organisational functions (human resources, sales, finance, procurement, information technology, legal, strategic development etc.) participate in the organisational risk management process. *Facilitation of continual improvement and enhancement of organisation* and *creates value for the organisation* both have a significant association of 0.775. The role of ERM is to enable organisations to determine what level of risk it is prepared to accept to achieve its strategic objectives, add value to activities and to achieve planned goals. This is achieved through a structured process to ensure that the outcome is coherent and that risk response measures are integrated. ERM can therefore guide the organisation to improve work according to the benefits of good risk management. Work improvement requires employees to obtain the necessary skills in order to monitor and control based on principles of efficiency and effectiveness. The next CSF in factor 2, *foster skills diversity and expertise* with an association of 0.724, points to the fact that employees, regardless of their hierarchical level in the organisation, should be aware of the importance of ERM to achieve planned results. The lowest association of 0.543 and 0.508 respectively are associated with the CSFs systematic, *planned and structured approach* and *joint practitioner and business contingency planning.* From the description of the other CSFs in factor 2, the structured approach and ERM knowledgeable employees are re-enforced and implied.

Factor grouping 3, *ERM business alignment,* consists of 4 CSFs – all with high loading. *Effectiveness agility and resilience dependent* with an association of 0.936 points to the key requirement that a dynamic approach to ERM should be based on an enhanced level of organisational agility. Furthermore, organisational resilience builds upon, and extends beyond, existing strategies for the management of unforeseen risk; it is based on a more organic capacity in the organisation. This CSF is a key mind set in terms of ERM principles. The following two CSFs with high loading (0.918 and 0.907 respectively) are *risk management practice should accommodate changing organisation* and *iterative and responsive to change*. Risk assessment is an essential component of the organisation, as the employees change, regulations change, suppliers change, etc. the objectives must be reviewed or new ones established. This change mind set on the organisational risk profile, informs the emergence of new risks and modification of existing risks. The last CSF in factor 3, *risk indicators tracking directly aligned to business performance indicators*, has a high association (0.834) and points to the philosophy that risk management is integrated and aligned to business strategy. A more proactive focus is required to ensure that key performance indicators (and the resulting outcomes) are achieved, by proactively identifying risks associated with those key performance indicators and managing those risks.

The three factor groupings with their CSFs will have a direct impact on the effectiveness and efficiency of ERM. ERM is a powerful tool that enables the organisation to have a view of the risks affecting the achievement of strategic and operational objectives. At the same time, ERM provides the process of identification, analysis and assessment of risks taking into account the events of and change in the organisation, which can take negative shape and are associated with risks or positive shape and are associated with opportunities.

6   Conclusion

In order to address the lack of guidelines on how to conduct risk management in a dynamic and responsive environment, this research identifies three factor groupings of 18 CSFs for effective ERM in responsive organisations. The three dimensions describe factors to consider in establishing and monitoring risk management policies and frameworks (ERM charter), defining risk management processes (ERM processes) and aligning risk management processes with business (ERM organisational alignment). These groupings give a holistic view of critical factors to take into account when responding to risk while transforming risk management practices to meet the dynamic needs of the organisation.

Although our starting point with identifying CSFs was related to responsive environments, one could argue that the CSF groupings identified are equally applicable to risk management in linear, traditional organisations. The existing risk management frameworks are not meant for dynamic, responsive organisations. Further research is therefore needed on how existing frameworks can be extended to be appropriate in continuously changing environments.

References

1. Sarah, B.Y., et al.: Agility ability. PM Netw. **26**(10), 54–61 (2012)
2. Overby, E., Bharadwaj, A., Sambamurthy, V.: Enterprise agility and the enabling role of information technology. Eur. J. Inf. Syst. **2006**(15), 120–131 (2006)

3. Burba, D.: When agile meets auditor. PM Netw. **29**(1), 60–67 (2015)
4. Teece, D., Peteraf, M., Leih, S.: Dynamic capabilities and organizational agility: risk, uncertainty, and strategy in the innovation economy. Calif. Manag. Rev. **58**(4), 13–35 (2016)
5. Blanco, C., Hinrichs, J., Mark, R.: Creating risk culture: a framework risk culture (2014). https://www.scribd.com/document/341453115/Creating-Risk-Culture-a-Framework. Accessed March 2019
6. Nyfjord, J., Kajko-Mattsson, M.: Outlining a model integrating risk management and agile software development. In: 34th Euromicro Conference Software Engineering and Advanced Applications. IEEE, Parma, Italy (2008)
7. Ganju, K.K., Pavlou, P.A., Banker, R.D.: Does information and communication technology lead to the wellbeing of nations? A country-level empirical investigation. MIS Q. **40**(2), 417–430 (2016)
8. Rocha, L., et al.: Cloud management tools for sustainable SMEs. Procedia CIRP **40**, 220–224 (2016)
9. Ismail, S., Malone, M.S., Van Geest, Y.: Exponential Organisations: Why New Organisations are Ten Times Better, Faster, and Cheaper than Yours (and What to do About it). Diversion Publishing Corporation, Diversion Books, New York (2014)
10. Knight, F.H.: Risk, Uncertainty and Profit. University of Illinois at Urbana-Champaign's Academy for Entrepreneurial Leadership Historical Research Reference in Entrepreneurship (2012). Accessed March 2019
11. ISO 31000 - Risk management. ISO 31000: 2018 Risk management – Guidelines (2018). https://www.iso.org/standard/65694.html. Accessed March 2019
12. Gatzert, N., Martin, M.: Determinants and value of enterprise risk management: empirical evidence from the literature 2013. Department for Insurance Economics and Risk Management Friedrich-Alexander-University (FAU) of Erlangen-Nürnberg, Nuremberg, Germany (2013)
13. Hopkin, P.: Fundamentals of Risk Management Understanding, Evaluating and Implementing Effective Risk Management. Kogan Page, London (2018)
14. Committee of Sponsoring Organizations of the Treadway Commission. Strengthening Enterprise Risk Management for Strategic Advantage (2017). http://www.coso.org. Accessed March 2019
15. Walczak, W., Kuchta, D.: Risks characteristic of agile project management methodologies and responses to them. Oper. Res. Decis. **23**(4), 75–95 (2013)
16. Nyfjord, J., Kajko-Mattsson, M.: Commonalities in risk management and agile process models. In: 2nd International Conference on Software Engineering Advances. IEEE (2007)
17. Mabey, C., Salaman, G., Storey, J.: Organizational structuring and restructuring. In: Understanding Business Organisations. Routledge, London (2001)
18. Ahmed, I., Manab, N.A.: Influence of enterprise risk management success factors on firm financial and non-financial performance: a proposed model. Int. J. Econ. Financ. Issues **6**(3), 1–7 (2016)
19. Soltanizadeh, S., et al.: Business strategy, enterprise risk management and organizational performance. Manag. Res. Rev. **39**(9), 1016–1033 (2016)
20. Nair, A., et al.: Enterprise risk management as a dynamic capability: a test of its effectiveness during a crisis. Manag. Decis. Econ. **35**(8), 555–566 (2013)
21. Aziz, N.A.A., Manab, N.A., Othman, S.N.: Critical success factors of sustainability risk management (SRM) practices in Malaysian environmentally sensitive industries. Soc. Behav. Sci. **2016**(219), 4–11 (2016)

22. McMillan, E.: Considering organisation structure and design from a complexity paradigm perspective. In: Frizzelle, G., Richards, H. (eds.) Tackling Industrial Complexity: the Ideas that Make a Difference, pp. 123–136. University of Cambridge, Cambridge, UK (2002)

23. Ambrose, C., Morello, D.: Designing the agile organization: design principles and practices. In: Strategic Analysis Report, pp. 1–25. Gartner Research (2004)

24. Yusuf, Y., Sarhadi, M., Gunasekaran, A.: Agile manufacturing: the drivers, concepts and attributes. Int. J. Prod. Econ. **62**(1–2), 33–43 (1999)

25. Boahin, P.: The changing nature of work and employability skills development in Higher Education Institutions in Ghana. Eur. J. Educ. Dev. Psychol. **6**(3), 21–32 (2018)

26. Coulson-Thomas, C.: IT and new forms of organisation for knowledge workers: opportunity and implementation. Empl. Relat. **13**(4), 22–32 (1991)

27. Dove, R.: Response Ability: The Language, Structure and Culture of the Agile Enterprise. Wiley, Hoboken (2001)

28. Roggi, O., Andersen, T.J.: Strategic risk management and corporate value creation. In: Andersen, T.J. (ed) The Routledge Companion to Strategic Risk Management, pp. 421–437. Routledge (2016)

29. Boehm, B., Turner, R.: Using risk to balance agile and plan-driven methods. IEEE Comput. Soc. **36**(6), 57–66 (2003)

30. Davis, F.W., Manrodt, K.B.: Service logistics: an introduction. Int. J. Phys. Distrib. Logist. Manag. **21**(7), 4–13 (1991)

31. Kaur, A., Sharma, P.C.: Social sustainability in supply chain decisions: Indian manufacturers. Environ. Dev. Sustain. **20**(4), 1707–1721 (2018)

32. McIntosh, R.I., et al.: Late customisation: issues of mass customisation in the food industry. Int. J. Prod. Res. **48**(6), 1557–1574 (2010)

33. Barclay, I., Poolton, J., Dann, Z.: Improving competitive responsiveness via the virtual environment, pp. 52–62. IEEE (1996)

34. Dove, R.: Knowledge management, response ability, and the agile enterprise. J. Knowl. Manag. **3**(1), 18–35 (1999)

35. Holbeche, L.: The Agile Organisation: How to Build an Innovative, Sustainable and Resilient Business. Kogan Page, London (2018)

36. Critical Success Factor: The Business Dictionary (2019)

37. Cormican, K.: Integrated enterprise risk management: from process to best practice. Mod. Econ. **5**, 401–413 (2014)

38. Shad, M.K., Lai, F.: A conceptual framework for enterprise risk management performance measure through economic value added. Glob. Bus. Manag. Res.: Int. J. **7**(2), 1–11 (2015)

39. Zhao, X., Hwang, B., Low, S.P.: Critical success factors for enterprise risk management in Chinese construction companies. Constr. Manag. Econ. **31**(12), 1199–1214 (2013)

40. Yaraghi, N., Langhe, R.G.: Critical success factors for risk management systems. J. Risk Res. **14**(5), 551–581 (2011)

41. Choi, Y., et al.: Optimizing enterprise risk management: a literature review and critical analysis of the work of Wu and Olson. Ann. Oper. Res. **237**(1–2), 281–300 (2016)

42. Wang, H., Barney, J., Reuer, J.: Stimulating firm-specific investment through risk management. Long Range Plann. **36**, 49–59 (2003)

43. Peteraf, M.A., Maritan, C.: Dynamic capabilities and organisational processes. In: Helfat, C. et al. (eds.) Dynamic Capabilities: Understanding Strategic Change in Organization, pp. 30–45. Blackwell Publishing, Oxford, UK (2007)

44. Kelley, K., et al.: Good practice in the conduct and reporting of survey research. Int. J. Qual. Health Care **15**(3), 261–266 (2003)

45. Oates, B.J.: Researching Information Systems and Computing. SAGE Publications, London (2008)

46. De Villiers, M.R.: Models for interpretive information systems research, part 2: design research, development research, design-science research, and design-based research - a meta-study and examples. In: Research Methodologies, Innovations and Philosophies in Software Systems Engineering and Information Systems, pp. 238–255 (2012)
47. Etikan, I.: Comparison of convenience sampling and purposive sampling. Am. J. Theor. Appl. Stat. **5**(5), 1–4 (2016)
48. Morling, B.: Research Methods in Psychology: Evaluating a World of Information. Norton, Canada (2015)
49. Williams, B., Onsman, A., Brown, T.: Exploratory factor analysis: a five-step guide for novices journal of emergency. Primary Health Care **8**(3), 1–13 (2010)
50. Akhtar-Danesh, N.: A comparison between major factor extraction and factor rotation techniques in Q-methodology. Open J. Appl. Sci. **7**, 147–156 (2017)

Structural Requirements for Digital Transformation – Insights from German Enterprises

Matthias Murawski[1]([⊠]), Tristan Thordsen[1], Malte Martensen[2], Christina Rademacher[3], and Markus Bick[1]

[1] ESCP Europe Business School Berlin, Berlin, Germany
{mmurawski,tthordsen,mbick}@escpeurope.eu
[2] IUBH University of Applied Sciences, Berlin, Germany
m.martensen@iubh.de
[3] Promerit AG, Munich, Germany
christina.rademacher@promerit.com

Abstract. German enterprises are often characterised by low levels of digital maturity. One reason for this is a lack of required structural changes on the path towards digital transformation. We consider a prescriptive framework, the digital transformation framework (DTF), which contains four structural requirements for digital transformation. Based on 16 interviews with German digitalisation experts, we aim at an evaluation of the DTF. The outcome is an enriched version of it containing seven structural requirements including the newly identified factors culture of change, agility of organizational structure, and integration of cloud computing and platforms. The extended DTF sheds light on additional facets of the digital transformation and thus supports managers in navigating their undertaking in this dynamic environment. Corresponding implications for research and practice are discussed.

Keywords: Digital transformation · Evaluation · Interviews ·
Prescriptive framework · Structural requirements

1 Introduction

Digital transformation is characterised by converging social, mobile, analytics, and cloud (SMAC) technologies and continuing miniaturisation with increasing processing power, storage capacity, and communication bandwidth [1]. Digital transformation denotes the changes digital technologies can cause with regards to a company's business model, resulting in adapted products or organizational structures [2]. Consequently, digital technologies have the power to complement and enrich existing products and services and enable entirely new business models [3]. In the context of this enormous and often radical change of the business landscape, new ways to cope with the situation and to develop strategic approaches are required by managers [4]. However, many companies struggle with their digital transformation. This is especially true for the German business landscape, which shows a relatively low level of digital transformation compared to other countries [e.g. 5].

© IFIP International Federation for Information Processing 2019
Published by Springer Nature Switzerland AG 2019
I. O. Pappas et al. (Eds.): I3E 2019, LNCS 11701, pp. 718–729, 2019.
https://doi.org/10.1007/978-3-030-29374-1_58

But what are the reasons for this lack of digital maturity of German business? In this paper we focus on one potential aspect: structural requirements. Structural requirements refer to the organisational setup of a company and refer to "organizational structures, processes and skill sets that are necessary to cope with and exploit new technologies" [2, p. 124]. Thus, the focus lies on the integration of digital technology into the organisational structure [6]. Related examples are new roles and responsibilities such as the Chief Digital Officer [7], or the recruitment of employees who possess and maintain high levels of digital competency [8]. Structural requirements are deemed necessary for an organisation's digital transformation [2]. Companies that fail to consider these aspects face a higher risk of failing in their efforts toward digital transformation [9].

However, there is little empirical research regarding specific structural requirements for digital transformation [10]; especially lacking are comprehensive overviews of these factors. For instance, Holotiuk and Beimborn [11] analysed 21 industry reports and identified organisational requirements and structural changes as critical success factors for a digital transformation, but also found that these factors require further in-depth analyses.

Structural requirements for digital transformation are primarily mentioned in studies dealing with the development of digital strategies [12–14]. On a more concrete level, Hess et al. [2] suggest four structural topics required in their digital transformation framework (DTF): operational change, responsibility for digital transformation, integration of new activities, and building of organisational competencies. Compared to most existing papers on digital transformation, the DTF is a guideline with a significant practical value, as it offers so-called strategic questions for managers regarding digital transformation.[1] Due to its outstanding practical value and the pioneer character of the DTF, we have chosen this framework as model of reference. The DTF can be considered as prescriptive since it supports managers in their decision making in the context of digital transformation. This is in line with recent calls for more relevance and practical value of IS research [15]. However, it must be noted that the empirical basis of the DTF are three case studies from the media industry. Although Hess et al. formulate their framework in a way that it is applicable to other industries as well, we believe that confronting the DTF with findings from other domains, and consequently a potential update of the DTF, would strengthen its applicability. Thus, the objective of this study is to assess and, if required, to extend the DTF by naturalistic evaluation, meaning that findings from other domain's experts are analysed and integrated. Therefore, while placing the focus on German organisations, we formulate three research questions:

RQ1: Which structural requirements identified in our cross-domain analysis are not part of the initial DTF of Hess et al. [2]?

RQ2: Which structural requirements identified in our cross-domain analysis are already part of the initial DTF of Hess et al. [2]?

---

[1] This statement can be underscored by the fact that we have used the DTF of Hess et al. for developing digital strategies during executive education programmes at our business school. Overall feedback of the executives on the DTF was positive, especially regarding its 'practical value'.

RQ3: Which structural requirements of the initial DTF of Hess et al. [2] could not be identified in our cross-domain analysis?

The paper is structured as follows. First, we present the theoretical basis – the digital transformation framework (DTF) of Hess et al. [2] – in the theoretical background section. In the research design section, we outline our research approach before results are described in the findings section. In the discussion, we debate our findings; our paper ends with a conclusion.

2   Theoretical Background

The role of technologies and their impact on firms has led to a substantial rethinking of the strategic role of IT among scholars and practitioners alike. In recent decades the so-called alignment view [16], which postulates IT strategy as aligned with but also subordinate to business strategy, has been the dominant perspective. Obviously, due to the transforming power of digital technologies [17, 18] and the corresponding increased importance of IT strategy, the alignment view no longer reflects the actual situation. Thus, IS scholars have argued for a fusion between IT strategy and business strategy, which is called digital business strategy (DBS) and defined as "organisational strategy formulated and executed by leveraging digital resources to create differential value" [19, p. 472].

Although DBS has attracted remarkable attention (e.g., a special issue of MIS Quarterly in 2013), its lack of transformational aspects has been criticised [2, 6]. Matt et al., for example, have proposed an enhancement of DBS, focusing on the digital transformation strategy (DTS). In contrast to DBS, which emphasises describing desired future opportunities or strategies, DTS "is a blueprint that supports companies in governing the transformations that arise owing to the integration of digital technologies, as well as in their operations after the transformation" [6, p. 340].

Furthermore, Matt et al. [6] transfer their DTS into a digital transformation framework (DTF). Given this conceptual basis, Hess et al. [2] suggest a DTF with concrete strategic questions – a prescriptive model – which can be used to develop a digital transformation strategy. The DTF consists of the four dimensions: use of technologies, changes in value creation, structural changes and financial aspects. Hess et al. [2] develop a set of corresponding strategic questions relevant for digital transformation. Moreover, they provide potential answer categories for each of the questions but emphasise that "there are no universal, definitive answers" to them [2, p. 137].

Given the research goal of our study, to explore structural requirements for digital transformation and to evaluate the DTF of Hess et al. [2], we place our focus on structural changes. This dimension refers to "variations in a firm's organisational setup, especially concerning the placement of the new digital activities within the corporate structures" [6, p. 341] which equals our understanding of structural requirements in our study. Hess et al. [2] suggest four structural requirements: responsibility for digital transformation, organisational positioning of new activities, operational changes, and building of competencies. In the following sections of this paper, we will refer to these structural requirements, e.g., during our content analysis.

3   Research Design

3.1   Data Collection

Recalling our three research questions and in line with the explorative approach of our study, we decided to interview experts in the field of digital transformation of German enterprises to find answers to our research questions. Experts are individuals who provide domain-specific knowledge and skills obtained through multiple years of professional experience in a certain field. These individuals provide an adequate perspective on a subject matter, especially for explorative questioning [20].

In order to assure the validity of our data collection, experts from three different domains were selected (triangulation): mid- or top-level industry managers and executives from German enterprises dealing with digital transformation, senior consultants working on German digital transformation projects cross-industry and experienced researchers who investigate digital transformation in German companies academically. We thus followed a purposeful sampling. To be specific, in our case we conducted a maximum variation approach allowing for both exploring different angles on the topic and identifying important shared patterns that cut across cases [21]. The wide range of industrial sectors (ranging from automotive to IT and telecommunications), as well as the different company sizes (ranging from 1,000 to 400,000 employees), ensured that various challenges of digitisation were brought up in the interviews. In total, 16 semi-structured expert interviews were conducted.

All of the semi-structured interviews were carried out via Skype or over the phone. To ensure flexibility while guiding the interviews, we chose a set of open-ended questions (e.g., What are the structural requirements in the context of the digital transformation of a company?; What are the challenges on the way towards a digital enterprise?; What changes need to be made in a company to take advantage of the opportunities offered by digitisation?). Interview participation was voluntary, and anonymity was promised. The interviews were transcribed and took, on average, 40 min.

After eleven of the 16 interviews, a theoretical saturation was perceived. Such saturation indicates a redundancy of information [22]. That is, many of the respondents' answers were quite similar, even across the different domains of expertise (i.e., research, industry and consultancy). Such redundancy of information in the analysis suggests an adequate sample size [23]. This observation also underpins the reasoning of Guest et al. [24] that, in a relatively homogenous sample (i.e., in our case, similar in terms of expertise level), a theoretical saturation can be expected to occur after six to 12 interviews.

3.2   Data Analysis

For the analysis of the interview transcripts, we applied the 'Gioia methodology' [25]. This approach aims to address issues related to 'qualitative rigor' and can be considered as an established approach for conducting qualitative research and is applied in various studies of high quality [e.g., 26].

The first analytic step according to Gioia et al. is building so-called first-order concepts. First-order concepts directly correspond with the interviewees' terminology; they should "adhere faithfully to informant terms" [25, p. 20]. Therefore, a passage of the text with a specific content was marked as a first-order concept. This was done for the entire corpus (i.e., 16 transcripts). For gaining a manageable number of first-order concepts, we searched for similarities and differences among the concepts and grouped them with suitable category labels. The QCAmap-Software[2] supported us during this step in the coding and categorisation process and facilitated a subsequent transparent determination of intercoder-reliability. The initial coding procedure was conducted by two researchers independently. They agreed in 86% of the cases and clarified the remaining cases during a discussion with a third researcher.

The first-order concept set developed in the previous step was analysed regarding its structure and with the objective of developing more abstract second-order themes. Second-order themes 'help us describe and explain the phenomena we are observing' [25]. This step is challenging, as we as researchers must think at multiple levels simultaneously: at the interviewee's level and at the abstract second-order level. Because of this challenge, we carefully considered the DTF and its structural requirements (operational change, responsibility for digital transformation, organisational positioning of new activities, and building of organisational competencies) for developing second-order themes. This included two steps. First, we assigned fitting first-order constructs to one of the four extant structural requirements (e.g., the first-order concept 'new positions and roles' was assigned to the DTF requirement 'responsibility for digital transformation'). Second, we developed new second-order themes for those first-order concepts we were unable to assign to one of the existing requirements. At this stage, we considered the abstraction level of the four extant structural requirements and applied the same abstraction level when developing new requirements at the second-order level.

Finally, it was investigated whether second-order themes might be aggregated. This step is of minor importance, compared to first-order concept and second-order theme development, since the latter already aims to answer the research question [25]. However, we apply the aggregate dimension view for illustrating which themes are established (i.e., already part of the initial DTF) or novel.

4   Findings

The process diagram in Fig. 1 depicts the outcomes of the various stages in the Gioia methodology. The illustration reveals all the structural requirements for digital transformation, mentioned by the interviewees, following our data analysis approach. In total, 18 distinct requirements (i.e., first-order concepts) have been highlighted.

Thirteen of the 16 experts deemed agility, in terms of organisational structure, as significant for organisations in mastering the digital transformation. Change, in the process of organisational thinking, was expressed by eleven participants as a structural

---

[2] https://www.qcamap.org/.

requirement for a digital transformation. Likewise, this code was mentioned most often, with a total of 22 instances in the 16 interviews. Nine of the 16 respondents identified a clear process structure as relevant in this context. The first-order concepts – i.e., IT infrastructure, continuous learning and new positions and roles – each came up in six of the expert interviews; the first-order concept digital HR was mentioned by seven experts. In each case, one-fourth of the respondents identified the following first-order concepts as requirements for organisations' digital transformation: focus on customer's needs, clear responsibilities, democratisation of decision making, a top-down process in decision implementation, flexibility, innovative learning methods, and data security.

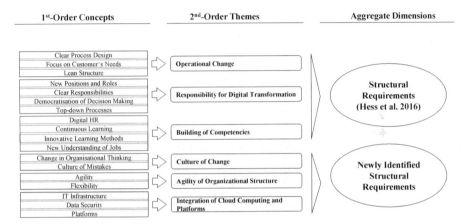

Fig. 1. Findings based on qualitative content analysis according to Gioia et al. [25]

5   Discussion

5.1   Comparison of Our Findings with the DTF

In the DTF [2], four structural requirements are formulated. We were able to identify three of these four (i.e., operational change, responsibility for digital transformation, and building of organisational competencies), while one requirement was neither directly nor indirectly mentioned (i.e., organisational positioning of new activities). This is basically the answer on two of the three research questions, namely the question regarding those structural requirements identified in our cross-domain analysis which are already part in the DTF (RQ2), and the question regarding structural requirements from the initial DTF which could not be identified in the cross-domain analysis (RQ3).

Hess et al. [2] discuss three different sub-topics of operational change: products and services, business processes, and skills. We found all three aspects during our analysis. Products and services relate to statements, which we have coded as customer focus. Many respondents emphasised the meaning of clear and lean processes, which can be linked to business processes in the initial DTF.

The second key topic we found is responsibility for digital transformation. Similar to the subtopics suggested in DTF (i.e., group CEO, business unit CEO, group CDO, and group CIO), many respondents mentioned specific top management roles, particularly the Chief Digital Officer (CDO); thus supporting recent studies in which the rapid emergence of this new role has been investigated [7]. Furthermore, many respondents named aspects such as top-down decision making and a clear leadership strategy regarding digital transformation as important.

Also, the topic of building competencies could be identified in our analysis. Considering the suggested subtopics of the DTF (i.e., internally, partnerships, company takeovers, external sourcing), we were able to find statements mostly related to the building of competencies 'internally'. The interviewees often mentioned the topic of innovative learning approaches, e.g., using MOOCs or other online formats. They also emphasised that only a digital HR approach can facilitate building organisational competencies internally. Another aspect with high priority among the interviewees are the individual digital competencies (or skills) of employees, which is in line with current research on this topic [e.g., 8]. In this context, the interviewees mentioned continuous learning, with a focus on digital competencies (i.e., new understanding of jobs), as one of the key challenges in today's business world. Furthermore, freedom and trust were mentioned as important complementary aspects when developing competencies.

Although we were able to identify significant parts of the structural requirements mentioned in the DTF of Hess et al. [2], one topic could not be found: organisational positioning of new activities (integrated vs. separated). This might be due to the different perspectives of the study by Hess et al. [2] and our research. The authors of the initial DTF had a stronger focus on business model aspects and digital transformation as a whole. We, instead, place focus on the specific aspect of structural requirements for digital transformation.

5.2   New Structural Requirements for Digital Transformation

In addition to the topics already suggested in the DTF of Hess et al. [2], we were able to elaborate three new structural requirements for digital transformation: culture of change, agility of organisational structure and integration of cloud computing and platforms (see also Fig. 2). This is the answer on RQ1, that asks for structural requirements identified in our cross-domain analysis which are not part of the initial DTF of Hess et al.

Eleven of the 16 interviewees mentioned a change of organisational culture as key for digital transformation. During the interviews, we asked how this rather abstract term might be made more concrete. We found that there seem to be two different understandings of a culture of change. The first meaning is similar to the recently popular notion of 'disruption'. But contrary to existing research on disruption [e.g., 27, 28], the interviewees use the term simply to describe fundamental changes. In this context, a change culture indicates that an organisation, specifically its managers, allow or even seek proactive, basic alterations. One of the experts expresses this view in the following statement: 'It is important for an organisation [in order to profit from the opportunities of digital transformation] to engage in a radical rethinking and reorientation, to be able to change things and leave old structures to find new ways' (Interviewee #7).

The second understanding of culture change that we could identify is a more evolutionary one. It is characterised by allowing mistakes and interpreting them as starting points for improvement, compared to a setting in which mistakes have a purely negative image. Besides this openness to experimentation and failing, no additional fundamental changes take place. A respondent formulates this idea as 'a culture and processes allowing that things go wrong, where you can experiment a lot, that is still positive, even if five projects fail' (Interviewee #11).

The next new factor we were able to identify is the agility of organisational structure. Again, two different subtopics emerged. First, many respondents mentioned innovative organisational structures such as the liquid organisation. The interviewees emphasised the disappearance of classical functions and departments, replaced by a more project-oriented framework, in which employees are grouped according to their complementary competencies: "They [organisations] should quit department structures and organise according to competencies" (Interviewee #10). Freelancing replaces classical employee-employer relationships. Leaders focus on outcomes and interpret themselves as moderators instead of supervisors. This goes along with new approaches and tools such as Design Thinking and SCRUM.

Second, the other understanding of agility refers to a more stable and hierarchical organisational structure. While digital aspects are more and more integrated, organisations stick to their classical organisational chart; however, they are often accompanied by new roles. An expert stated that in order to be agile it is crucial to 'create new positions', such as 'a data scientist, community manager or digital consultant' (Interviewee #14). In this context, these positions are not seen as being responsible for digital transformation, but of importance regarding organisational agility as they encourage quick responses to market opportunities.

Both experts' interpretations of agility of organisational structure rest on the firm's ability to adapt to new circumstances by realigning its structure and competencies. In line with recent definitions of agility in an organisational context [e.g., 29], the interviewees mention time-related aspects such as responding to new market opportunities quickly. Talking about agility, interviewees describe the structural requirements necessary for organisational agility such as specific approaches (e.g., Design Thinking and SCRUM) and related changes of the technological infrastructure, and new positions.

The last new structural requirement that we identified refers to the integration of cloud computing and platforms. The interviewees underlined the meaning of a 'sound and valuable' IT infrastructure (Interviewee #4) and the need for cloud computing and 'platforms for exchanging information' (Interviewee #7). Another very important aspect is data security: 'Data and IT security are obvious requirements for an organisation's digitalisation' (Interviewee #7). Two sub-categories regarding cloud computing and platforms can be identified in terms of the ownership. Today, infrastructure, platforms, software, and even entire business processes can be obtained from external vendors. In this context, [30, 31] goes as far as to interpret IT as a commodity that does not provide any competitive advantage.

On the other hand, obtaining infrastructure, platforms, and services externally goes along with risks and challenges. For instance, customers might not want their private data handled by third-party companies. Thus, while the need for cloud computing and platforms is indisputable from the interviewees' perspective, a company should carefully balance the question of ownership.

Based on our analysis, we suggest the following enriched structural changes section of the DTF (see Fig. 2). The shaded area indicates the new topics and respective strategic questions.

Structural changes (enriched)				
Responsibility for DT strategy?	Group CEO	Business Unit CEO	Group CDO	Group CIO
Organisational positioning of new activities?	Integrated		Separated	
Operational changes?	Products and services	Business processes		Skills
Building of competencies?	Internally	Partnerships	Company takeovers	External sourcing
Culture of change?	Disruptive		Evolutionary	
Agility of organisational structure?	Liquid organisation		Hierarchical organisation	
Cloud computing and platforms?	Ownership lies outside the firm		Ownership lies with the firm	

Fig. 2. Enriched structural changes section of the DTF proposed by Hess et al. [2]

6   Conclusion

While being one of the first empirical papers about the structural requirements for digital transformation of German companies, we have been able to explore new elements: culture of change, agility of organisational structure and integration of cloud computing and platforms. These requirements complement existing factors suggested by Hess et al. [2]. Thus, we can present a comprehensive set of structural requirements for digital transformation which is based on a cross-domain analysis, and we can develop an advanced version of the DTF, as shown in Fig. 2. We discuss subtopics that were extracted from the interviews, which can be applied by managers to carefully analyse their organisations in terms of digital transformation.

Corresponding managerial implications of our study are manifold. Our findings indicate that digital transformation is a rather complex and multifaceted process. From a leadership perspective, a substantial understanding of various internal and external aspects is required. The extended DTF supports managers to cope with such demands, but it can only provide a starting point. Digital transformation, as implied in the term, is a dynamic phenomenon. Managers need to understand that there will be a continuous need for learning (e.g., regarding technological innovations). Thus, they must ensure a learning-friendly environment. Beyond that, managers must answer the questions of whether and how technological innovations might improve the effectiveness and efficiency of their organisation. Thus, a digital transformation project, as is often announced in companies, might be misleading. Instead, leaders should aim at implementing a dynamic and open-digital mindset in their companies.

The goal of this study was to explore structural requirements for the digital transformation of a company. The factors (i.e., requirements) we were able to identify might serve as the starting point for developing theory [4, 25]. However, this would require careful elaboration of causal relations between the constructs as well as their underlying dynamics [32]; this was not part of our study. Thus, further research efforts should be invested in an improved understanding of such factors, with a focus on their completeness, their relations and underlying mechanisms.

Considering the DTF of Hess et al. [2], we have focussed on one specific aspect (i.e., structural requirements) which is one out of four categories. While we think that the structural requirements are the most fundamental aspect of the DTF, a more comprehensive naturalistic evaluation would be to analyse the other categories of the DTF, as well.

Another limitation lies in the cultural context. We interviewed experts from Germany. Considering the distinct features of the German culture (e.g., regarding uncertainty avoidance or long-term orientation [33]), we believe that integrating data from other cultures might lead to different results. For instance, the category of culture of mistakes can be expected to be more common and accepted in countries with a lower uncertainty avoidance (e.g., USA) than in Germany [34, 35]. Also, the dimension of data security is likely to differ among countries. In Europe, for example, data security is widely established and in the focus of the public whereas, in the USA, it is much less emphasised. Considering the high score of Germany for the dimension of long-term orientation [34, 35], it can be assumed that disruptive change is not favoured in this culture. The USA, again, is a suitable counterexample in terms of long-term orientation, as can be seen in the wide acceptance of disruptive behaviour in its culture [33]. Aside from cultural considerations on a country level, further research could focus on organisational culture [e.g., 36] which has also proved to be an important field of study in IS and management [37]. Therefore, future research in the field of digital transformation should focus on additional cultural contexts, as may serve as a basis for identifying and understanding such differences.

References

1. Legner, C., et al.: Digitalization: opportunity and challenge for the business and information systems engineering community. Bus. Inf. Syst. Eng. **59**, 301–308 (2017)
2. Hess, T., Matt, C., Benlian, A., Wiesböck, F.: Options for formulating a digital transformation strategy. MIS Q. Exec. **15**, 123–139 (2016)
3. Veit, D., et al.: Business models. Bus. Inf. Syst. Eng. **6**, 45–53 (2014)
4. Hinings, B., Gegenhuber, T., Greenwood, R.: Digital innovation and transformation. An institutional perspective. Inf. Organ. **28**, 52–61 (2018)
5. Windhagen, E., Bughin, J., Mischke, J., Baur, C., Mattern, F., Forman, S.: Stimulating digital adoption in Germany. Report McKinsey Global Institute (2017)
6. Matt, C., Hess, T., Benlian, A.: Digital transformation strategies. Bus. Inf. Syst. Eng. **57**, 339–343 (2015)
7. Horlacher, A., Hess, T.: What does a chief digital officer do? Managerial tasks and roles of a new C-Level position in the context of digital transformation. In: Bui, T.X., Sprague, R.H. (eds.) Proceedings of the 49th Annual Hawaii International Conference on System Sciences, 5–8 January 2016, Kauai, Hawaii, pp. 5126–5135. IEEE, Piscataway (2016)
8. Murawski, M., Bick, M.: Digital competences of the workforce – a research topic? Bus. Process Manag. J. **23**, 721–734 (2017)

9. Fitzgerald, M., Kruschwitz, N., Bonnet, D., Welch, M.: Embracing digital technology. A new strategic imperative. MIT Sloan Manag. Rev. **52**, 1–12 (2013)
10. Kahre, C., Hoffmann, D., Ahlemann, F.: Beyond business-IT Alignment - digital business strategies as a paradigmatic shift: a review and research agenda. In: Proceedings of the 50th Hawaii International Conference on System Sciences, pp. 4706–4715 (2017)
11. Holotiuk, F., Beimborn, D.: Critical success factors of digital business strategy. In: 13th Proceedings of International Conference on Wirtschaftsinformatik (WI 2017), pp. 991–1005 (2017)
12. Hansen, R., Kien, S.S.: Hummel's digital transformation toward omnichannel retailing: key lessons learned. MIS Q. Exec. **14**, 51–66 (2015)
13. Chanias, S., Hess, T.: Understanding digital transformation strategy formation: insights from Europe's automotive industry. In: Pacific Asia Conference on Information Systems 2016 Proceedings, p. 296 (2016)
14. Chanias, S.: Mastering digital transformation: the path of a financial services provider towards a digital transformation strategy. In: Proceedings of the 25th European Conference on Information Systems (ECIS), Guimarães, Portugal (2017)
15. Peppard, J., Galliers, R.D., Thorogood, A.: Information systems strategy as practice: micro strategy and strategizing for IS. J. Strat. Inf. Syst. **23**, 1–10 (2014)
16. Henderson, J.C., Venkatraman, N.: Strategic alignment: leveraging information technology for transforming organizations. IBM Syst. J. **32**, 4–16 (1993)
17. Brynjolfsson, E., McAfee, A.: The Second Machine Age. Work, Progress, and Prosperity in a Time of Brilliant Technologies. W. W. Norton & Company, New York (2014)
18. McAfee, A., Brynjolfsson, E.: Machine, Platform, Crowd. Harnessing Our Digital Future. W. W. Norton & Company, New York (2017)
19. Bharadwaj, A., El Sawy, O., Pavlou, P.A., Venkatraman, N.: Digital business strategy: toward a next generation of insights. MIS Q. **37**, 471–482 (2013)
20. Bernard, H.R.: Social Research Method. Qualitative and Quantitative Approaches. SAGE Publications, Thousand Oaks (2013)
21. Palinkas, L.A., Horwitz, S.M., Green, C.A., Wisdom, J.P., Duan, N., Hoagwood, K.: Purposeful sampling for qualitative data collection and analysis in mixed method implementation research. Adm. Policy Ment. Health **42**, 533–544 (2015)
22. Hennink, M., Hutter, I., Bailey, A.: Qualitative Research Methods. SAGE Publications Ltd., London (2011)
23. Mason, J.: Qualitative Researching. Sage, Los Angeles (2012)
24. Guest, G., Bunce, A., Johnson, L.: How many interviews are enough? Field Methods **18**, 59–82 (2006)
25. Gioia, D.A., Corley, K.G., Hamilton, A.L.: Seeking Qualitative rigor in inductive research. Organ. Res. Methods **16**, 15–31 (2013)
26. Smith, W.K.: Dynamic decision making. A model of senior leaders managing strategic paradoxes. Acad. Manag. J. **57**, 1592–1623 (2014)
27. Christensen, C.M.: Innovator's Dilemma: When New Technologies Cause Great Firms to Fail (Management of Innovation and Change Series). Harvard Business School Press, Brighton (1997). Harvard Business Review
28. Denning, S.: Christensen updates disruption theory. Strat. Leadersh. **44**, 10–16 (2016)
29. Ravichandran, T.: Exploring the relationships between IT competence, innovation capacity and organizational agility. J. Strat. Inf. Syst. **27**, 22–42 (2018)
30. Carr, N.G.: IT Doesn't Matter. Harvard Bus. Rev. **81**, 41–49 (2003)
31. Carr, N.G.: The Big Switch. Rewiring the World, from Edison to Google. W. W. Norton, New York (2009)

32. Whetten, D.A.: What constitutes a theoretical contribution? Acad. Manag. Rev. **14**, 490–495 (1989)
33. House, R.J., Dorfman, P.W., Javidan, M.: Strategic Leadership Across Cultures. The GLOBE Study of CEO Leadership Behavior and Effectiveness in 24 Countries. SAGE Publications, Los Angeles (2013)
34. Hofstede, G.: What about Germany? https://geert-hofstede.com/germany.html
35. Hofstede, G., Hofstede, G.J., Minkov, M.: Cultures and Organizations. Software for the Mind. McGraw-Hill, New York (2010)
36. Schein, E.H.: Organizational Culture and Leadership. Jossey-Bass, San Francisco (2010)
37. Kummer, T.-F., Leimeister, J.M., Bick, M.: On the importance of national culture for the design of information systems. Bus. Inf. Syst. Eng. **4**, 317–330 (2012)

Chief Digital Officers as Protagonists in Digital Transformation

Jostein Engesmo[1(✉)] [iD] and Niki Panteli[1,2] [iD]

[1] Department of Computer Science,
Norwegian University of Science and Technology, Sem Saelandsvei 9,
7491 Trondheim, Norway
jostein.engesmo@ntnu.no, niki.panteli@rhul.ac.uk
[2] School of Management, Royal Holloway, University of London,
Egham, Surrey TW20 0EX, UK

Abstract. With the popularity of digital transformation programmes becoming widerspread, our study is motivated by a need to understand who has the responsibility for digital transformation across different types of organisations and industries. We take a specific focus on the Chief Digital Officer which has been considered the most fast growing executive role in the recent years. In particular, in this paper, we present a research in progress study that aims to examine the role of Chief Digital Officer in enabling digital transformation in traditional, pre-digital organisations, and to identify its impact on the IT department of these organisations. The empirical study is based on the qualitative approach with its main dataset deriving from a series of semi-structured interviews. The study is expected to have both theoretical and practical implications on the management of digital transformation.

Keywords: Digital transformation · Digital technologies ·
Chief Digital Officer · Chief Information Officer · Leadership

1 Introduction

Digital transformation has been receiving an overwhelming attention by both academics and practitioners alike. While on the one hand, organisations such as digital start-ups are born with and because of digital technologies, known as born-digital, on the other hand, traditional, pre-digital, organisations have to find ways to embrace digital transformation into their operations and strategies whilst overcoming structural and cultural barriers. Reports have placed digital transformation high up on the business agenda [1]. In this paper we are interested in investigating the role of the Chief Digital Officer (CDO) in digital transformation, a fast growing role in the executive management team of many organisations [2], the impact that this role has on the transformation programme as well as on the IT department of the organisation.

In what follows, we review literature on digital transformation exploring the opportunities and challenges it provides to pre-digital organisations. We then discuss the role of Chief Information Officers (CIOs) who have traditionally been expected to lead IT-enabled change in organisations and introduce the emerging role of CDOs.

© IFIP International Federation for Information Processing 2019
Published by Springer Nature Switzerland AG 2019
I. O. Pappas et al. (Eds.): I3E 2019, LNCS 11701, pp. 730–737, 2019.
https://doi.org/10.1007/978-3-030-29374-1_59

Following these, we introduce the research design of the study and its expected contributions.

2 Literature Review

2.1 Digital Transformation: Concept, Opportunities and Challenges

With the emergence of digital technologies that encompass smart and interconnected systems, and the popularity of artificial intelligence, digital platforms, cloud computing, social media, as well as big data and data analytics [3], an increasing literature exists on the potentials of these technologies in transforming organisations. For example, the adoption of artificial intelligence creates new opportunities and challenges for employees and organisations by automating, transforming and possibly augmenting work and work boundaries, control, coordination and expertise [4, 5]. Further, the opportunities of platforms and platformization tend to cross organisational boundaries where network of actors (including platform owners and customers) together create value [6, 7]. Further, empirical studies have examined the role of digital platforms in promoting digital transformation among SMEs [8]. Many of the important innovations within digital technologies build on cloud computing [9], and with prior focus on cost reduction, cloud computing now also provides strategic impact [10]. Summing up research within business intelligence and analytics, it is evident that studies increasingly focus on big data [11, 12]. One opportunity arising here is for businesses to analyse data, including unstructured data, from use of social media and an increasing amount of sensors [13]. Lastly, studies of social media adoption points to both potential use internally [14, 15] and externally [16], as well as how to succeed with the adoption process [17]. Accordingly, digital transformation programmes often encompass a wide range of technologies adding to their complexity and challenges whilst opening up a range of opportunities for the organisations involved.

Different definitions have been given to digital transformation. Table 1 captures some of these definitions:

Table 1. Definitions of digital transformation.

Sources (in chronological order)	Definition
Bharadwaj, El Sawy, Pavlou, and Venkatraman [18]	Increasing scope and scale of digital business strategy, speed of decision making, and sources of value creation and capture
Westerman, Bonnet, and McAfee [19]	The use of technology to radically improve performance or reach of enterprises
Gruman [20]	The application of digital technologies to fundamentally impact all aspects of business
McAfee and Brynjolfsson [3]	Employing machine, platform, crowd and rebalance with human mind, product, core

(continued)

Table 1. (*continued*)

Sources (in chronological order)	Definition
Chianas, Myers and Hess [21]	A holistic form of business transformation enabled by information systems (IS) that is accompanied by fundamental economic and technological changes at both the organizational and industry-level
Hinings, Gegenhuber and Greenwood [22]	The combined effects of several digital innovations bringing about novel actors (and actor constellations), structures, practices, values, and beliefs that change, threaten, replace or complement existing rules of the game within organizations and fields
Vial [23]	A process where digital technologies create disruptions triggering strategic responses from organizations that seek to alter their value creation paths while managing the structural changes and organizational barriers that affect the positive and negative outcomes of this process

It follows from the table above that though some definitions on digital transformation have given an emphasis on the use and application of digital technologies, others have taken a broader focus that includes a strategic perspective of digital innovations and their impact on the wider business context and beyond. Siebel [24] posited that digital transformation is all about change, including change in the way products are designed all the way to how products are serviced. According to Cascio and Montealerge [25], the implications include: "…transforming the very foundations of global business and the organizations that drive it […] not just helping people to do things better and faster, but they are enabling profound changes in the ways that work is done in organizations" (p. 350). Digital transformation strategies are found to have dimensions of use of technologies, changes in value creation, structural changes and financial aspects, where the latter is necessary for the others to take place [26]. With these, digitalization transforms business models, operational processes and user experience [9].

Studies exist on the vital role that digital transformation plays in revamping organisations whilst also identifying the different dimensions of digital transformation [19] as well as how they gain wider stakeholders' approval and become institutionalised [22].

Westerman and Bonnet [27] posit that large traditional organisations need to rethink key managerial assumptions they often have about the type of customer service they offer, extend the automation and integration of their operations and their pre-digital strategic assets. In their view, these pre-digital assumptions may constrain developments in digital initiatives and therefore act as challenges in their implementation, and need to be revisited and adjusted in order to effectively embrace digital transformation. As such, according to Kane et al. [28], digital transformation should be guided by a business digital strategy as well as an organisational culture that encourages innovation and collaboration. Leadership has also been found to be another key factor for successfully transforming an organisation to being a digital organisation [29].

In this paper, we extend research in this area by taking a specific focus on the leadership of digital transformation programmes. It is our position that the nature of digital transformation that radically integrates digital technologies in business initiatives, processes and structures calls for a change in IT leadership to one that is a digital business integrator and not just an IT manger. For this, we examine the role of chief digital officers, a fast growing role in the senior management of numerous pre-digital organisations.

2.2   Chief Information Officers and Chief Digital Officers

Traditionally, IT-driven business change was a responsibility of the IT department and the Chief Information Officer (CIO). This was supported by an increasing acknowledgement in the information systems literature that the long term sustainable business value of IT resides in its complementarity and integration with business strategies, structures and competences [30]. According to Willcocks et al. [31] the IT department has four primary tasks which include: ensuring technical capability, managing external supply, eliciting and delivering on business requirements and IS governance and leadership. These tasks, which are inter-linked, contribute to nine associated core IT capabilities with IT leadership as the central one and ranging from architecture planning, IT implementation, business systems thinking, relationships building and vendor development.

Despite these capabilities and responsibilities linked to CIOs, recent research has posited that CIOs have not managed to gain strategic leadership positions in their organisations [32] as their role is perceived to be more technology rather than business-orientated. A study of time management for CIOs showed that the main priority for most CIOs is ensuring delivery of infrastructure, applications and projects, and that this makes it difficult to spend as much as time as they would like on more strategic activities [33]. This may therefore explain the emerging role of CDOs in leading company-wide digital transformation programmes.

According to an industry report, the role of CDOs presents the organisation's intention to embrace digital transformation [34]. Extant literature has emphasized the strategic involvement of CDOs in creating and implementing digital transformation projects. Further, according to a McKinsey report [35], the role should be given to someone who has obsession with the customer. Similarly, Horlacher and Hess [36] found that the CDOs they studied exhibit a strong customer focus and have an aim not just to improve but personalise customer experience.

Tumbas et al. [37] find that CDOs intentionally emphasize their skills and expertise in 'digital' as a way for distinguishing themselves from other senior management. They do so in order to gain legitimacy and strengthen their identity within the organisation. In this study, CDOs were also found to view the IT department as having more operational and cost saving function as opposed to their own role who they perceive as more revenue enhancing, transformational and customer facing. Singh and Hess [38] have also described CDOs as entrepreneurs who are highly customer focused, digital evangelists who are disseminating the digital strategy across the organisation, and cross-functional coordinators as they are expected to inter-link the whole company with digital technologies. Therefore apart from IT competency which is a critical skill for

CDOs, these post-holders should also show competency in change management skills, digital pioneering and inspiration skills (ibid).

In this paper, we adopt Goffman's [39] dramaturgical analogy which named roles in organisations according to the most common characters in a play: protagonists (the leading character in a play), deuteragonists (secondary character with supporting role), tritagonists (minor character). Accordingly, we view CDOs as protagonists for digital transformation in their organisations. As leading figures, CDOs are expected to be on central stage, take decisions and follow these through to their implementation.

Two research questions are driving the study: First, how is the role of Chief Digital Officers enabling digital transformation in traditional pre-digital organisations? And, second: How is the role of CDOs changing IT departments and IT leadership?

3   Research Design and Initial Findings

Our research approach comprises of an exploratory qualitative approach and includes two phases. Phase 1 of our data collection, involved the collection of job adverts of CDOs and related posts (e.g. Head of Digital, Digital Director) across different industries. LinkedIn was used for this purpose for a two month period (mid March- mid May) with the aim to understand the qualifications, experience and requirements of the role in different organisations and industries.

Phase 2, which will be taking place in early summer 2019, involves a series of semi-structured interviews with CDOs and CIOs across a selection of organisations. Particular emphasis in the interviews will be paid on the strategic role of each of these roles and their inter-relationships and the influence they exert or are expected to exert on each other. Thematic analysis will serve as our analytical approach. Data will be collected in both UK and Norway by both authors.

In Phase 1, we collected 25 adverts which were from a variety of industries and encompassed both public and private firms as well as large corporates (e.g. construction and media companies) and independent organisations (e.g. hotel boutiques and fashion houses). Tentative findings present CDOs as protagonists, though the nature of the transformation initiative may vary from strategic to marketing and technology. Our analysis show that public sector organizations tend to give a strategic focus to the position, expecting the person in the role to drive forward the digital transformation process/programme. Private companies, maybe due to being better resourced in terms of digital knowhow and capability, tend to give a narrower focus to their CDOs, often being linked to digital marketing and content management. Also where CDOs are expected to drive forward the strategic transformation of the organisation, there is also the expectation for them to work closely with other executives especially in marketing and IT and provide digital transformation technical leadership. Overall, what we can see is that emphasis on strategic direction varies across the different sectors covered in the job adverts.

4 Research Design and Initial Findings

This far, we have conducted a literature review in the areas of digital transformation, CIOs and CDOs in order to develop our research questions, and we have also started to collect data. At the time of the conference we will be presenting the initial results of both Phase 1 and 2 of our empirical study.

We expect to contribute to the Information systems literature with this research-in-progress paper, and in particular to the literature on digital transformation. Our study has implications for the management and leadership of digital transformation programmes as well as for IT departments which we will present at the conference.

References

1. Hess, T., Matt, C., Benlian, A., Wiesböck, F.: Options for formulating a digital transformation strategy. MIS Q. Exec. **15**(2), 123–139 (2016)
2. Grossman, R., Rich, J.: The Rise of the Chief Digital Officer. Russell Reynolds Associates, New York (2012)
3. McAfee, A., Brynjolfsson, E.: Harnessing Our Digital Future. Machine, Platform, Crowd. W. W. Norton & Company Ltd., New York (2017)
4. Barrett, M., Oborn, E., Orlikowski, W.J., Yates, J.: Reconfiguring boundary relations: robotic innovations in pharmacy work. Organ. Sci. **23**(5), 1448–1466 (2012). https://doi.org/10.1287/orsc.1100.0639
5. Faraj, S., Pachidi, S., Sayegh, K.: Working and organizing in the age of the learning algorithm. Inf. Organ. **28**(1), 62–70 (2018). https://doi.org/10.1016/j.infoandorg.2018.02.005
6. Constantinides, P., Henfridsson, O., Parker, G.: Introduction - platforms and Infrastructures in the digital age. Inf. Syst. Res. **29**(2), 381–400 (2019). https://doi.org/10.1287/isre.2018.0794
7. Henfridsson, O., Nandhakumar, J., Scarbrough, H., Panourgias, N.: Recombination in the open-ended value landscape of digital innovation. Inf. Organ. **28**(2), 89–100 (2018). https://doi.org/10.1016/j.infoandorg.2018.03.001
8. Li, L., Su, F., Zhang, W., Mao, J.Y.: Digital transformation by SME entrepreneurs: a capability perspective. Inf. Syst. J. **28**(6), 1129–1157 (2018). https://doi.org/10.1111/isj.12153
9. Henriette, E., Feki, M., Boughzala, I.: The shape of digital transformation: a systematic literature review. In: MCIS2015 Proceedings, vol. 10 (2016)
10. Junior, A., Biancolino, C., Maccari, E.: Cloud computing and information technology strategy. J. Technol. Manag. Innov. **8**, 178–188 (2013). https://doi.org/10.4067/S0718-27242013000300070
11. Chen, H., Chiang, R.H.L., Storey, V.C.: Business intelligence and analytics: from big data to big impact. MIS Q. **36**(4), 1165–1188 (2012). https://doi.org/10.1145/2463676.2463712
12. Gandomi, A., Haider, M.: Beyond the hype: big data concepts, methods, and analytics. Int. J. Inf. Manag. **35**(2), 137–144 (2015). https://doi.org/10.1016/j.ijinfomgt.2014.10.007
13. Brynjolfsson, E., McAfee, A.: Big data : the management revolution. Harvard Bus. Rev. 1–12 (2012). https://doi.org/10.1007/978-3-319-05029-4

14. Leonardi, P.M., Huysman, M., Steinfield, C.: Enterprise social media: definition, history, and prospects for the study of social technologies in organizations. J. Comput.-Mediat. Commun. **19**(1), 1–19 (2013). https://doi.org/10.1111/jcc4.12029

15. Kane, G.C.: The potential of enterprise social media. MIS Q. Exec. **14**(1), 1–16 (2015). https://doi.org/10.1111/jcc4.12029

16. Effing, R., Spil, T.A.M.: The social strategy cone: towards a framework for evaluating social media strategies. Int. J. Inf. Manag. **36**(1), 1–8 (2016). https://doi.org/10.1016/j.ijinfomgt.2015.07.009

17. Nolte, F., Guhr, N., Breitner, M.H.: Moderation of enterprise social networks – a literature review from a corporate perspective. In: Proceedings of the 50th Hawaii International Conference on System Sciences, pp. 1964–1973 (2017). https://doi.org/10.24251/hicss.2017.238

18. Bharadwaj, A., El Sawy, O.A., Pavlou, P.A., Venkatraman, N.: Digital business strategy: toward a next generation of insights. MIS Q. **37**(2), 471–482 (2013)

19. Westerman, G., Bonnet, D., McAfee, A.: The nine elements of digital transformation. MIT Sloan Manag. Rev. **55**(3), 1–6 (2014)

20. Gruman, G.: What digital transformation really means. InfoWorld (2016). http://www.infoworld.com/article/3080644/it-management/what-digital-transformation-really-means.html

21. Chanias, S., Myers, M.D., Hess, T.: Digital transformation strategy making in pre-digital organizations: the case of a financial services provider. J. Strat. Inf. Syst. **28**(1), 17–33 (2018). https://doi.org/10.1016/j.jsis.2018.11.003

22. Hinings, B., Gegenhuber, T., Greenwood, R.: Digital innovation and transformation: an institutional perspective. Inf. Organ. **28**(1), 52–61 (2018). https://doi.org/10.1016/j.infoandorg.2018.02.004

23. Vial, G.: Understanding digital transformation: a review and a research agenda. J. Strat. Inf. Syst. (2019, Forthcoming). https://doi.org/10.1016/j.jsis.2019.01.003

24. Siebel, T.M.: Why digital transformation is now on the CEO's shoulders. McKinsey Q. **4**(3), 1–7 (2017)

25. Cascio, W.F., Montealegre, R.: How technology is changing work and organizations. Annu. Rev. Organ. Psychol. Organ. Behav. **3**(1), 349–375 (2016). https://doi.org/10.1146/annurev-orgpsych-041015-062352

26. Matt, C., Hess, T., Benlian, A.: Digital transformation strategies. Bus. Inf. Syst. Eng. **57**(5), 339–343 (2015). https://doi.org/10.1007/s12599-015-0401-5

27. Westerman, G., Bonnet, D.: Revamping your business through digital transformation. MIT Sloan Manag. Rev. **56**(3), 10 (2015)

28. Kane, G.C., Palmer, D., Phillips, A.N., Kiron, D., Buckley, N.: Strategy, not technology, drives digital transformation. MIT Sloan Manag. Rev. Deloitte Univ. Press. **14**, 1–25 (2015)

29. Kontić, L., Vidicki, Đ.: Strategy for digital organization: testing a measurement tool for digital transformation. Strat. Manag. **23**(1), 29–35 (2018). https://doi.org/10.5937/StraMan1801029K

30. Sambamurthy, V.: Shaping agility through digital options: reconceptualizing the role of information technology in contemporary firms. MIS Q. **27**(2), 237–263 (2003). https://doi.org/10.2307/30036530

31. Willcocks, L., Reynolds, P., Feeny, D.: Evolving IS capabilities to leverage the external IT Services market. MIS Q. Exec. **6**(3), 127–145 (2007)

32. Gonzalez, P., Ashforth, L., McKeen, J.: The CIO stereotype: content, bias, and impact. J. Strat. Inf. Syst. **28**, 83–99 (2019). https://doi.org/10.1016/j.jsis.2018.09.002

33. Weill, P., Woerner, S.L.: The future of the CIO in digital economy. MIS Q. Exec. **12**, 65–76 (2013)

34. CIO.: Why the chief digital officer role is on the rise (2013). http://www.cio.com/article/2380788/careers-staffing/why-the-chief-digital-officer-role-is-on-the-rise.html

35. Rickards, T., Smaje, K., Sohoni, V.: Transformer in chief': the new chief digital officer (2015). http://www.mckinsey.com/business-functions/organization/our-insights/transformer-in-chief-the-new-chief-digital-officer

36. Horlacher, A., Hess, T.: What does a Chief Digital Officer do? Managerial tasks and roles of a new C-level position in the context of digital transformation. In: 2016 49th Hawaii International Conference on System Sciences (HICSS), pp. 5126–5135. IEEE (2016). https://doi.org/10.1109/hicss.2016.634

37. Tumbas, S., Berente, N., Brocke, J.V.: Digital innovation and institutional entrepreneurship: Chief Digital Officer perspectives of their emerging role. J. Inf. Technol. **33**(3), 188–202 (2018). https://doi.org/10.1057/s41265-018-0055-0

38. Singh, A., Hess, T.: How Chief Digital Officers promote the digital transformation of their companies. MIS Q. Exec. **16**(1), 1–17 (2017)

39. Goffman, E.: The Presentation of Self in Everyday Life. Doubleday Anchor, Garden City (1959)

A Role-Based Maturity Model
for Digital Relevance

Katja Bley[✉] and Hendrik Schön

Business Informatics, esp. IS in Trade and Industry, TU Dresden,
Dresden, Germany
{katja.bley,hendrik.schoen}@tu-dresden.de

Abstract. For several decades, maturity models have been regarded as a magic bullet for enterprises' economic growth processes. In these models, domains are structured and divided into (mostly linear) levels that are used as benchmarks for enterprise development. However, this approach has its shortcomings in the context of complex topics like digitalization. As we understand it, digitalization defines a conceptual approach to a phenomenon that is individually important and promising in different ways for different enterprises. Consequently, existing maturity models in their current form are not able to reproduce the full extent of digitalization for enterprises, as the models are too general—especially for SMEs of different sizes and from different sectors. In our research, we propose a maturity model approach that introduces the concept of roles as a possibility to depict enterprises' specific components, which are then added to a static core model. By doing so, the resulting maturity model is more flexible and scalable for SMEs' specific needs. Furthermore, we introduce a new assessment approach for defining whether improving digitalization is truly relevant and worthwhile for the enterprise.

Keywords: Maturity model · Individualization · Digitalization relevance · Role

1 Introduction

Recent developments, like the digitalization of economic processes, increase the pressure on enterprises of all sizes to adapt and digitally transform in order to remain competitive and efficient. Hence, companies search for tools that can help determine their current benchmarking position or that can assess their subsequent market position compared to a predefined best-practice performance. One famous example of these benchmarking tools is Maturity Models (MMs). An MM is primarily a structured, systematic elaboration of the best practices and processes within a domain that are related to the functioning and structure of an organization. An MM is divided into different levels, which are used as benchmarks for the maturity of an organization. Due to their general applicability and their simple development, many MMs have emerged in both science and practice over the last decade. MMs are especially favored when it comes to the defining, delimiting, and accounting for newly-emerging social or technical phenomena, such as digitalization or Industrial Internet/Industry 4.0 and its

© IFIP International Federation for Information Processing 2019
Published by Springer Nature Switzerland AG 2019
I. O. Pappas et al. (Eds.): I3E 2019, LNCS 11701, pp. 738–744, 2019.
https://doi.org/10.1007/978-3-030-29374-1_60

impact on enterprises. MMs are also favored for the classification of SMEs, as these companies are financially incapable of undergoing well-coordinated digitalization programs.

However, despite their wide range of applicability, MMs are not widely known of or implemented. A recent study revealed that scientific and consultancy Industry 4.0-MMs are quite unknown in business practice, although potential applicants stated a need for and interest in these models in general [1]. Apparently, if Industry 4.0 is considered a proxy for digitalization, a mismatch exists between the generated benefit of existing MMs and the needs of enterprises. Existing models fail in their ability to depict sector-specific organizational structures and characteristics. The definition/development of maturity level is generalized, vague, or not precise enough to be adapted by SMEs of different business sectors.

By designing a new concept of digital maturity within an MM that adapts to the specific components of a sector, we will be able to describe the benefit to an enterprise of moving along the maturity scale. With the application of this new concept for SMEs' individualization, our role-based relevance MM is able to adapt to specific SME characteristics, representing individual relevance of digital process improvement for each concrete SME.

2 Maturity Models: Concept and Criticism

Maturity, as a "state of being complete, perfect or ready" [2], is demonstrated by separating organizational growth process into linear levels. In staged MMs, each of these levels has a pre-defined set of characteristics that represent a certain level of maturity. Only after fulfilling all requirements in one level can a higher level be reached. In continuous MMs, the enterprise's maturity scoring can be executed on different levels. The final maturity score can be the weighted sum of single characteristics on different levels or several maturity levels in different dimensions [3]. The MM focus varies depending on workforce, processes, or management orientation, and on application areas such as software development, HR, and marketing. In addition to the wide range of applicable areas, its relatively rapid development promotes high dissemination.

Numerous best-practice articles exist on the development of MM, as the topic is widely discussed in research [e.g., 4–6]. However, some voices are critical of these somewhat-simplified, methodical, step-by-step development approaches. Pöppelbuß et al. [6], for instance, criticize the lack of an empirical foundation, which often leads to simply copying model structures without considering a conceptual grounding based in literature. Lasrado et al. [7] further criticize the lack of validation for selected variables and appropriate dimensions, as well as the lack of operationalization of maturity measurements. Moreover, they insist that a linear course of maturation must be a prerequisite for creating and applying an MM. The concept of equifinality (which postulates that an outcome can be achieved by more than one path) is rarely considered in MM development. Another critique is the lack of individualized MMs in terms of application and assessment. Taking up this aspect, our research focuses on a more individualized and flexible approach to an MM for digitalization; we consider this phenomenon as multi-dimensional, which cannot be captured by applying an existing (linear) approach to maturity. In order to meet this demand, we design a new type of MM, applying an empirical development approach and a different understanding of "moving along the maturity ladder." As a result, we become able to explain the benefits of improvement per level for distinct business sectors.

3 Towards a Conceptual Approach for a New Maturity Model

Considering the above-mentioned shortcomings of existing MMs, we intend to develop a new MM concept approach to measure digitalization, especially in SMEs. Digital transformation is a highly complex but promising process for all business sectors. Nevertheless—due to a variety of possible digitalization processes internal to, external to, and between enterprises of all sectors—the anatomy and individual progress of SME digitalization must be captured. Our research question (RQ), therefore is: how can the concept of an MM be concretized for static characteristics of SMEs (domain, size, and sector) as well as for dynamic components of individual SMEs (achieved and required digitalization conditions)? To answer this RQ, we develop a new MM concept, which evolves from a broad cross-enterprise to an individualized, enterprise-specific focus.

3.1 The Construction of the Maturity Model Framework

Due to the dual character of our MM concept, we combine static and dynamic conceptual components (Fig. 1). A Core Model unites the foundational concepts of MM (Fig. 1(i)): the maturity scale on the x-axis, the digitalization scale on the y-axis, and the pooling of digitalization-relevant factors for multiple SME sectors and for multiple sizes of a considered domain. A literature analysis and expert interviews may be used to detect digitalization-relevant factors for the pool, as these depend heavily on the practical experience of domain experts. At this stage, the maturity constructs are still unspecific, as the concepts are individualized to the research framework afterwards.

Since allocating concrete factors to maturity levels depends heavily on the sector characteristics of the SME, we utilize the idea of a role. A role is a common concept that has gained attention in the past few decades in multiple disciplines in software engineering but also in organizational modeling [e.g., 8]. In our model, a role specifies the selection and allocation of factors from the pool to the maturity levels in the maturity scale of the Core Model. As a role is utilized to represent a class or sector of enterprises (e.g., a role for the class of "small-sized non-international transport logistic enterprises"), it can be chosen or exchanged depending on the model user's intention. In particular, a user needs to select a role, which specifies the x-axis of the dimension chart. This contains information on the different levels l with the maturity characteristics for the SME. Thus, instead of using the same levels for different kinds of enterprises, the role-based approach allows us to more precisely identify maturity levels, depending on the requirements represented by a role. The levels of an "international logistics" enterprise may differ widely from a "national logistics" enterprise.

One possible method for assigning factors from the pool to the maturity levels of a role involves using a set-theoretic approach called Qualitative Comparative Analysis (QCA). This allows multiple combinations of necessary and sufficient conditions to be detected, which lead to a specific outcome (e.g., maturity level of an SME; blank bubbles per level (Fig. 1(ii))). A similar approach was taken by [9], who used set theory to create an MM. However, the role only has static information about the SME with regard to the level structure. Enterprise-specific information (such as the factors' fulfillment or the current level of the SME) are determined in the subsequent individualization (Fig. 1(iii)).

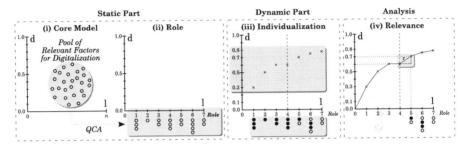

Fig. 1. Procedure model for the application and instantiation of the role-oriented MM.

3.2   The Individualization of the Maturity Model

The individualization of the MM (Fig. 1(iii)) represents the dynamic part of our MM, as it directly involves the user (SME) of the model. After the user has selected their corresponding role, the instantiated model appears with the predefined factors at the respective level (Fig. 1(ii)). Through user interviews and questionnaires, the SME is asked to specify its current equipment and development status. With this step, the already-fulfilled digitalization-related conditions, techniques, and processes (=factors) are queried and recorded in the x-axis of the model (Fig. 1(iii), filled bubbles). The level reached by the SME is the highest level at which all factors are fulfilled (e.g., level 4 in Fig. 1(iii)).

The individualized MM consists of the influence and calculation of a digitalization quotient d on the y-axis. It is determined by surveys on additional, not-yet-digitalized, enterprise-specific processes, deriving digitalization potential for possible improvement steps for the SME. The gradient is an abstraction of the enterprise's fulfillment of the targeted digitalization maturity levels. It relates the processes of the respective level to the overall digitalization processes of the enterprise (mapped between 0 and 1). A maturity curve is created by combining the digitalization quotients of the levels.

Thus, the increase of maturity between the levels reflects a relevance r of the SME's individual digitalization. This depends on the applied role as well as on the individual calculated digitalization quotient d per level (Fig. 2).

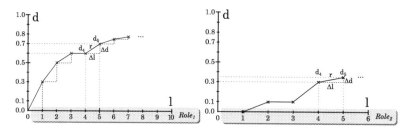

Fig. 2. Two domain-specific MMs, instantiated with different roles.

3.3 The Concept of Digitalization Relevance

The y-axis represents a scale for the value range of our metric, digitalization quotient d, which ranges from 0 to 1. The quotient expresses the degree to which the aggregation of the current and previous maturity levels affects the enterprise's digitalization. A high quotient can be understood as indicating that many processes have already benefited from digitalization on this maturity level, while a low quotient means that the enterprise has only marginally benefited from the levels achieved so far. The quotient is generally determined by the ratio of the sum of already-digitalized processes in current and previous levels with the total number of processes in the enterprise that can be digitalized:

$$d_l = \frac{\sum_{i=1}^{l}(p_i)}{p_n} \qquad (1)$$

where l is the approached level and n is the total number of maturity levels. However, the concrete mathematical calculation is still being researched. We could include, for example, process complexity with different weights. However, this is not the focus of this short paper. The plotting of the quotient d on the x-axis results in a monotonously increasing curve. Thus, calculating the derivation of the curve between two levels indicates the digitalization relevance,

$$r = \frac{\Delta d}{\Delta l} \qquad (2)$$

According to our understanding, relevance—as significance or meaningfulness—is a "complex but systematic and measurable concept if approached conceptually and operationally from the user's perspective" [10]. We incorporate this concept into our MM as we conceptually design the model and involve the SME's characteristics in creating the maturity path.

By the progression of the resulting curve, the maturity path for an SME is determined, and it represents the decisive component of the resulting MM. The relevance r defines the individual benefit of an SME moving from one maturity level to the next. Applied to the interpretation of the model, the derivation is an indicator of the relevance of digitalizing additional processes in an SME. With decreasing relevance (compared to the previous r), the enterprise can decide whether it is reasonable and profitable to digitize upcoming processes, in relation to costs/expenses/time to be invested. Since the curve—and, accordingly, the derivation—can vary in its significance, the relevance for each SME is unique. Thus, different SMEs may have different relevance values while achieving the same maturity level with identical roles. However, different SMEs can still be compared by the maturity level of their current relevance in digitalization.

The above-mentioned approach for a single, domain-specific MM can be extended to other domains by following the development approach, which will also be elaborated upon as part of our research (method artefact).

4   Contribution and Future Work

The top-down conceptual MM approach introduced here, from coarse orientation (core model) to an individualized focus (role and relevance orientation), allows for better assessment of digitalization for a decisive SME. Our concept would allow maturity to be graphically and arithmetically demonstrated, taking process path dependencies into account. It reveals up to which point it is reasonable for an SME to continue to digitalize itself. Contrary to the current trend of "the more digitalization, the better", our MM offers the opportunity to give concrete instructions to enterprises from different industries and sectors, taking their individual situations into consideration.

The next research steps will focus on a prototype of a domain-specific MM. We intend to define the desired domain and to conduct a literature analysis and expert interviews concerning the domain's digitalization-relevant business processes (factor pool). After that, the digitalization quotient formula must be refined to take into account the corresponding processes of the enterprises and their characteristics. Furthermore, we will construct a representative role, with its specific relevant factors, out of the pool. We will apply QCA to determine their assignment and maturity order, and we will test our digitalization algorithm in concrete SMEs. Several iterations and evaluations will help improve the formula and its impact for guided digitalization within SMEs.

References

1. Felch, V., Asdecker, B., Sucky, E.: Maturity models in the age of Industry 4.0 – do the available models correspond to the needs of business practice? In: Proceedings of the 52nd Hawaii International Conference on System Sciences (HICSS), pp. 5165–5174 (2019)
2. Simpson, J.A., Weiner, E.S.C.: The Oxford English Dictionary. Clarendon Press, Oxford (1989)
3. Lahrmann, G., Marx, F., Mettler, T., Winter, R., Wortmann, F.: Inductive design of maturity models: applying the Rasch algorithm for design science research. In: Jain, H., Sinha, Atish P., Vitharana, P. (eds.) DESRIST 2011. LNCS, vol. 6629, pp. 176–191. Springer, Heidelberg (2011). https://doi.org/10.1007/978-3-642-20633-7_13
4. De Bruin, T., Freeze, R., Kaulkarni, U., Rosemann, M.: Understanding the main phases of developing a maturity assessment model. In: 16th Australasian Conference on Information Systems (ACIS), Sydney (2005)

5. Becker, J., Knackstedt, R., Pöppelbuß, J.: Developing maturity models for IT management. Bus. Inf. Syst. Eng. **1**, 213–222 (2009)
6. Pöppelbuß, J., Röglinger, M.: What makes a useful maturity model? A framework of general design principles for maturity models and its demonstration in business process management. In: ECIS 2011 Proceedings, Helsinki (2011)
7. Lasrado, L., Vatrapu, R., Andersen, K.: Maturity models development in IS research: a literature review. In: Proceedings of the 38th Information System Research Seminar, Scandinavia (IRIS 38), vol. 6 (2015)
8. Bera, P., Burton-Jones, A., Wand, Y.: Improving the representation of roles in conceptual modeling: theory, method, and evidence. Requir. Eng. **23**(4), 465–491 (2017)
9. Lasrado, L., Vatrapu, R., Andersen, K.: A set theoretical approach to maturity models: guidelines and demonstration. In: Proceedings of the 37th International Conference on Information. System, ICIS Dublin (2016)
10. Schamber, L., Eisenberg, M.B., Nilan, M.S.: A re-examination of relevance: toward a dynamic, situational definition. Inf. Process. Manag. **26**(6), 755–776 (1990)

Digital Innovation and Business Transformation

Prioritizing Knowledge Transfer Conditions for Innovation Ecosystems: A Mixed-Method Approach

Emily Bacon$^{(\boxtimes)}$ ⓘ, Michael Williams ⓘ, and Gareth Davies ⓘ

School of Management, Swansea University,
Bay Campus, Swansea SA1 8EN, UK
{950171, m.d.williams, g.h.davies}@swansea.ac.uk

Abstract. Open innovation ecosystems rely upon inter-organisational knowledge transfer to support co-creation. Despite the significance of this process, and an abundance of open innovation research, empirical investigation and discussion of diverse knowledge transfer conditions across open innovation ecosystems remains unaddressed within existing literature. Using a mixed-method approach, this study investigates how knowledge, firm, and partner-relationship characteristics affect the successful exchange of knowledge between ecosystem partners. Interpretive Structural Modelling was employed to ascertain expert opinions regarding the interrelations between the transfer conditions. The combinatory nature of these conditions, and their integration into solutions for success, was further explored utilizing fuzzy-set Qualitative Comparative Analysis. Results indicate that conditions for knowledge transfer success are highly interrelated and co-dependent. Limitations and implications are discussed.

Keywords: Open innovation · Ecosystem · Knowledge transfer · fsQCA · ISM

1 Introduction

The rapid evolution of today's business environment necessitates the acquisition and integration of diverse, novel capabilities, generated through ecosystem engagement [1]. Innovation ecosystems engage multiple organisational actors to collaborate across a range of industries, coevolving their capabilities for innovative purposes [2] which relies upon inter-organisational knowledge transfer [3]. Despite the significance of this process, limited research has prioritized the conditions for knowledge transfer between ecosystem partners. Bacon, Williams and Davies [4] utilize fuzzy-set Qualitative Comparative Analysis (fsQCA) to analyze knowledge transfer conditions for open innovation but fail to concretely ascertain their importance. Innovation-related outcomes have been analyzed by other scholars utilizing fsQCA [5] as well as additional novel techniques such as Interpretive Structural Modelling (ISM) [6]. Existing literature reveals that individual-level analyses remain unexplored [7]: moreover, Ritala, Kraus and Bouncken [8] call for the application of more novel techniques for ecosystem analyses. Against this backdrop, this research aims to assess ecosystem

I. O. Pappas et al. (Eds.): I3E 2019, LNCS 11701, pp. 747–758, 2019.
https://doi.org/10.1007/978-3-030-29374-1_61

partner perceptions of the extent to which combinations of conditions are responsible for knowledge transfer success, in the context of innovation ecosystems. A mixed-method approach will be utilized to investigate two research questions: firstly, do specific conditions carry greater prominence when transferring knowledge success-fully? This will be determined through ISM. Secondly, are there multiple solutions for knowledge transfer success? Using the principles of complexity theory, this will be investigated through fsQCA.

The remainder of this paper is structured as follows. Section 2 explores current research surrounding knowledge transfer within innovation ecosystems. Section 3 presents the conditions applied within this research based upon a review of existing inter-organisational knowledge transfer literature. Section 4 identifies the sample and methods and explicates the chosen analytical techniques. Sections 5 and 6 demonstrate the main results arising from ISM and fsQCA respectively. Section 7 discusses these results.

2   Existing Literature

Open innovation [9] comprises a paradigm that supersedes traditional in-silo ideation, with organisations transferring knowledge across their organisational boundaries. Approaches to open innovation evidence its facilitation by a greater openness towards external knowledge sources [10]. Involving the movement of knowledge between actors, effective knowledge transfer is argued to be critical for innovation [11].

Extant research denotes that the increasingly complex nature of knowledge necessitates multiple partnerships with organisations who can deliver on distinct innovative requirements [11]. Knowledge is argued to transfer more readily between organisations who construct a solid inter-organisational network [12]. In the context of open innovation, ecosystems constitute an evolution of the inter-organisational network principle, and encompass a key resource for extrapolating external knowledge. Inno-vation ecosystems are comprised of multiple organisational actors, who collaborate within cooperative and competitive environments to generate new products and support innovative developments [2]. Ecosystem partnerships thus develop so that organisa-tions may share ideas [3] expediting the open innovation process through enabling firms to access high-quality, relevant knowledge from multiple sources.

Despite increasing research activity surrounding inter-organisational knowledge transfer for open innovation in the context of ecosystem-level analyses [13, 14] sig-nificant gaps remain. Holistic examinations of successful knowledge transfer within an ecosystem context are necessary [7] to potentially explicate the high failure rate of innovation partnerships: empirical examinations of factor interdependencies could address this detriment [7]. Determinants of inter-organisational knowledge transfer success remain well researched [15, 16] but hierarchical associations between con-stituents within ecosystem contexts are unexplored. What is absent from extant research is a directed focus toward the significance of knowledge transfer success, and importance of its determinants, in the context of open innovation ecosystems. Recent reviews of open innovation literature [14, 17] further emphasize that this area remains under-researched: this research addresses this gap.

3   Conceptual Outline

Based on a review of sixty-four articles examining factors for inter-organisational knowledge transfer [4], three predominant groupings arose from the most common conditions: knowledge, relationship, and firm-related. Due to existing research proposing many definitions of knowledge transfer success, with no generally accepted definition, this research outlines successful knowledge transfer to involve the '*resourceful exchange of knowledge between organisations, involving measurable and effective knowledge absorption, application and satisfaction by the recipient organisation*', in line with Bacon et al. [4].

3.1   Knowledge Characteristics

The nature of the knowledge exchanged between organisations can affect ease of transfer. Explicit knowledge, retaining more information-based qualities, arguably transfers more readily than tacit knowledge, which purports more personal attributes grounded upon individual experiences [18]. Explicit knowledge is designated as more translatable due to greater ease in articulation [18]: thus, the type of knowledge exchanged between organisations can impact the overall transfer process. Furthermore, the ability of the recipient organisation to understand the knowledge exchanged further facilitates transfer [15]. The degree of understanding possessed by the recipient organisation is mediated by the ambiguity of the knowledge itself [19]. This causal ambiguity perpetuates a lack of clarity surrounding the underlying origins and components of knowledge [20] which impedes the transfer process. Thus, knowledge-related conditions for transfer success include knowledge type, the degree of understanding possessed by the recipient organisation, and low causal ambiguity.

3.2   Relationship Characteristics

Existing literature suggests that characteristics of inter-organisational partnerships contribute to knowledge transfer success. Trustworthy partnerships arguably motivate organisations to collaborate and exchange information [21]. Trust refers to a positive expectation that partners will execute their obligations as a knowledge transferee and will reliably source the relevant information [21]. Further research [18] argues that trust strengthens a partnership. Relatedly, the strength of inter-organisational ties further affects the transfer process [10]. Strong ties encourage organisations to share detailed and complex knowledge, and correlate with increased knowledge exchange [16]. Trust and tie strength formulate the relationship characteristics category.

3.3   Organisational Characteristics

Recipient organisation characteristics further affect knowledge transfer success. Similarities between organisational cultures, in terms of shared beliefs, values and practices arguably enable knowledge transfer [10]. In order to learn from a partner, however, organisations must propagate an intent to do so. Learning intent acts as a driving force for pursuing inter-organisational partnerships, increasing knowledge transfer [19].

However, enthusiasm surrounding knowledge acquisition requires support to enable its absorption by the recipient firm. This final characteristic - absorptive capacity [22] - encompasses an organisational ability to recognize potential knowledge value, diffuse it internally, and utilize it beneficially, which in turn encourages knowledge transfer across organisational boundaries [15]. Hence, cultural similarity, learning intent, and absorptive capacity formulate organisational conditions for knowledge transfer.

3.4   Combinations of Conditions

Aside from the eight most prevalent conditions, many other factors were cited within existing research: this reinforces that no single condition can be identified as responsible for knowledge transfer success. Pappas [23] states that multiple and equally effective configurations of causal conditions can exist for a given outcome. In line with complexity theory, this research proposes that there is no single, optimum configuration that best represents knowledge transfer success: the construct cannot be reduced to a singular model of best-fit. The knowledge transfer conditions are expected possess equal importance (Fig. 1).

Fig. 1. Conceptual model

4   Research Method

4.1   Sample

This research adopts a mixed-method approach. During the first phase of data collection, a questionnaire was distributed to eleven key stakeholders, deemed experts in ecosystem engagement. Participants were sourced from a multinational keystone organisation, and included partner management coordinators, alliance managers, and strategic partnership managers. The majority of participants possessed over seven years of experience. The questionnaire extracted their opinions of the relationships between the transfer conditions. Each question was used to ascertain the pairwise relationship between the conditions, requiring participants to select from four options: (1) condition 1 influenced condition 2, (2) condition 2 influenced condition 1, (3) the conditions influenced each other, or (4) the conditions possessed no relationship. These questions were used to assess each of the pairwise relations, resulting in a total of thirty-four questions.

The second phase of data collection involved semi-structured telephone interviews, using a multi-industry sample of twenty ecosystem partners from a range of organisations, differing in size and scale. All organisations were engaged in inter-organisational partnerships within open innovation ecosystems and were sourced through purposive sampling. Participants were required to assess the presence of each condition within their ecosystem partnership on a seven-point semantic differential [24] scale. Additional unstructured questions supplemented the scales to present participants with the opportunity to offer further insights into their ratings. Knowledge transfer success was also measured using five-point semantic differential scales to assess the five separate components of the definition of transfer success – resourcefulness of transfer, measurable outcomes, effective absorption, effective application, and satisfaction.

4.2 Analytical Tools

The aim of the first phase of data analysis was to detect the interrelations between conditions, whilst pinpointing their hierarchical significance: ISM [25] was employed to achieve this. An interactive and interpretive method, ISM relies upon expert consensus to ascertain how variables are related. Within existing literature, expert opinions are often sought through questionnaires [26, 27]. ISM alleviates complexity through decomposing a given system into several elements, using this to generate a structural model and visual hierarchy of the conditions representing the system structure [28]. In this manner, ISM prioritizes and improves understanding of the key relationships between the conditions [28] which proved particularly fruitful in this context.

The second phase necessitated an analysis that would illuminate how the transfer conditions contributed to knowledge transfer success. FsQCA purports that a given combination of causal conditions can represent one of several paths to an outcome [29]. It enables the comparison of multiple cases, whilst capturing their diversity and complexity. FsQCA comprises a configurational approach, where individual cases are viewed as compositions of interrelated components [30]. FsQCA possesses particular suitability for this research due to its systematic comparisons of cases within a small-N sample [30]. The notion of equifinality, an underlying tenet of fsQCA, further elucidates its application, in that multiple configurations are expected for the outcome. Additionally, the notion of causal asymmetry, where conditions leading to the presence of an outcome differ from those leading to its absence, evidences the suitability of fsQCA for exploring the expectedly causally asymmetrical notion of success.

4.3 Stages in ISM

The application of ISM within any research context is comprised of a series of stages [28]. Firstly, the variables to be investigated are identified. The type of relationship between these variables is selected: in this study, a contextual relationship of 'influences' was chosen. Participants are asked to use their expertise to decide upon the pairwise relationships between the variables. Four notations indicate the direction of the relationship between two exemplary factors, i and j: V = i influences j; A = j influences i; X = i and j influence each other; O = no relationship. These VAXO notations are represented within a structural self-interaction matrix. The pairwise relations are then converted into 1s and 0s within a reachability matrix, based upon the following logic. If the (i, j) entry is V, then the (i, j) entry in the reachability matrix becomes 1, and the (j, i) entry becomes 0. If the (i, j) entry is A, then the (i, j) entry in the reachability matrix becomes 0 and the (j, i) entry becomes 1. If the (i, j) entry is X, then the (i, j) and (j, i) entries in the reachability matrix both become 1. If the (i, j) entry is O, then the (i, j) and (j, i) entries in the reachability matrix both become 0. The reachability matrix then requires further refinement based upon transitivity, which states that if A is related to B and B is related to C, then A and C are related. Transitivity alters the entries for variables which are indirectly related, resulting in a final reachability matrix, which displays the driving and dependence power of the variables. This produces a final digraph.

4.4 Stages in FsQCA

FsQCA requires that data be calibrated into fuzzy sets, which encompass variables that are continuous in nature: they can retain degrees of membership within a set. In this study, the type of knowledge transferred was split into tacit and explicit knowledge, and assigned three-value fuzzy set memberships of 1, 0.5, and 0. All other conditions were assigned seven-value fuzzy set memberships. In line with Ordanini et al. [31], the semantic differential scales were used to outline membership values: full membership was fixed at 6, the crossover point was set at 4.5, and non-membership was fixed at 3.

To calibrate the outcome, participant responses to outcome scales were averaged, and applied as baseline values. If participants had responded with a score higher than the average, their response was re-coded as 1; if it was lower, 0. Applying this principle across the five statements, these scores were then re-averaged for each participant, and used as the fuzzy-set values for outcome membership. Scores of above 0.8 constituted full-membership; 0.5 was a crossover point; and 0.2 was outlined as non-membership.

Following the calibration procedure, fsQCA produces a truth table, containing all logically possible combinations of cases. Cases with consistency values of less than 0.8 and frequency values of less than 1 [30] were removed from the analysis.

5 ISM Results

Based upon the expert opinions, the Structural Self-Interaction Matrix (SSIM) was developed utilizing the VAXO notations (Table 1).

Table 1. Structural self-interaction matrix

	Knowledge Type	Understanding	Causal Ambiguity	Trust	Tie Strength	Cultural Similarity	Learning Intent	Absorptive Capacity
Knowledge Type								
Understanding	X							
Causal Ambiguity	V	X						
Trust	V	X	X					
Tie Strength	X	O	X	X				
Cultural Similarity	X	X	X	V	V			
Learning Intent	X	X	X	O	A	X		
Absorptive Capacity	X	X	X	X	X	X	X	

The SSIM matrix was converted into the Initial Reachability Matrix (IRM) by converting the scores into 1s and 0s (see Sect. 4.3). It has been excluded here due to space limitations. The IRM was further refined based upon transitivity to obtain the Final Reachability Matrix (Table 2): all 0 values were converted to 1, with the conversions indicated by an Asterix.

Table 2. Final reachability matrix

	Knowledge Type	Understanding	Causal Ambiguity	Trust	Tie Strength	Cultural Similarity	Learning Intent	Absorptive Capacity	Dependence power
Knowledge Type	1	1	1*	1*	1	1	1	1	8
Understanding	1	1	1	1	1*	1	1	1	8
Causal Ambiguity	1	1	1	1	1	1	1	1	8
Trust	1	1	1	1	1	1*	1*	1	8
Tie Strength	1	1*	1	1	1	1*	1	1	8
Cultural Similarity	1	1	1	1	1	1	1	1	8
Learning Intent	1	1	1	1*	1*	1	1	1	8
Absorptive Capacity	1	1	1	1	1	1	1	1	8
Driving power	8	8	8	8	8	8	8	8	

Due to the driving and dependence power, and therefore the reachability and intersection sets, being the same for all conditions, there is only one level present in the final digraph (Fig. 2). As such, both the conical form of the reachability matrix, and the driving and dependence power diagram [6] have been excluded.

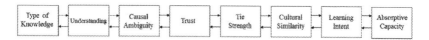

Fig. 2. Final ISM diagraph

6   FsQCA Results

Eight solutions are displayed for knowledge transfer success (Table 3). Large circles denote the presence of a core condition, indicating a strong causal relationship with the outcome, and small circles signify the presence of a peripheral condition, which exhibit weaker relationships with the outcome [32]. Circles with crosses indicate condition absence: blank spaces represent redundancy.

Table 3. Solutions for knowledge transfer success

Configuration	Solution							
	1	2	3	4	5	6	7	8
Tacit Knowledge	•	⊗	•	•	•	•	•	•
Explicit Knowledge	⊗	•	•	•	⊗	•	•	•
Under-standing	•		•	•	⊗	•	⊗	•
Causal Ambiguity	•	•	•	•	•	⊗	•	•
Trust	•	•	•		⊗	⊗	⊗	•
Tie Strength	•	•	•	•	•	⊗	•	•
Cultural Similarity	⊗	⊗	●	●	⊗	⊗	●	•
Learning Intent	•	•	●	●	⊗	•	●	⊗
Absorptive Capacity		•		•	⊗	•	⊗	•
Consistency	0.88	0.96	0.89	0.87	0.96	0.94	0.88	0.83
Raw Coverage	0.16	0.17	0.27	0.23	0.09	0.10	0.10	0.12
Unique Coverage	0.10	0.11	0.08	0.03	0.05	0.03	0.03	0.05
Overall solution coverage	0.68							
Overall solution consistency	0.93							

The solutions can be grouped according to their core and peripheral conditions. Solutions one and five display the absence of Explicit Knowledge as a core condition. However, while the absence of Cultural Similarity and Learning Intent are core conditions within solution five, Learning Intent is present within solution one. Solutions three, four and seven display the core causal configuration Cultfz*Learnfz. They differ on the redundancy of Trust within solution four, redundancy of Absorptive Capacity within solution three, and the absence of Understanding, Trust, and Absorptive Capacity within solution seven. Solutions two, six, and eight are unique.

The overall solution coverage score of 0.68 indicates that the solutions explicate a substantial proportion of the outcome. Overall consistency is high at 0.93 and demonstrates a highly significant subset relationship [30].

7 Discussion

Both the ISM and fsQCA results retain significant implications for knowledge transfer success. In response to the first research question of this study, the application of ISM within the first phase of analysis highlighted that no condition possessed greater prominence. Conditions for knowledge transfer are highly co-dependent. To further investigate the conditions, the fsQCA findings reveal eight distinct solutions for success, assisting both theoretical and practical endeavors in terms of increasing understanding of how knowledge is transferred successfully. In terms of the second research question, fsQCA confirmed that knowledge transfer success derives from multiple solutions. The fsQCA findings reflect equifinality, displaying eight distinct solutions: additionally, no configuration met the consistency threshold when analyzed against the absence of the outcome. The findings are therefore causally asymmetrical – the configurations for knowledge transfer success are distinct from those which contribute to its absence.

7.1 Theoretical Implications

This study complements and extends current research by presenting an alternative perspective of how knowledge transfer conditions combine. Previous studies have categorized conditions according to their characteristics, and utilized fsQCA to identify configurations for innovation-related outcomes [4, 5, 33]. This research provides empirical evidence for how different combinations of organisational, relationship and knowledge-related conditions are not only mutually inclusive, but causally significant for the outcome. The results of this research additionally verify extant studies that examine determinants of knowledge transfer success [4, 15, 16] whilst extending previous findings through revealing condition interrelations and their multiple effects upon the outcome, utilizing ecosystem partner perceptions as the unit of analysis.

Additionally, this study addresses a significant research gap, through amalgamating ISM and fsQCA as analytical techniques. ISM has also been integrated with other 'fuzzy' analyses [33–35] whilst fsQCA is commonly synthesized with statistical techniques such as Structural Equation Modelling [35]. However, fsQCA and ISM are seldom combined in the same study, particularly in innovation-related contexts.

7.2 Managerial Implications

The research findings also possess important practical implications. Both the ISM and fsQCA results reveal the interdependent nature of the knowledge transfer conditions. Organisations should thus reflect on the presence of such conditions, and cultivate them if missing. Additionally, an awareness of the strong interrelations between all conditions should be engendered: deficits in the presence of particular conditions could be addressed through the mediating effects of other conditions. However, the significance of individual conditions should not be overlooked. The fsQCA solutions demonstrate the pertinence of specific core and peripheral conditions: these should be noted, and their importance emphasized in practice.

7.3 Limitations and Future Research

A number of limitations are present within this study and could be addressed through further research. The fsQCA results reveal that 32% of the outcome remains unexplained: therefore, other conditions may be responsible, and could be identified through further research. Whilst ISM and fsQCA possess particular suitability for small-N analyses, the results are still grounded upon a small sample. Further studies could alleviate this through conducting larger scale studies employing quantitative techniques. Finally, this research was conducted on a sample of respondents from European ecosystems: cross-country analyses could be conducted to assess the role of ecosystem contexts.

References

1. MIT Sloan Management Review. https://sloanreview.mit.edu/article/the-myths-and-realities-of-business-ecosystems/. Accessed 03 June 2019
2. Moore, J.F.: Predators and prey: a new ecology of competition. Harvard Bus. Rev. **71**(3), 75–86 (1993)
3. Wulf, A., Butel, L.: Knowledge sharing and collaborative relationships in business ecosystems and networks: a definition and a demarcation. Ind. Manag. Data Syst. **117**(7), 1407–1425 (2017). https://doi.org/10.1108/IMDS-09-2016-0408
4. Bacon, E., Williams, M., Davies, G.H.: Recipes for success: conditions for knowledge transfer across open innovation ecosystems. In: Paper Presented at the World Open Innovation Conference, San Francisco (2018)
5. Kraus, S., Ribeiro-Soriano, D., Schüssler, M.: Fuzzy-set qualitative comparative analysis (fsQCA) in entrepreneurship and innovation research – the rise of a method. Int. Entrepreneurship Manag. J. **14**(1), 15–33 (2017). https://doi.org/10.1007/s11365-017-0461-8
6. Dwivedi, Y., et al.: Driving innovation through big open linked data (BOLD): exploring antecedents using interpretive structural modelling. Inf. Syst. Front. **19**(2), 197–212 (2016). https://doi.org/10.1007/s10796-016-9675-5
7. Milagres, R., Burcharth, A.: Knowledge transfer in interorganizational partnerships: what do we know? Bus. Process Manag. J. **25**(1), 27–68 (2019). https://doi.org/10.1108/bpmj-06-2017-0175

8. Ritala, P., Kraus, S., Bouncken, R.B.: Introduction to coopetition and innovation: contemporary topics and future research opportunities. Int. J. Technol. Manag. **71**, 1–9 (2016). https://doi.org/10.1504/ijtm.2016.077985

9. Chesbrough, H.W.: Open Innovation: The New Imperative for Creating and Profiting from Technology. Harvard Business Press, Boston (2003)

10. Van Wijk, R., Jansen, J.J., Lyles, M.A.: Inter-and intra-organizational knowledge transfer: a meta-analytic review and assessment of its antecedents and consequences. J. Manag. Stud. **45**(4), 830–853 (2008). https://doi.org/10.1111/j.1467-6486.2008.00771.x

11. Bogers, M.: The open innovation paradox: knowledge sharing and protection in R&D collaborations. Eur. J. Innov. Manag. **14**(1), 93–117 (2011). https://doi.org/10.1108/146010 61111104715

12. Argote, L., Ingram, P.: Knowledge transfer: a basis for competitive advantage in firms. Organ. Behav. Hum. Decis. Process. **82**(1), 150–169 (2000). https://doi.org/10.1006/obhd. 2000.2893

13. Miller, K., McAdam, R., Moffett, S., Alexander, A., Puthusserry, P.: Knowledge transfer in university quadruple helix ecosystems: an absorptive capacity perspective. R&D Manag. **46** (2), 383–399 (2016). https://doi.org/10.1111/radm.12182

14. de Vasconcelos Gomes, L.A., Facin, A.L.F., Salerno, M.S., Ikenami, R.K.: Unpacking the innovation ecosystem construct: evolution, gaps and trends. Technol. Forecast. Soc. Chang. **136**, 30–48 (2018). https://doi.org/10.1016/j.techfore.2016.11.009

15. Al-Salti, Z., Hackney, R.: Factors impacting knowledge transfer success in information systems outsourcing. J. Enterp. Inf. Manag. **24**(5), 455–468 (2011). https://doi.org/10.1108/ 17410391111166521

16. Cummings, J.L., Teng, B.S.: Transferring R&D knowledge: the key factors affecting knowledge transfer success. J. Eng. Technol. Manag. **20**(1–2), 39–68 (2003). https://doi.org/ 10.1016/s0923-4748(03)00004-3

17. Bogers, M., et al.: The open innovation research landscape: established perspectives and emerging themes across different levels of analysis. Ind. Innov. **24**(1), 8–40 (2017). https:// doi.org/10.1080/13662716.2016.1240068

18. Narteh, B.: Knowledge transfer in developed-developing country interfirm collaborations: a conceptual framework. J. Knowl. Manag. **12**(1), 78–91 (2008). https://doi.org/10.1108/ 13673270810852403

19. Simonin, B.L.: An empirical investigation of the process of knowledge transfer in international strategic alliances. J. Int. Bus. Stud. **35**(5), 407–427 (2004). https://doi.org/10. 1109/ieem.2007.4419560

20. Lippman, S., Rumelt, R.: Uncertain imitability: an analysis of interfirm differences in efficiency under competition. Bell J. Econ. **13**, 418 (1982). https://doi.org/10.2307/3003464

21. Inkpen, A.: Learning and knowledge acquisition through international strategic alliances. Acad. Manag. Perspect. **12**(4), 69–80 (1998). https://doi.org/10.5465/ame.1998.1333953

22. Cohen, W., Levinthal, D.: Absorptive capacity: a new perspective on learning and innovation. Adm. Sci. Q. **35**, 128 (1990). https://doi.org/10.2307/2393553

23. Pappas, I.O.: User experience in personalized online shopping: a fuzzy-set analysis. Eur. J. Mark. **52**(7/8), 1679–1703 (2018). https://doi.org/10.1108/ejm-10-2017-0707

24. Osgood, C.E., Suci, G.J., Tannenbaum, P.H.: The Measurement of Meaning. University of Illinois Press, Illinois (1957)

25. Warfield, J.N.: Intent structures. IEEE Trans. Syst. Man Cybern. (2), 133–140 (1973). https://doi.org/10.1109/tsmc.1973.5408494

26. Alawamleh, M., Popplewell, K.: Interpretive structural modelling of risk sources in a virtual organisation. Int. J. Prod. Res. **49**(20), 6041–6063 (2011). https://doi.org/10.1080/00207543. 2010.519735

27. Samantra, C., Datta, S., Mahapatra, S.S., Debata, B.R.: Interpretive structural modelling of critical risk factors in software engineering project. Benchmarking: Int. J. **23**(1), 2–24 (2016). https://doi.org/10.1108/bij-07-2013-0071

28. Pfohl, H., Gallus, P., Thomas, D.: Interpretive structural modeling of supply chain risks. Int. J. Phys. Distrib. Logist. Manag. **41**(9), 839–859 (2011). https://doi.org/10.1108/096000 31111175816

29. Pappas, I.O., Kourouthanassis, P.E., Giannakos, M.N., Chrissikopoulos, V.: Explaining online shopping behavior with fsQCA: the role of cognitive and affective perceptions. J. Bus. Res. **69**, 794–803 (2016)

30. Ragin, C.C.: Set relations in social research: evaluating their consistency and coverage. Polit. Anal. **14**(3), 291–310 (2006). https://doi.org/10.1093/pan/mpj019

31. Ordanini, A., Parasuraman, A., Rubera, G.: When the recipe is more important than the ingredients. J. Serv. Research. **17**(2), 134–149 (2013). https://doi.org/10.1177/1094670513 513337

32. Fiss, P.: Building better causal theories: a fuzzy set approach to typologies in organization research. Acad. Manag. J. **54**(2), 393–420 (2011). https://doi.org/10.5465/amj.2011.60263120

33. Mikalef, P., Boura, M., Lekakos, G., Krogstie, J.: Big data analytics and firm performance: findings from a mixed-method approach. J. Bus. Res. **98**, 261–276 (2019). https://doi.org/10. 1016/j.jbusres.2019.01.044

34. Khan, U., Haleem, A.: Smart organisations: modelling of enablers using an integrated ISM and fuzzy-MICMAC approach. Int. J. Intell. Enterp. **1**(3–4), 248–269 (2012). https://doi.org/ 10.1504/ijie.2012.052556

35. Mikalef, P., Pateli, A.: Information technology-enabled dynamic capabilities and their indirect effect on competitive performance: findings from PLS-SEM and fsQCA. J. Bus. Res. **70**, 1–16 (2017). https://doi.org/10.1016/j.jbusres.2016.09.004

Design Thinking for Pre-empting
Digital Disruption

Aurona Gerber[1,2(✉)] 📵 and Machdel Matthee[1] 📵

[1] Department of Informatics, University of Pretoria, Pretoria, South Africa
aurona.gerber@up.ac.za
[2] Department of Informatics and CAIR (Centre for AI Research),
University of Pretoria, Pretoria, South Africa

Abstract. *Digital disruption* is the phenomenon when established businesses succumb to new business models that exploit emerging technologies. Futurists often make dire predictions when discussing the impact of digital disruption, for instance that 40% of the Fortune 500 companies will disappear within the next decade. The digital disruption phenomenon was already studied two decades ago when Clayton Christensen developed a Theory of Disruptive Innovation, which is a popular theory for describing and explaining disruption due to technology developments that had occurred in the past. However it is still problematic to understand what is necessary to avoid disruption, especially within the context of a sustainable society in the 21st century. A key aspect we identified is the behavior of non-mainstream customers of an emerging technology, which is difficult to predict, especially when an organization is operating in an existing solution space. In this position paper we propose complementing the Theory of Disruptive Innovation with design thinking in order to identify the *performance attributes* that encourage the unpredictable and unforeseen customer behavior that is a cause for disruption. We employ case-based scenario analysis of higher education as evaluation mechanism for our extended disruptive innovation theory. Our position is that a better understanding of the implicit and unpredictable customer behavior that cause disruption due to additional performance attributes (using design thinking) could assist organizations to pre-empt digital disruption and adapt to support the additional functionality.

Keywords: Digital disruption · Design thinking ·
Theory of Disruptive Innovation

1 Introduction

Digital disruption was coined in the early 1980 to describe the phenomenon of failed companies such as Kodak that unexpectedly failed due to digitization and emerging technologies. The irony of this specific case is that Kodak developed the first digital camera that digitized photography but failed to capitalize on the technology that lead to their eventual closing down [1]. A similar case is that of the Smith-Corona typewriter company that was established in 1886 [2]. Smith-Corona was well positioned as a typewriter technology leader during the eighties when personal computers were introduced, for instance, introducing a cartridge ribbon in 1973 that eliminated the annoying problem of ink-stained fingers when replacing the inked ribbon [2].

© IFIP International Federation for Information Processing 2019
Published by Springer Nature Switzerland AG 2019
I. O. Pappas et al. (Eds.): I3E 2019, LNCS 11701, pp. 759–770, 2019.
https://doi.org/10.1007/978-3-030-29374-1_62

Smith-Corona failed to capitalize on the developments in word processing and viewed the personal computer market as a rival technology that they could counter with continued improvements in typewriter technology. This strategy lead to their demise about 20 years later when they were bought over by a private company during their second bankruptcy and ceased manufacturing of all typewriters [2].

The cases described are of companies that were large, well-managed and well positioned as technological leaders, however, they became victims of technological developments that created new customer bases and eroded their market share. This phenomenon was named in the 90's by Bower and Christensen in *Disruptive Technologies: Catching the Wave* [3] and *The Innovator's Dilemma* [4]. The original work subsequently developed into the Theory of Disruptive Innovation (TDI), which still remains one of the most significant theories regarding disruption two decades later [4, 5]. A key observation of DTI is that companies focus on their most-demanding mainstream customers as their most important sources of revenue, and this cause them to ignore emerging technologies[1] due to relative performance that does not satisfy the needs of these mainstream customers [3]. Mainstream customers demand better performance and therefore often oppose emerging innovations in favour of developments in existing technologies. In addition, company structures are built to support profit value networks and eliminate risk, and such value networks disregard emerging innovations representing risk and low profits. In the case of Kodak, digital photos could not match the quality of chemically developed photos for a while. In the case of Smith-Corona, large companies had typist pools with typists extremely capable on manual typewriters who regarded word processors as cumbersome and difficult to operate because, for example, a printer had to be installed before a typed document could be produced. However, in both cases the emerging innovations had additional functionality important to non-mainstream customers, which resulted in a fast growing adoption and new businesses that could refine the innovations until the performance matched those of the existing technologies. At this point and in spite of all the original opposition, the mainstream customer base typically abandoned existing technologies in favour of the emerging innovations causing disruption of the market and failure of the companies that was hooked into existing technologies [3–6].

Whilst TDI is useful in understanding disruption in retrospect, the impact of disruption is devastating and there is a need to develop such insights into disruption that it is possible to at least pre-empt full blown disruption that causes organizations to fail. This need is identified by scholars of disruptive innovations [5, 7, 8] and some of the more recent work on the TDI such as *Disruptive Strategy* attempts to address this challenge by assisting existing organizations to develop strategies for growth [5, 9]. However, we suggest that strategies that emerge from existing structures and value networks do not address the core challenges of disruption because it ignores the unpredictable behavior of low-profit adopter of a new technology with new functionalities. The investment, structures and legacy of organizations maintaining existing technology and functionality would still impede their capability to recognize and address disruptive innovations because they operate within an existing solution space.

---

[1] The recent work on Christensen's theory replaced the term *technology* with *innovation*.

Existing value networks has as core focus solving the explicit need of customers using sustaining innovations based on existing solutions. Disruptive innovations also solve the customer needs, but not as effective and what ultimately lead to rapid adoption of disruptive innovations, is the *additional functionality* that the low-demand users find particularly useful. This additional functionality is mostly *implicit*, causing unpredictable customer behavior and emerges with adoption of the innovation. The purpose of our work is to identify this additional functionality (represented by performance attributes in TDI) through design thinking.

An example that illustrates this adoption behavior is a known scholar that used several typewriters in addition to being an early adopter of a personal computer. When explicitly asked how he would generate his scientific reports, he stated that he *typed* them. However, the *additional functionality* provided by word processing programs such as the ability to easily correct mistakes and store digital versions of documents that could serve as a basis for further work at a later stage, lured him into using a word processor as a primary writing tool. This was an implicit choice and was never explicitly stated; he never got rid of his typewriters even after word processors were the status quo. What this case illustrates is that it is precarious to focus on what customers explicitly express as they would probably state the status quo. Discussing disruption within the context of the key solution space functionality (i.e. *writing* in the age of typewriters) would not necessarily expose the implicit user needs fulfilled by the additional functionality of disruptive innovations. We therefore investigated alternative mechanisms that promote an explicit focus on unpredictable, implicit user behavior decoupled from the existing status quo and solution space. Design thinking, especially given recent developments within IS, represents such a paradigm [10]. Design thinking is a human-centered method that adopts the principle that '*innovation is made by humans for humans*' and it focuses on understanding the human before thinking *solution* [10, 11], which is relevant to this study where focusing on existing solutions are part of the factors that were identified as contributing to disruption according to the TDI. We need to understand implicit customer needs and behavior without the solution space, and design thinking is appropriate for this as solution design only enter quite late into design thinking methodologies [12].

In this paper we report on initial work that use design thinking with the Theory of Disruptive Innovation in order to work towards an extended TDI. We propose that an understanding of implicit human needs and behavior due to additional performance attributes through design thinking could potentially expose why a disruptive innovation would be rapidly adopted. We used case-based scenario analysis as an evaluation method of the extended TDI. The remainder of this paper is structured as follows: the next sections provides background on TDI and design thinking, followed by Sect. 4 that describes extending TDI with design thinking. Section 5 introduces cased-based scenario analysis as evaluation while the final section concludes.

2 Theory of Disruptive Innovation

The Theory of Disruptive Innovation (TDI) (Fig. 1) is the core work of Christensen that focuses specifically on disruption caused by innovation, in contrast to the work on theories of digital innovation [13, 14]. TDI as described originally uses hard disk performance to differentiate between sustaining and disruptive technologies given *performance trajectories.* The Y-axis depicts a performance attribute [4]. Sustaining technologies maintain a steady rate of improvement that gives customers better performance on existing attributes. In contrast, disruptive technologies originally perform much worse on the key existing attribute (so they have a low value on the Y-axis) but they provide a different set of attributes [3, 4, 15]. Christensen's theory subsequently states that mainstream customer adoption of a technology requires high performance on key attributes, and because companies are structured to prioritize delivery to mainstream customers (or are 'held captive' by their best customers), they disregard low-profit customers that adopt low performance (potentially disruptive) technologies. A disruptive technology delivers on another set of attributes, which results in rapid adoption and subsequent growth with regards to performance on key performance attributes until it outperforms the existing sustaining technology. At this point the mainstream customer base abandons the existing technology and adopt the disruptive innovation resulting in the disruption of the company with the focus on the sustaining technology [3, 4, 15].

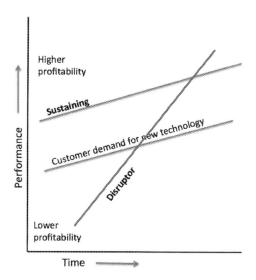

Fig. 1 The Disruptive Innovation Model (based on versions from [4, 5, 7, 15]) (Several versions of the model have been published [4, 5, 7, 15]. Disruption is depicted linearly but with different gradients and even sometimes as an exponential curve. In some latter versions a 'different measure of performance' is depicted on a third axis (Figs. 2 and 3, p. 44 [7]))

Later developments of TDI proposed refinements of the model as basis for a framework on disruptive innovation and the notion of *technology* is incorporated into *innovation* [5, 15]. Most of this work favors strategies and frameworks for companies to detect and manage disruption, as well as mechanisms that could be used to structure or reorganize companies for optimum disruptive growth [7, 9, 16]. An observation of TDI is that the model used as basis for discussion (refer to Fig. 1) is often ambiguous.

The trajectories initially indicate technology growth but are afterwards used to describe customer adoption and demand. This might lead to misinterpretation, which is the bases of some of the critique against the theory [17]. Some critics claim that the theory is outdated or that the cases on which the theory was based, such as disk drives, are selective. Others claim that *disruption* itself is a vague concept not well defined, and that the theory does not provide a satisfactory explanation thereof [18–20]. However, proponents of TDI insist that it remains one of the basis theories that explains disruption even though it is acknowledged that refinements, specifically with regards to the capability to pre-empt disruption, are necessary [8, 21]. The work reported on in this paper supports this research agenda and propose that understanding the human needs and behavior that drives adoption of an innovation is a significant indicator of its possibility to disrupt. We also propose that these needs are implicit and unpredictable, and therefore not readily distinguishable using established market analysis or requirements engineering (RE) techniques, especially ones that acknowledge an existing *solution space* or are bound to the status quo. Even though social goals or emotional goals are recognized and integrated into established RE techniques [22], these techniques have as basis approaches already working towards specific solutions. We adopt the position that any strategies that is based in existing solutions spaces and organizational structures do not address the core aspects of disruption. The focus on existing solutions and legacy functionality of existing organizations impedes their capability to recognize disruptive innovations with additional functionality that address implicit needs and behavior of emerging customers. We therefore do not attempt to augment ongoing work on DTI but propose a human centered approach that understands what human needs and behavior drive the rapid adoption of disruptive technologies. This is in line with the sentiment expressed by Yu and Hang [21] on future DTI research in that a question of 'tremendous interest' remains 'how to find emerging markets and understand the needs of new customers'. We identified design thinking as such a human centered approach because it emphasizes the understanding of human needs and behavior before proposing any solution.

3   Design Thinking

Design thinking refers to a process of creating artifacts through creation, prototyping, feedback and redesign. What distinguishes design thinking from other creative approaches, is its open-ended, often playful explorations "leading to solutions that avoid decisions and combines best possible choices" [12] (p. 336). This is in contrast to science and engineering where the design process is precise and repeatable within strict scientific boundaries, focusing on finding *solutions* [23].

Different design thinking methods exist but all center on the user and understanding the user with empathy [10]. Gasparini [24] considers empathy as an emotional response (one feels what others feel) and cognitive response (one understand what others experience from their perspective). Both these types of empathy inform design thinking. An emotional feeling can be transformed into an attribute whereas certain approaches can be used to foster cognitive empathy of designers. He furthermore shows how cognitive empathy can be gained by using 'experience prototyping', for example to understand the everyday challenges and feelings of a person that use a wearable medical device. This understanding implies more than just what a user *says*, but focus more on user needs and what a user *does*. For example, the International Standards Organization proposes a methodology that uses design thinking as starting point for requirements discovering and specification [23]. Hehn et al. [25] also shows promising results from the combination of design thinking and RE approaches when creating innovative software systems. Given digitization and digital disruption several advocates of design thinking believes that the focus on the user and really understanding user needs and motivation within complex and messy environments at least provides some measures to address the associated challenges.

A well known design thinking method, the Stanford d.School Design Thinking method, starts with a comprehensive *empathy mode* that has as core goal establishing empathy with the user without any bias towards specific solutions [25]. The empathy mode then flows into a *define mode* that precisely describing a problem with insight and preserving the emotion and need but without a considering any solution [26]. An example of a result of the define mode is a set of user statements of the form [USER] needs to [User's NEED] because [INISGHT] [27]. After the define mode, the method proposes the *ideate mode*, which is the mode that for the first time considers solutions, but the intent is to suggest "radical design alternatives" by "going wide" rather than focusing on a specific solution, followed by *prototyping* and *testing* modes. However, in contrast to known development methods, the prototyping and testing modes has as main purpose understanding and refining user needs, and not as such providing solutions. As stated, we believe that understanding user needs without any presupposed and existing solutions is core towards understanding disruption because user needs are the driving force for the adoption of emerging disruptive innovations.

4   Design Thinking and the Theory of Disruptive Innovation

By focusing on additional functionality of disruptive innovations, we complement the Theory of Disruptive Innovation in two ways: (1) Extending the *performance attribute* (PA) that serves as the basis of the theory by adding functionality performance values; and (2) using design thinking to determine existing and additional functionality performance values through the identification of implicit and explicit user needs.

We propose this complement as the first step to the development of a Theory of Disruptive Innovation that is pre-emptive in nature, and not just explanatory.

4.1   Extending the Performance Attribute of the Theory of Disruptive Innovation

As discussed, *performance* serves as the basis of TDI. The *performance attribute* (PA) is depicted on the Y-axis of all the models of the theory as rendered in Fig. 1 and is used to differentiate between sustaining and disruptive innovations, as well as the adoption behavior of mainstream or emerging customers. The current applications of the theory focus on assisting existing companies with identifying and managing innovations in order to sustain growth. We claim that strategies within existing paradigms and solutions impede the capability to recognize and address disruptive innovations because the *additional functionality* that the low-demand users find particularly useful emerges with the rapid adoption of the innovation.

Even though the *performance attribute* (PA) is key to DTI, limited in-depth investigations into what is meant with performance exist. When TDI centered around a single technology such as disk drives, performance was disk drive capacity [3]. However, when the innovation is Uber, performance is vaguely defined [15]. We argue that the vague meaning of this performance attribute leads to most disagreements about the nature of disruption, the value of the theory or critique against the theory, as well as the capability to pre-empt disruption.

A scrutiny of the PA discussions indicates that the performance is always mentioned within context of a functionality that responds to a specific user need. A disruptive innovation is described as an innovation that provides additional functionality (or as described as 'different measures of performance' (Figs. 2 and 3, p. 44 [7]). We therefore propose that the Performance Attribute (PA) implies a sum of a set of basis functionality performance values (f) and the sum of a set of additional functionality performance values (f'): $PA \rightarrow \{f_1 + f_2 +, \ldots, + f_n\} + \{f_1' + f_2', \ldots, + f_m'\}$.

A functionality performance value is defined as a response to a user need for example the speed-of-typing. When the innovation is sustaining, there would necessarily be no or few additional functionality performance for example $PA \rightarrow \{f_1 + f_2\}$ where f_1 may be the speed of typing and f_2 the size of the typewriter and when both have high values, the position on the Y-axis is high). When an innovation is disruptive, there are several additional functionality performance values (f'). Originally the sum of the values would be low as the innovation is not mature, but the combination of values are attractive enough for adoption by a large community of users. The innovation necessarily see rapid adoption from the community of users that find the additional functionality attractive resulting in PA rapidly growing as the sum of the different additional functionality performance values each increase until the determining functionalities are of sufficient value to disrupt existing innovations.

In order to determine functionality performance values (both basic and additional), it is necessary to understand user needs, and therefore we extend the performance attribute of TDI with design thinking as discussed in the next section.

4.2 Determining Functionality Performance Values Through Design Thinking

The predominant publications on TDI starts with discussions on the difference between sustaining and disruptive innovations by referring to its performance, and subsequently discuss customer adoption of these innovations, including how *additional functionality* or *different performance attributes* lead to disruptive innovations. *Innovator's Solution* states that being more predictable does not "entail learning to predict what **individuals** might do. Rather, it comes from understanding the **forces** that act upon the individuals involved in building businesses". The remainder of the work then focuses on individuals within businesses and presents several strategies for companies to innovate and grow based on the theory.

We propose that existing company structures that are representative of a specific *solution space* or paradigm prohibits its participants to effectively detect the different disruptive customer behavior that are the result of additional functionality of disruptive innovations. We suggest that the additional, often implicit and unspoken user needs that disruptive innovations address are core to understanding, and therefore pre-empting, disruptive innovations. Because these user needs are implicit and unknown, we employ solution independent design thinking that focus on thoroughly understanding the user through empathy. Using the extended Performance Attribute in the previous section $\left(PA \rightarrow \{f_1 + f_2 + , \ldots, + f_n\} + \{f_1' + f_2', \ldots, + f_m'\}\right)$ we therefore propose the following steps:

(1) Determine the context of the innovation and determine the basis functionality of the innovation (e.g. typing).
(2) Determine the set of basis functionality performance values (f) (e.g. speed of typing).
(3) Establish the basis PA as $PA \rightarrow \{f_1 + f_2 + , \ldots, + f_n\}$
(4) Using the basis functionality of the innovation as well as basis functionality performance values (steps 1 and 2), identify as many as possible *alternative innovations* that address or could possibly address the basis functionality (that would typically be low on the PA of step 3).
(5) Establish a *solution independent* design thinking team (the team should not in any way be proponents of existing sustaining innovations, therefore should not belong to organizations that support or maintain sustaining solutions).
(6) Use design thinking *empathy* to 'deeply' understand the needs and behavior (both explicit and implicit) of the early adopters and users of the *alternative innovations* as well as the forces and paradigms these users embrace. This could be in the form of the d-school define mode namely a set of user statements of the form [USER] needs to [User's NEED] because [INISGHT] [27].
(7) Determine the initial set of additional functionality performance values (f') in order to evaluate the disruptive innovation through:

$$\left(PA \rightarrow \{f_1 + f_2 + , \ldots, + f_n\} + \{f_1' + f_2', \ldots, + f_m'\}\right).$$

(8) Use the additional design thinking methods and steps (e.g. prototyping) to refine the user understanding, as well as propose radical and creative innovations (independent from existing solutions).
(9) Refine the set of additional functionality performance values (f') in order to evaluate the disruptive innovation through $(PA \rightarrow \{f_1 + f_2 + , \ldots, + f_n\} + \{f_1' + f_2', \ldots, + f_m'\})$.
(10) Feed the results back into the proposed strategies of the TDI for company growth and development (e.g. decisions of how such proposed innovations should be explored and developed (in-house or spin-off)).

5   Evaluation: Case-Based Scenario Analysis

As an initial evaluation of the proposed extended TDI for this paper, we adopted case-based scenario analysis. Scenario analysis is an approach that investigates alternative futures based on storyline-driven modeling [28, 29]. Such scenario analysis has been adopted in research that attempts to understand complex social contexts, especially where implicit knowledge has an impact such as in our research. We used the extended TDI as the storyline for the scenario analysis with higher education as case.

Higher education (HE) is defined as education beyond secondary level, usually provided by a higher education institution (HEI) such as a college or a university [30]. Given the emergence of several alternative mechanisms for higher education such as online courses and MOOCs [31], we initiated an investigation into disruptive innovation within the context of HE. Several discussions on whether MOOCs are potential disruptors for HEI abounds [32–35], and for this study we take the position that MOOCs provide *additional functionality* such as on-demand specific training when required by the changing nature of the workplace, as well as accessibility, customizability and affordability in contrast with classical HEI structures [34]. In the modern workplace claims are often made that a degree is already outdated when it is bestowed and that alternative life-long-learning training technologies will replace HEIs [36]. We used interviews with diverse role-players including middle management as well as enrolled students at HEIs to collect information and did a thematic analysis on the information acquired. We specifically investigated how the provision of higher education by HEIs differ from the alternative MOOC education mechanisms, and we identified *accredited certification* (degrees or diplomas) as the main differentiator, followed by *structured learning environments* (i.e. face-to-face lectures at specific venues at specific times and an established curriculum). For our scenario analysis we executed Steps 1–7 as Steps 8–10 represent design thinking iterations for the refinement of user needs analysis and proposed innovations. We executed Steps 1–7 as follow:

(1) The context of the innovation is the *provision of HE.*
(2) The basis functionality performance values (f) for this scenario analysis was identified to be *accredited certification* (degrees or diplomas) and *structured learning environments.*
(3) PA = *provision of HE* → f_1(*providing accredited certification*) + f_2(*providing structured learning environments*)
(4) For the scope of this paper, the scenario analysis will only consider MOOCs as an alternative possible disruptive innovation. MOOCs measure low on the PA of step 2 namely *the provision of accredited certification* and *structured learning environments* such as face-to-face lectures at specific locations and times.
(5) An initial execution of Step 5 was done by recruiting design thinking students. However, during the team brief we realized that these students (as participants in the education of an established HEI) are adopters of the 'existing solution' and their evaluation of MOOCs was therefore biased; they believed that a degree is necessary the solution to future job security in contrast with the HEI disruption sentiments. This supported our position that adopters of existing solutions do not

consider the potential of disruptive innovations, and we rephrased step 5 to be the establishment of a *solution independent* design thinking team. Limited opportunities within the scope of this study prohibited the establishment of a completely independent team, and we assigned a design thinking trainer knowledgeable about MOOCs and their possibilities to do an initial execution of Step 6.

(6) An initial empathy investigation into the needs of users that adopt MOOCs identified a number of user needs. The main reason why users enter HE is to be *employable*, and even though the mainstream advocates for employability still emphasize degrees, several additional voices emerge that emphasize alternative qualifications [37]. The exorbitant cost of HE is a huge challenge, and several people feel excluded and often angry because of the entry barrier. In addition, students can seldom work to support studies because they have to move to close proximity of a campus and the structured learning environment (i.e. face-to-face lectures). The accessibility of MOOCs as well as the freedom to learn wherever and whenever possible make them an attractive alternative to HE, however, uncertainty about the value of MOOC and online certifications still provide a barrier. The flexible course structure where users could.choose the most relevant courses are particularly attractive. The delivery mechanism that enable users to go back to video lectures assists with better learning because core concepts can be revisited. Users realize that continuous education and up-skilling will be a prerequisite to the future workplace and for such requirements, MOOCs are a key resource. Users do not necessarily complete courses, but use 'high value' MOOCs to obtain the skills necessary to better perform at existing jobs.

(7) An initial set of additional functionality performance values $\left(f'\right)$ therefore include: (1) providing ease of access to learning; (2) providing flexible course structures; (3) providing flexible learning environments (that support the freedom to learn wherever and whenever possible); (4) affordability; and (5) provide flexible delivery mechanisms of course content (for instance through videos).

The additional functionalities provided give insight into the reasons why users adopt MOOCs. The structured learning environments that are regarded as an advantage of existing HEI are actually considered a barrier by most online education adopters. Given the movement of MOOCs to provide acceptable and competitive accreditation mechanisms, which is one of the most valuable performance attributes determinants of HE, it is possible to argue that online education might possibly disrupt existing higher education, and existing HEIs could consider alternative mechanisms that support the identified additional functionalities that encourage user adoption.

6   Conclusion

In this paper we report on initial work to extend the Theory of Disruptive Innovation (TDI) using design thinking as a first step to identify additional functionality represented as performance attributes in order to pre-empt disruption. Our complement to the theory includes an extension of the performance attributes of the TDI in addition to a design thinking method that could be used to establish the often-implicit user needs and behavior that support the adoption of disruptive innovations. Further research includes refinement of the performance attribute and functionality performance values, as well as a refinement and extensive evaluation of the proposed design thinking method. The ability of the theory to better understand digital disruption would assist organizations to mediate and pre-empt the impact thereof.

References

1. Osborne, D.: The moment it all went wrong for Kodak (2012). http://www.independent.co.uk/news/business/analysis-and-features/the-moment-it-all-went-wrong-for-kodak-6292212.html
2. Smith Corona Corporation: History of Smith Corona Corporation. https://www.referenceforbusiness.com/history2/50/Smith-Corona-Corp.html
3. Bower, J.L., Christensen, C.M.: Disruptive Technologies: Catching the Wave. Harvard Business Review (1995)
4. Christensen, C.M.: The Innovator's Dilemma: When New Technologies Cause Great Firms to Fail. Harvard Business School Press, Boston (1997)
5. Christensen, C.M., McDonald, R., Altman, E.J., Palmer, J.: Disruptive Innovation: Intellectual History and Future Paths. Harvard Business School (2016)
6. Christensen, C.M.: Disruptive Innovation and Catalytic Change in Higher Education. Forum for the Future of Higher Education (2008)
7. Christensen, C.M., Raynor, M.E.: The Innovator's Solution: Creating and Sustaining Successful Growth. Harvard Business School Press, Boston (2003)
8. Christensen, C.M.: The ongoing process of building a theory of disruption. J. Prod. Innov. Manag. 23, 39–55 (2006). https://doi.org/10.1111/j.1540-5885.2005.00180.x
9. Christensen, C.M.: Online Course: Clayton Christensen Disruptive Strategy|HBX. https://hbx.hbs.edu/courses/disruptive-strategy/
10. Brenner, W., Uebernickel, F., Abrell, T.: Design thinking as mindset, process, and toolbox. In: Brenner, W., Uebernickel, F. (eds.) Design Thinking for Innovation, pp. 3–21. Springer, Cham (2016). https://doi.org/10.1007/978-3-319-26100-3_1
11. Cross, N.: Design Thinking: Understanding How Designers Think and Work. Berg Publishers, Oxford (2011)
12. Razzouk, R., Shute, V.: What is design thinking and why is it important? Rev. Educ. Res. 82, 330–348 (2012). https://doi.org/10.3102/0034654312457429
13. Nambisan, S., Lyytinen, K., Majchrzak, A., Song, M.: Digital innovation management: reinventing innovation management research in a digital world. MIS Q. 41, 223–238 (2017)
14. Tuomi, I.: Theories of Innovation: Change and Meaning in the Age of the Internet. Oxford University Press Inc., New York (2002)
15. Christensen, C.M., Raynor, M.E., McDonald, R.: What is disruptive innovation? (2015). https://hbr.org/2015/12/what-is-disruptive-innovation
16. Schmidt, G.M., Druehl, C.T.: When is a disruptive innovation disruptive? J. Prod. Innov. Manag. 25, 347–369 (2008)
17. Fitzgerald, J.: Clay Christensen explains, defends 'disruptive innovation' - The Boston Globe (2015). https://www.bostonglobe.com/business/2015/10/24/clay-christensen-explains-defends-disruptive-innovation/fmYOKlJXOSPPMquj8HQM1O/story.html
18. King, A.A., Baatartogtokh, B.: How useful is the theory of disruptive innovation? MIT Sloan Manag. Rev. 57, 77 (2015)

19. Markides, C.: Disruptive innovation: in need of better theory. J. Prod. Innov. Manag. **23**, 19–25 (2006)
20. Geller, L.W.: Howard Yu Disrupts Disruptive Innovation (2017). https://www.strategy-business.com/article/Howard-Yu-Disrupts-Disruptive-Innovation?gko=f75fc
21. Yu, D., Hang, C.C.: A reflective review of disruptive innovation theory: a reflective review of disruptive innovation theory. Int. J. Manag. Rev. **12**, 435–452 (2010). https://doi.org/10.1111/j.1468-2370.2009.00272.x
22. Curumsing, M.K., Fernando, N., Abdelrazek, M., Vasa, R., Mouzakis, K., Grundy, J.: Emotion-oriented requirements engineering: a case study in developing a smart home system for the elderly. J. Syst. Softw. **147**, 215–229 (2019). https://doi.org/10.1016/j.jss.2018.06.077
23. Shneiderman, B.: The New ABCs of Research: Achieving Breakthrough Collaborations. Oxford University Press (2016)
24. Gasparini, A.A.: Perspective and use of empathy in design thinking. In: The Eight International Conference on Advances in Computer-Human Interactions, Presented at the ACHI, Lisbon, Portugal (2015)
25. Hehn, J., Uebernickel, F.: Towards an understanding of the Role of Design Thinking for Requirements Elicitation - Findings from a Multiple-Case Study. In: Twenty-fourth Americas Conference on Information Systems. p. 10. AIS, New Orleans (2018)
26. Stanford d.School. https://dschool.stanford.edu/
27. Stanford d.School: POV Madlibs: 3. https://dschool-old.stanford.edu/groups/k12/revisions/22e39/3/
28. Garb, Y., Pulver, S., VanDeveer, S.D.: Scenarios in society, society in scenarios: toward a social scientific analysis of storyline-driven environmental modeling. Env. Res. Lett. **3**, 045015 (2008). https://doi.org/10.1088/1748-9326/3/4/045015
29. Beese, J., Haki, M.K., Aier, S., Winter, R.: Simulation-based research in information systems: epistemic implications and a review of the status quo. Bus. Inf. Syst. Eng. (2018). https://doi.org/10.1007/s12599-018-0529-1
30. Definition of Higher Education. https://www.merriam-webster.com/dictionary/higher+education
31. What is a MOOC? https://about.futurelearn.com/blog/what-is-a-mooc-futurelearn
32. Stepan, A.: Massive Open Online Courses (MOOC) Disruptive Impact on Higher Education. http://summit.sfu.ca/system/files/iritems1/13085/EMBA%25202013%2520Anita%2520Stepan.pdf
33. Flynn, J.T.: Moocs: disruptive innovation and the future of higher education. Christ. Educ. J. Res. Educ. Ministry **10**, 149–162 (2013). https://doi.org/10.1177/073989131301000112
34. Christensen, G., Steinmetz, A., Alcorn, B., Bennett, A., Woods, D., Emanuel, E.: The MOOC phenomenon: who takes massive open online courses and why? SSRN 25 (2013)
35. Pappano, L.: The Year of the MOOC (2012)
36. Blank, S.: College degrees are outdated for today's uncertain work environment (2011). https://www.businessinsider.com/college-and-business-will-never-be-the-same-2011-2
37. BusinessTech: These 10 jobs are the hardest to fill in South Africa (2018). https://businesstech.co.za/news/business/283662/these-10-jobs-are-the-hardest-to-fill-in-south-africa/

A Taxonomy for Personal Processes: Results from a Semi-structured Interview

Sercan Oruç[1]([✉]) [ID], P. Erhan Eren[1] [ID], Altan Koçyiğit[1] [ID],
and Sencer Yeralan[2] [ID]

[1] Graduate School of Informatics, Department of Information Systems,
Middle East Technical University, Ankara, Turkey
sercanoruc@gmail.com, {ereren,kocyigit}@metu.edu.tr
[2] Faculty of Engineering and Natural Sciences,
International University of Sarajevo, Sarajevo, Bosnia and Herzegovina
syeralan@ius.edu.ba

Abstract. There are few studies conducted on personal processes within the Business Process Management (BPM) domain. Personal processes are looser and more context- and person-dependent compared to the clearly defined business processes. This makes it more challenging to create solutions in this domain. In this study, a taxonomy is developed for personal processes. We used the data collected from semi-structured interviews that we have conducted with a diverse population. We built a taxonomy with 4 classes and 22 subclasses, further organized by 6 characteristics and 3 dimensions. The proposed taxonomy is intended to guide practitioners and researchers by identifying the range of processes, by understanding the relationship among process types, and by organizing the knowledge within the Personal Process Management (PPM) domain. As such, our work would lead to creating new methods, tools, and approaches for increased effectiveness of PPM solutions.

Keywords: Business Process Management · Personal Process Management · Taxonomy · Semi-structured interview

1 Introduction

Personal Process Management (PPM), as an extension to Business Process Management (BPM), focuses on the processes within people's personal lives. Planning a marriage event, choosing and registering for a college, making soup, or applying for a visa are some examples of personal processes. In many cases, personal processes highly depend on the context and the individuals involved.

Several taxonomies are suggested within the Business Process Management (BPM) domain, i.e. for BPM techniques [1], requirement changes attributes [2], unstructured workflows [3], execution exceptions [4], process flexibility [5, 6] and time rules [7]. Yet, no taxonomy has ever been developed with a focus on personal processes.

Taxonomies construct the knowledge core of domains which help the researchers to understand and analyze them and lead to an improvement in corresponding domains [8]. This statement also defines the main motivation behind this study: to create the

© IFIP International Federation for Information Processing 2019
Published by Springer Nature Switzerland AG 2019
I. O. Pappas et al. (Eds.): I3E 2019, LNCS 11701, pp. 771–782, 2019.
https://doi.org/10.1007/978-3-030-29374-1_63

knowledge core in the PPM domain and support the practitioners with an overview of personal processes so that different applications, methods or approaches can be developed for different classes. As study [8] highlights, it is necessary to create classifications for more advanced theories. Taxonomies not only reduce confusion but also aid understanding [9]. Nickerson et al. [10] list various studies showing the role of taxonomies in the information systems (IS) research literature and state that "classification is a fundamental mechanism for organizing knowledge".

The main objective of this paper is to propose a personal process taxonomy by using the method suggested by Nickerson et al. [10]. Accordingly, we conducted semi-structured interviews with 20 people of different ages and occupation groups. From those interviews, more than 60 process examples emerged. Using the responses, we applied an inductive approach of taxonomy development following [10]. We define the personal process taxonomy step by step by listing classes, subclasses, and their properties, and by illustrating each of them by giving examples.

This paper is organized as follows. In Sect. 2, we outline taxonomy studies conducted within the BPM domain. In Sect. 3, we justify and describe the method that we have used. In Sect. 4, we describe the resultant personal process taxonomy in detail. Finally, in Sect. 5, we conclude the paper with discussion of the contributions of this paper, and future work.

2 Taxonomy Studies in BPM Domain

In the BPM domain, there are several studies proposing taxonomies from various perspectives. [11] shows an ontological model and a taxonomy of BPM systems. It also shows the hierarchy of interface, execution engine, metrics and their subclasses pertinent to software industry BPM systems. Shaw et al. [12] propose a BPM system architecture showing core technologies as building blocks. They list the full set of levels and core technologies and how they merge into a BPM system along with the transmission and processing of modeling characteristics. [9] highlights a taxonomy that would be used in expressing the purpose of any evaluated BPM technology.

Study [1] gives a taxonomy of business process modeling and IS modeling techniques. It states that the taxonomy can be used in evaluating and selecting suitable modeling techniques by the decision makers, depending on the needs of the projects. On the other hand, in [13], project types in BPM are classified and three major and two minor classes by using multivariate data analysis techniques are suggested.

In study [14], a list of BPM and flow automation definitions are made and a standard set of terms and concepts to support clear communication in industry are given. Five BPM categories are listed to make the clarification: Administrative and Task Support (Visual), Team Process Support Tools (Collaborative), Application Specific (Preconfigured), Integration-Focused, and Application Independent.

In study [7], Arevalo et al. focus on the temporal dimension of business processes and define a time rule taxonomy which leads to "business temporal rules with current BPMN standard" in a declarative way.

In study [4], Zhao et al. try to find solution to the deficiency in support for exception handling for current business process programming languages for semantic web services by providing an exception taxonomy.

In [2], a taxonomy of change with four main classes are suggested: "time of change", "origin of change", "type of change", and "structural effect of change" that can be used in detecting changes before they are reported. A taxonomy for BPM flexibility with a focus of change is also suggested in study [6]: abstraction level of change, subject of change, and properties of change.

[5] gives a taxonomy of process flexibility by listing four types: flexibility by design, deviation, underspecification, and change. This distinction is made based on the conducted literature study. These four categories are evaluated, and it is seen that these types can be found in the literature and in practice.

In summary, within the BPM domain, there is a wide spectrum of taxonomy studies including taxonomies of technologies, modeling techniques, project types, definitions, temporal dimension of processes, exceptions, change, and flexibility. Yet, these examples do not suggest a taxonomy directly from the processes themselves.

There are two studies which have similarity with ours by directly focusing on the processes themselves. The first one is presented by [3] which gives a taxonomy of unstructured workflows with the aim of analyzing those workflows and determining if they can be changed into equivalent structured forms. Yet, this study creates the taxonomy using the relationship of the control elements of the workflows, regardless of the context or the domain of the process.

In the second study [15], a systematic literature review is conducted and organizational information-processing theory is employed to identify the differences among processes. The goal is to minimize the wasted efforts by understanding different management requirements for different processes. By using the data obtained from other studies within the literature, this study considers context-specific BPM practices. Yet, its scope covers business processes within organizations. None of these studies outlines a taxonomy of processes within everyday life considering contextual factors.

3   Method

In this study, first we conducted semi-structured interviews with 20 respondents to bring up a set of personal processes. Then, we used the responses from the interviews in developing a personal process taxonomy. In taxonomy development, we followed the seven-step method proposed in study [10] which is also used by many IS research, i.e. [15–18]. Study [10] presents a better alternative to ad hoc way of developing taxonomy in the IS domain by showing that the proposed method has requisite qualities developed based on well-established taxonomy development literature.

3.1   Data Collection: Semi-structured Interview

To understand things that cannot be observed like experiences, attitudes, thoughts, intentions, comments, perceptions, and reactions; qualitative researchers use interviewing as an effective method [20]. We used semi-structured interviews to gather information from a diverse population. As it is stated in [19], "the semi-structured interview provides a repertoire of possibilities". While the interview is structured enough to point to a specific topic, it also leaves space to the participants to offer new ideas. The questions are mostly open-ended, which allows the discovery and gathering of unforeseen or unpredicted information.

The Sample of the Study. In this study, we used diversity (maximum variation) sampling, which is a type of purposive (judgmental) sampling. We interviewed 20 people from 18 distinct occupations. The minimum conditions for selecting the participants were that the participant should be using a mobile device and that should be actively managing the daily life processes of themselves. We tried to reflect the diversity of the population within the sample by choosing from different genders, age groups, occupations, and education degrees. The age distribution of participants can be seen in Fig. 1. The youngest participant is 22 years old whereas the oldest one is 60. The education levels of the participants can be seen in Fig. 2.

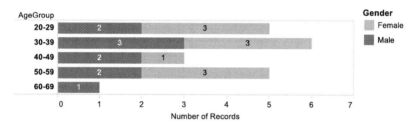

Fig. 1. Age distribution

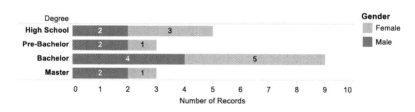

Fig. 2. Educational degree distribution

3.2 Seven Steps of Taxonomy Development

To develop a taxonomy by the personal processes gathered from the semi-structured interview, we followed the seven-step method proposed by Nickerson, Varshney and Muntermann [10]. Figure 3 shows the steps of the taxonomy development method.

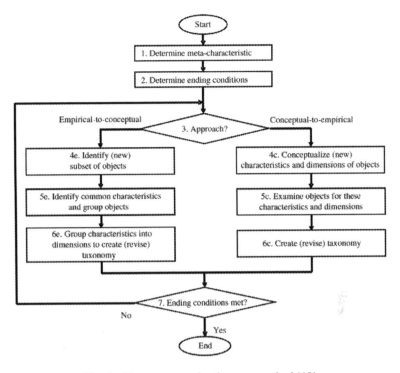

Fig. 3. The taxonomy development method [10].

Step 1 – Determine Meta-characteristics. Meta-characteristic is defined in [10] as "the most comprehensive characteristic that will serve as the basis for the choice of characteristics in the taxonomy". Our goal is to structure personal processes related knowledge. The target users are both researchers and practitioners interested in personal processes who may create new applications, methods or approaches for managing personal processes. The scope of the taxonomy is limited to processes of people using a mobile device and actively managing the daily life processes of themselves. In these terms, processes of a person such as a child using a mobile phone yet having a life highly dependent on parents, or an elder living independently in a community yet not using a mobile device does not fall within the scope of this study. Considering all these aspects, we define the meta-characteristics of our taxonomy as *'connection between the management approach of the process owner and the personal process'*.

Step 2 – Determine Ending Conditions. We used eight objective and five subjective ending conditions proposed in study [10]. These conditions determine when to end the process of developing the taxonomy.

Step 3 – Approach. We used inductive (empirical-to-conceptual) approach for all three iterations.

Steps 4, 5 and 6 – Identify a Subset of Objects, Identify Common Characteristics and Group Objects, Group Characteristics into Dimensions to Create Taxonomy. In each iteration, we evaluated a new subset of personal processes gathered from the semi-structured interview. At the end of the three iterations, we finished evaluating all the personal processes gathered from the interviews. The outcome is the following common characteristics:

- Essential: Some processes are essential to have an independent daily life.
- Optional: Some processes are optional in terms of having an independent daily life.
- Routine: Some processes routinely take part in personal lives.
- Ad Hoc: Some processes occur in an ad hoc manner.
- Obliged: Some processes are completed to fulfill some obligations. These processes emerge from something the person owns or is responsible for.
- Not Obliged: Some processes emerge from something other than the things that the person owns or is responsible for.

We grouped these characteristics into three dimensions:

- D1: Necessity (Essential, Optional)
- D2: Occurrence (Routine, Ad Hoc)
- D3: Obligation (Obliged, Not Obliged)

Step 7 – Ending Conditions Met? At the end of the third iteration, ending conditions are met and we concluded the taxonomy development.

4 Taxonomy of Personal Processes

Using the characteristics in the previous section, we defined a personal process taxonomy as in Table 1. We grouped the process examples that we have collected from the semi-structured interviews, in four groups: Diversions, Emergencies, Instrumental Activities of Daily Living (IADL), and Responsibilities. Those four classes have 22 subclasses in total. During the development process of the taxonomy, we kept in mind to bring the qualitative attributes listed in [10] to the taxonomy: concise, robust, comprehensive, extendible, and explanatory.

4.1 Instrumental Activities of Daily Living

Activities of Daily Living (ADL), Basic Activities of Daily Living (BADL) and IADL terms are well known terms used in healthcare. BADL are needed for fundamental functioning of a person whereas IADL are needed additionally to have an independent life in a community. We considered using IADL not BADL, as we interpreted that managing BADL with some IS would not be effective. BADL consist of the following 'toilet hygiene', 'self-feeding', 'dressing', 'grooming', 'physical ambulation', and 'bathing' [21].

Table 1. Personal process taxonomy

		D1: Necessity		D2: Occurrence		D3: Obligation	
		Essential	Optional	Routine	Ad Hoc	Obliged	Not Obliged
Diversions	Exercising		X	X	X		X
	Hobbies		X	X	X		X
	Social activities		X	X	X		X
	Travelling		X	X	X		X
Emergencies	Accidents	X			X		X
	Injuries and sickness	X			X		X
	Missing flight/train/bus case	X			X		X
	Lost wallet case	X			X		X
IADL	Handling finances	X		X			X
	Housework	X		X			X
	Mode of transportation	X		X			X
	Preparing meals	X		X			X
	Shopping	X		X			X
	Taking medication as prescribed	X		X			X
	Use forms of communication	X		X			X
Responsibilities	Business processes		X	X	X	X	
	Care of pets		X	X	X	X	
	Child rearing		X	X	X	X	
	Citizenship responsibilities		X	X	X	X	
	Garden care		X	X	X	X	
	Real estate care		X	X	X	X	
	Vehicle care		X	X	X	X	

A modification of IADL listed in [21] has 7 subclasses:

- Handling finances (stated as "ability to handle finances" in [21]).
- Housework, (stated as "housekeeping" and "laundry" in [21])
- Mode of transportation,
- Preparing meals (stated as "food preparation" in [21]),
- Shopping,
- Taking medication as prescribed (stated as "responsibility for own medications" in [21]),
- and Use a form of communication (stated as "ability to phone" in [21]).

Handling Finances: Although money management is mostly about decision making, processes can also be very vital as in the example of invoice payment timings.

Housework: An example process emerges after a dinner consist of activities: clearing the table, loading the dishwasher, starting the dishwasher, wiping the table, sweeping the floor, emptying the dishwasher, putting the dishes into the cupboards.

Mode of Transportation: Using different means of transportation may lead to different processes. For instance, going from one point to another in a city by mass transportation may have activities like getting on a bus number X, then going 3 stations by tram, finally walking 400 m.

Preparing Meals: Any dish recipe, which list actions to be completed in a given order, is a good example for a "Preparing Meals" type of process.

Shopping: The person may have a long shopping list. There could be many shop and product alternatives. Also, the timing, following the discounts, or closeness to the shops could be some possible concerns of the person. If the person wants to optimize the time and money he spends, or the quality he buys, then the process of shopping becomes computationally complex.

Taking Medication as Prescribed: Taking medication is a common part of any medical care. Usually the timing and dosage of taking medication are significantly important. So, tracking the process becomes more important.

Use a Form of Communication: This subclass is composed of many atomic activities like making a phone call or sending an e-mail. Combining these activities with other surrounding activities, we get some simple processes. For instance, we can think of a person starting her computer and sending an e-mail (signing in, writing the e-mail, entering to-cc-bcc lists, sending the e-mail).

4.2   Responsibilities

This class consists of processes that emerge from the things that the person owns or is responsible for. For instance, if the person owns a dog, then she should handle the processes regarding dog care like tracking the vaccination guidelines or meeting the daily needs of walking or feeding. Although there are fewer than 10 subclasses listed under the class "responsibilities", the number can easily increase depending on the variety of belongings the person has.

Business Processes: Business processes serve for organizational goals. This collection of activities takes place in a person's life in case that person has a business. From the perspective of that single person, business processes that she is involved in are processes as a set of responsibilities in her personal life. Depending on the organizational culture and policies, sometimes these processes intertwine with other, more personal processes. In the first case, there could be a more effective way of managing this collection of processes by dealing with them all together.

Care of Pets: Some examples would be taking the dog to walks periodically or following vaccination schedules of the pet.

Child Rearing: Some activities that would exemplify such processes would be feeding, playing, or taking the child to a doctor.

Citizenship Responsibilities: Having a citizenship from a country comes with many processes to be completed. Some examples could be voting or compulsory military service in countries or serving jury duty.

Garden Care: Watering the grass, disinfecting the tools, controlling the weeds, and mulching are some activities that may take place in garden care processes.

Real Estate Care: For instance, a person having a house should complete house maintenance tasks in the lifespan of that house, like inspecting the fire extinguisher, getting the air conditioner ready for the summer, getting the chimney cleaned, or paying the taxes of the house.

Vehicle Care: Some examples would be changing the tires, getting the car cleaned, or keeping up with insurance payments.

4.3 Diversions

"Diversions" are the processes that divert from basic or instrumental daily living processes and responsibilities. The causes or motivations behind those processes are intangible things like happiness, health, curiosity, etc. "IADL" processes should take place in a person's life in order for him to have an independent life in a community.

Exercising: This subclass consists of mostly structured processes. These processes could be created by domain experts and followed by the person.

Hobbies: Following a guitar lesson, doing ear training, improving the technique, practicing scales, chords, or arpeggios could be given as example activities that would form a personal process of learning guitar.

Social Activities: This subclass consists of social events like organizing a home party or some gathering activity with some friends. Processes related with social activities are mostly people centric as the main purpose of social activities are consorting with or joining with other people.

Traveling: Arranging for flight and hotel, listing the attraction points in a city, and the order of visiting these attraction points can be given as examples of activities and relations that would create traveling type of processes.

4.4 Emergencies

The fourth class consists of processes that are completed in unplanned occasions like "what should a person do when he has lost his wallet?" or "what should a person do when she misses her flight?". Following four examples are collected from the semi-structured interviews that we have conducted. The number of subclasses can be increased by collecting new example cases.

Accidents: The activities that should be performed when an accident occurs would create processes to be considered under the accidents subclass.

Injuries: The activities that should be performed when an injury occurs would create processes to be considered under the injuries subclass.

Lost Wallet Case: If a wallet is lost, what should the person do? The answer would create a process. As an example answer: the person should think of the last time he saw the wallet, and ask the people who might have seen it and check the places he passed since then. If he couldn't get a positive response, he should call the banks depending on the credit or bank cards in his wallet, so that he can cancel those cards. He should inform the police that he has lost his ID cards. Depending on the items he has lost with his wallet, new activities can be added to the process. The order of the activities would mostly be affected by the importance and urgency of the activities.

Missing Flight/Train/Bus Case: The activities that should be performed when a person misses a flight, train, bus, etc.

5 Discussions and Conclusions

In this paper, we propose a taxonomy for personal processes by using the method presented by [10] as it is "based on well-established literature in taxonomy development". As the input data for the taxonomy development, we used the empirical results of semi-structured interviews that we have conducted with a diverse population. As a result, in this taxonomy, there are four main classes which are composed of 22 subclasses in total. The taxonomy is open for extension in terms of new classes and subclasses. The following questions would help in defining the properties or attributes of corresponding subclasses and the related processes.

How Frequently is the Process Executed? The number of times in a period that a person completes a process would also be considered as an important dimension. Some personal processes are completed just once or twice in a lifetime (low frequency) as in the example of marriage. Some personal processes are completed much more frequently (high frequency) like preparing breakfast. There are also some other processes that are in between high and low frequency personal processes (medium frequency) as in the example of course registration in a university. For instance, in some universities, a student completes course registration twice in a year for 4 years. There are two important points here in this question:

- Although it is not necessarily needed, it is difficult to set specific boundaries (number over time) to define which processes are in classes high, medium, or low frequencies. The borders may even change from person to person.
- Having fuzzy boundaries between frequency classes does not affect the importance of having those classes.

How Important/Critical/Serious Is the Process? Some processes are more critical than the others. The actions of that process must be followed completely without any errors. The process of following medical treatment routines is more critical than the process of traveling. Some actions in seeing a city may be skipped without any critical consequences. Yet, it would not be the same for skipping an action in the process of some medical treatment.

Does the Process Have a Legislative, a Regulation, or Some Other Strict Process Definition? If the process is executed depending on a legislative process, then it is assumed that the steps cannot be changed. The case whether the process has a legislative or not would affect the flexibility of it. This type of processes also takes significant amount of time in personal lives. Driver's license registration or child adoption processes can be given as examples.

Is the Process Data Driven or Judgment Driven? Some processes can be managed more effectively by solely using the available data and some predefined objectives like minimizing time, money, or energy consumption. On the other hand, other processes are affected more by the judgments of the person. The process of profession selection is more like a judgment driven process than a data driven process whereas visa application process is a data driven process.

The sample size and extent of the semi-structured interview is rather limited, as we consider our work as an initial investigation of the validity of the approach, and to assess its expected success. As the development of any class of mobile and computer applications is an evolutionary process, the initial first steps are usually taken in small increments, while the validity and the appropriateness of the approach are frequently and carefully monitored and evaluated. Corrections at the beginning are clearly easier, more efficient, and less intrusive than latter ones. Given the encouragement of the initial limited survey, and now equipped with the experiences from this initial probe, we are now confident to extend and expand our investigation. The purpose of the dissemination of our findings is to avail others from joining our effort and giving them head start so that they do not need to start from scratch.

The role of this taxonomy is to guide practitioners and researchers by structuring personal process classes, making the relationship among process types clear, and arranging the knowledge within the PPM domain. This understanding would eventually help practitioners and researchers in suggesting methodologies or techniques to be used in effective management of personal processes.

As in any academic study, we take a promising idea and push it to its logical and practical limits to evaluate its usefulness. The current study is an attempt to best address the robust development of the emerging field, and subsequent applications of PPM. As in any academic study, one cannot guarantee the eventual unqualified success of the approach taken. However, reporting on the results of the diligent and honest scientific efforts is an enriching contribution to the body of academic literature. Our initial study and experience indicate that our work has so far provided encouragement for its usefulness and eventual benefits.

The paper is a report on the work accomplished so far. The development of a PPM system is a complex issue which will most likely take time to evolve and mature before it settles into a universally accepted technology. Our approach is to embark on this process following the most scientifically rigorous methodologies available. Accordingly, we dwell on a taxonomy, which we hope will not only start the research and development process on a scientific footing, but also facilitate the emergence of heterodoxical approaches not immediately available through customary software development efforts.

References

1. Giaglis, G.M.: A taxonomy of business process modeling and information systems modeling techniques. Int. J. Flex. Manuf. Syst. **13**(2), 209–228 (2001)
2. Mathisen, E., Ellingsen, K., Fallmyr, T.: Using business process modelling to reduce the effects of requirements changes in software projects. In: 2009 2nd International Conference on Adaptive Science & Technology (ICAST), pp. 14–19 (2009)
3. Liu, R., Kumar, A.: An analysis and taxonomy of unstructured workflows. In: van der Aalst, W.M.P., Benatallah, B., Casati, F., Curbera, F. (eds.) BPM 2005. LNCS, vol. 3649, pp. 268–284. Springer, Heidelberg (2005). https://doi.org/10.1007/11538394_18
4. Zhao, K., Zhang, L., Ying, S.: Ontology-based exception handling for semantic business process execution. J. Softw. **7**(8), 1791–1798 (2012)
5. Schonenberg, M.H., Mans, R.S., Russell, N.C., Mulyar, N.A., van der Aalst, W.M.P.: Towards a taxonomy of process flexibility (extended version). BPMcenter.org (2007)
6. Regev, G., Soffer, P., Schmidt, R.: Taxonomy of flexibility in business processes. In: BPMDS (2006)
7. Arevalo, C., Escalona, M.J., Ramos, I., Domínguez-Muñoz, M.: A metamodel to integrate business processes time perspective in BPMN 2.0. Inf. Softw. Technol. **77**, 17–33 (2016)
8. Glass, R.L., Vessey, I.: Contemporary application-domain taxonomies. IEEE Softw. **12**(4), 63–76 (1995)
9. SAP and Accenture: BPM Technology Taxonomy (2009)
10. Nickerson, R.C., Varshney, U., Muntermann, J.: A method for taxonomy development and its application in information systems. Eur. J. Inf. Syst. **22**(3), 336–359 (2013)
11. Manoilov, G., Deliiska, B., Todorov, M.D.: Ontological model of business process management systems. In: AIP Conference Proceedings, vol. 1067, no. 1, pp. 491–499 (2008)
12. Shaw, D.R., Holland, C.P., Kawalek, P., Snowdon, B., Warboys, B.: Elements of a business process management system: theory and practice. Bus. Process Manag. J. **13**(1), 91–107 (2007)
13. Bucher, T., Winter, R.: Project types of business process management. Bus. Process Manag. J. **15**(4), 548–568 (2009)
14. Sinur, J., Bell, T.: Gartner a BPM taxonomy: creating clarity in a confusing market (2003)
15. Zelt, S., Schmiedel, T., vom Brocke, J.: Understanding the nature of processes: an information-processing perspective. Bus. Process Manag. J. **24**(1), 67–88 (2018)
16. Seyffarth, T., Kühnel, S., Sackmann, S.: A taxonomy of compliance processes for business process compliance. In: Carmona, J., Engels, G., Kumar, A. (eds.) BPM 2017. LNBIP, vol. 297, pp. 71–87. Springer, Cham (2017). https://doi.org/10.1007/978-3-319-65015-9_5
17. Reman, G., Hanelt, A., Tesch, J.F., Kolbe, L.M.: The business model pattern database—a tool for systematic business model innovation. Int. J. Innov. Manag. **21**(01), 1750004 (2017)
18. Lehnert, M., Linhart, A., Roeglinger, M.: Exploring the intersection of business process improvement and BPM capability development. Bus. Process Manag. J. **23**(2), 275–292 (2017)
19. Galletta, A.: Mastering the Semi-structured Interview and Beyond: From Research Design to Analysis and Publication. NYU Press, New York (2013)
20. Yıldırım, A., Şimşek, H.: Research Methods in Social Sciences. Seçkin Yayıncılık (2006)
21. Lawton, M.P., Brody, E.M.: Assessment of older people: self-maintaining and instrumental activities of daily living. Gerontologist **9**(3 Part 1), 179–186 (1969)

Online Communities

Learning to Lead Online Collaborations: Insights from Student-Based Global Virtual Teams Between UK and Norway

Niki Panteli[1], Tor Atle Hjeltnes[2], and Knut Arne Strand[2(✉)]

[1] Royal Holloway University of London, London, England, UK
[2] Norwegian University of Science and Technology, Trondheim, Norway
knut.a.strand@ntnu.no

Abstract. In this paper we present a virtual collaborative student project across two universities in the UK and Norway. The students involved were all Master students in Digital Innovation & Analytics and Digital Collaboration retrospectively. The project also had an industry partner, Cisco, and was set up as part of students' learning in their corresponding universities. Five student-based Global virtual teams (GVTs) were formed. We draw on the experiences of these GVTs to gain better understanding of students' experiences in dispersed collaboration giving particular focus on the leadership practices adopted in student-based GVTs. Our analysis of the GVT members' experiences and reflections show that the way leadership was enacted had a role to play in the collaboration within the GVT. Overall, students appreciated being given the opportunity to be part of a globally dispersed project and were able to identify lessons learned and skills that they gained from the experience. Further, students were able to get practical experience in being part of virtual teams and to implement some of the ideas and approaches that they have learned from theory and in class discussions. For example, personal qualities that are central to success in virtual teams, i.e. communication skills, intercultural skills, interpersonal skills, methodological and technical skills, team working skills and leadership skills.

Keywords: Global virtual teams · Collaboration · Leadership · Dispersed projects · Pedagogy

1 Introduction

Technological advancements as well as an organisational interest in recruiting talent regardless of location, has contributed to the increasing use of globally dispersed virtual teams. It is therefore not surprising that university lecturers, especially within the Information Systems discipline, have been setting up global virtual student projects in order to expose students to the opportunities and challenges of working in virtual teams. Such projects necessitate a virtual collaboration where students from different universities are often asked to work on a project as part of their assessment within a specific timeframe. The task mandates the use of web-based technologies and a cooperative effort on the part of all team members who are then often assessed as a group. Organising student-based global virtual teams (GVTs) offer opportunities for

© IFIP International Federation for Information Processing 2019
Published by Springer Nature Switzerland AG 2019
I. O. Pappas et al. (Eds.): I3E 2019, LNCS 11701, pp. 785–796, 2019.
https://doi.org/10.1007/978-3-030-29374-1_64

enhancing teaching and learning practice as well as for enabling students to gain skills in managing and leading effectively in the online space [8] which ultimately contribute to increasing their employability and career development. In this paper, we present one such project between a university in the UK and a university in Norway that have among others the purpose of encouraging students to learn about leading online collaborations and developing effective dispersed collaborations in general. Drawing on this project, we aim to develop a better understanding of the leadership practices adopted in student based GVTs in order to develop effective collaborations in the dispersed setting. Though numerous pedagogical studies exist to-date on student-based globally dispersed teams, this is the first study to our knowledge that takes a focus on leadership specifically examining how students may develop their leadership capability in the online setting.

Following this introduction, we review the relevant literature on student-based GVTs, collaboration and leadership in the virtual team context. We then describe our GVT and the involvement of the two universities in this endeavour and explore the key themes that we have encountered in this project, illustrated by student comments and insights. Finally, we present what we consider are effective leadership approaches in the student-based GVTs and identify recommendations to other instructors for organising successful GVTs.

2 Student-Based Global Virtual Teams

Many university instructors now engage with their students through diverse virtual learning platforms. These mediated environments may be restricted to within country designs [2, 14] or to between two or more countries [7, 15, 23, 24] as part of a student's learning process. The latter contribute to the emergence of global virtual teams. These are teams that consist of globally dispersed students who work on a joint project in a technology-mediated environment. In this way, collaboration in student-based GVTs are carried out across time and space as well as across organizational boundaries adding diversity to students' project teams. For the instructors, online collaborative tools such as Blackboard, Moodle and WebCT among others, have enabled the design of numerous virtual student-based projects often at a global scale providing opportunities for innovations in teaching and learning.

A study by Alavi et al. [2] that compared two distributed courses (one with campus-based students and the other with non-proximate distant students) with a traditional classroom based course, found that the students involved in the distant distributed course shown higher levels of critical thinking skills. Similarly, Piccoli et al. [18] in a study on the effectiveness of web-based learning environments found that learning in such environments has fostered increased computer self-efficacy among students. Virtual student teams are important for enhancing students' learning as well as for giving insights into virtual team dynamics by simulating work based scenarios that our students are likely to experience in the 'real' world. In this way, such practices equip students with necessary skills in how to manage effectively virtual team projects and online collaborations [8]. In what follows, we discuss two key factors for the success of GVTs: collaboration and leadership.

3   Collaboration

In a globally distributed environment collaboration between the dispersed team members rely heavily on digital technologies to achieve common outputs. Within this setting, limited social cues restrict the occurrences of familiarity and trust development whilst raise the likelihood of misunderstanding and conflicts that have negative effect on effectiveness and efficiency of collaborative teamwork and team dynamics [12]. Though misunderstandings occur in collocated teams too, it is aspects of virtual teams such as time differences, delays in information exchange and limited social cues that can exacerbate conflict [6]. It is often assumed that due to the greater diversity of members' backgrounds in GVTs [22], but also the computer-mediated nature of GVT's communications [1], the likelihood for conflicting goals and opinions are greater. Research has also suggested that such teams are more likely to suffer from problems of information distribution [5], more likely to face difficulties in creating and maintaining good working relationships, and more likely to have problems developing trust in each other [10]. It follows, therefore, that developing effective collaborations over distance in a technology-mediated setting becomes a major challenge for GVTs.

Collaboration implies that a shared end result is achieved by mutual effort of different parties (individuals, teams, organisations) involved in a collaboration process. However, there are different ways to collaborate towards achieving the shared end result. For example, teams involved in collaborative projects can work together or separately. Linked to this, existing literature has distinguished between two different collaboration patterns: interdependent mutual engagement (i.e. working together) and independent cooperative work (i.e. working separately). The former implies joint orchestrated effort and involves communication in sense of dialogue and group discussion. The latter implies that the process of achieving the shared outcome is subdivided in tasks and takes the form of cooperative working achieved through division of labour [21]. Nevertheless, regardless of the differences between these patterns, effective collaboration should maintain mutual influence between the different parties involved in the collaborative arrangement. To reinforce this, we adopt Robey et al.'s [20] 'intertwine' concept. According to them: "First, intertwining literally refers to the weaving, braiding, and entangling of filaments such as silk, wool or hair. … Second, intertwining figuratively means 'mutually involved' …[this] not only suggests that separate elements are engaged, but also that each element's contribution depends on its reciprocal involvement with the other element" [20, p. 118]. In their study, they identify four key features of intertwining: reinforcement, complementarity, synergy and reciprocity. Their approach in relation to our present study suggests that the different parties that engage in collaborative activities are not substitutes, but interacting influences. Table 1 presents the key dimensions of the intertwining effect and shows their relevance to GVT students' collaborations.

Table 1. Key features of intertwining and relevance to VT students' collaborations.

Feature	Definition	Relevance to GVT collaborative projects
Reinforcement	Each element amplifies the effect of the other element	The combination of the different parties' activities and idea which provide potentials for new ideas and activities
Complementarity	The strengths of the one complement the other's weakness	The strength is the ability to exchange information and knowledge regardless of time and space
Synergy	The combination of elements create new properties which did not previously exist	Going beyond the boundaries of their university programme and which encompasses characteristics of each different subgroup, contributing to new ideas and opportunities
Reciprocity	The elements are mutually interdependent and that there is an equal partnership between them, rather than a leader-follower relationship	Both parties co-exist equally; the one is not more important than the other

Our first proposition following the above discussion is:

Proposition 1: Effective collaboration in student-based GVTs has an intertwining effect.

4   Leadership

Literature on leadership and virtual teams has identified three types of leaders within this context: appointed or designated leaders, emergent leaders and shared leaders. With regard to the former, for example, Kayworth and Leidner [11] studied 13 student-based virtual teams which contained at least one designated team leader from each participant university. They explain the choice of the appointed leaders as follows: "high levels of prior work experience among team leaders helped to ensure a more realistic setting for the study" (p. 13). Having an appointed leader also has disadvantages: Firstly it means that the researchers (or instructors as it was in this case) do not allow any team member to gradually and naturally emerge as a leader; and secondly by allocating team leaders' roles in a team, this has an immediate effect on team interactions.

Further, other studies have elicited that leaders emerge from the interactions that take place within the virtual team (e.g. [3]). These authors suggest that for a member to become a leader, he or she should actively participate in several activities within the group, make fruitful contributions to discussions and exert leadership and management skills such as encouraging other members to take part and develop coordination among members' interaction [19]. The frequency with which virtual team leaders [25] communicate with their team members has been seen as an indication of effective leadership.

More recently, studies have also pointed to evidence of shared leadership. Chamakiotis and Panteli [4] for instance have shown in their study of GVTs in an industry-academia collaboration project that several individuals may enact the role of a leader depending on their expertise and the stage of the project. They also shown that different leaders may co-exist to support different aspects of the project. From a learning perspective, it is our view that all students should be given the opportunity to develop leadership skills online as this will be important for their employability and career development in an increasingly global and virtual workplace.

Moreover, in their attempt to identify effective leadership practices, some researchers have referred to key phases of the virtual team lifecycle, describing the practices that leaders should adopt during each phase in terms of facilitating interactions, developing synergies and improving the overall team performance [26, 27]. According to this literature, the three phases of the virtual project lifecycle include: the welcoming, performing and wrapping up phases. In the welcoming phase, the general purpose or mission of the team is clarified, with resources and roles being allocated. Due to the members' diversity and dispersion, it is important at this early stage to embark on a socialisation process so as to promote synergies and shared understanding of the goals of the team. During the performing phase, team members are expected to complete the tasks assigned, attend meetings, report back to the team and share their work in progress with other members. The performing phase also involves the team moving the goal forward and meeting deadlines. Once action is underway, the virtual leader will provide the team with feedback about the task and their performance. Motivating the team should occur on a continual basis. Further, there should be acknowledgement of and communication about what has been completed towards reaching the team's goals during this phase. Finally, during the wrapping up phase the overall success of the team is celebrated and members are prepared for redeployment to another team. The extant literature has emphasised the role of the virtual team leader during all three stages of the virtual team lifecycle. For example, the ability to develop trust [9, 16] has been showed to be an essential characteristic of effective GVT leaders [13, 27]. Following from this discussion the second proposition of our paper is:

Proposition 2: Leadership has a significant impact on the effectiveness of student-based GVT collaborations.

We examine these issues by focusing on a specific GVT project that involved students from two universities, in the UK and Norway.

5   The Student Based Global Virtual Team Project Between UK and Norway

The project was a collaboration between Royal Holloway University of London (RHUL) and the Norwegian University of Science and Technology (NTNU) and took place in the Spring Term of the academic year 2018–19. In particular, Master programme students from both universities (Master in Digital Innovation and Analytics and Master in Digital Collaborations respectively) were asked to work on a group project. The project had a four week duration; it officially started on February 1st and the deliverable was due on February 27th. In total, there were 32 students involved, 22 at RHUL and 10 at NTNU. The RHUL students belonged to multiple ethnicities and consisted of an international cohort from countries including India, China, Thailand, South Korea, Singapore, Brazil, Japan, Russian, Romania and UK. The 32 students were split into five teams; 3 of the teams consisted for 6 members (4 RHUL and 2 NTNU) whilst two teams consisted of 5 RHUL and 2 NTNU members). The teams had no prior history and were not expected to work together again in the future. CISCO became the industry·partner for this collaborative project. The partner had a dual role; first it offered access to a cisco web-conferencing system, Cisco webex; and second, it provided topics for the students to work on. The themes allocated involved topical issues that the business world faces and all related to different aspects of collaboration technologies.

Both sets of students were attending a course or degree programme on Digital Collaborations. They were told that the purpose of the project was to encourage them to acquire specialized knowledge by applying what was covered in the course whilst giving them the opportunity to extend them academic knowledge of the subject by working on a specific online collaborative team project. The project was not just for assessment - it was part of deepening what they have learnt during the lectures whilst giving them the opportunity to gain practical skills by working on a real virtual project.

Each group worked on a topic sponsored by Cisco and had access to Cisco Webex for their online group collaborations. Under current GDPR (General Data Protection Regulation) they needed to opt in to use the Cisco tool. Each team was given a different topic to work on, but all topics were on different aspects and or different sectors where digital collaborations were used. The groups also had the opportunity to organise one virtual coaching session with a Cisco collaboration Technology expert to get formative feedback on their progress. It was up to each group to make the arrangements for this meeting themselves. The formal deliverable of the project was a 20 min presentation on their assigned VPT topic. The RHUL students were assessed on this presentation as well as on their ability to respond to questions linked to the presentation. Overall, the performance of all five teams that participated in the collaborative project was rated by the RHUL instructor between good to excellent; no team was assessed poorly.

Drawing on their VPT experience, the RHUL students were asked to write an individual reflection report with a focus on: "Leading successful virtual teams whilst promoting collaboration and creativity among its members", which they submitted a month after the group presentations took place. The NTNU students were asked to give a presentation on the VPT experience and to clearly identify the opportunities and challenges of being part of a VPT and lessons learned. All the VPTs gave a good presentation that gave clarity to how they experienced working in a VPT. The students from NTNU all said that working in a VPT was interesting and relevant to their education and future job, regardless of the opportunities and challenges they had met.

5.1 Communication Medium

With Cisco as the industry partner for this GVT project, the students were given access to the Cisco web conferencing tool: Webex Teams. A link was sent to all students prior to the commencement of the project that was guided them to an online training on how to use the medium. The students were encouraged to use this medium for their video-conferencing meetings with their dispersed partners. However, their communication was not restricted to this medium and each VPT could incorporate other media too:

"The team used Web-ex to carry out video calls, however, the platform had minor glitches and Messenger was used as a supporting communication tool. Additionally, the team used Google Docs to share and live-update files as Web-ex did not have that option" (GVT5, Y).

5.2 Leadership and Collaboration in the RHUL – NTNU GVT Project: Evidence from the Five GVTs

The study examined the case of five global virtual teams were examined formed as a result of a collaborative project between two universities in the UK and Norway. The GVTs were characterised by a high degree of geographical and cultural dispersion and experienced time and language differences, limited homogeneity among team members in different organizations and temporality. By drawing on the intertwining concept (Table 1) and its core dimensions, it is notable that there was evidence of the reciprocity and complementarity dimensions in most if not all of the teams. In their group presentations, two of the groups clearly identified the contribution made by their Norwegian collaborators, e.g. technology or industry examples: "These examples were provided to us by our Norwegian members" (GVT 1). In the case of GVT4, there was also evidence of complementarity and synergy developing their collaboration where expertise from the different subgroups in the two university was united to develop new ideas and knowledge: "Our Norwegian collaborator guided us through the topic as he had prior experience with it" (GVT 4, Yu).

5.3 Self-appointed, Emergent and Shared Leaders Were Evident Across the Five GVTs

In GVT 1, no single individual emerged as a leader. Instead there was an attempt to develop shared leadership with every member taking on responsibility for the project. As one put it: "It was natural for us to expect a democratic co-leadership in university assignments" (GVT 1, UK). However, it was recognised that this was not working well because of the lack of a leader to take responsibility of the big picture in the team process. A Japanese RHUL member noted: "in my culture, it is a nature process for members to follow a leader and only in rare occasion where the leader needs to get a second opinion, another person may get involved".

In GVT 2, the UK based members made a conscious effort develop shared leadership. For this, they agreed in their first meeting that each meeting will be facilitated by a different member. This led to very good working relations among the dispersed members, to the point that a Norwegian student said: "I wish I was attending the presentation in the UK – I am curious to see how it all went".

"Though I have had industry experience I never worked in a virtual team setting; … it is was an interesting and important project which added to my experiential projects … a very useful experience for a future career in business" (GVT 2 UK, M).

In GVT 3, some delays were exhibited in terms of starting the project with the first week gone and no communication was arranged among the VPT members. When this finally happened, the leadership role was shared among 2 members both in RHUL during the welcoming stage of the project. One of these individuals led the socialisation process and set up ice-breaker activities, while the second encourage communication about the skills that each member brought to the team and task allocation. When the second individual was absent in the second group meeting, the first individual took on the leadership role till the end of the project. The group was found to have worked well with their dispersed members and the Norwegian students' input to the presentation was clearly acknowledge and valued. Where collaboration suffered was among the UK-based members and it believed to be due to the cultural diversity of this group, with the Chinese and Indian students being particularly quiet: One of the emergent leaders acknowledged that though "The VPT was successful in socialising with the Norwegian students, we were less successful in socialising with the local students" (GVT3, UK, A). "This project was a good opportunity to improve our employability and career development" (GVT 3, UK F).

In GVT 4, an individual emerged as a leader early on in the project. His leadership style described by himself and others was seen as a transactional style due to being goal-orientated and task driven, aiming to direct, coordinate and correct members: "Our leader showed organisational skills and an ability to bring team members together through communication and enthusiasm" (GVT4, UK, M). The three stages of the VT lifecycle was acknowledged by team members, which reflected on the activities that took place within each stage. It was acknowledged that not enough effort was put in developing rapport and icebreaking activities in the welcoming stage, however according to another member, the leader was found to start each meeting by asking each member what they have been up to, thus making an effort on build social relations with other members. Also, it was felt that opportunities should have been created for other members to enact the leadership role too: "I should have allowed different members to take responsibility or facilitate the different meetings each week; as well as enhancing their skills, it would have enhanced their motivation and creativity too" (GVT 4, UK, Yu). "The Norwegian student stayed active and energetic throughout the project and we had the chance to embrace diversity in opinion, skills and background" (GVT 4, UK, M).

In GVT 5, a UK based member was appointed as the team leader: "I was chosen as a leader by the RHUL members"; this indicates that the appointed was not discussed with the NTNU members according to whom: "Y put herself forward as the leader and we accepted it". It was acknowledged that this role was not discussed and that this was a case of a self-appointed leader early in the project. It was acknowledged that in this GVT, not enough time was spent in the welcoming stage and getting to know each other: "When given the opportunity to work in a VPT, if time allows, building rapport would be beneficial. Gaining a greater understanding of individual skill sets will also allow for better division of work ... as well as clearer expectations for all members involved" (GVT5, UK M).

5.4 Students' Reflections on the Student-Based GVTs

All students had the opportunity to reflect, both verbally and in writing, on the GVT collaboration following the completion of the project:

"The virtual project was a very valuable experience and it provided the opportunity to implement leadership theory and put into practice" (GVT 3, UK A).

"This experience can only make one wiser and make them more knowledgeable for future events" (GVT 4, UK S).

"The way we build trust among the group members was by meeting the deadlines the group agreed upon" (GTV 2, Norway).

"Online start-up meeting were extremely useful to get to know each other and establish team roles" (GTV 4, Norway).

UK students also reflected specifically on the e-leadership roles enacted within their GVT, commenting on their own leadership style and that by their fellow members. Some members showed a very good awareness of this role. For example: "our objective was to draw on the strengths and to overcome the challenges of working in a virtual setting... with leadership our team increased in productivity and we were able to become more cohesive as a group" (GVT 3, UK A). Where a GVT only adopted the shared leadership style, it was felt that this did not work very effectively. Instead, in the case where shared leadership was accompanied by an emergent leader, the results were more positive both in terms of team performance and team dynamics.

Overall, it was shown in their reflections that students would welcome a more flexible, fluid and shared leadership approach where more members take on the role of the leader. They appreciated that this would enhance everyone's learning and improve their skills in working in the virtual team environment:

"When carrying out the role of an e-leader, I understood the underlying difference in contrast to working only locally" (appointed leader, GVT 5, UK Y). The same appointed leader however acknowledged in her reflection that the leadership role should be a more fluid one: "If provided, we had more time for project completion, this fluid inter-transferrable leadership position would be possible as well as exploration of more ideas and research topic wise" (GVT 5, UK Y).

6 Pedagogical Issues on Using GVTs in Teaching

Following their GVT experience, students were asked to make recommendations for improving these kind of projects. They identified three areas where in their views change was needed. We present these below and also add our response as instructors:

Students' recommendation 1: More time to be allocated to the project.

Instructors' Response: The project had four weeks duration. Four out of five GVTs did not start the GVT meeting until the second week of the project and after being prompted by the instructor. In one case, the UK-based members had an initial meeting without inviting their Norwegian collaborators. A pedagogical implication of this is that students need to be reminded that virtual teams often operate on a temporary, short term basis. Nevertheless, all three stages of the VT lifecycle should be implemented with particular emphasis being given to the welcoming stage where all members need to be included. Developing rapport and social relations are crucial at this early stage of the team process for promoting team identity and collaboration.

Student Recommendation 2: The meeting with the industry expert to take place earlier in the project in order to clarify project aims.

Instructors' Response: Though the need to clarify project aims at the earliest possible as this is important for the project development, it is also acknowledged that students should be given the chance to figure out the project aims themselves. In this case the aims had flexibility and therefore students could bring their own ideas as to how to approach the project. The industry expert also agreed with this view by adding: "part of the journey to success is realising which resources are available and (how) to make best use of them ☺" (industry expert, email).

A criticism given to existing studies that used student-based GVTs is that these are not always realistic team settings as the students tend to get very clear instructions as to what the task is about and therefore what is expected of them in order to fulfil the task. The reason for giving clear instructions is of course linked to the need to systematically measure students' performance. Outside academia however, virtual team members may not have clear goals. Instead, project members need to spend time developing the goals of their team. For example, it has been argued that student-based VTs experience limited team dynamics and interactions which may be necessitate efforts to clarify team goals and expectations and therefore cannot represent real-life business environments where power dynamics prevail [4]. Similarly, research has shown that it is more likely for a virtual team to experience high levels of trust when its members work together to develop the goals of their team than those teams whose members do not spend time to develop a shared understanding of what the team goals are [17].

Student Recommendation 3: The need for the project deliverables to be the same across the different member groups in the different universities.

Instructors' Response: We readily acknowledge that this is important. In our case, this was not possible for the specific project as the instructors in Norway had already made arrangements for alternative assessments. Therefore whilst the UK based students were assessed on the group presentation, the Norwegian students were not, even though they were asked to make a contribution and collaborate with the UK based members to jointly develop the presentation.

These pedagogical issues can be summarised as follows:

- Instructors should emphasize the temporal dimension of VPTs and that students need to make the most of the time they have available working on the project.

- To make it more realistic for students, instructors should give a degree of flexibility to students to set up their own specific objectives, guided by the general goals of the project.
- The universities involved should agree on common deliverables and assessment methods.

7   Conclusions and Implications

The main aim of this study has been to develop a better understanding of the leadership practices adopted in student based GVTs. It has been driven by our position that leadership has an impact on effective collaborations in the dispersed setting. Using the case of a virtual collaborative project set up between a university in the UK and a university in Norway, it was found that the way leadership was enacted had a role to play in the collaboration within the GVT. The teams with self-appointed leaders were found not to have put significant effort in developing team relationships and trust which are prerequisites for effective collaborations. For all team members, this was the first time that they had worked on a virtual collaborative project. In their reflections, they all acknowledged that despite the problems and difficulties experienced, through the GVT project, they were able to understand the role and important of effective leadership practices and appreciate some of the norms needed to facilitate virtual team success. Moreover, the findings suggest that GVT leaders, either appointed or emergent, should encourage social interactions at an early stage of the GVT in order to enhance team dynamics, avoid isolation and improve interpersonal relations among virtual team members. Such practices are effective ice-breakers and can increase the opportunities for collaboration.

Overall, giving the opportunity to students to lead and not just be part of GVTs can contribute to invaluable experiences and can enhance students' employability and career development.

References

1. Ahuja, M.K., Galvin, J.E.: Socialization in virtual groups. J. Manag. **29**, 161 (2003)
2. Alavi, M., Wheeler, B.C., Valacich, J.S.: Using IT to reengineer business education: an exploratory investigation of collaborative telelearning. MIS Q. **19**, 293–312 (1995)
3. Carte, T.A., Chidambaram, L., Becker, A.: Emergent leadership in self-managed virtual teams. Group Decis. Negot. **15**(4), 323–343 (2006)
4. Chamakiotis, P., Panteli, N.: Leading the creative process: the case of virtual product design. New Technol. Work Employ. **32**(1), 28–42 (2017)
5. Cramton, C.D.: Information problems in dispersed teams. In: Annual Meeting of the Academy of Management (Best Papers Proceedings), Boston, MA (1997)
6. Cramton, C.D.: Attribution in distributed work groups. In: Kiesler, S. (ed.) Distributed Work, p. 191. The MIT Press, Cambridge (2002)
7. Davison, R.M., Fuller, M.A., Hardin, A.: E-consulting in virtual negotiations. Group Decis. Negot. **12**(6), 517–535 (2003)

8. Davison, R.M., Panteli, N., Hardin, A.M., Fuller, M.A.: Establishing effective global virtual student teams. IEEE Trans. Prof. Commun. **60**(3), 317–329 (2017)
9. Germain, M.L., McGuire, D.: The role of swift trust in virtual teams and implications for human resource development. Adv. Dev. Hum. Resour. **16**(3), 356–370 (2014)
10. Jarvenpaa, S.L., Leidner, D.E.: Communication and trust in global virtual teams. J. Comput. Mediat. Commun. **3**(4) (1998). http://www.ascusc.org/jcmc
11. Kayworth, T.R., Leidner, D.E.: Leadership effectiveness in global virtual teams. J. Manag. Inf. Syst. **18**(3), 7–40 (2002)
12. Kotlarsky, J., Oshri, I.: Social ties, knowledge sharing and successful collaboration in globally distributed system development projects. Eur. J. Inf. Syst. **14**(1), 37–48 (2005)
13. Malhotra, A., Majchrzak, A., Rosen, B.: Leading virtual teams. Acad. Manag. Perspect. **21**, 60–70 (2007)
14. Northcraft, G.B., Griffith, T.L., Fuller, M.A.: Virtual study groups: a challenging centerpiece for "Working Adult" management education. In: Ferris, S.P., Godar, S.H. (eds.) Teaching and Learning with Virtual Teams. Idea Group Publishing, Hershey (2006)
15. Panteli, N., Davison, R.M.: The role of subgroups in the communication patterns of global virtual teams. IEEE Trans. Prof. Commun. **48**(2), 191–200 (2005)
16. Panteli, N., Duncan, E.: Trust and temporary virtual teams: alternative explanations and dramaturgical relationships. Inf. Technol. People **17**(4), 423–441 (2004)
17. Panteli, N., Tucker, R.: Power and trust in global virtual teams. Commun. ACM **52**(12), 113–115 (2009)
18. Piccoli, G., Ahmad, R., Ives, B.: Web-based virtual learning environments: a research framework and a preliminary assessment of effectiveness in basic IT skills training. MIS Q. **25**, 401–426 (2001)
19. O'Mahony, S., Ferraro, F.: The emergence of governance in an open source community. Acad. Manag. J. **50**(5), 1079–1106 (2007)
20. Robey, D., Schwaig, K.S., Jin, L.: Intertwining material and virtual work. Inf. Organ. **13**(2), 111–129 (2003)
21. Roschelle, J., Teasley, S.: The construction of shared knowledge in collaborative problem solving. In: O'Malley, C.E. (ed.) Computer Supported Collaborative Learning, vol. 128, pp. 69–97. Springer, Heidelberg (1995). https://doi.org/10.1007/978-3-642-85098-1_5
22. Qureshi, S., Bogenrieder, I., Kumar, K.: Managing participative diversity in virtual teams: requirements for collaborative technology support. In: 33rd Hawaii International Conference on Systems Sciences. IEEE (2000)
23. Sarker, S., Sahay, S.: Understanding virtual team development: an interpretive study. J. Assoc. Inf. Syst. **4**(1), 1 (2003)
24. Vogel, D.R., Genuchten, M., Lou, D., van Eekhout, M., Verveen, S., Adams, T.: Exploratory research on the role of national and professional cultures in a distributed learning project. IEEE Trans. Prof. Commun. **44**(2), 114–125 (2001)
25. Yoo, Y., Alavi, M.: Emergent leadership in virtual teams: what do emergent leaders do? Inf. Organ. **14**(1), 27–58 (2004)
26. Zander, L., Mockaitis, A.I., Butler, C.L.: Leading global teams. J. World Bus. **47**(4), 592–603 (2012)
27. Zander, L., Zettinig, P., Makela, K.: Leading global virtual teams to success. Organ. Dyn. **42**(3), 228–237 (2013)

Fighting Crime: Harnessing the Power of Virtual Social Communities

Marie J. Hattingh$^{(\boxtimes)}$ ⓘ and Sunet Eybers ⓘ

University of Pretoria, Private Bag X20, Hatfield, Pretoria 0028, South Africa
{marie.hattingh, sunet.eybers}@up.ac.za

Abstract. Crime is a reality that effects everyone in the world. Even developed countries such as the United Kingdom, Canada and Germany are not exempted from crime occurrences. Although these indicators are substantially less than developing countries such as South Africa, the existence of crime is a worldwide phenomenon. In this paper we explore the extent to which social media, in particular Facebook are used in the fight against crime.

The study adopts a social technical approach in its investigation, considering the symbiotic relationship between communities (the organisation), Facebook and the utilisation of Facebook to complete tasks (technical subsystem), team members and structure to report crime in virtual communities (social subsystem) and current governance structures (environmental system). Based on a study of 297 crime fighting Facebook communities in South Africa, we found a positive correlation between the number of Facebook crime fighting communities per region and the crime rates for a particular region. Furthermore, we noticed that the regions with the most crime communities also had the most Internet connectivity per household. Both findings are indicative of a functional symbiotic relationship between the technical subsystem and the social subsystem. However, it highlights the fact that these structures are initiated by communities therefore lacking strong intervention from the environmental system, in this instance governmental bodies. We propose that governmental agencies formally recognise social media platforms as social crime fighting tool. Secondly, we suggest that governmental entities should focus on infrastructure related challenges as part of their attempt to combat crime.

Keywords: Social media · Crime prevention · Facebook ·
Cohesive community

1 Introduction

Crime is a reality that affects everyone in the world, irrespective of their developmental classification status. Although a substantial difference between the number of crime occurrences and crime type exist between countries from different developmental classifications, the fact remains that crime occur. For example, when violent crimes (such as murder) are investigated, a country such as South Africa is listed as having three cities in the top 50 in 2017/2018 [1]. On the other hand, developed countries such as United Kingdom, Canada or Germany do not appear on the list.

© IFIP International Federation for Information Processing 2019
Published by Springer Nature Switzerland AG 2019
I. O. Pappas et al. (Eds.): I3E 2019, LNCS 11701, pp. 797–808, 2019.
https://doi.org/10.1007/978-3-030-29374-1_65

In a developing country such as South Africa, local authorities have called for local communities to work together to actively participate to combat crime. After the release of the 2014/2015 crime statistics the local Police Minister, Nkosinathi Nhleko, said that businesses, communities and the police need to work together to curtail crime in South Africa [2]. This call is a repeat of an earlier call by the Member of the Executive Council (MEC), Nomusa Dube-Ncube, who expressed his shock at the brutal killing of one of its members [3]. He stated that *"It is incidents such as this heinous crime that remind us that crime and violence remain a grave challenge in our communities and that as society we need to galvanise each other's strength to isolate the criminal elements that threaten social cohesion and harmony in our communities"* [3].

Communities have been 'taking up the fight' against crime in the form of Social Networking Crime Fighting communities – specifically Facebook. These "crime fighting communities" were established with the specific purpose to combat crime in the area. In [4] it was reported how a CPF uses Facebook to execute their mandate and found that the CPF community shares two types of information: firstly information relating to the building of a cohesive community. Secondly, information related to the creating of awareness of crime in the area. In a second study [5] investigated how Facebook is used to locate people who have been reported missing by family or friends in South Africa. Graphs were used to indicate differentiated roles of the Facebook communities. Whilst some communities act mainly as originators of the messages, others act more as distributors or end points of the messages.

On an international level similar studies, where communities act both as originators and distributors of messages to contribute to a specific cause, have been conducted. One such instance was the utilisation of a Facebook group to assist with the finding of an Australian woman, Gillian "Jill" Meagher that went missing after an evening out. Although the study reported on the *"collective practices of meaning-making in response to public crime events"* [6], it was a good example of how Facebook communities were utilised. This is in line with the findings of Hattingh [4] and Powell et al. [6] that confirms that social networking sites, such as Facebook, are used in the fight against crime and crime related activities.

This paper will extend on previous studies by answering questions regarding the representation and focus of communities on Facebook and the probable correlation between said communities and crime levels. The study will furthermore add to the existing understanding of the use of technology and community participation in the fight against crime in developing countries. This will be achieved through a structured review (using specific keywords) of Facebook communities/groups. The study is based on a socio-technical approach as the main theoretical underpinning considering the assumed symbiotic relationship between communities (the organisation), Facebook and utilization of the Facebook environment to complete tasks (technical subsystem), team members and structure in the virtual community (social subsystem) and current governance structures (the environment). This will hopefully expose the weak points in the socio-technical value chain.

The remainder of the paper follows the following structure: in Sect. 2 we provide an introduction to the socio-technical theory [7]. In Sect. 3 the literature will be presented in accordance with the socio-technical theory introducing the environment, the organizational system and the social and technical subsystems. The approach to this study is discussed in Sect. 4 where after we discuss the results in Sect. 5. We conclude the study in Sect. 6.

2 Social Technical Theory

Socio-technical theory focus on the interrelationship between technical subsystems and social subsystems with the main objective of creating a balanced, effective, symbiotic relationship in the context of an organisation or social system governed by the rules and regulations of a bigger environmental system [7]. It is postulated that, the more effective the interrelationship, the greater the benefits as a result of the interaction between the subsystems [7]. Socio-technical systems refer to the interaction between team members in a social system or organisation whilst the technical system refers to the utilisation of technical tools and techniques that enable the interaction (referred to as tasks) [7].

In the instance of Facebook communities, the organisation sub system refers to a virtual community, i.e. CPF in Facebook. The community interacts within the virtual community through the utilisation of Facebook, in this instance the social networking site (or Web 2.0 tool) [8] enabling connectivity and information sharing amongst members. The virtual community share the same values, i.e. to contribute to a safer community through collaboration. These values are built into the use and capabilities of technology (the technical subsystem). For example, strict security measures by means of membership only groups can be enforced in order to vet members for membership eligibility prior to joining the group. As a result, potential members with criminal intent is identified prior to the allowing membership.

This virtual FB community is a classic example of a self-organising community [9] with a shared interest of contributing to a safer local community. The environmental system provides the overall governance and unspoken rules to the other systems/subsystems (organisation, technical and social). For example, the prevention and possible prosecution of 'hate speech' when using the virtual community is governed by the inherent rules and regulations of the local government.

3 The Organisational System: Cohesive Communities

The causes, impact and response to crime as well as the relationship between these factors have been a much researched area internationally [10–12]. One study of much importance is research conducted by Leverentz and Williams [10] that investigated how physical communities react to, and subsequently attempt to control crime by adopting various crime-control strategies. They have identified three responses or strategies to crime namely "reliance on public alliances, tentative public-parochial partners and grassroots public engagement". Bendler et al. [13] has investigated the utilisation of social media data (Twitter) to predict crime related activities using predictive analysis and virtually published their results as part of a "virtual neighborhood watch" group. Using predictive analysis to predict crime based on historic events are perceived by many authors as key to combat future crime.

Research on the impact of crime in South Africa has increased significantly, particularly with publications such as this one, dedicated to report on the state of, and the progress in the fight against crime in South Africa. Crime patterns are not evenly distributed which makes it difficult to predict and manage [14]. Recent statistics indicated that the Western Cape has the highest level of reported crime experience at 9.7%, followed by Gauteng with 9.1%. The lowest level of reported crime experienced was in Limpopo with 4.2%. There has been a focus on two main areas in the fight against crime: Cohesive community participation and the use of technology. A cohesive community is defined as a community where "there is a common vision and sense of belonging for all communities, the diversity of people's different backgrounds and circumstances is appreciated and positively valued" [15]. The cohesive community is also referred to as the organisation in the social-technical theory, whilst the use of technology forms part of the technical subsystem. In the sections to follow each of these two areas or subsystems will be elaborated upon. However, first the environment in which these two subsystems exist need to be considered and will be discussed next.

3.1   Environment: Governance Structures

Any community initiative needs to occur within the confines of the law. This include community initiatives that support the fight of crime. In support of the CPF initiative of the SAPS, Choi, Lee and Chun [16] state that the police force (the environmental system) needed the support of communities in order to be effective in providing community safety. In their extensive literature survey they identify a number of factors that motivate citizens to participate in crime prevention activities: (1) confidence in the police, (2) personal safety, (3) attachment to the area, and (4) crime problems in the community.

The importance of CPFs are further highlighted in research by Rey [17] where the author focused on the identification and measuring of online crime prevention communities to ensure the healthy (and therefore effective) only communities.

Even though the South African Police Service (SAPS) has a social media presence, the platforms are only used to engage with citizens. They urge citizens not to use social media platforms to report a crime as the type of information required (normally by an operator) is too specific and the response time to these posts cannot be guaranteed [18].

3.2   Social Subsystem: Using Cohesive Communities to Combat Crime

Sampson and Raudenbush [15] found that cohesive communities display lower levels of crime and social disorder due to the collective effort by the community to meet their common goal. Lee [19] found that socioeconomic status, lifestyle and neighborhood characteristics have no influence on the possibility of becoming a victim of violent crime, such as robbery and assault, when one is part of a cohesive community because of high levels of social control. Even though Roberts and Gordon [12] found that social cohesion can pull citizens apart due to the fear of crime, it was found in a previous study [4] that community cohesion had a positive effect on the community. This was also supported by an earlier study conducted by Wedlock [11] found that there was a 3% decrease in residential burglary, 4% decrease in motor theft, 2% decrease in theft from motor vehicles and 3% decrease in violent crime with every 1% increase of sense of community experienced by neighborhood communities.

3.3 Technical Subsystem: Using Technology to Analyse and Predict Crime

The use of technology in the fight against crime can take two forms: using technology in the analysis of crime statistics and using it to predict the possibility of crime occurrence. Firstly an example of the former is the interactive crime statistics map(s) based on the annual crime statistics released by the SAPS and created by the Institute for Security Studies. The visual representation of the SAPS crime statistics allow citizens to view the crime trends since 2004 per category, per municipality and per police station. In addition to the SAPS' statistics the Crime Hub provides information on public violence per region [20].

Secondly technology allows for the prediction of crime. Cherian and Dawson [21] employed machine learning and other statistical techniques to classify and predict average crime incidents in the coming weeks and months. Also, the illustrative study of Lancaster and Kamman [22] proposed a data linking methodology that can analyse the demographic characteristics of police precincts to predict the murder rate at precinct level. This methodology allows for more sophisticated measurements to investigate certain associations between the risk factors identified in the ecological framework (consisting of the individual, relationship, community and societal). One of the most important indicators that could be identified using this methodology will be that between crime and the community which includes "feelings of belonging or perceptions of social or group integration, and a willingness to show solidarity". This connects the "technology" aspect to the community aspect.

The previous discussions have considered community participation independent of the usage of technology to combat crime. Web 2.0 technologies and more specifically social networking platforms allows normal citizens to partake of the content creation platforms, especially in the form of social networking participation. In the following section we will discuss how communities utilize Web 2.0 technologies to combat crime.

3.4 Interaction Between Social and Technical Subsystems: Communities Using Web 2.0 Technology to Combat Crime

The increased Internet access of South Africans have enabled more citizens to take part in digital activities. According to World Wide Worx and Ornico's South African Social Media Landscape 2018 study there has been a sharp increase in social media uptake. 31% (16.74 million) of all South Africans now use WhatsApp and 26% (14.04 million) of all South Africans use Facebook [8]. Social networking platforms such as Facebook provide an ideal tool for citizens to participate in the fight against crime. Citizens can now "post" about an event or upload photos and videos with GPS coordinates without much effort. The most prominent use of social media in the fight against crime was during the Boston Marathon bombings where it was used to identify the bombers successfully. In response to this successful use of social media McCullagh [23] stated that "a traditional manhunt becomes something much different in the age of Twitter, Instagram, and face recognition".

Twitter has been used in the fight against crime. Wang, Gerber and Brown [24] developed a model that predicts hit-and-run incidents uniformly across all days. Bendler, Brandt, Wagner, and Neuman's [13] research focused on how Twitter can be used to create a sort of virtual neighborhood watch (NHW) which will create a secure environment for tourists and residents. It will also help the police and authorities in identifying patrol spots. The latter is accomplished through the live prediction from media streams. Gerber [25] further analysed the use of Twitter to predict crime by analysing the tweets using kernel density estimation. He identified a number of "performance bottlenecks" that could have an impact on the use of Twitter in an actual decision support system.

In South Africa Featherstone [26] investigated how Twitter can make communication more useful in terms of data gathering, prediction and plotting broader patterns. She showed in a second paper how Twitter can be used to identify vehicle descriptions to assist in reducing or predicting crime [27].

In [14] the Internet access at home, at work, using mobile devices and at other facilities were reported. It should be noted that a citizen can access the Internet at more than one location, therefore the total percentage of Internet access can exceed 100%. Taking this into account, Gauteng has the highest level of Internet access with 119.7% followed by Western Cape with 113%, Kwa-Zulu Natal with 76.7%, Free State with 75.4%, Mpumalanga with 75.1%, Northern Cape with 73.4%, Eastern Cape with 69%, North West with 67.7% and Limpopo with lowest level of access at 49.4%.

Mobile Internet access is by far the most accessible option of accessing the Internet as it can happen anytime, anywhere. This is not surprising as currently there are 20.8 million smart phone users in South Africa [28].

4   Research Methodology

The aim of this research project is to explore the extent to which communities fight crime using Facebook groups/pages as part of a bigger socio-technical system. In reaching the aim the following questions need to be answered: (1) To what extent are crime fighting communities represented on Facebook? (2) What is the focus of these communities? (3) Is there a correlation between the number of crime fighting Facebook communities, the membership rate of the crime fighting Facebook communities and the crime rate on provincial level? (4) What are the weak areas considering the various subsystems (organisation, technical, social and environmental) in the bigger socio-technical system?

In answering the first research question the researchers conducted a review of Facebook communities between 22 March and 30 May 2016. Facebook's built-in search engine was used to search the following key words to identify "crime fighting communities" on Facebook: "CPF", "Community police (to pick up "Policing" and "Police")", "Crime", "Concerned citizens", "Crisis", "Emergency", "Intelligence bureau", "Neighborhood watch". The search was restricted to South African groups/pages that were in English. The keywords were derived by following a snowball sampling approach, where the first keyword "CFP" derived from the first study [4] was used as the initial community. The researchers then observed which pages/groups were linked to the initial community to derive the remaining keywords.

The researchers recorded, in an MS Excel spreadsheet, the keyword used in the search, whether it was a group or page, the title of the group/page, membership numbers, the description of the group/page, which province the group/page covered and whether mention was made of any other means of communication, like WhatsApp and interesting observations. The researchers also captured the latitude and longitude of each area obtained from the LatLong.net in the spreadsheet which helped them to plot all the Facebook communities that were identified through the search, on a map of South Africa. This map is generated by MS Excel Powerview and is illustrated in Fig. 1. The size of the bubble is related to the number of communities in that particular area. The overlapping bubbles indicate the concentration of members in a specific area as an individual can be a member of more than one community and the number of communities in a very small area.

Fig. 1. Facebook communities in South Africa

In order to answer the second research question thematic content analysis [26] was used to analyse the descriptions (as stated on their Facebook profiles) of the top member groups, as well as all the posts for the past week (6 July 2016–13 July 2016) which will be used to obtain an understanding of the focus of each group/page. In order to answer the third research question the researchers utilised the results illustrated in Fig. 1. No further data was gathered to answer the fourth research question as data gathered to answer question one to three will be used to apply to the concept of a socio-technical system.

5   Discussion of Results

The aim of this paper was four-fold: firstly, to identify the number of crime fighting communities on Facebook in South Africa, secondly to understand the focus of said communities thirdly to determine if there is any correlation between the communities and the crime levels and fourthly to use the data gathered in order to identify possible weak links in the various subsystems of the socio-technical system. The results will be discussed in accordance with these question.

5.1   The Number of "Crime Fighting Communities" on Facebook in SA

In meeting the first aim, the Facebook search, using the keywords stated above, have revealed 297 dedicated crime fighting Facebook communities throughout South Africa. The Eastern Cape has 18 communities (91 364 members), Free State has 7 communities (12 645 members), Gauteng has 114 communities (299 336 members), Kwa Zulu Natal has 29 communities (65 935 members), Mpumalanga has 10 communities (16 884 members), North West has 11 communities (23 44 members), Western Cape has 71 communities (153 712 members) and Limpopo has 6 communities (3820 members). Furthermore, there were 31 national communities which are not associated with any specific area/province. In total more than 1.1 million in South Africans belong to crime fighting communities. (It is possible for a citizen to belong to more than one community simultaneously). The communities considered is by no means an exhaustive list of crime fighting communities, it was observed that a number of the communities also had websites, WhatsApp groups, Zello accounts, Twitter accounts or use "old fashioned" citizen band radios. The usage of multiple (mainly) social media platforms by the communities are in line with a previous study by Hattingh [4] where a single CPF used multiple platforms.

Although the number of communities dedicated to crime in SA was impressive the most interesting finding of this study is that, by using the keyword listed previously, no Facebook crime fighting communities were found for the Northern Cape Province.

5.2   The Focus of the "Crime Fighting" Facebook Communities

Facebook Communities typically had a description that invites community members to partake in the fight against crime. From the quotes below, it can be seen that these communities were dedicated to "fighting crime".

> *"Reporting and fighting crime - by the community for the community"* [Concerned Citizens page, GP]

Communities are now standing together to make headway in the fight against crime by supporting one another. The following post illustrates the call from the community for the community to assist.

> *"The Time Has Come......we have to all pull together and watch over each Other. Crime is out of hand and out of touch. Everyone needs an immediate update of Crime and emergencies in your Area, so that anyone in the Vicinity can Respond and assist immediately, like all Good and caring Citizens should ..."* [Crime group, KZN]

In addition to identifying the "mission" of each Facebook community by reviewing their descriptions, a total of 210 posts were reviewed across the top five communities. The analysis have generated a number of themes which supported those that have been identified in a previous study [4] which included "reporting", "awareness", "alertness", and "update". The cohesive community principle of cohesive community as introduced in [4] was extended by requesting "assistance" from the community members. For example, community input was requested on a vehicle accident that occurred (assistance theme), general information regarding awareness tips (awareness theme), information sharing regarding activities in the community to "Be On the LookOut" (BOLO) for armed robbery suspects, missing people, suspects involved with a murder/robber/vehicle theft etc. (alertness theme). The reporting and updating activities in followed in the same vein as previous studies. However, there have been much more updates provided to the community members compared to the first study. 12% of the posts were updates to "crime events" that occurred. This includes updates regarding armed robberies, vehicle theft, ATM bombings etc. Research has shown that updates are important and seen as "rewards" for communities when communities help by providing the intelligence when solving a problem [4].

The data revealed a few more crime categories identified compared to the first study. This includes posts related to drugs which includes updates on successful drug busts but also awareness regarding the dangers of using drugs and who to contact when help is needed with regards to rehabilitation. Furthermore, hijacking's, ATM bombing and public violence/protests were the other new crime categories that were identified. The new crime categories can be a result of firstly, the larger "affected area" as three of the five groups under consideration were "National groups" (i.e. not related to a specific area) and secondly due to the time the snapshot of posts were taken – just before the government elections.

Finally, even though three of the five groups were "National", the theme of cohesive community, identified in the previous study persist as there were 73 information sharing posts which included posts with photos/videos/newspaper articles on incidents such as drug busts, substation being on fire, road collisions that happened in the past week etc. These posts were not updates per say (an update is defined as a response to a specific incident) but it kept the communities informed about activities in their area/surrounding areas.

5.3   Correlation Between the Communities and the Crime Levels

When comparing the number of communities to the crime statistics as presented above, it shows that Limpopo province has the lowest level of experienced crime events [14]. Limpopo only has six crime fighting communities with a mere 3820 members in total. With a population of more than 5.72 million [14] people the Facebook crime fighting communities are only accounting for 0.0007% of the population of Limpopo. One reason for this might be that Limpopo has the lowest Internet access level of 49.4% [14].

On the opposite end of the scale, Gauteng, the smallest province have a total of 114 different crime fighting Facebook communities, with a total membership of more than 299 000. Gauteng also has the second highest experienced crime level and has the largest Internet access level. The high crime rate, high population and high Internet access level might explain why Gauteng has by far the most crime fighting communities on Facebook, in South Africa. It can therefore be argued that there is a correlation between the crime levels, the number of social media crime fighting communities and to a lesser extent the availability of Internet access in the province.

5.4   Possible Weak Links in the Various Subsystems of the Socio-technical System

Based on the discussion above it is therefore evident, and safe to say, that the organisation system is a strong, functional subsystem although it was anticipated that a stronger focus on the objective of crime fighting would prevail. The majority of the communities work together with the SAPS and security companies (as illustrated in the quote below) in the fight against crime.

> *"Independent Group to report Crime, creating a vigilant community helping each other bringing the Community, Police, Sector Police and Security companies together in fighting crime".* [Crime group, WC].

Figure 2 illustrates the socio-technical system of crime fighting communities on Facebook.

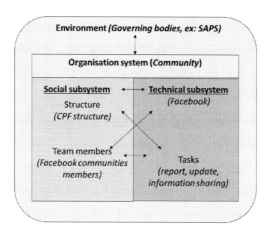

Fig. 2. Facebook as a socio-technical used by crime fighting communities

However, the utilisation of the technical subsystem by means of a computer mediated communication platform (Facebook) has enabled members to contribute to a greater, common cause despite geographical dispersed challenges.

The technical subsystem, (the social media platform, in this instance Face-book), is an effective tool to use in the fight against crime. Internationally social media platforms are used as a crime prevention tool [29]. Citizens of South Arica, through the utilization of Facebook Communities and other social media platforms have already showed a willingness to work with the SAPS and other security organisations, however the impression is that this initiative is driven from the citizens' side. The environmental system (SAPS and other governmental institutions) perhaps need to formally recognize the potential of social media as a crime fighting tool and dedicate resources to assist citizens in the monitoring of social media crime reports and deploy the necessary members to act on these reports. If this issue can be addressed it can contribute to a stronger environmental subsystem to the benefit of the organisation subsystem. Social media platforms or the technical subsystem is an inexpensive medium to formulate a crime fighting network.

6   Conclusion

This paper has confirmed and extended previous findings on the successful use of Facebook as a crime fighting tool by communities in South Africa. The paper has found that 297 Facebook communities, over eight provinces, exist that are dedicated to the fight against crime. The findings indicated a correlation between the number of crime communities and crime rates. As the power of social media as a crime fighting and prevention tool has been confirmed in this study and previous studies, it is recommend that the SAPS formally recognise and adopt social media platforms as a crime fighting and prevention tool. Government needs to develop a formal strategy, incorporating all relevant departments, to enable citizens through the provision of affordable data and infrastructure to participate in the fight against crime. It is envisaged that, if these challenges are addressed, the environmental subsystem, which have been identified as a weak link, will contributed to a stronger, much more effective socio-technical system.

References

1. Cape Town is one of the most violent cities in the world. BusinessTech (2018). https:// businesstech.co.za/news/lifestyle/230123/cape-town-is-one-of-the-most-violent-cities-in-the-world/. Accessed 31 Mar 2018
2. Police and communities must fight crime together. North Natal Courier (2015). https:// northernnatalcourier.co.za/30679/speaker-shooting-mec-condemns-brutal-murder/. Accessed 05 Mar 2018
3. South African Government: MEC Nomusa Dube-Ncube Condemns the Brutal Murder of Councillor Vusi Ntombela. South African Government (2015)
4. Hattingh, M.J.: The use of Facebook by a Community Policing Forum to combat crime. In: Proceedings of SAICSIT 2015, vol. 2, no. 2, pp. 1–10 (2015)
5. Hattingh, M.J., Matthee, M.C.: Using facebook to find missing persons: a crowd-sourcing perspective. In: Dwivedi, Y.K., et al. (eds.) I3E 2016. LNCS, vol. 9844, pp. 685–694. Springer, Cham (2016). https://doi.org/10.1007/978-3-319-45234-0_61
6. Powell, A., Overington, C., Hamilton, G.: Following #JillMeagher: collective meaning-making in response to crime events via social media. Crime Media Cult. Int. J. **14**, 409–428 (2017). https://doi.org/10.1177/1741659017721276
7. Bostrom, R.P., Heinen, J.S.: STS perspective: MIS problems and failures: a socio-technical perspective. Part I: the causes. MIS Q. **1**(3), 17–32 (2016)
8. World Wide Worx and Ornico: 2018 The Social Media Landscape in South Africa (2017). http://gullanandgullan.com/wp-content/uploads/2017/10/13907_GG-Breakthrough-infographic.pdf. Accessed 02 Mar 2018

9. Starbird, K., Palen, L.: Self-organizing by digital volunteers in times of crisis. In: 29th Annual CHI Conference on Human Factors in Computing Systems 2011 Proceedings (2011)
10. Leverentz, A., Williams, M.: Contextualizing community crime control: race, geography, and configurations of control in four communities. Criminology **55**(1), 112–136 (2017)
11. Wedlock, E.: Crime and cohesive communities (2006). http://citeseerx.ist.psu.edu/viewdoc/download?doi=10.1.1.510.6857. Accessed 02 Mar 2018
12. Roberts, B., Gordon, S.: Pulling us apart? The association between fear of crime and social cohesion in South Africa. S. Afr. Crime Q. **55**, 49–60 (2016)
13. Bendler, J., Brandt, T., Wagner, S., Neumann, D.: Investigating crime-to-twitter relationships in urban environments - facilitating a virtual neighborhood watch. In: Twenty Second European Conference on Information Systems, pp. 1–16 (2014)
14. Statistical Release General Household Survey 2016, May 2018. https://www.statssa.gov.za/publications/P0318/P03182016.pdf. Accessed 02 Apr 2018
15. Sampson, R.J., Raudenbush, S.W., Earls, F.: Neighborhoods and violent crime: a multilevel study of collective efficacy. Science **277**(5328), 918–924 (1997)
16. Choi, K., Lee, J., Chun, Y.: Why do citizens participate in community crime prevention activities? 287–298 (2014)
17. Rey, P.J.: Defining and measuring success for online crime-prevention communities. In: AMCIS 2011 Proceedings - All Submissions (2011)
18. SAPS: Services|SAPS (South African Police Service). https://www.saps.gov.za/faqdetail.php?fid=13. Accessed 24 Mar 2018
19. Lee, M.R.: Community cohesion and violent predatory victimization: a theoretical extension and cross-national test of opportunity theory. Soc. Forces **79**, 683–706 (2000). https://doi.org/10.1093/sf/79.2.683
20. Institute for Security Studies (2016). https://www.issafrica.org/crimehub/. Accessed 11 July 2016
21. Cherian, J., Dawson, M.: RoboCop : crime classification and prediction in San Francisco (2014)
22. Lancaster, L., Kamman, E.: Risky localities: exploring a methodology for measuring socio-economic characteristics of high murder areas. S. Afr. Crime Q. (56) (June 2016). https://doi.org/10.17159/2413-3108/2016/v0n56a51
23. McCullagh, C.: Men! F seeks crowdsourcing help in B bombing case: I these two. In: CNET (2013). https://www.cnet.com/news/fbi-seeks-crowdsourcing-help-in-boston-bombing-case-id-these-two-men/. Accessed 25 Mar 2018
24. Wang, X., Gerber, M.S., Brown, D.E.: Automatic crime prediction using events extracted from twitter posts. In: Yang, S.J., Greenberg, A.M., Endsley, M. (eds.) SBP 2012. LNCS, vol. 7227, pp. 231–238. Springer, Heidelberg (2012). https://doi.org/10.1007/978-3-642-29047-3_28
25. Gerber, M.S.: Predicting crime using Twitter and kernel density estimation. Decis. Support Syst. **61**(1), 115–125 (2014)
26. Featherstone, C.: The relevance of social media as it applies in South Africa to crime prediction. Inst. Electr. Electron. Eng. 1–7 (2013)
27. Featherstone, C.: Identifying vehicle descriptions in microblogging text with the aim of reducing or predicting crime. In: IEEE International Conference on Adaptive Science and Technology, ICAST (2013)
28. Number of smartphone users in South Africa from 2014 to 2022 (in millions). Statista (2018). https://www.statista.com/statistics/488376/forecast-of-smartphone-users-in-south-africa/. Accessed 02 Apr 2018
29. United Nation: The role of the public in strengthening crime prevention and criminal justice. In: 13th United Nation Congress on Crime Prevention and Criminal Justice, p. 2 (2015)

Author Index